Assembly Modeling with SolidWorks 2008

For the SolidWorks user who needs to understand Assembly Modeling

David C. Planchard & Marie P. Planchard

ISBN: 978-1-58503-467-3

Schroff Development Corporation
www.schroff.com

Better Textbooks. Lower Prices.

Trademarks and Disclaimer

SolidWorks and its family of products are registered trademarks of the Dassault Système. Microsoft Windows, Microsoft Office and its family of products are registered trademarks of the Microsoft Corporation. Pro/ENGINEER is a registered trademark of PTC Corporation. AutoCAD is a registered trademark of AutoDesk Corporation.
Other software applications and parts described in this book are trademarks or registered trademarks of their respective owners.
The authors modified model dimensions for illustration purposes. They made every effort to provide an accurate text. The authors and the manufacturers shall not be held liable for any parts, assemblies or drawings developed or designed with this book or any responsibility for inaccuracies that appear in the book. Web and company information was valid at the time of this printing.

Examination Copies

Books received as examination copies are for review purposes only and may not be made available for student use. Resale of examination copies is prohibited.

Electronic Files

Any electronic files associated with this book are licensed to the original user only. These files may not be transferred to any other party.

INTRODUCTION

Assembly Modeling with SolidWorks 2008 is written to assist the beginning SolidWorks user with a few months of design experience to the *intermediate* SolidWorks user who desires to enhance their skill sets in assembly modeling. The book provides a solid foundation in assembly modeling using competency-based projects. In step-by-step instructions, the book provides examples to:

- Start a SolidWorks session and to understand the following interfaces: Menu bar toolbar, Menu bar menu, Drop-down menus, Context toolbars, Consolidated drop-down toolbars, System feedback icons, Confirmation Corner, Heads-up View toolbar, CommandManager, and more.
- Set System Options and Document Properties as they applied to a part and assembly template. Create new SolidWorks folder locations: Document Templates, Reference Documents, and Design Library.
- Download components from 3D ContentCentral and rename and save components using SolidWorks Explorer.
- Apply the Bottom-up assembly approach with two levels of configurations using the Configure component tool, the Configure dimension tool, Design Tables, and the Add Configuration tool.
- Create new parts based on component features utilizing the Bottom-up assembly approach.
- Apply Standard Mates, SmartMates, and the Design Library Toolbox.
- Apply the Top-down assembly approach with two levels of configurations with In-Context components.
- Understand the following: Out-of-Context components, External References, InPlace Mates, redefining and replacing components and motion studies.
- Apply the Derived Feature Component Pattern tool, Linear Component Pattern tool, and the Mirror Component tool along with the Explode Line Sketch tool.
- Create a multi sheet, multi view assembly drawing. Knowledge of Custom Properties in a part/assembly and linked notes, with the ability to incorporate configurations of an Exploded view, Bill of Materials, Revision tables, and more.
- Address the Layout-based assembly approach and Link Values and Equations to control relationships.

Each project begins with the desired outcomes and usage competencies. Explore assembly modeling techniques through a series of design situations, industry scenarios, projects and objectives.

Initial and final models are provided on the enclosed CD.

The book compliments and enhances the **SolidWorks Reference Guide** and **SolidWorks Tutorials**. Although over 150 SolidWorks tools and commands are utilized in **Assembly Modeling with SolidWorks 2008,** the book is not a reference guide.

The book is a self-paced tutorial in a realistic design setting. Complex models expose you to large assembly modeling techniques. You focus on the design process while learning the commands relative to assemblies.

To obtain the most from this text, you should be familiar with the SolidWorks User Interface or other parametric modeling software application. Your skill sets should include the ability to create simple parts, assemblies, and drawings and manipulate documents through the Windows operating system.

The authors developed the industry scenarios by combining their own industry experience with the knowledge of engineers, department managers, vendors and manufacturers. These professionals are directly involved with SolidWorks everyday. They create assemblies with thousands of components and drawings with hundreds of sheets. Their responsibilities go far beyond the creation of just a 3D model.

About the Authors

David Planchard is the President of D&M Education, LLC. Before starting D&M Education LLC, he spent over 25 years in industry and academia holding various engineering, marketing, and teaching positions and degrees. He has five U.S. patents and one International patent. He has published and authored numerous papers on equipment design. David is also a technical editor for Cisco Press. He is a member of the New England Pro/Users Group, New England SolidWorks Users Group, and the Cisco Regional Academy Users Group. David holds a BSME and a MSM. David is a SolidWorks Research Partner and a SolidWorks Solution Partner and holds the Certified SolidWorks Associate CSWA Certification.

Marie Planchard is the Director of World Education Markets at SolidWorks Corporation. Before she joined SolidWorks, Marie spent over 10 years as an engineering professor at Mass Bay College in Wellesley Hills, MA. She has 18 plus years of industry software experience and held a variety of management and engineering positions. Marie holds a BSME, MSME, and the Certified SolidWorks Professional (CSWP) Certification.

David and Marie Planchard are co-authors of the following books:

- **Official Certified SolidWorks Associate CSWA Exam Guide**, Version 1
- **The Fundamentals of SolidWorks: Featuring the VEXplorer robot, 2008**,2007
- **A Commands Guide for SolidWorks 2008**
- **A Commands Guide Reference Tutorial for SolidWorks 2007**

- **Engineering Design with SolidWorks 2008**, 2007, 2006, 2005, 2004, 2003, 2001Plus, 2001, and 1999
- **SolidWorks Tutorial with Multimedia CD 2008**, 2007, 2006, 2005, 2004, 2003, and 2001/2001Plus
- **SolidWorks The Basics, with Multimedia CD 2008**, 2007, 2006, 2005, 2004, and 2003
- **Assembly Modeling with SolidWorks 2008**, 2006, 2005-2004, 2003, and 2001Plus
- **Drawing and Detailing with SolidWorks 2008**, 2007, 2006, 2005, 2004, 2003, 2002, and 2001/2001Plus
- **Applications in Sheet Metal Using Pro/SHEETMETAL & Pro/ENGINEER**

Dedication

A special acknowledgment goes to our loving daughter Stephanie Planchard who supported us during this intense and lengthy project. Stephanie continues to support us with her patience, love, and understanding.

Contact the Authors

This is the 5th edition of the book. We realize that keeping software application books current is imperative to our customers. We value the hundreds of professors, students, designers, and engineers that have provided us input to enhance our book. We value your suggestions and comments. Please contact us with any comments, questions, or suggestions on this book or any of our other SolidWorks books. David Planchard, D & M Education, LLC, dplanchard@verizon.net or visit our website at **www.dmeducation.net**.

Note to Instructors

Please contact the publisher: http://www.schroff.com for additional materials that will support the usage of this text in your classroom.

Trademarks, Disclaimer, and Copyrighted Material

SolidWorks and its family of products are registered trademarks of the Dassault Système. Microsoft Windows, Microsoft Office and its family of products are registered trademarks of the Microsoft Corporation. Pro/ENGINEER is a registered trademark of PTC Corporation. AutoCAD is a registered trademark of AutoDesk Corporation.

Other software applications and parts described in this book are trademarks or registered trademarks of their respective owners.

The authors modified model dimensions for illustration purposes. They made every effort to provide an accurate text. The authors and the manufacturers shall not be held liable for any parts, assemblies or drawings developed or designed with this book or any responsibility for inaccuracies that appear in the book.

References:

References used in this text:

- SolidWorks Users Guide, SolidWorks Corporation, 2008.
- SolidWorks Reference Guide[1.], SolidWorks Corporations, 2008.
- COSMOS/Works On-line help 2008.
- ASME Y14 Engineering Drawing and Related Documentation Practices.
- Gradin, Hartley, Fundamentals of the Finite Element Method, Macmillan, NY 1986.
- Jensen, Cecil, Interpreting Engineering Drawings, Glencoe 2002.
- Norton, Robert, Design of Machinery, 2ed. McGraw Hill, Boston, MA.
- Hibbler, R. C. Engineering Mechanics Statics and Dynamics, 8th ed. Prentice Hall, Saddle River, NJ.
- Beer & Johnson, Vector Mechanics for Engineers, 6th ed. McGraw Hill, Boston, MA.
- Planchard & Planchard, Drawing and Detailing with SolidWorks 2008, SDC Pub., Mission, KS.
- 80/20 Product Manual, 80/20, Inc., Columbia City, IN, 2008.
- Reid Tool Supply Product Manual, Reid Tool Supply Co., Muskegon, MI, 2008.
- SMC Corporation of America, Product Manuals, Indiana, USA, 2008.

[1.] The SolidWorks Reference Guide 2008 is a .pdf document available to subscription users to download from the SolidWorks website.

Table of Contents

What is SolidWorks?

SolidWorks is a design automation software package used to produce parts, assemblies and drawings. SolidWorks is a Windows native 3D solid modeling CAD program. SolidWorks provides easy to use, highest quality design software for engineers and designers who create 3D models and 2D drawings ranging from individual parts to assemblies with thousands of parts.

The SolidWorks Corporation, headquartered in Concord, Massachusetts, USA develops and markets innovative design solutions for the Microsoft Windows platform. Additional information on SolidWorks and its family of products can be obtained at their URL, www.SolidWorks.com.

In SolidWorks, you create 3D parts, assemblies, and 2D drawings. The part, assembly and drawing documents are related.

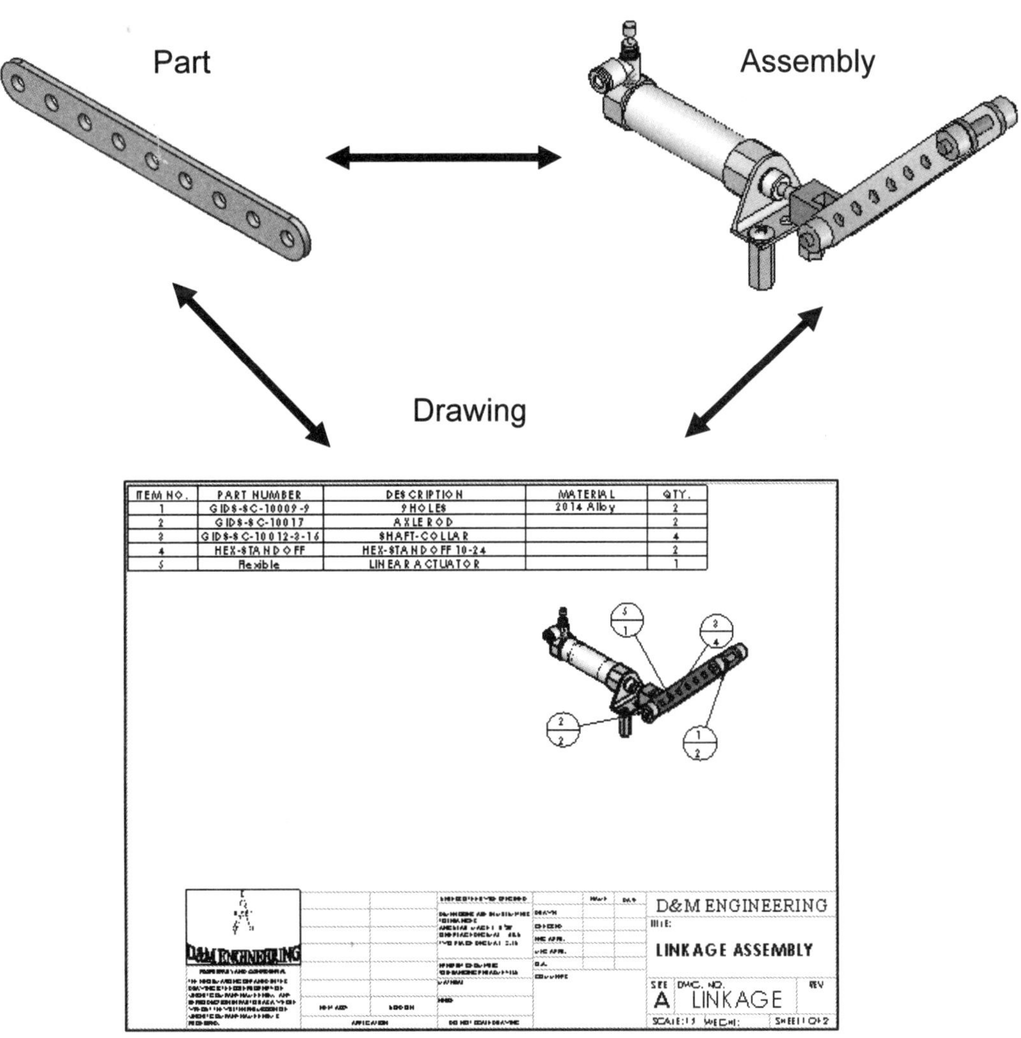

Part
Assembly
Drawing
ITEM NO. | PART NUMBER | DESCRIPTION | MATERIAL | QTY.
1 | GIDS-SC-10009-9 | 9 HOLES | 2014 Alloy | 2
2 | GIDS-SC-10017 | AXLE ROD | | 2
3 | GIDS-SC-10012-3-16 | SHAFT-COLLAR | | 4
4 | HEX-STANDOFF | HEX-STANDOFF 10-24 | | 2
5 | Flexible | LINEAR ACTUATOR | | 1
D&M ENGINEERING
LINKAGE ASSEMBLY
A
LINKAGE

Features are the building blocks of parts. Use features to create parts, such as: Extruded Boss/Base and Extruded Cut. Extruded features begin with a 2D sketch created on a Sketch plane.

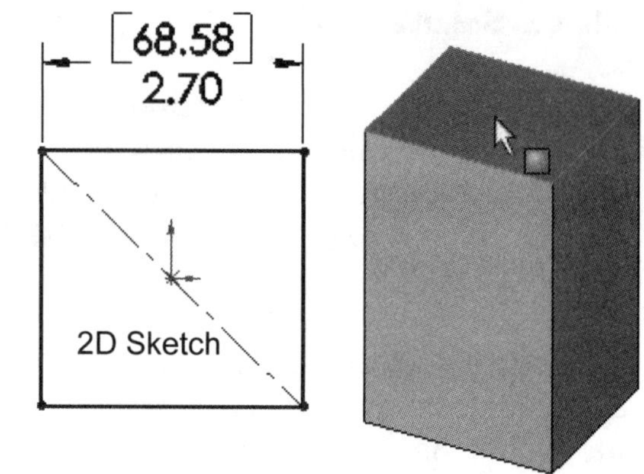

The 2D sketch is a profile or cross section. Sketch tools such as: lines, arcs, and circles are used to create the 2D sketch. Sketch the general shape of the profile. Add Geometric relationships and dimensions to control the exact size of the geometry.

Create features by selecting edges or faces of existing features, such as a Fillet. The Fillet feature rounds sharp corners.

Dimensions drive features. Change a dimension, and you change the size of the part.

Apply Geometric relationships: Vertical, Horizontal, Parallel, etc. to maintain design intent.

Create a hole that penetrates through a part. SolidWorks maintains relationships through the change.

The step-by-step approach used in this text allows you to create parts, assemblies, and drawings.

The book provides the knowledge to modify all parts and components in a document. Change is an integral part of design.

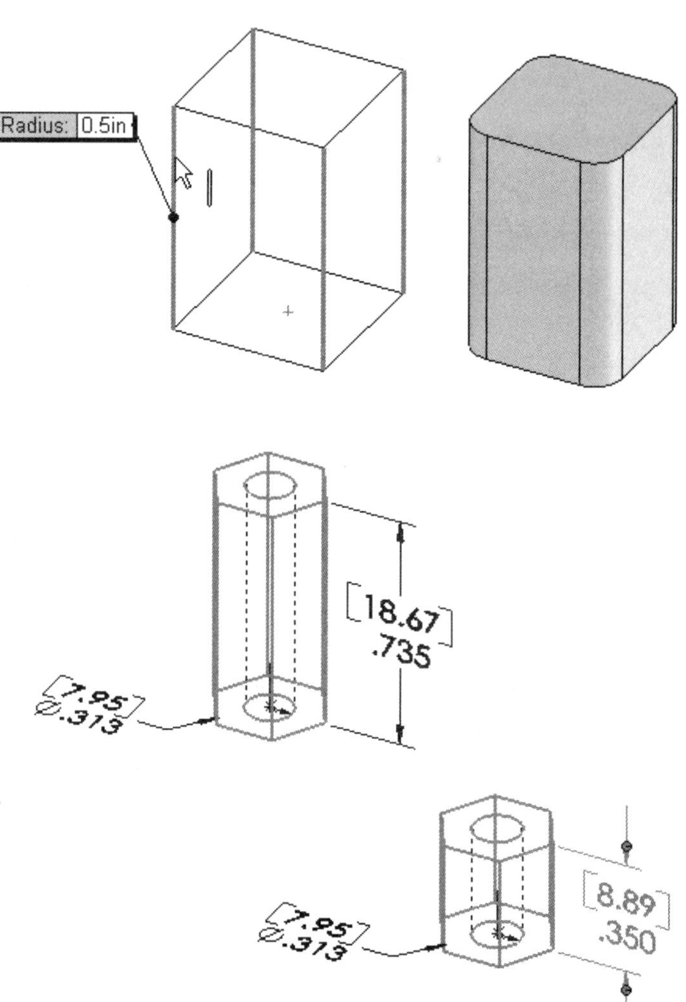

Design Intent

The SolidWorks definition of design intent is the process in which the model is developed to accept future changes.

Models behave differently when design changes occur. Design for change.

Utilize geometry for symmetry, reuse common features and reuse common parts.

Build change into the following areas:

1. Sketch.
2. Feature.
3. Part.
4. Assembly.
5. Drawing.

1. Design Intent in the Sketch

Build the design intent in the sketch as the profile is created.

A profile is determined from the sketch tools, Example: rectangle, circle and arc.

Build symmetry into the profile through a sketch centerline, mirror entity and position about the Reference planes and Origin.

Build design intent as you sketch with automatic relationships.

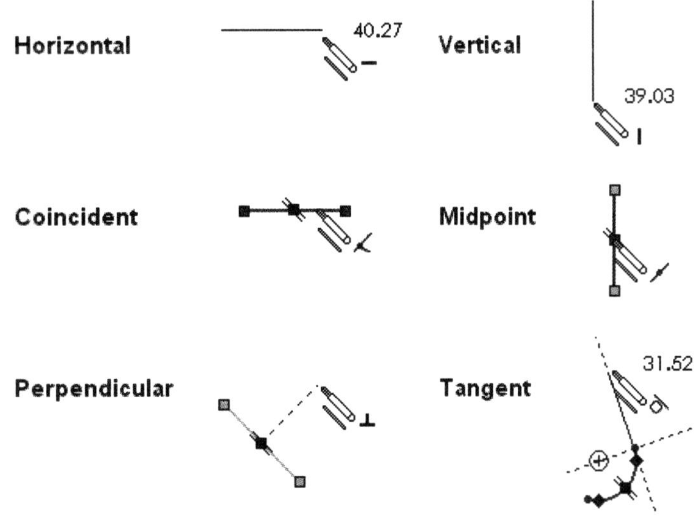

A rectangle contains horizontal, vertical and perpendicular automatic relations.

Build design intent using added geometric relations. Example: horizontal, vertical, coincident, midpoint, intersection, tangent and perpendicular.

Example A: Develop a square profile. Build the design intent to create a square profile.

Apply the Corner Rectangle tool. Insert a centerline. Add a midpoint relation. Add an equal relation between the two perpendicular lines. Insert a dimension to define the width of the square. Note: You can also apply the Center Rectangle tool which automatically addresses the midpoint relation.

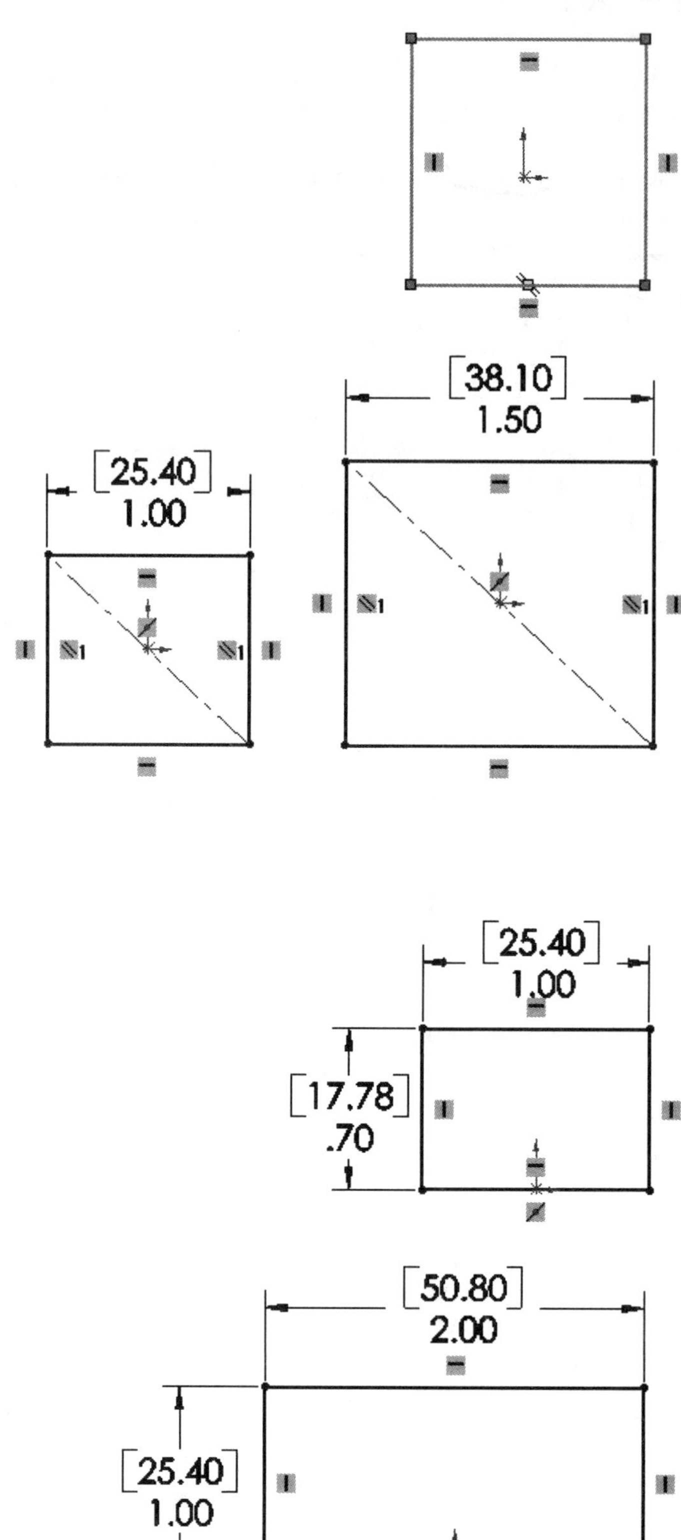

New in 2008 is the Consolidated Rectangle PropertyManager.

Example B: Develop a rectangular profile. The bottom horizontal midpoint of the rectangular profile is located at the Origin.

Sketch a rectangle.

Add a midpoint relation between the horizontal edge of the rectangle and the Origin.

Insert two dimensions to define the width and height of the rectangle.

2. Design Intent in the Feature

Build design intent into a feature by addressing symmetry, feature selection and the order of feature creations.

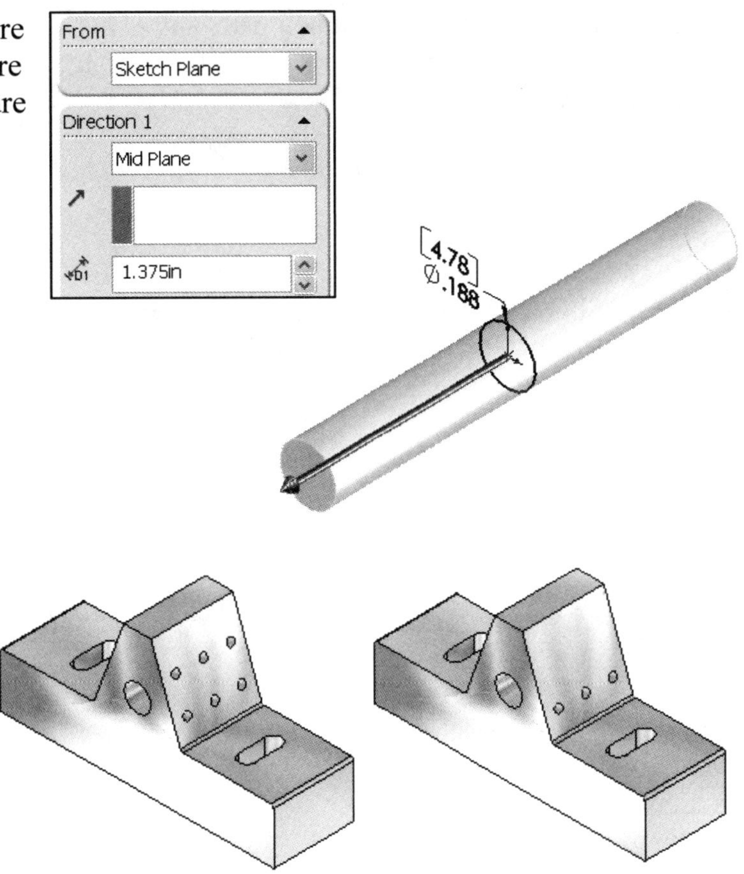

Example A: Extruded feature remains symmetric about a plane.

Utilize the Mid Plane Depth option. Modify the depth and the feature remains symmetric about the Front Plane.

Example B: Create six holes for a pattern.

Do you create six separate Extruded Cuts? No. Create one hole with the Hole Wizard.

Insert a Linear Pattern feature.

Modify the number of holes from six to three.

3. Design Intent in the Part

Utilize symmetry, feature order and reusing common features to build design intent into the part.

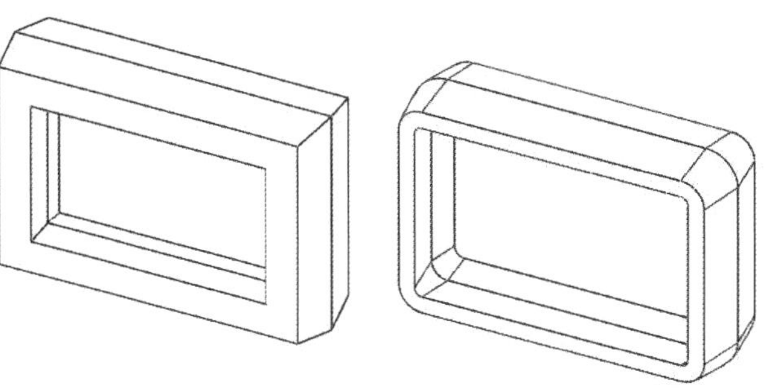

Example A: Feature Order.

Is the entire part symmetric?

Feature order affects the part. Apply the Shell feature before the Fillet feature and the inside corners remain perpendicular.

4. Design Intent in the Assembly

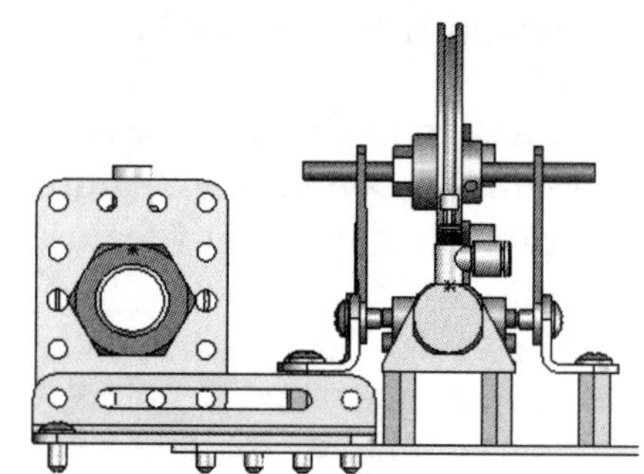

Utilizing symmetry, reusing common parts and using the Mate relationship between parts builds the design intent into an assembly.

Example A: Reuse Geometry in an assembly.

The PNEUMATIC-TEST-MODULE Assembly contains a Linear Pattern of holes. Insert one SCREW into the first hole. Utilize the Component Pattern tool to copy the original SCREW to the other holes. Note: The original SCREW is known as the seed feature.

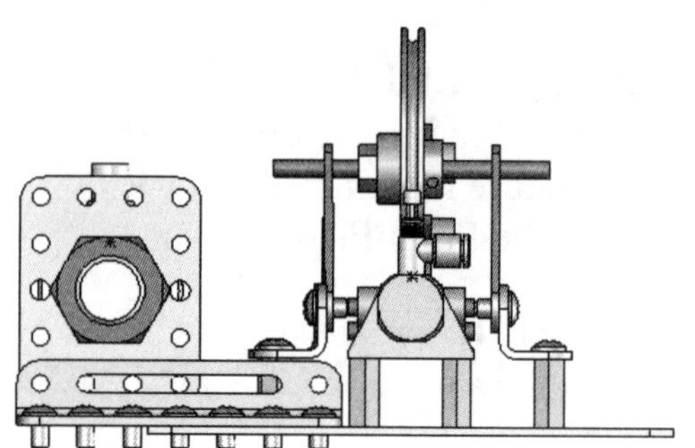

5. Design Intent in the Drawing

Utilize dimensions, tolerance and notes in parts and assemblies to build the design intent into the Drawing.

Example A: Tolerance and material in the drawing.

Insert an outside diameter tolerance +.000/-.002 into the TUBE part. The tolerance propagates to the drawing.

Define the Custom Property MATERIAL in the Part. The MATERIAL Custom Property propagates to the drawing.

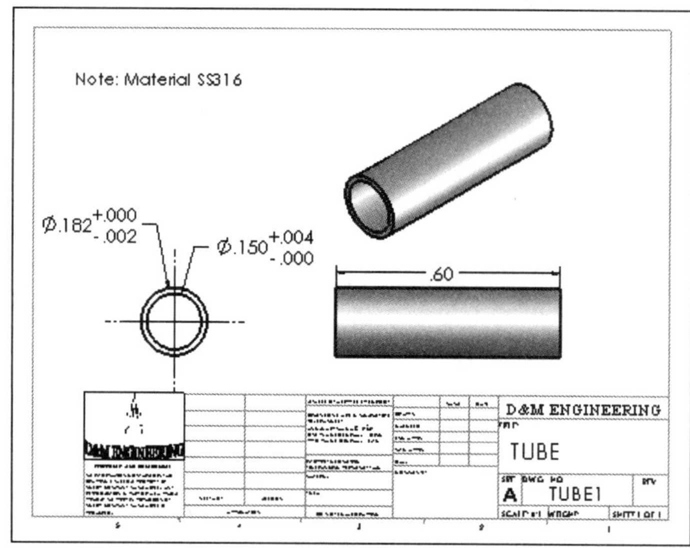

Additional information on the design process and design intent is available in SolidWorks Online Help.

Overview of Projects:

Project 1 - SolidWorks 2008 User Interface

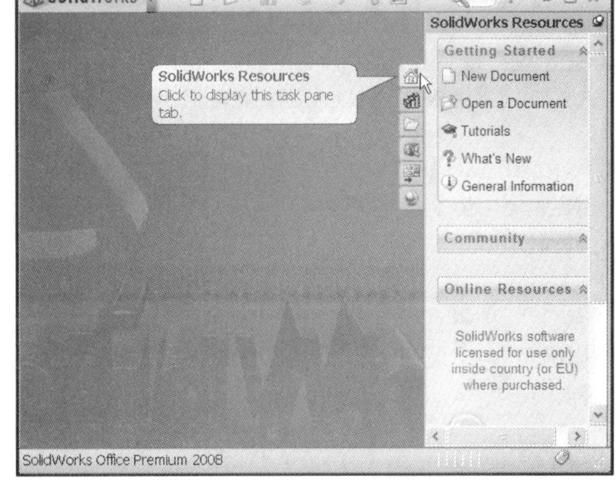

SolidWorks is a design software application used to model and create 2D and 3D sketches, 3D parts and assemblies, and 2D drawings. Project 1 introduces you to the SolidWorks 2008 User Interface and CommandManager: Menu bar toolbar, Menu bar menu, Drop-down menus, Context toolbars, Consolidated drop-down toolbars, System feedback icons, Confirmation Corner, Heads-up View toolbar, Document Properties, and more.

Project 2 – File Management, System Options, Templates, SolidWorks Explorer, and more

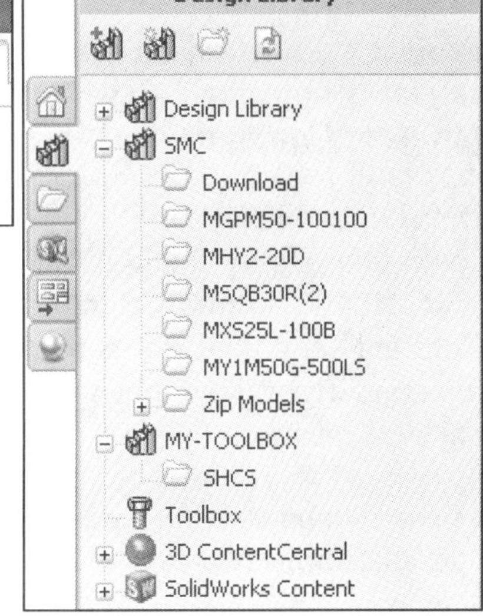

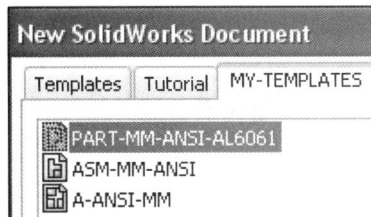

Create two templates:
ASM-MM-ANSI Assembly template and the PART-MM-ANSI-AL6061 Part template.

Create new SolidWorks File Locations: Document Templates, Reference Documents, and Design Library folders in the Task Pane.

Download a component from 3DContentCentral. Rename and save components using SolidWorks Explorer.

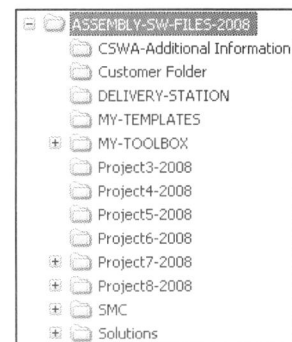

All initial and final models are located on the enclosed CD. All required 3DContentCentral components are located on the CD in the SMC folder.

Project 3 – Assembly Modeling – Bottom-up design approach

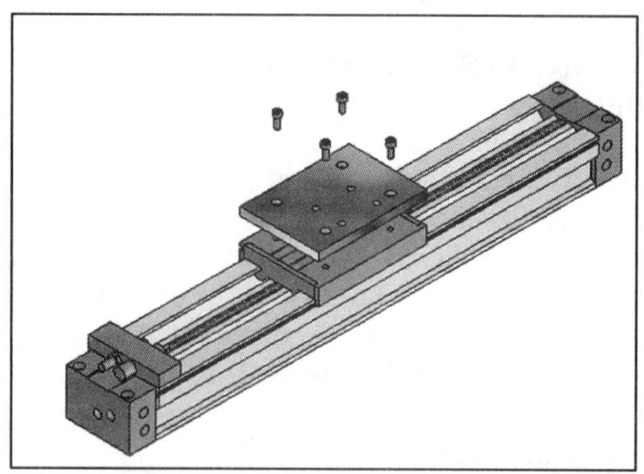

Develop the LINEAR-TRANSFER assembly. The LINEAR-TRANSFER assembly is the first assembly in the 3AXIS-TRANSFER assembly.

Create the following models: PLATE-A part, and the LINEAR-TRANSFER assembly.

Insert Standard Mates and SmartMates, along with four M8 x 1.25 Socket Head Cap Screws.

Apply the Design Library Toolbox and the Measure tool.

Project 4 – Bottom-up design assembly approach – Two Levels of Configurations

Modify Configurations

	RODLESS-CYLINDER-1@test1		Socket Head Cap Screw AM-1@test1	
	Suppress	Configuration	Suppress	Configuration
Default	☐	MY1M50G-	☑	B18.3.1M -
Extended	☐	Extended	☑	B18.3.1M -
Fastener	☐	MY1M50G-	☐	B18.3.1M -
Normal	☐	Normal	☑	B18.3.1M -
< Creates a new configuration. >				

OK Cancel Help

Develop two levels of configurations for the RODLESS-CYLINDER assembly using the Configure component tool to illustrate dynamic motion and physical location.

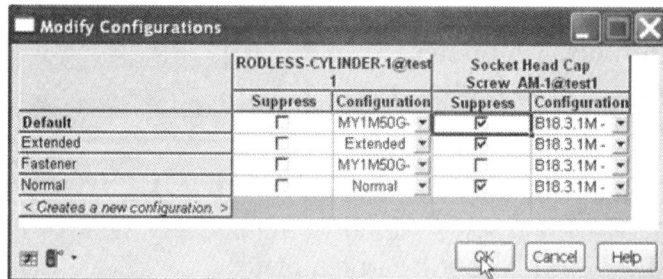

Create two new RODLESS-CYLINDER configurations: *Normal*, and *Extended.*

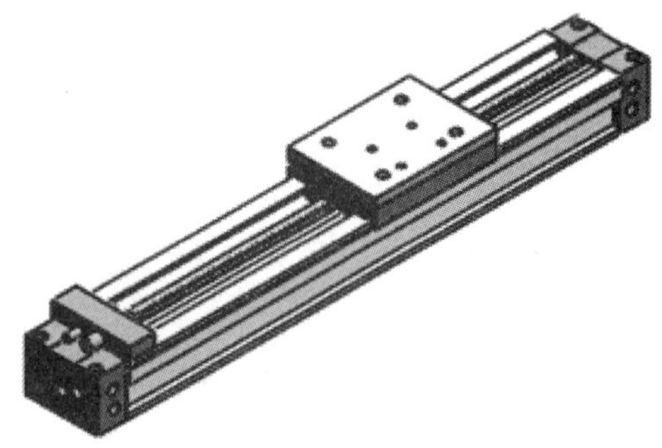

Create three new configurations for the LINEAR-TRANSFER assembly: *Normal, Extended*, and *Fastener*.

Insert a Derived Feature Component Pattern and apply the Collision Detection tool.

Project 5 – Top-down design assembly approach – Two Components with Configurations

Modify Configurations

	GUIDE CYLINDER-1@2AXIS-TRANSFER		SLIDE-TABLE-1@2AXIS-TRANSFER	
	Suppress	Configurati	Suppress	Configurati
Default		MGPM50-1		MXS25L-1
Extended-Extended		Extended		Extended
Extended-Normal		Extended		Normal
Normal-Extended		Normal		Extended
Normal-Normal		Normal		Normal
< Creates a new configuration. >				

OK Cancel Help

Create the 2AXIS-TRANSFER assembly. Design the PLATE-B part In-Context of the GUIDE-CYLINDER and SLIDE-TABLE assemblies.

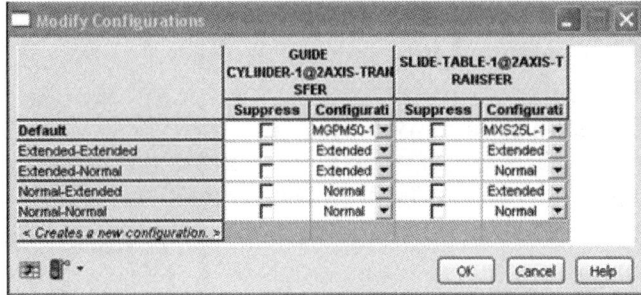

Utilize the Configure dimension tool to create new configurations for the GUIDE-CYLINDER and SLIDE-TABLE.

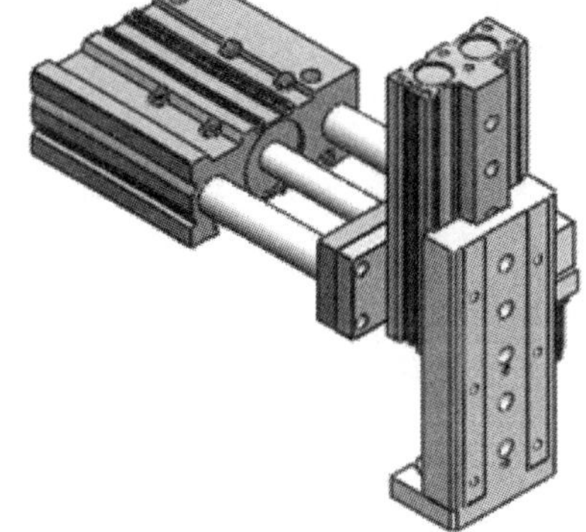

Utilize the Configure component tool to create configurations for the new 2AXIS-TRANSFER assembly. The 2AXIS-TRANSFER assembly is the second component in the 3AXIS-TRANSFER assembly.

Obtain knowledge of In-Context methods used in Top-down Assembly modeling, Out-of-Context components, External References and InPlace Mates.

Project 6 – Part and Assembly Configurations, Custom Properties, Design Tables, & References

Create the ROTARY-GRIPPER assembly. The ROTARY-GRIPPER assembly is the third component in the 3AXIS-TRANSFER assembly.

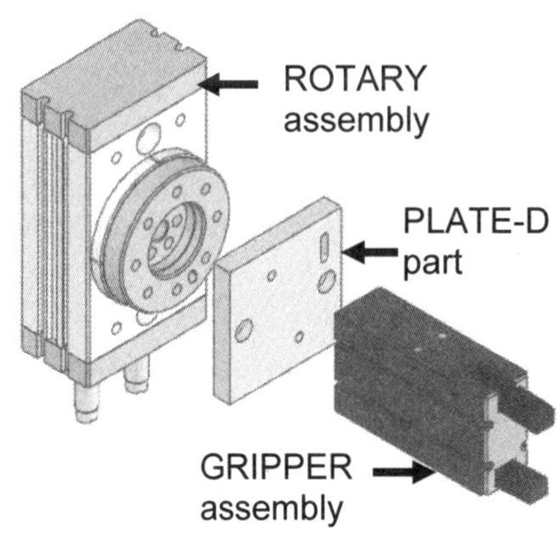

ROTARY-GRIPPER assembly

Create the PLATE-C part. Insert the PLATE-C part into the 2AXIS-TRANSFER assembly with no External References.

Create the PLATE-D part In-Context of the ROTARY and GRIPPER assembly. Delete all InPlace Mates.

Utilize the Add Configuration tool and the Design Table tool to create multi configurations in the ROTARY assembly, ROTARY-GRIPPER assembly, and the PLATE-D part.

Develop Custom Properties for the PLATE-D part.

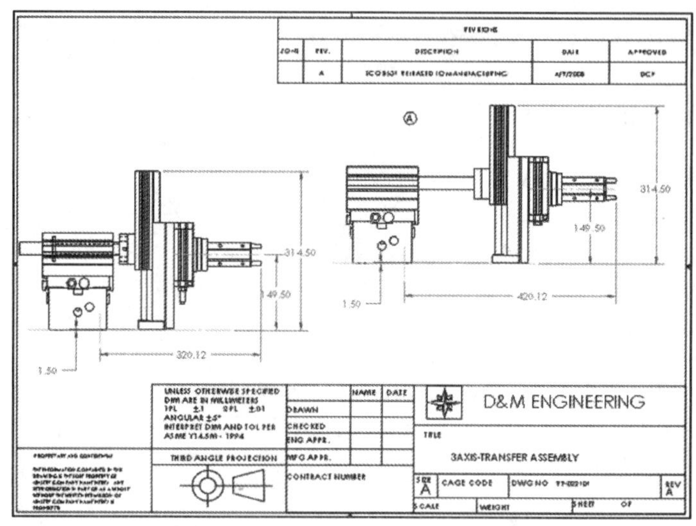

Project 7 – Assembly Drawings with Revision Table and Bill of Materials – Multiple Sheets, Views, and Custom Properties

Create the 3AXIS-TRANSFER assembly. Utilize the Configure Component tool to create eight position configurations and a Fastener configuration using the following assemblies: *LINEAR-TRANSFER, 2AXIS-TRANSFER,* and the *ROTARY-GRIPPER.*

Create the 3AXIS-TRANSFER drawing. Insert Fasteners into the 3AXIS-TRANSFER assembly.

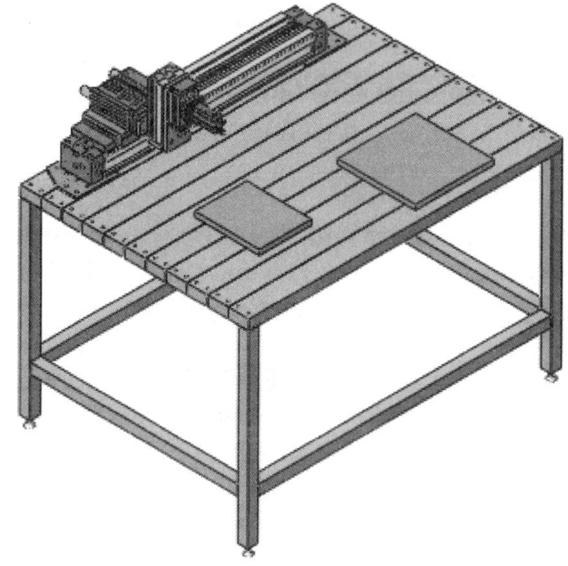

Insert Custom Properties to the components in the 3AXIS-TRANSFER assembly. Apply the Replace Component tool to the 3AXIS-TRANSFER assembly. Develop an Exploded Isometric View, Linked Notes, Revision Table, and Bill of Materials in the drawing. Create multiple configurations and multiple sheets.

Project 8 – Top-down design, Layout Sketches, Block, Motion, and more

Create the final DELIVERY-STATION assembly utilizing the Top-down assembly approach. Create the INPUT-BASE-PLATE part and reordered components in the assembly.

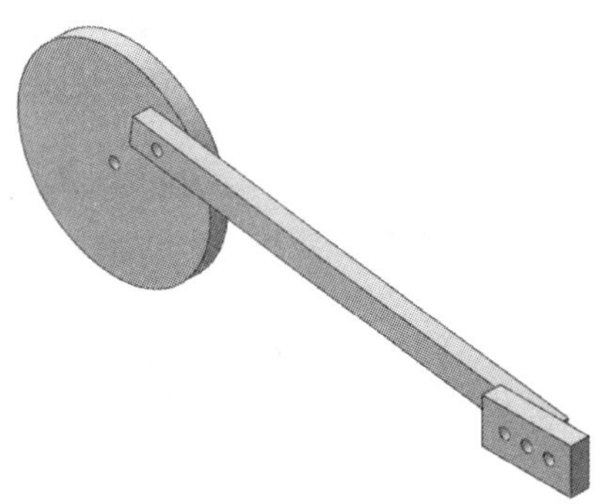

Create Link Values and apply Equations to control relationships along with using the Component Pattern tool, Mirror Components tool, Explode Line Sketch tool, Join feature, and Split feature.

Create two Motion Studies using the Linear motor, Rotary motor, and gravity options.

Apply the Layout-based assembly design with blocks to create motion. The AssemblyXpert tool, and envelopes are explored.

About the Book

The following conventions are used throughout this book. The term document is used to refer a SolidWorks part, drawing, or assembly file.

The list of items across the top of the SolidWorks interface is the Menu bar menu or the Menu bar toolbar. Each item in the Menu bar has a pull-down menu. When you need to select a series of commands from these menus, the following format is used: Click **View**, check **Origins** from the Menu bar menu. The Origins are displayed in the Graphics window.

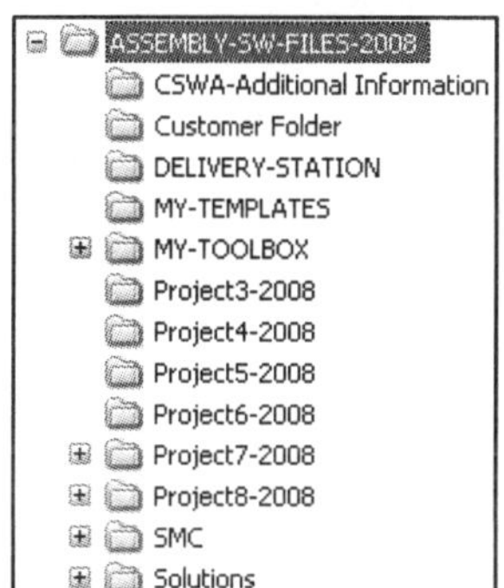

The book is organized into eight Projects. Each Project is focused on a specific subject or feature: Example: Top-down, Bottom-up, Configurations, Design Tables, drawings, etc.

Copy the files and folders from the CD in the book. Work from your hard drive. The CD provides the needed initial and final (solution) models for each Projects.

The book was written using Windows XP Professional SP2 with SolidWorks Premium 2008 version SP2.1.

An additional section on the CSWA exam in a pdf format is provided in the CSWA-Additional Information folder.

You can either take the CSWA exam in SolidWorks 2007 or SolidWorks 2008.

Command Syntax

The following command syntax is utilized throughout the text. Commands that require you to perform an action are displayed in **Bold** text.

Format:	Convention:	Example:
Bold	All commands actions. Selected icon button. Selected geometry: line, circle. Value entries.	Click **Options** from the Menu bar toolbar. Click **Corner Rectangle** from the Sketch toolbar. Click the **center point**. Enter **3.0** for Radius.
Capitalized	Filenames. First letter in a feature name.	**Save** the 2AXIS-TRANSFER assembly. Click the **Extruded Base** tool from the Features toolbar.

Windows Terminology

The mouse buttons provide an integral role in executing SolidWorks commands. The mouse buttons execute commands, select geometry, display Shortcut menus and provide information feedback. The table below contains a summary of mouse button terminology:

Item:	Description:
Click	Press and release the left mouse button.
Double-click	Double press and release the left mouse button.
Click inside	Press the left mouse button. Wait a second, and then press the left mouse button inside the text box. Use this technique to modify Feature names in the FeatureManager design tree.
Drag	Point to an object, press and hold the left mouse button down. Move the mouse pointer to a new location. Release the left mouse button.
Right-click	Press and release the right mouse button. A Shortcut menu is displayed. Use the left mouse button to select a menu command.
ToolTip	Position the mouse pointer over an Icon (button). The tool name is displayed below the mouse pointer.
Large ToolTip	Position the mouse pointer over an Icon (button). The mouse pointer displays the tool name and a description of its functionality below the Icon.
Mouse pointer feedback	Position the mouse pointer over various areas of the sketch, part, assembly or drawing. The cursor provides feedback depending on the geometry.
Window-select	To select multiple items, position the mouse pointer in an upper corner location. Drag the mouse pointer to the opposite corner. Release the mouse pointer. The bounding box contains the selected items.

A mouse with a center wheel provides additional functionality in SolidWorks. Roll the center wheel downward to enlarge the model in the Graphics window. Hold the center wheel down. Drag the mouse in the Graphics window to rotate the model. Review various Windows terminology that describes: menus, toolbars, and commands that constitute the graphical user interface in SolidWorks.

SolidWorks System requirements for Microsoft Windows Operating Systems and hardware are as illustrated.

System Requirements

System requirements for our **Mechanical Design** (SolidWorks), **Design Validation** (COSMOS), **File Management** (SolidWorks Explorer) and **Collaboration** (eDrawings)(3).

For **Data Management** (PDMWorks Wrokgroup and Enterprise) products, **Click Here**.

Microsoft® Windows® Supported Operating Systems (9)

	SolidWorks 2005	SolidWorks 2006	SolidWorks 2007	SolidWorks 2008
Vista (32-bit)	✗	✗	✗	✓
XP Professional (32-bit) (1)	✓	✓	✓	✓
XP Professional (64-bit)	✓ (4, 5, 7)	✓ (4)	✓	✓
2000 Professional (2)	✓	✓	✗	✗

Your default system document templates may be different if you are a new user of SolidWorks 2008 vs. an existing user who has upgraded from a previous version.

There are slight screen and toolbar variations between the various versions and products of SolidWorks: Student Edition, SolidWorks Office, SolidWorks Office Professional, and SolidWorks Office Premium.

Notes:

Project 1

SolidWorks 2008 User Interface

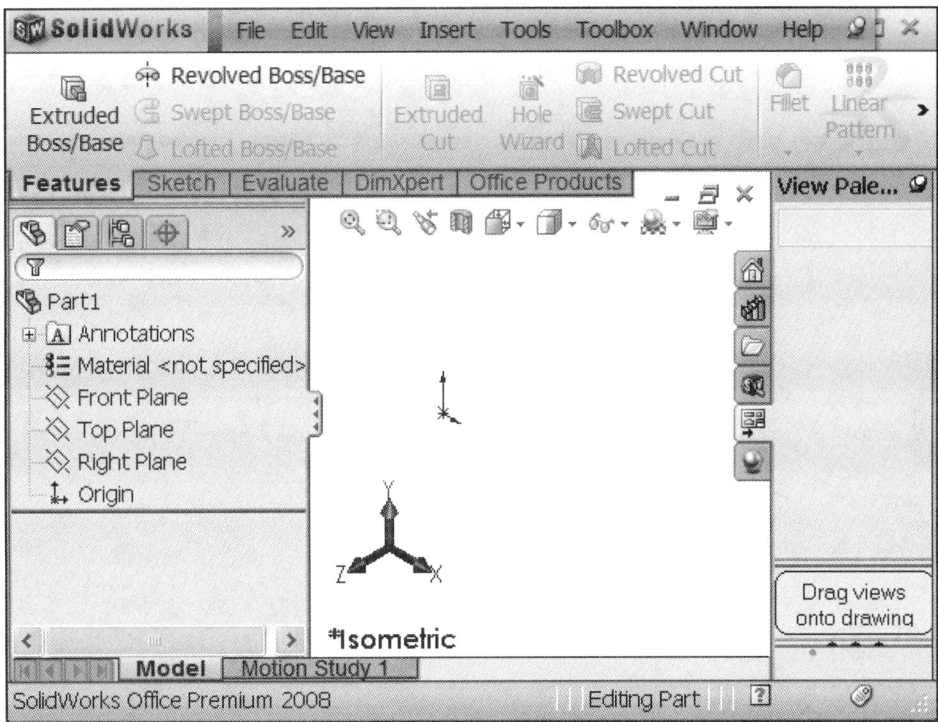

Below are the desired outcomes and usage competencies based on the completion of Project 1.

Project Desired Outcomes:	Usage Competencies:
• A comprehensive understanding of the SolidWorks 2008 User Interface and CommandManager.	• Ability to establish a SolidWorks session. • Aptitude to apply and use the following: Menu bar toolbar, Menu bar menu, Drop-down menus, Context toolbars, Consolidated drop-down toolbars, System feedback icons, Confirmation Corner, Heads-up View toolbar, Document Properties and more.

Notes:

Project 1-SolidWorks 2008 User Interface

Project Overview

SolidWorks is a design software application used to model and create 2D and 3D sketches, 3D parts and assemblies, and 2D drawings. Project 1 introduces you to the SolidWorks 2008 User Interface and CommandManager: *Menu bar toolbar, Menu bar menu, Drop-down menus, Context toolbars, Consolidated drop-down toolbars, System feedback icons, Confirmation Corner, Heads-up View toolbar, Document Properties and more.*

On the completion of this project, you will be able to:

- Establish a SolidWorks session.
- Know the SolidWorks 2008 User Interface.
- Recognize the default Reference Planes in the FeatureManager.
- Comprehend and apply the Task Pane.
- Recognize the default CommandManager for a Part, Assembly, and Drawing document.
- Create a Motion Study.

Start a SolidWorks Session

The SolidWorks application is located in the Programs folder. SolidWorks displays the Tip of the Day box. Read the Tip of the Day every day to obtain additional information on SolidWorks.

Create a new part. Click **File, New** from the Menu bar menu or click **New** from the Menu bar toolbar. There are two options for a new document: *Novice* and *Advanced.* Select the Advanced option. Select the Part document.

Activity: Start a SolidWorks Session

Start a SolidWorks 2008 session.

1) Click **Start** on the Windows Taskbar.

2) Click **All Programs**.

3) Click the **SolidWorks 2008** folder.

4) Click **SolidWorks 2008** application. The SolidWorks program window opens. Note: Do not open a document at this time.

If available, double-click the SolidWorks 2008 icon on the Windows Desktop to start a SolidWorks session.

Read the Tip of the Day dialog box.

5) If you do not see this screen, click the SolidWorks **Resources** icon on the right side of the Graphics window located in the Task Pane.

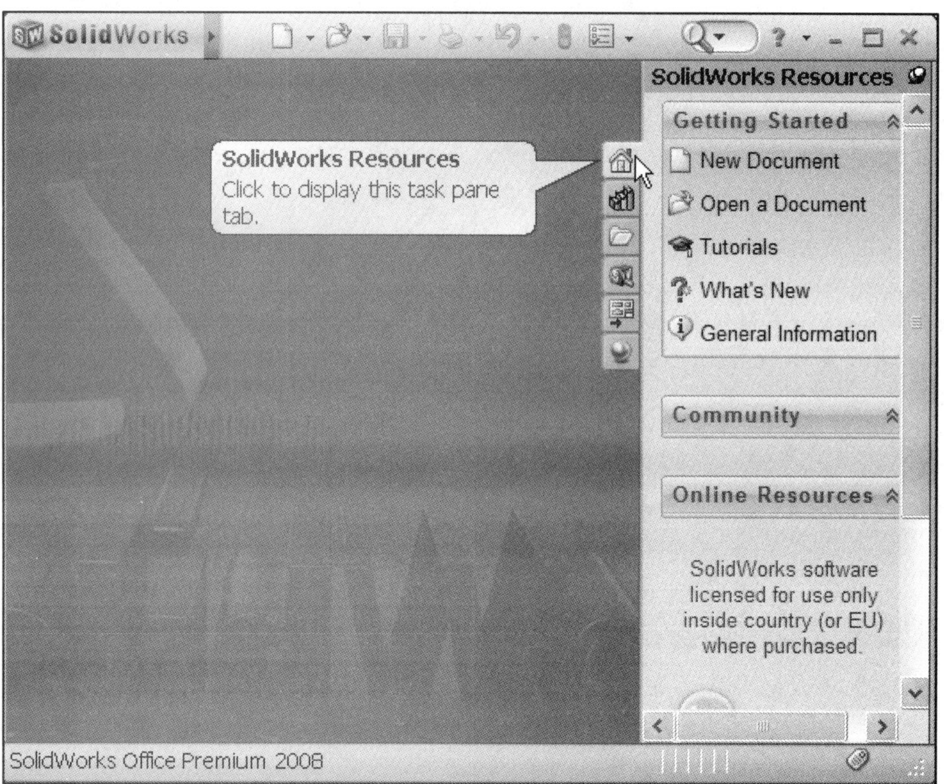

Activity: Understanding the SolidWorks UI and CommandManager

Menu bar toolbar

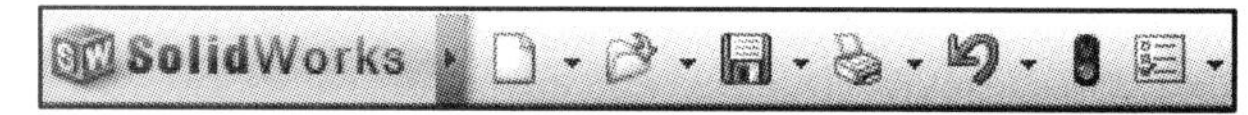

SolidWorks 2008 (UI) is redesign to make maximum use of the Graphics window area. The default Menu bar toolbar contains a set of the most frequently used tool buttons from the Standard toolbar. The available tools are:

- **New** – Creates a new document.
- **Open** – Opens an existing document.
- **Save** – Saves an active document.
- **Print** – Prints an active document.

- **Undo** – Reverses the last action.
- **Rebuild** – Rebuilds the active part, assembly, or drawing.
- **Options** – Changes system options and Add-Ins for SolidWorks.

Menu bar menu

Click SolidWorks in the Menu bar toolbar to display the Menu bar menu. SolidWorks provides a Context-sensitive menu structure. The menu titles remain the same for all types of documents; (part, assembly, and drawing) but the menu items change depending on which type of document is active.

Example: The Insert menu includes features in part documents, mates in assembly documents, and drawing views in drawing documents. The display of the menu is also dependent on the work flow customization that you have selected. The default menu items for an active document are: *File*, *Edit*, *View*, *Insert*, *Tools*, *Window*, *Help*, and *Pin*.

The Pin tool displays the Menu bar toolbar and the Menu bar menu as illustrated. Throughout the book, the Menu bar menu and the Menu bar toolbar is referred to as the Menu bar.

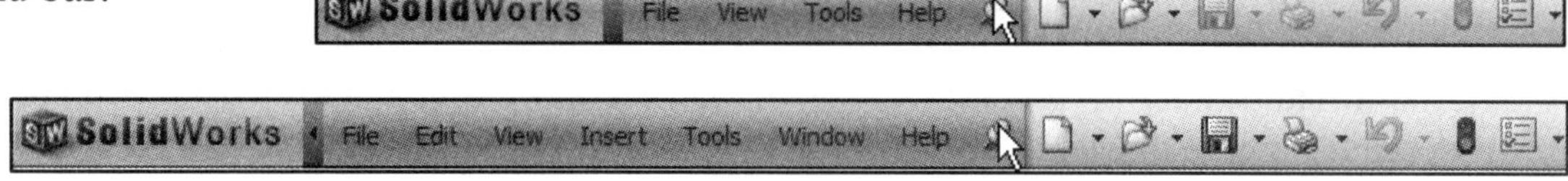

Drop-down menus

SolidWorks takes advantage of the familiar Microsoft® Windows® user interface. Communicate with SolidWorks either through the drop-down menu, pop-up menu, shortcut toolbar, flyout toolbar or the CommandManager. A command is an instruction that informs SolidWorks to perform a task.

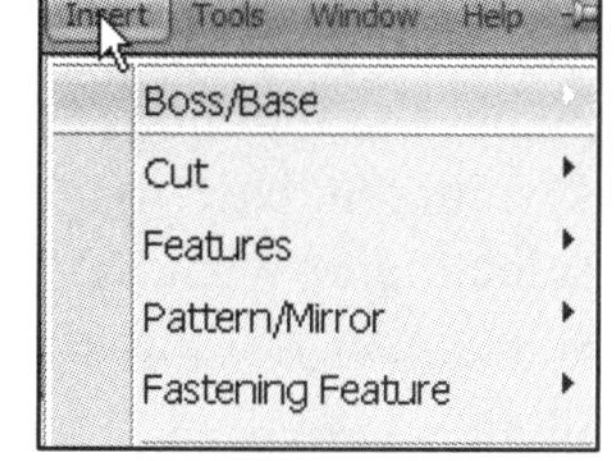

In SolidWorks, each part, assembly, and drawing is referred to as a document, and each document is displayed in a separate window.

To close a SolidWorks drop-down menu, press the Esc key. You can also click any other section in the SolidWorks Graphics window, or click another drop-down menu.

Right-click Pop-up menus

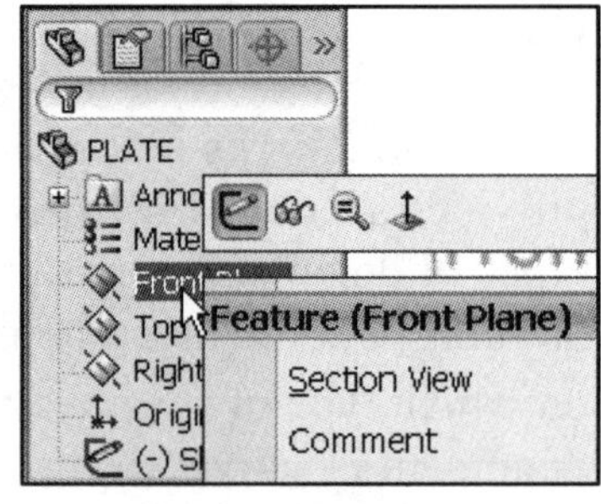

Right-click in the Graphics window either on a model, or in the FeatureManager on a feature or sketch to display a Context-sensitive shortcut toolbar. If you are in the middle of a command, the toolbar displays a list of options specifically related to that command.

Flyout tool buttons / Consolidated menus

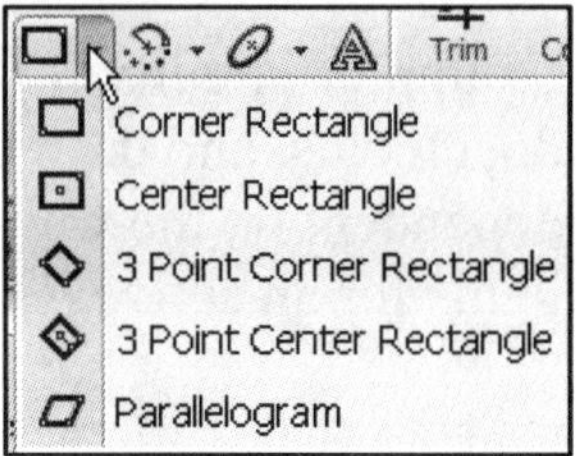

Similar commands are grouped into flyout buttons on toolbars and the CommandManager. Example: Variations of the rectangle tool are consolidated together in a button with a flyout control as illustrated. Select the drop-down arrow and view the available tools.

If you select the flyout button without expanding:

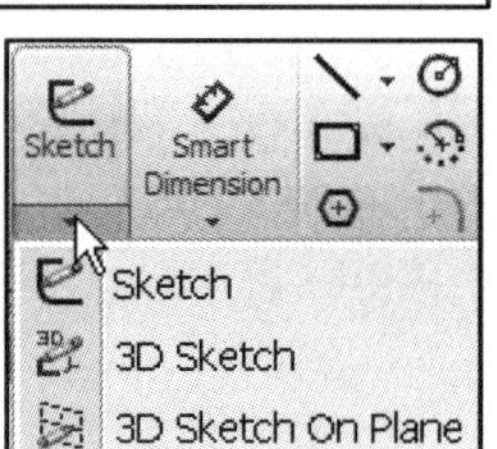

- For some commands such as Sketch, the most commonly used command is performed. This command is the first listed and the command shown on the button.
- For commands such as rectangle, where you may want to repeatedly create the same variant of the rectangle, the last used command is performed. This is the highlighted command when the flyout tool is expanded.

System feedback icons

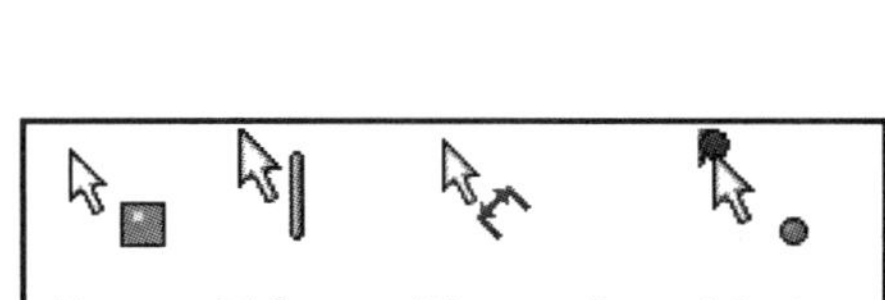

SolidWorks provides system feedback by attaching a symbol to the mouse pointer cursor arrow. The system feedback symbol indicates what you are selecting or what the system is expecting you to select. As you move the mouse pointer across your model, system feedback is provided.

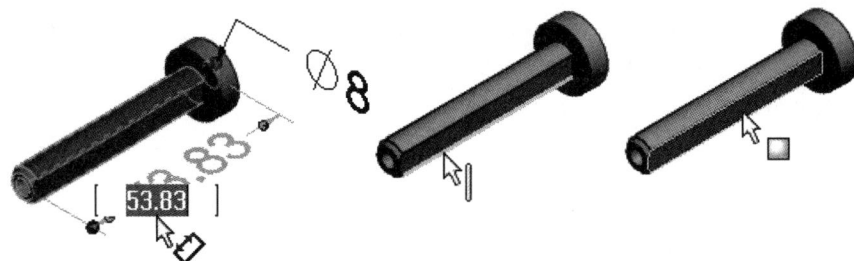

Confirmation Corner

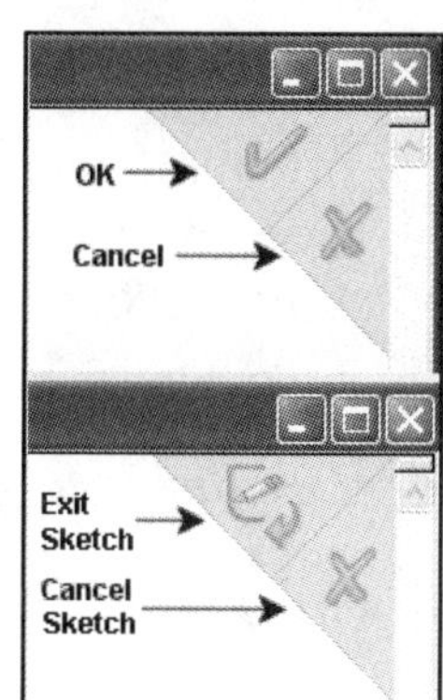

When numerous SolidWorks commands are active, a symbol or a set of symbols are displayed in the upper right corner of the Graphics window. This area is called the Confirmation Corner.

When a sketch is active, the confirmation corner box displays two symbols. The first symbol is the sketch tool icon. The second symbol is a large red X. These three symbols supply a visual reminder that you are in an active sketch. Click the sketch symbol icon to exit the sketch and to saves any changes that you made.

When other commands are active, the confirmation corner box provides a green check mark and a large red X. Use the green check mark to execute the current command. Use the large red X to cancel the command.

Heads-up View toolbar

SolidWorks provides the user with numerous view options from the Standard Views, View, and Heads-up View toolbar.

The Heads-up View toolbar is a transparent toolbar that is displayed in the Graphics window when a document is active. You can't hide nor move the Heads-up View toolbar. The following views are available:

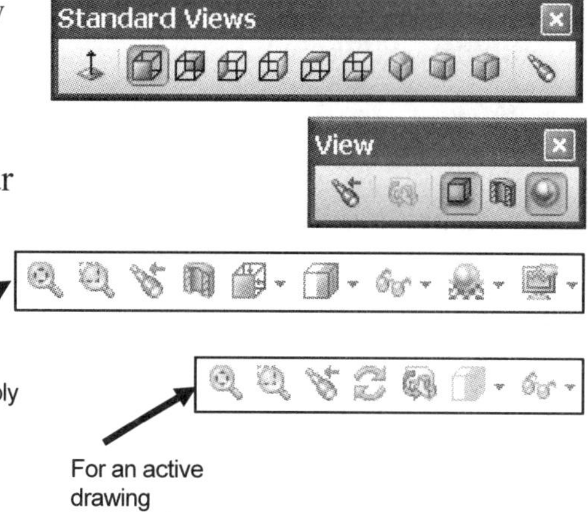

Views in the Heads-up View toolbar are document dependent.

- *Zoom to Fit* : Zooms the model to fit the Graphics window.
- *Zoom to Area* : Zooms to the areas you select with a bounding box.
- *Previous View* : Displays the previous view.
- *Section View* : Displays a cutaway of a part or assembly, using one or more cross section planes.

- *View Orientation*: Provides the ability to select a view orientation or the number of viewports. The available options are: *Top, Isometric, Trimetric, Dimetric, Left, Front, Right, Back, Bottom, Single view, Two view - Horizontal, Two view - Vertical, Four view.*

- *Display Style*: Provides the ability to display the style for the active view. The available options are: *Wireframe, Hidden Lines Visible, Hidden Lines Removed, Shaded, Shaded With Edges.*

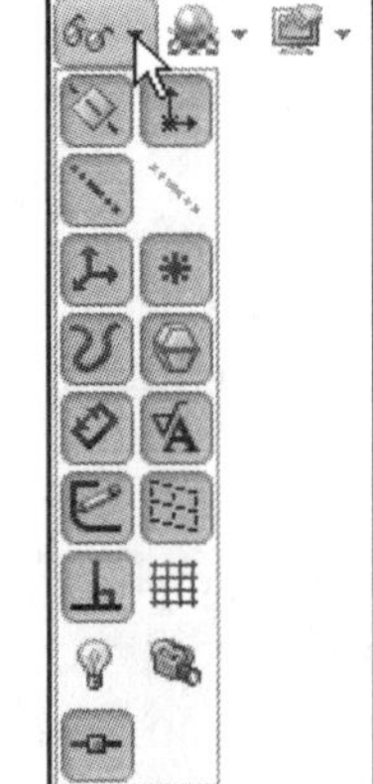

- *Hide/Show Items*: Provides the ability to select items to hide or show in the Graphics window. Note: The available items are document dependent.

- *Apply Scene*: Provides the ability to apply a scene to an active part or assembly document. View the available options.

- *View Setting*: Provides the ability to select the following: *RealView Graphics, Shadows in Shaded Mode*, and *Perspective.*

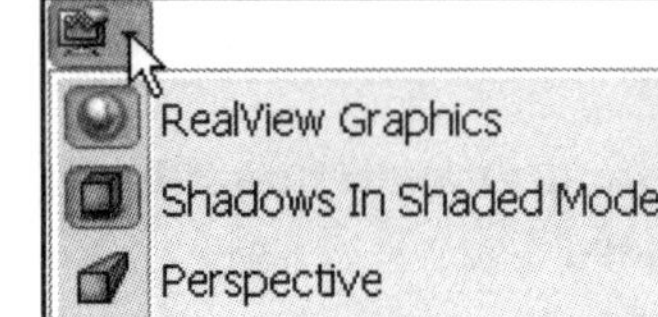

- *Rotate*: Provides the ability to rotate a drawing view.

- *3D Drawing View*: Provides the ability to dynamically manipulate the drawing view to make a selection.

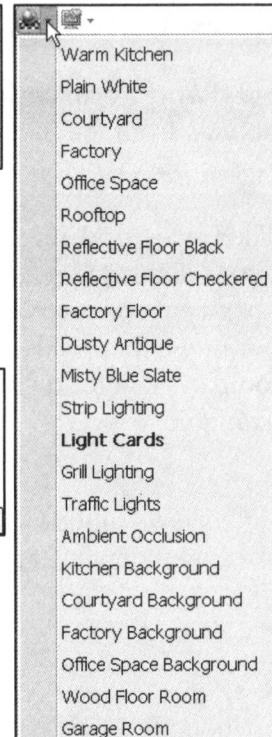

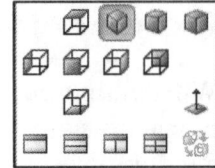

For 2008 the Heads-up View toolbar replaces the Reference triad in the lower left corner of the Graphics window.

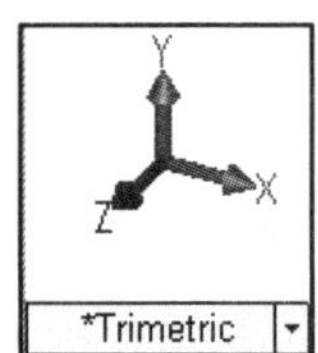

The default document setting displays reference planes and the grid in the Graphics window. To deactivate the reference planes for an active document, click **View**, uncheck **Planes** from the Menu bar. To deactivate the grid, click **Options**, **Document Properties** tab. Click **Grid/Snaps**, uncheck the **Display grid** box.

To deactivate a single reference plane in an active document, right-click the **selected plane**, click **Hide**.

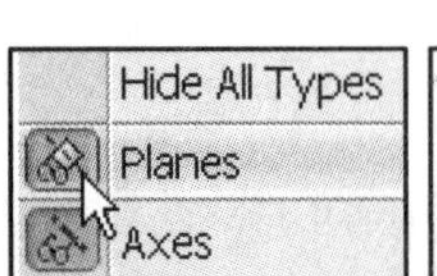

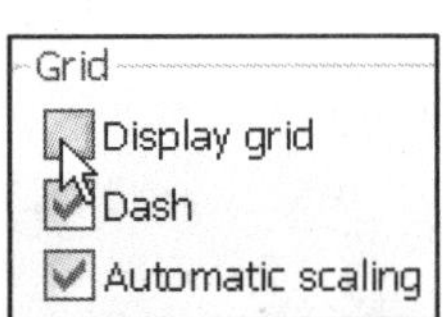

CommandManager

The CommandManager is document dependent. Drop-down tabs are located on the bottom left side of the CommandManager and display the available toolbars and features for each corresponding tab. The default part tabs are: *Features*, *Sketch*, *Evaluate*, *DimXpert*, and *Office Products*.

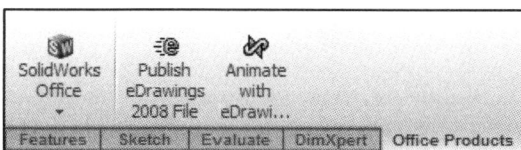

Below is an illustrated CommandManager for a default Part document.

The Office Products toolbar display is dependent on the activated Add-Ins.. during a SolidWorks session.

If you have SolidWorks Office, SolidWorks Office Professional, or SolidWorks Office Premium, the Office Products tab is displayed in the CommandManager. The book was written with SolidWorks Office Premium using version SP2.1.

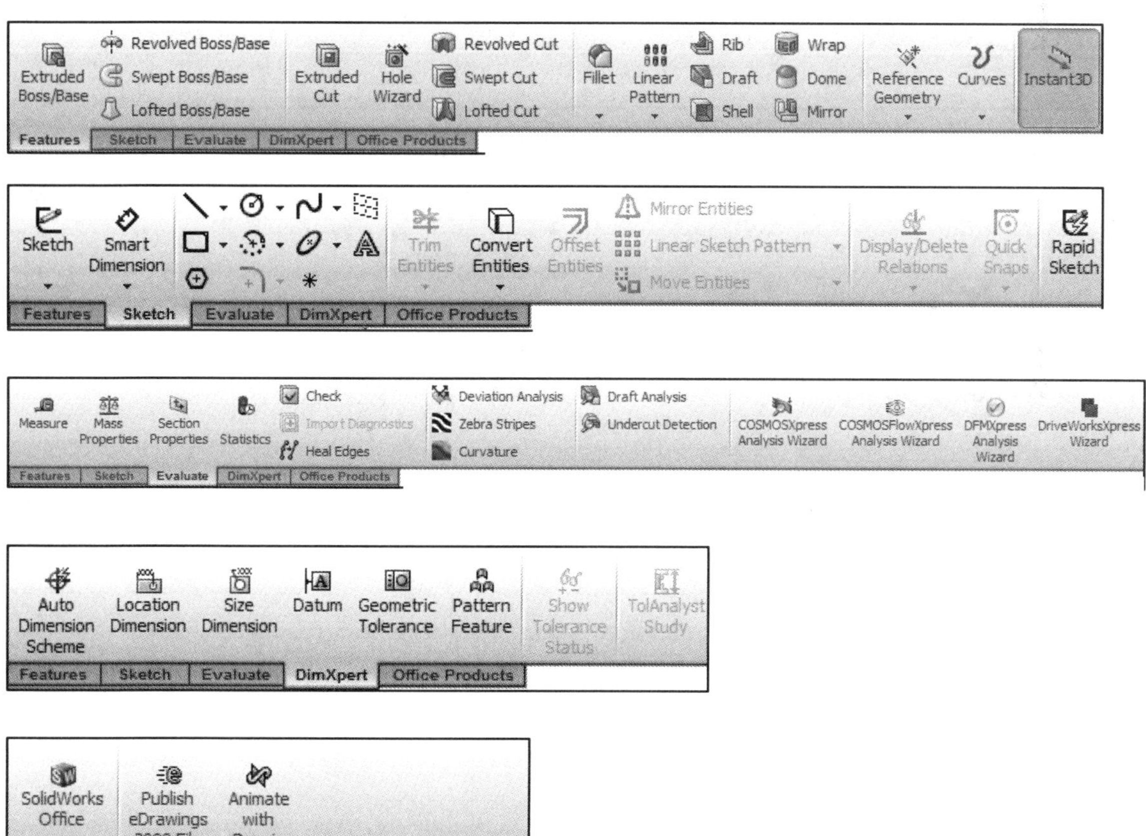

Below is an illustrated CommandManager for a default Assembly document. The default tabs are: *Assembly, Layout*, *Sketch*, *Evaluate*, and *Office Products*.

The Office Products toolbar display is dependent on the activated Add-Ins.. during a SolidWorks session.

If you have SolidWorks Office, SolidWorks Office Professional, or SolidWorks Office Premium, the Office Products tab is displayed in the CommandManager. The book was written with SolidWorks Office Premium using version SP2.1.

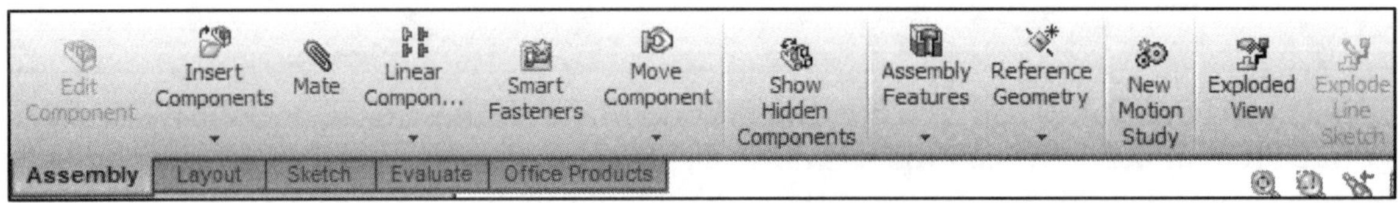

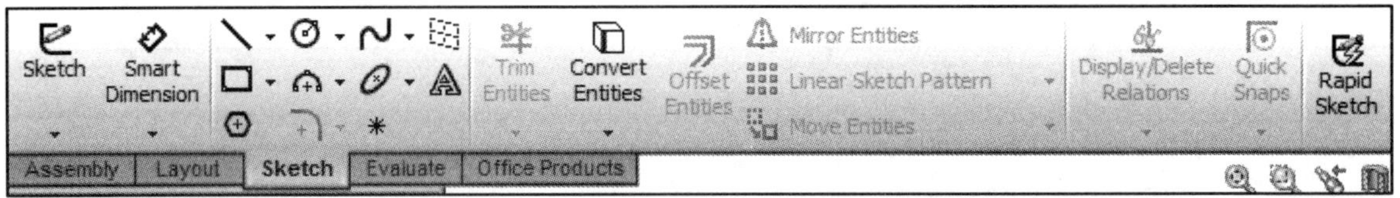

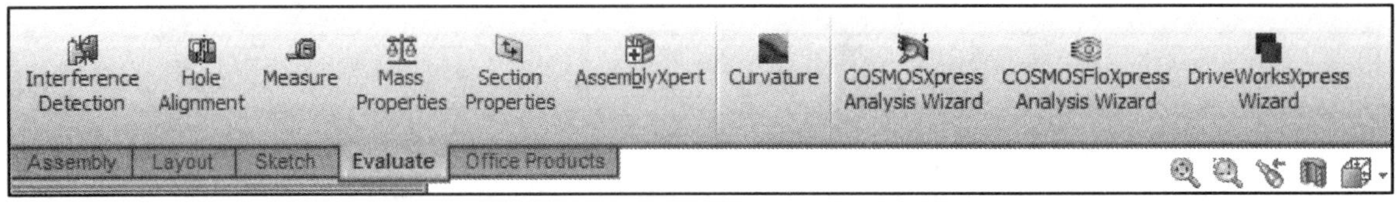

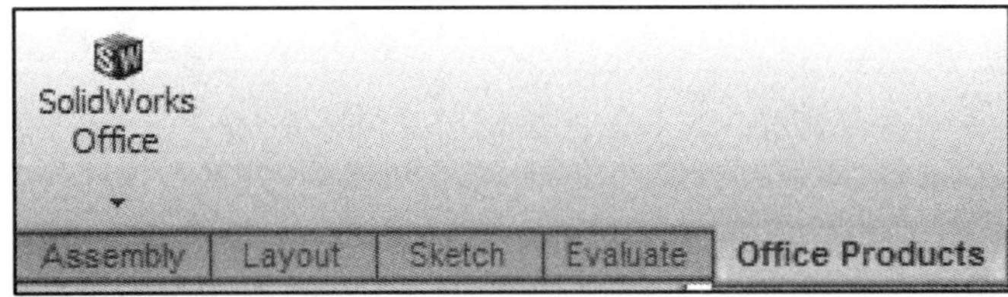

Below is an illustrated CommandManager for a default Drawing document. The default tabs are: *View Layout*, *Annotation*, *Sketch*, *Evaluate*, and *Office Products*.

The Office Products toolbar display is dependent on the activated Add-Ins.. during a SolidWorks session.

If you have SolidWorks Office, SolidWorks Office Professional, or SolidWorks Office Premium, the Office Products tab is displayed in the CommandManager. The book was written with SolidWorks Office Premium using version SP2.1.

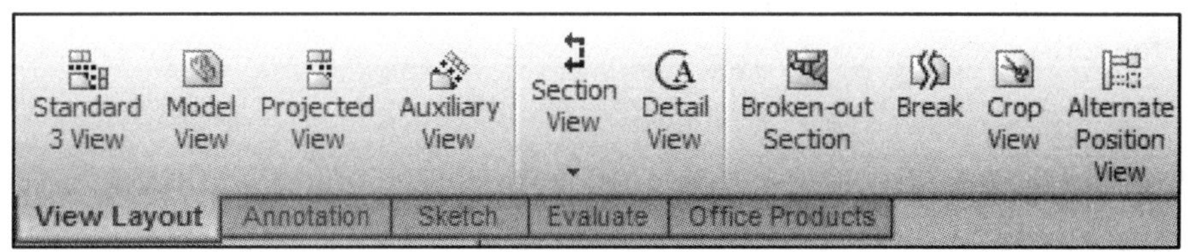

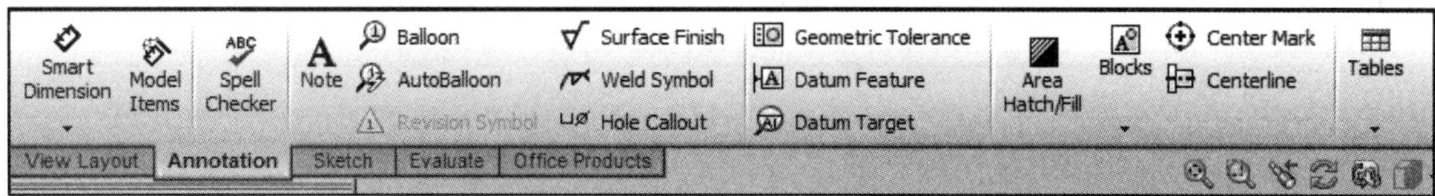

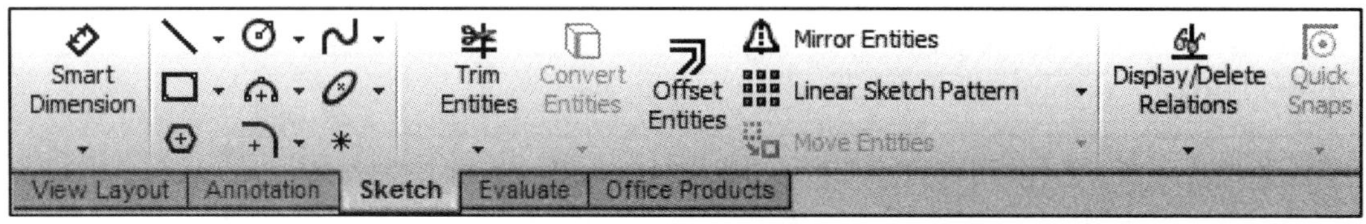

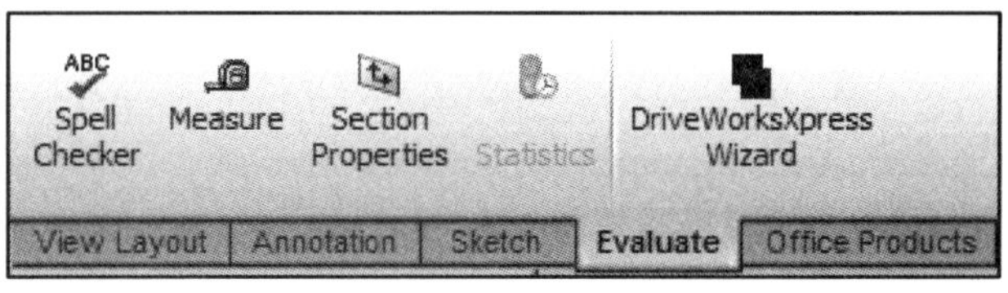

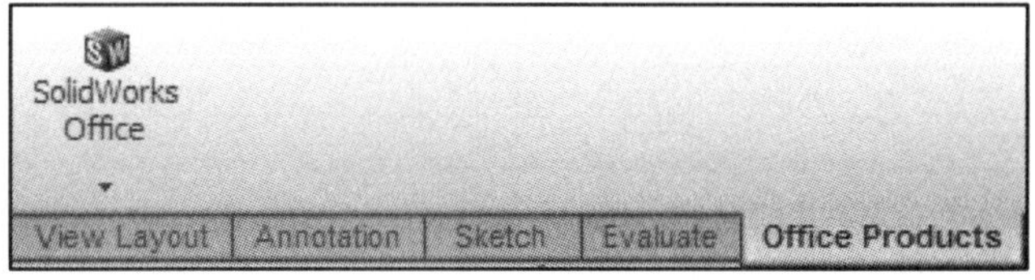

The tabs replace the Control areas buttons from pervious SolidWorks versions. The tabs that are displayed by default depend on the type of document open and the work flow customization that you have selected.

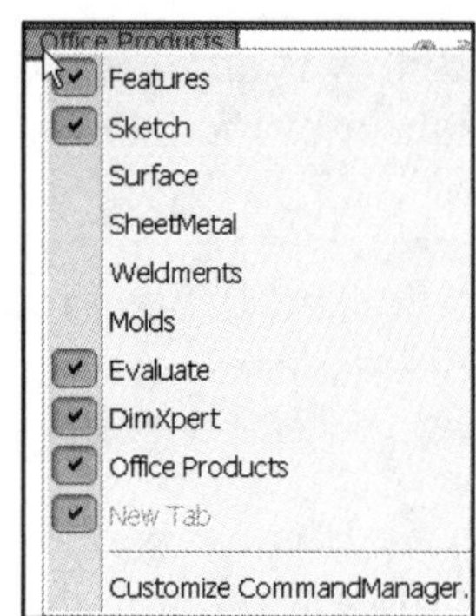

To customize the CommandManager tabs, right-click on a tab, and select the required custom option or select Customize CommandManager to access the Customize dialog box.

DimXpert for parts provides the ability to graphically check if the model is fully dimensioned and toleranced.

Both DimXpert for parts and drawings automatically recognize manufacturing features. Manufacturing features are *not SolidWorks features*. Manufacturing features are defined in 1.1.12 section of the ASME Y14.5M-1994 Dimensioning and Tolerancing standard as: "The general term applied to a physical portion of a part, such as a surface, hole or slot.

FeatureManager Design Tree

The FeatureManager design tree is located on the left side of the SolidWorks Graphics window. The design tree provides a summarize view of the active part, assembly, or drawing document. The tree displays the details on how the part, assembly, or drawing document is created.

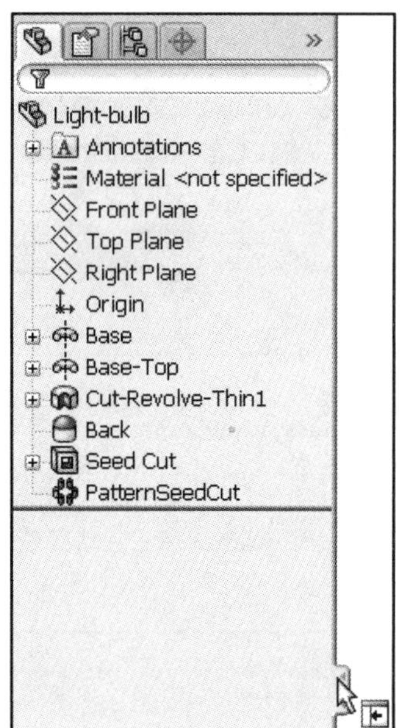

Understand the FeatureManager design tree to troubleshoot your model. The FeatureManager is use extensively throughout this book.

The FeatureManager consist of four default tabs:

- *FeatureManager design tree.*
- *PropertyManager.*
- *ConfigurationManager.*
- *DimXertManager.*

Select the Hide FeatureManager Tree Area arrows tab from the FeatureManager to enlarge the Graphics window for modeling.

Various commands provide the ability to control what is displayed in the FeatureManager design tree. They are:

1. Show or Hide FeatureManager items.

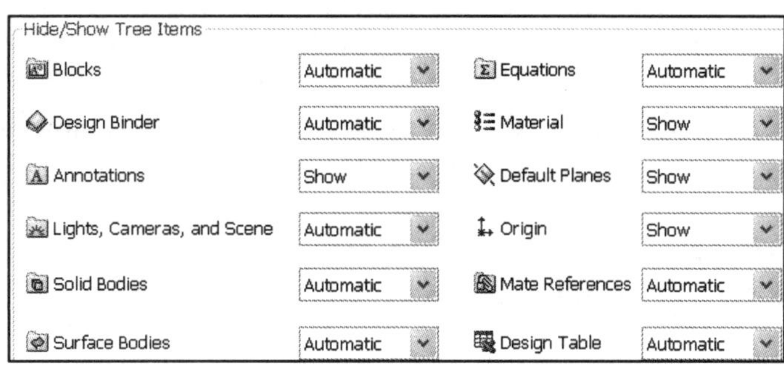

Click **Options** from the Menu Bar toolbar. Click **FeatureManager** from the System Options tab. Customize your FeatureManager from the Hide/Show Tree Items dialog box.

2. Filter the FeatureManager design tree. Enter information in the filter field. You can filter by: *Type of features, Feature names, Sketches, Folders*, *Mates*, *User-defined tags*, and *Custom properties*.

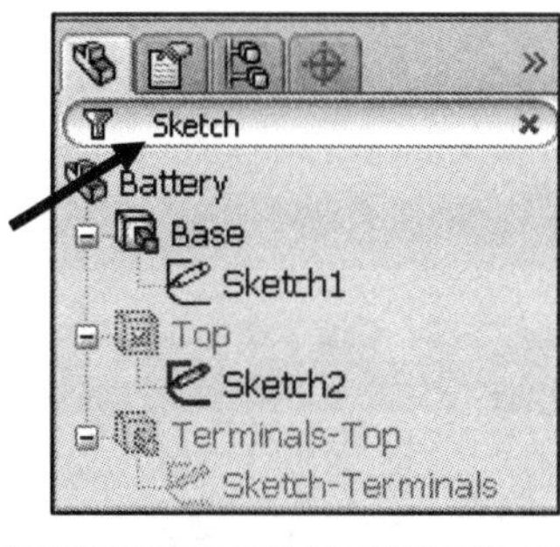

Tags are keywords you can add to a SolidWorks document to make them easier to filter and to search. The Tags icon is located in the bottom right corner of the Graphics window.

To collapse all items in the FeatureManager, **right-click** and select **Collapse items**, or press the **Shift +C** keys.

The FeatureManager design tree and the Graphics window are dynamically linked. Select sketches, features, drawing views, and construction geometry in either pane.

Split the FeatureManager and either display two FeatureManager instances, or combine the FeatureManager design tree with the ConfigurationManager or PropertyManager.

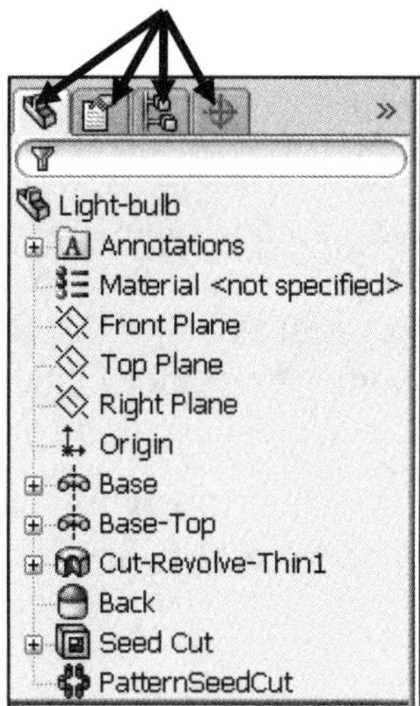

Move between the FeatureManager, PropertyManager, ConfigurationManager, and DimXertManager by selecting the tabs at the top of the menu.

The ConfigurationManager tab is located to the right of the FeatureManager tab. Use the ConfigurationManager to create, select, and view multiple configurations of parts and assemblies.

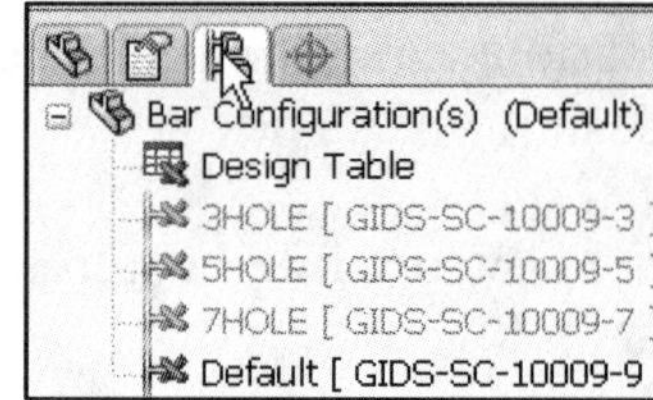

The icons in the ConfigurationManager denote whether the configuration was created manually or with a design table.

The DimXpertManager tab provides the ability to insert dimensions and tolerances manually or automatically.

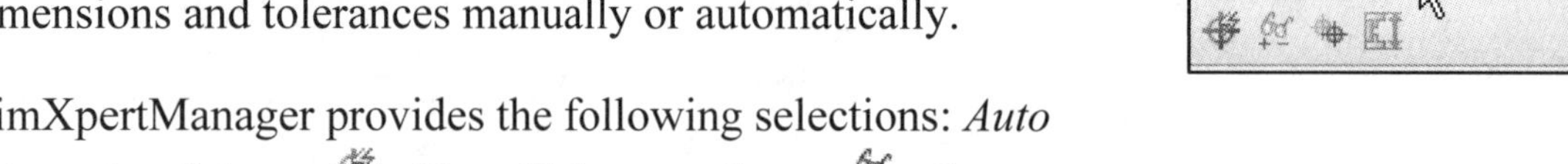

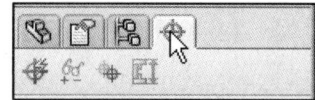

DimXpertManager provides the following selections: *Auto Dimension Scheme*, *Show Tolerance Status*, *Copy Scheme*, and *TolAnalyst Study*.

Fly-out FeatureManager

The fly-out FeatureManager design tree provides the ability to view and select items in the PropertyManager and the FeatureManager design tree at the same time.

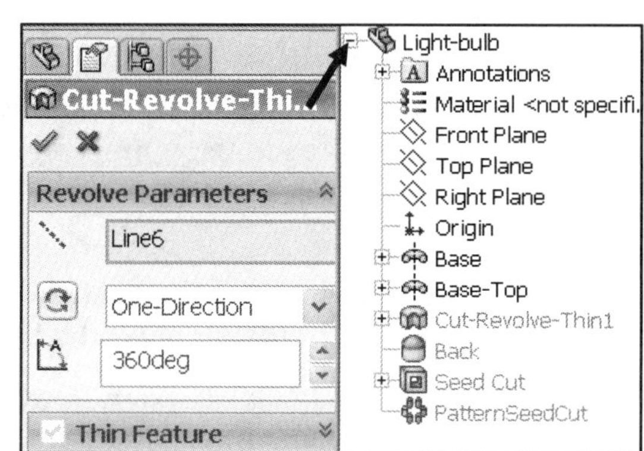

The fly-out FeatureManager provides the ability to select items which may be difficult to view or select from the Graphics window.

Throughout the book, you will select commands and command options from the drop-down menus, fly-out FeatureManager, shortcut toolbars, or from the SolidWorks toolbars.

Another method for accessing a command is to use the accelerator key. Accelerator keys are special keystrokes which activates the drop-down menu options. Some commands in the menu bar and items in the drop-down menus have an underlined character.

Press the Alt key followed by the corresponding key to the underlined character activates that command or option.

Task Pane

The Task Pane is displayed when a SolidWorks session starts. The Task Pane contains the following default tabs: *SolidWorks Resources*, *Design Library*, *File Explorer*, *SolidWorks Search*, *View Palette*, *RealView*, and *Document Recovery*.

The Document Recovery tab is only displayed in the Task Pane if your system terminates unexpectedly with an active document and if auto-recovery is enabled in the System Options section.

SolidWorks Resources

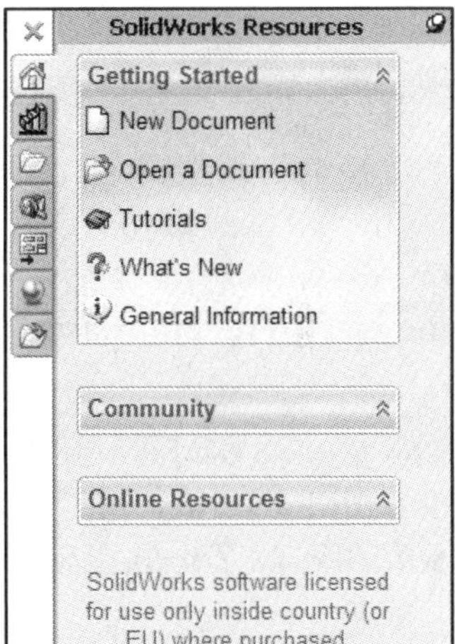

The basic SolidWorks Resources menu displays the following default selections: *Getting Started*, *Community*, *Online Resources*, and *Tip of the Day*.

Other user interfaces are available during the initial software installation selection: *Machine Design*, *Mold Design*, or *Consumer Products Design*.

Design Library

The Design Library contains reusable parts, assemblies, and other elements, including library features.

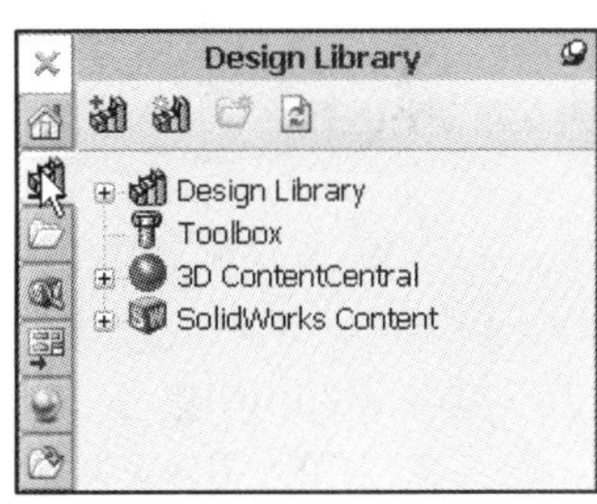

The Design Library tab contains four default selections. Each default selection contains additional sub categories. The default selections are*: Design Library*, *Toolbox*, *3D ContentCentral*, and *SolidWorks Content*.

Click **Tools, Add-Ins…, SolidWorks Toolbox** and **SolidWorks Toolbox Browser** to active the SolidWorks Toolbox.

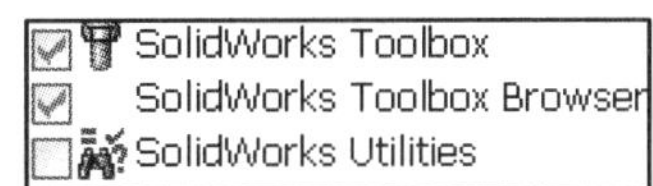

To access the Design Library folders in a non network environment for a new installation, click **Add File Location**, enter: **C:\Documents and Settings\All Users\Application Data\SolidWorks\SolidWorks 2008\design library**. Click **OK**. In a network environment, contact your IT department for system details.

File Explorer

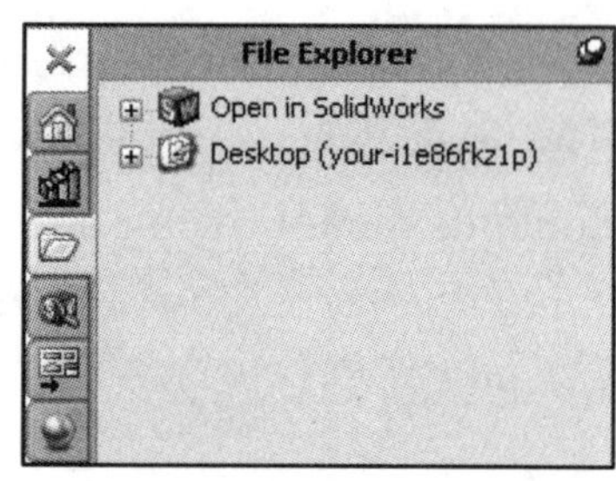

File Explorer duplicates Windows Explorer from your local computer and displays the following directories: *Recent Documents*, and *Open in SolidWorks*.

Search

SolidWorks Search is installed with Microsoft Windows Search and indexes the resources once before searching begins, either after installation, or when you initiate the first search.

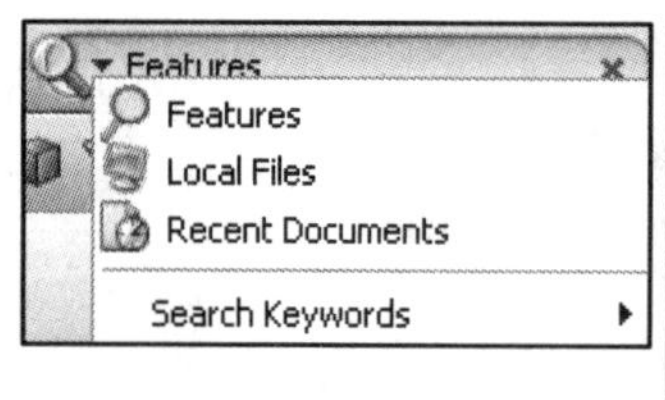

The SolidWorks Search box is displayed in the upper right corner of the SolidWorks Graphics window. Enter the text or key words to search. Click the drop-down arrow to view the last 10 recent searches.

The Search tool in the Task Pane searches the following default locations: *All Locations*, *Local Files*, *Design Library*, *SolidWorks Toolbox*, and *3D ContentCentral*.

Select any or all of the above locations. If you do not select a file location, all locations are searched.

View Palette

The View Palette tool located in the Task Pane provides the ability to insert drawing views of an active document, or click the Browse button to locate the desired document.

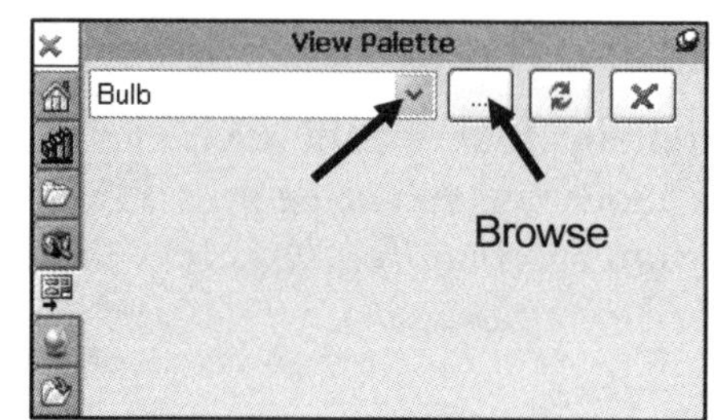

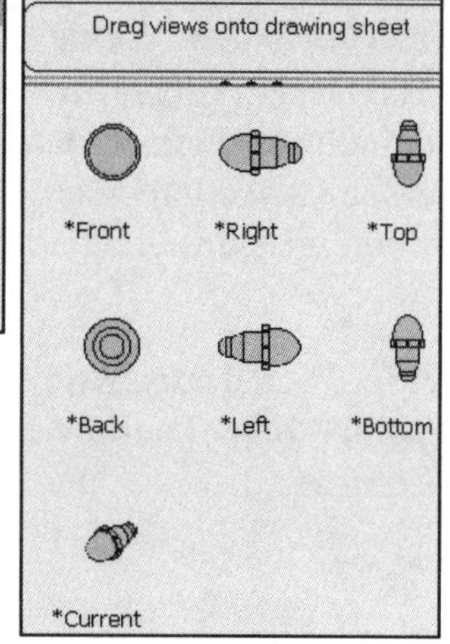

Click and drag the view from the View Palette into an active drawing sheet to create a drawing view.

The (A) next to the drawing view informs the user that DimXpert Annotations are present.

RealView

RealView provides a simplified way to display models in a photo-realistic setting using a library of appearances and scenes. Note: RealView requires graphics card support and is memory intensive!

On RealView compatible systems, you can select Appearances and Scenes to display your model in the Graphics window. Drag and drop a selected appearance onto the model or FeatureManager. View the results in the Graphics window.

PhotoWorks needs to be active to apply the scenes tool.

RealView graphics is only available with supported graphics cards. For the latest information on graphics cards that support RealView Graphics display, visit: *www.solidworks.com/pages/services/videocardtesting.html.*

Document Recovery

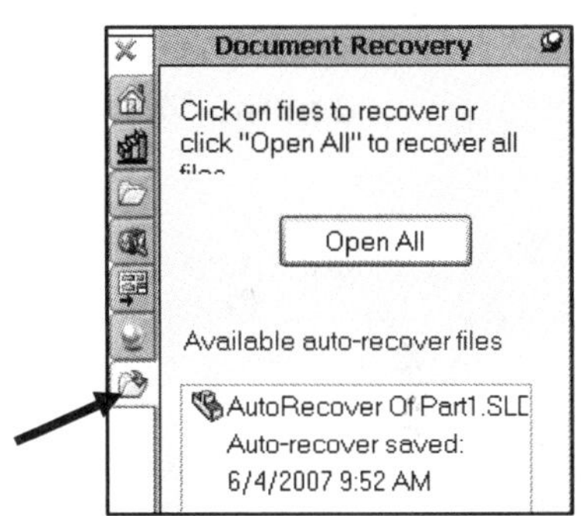

Document Recovery provides the ability to save information files if the system terminates unexpectedly with an active document. The saved files are available on the Task Pane Document Recovery tab the next time you start a SolidWorks session. Note: Auto recovery is activated by default in the System Options section.

Motion Study tab

The Motion Study tab is located in the bottom left corner of the Graphics window. Motion Study uses a key frame-based interface, and provides a graphical simulation of motion for the selected model.

Click the Motion Study tab to view the MotionManager.

Click the Model tab to return to the FeatureManager design tree.

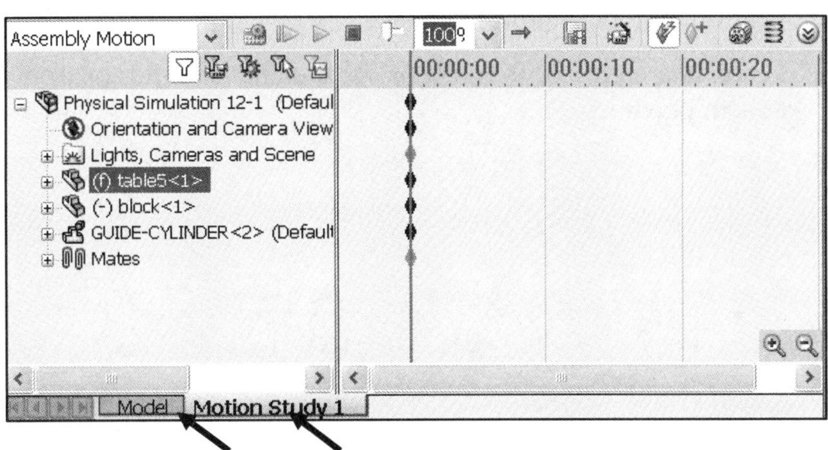

The MotionManager displays a timeline-based interface, and provides the following selections:

1. *All levels*. Provides the ability to change viewpoints, display properties, and create animations displaying the assembly in motion.

2. *Assembly Motion*. (Available in core SolidWorks.) Provides the ability to animate the assembly and to control the display at various time intervals. The Assembly Motion option computes the sequences required to go from one position to the next.

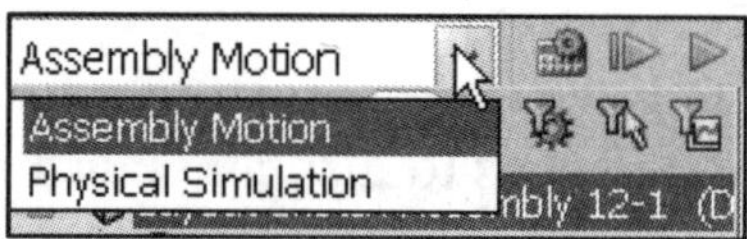

3. *Physical Simulation*. (Available in core SolidWorks.) Provides the ability to simulating the effects of motors, springs, dampers, and gravity on assemblies. This options combines simulation elements with SolidWorks tools such as mates and Physical Dynamics to move components around the assembly.

4. *COSMOSMotion*. (Available in SolidWorks Office Premium.) Provides the ability to simulate, and analyze the effects of forces, contacts, friction, and motion on an assembly.

If the Motion Study tab is not visible, click **View**, **MotionManager** from the Menu bar. Note: On a model that was created before SolidWorks 2008, the Annotation tab may be displayed in the Motion Study location.

To create a new Motion Study, click **Insert, New Motion Study** from the Menu bar menu.

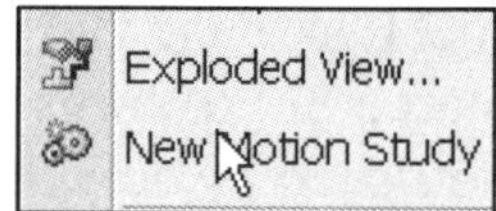

Activity: Open a Part document

A part is a 3D model which consists of features. What are features?

- Features are geometry building blocks.
- Features add or remove material.
- Features are created from 2D or 3D sketched profiles or from edges and faces of existing geometry.

There are two modes in the New SolidWorks Document dialog box: *Novice* and *Advanced*. The Novice option is the default option with three templates. The Advanced option contains access to additional templates. Use the Advanced option in this book.

Create a new part.

6) Click **New** from the Menu bar toolbar. The New SolidWorks Document dialog box is displayed.

Select the Advanced mode.

7) Click the **Advanced** button. The advanced mode is set.

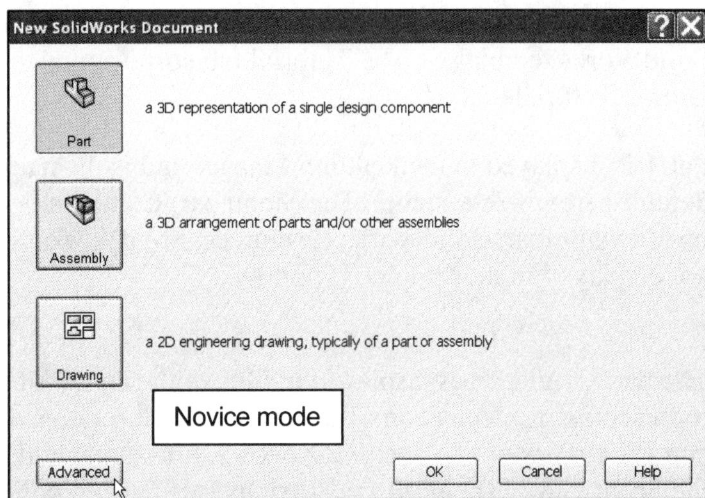

The Templates tab is the default tab. Part is the default template from the New SolidWorks Document dialog box.

8) Click **OK** from the New SolidWorks Document dialog box.

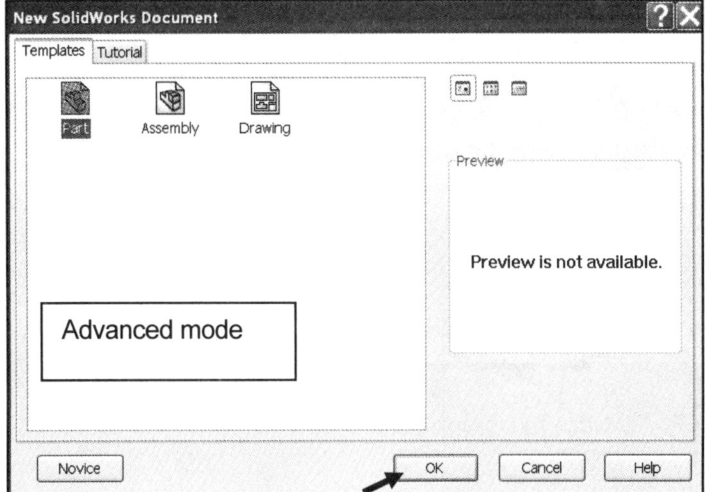

The Advanced mode remains selected for all new documents in the current SolidWorks session. When you exit SolidWorks, the Advanced mode setting is saved.

The default SolidWorks installation contains two tabs in the New SolidWorks Document dialog box; *Templates* and *Tutorial*. The Templates tab corresponds to the default SolidWorks templates. The Tutorial tab corresponds to the templates utilized in the Online Tutorials.

Part1 is displayed in the FeatureManager and is the name of the document. Part1 is the default part window name. The Menu bar, CommandManager, FeatureManager, Heads-up View toolbar, SolidWorks Resources, SolidWorks Search, Task Pane, and the Origin are displayed in the Graphics window.

The part Origin is displayed in blue in the center of the Graphics window. The Origin represents the intersection of the three default reference planes: *Front Plane*, *Top Plane*, and *Right Plane*. The positive X-axis is horizontal and points to the right of the Origin in the Front view. The positive Y-axis is vertical and point upward in the Front view. The FeatureManager contains a list of features, reference geometry, and settings utilized in the part.

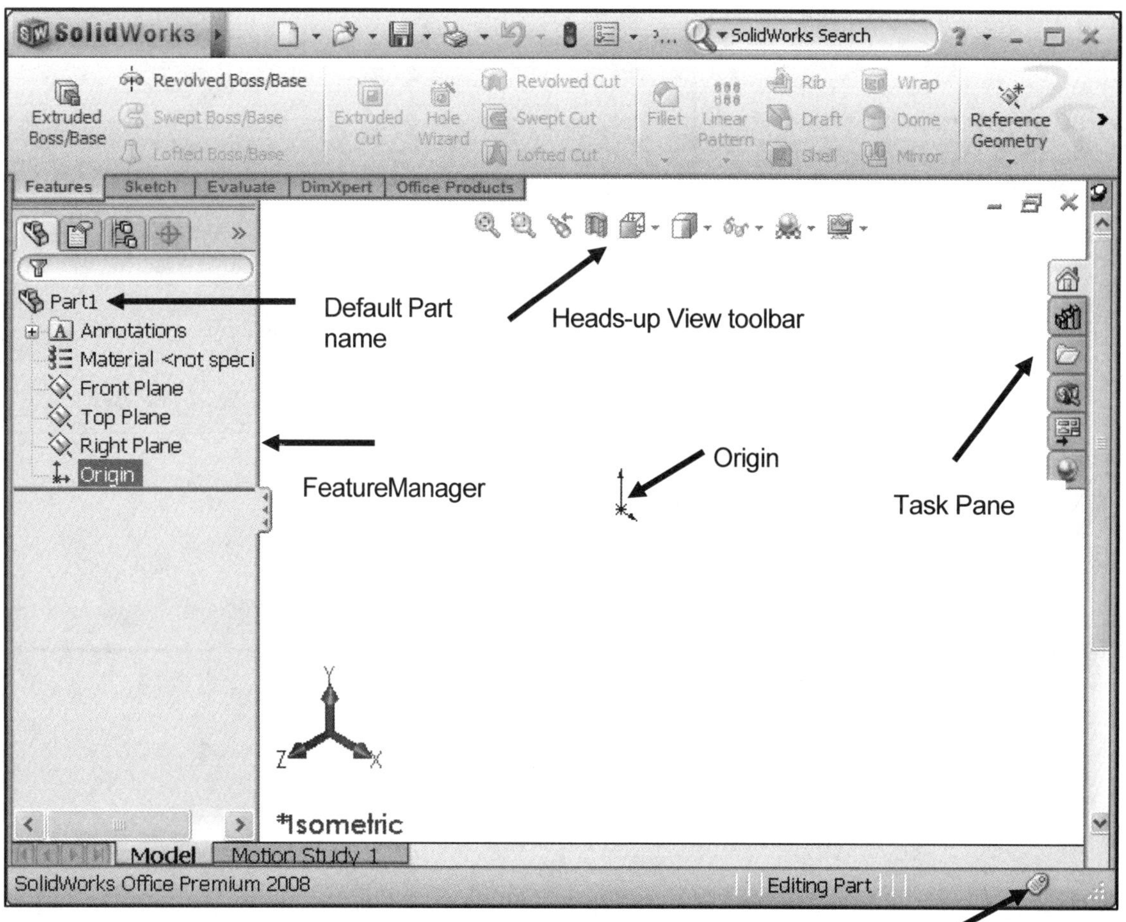

The Tags icon is displayed in the bottom right corner of the Graphics window. Tags are keywords you add to SolidWorks documents and features to make them easier to filter and search for.

In this book, Reference planes and Grid/Snaps are deactivated in the Graphics window for improved model clarity.

Activity: Menu Bar toolbar, Menu Bar menu, Heads-up View toolbar

Display tools and tool tips.

9) Position the **mouse pointer** over the Heads-up View toolbar and view the tool tips.

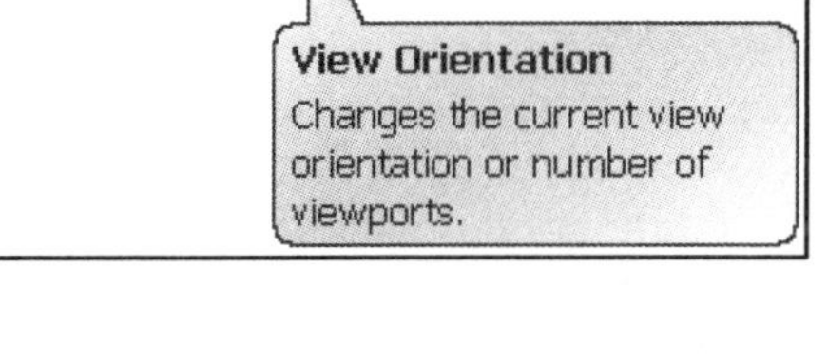

View Orientation
Changes the current view orientation or number of viewports.

10) **Read** the large tool tip.

11) Select the **drop-down arrow** to view the available view tools.

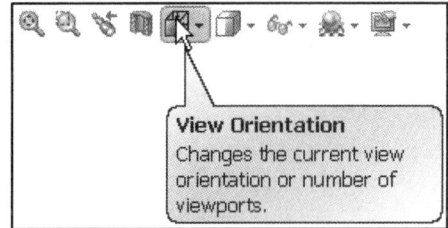

Display the View toolbar and the Menu bar.

12) Right-click in the **gray area** of the Menu bar.

13) Click **View**. The View toolbar is displayed.

14) Click and drag the **View toolbar** off the Graphics window.

15) Click **SolidWorks** as illustrated to expand the Menu bar menu.

16) **Pin** the Menu bar as illustrated. Use both the Menu bar menu and the Menu bar toolbar in this book.

The SolidWorks Help Topics contains step-by-step instructions for various commands. The Help icon is displayed in the dialog box or in the PropertyManager for each feature.

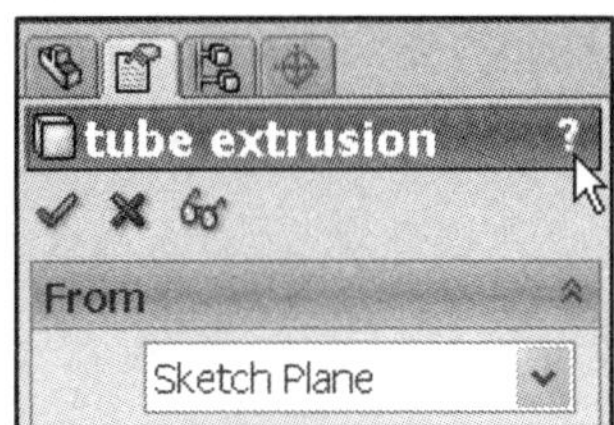

Display SolidWorks Help. Use SolidWorks Help to locate information on sketches, features, and tools.

Display SolidWorks Help

17) Click **Help** from the Menu bar menu. The Help options are displayed.

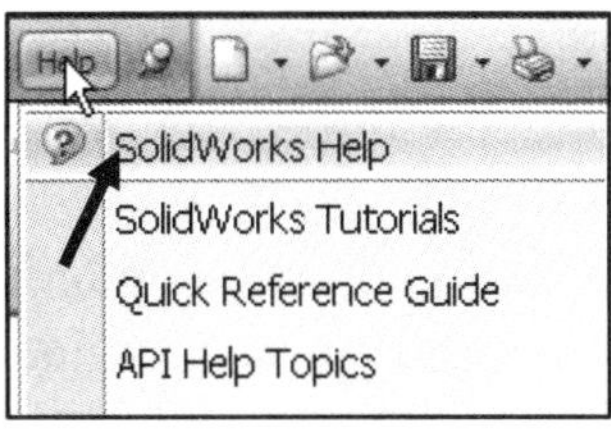

18) Click **SolidWorks Help**. The SolidWorks Help dialog box is displayed.

The SolidWorks Help dialog box contains the following tabs:

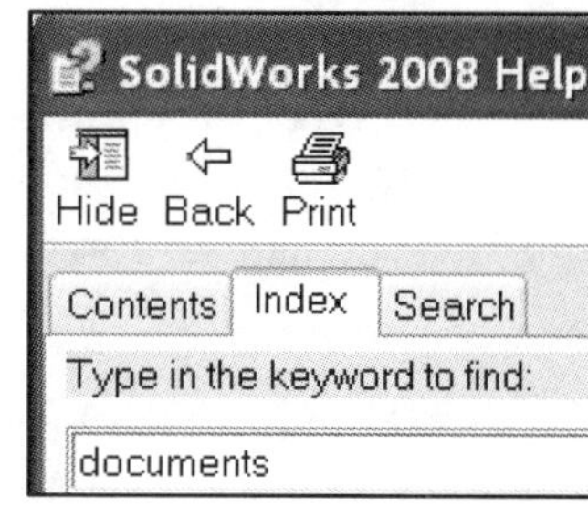

- **Contents** tab: Contains the SolidWorks Online User's Guide documents.
- **Index** tab: Contains additional information on key words.
- **Search** tab. Locates needed information.

19) **Close** the SolidWorks Help dialog box.

Display and explore the SolidWorks Tutorials.

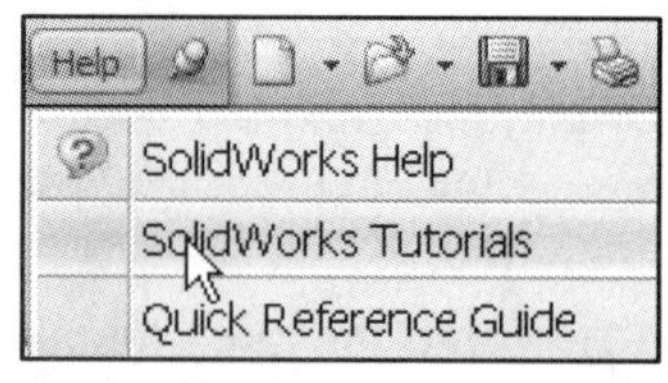

20) Click **Help** from the Menu bar.

21) Click **SolidWorks Tutorials**. The SolidWorks Tutorials are displayed. The SolidWorks Tutorials are presented by category.

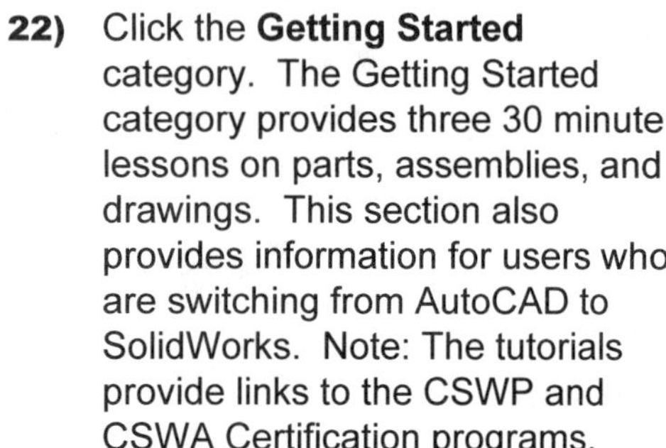

22) Click the **Getting Started** category. The Getting Started category provides three 30 minute lessons on parts, assemblies, and drawings. This section also provides information for users who are switching from AutoCAD to SolidWorks. Note: The tutorials provide links to the CSWP and CSWA Certification programs.

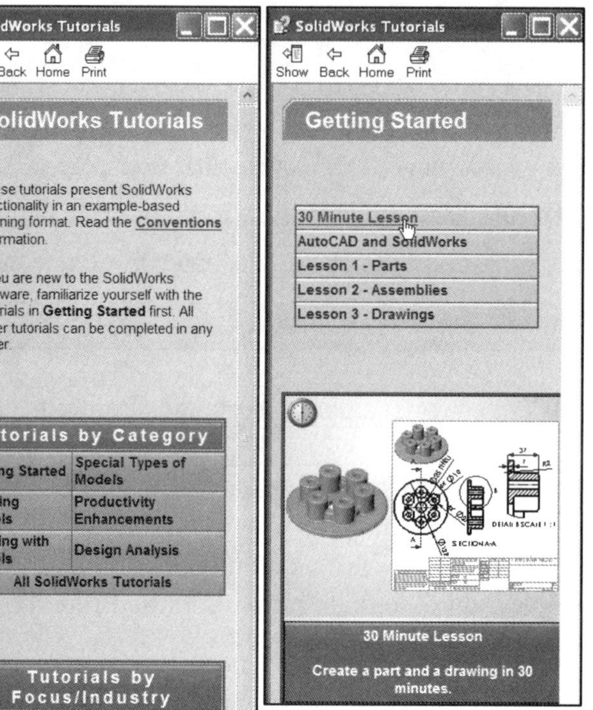

SolidWorks Corporation offers two levels of certification representing increasing levels of expertise in 3D CAD design as it applies to engineering: Certified SolidWorks Associate CSWA, and the Certified SolidWorks Professional CSWP.

The CSWA certification indicates a foundation in and apprentice knowledge of 3D CAD design and engineering practices and principles.

The main requirement for obtaining the CSWA certification is to take and pass the three hour, seven question on-line exam at a Certified SolidWorks CSWA Provider, "university, college, technical, vocational, or secondary educational institution" and to sign the SolidWorks Confidentiality Agreement.

Passing this exam provides students the chance to prove their knowledge and expertise and to be part of a world wide industry certification standard.

Return to the SolidWorks Graphics window.

23) **Close** the Online Tutorial dialog box.

Close all models.

24) Click **Windows**, **Close All** from the Menu bar menu.

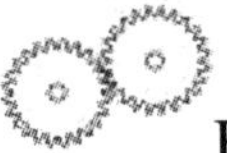

Review of the SolidWorks User Interface and CommandManager

The SolidWorks 2008 User Interface and CommandManager consist of the following options: *Menu bar toolbar, Menu bar menu, Drop-down menus, Short-cut toolbars, Consolidated flyout menus, System feedback icons, Confirmation Corner, and Heads-up View toolbar.*

There are two modes in the New SolidWorks Document dialog box: *Novice* and *Advanced*. The Novice option is the default option with three templates. The Advanced option contains access to more templates

The FeatureManager design tree consist of four default tabs: *FeatureManager design tree, PropertyManager, ConfigurationManager, and DimXertManager.*

The CommandManager is document dependent. The CommandManager tabs are located on the bottom left side of the CommandManager and display the available toolbars and features for each corresponding tab.

The default Part tabs are: *Features*, *Sketch*, *Evaluate*, *DimXpert*, and *Office Products.*

The default Drawing tabs are: *View Layout*, *Annotation*, *Sketch*, *Evaluate*, and *Office Products*.

The default Assembly tabs are: *Assembly*, *Layout*, *Sketch*, *Evaluate*, and *Office Products.* The Office Products toolbar display is dependent on the activated Add-Ins.. during a SolidWorks session.

The Task Pane contains the following default tabs: *SolidWorks Resources*, *Design Library*, *File Explorer*, *SolidWorks Search*, *View Palette*, *RealView*, and *Document Recovery*.

Project Terminology

Assembly: An assembly is a document in which parts, features, and other assemblies (sub-assemblies) are put together. A part in an assembly is called a component. Adding a component to an assembly creates a link between the assembly and the component. When SolidWorks opens the assembly, it finds the component file to show it in the assembly. Changes in the component are automatically reflected in the assembly. The filename extension for a SolidWorks assembly file name is .SLDASM.

CommandManager: The CommandManager is a Context-sensitive toolbar that dynamically updates based on the toolbar you want to access. By default, it has toolbars embedded in it based on the document type. When you click a tab below the Command Manager, it updates to display that toolbar. For example, if you click the **Sketches** tab, the Sketch toolbar is displayed.

ConfigurationManager: The ConfigurationManager is located on the left side of the SolidWorks window and provides the means to create, select, and view multiple configurations of parts and assemblies in an active document. You can split the ConfigurationManager and either display two ConfigurationManager instances, or combine the ConfigurationManager with the FeatureManager design tree, PropertyManager, or third party applications that use the panel.

Coordinate System: SolidWorks uses a coordinate system with origins. A part document contains an original Origin. Whenever you select a plane or face and open a sketch, an Origin is created in alignment with the plane or face. An Origin can be used as an anchor for the sketch entities, and it helps orient perspective of the axes. A three-dimensional reference triad orients you to the X, Y, and Z directions in part and assembly documents.

Cursor Feedback: The system feedback symbol indicates what you are selecting or what the system is expecting you to select. As you move the mouse pointer across your model, system feedback is provided.

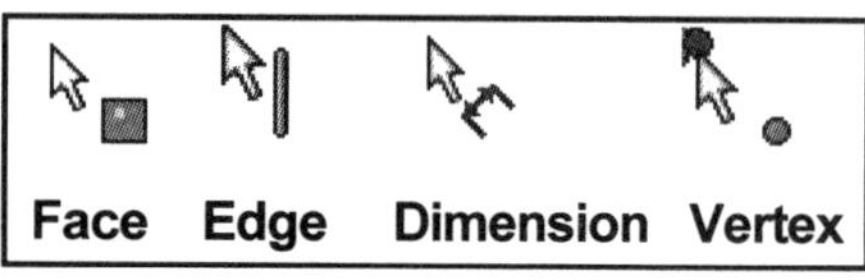

Dimension: A value indicating the size of the 2D sketch entity or 3D feature. Dimensions in a SolidWorks drawing are associated with the model, and changes in the model are reflected in the drawing, if you DO NOT USE DimXpert.

DimXpertManager: The DimXpertManager lists the tolerance features defined by DimXpert for a part. It also displays DimXpert tools that you use to insert dimensions and tolerances into a part. You can import these dimensions and tolerances into drawings. DimXpert is not associative.

Document: In SolidWorks, each part, assembly, and drawing is referred to as a document, and each document is displayed in a separate window.

Drawing: A 2D representation of a 3D part or assembly. The extension for a SolidWorks drawing file name is .SLDDRW. Drawing refers to the SolidWorks module used to insert, add, and modify views in an engineering drawing.

Feature: Features are geometry building blocks. Features add or remove material. Features are created from 2D or 3D sketched profiles or from edges and faces of existing geometry.

FeatureManager: The FeatureManager design tree located on the left side of the SolidWorks window provides an outline view of the active part, assembly, or drawing. This makes it easy to see how the model or assembly was constructed or to examine the various sheets and views in a drawing. The FeatureManager and the Graphics window are dynamically linked. You can select features, sketches, drawing views, and construction geometry in either pane.

Graphics window: The area in the SolidWorks window where the part, assembly, or drawing is displayed.

Heads-up View toolbar: A transparent toolbar located at the top of the Graphic window.

Model: 3D solid geometry in a part or assembly document. If a part or assembly document contains multiple configurations, each configuration is a separate model.

Motion Studies: Graphical simulations of motion and visual properties with assembly models. Analogous to a configuration, they do not actually change the original assembly model or its properties. They display the model as it changes based on simulation elements you add.

Origin: The model origin is displayed in blue and represents the (0,0,0) coordinate of the model. When a sketch is active, a sketch origin is displayed in red and represents the (0,0,0) coordinate of the sketch. Dimensions and relations can be added to the model origin, but not to a sketch origin.

Part: A 3D object that consist of one or more features. A part inserted into an assembly is called a component. Insert part views, feature dimensions and annotations into 2D drawing. The extension for a SolidWorks part filename is .SLDPRT.

Plane: Planes are flat and infinite. Planes are represented on the screen with visible edges.

PropertyManager: Most sketch, feature, and drawing tools in SolidWorks open a PropertyManager located on the left side of the SolidWorks window. The PropertyManager displays the properties of the entity or feature so you specify the properties without a dialog box covering the Graphics window.

RealView: Provides a simplified way to display models in a photo-realistic setting using a library of appearances and scenes. RealView requires graphics card support and is memory intensive.

Rebuild: A tool that updates (or regenerates) the document with any changes made since the last time the model was rebuilt. Rebuild is typically used after changing a model dimension.

Relation: A relation is a geometric constraint between sketch entities or between a sketch entity and a plane, axis, edge or vertex.

Rollback: Suppresses all items below the rollback bar.

Sketch: The name to describe a 2D profile is called a sketch. 2D sketches are created on flat faces and planes within the model. Typical geometry types are lines, arcs, corner rectangles, circles, polygons, and ellipses.

Task Pane: The Task Pane is displayed when you open the SolidWorks software. It contains the following tabs: SolidWorks Resources, Design Library, File Explorer, Search, View Palette, Document Recovery, and RealView/PhotoWorks.

Toolbars: The toolbars provide shortcuts enabling you to access the most frequently used commands. When you enable add-in applications in SolidWorks, you can also display their associated toolbars.

Units: Used in the measurement of physical quantities. Decimal inch dimensioning and Millimeter dimensioning are the two types of common units specified for engineering parts and drawings.

Project 2

File Management, System Options, Templates, SolidWorks Explorer, and more

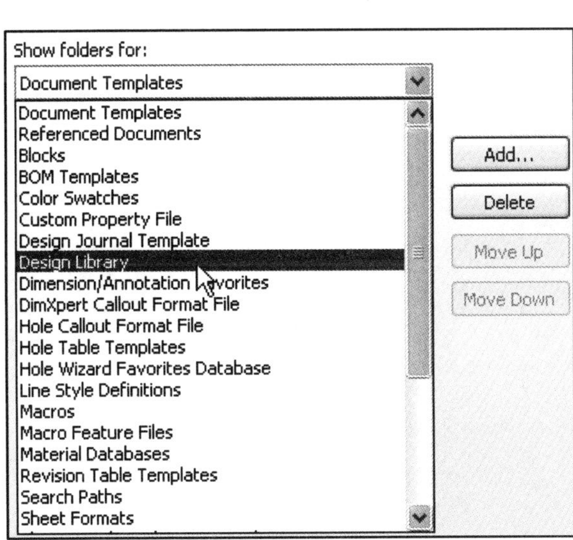

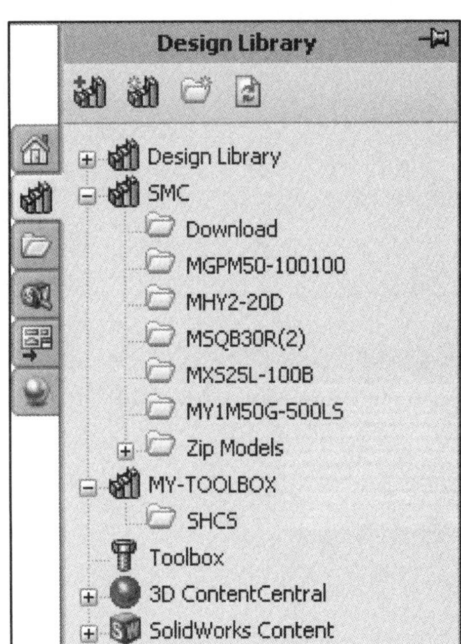

Below are the desired outcomes and usage competencies based on the completion of this Project.

Project Desired Outcomes:	Usage Competencies:
Create two templates: • ASM-MM-ANSI Assembly template. • PART-MM-ANSI-AL6061 Part template.	• Set System Options and Document Properties as they applied to a Part and Assembly template. • Create new SolidWorks File Locations: Document Templates, Reference Documents, and Design Library folders.
• Apply 3DContentCentral. • Use SolidWorks Explorer. • Utilize the Measure tool.	• Ability to download components using 3D ContentCentral. • Rename and save components using SolidWorks Explorer.

Notes:

Project 2 – File Management, System Options, Templates, SolidWorks Explorer, and more

Project Objective

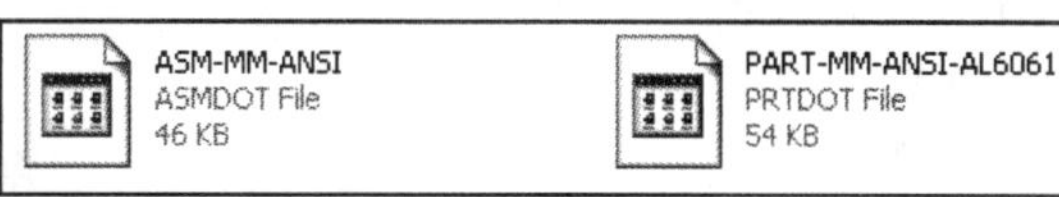

Obtain a general knowledge of Top-down and Bottom-up assembly modeling. Create two templates: *ASM-MM-ANSI Assembly template* and the *PART-MM-ANSI-AL6061 Part template*.

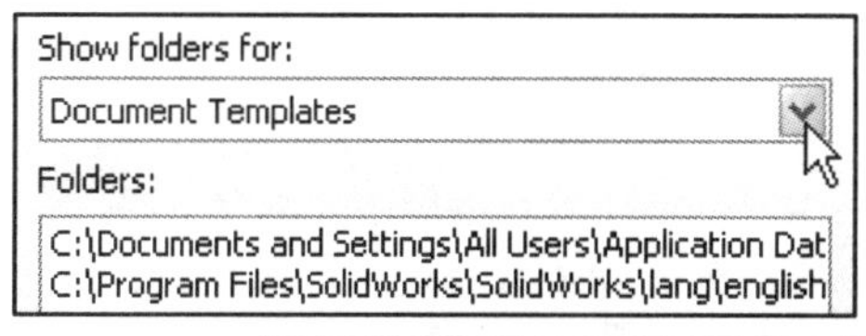

Create new SolidWorks File Locations: *Document Templates*, *Reference Documents*, and *Design Library folders* in the Task Pane.

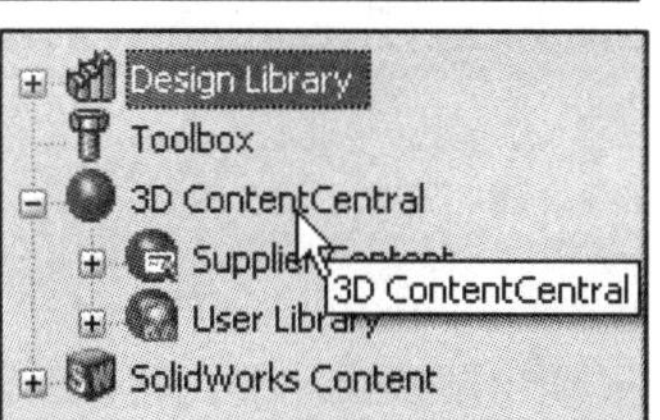

Download a component from 3DContentCentral. Rename SMC components using SolidWorks Explorer. Apply the Measure tool.

On the completion of this project, you will be able to:

- Develop an Assembly Task List and Assembly Layout Diagram.
- Obtain a general understanding of the two key design methods for an assembly:
  - o Top-down assembly modeling.
  - o Bottom-up assembly modeling.
- Set System Options as they relate to assemblies.
- Create an Assembly template with document properties.
- Create a Part template and apply material properties.
- Modify File Location references for the Document Templates, Reference Documents, and the Design Library Download components from 3D ContentCentral.
- View and rename sub-assemblies in SolidWorks Explorer required for the 3AXIS-TRANSFER assembly.
- Obtain and confirm geometric and functional requirements from the vendor's component specifications using the Measure tool from the Evaluate toolbar.
- Utilize and apply the following SolidWorks tools and commands: Measure tool, SolidWorks Explorer, Filer Explorer, Large Assembly mode, Lightweight mode, and 3DContext Central.

Project Overview

You are part of a design team to develop the DELIVERY-STATION assembly for a customer's industrial application. The DELIVERY-STATION assembly contains hundreds of components.

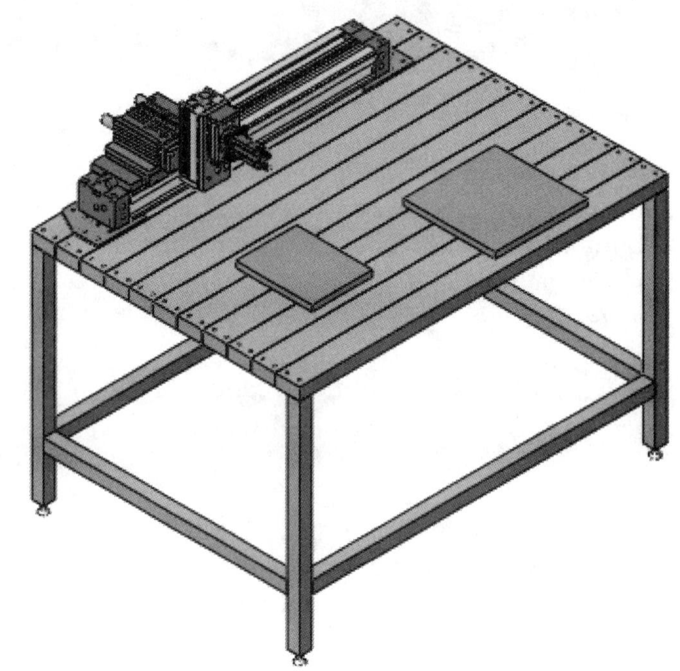

You attend a design review meeting to discuss the customer requirements with your colleagues.

The two fingers of the GRIPPER assembly obtain an object from the INPUT assembly.

The 3AXIS-TRANSFER assembly rotates the object 90 degrees and linearly translates 500mm along the RODLESS CYLINDER assembly.

The 3AXIS-TRANSFER assembly raises the object 100mm. The 3AXIS-TRANSFER assembly moves the object outward 100mm. The two fingers of the GRIPPER assembly places the object into the OUTPUT assembly.

A senior engineer on your project team provides a list of five purchased pneumatic parts for the program.

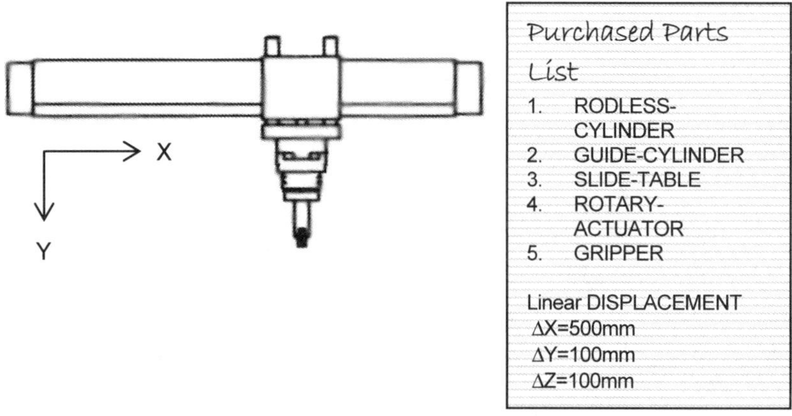

X
Y
Purchased Parts List
1. RODLESS-CYLINDER
2. GUIDE-CYLINDER
3. SLIDE-TABLE
4. ROTARY-ACTUATOR
5. GRIPPER
Linear DISPLACEMENT
ΔX=500mm
ΔY=100mm
ΔZ=100mm

Rough Sketch - Top view and Purchased Parts List
3AXIS-TRANSFER Assembly (Your Task)

The senior engineer provides key dimensions for linear displacement and a rough sketch of the top view for the 3AXIS-TRANSFER assembly.

Your responsibilities include:

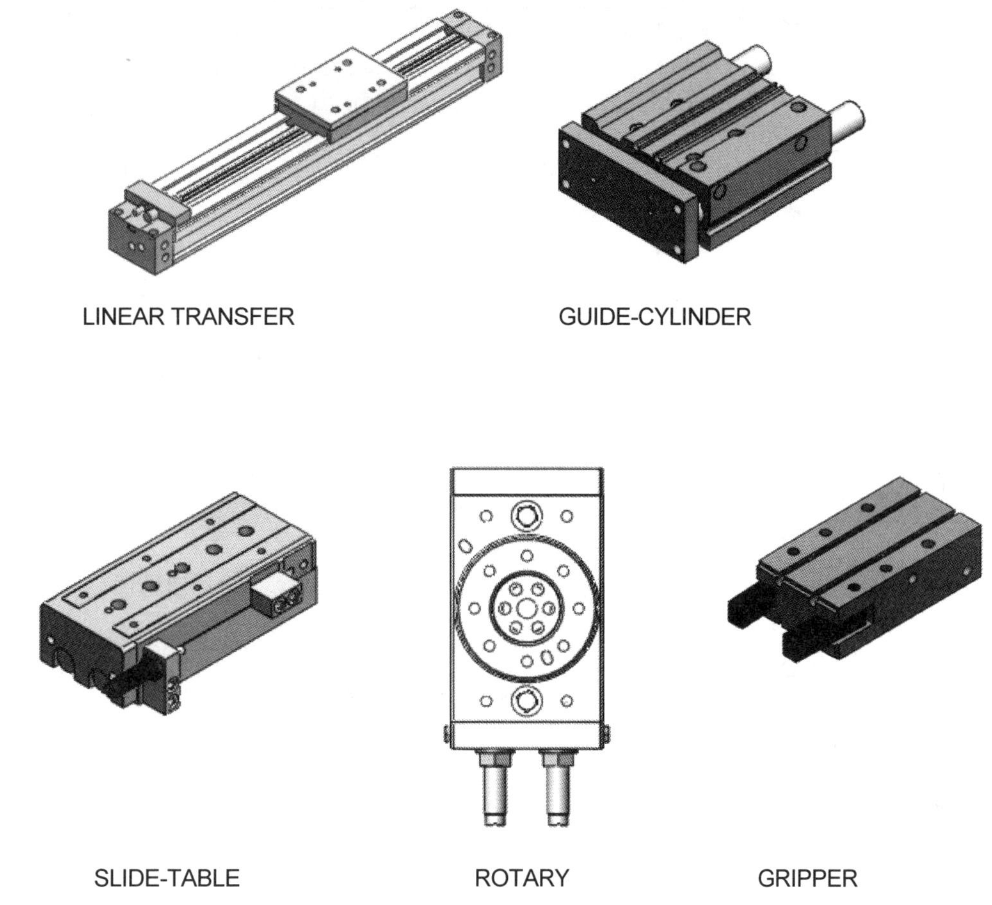

Purchased Pneumatic Parts
Courtesy of SMC Corporation of America

- Obtain the five component models from a manufacturer, (SMC).
- Extract information required from each component.
- Create the 3AXIS-TRANSFER assembly from purchased components and created parts.

In the following projects, develop the 3AXIS-TRANSFER assembly utilizing SolidWorks features, tools, and commands. Work between part, assembly and drawing documents.

SolidWorks Document Definitions

File type:	Extension:	Definition:
Part	.sldprt	A part is a single 3D object that consists of various features.
Assembly	.sldasm	An assembly combines two or more parts. A part inserted into an assembly is called a component. A sub-assembly is a component contained within an assembly.
Part template	.prtdot	The foundation for a SolidWorks part is the Part template. Define part drawing standards, units and other properties in the Part template.
Assembly template	.asmdot	The foundation for a SolidWorks assembly is the Assembly template. Define drawing standards, units and other properties in the Assembly template.

Assembly Task List – Before you begin

You are required to perform numerous tasks before you create a SolidWorks assembly. Review the following list. Mark this page for future reference.

Assembly Task List – Before you Begin:		
Task:	**Comments:**	**Complete:**
Review the Assembly Layout Diagram with your colleagues. Group components into sub-assemblies.	My task – 3AXIS-TRANSFER assembly	✓
Comprehend the geometric and functional requirements of the purchased components. How do the components interact with other components in the assembly? Know the fit and function of each component. Obtain model files and data specifications from the vendors.		
Place yourself in the position of the machinist, manufacturing technician, field service engineer, or customer. Identify potential obstacles or design concerns.		

Task:	**Comments:**	**Complete:**
Plan and create the Assembly, Part, and Drawing templates. Identify units, dimensioning standards, and other document properties.		
Organize documents into file folders. Place templates, vendor components, library components, parts, assemblies, and drawings in a specific location.		
Obtain unique part numbers for components. A unique part number avoids duplication problems in the assembly. Note: In this project, utilize a part description filename. In a later Project, rename part description filenames to your company's unique part number filename.		

DELIVERY-STATION Assembly Layout Diagram

The project leader developed a layout diagram for the DELIVERY-STATION assembly structure. Review the DELIVERY-STATION assembly layout diagram.

Before you begin an assembly, organize the components. The DELIVERY-STATION assembly is comprised of the following components:

- *3AXIS-TRANSFER assembly*
- *MOUNTING-PLATE component*
- *INPUT assembly*
- *OUTPUT assembly*

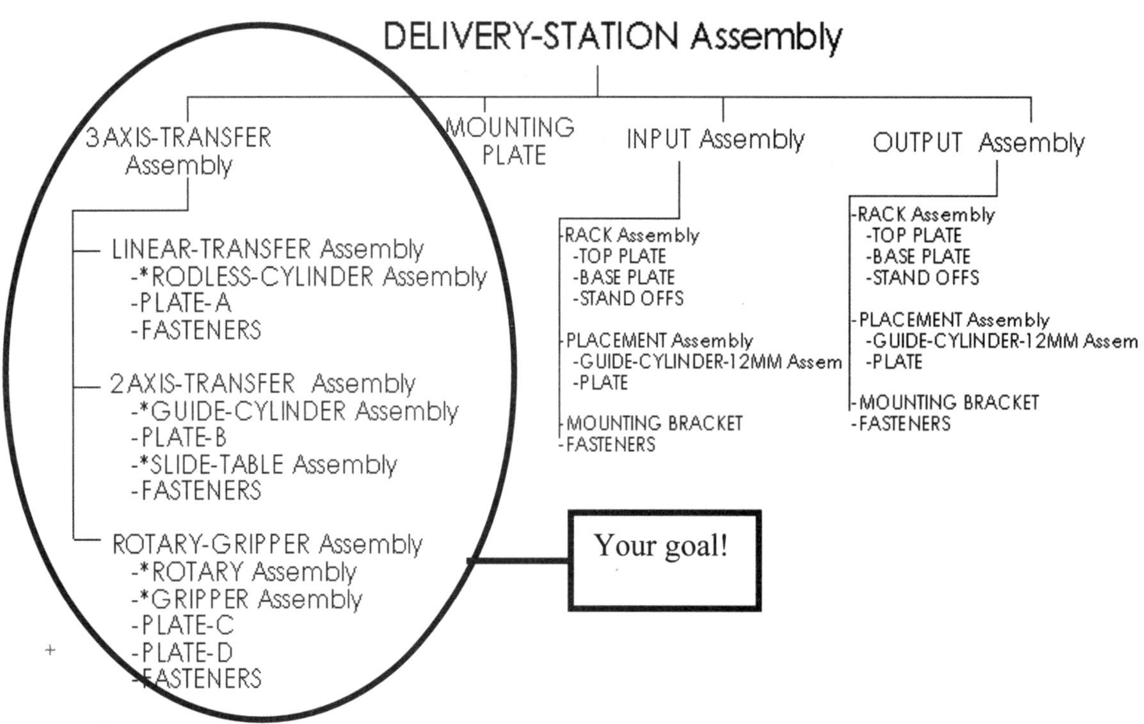

DELIVERY-STATION Assembly Layout Diagram

*Purchased SMC Components.

Assembly Layout modeling methods

There are two key methods to document an assembly layout:

- *Top-down assembly modeling*
- *Bottom-up assembly modeling*

You will first address the Top-down assembly modeling approach. In Top-down assembly design, one or more features of a part are defined by something in an assembly, such as a layout sketch or the geometry of another part.

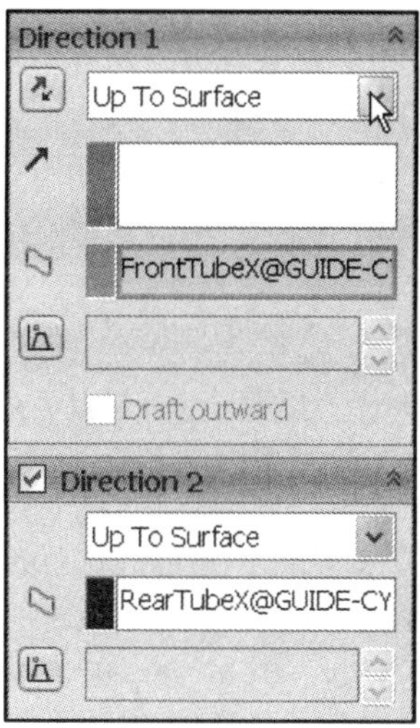

The design intent (sizes of features, placement of components in the assembly, proximity to other parts, etc.) comes from the top (the assembly) and moves down (into the parts), hence the phrase "top-down."

For example, when creating a locating pin on a plastic part using the *Extruded Boss/Base* command, you might choose the *Up to Surface* option and select the bottom of a circuit board (a different part). This selection would make the locating pin exactly long enough to touch the board, even if the board were moved in a future design change. Thus the length of the pin is defined in the assembly, not by a static dimension in the part.

Methods

There are three key methods in Top-down assembly modeling. You can use some or all of these methods. They are: *Individual features, Complete parts*, and *An entire assembly.* These methods are addressed later in the book.

Considerations

- Whenever you create a part or feature using Top-down modeling techniques, External references are created to the geometry you referenced. An External reference is created when one document is dependent on another document for its solution. If the referenced document changes, the dependent document changes. In other words, External References are used to create and maintain relations between parts at the assembly level.
- In some cases, assemblies with large numbers of In-Context features (which form the basis of Top-down design) can take longer to rebuild than the same assembly without them.

- When creating In-context features, it is important to not to create mating conflicts because they can cause long rebuild times and unexpected geometry behavior. You can generally avoid these conflicts by not creating mates to geometry created by In-context features.

In a planning meeting, team members review the DELIVERY-STATION assembly layout diagram. Other members of the design team are concurrently developing the MOUNTING-PLATE part, INPUT assembly, and OUTPUT assembly.

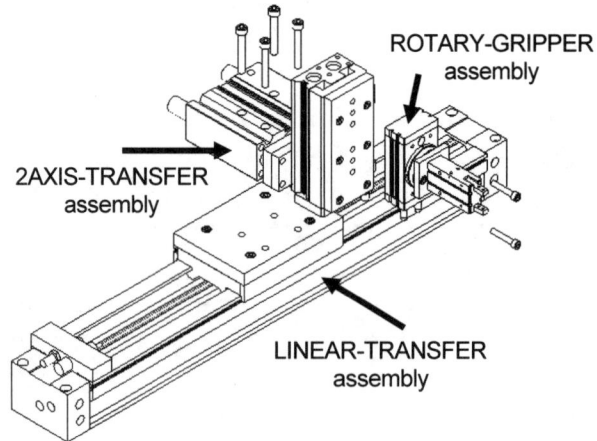

The goal is to create the 3AXIS-TRANSFER assembly. The 3AXIS-TRANSFER assembly consists of three sub-assemblies. They are:

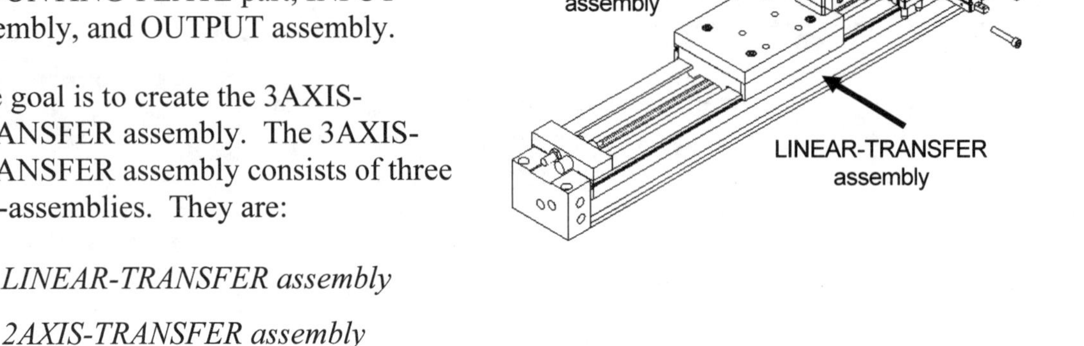

- *LINEAR-TRANSFER assembly*
- *2AXIS-TRANSFER assembly*
- *ROTARY-GRIPPER assembly*

The three modular sub-assemblies provide different examples of SolidWorks assembly modeling techniques. Resource allocations change during the product development cycle. In an engineering environment, create modular sub-assemblies.

File Organization

File organization is essential to a successful design. A common file structure relates components in an assembly. Changes in the part affect the assembly and vice a versa. Managing assembly information is a complex undertaking and goes far beyond just creating SolidWorks parts, assemblies, and drawings.

Companies develop Engineering Change Orders, "ECO" and manufacturing procedures to document product revisions. Companies utilize Product Data Management (PDM) systems to control engineering documents.

The projects in this book focus on using SolidWorks parts, assemblies, and drawings along with SolidWorks Explorer.

SolidWorks Explorer is a file management tool designed to help you perform such tasks as *renaming, replacing*, and *copying* SolidWorks files. You can display a document's references, search for documents using a variety of criteria, and list all the places where a document is used.

Renamed files are still available to those documents that reference them.

You can use SolidWorks Explorer with or without the SolidWorks application and with or without PDMWorks Workgroup added in.

SolidWorks Explorer is not a PDM (Product Data Management) tool; however, it does perform many useful tasks and simplifies many file management processes. You can add in The PDMWorks Workgroup Contributor application to run as a standalone application inside SolidWorks Explorer.

How do you organize components in an assembly? Answer: Before you begin an assembly, utilize file organization to create an assembly layout diagram. The following examples describe assembly layout structures.

Example 1:

Take a closer look at the 3AXIS–TRANSFER assembly. Why is this example a difficult layout structure? Answer: All of the sub-assemblies and parts are at the top level.

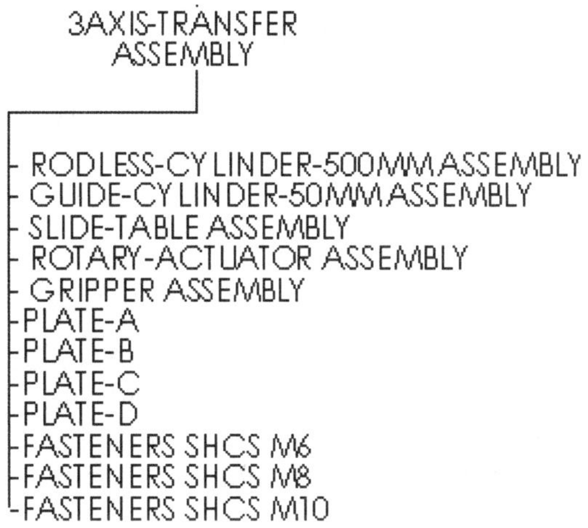

3AXIS-TRANSFER ASSEMBLY
- RODLESS-CYLINDER-500MM ASSEMBLY
- GUIDE-CYLINDER-50MM ASSEMBLY
- SLIDE-TABLE ASSEMBLY
- ROTARY-ACTUATOR ASSEMBLY
- GRIPPER ASSEMBLY
- PLATE-A
- PLATE-B
- PLATE-C
- PLATE-D
- FASTENERS SHCS M6
- FASTENERS SHCS M8
- FASTENERS SHCS M10

The 3AXIS-TRANSFER assembly consists of more parts than sub-assemblies. This structure can be difficult to create, modify, and resolve problems. Dividing a larger assembly into smaller sub-assemblies provides the ability to:

- Identify problems and address issues quicker.
- Provide and divide work between teammates.

Maximize sub-assemblies at each assembly level. Minimize parts at the assembly level.

Example 2:

Create three sub-assemblies:

- *LINEAR-TRANSFER assembly*
- *2AXIS-TRANSFER assembly*
- *ROTARY-GRIPPER assembly*

3AXIS-TRANSFER

LINEAR-TRANSFER-500MM Assembly
-*RODLESS-CYLINDER-500MM Assembly
-PLATE-A
-FASTENERS

2AXIS-TRANSFER Assembly
-*GUIDE-CYLINDER-50MM Assembly
-PLATE-B
-*SLIDE-TABLE Assembly
-FASTENERS

ROTARY-GRIPPER Assembly
-*ROTARY-ACTUATOR Assembly
-*GRIPPER Assembly
-PLATE-C
-PLATE-D
-FASTENERS

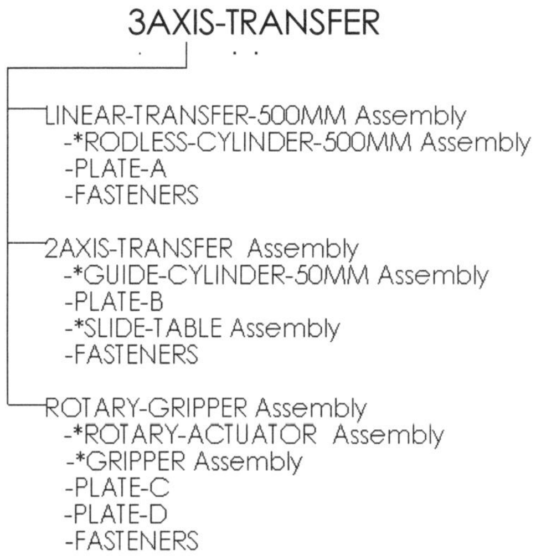

Utilize three sub-assemblies to simplify the layout structure. Each sub-assembly is self-contained.

You are responsible for the 3AXIS-TRANSFER assembly. You must be cognizant of your teammates working on the INPUT assembly and OUTPUT assembly. Both the INPUT assembly and OUTPUT assembly requires a TOP PLATE part, BOTTOM PLATE part, and a STAND OFFS part. The STAND OFFS part separates the TOP PLATE part from the BOTTOM PLATE part

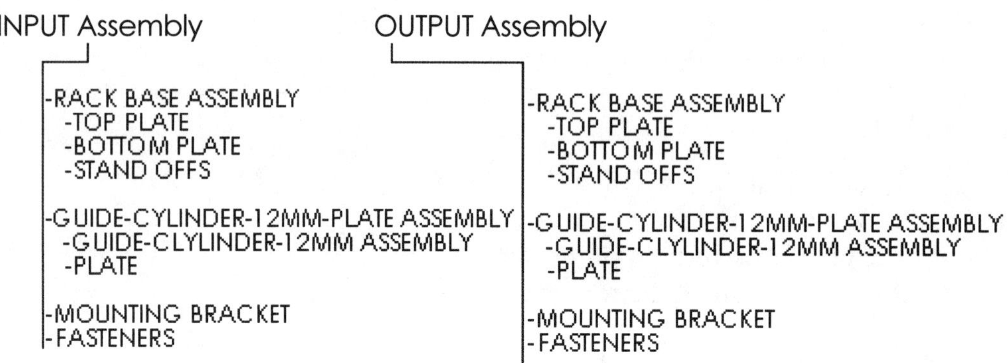

Reuse existing geometry. Design parts and assemblies to reuse and manipulate common information with Design Tables.

Review the 3AXIS-TRANSFER Assembly Layout diagram. Determine the required document templates.

Conserve design time. Develop Assembly templates and Part templates before you create new assemblies and parts.

Determine the required models to create in SolidWorks. Obtain purchased component models from the web or directly from the vendor.

Conserve design time. A model obtained from another source is one you do not have to create.

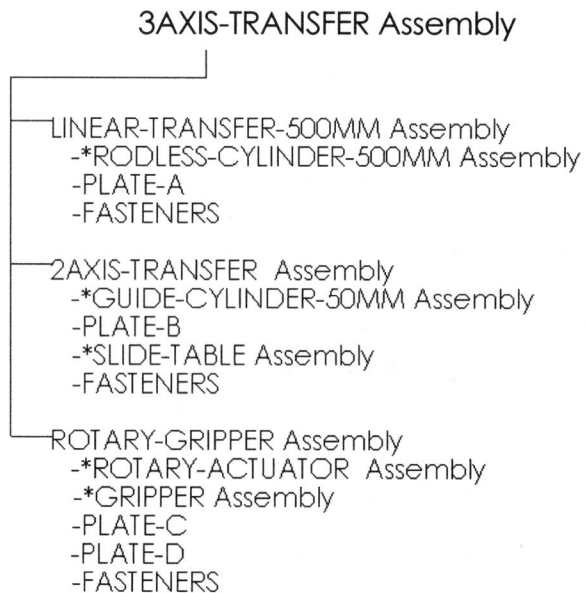

3AXIS-TRANSFER Assembly

- LINEAR-TRANSFER-500MM Assembly
  - -*RODLESS-CYLINDER-500MM Assembly
  - -PLATE-A
  - -FASTENERS
- 2AXIS-TRANSFER Assembly
  - -*GUIDE-CYLINDER-50MM Assembly
  - -PLATE-B
  - -*SLIDE-TABLE Assembly
  - -FASTENERS
- ROTARY-GRIPPER Assembly
  - -*ROTARY-ACTUATOR Assembly
  - -*GRIPPER Assembly
  - -PLATE-C
  - -PLATE-D
  - -FASTENERS

File Management

Why do you require file management? In a large assembly, there could be hundreds or even thousands of parts. To facilitate time, distribute parts and sub-assemblies between team members. Design changes occur frequently in the development process. How do you manage and control these changes? Answer: Through file management. File management is a very important tool in the development process.

The DELIVERY-STATION assembly consists of multiple folders. Utilize folders for projects, vendor components, templates and libraries. Folders exist on your local hard drive, example C:\. Folders can also exist on a network drive, example Z:\.

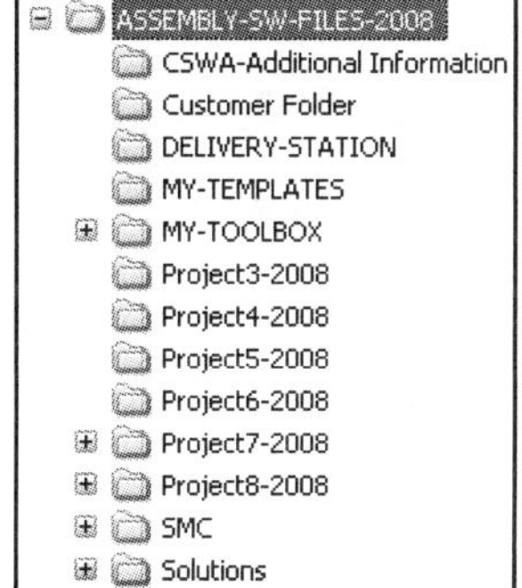

The CD included in the book contains the following top folders as illustrated.

The Projects in the book requires the documents contained in theses folders. Copy information from the CD to your computer. Final solutions for the models in this book are provided in the Project and Solutions folder.

Review the documents contained in the ASSEMBLY-SW-FILES-2008 folder. In the next section, utilize the MY-TEMPLATES folder to store the Assembly template and Part template that you create in this project. The SMC folder contains the needed components obtained from 3D ContentCentral.

Activity: Create New File Folders

Copy the file folders.

1) Place the **CD** into the CD drive.

2) Copy the **folders** onto your hard drive, "My Documents" location. Remove and save the **CD**. The CD is required for future projects.

ASSEMBLY-SW-FILES-2008
CSWA-Additional Information
Customer Folder
DELIVERY-STATION
MY-TEMPLATES
MY-TOOLBOX
Project3-2008
Project4-2008
Project5-2008
Project6-2008
Project7-2008
Project8-2008
SMC
Solutions

Review the folder contents.

3) **Expand** the ASSEMBLY-SW-FILES-2008 folder. The DELIVERY-STATION file folder is empty. Store the parts that you create in the DELIVERY-STATION file folder.

Review the MY-TEMPLATES file folder.

4) Click the **MY-TEMPLATES** file folder. View the two files.

5) Click the **Back** Back icon.

The MY-TEMPLATES file folder contains the A-ANSI-MM.drwdot Drawing template and the a-format.slddrt Sheet format.

Store the project Assembly template and Part template in the MY-TEMPLATES folder.

Utilize the MY-TOOLBOX folder to store copies of the SolidWorks\Toolbox parts.

System Options – File Locations

System Options are stored in the registry of the computer. System Options are not part of the document. Changes to the System Options affect current and future documents.

Review and modify System Options in this project. If you work on a local drive, C:\, the System Options are stored on the computer.

If you work on a network drive, Z:\ and change computers during this project, the System Options will reset. Conserve modeling time. Set the System Options before you begin an assembly.

Add folder search pathnames to the Document Templates and Reference Documents options in the next activity.

File Locations, Document Templates

Tabs for the New SolidWorks Document dialog box are listed under **Options**, **System Options**, **File Locations** as illustrated.

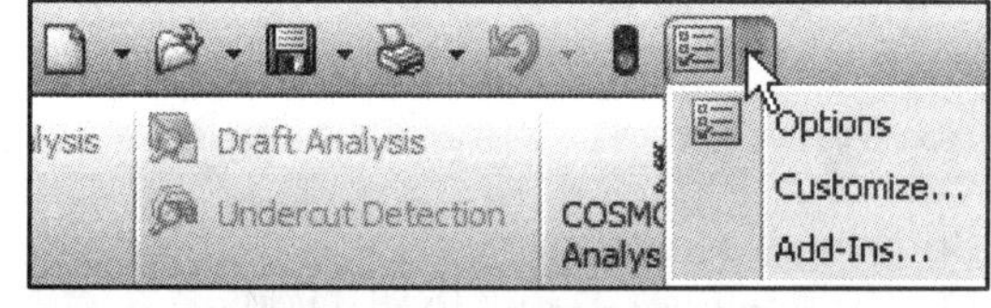

Each template produces a corresponding tab in the New SolidWorks Document dialog box.

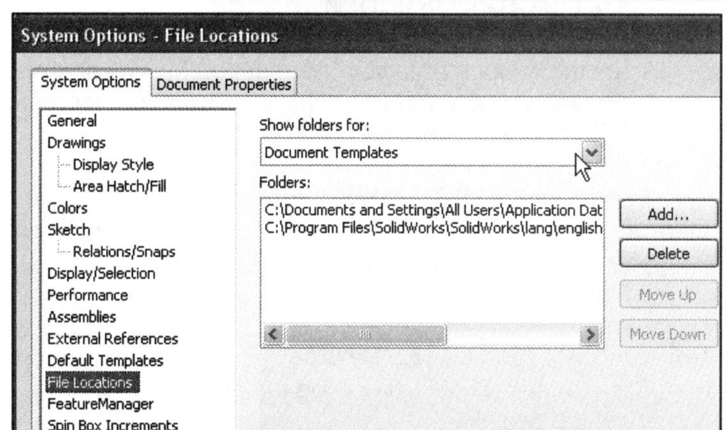

The MY-TEMPLATES tab is visible ***ONLY*** when the folder contains one or more SolidWorks documents: Part, Assembly, or Drawing templates.

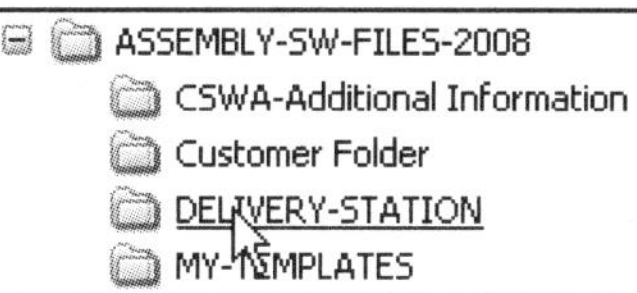

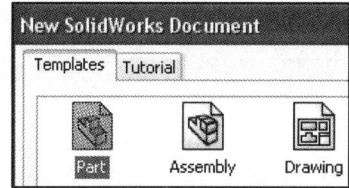

The order in the folders determines the tab order in the New SolidWorks Document dialog box.

File Locations, Reference Documents

SolidWorks utilizes a compound file structure that creates file references between documents. Example; when you open an assembly drawing, SolidWorks searches for the referenced assembly document. If the assembly document cannot be located, SolidWorks performs a search to locate the missing document. In the file open process, the search order is as follows:

- Documents loaded in memory.
- Optional user-defined search lists.

Utilize the first pathname under the Referenced Documents, Folders box. Example: \ASSEMBLY-SW-FILES-2008\DELIVERY-STATION.

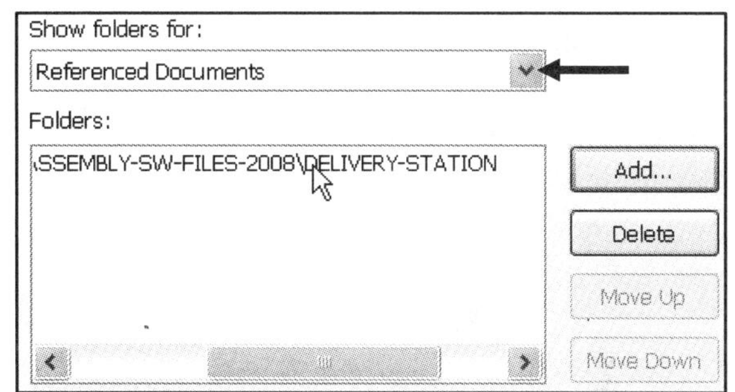

To activate a search, click System Options, External References. Check the Search file locations for the external references box.

- Current folder of the drawing or assembly documents.
- Same folder as the last found referenced.
- Stored pathname saved in the assembly document. SolidWorks searches the current drive and then the stored drive.
- Prompt the user to search for the file location.

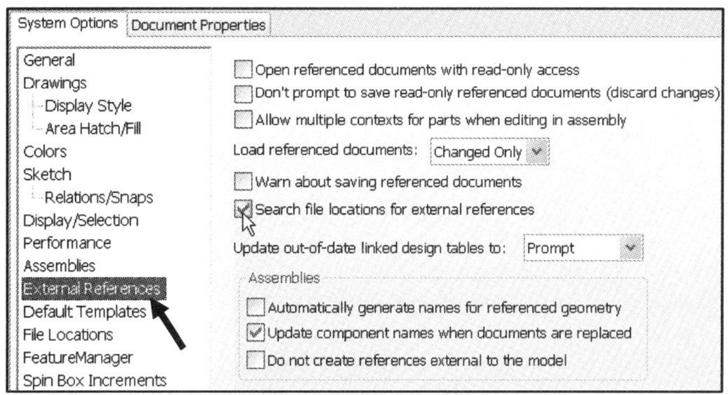

A file reference differs from an External reference. A file reference is the file pathname. The File, Find References option lists the pathname of the referenced documents.

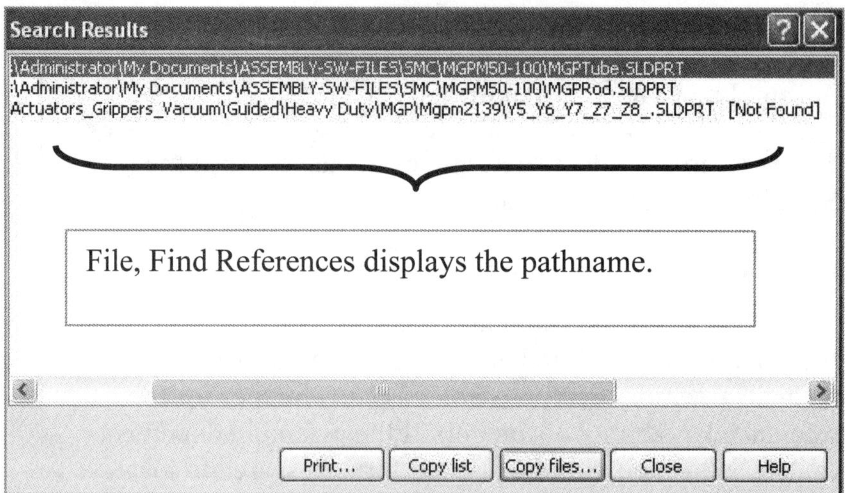

An External reference is geometry from one entity that is dependent on geometry in another component.

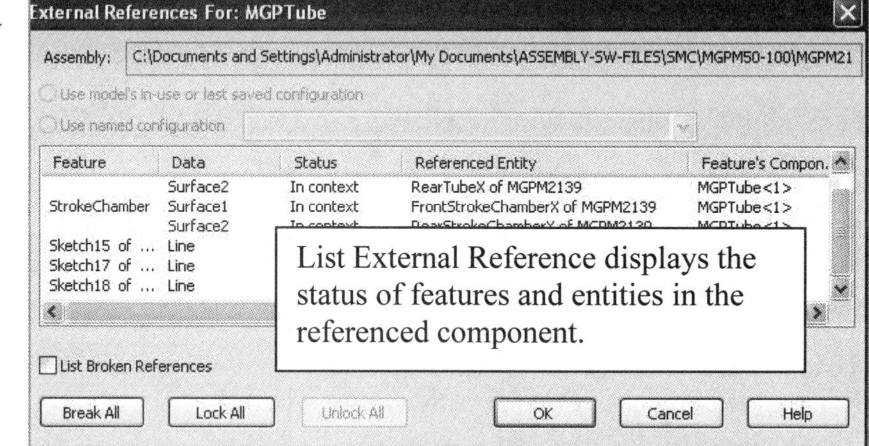

Utilize the List External References option in a later Project

During the search process, SolidWorks uses an absolute pathname including drive letter, folder location, and filename.

Example:

Absolute pathname

D:\Project-A\Transmission\Gear-A-Assembly\p2357-21.sldprt.

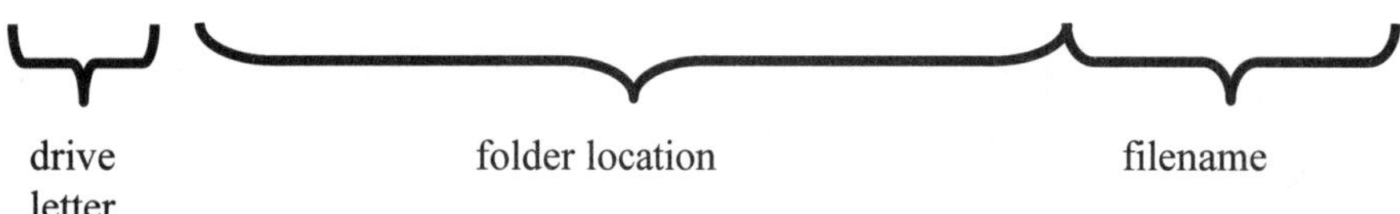

Avoid problems with file references. Utilize unique filenames.

File Locations and Design Library

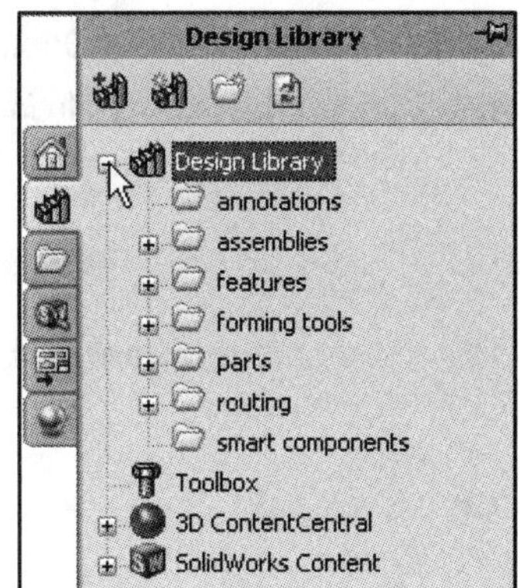

The Design Library in the Task Pane provides a central location for reusable elements such as parts, assemblies, and sketches. It does not recognize non-reusable elements such as SolidWorks drawings, text files, or other non-SolidWorks files.

The Design Library includes the following default entries: *design library*, *Toolbox*, *3D ContentCentral*, and *SolidWorks Content*.

Add the MY-TOOLBOX and SMC folders to the Design Library.

Activity: Set System Options and File Locations

Start a SolidWorks 2008 session.

6) Click **Start** from the Windows Taskbar

7) Click **All Programs.**

8) Click the **SolidWorks 2008** folder.

9) Click the **SolidWorks 2008** application. The SolidWorks program window opens. Note: Do not open a document.

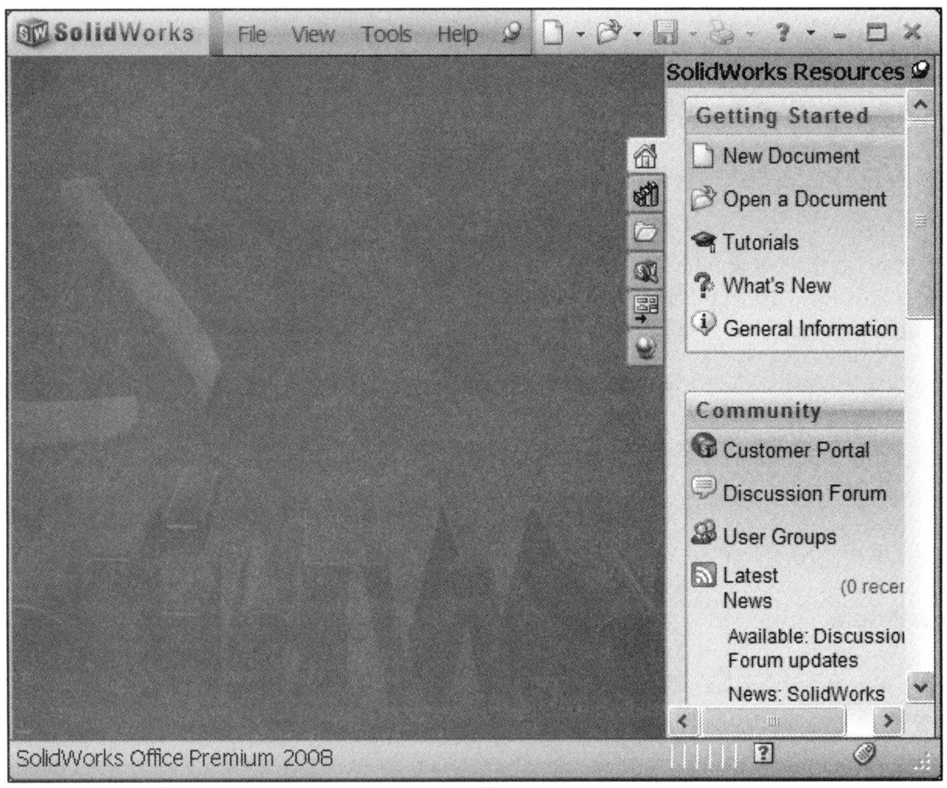

System Options. Add a Document template folder.

10) Click **Options** from the Menu bar toolbar. The System Options – General dialog box is displayed.

11) Click **File Locations**.

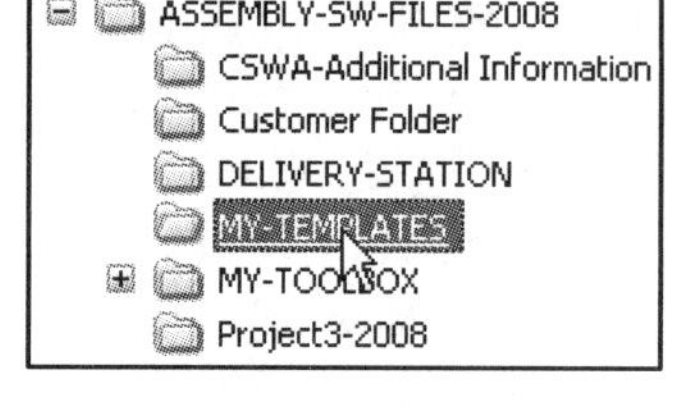

12) Select **Document Templates** from the Show folders drop-down menu.

13) Click **Add**.

14) Browse and select the **ASSEMBLY-SW-FILES-2008\MY-TEMPLATES** folder.

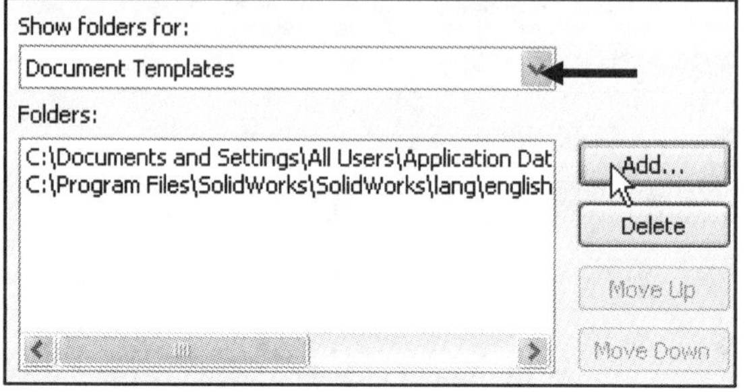

15) Click **OK** from the Browse For Folder dialog box.

16) If required, click the **Move Down** button to position the MY-TEMPLATES folder at the bottom of the Folders list. Note: The MY-TEMPLATES folder will be the third tab in the New dialog box.

Add a Referenced Document folder.

17) Select **Referenced Documents** from the Show folders drop-down menu.

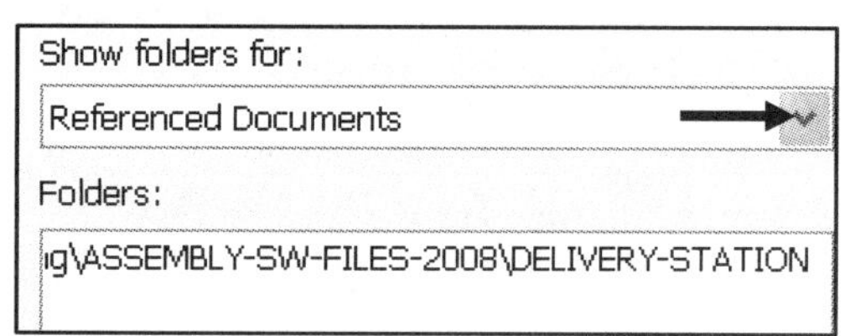

18) Click **Add**.

19) Select the **ASSEMBLY-SW-FILES-2008\DELIVERY-STATION** folder.

20) Click **OK** from the Browse For Folder dialog box.

Add two folders to the Design Library.

21) Select **Design Library** from the Show folders drop-down menu.

22) Click **Add**.

23) Select the **ASSEMBLY-SW-FILES-2008\MY-TOOLBOX** folder.

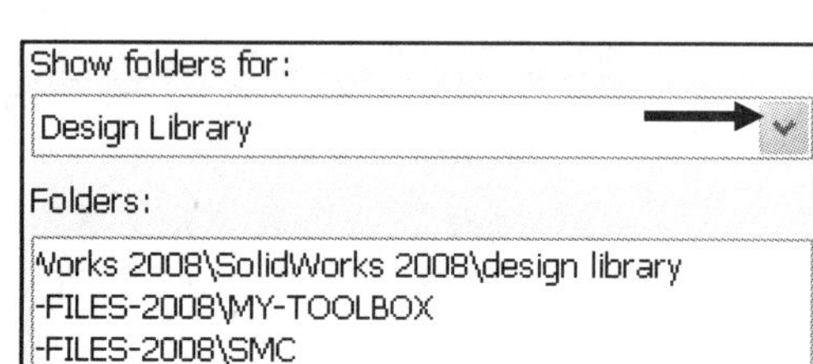

24) Click **OK**.

25) Click **Add**.

26) Select the **ASSEMBLY-SW-FILES-2008\SMC** folder.

27) Click **OK** from the Browse For Folder dialog box.

System Options - Large Assembly Mode

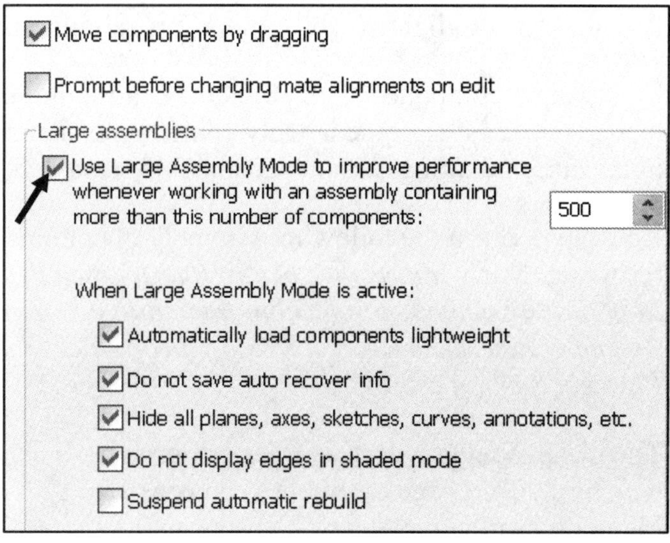

Large Assembly mode is a collection of system settings that improves the performance of assemblies. Automatically load components lightweight is check by default.

Set a threshold for the number of components, and have Large Assembly mode active automatically when that threshold is reached. The default setting for the Large Assembly mode is 500 components as illustrated.

Fully Resolved vs. Lightweight vs. Quick view / Selective open

You can load an assembly with its active components *fully resolved* or in a *lightweight* or *Quick view mode*. Both parts and assemblies can be opened with either mode.

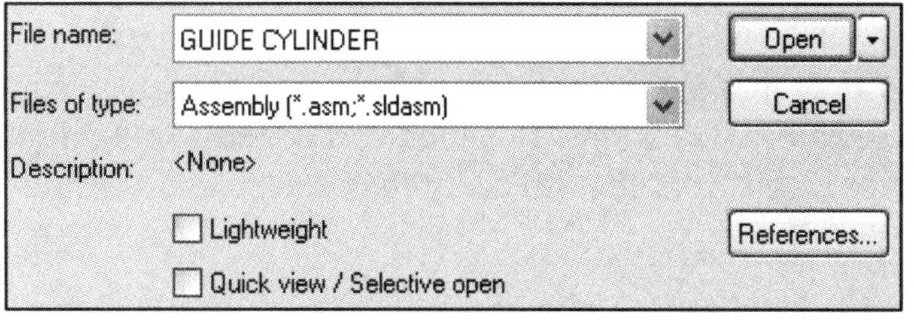

When a component is *fully resolved*, all its model data is loaded in memory.

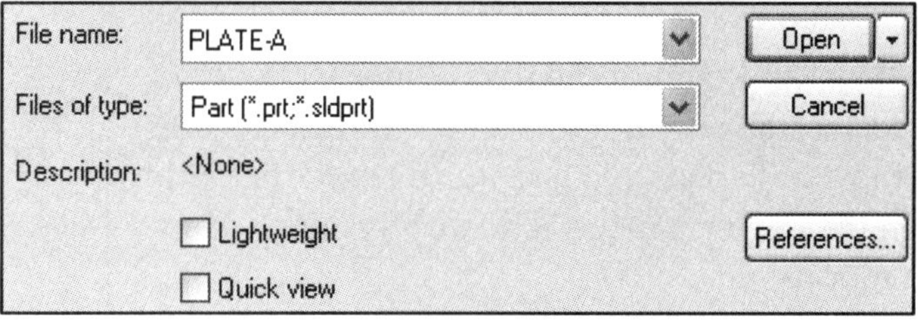

When a component is *lightweight*, only a subset of its model data is loaded in memory. The remaining model data is loaded on an as-needed basis. A feather is displayed in the FeatureManager.

Improve performance of large assemblies significantly by using lightweight components. Loading an assembly with lightweight components is faster than loading the same assembly with fully resolved components.

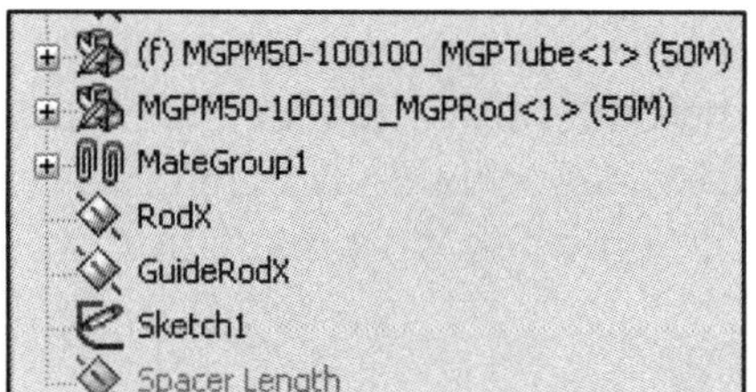

Assemblies with lightweight components rebuild faster because less data is evaluated.

Lightweight components are efficient because the full model data for the components is loaded only as it is needed. Only components that are affected by changes that you make in the current editing session become fully resolved.

You can perform the following assembly operations on lightweight components without resolving them: *Add/remove mates, Interference detection, Collision detection, Edge/Face/Component selection, Annotations, Measure, Dimensions, Section Properties, Assembly Reference Geometry, Mass Properties, Section View, Exploded View, and Physical Simulation.*

The Quick View / Selective Open option is new for 2008. Large assemblies can consist of hundreds of components. Reasons to simplify a large assembly include:

- Improve performance and reduce rebuild times.
- Improve display speed during dynamic view operations (zoom, pan, rotate, etc).
- Focus your work on a subset of components.

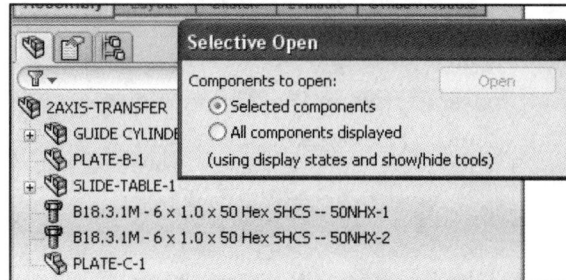

The Quick View / Selective Open option opens a simplified representation of the assembly. You specify which components to load; other components are not loaded and not visible, but the effects of their mates are / should be retained.

The Quick View / Selective Open option is not used in this book.

The Level of detail option affects performance. Drag the slider to the right for a faster display and a reduced level of detail in the Performance section of System Options.

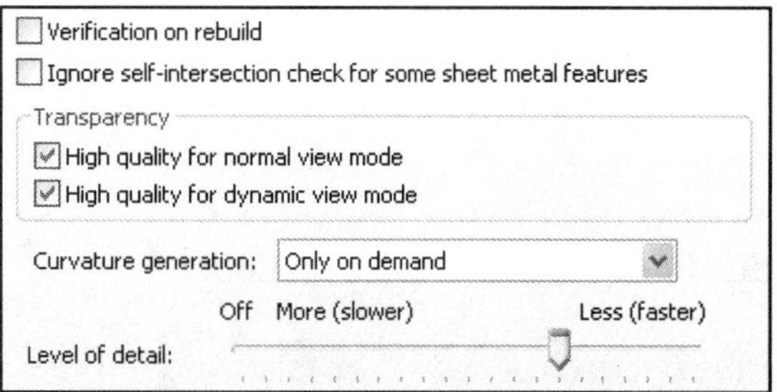

The Large Assembly Mode by default hides all planes, axes, sketches, curves, and annotations. Uncheck the Hide all planes, axes, sketches, curves, annotations, etc. option when working with Layout Sketches.

Incorporate Layout Sketches with the Top-down design assembly modeling approach in Project 8.

Large Assembly Mode controls various Drawing options as illustrated.

Selected lightweight components in a drawing remain in a lightweight state.

Modify Display modes at any time in the assembly, part, or drawing.

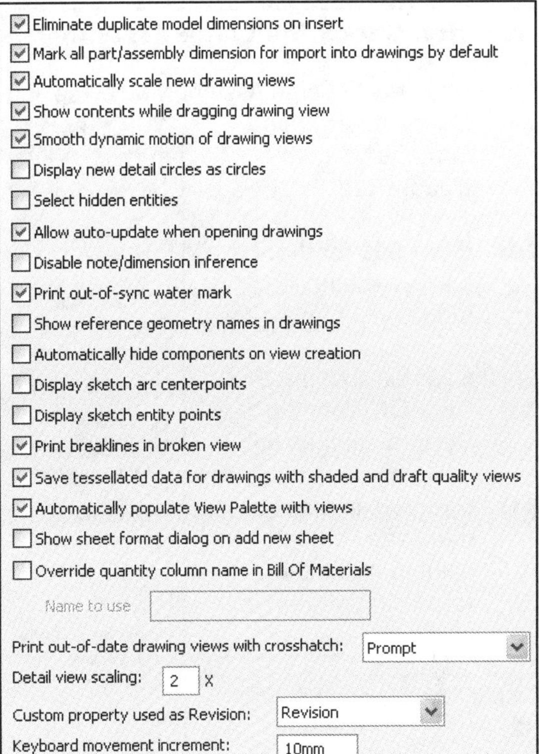

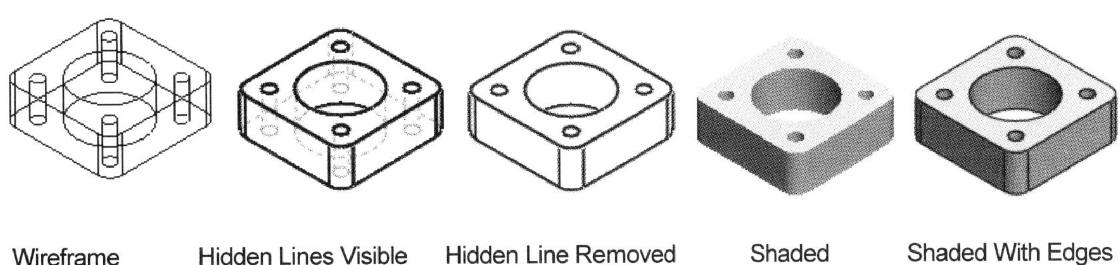

Save models in the Shaded With Edges or Shaded display mode from the Heads-up View toolbar in the Graphics window.

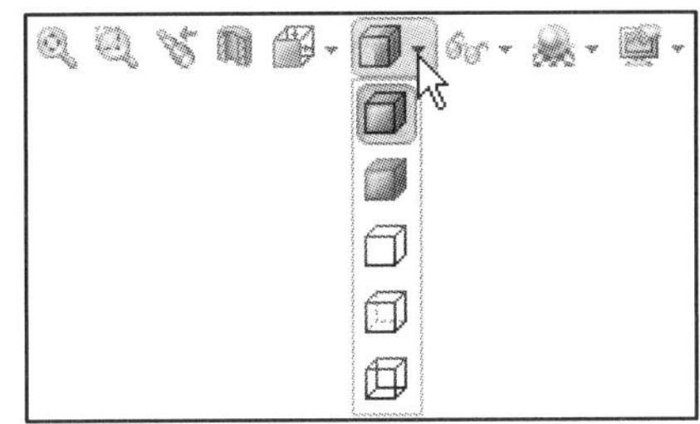

How large is a large assembly? Answer: There is no right or wrong answer. The goal in the project is to develop sound assembly modeling techniques and to understand the various assembly options in SolidWorks.

Activity: Check the Large Assembly Mode Setting

Check the default Large Assembly Mode setting.

28) Click **Assemblies** from the System Options tab.

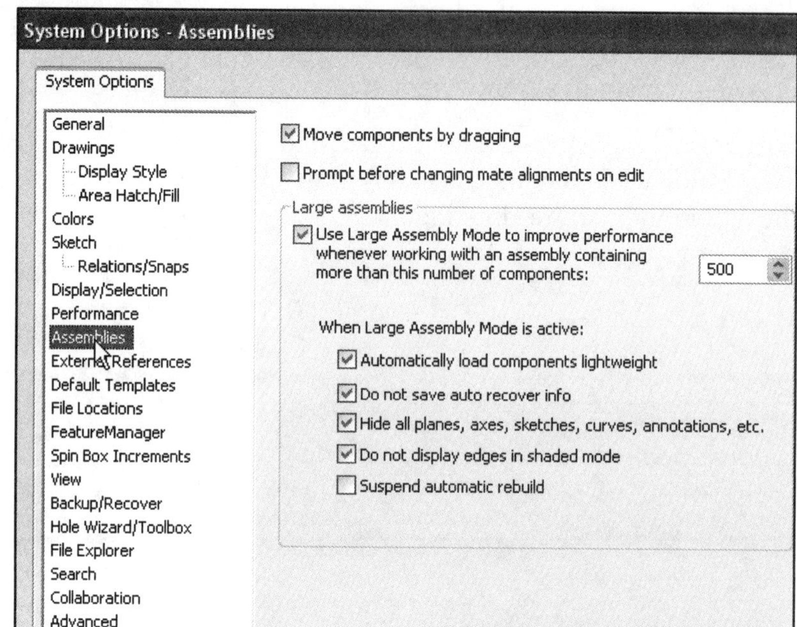

29) Enter **500** for the Large assemblies mode.

Set the System Options.

30) Click **OK** from the System Options box.

31) Click **OK** to the message, "Do you want to make the following path changes?"

Display the Design Library.

32) Click the **Design Library** icon from the Task Pane. View the added folders: *MY-TOOLBOX and SMC.*

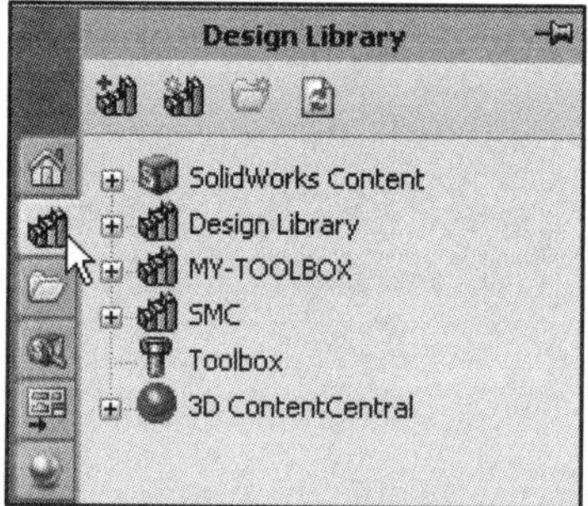

Assembly Template, Part Template, and Document Properties

Templates are the foundation for assemblies, parts, and drawings. Document Properties address: dimensioning standards, units, text style, center marks, witness lines, arrow styles, tolerance, precision, and other parameters. Document Properties apply only to the current document.

The foundation of a SolidWorks assembly is the Assembly template. The custom Assembly template begins with the default Assembly template.

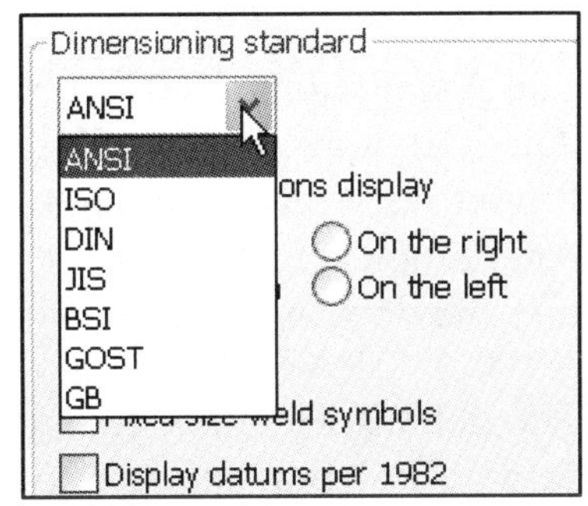

Conserve modeling time. Store Document Properties in the Assembly Template. Set the parameters for the Dimensioning standard and Units. New documents that utilize the same template contain the saved parameters.

The Dimensioning standard options are: *ANSI*, *ISO*, *DIN*, *JIS*, *BSI*, *GOST*, and *GB*. The SMC engineers dimensioned the components using the ISO standard. Display sub-assemblies you create for the DELIVERY-STATION assembly project using the ANSI standard.

Modify Document Properties, and Annotations settings. Save the custom Assembly template in the MY-TEMPLATES folder.

ASSEM1.sldasm is the default document name. Assembly documents end with the extension ".sldasm." Assembly templates end with the extension, ".asmdot."

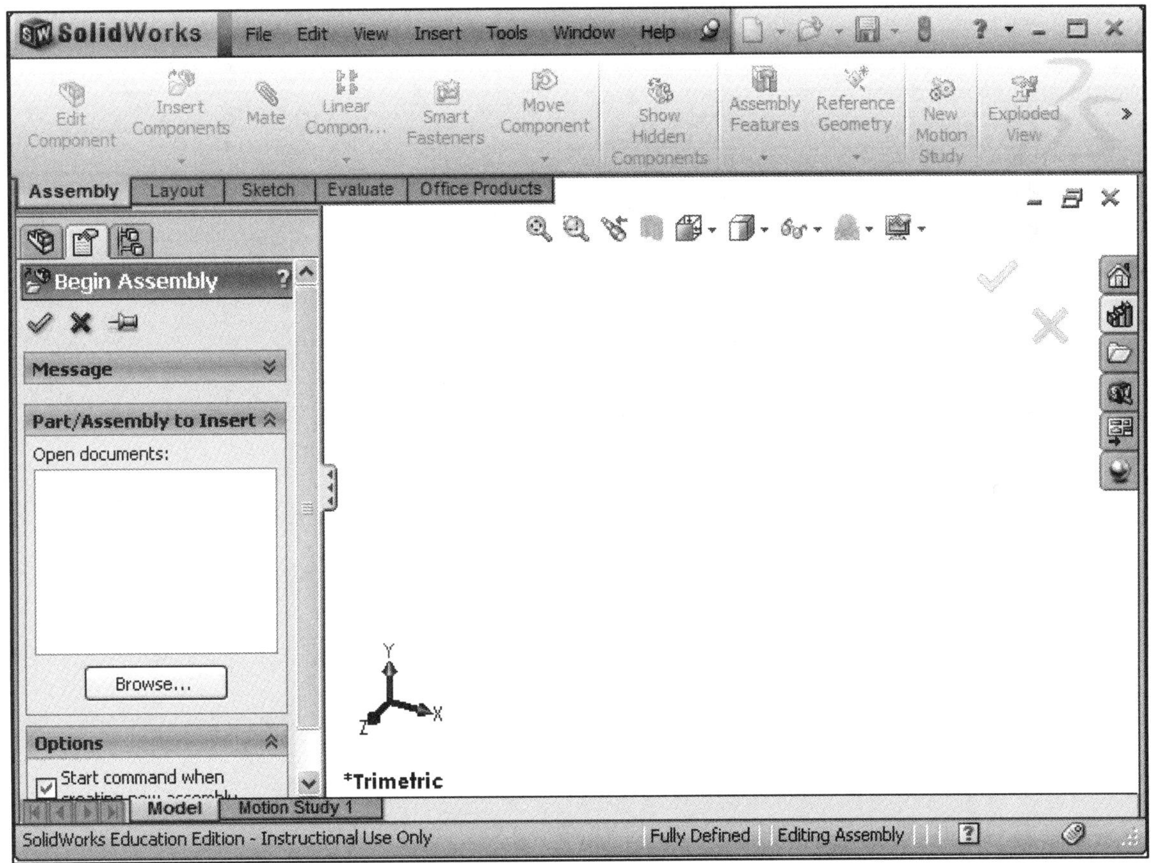

The Begin Assembly PropertyManager is displayed if the Start command when creating new assembly box is checked.

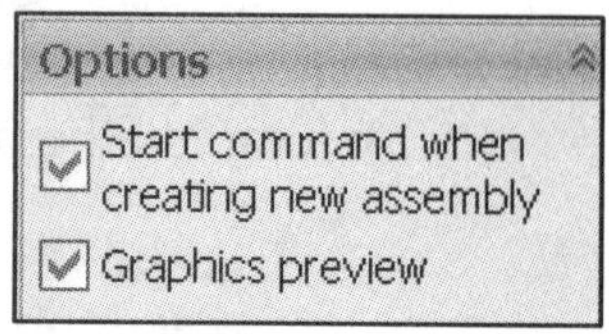

The Annotations, Details option contains the Annotation Properties. Store the Annotation Properties with the Assembly template. Insert Annotations created in the assembly and part into the drawing.

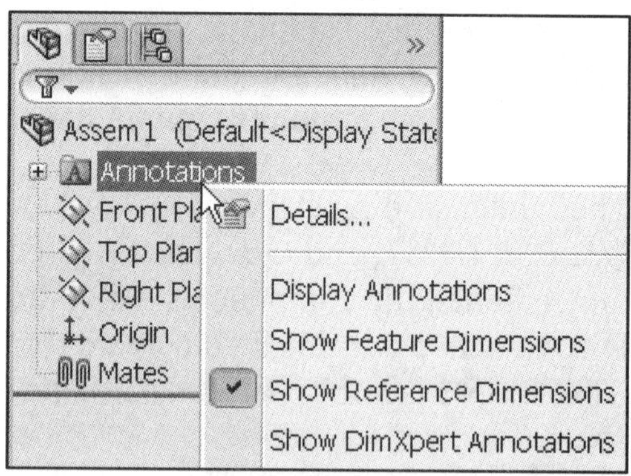

The default Assembly template contains the assembly Origin and three default assembly Reference planes:

- *Front Plane*
- *Top Plane*
- *Right Plane*

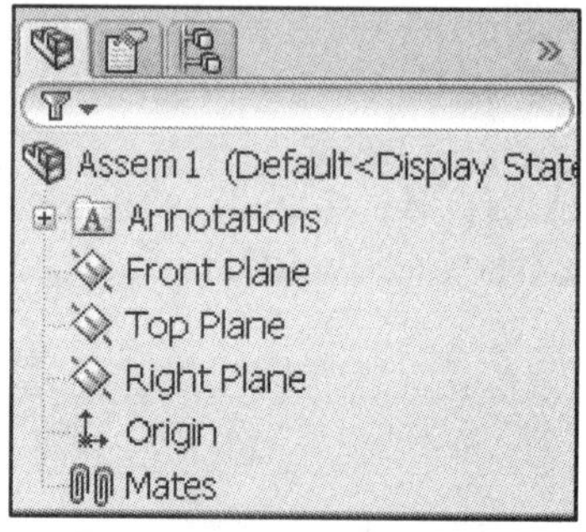

New parts require a Part template. The foundation for a SolidWorks part is a Part template. Modify the Documentation Properties Units and Dimensioning standard. Templates store material properties.

Utilize the Materials Editor and select Aluminum, 6061 Alloy. The material parameters pass to the Mass Property calculations in the part and the Section view hatching in the drawing.

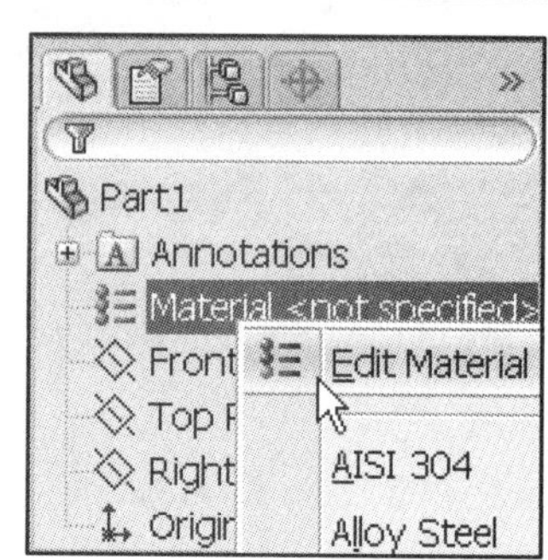

Reuse information. Create Assembly templates and Part templates before you begin a project!

In this book, the planes are Snap/grid are deactivated to improve illustration visibility.

The MY-TEMPLATES folder contains the Drawing template, A-ANSI-MM. Text height, arrows, and line styles are defined in millimeter values according to the ASME Y14.2-1992(R1998) Line Conventions and Lettering standard.

The Drawing template contains a Sheet format. A Sheet format contains Title block, Company logo, and Custom Properties. The SolidWorks drawing combines the Drawing template, Sheet format, and views of a part or assembly. The Drawing file extension is ".slddrw."

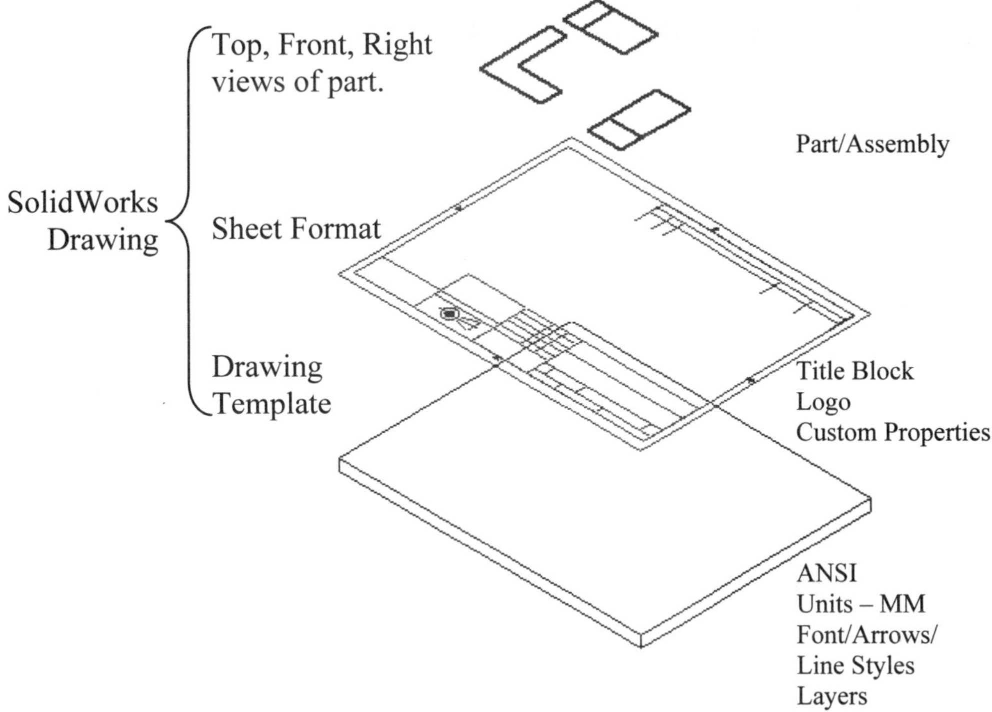

For additional information on Drawing Templates, see Planchard and Planchard, **Drawing and Detailing with SolidWorks 2008**, SDC Publications.

Activity: Create an Assembly Template, Part Template, with Document Properties

Create a new assembly.

33) Click **New** from the Menu bar toolbar. Note: The Menu bar toolbar and the Menu bar menu are pinned in this book.

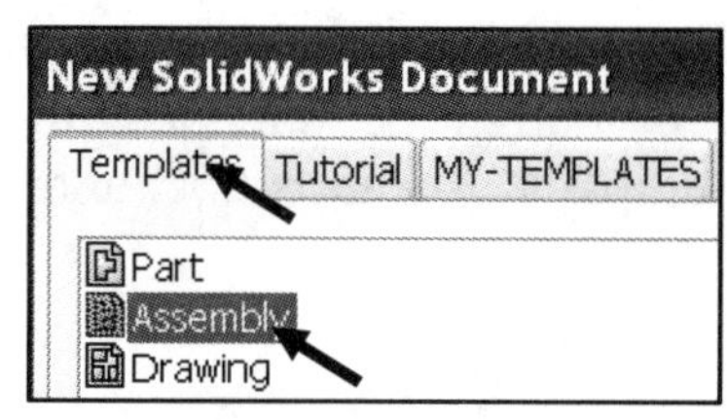

34) Click the default **Templates** tab.

35) Double-click **Assembly** from the New SolidWorks Document dialog box. The Begin Assembly PropertyManager is displayed if the Start command when creating new assembly box is checked.

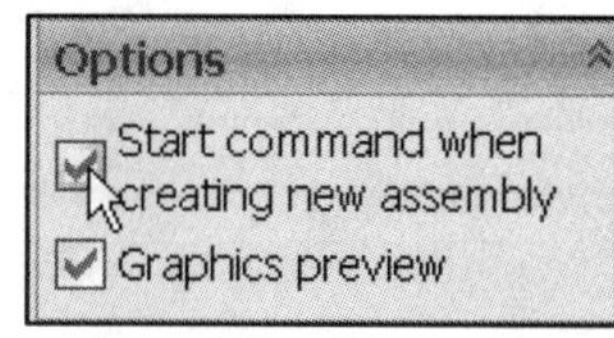

36) Click **Cancel** from the Begin Assembly PropertyManager. Assem1 is displayed.

Set document properties.

37) Click **Options**, **Document Properties** tab from the Menu bar toolbar.

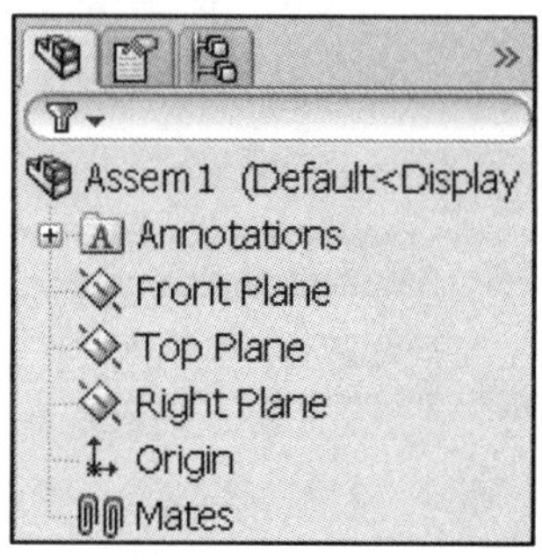

38) Select **ANSI** from the Dimensioning standard drop-down menu.

Set Template units.

39) Click **Units** from the left text box.

40) Click **MMGS (millimeter, gram, second)** for Unit system.

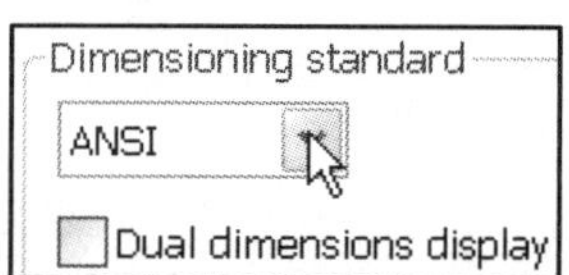

41) Select **.12** for Length units Decimal places.

42) Click **OK** from the Document Properties - Units dialog box.

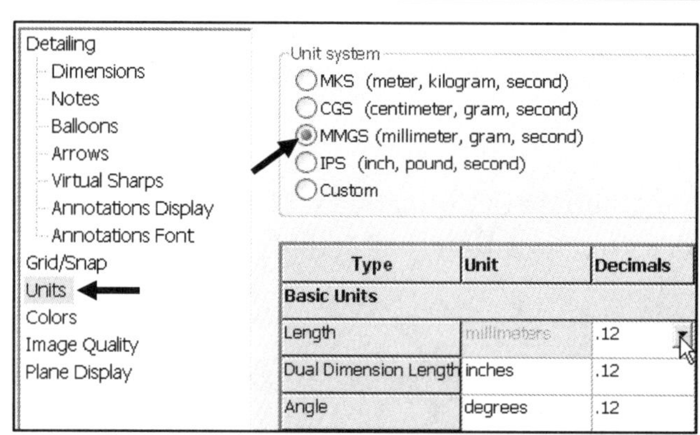

Display the Annotation Properties.

43) Right-click **Annotations** from the Assembly FeatureManager.

44) Click **Details**. Review the default settings.

45) Click **OK** from the Annotations Properties box.

Planes are deactivated in the Graphics window for improved visibility.

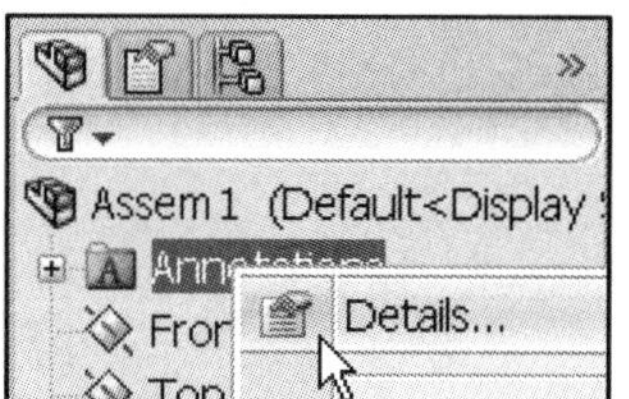

Save the Assembly template.

46) Click **Save** .

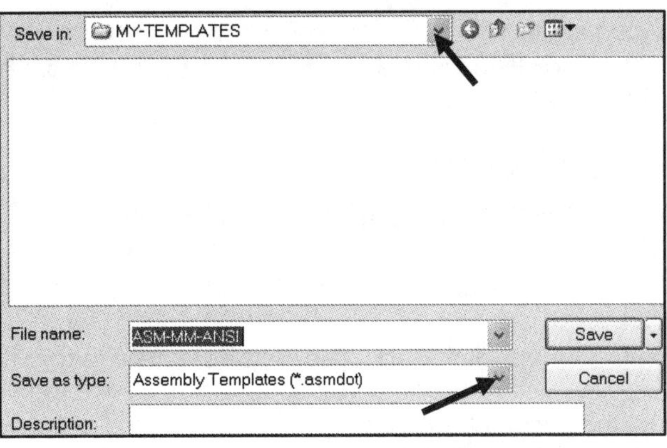

47) Select **Assembly Templates(*.asmdot)** for Save as type.

48) Select the **ASSEMBLY-SW-FILES-2008\MY-TEMPLATES** folder.

49) Enter **ASM-MM-ANSI** for File name.

50) Click **Save**.

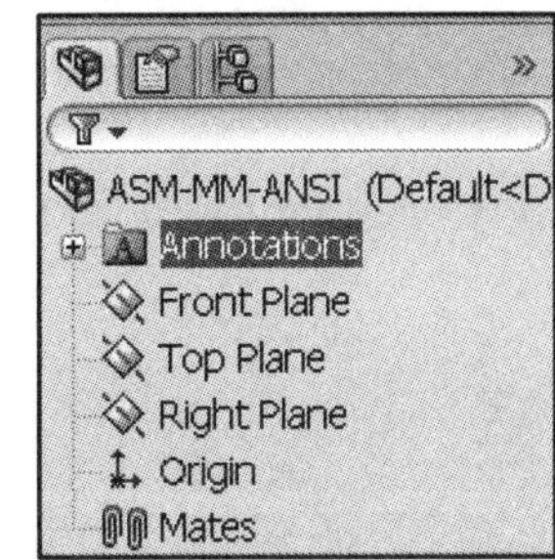

Close all files.

51) Click **Window**, **Close All** from the Menu bar menu.

Create a New Assembly.

52) Click **New** from the Menu bar toolbar.

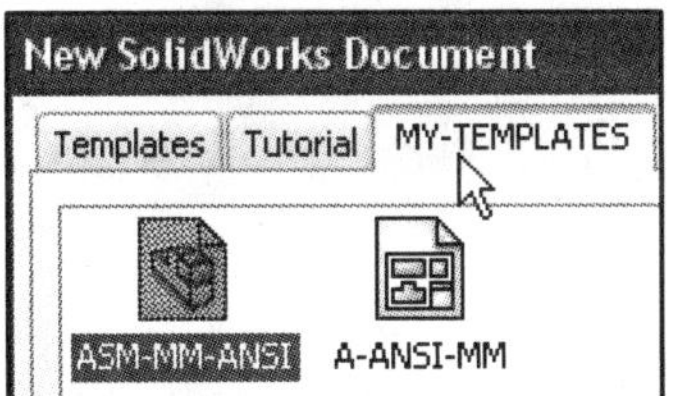

53) Click the **MY-TEMPLATES** tab.

54) Double-click **ASM-MM-ANSI**.

55) Click **Cancel** from the Begin Assembly PropertyManager. Assem2 is displayed.

Close all files.

56) Click **Windows**, **Close All** from the Menu bar menu. Do not exit SolidWorks.

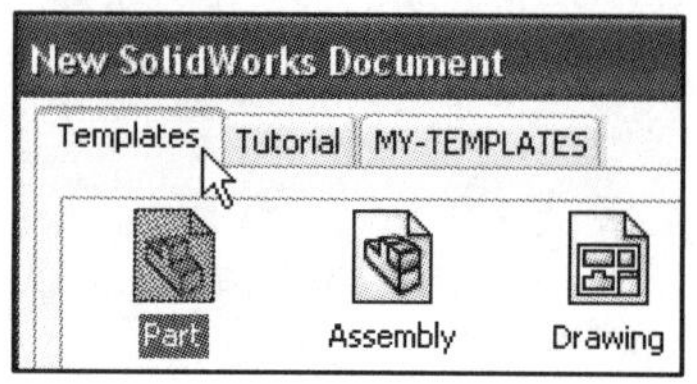

Create a new Part template.

57) Click **New** from the Menu bar toolbar.

58) Click the default **Templates** tab.

59) Double-click **Part**. The Part FeatureManager is displayed.

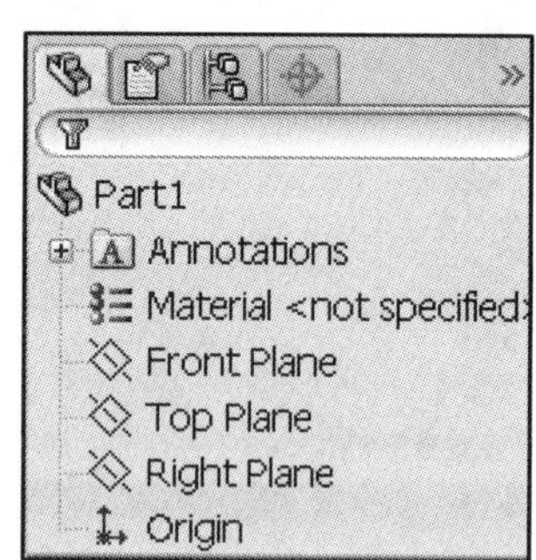

Set the document properties.

60) Click **Options**, **Document Properties** tab from the Menu bar toolbar.

61) Select **ANSI** for Dimensioning standard.

Set Linear units.

62) Click **Units** from the left text box.

63) Click **MMGS (millimeter, gram, second)** for Unit system.

64) Select **.12** for Length units Decimal places.

65) Click **OK** from the Document Properties - Units dialog box.

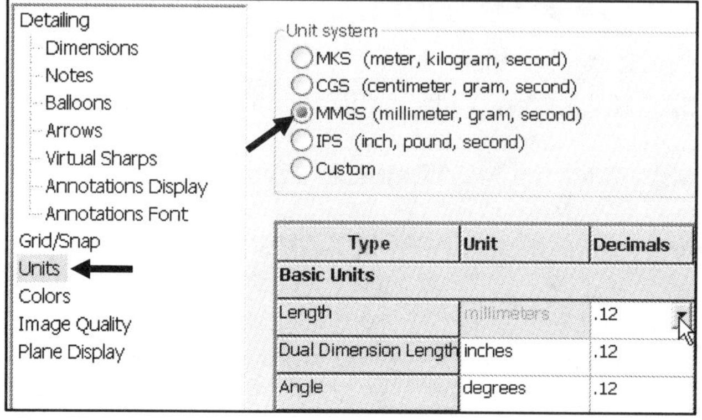

Apply material to the Part template.

66) Right-click **Material** from the Part1 FeatureManager.

67) Click **Edit Material**.

68) **Expand** Aluminum Alloys.

69) Click **6061 Alloy**.

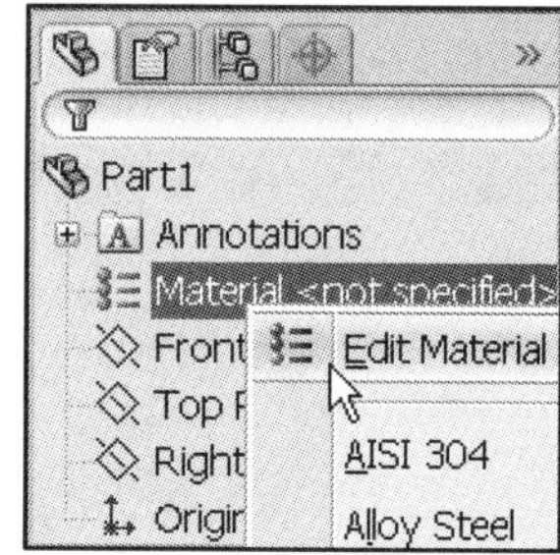

70) Click **OK** from the Materials Editor PropertyManager. 6061 Alloy is displayed in the Part1 FeatureManager.

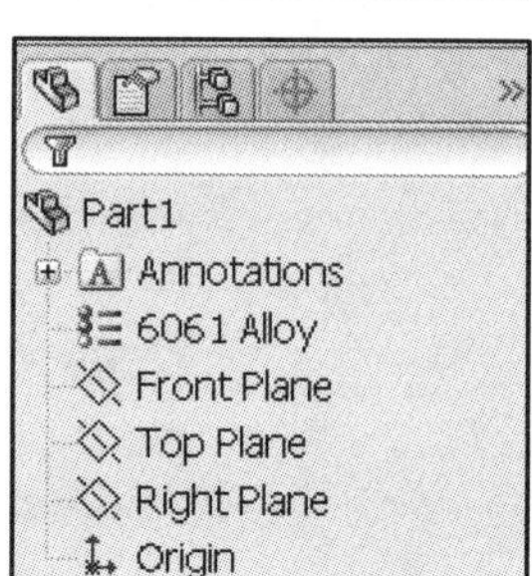

Save the Part template.

71) Click **Save** .

72) Click **Part Templates (*.prtdot)** from the Save As type box.

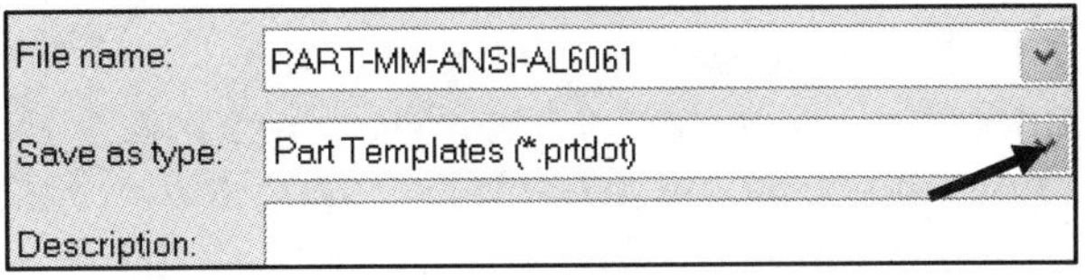

73) Select **ASSEMBLY-SW-FILES-2008\MY-TEMPLATES** folder.

74) Enter **PART-MM-ANSI-AL6061** in the File name box.

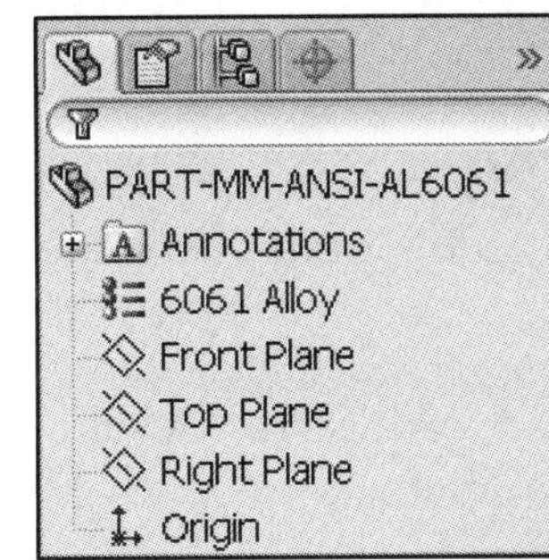

75) Click **Save**. The PART-MM-ANSI-AL6061 FeatureManager is displayed.

Close all documents.

76) Click **Window**, **Close All** from the Menu bar menu.

Create a New Part.

77) Click **New** from the Menu bar toolbar

78) Click the **MY-TEMPLATES** tab.

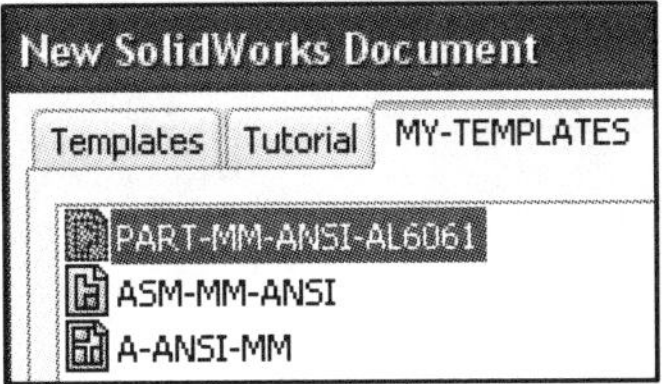

79) Double **PART-MM-ANSI-AL6061**. The Part2 FeatureManager is displayed with the Part-MM-ANSI-AL6061 template.

Close all models.

80) Click **Window**, **Close All** from the Menu bar menu.

Download an SMC Component from 3D ContentCentral

The senior engineer on the team specified SMC assemblies based on the application and loading conditions. The SMC folder contains the un-zipped assembly models required for the 3AXIS-TRANSFER assembly project which were obtained from 3D ContentCentral.

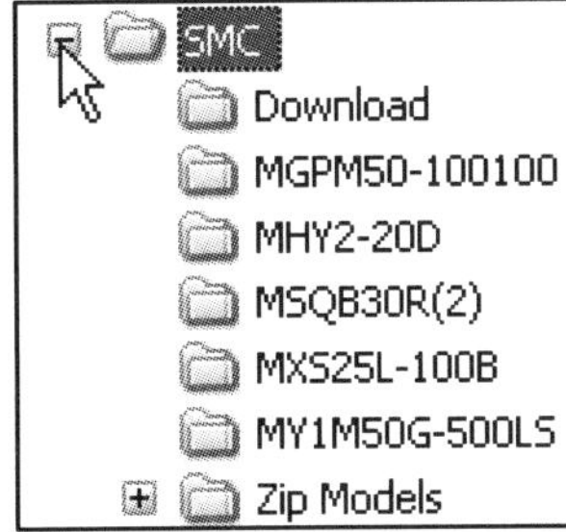

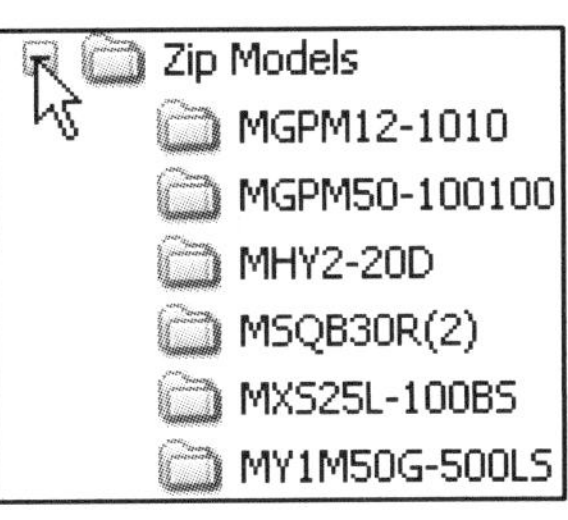

The Zip Models folder contains the SMC models, obtained from 3D ContentCentral in a zip format.

Utilize 3D ContentCentral to download the Guided Actuator *MGPM12-1010*.

If you do not have access to the Internet, locate the folder, SMC\Zip Models from the CD in the book and copy the *MGPM12-1010* files into the SMC\Download folder. The next activity is an exercise to download an assembly from 3D ContentCentral.

You are required to **Login** and **register** to download models from 3D ContentCentral.

All SMC files are provided: *MHY2-20D* "Gripper Actuator", *MSQB30R* "Rotary Actuator", *MXS25L-100B* "Slide Table", MY1M50G-500LS, "RODLESS CYLINDER", and *MGPM12-1010*, "Guided Actuator" in the SMC\Zip Models folder.

Activity: Download a Component from 3D ContentCentral

Perform this next activity if you want to download the *MGPM12-1010* Zip folder from 3D ContentCentral verses coping the files from the SMC\Zip Models\MGPM12-1010 folder to the SMC\Download folder.

Download an assemlby from 3D ContentCentral. Note: The other components in the SMC folder were downloaded from this site.

81) Click the **Design Library** tab from the Task Pane.

82) **Expand** the SMC folder. View the folders containing assemblies and parts.

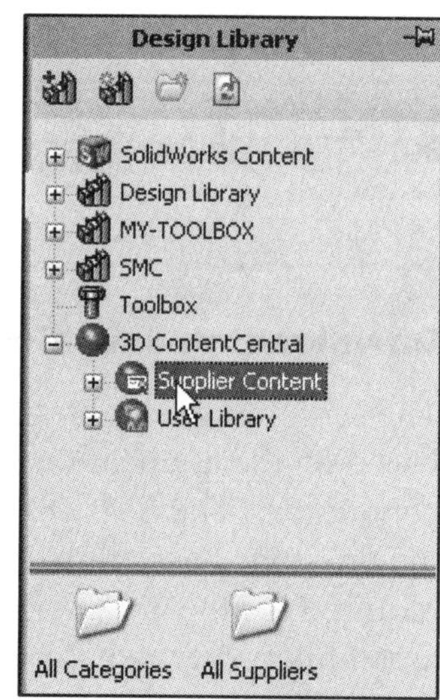

Invoke the 3D ContentCentral.

83) **Expand** 3D ContentCentral. Note: You need to be connected to the internet for this next section.

84) Click the **Supplier Content** icon. Two folders are displayed: All Categories, and All Suppliers.

85) Double-click the **All Supplies** folder.

86) Click the **Click here for all supplies** icon. 3DContentCentral is displayed.

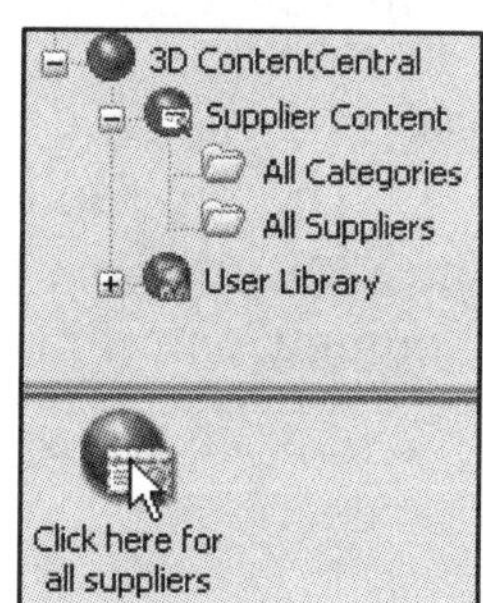

87) Click the **SMC Corporation of America** hyperlink. The SMC Corporation of America web site is displayed. Part is the active tab.

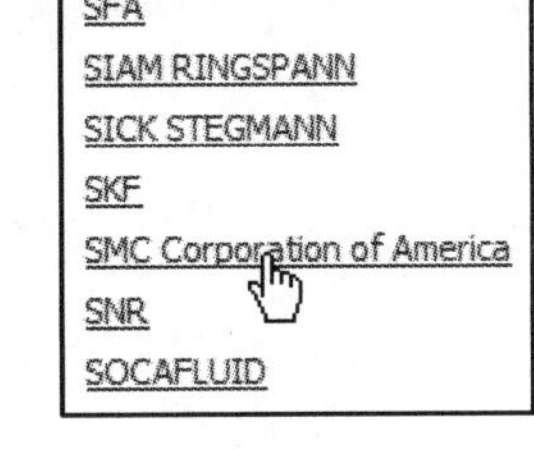

88) Click the **Actuators** folder as illustrated.

89) Click the **Guided Actuators** folder as illustrated.

90) Click the **Heavy Duty** folder as illustrated.

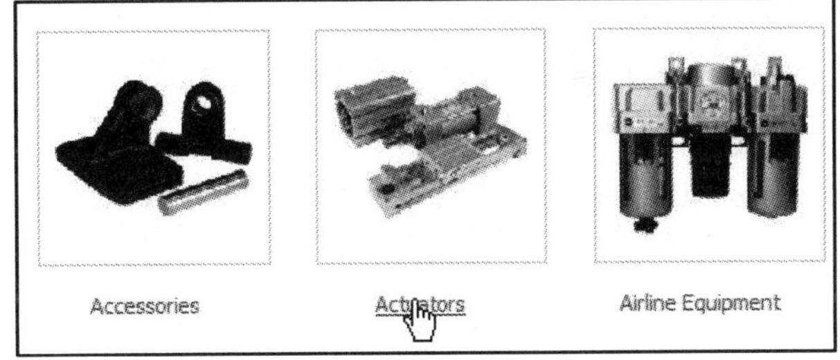

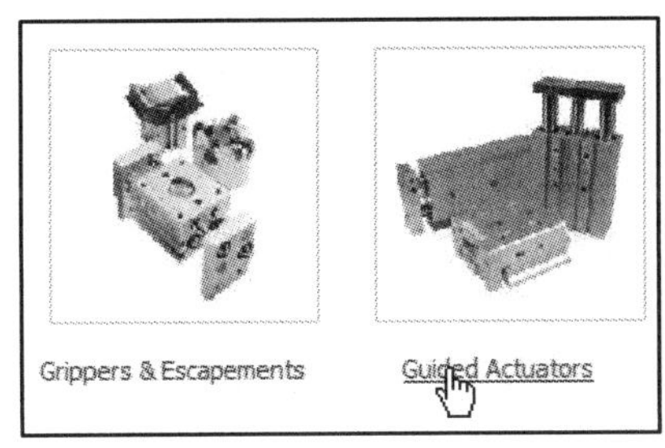

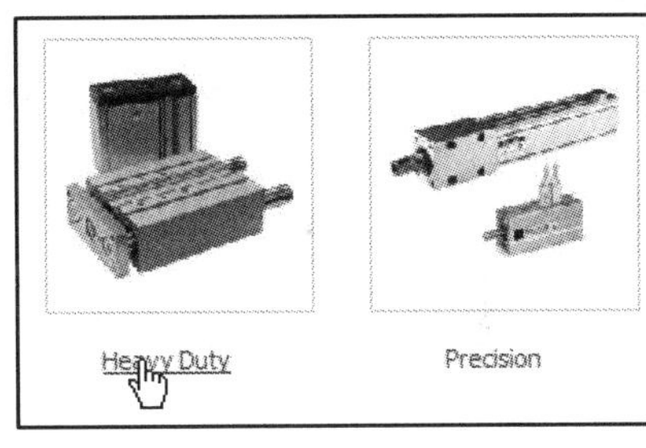

Select the Guide Cylinder.

91) Click the **MGP** folder.

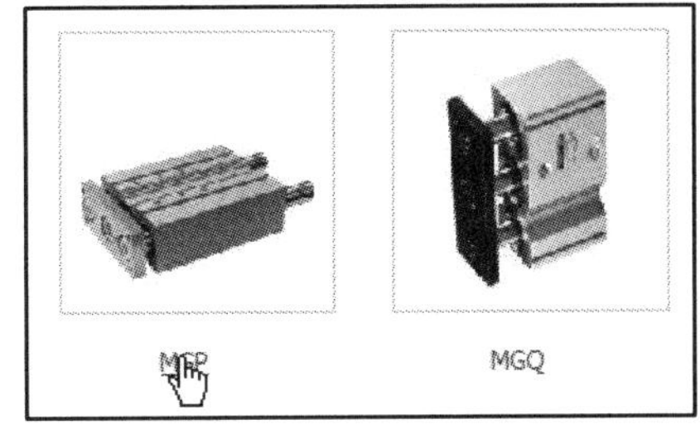

92) Click the **MGPM, Compact Guide Cylinder, Slide Bearing** folder.

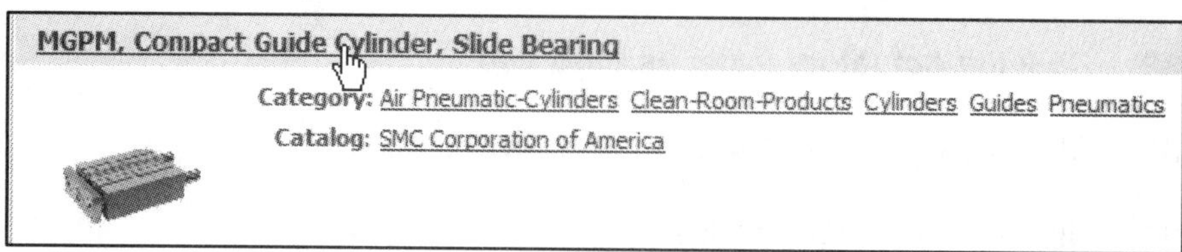

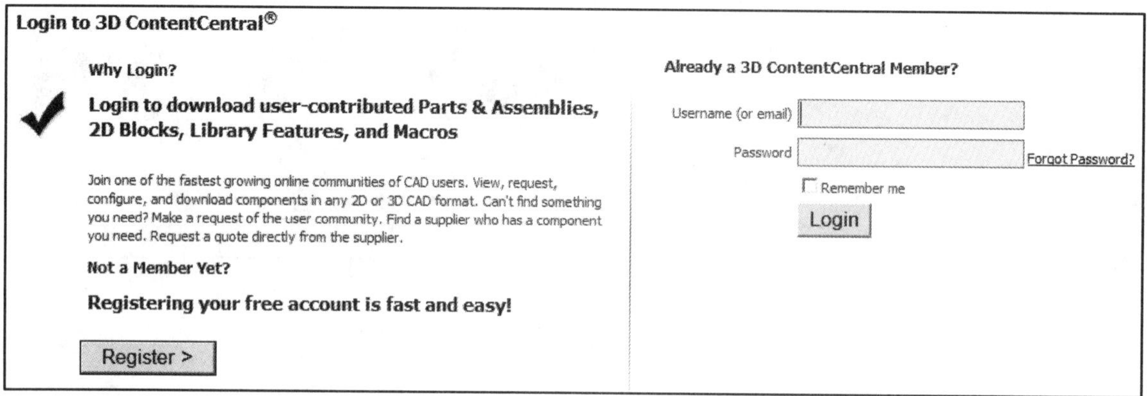

Login to 3D ContentCentral®
Why Login?
Login to download user-contributed Parts & Assemblies, 2D Blocks, Library Features, and Macros
Join one of the fastest growing online communities of CAD users. View, request, configure, and download components in any 2D or 3D CAD format. Can't find something you need? Make a request of the user community. Find a supplier who has a component you need. Request a quote directly from the supplier.
Not a Member Yet?
Registering your free account is fast and easy!
Register >
Already a 3D ContentCentral Member?
Username (or email)
Password
Forgot Password?
Remember me
Login

93) **Login** or **register** to download the assembly.

94) Select **12** for Bore Size.

95) Select **RC (Or M5x08 for 12)** for Port Type.

96) Select **10**mm for Stroke.

97) Select **10**mm for Stroke.

98) Select **No Switch**.

99) Select **2 pcs**.

100) Click **Update Preview**. View the model.

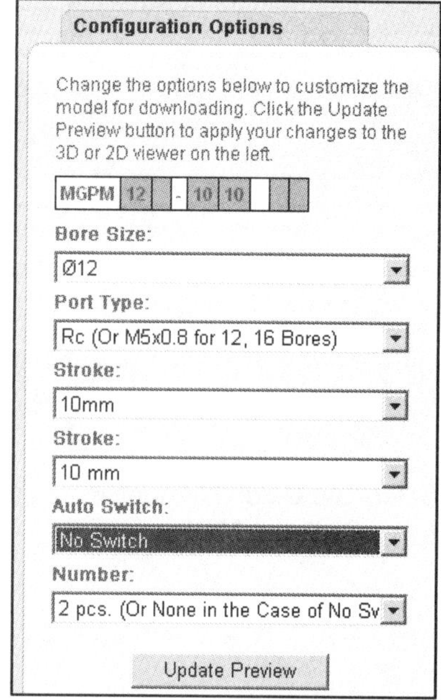

Configuration Options
Change the options below to customize the model for downloading. Click the Update Preview button to apply your changes to the 3D or 2D viewer on the left.
MGPM 12 - 10 10
Bore Size:
Ø12
Port Type:
Rc (Or M5x0.8 for 12, 16 Bores)
Stroke:
10mm
Stroke:
10 mm
Auto Switch:
No Switch
Number:
2 pcs. (Or None in the Case of No Sv
Update Preview

Download the zip file.

101) Select **SolidWorks Part/Assembly (.sldpt)** from the drop-down menu.

102) Select **2008** for Version. The Zipped box is checked.

103) Click the **Download Files** button.

File Download

Downloading is complete.

Click to download

Close

104) Click the **Click to download** hyperlink as illustrated.

105) Select the **SMC\Download** folder from the Browse For Folder dialog box.

106) Click **OK**. The MGPM-12-1010.zip folder is downloaded to your computer.

107) **Return** to SolidWorks.

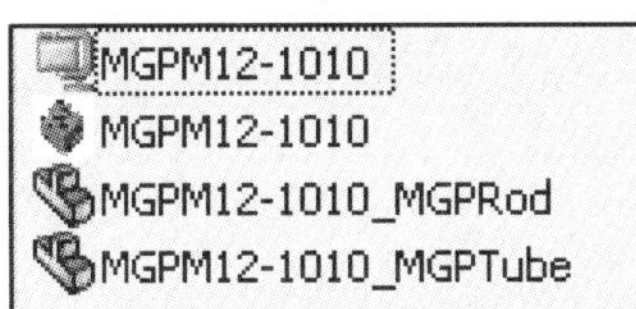

Extract the assembly and parts in the SMC/Download folder.

108) Double-click **MGPM12-1010.zip** from the ASSEMBLY-SW-FILES-2008\SMC\Download folder.

109) Click **Extract all files**.

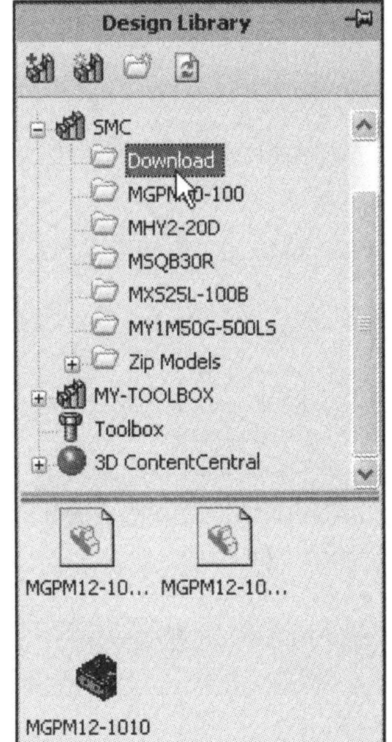

Return to SolidWorks. Use the downloaded information or the models on the CD in the SMC folder.

110) Click the **SMC\Download** folder from the Design Library. View the models.

111) Position the mouse pointer on the **MGPM12-1010** icon. The icon displays a large thumbnail of the assembly.

112) Click and drag the **MGPM12-1010** icon into the Graphics window. The MGPM12-1010 assembly is displayed in the Graphics window.

113) Click **Yes** to update. View the model in the FeatureManager.

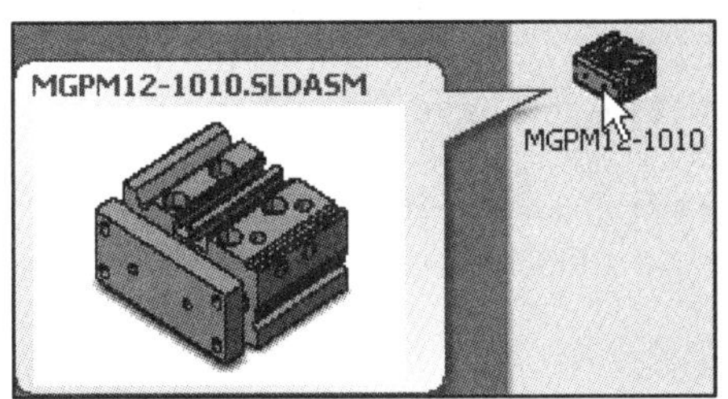

Review the FeatureManager component names.

114) **View** the FeatureManager and the two component icons MGPM12-1010_MGPTube and MGPM12-1010_MGPRod in the assembly.

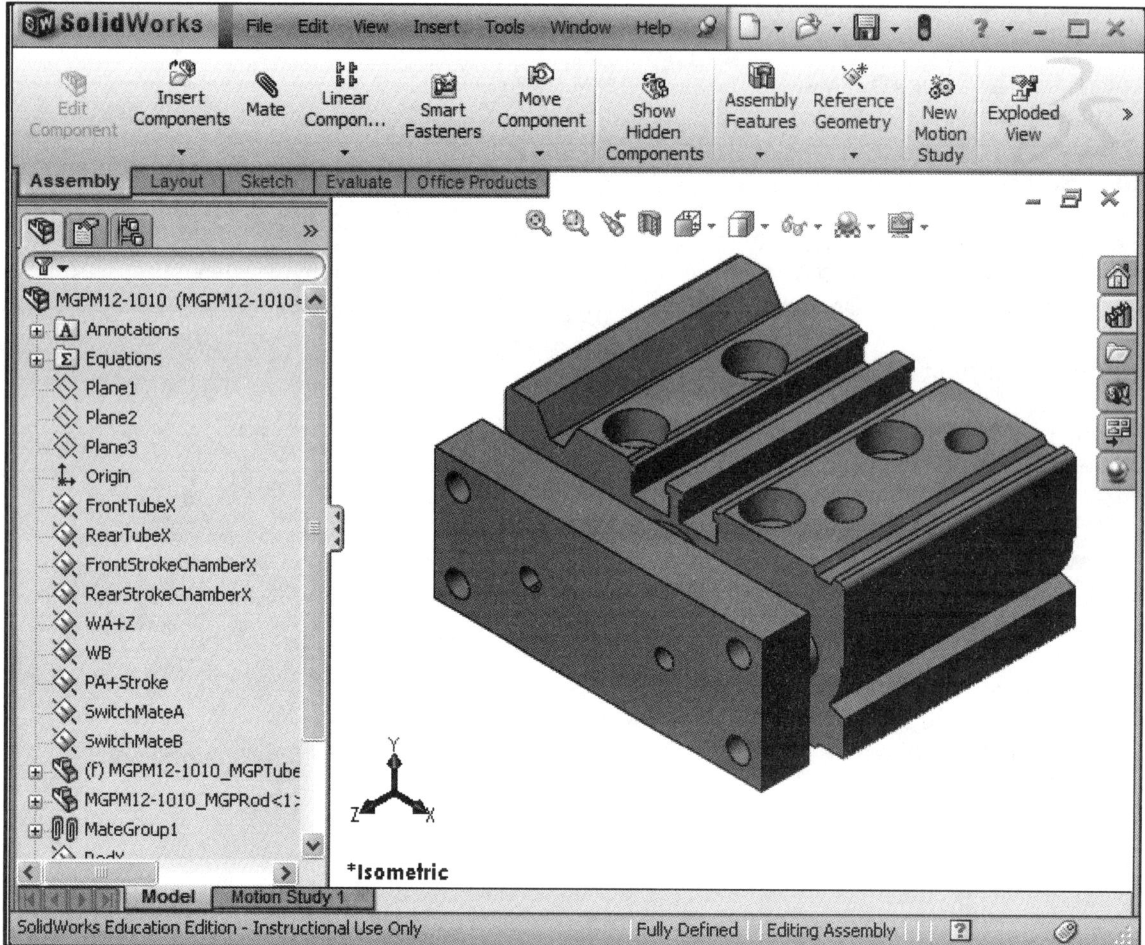

Close all documents.

115) Click **Save**.

116) Click **Windows**, **Close All** from the Menu bar menu. You downloaded a component from 3D ContentCentral. Explore the available models on 3D ContentCentral.

How do you distinguish the difference between an assembly and a part in the FeatureManager? Answer: The assembly icon contains a green square block and an upside down yellow "T" extrusion. The part icon contains an upside down yellow "T" extrusion.

SolidWorks Explorer

SolidWorks Explorer is a file management tool designed to help you perform such tasks as renaming, replacing, and copying SolidWorks files. You can display a document's references, search for documents using a variety of criteria, and list all the places where a document is used. Renamed files are still available to those documents that reference them.

Execute SolidWorks Explorer within SolidWorks or directly from the desktop. The SolidWorks documents remain closed while manipulating names in SolidWorks Explorer.

You can use SolidWorks Explorer with or without the SolidWorks application and with or without PDMWorks Workgroup added in.

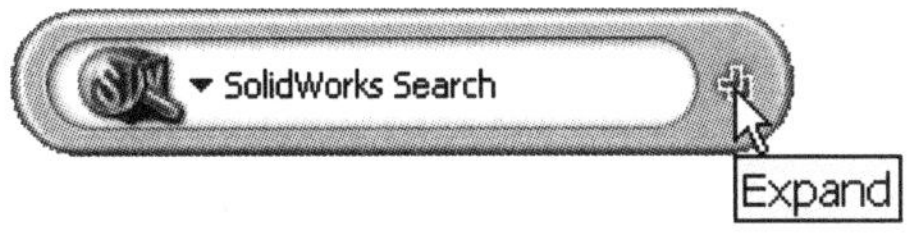

The first time you open SolidWorks Explorer, it is displayed in its collapsed view, with only the SolidWorks Search box visible.

In the collapsed view, you can:

- Search for text strings and tags in all indexed documents, including SolidWorks and Microsoft Office documents.
- Click the **Expand** icon to display the File Explorer pane.
- Right-click near the outer edge and select **Close** or **Minimize.**
- Leave the collapsed view open on your desktop. It becomes transparent while you use other applications.
- Insert tags in documents to use as search criteria. Remember, tags provide the ability to associate keywords with documents to make it easier to search for them.

When you perform a search or click the **Expand** icon, the view expands to display the File Explorer pane, which has two tabs:

- *File Explorer:* The File Explorer tab displays the folders and documents on your computer. If PDM Works Workgroup Contributor is added in, the vault view is displayed at the bottom of the pane.

- *Results*: Displays results of the searches.

The SMC engineers assign unique part numbers to their assemblies. Your Engineering department requests a new part number for the assemblies.

Assembly names are comprised of alphanumeric characters. Companies utilize part names, part numbers, or a combination of both. Utilize descriptive part names for the DELIVERY-STATION assembly. Do not use spaces in document names.

Utilize SolidWorks Explorer to rename the MGPM12-1010 assembly contained in the Downloaded folder. Update the assembly and part references using SolidWorks Explorer.

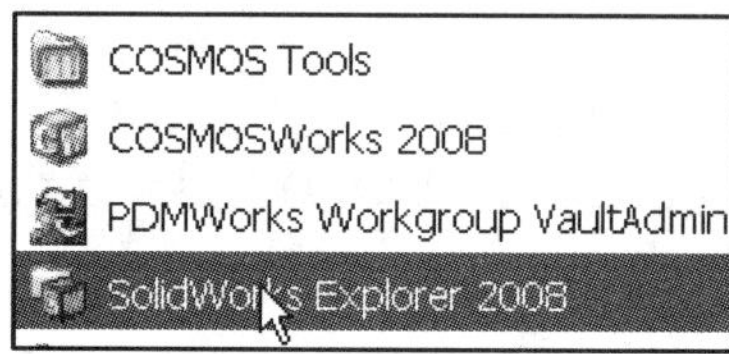

Activate SolidWorks Explorer from the SolidWorks Tools menu or from the Windows Start menu. The application is located on the SolidWorks installation CD's or on the SolidWorks website.

Activity: SolidWorks Explorer – Rename and Save Components

Activate SolidWorks Explorer.

117) Click **Tools**, **SolidWorks Explorer** from the Menu bar menu. SolidWorks Explorer is displayed.

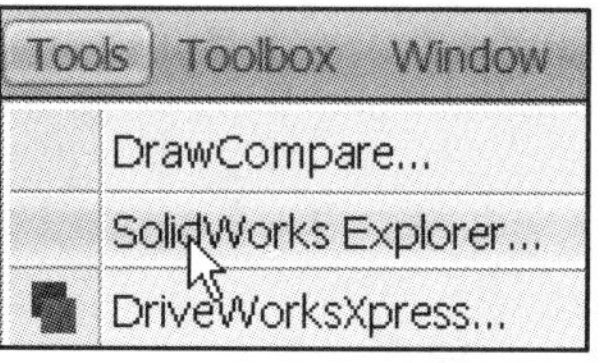

118) Click **Cancel** from the PDMWorks Workgroup 2008 - Login box dialog box. The SolidWorks Search icon is displayed.

119) Click **Expand** as illustrated if this is your first time using SolidWorks Explorer.

Display the MGPM12-1010 assembly.

120) **Expand** ASSEMBLY-SW-FILES-2008\SMC\Downloaded folder.

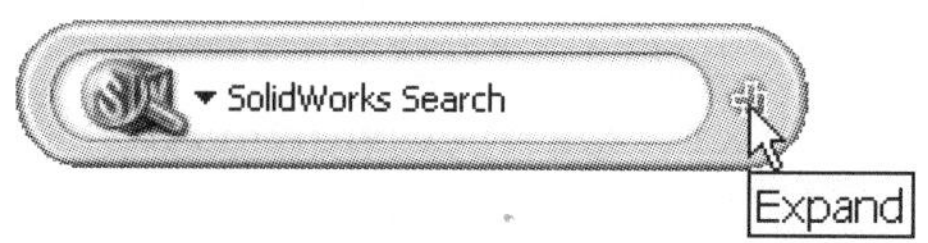

121) Click the **MGPM12-1010** assembly. The MGPM12-1010 assembly is displayed in the main window. Note: If you double-click MGPM12-1010, the assembly opens in the SolidWorks Graphics window. Do not open the assembly at this time.

122) Click the **Info** tab. View the results.

123) Click the **Properties** tab. View the results.

124) Click the **References** tab. View the results. Explore the other tabs.

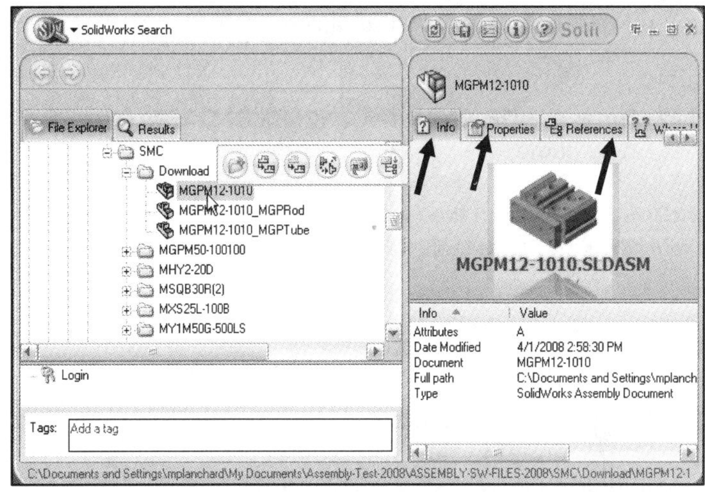

Depending on the type of item selected, different tabs are displayed in the expanded view, where you can perform data management tasks. Each tab can contain several columns of information.

The MGPM12-1010 assembly contains the MGPRod part and the MGPTube part.

Display assembly references with the References tab.

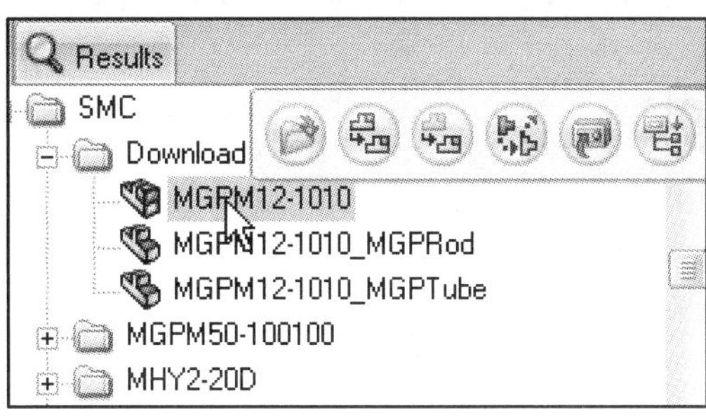

Display to pop-up toolbar.

125) Click the **MGPM12-1010** assembly as illustrated. The pop-up toolbar is displayed.

When you select a document, a pop-up toolbar helps you perform additional tasks. The pop-up toolbar provides the following tools:

- *Open a document*. Opens the selected document.
- *SolidWorks Pack and Go*: Gathers all related files for a model design (parts, assemblies, drawings, references, design tables, Design Binder content, PhotoWorks content, and COSMOS results) into a folder or zip file.
- *Rename*: Renames one or more selected documents and updates all the references.
- *Replace*: Replaces a selected part or assembly document and updates its references.
- *Check In*: Checks the document into the vault.
- *Find in Vault*: Locates the document in the vault.

Rename the document with SolidWorks Explorer. SolidWorks Explorer updates file references and requires less work. Microsoft Windows Explorer does not update file references. You are required to locate individual file references.

Rename the MGPM12-1010 assembly.

126) Click the **Rename** icon in the pop-up toolbar. The Rename Document dialog box is displayed.

127) Enter **GUIDE-CYLINDER-12MM.SLDASM** for new name.

128) Click **OK** from the Rename Document dialog box. View the results.

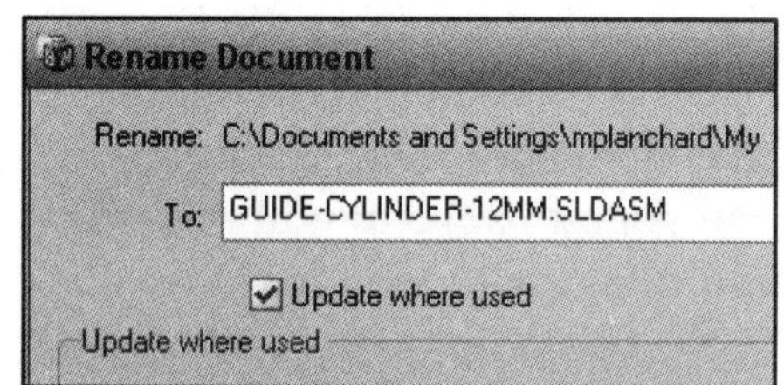

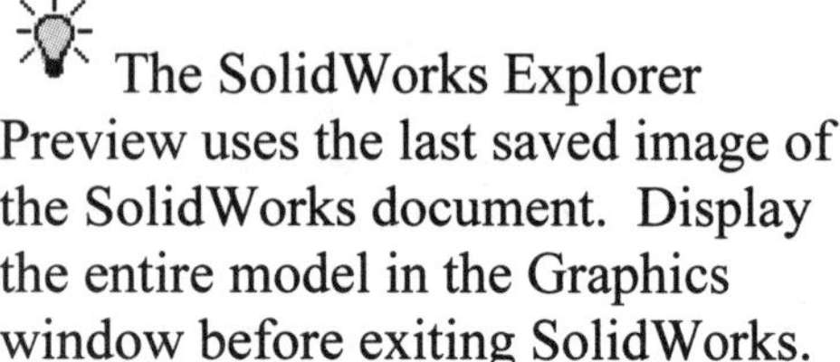

The SolidWorks Explorer Preview uses the last saved image of the SolidWorks document. Display the entire model in the Graphics window before exiting SolidWorks.

If SolidWorks Explorer displays no Preview image, open the document in SolidWorks. Fit the model to the screen. Save and Close the document.

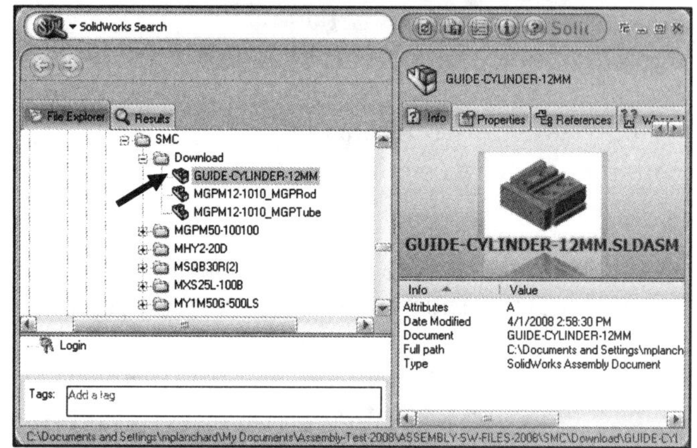

Rename the MGPM50-100100 SMC component.

129) **Expand** the MGPM50-100100 folder.

130) Click **MGPM50-100100** as illustrated.

131) Click the **Rename** icon in the pop-up toolbar. The Rename Document dialog box is displayed

132) Enter **GUIDE CYLINDER.SLDASM**.

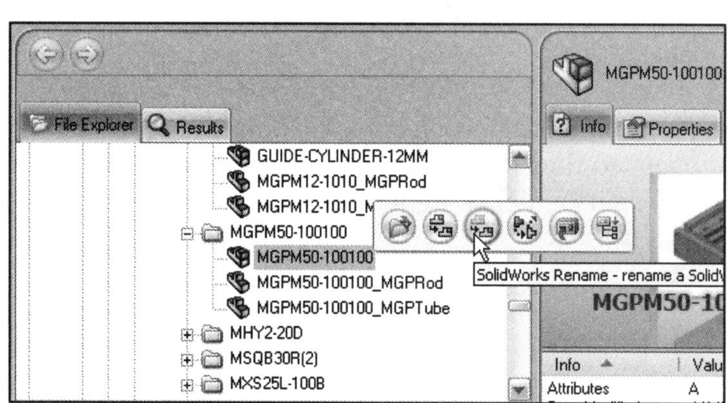

133) Click **OK** from the Rename Document dialog box. View the results.

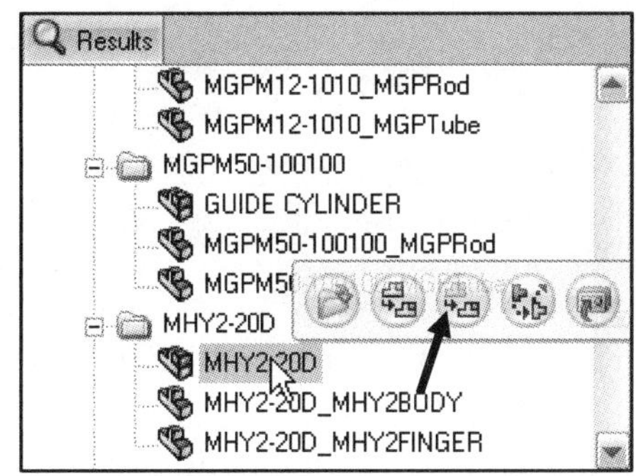

Rename MHY2-20D.

134) Expand the MHY2-20D folder.

135) Click **MHY2-20D** as illustrated.

136) Click the **Rename** icon in the pop-up toolbar. The Rename Document dialog box is displayed.

137) Enter **GRIPPER.SLDASM**.

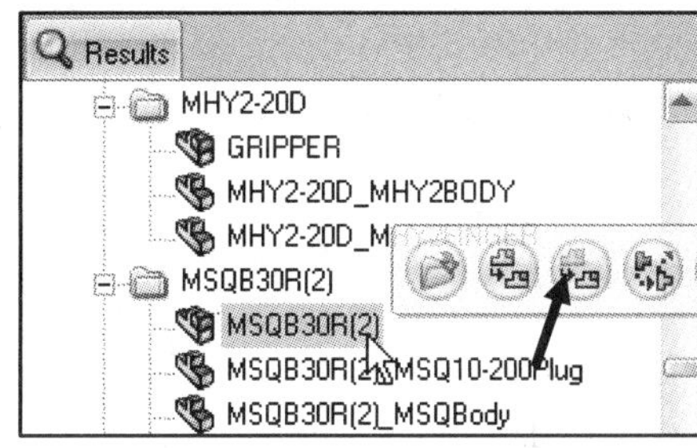

138) Click **OK** from the Rename Document dialog box. View the results.

Rename MSQB30R(2).

139) Expand the MSQB30R(2) folder.

140) Click **MSQB30R(2)** as illustrated.

141) Click the **Rename** icon in the pop-up toolbar. The Rename Document dialog box is displayed.

142) Enter **ROTARY.SLDASM**.

143) Click **OK** from the Rename Document dialog box. View the results.

Rename MXS25L-100B.

144) Expand the MXS25L-100B folder.

145) Click **MXS25L-100B** as illustrated.

146) Click the **Rename** icon in the pop-up toolbar. The Rename Document dialog box is displayed.

147) Enter **SLIDE-TABLE.SLDASM**.

148) Click **OK** from the Rename Document dialog box. View the results.

Rename MY1M50G-500LS.

149) Expand the MY1M50G-500LS folder.

150) Click **MY1M50G-500LS** as illustrated.

151) Click the **Rename** icon in the pop-up toolbar. The Rename Document dialog box is displayed.

152) Enter **RODLESS-CYLINDER.SLDASM**.

153) Click **OK** from the Rename Document dialog box. View the results.

How do you save an assembly with multi components and references? You can either apply SolidWorks Explorer or the Save As command from the Menu bar menu.

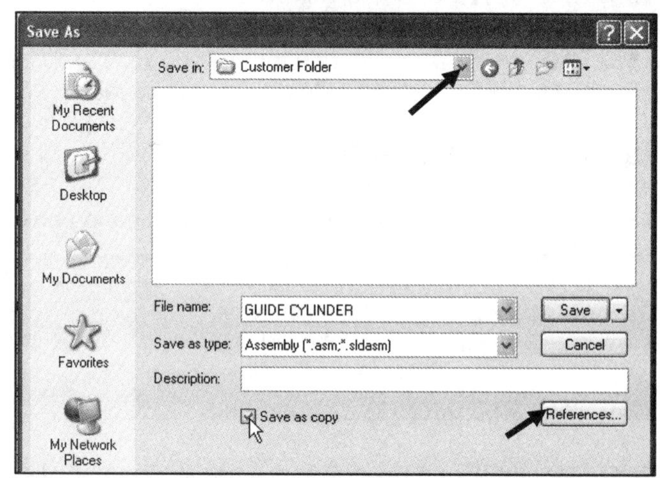

To apply the Save As command, click Save As from the Menu bar menu. The Save As dialog box is displayed.

Check the Save as copy box. Select the assembly folder location. In this example, the assembly is GUIDE CYLINDER and the location is Customer Folder.

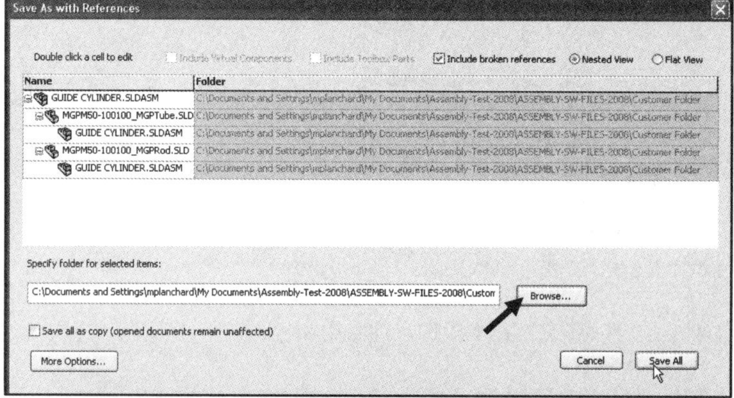

Click the References button. The Save As with Reference dialog box is displayed.

Click the Browse button to locate the Destination folder. Again, in this example it is Customer Folder. Locate your folder.

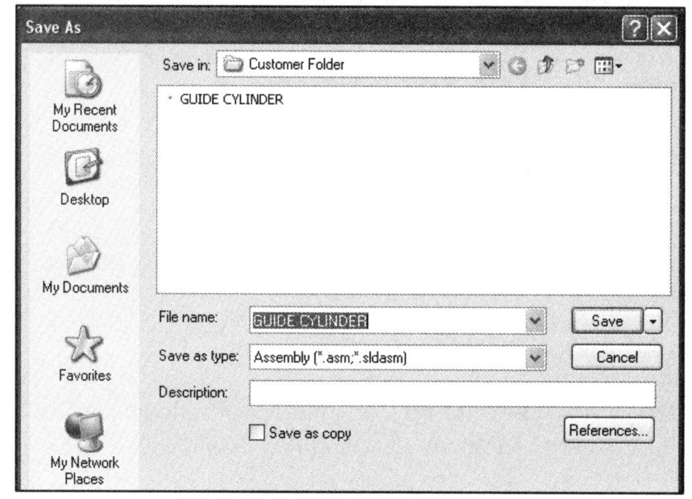

Click OK from the Browse For Folder dialog box.

Click the Save All button from the Save As with References dialog box. You saved the GUIDE CYLINDER assembly with all of it's components and references to the Customer Folder location.

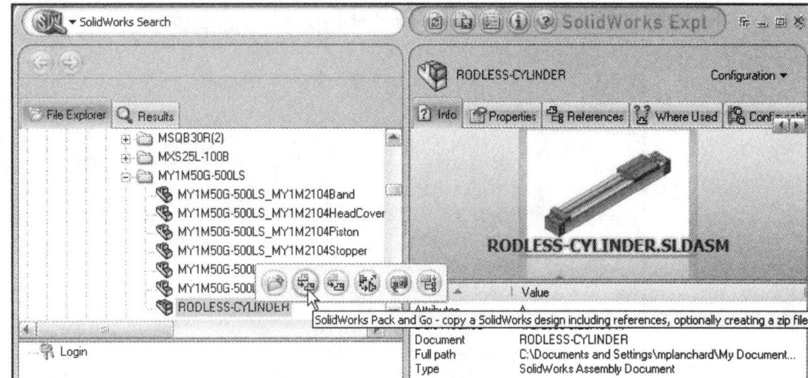

To use SolidWorks Explorer, select the assembly that you want to save, in this example it is RODLESS-CYLINDER. Click the selected assembly. The Pop-up toolbar is displayed.

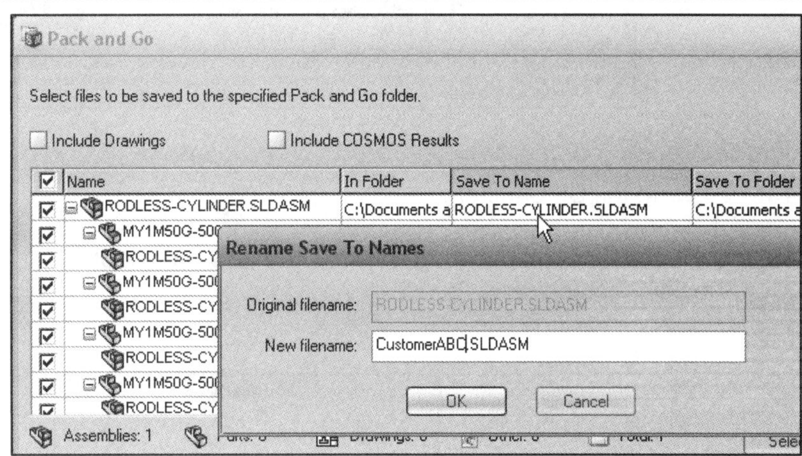

Click the SolidWorks Pack and Go icon. The Pack and Go dialog box is displayed.

Double-click RODLESS-CLINDER in the Save To Name column. The Rename Save to Names dialog box is displayed.

Enter a new name. In this example it is Customer ABC.SLDASM.

Click OK from the Rename Save To Names box.

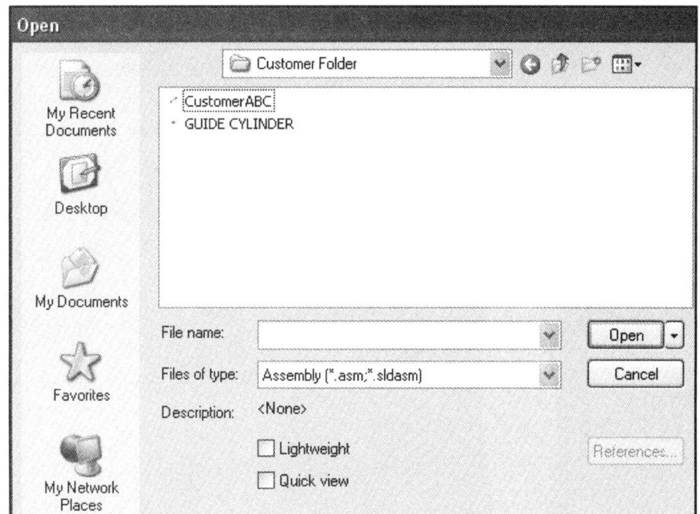

Click the Browse button to locate the Destination folder. In this example, it is Customer Folder. Locate your folder.

Click OK from the Browse For Folder dialog box.

Click Save from the Pack and Go dialog box. You saved the RODLESS-CYLINDER assembly with all of it's components and references to the Customer Folder location.

154) Close SolidWorks Explorer and return to SolidWorks.

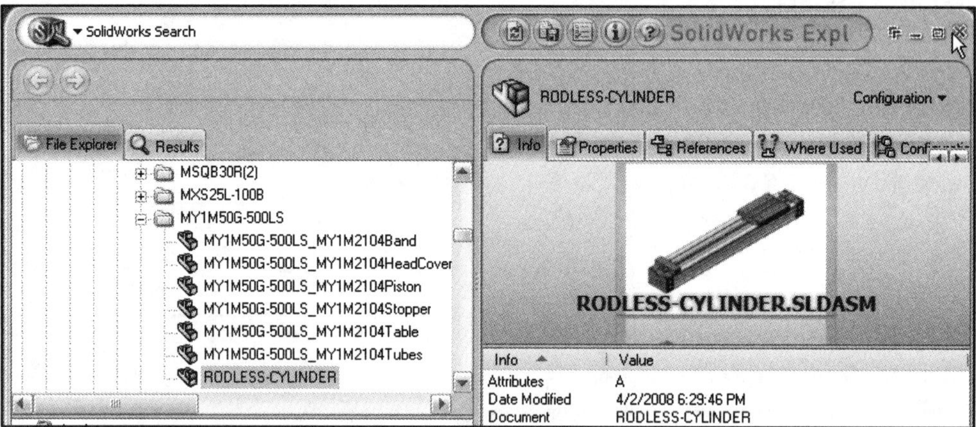

View the results in the Task Pane.

155) Expand the SMC folder.

156) Double-click **each sub-folder**. View the new names of the SMC components.

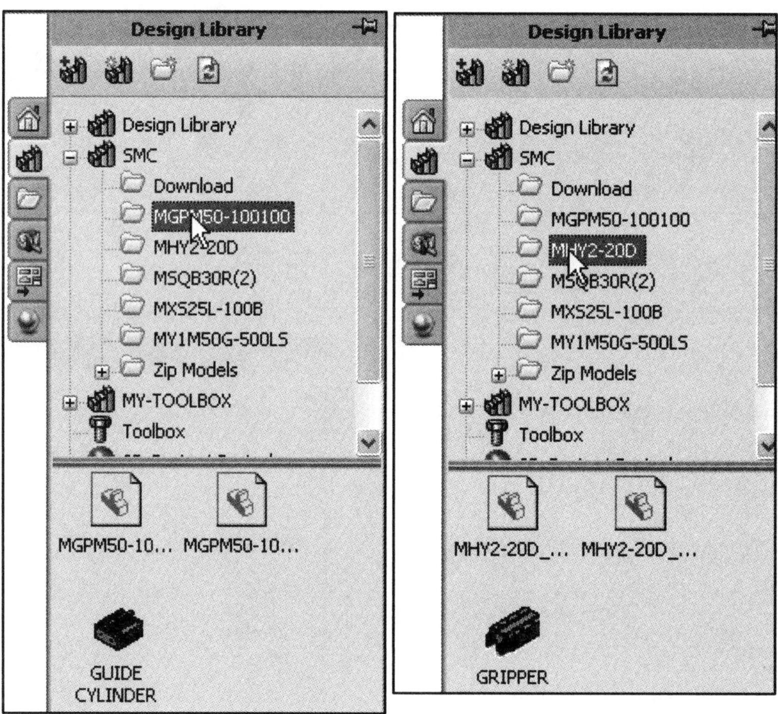

Summary of SMC Components from 3D ContentCentral

A summary of the SolidWorks Explorer document renaming convention is as follows:

Assembly Shaded Images: **Note: Not to Scale.**	**New Assembly Name:**	**Folder Location: (SMC Part Number)**
	GUIDE-CYLINDER	MGPM12-1010
	GRIPPER	MHY2-20D
	ROTARY	MSQB30R(2)
	SLIDE-TABLE	MXS25L-100Bs

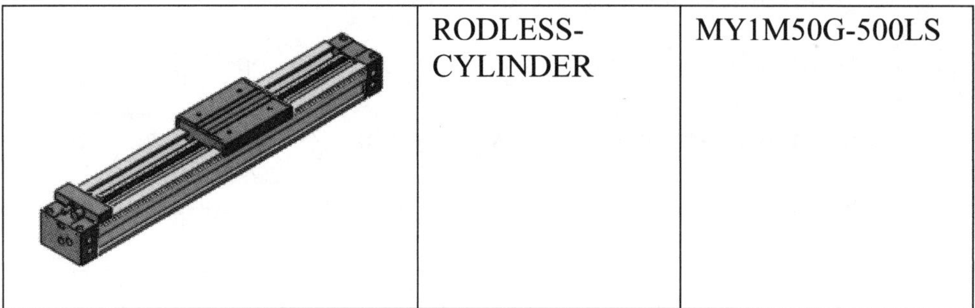

	RODLESS-CYLINDER	MY1M50G-500LS

FeatureManager and Component States

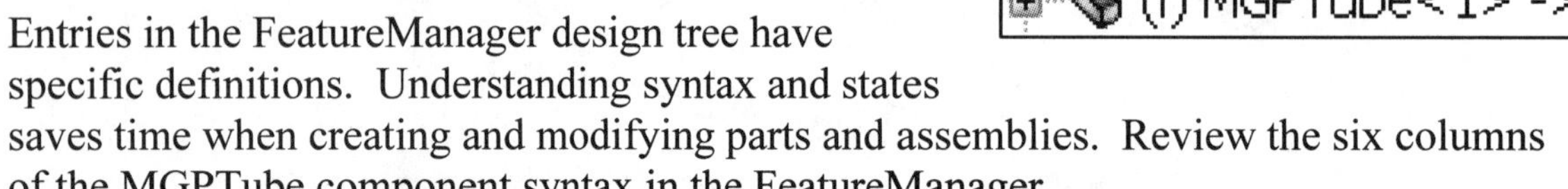

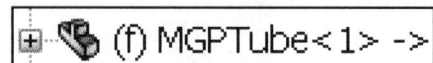

Entries in the FeatureManager design tree have specific definitions. Understanding syntax and states saves time when creating and modifying parts and assemblies. Review the six columns of the MGPTube component syntax in the FeatureManager.

Column 1: A resolved component (not in lightweight state) displays a plus icon. The plus icon indicates that additional feature information is available. A minus icon displays the fully expanded feature list.

Column 2: Identifies a component's (part or assembly) relationship with other components in the assembly.

Component or Part States:	
Symbol:	**State:**
	Resolved part: A yellow part icon indicates a resolved state. A blue part icon indicates a selected, resolved part. The component is fully loaded into memory and all of its features and mates are editable.
	Lightweight part: A blue feather on the part icon indicates a lightweight state. When a component is lightweight, only a subset of its model data is loaded in memory.
	Out-of-Date Lightweight: A red feather on the part icon indicates out-of-date references. This option is not available when the Large Assembly Mode is activated.
	Suppressed: A gray icon indicates the part is not resolved in the active configuration.

	Hidden: A clear icon indicates the part is resolved but invisible.
	Hidden Lightweight: A transparent blue feather over a transparent component icon indicates that the component is lightweight and hidden.
	Hidden, Out-of-Date, Lightweight: A red feather over a clear part icon indicates the part is hidden, out-of-date, and lightweight.
	Hidden Smart Component: A transparent star over a transparent icon indicates that the component is a Smart Component and hidden.
	Smart Component: A star overlay is displayed on the icon of a Smart Component.
	Rebuild: A rebuild is required for the assembly or component.
	Flexible state: By default, when you create a sub-assembly, it is in the rigid state.
	Resolved assembly: Resolved (or unsuppressed) is the normal state for assembly components. A resolved assembly is fully loaded in memory, fully functional, and fully accessible.

When you insert the Smart Component into an assembly, you can choose whether or not to insert the associated components and features. The following features can be associated with a Smart Component: Simple holes, Hole Wizard holes, Extruded Boss and Cut, and Revolved Boss and Cut.

Column 3: The MGPTube part is fixed (f). You can fix the position of a component so that it cannot move with respect to the assembly Origin. By default, the first part in an assembly is fixed; however, you can float it at any time.

It is recommended that at least one assembly component is either fixed, or mated to the assembly planes or Origin. This provides a frame of reference for all other mates, and helps prevent unexpected movement of components when mates are added.

The Component Properties are:

Component Properties in an assembly:	
Symbol:	**Relationship:**
(-)	A minus sign (–) indicates that the part or assembly is under-defined and requires additional information.
(+)	A plus sign (+) indicates that the part or assembly is over-defined.
None	The Base component is mated to three assembly reference planes.
(f)	A fixed symbol (f) indicates that the part or assembly does not move.
(?)	A question mark (?) indicates that additional information is required on the part or assembly.

Column 4: MGPTube - Name of the part.

Column 5: The symbol <#> indicates the particular inserted instance of a component. The symbol <1> indicates the first inserted instance of a component, "MGPTube" in the assembly. If you delete a component and reinsert the same component again, the <#> symbol increments by one.

Column 6: The Resolved state displays the MGPTube icon with an external reference symbol, "–>". The state of external references is displayed as follows:

- If a part or feature has an external reference, its name is followed by –>. The name of any feature with external references is also followed by –>.
- If an external reference is currently out of context, the feature name and the part name are followed by –>?
- The suffix –>* means that the reference is locked.
- The suffix –>x means that the reference is broken.

There are modeling situations in which unresolved components create rebuild errors. In these situations, issue the forced rebuild, Ctrl+Q. The Ctrl+Q option rebuilds the model and all its features. If the mates still contain rebuild errors, resolve all the components below the entry in the FeatureManager that contains the first error.

Comparison of Component States

A complete list of component suppression states is displayed in: SolidWorks Help Topics \ Lightweight\Comparison of Components Suppression.

	Resolved	Lightweight	Suppressed	Hidden
Loaded in memory	Yes	Partially	No	Yes
Visible	Yes	Yes	No	No
Features available in FeatureManager design tree	Yes	No	No	No
Faces and edges accessible for adding mates	Yes	Yes	No	No
Mates solved	Yes	Yes	No	Yes
In-context features solved	Yes 1	Yes	No	Yes
Assembly features solved	Yes	Yes	No	Yes
Considered in global operations 2	Yes	Yes 3	No	Yes
May be edited in-context	Yes	Yes 4	No	No
Load and rebuild speed	Normal	Faster	Faster	Normal
Display speed	Normal	Normal	Faster	Faster

Geometric and Functional Requirements

The senior engineer on the design team specified the geometric and functional requirements for the GUIDE-CYLINDER assembly.

Geometric Requirements:

The GUIDE-CYLINDER assembly mounts to the RODLESS-CYLINDER assembly. The RODLESS-CYLINDER assembly contains a table with the following dimensions: 200mm x 144mm x 30mm.

Functional Requirements:

The GUIDE-CYLINDER assembly Stroke distance is 100mm. The force and pressure conditions determine the Bore diameter of the GUIDE-CYLINDER assembly. The Bore diameter is 50mm.

Conserve time. Validate that a vendor component meets both your geometric and functional requirements. Review the model configuration parameters and key dimensions.

The SMC components are modeled using part and assembly configurations. Configurations are different variations of a component based on a series of parameters. Review the configuration information for Bore size and Stroke parameters for the GUIDE-CYLINDER assembly. Measure key features and compare dimensions with the specification data sheets.

Review the Configuration Properties of the GUIDE-CYLINDER assembly. The Configuration Properties dialog box displays the Configuration Name. The Custom button contains configuration specific information.

Record the Stroke distance 100mm and the Bore Size 50mm in the Configuration Specific Properties.

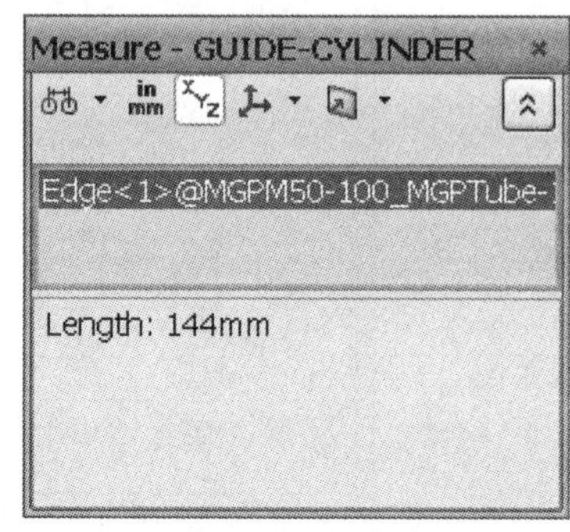

Measure the overall dimensions of the MGPTube. The depth is 144mm, the width is 148mm and the height is 63mm. Note: Do not select a fillet.

These dimensions meet the geometric requirements for the 3-AXIS-TRANSFER assembly. Common measurements are displayed in the Status bar in the lower right corner of the Graphics window.

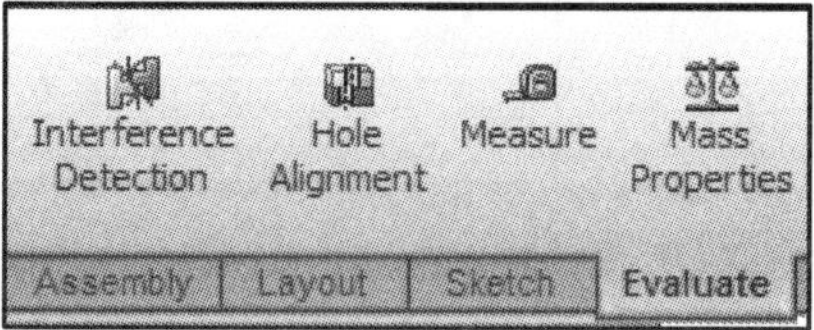

Apply the Measure tool located in the Evaluate toolbar.

Activity: Measure Geometric and Functional Requirements

Review the GUIDE-CYLINDER Configuration Properties.

157) If needed **open** the GUIDE-CYLINDER assembly.

158) Click the **ConfigurationManager** icon.

159) Right-click **MGPM50-100**.

160) Click **Properties**. The Configuration Properties PropertyManager is displayed,

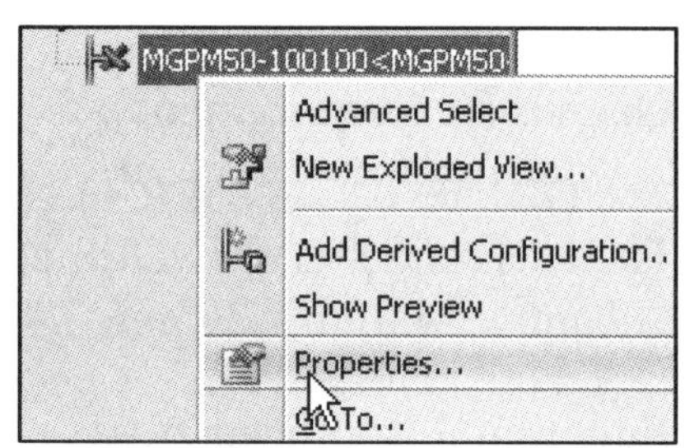

161) Click **Custom Properties** from the Configuration Properties PropertyManager. The Summary Information box is displayed.

162) Click the **Configuration Specific** tab.

163) Drag the Properties **scroll bar** downward in the table to display the values for the Stroke (100) and Bore Size (50).

164) Click **OK** from the Summary Information box.

165) Click **OK** ✔ from the Configuration Properties PropertyManager.

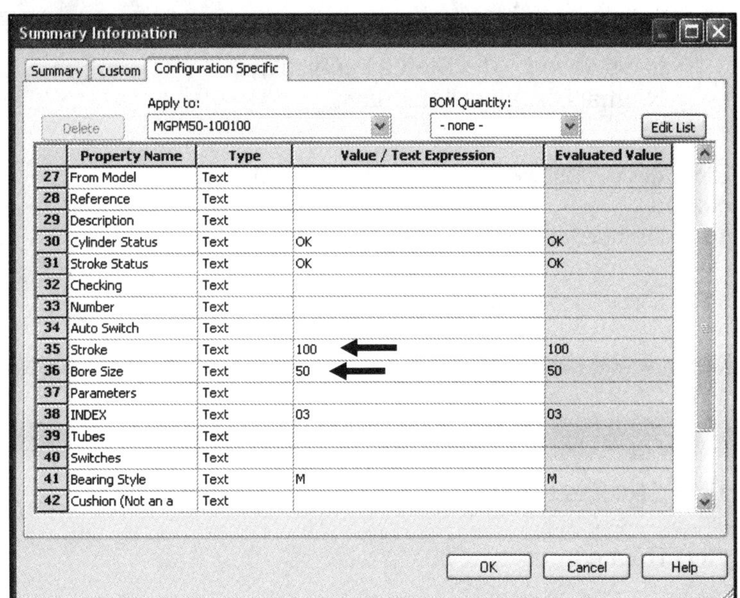

	Property Name	Type	Value / Text Expression	Evaluated Value
27	From Model	Text		
28	Reference	Text		
29	Description	Text		
30	Cylinder Status	Text	OK	OK
31	Stroke Status	Text	OK	OK
32	Checking	Text		
33	Number	Text		
34	Auto Switch	Text		
35	Stroke	Text	100	100
36	Bore Size	Text	50	50
37	Parameters	Text		
38	INDEX	Text	03	03
39	Tubes	Text		
40	Switches	Text		
41	Bearing Style	Text	M	M
42	Cushion (Not an a	Text		

Return to the Assembly FeatureManager.

166) Click the **FeatureManager** icon.

Measure the feature geometry.

167) Click **Top** view from the Heads-up View toolbar.

168) Click the **Evaluate** tab from the CommandManager. The Evaluate toolbar is displayed.

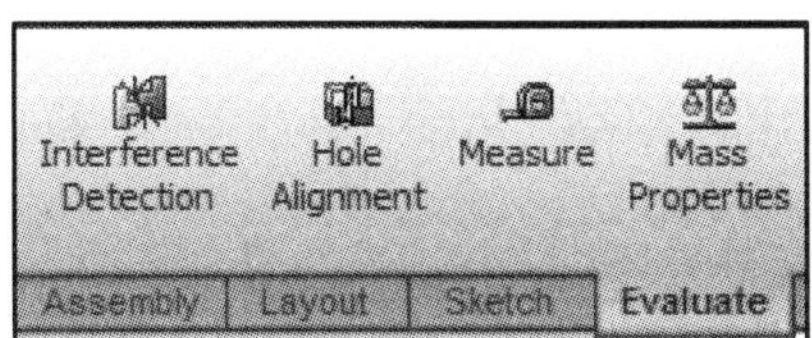

169) Click the **Measure** tool from the Evaluate toolbar.

170) Click the **vertical left edge** of the MGPTube part. The Status bar displays Length: 144mm.

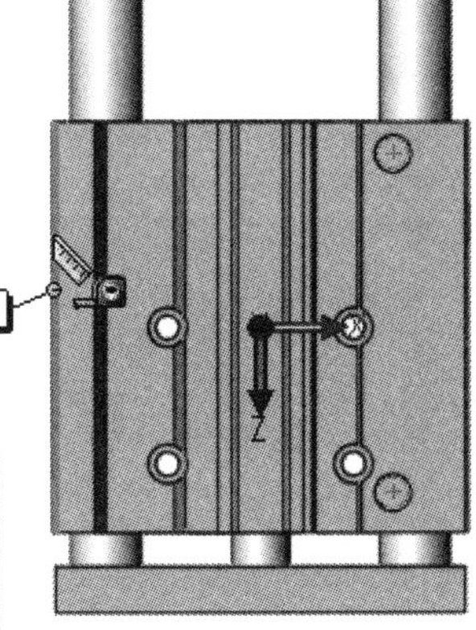

Clear the vertical left edge selection from the Measure box.

171) Right-click in the **highlighted blue** box as illustrated.

172) Click **Clear Selection**.

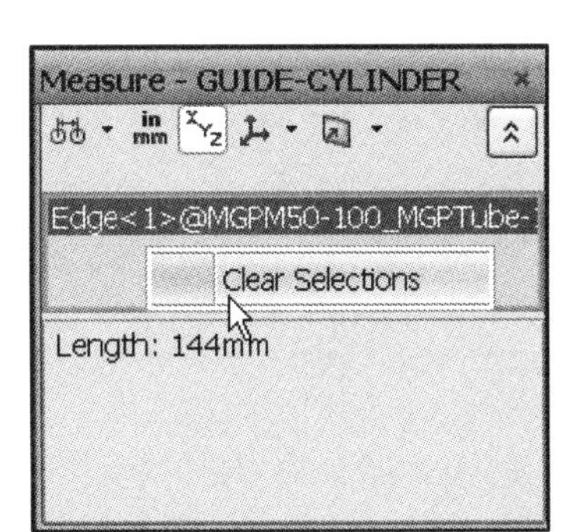

Display an Isometric view.

173) Click **Isometric** view from the Heads-up View toolbar.

Measure the overall width.

174) Click the **right face**. Face<1> is displayed.

175) Rotate the **model 90º**.

176) Click the **left face as** illustrated. Face<2> is displayed. The Status bar displays: Normal Distance: 148.00mm.

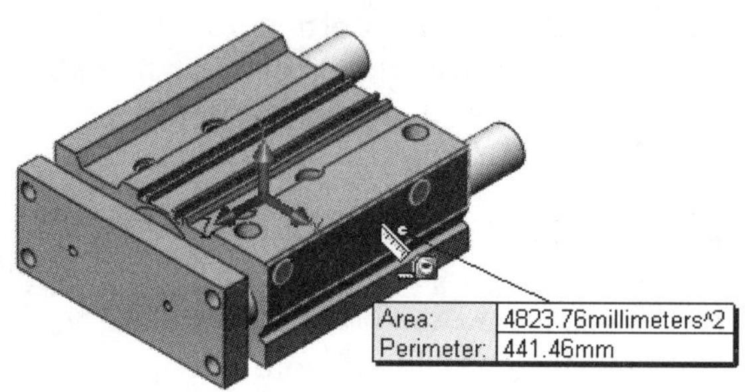

Clear the overall width selection from the Measure box.

177) Right-click in the **highlighted** box.

178) Click **Clear Selection**.

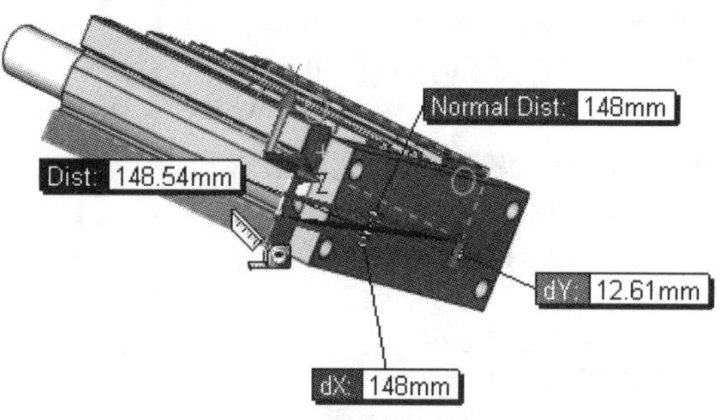

Measure the overall height.

179) Click **Isometric** view from the Heads-up View toolbar.

180) Click the **top face**. Face <3> is displayed.

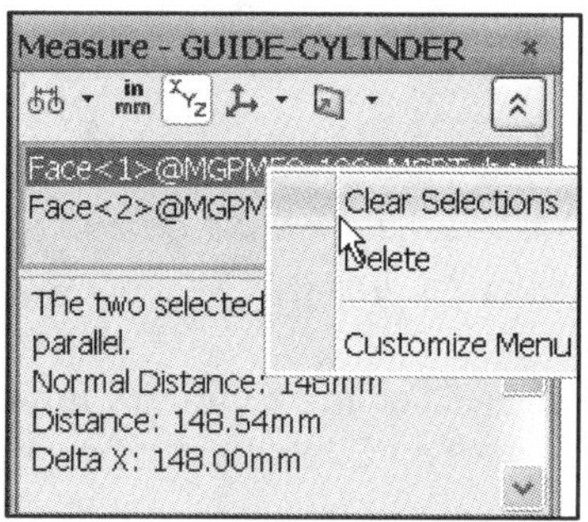

181) Rotate the **model 90º**.

182) Click the **bottom face**. Face<4> is displayed. The Status bar displays: Normal Distance: 63mm.

183) Click **Close** from the Measure box.

Display an Isometric view and save the model.

184) Click **Isometric** view.

185) Click **Shaded With Edges** .

186) Click **Save** .

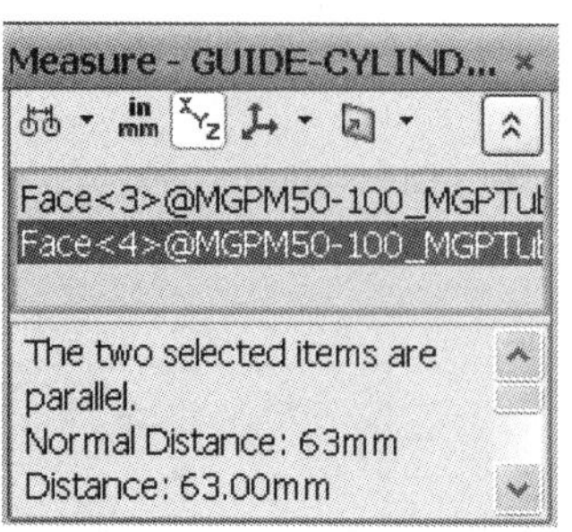

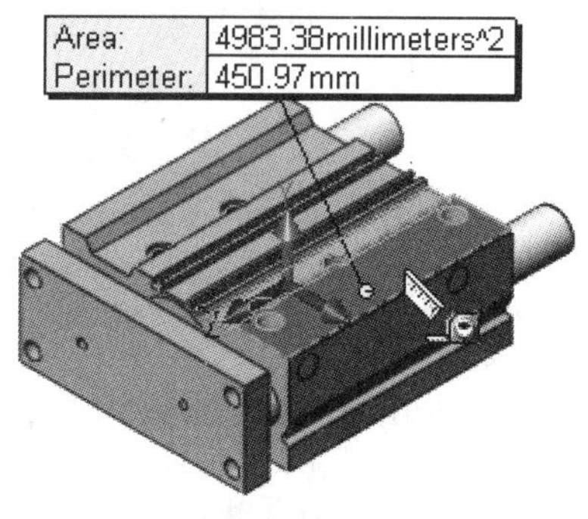

View Thumbnails easily. Before you exit SolidWorks, save assemblies in their Isometric view, Shaded With Edges display.

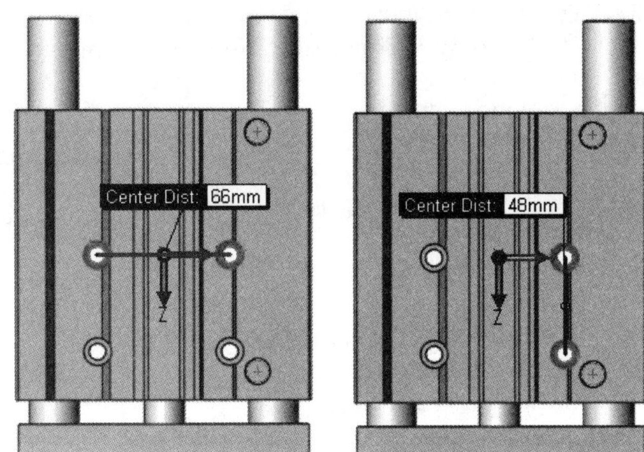

The Isometric view option enlarges the model to fit the Graphics window.

As an exercise, measure the distance between the two sets of Counterbore faces.

The Status area displays the Distance between cylindrical axes.

SolidWorks Toolbox Configuration

The SolidWorks Toolbox is a library of feature based design automation tools for SolidWorks. The SolidWorks Toolbox uses the Microsoft Window's click, drag, and drop functionality.

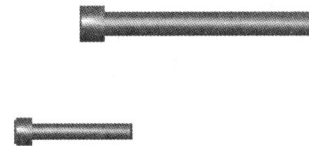

There are three options to apply fasteners in the 3AXIS-TRANSFER assembly.

- Utilize SolidWorks Toolbox for fasteners.
- Utilize the Socket Head Cap Screw part file that is located in the MY-TOOLBOX folder.
- Utilize your own fasteners.

The book utilizes SolidWorks Toolbox fasteners. Configure the SolidWorks Toolbox to create a copy of the library part. Store the SolidWorks Toolbox parts in the ASSEMBLY-SW-FILES-2008\MY-TOOLBOX folder.

Activity: SolidWorks Toolbox

Add SolidWorks Toolbox to the Menu bar menu.

187) Click **Add-Ins** from the Menu bar toolbar. The Add-Ins dialog box is displayed.

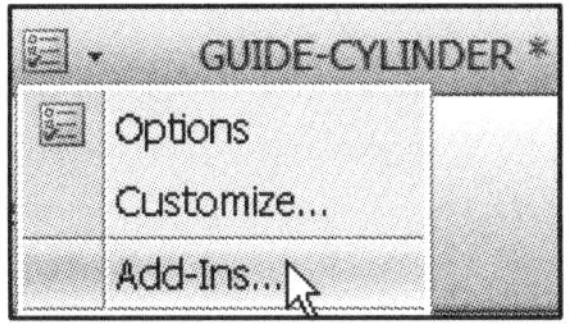

188) Check the **SolidWorks Toolbox** box.

189) Check the **Toolbox Browser** box.

190) Click **OK**. Toolbox is added.

Configure the SolidWorks Toolbox Browser.
191) Click **Toolbox**, **Configure...** from the Menu bar menu.

Set the Storage folder to copy the Toolbox parts.
192) Click the **Settings** tab.

193) Check the **Create Parts** box.

194) Click **Browse**.

195) Select the **ASSEMBLY-SW-FILES-2008\MY-TOOLBOX** folder for Copy Directory.

196) Click **OK from the Browse for folder dialog box**.

197) Click **OK** from the Configure Browser box.

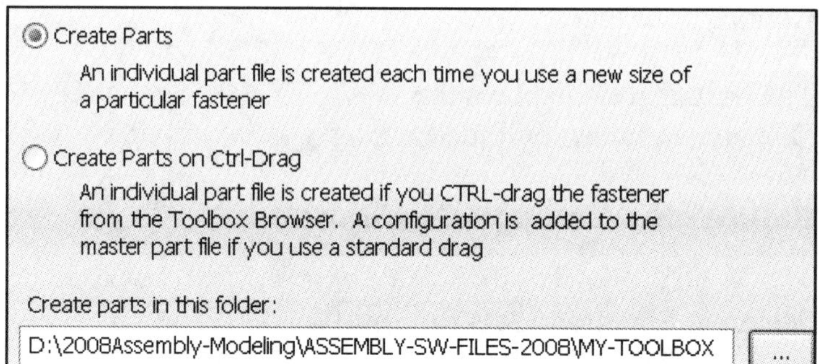

Create Parts
An individual part file is created each time you use a new size of a particular fastener
Create Parts on Ctrl-Drag
An individual part file is created if you CTRL-drag the fastener from the Toolbox Browser. A configuration is added to the master part file if you use a standard drag
Create parts in this folder:
D:\2008Assembly-Modeling\ASSEMBLY-SW-FILES-2008\MY-TOOLBOX

Close all models.
198) Click **Windows**, **Close All** from the Menu bar menu.

Project Summary

You obtained a general knowledge of Top-down and Bottom-up assembly modeling.

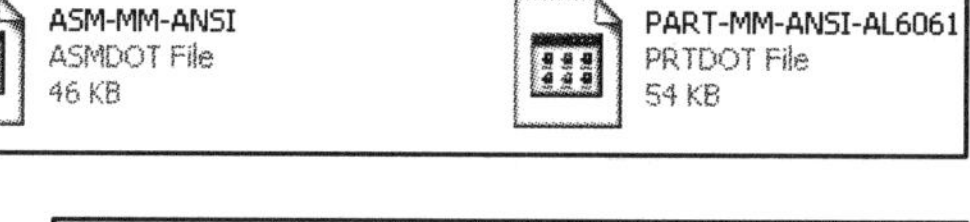

You created two templates: *ASM-MM-ANSI Assembly template* and the *PART-MM-ANSI-AL6061 Part template* and created new SolidWorks File Locations: *Document Templates*, *Reference Documents*, and *Design Library folders* in the Task Pane.

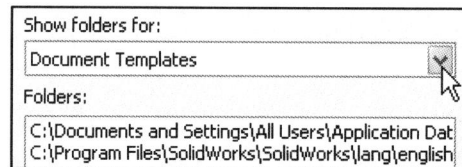

You either downloaded or copied SMC components and applied SolidWorks Explorer to rename the SMC default component names.

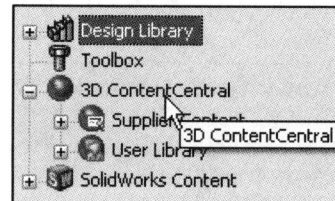

You obtained and confirmed geometric and functional requirements utilizing the Measure tool from the Evaluate toolbar.

Develop the LINEAR-TRANSFER assembly in the next Project using the Bottom-up design approach. The LINEAR-TRANSFER assembly is the first assembly in the 3AXIS-TRANSFER assembly.

In Project 4, develop configurations for the RODLESS-CYLINDER assembly to illustrate dynamic motion and physical location. Create two new RODLESS-CYLINDER configurations: *Normal*, and *Extended.*

Create three new configurations for the LINEAR-TRANSFER assembly. The LINEAR-TRANSFER configurations are named *Normal, Extended*, and *Fastener.*

Questions

1. Why is file management critical in the design and development process?
2. Identify the document that is the foundation for a SolidWorks assembly.
3. Describe the difference between an assembly and a part.
4. Describe the difference between a component and a part.
5. List the three SolidWorks default Templates in the New dialog box.
6. Why should you use unique part numbers and assembly filenames? Provide an example.
7. True or False. Maximize the amount of parts at the top level of the assembly. Explain.
8. True or False. Design parts and assemblies to reuse information. Explain.
9. An Assembly Template file extension is ______________, a Part Template file extension is ______________.
10. True or False. System Options are stored with the current SolidWorks document. Explain.
11. Utilize ________________ Explorer to rename parts and assemblies.
12. Provide an example of a geometric requirement for the GUIDE-CYLINDER assembly. Provide an example of a functional requirement.
13. Identify the symbol used to represent the Lightweight State in the FeatureManager.
14. Identify the following component states for the FeatureManager.

	a)		e)
	b)		f)
	c)		g)
	d)		

Project 3

Assembly Modeling – Bottom-up design approach

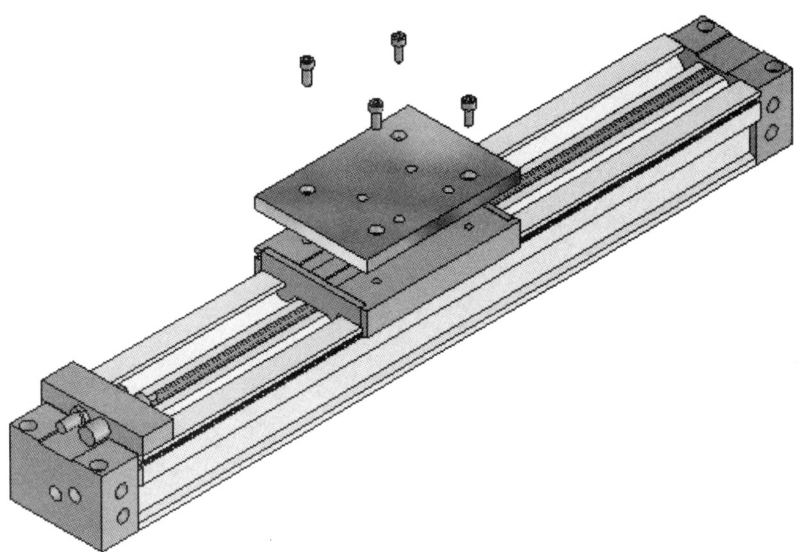

Below are the desired outcomes and usage competencies based on the completion of this Project.

Project Desired Outcomes:	Usage Competencies:
• PLATE-A part.	• Knowledge to create new parts based on component features utilizing the Bottom-up design approach.
• LINEAR-TRANSFER assembly.	• Ability to Insert components and to apply the Measure tool.
• Insert Standard and SmartMates Mates.	• Aptitude to apply the Mate and SmartMate tools.
• Four M8 x 1.25 Socket Head Cap Screws.	• Capacity to apply the Design Library Toolbox.

Notes:

Project 3 – Assembly Modeling – Bottom-up design approach

Project Objective

Develop the LINEAR-TRANSFER assembly. The LINEAR-TRANSFER assembly is the first assembly in the 3AXIS-TRANSFER assembly.

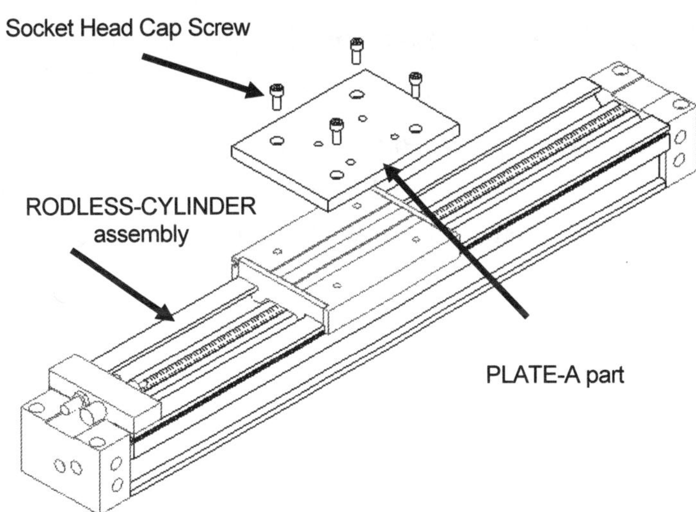

LINEAR-TRANSFER assembly

Create the following models in this project:

- PLATE-A part.
- LINEAR-TRANSFER assembly.

On the completion of this project, you will be able to:

- Apply the Bottom-up design assembly modeling approach.
- Identify Standard, Advanced, and Mechanical Mate types.
- Utilize SmartMates to assemble the PLATE-A part to the RODLESS-CYLINDER assembly.
- Obtain the required dimensions, and identify the required features in mating components.
- Insert components into an assembly.
- Modify a Distance Mate.
- Address Suppress/Un-suppress and Rigid/Flexible states in a configuration.
- Work with the SolidWorks Design Library.
- Utilize and apply the following SolidWorks tools and commands:
  - Mate, Mate Types, Mate Reference and SmartMate.
  - Rotate Component and Move Component.
  - Hide / Show components.

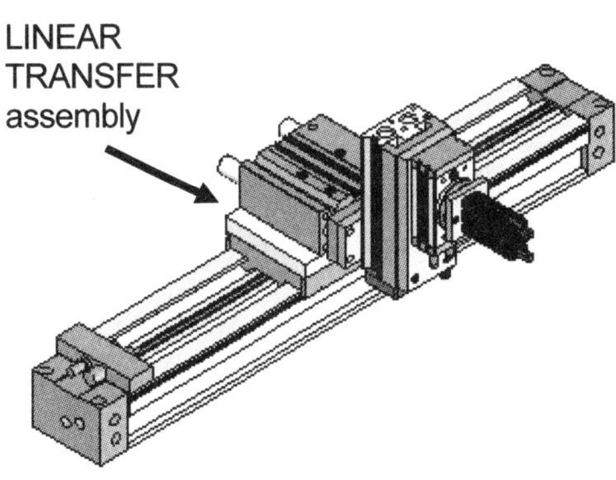

3AXIS-TRANSFER assembly

- Flexible and Rigid states.
- Collision Detection.
- Linear Pattern, and Derived Component Pattern.
- SolidWorks Task Pane, Design Library and Toolbox.
- Insert Part and Insert Component.
- Sketch tools: Corner Rectangle, Center Rectangle, Centerline, and Dimension.
- Geometric relations: Midpoint, Equal, Vertical, and Horizontal.
- Views: Section, Isometric, Front, Top, and Right.
- Features: Extruded Base, Extruded Boss, Extruded Cut, and Hole Wizard.

Project Overview

Bottom-up design is the traditional assembly method. You first design and model parts, then insert them into an assembly and apply Mates to position the parts. To modify the parts, you must edit them individually. These changes are then seen in the assembly.

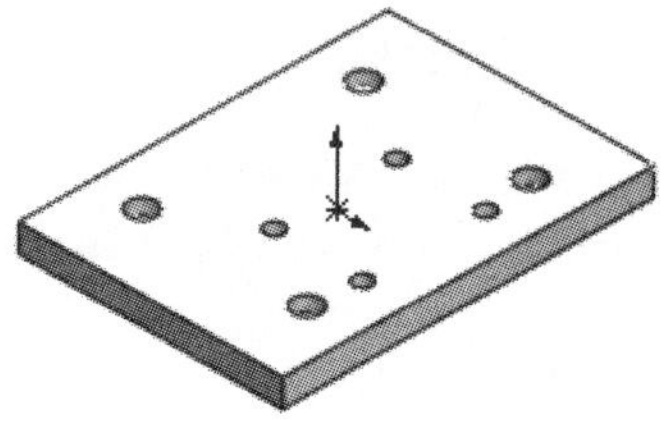

PLATE-A

The three major steps in a Bottom-up design approach are:

1. Create each component independent of any other component in the assembly.
2. Insert the components into the assembly.
3. Mate the components in the assembly as they relate to the physical constraints of the design.

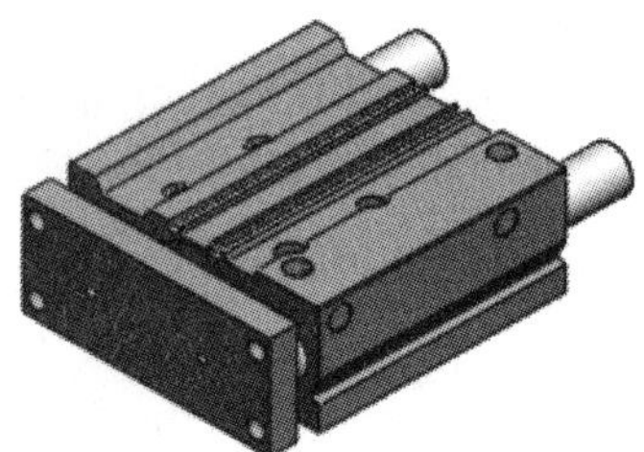

GUIDE-CYLINDER

The geometry and functionality of the PLATE-A part is dependent on the GUIDE-CYLINDER assembly and the RODLESS-CYLINDER assembly.

The GUIDE-CYLINDER and RODLESS-CYLINDER assemblies are located in the SMC folder in the Task Pane.

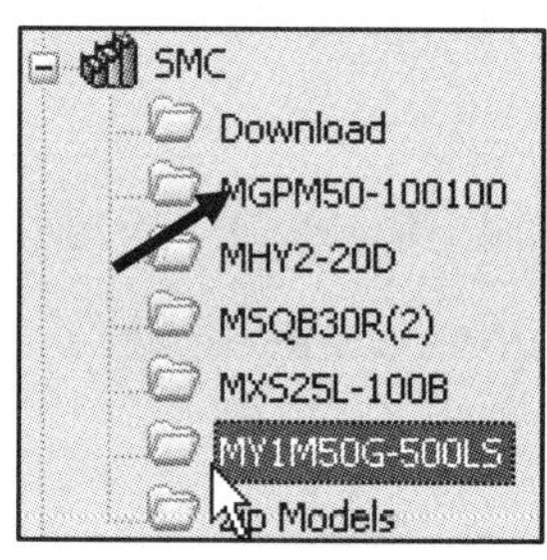

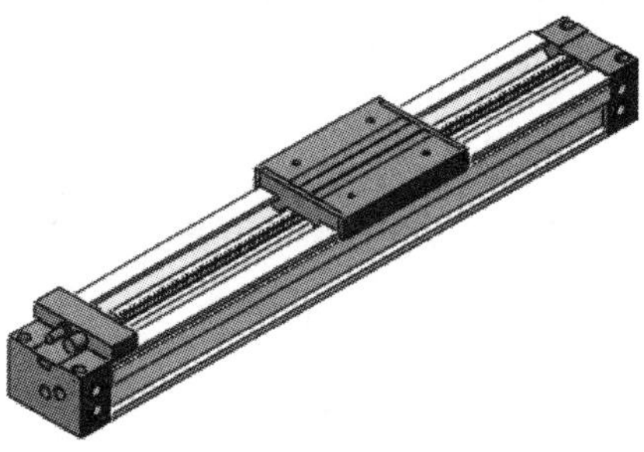

RODLESS-CYLINDER

The mounting holes in the GUIDE-CYLINDER are not aligned to the mounting holes of the RODLESS-CYLINDER.

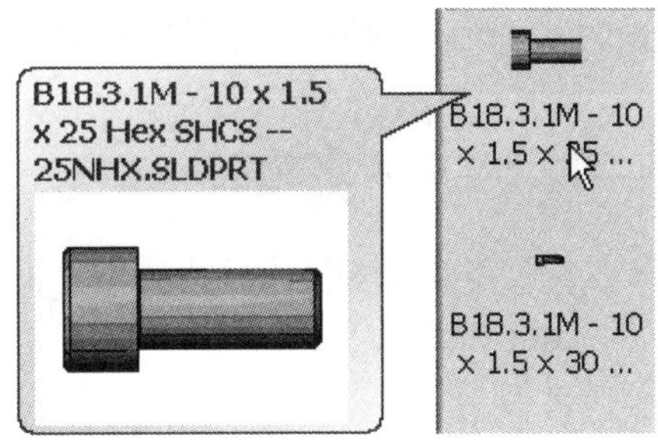

The new PLATE-A part utilizes design criteria from the two assemblies to locate two sets of holes.

Utilize a Bottom-up design approach to develop the LINEAR-TRANSFER assembly. The LINEAR-TRANSFER assembly consists of the following:

- RODLESS-CYLINDER assembly, (located in the SMC file folder).
- PLATE-A part, (create the new part in SolidWorks).
- Four M8 x 1.25 Socket Head Cap Screws, (located in the SolidWorks Toolbox).
- Identify the design components.
- Identify the purchased components.
- Identify the library components.

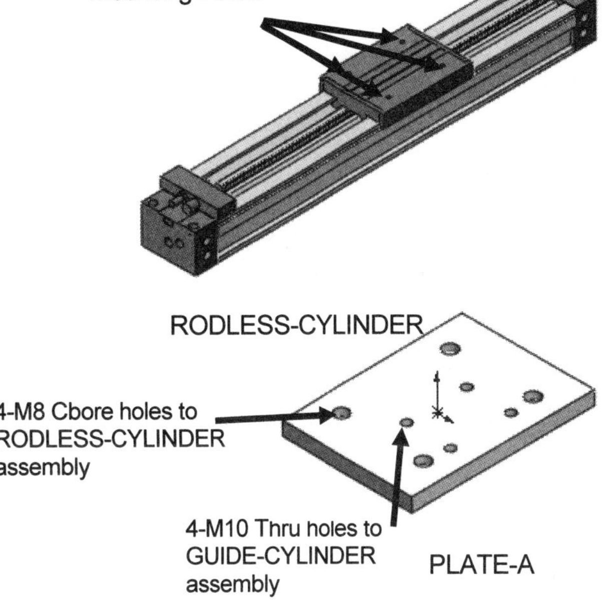

To use the SolidWorks Toolbox, click **Add-Ins..** from the Menu bar toolbar. Check **SolidWorks Toolbox** and **SolidWorks Toolbox Browser** from the Add-Ins dialog box. Click **OK**.

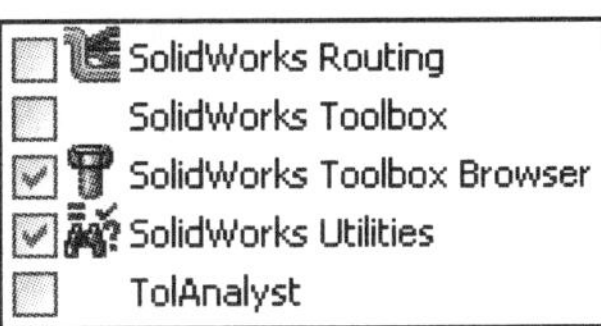

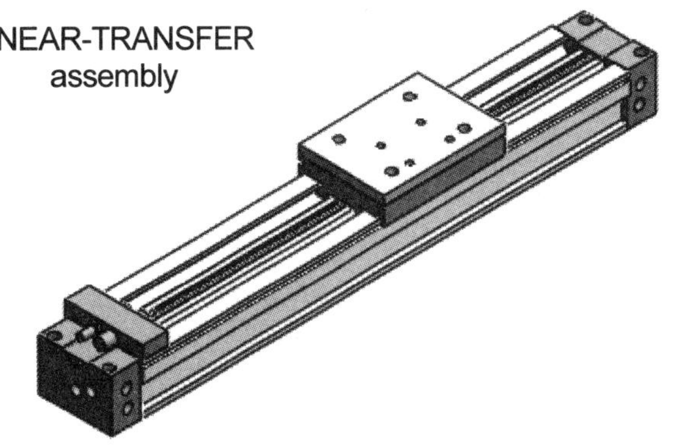

Create the PLATE-A part. Assemble PLATE-A to the RODLESS-CYLINDER assembly. Use four, M8 x 1.25 Socket Head Cap Screw (SHCS) to fasten the PLATE-A part to the RODLESS-CYLINDER assembly.

Determine the required length of the SHCS by analyzing the components in the LINEAR-TRANSFER assembly. The M8 x 1.25 SHCS is defined as follows:

- M8 represents a metric screw: 8mm major outside diameter.
- 1.25 thread pitch (mm per thread).

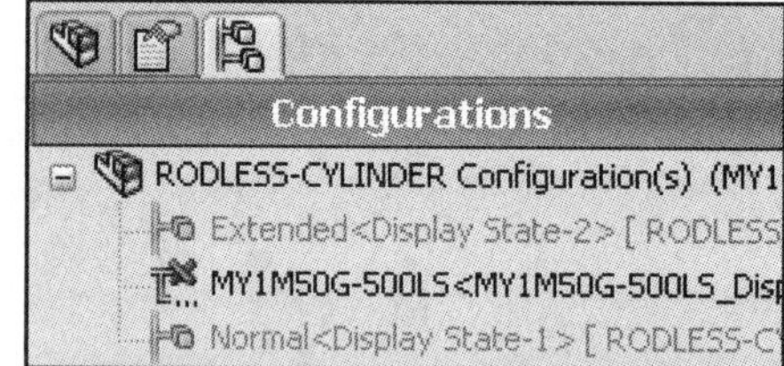

In the next Project, develop three configurations for the RODLESS-CYLINDER assembly and three configurations for the LINEAR-TRANSFER assembly.

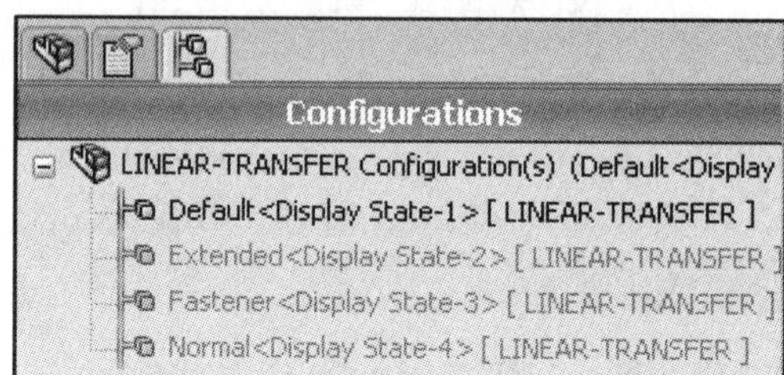

Geometric and Functional Requirements of the PLATE-A part

The PLATE-A part contains five features as illustrated by the illustrated FeatureManager.

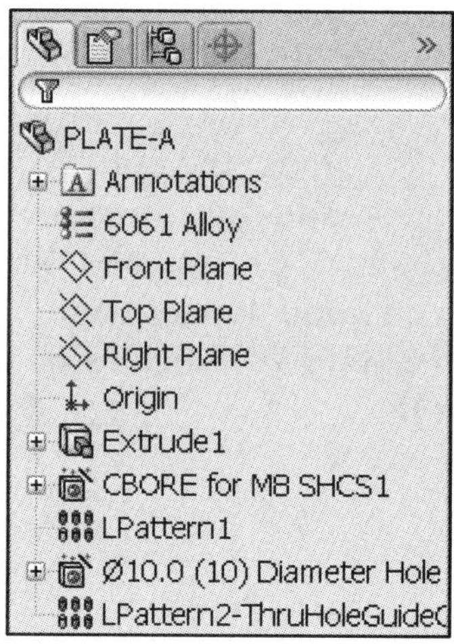

Determine the geometric and functional requirements for PLATE-A.

Remember, you will assemble PLATE-A to the RODLESS-CYLINDER assembly.

This project contains thousands of assemblies, parts, features, Mate types, and sketches. Know and understand your file and folder locations.

Use the FeatureManager to understand your present model condition.

Example 1: The PLATE-A part is contained in the LINEAR-TRANSFER assembly. The FeatureManager full name of the PLATE-A part is: LINEAR-TRANSFER\PLATE-A.

- LINEAR-TRANSFER is the assembly name.
- PLATE-A is the component name.

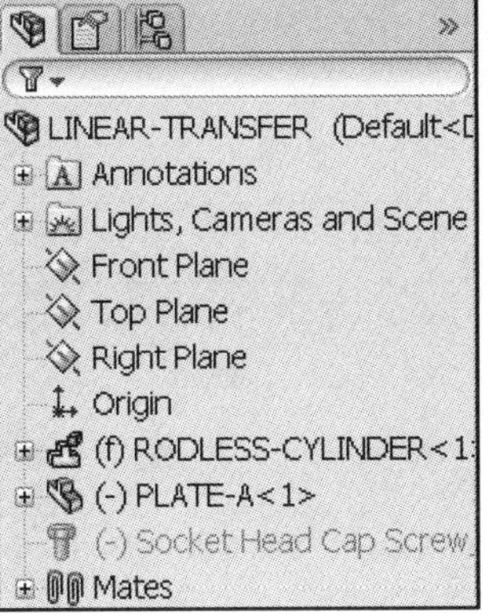

Example 2: Sketch3 is the sketch name of the M8 Cbore Hole. The FeatureManager full name of Sketch3 is LINEAR-TRANSFER\PLATE-A\CBORE for M8 SHCS1\Sketch3.

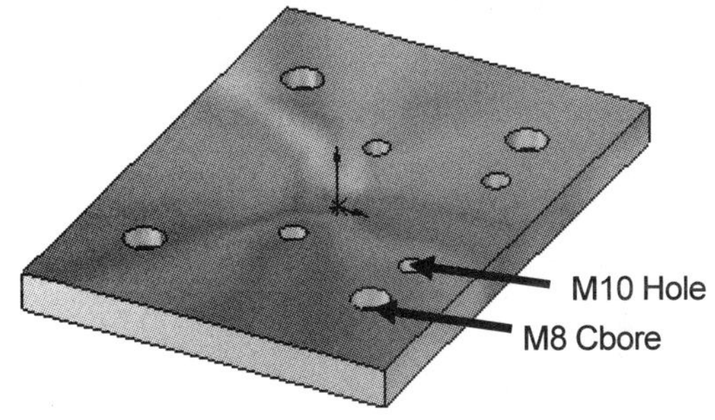

PLATE-A

- LINEAR-TRANSFER is the assembly name.
- PLATE-A is the part name.
- CBORE for M8 SHCS1 is the feature name.
- Sketch3 is the sketch name.

CBORE is the abbreviation for Counterbore.

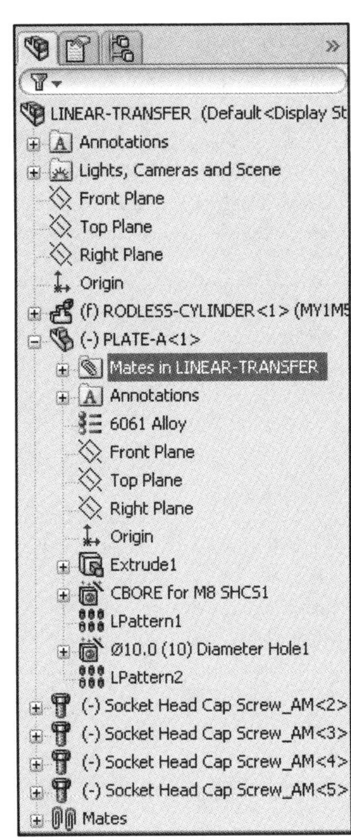

Before you begin a part, review the following New Part Task List.

New Part Task List – Before you begin:		
Task:	**Comments:**	**Complete:**
Identify the part function.	PLATE-A combines the RODLESS-CYLINDER with the GUIDE-CYLINDER in the LINEAR-TRANSFER assembly.	✓
Identify the components that directly affect the part.	RODLESS-CYLINDER, GUIDE-CYLINDER, and M8 SHCS parts	✓
Research the company component database. Identify if PLATE-A, or a similar part exists.	No. Always verify that the existing part does not exist. Copy similar parts to save model time.	✓
Identify the Mate references in the assembly.	Utilize two Concentric Mates between mating holes. Utilize a Coincident Mate between the bottom face of PLATE-A and the top face of the RODLESS-CYLINDER.	✓
Define the material, units, tolerance and precision. Utilize the Custom Part Template.	Aluminum. Use company default standard tolerance and precision values for all machined parts.	✓
Identify the geometric requirements of the part; width, height, depth, hole locations, etc.	Utilize the Measure tool	partial
Is the part symmetrical? Yes, design with symmetry in the sketch of the base feature.		
Design for changes.		
Identify Features and Mates with descriptive names.		
Group Fillets, Draft, and Patterns together. Reuse geometry. Locate the seed feature in a pattern to be utilized in a component pattern.		
Will this part be used in another assembly? Design for multiple configurations. Create a simplified version with no Fillets, no Draft or on unnecessary features.		
Utilize patterns to be referenced in the assembly and suppressed.		
Obtain a unique filename.	PLATE-A (45-63421). Utilize PLATE-A assigned part number.	✓

Six of the new part tasks are completed. You have some work to do! Determine the Geometric requirements for the PLATE-A part from the size and shape of the following features:

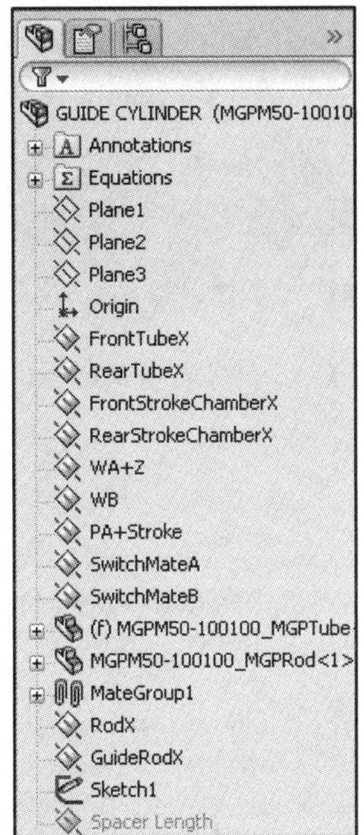

- *GUIDE-CYLINDER\MGPM50-100100_MGPTube\Cbores*
- *GUIDE-CYLINDER\MGPM50-100100_MGPTube\ThruHoles*
- *RODLESS-CYLINDER\MY1M50G-500LS_MY1M2104Table\Table*
- *RODLESS-CYLINDER MY1M50G-500LS_\MY1M2104Table\Table_Holes*

In the first activity, determine the location of the *MGPM50-*100100_MGPTube\Cbores and MGPM50-100100_MGPTube\ThruHoles.

In the second activity, determine the proper overall size of the RODLESS-CYLINDER\MY1M50G-500LS_MY1M2104Table\Table and the location of the Table_Holes.

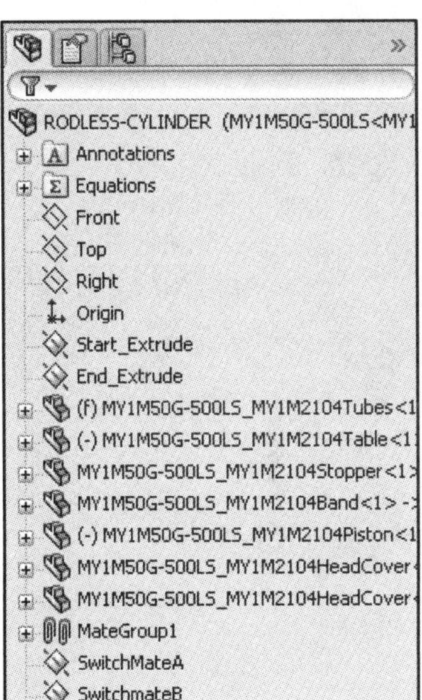

Quickly locate entries in the FeatureManager by using the filter tool. Rename Features, Mates, and Reference Geometry with descriptive names.

The ThruHoles feature defines the Thru Hole position and diameter. Record the dimensions for the CBORES and ThruHoles features. Avoid precision and tolerance stack-up issues. Perform the following tasks:

- *Set the precision to the appropriate number of decimal places*
- *Mate two diagonal holes between PLATE-A and the MGPTube\ThruHoles*

In modeling, utilize Concentric Mates (places the selections so that they share the same center line) with any two sets of holes. Mating the diagonal holes simulates the shop floor practice to utilize diagonal holes for the best stability and clamping.

The SMC components (downloaded from 3D ContentCentral) utilize an ISO dimensions standard.

Large assemblies can contain models with legacy data (inherited older models).

Activity: Geometric and Functional Requirements – PLATE-A and GUIDE-CYLINDER Assembly

Open the GUIDE-CYLINDER assembly.

1) Click the **Design Library** tab.

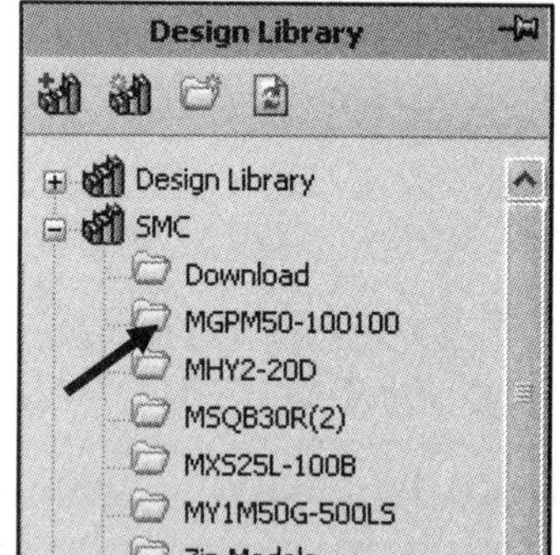

2) **Expand** the SMC folder.

3) Click the **MGPM50-100100** folder.

4) Click and drag the **GUIDE-CYLINDER** icon into the Graphic window. The GUIDE-CYLINDER assembly is displayed.

Open the MGPTube part.

5) Right-click **MGPTube** from the FeatureManager.

6) Click **Open Part** from the Context toolbar. The MGPTube is displayed in the Graphics window.

Locate the Cbores and ThruHoles features.

Expand the features.

7) **Expand** ThruHoles and Cbores. Sketch15 and Sketch16 are fully defined. Sketch 15 contain External References as indicated by the '->' symbol.

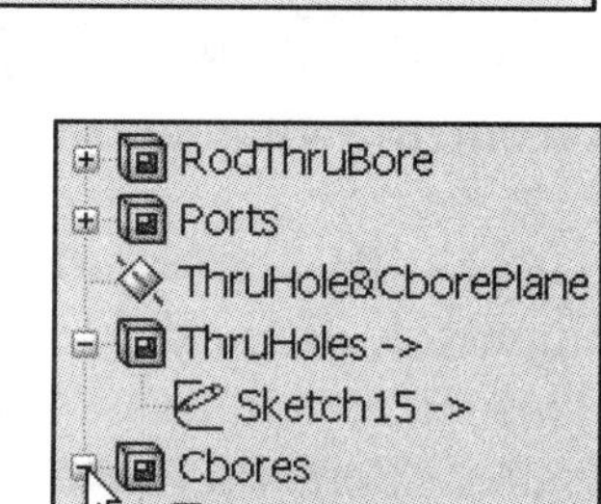

An External reference is created when one document is dependent on another document for its solution. If the referenced document changes, the dependent document changes also.

To create a new feature or part in an assembly without External References, check **Options**, **External References**, **Do not create references external to the model** from the System Options dialog box.

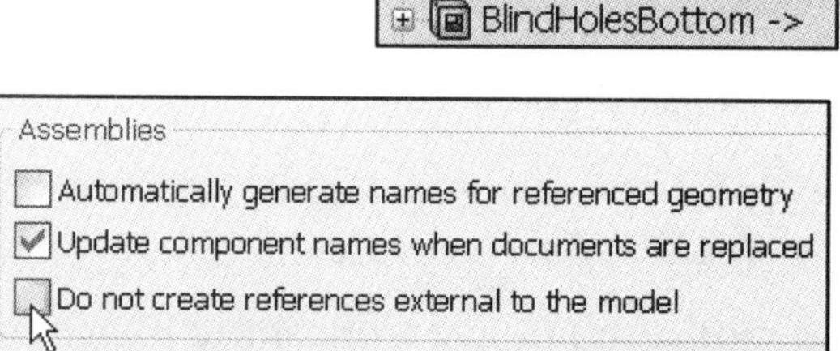

Know the default SW colors. A selected feature in the Graphics window is displayed in blue. The corresponding feature entry in the FeatureManager is displayed in blue. Fully defined sketched dimensions are displayed in black. Extruded depth dimensions are displayed in blue. Modify default colors, check **Options**, **System Options**, **Colors**, **System colors** from the System Options dialog box.

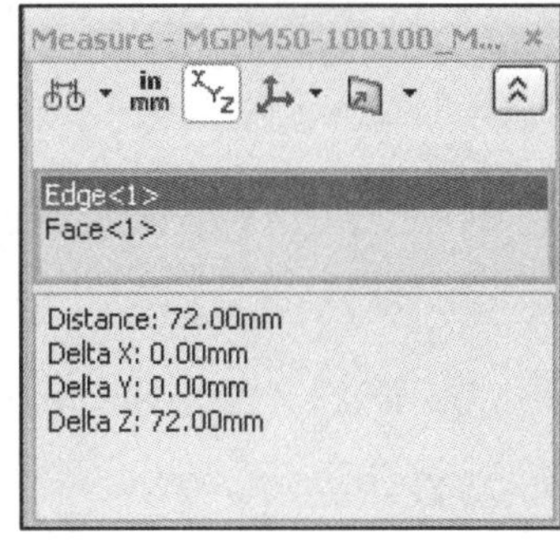

Measure the distance between the front face to the back left Cbore.

8) Click the **Evaluate** tab from the CommandManager.

9) Click the **Measure** tool from the Evaluate toolbar.

10) Click the **front face**. Face<1> is displayed.

11) Click the **back left Cbore inside cylindrical face** as illustrated. Face<2> is displayed. The center distance is 72mm.

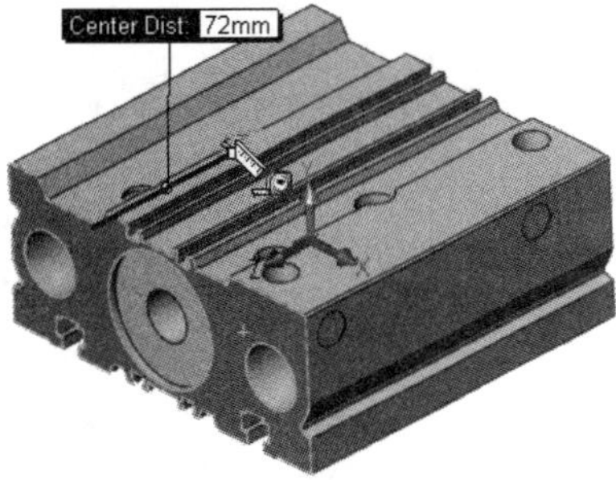

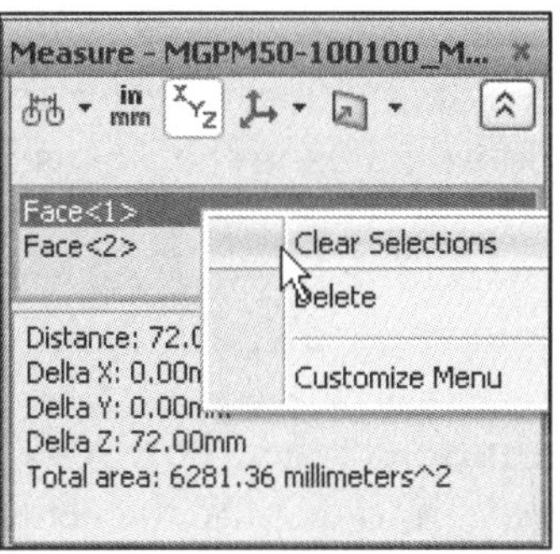

Deselect all faces.

12) Right-click in the **selected box**.

13) Click **Clear Selections**.

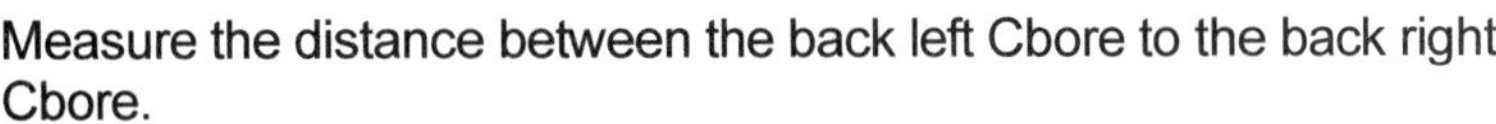

Measure the distance between the back left Cbore to the back right Cbore.

14) Click the **back left Cbore cylindrical face**.

15) Click the **back right Cbore cylindrical face**. The center distance is 66mm.

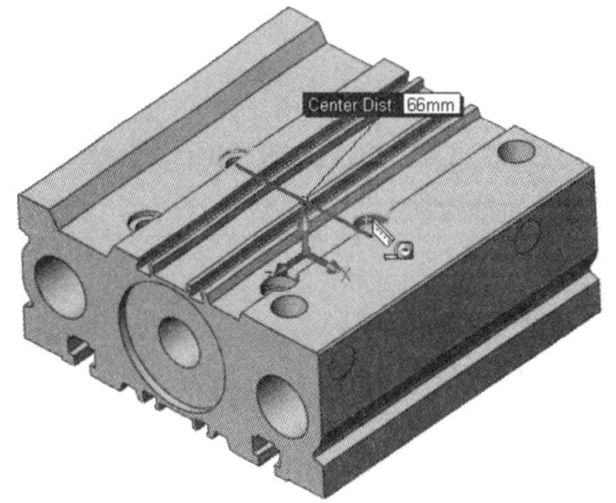

Close the open documents.

16) Click **Close** from the Measure box.

17) Click **Window**, **Close All** from the Menu bar menu.

18) Click **No** to Save changes.

Review the hole placement. Vertical: 72mm – 24mm = 48mm. Horizontal: 66mm on center.

Review the hole type: Cbore: ∅14. Thru Hole:∅8.6. Common Metric fastener required.

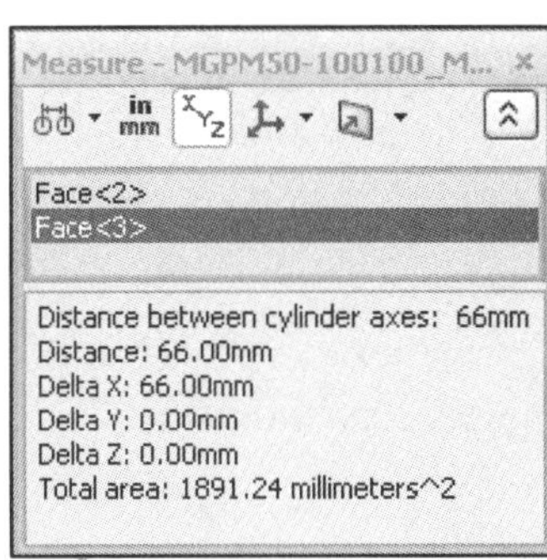

The SolidWorks Measure tool contains the following options:

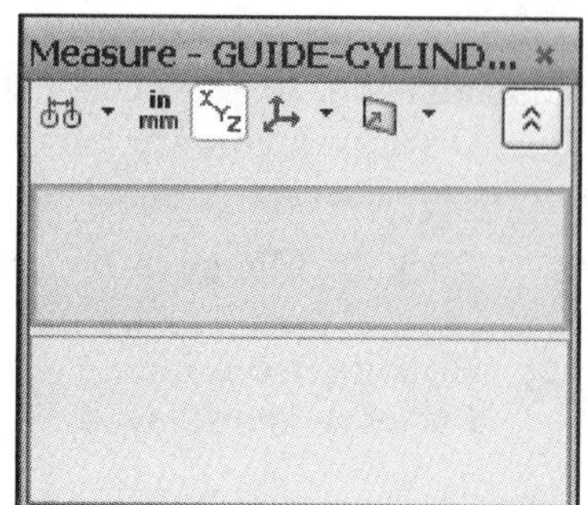

- *Arc/Circle Measurements*
- *Units/Precision*
- *Show XYZ Measurements*
- *XYZ Relative To*
- *Projected On*

The XYZ coordinates display different results. Select a vertex to display the XYZ coordinates in the Status bar.

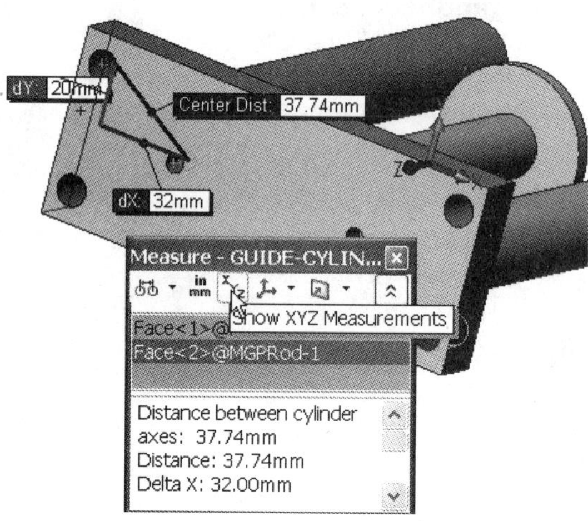

Select the Show XYZ Measurements option to display dX, dY, or dZ.

Un-Select the Show XYZ Measurements option to display the center distance between two selected entities.

Activity: Geometric and Functional Requirements – PLATE-A and RODLESS-CYLINDER

Open the RODLESS-CYLINDER assembly.

19) Click the **SMC\MY1M50G-500LS** folder from the Design Library.

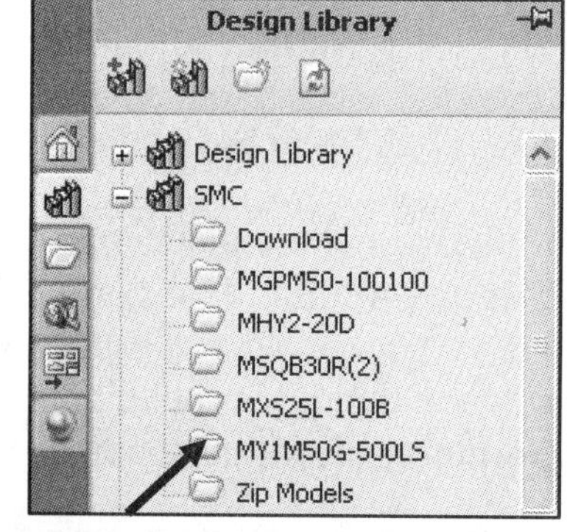

20) Click and drag the **RODLESS-CYLINDER** icon into the Graphic window.

21) Click **Yes** to rebuild. The RODLESS-CYLINDER assembly is displayed.

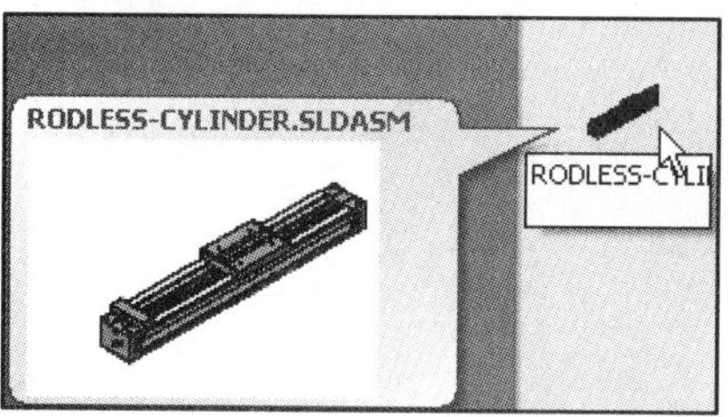

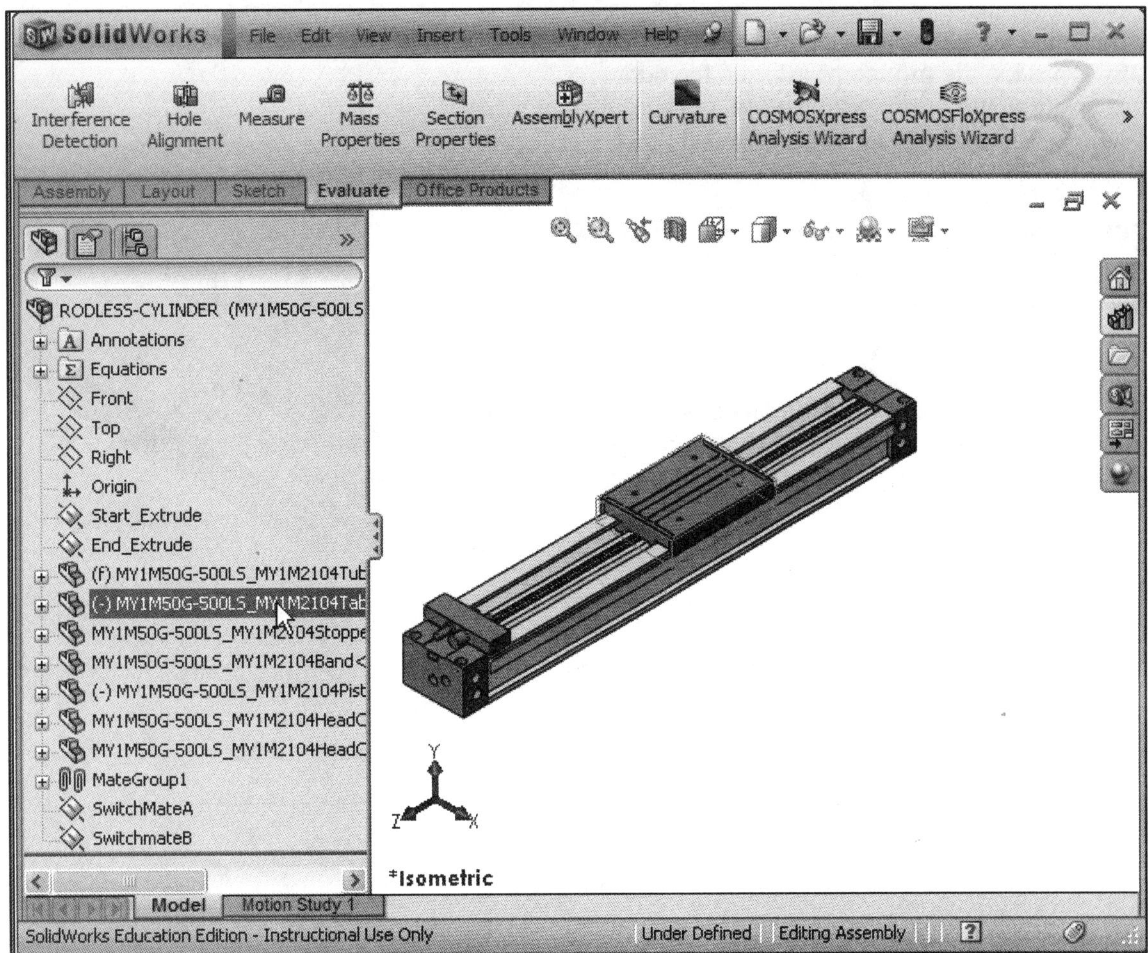

Open the MY1M2104Table.

22) Right-click **MY1M50G-500LS_MY_1M2104Table<1>** from the FeatureManager.

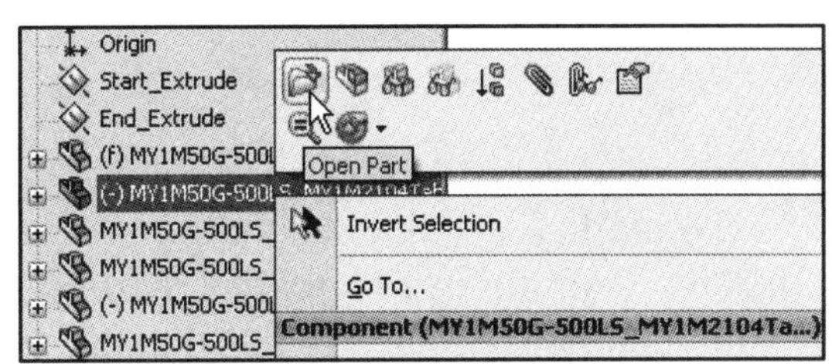

23) Click **Open Part** from the Context toolbar. The table is displayed in the Graphics window.

Display an Isometric view in the Graphics window.

24) Click **Isometric** view from the Heads-up View toolbar.

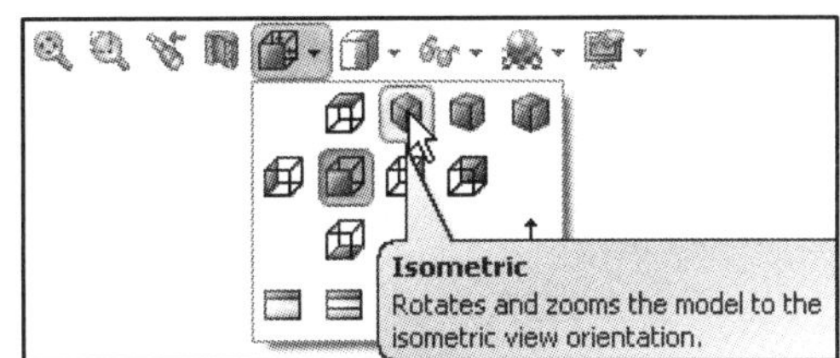

Locate the Table features.

25) Position the **mouse pointer** on the right side of the Table. The feature tool tip Table is displayed. Table is an Extruded Base feature.

26) Position the **mouse pointer** on the top-hole circumference. The feature tool tip Table_Holes is displayed.

Close the MY1M2104Table.

27) Click **File**, **Close** from the Menu bar menu. The RODLESS-CYLINDER remains open.

28) Click **No** to save changes.

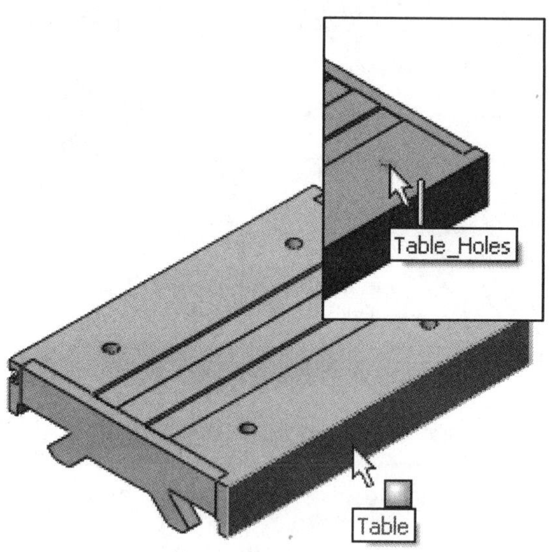

PLATE-A part

The dimensions in the mating parts determine the feature dimensions in PLATE-A. At this time, the Table_Holes are not aligned with the GUIDE-CYLINDER Cbore Holes. PLATE-A requires two patterns of holes.

To flip a dimension arrow, click the **dimension**, click the **blue dot**. View the illustrated dimension arrow direction icons.

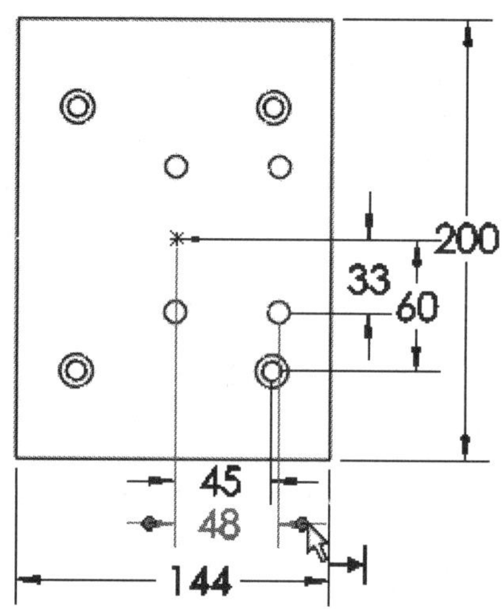

To modify the dimension font size, click **Options**, **Document Properties**, **Annotations Display**, and check the **Always display text at the same size** box. Adjust the Font size using the **Options**, **Document Properties**, **Annotation Font** option.

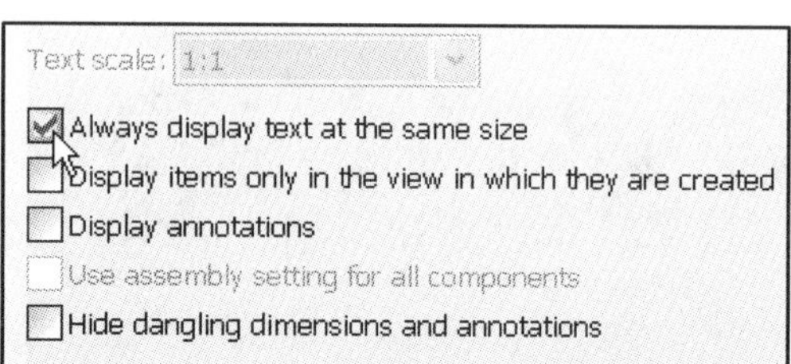

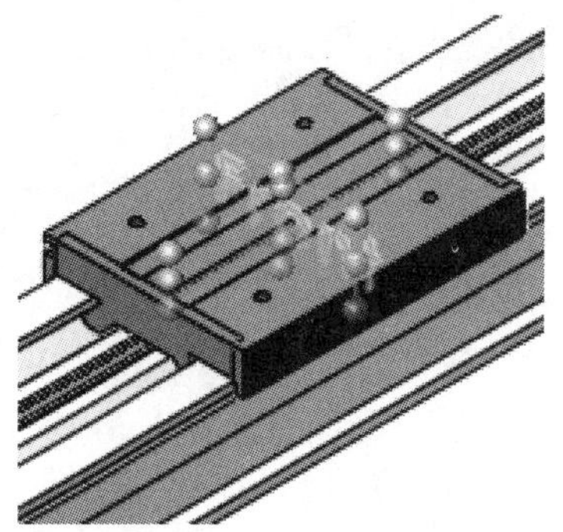

Where should the PLATE-A reference planes be located? Answer: Review the RODLESS-CYLINDER\MY1M2104Table part to locate the planes of symmetry.

The MY1M2104Table part identifies the overall sketch dimensions and orientation of the PLATE-A part.

The MY1M2104Table part is centered on the Front and Right Plane.

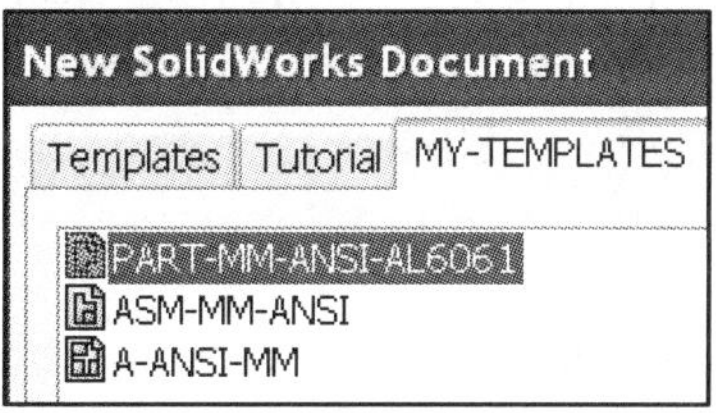

The first feature of the PLATE-A part is an Extruded Base feature. The Top Plane is the Sketch plane. Center the rectangular sketch on the Front and Right Plane.

Utilize 15mm Aluminum plate stock. The PLATE-A part utilizes the custom PART-MM-ANSI-AL6061 Template created in Project 2.

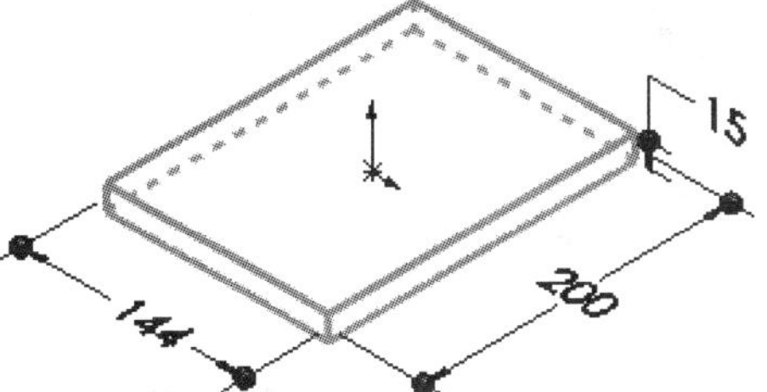

Plan Mate types before creating the Base feature of the part. Mates create geometric relationships between assembly components. As you add mates, you define the allowable directions of linear or rotational motion of the components. You can move a component within its degrees of freedom, visualizing the assembly's behavior.

Review the Mates between the PLATE-A part and the MY1M2104Table part.

Mate Type:	PLATE-A part:	RODLESS-CYLINDER\ MY1M2104Table part:
Coincident	Bottom face	Top face
Concentric	Lower right hole	Lower right hole
Concentric	Upper left hole	Upper left hole

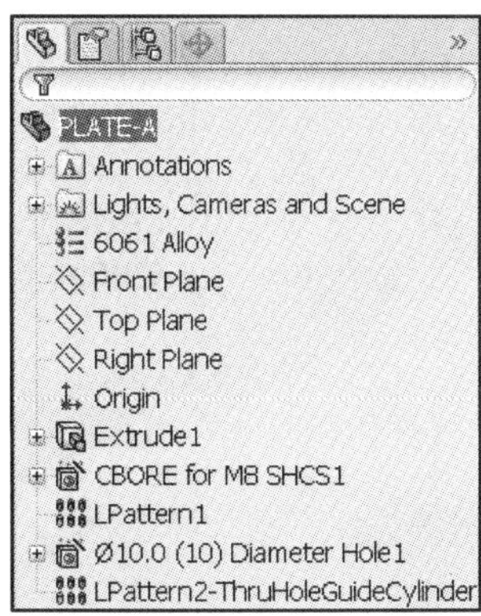

Align the component in the same orientation as the assembly to avoid unnecessary use of Rotate Component in the assembly. Create the Extruded Base feature vertical and horizontal dimensions in the same orientation as the MY1M2104Table Extruded Base feature.

The PLATE-A part requires two sets of four holes. The first set contains four Cbores.

The second set contains four Thru Holes.

Create a 2x2 Linear Pattern for both hole types. Utilize the Hole Wizard tool.

The seed feature of the Linear Pattern is the first Cbore. The PLATE-A part positions the seed feature in its lower right corner. Utilize the seed feature and Linear Pattern tool in the assembly.

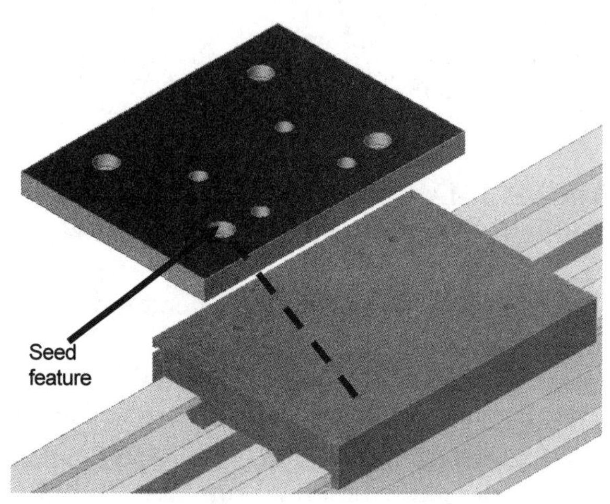

Display Cbore Holes and the Thru Holes in the ANSI Metric standard. Other standards may be selected when using the Hole Wizard or SolidWorks\Toolbox.

Prepare for future design changes. If the overall size of PLATE-A changes, the hole location remains constant. Select the Front and Right Plane for a Symmetric Reference for the Cbore.

Select the Front Plane for a Symmetric Reference for the Thru Holes.

Select the Right plane for a Coincident Reference.

Activity: Create PLATE-A In-Context of the Assembly

Display the RODLESS-CYLINDER reference planes.

29) **Expand** MY1M2104Table from the RODLESS-CYLINDER FeatureManager as illustrated.

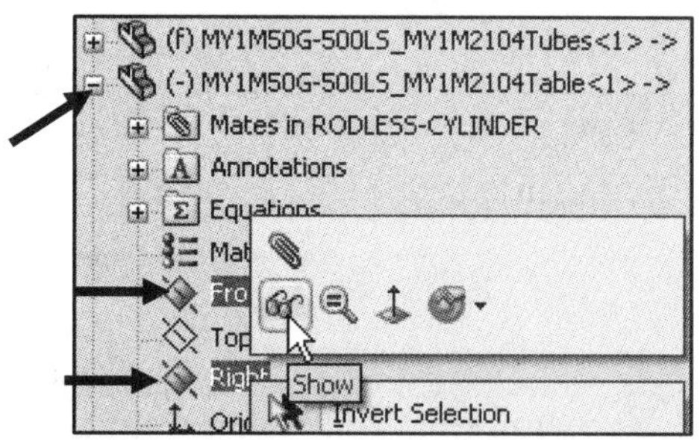

30) Click **Front** Plane from the FeatureManager.

31) Hold the **Ctrl** key down.

32) Click **Right** Plane from the FeatureManager.

33) Release the **Ctrl** key.

34) Right-click **Show** from the Context toolbar. The Front and Right Planes are displayed in the Graphics window.

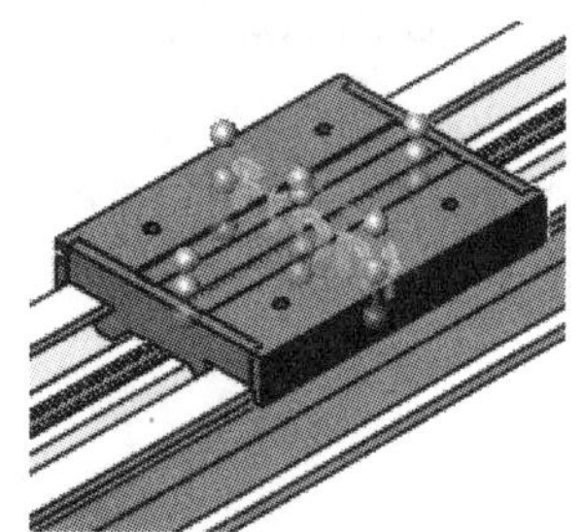

Create a New Part.

35) Click **New** from the Menu bar menu.

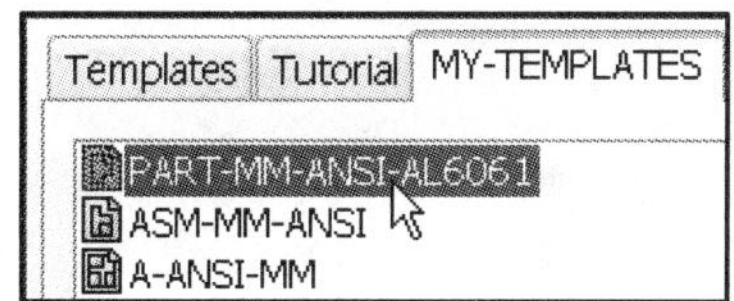

36) Click the **MY-TEMPLATES** tab.

37) Double-click the **PART-MM-ANSI-AL6061** Part template. The Part FeatureManager is displayed.

Save the New Part.

38) Click **Save**.

39) Select the **DELIVERY-STATION** folder.

40) Enter **PLATE-A** for File name.

41) Click **Save**. The PLATE-A FeatureManager is displayed.

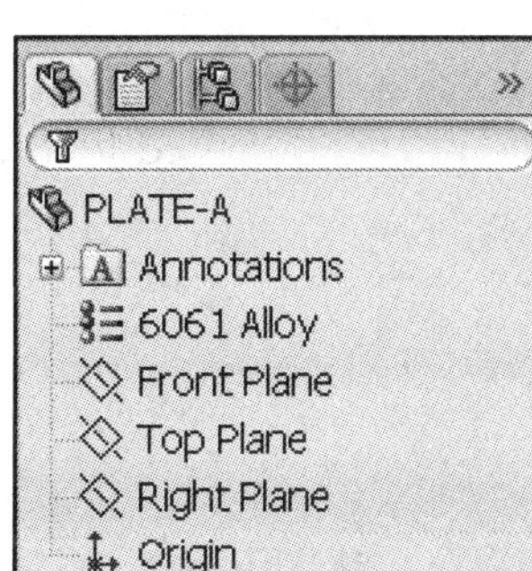

By default, the Bill of Materials utilizes the File name field for the Part Number column and the Description field for the Description column.

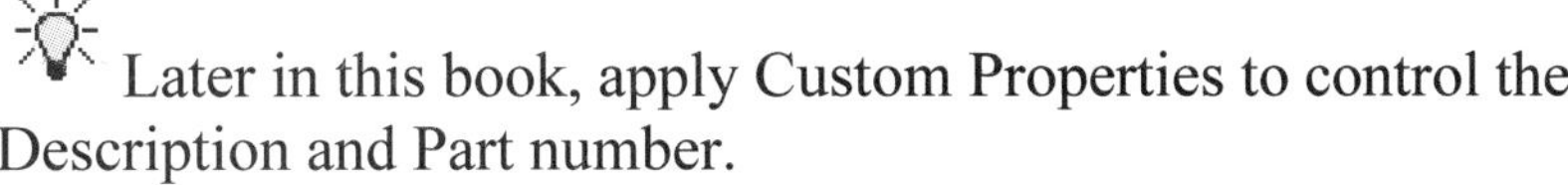

Later in this book, apply Custom Properties to control the Description and Part number.

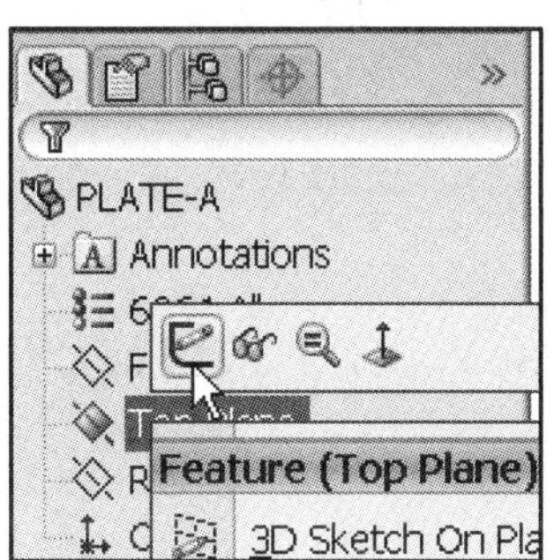

Sketch the profile.

42) Right-click **Top Plane** from the FeatureManager for the Sketch plane.

43) Click **Sketch** from the Context toolbar. The Sketch toolbar is displayed

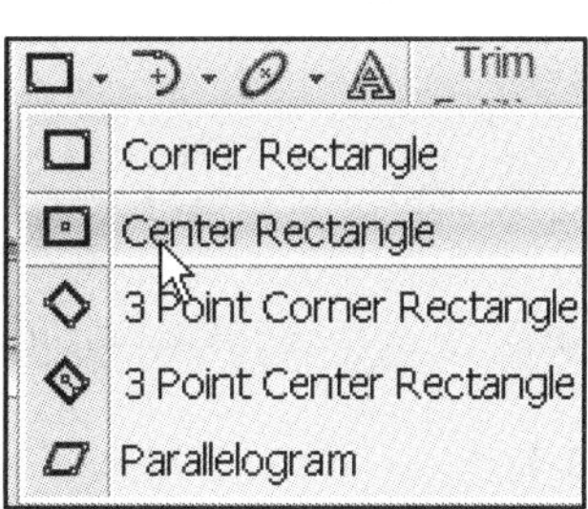

44) Click the **Center Rectangle** tool from the Sketch toolbar. Note: The Center Rectangle tool sketches rectangles at a center point.

45) Click the **Origin**.

46) **Sketch** a center rectangle as illustrated.

47) Right-click **Select** to deselect the Center Rectangle Sketch tool.

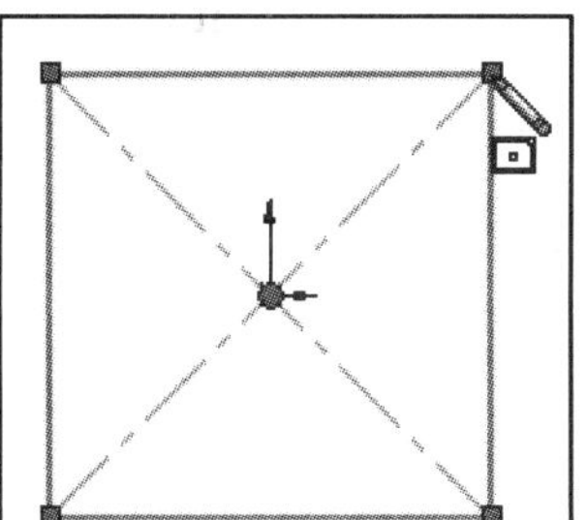

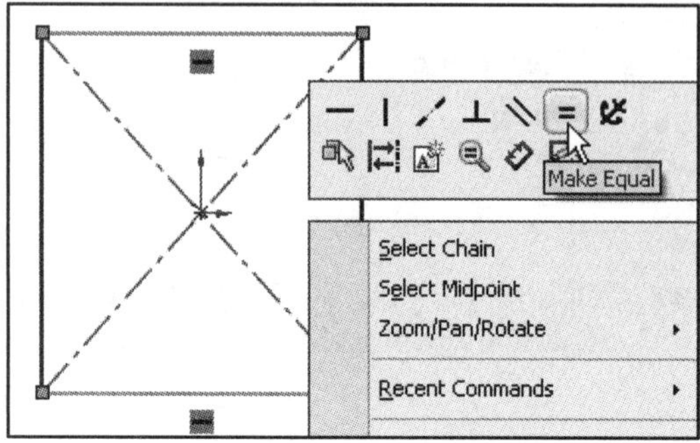

Insert an Equal relation if needed.

48) Insert an **Equal** relation between the top horizontal line and the bottom horizontal line.

49) Insert an **Equal** relation between the left vertical line and the right vertical line.

Add a vertical dimension.

50) Click the **Smart Dimension** tool from the Sketch toolbar.

51) Click the **right vertical** line.

52) Click a **position** to the right of the vertical line.

53) Enter **200**.

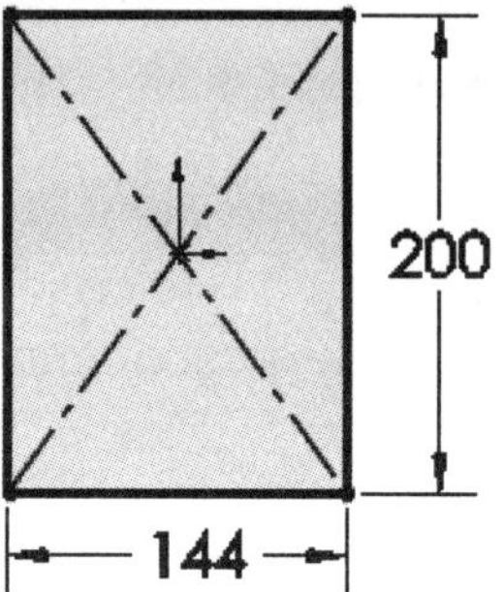

Add a horizontal dimension.

54) Click the **bottom horizontal** line.

55) Click a **position** below the horizontal line.

56) Enter **144**.

57) Click **OK** from the Dimension PropertyManager. Sketch1 is fully defined.

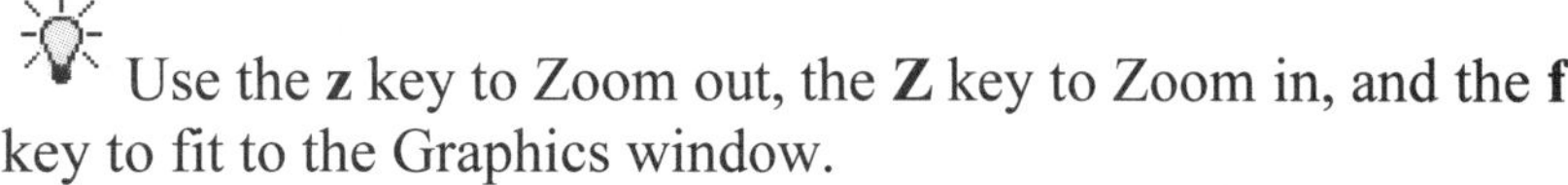

Use the **z** key to Zoom out, the **Z** key to Zoom in, and the **f** key to fit to the Graphics window.

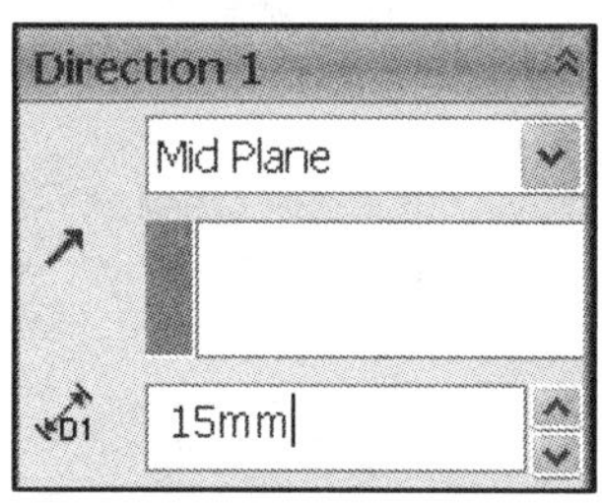

Extrude the sketch.

58) Click the **Features** tab from the CommandManager.

59) Click the **Extruded Boss/Base** tool from the Features toolbar. The Extrude PropertyManager is displayed.

60) Select **Mid Plane** for End Condition in Direction 1.

61) Enter **15**mm for Depth.

62) Click **OK** from the Extrude PropertyManager. Extrude1 is displayed in the FeatureManager

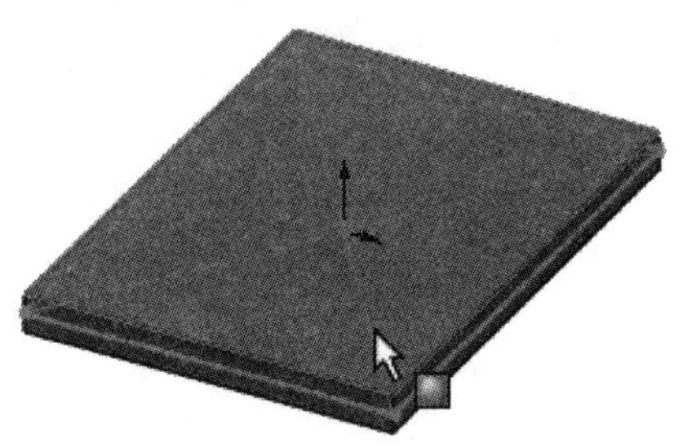

Apply the Hole Wizard tool. Create a M8 CBORE hole.

63) Click the **top face** of PLATE-A in the lower right corner as illustrated. Extrude1 is highlighted in the FeatureManager.

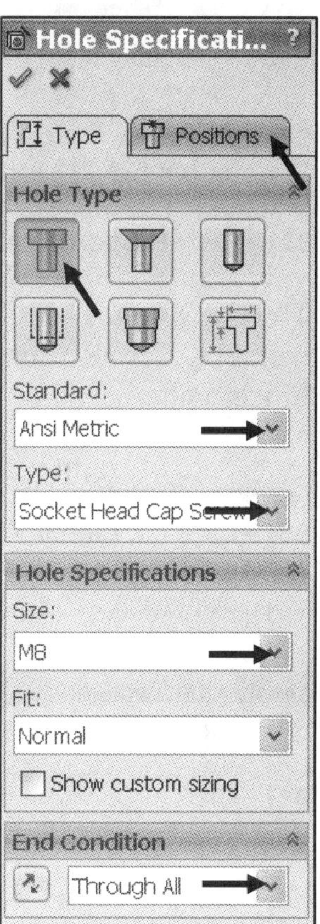

64) Click the **Hole Wizard** tool from the Features toolbar. The Hole Specification PropertyManager is displayed. The Type tab is selected by default.

65) Click **Counterbore** for Hole Type.

66) Select **Ansi Metric** for Standard.

67) Select **Socket Head Cap Screw** for Type.

68) Select **M8** for Size.

69) Select **Through All** for End Condition.

70) Click the **Positions** tab.

The Point icon is displayed.

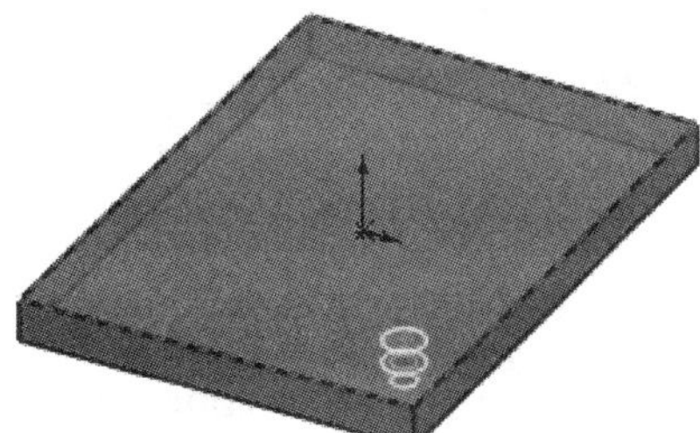

Insert dimensions.

71) Click the **Smart Dimensions** tool from the Sketch toolbar.

72) Click the **Origin**.

73) Click the **Cbore center point**.

74) Click a **position** below the horizontal profile line.

75) Enter **45**mm.

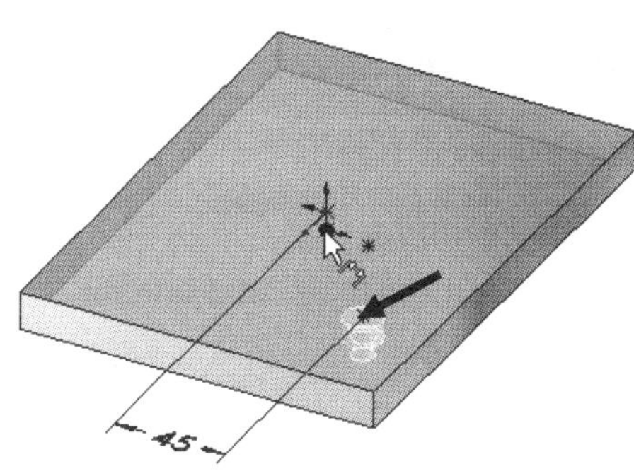

76) Click the **Origin**.

77) Click the **Cbore center point**.

78) Click a **position** to the right of the vertical profile line.

79) Enter **60**mm.

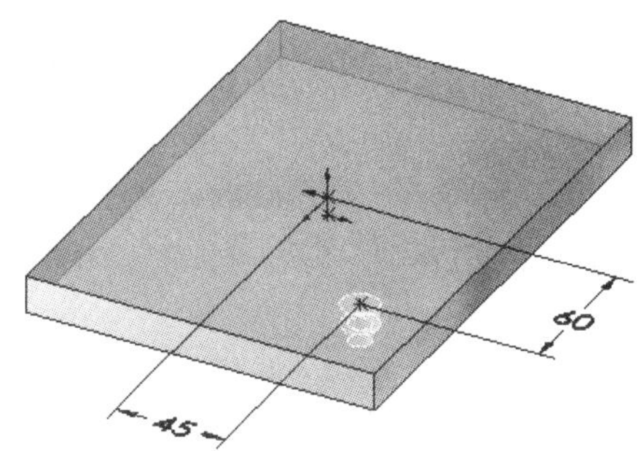

80) Click **OK** from the Dimension PropertyManager

81) Click **OK** from the Hole Position PropertyManager. CBORE for M8 SHCS1 is displayed in the FeatureManager.

82) Click **Hidden Lines Visible** from the Heads-Up View toolbar.

The CBORE for M8 SHCS1 is displayed in the Graphics window. CBORE for M8 SHCS1 is the seed feature for the first Linear Pattern.

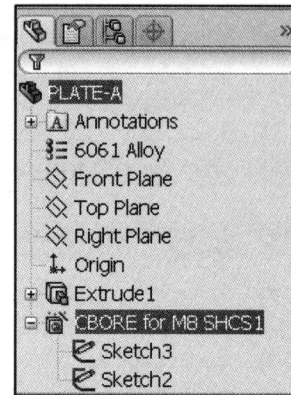

Create a Linear Pattern Feature.

83) Click the **Linear Pattern** tool from the Features toolbar. The Linear Pattern PropertyManager is displayed.

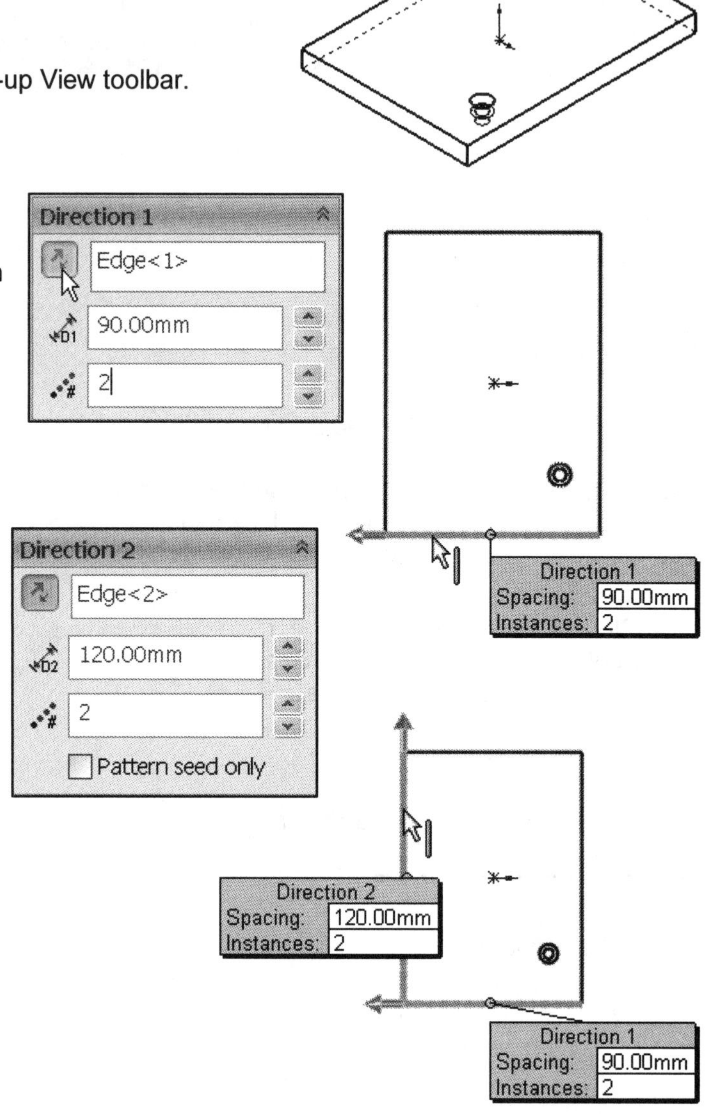

Display the Top view.

84) Click **Top** view from the Heads-up View toolbar.

85) Click the **bottom edge** of PLATE-A for Direction 1.

86) If required, click the **Reverse Direction** button. The direction arrow points to the left.

87) Enter **90**mm for Spacing in Direction 1.

88) Enter **2** for Instances.

89) Click the **left vertical line** for Direction 2.

90) If required, click the **Reverse Direction** button. The direction arrow points upward.

91) Enter **120**mm for Spacing in Direction 2.

92) Enter **2** for Instances.

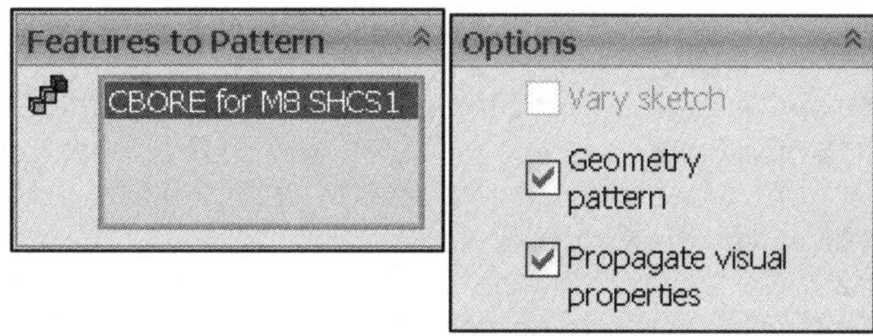

93) Check **Geometry pattern** from the Options box.

94) If required, click inside the **Features to Pattern** box. **Expand** PLATE-A in the flyout FeatureManager. Click **CBORE for M8 SHCS1**. CBORE for M8 SHCS1 is displayed in the Features to Pattern box.

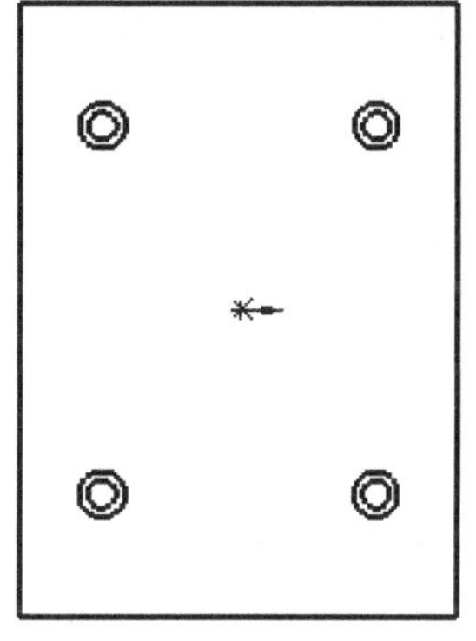

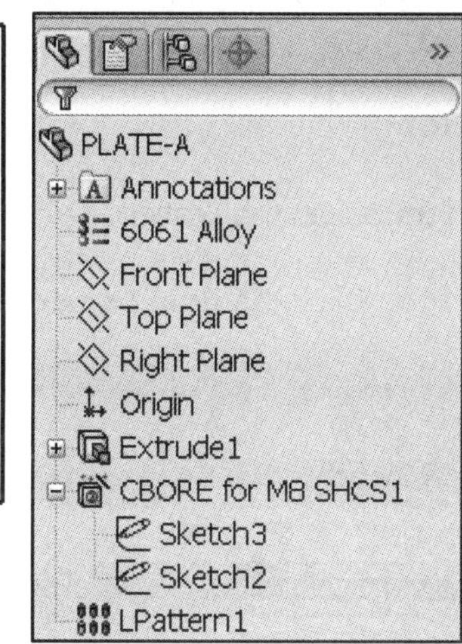

95) Click **OK** from the Linear Pattern PropertyManager. LPatten1 is created in the FeatureManager.

The checked Geometry pattern option copies only the geometry (faces and edges) of the features. The unchecked Geometry pattern option results in a calculated solution for every instance in the pattern.

The geometry pattern option usually decreases the time required to create and rebuild a pattern.

Apply the Hole Wizard tool. Create an M10 Thru Hole.

96) Click the **top face** of PLATE-A in the lower right hand corner. Extrude1 is highlighted in the FeatureManager.

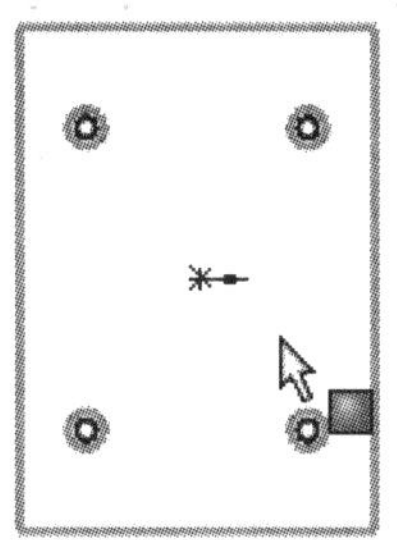

97) Click the **Hole Wizard** tool from the Features toolbar. The Hole Specification PropertyManager is displayed.

98) Click **Hole** for Hole Type.

99) Select **Ansi Metric** for Standard.

100) Select **Drill sizes** for Type.

101) Select **10** for Size.

102) Select **Through All** for End Condition.

103) Click the **Positions** tab. The Point icon is displayed.

Dimension the hole.

104) Click the **Smart Dimensions** tool from the Sketch toolbar.

105) Click the **Origin**.

106) Click the **hole center point** as illustrated.

107) Click a **position** below the horizontal profile line.

108) Enter **48**mm.

109) Click the **Origin**.

110) Click the **hole center point**.

111) Click a **position** to the right of the vertical profile line.

112) Enter **33**mm.

113) Click **OK** from the Dimension PropertyManager.

114) Click **OK** from the Hole Position PropertyManager. The hole is the seed feature for the second Linear Pattern.

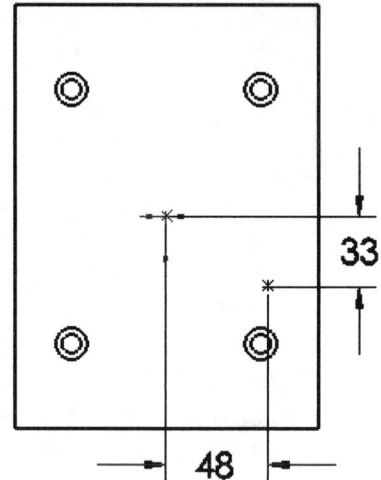

Create the second Linear Pattern.

115) Click the **Linear Pattern** tool from the Features toolbar. The Linear Pattern PropertyManager is displayed.

116) Click the **bottom edge** for Direction1. Edge<1> is displayed. If required, click the **Reverse Direction** button. The direction arrow points to the left.

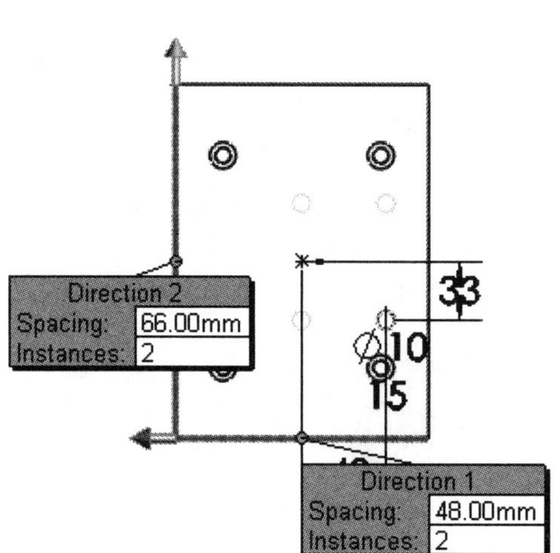

117) Enter **48**mm for Spacing in Direction 1.

118) Enter **2** for Instances.

119) Click the **left vertical edge** for Direction 2. The direction arrow points upward. If required, click the **Reverse Direction** button.

120) Enter **33*2** for Spacing in Direction 2.

121) Enter **2** for Instances.

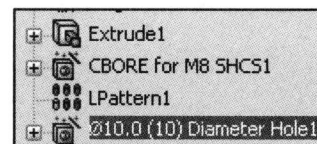

122) If required, click inside the **Features to Pattern** box. **Expand** PLATE-A in the Graphics window. Click **10.0 (10) Diameter Hole1** from the fly-out FeatureManager.

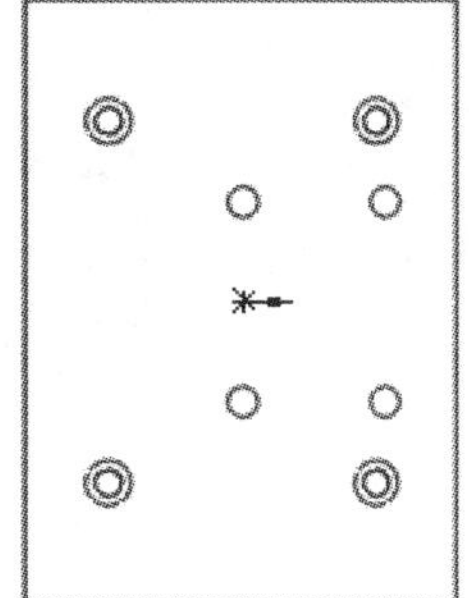

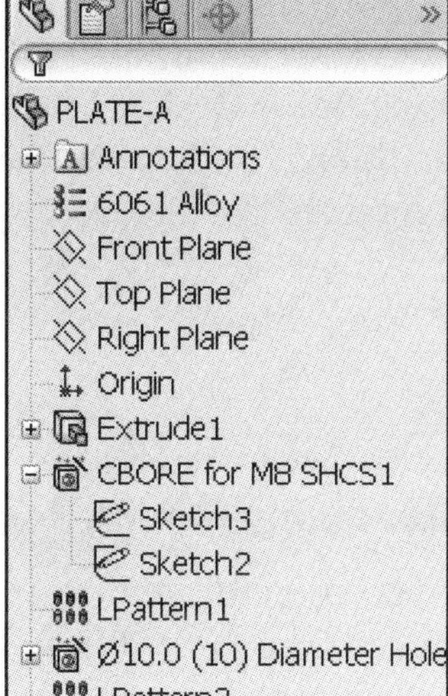

123) Click **OK** from the Linear Pattern PropertyManager. LPattern2 is displayed in the FeatureManager.

Display an Isometric view.

124) Click **Isometric** view from the Heads-up View toolbar.

Save the PLATE-A part.

125) Click **Save.**

Activity: Create a New Folder in the SolidWorks Design Library

Create a new parts folder in the SolidWorks Design Library.

126) **Expand** the Design Library folder.

127) Click the **Push Pin** icon to pin the Design Library open.

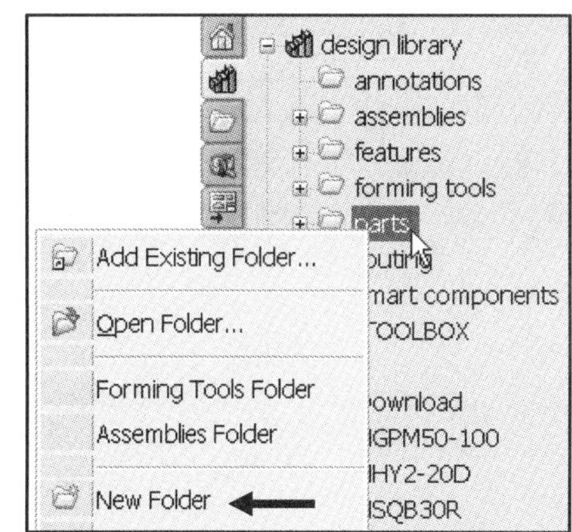

128) Right-click on **parts** in the folder area.

129) Click **New Folder** as illustrated.

130) Enter **plates** for Folder name.

131) Double-click the **plates** folder. The folder is empty.

Insert PLATE-A into the plates file folder.

132) Drag the **PLATE-A** PLATE-A part icon from the top of the FeatureManager into the plates folder. The Add to Library PropertyManager is displayed.

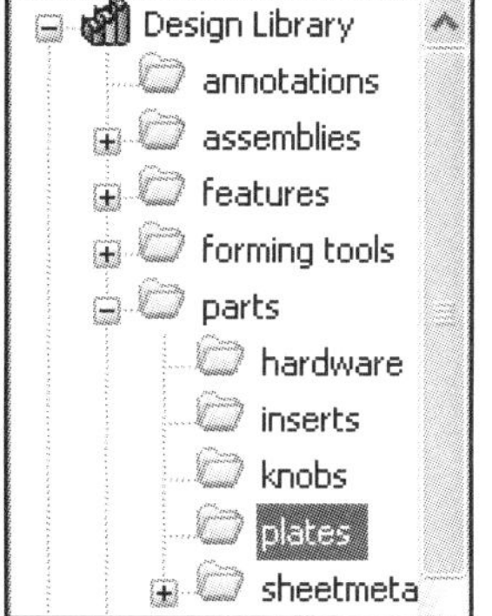

133) Click **OK** from the Add to Library PropertyManager. PLATE-A is contained in the parts\plates folder.

Utilize **Options, File Locations, Design Library** to insert additional folders into the Design Library.

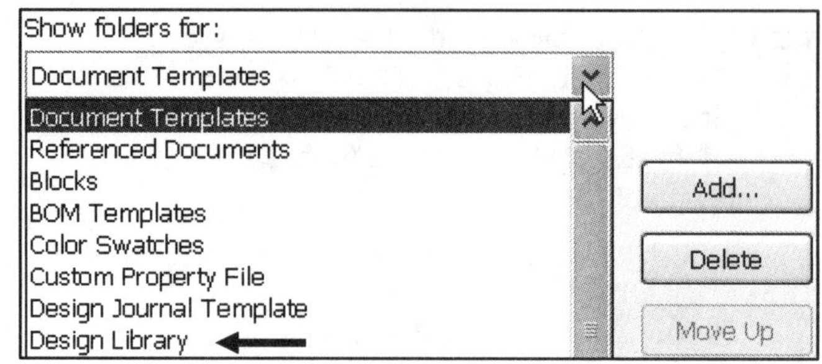

Assembly Mating Techniques

The action of assembling components in SolidWorks is defined as Mates. Mates simulate the construction of the assembly in a manufacturing environment. In dynamics, components possess linear motion along the x, y, and z-axes and rotational motion around the x, y, and z-axes. In an assembly, each component contains six degrees of freedom: three translational (linear) and three rotational. All components behave as rigid bodies. Components do not flex or deform.

In a static analysis, there is no motion. How do static and dynamic principles translate to component Mates? Answer: Mates remove degrees of freedom.

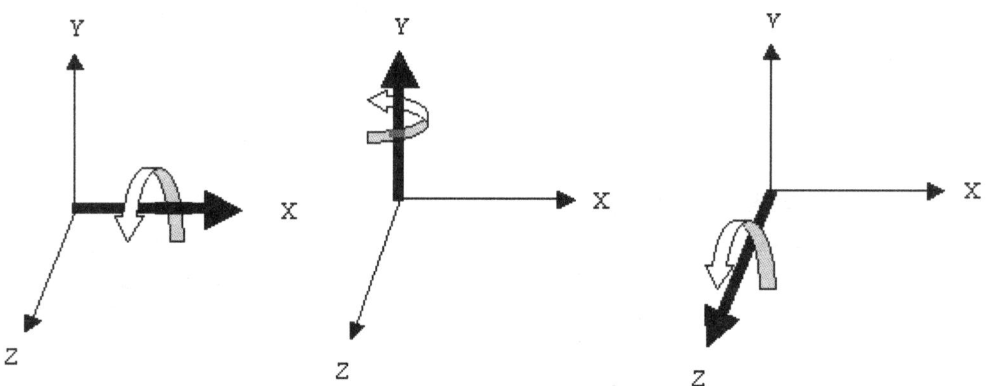

Understand the engineering mechanics of the component before creating Mates.

Example 1:

Static: Fasten the DELIVERY-STATION assembly to the MOUNTING-PLATE part. The MOUNTING PLATE part is fixed to the Origin of the final assembly. The MOUNTING-PLATE part does not translate or rotate.

Example 2:

Dynamic: Assemble the PLATE-A part to the RODLESS-CYLINDER\ MY1M2104Table part. The MY1M2104Table part slides along the MY1M2104Tubes part. The PLATE-A part travels at the same velocity as the MY1M2104Table part. Insert the Mates between the PLATE-A part and the MY1M2104Table part.

Assembly modeling requires practice and time. Below are a few helpful techniques to address component mating. Utilize these techniques throughout the development of the 3AXIS-TRANSFER assembly and sub-assemblies.

Mating Techniques:
Right-click in the assembly Graphics window to avoid mouse pointer "movement" to the assembly toolbar and the assembly FeatureManager.
Use the Zoom and Rotate tools to select the geometry in the mate process. Zoom in to the correct face. Right-click Select Other for hidden geometry.
Use View Orientation, Named Views to display a key area of the model.
Apply various colors to features and components to improve display.
Utilize Reference Planes and axes to assemble complex geometry.
Activate Temporary axes and Show Planes when required for Mates, otherwise Hide All Types from the View menu. Create Shortcut keys to activate View commands.
Select Reference Planes from the FeatureManager for complex components. Expand the FeatureManager to view the correct plane.
Remove display complexity. Hide components when visibility is not required.
Suppress components when Mates are not required. Group fasteners at the bottom of the FeatureManager. Suppress fasteners and their assembly patterns to save rebuild time and file size. Utilize caution with suppressed components. Suppressed Mates may cause related components to translate and rotate. Use View Mates to understand mating dependencies.
Utilize Section views to select internal geometry. Utilize Transparency to see through components required for mating.
Use the Move Component and Rotate Component commands before Mating. Position the component in the correct orientation.
Use a Coincident Mate when the distance value between two entities is zero. Utilize a Distance Mate when the distance value between two entities is not zero.
Cylindrical components require a Concentric and Coincident Mate. They are not fully defined.

Verify the position of the components. Use Top, Front, Right and Section views.
Rename Mates, key features and Reference Geometry with descriptive names.
Avoid unwanted references. Confirm the geometry name you selected in the Mate Property Manager.
Uncheck the Show preview option to prevent components from moving out of the Graphics window during mating.

LINEAR-TRANSFER Assembly

The RODLESS-CYLINDER assembly is the Base (first) component in the LINEAR-TRANSFER assembly.

All components of the RODLESS-CYLINDER assembly remain stationary, except for the MY1M2104Table part.

The MY1M2104Table part linearly translates along the MY1M2104Tubes part.

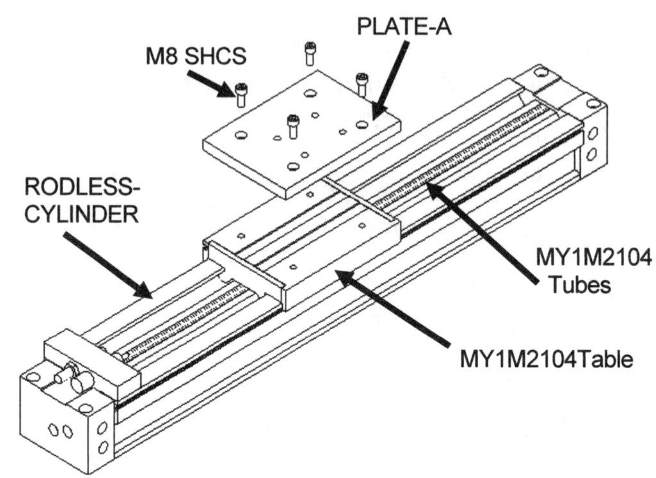

LINEAR-TRANSFER assembly

Perform the following tasks to complete the LINEAR-TRANSFER assembly.

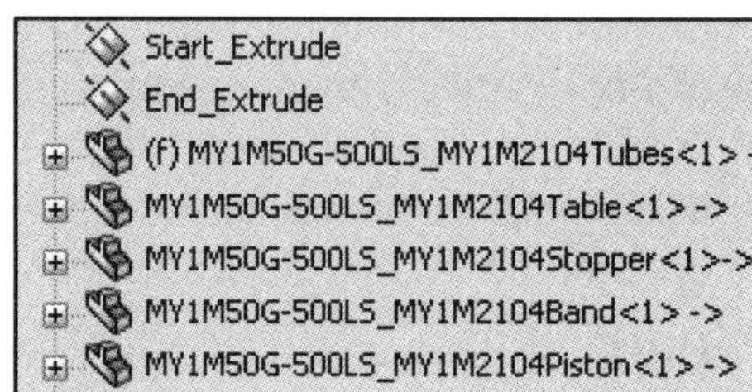

- Create the LINEAR-TRANSFER assembly.
- Fix the RODLESS-CYLINDER assembly to the Origin of the LINEAR-TRANSFER assembly.
- Assemble the PLATE-A part to the RODLESS-CYLINDER\MY1M2104Table part.
- Determine the diameter and length of the SHCS using the Measure tool. Mate the SHCS with the SolidWorks\Toolbox.

The PLATE-A part, and RODLESS-CYLINDER assembly are active documents.

Activity: Insert Multiple Components at Once in an Assembly

Create the LINEAR-TRANSFER assembly.

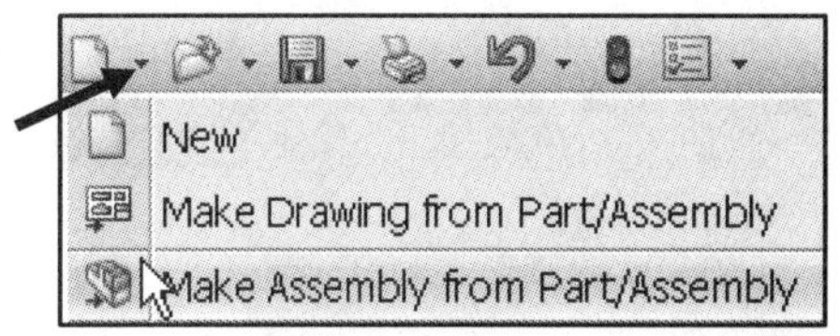

134) Click **Make Assembly from Part/Assembly** from the Menu bar toolbar.

135) Click the **MY-TEMPLATES** tab.

136) Double-click **ASM-MM-ANSI**.

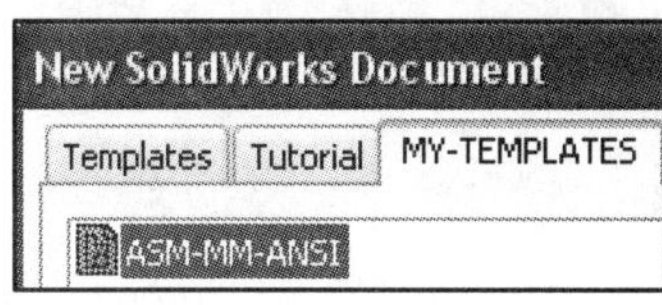

The Begin Assembly PropertyManager is displayed. In order to select multiple components from the Part/Assembly to Insert, box, select the Push Pin as illustrated. The Begin Assembly PropertyManager remains open. Utilize the Browse button to select components not displayed in the Open documents box.

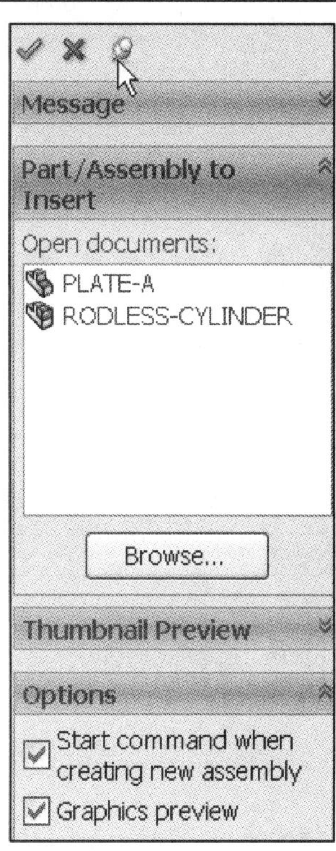

Inset the ROD-CYLINDER assembly.

137) Click the **Push Pin** icon from the Begin Assembly PropertyManager.

138) Click **RODLESS-CYLINDER** from the Open documents box.

139) Click **inside** the Graphics window. The first inserted component is fixed to the Origin.

140) Click **PLATE-A** in the Open documents box.

141) Click a **position** above the RODLESS-CYLINDER as illustrated.

142) Click **OK** from the Insert Begin Assembly PropertyManager. View the results.

Hide the Origins.

143) Click **View,** uncheck **Origins** from the Menu bar menu.

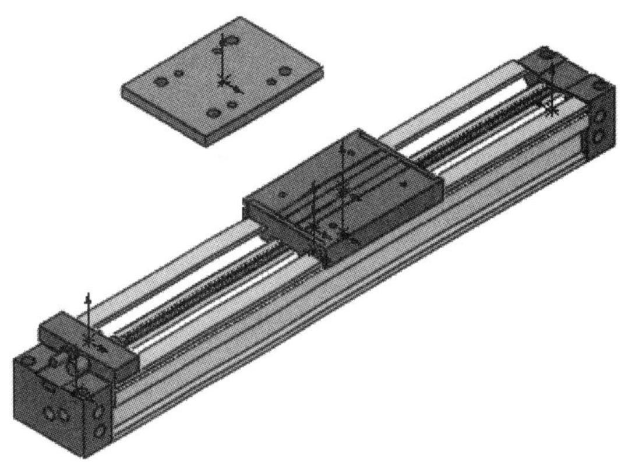

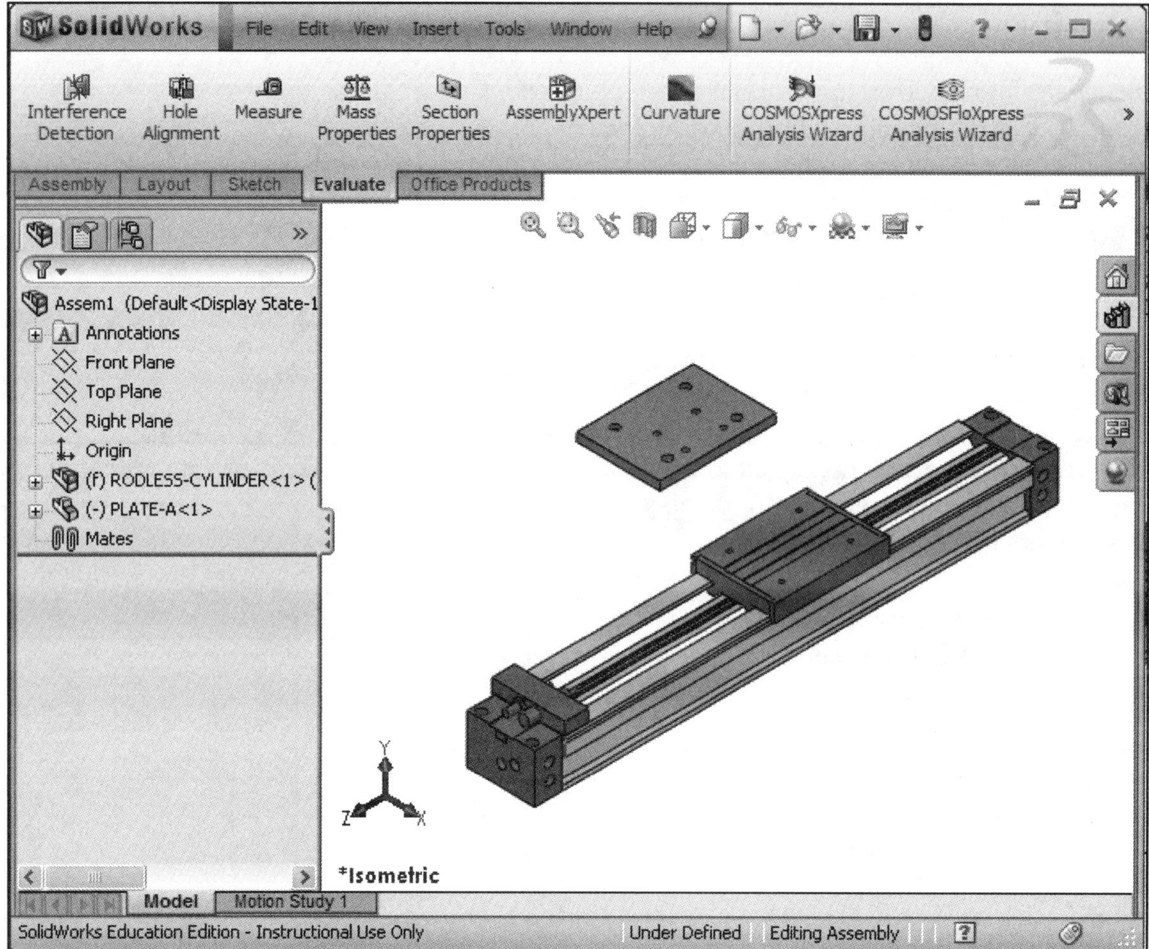

Save the assembly.

144) Click **Save**.

145) Select the **DELIVERY-STATION** for Save in folder.

146) Enter **LINEAR-TRANSFER** for File name.

147) Click **Save**. The LINEAR-TRANSFER assembly FeatureManager is displayed.

Customize the Keyboard

Customize your keyboard to create Shortcut keys for reference geometry. Create Shortcut keys to check or uncheck Hide All Types, Planes, Axes, Temporary Axes, and Origins. Large Assembly Mode hides all Reference geometry by default.

Create a new view in the View Orientation dialog box. An enlarged view saves time in assembling the MY1M2104Table holes to the PLATE-A holes.

Activity: Customize the Keyboard

Create four View Shortcut keys.

148) Click **Tools**, **Customize** from the Menu bar menu.

149) Click the **Keyboard** tab.

150) Click **View** from the Categories box.

Create the Planes Shortcut key.

151) Select **Planes** from the Commands box.

152) Enter **Shift + P** in the Press new Shortcut key.

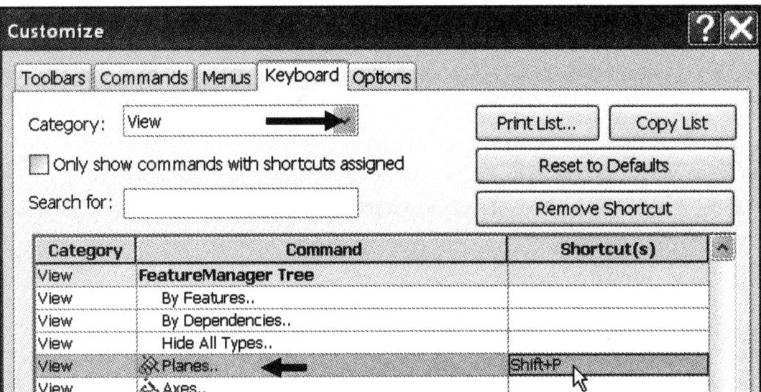

Create the Axes Shortcut key.

153) Select **Axes** from the Commands box.

154) Enter **Shift + A** in the Press new Shortcut key.

Create the Temporary Axes Shortcut key.

155) Select **Temporary Axes** from the Commands list box.

156) Enter **Shift + T** in the Press new Shortcut key.

Create the Origins Shortcut key.

157) Select **Origins** from the Commands list box.

158) Enter **Shift + O** in the Press new Shortcut key.

159) Click **OK** from the Customize dialog box.

Activity: Create a New View

Create a New View.
160) Zoom in on the MY1M2104Table.

161) Rotate the **MY1M2104Table** as illustrated.

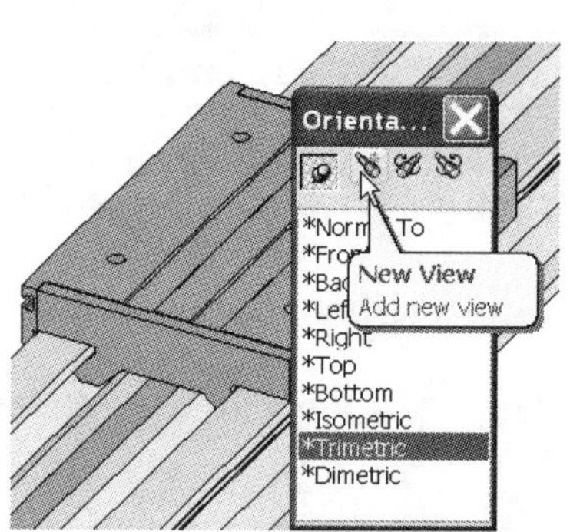

162) Press the **Space Bar** to display the View Orientation dialog box.

163) Click **Pin** from the Orientation box.

164) Click **New View**.

165) Enter **table-view** for view name.

166) Click **OK** from the Named View box.

167) Uncheck Pin from the Orientation box.

Display an Isometric view.
168) Click **Isometric** view from the Heads-up View toolbar.

Display the table-view.
169) Click **table-view** from the Heads-up View toolbar.

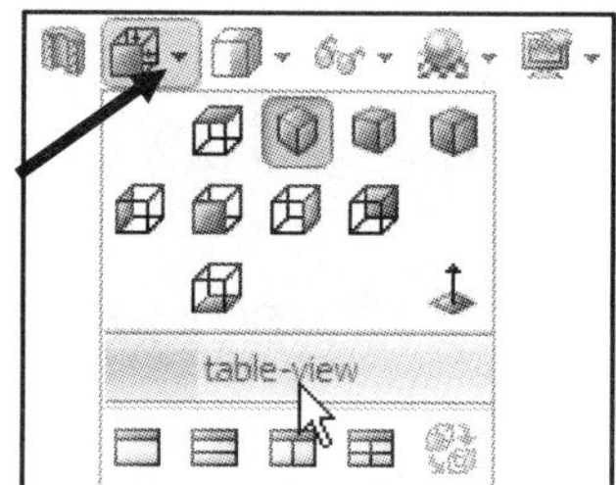

Note: Custom Shortcut keys are set on the current keyboard. To save/restore settings to another computer, utilize the Start, All Programs, SolidWorks, SolidWorks Tools, Copy Settings Wizard. For best practice, System Administrators copy settings to network computers and roaming user profiles.

Modify the Base component: Fix / Float options

By default, the first component in an assembly is fixed with respect to the assembly Origin. Click OK from the Begin Assembly PropertyManager to fix the first component to the Origin. The component receives an (f) in the FeatureManager.

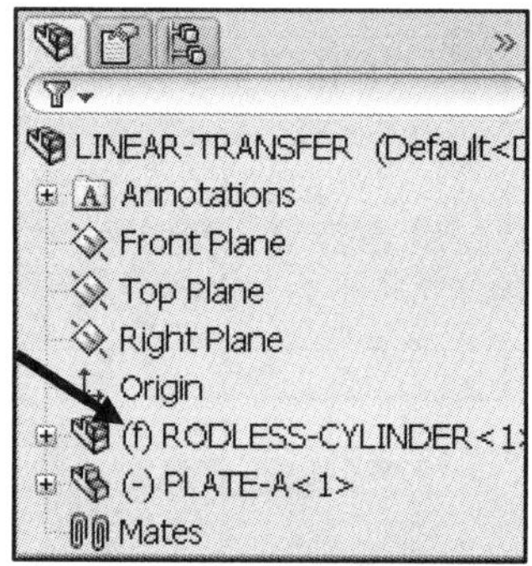

The Float state displays a minus (-) in the FeatureManager.

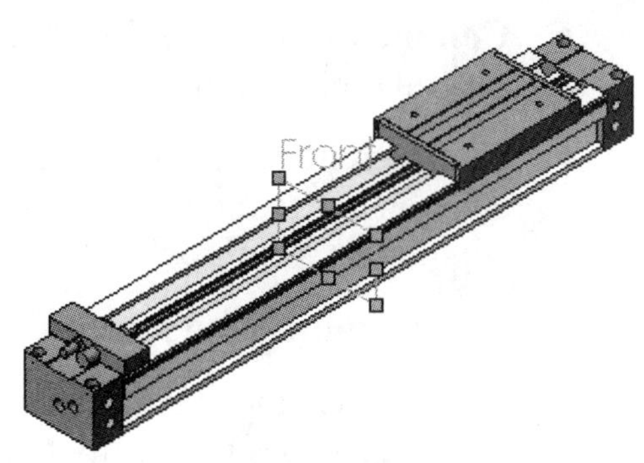

As components increase in complexity, visualizing the icon becomes more challenging. In many design situations, the first component orientation and position with respect to the assembly Origin requires modification.

How do you address these issues? Answer: Modify the Fixed state to a Float state.

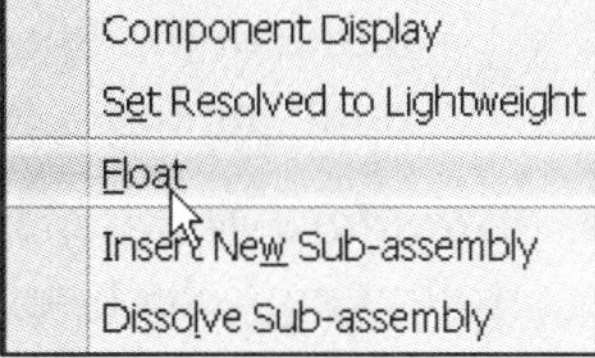

The Float state displays a minus (-) in the FeatureManager. Move and rotate the component with respect to the assembly Origin.

Mate the first component to reference assembly geometry.

Mate PropertyManager

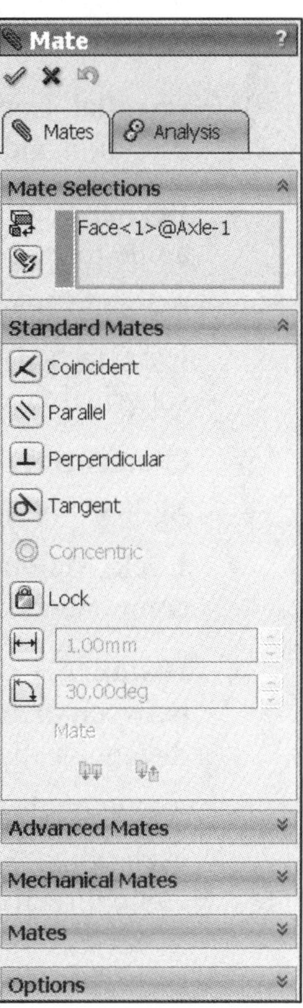

Mates provide the ability to create geometric relationships between assembly components. Mates define the allowable directions of rotational or linear motion of the components in the assembly. Move a component within its degrees of freedom in the Graphics window, to view the behavior of an assembly.

Mates are solved together as a system. The order in which you add mates does not matter. All mates are solved at the same time. You can suppress mates just as you can suppress features.

The Mate PropertyManager provides the ability to select either the Mates or Analysis tab. Each tab has a separate menu. The Analysis tab requires the ability to run COSMOSMotion. The Analysis tab will not be covered in detail. The Mate PropertyManager displays the appropriate selections based on the type of geometry you select.

Mate PropertyManager: Mates tab

The Mates tab is the default tab. The Mates tab provides the ability to insert a Standard, Advanced, or Mechanical Mate.

- ***Mate Selections***. The Mate Selections box provides the following selections:
  - **Entities to Mate**. Displays the selected faces, edges, planes, etc. that you want to mate.
  - **Multiple mate mode**. Mates multiple components to a common reference in a single operation. When activated, the following selections are available:

- **Common references**. Displays the selected entity to which you want to mate several other components.
- **Component references**. Displays the selected entities on two or more other components to mate to the common reference. A mate is added for each component.
- **Create multi-mate folder**. Groups the resulting mates in a Multi-Mates folder.
- **Link dimensions**. Only available for Distance and Angle mates in a multi-mate folder. Provides the ability to link dimensions. The variable name in the Shared Values dialog box is the same as the multi-mate folder name.

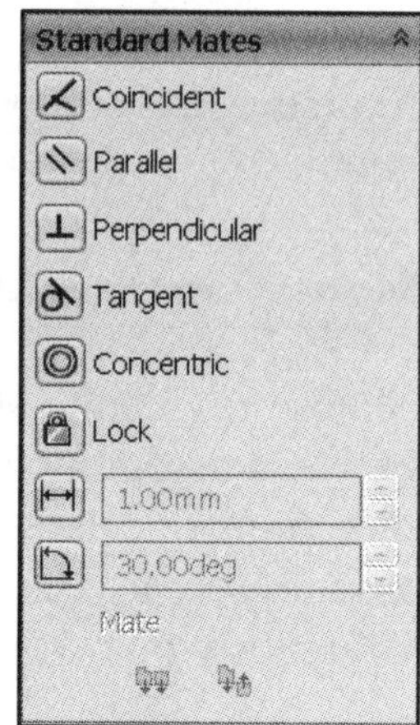

- ***Standard Mates***. The Standard Mates box provides the following selection:
  - **Coincident**. Locates the selected faces, edges, or planes so they use the same infinite line. A Coincident mate positions two vertices for contact.
  - **Parallel**. Locates the selected items to lie in the same direction and to remain a constant distance apart.
  - **Perpendicular**. Locates the selected items at a 90 degree angle to each other.
  - **Tangent**. Locates the selected items in a tangent mate. At least one selected item must be either a conical, cylindrical, spherical face.
  - **Concentric**. Locates the selected items so they can share the same center point.
  - **Lock**. Maintains the position and orientation between two components.
  - **Distance**. Locates the selected items with a specified distance between them. Use the drop-down arrow box or enter the distance value directly.
  - **Angle**. Locates the selected items at the specified angle to each other. Use the drop-down arrow box or enter the angle value directly.

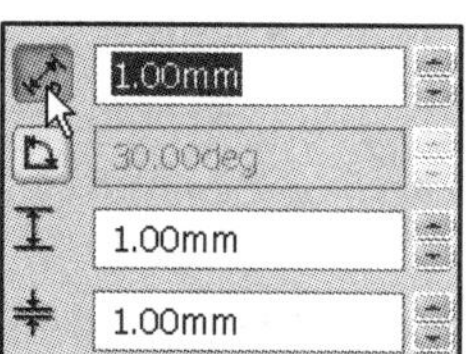

- **Mate alignment**. Provides the ability to toggle the mate alignment as necessary. There are two options. They are:
    - **Aligned**. Locates the components so the normal or axis vectors for the selected faces point in the same direction.
    - **Anti-Aligned**. Locates the components so the normal or axis vectors for the selected faces point in the opposite direction.

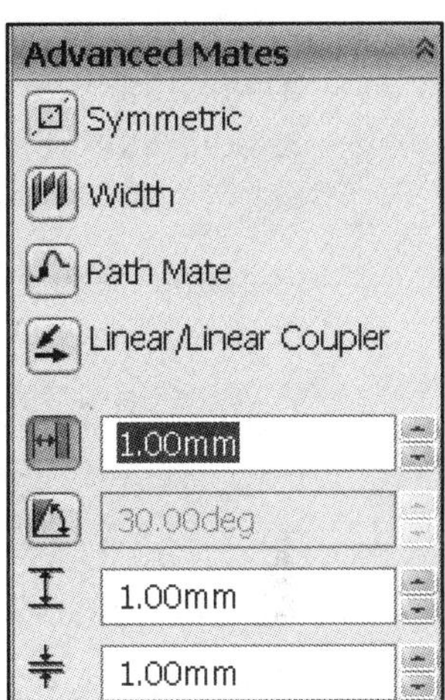

- *Advance Mates*. The Advance Mates box provides the following selections:
    - **Symmetric**. Forces two similar entities to be symmetric about a planar face or plane.
    - **Width**. Centers a tab within the width of a groove.
    - **Path Mate**. Constrains a selected point on a component to a path.
    - **Linear/Linear Coupler**. Establishes a relationship between the translation of one component and the translation of another component.
    - **Limit**. Provides the ability to allow components to move within a range of values for distance and angle. Select the angle and distance from the provided boxes. Specify a starting distance or angle as well as a maximum and minimum value.
        - **Distance**. Locates the selected items with a specified distance between them. Use the drop-down arrow box or enter the distance value directly.
        - **Angle**. Locates the selected items at the specified angle to each other. Use the drop-down arrow box or enter the angle value directly.

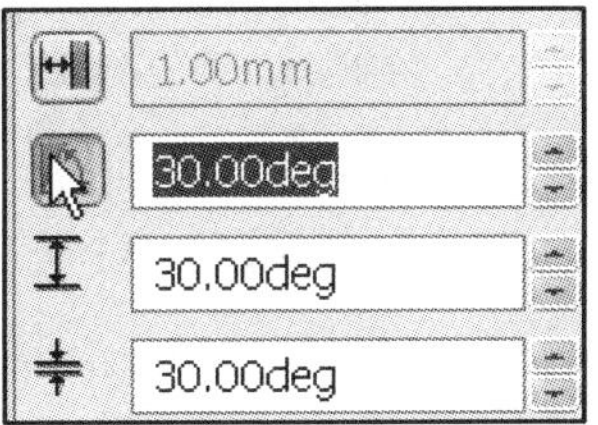

    - **Mate alignment**. Provides the ability to toggle the mate alignment as necessary. There are two options. They are:
        - **Aligned**. Locates the components so the normal or axis vectors for the selected faces point in the same direction.
        - **Anti-Aligned**: Locates the components so the normal or axis vectors for the selected faces point in the opposite direction.

- ***Mechanical Mates***. The Mechanical Mates box provides the following selections:
  - **Cam**. Forces a plane, cylinder, or point to be tangent or coincident to a series of tangent extruded faces.
  - **Gear**. Forces two components to rotate relative to one another around selected axes.
  - **Rack and Pinion**. Provides the ability to have Linear translation of a part, rack causes circular rotation in another part, pinion, and vice versa.
  - **Screw**. Constrains two components to be concentric, and also adds a pitch relationship between the rotation of one component and the translation of the other.
  - **Universal Joint**. The rotation of one component (the output shaft) about its axis is driven by the rotation of another component (the input shaft) about its axis.
- ***Mates***. The Mates box displays the activated selected mates.
- ***Options***. The Options box provides the following selections:

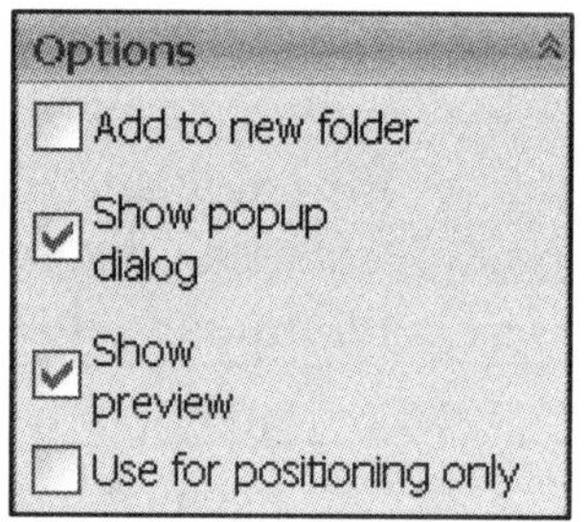

  - **Add to new folder**. Provides the ability for new mates to be added and to be displayed in the Mates folder in the FeatureManager design tree.
  - **Show popup dialog**. Selected by default. Displays a standard mate, when added in the Mate pop-up toolbar. When cleared, adds the standard mates in the PropertyManager.
  - **Show preview**. Selected by default. Displays a preview of a mate when enough selections for a valid mate occur.
  - **Use for positioning only**. When selected, components move to the position defined by the mate. A mate is not added to the FeatureManager design tree. A mate is displayed in the Mates box. Edit the mate in the Mate box. The mate is not displayed in the FeatureManager design tree.

The Use for positioning only box is an alternative to adding numerous mates, then afterward deleting those mates in the FeatureManager design tree.

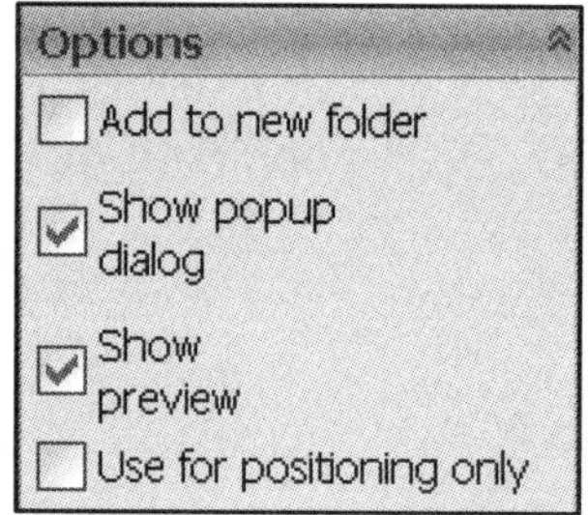

Mate PropertyManager: Analysis tab

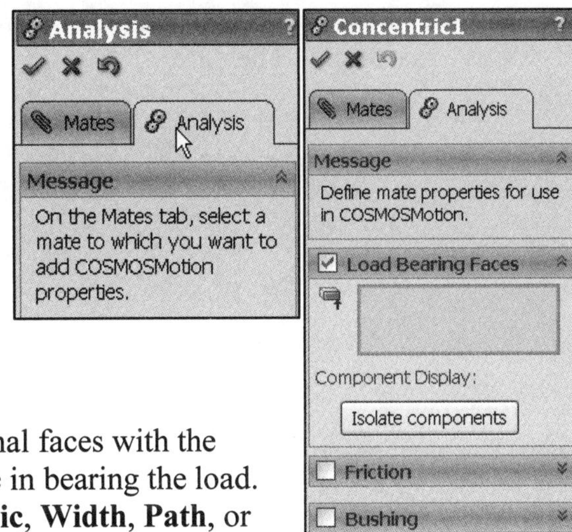

You can assign mate properties for use in COSMOSMotion analysis.

You can add the properties without having COSMOSMotion added in.

The Analysis tab provides the following options for a selected mate:

- ***Load Bearing Faces***. Associates additional faces with the selected mate to define which faces share in bearing the load. This option is not available for **Symmetric**, **Width**, **Path**, or **Cam** mates.
  - **Isolate components**. Provides the ability to only display the components referenced by the mate.
  - **Friction**. Provides the ability to associate friction properties with some types of mates. The following options are available:
    - **Parameters**. Select how to define the friction properties of the mate.
    - **Specify materials**. Select the materials of the components from the first and second lists.
    - **Specify coefficient**. Provides the ability to specify the following:
      - **Dynamic Friction Coefficient** by typing a number or moving the slider between:
        - **Slippery** and **Sticky.**

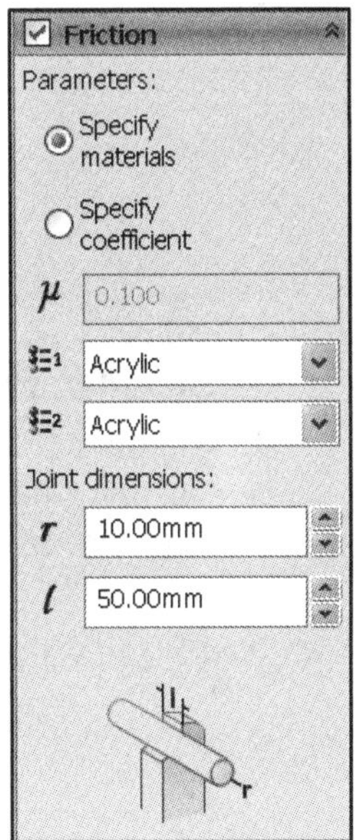

- **Joint dimensions**. Available dimensions vary depending on geometry and mate type. They are:

Geometry	Dimensions	Mate Types
Spherical	d	• **Coincident** mate between any two vertices, sketch points, or reference points • **Concentric** mate between two spherical faces
Cylindrical	l, r	• **Concentric** mate between two cylindrical faces • **Coincident** mate between two linear entities (edges, axes, temporary axes, sketch lines)
Translational	w, h, l	**Coincident** mate between two planar faces
Planar	r, l, w	**Coincident** mate between two planar faces
Universal Joint	w, r	**Universal Joint** mate

- **Bushing**. Provides the ability to associate bushing properties with a mate. Bushing properties make a mate somewhat flexible by giving it spring and damper characteristics. Mates with bushing properties can produce a more realistic distribution of forces in COSMOSMotion analyses.

See SolidWorks help for additional information.

SolidWorks Help Topics list the rules governing Mate Type valid geometry. The valid geometry selection between components in a Coincident Mate is displayed in the Coincident Mate Table.

Mates reflect the physical behavior of a component in an assembly. In this project, the two most common Mate types are Concentric and Coincident.

Concentric Mate - 2 Conical faces

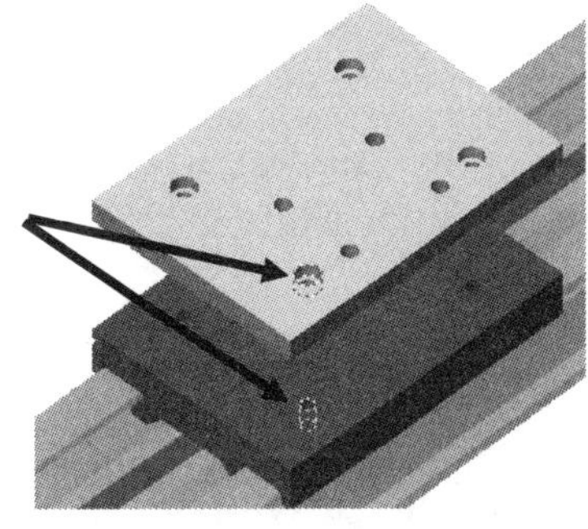

Concentric Mate – 2 Conical faces

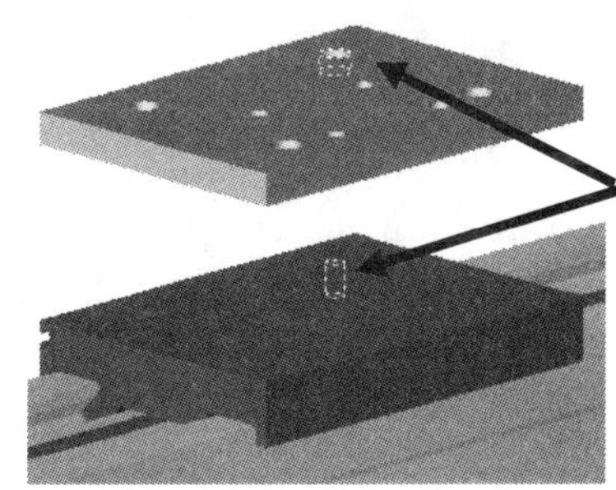

Mates reflect the physical behavior of a component in an assembly. In this project, the two most common Mate Types are Concentric and Coincident.

Utilize two Concentric Mates between the two sets of holes from the PLATE-A part and the RODLESS-CYLINDER assembly.

Coincident Mate – 2 Planar faces

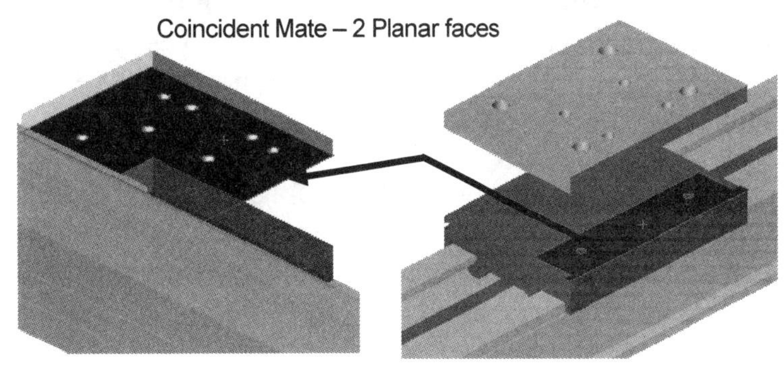

Utilize one Coincident Mate between the two planar faces from the PLATE-A part and the RODLESS-CYLINDER assembly.

The two Concentric Mates and the one Coincident Mate remove all six degrees of freedom for the PLATE-A part.

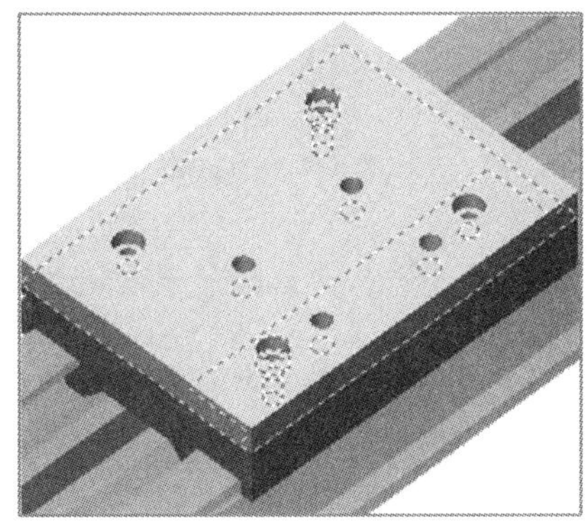

The PLATE-A part is fully defined in the LINEAR-TRANSFER assembly.

The Mates entry in the FeatureManager displays the Mates types.

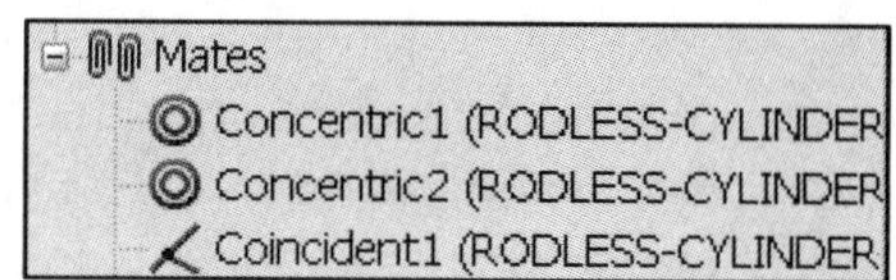

Organize your Mates in the FeatureManager. A Mates list for a 100 component assembly has 200 – 300 Mate Types. Group Mates from the same component. Utilize folders to organize Mates. Select the free component entity to assemble and then select the target assembly entity.

SmartMates:

The SmartMates tool saves time by allowing you to create commonly used mates without using the Mate PropertyManager. A SmartMate is a Mate that automatically occurs when a component is placed into an assembly.

Types of SmartMates

There are various SmartMates types that are available to you in SolidWorks. The available SmartMates types are depended on the application and your situation. In most cases, the application creates a single mate. The type of SmartMate created depends on the geometry that is selected, "to drag" and the type of geometry which you drop the component.

Use one of the following entities to drag the component: a linear or circular edge, a temporary axis, a vertex, a planar face, or a cylindrical/conical face. The following types of automatic SmartMates are supported and are displayed on your mouse pointer. They are:

- *Coincident SmartMate.*
    - Mate two linear edges .
    - Mate two planar faces .
    - Mate two vertices .
    - Mate two axes, two conical faces, or a single conical face and a single axis .
- *Concentric & Coincident SmartMate.*
    - Mate two circular edges, (Peg-in-Hole SmartMate). The edges do not have to be complete circles . There are a few conditions that you need to know to apply the Peg-in-Hole SmartMate. They are:
        - One feature must be a Base or Boss.

- The other feature must be a Hole or a Cut.
- The features must be Extruded or Revolved.
- The faces that are selected in the mate must both be of the same type, either a cylinder or a cone or a cylinder. Both need to be the same. You can not have one of each type.

Review the following table on three options to create a SmartMate.

Methods to Invoke Smart Mates:	
Option 1: Within the assembly	Hold the Alt key down. Click the mating entity of the free component. Drag the component to the assembly reference. Release the Alt key.
Option 2: Within the assembly	Click the Move Component tool. Click SmartMates from the Move Component PropertyManager. Option A: Double-click and drag the mating entity of the free component to the target mating entity of the assembly. Release the left mouse button. Option B: Double-click the mating entity of the free component. Single click on the target mating entity of the assembly.
Option 3: From an open document	Tile Horizontally with the free component and the target assembly. Select a face, edge or vertex on the free component. Drag to the target mating entity of the assembly in the second window.

Press the Tab key after the Concentric/Coincident icon is displayed to control the Aligned or Anti-Aligned option.

Tab key Aligned/Anti-Aligned

InPlace Mates

Components added In-Context of the assembly automatically receives an InPlace Mate within the Mates entry in the FeatureManager. The InPlace Mate is a Coincident Mate created between the Front Plane of a new component and the selected planar geometry of the assembly.

The component is fully defined by the InPlace Mate. No additional Mates are required to position the component. The InPlace1 Mate is added to the FeatureManager.

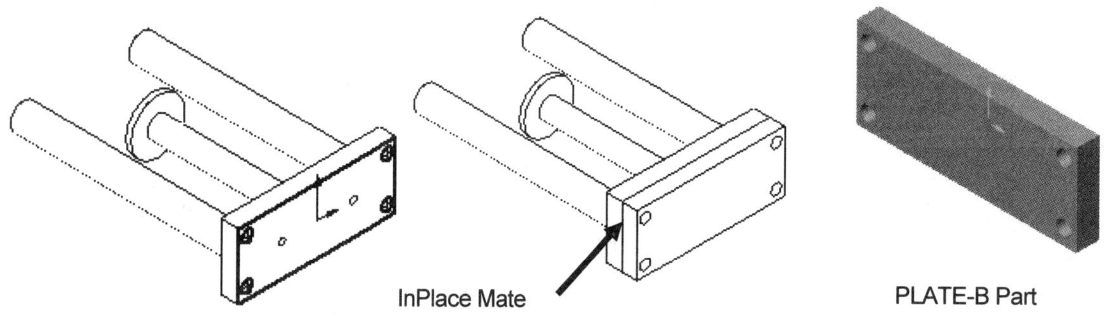

The PLATE-B part is created In-Context of the GUIDE-CYLINDER assembly.

The InPlace Mate is created between the PLATE-B Part Front Plane and the GUIDE-CYLINDER assembly right face.

InPlace Mates are explored later in this book. The next activity utilizes SmartMate Geometry based techniques to assemble the PLATE-A part to the MY1M2104Table part.

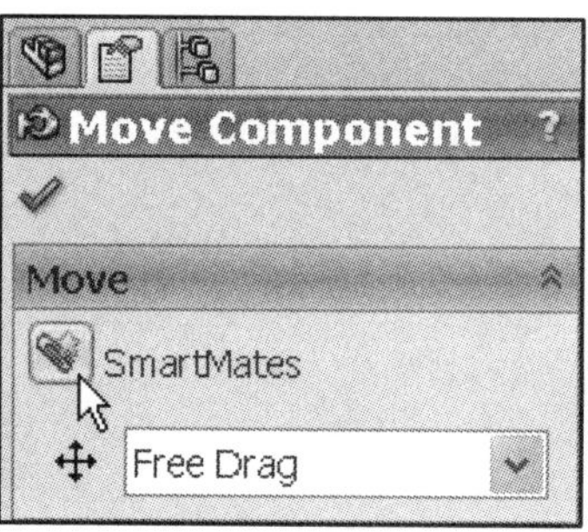

Utilize SmartMates with the Alt key to create two Concentric Mates. Utilize the SmartMates tool in the Move Component PropertyManager to create a single Coincident Mate. The SmartMate icon indicates the SmartMate mode. Practice the different methods and options.

Move Component tool

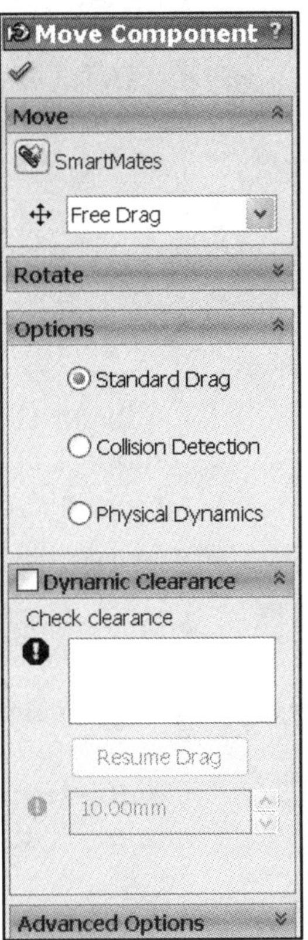

The Move Component tool provides the ability to drag and move a component in the Graphics window. The component moves within its degrees of freedom.

The Move Component tool uses the Move Component PropertyManager. The Move Component PropertyManager provides the following capabilities: *Move a component, Add SmartMates while moving a component, Rotate a component, Detect collision with other components, Activate Physical Dynamics, and Dynamically detect the clearance between selected components*.

The available selections are dependent on the selected options. The Move Component PropertyManager provides the following selections:

- ***Move***. The Move box provides the ability to move the selected component with the following options:
  - **SmartMates**. Creates a SmartMate while moving a component. The SmartMates PropertyManager is displayed.
  - **Move**. The Move box provides the following options: *Free Drag, Along Assembly XYZ, Along Entity, By Delta XYZ, and To XYZ Position.*
- ***Rotate***. Provides the ability to rotate a component in the Graphics window. The Rotate box provides the following selections:
  - **Free Drag**. Provides the ability to drag a selected component in any direction.

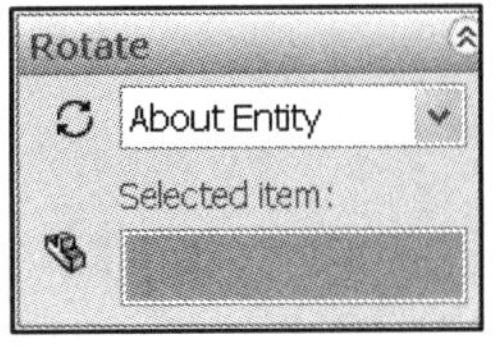

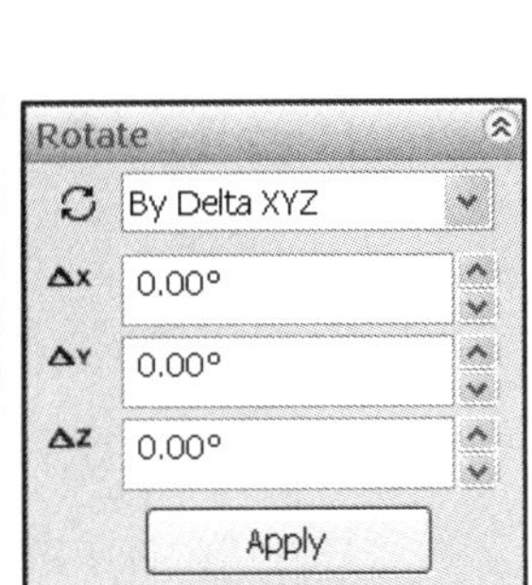

- **About Entity**. Select a line, an edge, or an axis. Drag a component from the Graphics window around the selected entity.

- **By Delta XYZ**. Moves a component around an assembly axes by a specified angular value. Enter an X, Y, or Z value in the Move Component PropertyManager. Click Apply.

- ***Options***. The Options box provides the followings selections:

  - **Standard Drag**. Provides a standard drag to the mouse pointer.

  - **Collision Detection**. Detects collisions with other components when moving or rotating a component. Locate collisions for either the selected components or for all of the components that move as a result of mates to the selected components.

  - **Physical Dynamics**. View the motion of the assembly components. Drag a component. The component applies a force to components that it touches.

- ***Dynamic Clearance***. The Dynamic Clearance box provides the following selections:

  - **Components for Collision Check**. Displays the dimension indicating the minimum distance between the selected components when moving or rotation a component in the Graphics window.

  - **Clearance.** Specify a distance between two components when moving or rotating.

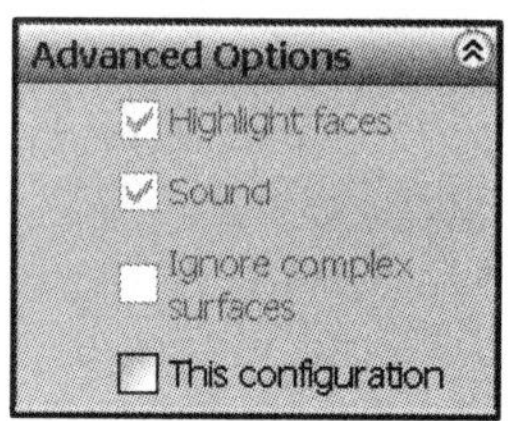

- ***Advanced Option***. The Advance Option box provides the following selections:

  - **Highlight faces**. Selected by default. Faces in the Graphics window are highlighted.

  - **Sound**. Selected by default. The computer beeps when the minimum distance in the Clearance box is reached.

  - **Ignore complex surfaces**. Clearances are only detected on the following surface types: planar, cylindrical, conical, spherical, and torodial.

  - **This configuration**. Apply the movement of the components to only the active configuration.

The "This configuration" check box does not apply to Collision Detection, Physical Dynamics, or Dynamic Clearance. It applies only to Move Component or Rotate Component.

Rotate Component tool

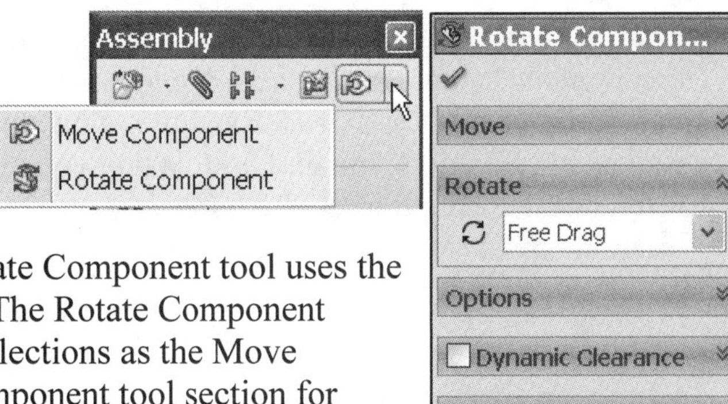

The Rotate Component tool provides the ability to rotate a component within the degrees of freedom defined by its mates. The Rotate Component tool uses the Rotate Component PropertyManager. The Rotate Component PropertyManager provides the same selections as the Move PropertyManager. View the Move Component tool section for detail PropertyManager information.

Show Hidden Components

The Show Hidden Components tool provides the ability to toggle the display of hidden and shown components in an assembly. The tool provides the ability to select which hidden component to be displayed in the Graphics window.

Assembly Features

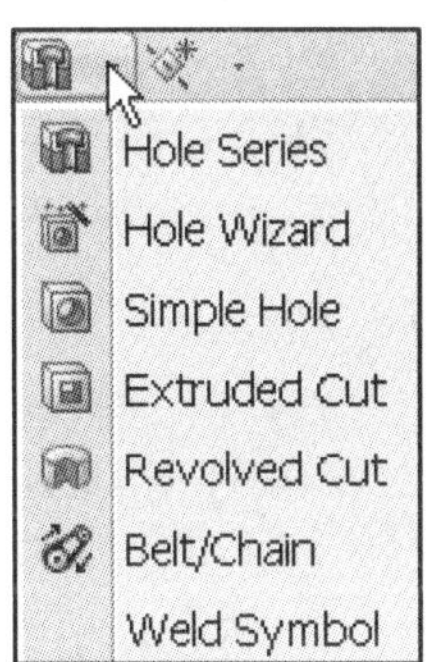

The Assembly Features tool provides the ability to access the following tools for an assembly: *Hole Series*, *Hole Wizard*, *Simple Hole*, *Extruded Cut*, *Revolved Cut*, *Belt/Chain*, *Weld Symbol.*

Mate Reference

Mate references specify one or more entities of a component to use for automatic mating. When you click and drag a component with a mate reference into an assembly, the software tries to locate other combinations of the same mate reference name and type. If the name is the same, but the type does not match, the software does not add the mate.

The Mate Reference tool is located in the Reference Geometry toolbar and in the Assembly toolbar. Below are a few items to be aware of when using the Mate Reference tool:

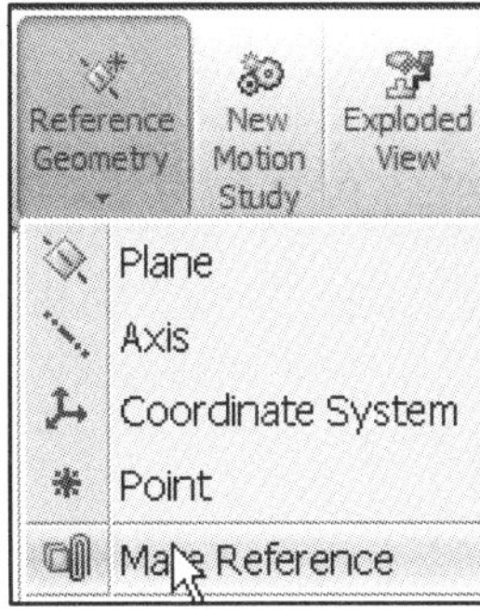

- *Components*. You can add mate references to parts and assemblies. Select assembly geometry, example: a plane in the assembly or component geometry, example: the face of a component.

- *Multiple mate references*. More than a single mate reference can be contained in a component. All mate references are located in the Mate References folder in the FeatureManager design tree. Example: You have a component in an assembly with two mate references: nut and bolt. When you click and drag a fastener with a mate reference named nut into your assembly, mates are inserted between the entities with the same mate reference name.
- *Multiple mated entities*. Each mate reference may contain one to three mated entities. The mated entities are: a primary for the first, a secondary for the second, and tertiary for the three reference entity. Each of the entities can have an assigned mate type and alignment. For two components to mate automatically, their mate references must have the same: *Number of entities*, *Name*, and *Mate type for corresponding entities*.
- *SmartMates*. When the SmartMate PropertyManager is active, the software adds mates through the Mate References tool before it adds geometric SmartMates.

The Mate Reference tool uses the Mate Reference PropertyManager. The Mate Reference PropertyManager provides the following selections:

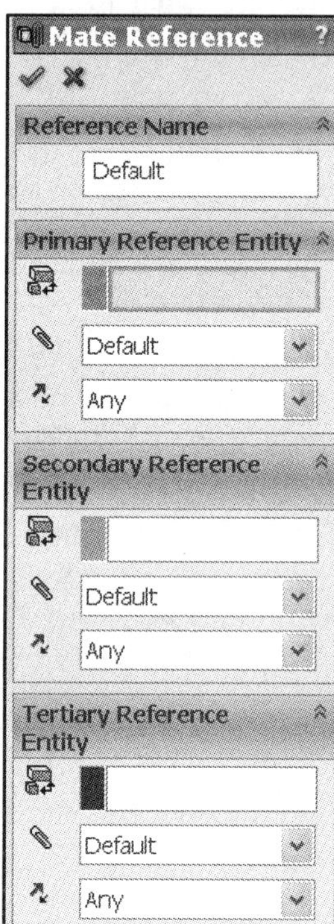

- ***Reference Name***. Displays the name for the mate reference. Default is the default name reference. Accept Default or type a name in the mate reference box.
- ***Primary Reference Entity***. Displays the selected face, edge, vertex, or plane for the Primary reference entity. The selected entity is used for potential mates when dragging a component into an assembly.
  - **Mate Reference Type**. Provides the ability to select the following mate types: **Default**, **Tangent**, **Coincident**, **Concentric**, or **Parallel**.
  - **Mate Reference Alignment**. Provides the ability to define the default mate for the reference entity. The following Alignment options are available: **Any**, **Aligned**, **Anti-Aligned**, and **Closest**.

Secondary and tertiary entities options are the same as the Primary Reference Entity box.

Mate Errors

The following error and warning icons in the FeatureManager design tree indicate a Mate error and type:

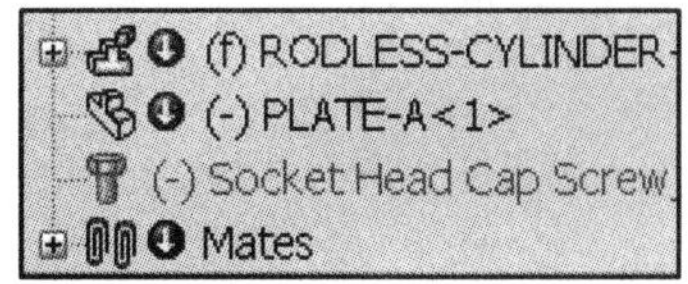

- : When displayed on the Mates folder , it indicates that one or more mates are not satisfied.

- : When displayed on the Mates folder , it indicates that all the mates are satisfied, but one or more mates are over defined.

Expand the Mates folder to view each mate error icon and the mate status:

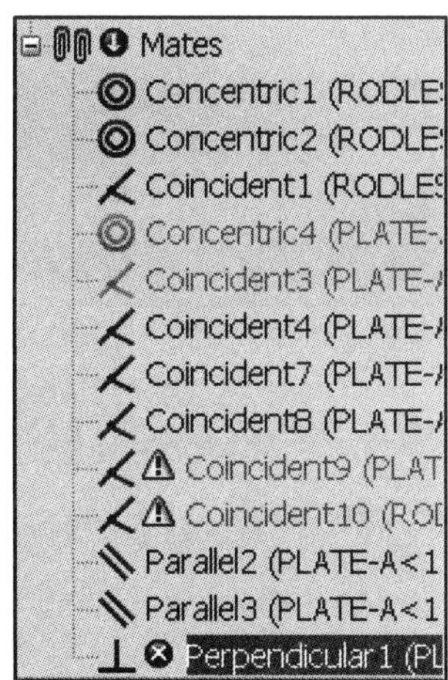

- No icon: Satisfied. Mate entities exist and a valid mate is possible.

- : Not satisfied. A valid mate is not possible for geometric reasons, or mate entities do not exist, which results in dangling mates.

- : Satisfied, but over defines the assembly.

MateXpert

MateXpert is a tool that provides the ability to identify mating problems in an assembly. You can examine the details of mates that are not satisfied, and identify groups of mates which over define the assembly.

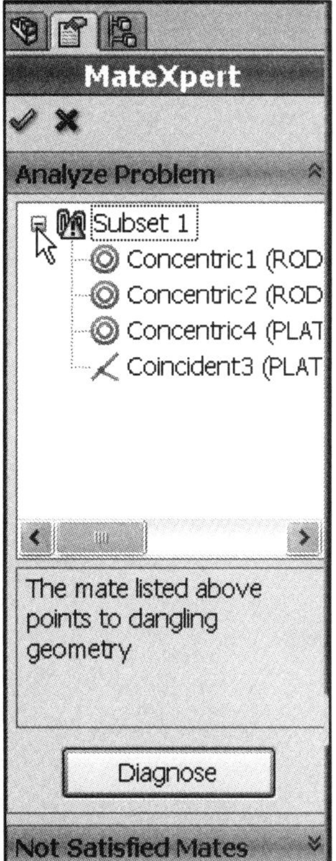

Diagnose Mating Problems

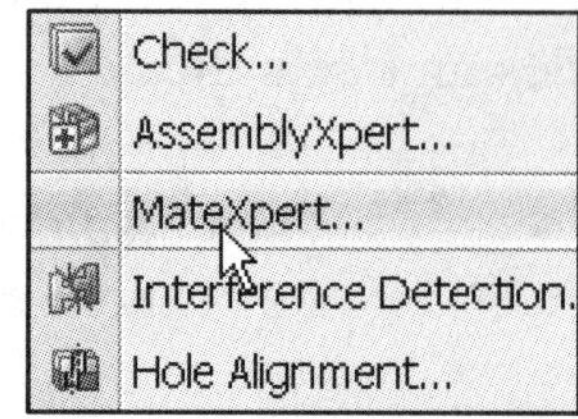

- Click **Tools**, **MateXpert**, or right-click the assembly, **Mates** folder, or any mate in the **Mates** folder, and click **MateXpert**.
- In the PropertyManager, under **Analyze Problem**, click **Diagnose.** One or more subsets of mates with problems are displayed. In the Graphics window, components that are not related to the current subset become transparent. A message is displayed with information on the mating problem.

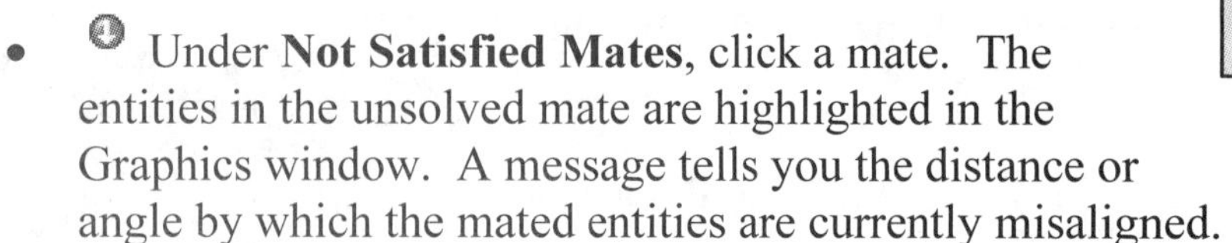

- Under **Not Satisfied Mates**, click a mate. The entities in the unsolved mate are highlighted in the Graphics window. A message tells you the distance or angle by which the mated entities are currently misaligned.

Mates that appear under both **Analyze Problem** and **Not Satisfied Mates** appear in bold.

Activity: Insert SmartMates between PLATE-A and the RODLESS-CYLINDER Assembly

Hide the MYM1M2104Tubes part.

170) Right-click **MY1M2104Tubes** from the FeatureManager.

171) Click **Hide components** from the Context toolbar. View the results.

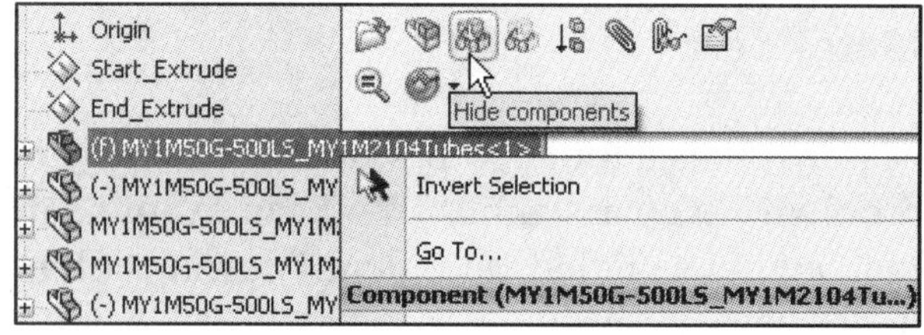

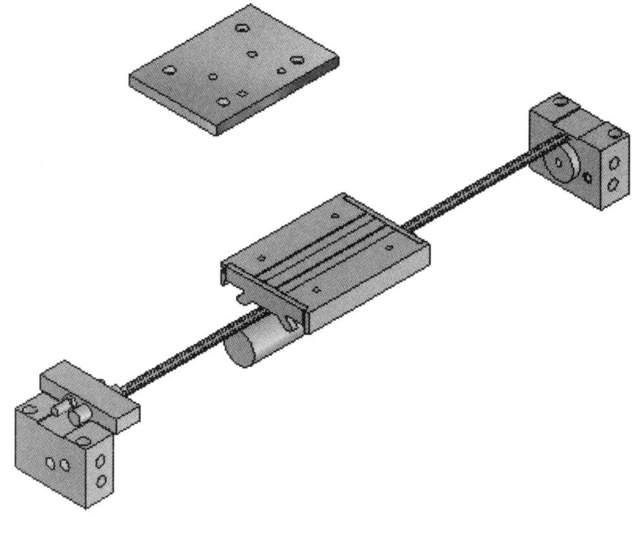

Insert a Concentric SmartMate.

172) Hold the **Alt** key down.

173) Click and drag the PLATE-A **CBORE face** to the front right Table_Hole face, as illustrated. The Concentric icon is displayed. Note: Zoom in on the selected area.

174) Release the **Alt** key. Concentric is selected by default from the Mate Pop-up menu.

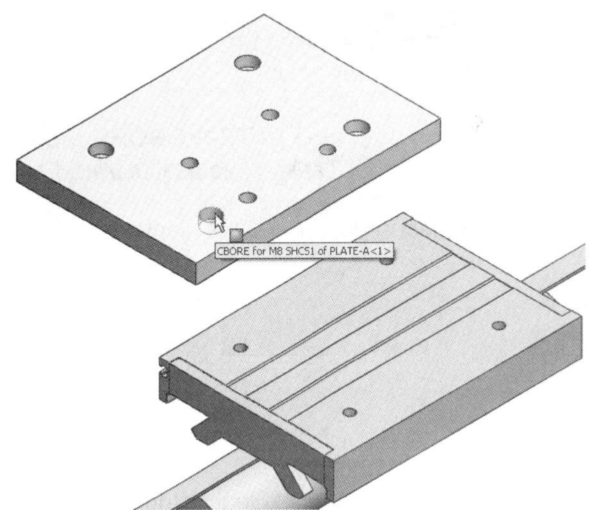

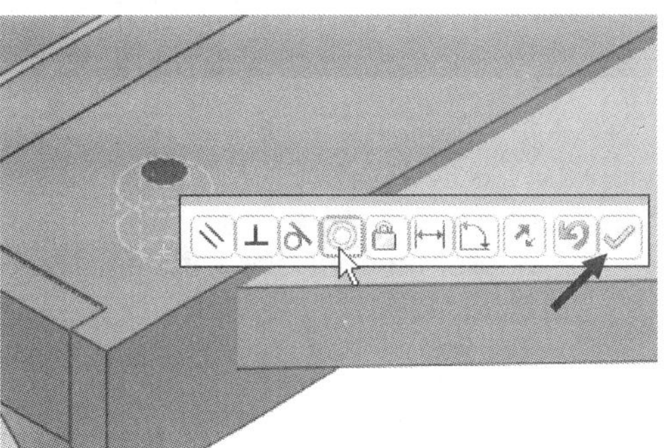

175) Click the **Green Check mark**.

176) **Expand** the Mates folder from the FeatureManager. View the created mate.

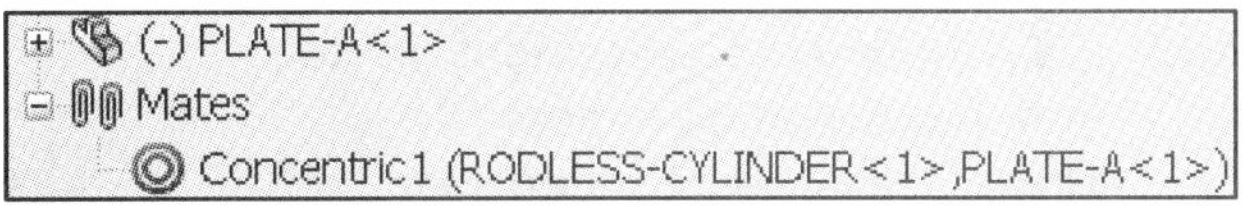

Move the PLATE-A part.

177) Drag the **PLATE-A part** upward until you view the upper left CBORE as illustrated.

Fit the model to the Graphics window. Zoom out.

178) Press the lower case **z** key until the MYM2104Table part and the PLATE-A part are displayed in the Graphics window.

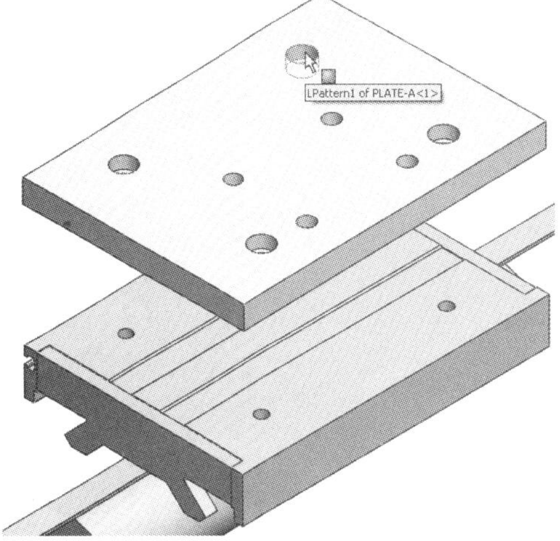

Insert the second Concentric SmartMate.

179) Hold the **Alt** key down.

180) Click and drag the PLATE-A **CBORE face** to the back left Table_Hole as illustrated.

The Concentric icon is displayed.

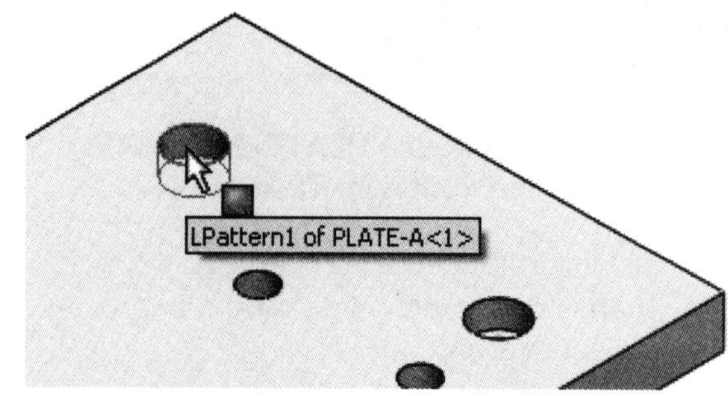

181) Release the **Alt** key. Concentric is selected by default from the Mate Pop-up menu.

182) Click the **Green Check mark**.

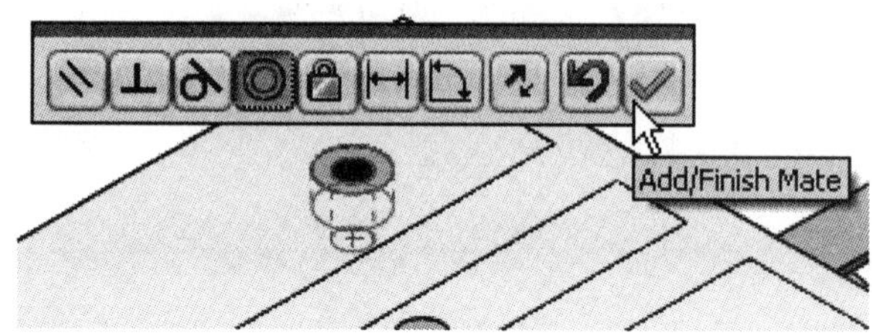

View the created Mate.

183) **Expand** the Mates folder from the FeatureManager. View the second inserted Concentric Mate.

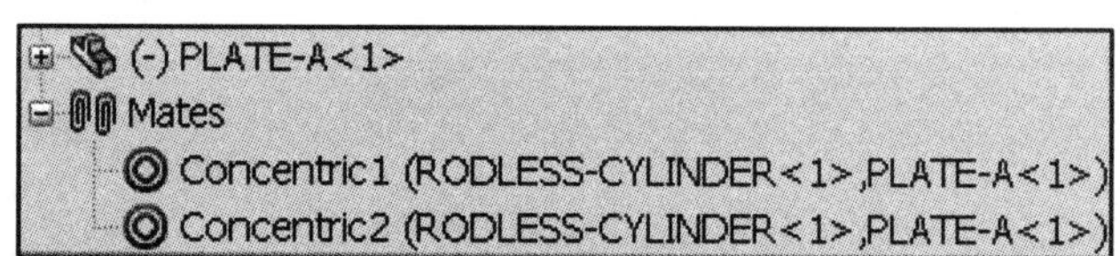

Insert a Coincident SmartMate.

184) Click and drag **PLATE-A** upward and rotate until its bottom face is visible.

185) Click the **Move Component** tool from the Assembly toolbar. The Move Component PropertyManager is displayed.

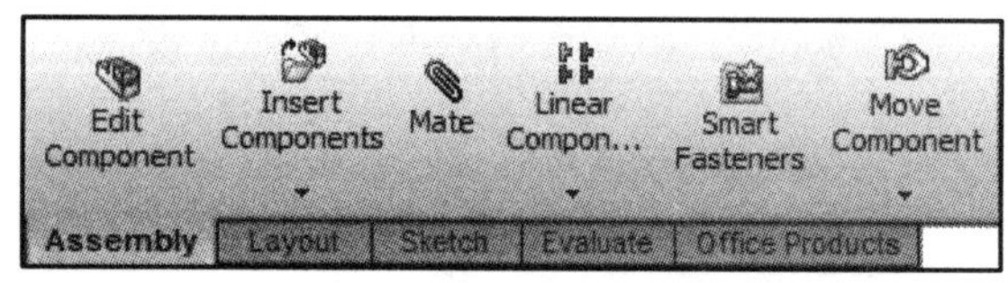

186) Click the **SmartMates** icon in the Move box.

187) Double-click the **bottom face** of PLATE-A. The SmartMate icon is displayed.

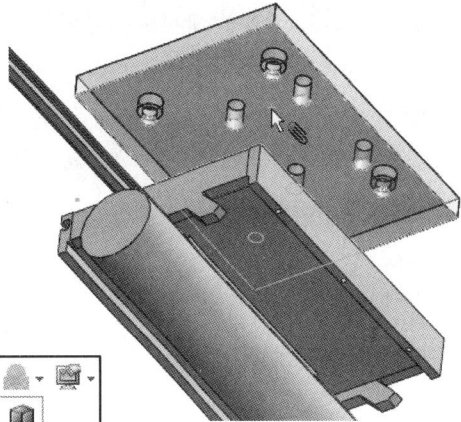

188) Click **table-view** from the Heads-up View toolbar. Note: The table-view was created in the previous project.

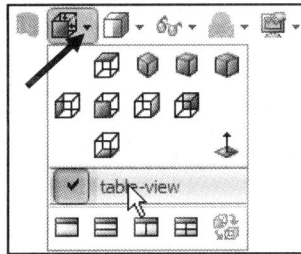

189) Click the **top face** of the MYM2104Table as illustrated. Coincident is selected by default from the Mate Pop-up.

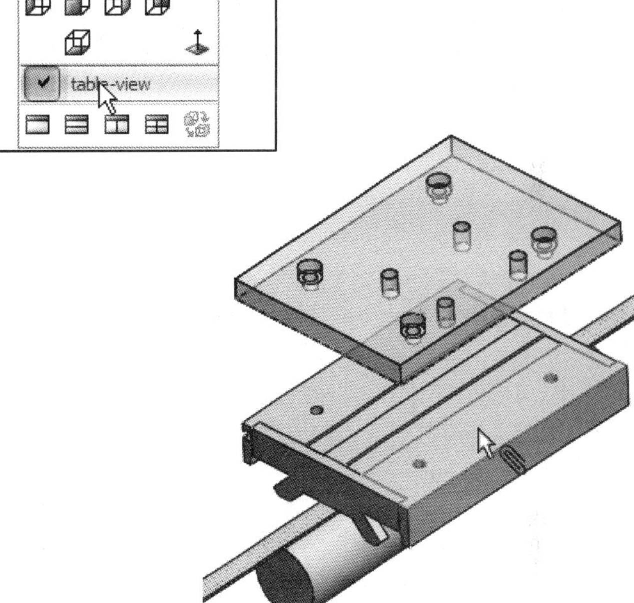

190) Click the **Green Check mark**.

191) Click **OK** from the SmartMates PropertyManager.

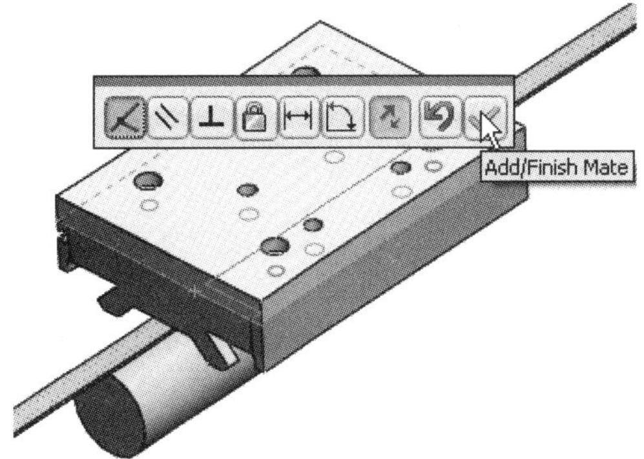

Show the MYM1M2104Tubes part.

192) Right-click **MY1M2104Tubes** from the FeatureManager.

193) Click **Show components** from the Context toolbar.

194) **Rebuild** the model.

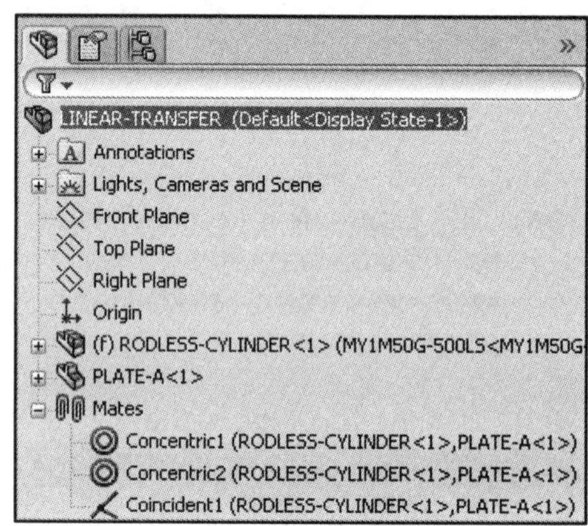

Expand the LINEAR-TRANSFER\Mates entry.

195) **Expand** the Mates folder from the LINEAR-TRANSFER FeatureManager. View the created Mates.

The three SmartMates created two Concentric Mates and one Coincident Mate. The PLATE-A part cannot translate or rotate.

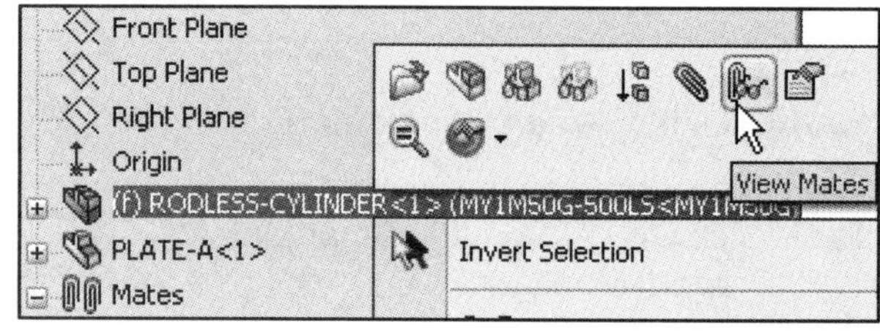

Design for change. For easier recognition, Mates that require future modification should be renamed to a descriptive name.

Note: Mate name numbers increment by one. If you delete a Mate and insert a new Mate in the same session of SolidWorks, the new Mate name is incremented by one.

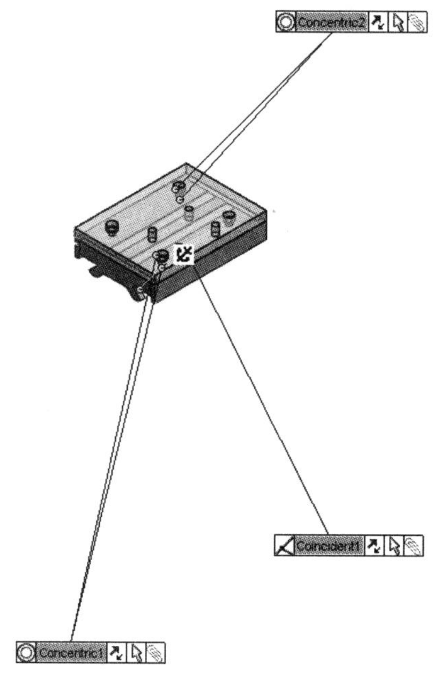

The View Mates option displays all the Mates for a selected component. Right-click on a component name and select View Mates. The FeatureManager splits into two sections.

How do you enable the PLATE-A part to translate in the LINEAR-TRANSFER assembly? Answer: Modify the Component Property Solve as option from Rigid to Flexible.

Rigid and Flexible

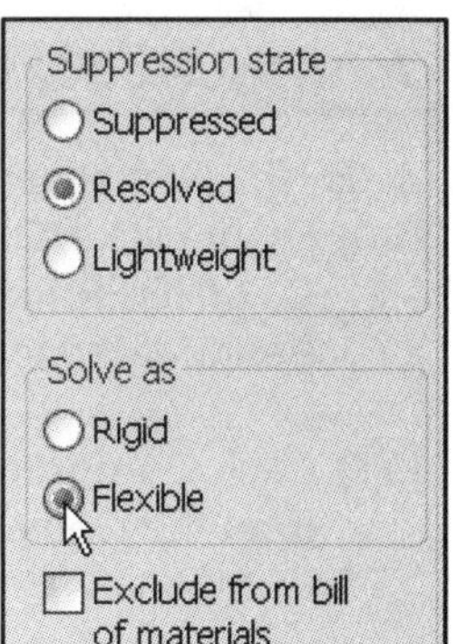

There are two states to solve Mates in an assembly:

- *Rigid*
- *Flexible*

By default, components inserted into an assembly solve Mates as Rigid. Rigid components do not translate or rotate.

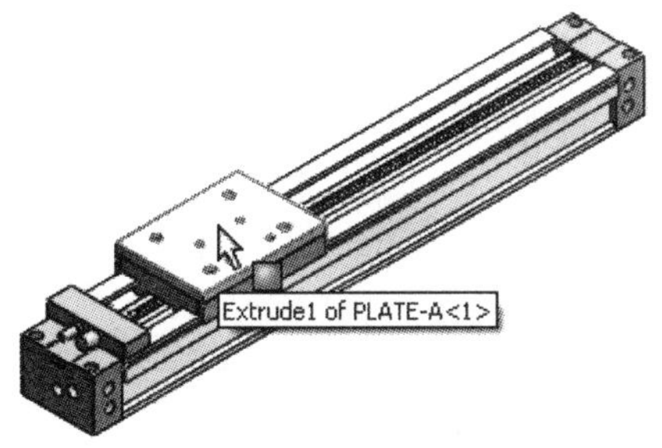

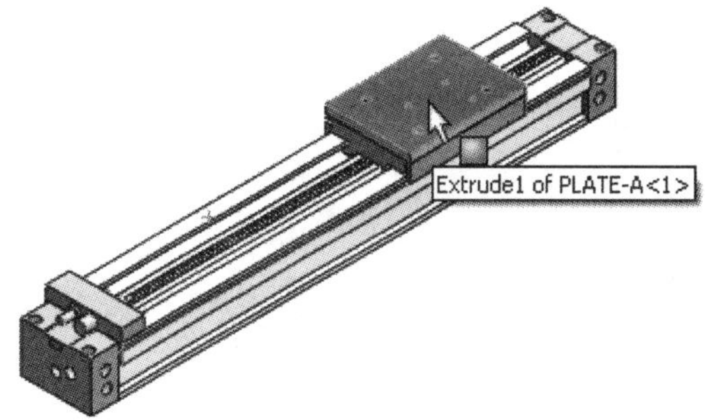

Flexible components translate or rotate based on the behavior of their Mates.

In the flexible state, the MY1M2104Table part and PLATE-A part are free to translate in the LINEAR-TRANSFER assembly.

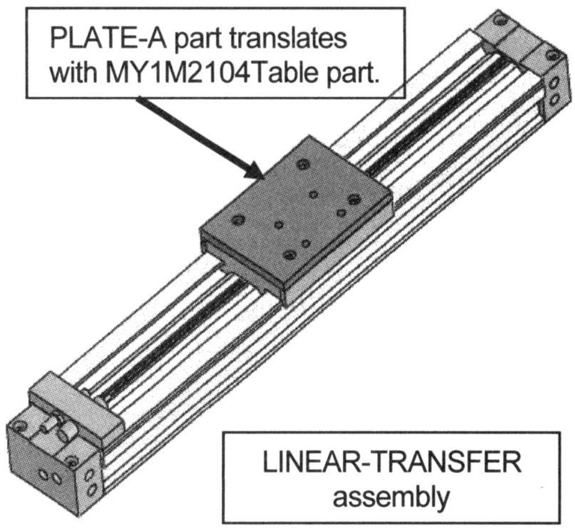

Activity: Modify the Rigid State to a Flexible State

Modify the Component Properties.

196) Right-click **RODLESS-CYLINDER** from the FeatureManager.

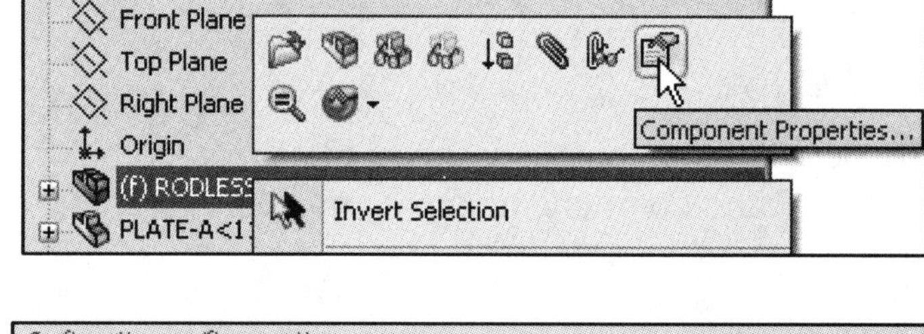

197) Click **Component Properties** from the Context toolbar. The Component Properties dialog box is displayed.

198) Check the **Flexible** box in the Solve as section as illustrated.

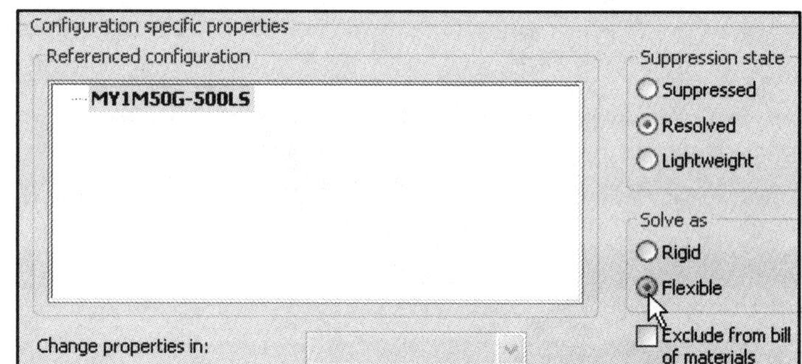

199) Click **OK** from the Component Properties dialog box. The flexible state parameter is displayed in the FeatureManager at the component level.

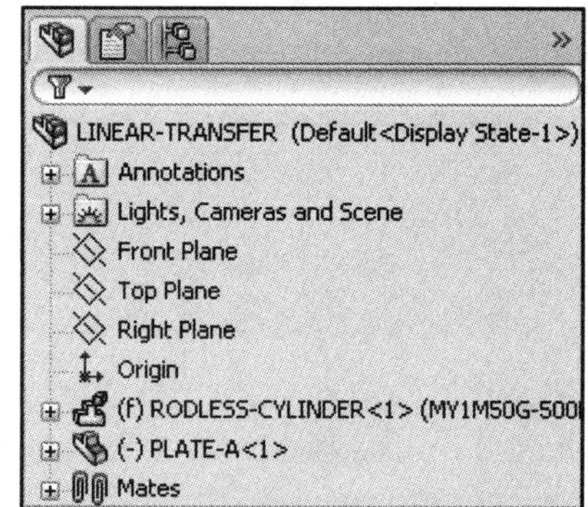

Move PLATE-A.

200) Click and drag the **PLATE-A** part in the LINEAR-TRANSFER assembly from left to right. .

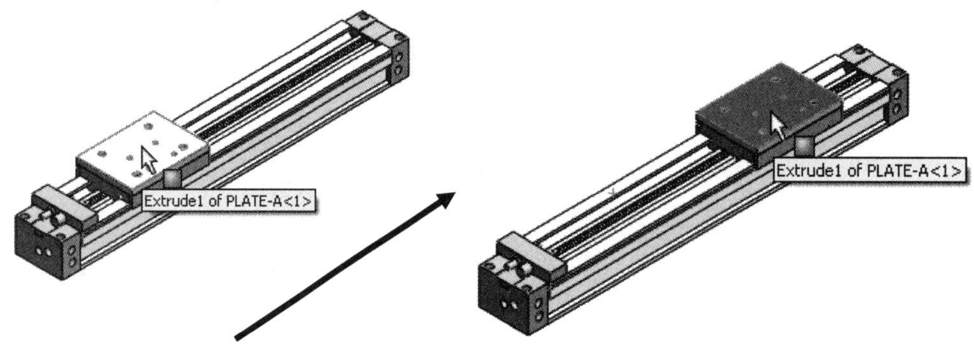

Save the LINEAR-TRANSFER assembly.
201) Click **Isometric** view.

202) Click **Save**.

Fasteners

Screws, bolts, and fasteners are used to join parts. Use standard available fasteners whenever possible. This will decrease product cost and reduce component purchase lead times. The American Society for Mechanical Engineers, (ASME) and the International Standardization Organization, (ISO) provides standards on various hardware components.

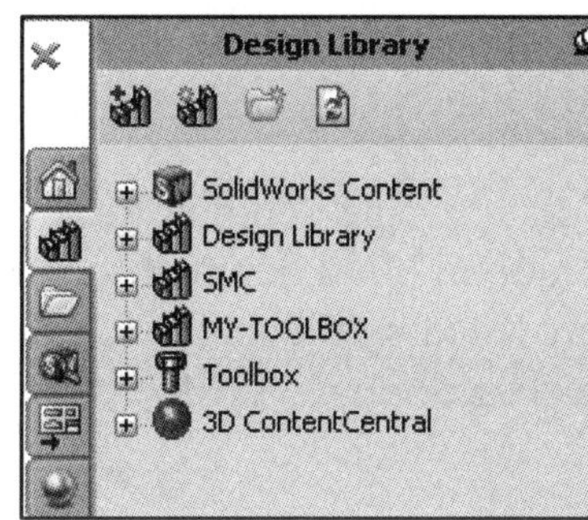

Below are general selection and design guidelines that are utilized in this text:

- Use standard industry fasteners where applicable.
- Utilize industry fasteners that are supplied by qualified vendors and suppliers.
- Know the customer geographic location of the assembly and the fastener when dealing with both millimeter and inch units.
- Reuse common fastener types where applicable. Dissimilar screws and bolts may require additional tools for assembly, additional part numbers and increase inventory storage and cost.
- Decide on the fastener type before creating holes. Dissimilar fastener types require different geometry.
- Create notes on all fasteners. This will assist in the development of a Parts list and Bill of Materials.
- Caution should be used in positioning holes. Do not position holes too close to an edge. Review manufacturer's specifications for punching and machining to determine minimum hole spacing.
- Design for service support. Insure that the model can be serviced in the field and or on the production floor.

Use a standard M8 x 1.25 SHCS in this exercise. Note: The Threads are suppressed in this section.

- M8 represents a metric screw: 8mm major outside diameter.
- 1.25 thread pitch (mm per thread).

Determine the proper overall length with the Measure tool from the Evaluate toolbar.

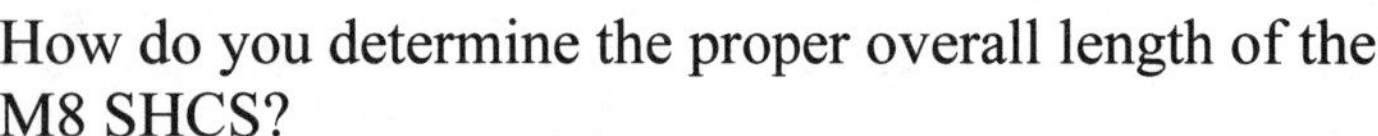

How do you determine the proper overall length of the M8 SHCS?

Answer: The depth of PLATE-A (15mm) plus the required blind depth of the Table-Hole (15mm) provided by the manufacturer. The SHCS top is recessed, below the top face of the Table.

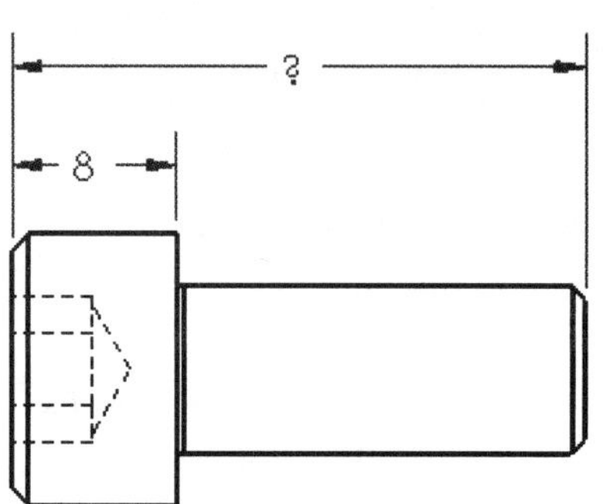

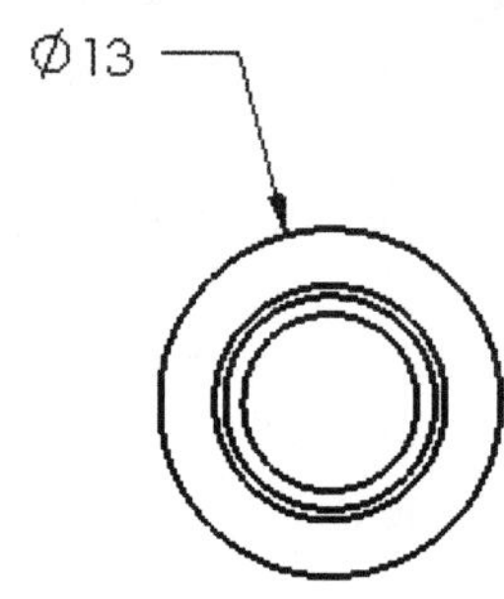

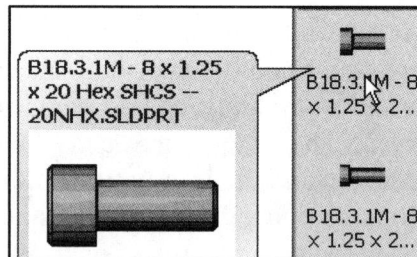

When using fasteners to connect plates, a rule of thumb is to use at least 75% - 85% of the second plate blind depth to avoid fastener failure.

In some processes, it is easier to manufacture a thru thread, rather than a blind one. In this instance, have a least enough thread engagement to equal the diameter of the fastener.

The metric fasteners from your supplier are available in 5mm increments for lengths greater than 20mm.

Determine the length of the fastener.

- PLATE-A thickness = 15mm.
- Table-Hole blind depth = 15mm.
- Height of the 8M x 1.25 Socket Head = 8mm.
- Length = (PLATE-A thickness + Table_Hole blind depth) – Height Socket Head.
- Length = 15mm +15mm – 8mm = 22mm.

What length do you utilize; 20mm or 25mm? Answer: 20mm. The 20mm SHCS is engaged within 75% - 85% of the Table_Hole blind depth. The 25mm is too long since the holes are drilled and tapped at the vendor's facility.

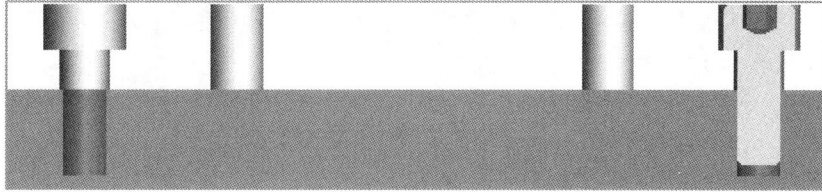

A few screw manufacturers produce a 22mm SHCS, however, your machine shop does not stock this size. Integrating a new part number for hardware costs time and money.

You decide the 20mm SHCS is your choice. SolidWorks Toolbox automatically creates two SmartMates between the SHCS and the CBORE Hole. Copies of the SolidWorks Toolbox SHCS required for this project are located in the MY-TOOLBOX\SHCS folder.

Utilize the SHCS copies in the next activity to explore SmartMates between Graphic windows. Review the optional method of utilizing SolidWorks\Toolbox directly.

Toolbox parts are listed in the FeatureManager in two ways:

- Configuration Name: B18.31M-8x1.25x20Hex SHCS-20NHX.
- User defined name: SHC-91.

The B18.3.1M-8x1.25x20 Hex SHCS – 20NHX configuration name is defined as follows:

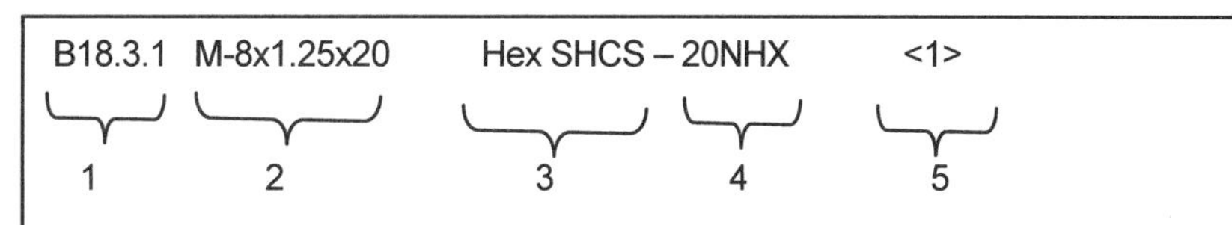

1. B18.3.1M is the ASME B18.3.1M Socket Head Cap Screw Metric Standard.
2. M-8×1.25×20:
   - M is Metric, 8mm is the diameter; 1.25 is the thread pitch, 20 is the length.
3. Hex SHCS is the fastener type.
4. 20NHX is the length of thread.
5. <1> is the first instance of the SHCS.

The User defined name corresponds to the part number utilized by Manufacturing, Purchasing and Inventory personnel.

Open the B18.3.1M-8x1.25x20 Hex SHCS – 20 NHX part. Drag the SHCS part into the LINEAR-TRANSFER assembly. Utilize the Concentric/Coincident SmartMates to position the SHCS in the PLATE-A Cbore.

The Concentric Mate aligns the SHCS to the cylindrical face of the Cbore. The Coincident Mate aligns the screw head bottom edge to the PLATE-A Cbore bottom edge.

Component Patterns

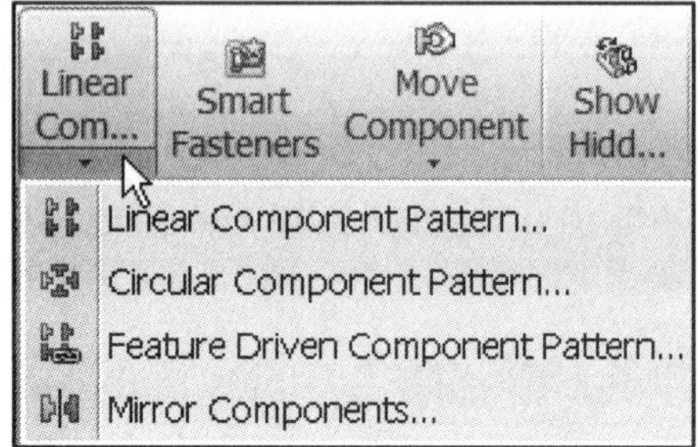

A pattern repeats the selected features in an array based on a seed feature. You can create a Linear pattern, Circular pattern, Curve Driven pattern, Fill pattern, or use sketch points or table coordinates to create your own pattern.

You can create a pattern of components in the assembly in one of the following ways:

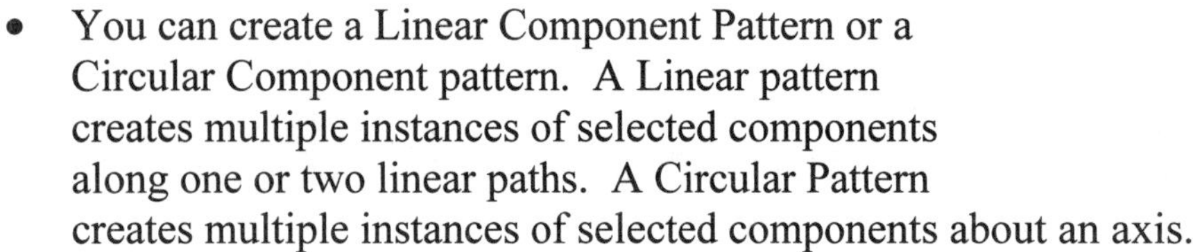

- You can create a Linear Component Pattern or a Circular Component pattern. A Linear pattern creates multiple instances of selected components along one or two linear paths. A Circular Pattern creates multiple instances of selected components about an axis.

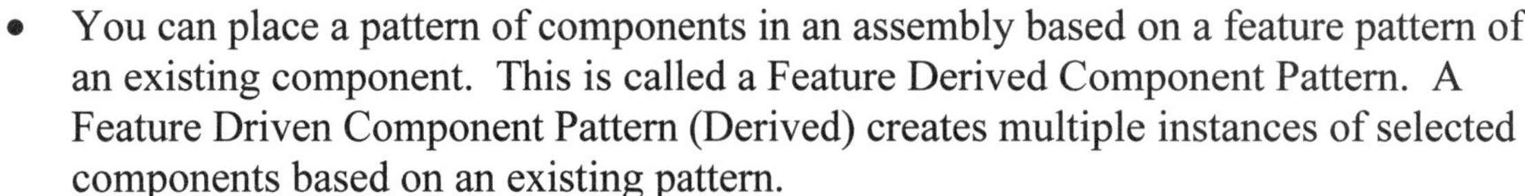

- You can place a pattern of components in an assembly based on a feature pattern of an existing component. This is called a Feature Derived Component Pattern. A Feature Driven Component Pattern (Derived) creates multiple instances of selected components based on an existing pattern.

Mirror copies the selected features or all features, mirroring them about the selected plane or face.

To toggle the visibility or suppression state of all of the components in the pattern, right-click the pattern feature in the FeatureManager design tree, and select **Hide components**, **Show components**, **Suppress**, **Unsuppress**, or **Isolate components**.

Utilize a Feature Driven Component Pattern to copy the SHCSs based on the PLATE-A Linear Pattern of Cbores.

Activity: Apply Toolbox -Fasteners – SmartMate

Open the SHCS folder in the Design Library.

203) Expand the MY-TOOLBOX folder in the Design Library.

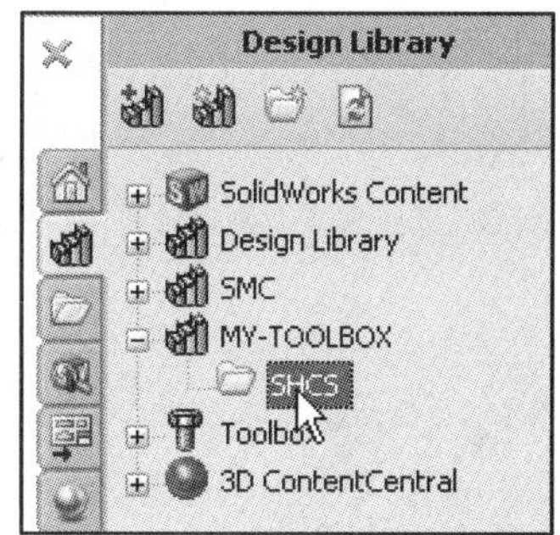

204) Click the **SHCS** folder.

205) Right-click on the **B18.3.1M-8x1.25x20 Hex SHCS – 20 NHX** icon.

206) Click **Open**. The Hex SHCS is displayed in the Graphics window.

Display an Isometric view.

207) Click **Isometric** view from the Heads-up View toolbar.

Insert the Hex SHCS.

208) Click **Window**, **Tile Horizontally** from the Menu bar menu.

209) Zoom in and **Rotate** the LINEAR-TRANSFER assembly until the inside seed Cbore is displayed.

210) Click and drag the **bottom circular edge** of the SHCS to the inside bottom circular edge of the Cbore. The mouse pointer displays the Concentric/Coincident SmartMates.

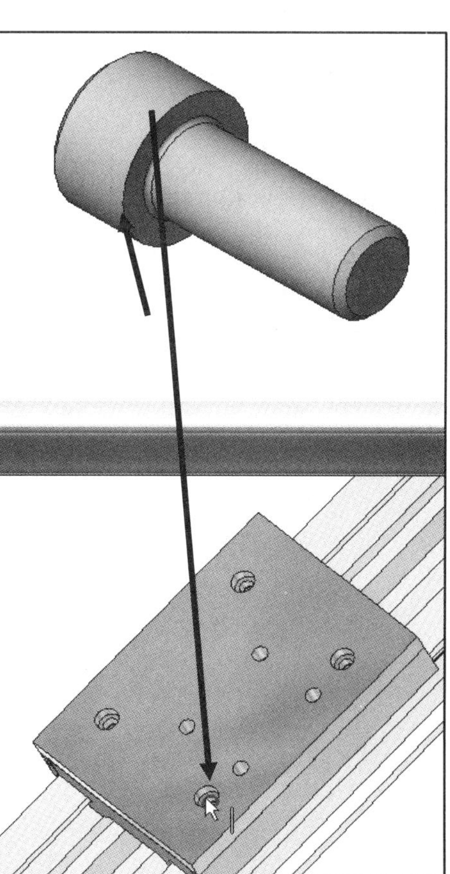

211) Release the **left mouse button** to create the two SmartMates.

212) Maximize the LINEAR-TRANSFER assembly.

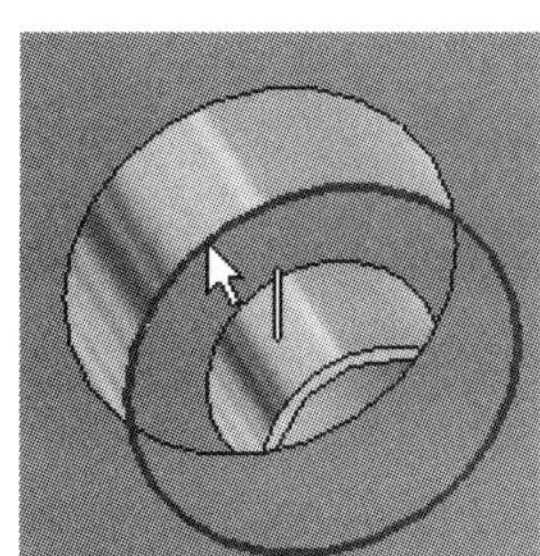

Fit the Model to the Graphics window.

213) Press the **f** key.

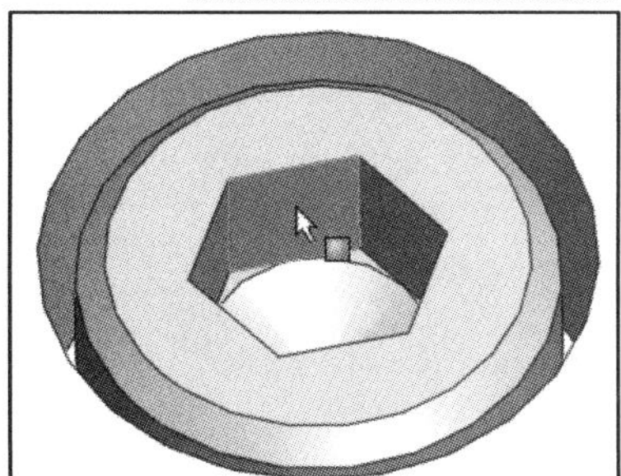

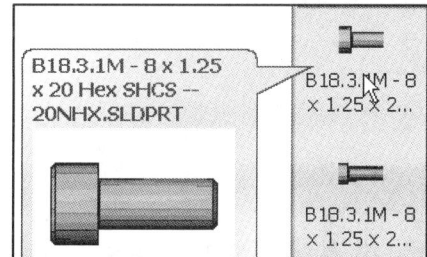

Review the Inserted mates.

214) Expand the Mates folder from the FeatureManager. View the created mates.

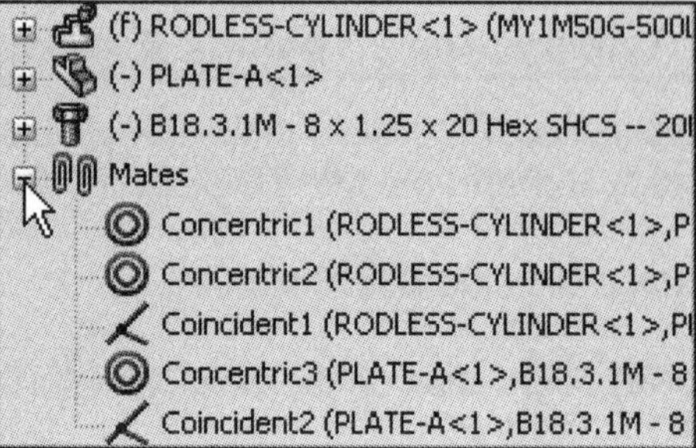

The SHCS is free to rotate about its axis. Multiple Hex-shaped fasteners require a Parallel Mate to orient faces in the same direction. Fully defined fasteners rotate together.

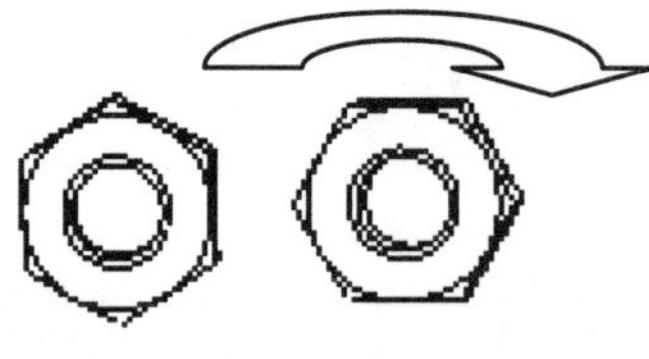

Under defined Mates, Free to rotate

An additional Parallel Mate between the Hex head face and the PLATE-A narrow face prevents rotation.

Fully defined

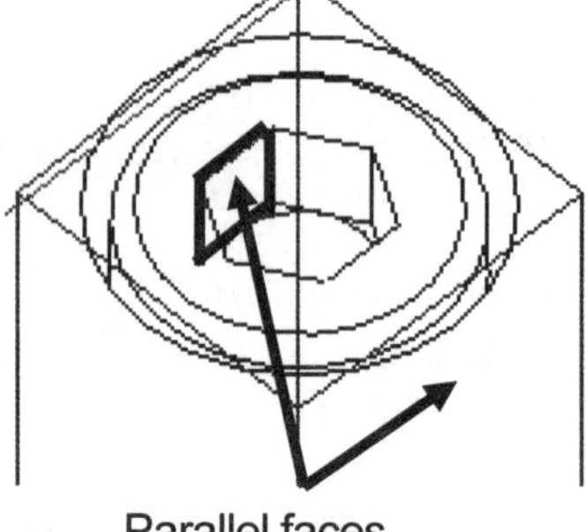

Parallel faces prevent rotation

The SHCS top face is positioned below the PLATE-A top face, there are no interferences. No Parallel Mate is created to fully define the SHCS.

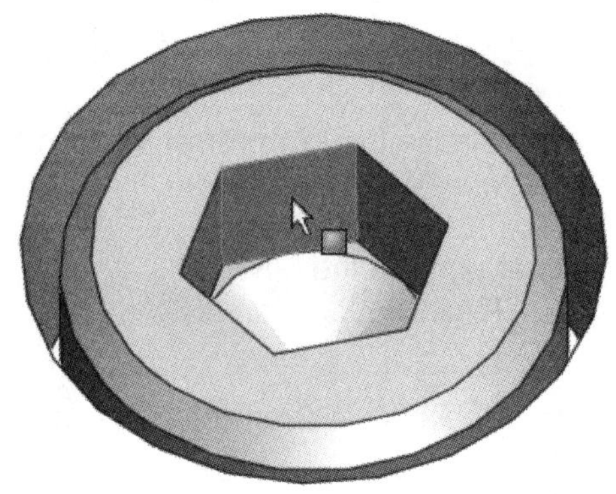

Save mate time and rebuild time. Utilize a Concentric/Coincident Mate for screws, nuts, washers, and bolts. Utilize the Parallel Mate to locate the head direction for hex geometry when required for interference detection or appearance.

Create a Feature Driven Component Pattern.

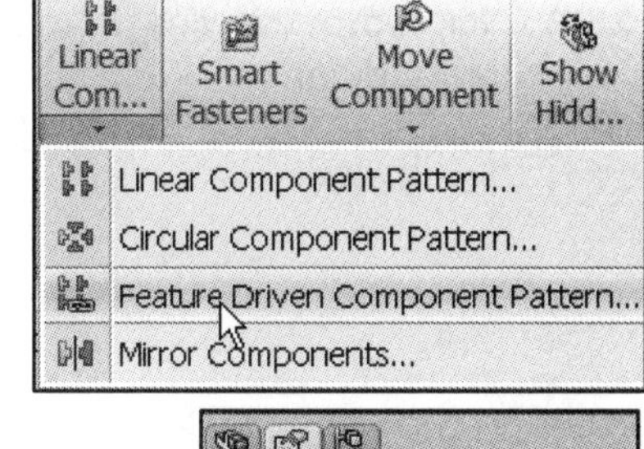

215) Click the **Feature Driven Component Pattern** tool from the Consolidated Assembly toolbar. The Feature Driven PropertyManager is displayed. B18.3.1M-8x1.25x20 Hex SHCS – 20 NHX is displayed in the Components to Pattern box.

216) Click a **position** inside the Driving Feature box.

217) **Expand** PLATE-A<1> from the Flyout FeatureManager.

218) Click **LPattern1**. LPattern1 is displayed in the Driving Feature box.

219) Click **OK** from the Feature Driven PropertyManager.

DerivedLPattern1 is listed in the assembly FeatureManager and contains three instances of the SHCS.

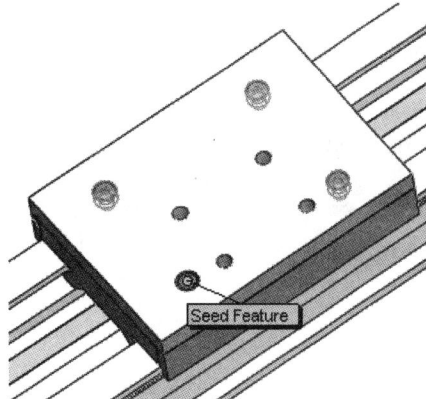

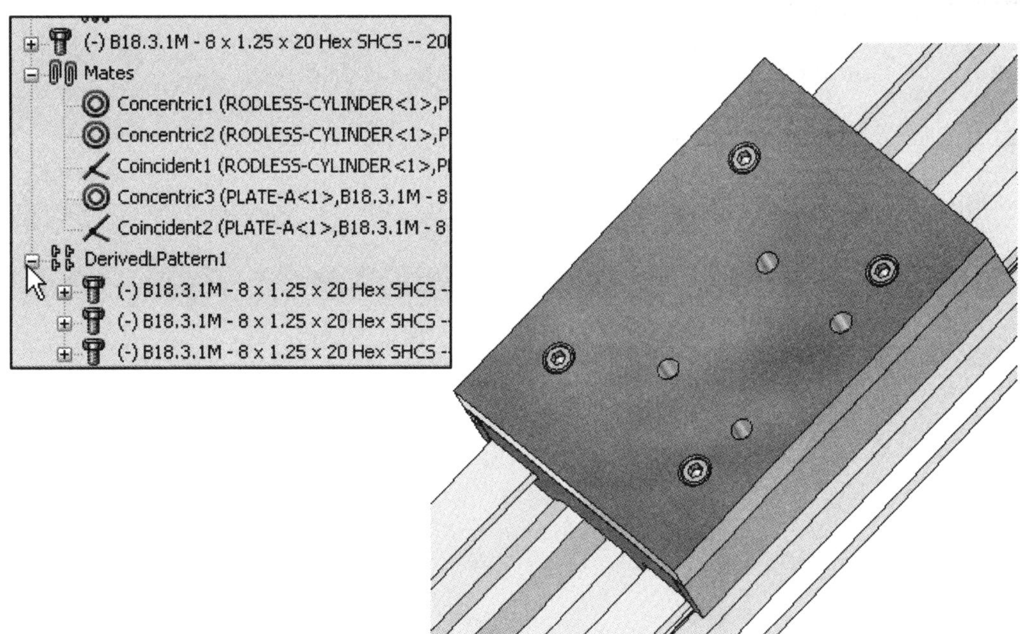

Save the LINEAR-TRANSFER assembly.

220) Click **Isometric** view from the Heads-up View toolbar.

221) Click **Save**.

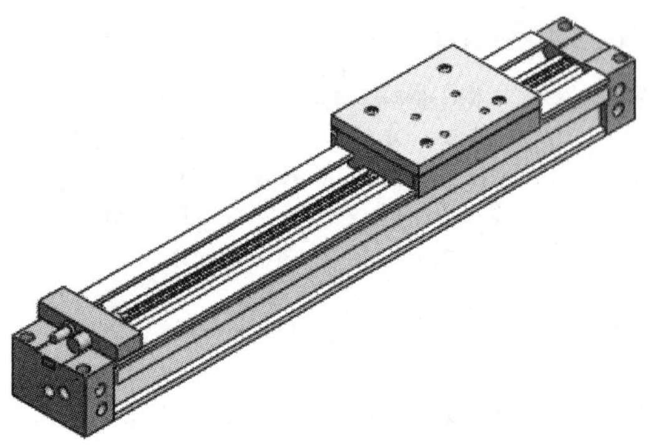

Activity: Set the Toolbox directory

Activate the Toolbox Browser.

222) Click **Add-Ins** from the Menu bar toolbar.

223) Check the **SolidWorks Toolbox** box and the **Toolbox Browser** box.

224) Click **OK** from the Add-Ins box.

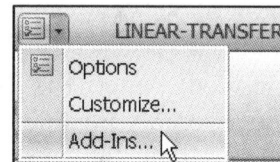

Set the Toolbox directory.

225) Click **Toolbox** from the Menu bar menu.

226) Click **Configure.** The Configure Data dialog box is displayed.

227) Click the **settings** tab.

228) Check the **Create Parts on Ctrl-Drag** box.

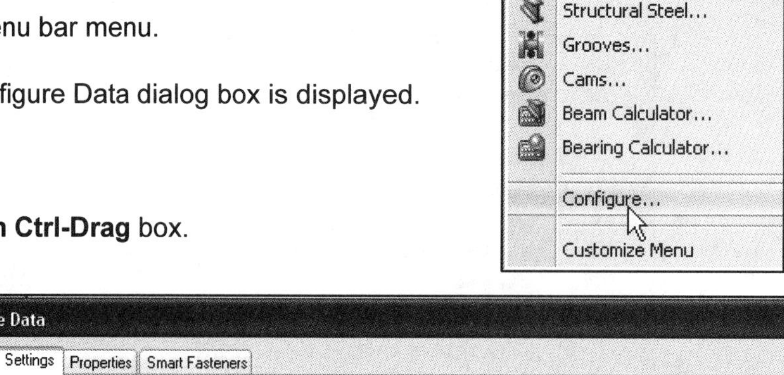

229) Click **Browse**.

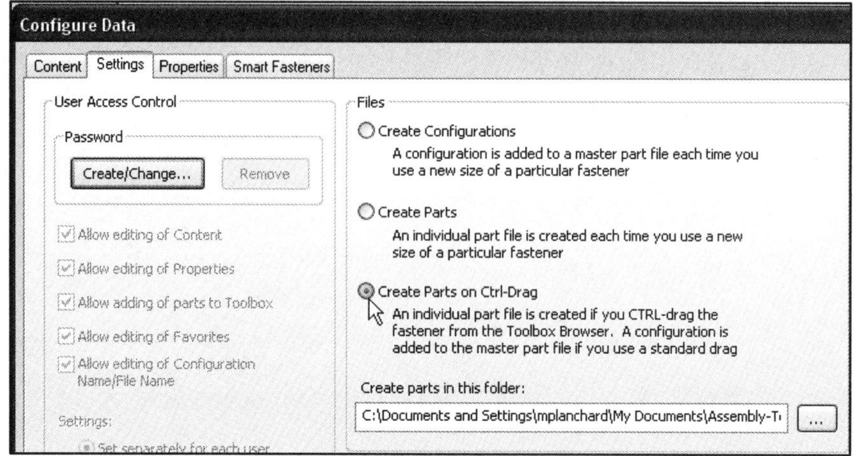

230) Select **\ASSEMBLY-SW-FILES-2008\MY-TOOLBOX**.

231) Click **OK** from the Browse For Folder dialog box.

232) Click **Close** from the Configure Data box.

An individual part file is created if you CTRL-drag the fastener fro the Toolbox Browser.

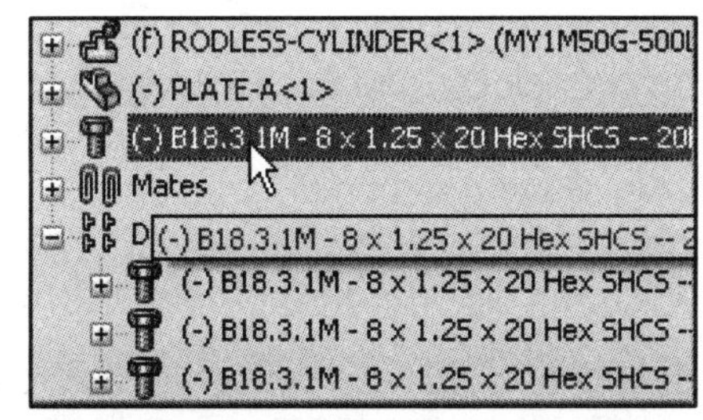

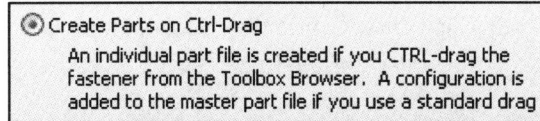

Delete the existing SHCS and the Mates.

233) Right-click the **B18.3.1M-8x1.25x20 Hex SHCS – 20 NHX** from the FeatureManager.

234) Right-click **Delete**.

235) Click **Yes** to delete dependent entities and mates. Note: DerivedLPattern1 is also deleted.

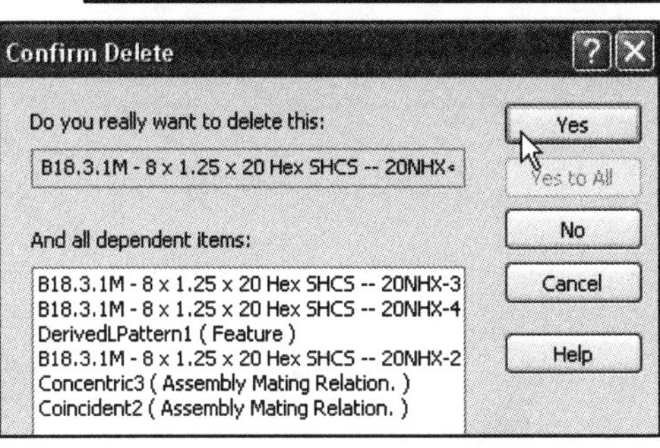

Insert a M8x1.25x20 Hex SHCS into the LINEAR-TRANSFER assembly.

236) **Zoom in** on the CBORE face of the lower right seed feature in the Graphics window

237) **Expand** Toolbox from the Design Library.

238) **Expand** Ansi Metric.

239) **Expand** Bolts and Screws.

240) Click **Socket Head Screws**.

241) Click and drag the **Cap (B18.3.1M)** icon into the assembly Graphics window.

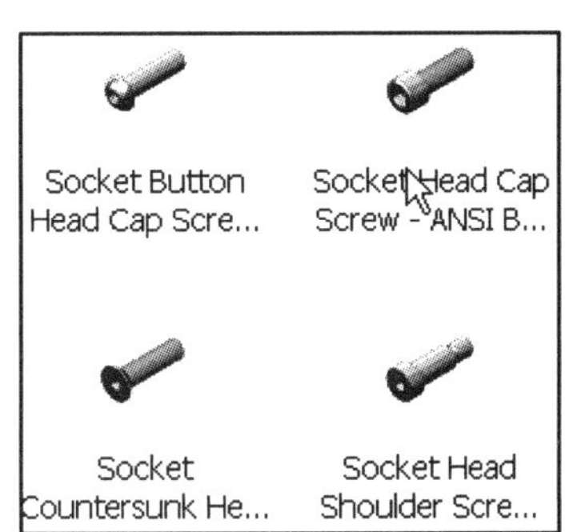

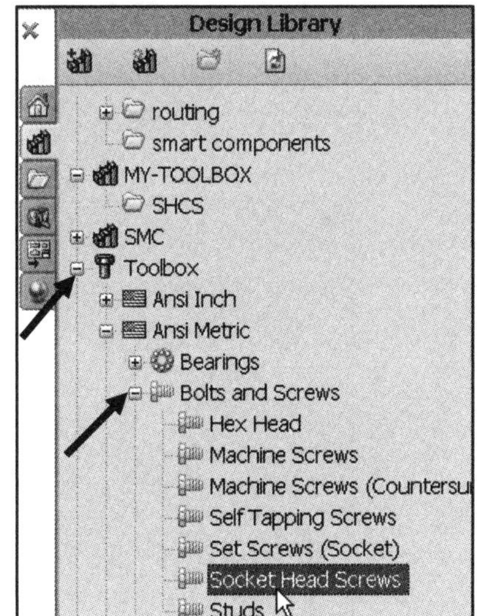

242) Release the **mouse pointer** on the CBORE face of the lower right seed feature. The Socket Head Cap Screw Properties dialog box is displayed.

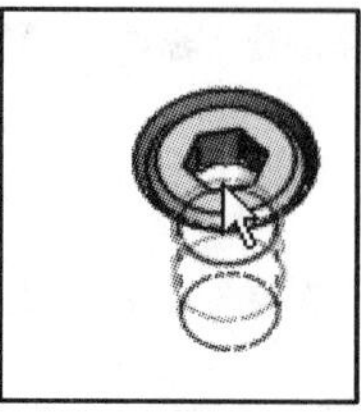

243) Enter **M8** for Size.

244) Enter **20** for Length. Accept the default values.

245) Click **OK** from the Socket Head Cap Screw PropertyManager.

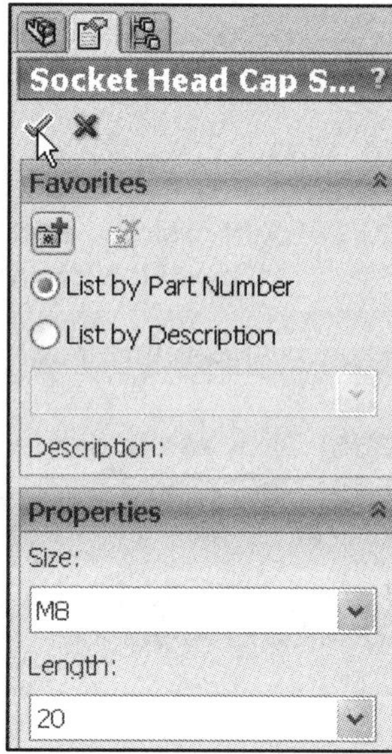

246) Insert the **second**, **third** and **fourth** M8x1.25x20 Hex SHCS into the LINEAR-TRANSFER assembly as illustrated.

247) Click **Cancel** from the Insert Component PropertyManager.

248) **Save** the model.

View the results in the FeatureManager and Graphics window.

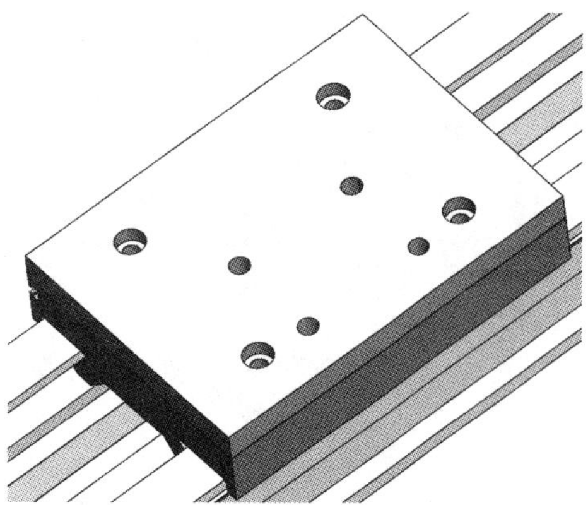

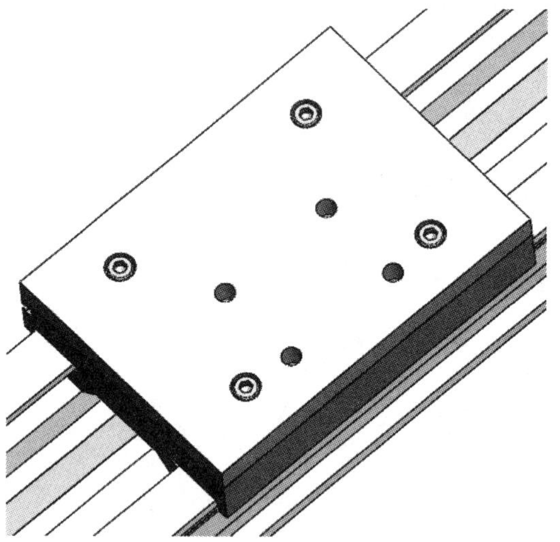

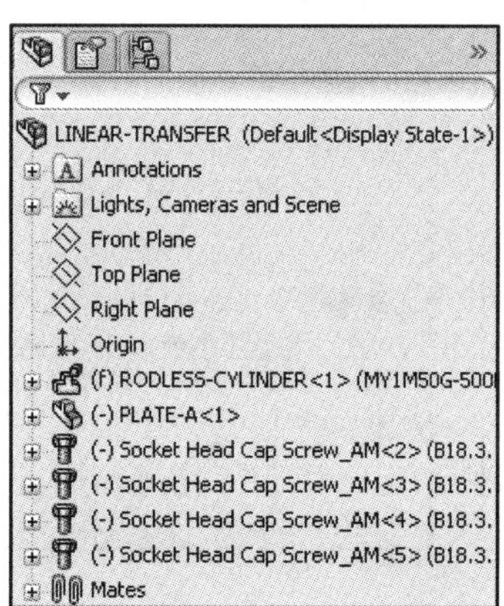

Project Summary

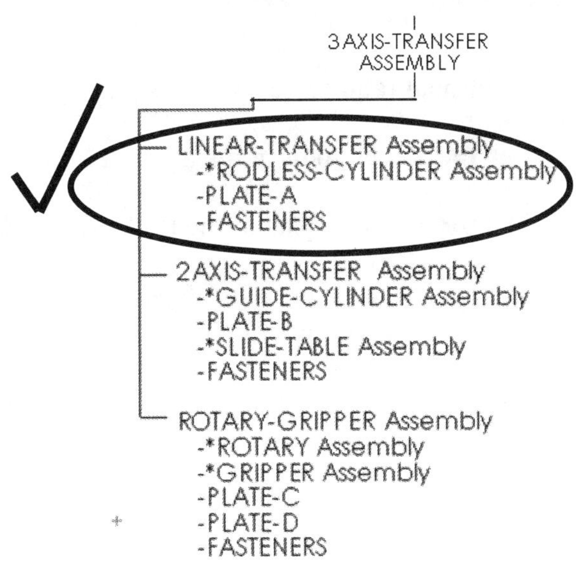

The Bottom-up design assembly modeling approach was utilized to create the LINEAR-TRANSFER assembly. The LINEAR-TRANSFER assembly is the first assembly in the 3AXIS-TRANSFER assembly.

You created the PLATE-A part based on the features of the RODLESS-CYLINDER\MY1M2104Table part and the GUIDE-CYLINDER assembly.

You utilized the Design Library Toolbox and inserted four M8x1.25x20 SHCS using SmartMates to assemble the PLATE-A part to the RODLESS-CYLINDER assembly

The LINEAR-TRANSFER assembly consisted of the RODLESS-CYLINDER assembly, the PLATE-A part and four M8x1.25x20 SHCS.

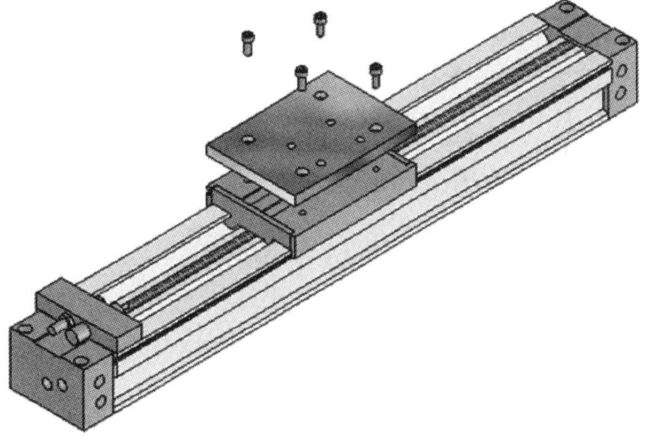

You utilized and applied the following SolidWorks tools and commands: *Mate, Mate Reference, SmartMate, Rotate Component, Move Component, Hole Wizard tool, Hide / Show components, Flexible, Rigid, Linear Pattern, Derived Component Pattern, Insert Part, Insert Component, Corner Rectangle, Extruded Base, and Extruded Boss.*

Questions

1. Describe the components and features utilized to determine the geometric and functional requirements of the PLATE-A part.

2. List the sketch tools and feature options that build symmetry into a part.

3. Identify the locations of the PLATE-A Reference planes.

4. True or False. The Hole Wizard does not require dimensions or relationships to define the position of a hole.

5. Assembling components in SolidWorks is defined as _________

6. Each component has ________________ degrees of freedom.

7. Identify the view type that displays internal geometry.

8. Describe the difference between a Distance Mate with a 0 value and a Coincident Mate.

9. Describe the SHCS abbreviation. What does it stand for?

10. Identify the two SmartMates that are used to assemble a SHCS to a hole in the PLATE-A part.

11. Identify the command utilized to create a Component Pattern in an assembly that references an existing feature for another component.

12. A sub-assembly named Flexible is inserted into an assembly. The Flexible sub-assembly is Rigid. Identify the option that would regain a flexible state?

13. Review the SmartMate .avi files with SW help. Identify other types of Smart Mates. Explain.

Mating entities	Type of mate	Pointer	Click for example
2 linear edges	Coincident		Show Me
2 planar faces	Coincident		Show Me
2 vertices	Coincident		Show Me
2 conical faces, or 2 axes, or 1 conical face and 1 axis	Concentric		Show Me
2 circular edges (the edges do not have to be complete circles)	Concentric (conical faces) - and - Coincident (adjacent planar faces)		Show Me

Project 4

Bottom-up Design Approach – Two Levels of Configurations

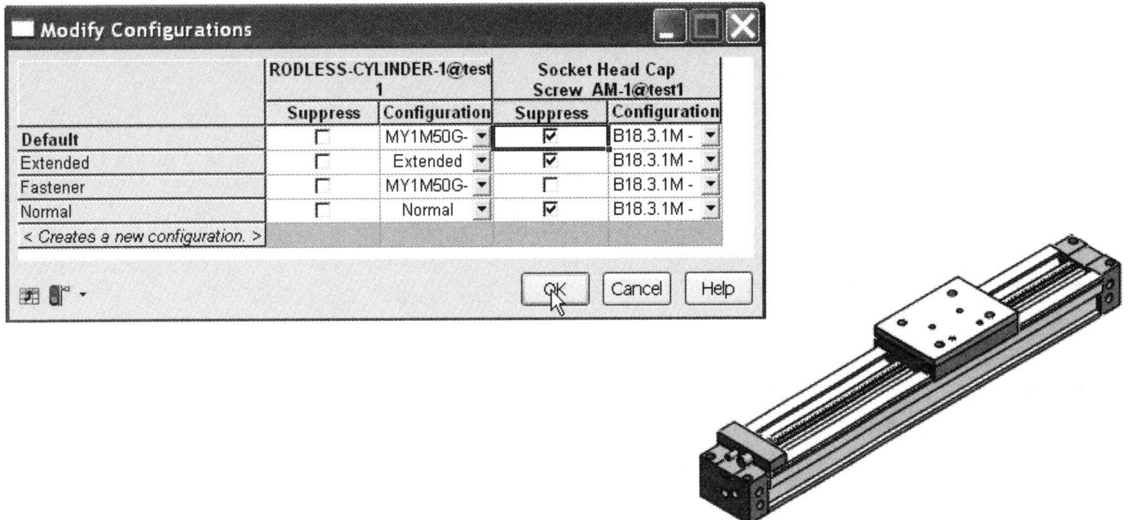

Below are the desired outcomes and usage competencies based on the completion of this Project.

Project Desired Outcomes:	Usage Competencies:
• Two RODLESS-CYLINDER configurations: *Normal* and *Extended.*	• Understand the different ways to create assembly configurations. • Comprehend and apply the Configure Component tool.
• Two Levels of Configuration using the Bottom-up design approach of the LINEAR-TRANSFER assembly: *Normal*, *Extended*, and *Fastener*.	• Aptitude to manage components and to create configurations at various levels of the assembly. • Create a Derived Feature Component Pattern. • Ability to apply the Collision Detection tool.

Notes:

Project 4 – Bottom-up Design – Two Levels of Configurations

Project Objective

Develop two configurations for the RODLESS-CYLINDER assembly to illustrate dynamic motion and physical location. Create the *Normal*, and *Extended* configurations.

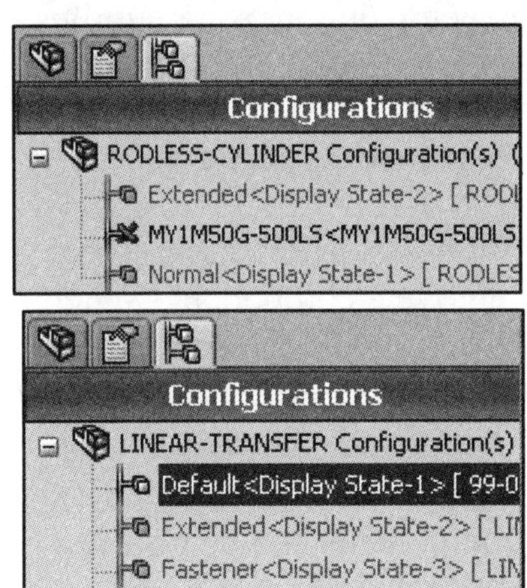

Create three new configurations for the LINEAR-TRANSFER assembly. The LINEAR-TRANSFER configurations are named *Normal, Extended*, and *Fastener*.

Prepare for the next assembly in Project5.

On the completion of this project, you will be able to:

- Understand the different ways to create assembly configurations:
  - Manual(Add Configuration command).
  - Configure component /Configure dimension tool.
  - Design Tables.
- Create a two level configuration of an assembly using the following method:
  - Configure component tool.
  - Configure dimension tool.
- Create a Derived Feature Component Pattern
- Insert and Edit a Distance Mate.
- Suppress/unSuppress Mates.
- Customize the Pop-up menu.
- Apply the Collision Detection tool.
- Understand Parent/Child component relationships.
- Rename Features and Mates.

Configurations

Configurations in SolidWorks provide the ability to create multiple variations of a part or assembly model within a single document. Configurations are a convenient way to develop and manage families of models with different dimensions, components, or other parameters.

Terminology Review

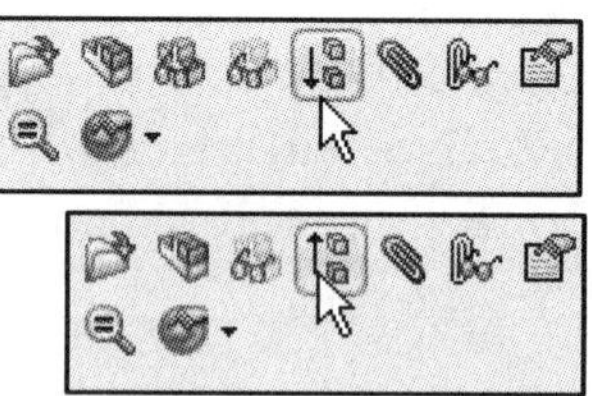

Suppress: The Suppress tool provides the ability to temporarily remove a component. When a component is suppressed, the system treats the component as if it does not exist. That means other components and mates that are dependent o it will be also suppressed. In addition, suppressed components are removed from memory, freeing up system resources. Suppressed components can be resolved (un-suppressed) as any time.

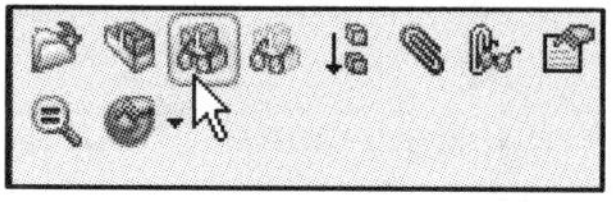

Hide/Show: The Hide tool provides the ability to remove a component's graphics without removing the component or its dependents. Mates associated with hidden components are still evaluated. Hidden components remain in memory, and can be shown at any time. Note: The Hide and show states are captured by the Display State.

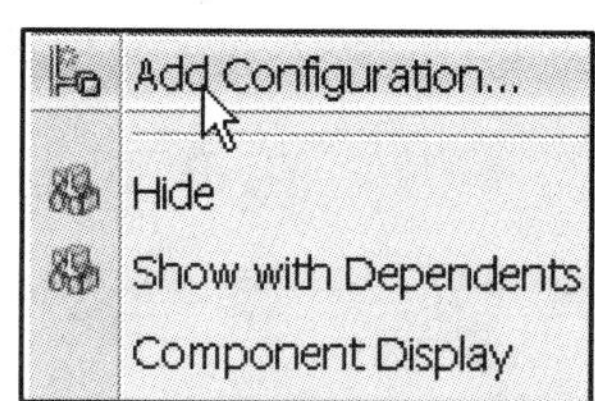

There are several way to create assembly configurations. All three are valuable and are explored in this book.

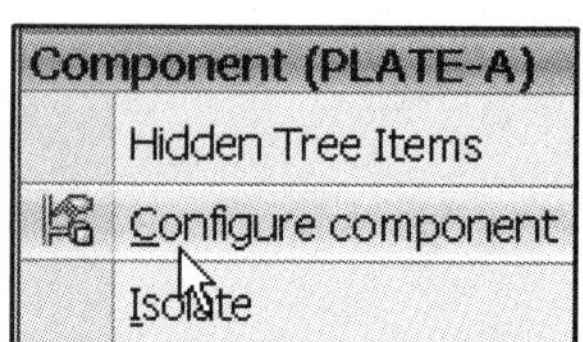

- *Manual(Add Configuration command)*
- *Configure component /Configure dimension tool*
- *Design Tables*

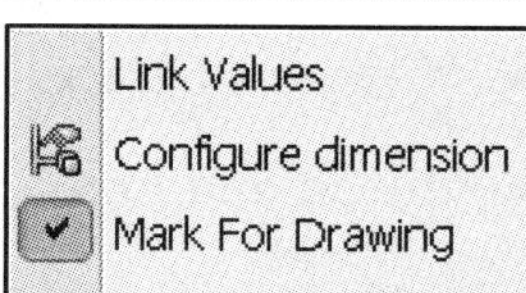

Manual (Add Configuration command)

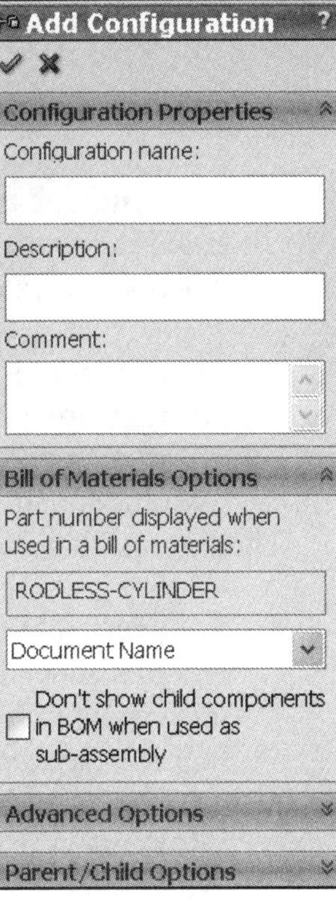

The Manual (Add Configuration command) method uses the Add Configuration PropertyManager. Right-click the assembly name in the ConfigurationManager and click the Add Configuration options. The Add Configuration PropertyManager provides the following options:

- ***Configuration Properties*:** The Configuration Properties box provides the following dialog boxes:
  - **Configuration name**. Type a name for the configuration. The name must not include the forward slash (/) or "at" sign (@). A warning message is displayed when you close the dialog box if the name field contains either of these characters, if the field is blank, or if the name already exists. You can display component configuration names in the FeatureManager design tree.
  - **Description** (optional). Type a description that identifies the configuration. You can display component configuration descriptions in the FeatureManager and the ConfigurationManager.
  - **Comment** (optional). Type additional descriptive information about the configuration.
  - **Custom Properties** (available only when editing properties of an existing configuration). Click to access Configuration Specific properties in the Summary Information dialog box.
- ***Bill of Materials Options***: The Bill of Materials Options box provides the following dialog boxes:
  - **Part number displayed when used in a bill of materials**. Provides the ability to specify how the assembly or part is listed in a Bill of Materials. Select one of the following:
    - **Document Name**. The part number is the same as the document name.
    - **Configuration Name**. The part number is the same as the configuration name.
    - **Link to Parent Configuration**. (For derived configurations only.) The part number is the same as the parent configuration name.

- **User Specified Name**. The part number is a name that you type.

- **Don't show child components in BOM when used as sub-assembly** (assemblies only). When selected, the sub-assembly is always displayed as a single item in the Bill of Materials. Otherwise, the child components might be listed individually in the BOM, depending on the BOM properties you select when you create the BOM.

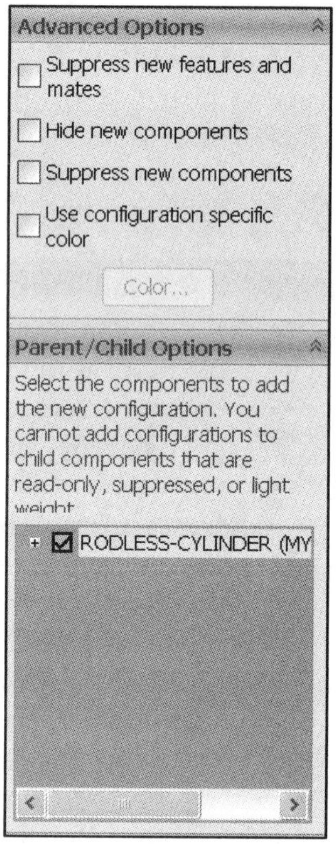

- ***Advanced Options***: The Advanced Options box provides the following dialog boxes: Note: The following properties control what happens when you add new items to another configuration, and then activate this configuration again. The options that are available depend on the document type.

  - **Suppress features** (parts only). When selected, new features added to other configurations are suppressed in this configuration. Otherwise, new features are included (not suppressed) in this configuration.

  - **Suppress new features and mates** (assemblies only). When selected, new mates and features added to other configurations are suppressed in this configuration. Otherwise, new mates and features are included (not suppressed) in this configuration. New features in assemblies include assembly feature cuts and holes, component patterns, reference geometry, and sketches that belong to the assembly (not to one of the assembly components).

  - **Hide new components** (assemblies only). When selected, new components added to other configurations are hidden in this configuration. Otherwise, new components are displayed in this configuration.

  - **Suppress new components** (assemblies only). When selected, new components added to other configurations are suppressed in this configuration. Otherwise, new components are resolved (not suppressed) in this configuration.

  - **Use configuration specific color**. Provides the ability to specify a color for the configuration. Select the check box, then click **Color** to choose a color from the color palette.

- ***Parent/Child Options***: The Parent/Child Options box is only available in assemblies and only when adding a new configuration to the assembly or one of its components. Select the components to which you want to add the new configuration.

Configure component / Configure dimension tool

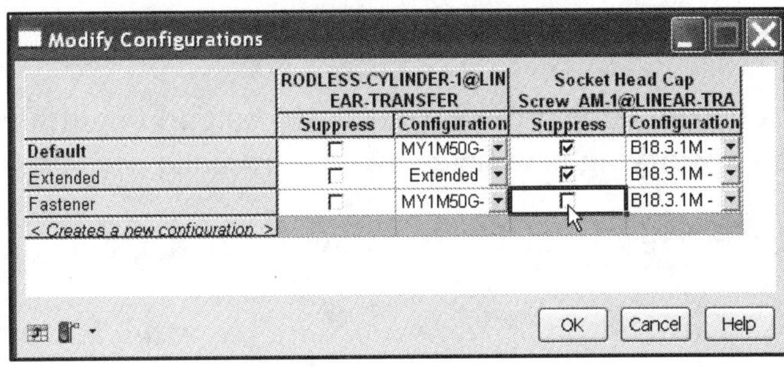

The Configure component / Configure dimension tool provides access to the Modify Configurations dialog box. The Modify Configurations dialog box facilitates creating and modifying configurations for commonly configured parameters in parts and assemblies. You can add, delete, and rename configurations and modify which configuration is active.

For features and sketches in parts, you can configure the following: Dimensions, and Suppression states. In assemblies, you can configure the following: Which configurations of components to use, Suppression states of components, Assembly features, and mates, and dimensions of assembly features and mates.

The Modify Configurations dialog box provides the following options:

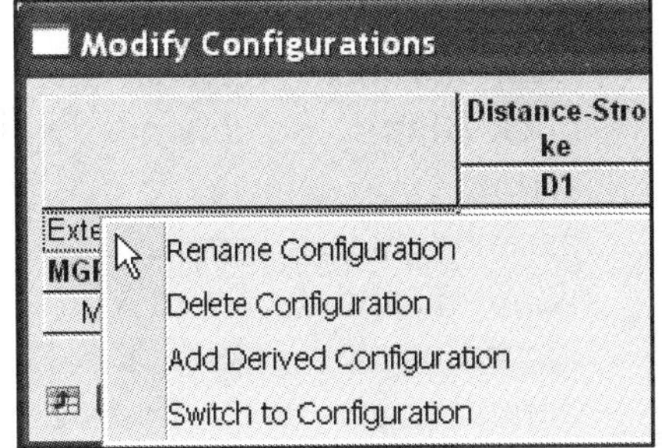

- ***First Column***: Lists the configurations of the model and the configurable parameters of the selected item in the other columns. Note: Right-click any configuration and select the following: *Rename Configuration, Delete Configuration, Add Derived Configuration, Switch to Configuration.*

Derived configurations provides the ability to create a Parent-Child relationship within a configuration. By default, all parameters in the child configuration are linked to the parent configuration. If you change a parameter in the parent configuration, the change automatically propagates to the child.

Click the **Rebuild active configuration** icon to update the active configuration.

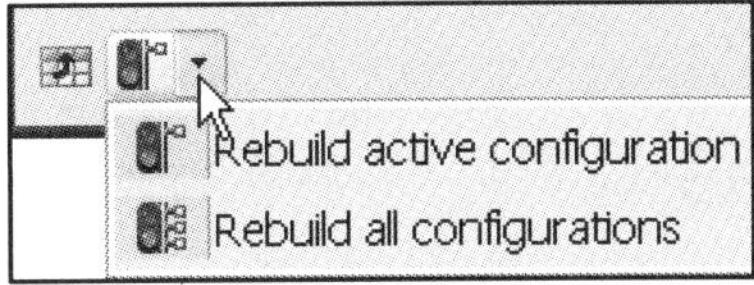

- ***Parameter Columns***: Provides the ability to click in a cell and: *Type to change the numeric values*, *Select from a list of component configurations*, or to *Change the suppression state of features, sketches, components and mates.*

Design Tables

A design table provides the ability to build multiple configurations of parts or assemblies by specifying parameters in an embedded Microsoft Excel worksheet.

There are several different ways to insert a design table. You can:

- *Have the SolidWorks Software automatically insert one for you.* In a part or assembly document, click **Design Table** on the Tools toolbar, or click **Insert**, **Design Table** from the Menu bar menu. In the PropertyManager, under Source, select **Auto-create**. Set any needed settings or options. Click **OK**. Depending on the settings you selected, a dialog box may appear that asks which dimensions or parameters you want to add. An embedded worksheet is displayed in the Graphics window, and the SolidWorks toolbars are replaced with Excel toolbars. Cell **A1** identifies the worksheet as **Design Table for:** <*model_name*>. Click anywhere outside of the worksheet, in the Graphics area to close the design table. A message lists the configurations that were created. The Design Table is displayed in the ConfigurationManager.

- *Insert a blank design table.* In a part or assembly document, click **Design Table** on the Tools toolbar, or click **Insert**, **Design Table** from the Menu bar menu. The Design Table PropertyManager is displayed. In the PropertyManager, under Source, click **Blank**. Set any needed settings or options. Click **OK**. Depending on the settings you selected, a dialog box may appear that asks which dimensions or parameters you want to add. An embedded worksheet is displayed in the Graphics window, and the SolidWorks toolbars are replaced with Excel toolbars. Cell **A1** identifies the worksheet as **Design Table for:** <*model_name*>. Cell **A3** contains the default name for the first new configuration, **First Instance**. In row **2**, type the parameters that you want to control. Leave cell **A2** blank. Notice that cell **B2** is active. In column **A** (cells **A3**, **A4**, etc), type the names of the configurations that you want to create. The names can include numerics but must not include the forward slash (/) or at (@) characters. Type the parameter values in the worksheet cells. When you finish adding information to the worksheet, click outside the table to close it. A message lists the configurations that were created. Click **OK**. The Design Table is displayed in the ConfigurationManager.

You can also enter parameters by double-clicking the feature or dimension in the graphics area or in the FeatureManager design tree. When you double-click a feature or dimension, its associated value is displayed in the **Default** row.

- *Insert an external MS Excel table as a design table.* In a part or assembly document, click **Design Table** on the Tools toolbar, or click **Insert**, **Design Table** from the Menu bar menu. The Design Table PropertyManager is displayed. In the PropertyManager, under Source, click **From file**, then click **Browse** to locate the Excel file.

To link the design table to the model, select the **Link to file** check box. A linked design table reads all of its information from an external Excel file. NOTE: If you update a linked design table in Microsoft Excel, then open the SolidWorks model, you can choose to update either. Click **OK**. An embedded worksheet appears in the window, and the SolidWorks toolbars are replaced with Excel toolbars. Click anywhere outside of the worksheet (but in the graphics area) to close the design table.

Develop two configurations for the RODLESS-CYLINDER and LINEAR-TRANSFER assembly

Develop new configurations for the RODLESS-CYLINDER assembly and the LINEAR-TRANSFER assembly. Apply the Configure dimension tool to the RODLESS-CYLINDER and the Configure Component tool to the LINEAR-TRANSFER assembly.

Create two new configurations for the RODLESS-CYLINDER assembly to illustrate dynamic motion and physical location: *Normal and Extended.*

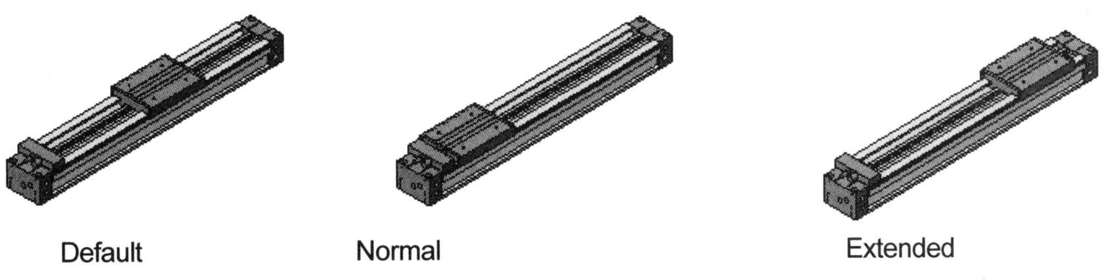

By default, all assemblies contain a default configuration. The MY1M50G-500LS (Default) configuration was named by SMC which was downloaded.

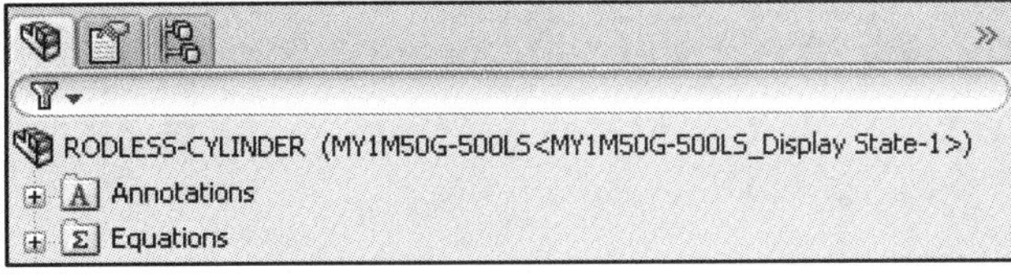

The Normal and Extended configuration names represent the first and second position for a pneumatic component.

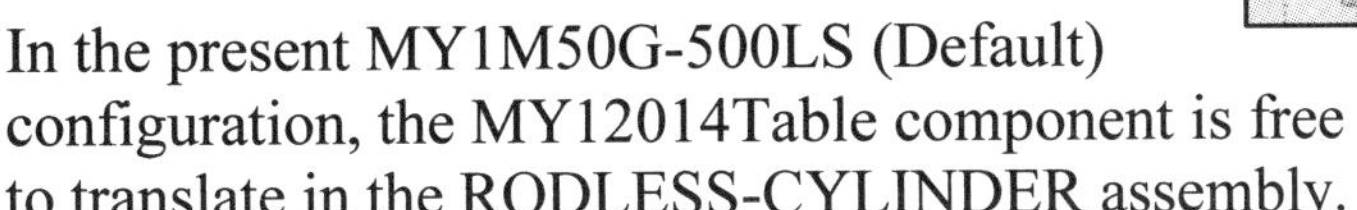
In the present MY1M50G-500LS (Default) configuration, the MY12014Table component is free to translate in the RODLESS-CYLINDER assembly.

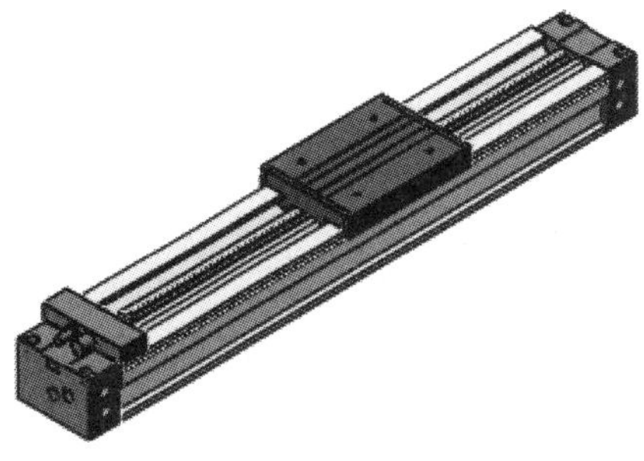

The MY1M50G-500LS (Default) Flexible configuration is a derived configuration that allows the PLATE-A part to translate.

SolidWorks creates this configuration when the Solve as state changes from Rigid to Flexible.

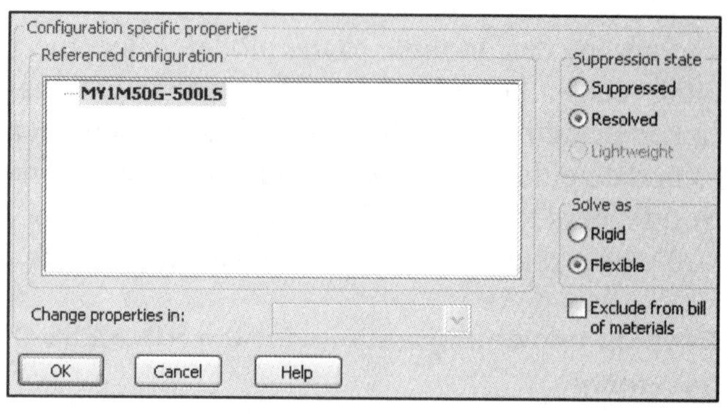

By default, when you create a sub-assembly, it is rigid. Within the Parent assembly, the sub-assembly acts as a single unit and its components do not move relative to each other.

The MY1M50G-500LS (Default) Flexible derived configuration is not displayed in the Design Table. The Default (Flexible) derived configuration name and parameters are determined from the Default configuration.

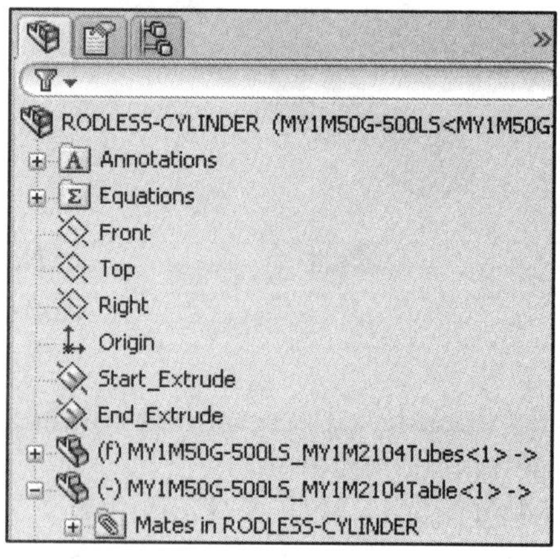

Review the RODLESS-CYLINDER assembly. The MY1M2104Table part slides along the MY1M2104Tubes part.

Apply the Collision Detection tool to determine the physical location of the MY1M2104 Table part in the *Normal* and *Extended* configurations.

Insert a Distance Mate between the MY1M2104Piston Part and the MY1M2104HeadCover Part.

The RODLESS-CYLINDER assembly is in the Normal position when the Distance Mate value equals 0.

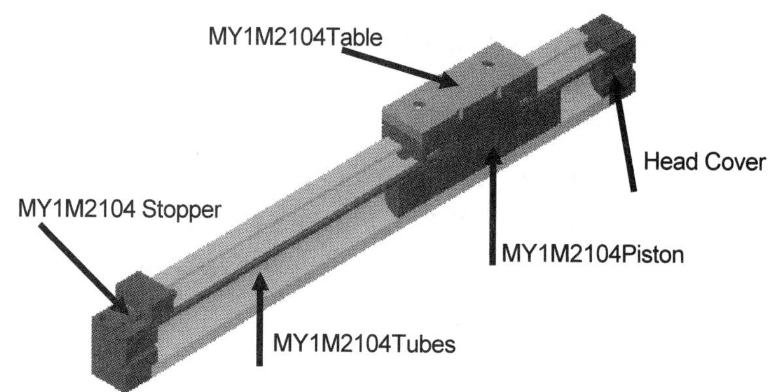

The RODLESS-CYLINDER assembly is in the Extended position when the Distance Mate value equals 500. Collisions occur when one component impacts another component. You can detect collisions with other components when moving or rotating a component.

Customize the Pop-up menu to include the Move option. The Move option provides access to the Move PropertyManager and the Collision Detection option.

Activity: Apply the Collision Detection tool

Open the RODLESS-CYLINDER assembly.

1) Right-click **(f)RODLESS-CYLINDER** from the LINEAR-TRANSFER FeatureManager.

2) Click **Open Assembly** from the Context toolbar. The RODLESS-CYLINDER Assembly is displayed.

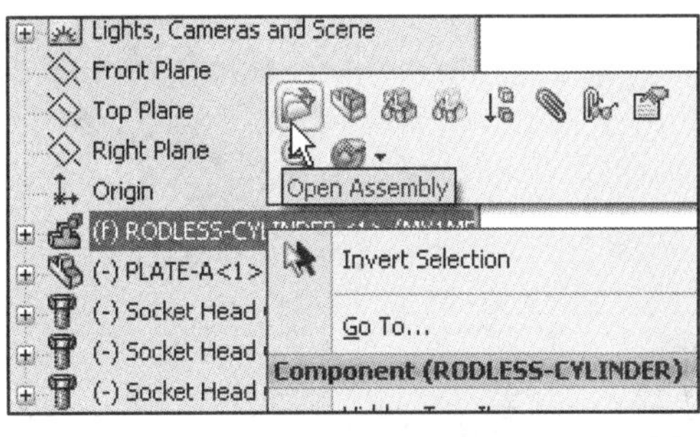

Customize the Pop-up menu.

3) Right-click **MY1M2104Table** from the FeatureManager.

4) Click **Customize Menu**.

5) Check the **Move** box.

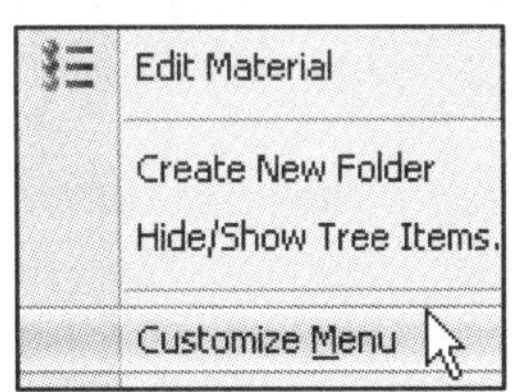

Locate the collision between the bottom components of the Table.

6) Right-click **MY1M2104Table** from the FeatureManager.

7) Click **Move**. The Move Component PropertyManager is displayed.

8) Check the **Collision Detection** box.

9) Check the **Stop at collision** box.

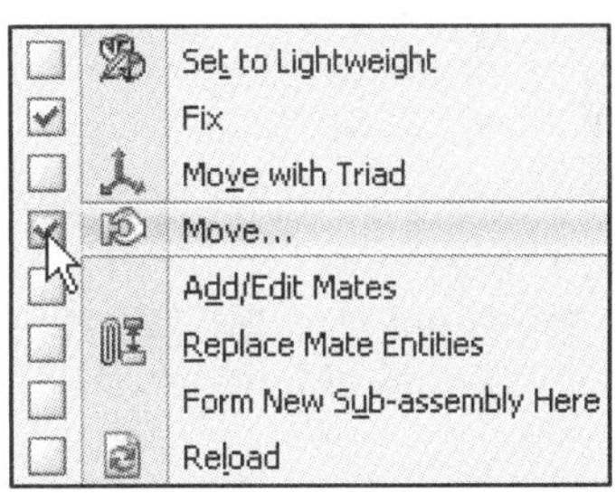

10) Check the **Dragged part only** box.

11) Drag the **MY1M2104Table** part until it meets the MY1M2104Stopper part as illustrated.

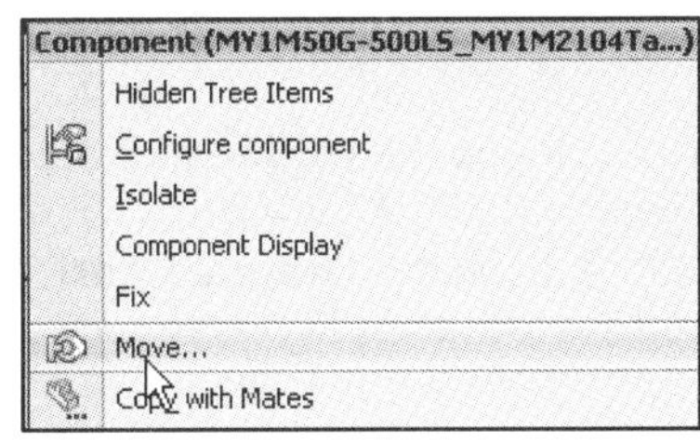

12) Click **OK** from the Move Component PropertyManager.

13) **Save** the model.

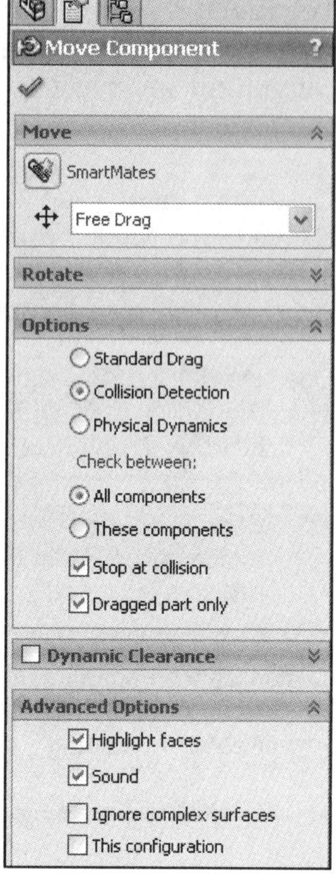

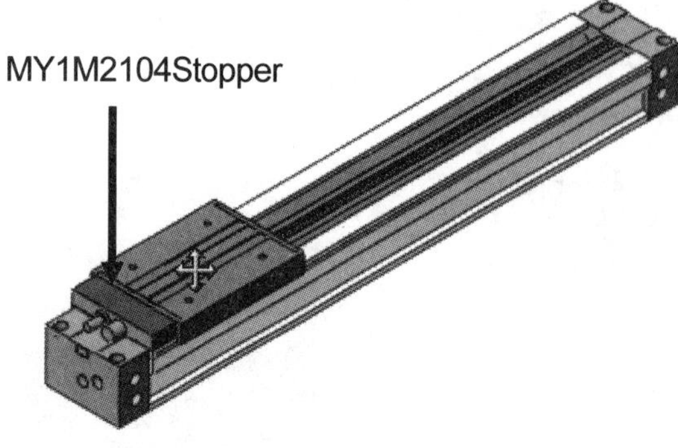

Display the Section view.

14) Click **Right Plane** from the FeatureManager. Right Plane is highlighted in the FeatureManager.

15) Click **Section view** from the Heads-up View toolbar. The Section View PropertyManager is displayed. View the section view in the Graphics window.

16) Click **OK** from the Section View PropertyManager.

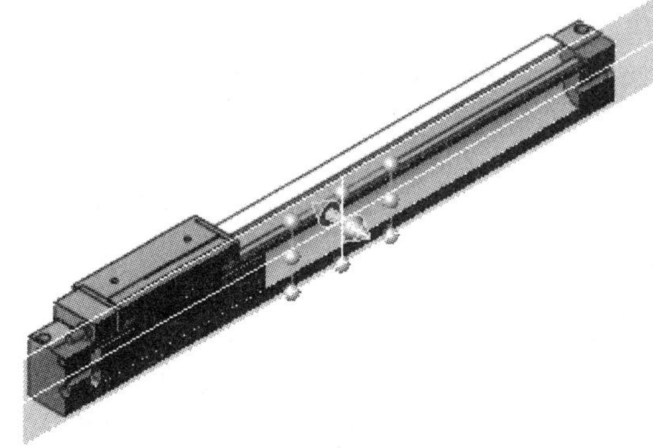

Locate the collision between the top components of the Table.

17) Right-click **MY1M2104Table** from the FeatureManager.

18) Click **Move**. The Move Component PropertyManager is displayed.

19) Check the **Collision Detection** box.

20) Check the **Dragged part only** box.

21) Check the **Stop at Collision** box.

22) Drag the **MY1M2104Table** part until it meets the MY1M2104HeadCover part as illustrated.

23) Click **OK** ✔ from the Move Component PropertyManager.

24) **Save** the model.

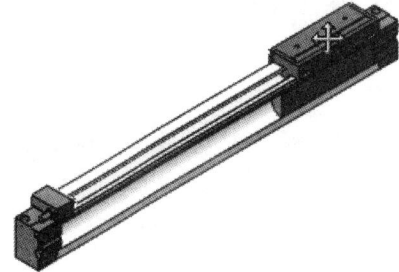

Expand MateGroup1.

25) **Expand** the MateGroup1 folder. View the created mates.

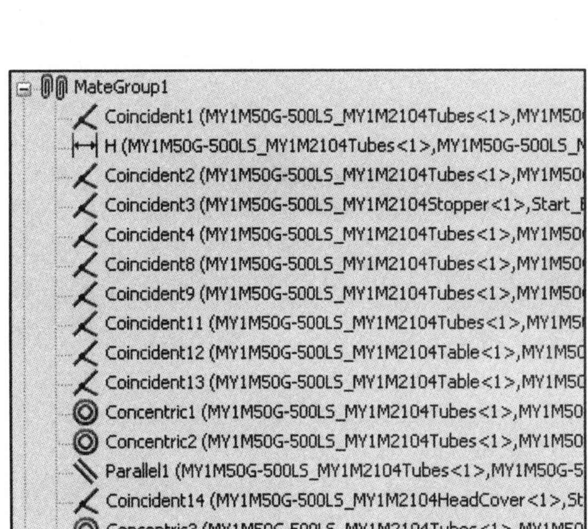

The list contains two Mates for the MY1M2104Tubes part and the MY1M2104Table part.

The MY1M2104Table part is free to translate along the MY1M2104Tubes part.

 H is a renamed Distance Mate.

The MY1M2104Piston part translates along the MY1M2104 Tubes part with a Concentric Mate.

View the internal components with a Section view.

Activity: Create a Distance Mate

Create a Distance Mate.

26) Right-click the **MY1M50GPiston** front face as illustrated.

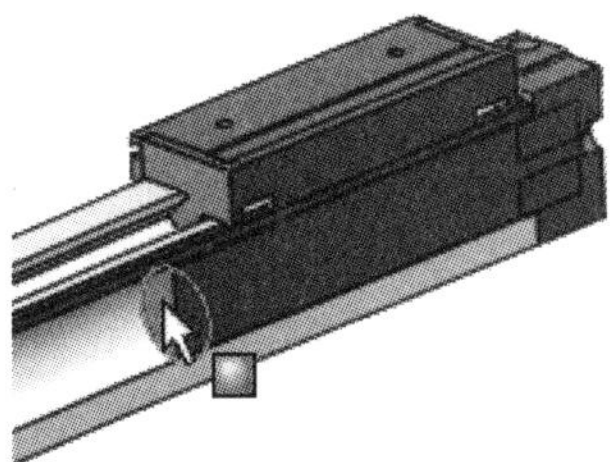

27) Click **Mate** from the Context toolbar. The selected face is displayed in the Mate Selections box.

28) Click the **MY1M50GHeadCover** left inside face as illustrated. The selected face is displayed in the Mate Selections box.

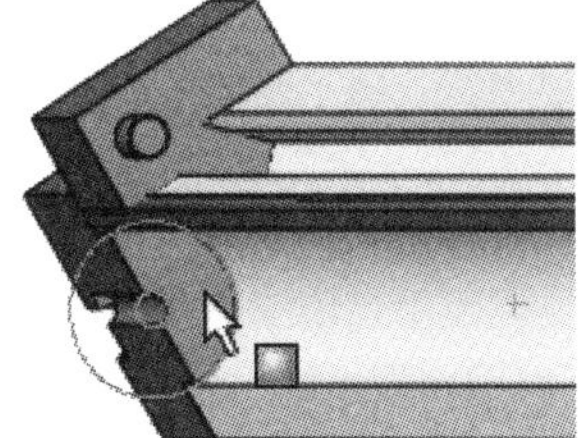

29) Click **Distance**.

30) Enter **0**.

31) Click the **Green Check Mark** ✓.

32) Click **OK** ✓ from the Mate PropertyManager.

Display an Isometric view

33) Click **Isometric** view from the Heads-up View toolbar. View the results. Remember, the RODLESS-CYLINDER assembly is in the new Normal configuration when the Distance Mate value equals 0.

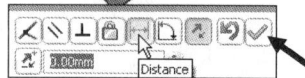

Modify the Distance1 Mate.

34) Right-click the **Distance1** mate from the FeatureManager.

35) Click **Edit Feature**. The Distance1 PropertyManager is displayed.

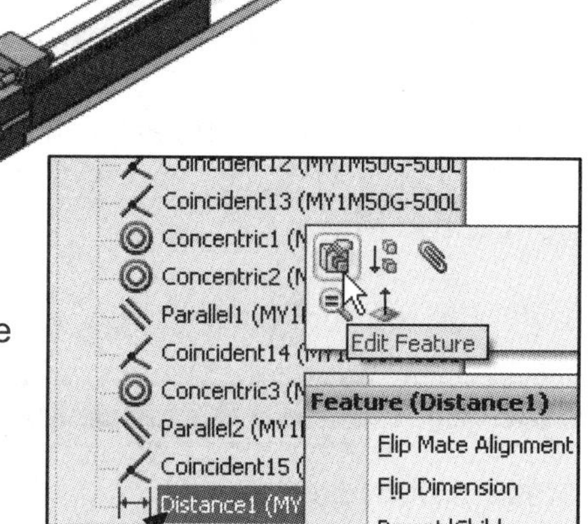

36) Enter **500**mm for new distance. View the results in the Graphics window,

37) Click **OK** ✓ from the Distance1 PropertyManager.

38) Click **OK** ✓ from the Mate PropertyManager.

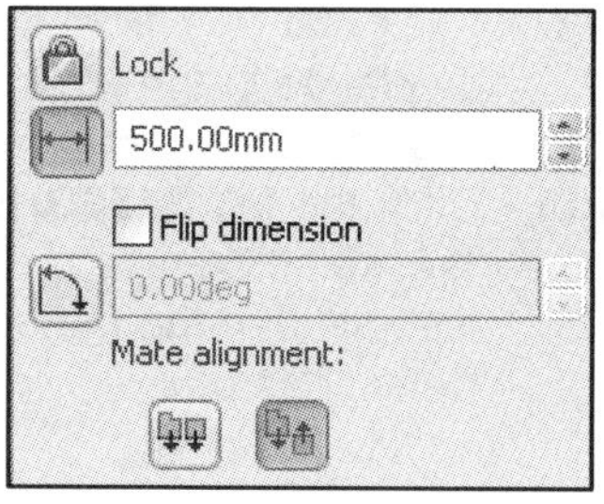

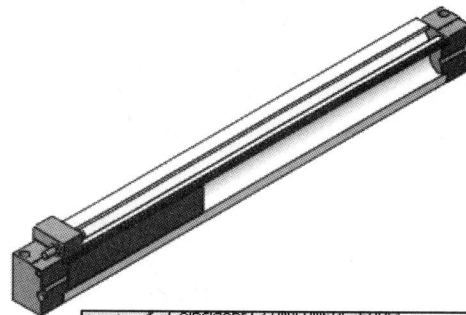

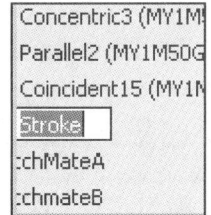

Rename Distance1 Mate.

39) Double-click **Distance1** in the FeatureManager.

40) Click **inside** the text box.

41) Enter **Stroke**. Spelling must be exact. Do not leave spaces in Mate names. The variable is utilized in the configurations.

Display a full view.

42) Click **Section view** from the Heads-up View toolbar.

Locate and modify the Stroke value. Utilize the FeatureManager. Position the dimension off the profile.

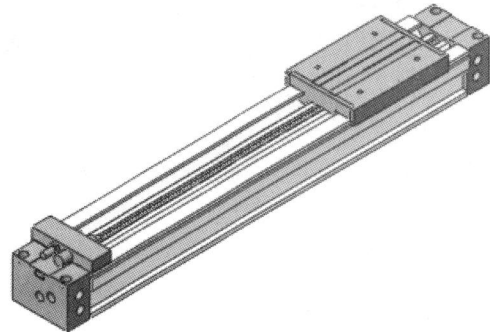

Activity: Modify the Distance Mate

Modify the distance value.

43) Double-click **Stroke** from the FeatureManager. The value 500 is displayed.

44) Drag the **500** dimension off of the model as illustrated.

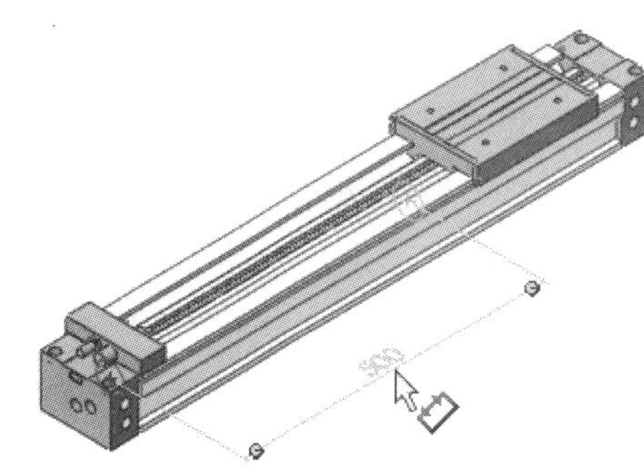

45) Double-click **500**.

46) Enter **0**.

47) Click **Rebuild** from the Modify box. The MY1M2104Table part moves to the left.

48) Click the **Green Check Mark** ✓.

49) Click **OK** ✓ from the Dimension PropertyManager.

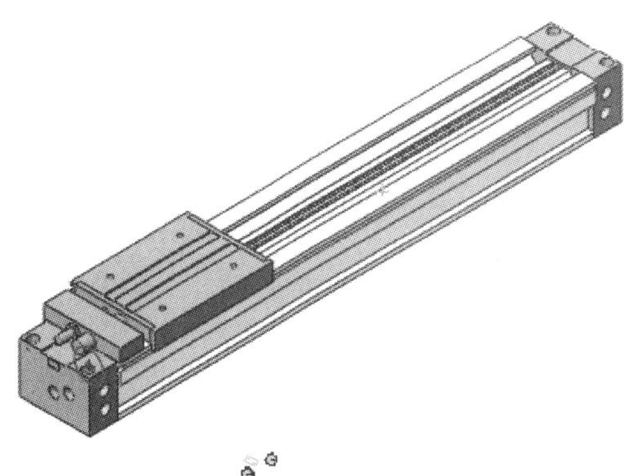

Save the RODLESS-CYLINDER assembly.

50) Click **Save**.

Drag the distance dimension outward to improve visibility. The "0" value contains no dimension lines. Utilize a Distance Mate to modify the value between mating component entities.

Activity: RODLESS-CYLINDER Configurations: Configure dimension tool

Display the ConfigurationManager.

51) Click the **ConfigurationManager** tab. Remember, the default configuration was renamed by SMC to MY1M50G-500LS.

52) **Return** to the FeatureManager.

Add the RODLESS-CYLINDER assembly (Normal) configuration.

53) Double-click **Stroke** from the FeatureManager. View the 0 dimension.

54) Right-click the **0** dimension in the Graphics window.

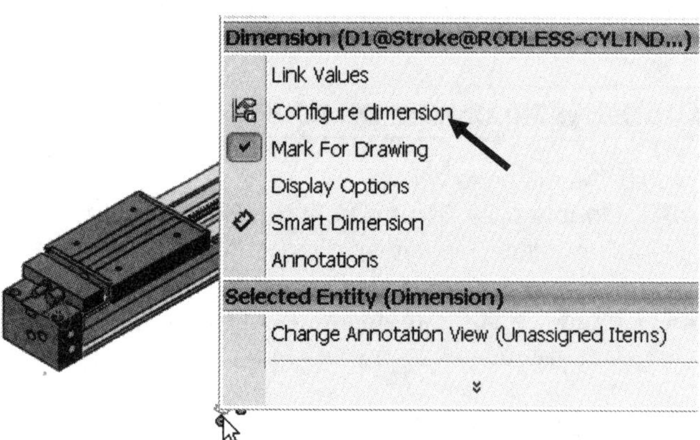

55) Click the **Configure dimension** tool. The Modify Configurations dialog box is displayed.

56) Click inside the **Creates a new configuration** box.

57) Enter **Normal** for Configuration name.

58) Press the **Tab** key.

59) Enter **0**.

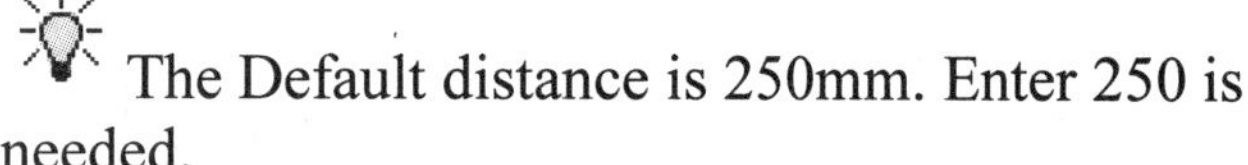

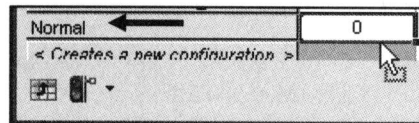

The Default distance is 250mm. Enter 250 is needed.

Add the RODLESS-CYLINDER (Extended) configuration.

60) Click inside the **Creates a new configuration** box.

61) Enter **Extended** for Configuration Name.

62) Press the **Tab** key. Enter **500**.

63) Click **OK** from the Modify Configurations dialog box.

64) Click **OK** from the Dimension PropertyManager.

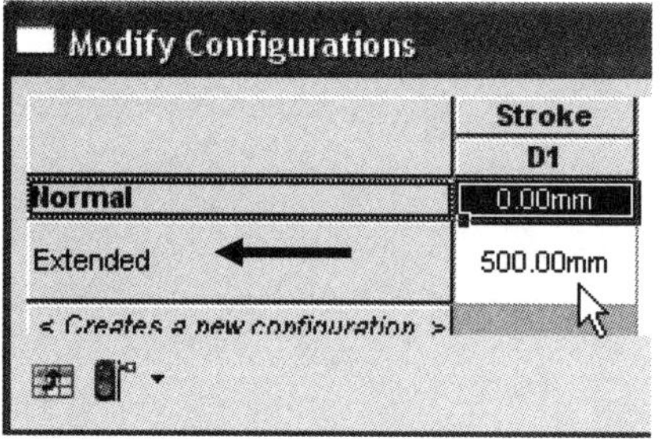

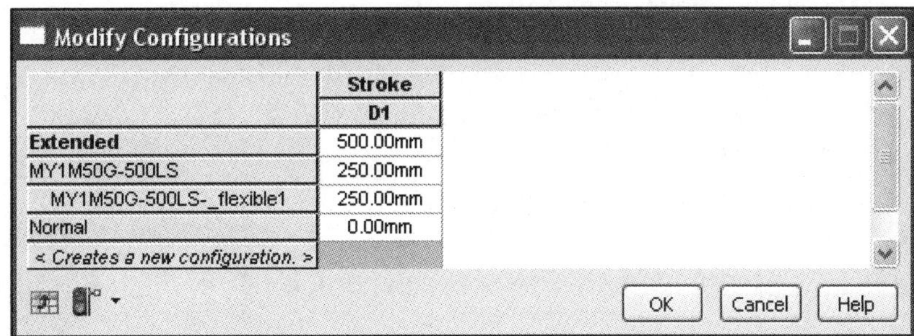

View the inserted dimensions for the Configurations.

65) Double-click **Stroke** from the FeatureManager. View the 500 dimension.

66) Right-click the **500** dimension in the Graphics window.

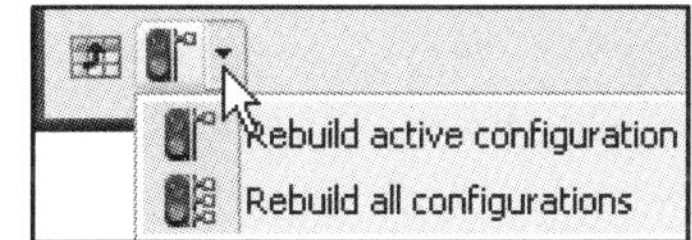

67) Click the **Configure dimension** tool. The Modify Configurations dialog box is displayed. View the two new configurations and the default configuration.

68) Click **Rebuild all configurations**.

69) Click **OK** from the Modify Configurations dialog box.

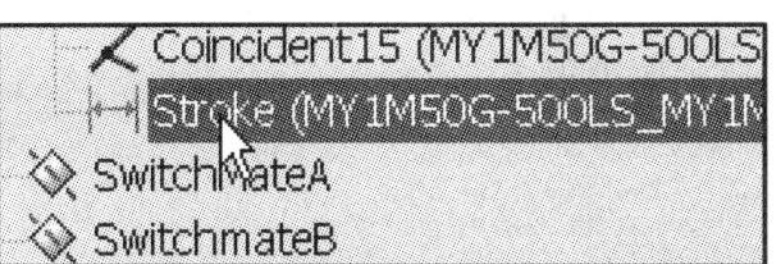

70) Click **OK** from the Dimension PropertyManager.

Verify the three Configurations.

71) Click the **ConfigurationManager** tab.

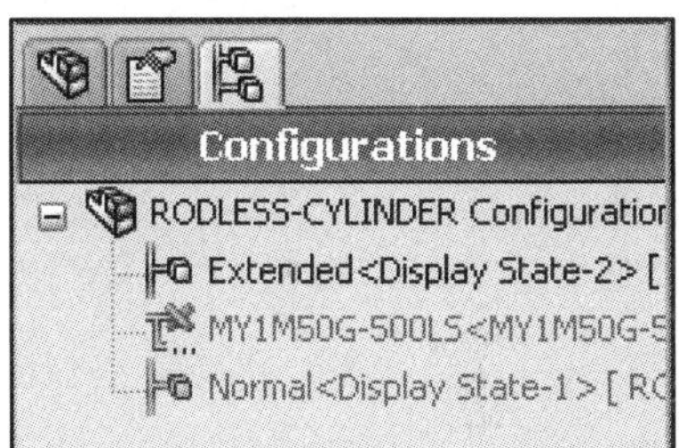

72) Double-click the **MY1M50G-500LS** configuration. View the results.

73) Double-click the **Normal** configuration. View the results.

74) Double-click the **Extended** configuration. View the results.

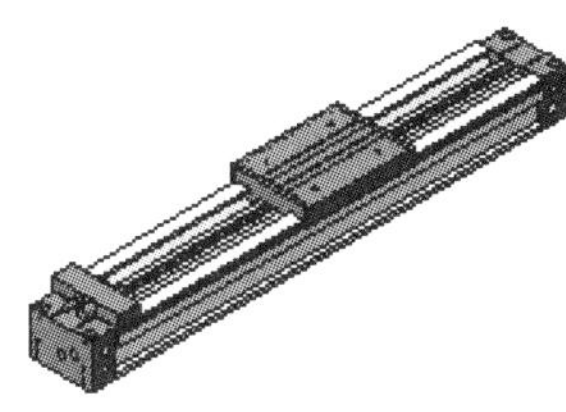

Default

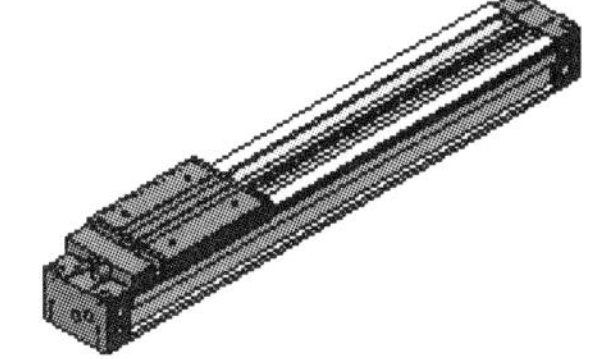

Normal

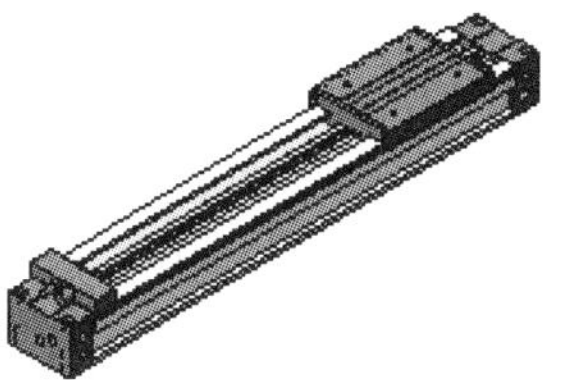

Extended

Return to the Default configuration.

75) Double-click the **Default** configuration.

76) **Suppress** Stroke in the MateGroup1 folder. This will make the table flexible.

Return to the Assembly FeatureManager.

77) Click the **Assembly FeatureManager** tab.

78) **Save** the assembly.

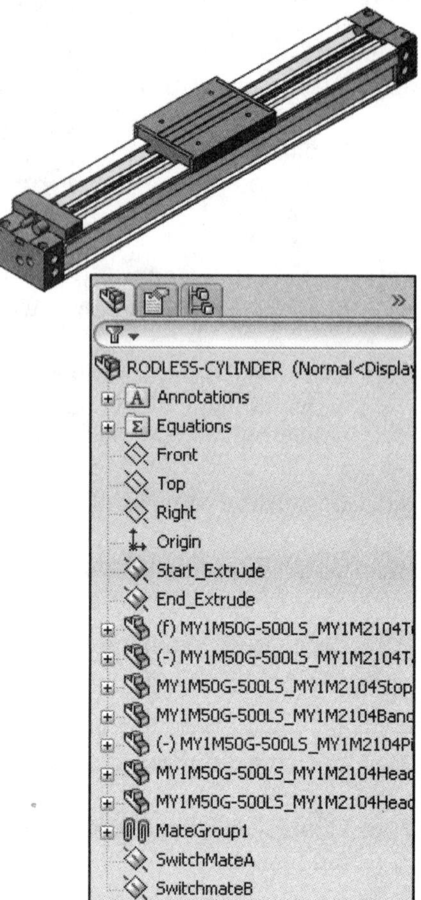

Parent/Child relation in an assembly

A Parent is an existing feature on which other features are dependent. A Child is a dependent feature related to a previously built feature (its parent). During a Parent modification, a Child is modified automatically. Parent\Child relationships in the assembly are available from the FeatureManager or Pop-up Component menu.

Example: Right-click **MY1M2104Table** from the FeatureManager. Click **Parent/Child**.

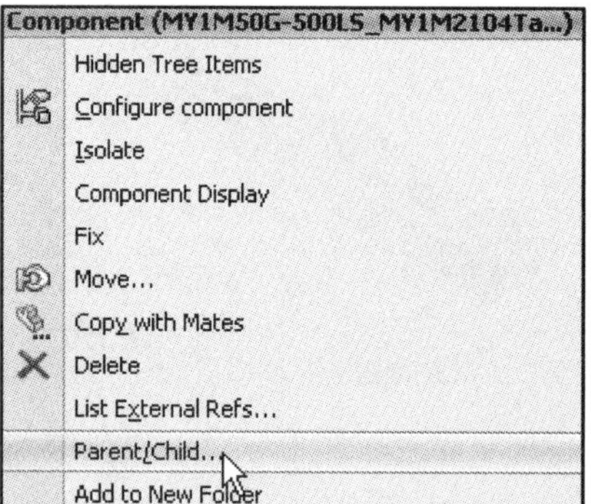

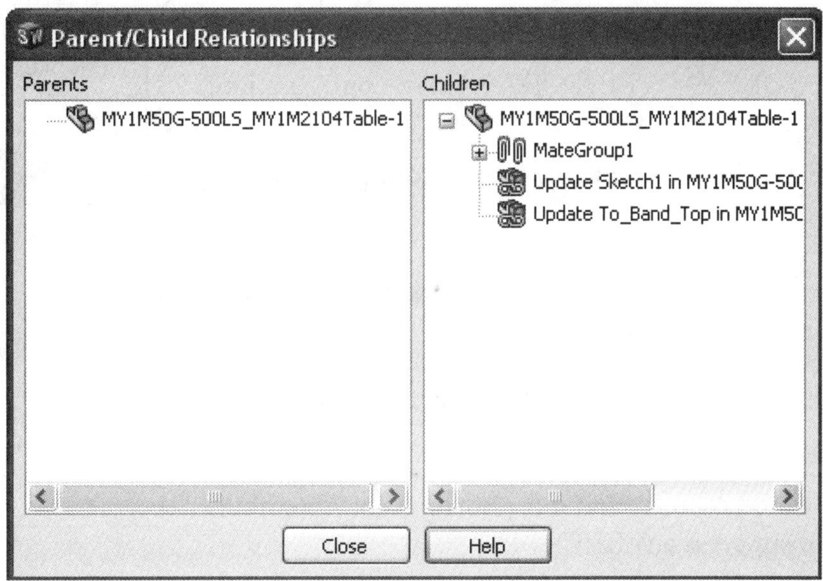

Review the Parent/Child relationships in an assembly before you develop configurations that require Suppress/Unsuppress states. When you suppress a component, the corresponding Mates are suppressed.

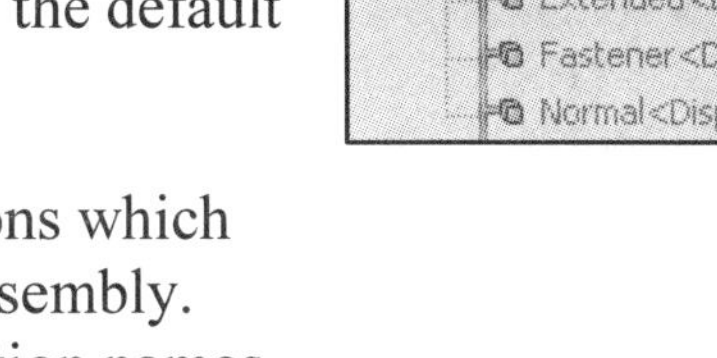

LINEAR-TRANSFER Configurations

Create three new configurations to the LINEAR-TRANSFER assembly. Note: At this time, only the default configuration is present.

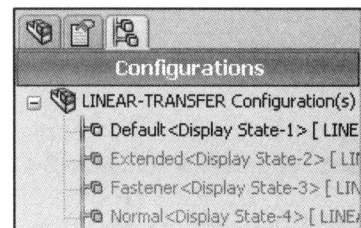

Utilize the RODLESS-CYLINDER configurations which you just created in the LINEAR-TRANSFER assembly. The three new LINEAR-TRANSFER configuration names are: *Normal, Extended, and Fastener*

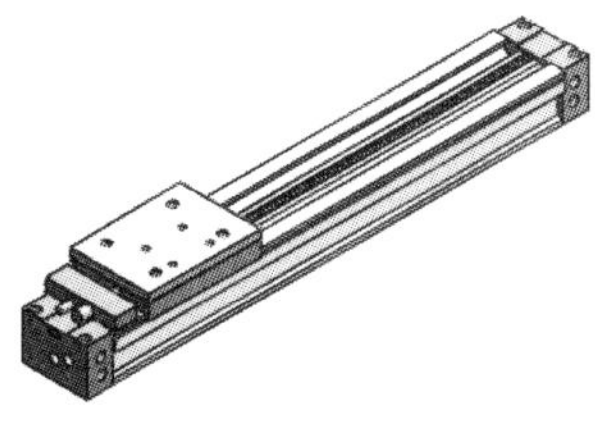

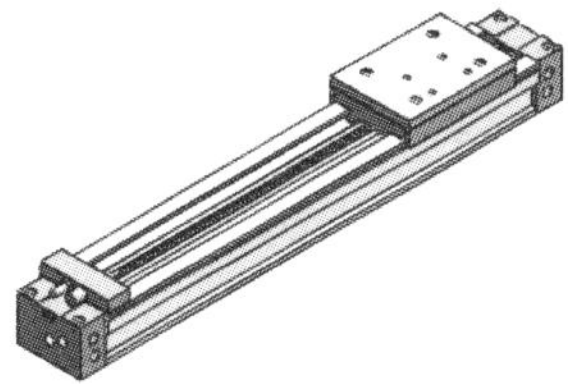

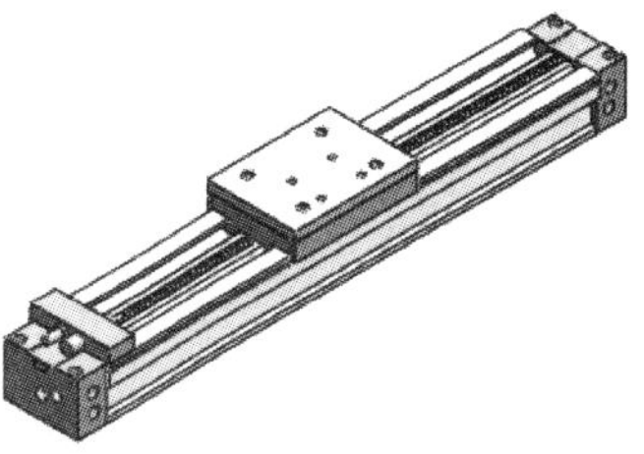

Physical dynamics analysis and finite element analysis are computer intensive. Utilize configurations to develop simplified parts and assemblies. Develop simplified parts by suppressing fillet and draft features. Develop simplified assemblies by suppressing hardware and insignificant components.

The LINEAR-TRANSFER (Normal) configuration utilizes:

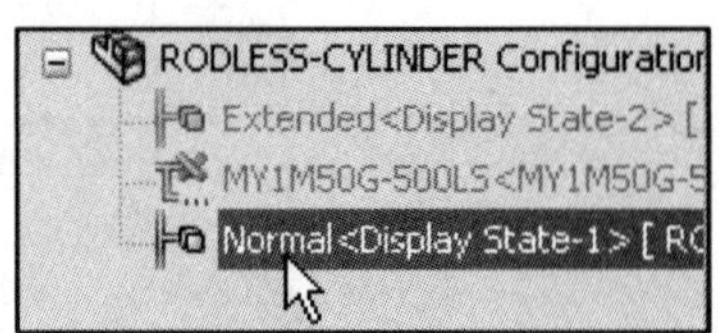

- The RODLESS-CYLINDER (Normal) configuration. Do not suppress any SHCSs

The LINEAR-TRANSFER (Extended) configuration utilizes:

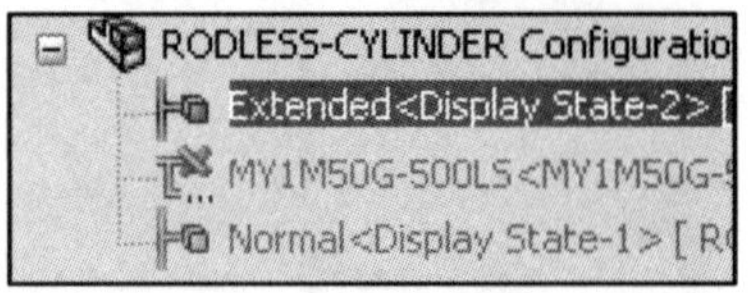

- The RODLESS-CYLINDER (Extended) configuration and a suppressed SHCS.

The LINEAR-TRANSFER (Fastener) configuration utilizes:

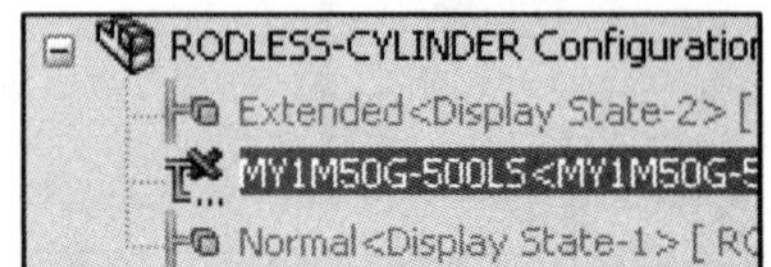

- The RODLESS-CYLINDER (Default) configuration. Do not suppress any SHCSs.

Activity: Create Three New LINEAR-TRANSFER Configurations

Review the LINEAR-TRANSFER FeatureManager.

79) Open the **LINEAR-TRANSFER** assembly. The LINEAR-TRANSFER assembly is displayed in the Graphics window.

View the Component Properties.

80) Right-click **RODLESS-CYLINDER** from the LINEAR-TRANSFER FeatureManager.

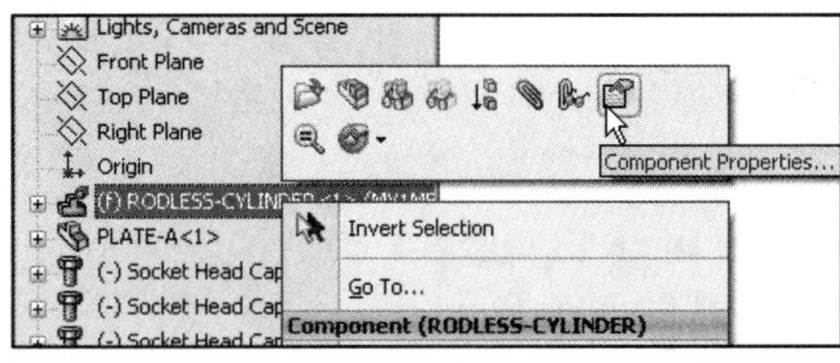

81) Click **Component Properties**. The Configuration name is MY1M50G-500LS which is the default. The Extended and Normal configurations are displayed in the Referenced configuration box.

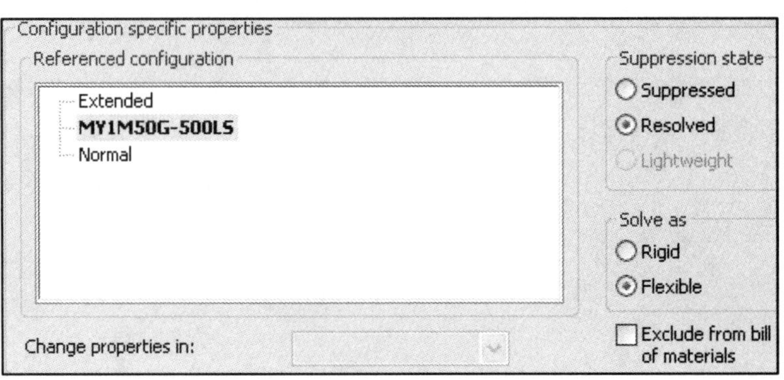

82) Click **OK** from the Component Properties box.

Apply the Configure component tool

83) Right-click **RODLESS-CYLINDER** from the FeatureManager.

84) Click **Configure component**. The Modify Configurations dialog box is displayed.

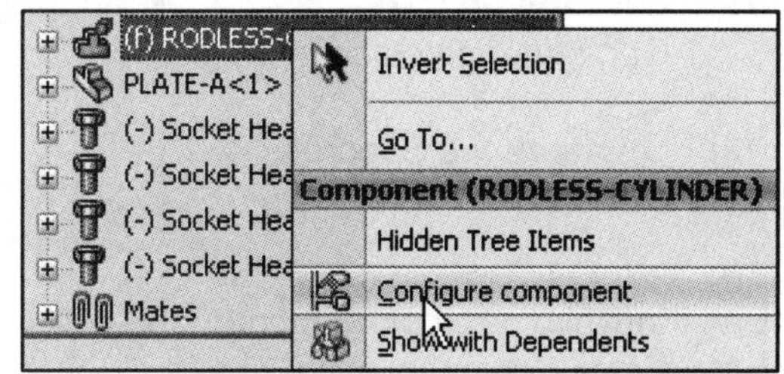

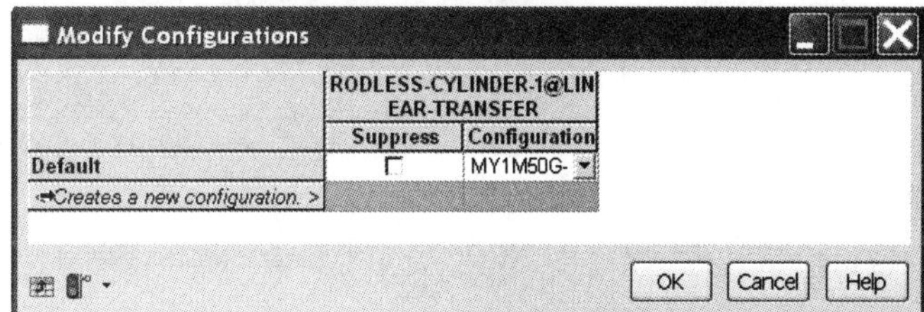

Enter a new configuration.

85) Enter **Extended** in the Creates a new configuration box.

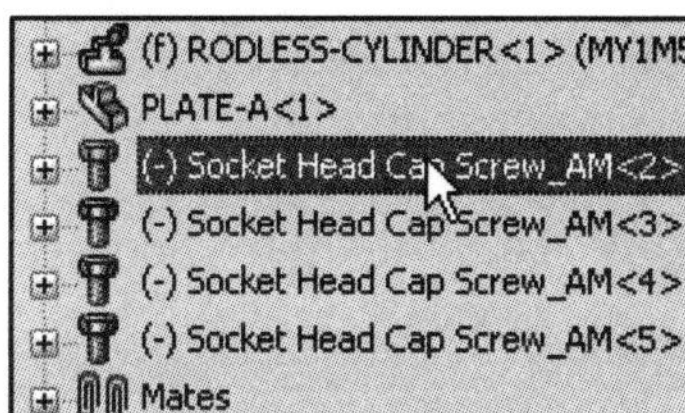

86) Double-click the first **Socket Head Cap Screw** from the FeatureManager as illustrated. The Socket Head Cap column is displayed in the Modify Configuration dialog box.

87) Check the **Suppress** box for the Default configuration.

88) Check the **Suppress** box for Extended configuration.

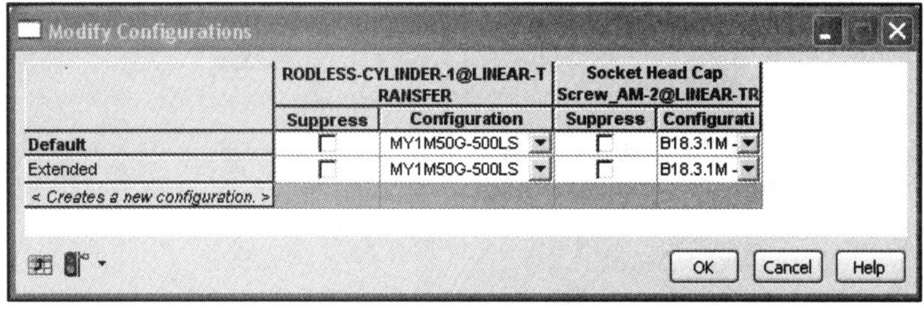

89) Select **Extended** from the Configuration drop-down menu as illustrated for the Extended configuration.

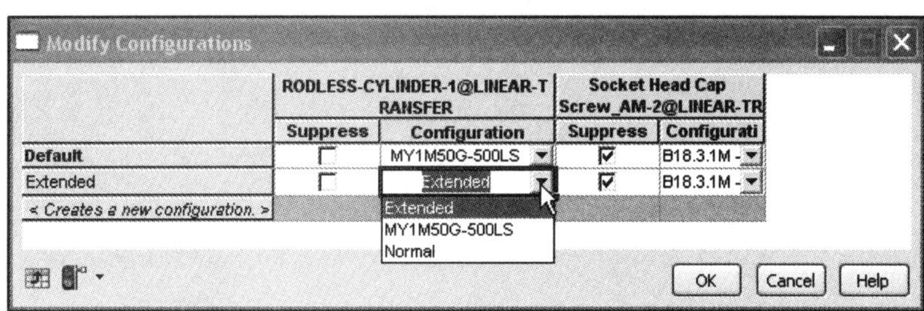

Enter the second new configuration.

90) Enter **Fastener** in the Creates a new configuration box as illustrated. The default configuration of the ROLDLESS CYLINDER is displayed.

91) Click **inside** the Configuration column.

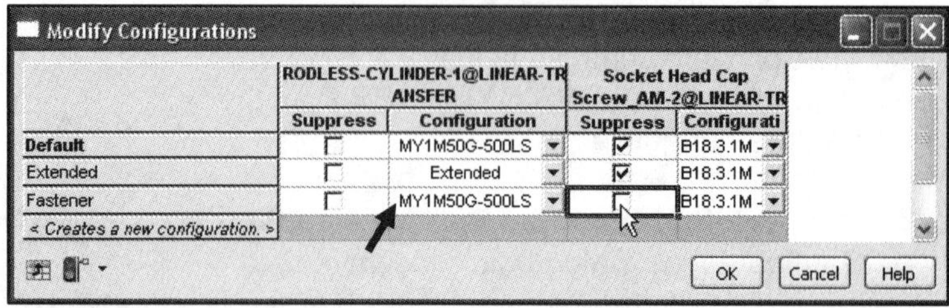

92) **Uncheck** the Suppress box.

Enter the third new configuration.

93) Enter **Normal** in the Creates a new configuration box as illustrated.

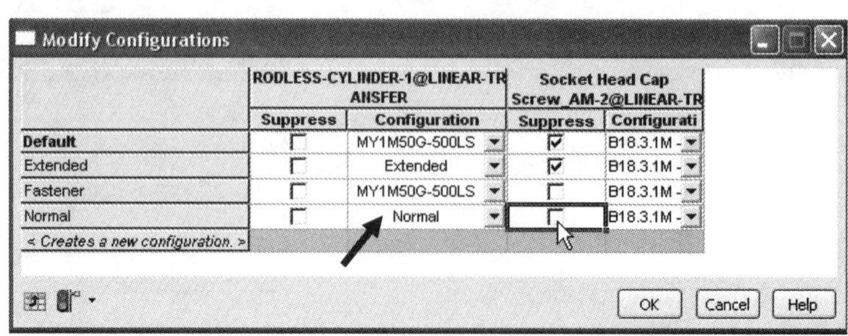

94) Select **Normal** from the Configuration drop-down menu.

95) Click **inside** the Configuration column.

96) **Uncheck** the Suppress box.

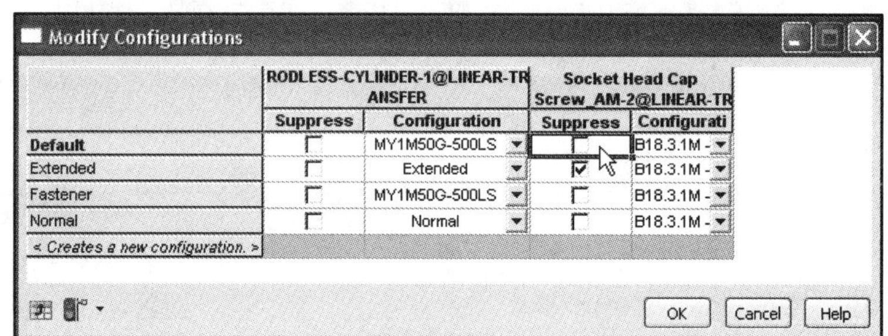

Modify the Default / Default configuration.

97) **Uncheck** the Suppress box.

98) Click **OK** from the Modify Configurations dialog box. The FeatureManager is displayed. View the results.

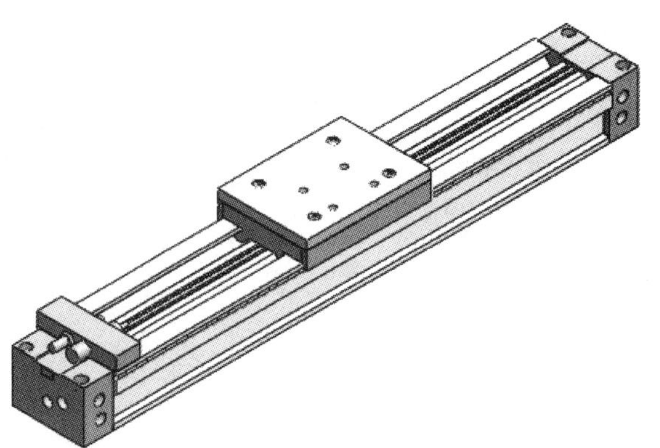

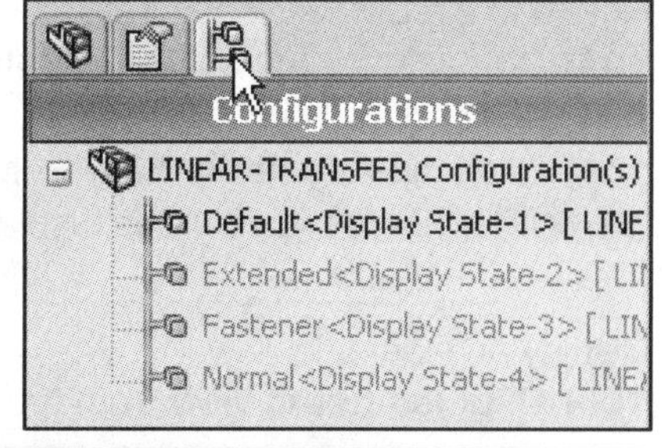

View the configurations.

99) Click the **Configurations Manager** tab.

100) Double-click the **Default** configuration. View the results. The SHCSs are displayed.

101) Double-click the **Extended** configuration. View the results. Note: The first SHCS is suppressed.

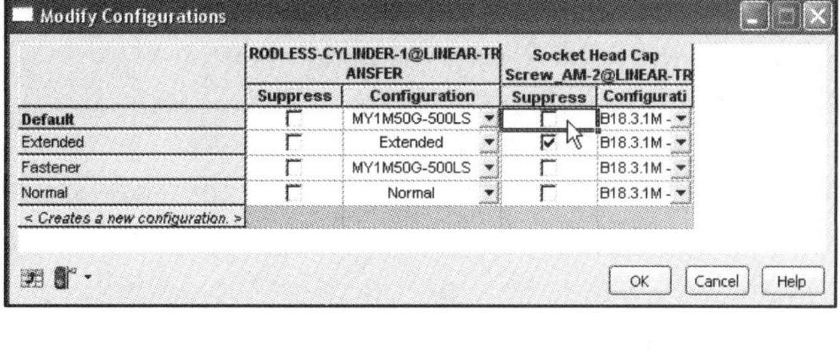

102) Double-click the **Fastener** configuration. View the results. The SHCSs are displayed.

103) Double-click the **Normal** configuration. View the results. The SHCSs are displayed.

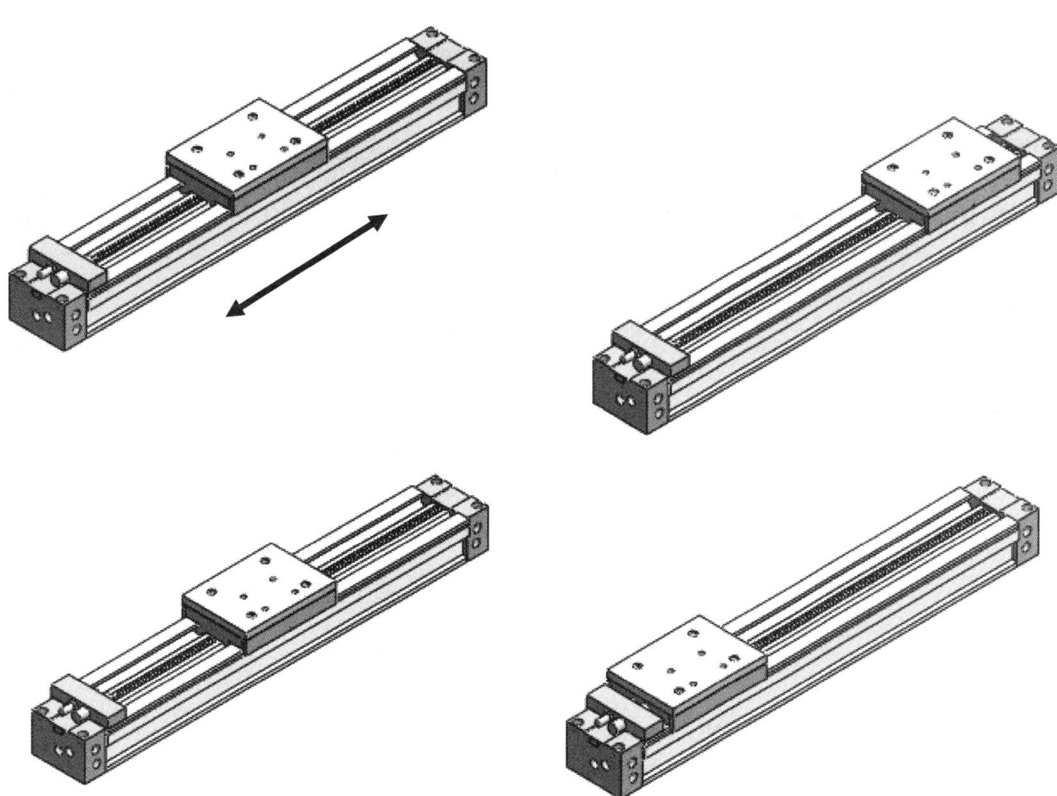

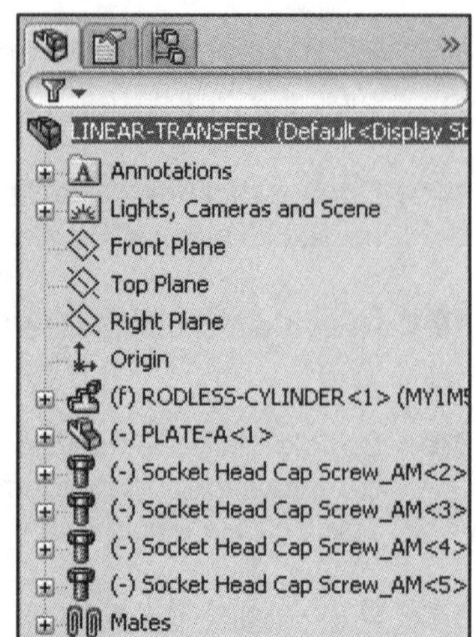

Return to the Default configuration.

104) Double-click the **Default** Configuration.

105) Click the **Assembly FeatureManager** tab. LINEAR-TRANSFER (Default) is displayed.

Display an Isometric view.

106) Click **Isometric** view from the Heads-up View toolbar.

Save the LINEAR-TRANSFER assembly.

107) Click **Save**.

The configurations are complete for the LINEAR-TRANSFER assembly. The LINEAR-TRANSFER assembly is the first component in the 3AXIS-TRANSFER assembly.

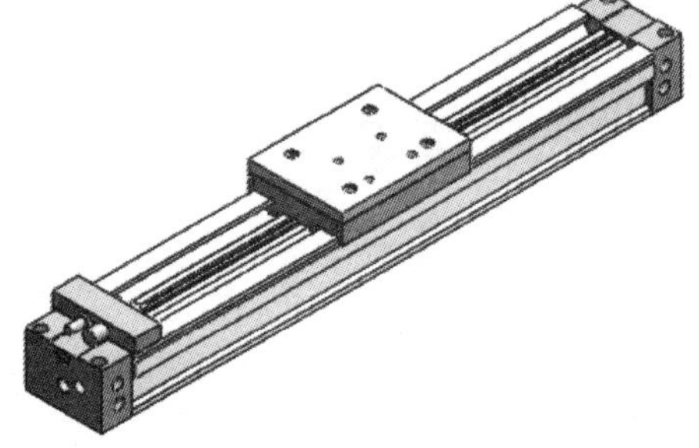

Preparing for the Next Assembly

Determine the components and features in the LINEAR-TRANSFER assembly that are utilized in the next assembly.

What key component and feature is required for the next phase of the project?

Answer: The GUIDE-CYLINDER assembly is the next key component. The next key feature is the four Thru Holes.

Mount the GUIDE-CYLINDER assembly to the four PLATE-A Thru Holes.

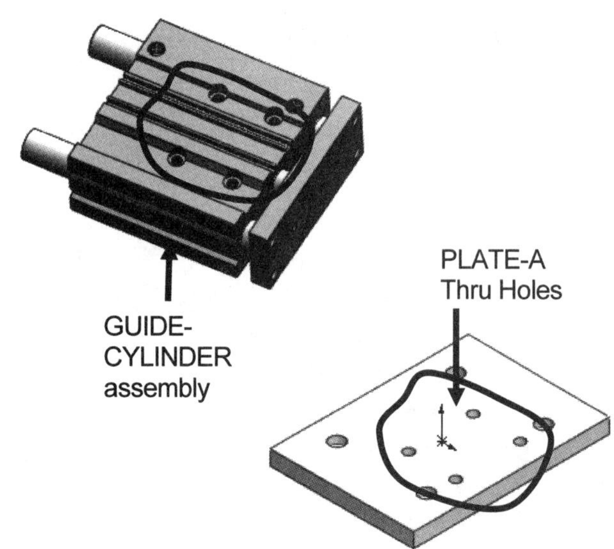

Rename the Thru Hole LPattern2 feature for clarity in the next step.

The GUIDE-CYLINDER is the base (first) component in the 2AXIS-TRANSFER assembly.

The project leader incorporates the GUIDE-CYLINDER into the 2AXIS-TRANSFER assembly versus the LINEAR-TRANSFER assembly for modularity.

The LINEAR-TRANSFER assembly becomes a future sub-assembly in another application.

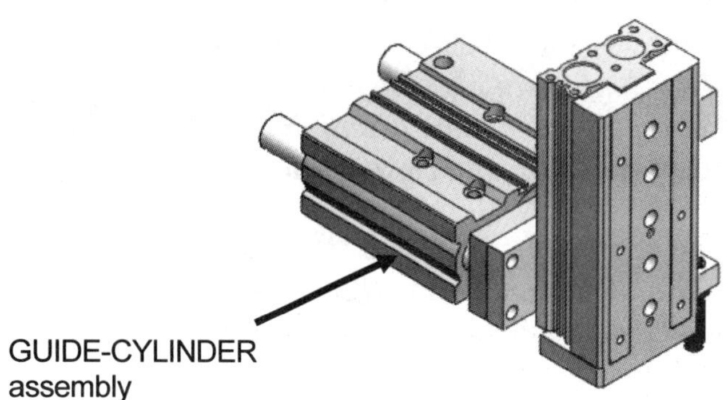

2AXIS-TRANSFER assembly

Activity: Preparing for the Next Assembly

Open the PLATE-A part.

108) Right-click **PLATE-A** from the Linear-Transfer FeatureManager.

109) Click **Open Part**. PLATE-A is displayed in the Graphics window.

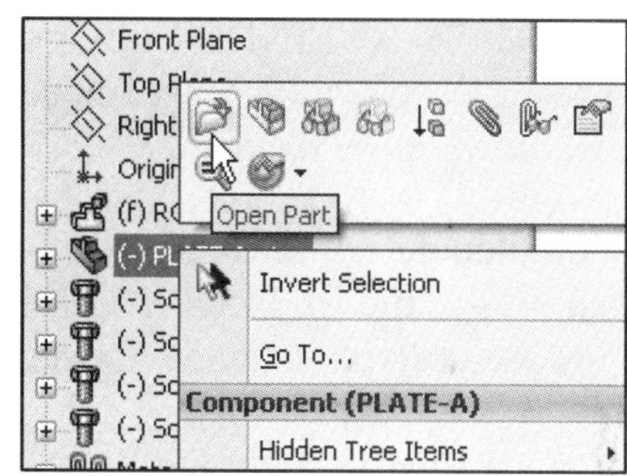

Display an Isometric view.

110) Click **Isometric** view from the Heads-up View toolbar.

Rename LPattern2 in the PLATE-A part.

111) Double-click **LPattern2** from the FeatureManager.

112) Click **inside** the name text box.

113) Enter **LPattern2-ThruHoleGuideCylinder**.

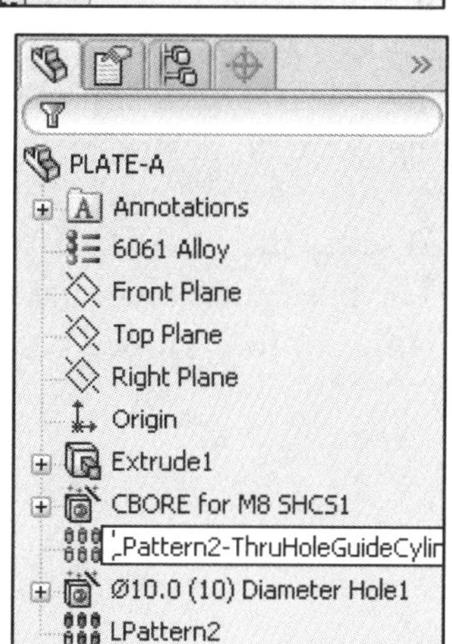

Save the PLATE-A part.

114) Click **Save**.

Close all parts and assemblies.

115) Click **Windows**, **Close All** from the Menu bar menu.

Project Summary

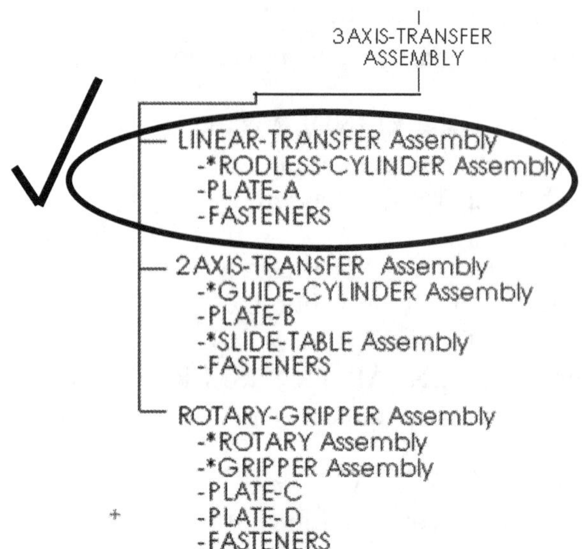

You reviewed the three different ways to create assembly configurations: *Manual (Add Configuration command)*, *Configure component /Configure dimension tool*, and *Design Tables*.

You applied the Collision Detection tool to the RODLESS-CYLINDER assembly and created a modified a Distance Mate.

You then applied the Configure dimension tool to create two new configurations for the RODLESS-CYLINDER: *Normal* and *Extended.*

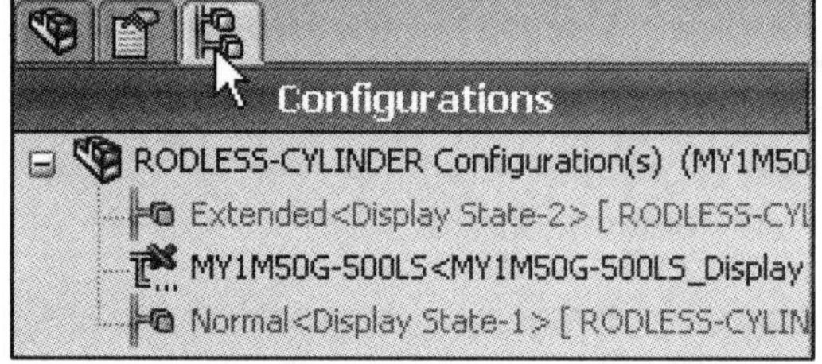

You applied the Configure Component tool to create three new configurations for the LINEAR-TRANSFER assembly using the RODLESS-CYLINDER sub-assembly and the Socket Head Cap Screw component: *Normal, Extended*, and *Fastener*.

You then determined the components and features in the LINEAR-TRANSFER assembly that are utilized in the next assembly.

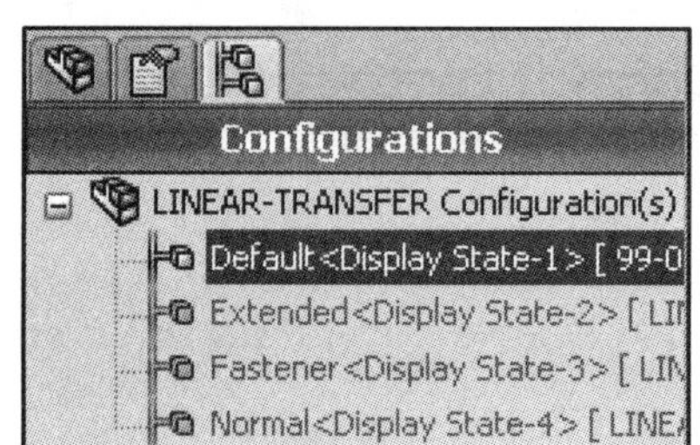

Discuss the assemblies with your project team leader. Ask if the customer has provided any additional input that would constitute a design change. For now, there are no design changes.

Discuss the PLATE-A part fabrication with a machinist. The machinist recommends modifying the four Thru Holes to four tapped holes.

Questions

1. Describe the components and features utilized to determine the geometric and functional requirements of the PLATE-A part.

2. List the sketch tools and feature options that build symmetry into a part.

3. Identify the locations of the PLATE-A Reference planes.

4. True or False. The Hole Wizard does not require dimensions or relationships to define the position of a hole.

5. Assembling components in SolidWorks is defined as ________

6. Each component has ________________ degrees of freedom.

7. Identify the view type that displays internal geometry.

8. Describe the difference between a Distance Mate with a 0 value and a Coincident Mate.

9. Describe the SHCS abbreviation. What does it stand for?

10. Identify the two SmartMates that are used to assemble a SHCS to a hole in the PLATE-A part.

11. Identify the command utilized to create a Component Pattern in an assembly that references an existing feature for another component.

12. Describe configurations. Are they useful? Explain your answer.

13. A sub-assembly named Flexible is inserted into an assembly. The Flexible sub-assembly is Rigid. Identify the option that would regain a flexible state?

14. Review the SmartMate .avi files with SW help. Identify other types of Smart Mates. Explain.

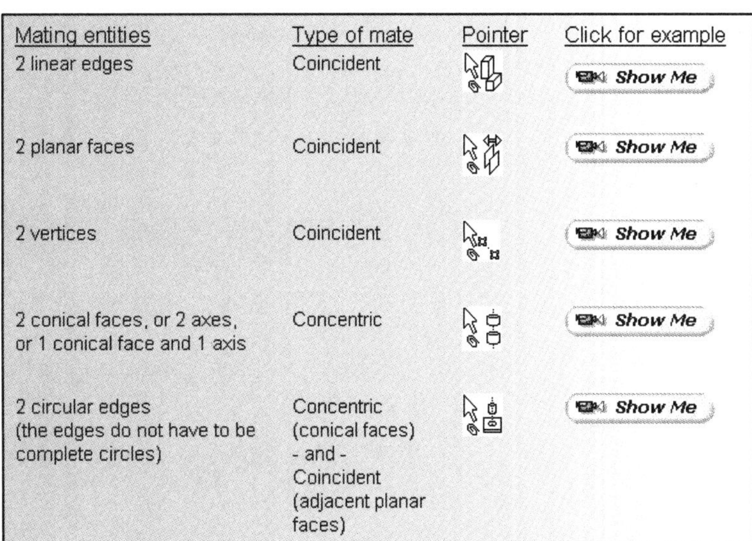

Mating entities	Type of mate	Pointer	Click for example
2 linear edges	Coincident		Show Me
2 planar faces	Coincident		Show Me
2 vertices	Coincident		Show Me
2 conical faces, or 2 axes, or 1 conical face and 1 axis	Concentric		Show Me
2 circular edges (the edges do not have to be complete circles)	Concentric (conical faces) - and - Coincident (adjacent planar faces)		Show Me

Notes:

Project 5

Top-down Design Approach - Two Components with Configurations

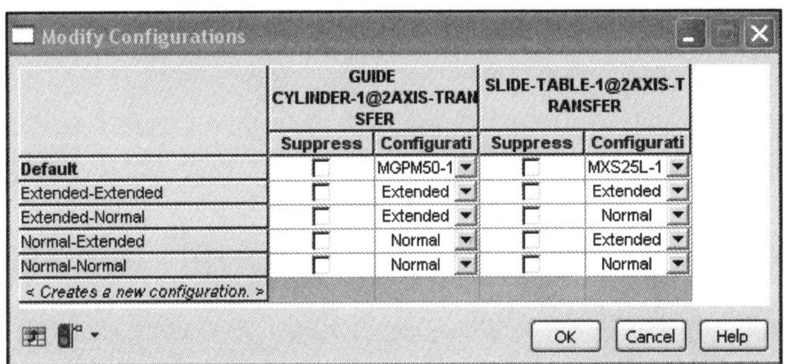

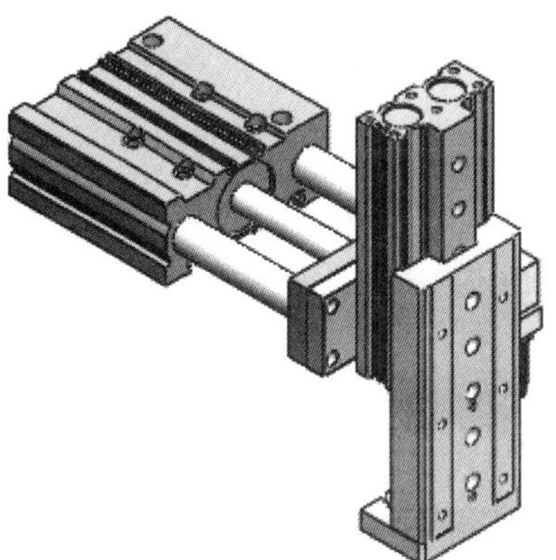

Below are the desired outcomes and usage competencies based on the completion of this Project.

Project Desired Outcomes:	Usage Competencies:
• 2AXIS-TRANSFER assembly.	• Apply In-Context methods used in Top-down assembly modeling. • Understanding of Out-of-Context components. • Comprehension of External References and InPlace Mates.
• PLATE-B part.	• Ability to create, lock, break, and redefine External References.
• Configurations for the GUIDE-CYLINDER, SLIDE-TABLE, and 2AXIS-TRANSFER assemblies. • Insert Smart Fasteners.	• Knowledge to develop and incorporate assembly configurations at various levels with the Configure component /Configure dimension tool. • Create a Linear Component Pattern. • Ability to create and modify Mates related to configurations.

Notes:

Project 5 – Top-down Design Approach – Two Components with Configurations

Project Objective

Create the 2AXIS-TRANSFER assembly. Design the PLATE-B part In-Context of the GUIDE-CYLINDER and SLIDE-TABLE assemblies.

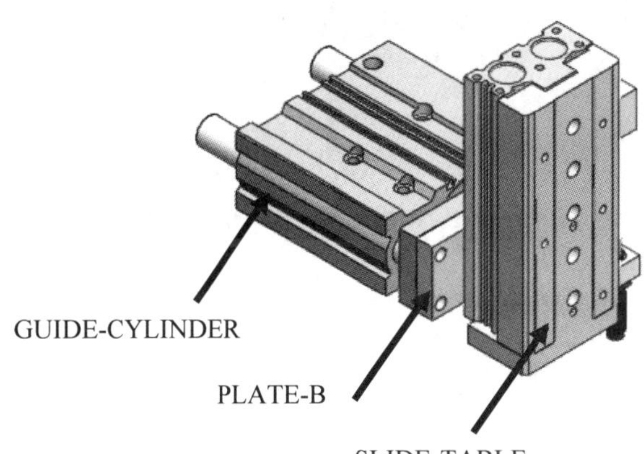

Utilize the Configure dimension tool to create new configurations for the GUIDE-CYLINDER and SLIDE-TABLE.

Utilize the Configure component tool to create configurations for the new 2AXIS-TRANSFER assembly. The 2AXIS-TRANSFER assembly is the second component in the 3AXIS-TRANSFER assembly.

On the completion of this project, you will be able to:

- Apply a Top-down design assembly modeling approach to develop components In-Context of the assembly.
- Edit and create External References and InPlace Mates.
- Select appropriate hole types and Smart fasteners.
- Measure, obtain the required dimensions, and insert components.
- Calculate the interference between components.
- Redefine all External references.
- Redefine and Replace Components.
- Create a Linear Component Pattern.
- Apply the Configure component / Configure dimension tool to add configurations to an assembly.
- Customize the Assembly toolbar.

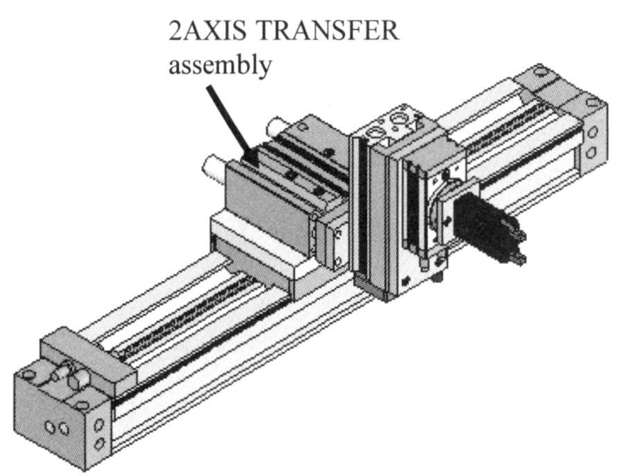

3AXIS-TRANSFER assembly

Project Overview

The 2AXIS-TRANSFER assembly is the second sub-assembly for the 3AXIS-TRANSFER assembly.

The 2AXIS-TRANSFER assembly combines the GUIDE-CYLINDER assembly and the SLIDE-TABLE assembly.

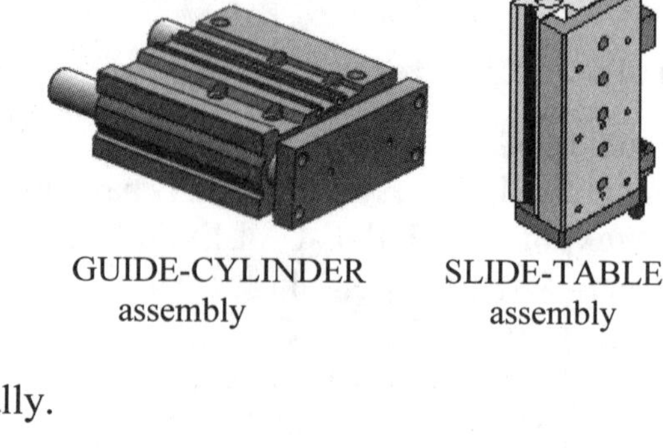

GUIDE-CYLINDER assembly   SLIDE-TABLE assembly

The SLIDE-TABLE assembly vertically lifts the GRIPPER 100mm. The GUIDE-CYLINDER assembly moves 100mm horizontally.

The SLIDE-TABLE assembly cannot be fastened directly to the GUIDE-CYLINDER assembly.

Design the PLATE-B part as an interim part to address this issue. Create PLATE-B In-Context of the GUIDE-CYLINDER assembly.

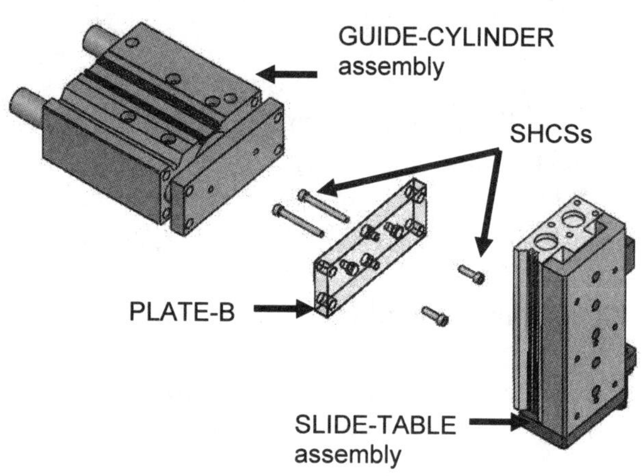

2AXIS-TRANSFER assembly

The 2AXIS-TRANSFER assembly consists of the following models:

- *GUIDE-CYLINDER assembly*
- *PLATE-B part*
- *SLIDE-TABLE assembly*
- *SHCS*

Add the configurations for the GUIDE-CYLINDER, SLIDE-TABLE, and 2AXIS-TRANSFER assemblies to represent physical positions.

Utilize the Configure dimension tool to create the GUIDE-CYLINDER configurations: *Normal*, and *Extended.*

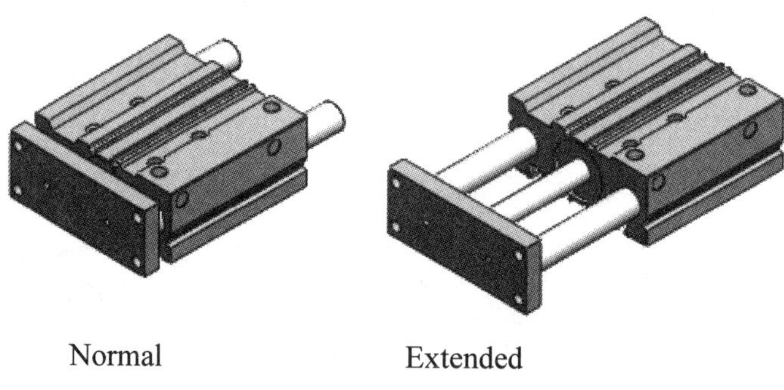

Normal   Extended

GUIDE-CYLINDER Configuration

The Default name was supplied by SMC as MGPM50-100. The part was either obtained from 3D ContentCentral or from the CD in the book.

Utilize the Configure dimension tool to create the following SLIDE-TABLE configurations: *Normal*, and *Extended*.

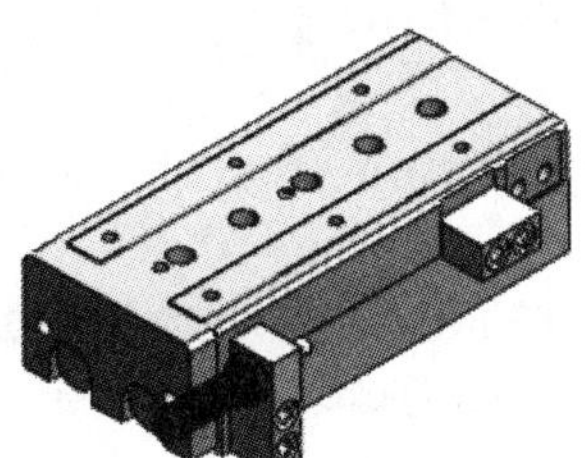

Normal

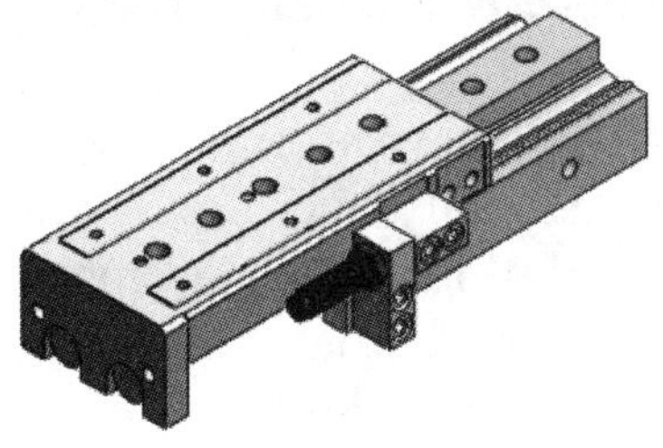

Extended

SLIDE-TABLE Configurations

Combine the GUIDE-CYLINDER *Normal* configuration and *Extended* configuration with the SLIDE-TABLE *Normal* configuration and *Extended* configuration to create the following four new 2AXIS-TRANSFER configurations: *Normal-Normal, Normal-Extended, Extended-Normal, Extended-Extended.*

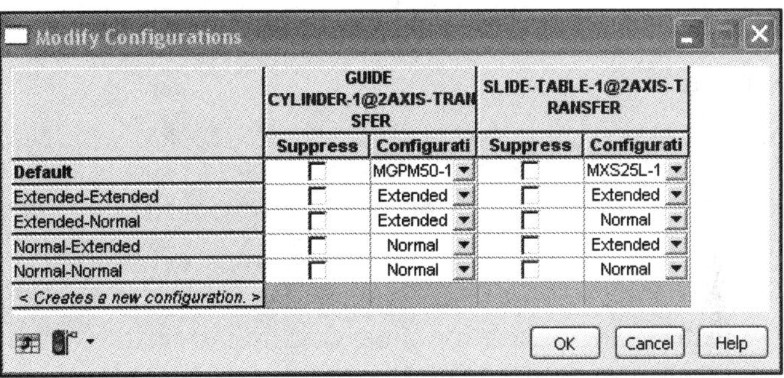

Modify Configurations

	GUIDE CYLINDER-1@2AXIS-TRAN SFER		SLIDE-TABLE-1@2AXIS-T RANSFER	
	Suppress	Configurati	Suppress	Configurati
Default	☐	MGPM50-1	☐	MXS25L-1
Extended-Extended	☐	Extended	☐	Extended
Extended-Normal	☐	Extended	☐	Normal
Normal-Extended	☐	Normal	☐	Extended
Normal-Normal	☐	Normal	☐	Normal
< Creates a new configuration. >				

OK Cancel Help

The GUIDE-CYLINDER configuration is listed first, followed by the SLIDE-TABLE configuration.

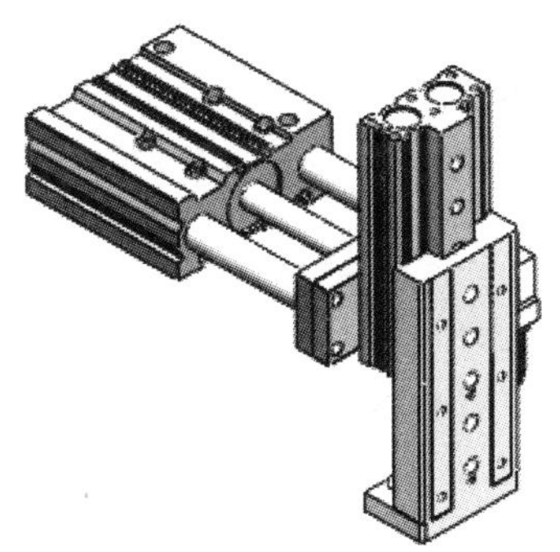

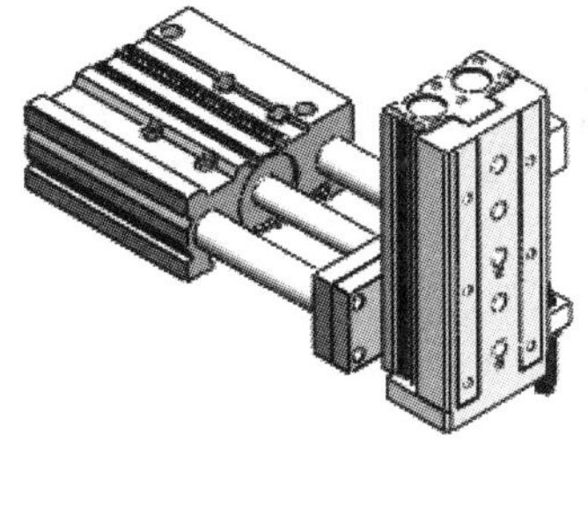

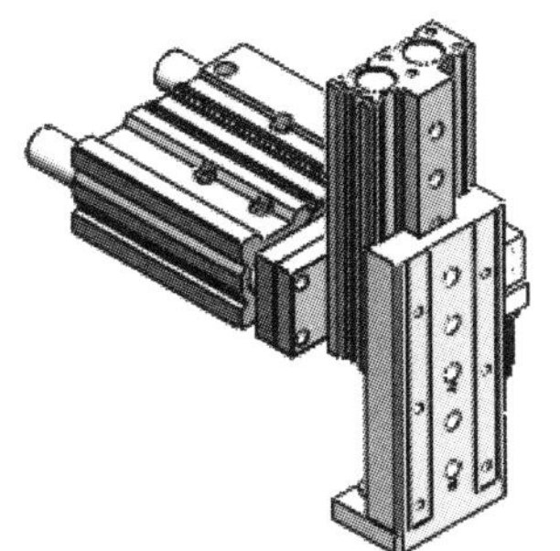

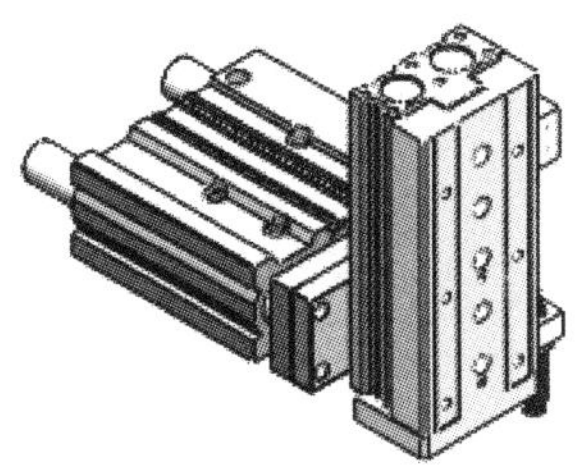

Top-down Design Assembly Modeling Approach

In Top-down assembly design, one or more features of a part are defined by something in an assembly, such as a layout sketch or the geometry of another part. The design intent (sizes of features, placement of components in the assembly, proximity to other parts, etc.) comes from the top (the assembly) and moves down (into the parts), hence the phrase “Top-down."

Whenever you create a part or feature using Top-down techniques, External references are created to the geometry you referenced.

There are three methods to start a Top-down design assembly approach:

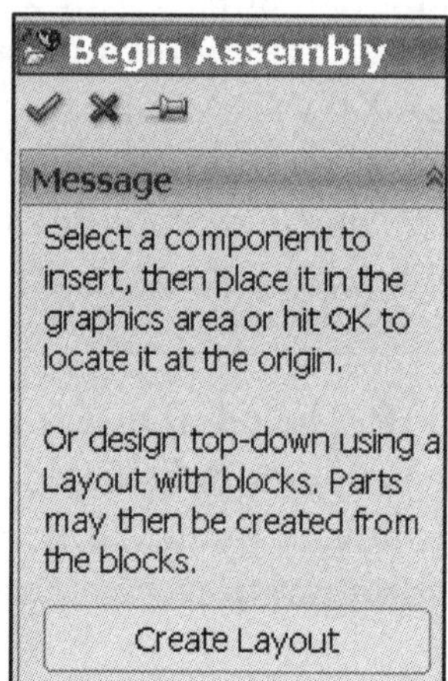

- **Method 1**: Start with a *Layout Sketch* in the assembly. An entire assembly can be designed from the Top-down, by first building a layout sketch that defines component locations, key dimensions, etc. Then build 3D parts, so the 3D parts follow the sketch for their size and location. The speed and flexibility of the sketch provides the ability to quickly try several versions of the design before building any 3D geometry. Even after you build the 3D geometry, the sketch allows you to make a large number of changes in one central location.
- **Method 2**: Start with a *component* in the assembly. Complete parts can be built with Top-down assembly methods by creating new components In-Context of the assembly. The component you build is actually attached (mated) to another existing component in the assembly. The geometry for the component you build is based on the existing component. This method is useful for parts like brackets and fixtures, which are mostly or completely dependent on other parts to define their shape and size.
- **Method 3**: Start with an *individual feature*. Individual features can be designed with Top-down assembly methods by referencing other parts in the assembly. In Bottom-up assembly design, a part is built in a separate window where only that part is visible. However, SolidWorks also allows you to edit parts while working in the assembly window. This makes all of the other components' geometry available to reference.

This method is helpful for those parts that are mostly static but have certain features that interface with other assembly components.

In Method 1, all major components are positioned based on a 2D sketch. Relationships between sub-assemblies must be maintained for proper fit. Utilize Method 1 later in this book.

In Method 2, relationships are derived from an existing component in the assembly. Utilize Method 2 for the PLATE-B part in this section.

Develop the PLATE-B part In-Context of the existing GUIDE-CYLINDER assembly. The PLATE-B part contains In-Context relations.

In-Context

You can create a new part in the context of an assembly. That way you can use the geometry of other assembly components while designing the part. The new part is saved as a virtual component. Virtual components are saved internally in the assembly file in which they are created, instead of in a separate part file. When you create components in the context of an assembly, the software saves them inside the assembly file as virtual components. Later, you can save the components to external files or delete them.

During the conceptual design process, when you frequently experiment with and make changes to the assembly structure and components, using virtual components has several advantages over the Bottom-up assembly method:

- You can rename these virtual components in the FeatureManager design tree, avoiding the need to open, save as a copy, and use the Replace Components command.
- You can make one instance of a virtual component independent of other instances in a single step.
- The folder where you store your assembly is not cluttered with unused part and assembly files resulting from iterations of component designs.

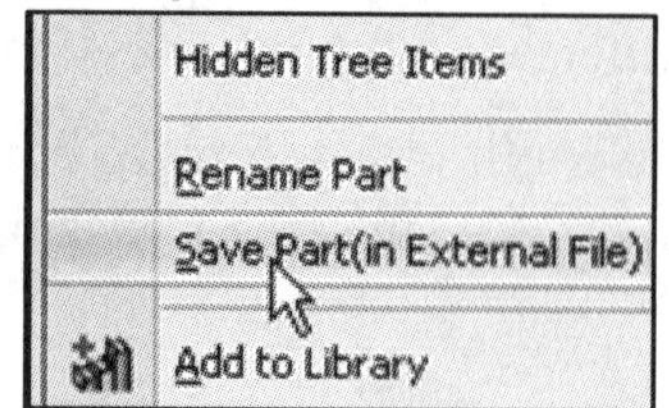

To save a virtual component to its own external file, right-click the component and select **Save Part(in External File)** or **Save Assembly(in External file)**. See Project 8 for examples.

You can also create a new sub-assembly in the context of the top-level assembly.

External References

External references are created when one document is dependent on another document for its solution. In an assembly, you can create an In-Context feature on one component that references the geometry of another component. This In-context feature has an External reference to the other component. If you modify the geometry on the referenced component, the associated In-context feature changes accordingly.

An In-context feature updates automatically if the update path is available. The update path is contained in the assembly where you create the reference. If the update path is not available (for example, if the assembly document is closed), updating occurs the next time you open the assembly that contains the update path.

Update paths for In-context features are displayed in the FeatureManager design tree of the assembly with this icon.

You can hide or show all of these Updated paths In-context icons by right-clicking the top-level assembly icon and selecting **Hide Update Holders** or **Show Update Holders**.

You also have the option to not create External references when designing in the context of an assembly.

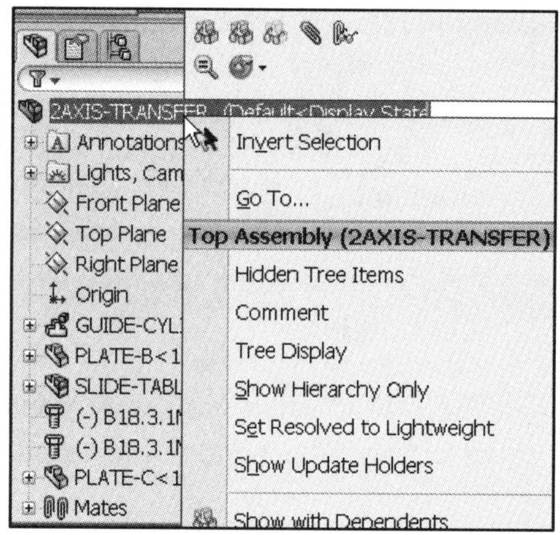

External References - Suffix

In the FeatureManager design tree, any item with an External reference has a suffix that indicates the status of the reference.

- The suffix -> means that the reference is In-Context. It is solved and up-to-date.
- The suffix **->?** means that the reference is out-of-context. The feature is not solved or not up-to-date. To solve and update the feature, open the assembly that contains the update path.
- The suffix ->* means that the reference is locked.
- The suffix ->**x** means that the reference is broken.

External References – Lock / Break

You can lock, unlock, or break the External references of a component. When you *lock* the external references on a component, the existing references no longer update and you cannot add any new references to that component.

Once you *unlock* the External references, you can add new references or edit the existing references.

When you *break* the External references, the existing external references no longer update and you can add new references to the component.

To list the External references in a part or feature: **Right-click** the part or the feature with the External reference or right-click **the update holder**, and select **List External Refs**. The referenced components, features, and entities are listed, as well as the status of each reference.

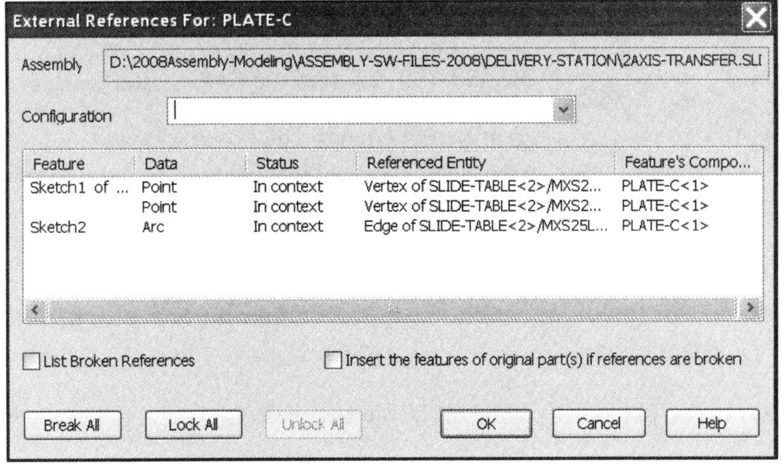

2AXIS-TRANSFER Assembly

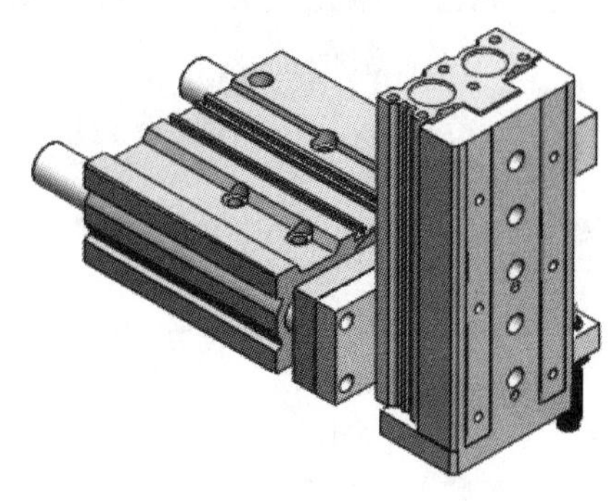

Create an assembly called 2AXIS-TRANSFER assembly. Determine the specific features required to create the PLATE-B part using the Top-down design assembly approach.

Utilize the New Part tool from the Consolidated Insert Components toolbar to create PLATE-B In-Context of the GUIDE-CYLINDER assembly. Redefine the orientation of the GUIDE-CYLINDER assembly. The Float option removes the Fixed constraint in the FeatureManager.

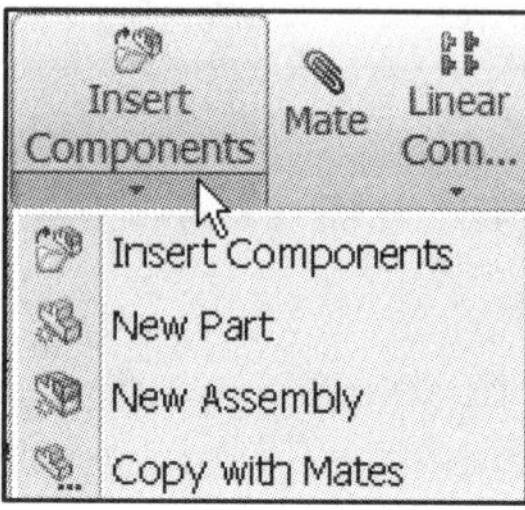

Utilize the 2AXIS-TRANSFER default reference planes: Front Plane, Top Plane, and Right Plane.

The reference planes provide an accurate method to locate the first component in an assembly at the required orientation.

To rotate a component by an exact value, select Rotate Component. Select the By Delta XYZ option. Enter an angular value.

Activity: Create the 2AXIS-TRANSFER Assembly

Close all documents.

1) Click **Window**, **Close** All from the Menu bar menu.

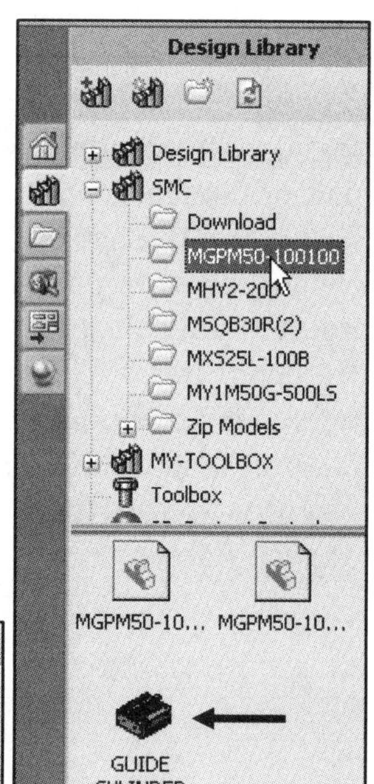

Open the GUIDE-CYLINDER assembly from the Design Library.

2) Double-click **MGPM50-100100** from the SMC folder.

3) Click and drag **GUIDE-CYLINDER** into the Graphics window. The GUIDE-CYLINDER assembly is displayed in the Graphic window.

Create a new assembly.

4) Click **Make Assembly from Part/Assembly** from the Menu bar toolbar.

5) Select the **MY-TEMPLATES** tab.

6) Double-click **ASM-MM-ANSI**. The Begin Assembly PropertyManager is displayed.

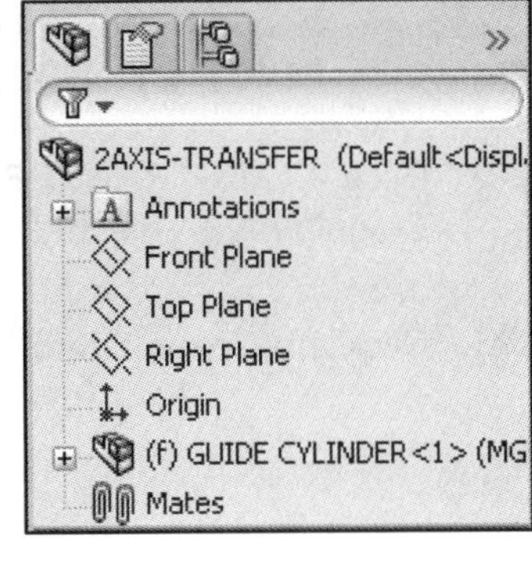

7) Click **OK** from the Begin Assembly PropertyManager. The GUIDE-CYLINDER is fixed to the Origin. Note: If required, click **View**, uncheck **Planes** to hide all planes.

Display an Isometric view.

8) Click **Isometric** view from the Heads-up View toolbar.

Save the assembly.

9) Click **Save**.

10) Select **DELIVERY-STATION** for the save folder.

11) Enter **2AXIS-TRANSFER** for file name.

12) Click **Save**. The 2AXIS-TRANSFER FeatureManager is displayed.

13) Click **View**, un-check **Origins** from the Menu bar menu.

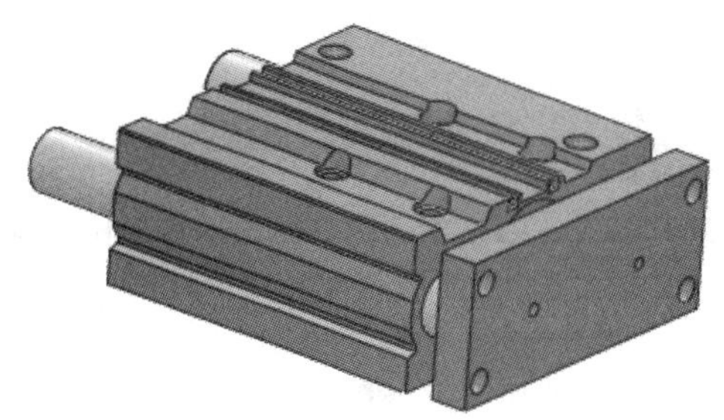

Float the GUIDE-CYLINDER.

14) Right-click **(f)GUIDE-CYLINDER** from the FeatureManager.

15) Click **Float**. The GUIDE-CYLINDER entry changes from fixed, (f) to under-defined, (-).

16) **Rotate** the model as illustrated.

Mate the GUIDE-CYLINDER. Create a Coincident mate.

17) **Expand** GUIDE-CYLINDER from the FeatureManager.

18) Right-click **GUIDE-CYLINDER\Plane3**.

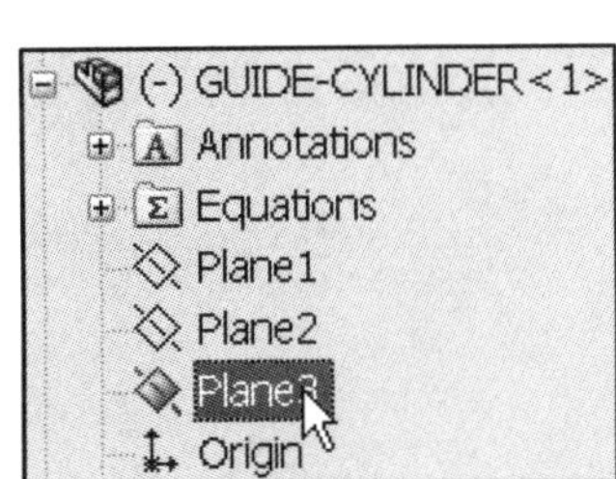

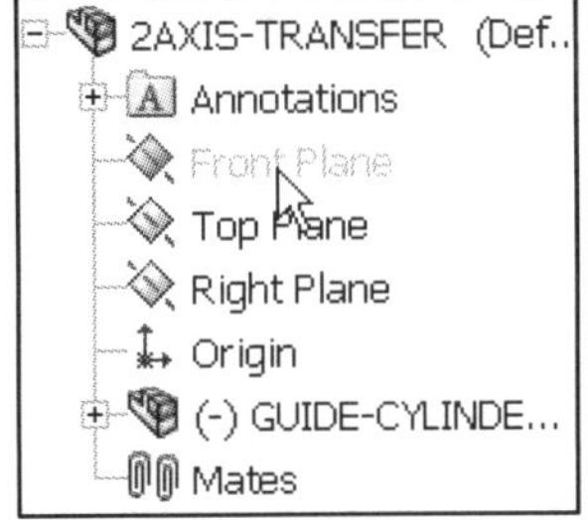

19) Click the **Mate** tool from the Context toolbar. The Mate PropertyManager is displayed.

20) Click **2AXIS-TRANSFER\Front Plane** from the fly-out FeatureManager. Coincident is selected by default.

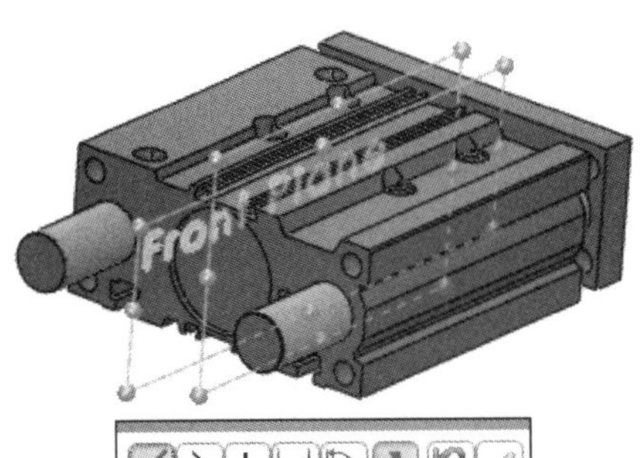

21) Click the **Green Check mark**.

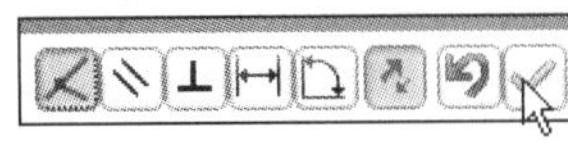

Create the second Coincident mate.

22) Click **GUIDE-CYLINDER\Plane2**.

23) Click **2AXIS-TRANSFER\Top Plane**. Coincident is selected by default.

24) Click the **Green Check mark** ✔.

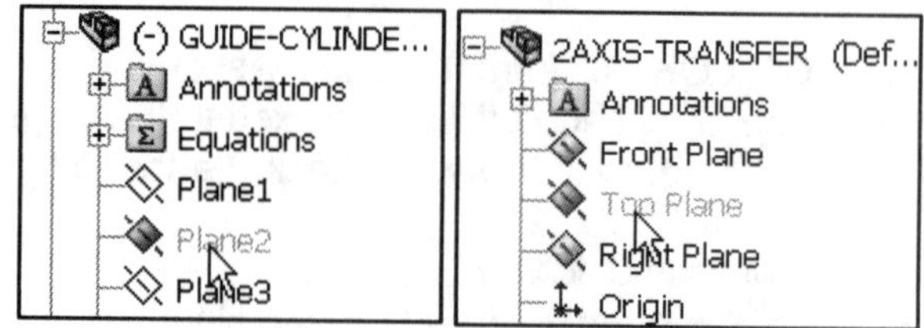

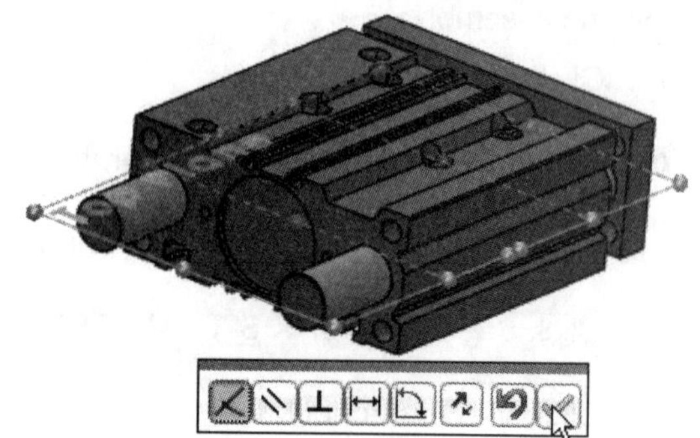

Create the third Coincident mate.

25) Click **GUIDE-CYLINDER\Plane1**.

26) Click **2AXIS-TRANSFER\Right Plane**. Coincident is selected by default.

27) Click the **Green Check mark** ✔.

28) Click **OK** ✔ from the Mate PropertyManager.

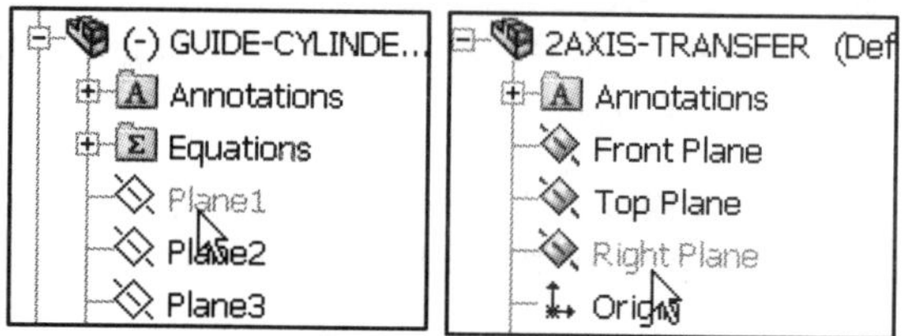

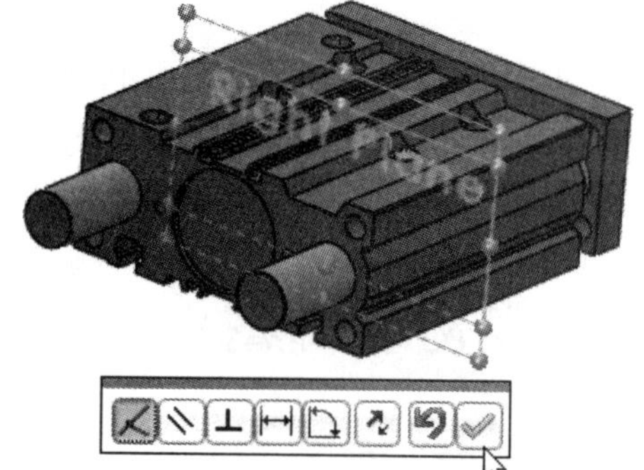

View the created mates.

29) **Expand** the Mates folder from the FeatureManager. View the 3 Mates. The GUIDE-CYLINDER is fully defined in the 2AXIS-TRANSFER assembly.

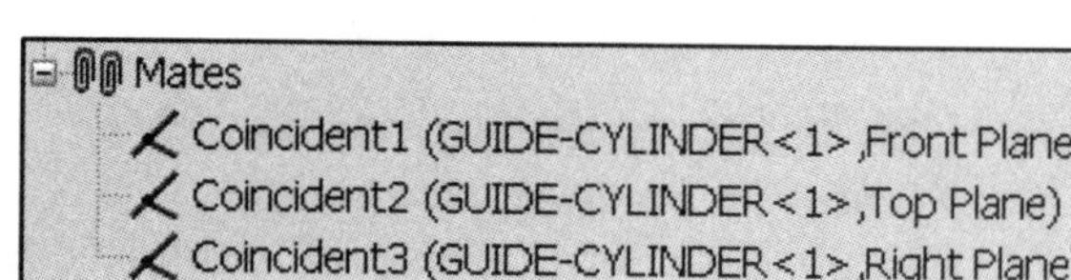

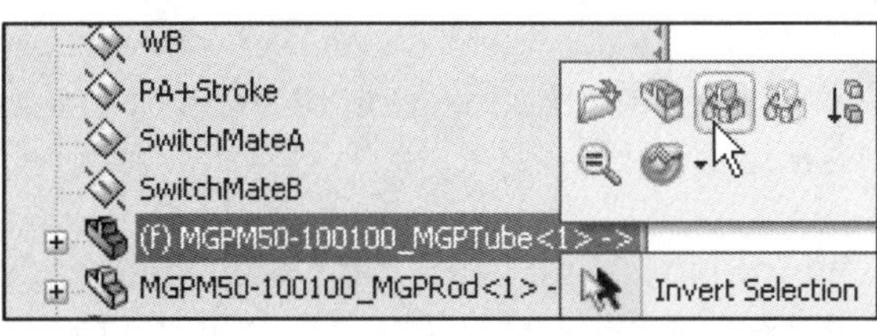

The Fix option provides a fast technique in assembly modeling. As models become more complex, it is difficult to determine where the component Origin is in space. Mating the first component to three planes takes more time but provides orientation flexibility and greater accuracy.

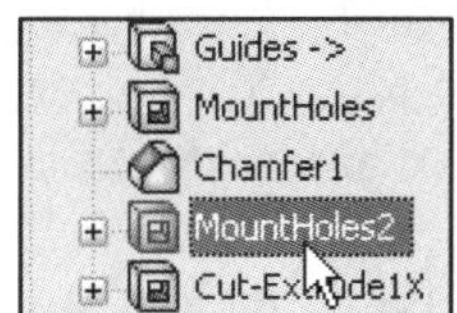

Hide the MGPTube component.

30) Right-click **MGPTube<1>** from the FeatureManager.

31) Click **Hide components**.

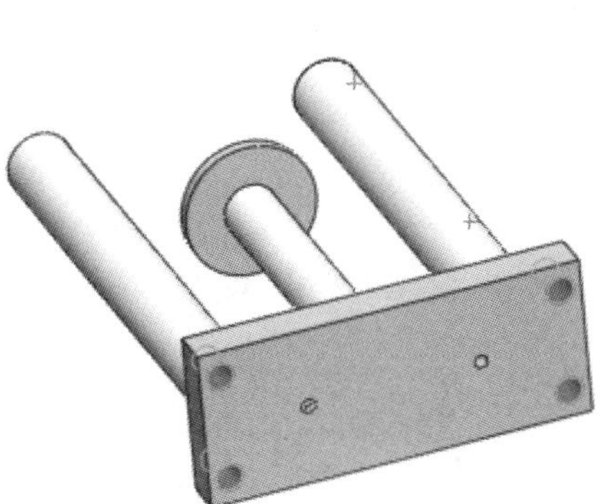

Expand the MGPRod part.

32) **Expand** MPGRod<1> from the 2AXIS-TRANSFER FeatureManager. If require, Set to Resolve.

33) Click **MountHoles2** from the FeatureManager. The four holes are selected in the Graphics window and are displayed in blue.

The PLATE-B part references the MountHoles2 feature.

External References - InPlace Mates

An External reference is a relationship that exists between a sketch entity and geometry outside the sketch. Example: The GUIDE-CYLINDER utilizes reference planes to develop the Base Extrude feature for the MGPTube. An External reference develops an In-context relationship when geometry is referenced outside the part. Example: Create the new PLATE-B part in the context of the 2AXIS-TRANSFER assembly that references the MGPRod component.

If you Do NOT want to create any External references in your part, click **Options**, **External References** and check the **Do not create references external to the model** box.

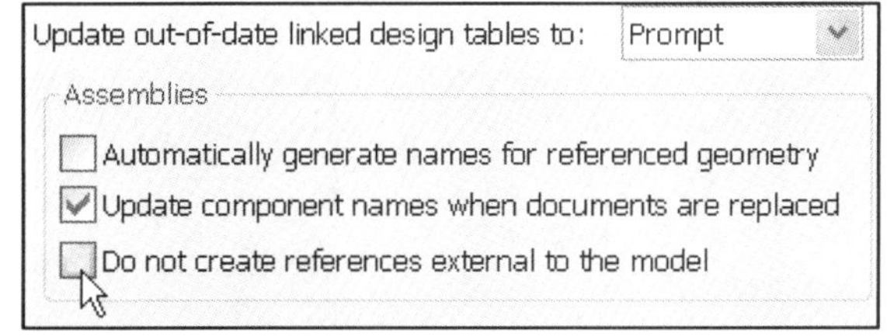

InPlace mates are created automatically for in-context components. InPlace mates are created to prevent movement of the component. This is because the In-context component is attached to geometry of components in the assembly through External references, references that cross between component at the assembly level.

Changing the location of the part can cause changes to the geometry that may not be desired.

The InPlace Mate is a Coincident Mate created between the Front Plane of a new component and the selected planar geometry of the assembly. The component is fully defined; no additional Mates are required to position the component. By default, SolidWorks uses the default templates for new parts and assemblies developed In-context of an existing assembly.

To select a custom Template, define the System Options, Document Templates option before you insert a new component into the assembly.

Create the PLATE-B part In-context of the 2AXIS-TRANSFER assembly, click New Part from the consolidated Insert Components toolbar located in the Assemble toolbar.

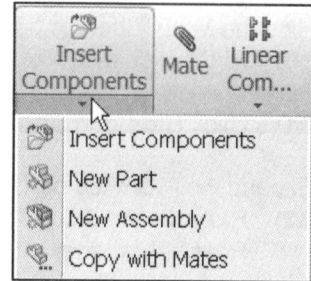

Select the custom Part Template from the MY-TEMPLATES folder. The new part is displayed in the FeatureManager design tree with a name in the form **[Part*n*^*assembly_name*]**. The square brackets indicate that the part is a virtual component. The new Component Pointer icon is displayed. The default component is empty and requires a Sketch plane. The Right face is the Sketch plane. Select the MGPRod right face to create an InPlace Mate reference with the PLATE-B Front Plane. SolidWorks automatically selects the Edit Component icon when inserting a new component.

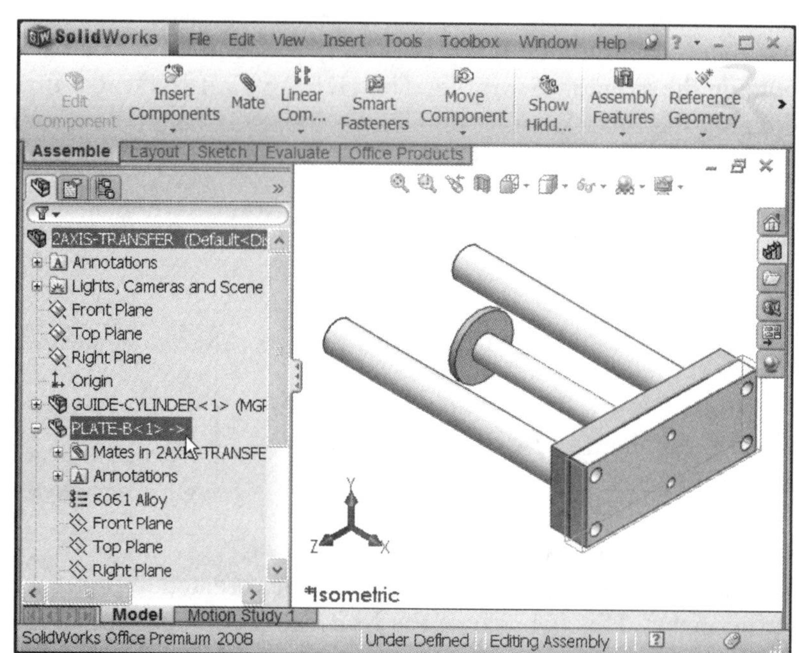

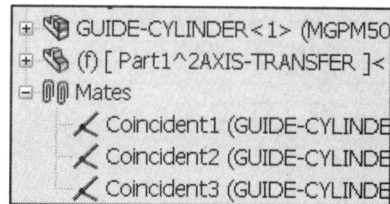

Save the new part as PLATE-B. The PLATE-B blue text is displayed in the FeatureManager. The default blue color indicates that the part is actively being edited.

The right face of the MGPRod part is the current Sketch plane. The current sketch name is Sketch1. The current Graphics window title displays the sketch and name.

Example: "Sketch1 of PLATE-B -in- 2AXIS-TRANSFER."

PLATE-B is the name of the component created In-Context of the 2AXIS-TRANSFER assembly. SolidWorks automatically selects the Sketch tool.

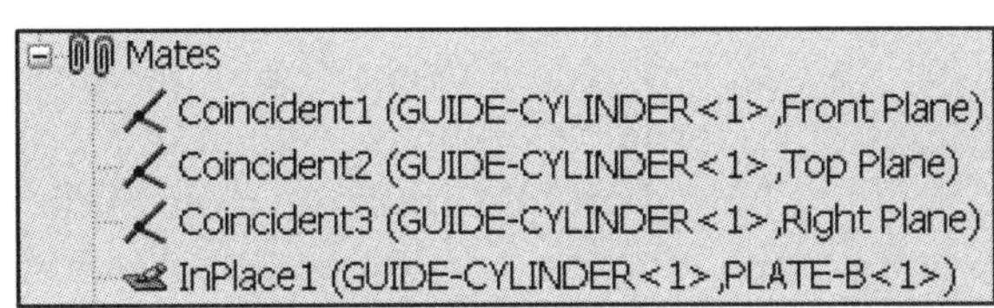

The Mate, InPlace1 (GUIDE-CYLINDER<1>, PLATE-B<1>) fully defines PLATE-B in the 2AXIS-TRANSFER assembly.

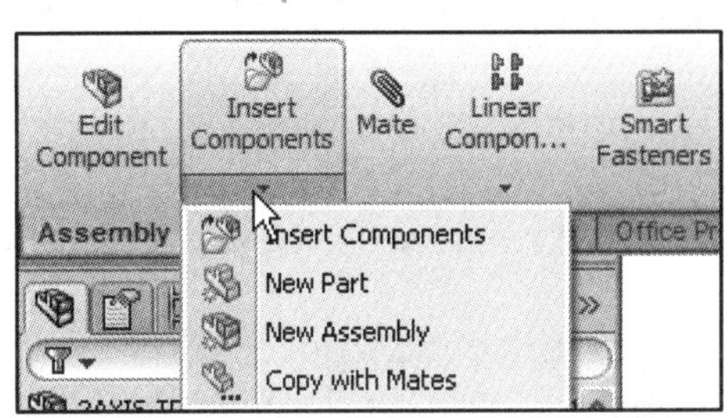

The Assembly toolbar, FeatureManager, and Pop-up Assembly menu display different options.

Review Edit Component, Edit Part, and Edit Sub-assembly tools.

- For components and assemblies, utilize the Edit Component from the Assembly toolbar.
- For components only in an assembly, utilize the Edit Part and the Open Part tools from the Context toolbar.
- For sub-assemblies only, utilize Edit Sub-Assembly and the Open Assembly tools from the Context toolbar.

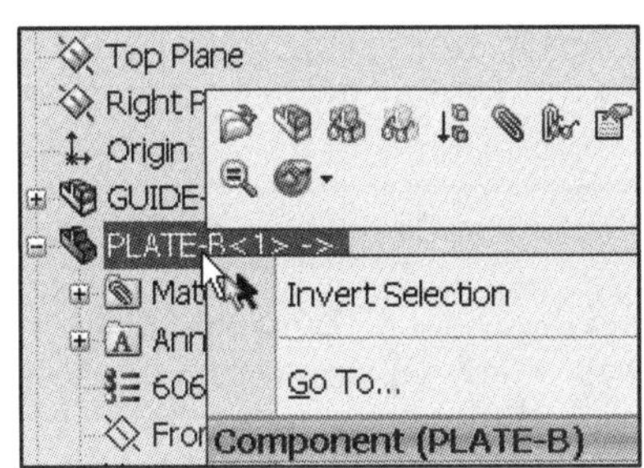

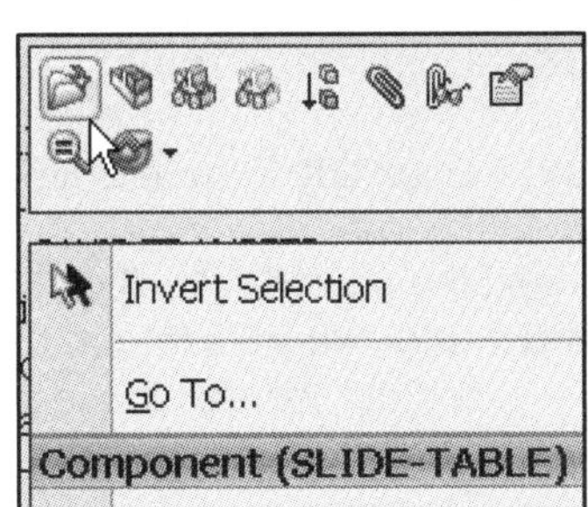

SolidWorks creates External references from the PLATE-B part to the GUIDE-CYLINDER assembly.

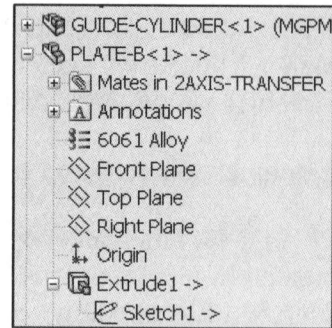

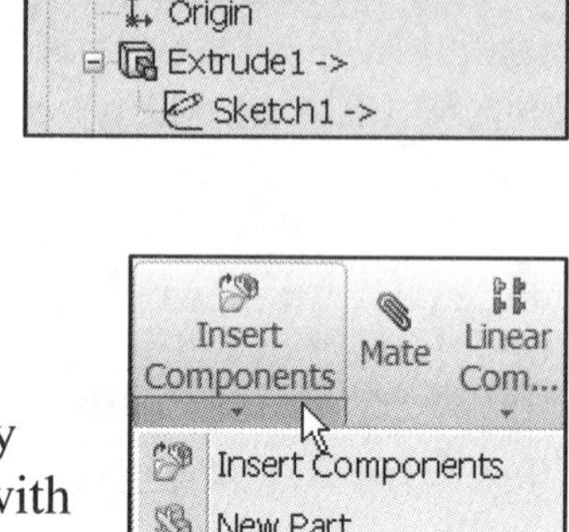

Example: The Extrude1 feature develops an External reference from the Sketch plane. Sketch1 develops External references from the Convert Entities Sketch tool.

The No External References tool develops no InPlace Mates or External references. Select this option before you select the Now Part tool from the Consolidated Insert Components toolbar. Customize the Assemble toolbar in the next activity to include this important option.

The procedure to create a component In-Context of an assembly with no External references is the same as creating a new part with External references. Select a Sketch plane and create the sketch.

If you utilize the Convert Entities tool and Offset Entities Sketch tool, no External references are developed. The new part requires dimensions and relations to fully define the geometry and Mates to constrain its position in the assembly. The Do not create External references option toggles on and off. Insert this tool into the Assemble toolbar.

Activity: Create In-Context, External References, and InPlace Mates

Set the Default Template option.

34) Click **Options** from the Menu bar menu.

35) Click **Default Templates**.

36) Check the **Prompt user to select document template** box.

37) Click **OK** from the System Options box.

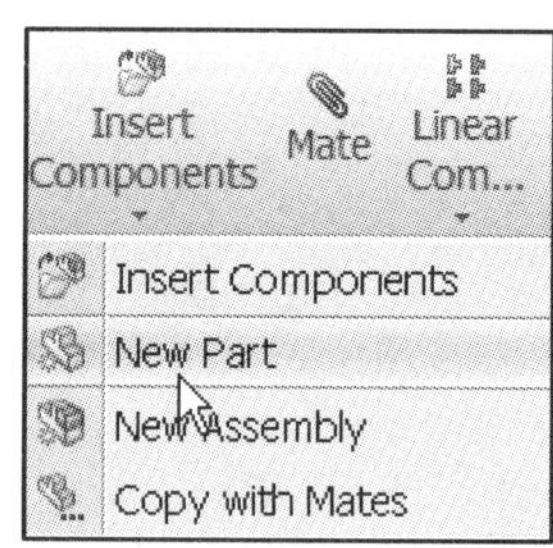

Insert the new PLATE-B part.

38) Click **New Part** from the Consolidated Insert Components toolbar located in the Assembly toolbar.

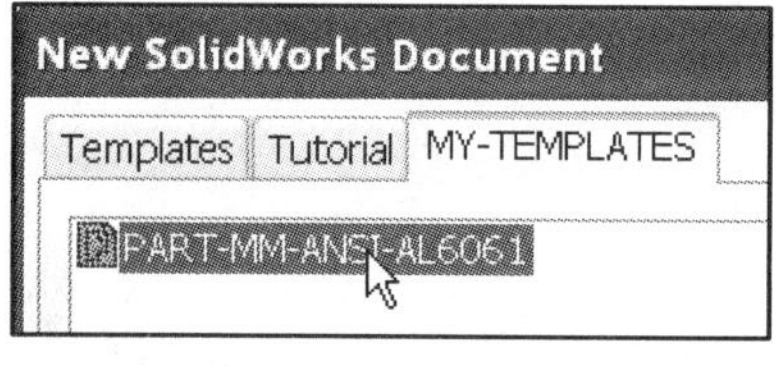

39) Double-click **PART-MM-ANSI-AL6061**. The new part is displayed in the FeatureManager design tree with a name in the form [Part*n*^*assembly_name*]. The square brackets indicate that the part is a virtual component. The new Component Pointer icon is displayed. The default component is empty and requires a Sketch plane. The Right face is the Sketch plane.

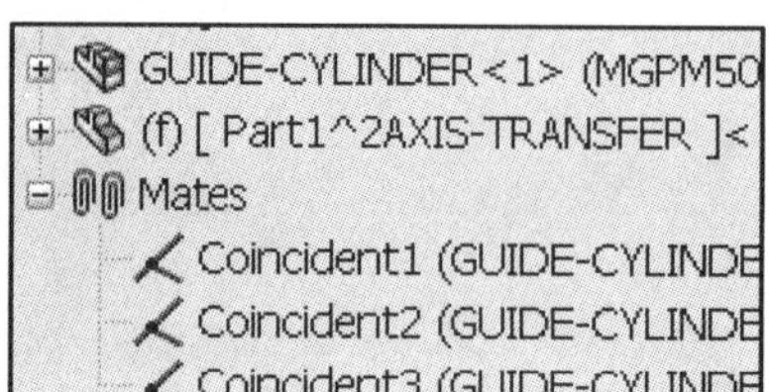

To rename the virtual component in the assembly, right-click the **virtual component** and click **Rename Part.**

To save the virtual component in the assembly, right-click the **virtual component** and click **Save Part (in External File)** to save the part to a true part file(*sldprt) outside the assembly. Saving the assembly will generate the same option. See Project 8 for details.

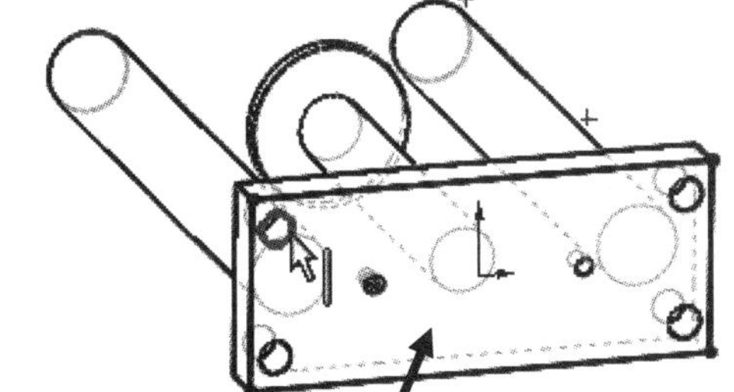

Locate the new part with an InPlace Mate.

40) Click the **right face** of the MGPRod part as illustrated for your Sketch plane. SolidWorks creates the InPlace1 Mate.

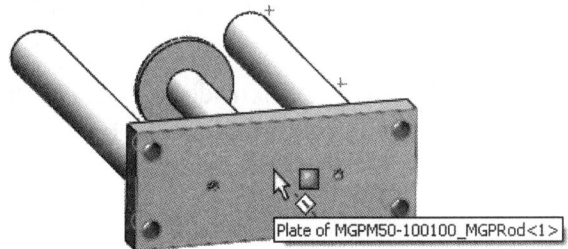

41) Click **Hidden Lines Visible** from the Heads-up View toolbar. If required, **deactivate** the Grid in the Graphics window.

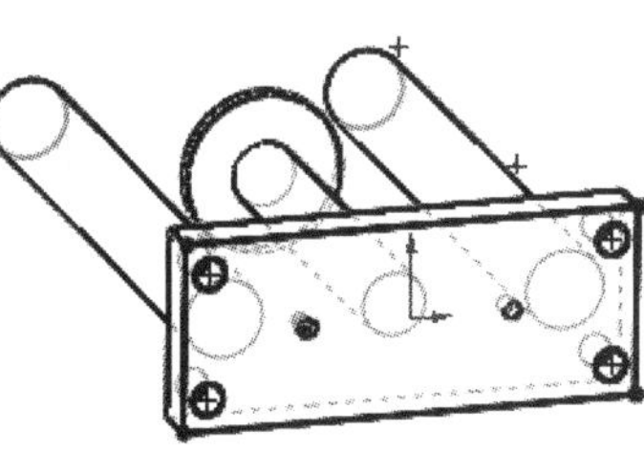

Convert existing edges.

42) Click the **right face** as illustrated.

43) Click the **Convert Entities** tool from the Sketch toolbar.

44) Click the **top left MountHoles2 circle**.

45) Hold the **Ctrl** key down.

46) Click the three other **MountHoles2 circles**. The holes are selected and are displayed in blue.

47) Release the **Ctrl** key.

48) Click the **Convert Entities** tool from the Sketch toolbar.

Direction 1

Blind

15.00mm

Draft outward

Extrude the Sketch.

49) Click **Extruded Boss/Base** from the Features toolbar.

50) Enter **15** for Depth. Blind is the default End Condition in Direction 1.

51) Click **OK** from the Extrude PropertyManager. The part is edited In-Context of the 2AXIS-TRANSFER assembly.

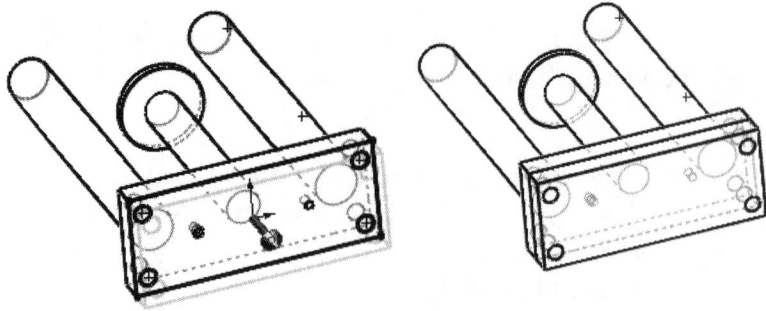

The default or virtual component [Part1^2AXIS-TRANSFER]<1> ->, Extrude1 ->, and Sketch1 -> all contain the "->" symbol indication External references to the 2AXISA-TRANSFER assembly.

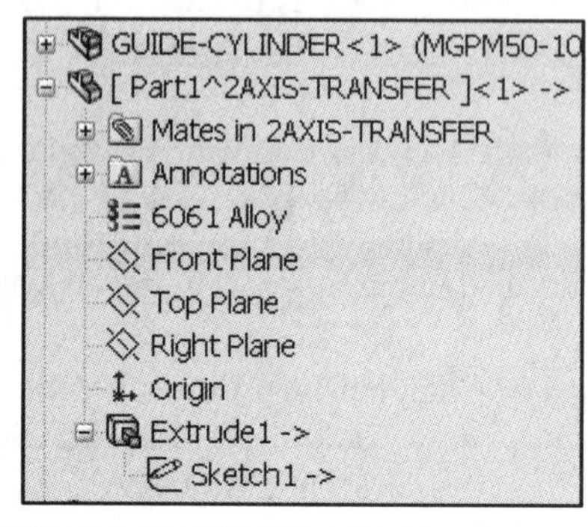

The Edit Component tool acts as a switch between the assembly and the component edited In-Context.

Return to the 2AXIS-TRANSFER assembly.

52) Right-click a **position** in the Graphics window.

53) Click the **Edit Component** tool to return to the assembly.

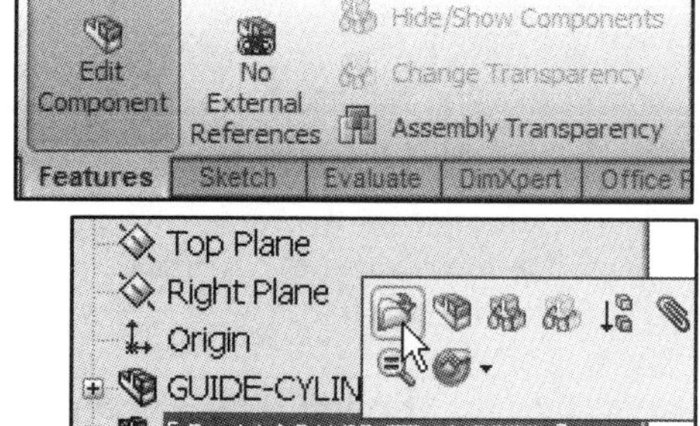

54) **Rebuild** the model.

55) Click **Save**.

Rename the virtual component to PLATE-B.

56) Right-click the **virtual component name**.

57) Click **Open Part** from the Context toolbar.

58) Click **Save As** from the Menu bar toolbar.

59) Click **OK** to the message dialog box.

60) Enter **PLATE-B** in the DELIVERY STATION folder.

61) Click **Save**.

62) **Close** the part. The 2AXIS-TRANSFER assembly is displayed.

63) Click **Save**.

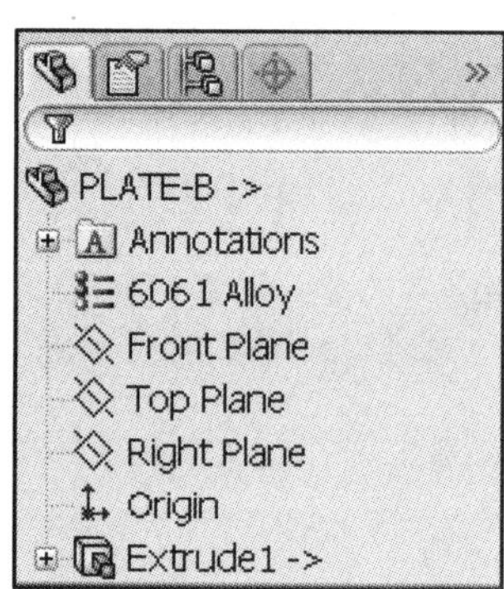

View the In-Place Mate.

64) Right-click **PLATE-B<1> ->** from the FeatureManager.

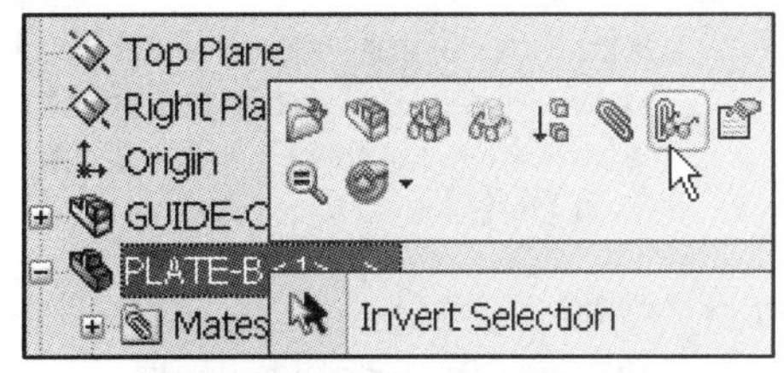

65) Click **View Mates** from the Context toolbar. The InPlace1 Mate lists the component reference: GUIDE-CYLINDER<1>.

66) Click a **position** inside the Graphics window.

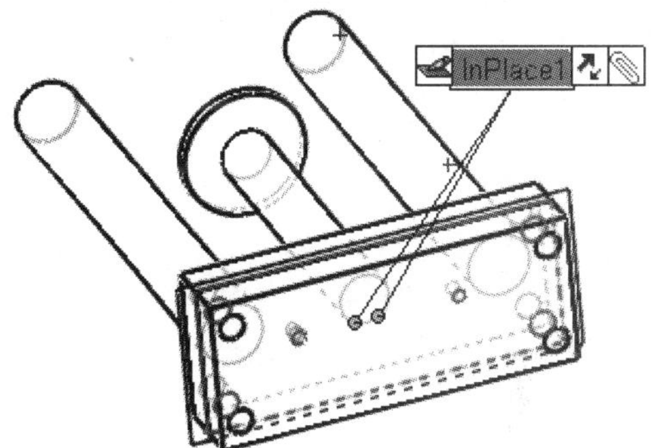

Display the MGPTube part.

67) **Expand** GUIDE-CYLINDER<1> from the FeatureManager.

68) Right-click **MGPTube** from the FeatureManager.

69) Click **Show components** from the Context toolbar.

70) Click **Shaded With Edges** from the Heads-up View toolbar.

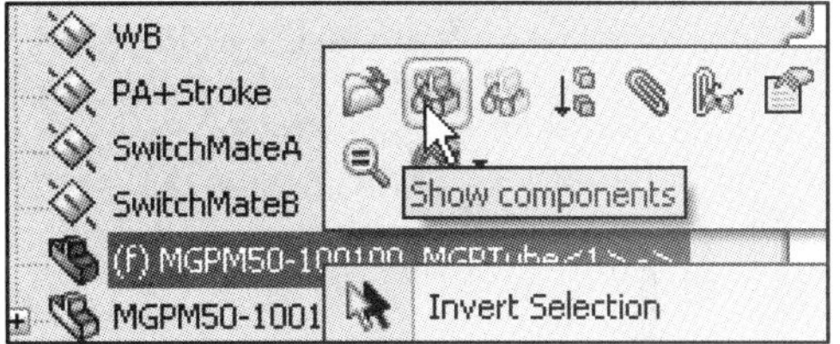

Save the 2AXIS-TRANSFER assembly.

71) Click **Isometric** view from the Heads-up View toolbar.

72) **Rebuild** the model.

73) Click **Save**.

Activity: Review External References in PLATE-B

Open PLATE-B.

74) Right-click **PLATE-B** from the FeatureManager.

75) Click **Open Part** from the Context toolbar. PLATE-B is displayed in the Graphics window. PLATE-B is displayed in the Graphics window.

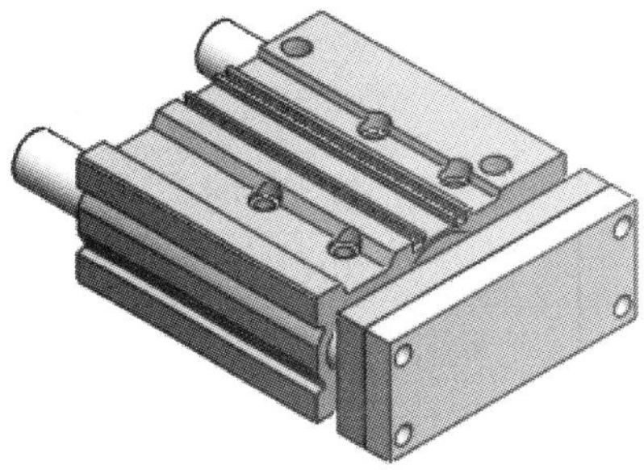

Review External references in PLATE-B.

76) The "->" symbol indicates that there are External references for the PLATE-B part. Right-click **PLATE-B->**.

77) Click **List External Refs**. The External Reference list contains the Feature, Data, Status, Reference Entity, and Feature Component. All External references are defined.

78) Click **OK**.

79) **Close** the part. Return to the 2AXIS-TRANSFER assembly.

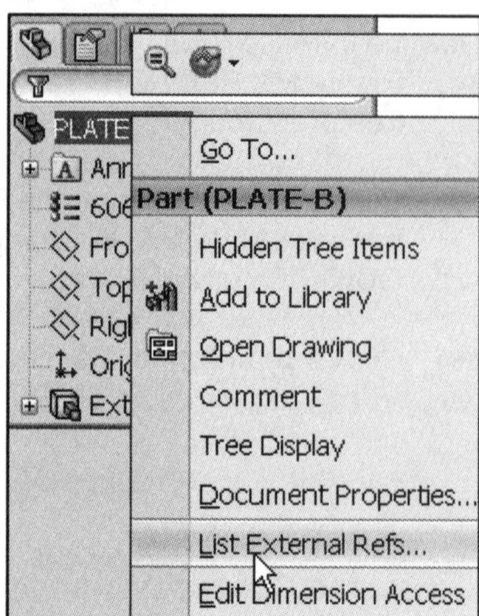

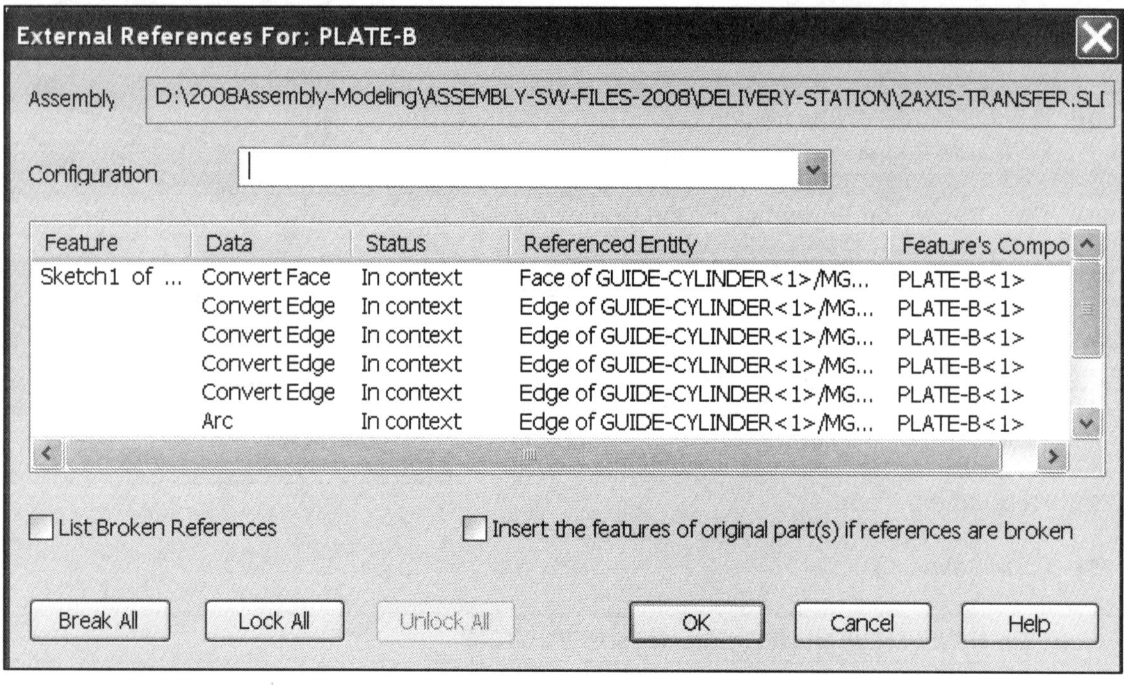

Activity: Customize the Assembly toolbar in the CommandManager

Customize the Assembly toolbar.

80) Click **Tools**, **Customize** from the Menu bar menu. The Customize box is displayed.

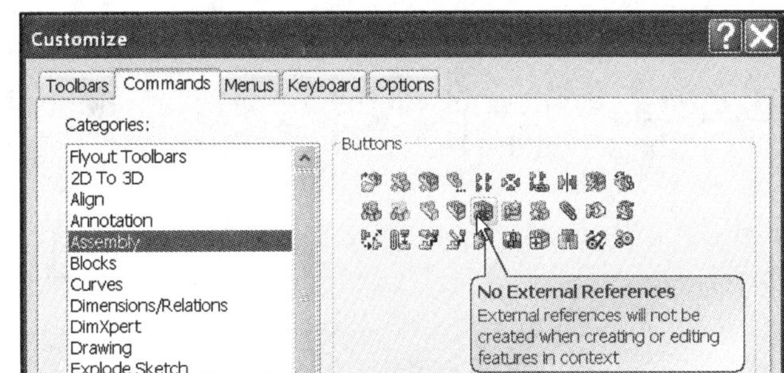

81) Click the **Commands** tab.

82) Select **Assembly** from the Categories list.

83) Drag the **No External References** icon into the Assembly toolbar.

84) Click **OK**. View the updated Assembly toolbar in the CommandManager.

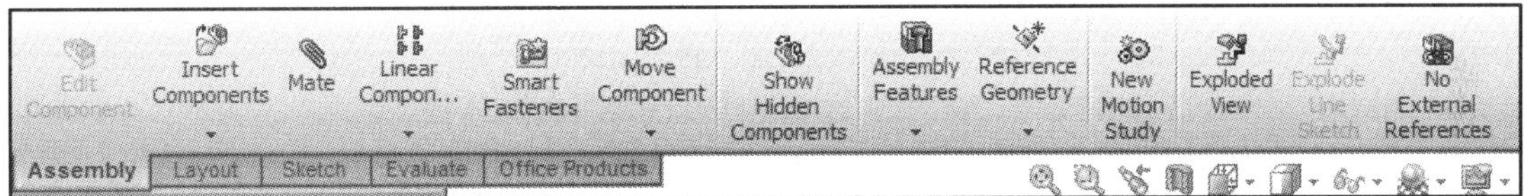

Convert Face entry occurs when you select the sketch plane. Convert Edge and Arc entries occur when you select Convert Entities in Sketch1. The Data column lists External references.

- *Convert Face*
- *Convert Edge*
- *Arc*

The Convert Entities of the MGPRod's right face results in four Convert Edge references. The four Convert Edge references are:

- *Bottom Horizontal Line*
- *Right Vertical Line*
- *Top Horizontal Line*
- *Left Vertical Line*

There are four Arc references. The Convert Entities of the four MountHoles2 circles created the Arc references. From the 2AXIS-TRANSFER assembly, utilize two additional methods to access External references.

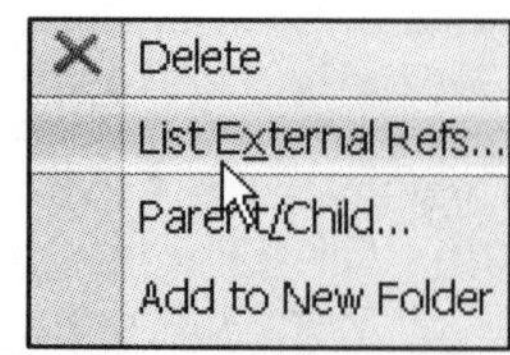

Method 1: Right-click on an In-Context component in the FeatureManager or in the Graphics window. Click List External Refs.

Method 2: Right-click on the top level assembly icon. Click Show Update Holders.

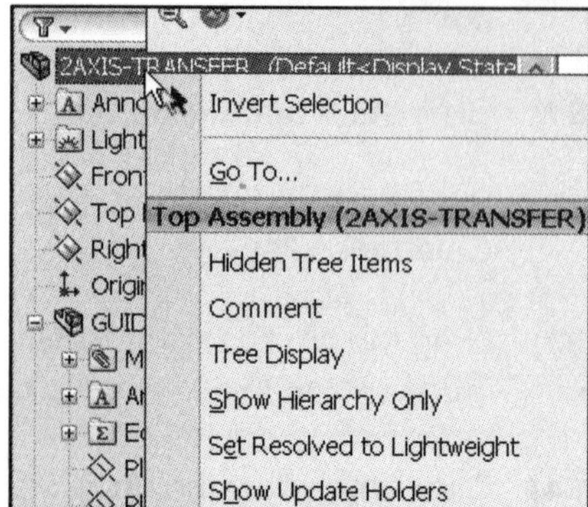

SolidWorks creates an Update Holder for each External sketch reference. The Update Holders are displayed at the bottom of the FeatureManager.

The Update Holder entry contains the option to List External Refs. Reduce the size of the FeatureManager. Select the default Hide Update Holders.

Hole Selection

Hole selection becomes an important decision in machine design. You decide on the hole type, placement, and feature selection. Four Ø10mm SHCSs fasten the PLATE-B part to the GUIDE-CYLINDER assembly.

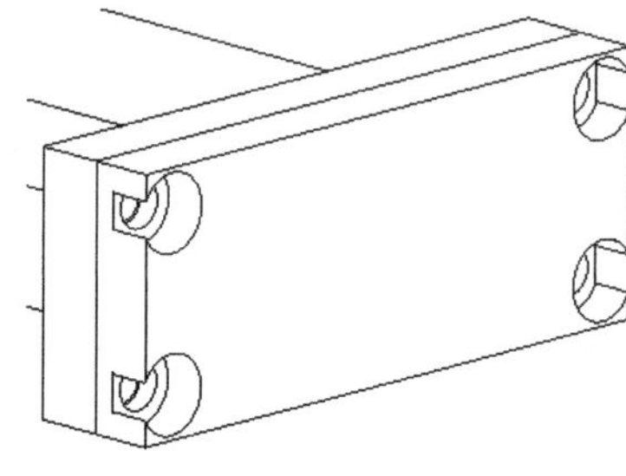

Should the holes utilize a counterbore? Answer: No. The holes are too close to the edge of the PLATE-B part. Do you enlarge PLATE-B to accommodate the counterbore? Answer: No. Increasing the part size adds additional weight and cost.

You must decide whether to create the PLATE-B holes in a Top-down design approach with External references, or a Bottom-up design approach with no External references.

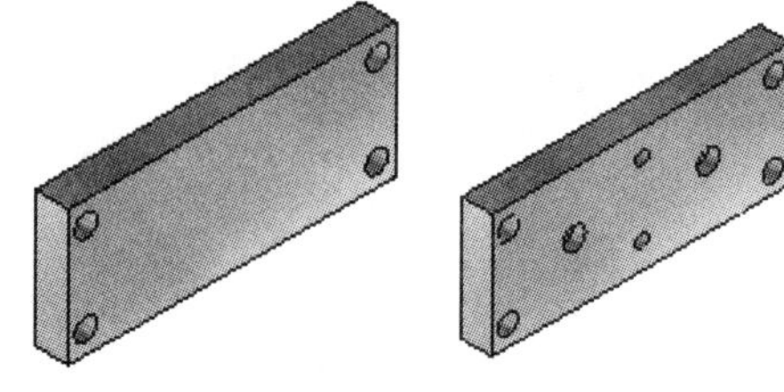

PLATE-B

Examine the SLIDE-TABLE assembly to determine the fastener type. Are additional holes required to mount the SLIDE-TABLE assembly to PLATE-B? Answer: Yes. Add two additional holes.

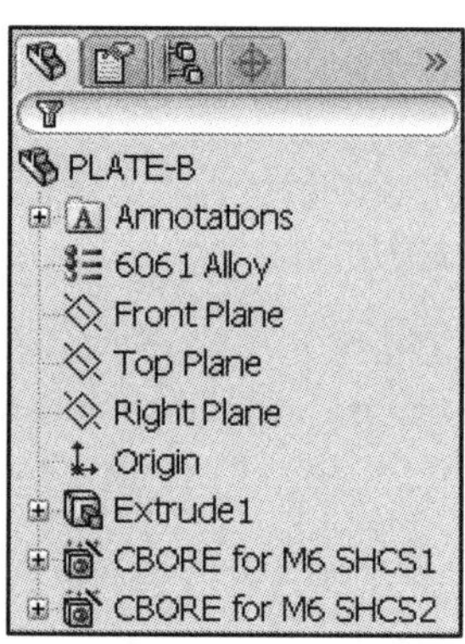

There are two major components in the SLIDE-TABLE assembly:

1.) MXSL-Body

2.) MXSL-Table

The MXSL-Body back face mates to the PLATE-B front face. Simplify the mate process. Hide the MXSL-Table. Utilize BodyThruHole4 and BodyThruHole5, closest to the bottom face. Create two M6 Cbores in the PLATE-B part that correspond to the ThruHoles in the MXSLTable. No External references are created in this Bottom-Up approach.

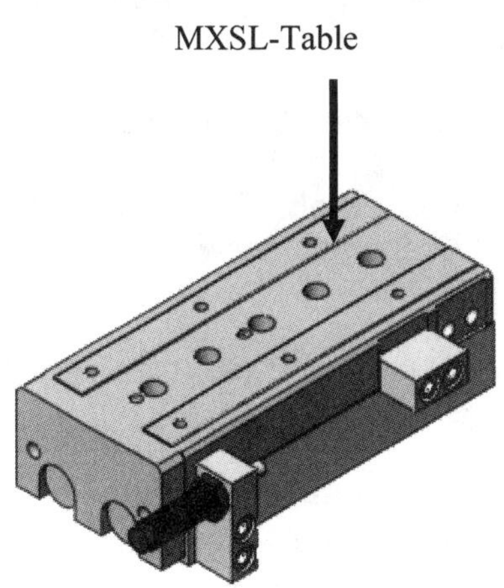

SLIDE-TABLE assembly

Minimize the use of External references from multiple parts. Multiple part references lead to problems in higher levels of the assembly. External references require additional modification when dissolving components and forming sub-assemblies used in other projects.

Remember, if you Do NOT want to create any External references in your part, click **Options, External References** and check the **Do not create references external to the model** box. We will create them to show how to delete External references in this section.

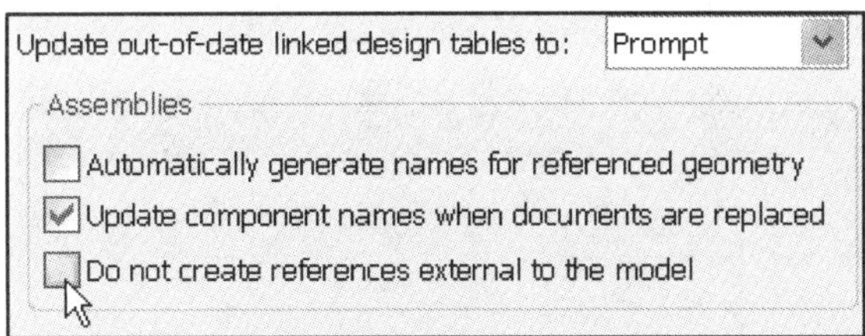

Avoid unnecessary references. Do not work continuously in the Edit Component mode for individual parts. Open the part. Insert additional features at the part level. The individual part is less complex than an assembly. Rebuild time is quicker.

Activity: Hole Selection for the PLATE-B Part to the GUIDE-CYLINDER Assembly

Hide the GUIDE-CYLINDER assembly.

85) Right-click **GUIDE-CYLINDER** from the FeatureManager.

86) Click **Hide components** from the Context toolbar. PLATE-B is displayed in the Graphics window.

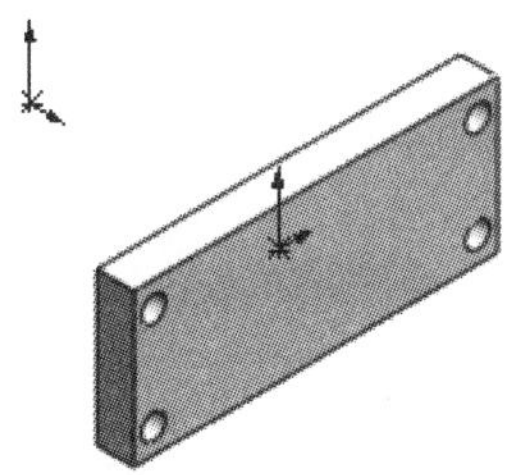

Display the Origin.

87) Click **View**, check **Origins** from the Menu bar menu.

Do not suppress the GUIDE-CYLINDER assembly. The Mates will be suppressed and the 2AXIS-TRANSFER assembly will no longer be constrained.

The 2AXIS-TRANSFER assembly determines the location of the PLATE-B Origin.

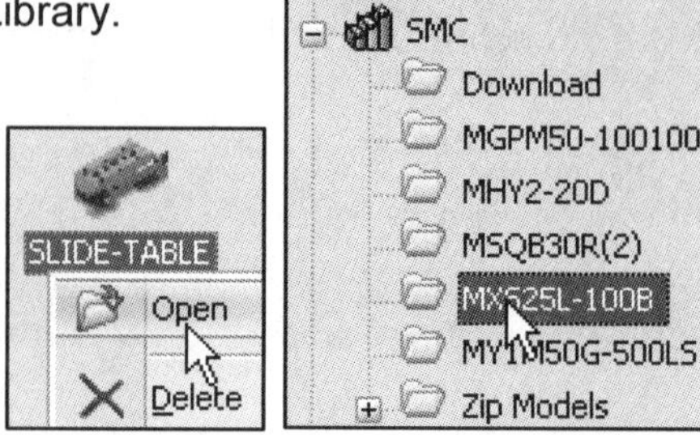

Open the SLIDE-TABLE assembly.

88) Click the **SMC\MXS25L-100B** folder from the Design Library.

89) Right-click **SLIDE-TABLE**.

90) Click **Open**. The SLIDE-TABLE is displayed in the Graphics window.

View the holes.

91) Right-click **MXSL-Table(25-100L)<1>** from the FeatureManager.

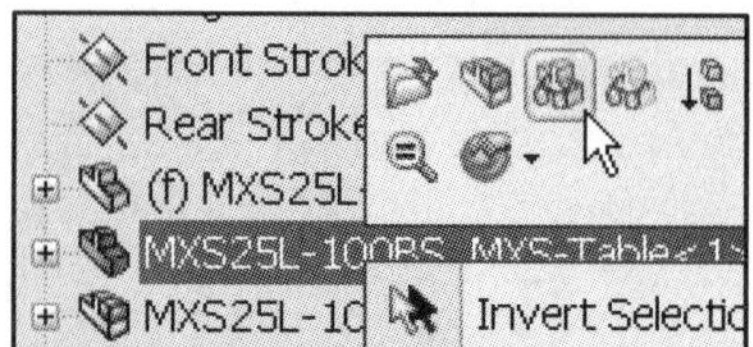

92) Click **Hide components** from the Context toolbar. View the holes and their location. Note: As an exercise, apply the Measure tool to the holes and their locations.

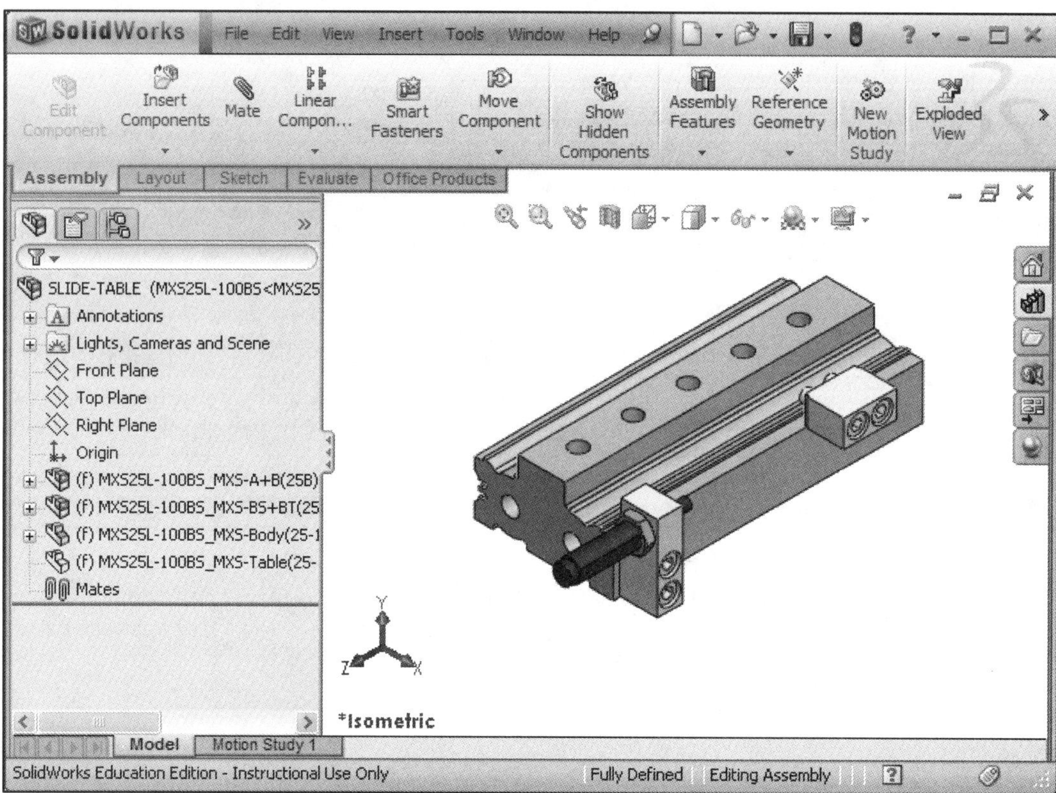

Display the MXSL-Table(25-100L)<1> from the FeatureManager.

93) Right-click **MXSL-Table(25-100L)<1>.**

94) Click **Show components.**

Display an Isometric view.

95) Click **Isometric** view from the Heads-up View toolbar.

96) Click **Save**.

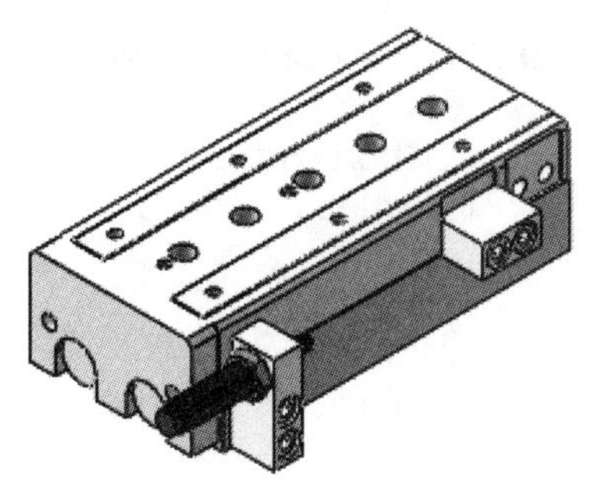

Open the PLATE-B part.

97) Open the **PLATE-B** part. PLATE-B is displayed.

98) Click **Hidden Lines Visible** from the Heads-up View toolbar.

Add two Cbore Holes to the back face of the PLATE-B part. Use the Hole Wizard tool.

99) Click **Back** view from the Heads-up View toolbar.

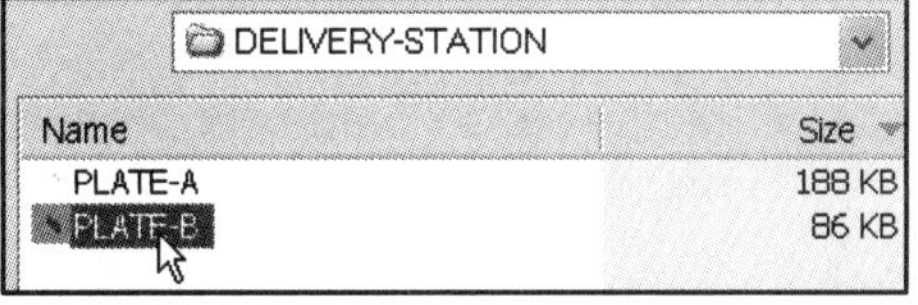

100) Click the **back face** above the Origin.

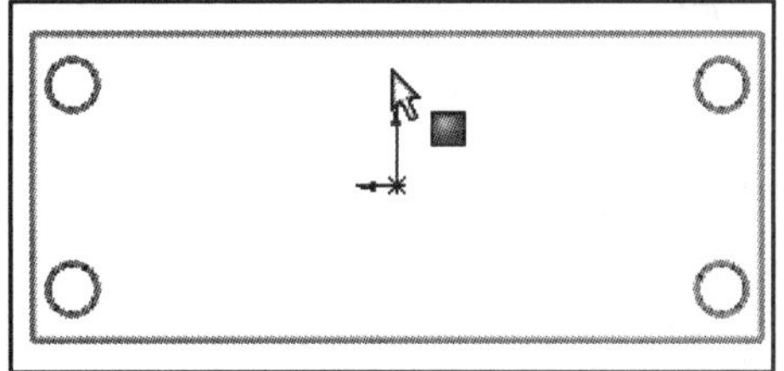

101) Click the **Hole Wizard** tool from the FeatureManager. The Hole Specification PropertyManager is displayed.

Create Cbore Hole1.

102) Click **Counterbore** for Hole Type.

103) Select **Ansi Metric** for Standard.

104) Select **Socket Head Cap Screw** for Type.

105) Select **M6** for Size.

106) Select **Through All** for End Condition.

107) Click the **Positions** tab. The Point icon is displayed.

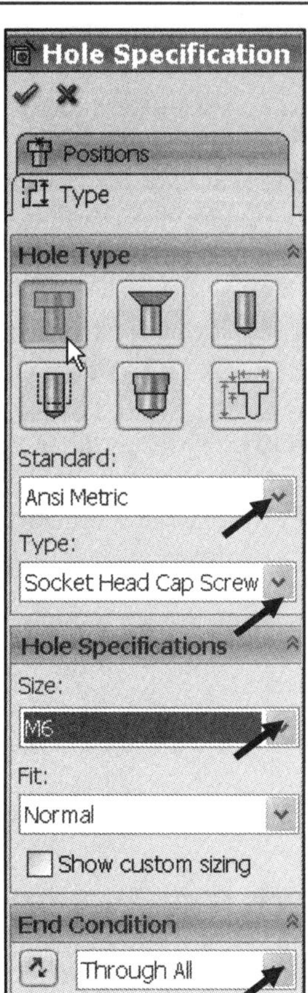

Create a Cbore Hole2.

108) Click a **position** below the Top plane, aligned with the Origin as illustrated. The center point of Cbore Hole2 is displayed in blue. Note: Blue indicates that dimensions and relations are required.

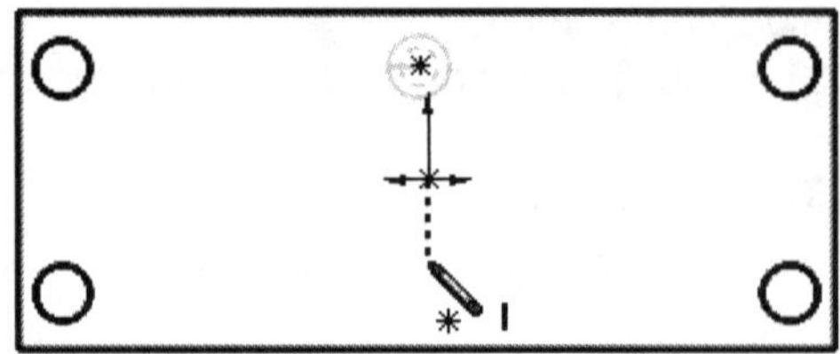

Add a Vertical relation.

109) Right-click **Select** in the Graphics window to deselect the Point Sketch tool.

110) Click the **Origin**. Hold the **Ctrl** key down.

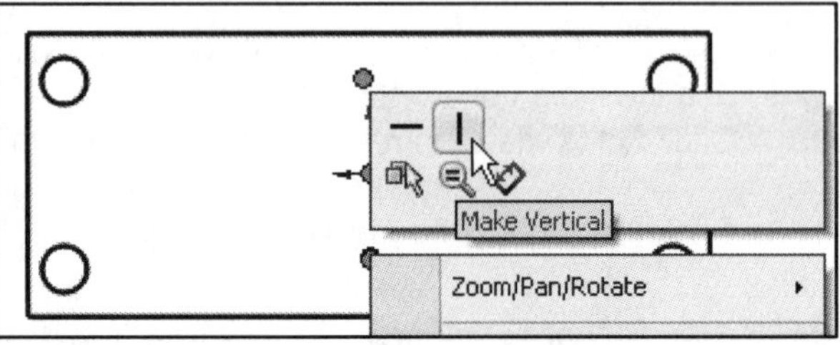

111) Click the **Hole1 center point** and **Hole2 center point**.

112) Release the **Ctrl** key. Right-click **Make Vertical** from the Context toolbar.

113) Click **OK** ✓ from the Properties PropertyManager.

Create a Centerline.

114) Click the **Centerline** ¦ tool from the Sketch toolbar. The Insert Line PropertyManager is displayed.

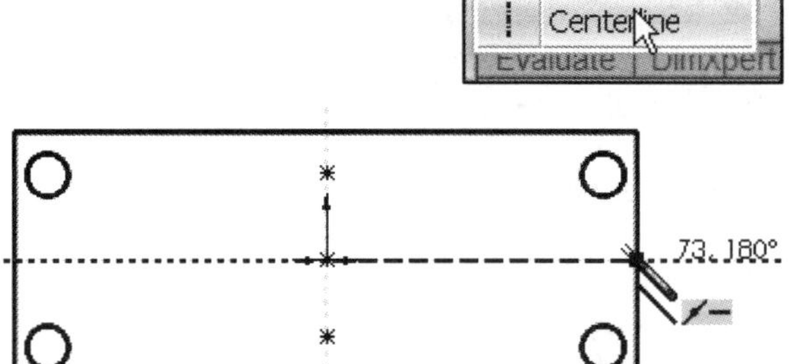

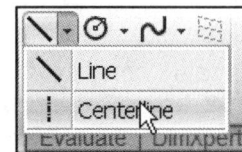

115) Sketch a **horizontal centerline** from the Origin to the midpoint of the right vertical edge as illustrated.

116) Right-click **Select** to deselect the Centerline tool.

Add a Symmetric relation.

117) Click the **centerline**. Hold the **Ctrl** key down.

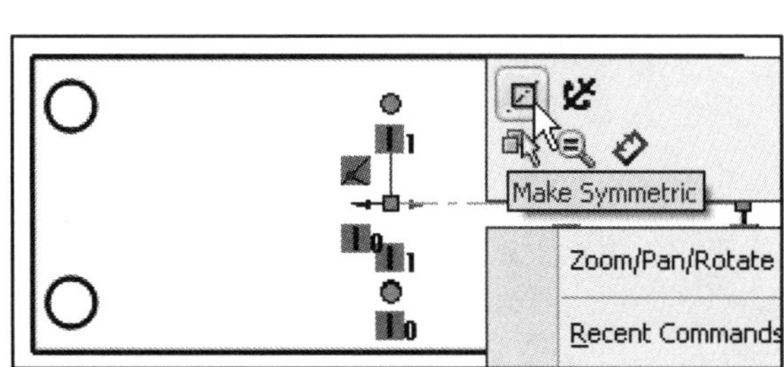

118) Click the **Hole1 center point** and the **Hole2 center point**.

119) Release the **Ctrl** key.

120) Right-click **Make Symmetric** from the Context toolbar.

121) Click **OK** ✓ from the Properties PropertyManager.

Add a vertical dimension.

122) Click the **Smart Dimension** tool from the Sketch toolbar.

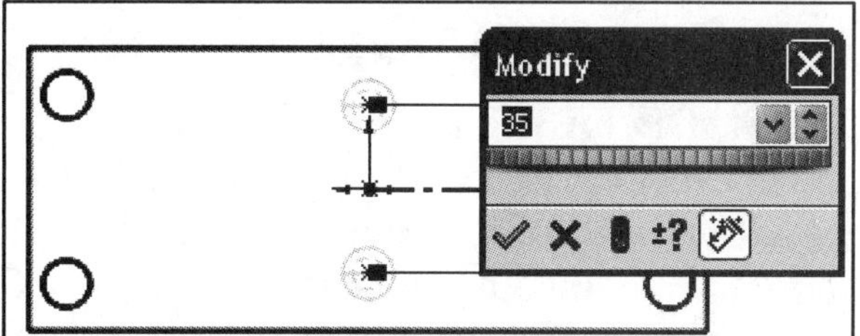

123) Click the **Hole1 center point** and the **Hole2 center point**.

124) Enter **35**.

125) Click the **Green Check mark** ✔. The hole center points are fully defined.

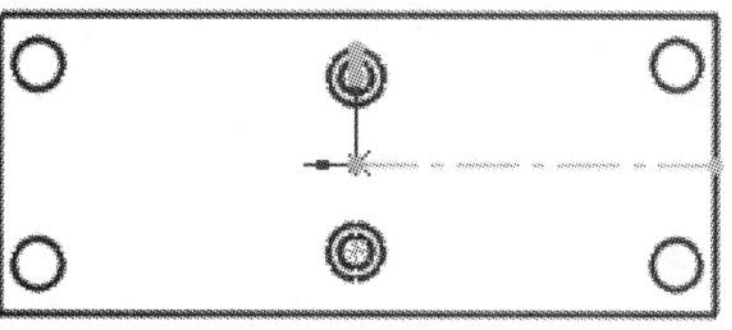

126) Click **OK** ✔ from the Dimension PropertyManager.

127) Click **OK** ✔ from the Hole Position PropertyManager.

Display an Isometric view.
128) Click **Isometric** view.

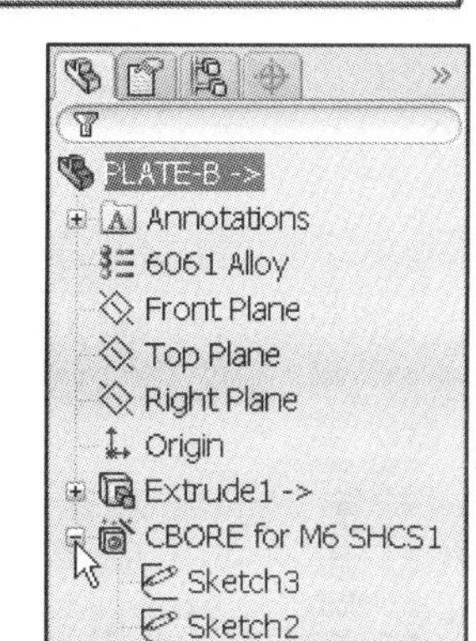

Save the PLATE-B part.
129) Click **Save**.

Return to the 2AXIS-TRANSFER assembly.
130) Click **Window**, **2AXIS-TRANSFER** from the Menu bar menu.

131) Click **Yes** to the Rebuild now message.

PLATE-B changed by adding two Cbore Holes. The 2AXIS-TRANSFER assembly contains the PLATE-B part. Utilize a Section view to display the new Cbores.

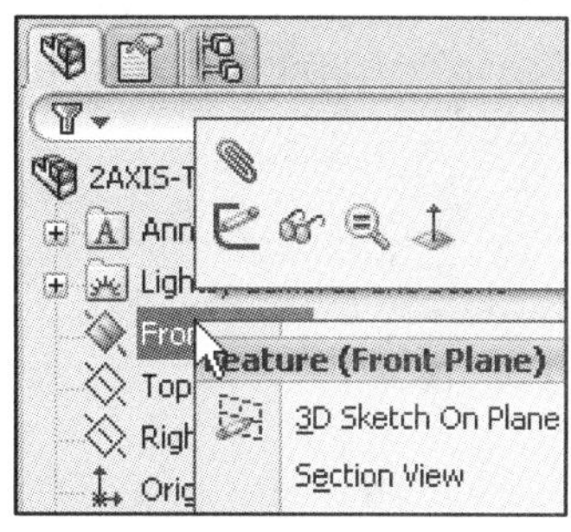

Update the 2AXIS-TRANSFER assembly.
132) Right-click **GUIDE-CYLINDER** from the FeatureManager.

133) Click **Show components**.

View the Cbore Hole in the 2AXIS-TRANSFER assembly.

134) Right-click **Front Plane** from the 2AXIS-TRANSFER FeatureManager.

135) Click **Section View** from the Pop-up toolbar. The Cbores are on the back face of the PLATE-B part.

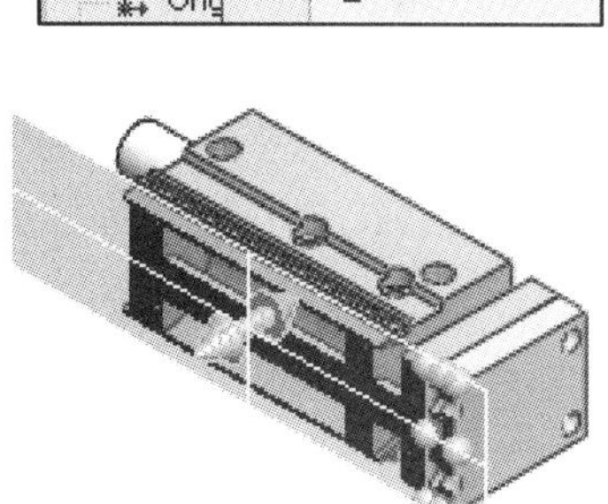

136) Click **Cancel** ✖ from the Section View PropertyManager to display the Full view.

Conserve design time. There are numerous Front Plane, Top Plane, and Right Plane entries in an assembly FeatureManager. Each component contains these reference planes. How do you select the correct Plane? Answer: Locate the component in the FeatureManager. Expand the component entry. Select the reference plane directly below the component name.

Mating the SLIDE-TABLE Assembly

The SLIDE-TABLE assembly fastens to the PLATE-B Cbores. Open the SLIDE-TABLE and 2AXIS-TRANSFER assemblies if required. Utilize the Tile Horizontally command and drag the SLIDE-TABLE assembly icon into the 2AXIS-TRANSFER assembly. Position the SLIDE-TABLE in its approximate orientation before creating a Mate.

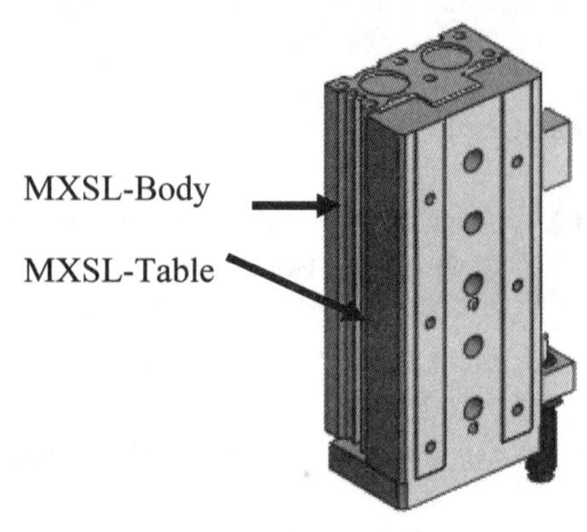

Hide components when not required. Do not suppress the GUIDE-CYLINDER assembly. Suppressing components suppresses Mates, resulting in parts being free to move and rotate.

There are many holes on the MXSL-Body part. What holes do you assemble to PLATE-B? Answer: The two bottom holes on the MXSL-Body part.

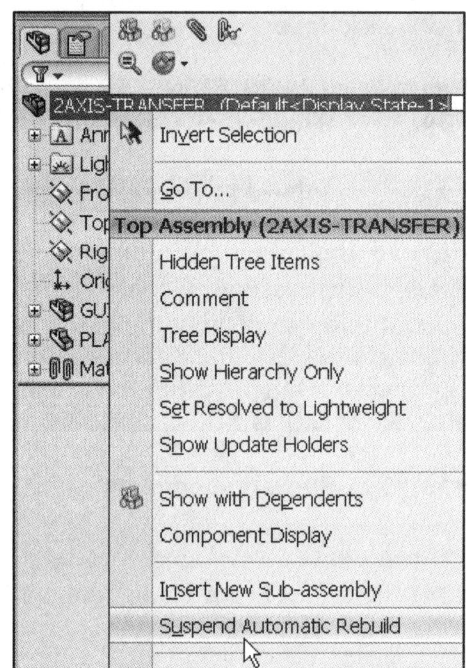

Investigate the physical behavior of the SLIDE-TABLE assembly. What part moves? What part remains static? Answer: The MXSL-Table part linearly translates and the MXSL-Body part is fixed.

The Suspend Automatic Rebuild defers the updating of Mates in the top level 2AXIS-TRANSFER assembly.

Utilize this option to create and change multiple Mates. The Rebuild command from the Menu bar toolbar controls the update of the deferred Mates.

Utilize a Section view to view the PLATE-B Cbores and the BodyThruHole4 and BodyThruHole5.

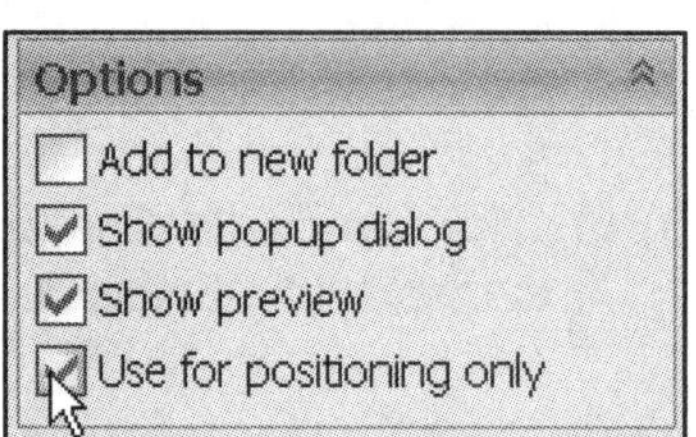

Utilize the Use for positioning only option to move and rotate components based on the Mate type. The Mate is not created or added to the FeatureManager.

Activity: Mating the SLIDE-TABLE sub-assembly to the 2AXIS-TRANSFER

Insert the SLIDE-TABLE assembly.

137) Click **Window**, **Tile Horizontally** from the Menu bar menu.

138) Click and drag the **SLIDE-TABLE assembly icon** into the 2AXIS-TRANSFER assembly.

139) Click a **position** in front of the PLATE-B part.

140) **Maximize** the 2AXIS-TRANSFER assembly. View the results.

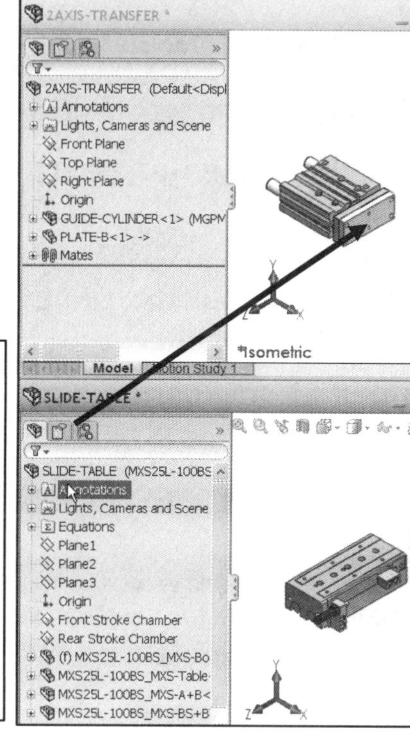

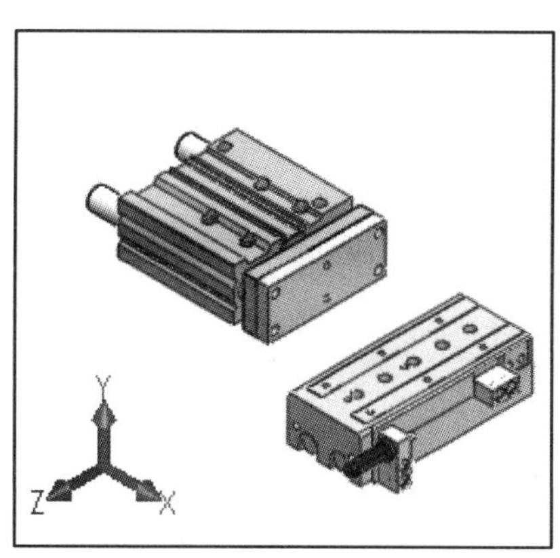

Move and Rotate the SLIDE-TABLE assembly.

141) Right-click **SLIDE-TABLE** from the FeatureManager.

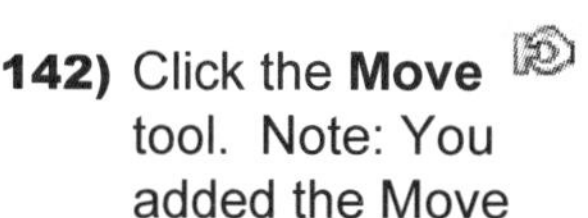

142) Click the **Move** tool. Note: You added the Move tool earlier in this book. The Move Component PropertyManager is displayed.

143) Right-click in the **Graphics window**.

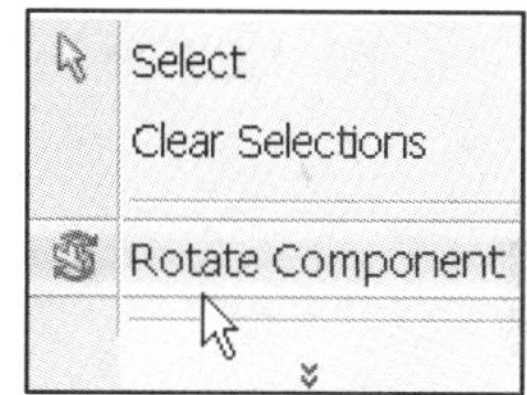

144) Click **Rotate Component**. The Rotate icon is displayed in the Graphics window.

145) Rotate the **SLIDE-TABLE** assembly as illustrated in front of the PLATE-B part.

146) Click **OK** from the Rotate Component PropertyManager.

147) **Rebuild** the model.

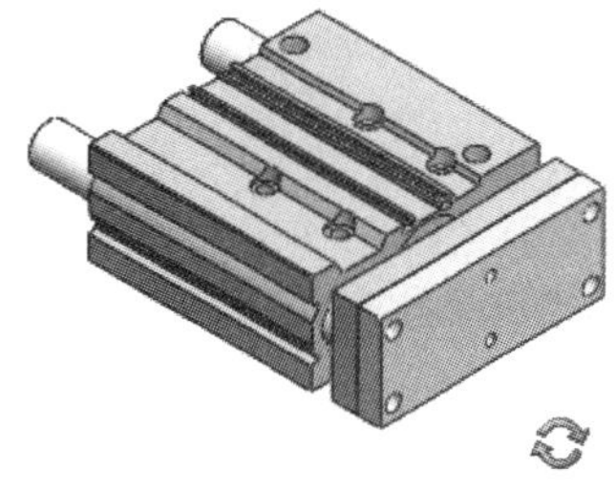

Hide Components that are not required.

148) Expand SLIDE-TABLE from the FeatureManager.

149) Click **MXSL-Table(25-100L)**.

150) Hold the **Ctrl** key down.

151) Click **MXS-BS+BT(25BSL)**.

152) Click **MXS-A+B(25B)**.

153) Click the **GUIDE-CYLINDER** assembly from the FeatureManager.

154) Release the **Ctrl** key.

155) Right-click **Hide components**. View the results in the Graphics window.

Display an Isometric view.

156) Click **Isometric** view from the Heads-up View toolbar.

Create a Coincident mate.

157) Right-click **Front Plane** from the 2AXIS-TRANSFER FeatureManager.

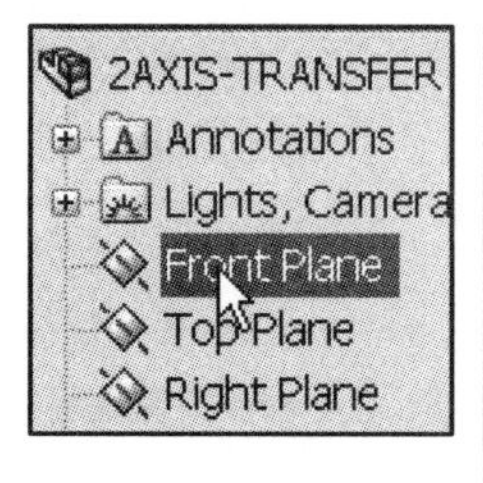

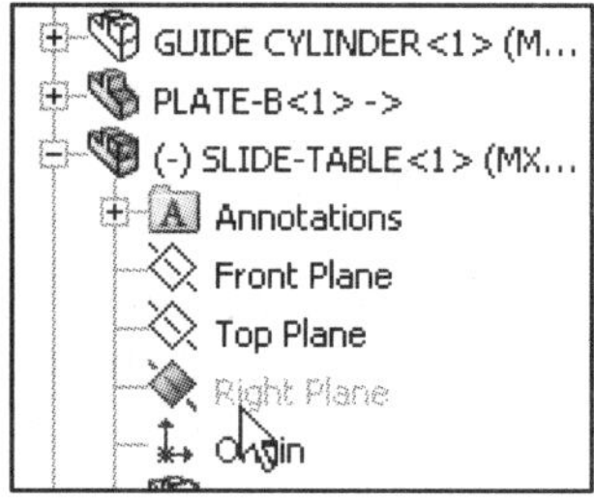

158) Click the **Mate** tool from the Context toolbar. The PropertyManager is displayed.

159) Click **SLIDE-TABLE/Right Plane** from the fly-out FeatureManager.

160) Click the **Use for positioning only** option. Coincident is selected by Default.

161) Click the **Green Check mark**. Do not move or rotate the MXSL-Body.

162) Click **OK** from the Mate PropertyManager.

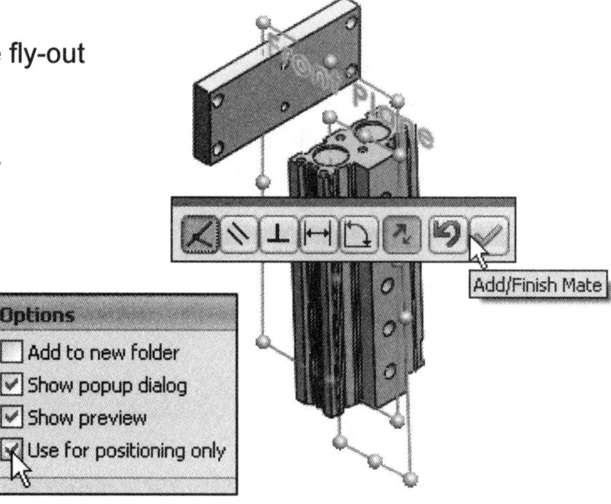

Defer the Mates.

163) Right-click **2AXIS-TRANSFER** from the FeatureManager.

164) Click **Suspend Automatic Rebuild**.

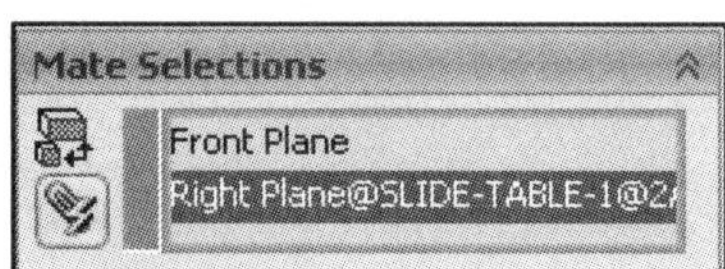

Display the Section view.

165) Right-click **Front Plane** from the 2AXIS-TRANSFER FeatureManager.

166) Click **Section view**.

167) Click **OK** ✔ from the Section View PropertyManager.

Insert a Concentric Mate.

168) Click the **MSXBody cylindrical face** as illustrated.

169) Click the **Mate** tool from the Assembly toolbar.

170) Click the top **PLATE-B Cbore cylindrical face**. Concentric is selected by default.

171) Click the **Green Check mark** ✔.

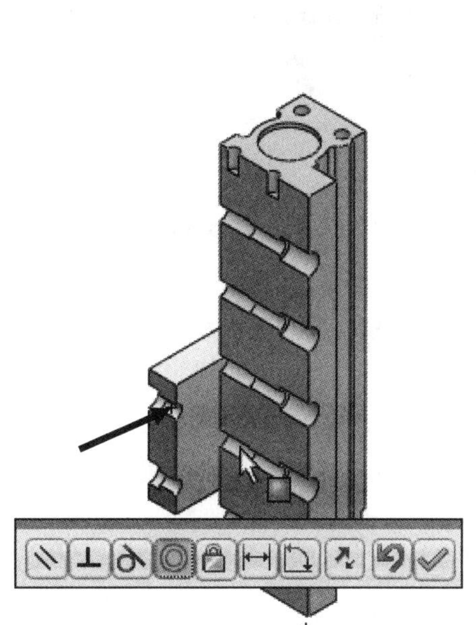

Insert the second Concentric Mate.

172) Click the **MSXBody cylindrical face** as illustrated.

173) Click the bottom **PLATE-B Cbore cylindrical face**. Concentric is selected by default.

174) Click the **Green Check mark** ✔.

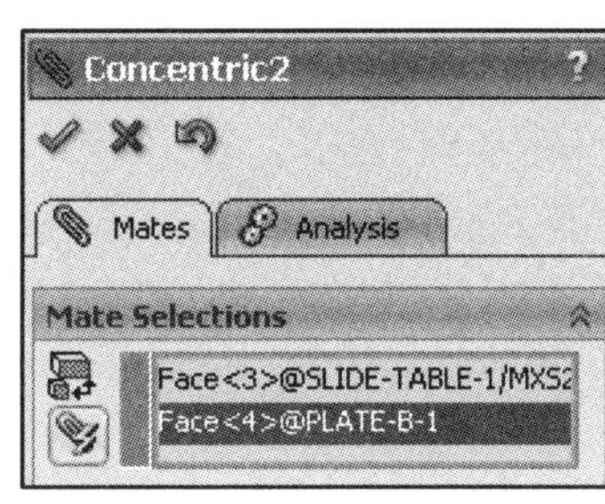

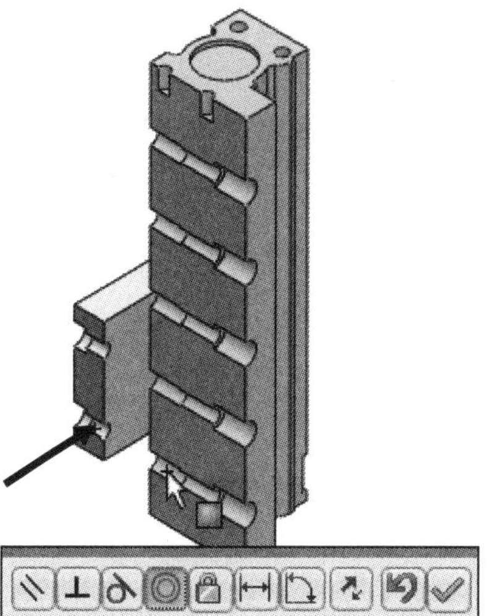

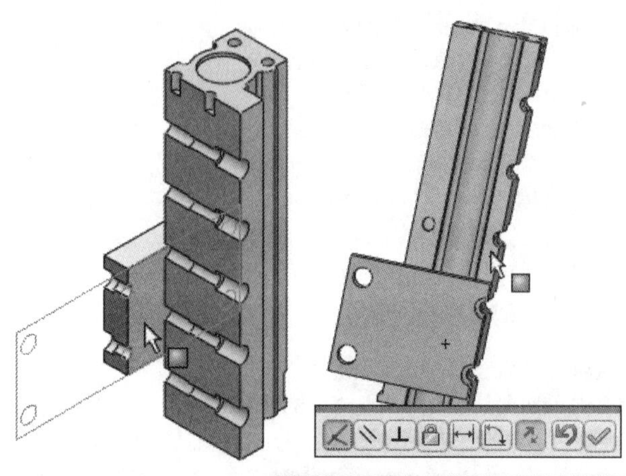

Insert a Coincident Mate.

175) Click the **PLATE-B face** as illustrated.

176) Click the **MXSL-Body back face** as illustrated. Coincident is selected by default.

177) Click the **Green Check mark** ✔.

178) Click **OK** ✔ from the Mate PropertyManager. The SLIDE-TABLE is fully defined.

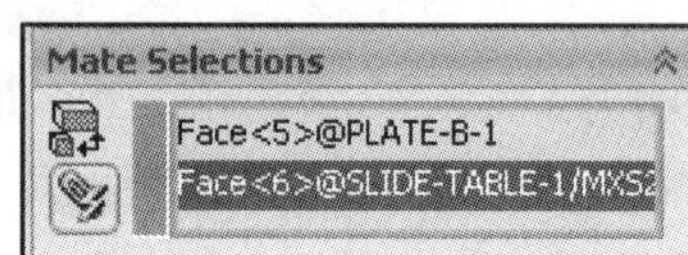

Display an Isometric view.

179) Click **Isometric** view from the Heads-up View toolbar.

180) Click **Section view** .

Save the 2AXIS-TRANSFER assembly.

181) Click **Save**.

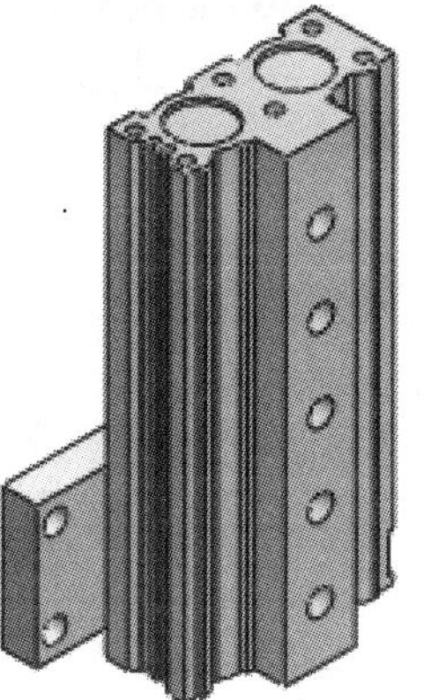

Smart Fasteners

Smart Fasteners automatically adds fasteners to your assembly if there is a hole, hole series, or pattern of holes, that is sized to accept standard hardware. It uses the SolidWorks Toolbox library of fasteners, which has a large variety of ANSI Inch, Metric and other standard hardware.

The 2AXIS-TRANSFER assembly requires two different length fasteners.

- Insert two M6x1.0 SHCSs between the PLATE-B part and the SLIDE-TABLE assembly.
- Insert two M6x1.0 SHCSs between the PLATE-B part and the GUIDE-CYLINDER assembly.
- Create an assembly-sketched pattern for the fasteners.

Inserting fastener components simulates the assembly process in manufacturing. Assemble the PLATE-B part to the SLIDE-TABLE assembly. The individual SHCSs were created from SolidWorks Toolbox and stored in the MY-TEMPLATE\SHCS folder.

The Mate References in the SHCS create the Concentric\Coincident SmartMate when dragged to the PLATE-B hole. Utilize the components located in the SHCS folder instead of SolidWorks\Toolbox to practice Replace and Redefine options.

Activity: Measure and Insert Smart Fasteners from the MY-Toolbox Folder

Measure the thread length distance.

182) Click **Top** view from the Heads-up View toolbar.

183) Click **Hidden Lines Visible** from the Heads-up View toolbar.

184) Click the **Measure** tool from the Evaluate toolbar. The Measure dialog box is displayed.

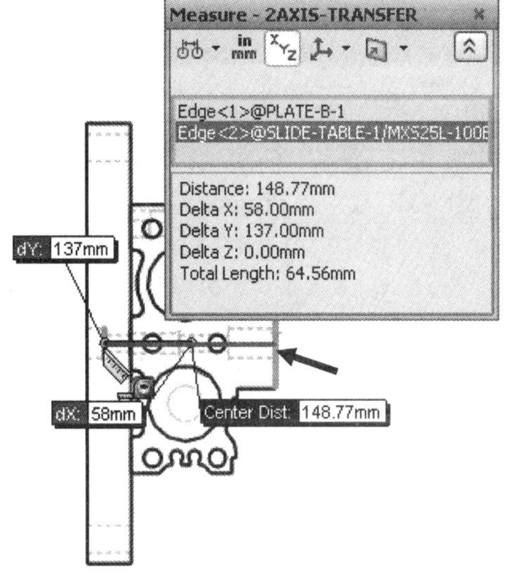

185) Click the **inside edge** of the PLATE-B Cbore Hole as illustrated.

186) Click the **bottom edge** of the hole as illustrated. The Delta X distance is 58mm. Utilize a 50mm thread length for the SHCS.

187) Click **Close**.

188) Click **Shaded With Edges**.

Position the model.

189) **Rotate** the model as illustrated.

190) **Zoom in** on the bottom Cbore.

Insert two M6 Hex SHCS from the Design Library.

191) Click the **MY-TOOLBOX\SHCS** folder.

Insert the first Hex SHCS.

192) Click and drag the **B18.3.1M-6x1.0x50 Hex SHCS** to the bottom Cbore. The Coincident\Concentric icon is displayed.

193) Release the mouse pointer on the **inside circular edge** as illustrated.

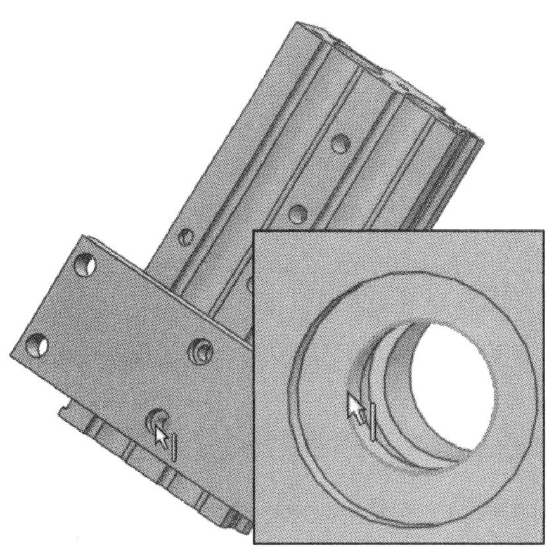

Insert the second M6Hex SHCS from the Design Library.

194) Drag the **B18.3.1M-6x1.0x50 Hex SHCS** to the top Cbore.

195) Click on the **inside circular edge** as illustrated.

196) Select **Default**.

197) Click **Yes.**

198) Click **Cancel** ✖ from the Insert Component PropertyManager.

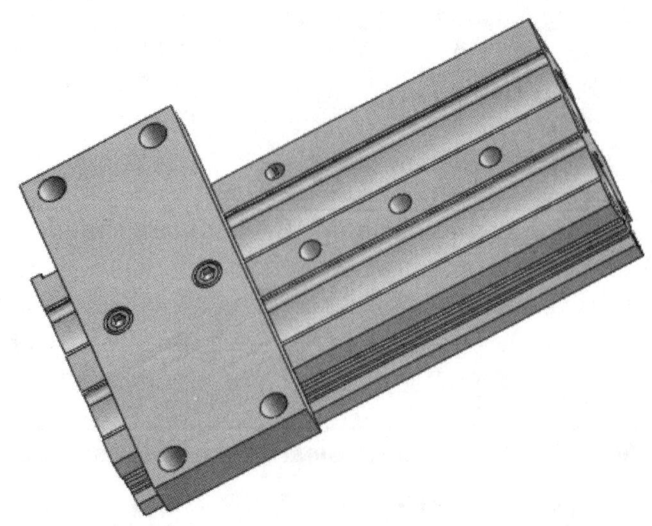

Fit the Model to the Graphics window.

199) Press the **f** key.

View the created Mates.

200) **Expand** the Mates folder from the FeatureManager. View the results.

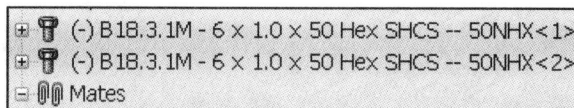

(-) B18.3.1M - 6 x 1.0 x 50 Hex SHCS -- 50NHX<1>
(-) B18.3.1M - 6 x 1.0 x 50 Hex SHCS -- 50NHX<2>
Mates

Mates
Coincident1 (GUIDE-CYLINDER<1>,Front Plane)
Coincident2 (GUIDE-CYLINDER<1>,Top Plane)
Coincident3 (GUIDE-CYLINDER<1>,Right Plane)
InPlace1 (GUIDE-CYLINDER<1>,PLATE-B<1>)
Coincident4 (SLIDE-TABLE<1>,Front Plane)
Concentric1 (PLATE-B<1>,SLIDE-TABLE<1>)
Concentric2 (PLATE-B<1>,SLIDE-TABLE<1>)
Coincident5 (PLATE-B<1>,SLIDE-TABLE<1>)
Concentric3 (SLIDE-TABLE<1>,B18.3.1M - 6 x 1.0 x 50 Hex SHCS
Coincident6 (SLIDE-TABLE<1>,B18.3.1M - 6 x 1.0 x 50 Hex SHCS
Concentric4 (SLIDE-TABLE<1>,B18.3.1M - 6 x 1.0 x 50 Hex SHCS
Coincident7 (SLIDE-TABLE<1>,B18.3.1M - 6 x 1.0 x 50 Hex SHCS

Two instances of the M – 6 x 1.0 x 50 SHCS have been added to the FeatureManager. The B18.3.1M -6 x 1.0 x 50 Hex SHCS<1> is the first instance. The B18.3.1M – 6 x 1.0 x 50 Hex SHCS<2> is the second instance. Each time you insert a SHCS, in the same session of SolidWorks, the instance number is incremented.

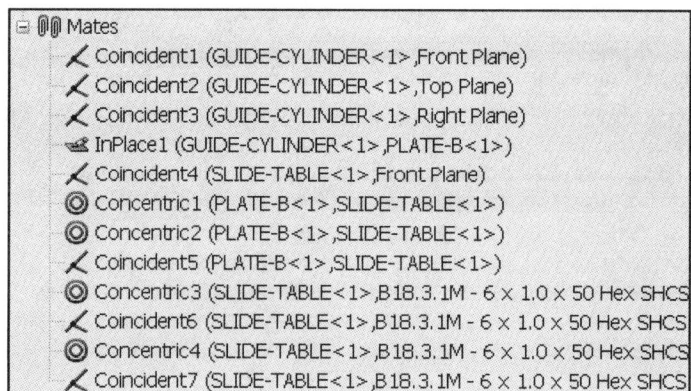

Your instance numbers <1>, <2>, may be different if a SHCS was deleted.

Dragging the SHCS into the assembly and referencing the Cbore circular edge created four SmartMates.

Your numbers may be different if a Mate was deleted.

Hide and Show components.

201) Click **Isometric** view from the Heads-up View toolbar.

202) Click **SLIDE-TABLE** from the FeatureManager.

203) Hold the **Ctrl** key down.

204) Click **B18.3.1M-6x1.0x50Hex SHCS <1>** from the FeatureManager.

205) Click **B18.3.1M-6x1.0x50Hex SHCS<2>** from the FeatureManager. Release the **Ctrl** key.

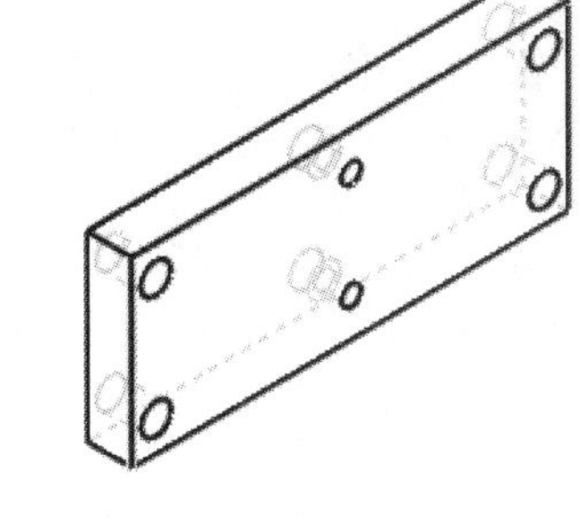

206) Right-click **Hide components**.

207) Click **Hidden Lines Visible** from the Heads-up View toolbar.

208) Right-click **GUIDE-CYLINDER** from the FeatureManager.

209) Click **Show components**.

210) Right-click **GUIDE-CYLINDER\MGPTube** from the FeatureManager.

211) Click **Hide components**. PLATE-B and the MGPRod parts are displayed.

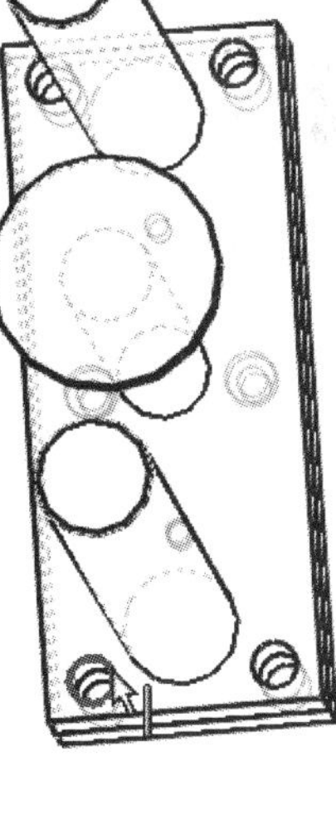

Add an M10x1.5 SHCS to PLATE-B from the Design Library.

212) Click the **MY-TOOLBOX\SHCS** folder.

213) **Zoom in** on the front left hole as illustrated.

214) Click and drag the **B18.3.1M-10x1.5x25 Hex SHCS** to the front left hole as illustrated.

215) Release the mouse pointer on the **outside circular edge**. The B18.3.1M-10x1.5x25 Hex SHCS is displayed.

216) Click **Cancel** ✖ from the Insert Component PropertyManager.

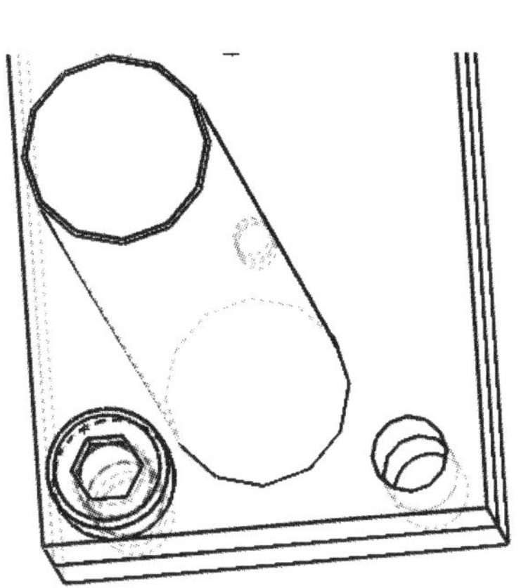

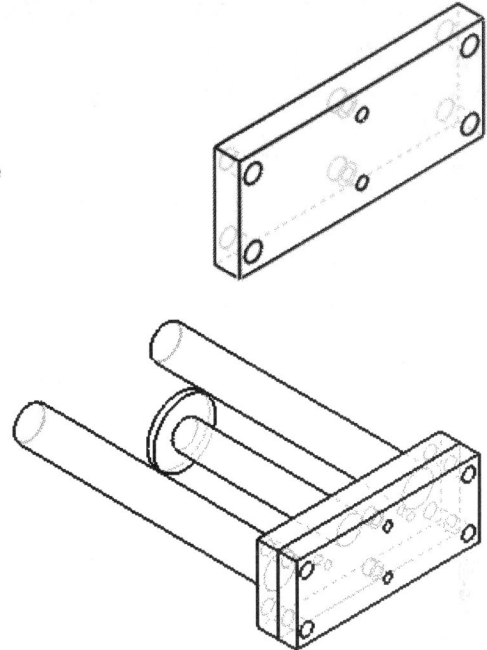

Edit Mates and Redefine Components

Assemblies require the ability to modify Mates and redefined components.

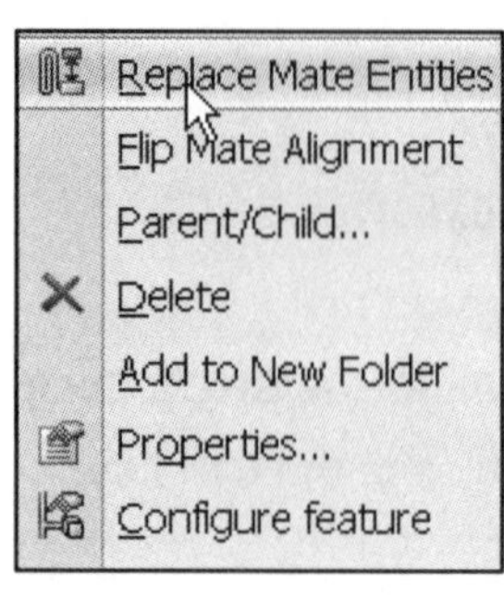

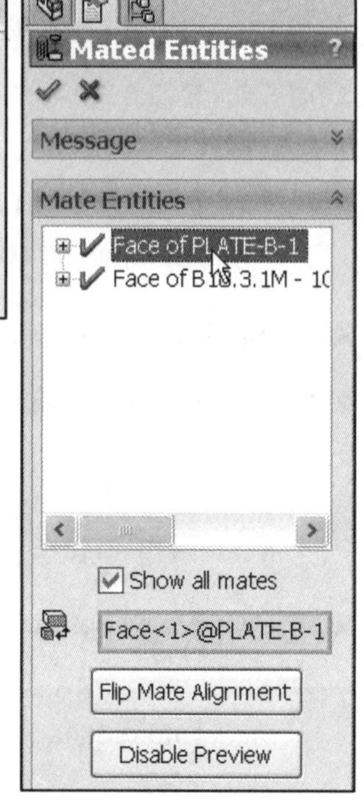

The 2AXIS-TRANSFER assembly requires four M10 SHCSs to fasten the PLATE-B part to the GUIDE-CYLINDER assembly.

A Concentric Mate and Coincident Mate defines the SHCS placement. Modify the Concentric Mate selections from the GUIDE-CYLINDER bottom left hole to the PLATE-B bottom front hole with the Replace Mate Entities tool. The Replace Mate Entities tool redefines the selected Coincident Mate.

What is the required thread length? Answer: 25mm or 30mm. Try a 25mm SHCS. The 25mm SHCS thread does not provide the minimum engagement of 75% for the MGPRod Plate hole.

Utilize the Replace Component tool to modify the 25mm SHCS to a 30mm.

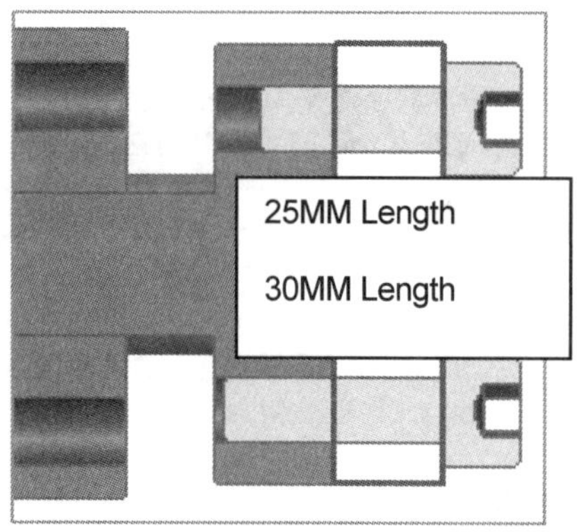

An assembly and its components may go through many revisions during the course of a design cycle. This is especially true in a multi-user environment where several users can work on the individual parts and sub-assemblies. A safe, efficient way to update the assembly is to replace the components as needed.

The SHCS fastens PLATE-B to the GUIDE-CYLINDER assembly. Create a Local Assembly Pattern that corresponds to the MountHoles2 position. Record the dimensions between the holes.

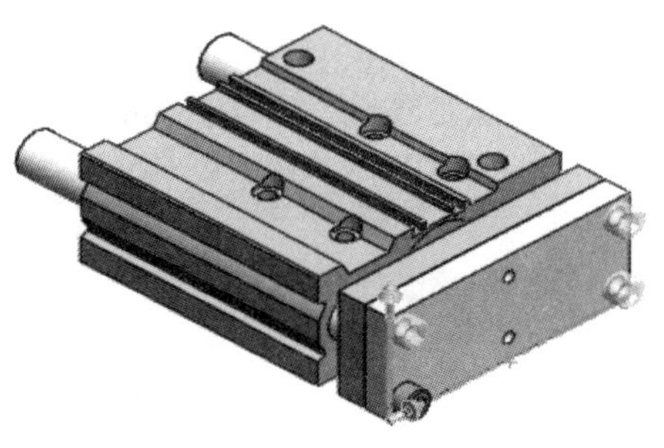

The Local Assembly Pattern of the M10 SHCS requires the 130mm and 40mm dimensions.

Identify the location of the pattern. Locate the pattern at the top level of the 2AXIS-TRANSFER assembly.

There is a visual interference between the lower right fastener and the SLIDE-TABLE assembly. What is the solution? Answer: Utilize the second set of MGPRod M6 holes, named MountHoles.

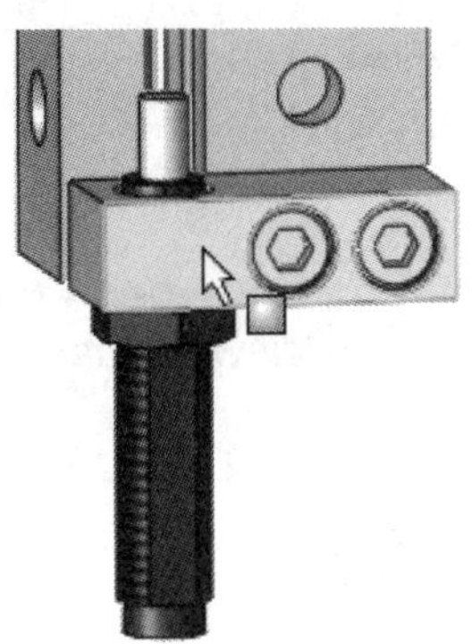

Activity: Redefine and Replace Components

Apply the Replace Mate Entities tool.

217) Right-click the last **Coincident** mate from the Mates folder in the FeatureManager as illustrated.

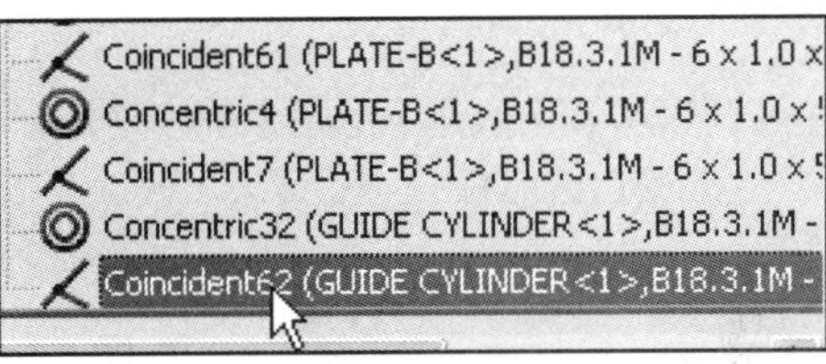

218) Click **Replace Mate Entities**. The Mated Entities PropertyManager is displayed.

219) Click the **Face of GUIDE-CYLINDER** from the Mate Entities box.

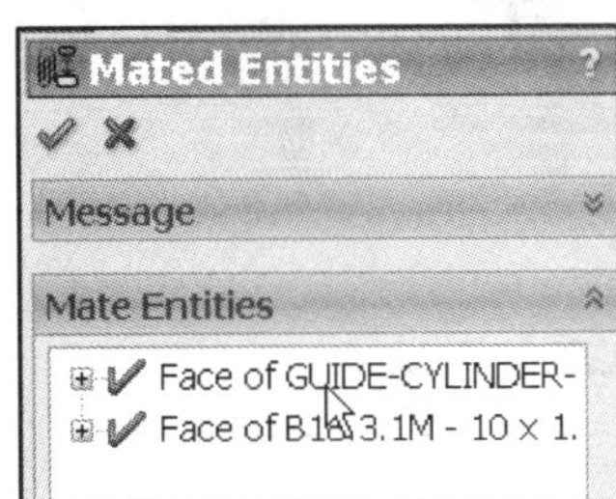

220) Click the **PLATE-B front face** as illustrated. The SHCS head changes direction. Click the **Flip Mate Alignment** button if required. Note the update in the Mate Entities box.

221) Click **OK** from the Mated Entities PropertyManager.

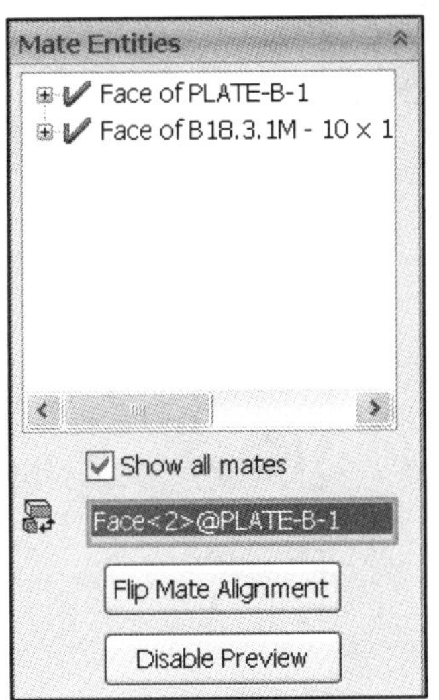

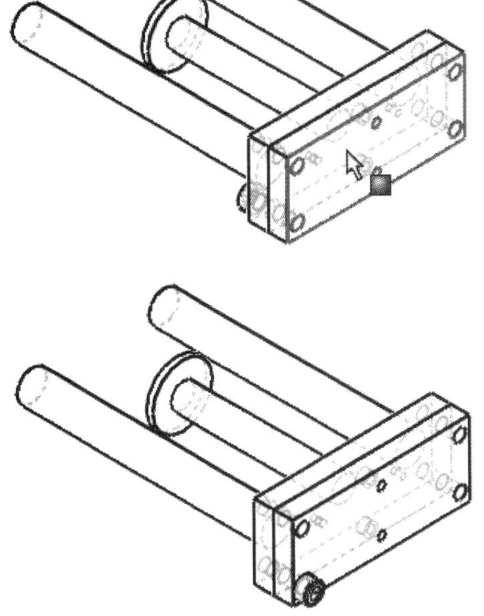

Display an Isometric view.

222) Click **Isometric** view from the Heads-up View toolbar.

223) Click **Shaded With Edges** from the Heads-up View toolbar. View the results.

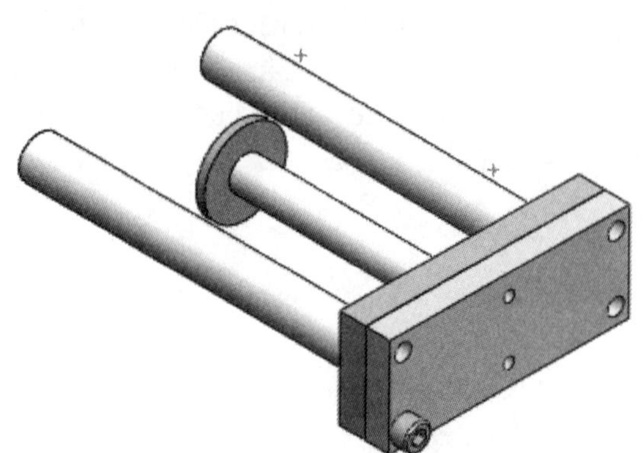

Create a Section view to view the engagement of the MGPRod Plate hole.

224) Click the **Front** face of PLATE-B.

225) Click **Section View** from the Heads up View toolbar.

226) Enter **-8** for Offest Distance.

227) Click **OK** from the Section View PropertyManager.

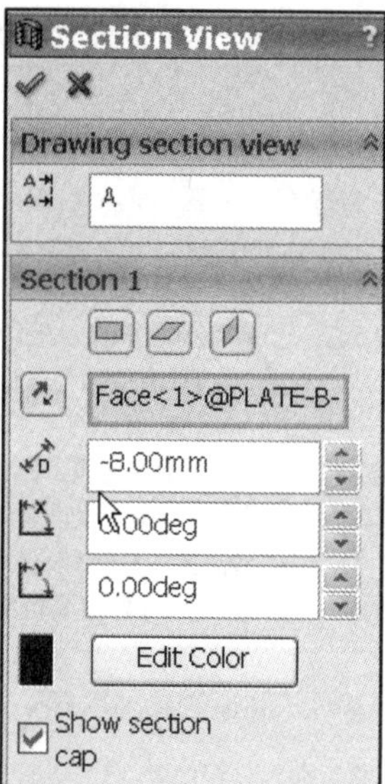

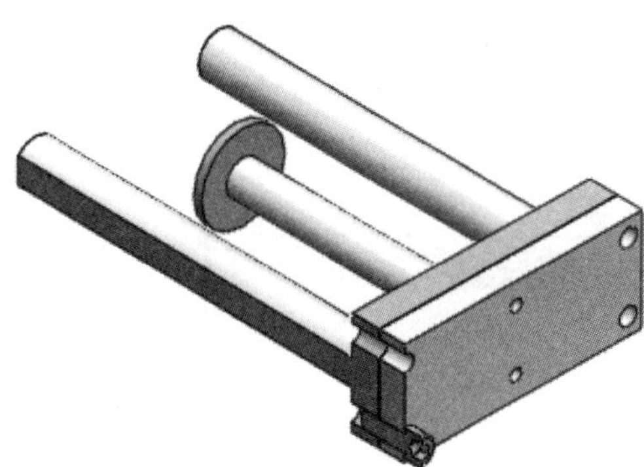

Replace the SHCS.

228) Right-click **B18.3.1M-10x1.5x25 Hex SHCS** from the FeatureManager.

229) Click the **Replace Components** tool. The Replace PropertyManager is displayed.

230) Click **Browse** from the Replace PropertyManager.

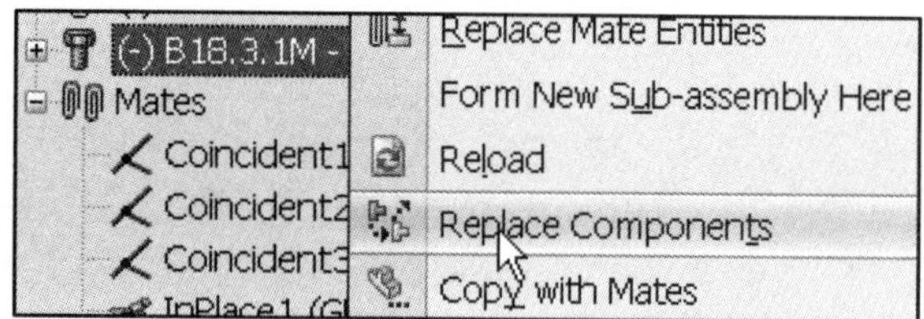

231) Select **B18.3.1M-10x1.5x30 Hex SHCS** from the MY-TOOLBOX\SHCS folder.

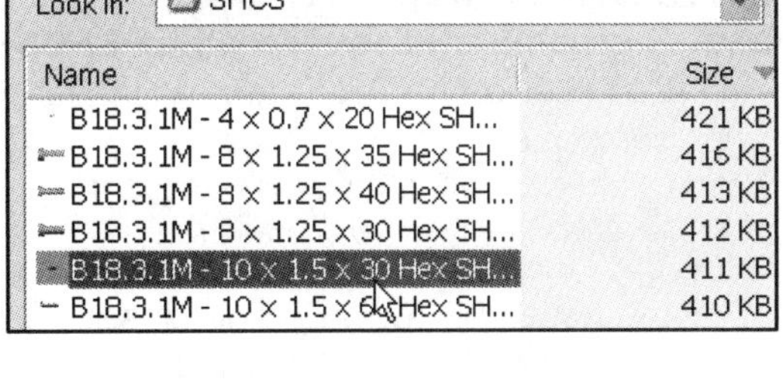

232) Click **Open**.

233) Click **OK** from the Replace PropertyManager.

234) Click **OK** from the Mated Entities PropertyManager. View the engagement of the component in the model.

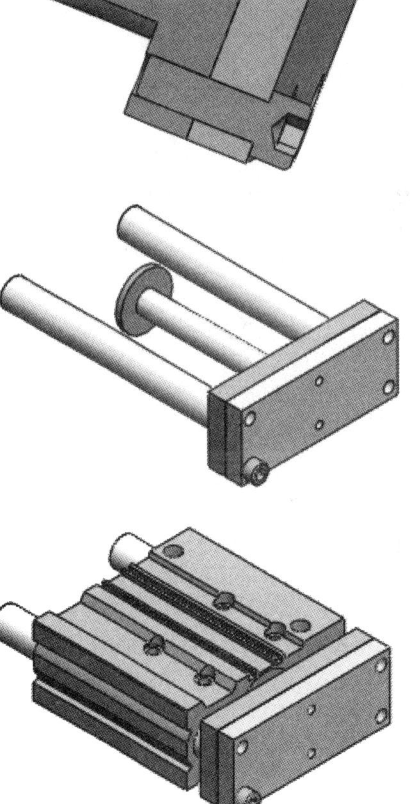

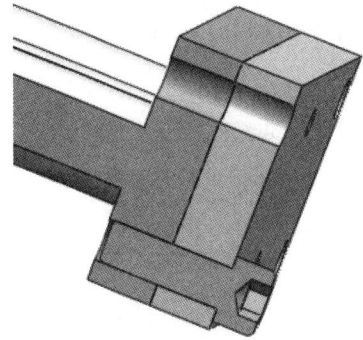

Display the full view.

235) Click **Section View** from the Heads-up View toolbar.

Show the MGPTube.

236) Right-click **MGPTube** from the FeatureManager.

237) Click **Show components** from the Context toolbar.

238) **Save** the model.

The Mated Entities PropertyManager displays the Concentric and Coincident references for the Mates.

The SHCS updates in the Graphics window.

The FeatureManager displays the new entries with the part icon and Mates entries.

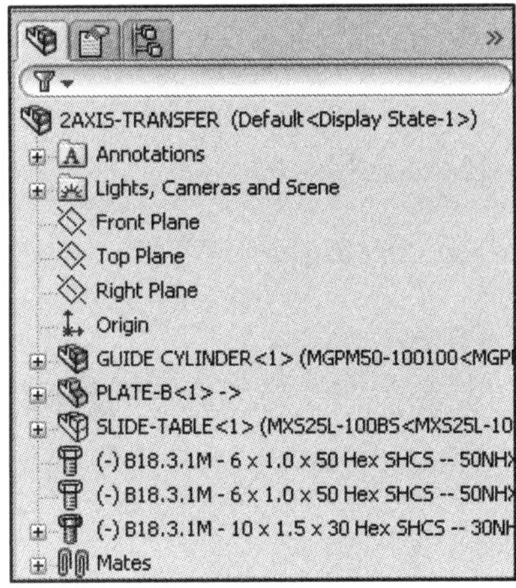

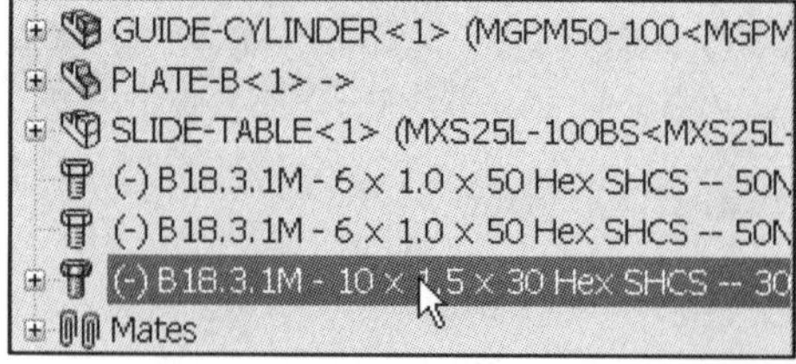

Create a Linear Component Pattern.

239) Click **B18.3.1M-10x1.5x30Hex SHCS** from the 2AXIS-TRANSFER FeatureManager for the seed component.

240) Click the **Linear Component Pattern** tool from the Assembly toolbar. The Linear Pattern PropertyManager is displayed.

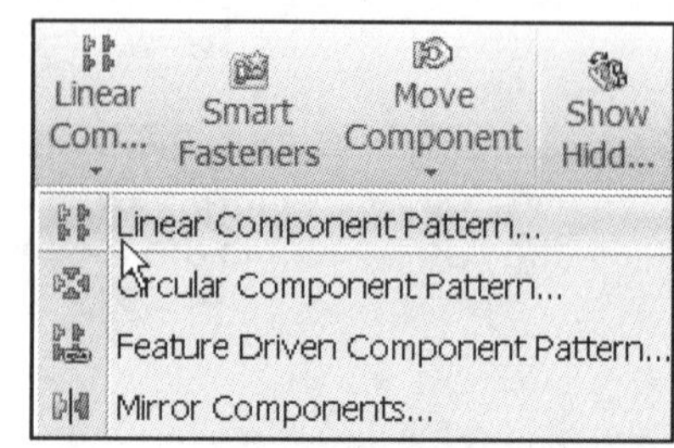

241) Click the **bottom horizontal edge** for Direction 1. The arrow points to the right

242) Enter **130** for Spacing.

243) Enter **2** for Instances.

244) Click the **left vertical edge** for Direction 2. The arrow points upward.

245) Enter **40** for Spacing.

246) Enter **2** for Instances.

247) Click **OK** from the Linear Pattern PropertyManager. LocalPattern1 is displayed in the FeatureManager.

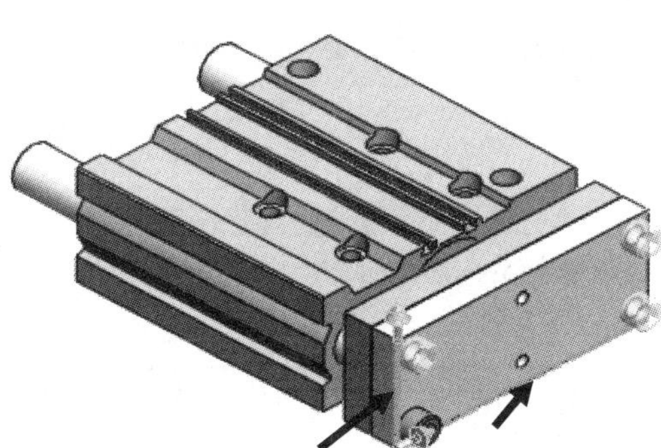

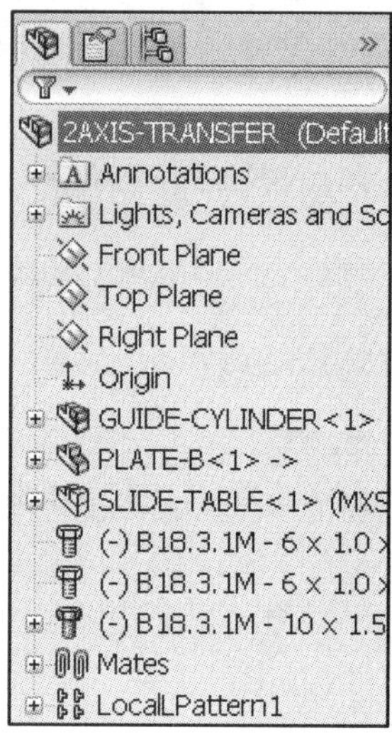

Show the SLIDE-TABLE components.

248) Right-click **SLIDE-TABLE** from the FeatureManager.

249) Click **Show components** from the Context toolbar.

250) **Expand** SLIDE-TABLE from the FeatureManager.

251) Click **MXS-A+B(25B)<1>**.

252) Hold the **Ctrl** key down.

253) Click **MXS-BS+BT(25BSL)<1>.**

254) Release the **Ctrl** key.

255) Right-click **Show components** from the Context toolbar.

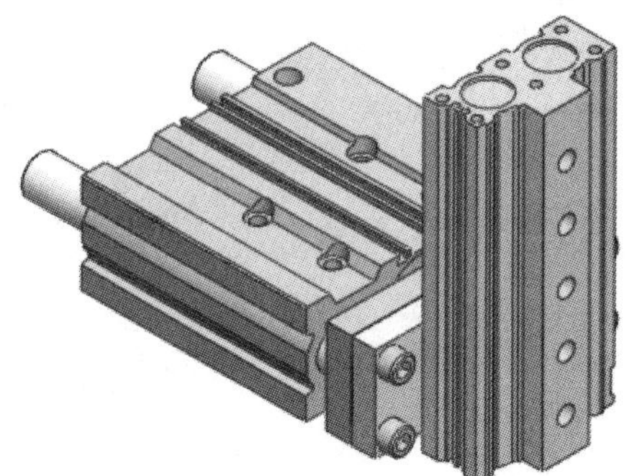

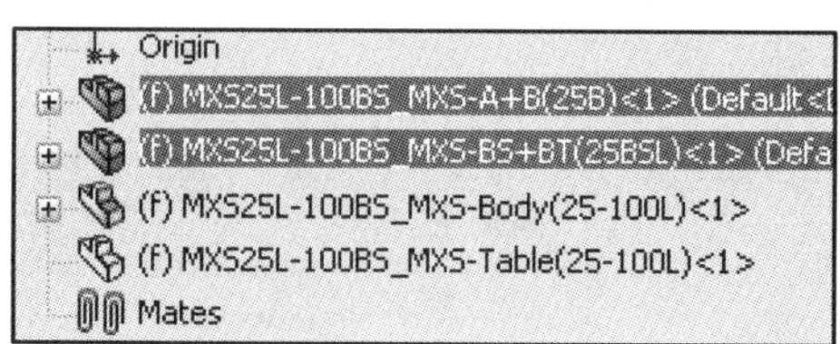

Rotate the 2AXIS-TRANSFER assembly.

256) Rotate the 2AXIS-TRANSFER assembly to view the **MXS-BS+BT(25BSL)<1>** as illustrated. Note the interference issue.

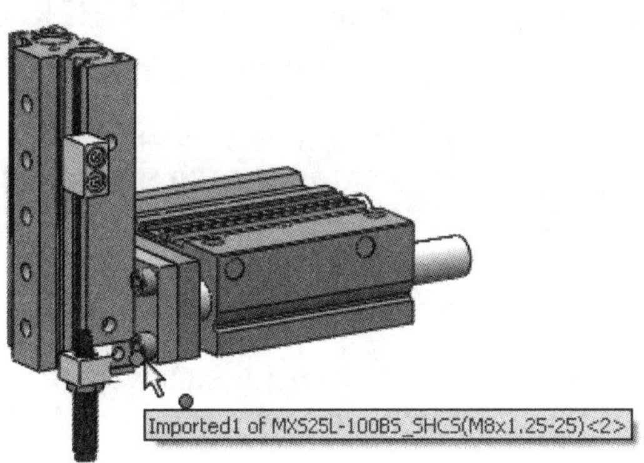

Activity: Apply the Interference Detection tool

Perform an Interference Detection on the assembly.

257) Click the **Interference Detection** tool from the Evaluate toolbar.

258) Right-click a **position** in the Selected Components box.

259) Click **Clear Selections**.

260) Click **B18.3.1M-10x1.5x30 Hex SHCS** from the Graphics window.

261) Click **MXS-BS+BT Plate** from the Graphics window as illustrated.

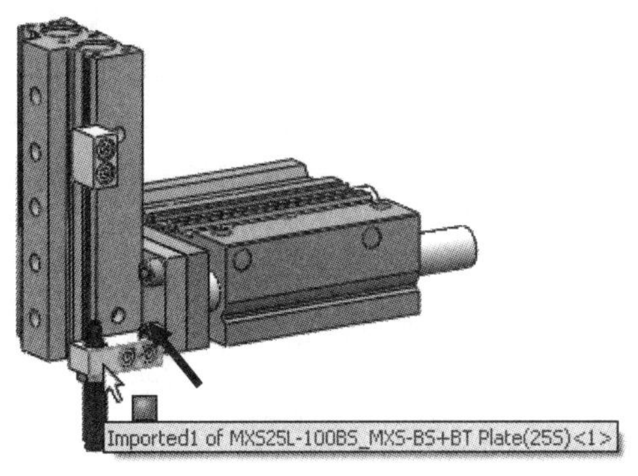

262) Click **Calculate**. The results display the Interference1 volume.

263) Click **OK** from the Interference Detection PropertyManager.

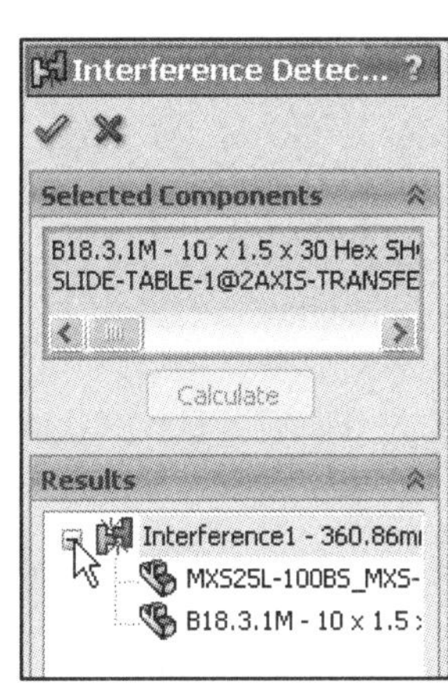

The Interference results in a design decision. Review the four options:

1.) *Modify the positions of the PLATE-B four holes.*

2.) *Mount the SLIDE-TABLE to PLATE-B utilizing BodyHole3 and BodyHole4.*

3.) *Increase the overall size of PLATE-B and modify the four through holes to countersink or counterbore.*

4.) *Locate additional holes on the MGPRod component.*

The first option results in modification of a purchased part. The second and third options cause interference with other components. Proceed with the fourth option.

Locate two MountHoles on the MGPRod. Insert two M6 Cbores in PLATE-B with the Holes Wizard tool.

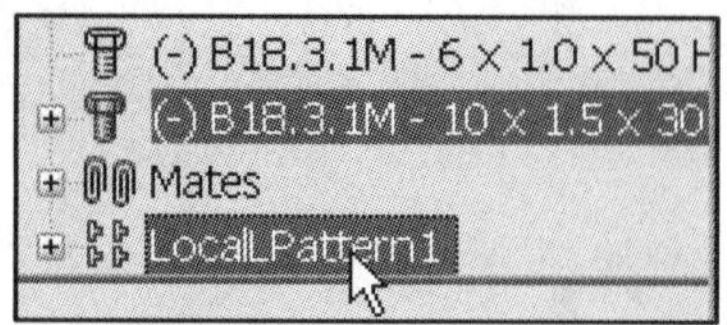

Delete the M10 SHCS and LocalPattern1.

264) Click **B18.3.1M-10x1.5x30 Hex SHCS** from the 2AXIS-TRANSFER FeatureManager.

265) Hold the **Ctrl** key down.

266) Click **LocalPattern1** from the FeatureManager.

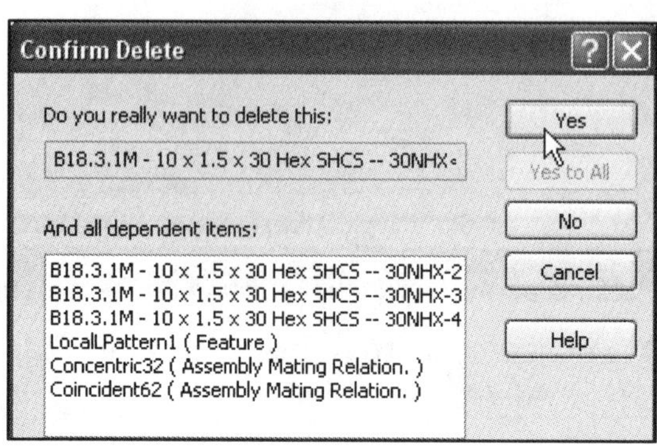

267) Release the **Ctrl** key. Right-click **Delete**.

268) Click **Yes** to delete the dependent items.

269) **Rebuild** the model.

Hide the SLIDE-TABLE and the GUIDE-CYLINDER/MGPTube.

270) Click **SLIDE-TABLE** from the FeatureManager.

271) Hold the **Ctrl** key down.

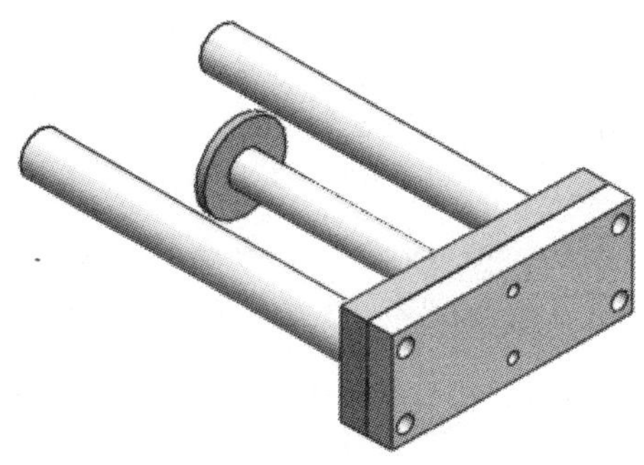

272) Click **GUIDE-CYLINDER/MGPTube** from the FeatureManager.

273) Release the **Ctrl** key.

274) Right-click **Hide components**.

275) Click **Hidden Lines Visible**.

Edit PLATE-B In-Context of the 2AXIS-TRANSFER assembly.

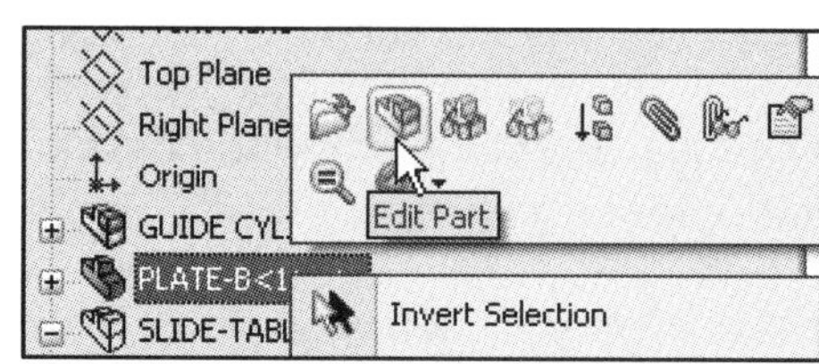

276) Right-click **PLATE-B** from the FeatureManager.

277) Click **Edit Part** from the Context toolbar. The PLATE-B part name is displayed in blue.

Display Temporary Axes.

278) Click **View**, check **Temporary Axes**.

Display the Origins.

279) Click **View**, check **Origins**.

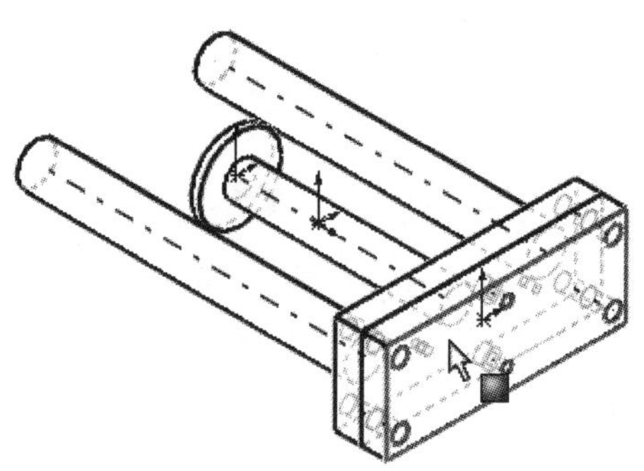

Insert a M6 Cbore. Use the Hole Wizard tool.

280) Click the **PLATE-B face** to the left of the Origin as illustrated.

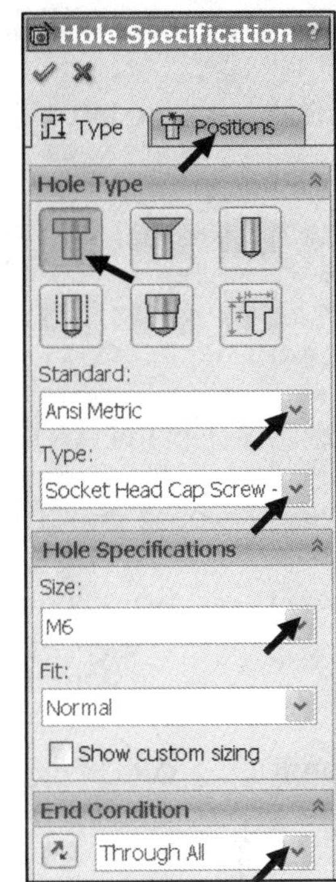

281) Click the **Hole Wizard** tool from the FeatureManager.

282) Click **Countbore** for Hole Specification.

283) Select **Ansi Metric** for Standard.

284) Select **Socket Head Cap Screw** for Type. Select **M6** for Size.

285) Select **Through All** for End Condition.

286) Click the **Positions** tab. The Point icon is displayed.

Position the second M6 hole center point.

287) Click **Right** view.

288) Click a **position** to the right of the Origin as illustrated.

289) Right-click **Select** to deselect the Point Sketch tool.

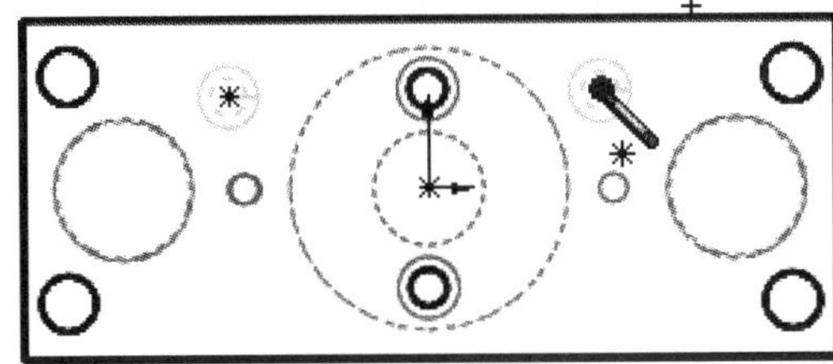

There are two methods to reference the center point of a Hole Wizard hole or Circle Sketch tool. The first method is to "wake up" the center point of an existing hole by dragging the mouse pointer over circular geometry.

A Coincident relationship is inferred. This method requires that the referenced circular geometry and the new center point are on the same plane or face. The second method utilizes the Temporary axis of an existing hole and the new center point. Work in an Isometric view to display the Temporary axis and the center point. Utilize this method in the next step.

Select the Axis filter.

290) Click **Filter Axes** from the Selection Filter toolbar. The filter icon is displayed. The Filter icon is displayed.

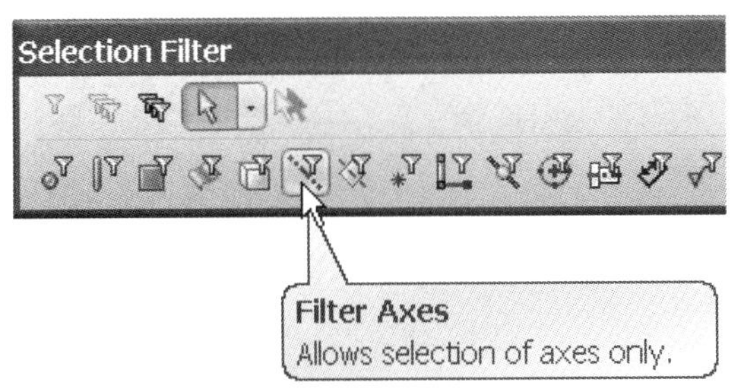

291) Click **Isometric** view.

Click **View**, **Toolbars**, **Selection Filter** to display the Selection Filter toolbar.

Add a Coincident relation to the left Cbore.

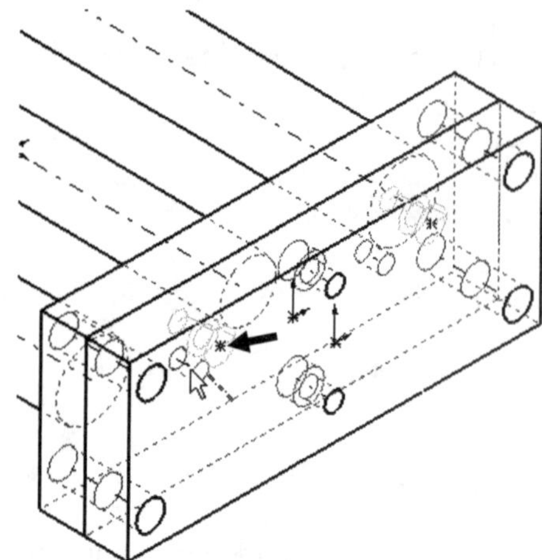

292) Click the **left MGPRod/MountHole Temporary Axis** as illustrated.

293) Click **Clear All Filters** from the Selection Filter toolbar.

294) Hold the **Ctrl** key down.

295) Select the **left Cbore center point**.

296) Release the **Ctrl** key.

297) Click **Coincident** from the Add Relations box. The hole is fully defined. Note: You can also right-click and click Coincident from the Context toolbar.

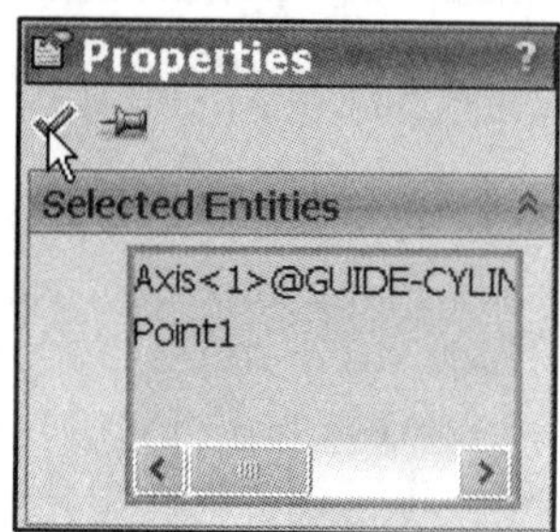

298) Click **OK** from the Properties PropertyManager.

Add a Coincident relation to the right Cbore.

299) Click **Filter Axes** from the Selection Filter toolbar.

300) Click the **right MGPRod/MountHole Temporary Axis.**

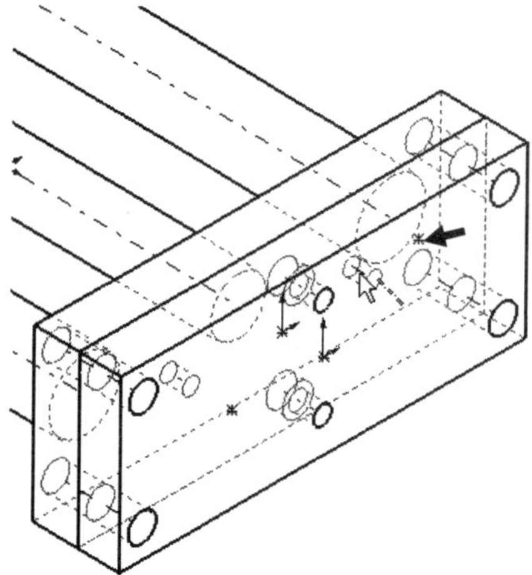

301) Click **Clear All Filters** from the Selection Filter toolbar.

302) Hold the **Ctrl** key down.

303) Click the **right Cbore center point**.

304) Release the **Ctrl** key.

305) Click **Coincident** from the Add Relations box. The hole is fully defined.

306) Click **OK** from the Properties PropertyManager.

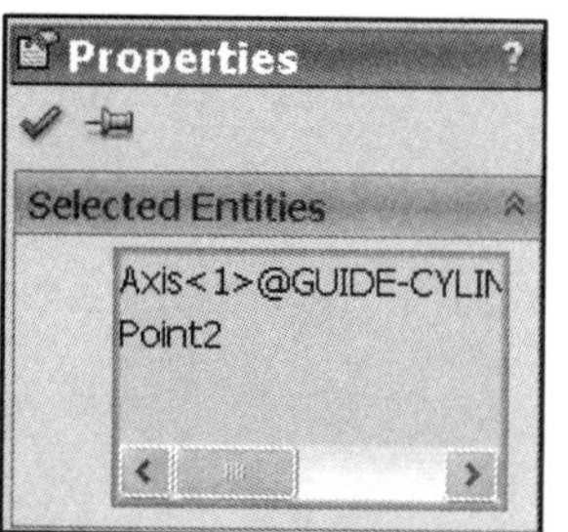

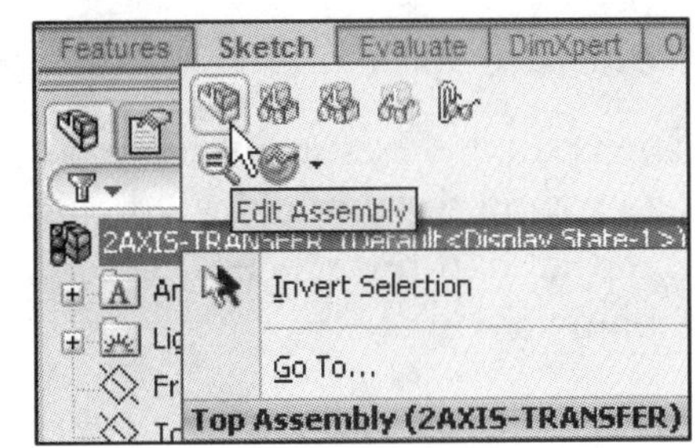

Return to the 2AXIS-TRANSFER assembly.

307) Click **OK** ✔ from the Hole Position PropertyManager.

308) Click **Shaded With Edges** from the Heads-up View toolbar.

309) Click the **Edit Assembly** tool.

310) Deactivite the **Origins** and **Temporary Axis**.

311) **Rebuild** the model.

Save the 2AXIS-TRANSFER assembly.

312) Click **Save**.

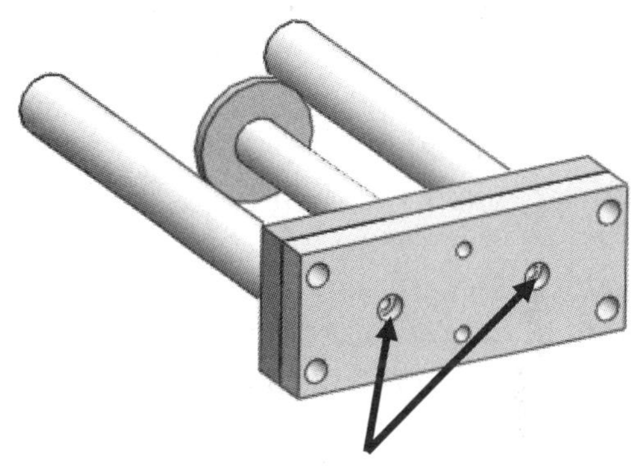

As an exercise after this project, sized and insert two M6 SHCSs as illustrated. Note: Utilize the four outside mounting holes in a different assembly.

Display the Hidden components.

313) Display the **hidden components** as illustrated.

314) Display an **Isometric** view.

315) **Rebuild** the model.

Save the model.

316) Click **Save**. View the updated PLATE-B<1> -> feature.

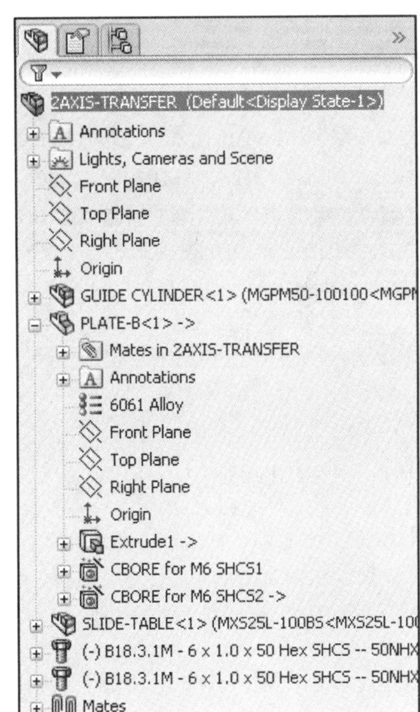

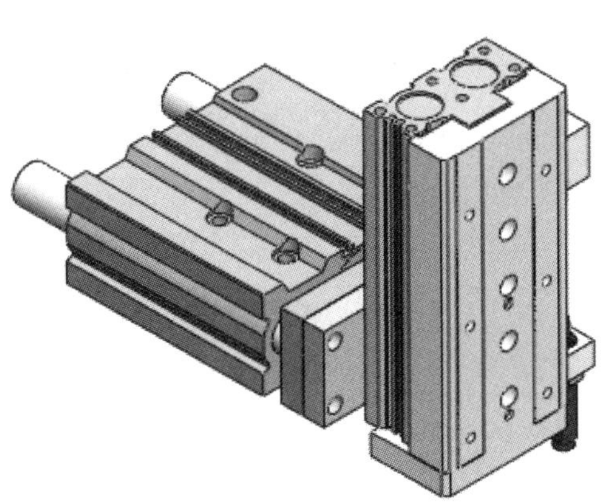

Redefine External References

The company has instituted a policy. Utilize InPlace Mates and External references when required in the initial design phase of an assembly. Redefine all InPlace Mates and External part references before the assemblies, parts, and drawings are released to manufacturing.

PLATE-B requires that the GUIDE-CYLINDER be loaded into memory. How can a component developed In-Context of an assembly be modified for the independent Bottom-up design assembly modeling approach? Answer: Redefine all External references. Delete all InPlace Mates. Add dimensions and relations to fully define the PLATE-B sketches. Insert Mates to constrain PLATE-B in the 2-AXIS TRANSFER assembly.

You can lock all, unlock all, or break all the external references of a component. The Lock All command protects the part. When you lock all the External references on a component, the existing references no longer update and you cannot add any new references to that component.

When you break all the external references, the existing external references no longer update and you can add new references to the component.

When you lock the PLATE-B component, the PLATE-B FeatureManager displayed the suffix for the component from -> to ->*.

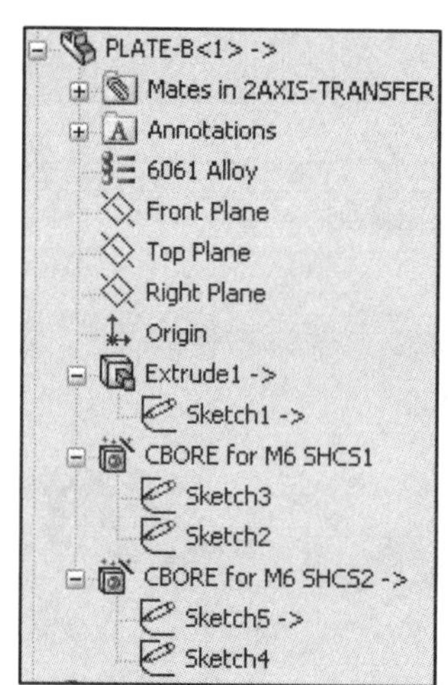

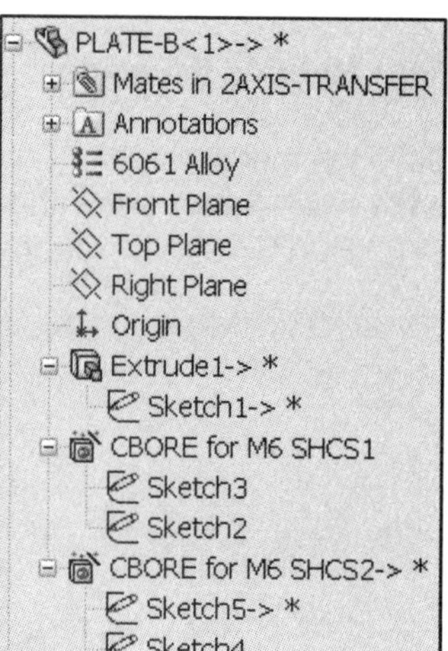

Redefine External references with a systematic approach. Review both the feature and the sketch.

Start with Sketch1 of the Extrude1 feature. Review geometric relations with the Display/Delete Relations tool. Delete external references. Redefine design intent such as symmetry, dimensions, and geometric relations.

Work through the FeatureManager until all External references developed In-Context of an assembly are redefined.

External Reference - Out of Context

Look at the External reference symbols. If you see the notation “->? appended to a component, the ? indicates that the External reference is out of context.

To put an out of context component back into context, open the externally referenced document. The Edit In Context automatically opens the document that is referenced by an external reference. This is quite a time saver because you do not have to query the feature to identify the references file, browse to the locate it, and then open it manually.

Activity: Redefine External References – Out of Context

Redefine the PLATE-B references.

317) Right-click **PLATE-B** from the 2AXIS-TRANSFER FeatureManager.

318) Click **List External Refs**. The features and sketches referenced from the 2AXIS-TRANSFER/PLATE-B are displayed.

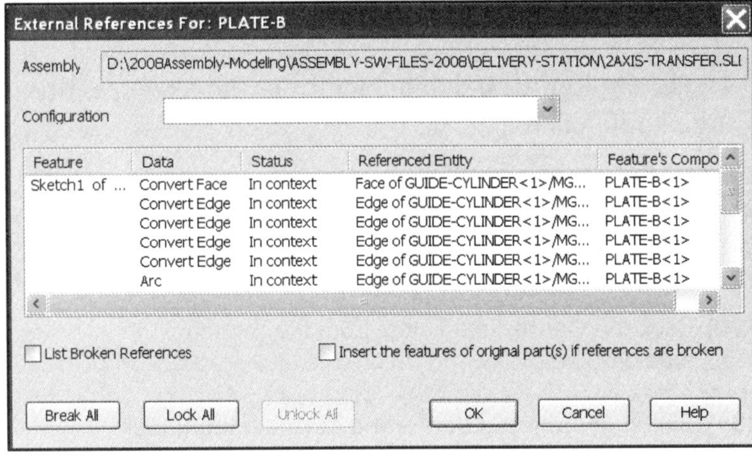

Lock all GUIDE-CYLINDER assembly references.

319) Click the **Lock All** button.

320) Click **OK**. The warning message is displayed, “All external references for the model, PLATE-B will be locked. You will not be able to add any new external references until you unlock the existing references.”

321) Click **OK**. The “->*” symbol is displayed next to the part name, PLATE-B in the FeatureManager. PLATE-B contains External references that are locked.

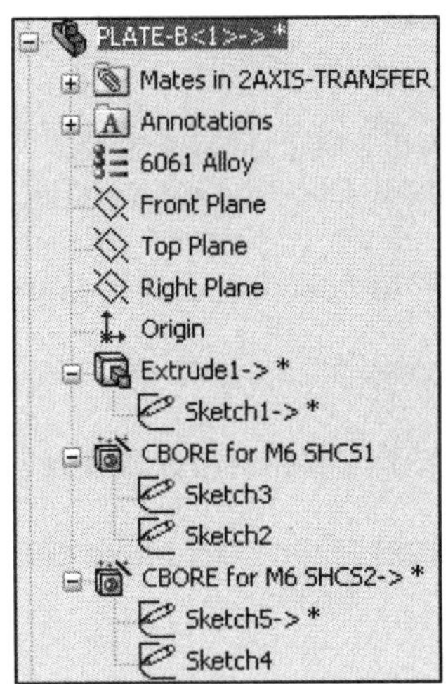

Open the PLATE-B part.

322) Right-click **PLATE-B** from the 2AXIS-TRANSFER FeatureManager.

323) Click **Open Part** from the Context toolbar. PLATE-B is displayed in the Graphics window.

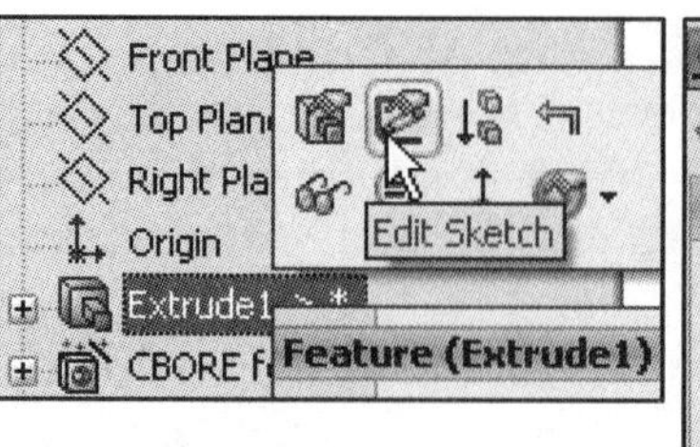

Delete the Sketch1 External references.

324) Right-click **Extrude1** from the FeatureManager.

325) Click **Edit Sketch** from the Context toolbar.

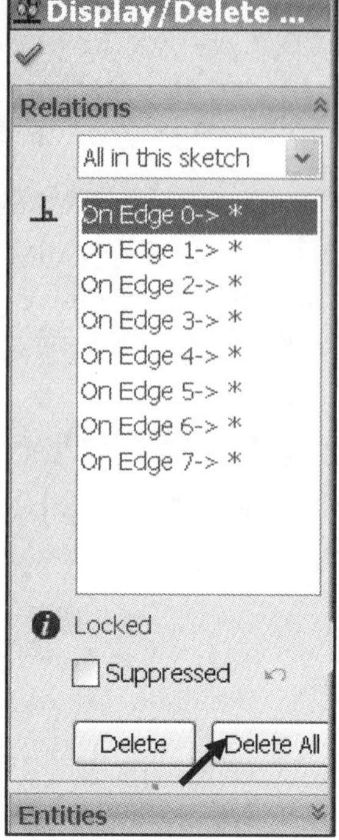

Delete the Locked references.

326) Click the **Display/Delete Relations** tool from the Sketch toolbar. The PropertyManager is displayed.

Delete the 8 On Edge references. The "*" symbol indicates the Lock All command was activated.

327) Click the **Delete All** button from the Relations box.

328) Click **OK** from the Display/Delete Relations PropertyManager.

The On Entity symbol indicates the Sketch entities with External references.

Redefine the Geometry relations and dimensions.

329) Click **Front** View from the Heads-up View toolbar.

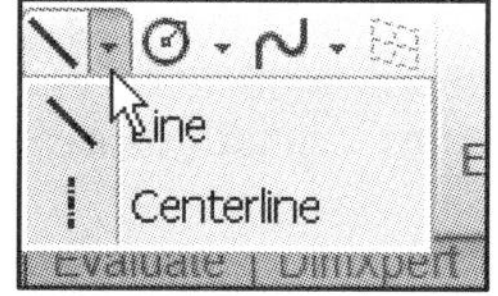

330) Click the **Centerline** tool from the Sketch toolbar.

331) Sketch a **diagonal centerline** between the upper left corner and the lower right corner.

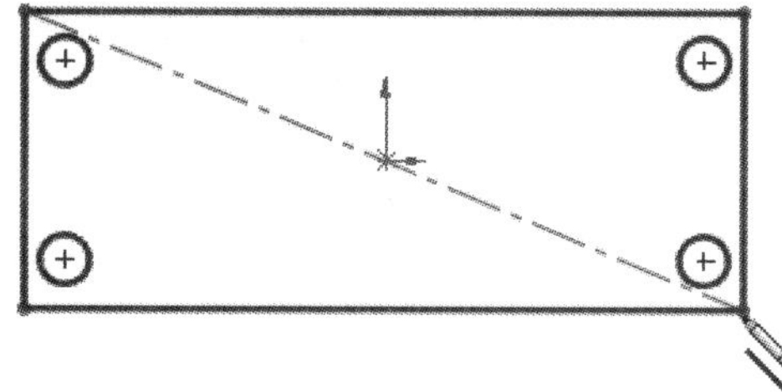

332) Right-click **Select.**

333) Click **View**, **Sketch Relations** from the Menu bar menu.

Add a Midpoint relation.

334) Click the **centerline**.

335) Hold the **Ctrl** key down.

336) Click the **Origin**.

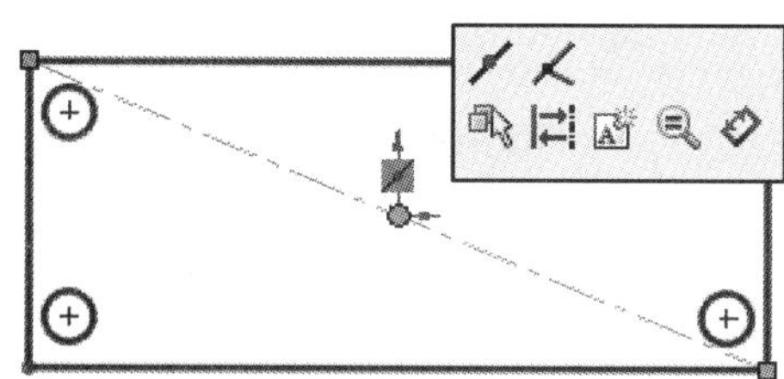

337) Release the **Ctrl** key.

338) Right-click **Make Midpoint** from the Context toolbar.

Add a Horizontal relation.

339) Click the **top horizontal** line. Hold the **Ctrl** key down.

340) Click the **bottom horizontal line**. Release the **Ctrl** key.

341) Right-click **Make Horizontal** from the Context toolbar.

Add a Vertical relation.

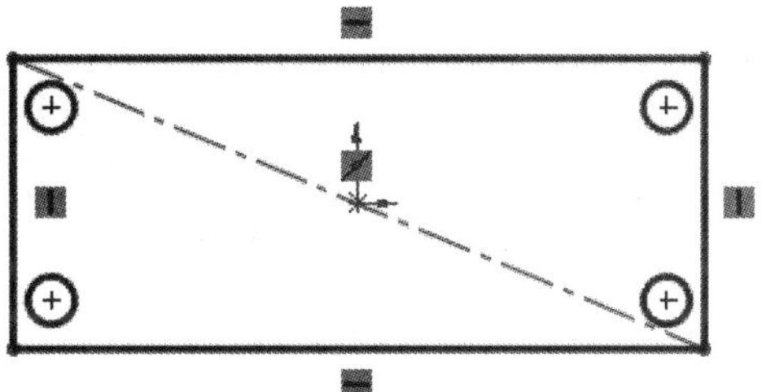

342) Click the **right vertical** line. Hold the **Ctrl** key down.

343) Click the **left vertical** line. Release the **Ctrl** key.

344) Right-click **Make Vertical**. Click **OK** from the Properties PropertyManager.

Add dimensions.

345) Click the **Smart Dimension** tool from the Sketch toolbar.

346) **Dimension** the model as illustrated.

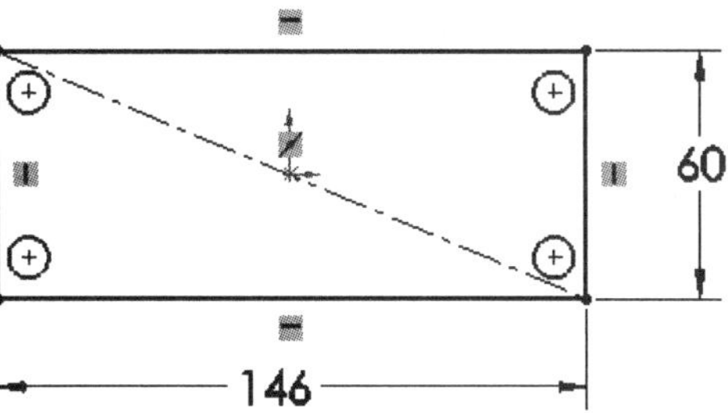

347) **OK** from the Dimension PropertyManager. The rectangular sketch is fully defined and is displayed in black. The four circles are undefined and are displayed in blue.

348) Click **View**, uncheck **Sketch Relations**.

Sketch the Construction geometry.

349) Click the **Centerline** tool from the Sketch toolbar.

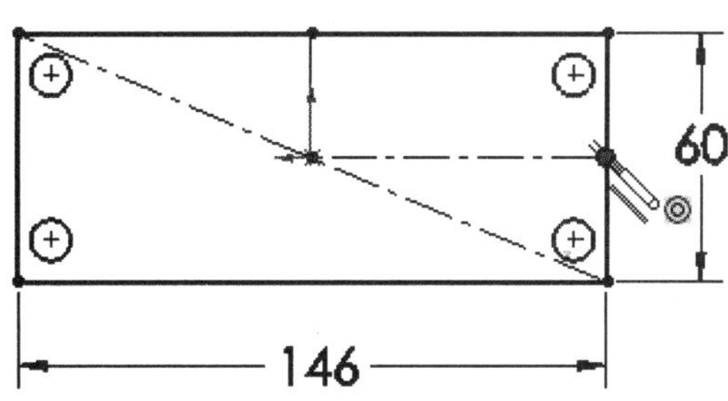

350) Sketch a **horizontal centerline** from the Origin to the midpoint of the right vertical line.

351) Sketch a **vertical centerline** from the Origin to the midpoint of the top horizontal line.

Add an Equal relation to the four circles.

352) Right-click **Select**.

353) Click the **circumference** of the upper right circle.

354) Hold the **Ctrl** key down.

355) Click the **circumference** of the remaining three circles.

356) Release the **Ctrl** key.

357) Right-click **Make Equal** from the Context toolbar.

Add a Symmetric relationship to the top right and bottom right circles.

358) Click the **horizontal centerline**.

359) Hold the **Ctrl** key down.

360) Click the **top right circle**.

361) Click the **bottom right circle**.

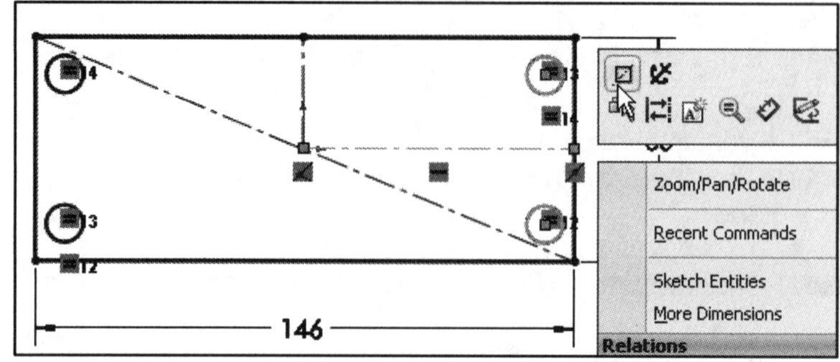

362) Release the **Ctrl** key.

363) Right-click **Make Symmetric**.

Add a Symmetric relationship between the top right circle and the top left circle.

364) Click the **vertical centerline**.

365) Hold the **Ctrl** key down. Click the **top right circle**.

366) Click the **top left circle**. Release the **Ctrl** key.

367) Right-click **Make Symmetric**.

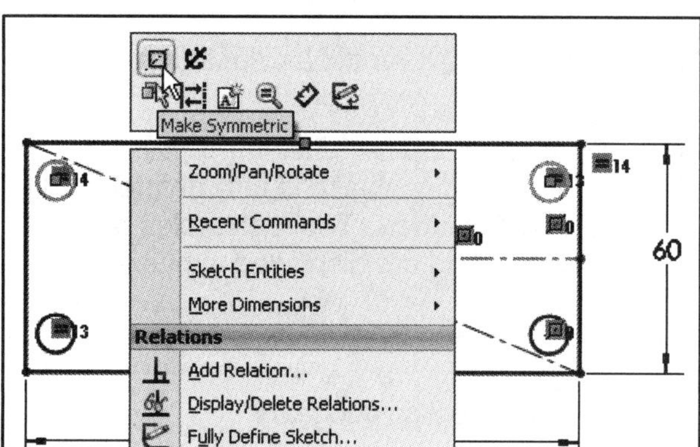

Add a Symmetric relationship between the top left circle and the bottom left circle.

368) Click the **horizontal centerline**.

369) Hold the **Ctrl** key down.

370) Click the **top left circle**.

371) Click the **bottom left circle**. Release the **Ctrl** key.

372) Right-click **Make Symmetric**.

373) Click **OK** ✔ Properties PropertyManager.

Add dimensions.

374) Click the **Smart Dimensions** tool.

375) Click the **center points** of the two top circles.

376) Drag the dimension **130** above the profile.

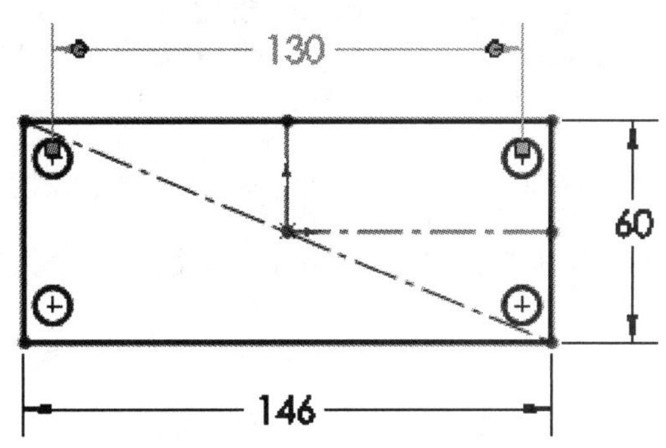

377) Click the **Green Check mark** ✔.

378) Click the **center points** of the two right circles.

379) Drag the dimension **40** to the right of the profile.

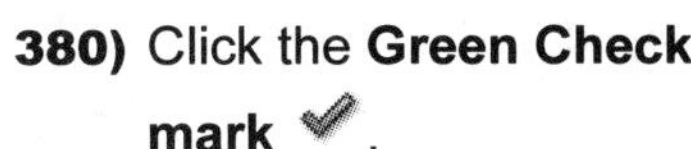

380) Click the **Green Check mark** ✔.

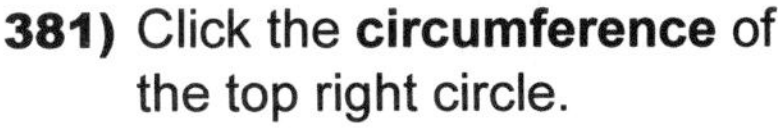

381) Click the **circumference** of the top right circle.

382) Drag the diameter **10** off the profile.

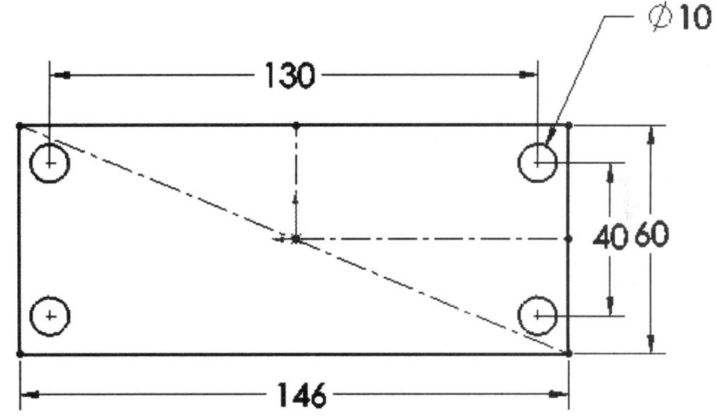

383) Click the **Green Check mark** ✔.

384) Click **OK** ✔ from the Dimension PropertyManager. The sketch is fully defined and is displayed in black.

385) **Rebuild** the model. View the updated PLATE-B FeatureManager.

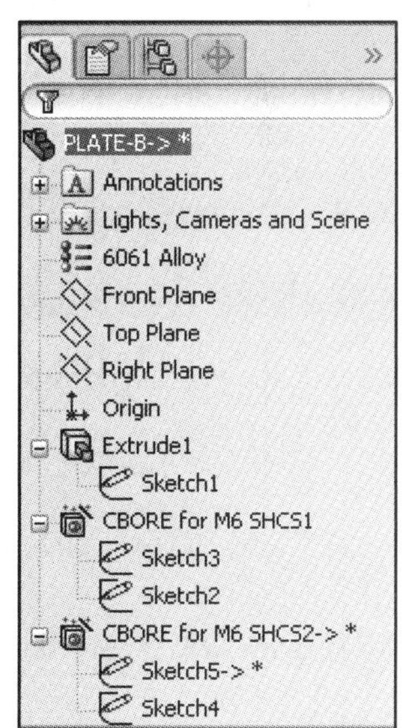

Color indicates that a sketch is under defined (blue), fully defined (black) or over defined (red). The status of a sketch is displayed in the lower right corner of the Graphics window.

The External references are deleted from Extrude1 and Sketch1. Sketch1 is fully defined in the FeatureManager. The In-Context locked "->*" symbol is removed from Sketch1.

Redefine the CBORE for M6 SHCS2.

386) **Expand** CBORE for M6 SHCS2 from the FeatureManager.

387) Right-click **Sketch5->***.

388) Click **Edit Sketch** from the Context toolbar.

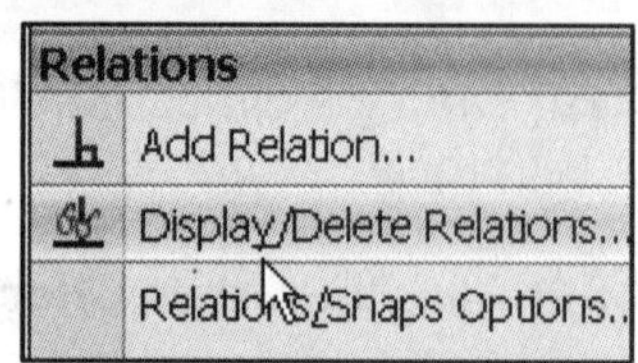

389) Right-click **Display/Delete Relations.**

Delete the locked Coincident0->* and Coincident1->* relations.

390) Click the **Delete All** button.

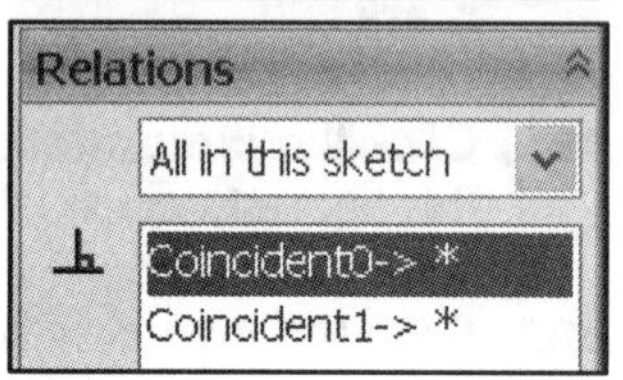

391) Click **OK** from the PropertyManager.

Sketch a vertical centerline.

392) Sketch a **vertical centerline** from the Origin to the midpoint of the top horizontal line as illustrated.

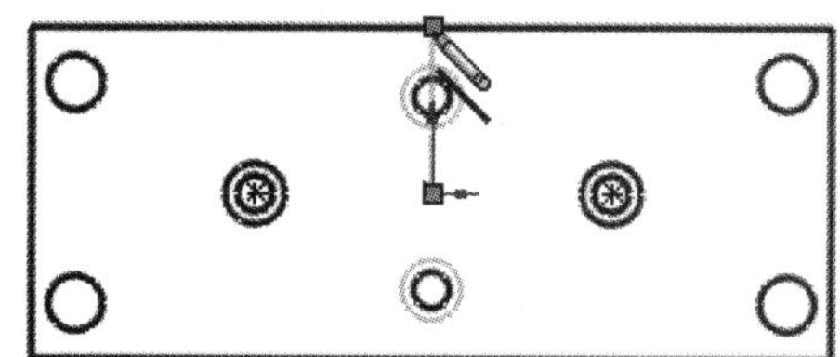

Add a Symmetric relation.

393) Right-click **Select**.

394) Click the **left center point**.

395) Hold the **Ctrl** key down.

396) Click the **right center point**.

397) Click the **centerline**. Release the **Ctrl** key.

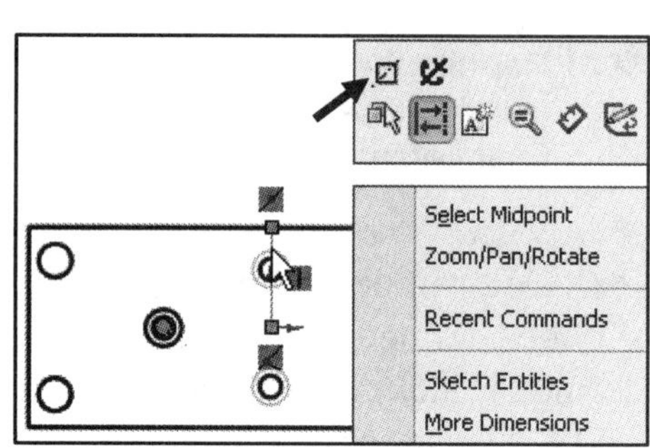

398) Right-click **Make Symmetric**.

Add a Horizontal relation.

399) Click the **Origin**.

400) Hold the **Ctrl** key down.

401) Click the **two center points**.

402) Release the **Ctrl** key.

403) Right-click **Make Horizontal**.

404) Click **OK** from the Properties PropertyManager.

Add a 66mm dimension.

405) Click the **Smart Dimensions** tool.

406) Click the **two center points**.

407) Enter the **66 dimension** above the top horizontal line.

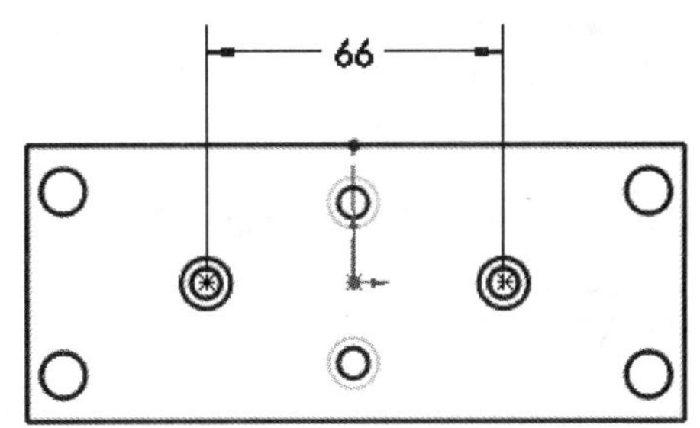

408) Click the **Green Check mark** ✓.

409) Click **OK** ✓. The center points are fully defined. The External references for PLATE-B are redefined.

Close the Sketch.

410) Click **Exit Sketch**.

Save PLATE-B.

411) Click **Save**.

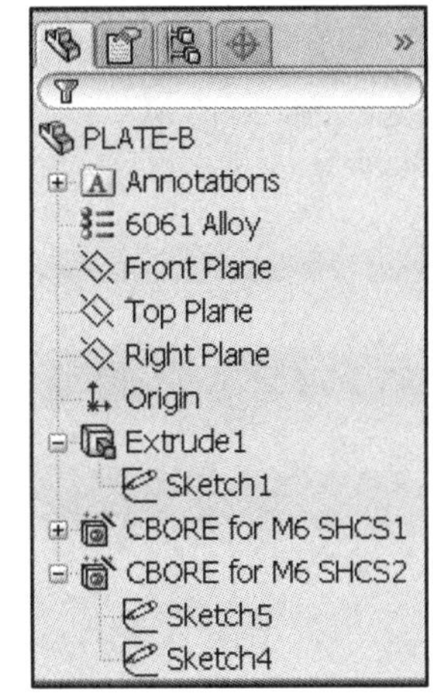

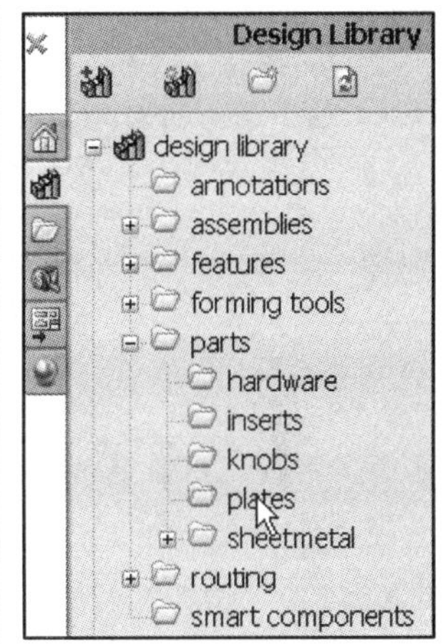

Insert PLATE-B into the plates folder.

412) Click and drag the **PLATE-B** part icon into the plates folder. If required, Pin the Design Library.

413) Click **OK** ✓ from the Add to Library PropertyManager.

414) Click **Save**.

Utilize PLATE-B in other assemblies. PLATE-B contains no External references or InPlace Mates.

Return to the 2AXIS-TRANSFER assembly.

415) Click **Window**, **2AXIS-TRANSFER**.

416) Click **Yes** to update the models.

Activity: Locate InPlace Mates with the Filter FeatureManager tool

Locate the InPlace Mates in the 2AXIS-TRANSFER assembly.

417) Enter **InPlace** in the Filter FeatureManager location as illustrated. View the results.

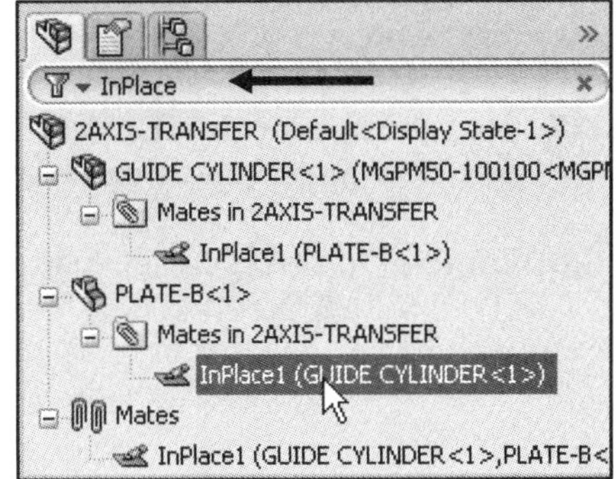

Delete the InPlace text in the Filter FeatureManager section.

418) Right-click **InPlace1 (GUIDE-CYLINDER<1>)** from the FeatureManager as illustrated.

419) Click **Delete**.

420) Click **Yes** to confirm delete.

421) Delete the **InPlace text** in the Filter FeatureManager location. Return to the standard FeatureManager

Hide components.

422) Hide the **following components** as illustrated.

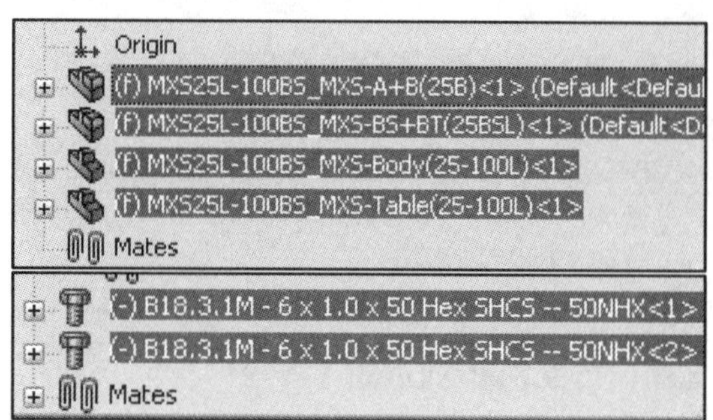

PLATE-B is free to translate and rotate. Create three new Smart Mates to fully define PLATE-B in the 2AXIS-TRANSFER assembly.

Move PLATE-B.

423) Click and drag **PLATE-B** in the Graphics window to create a gap between the GUIDE-CYLINDER assembly and the PLATE-B part as illustrated.

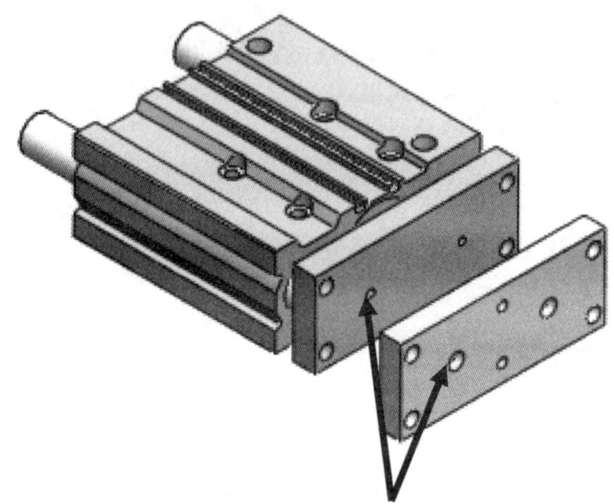

Activity: Insert Standard Mates between PLATE-B and the GUIDE-CYLINDER

Insert Standard Coincident and Concentric Mates between the PLATE-B Part and the GUIDE-CYLINDER Assembly.

Create a Concentric mate.

424) Click the **Mate** tool from the Assembly toolbar. The Mate PropertyManager is displayed.

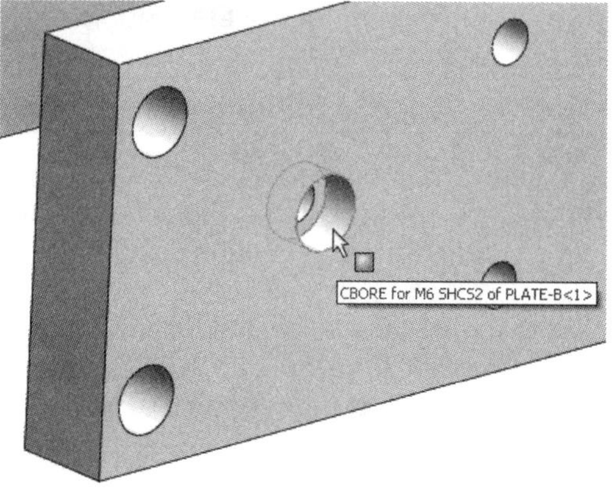

425) Click the **left inside CBORE PLATE-B** cylindrical hole face as illustrated.

426) **Zoom in** to select the left inside cylindrical face of the MGPROD<1>.

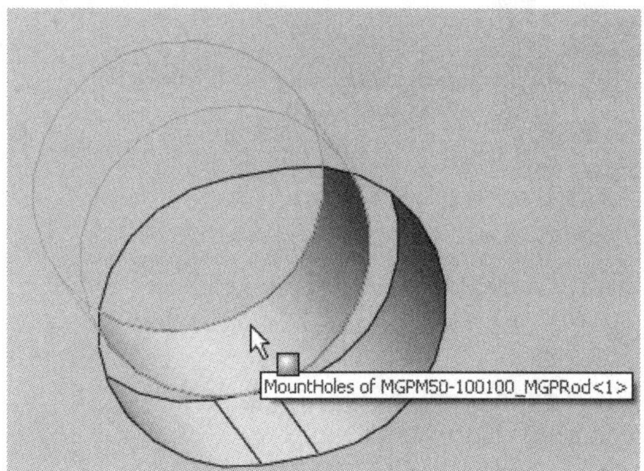

427) Click the **left inside MountHoles of the MGPM50** cylindrical face as illustrated. Note: _It is very important that you pick the correct inside cylindrical face_. Concentric is selected by default.

428) Click the **Green Check mark** ✔.

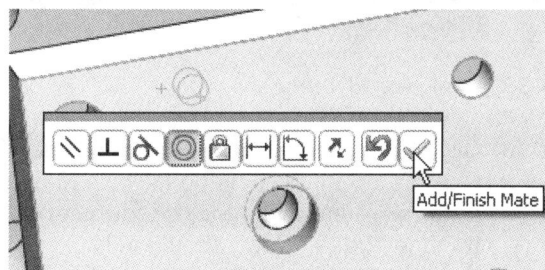

Create the second Concentric mate.

429) Click the **right inside CBORE PLATE-B** cylindrical hole face.

430) Click the **right inside MountHoles of the MGPM50** cylindrical face. Note: It is very important that you pick the correct inside cylindrical face. Concentric is selected by default.

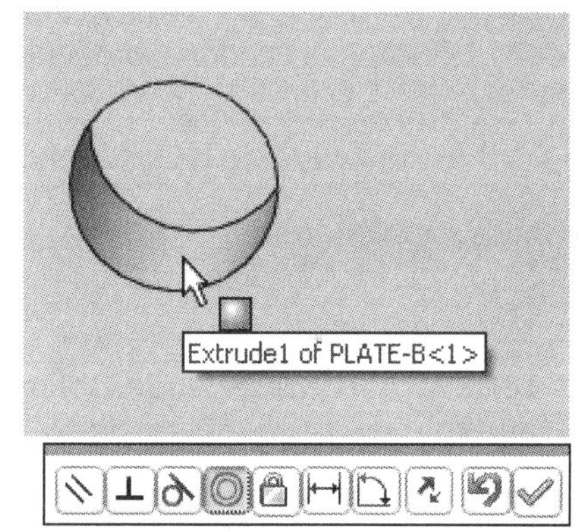

431) Click the **Green Check mark** ✔.

432) Click and drag **PLATE-B** in the Graphics window to create a gap between the GUIDE-CYLINDER assembly and the PLATE-B part

Create a Coincident mate.

433) Click the **back face** of PLATE-B as illustrated.

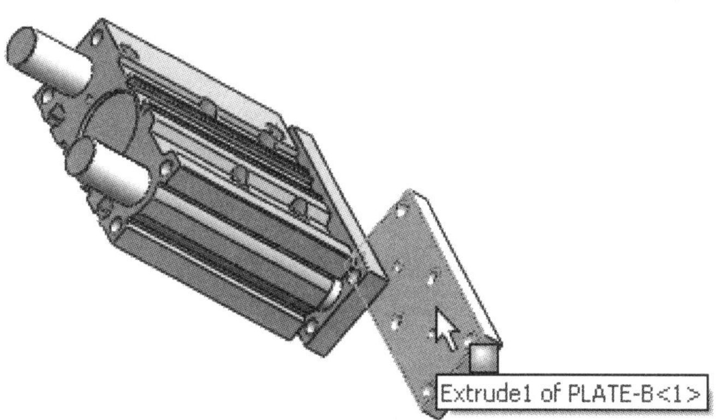

434) Click the **front face** of the GUIDE-CYLINDER. Coincident is selected by default.

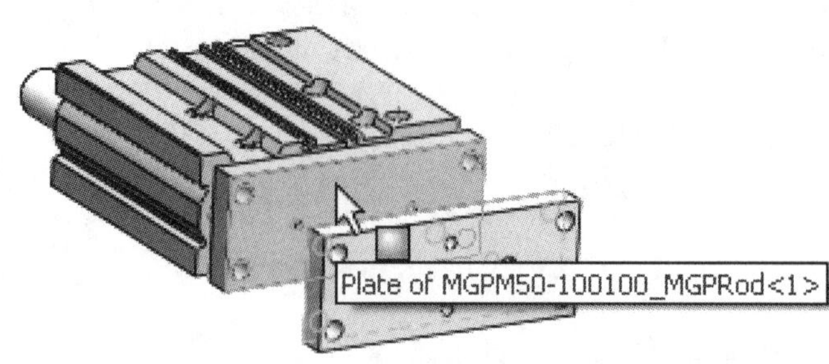

435) Green Check mark ✓.

436) Click **OK** ✓ from the Mate FeatureManager.

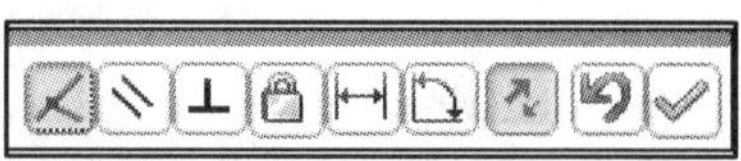

View dependent InPlace Mates and External references.

437) Right-click **2AXIS-TRANSFER** from the FeatureManager.

438) Click **Tree Display**.

439) Click **View Mates and Dependencies**. The PLATE-B part contains no InPlace Mates or External references. Search for other InPlace Mates. None should exist.

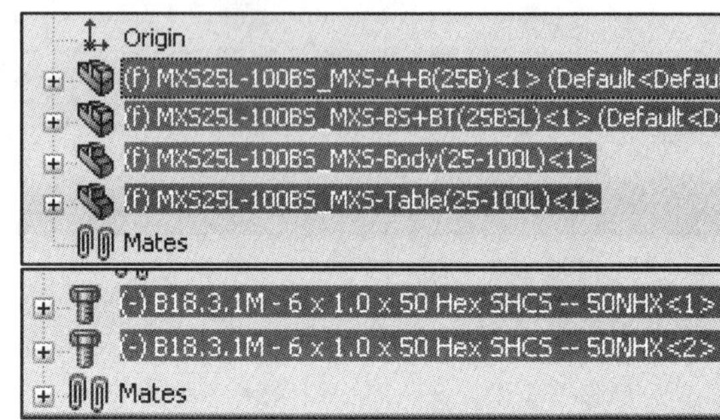

Display the All Hidden Components.

440) Display all Hidden Components.

Activity: Apply the Interference Detection tool

Check for Interference.

441) Click **PLATE-B** from the FeatureManager.

442) Click the **Interference Detection** tool from the Evaluate toolbar.

443) Click **MXS-BS-BT Plate(255)** from the Graphics window.

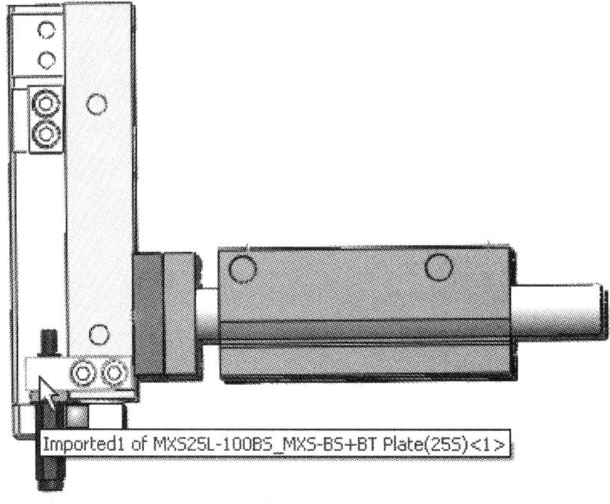

444) Click **Calculate**. There are No Interferences.

445) Click **OK** ✓ from the Interference Detection PropertyManager.

Display an Isometric view.

446) Click **Isometric** view from the Heads-up View toolbar.

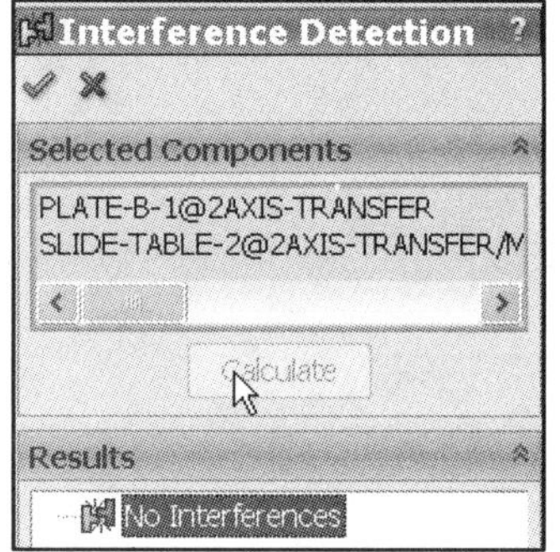

Save the 2AXIS-TRANSFER assembly.

447) Click **Save**.

The 2AXIS-TRANSFER assembly is complete. The Default configuration displays the GUIDE-CYLINDER assembly, the PLATE-B part, and the SLIDE-TABLE assembly.

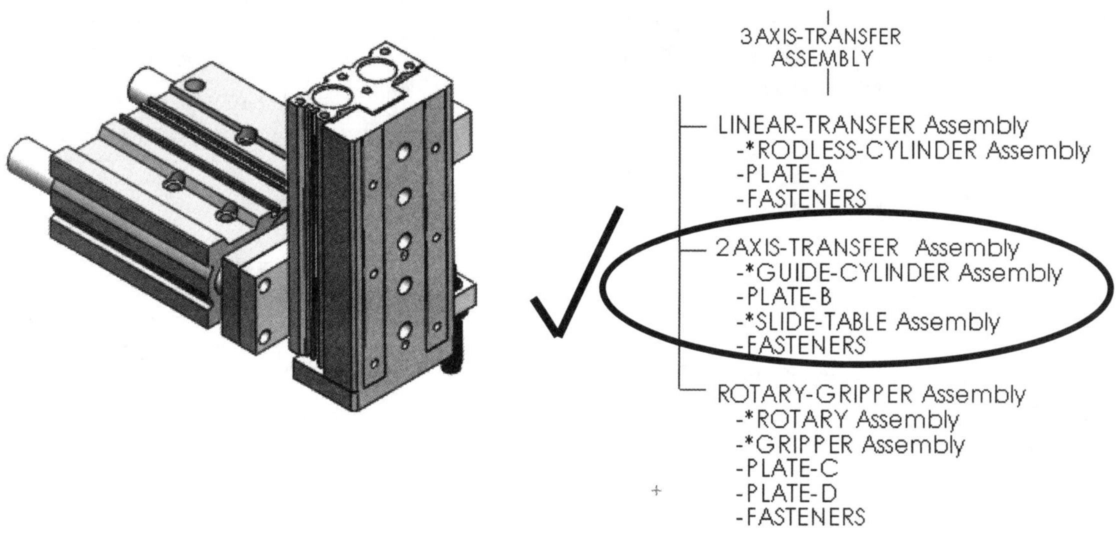

Develop the 2AXIS-TRANSFER configurations. Utilize assembly configurations to control visualization of components, Suppress/Resolve states, Color, Mate characteristics, sub-assembly configurations, and part configurations.

Organize hardware components. Create folders for fasteners in an assembly. Utilize assembly configuration to control the Suppress state and Display state of fasteners, washers, nuts, and other hardware.

Configurations

As discussed in previous projects, there are three ways to create assembly configurations: *Manual (Add Configuration command), Configure component /Configure dimension tool,* and *Design Tables.*

Utilize the Configure dimension tool to create two new configurations for the GUIDE-CYLINDER assembly and the SLIDE-TABLE assembly.

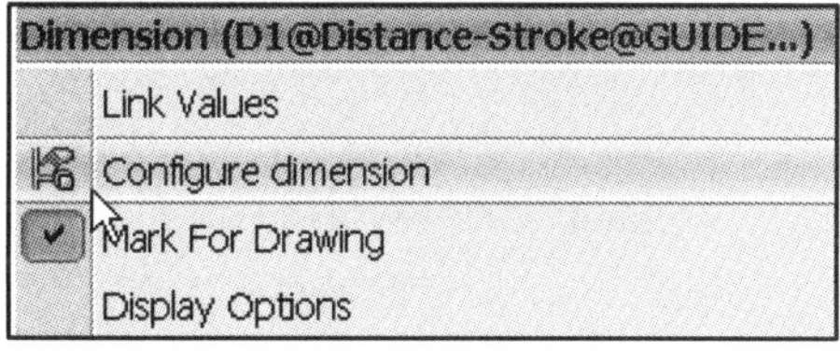

Utilize the Configure component tool to combine the GUIDE-CYLINDER assembly configurations and the SLIDE-TABLE assembly configurations to create the 2AXIS-TRANSFER configurations.

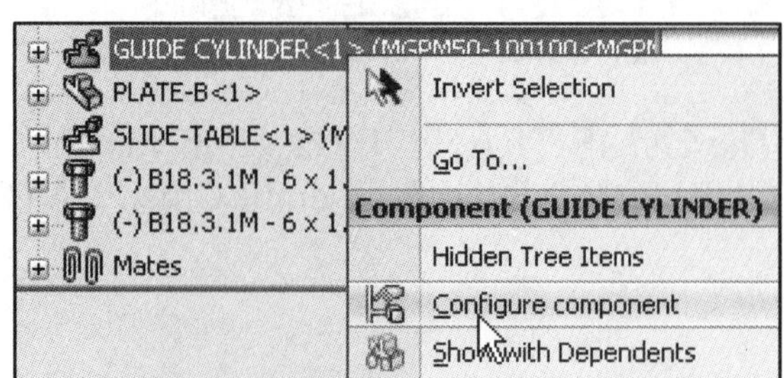

The GUIDE-CYLINDER assembly configurations require a Distance Mate between the GUIDE-CYLINDER\MGPTube part and the GUIDE-CYLINDER\MGPRod part.

Review the existing Mates. Modify the existing Coincident Mate to a Distance Mate.

The GUIDE-CYLINDER assembly is in the Default(MGPM50-100100) configuration.

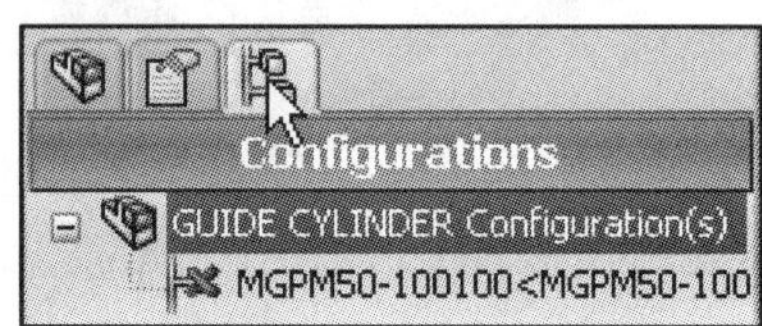

The current configuration of the GUIDE-CYLINDER assembly is named MGPM50-100100. The Distance Mate value equals 0.

Create two new GUIDE-CYLINDER configurations: *Normal* and *Extended*

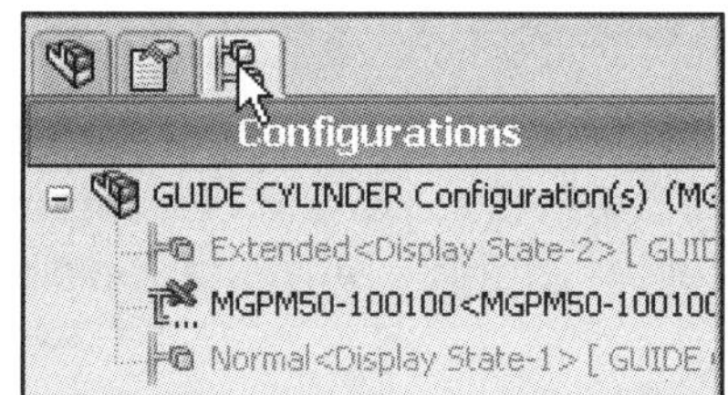

The GUIDE-CYLINDER assembly is in the Normal configuration when the Distance Mate value equals 0.

The GUIDE-CYLINDER is in the Extended configuration when the Distance Mate value equals 100.

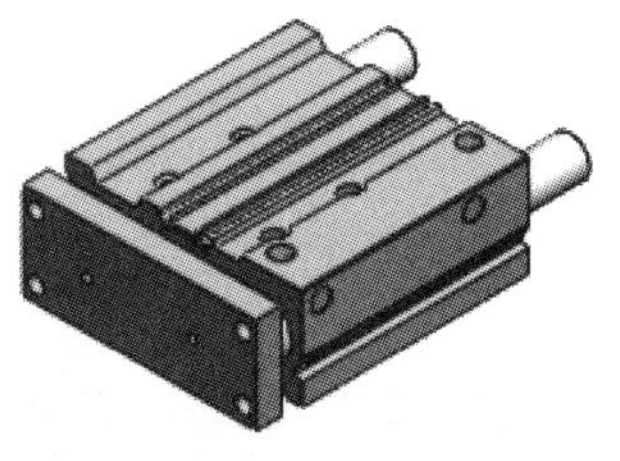

Default (MGPM50-100100)

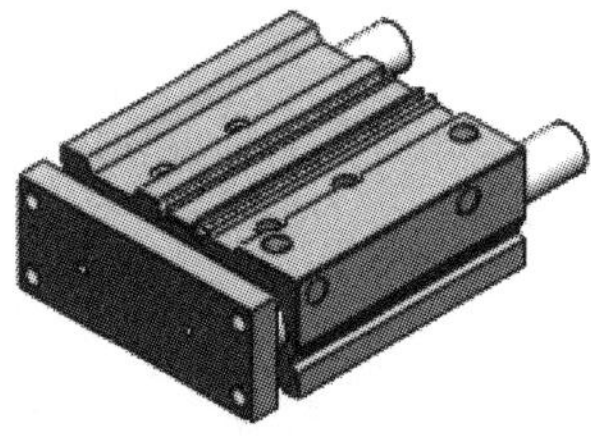

Normal

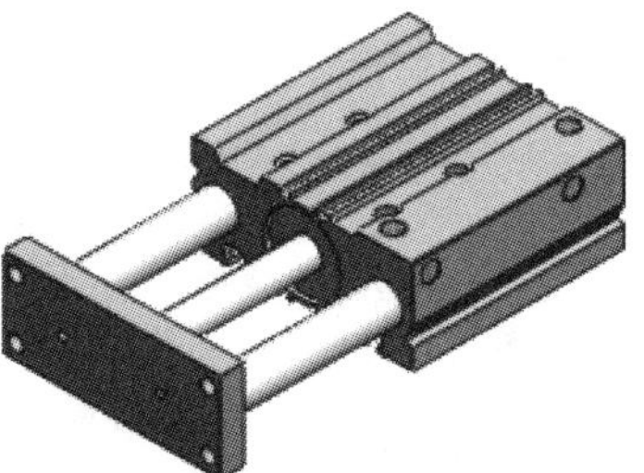

Extended

GUIDE-CYLINDER Configurations

Why maintain a Default(MGPM50-100100) configuration and a Normal configuration when both positions are the same? Answer: The Default(MGPM50-100100 configuration remains a “safety fall back” configuration.

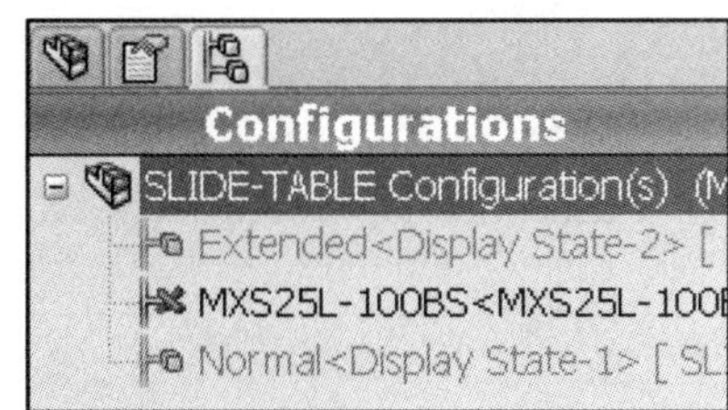

The SLIDE-TABLE requires a Distance Mate between the SLIDE-TABLE/MXSL-Body part and SLIDE-TABLE/MXSL-Table part.

Modify the existing Coincident Mate to a Distance Mate.

The SLIDE-TABLE assembly is currently in the Default(MXS25L-100BS) configuration.

The current configuration of the SLIDE-TABLE assembly is MXS25L-100BS. The Distance Mate is 0.

Create two SLIDE-TABLE assembly configurations:

- *Normal*
- *Extended*

The SLIDE-TABLE assembly is in the Normal configuration when the Distance Mate is 0.

The SLIDE-TABLE assembly is in the Extended configuration when the Distance Mate is 100.

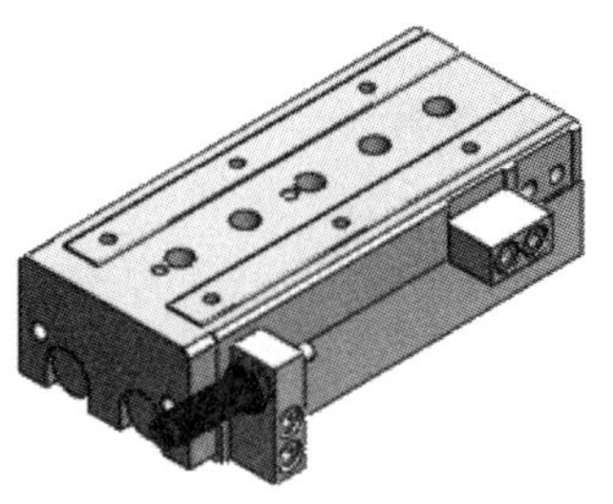

Default(MXS25L-100BS)

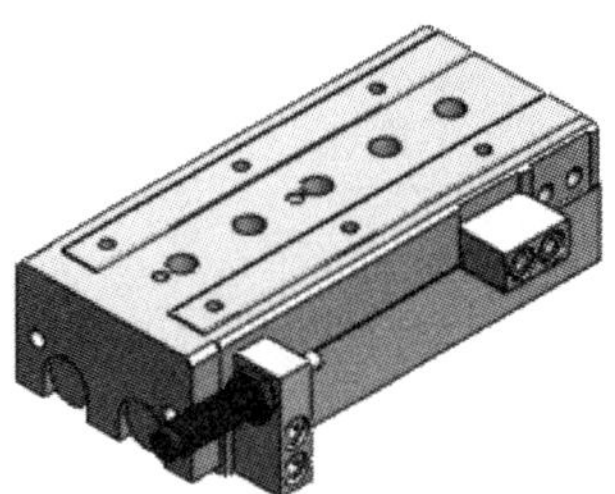

Normal

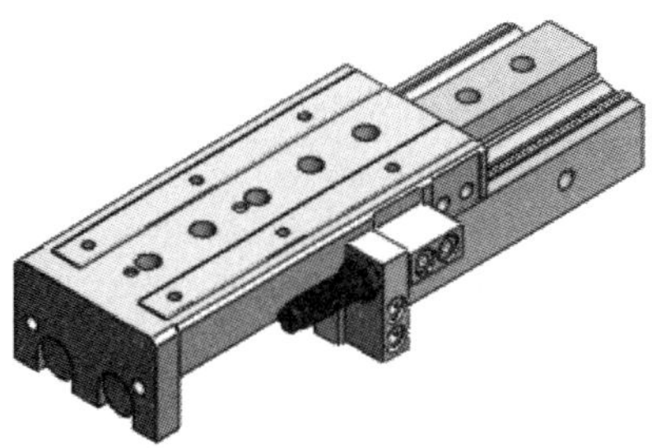

Extended

SLIDE-TABLE Configurations

Create four 2AXIS-TRANSFER assembly configurations:

- *Normal-Normal*
- *Normal-Extended*
- *Extended-Normal*
- *Extended-Extended*

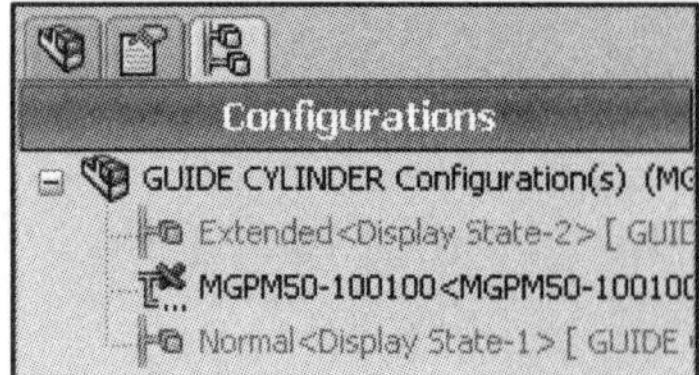

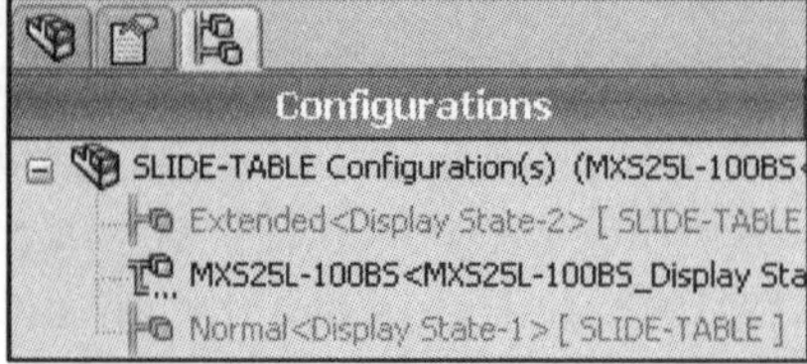

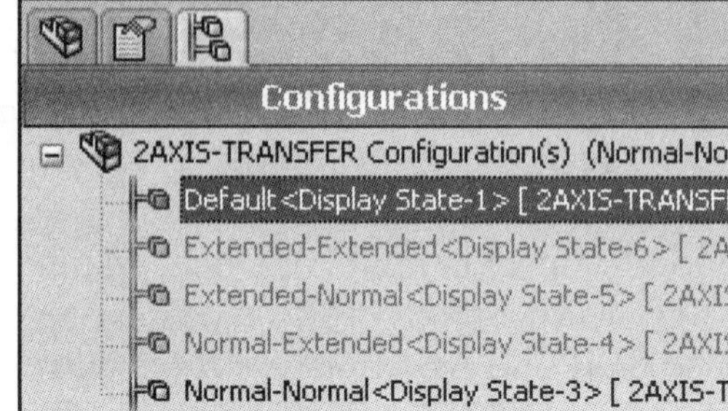

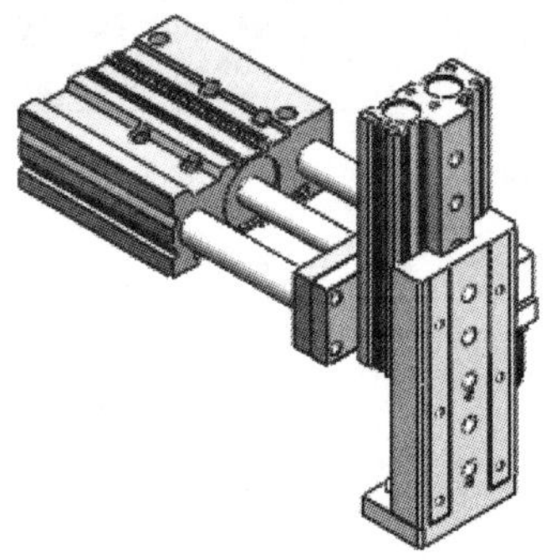

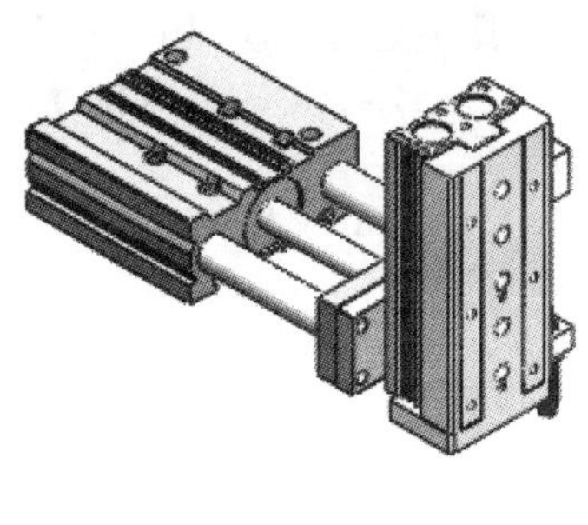

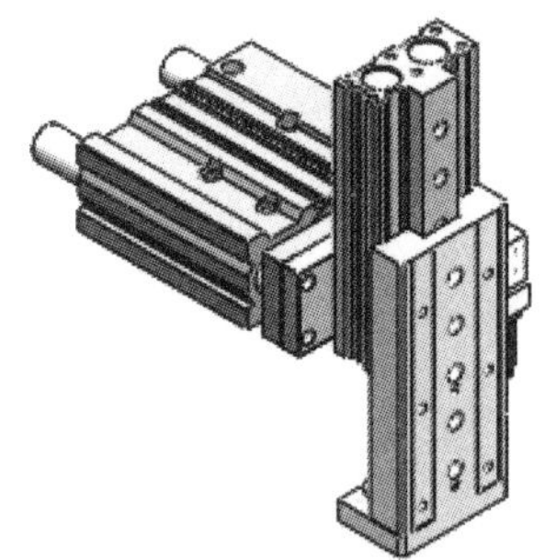

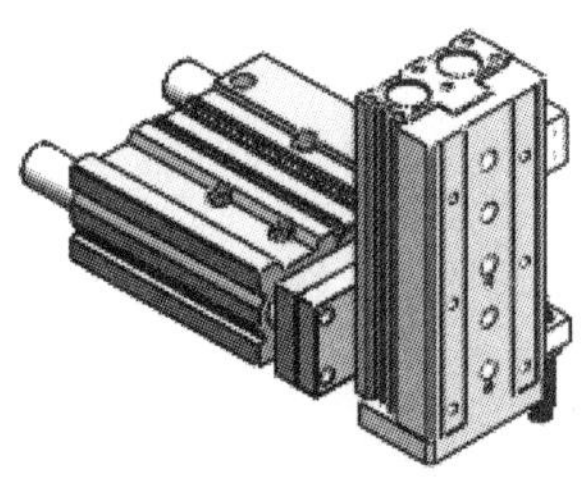

In the 2AXIS-TRANSFER assembly configurations, the configuration name of the GUIDE-CYLINDER assembly is listed first followed by the configuration name of the SLIDE-TABLE assembly.

If using a design table, before creating the new configurations with models obtained from other sources, review Design Table properties.

Avoid problems with configurations. Utilize unique names in your configurations that do not conflict with names selected by the manufacturer.

The 2AXIS-TRANSFER assembly requires the Stroke distance to be controlled through two positions.

Rename the Distance Mate to Distance-Stroke.

Activity: Create two new GUIDE-CYLINDER Configurations

Set the Flexible state and open the GUIDE-CYLINDER assembly.

448) Right-click **GUIDE-CYLINDER** from the 2AXIS-TRANSFER FeatureManager.

449) Click the **Component Properties** tool from the Context toolbar.

450) Check the **Flexible** box.

451) Click **OK** from the Components Properties dialog box.

452) Right-click **GUIDE-CYLINDER** from the 2AXIS-TRANSFER FeatureManager.

453) Click **Open Assembly**. The GUIDE-CYLINDER is displayed in the Graphics window.

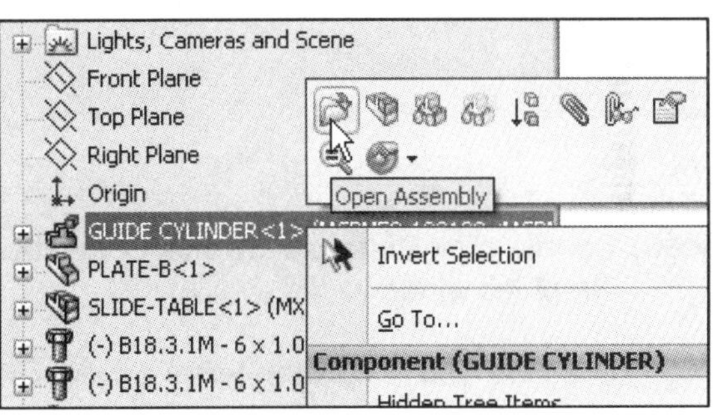

454) Right-click **MGPM50-100100_MGPRod** in the FeatureManager.

455) Click **List External References**.

456) Click the **Break All** button.

457) Click **OK**.

458) Click **OK**.

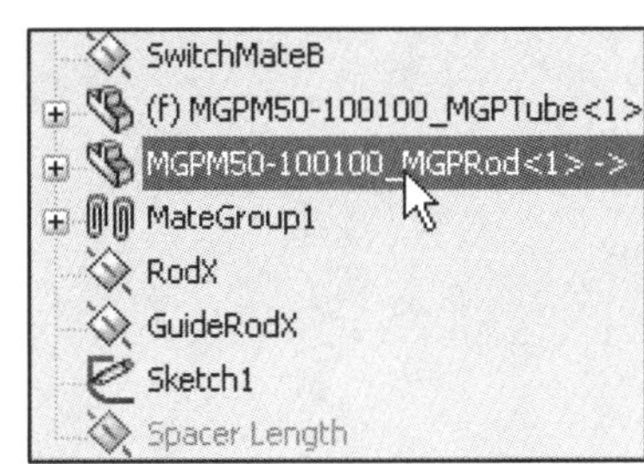

Locate and Redefine the GUIDE-CYLINDER Coincident Mate.

459) **Expand** the MateGroup1 folder.

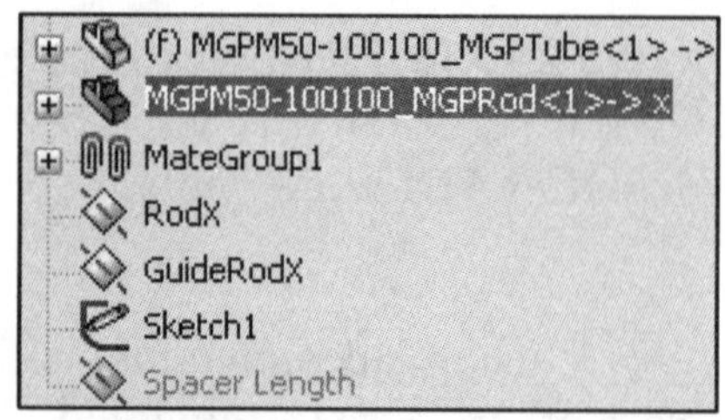

460) Right-click **Coincident1** as illustrated. The Coincident1 Mate is between the face of the MGPTube part and the face of the MGPRod part.

461) Click **Edit Feature** from the Context toolbar.

462) Click **Distance** from the Standard Mates box. The Distance value is 0.

463) Enter **100**.

464) Click **OK** ✔ from the Distance1 PropertyManager.

465) Click **OK** ✔ from the Mate PropertyManager.

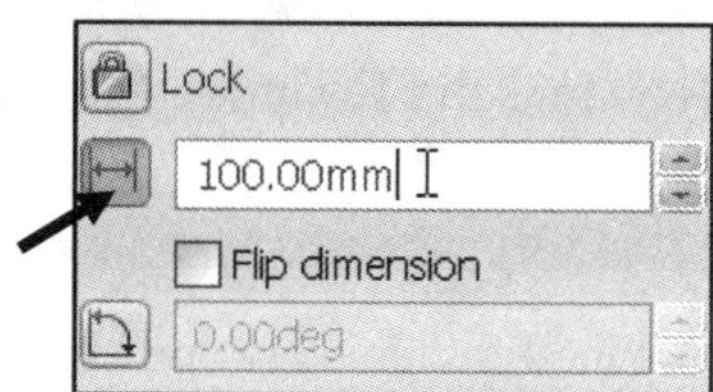

Rename the Distance Mate.

466) Rename the **Distance1** Mate to **Distance-Stroke**.

467) Click **Hidden Lines Removed**.

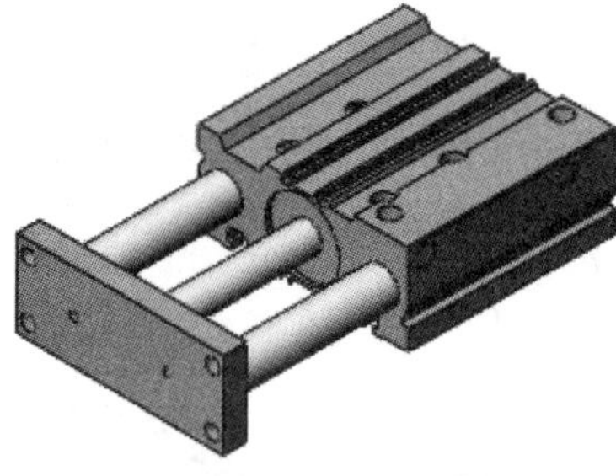

468) Double-click **Distance-Stroke**. View the dimension in the Graphics window.

469) Drag the **100** dimension text off the profile.

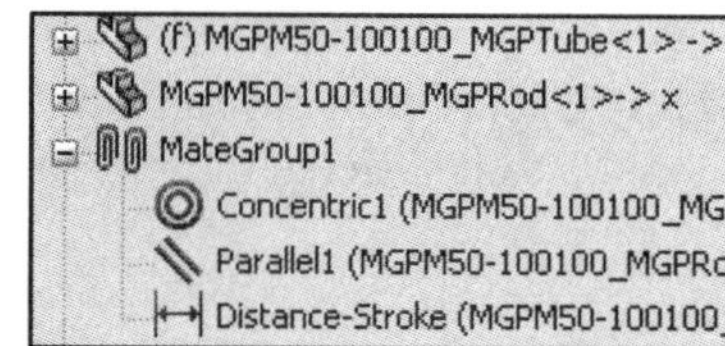

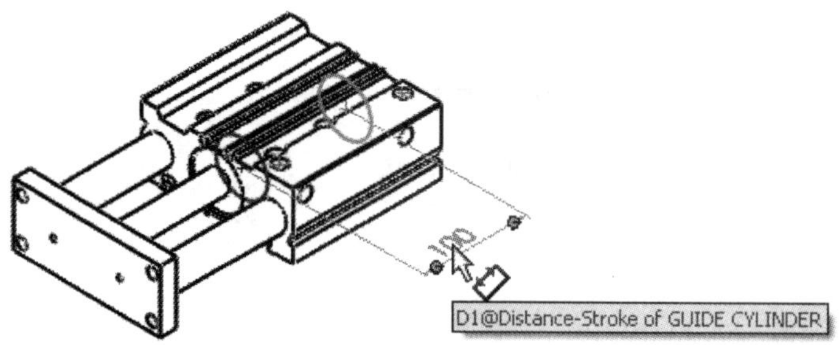

Modify the Distance.

470) Double-click the **100** dimension text.

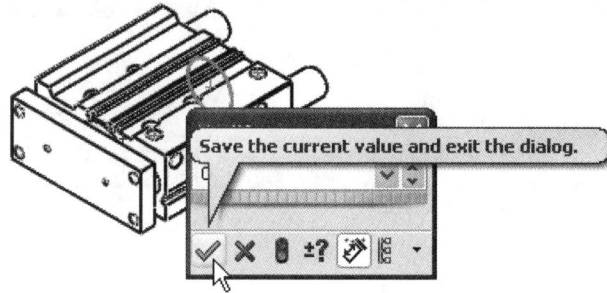

471) Enter **0**.

472) Click **Rebuild**.

473) Click the **Green Check mark** ✔.

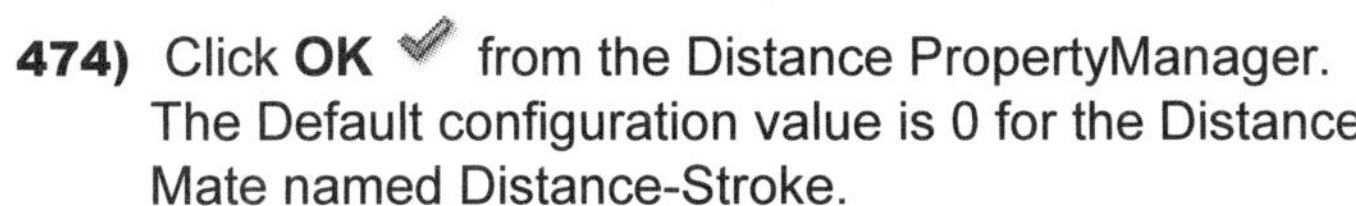

474) Click **OK** ✔ from the Distance PropertyManager. The Default configuration value is 0 for the Distance Mate named Distance-Stroke.

Create the GUIDE-CYLINDER *Normal* and *Extended* Configurations. Utilize the Configure dimension tool.

475) Double-click **Distance-Stroke**.

476) Right-click the **0** dimension text in the Graphics window.

477) Click the **Configure dimension** tool. The Modify Configuration dialog box is displayed. Note Start with the displayed information. The component is in the Default flexible configuration.

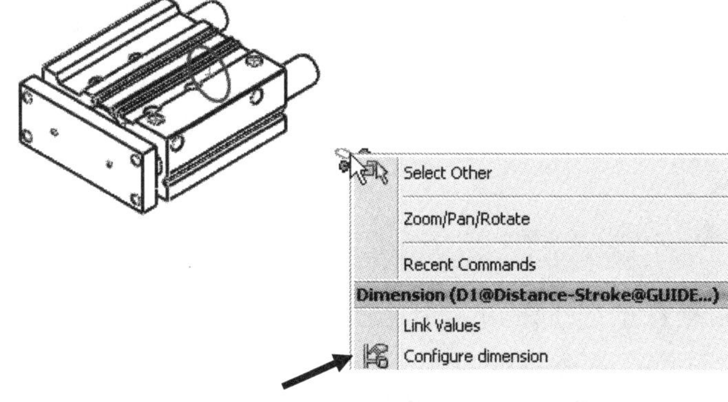

Create the first Configuration.

478) Click inside the **Creates a new configuration** box.

479) Type **Normal**.

480) Press the **Tab** key.

481) Enter **0**.

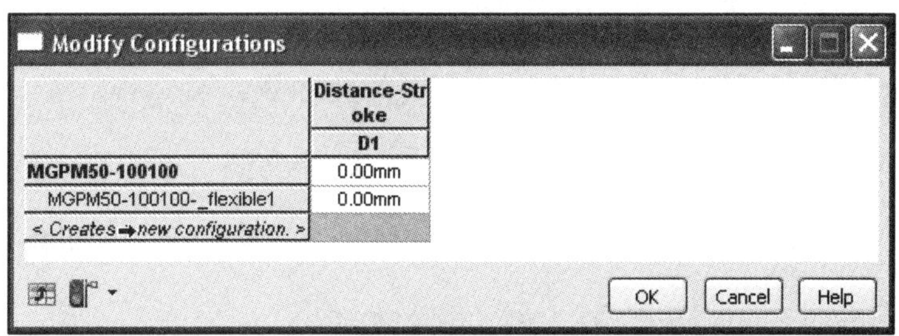

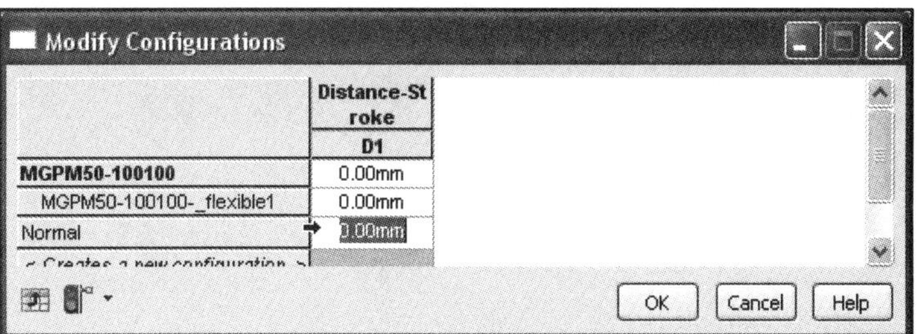

Create the second Configuration.

482) Click inside the **Creates a new configuration** box.

483) Type **Extended**.

484) Press the **Tab** key.

485) Enter **100** as illustrated. You created two new configurations: Normal and Extended. Remember all assemblies have a default configuration. MGPM50-100100 was named by SMC of America. The default configuration is in the flexible state.

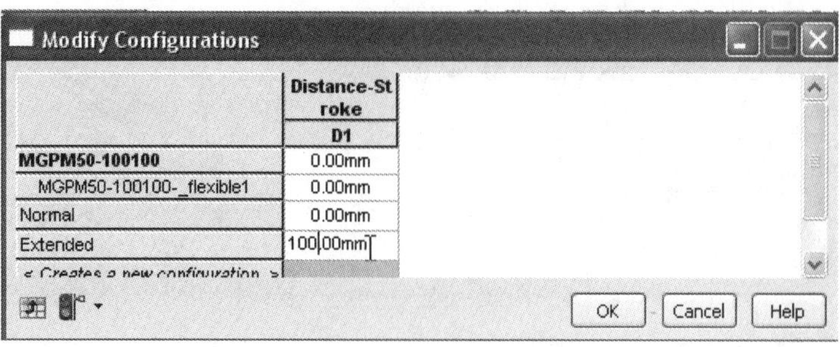

You can rebuild an active configuration or all configurations from the Modify Configuration dialog box.

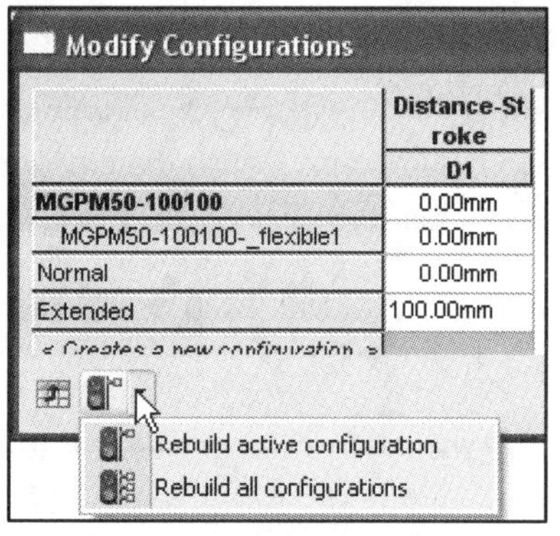

486) Click **OK** from the Modify Configurations dialog box.

487) Click **OK** from the Dimension PropertyManager.

488) Click **Shaded With Edges**.

489) **Rebuild** the assembly.

490) Click **Save**.

Test the configurations.

491) Click the **ConfigurationManager** icon.

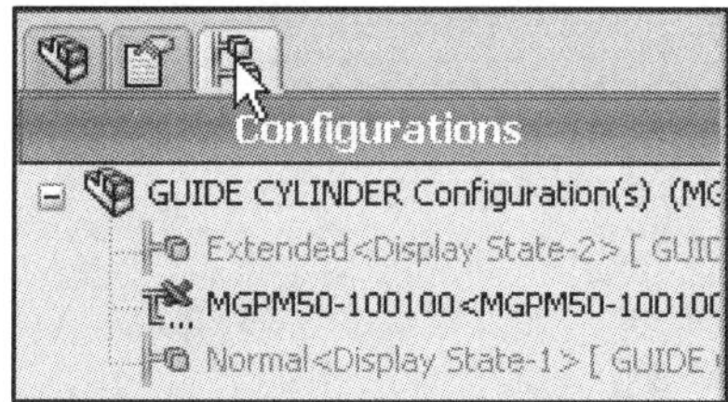

492) Double-click **Normal**. View the results.

493) Double-click **Extended**. View the results.

494) Double click the (Default) **MGPM50-100100** configuration.

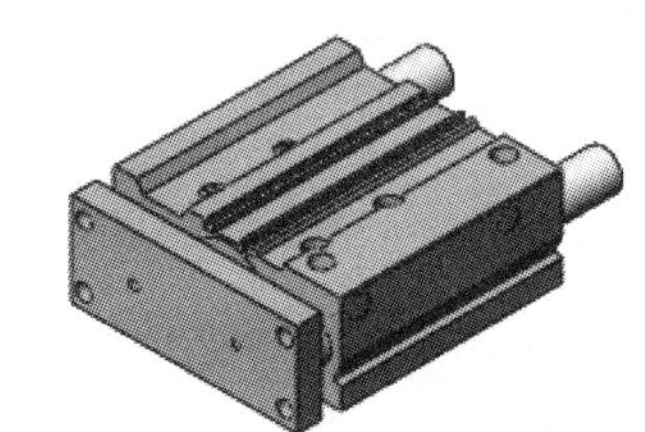

Return to the assembly FeatureManager.

495) Click the **FeatureManager** icon.

Save the GUIDE-CYLINDER assembly.

496) Click **Save**.

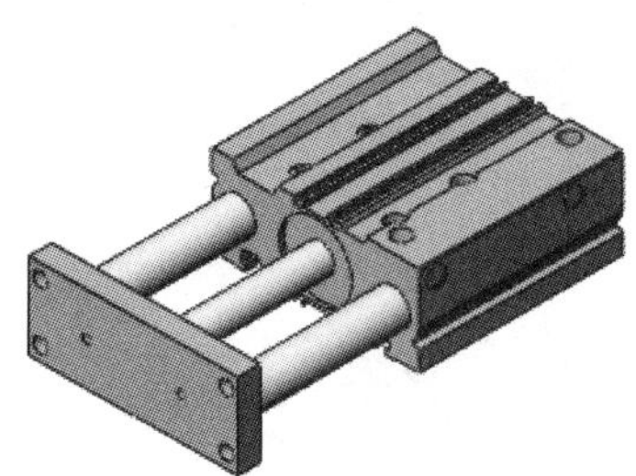

Activity: Create two new SLIDE-TABLE Configurations

Return to the 2AXIS-TRANSFER assembly.

497) Click **File**, **Close**. The 2AXIS-TRANSFER assembly is displayed.

Set the Flexible state and open the SLIDE-TABE assembly.

498) Right-click **SLIDE-TABLE** from the 2AXIS-TRANSFER FeatureManager.

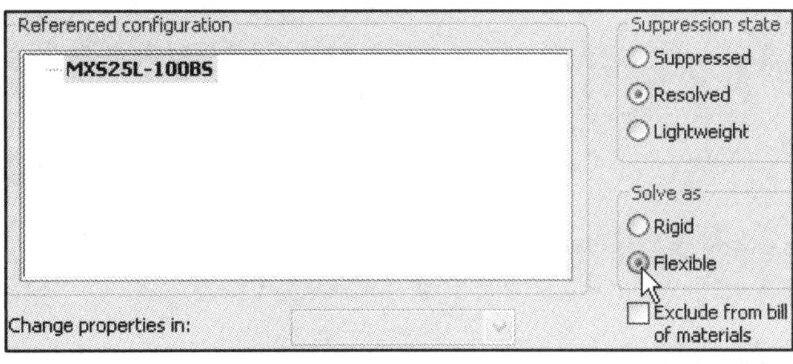

499) Click the **Component Properties** tool from the Context toolbar.

500) Check the **Flexible** box.

501) Click **OK** from the Components Properties dialog box.

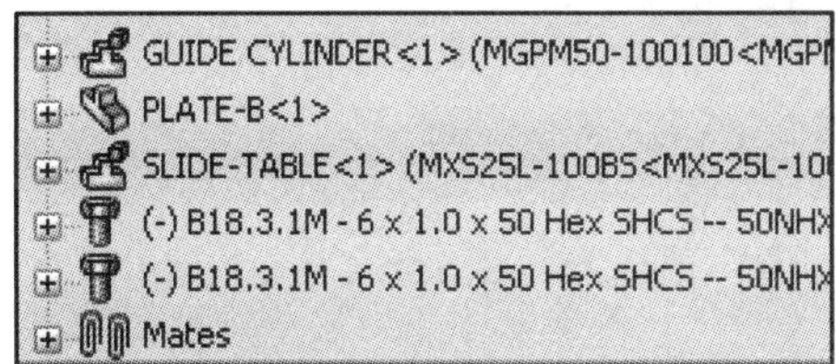

502) Right-click **SLIDE-TABLE** from the 2AXIS-TRANSFER FeatureManager.

503) Click **Open Assembly**. The SLIDE-TABLE is displayed in the Graphics window.

Locate and Redefine the SLIDE-TABLE Distance1 Mate.

504) **Expand** the Mates folder.

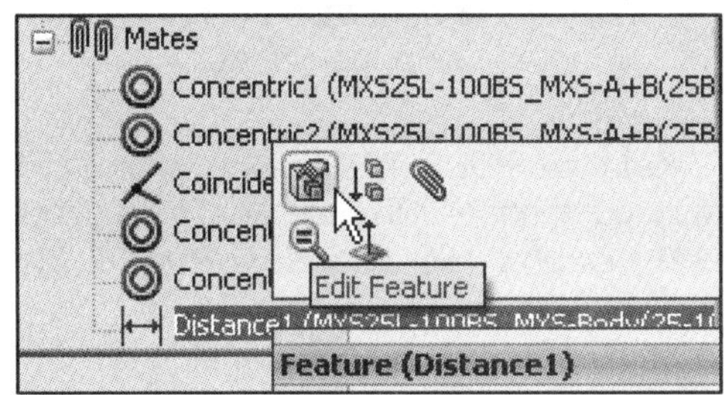

505) Right-click **Distance1** as illustrated. The Distance1 Mate is between the face of the MXS-Body and the face of the MXS-Table.

506) Click **Edit Feature** from the Context toolbar. The Distance1 PropertyManager is displayed.

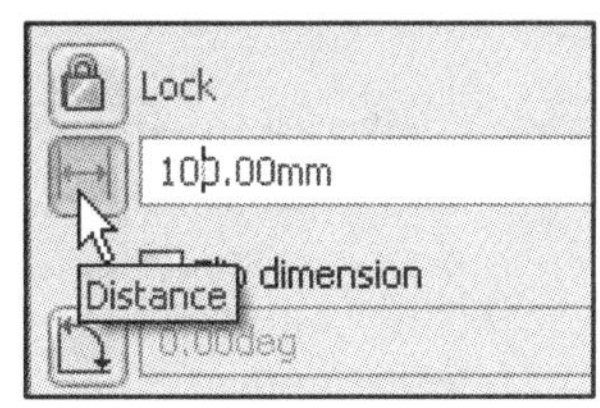

507) Click **Distance** from the Standard Mates box. The Distance value is 0.

508) Enter **100**. View the results in the Graphics window.

509) Click **OK** ✔ from the Distance1 PropertyManager.

510) Click **OK** ✔ from the Mate PropertyManager.

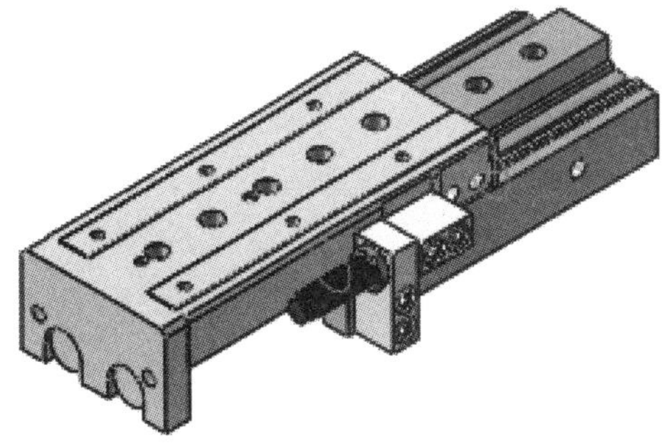

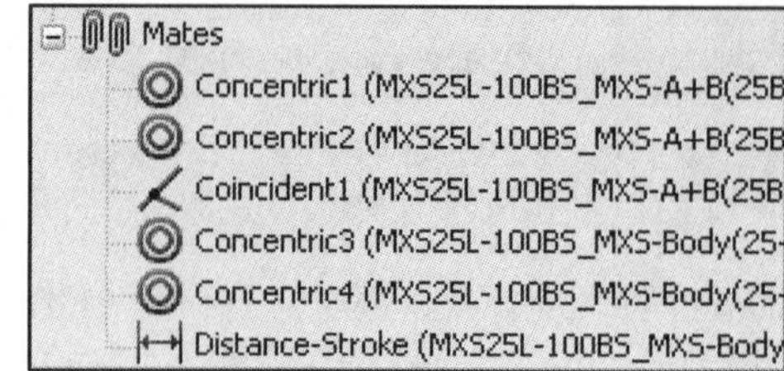

Rename the Distance Mate.

511) Rename the **Distance1** Mate to **Distance-Stroke**.

512) Click **Hidden Lines Removed** from the Heads-up View toolbar.

513) Double-click **Distance-Stroke**. View the dimension in the Graphics window.

514) Drag the **100** dimension text off the profile as illustrated.

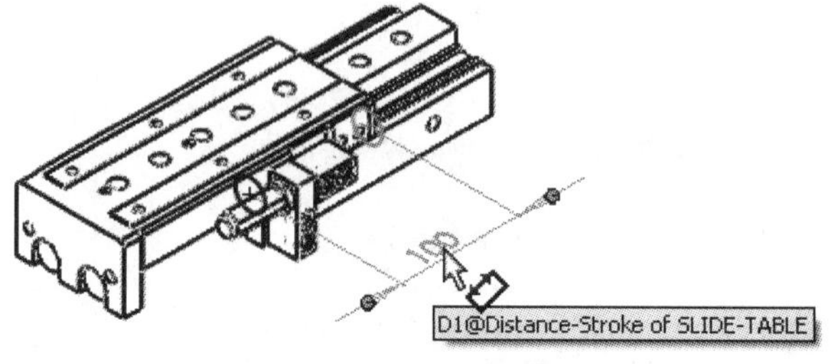

Modify the Distance.

515) Double-click the **100** dimension text.

516) Enter **0**.

517) Click **Rebuild**.

518) Click the **Green Check mark** ✓.

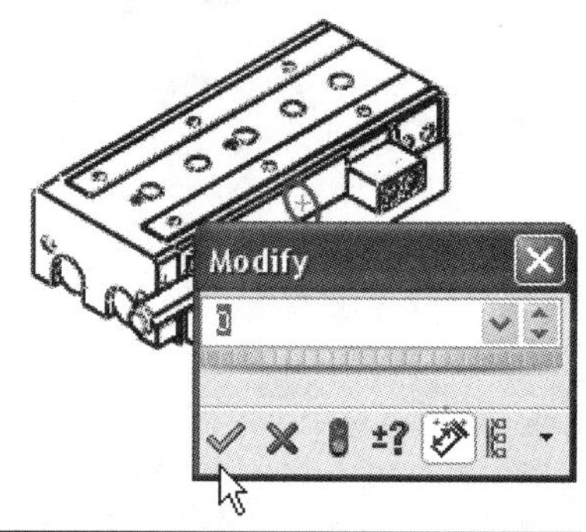

519) Click **OK** ✓ from the Distance PropertyManager. The default configuration value is 0 for the Distance Mate named Distance-Stroke.

Create the SLIDE-TABLE *Normal* and *Extended* configurations. Utilize the Configure dimension tool.

520) Double-click **Distance-Stroke**.

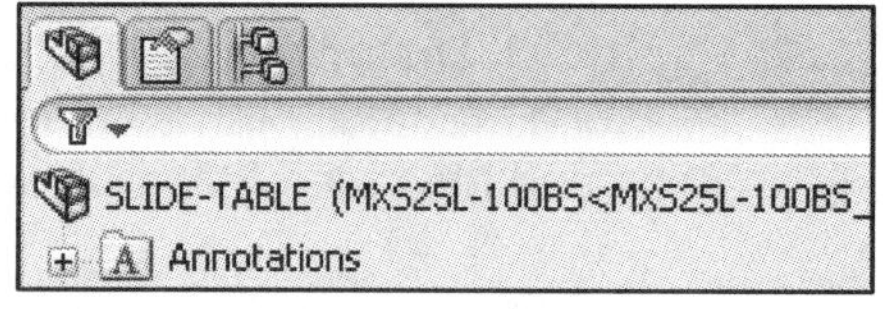

521) Right-click the **0** dimension text in the Graphics window.

522) Click the **Configure dimension** tool. The Modify Configuration dialog box is displayed. Note Start with the displayed information. The component is in the default flexible configuration.

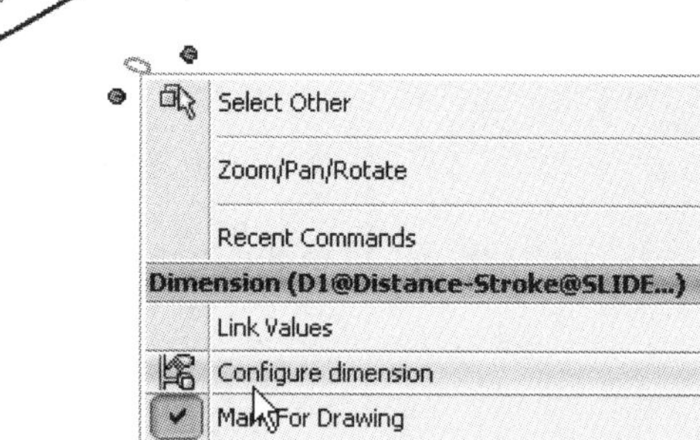

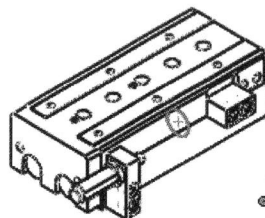

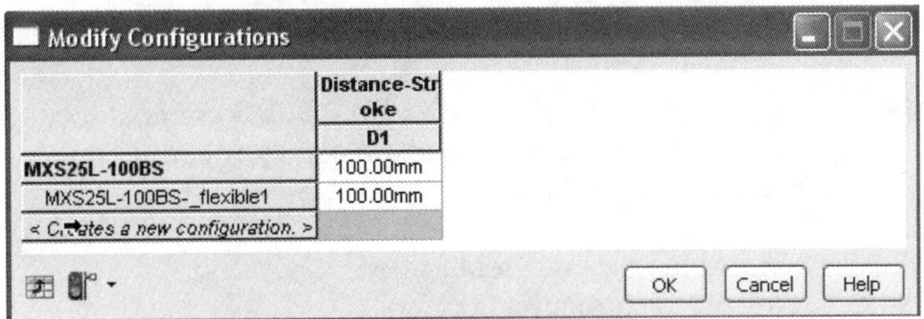

Create the first Configuration.

523) Click inside the **Creates a new configuration** box.

524) Type **Normal**.

525) Press the **Tab** key.

526) Enter **0**.

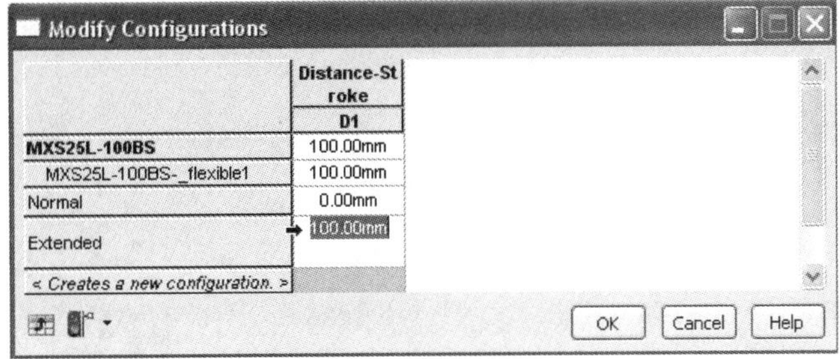

Create the second Configuration.

527) Click inside the **Creates a new configuration** box.

528) Type **Extended**.

529) Press the **Tab** key.

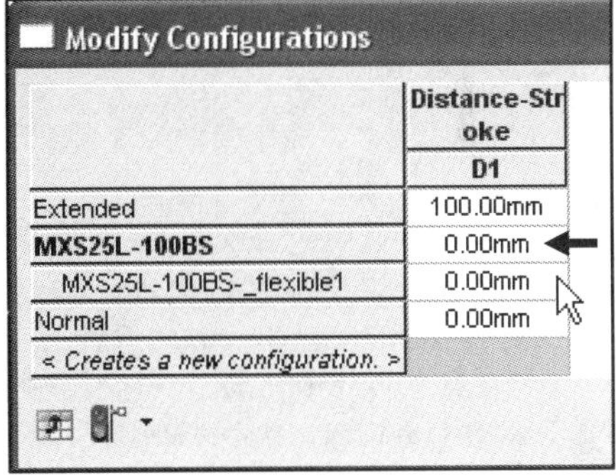

530) Enter **100** as illustrated. You created two new configurations: Normal and Extended. Remember all assemblies have a default configuration. MXS25L_100BS was named by SMC of America. The default configuration is in the flexible state.

531) Enter **0** for Distance-Strike for the MXS25L-100BS configurations as illustrated.

532) Click **Rebuild all configurations**.

533) **Save** the model.

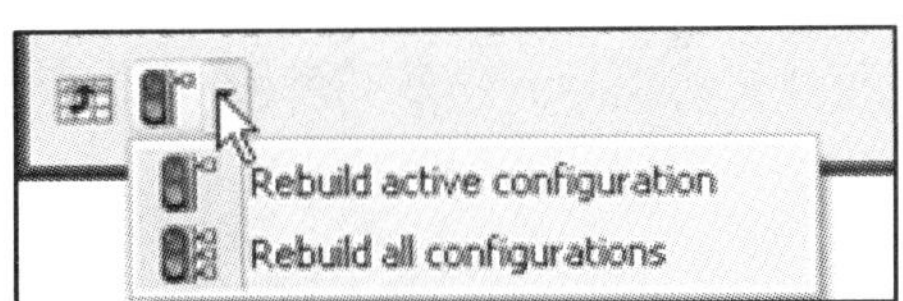

You can rebuild an active configuration or all configurations from the Modify Configuration dialog box.

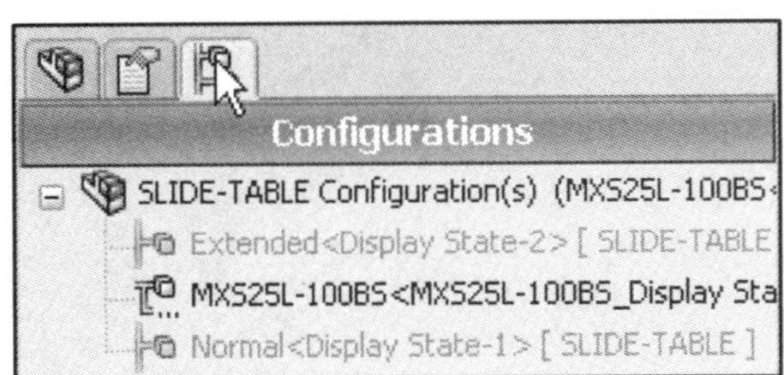

534) Click **OK** from the Modify Configurations dialog box.

535) Click **OK** ✔ from the Dimension PropertyManager. Click **Shaded With Edges**.

536) **Rebuild** the assembly.

537) Click **Save**.

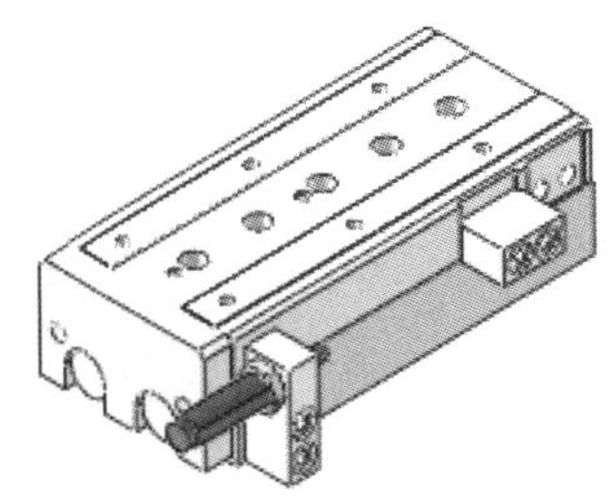

Test the configurations.

538) Click the **ConfigurationManager** icon.

539) Double-click **Normal**. View the results.

540) Double-click **Extended**. View the results.

541) Double click the (Default) **MXS25L-100BS** configuration. Remember, Normal is the backup configuration for the default configuration.

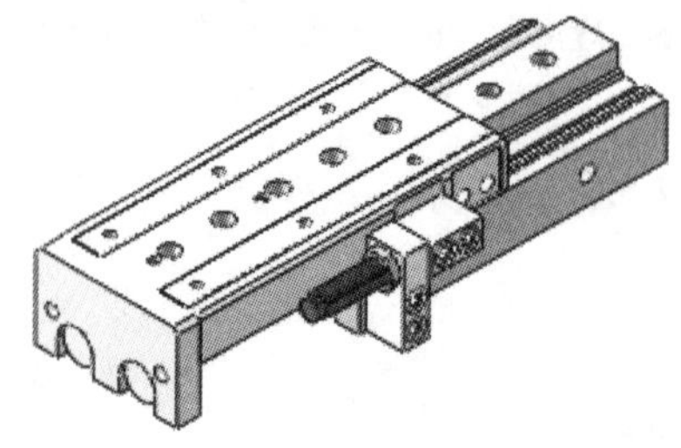

Return to the assembly FeatureManager.

542) Click the **FeatureManager** icon.

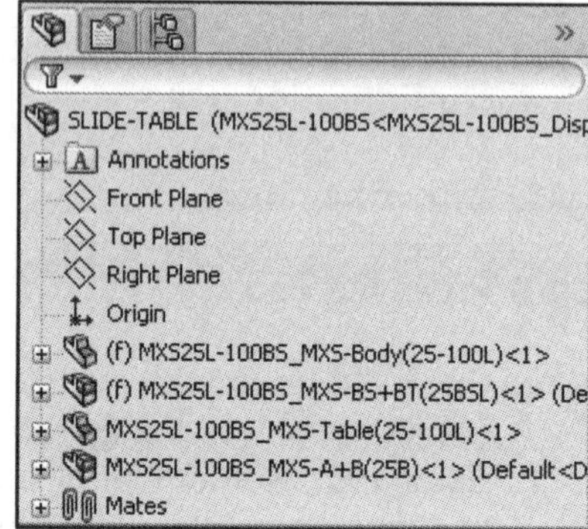

Save the SLIDE-TABLE assembly.

543) Click **Save**.

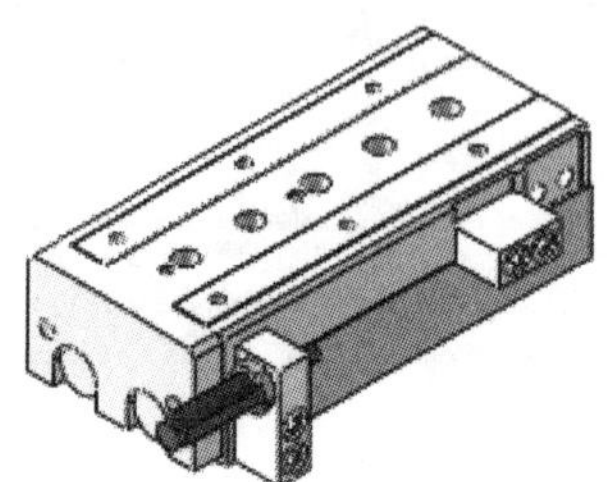

Return to the 2AXIS-TRANSFER assembly.

544) Click **Window**, **2AXIS-TRANSFER**. The GUIDE-CYLINDER Default(MGPM50-100100) and SLIDE-TABLE Default(MXS25L-100BS) are the current configurations in the 2AXIS-TRANSFER assembly FeatureManager.

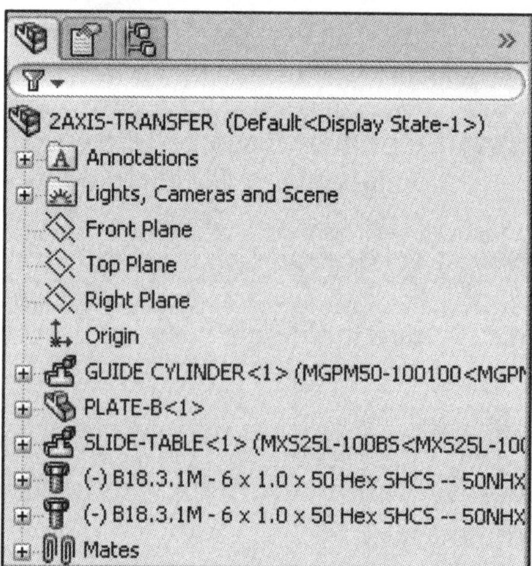

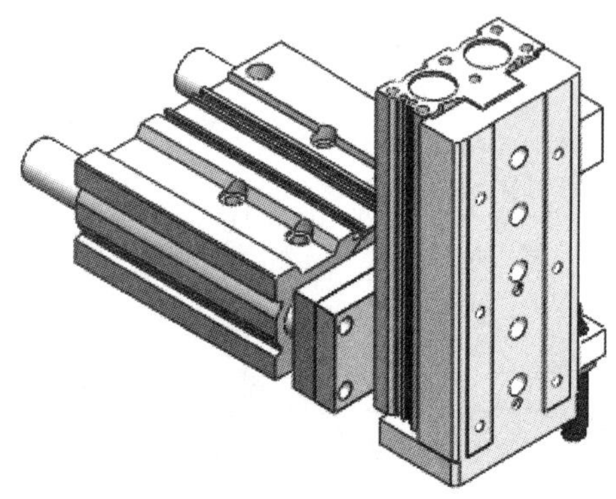

Create the Top level 2AXIS-TRANSFER Configurations

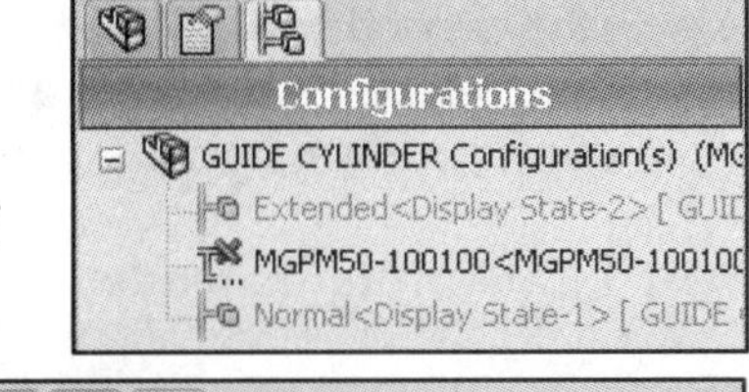

You just created the *Extended* and *Normal* configuration of the GUIDE-CYLINDER assembly and the *Extended* and *Normal* configurations of the SLIDE-TABLE assembly.

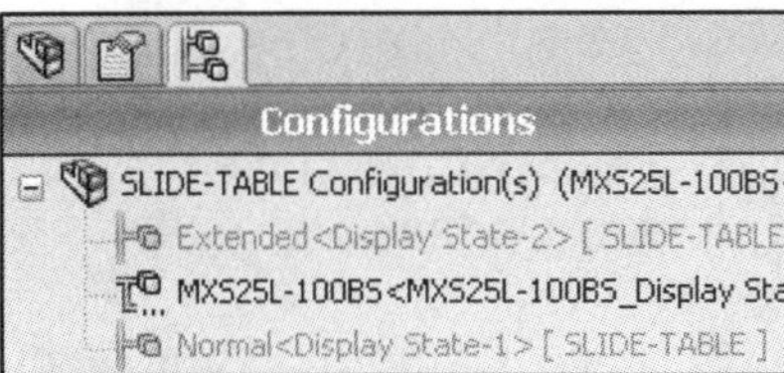

Create the following 2AXIS-TRANSFER configurations for the GUIDE-CYLINDER and the SLIDE-TABLE: *Normal-Normal, Normal-Extended, Extended-Normal*, and *Extended-Extended.* Apply the Configure Component tool.

Activity: Create the Top Level 2AXIS-TRANSFER Configurations

Return to the 2AXIS-TRANSFER assembly.

545) Click **File**, **Close**. The 2AXIS-TRANSFER assembly is displayed.

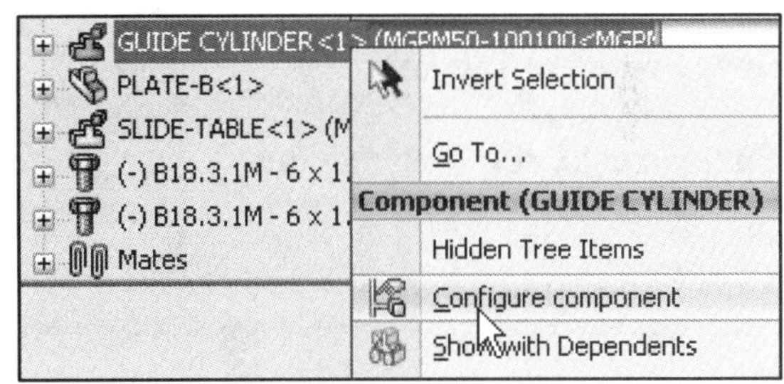

Create the first configuration: Normal-Normal.

546) Right-click **GUIDE CYLINDER** from the 2AXIS-TRANSFER FeatureManager.

547) Click the **Configure component** tool from the pop-up toolbar.

548) Click inside the **Creates a new configuration** box.

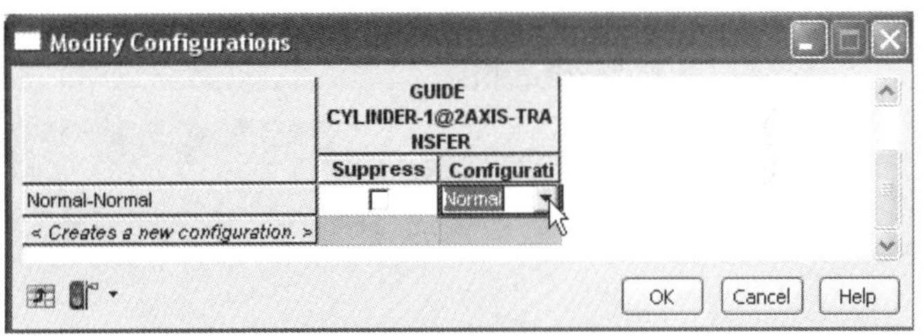

549) Type **Normal-Normal**.

550) Press the **Tab** key.

551) Select **Normal** from the drop-down menu

552) Double-click **SLIDE-TABLE** from the 2AXIS-TRANSFER FeatureManager. The SLIDE-TABLE column is displayed in the Modify Configurations dialog box.

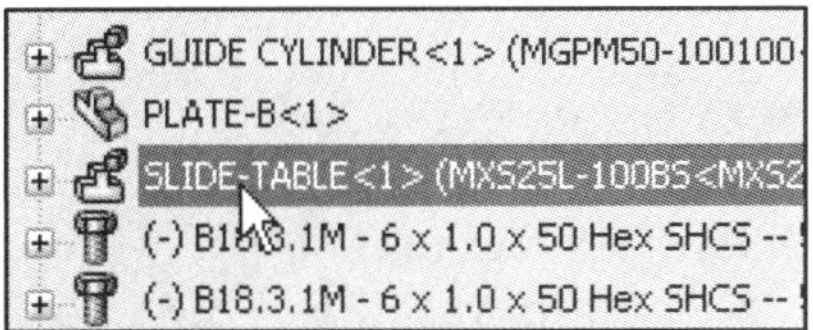

553) Select **Normal** from the drop-down menu as illustrated.

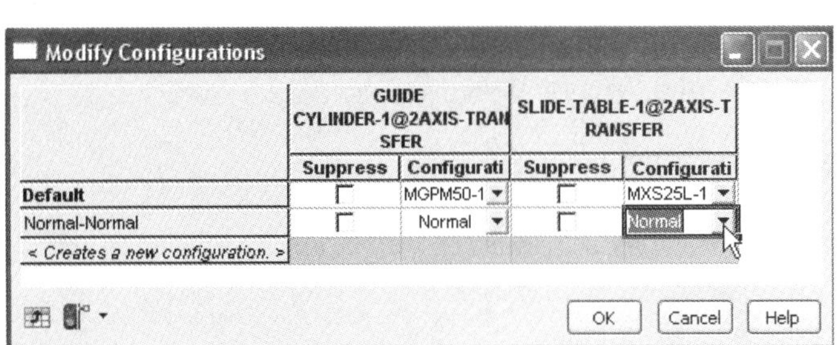

Create the second configuration.

554) Click inside the **Creates a new configuration** box.

555) Type **Normal-Extended**.

556) Press the **Tab** key.

557) Select **Normal** from the drop-down menu.

558) Select **Extended** from the drop-down menu as illustrated.

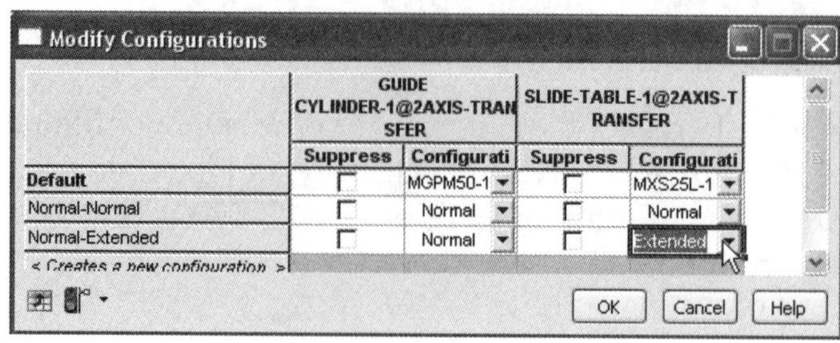

Create the third configuration.

559) Click inside the **Creates a new configuration** box.

560) Type **Extended-Normal**.

561) Press the **Tab** key.

562) Select **Extended** from the drop-down menu.

563) Select **Normal** as illustrated.

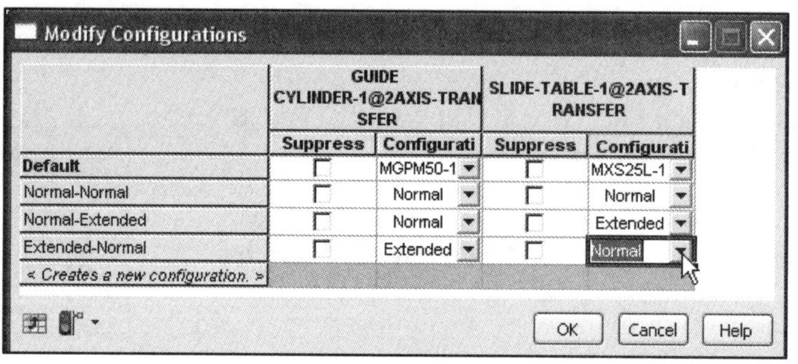

Create the fourth configuration.

564) Click inside the **Creates a new configuration** box.

565) Type **Extended-Extended**.

566) Press the **Tab** key.

567) Select **Extended**.

568) Select **Extended**.

569) Click **Rebuild all configurations**.

570) Click **OK** from the Modify Configurations dialog box.

571) **Save** the model.

572) Click **Yes** to rebuild.

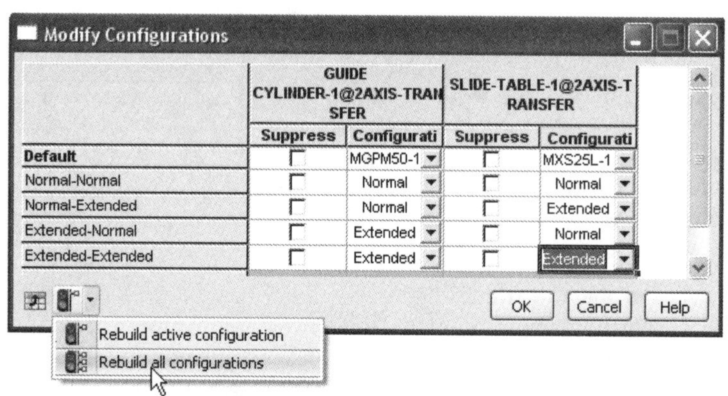

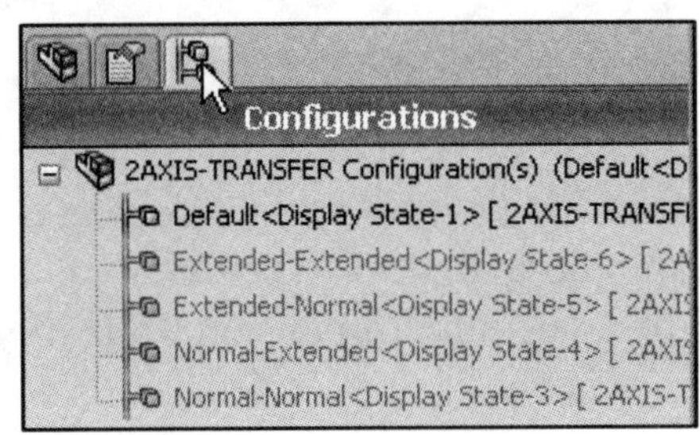

Test the configurations.

573) Click the **ConfigurationManager** icon.

574) Double-click **Extended-Extended**. View the results.

575) Double-click **Extended-Normal**. View the results.

576) Double-click **Normal-Extended**. View the results.

577) Double-click **Normal-Normal**. View the results.

Return to the default configuration.

578) Double-click **Default**. View the results.

Return to the FeatureManager.

579) Click the **FeatureManager** icon.

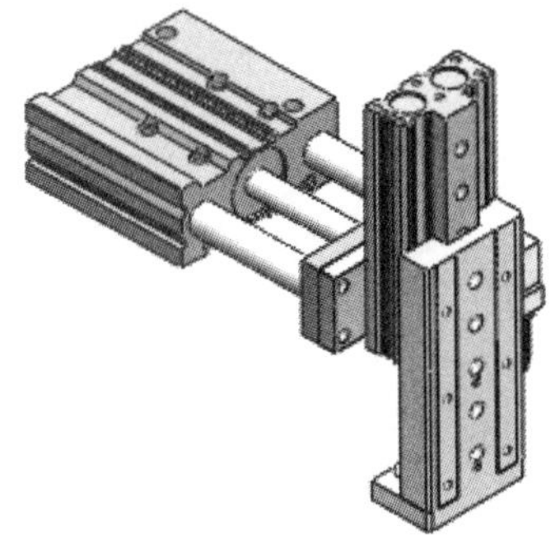

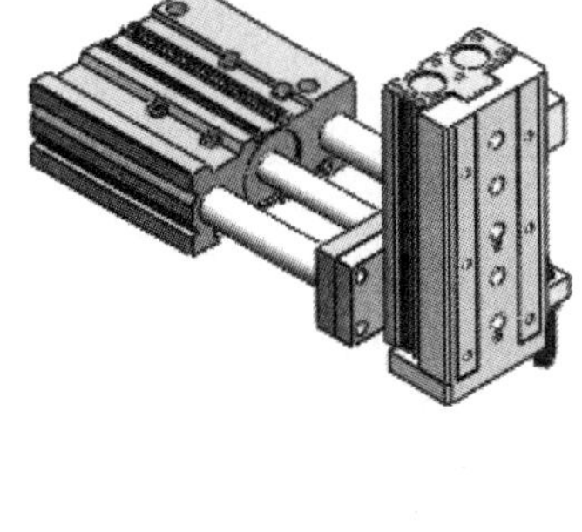

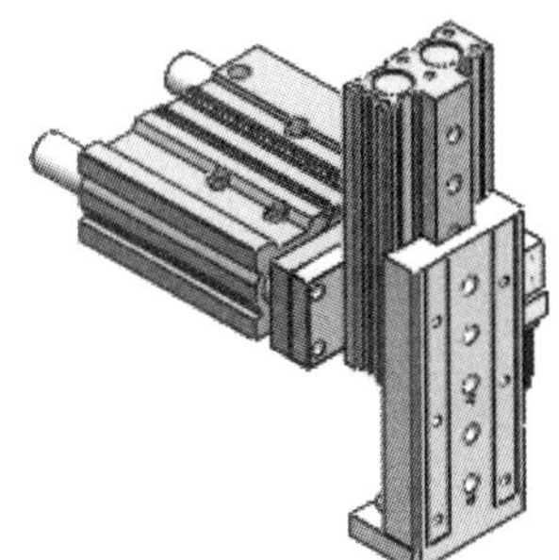

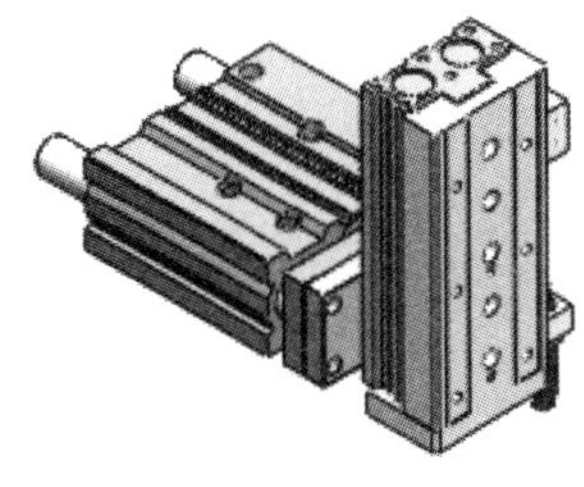

Design Table

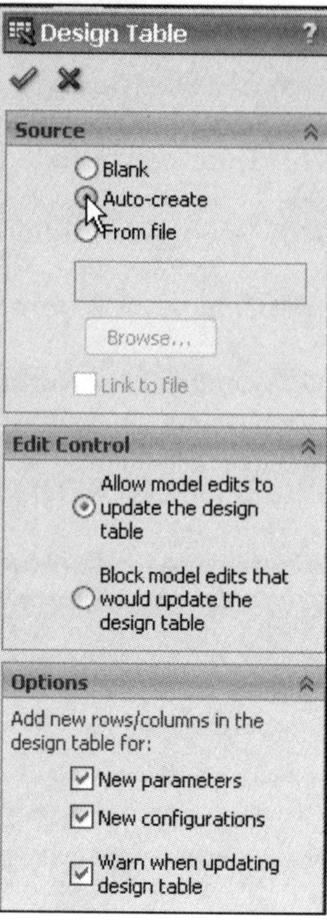

A design table could be applied to control the *Normal* and *Extended* configurations for the GUIDE-CYLINDER assembly and the SLIDE-TABLE assembly. Instead, this project applied the Configure dimension tool. You will use design tables later in this book.

You could also have applied a design table for the 2AXIS-TRANSFER configurations, instead you applied the Configure Configuration tool. The 2AXIS-TRANSFER design table would control the parameters $Configuration and $STATE for each component in the assembly. The $Configuration parameter is the configuration name. The $STATE parameter is the Suppressed/Resolved state of a component in the assembly.

The model name associated with the Design Table would be located in Cell A1. You would define the 2AXIS-TRANSFER configuration names in the first column of an Excel spreadsheet. Define the parameters in the second row. Enter values in the Cells that correspond to the configuration name and the parameter name.

Entering individual configurations in the design table is a cumbersome task. Avoid spelling issues. Utilize the Auto-create option to insert SHCS $STATE parameters into the design table.

Additional part and assembly parameters control Dimensions, Color, and Comments. All parameters begin with a $, except Dimension.

Enter parameters carefully. The “$”, “@” and “<>” symbol format needs to match exactly for the result to be correct in the BOM.

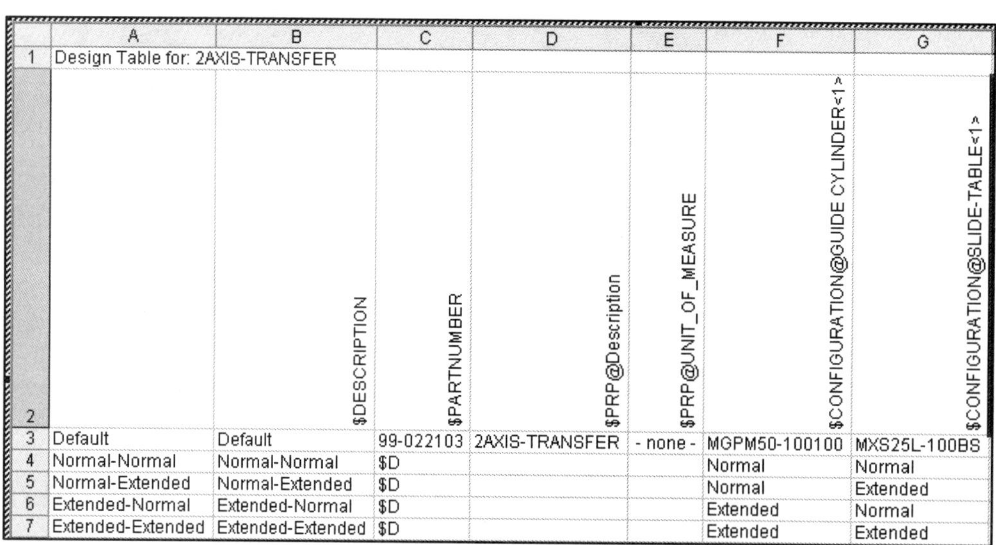

	A	B	C	D	E	F	G
1	Design Table for: 2AXIS-TRANSFER						
2		$DESCRIPTION	$PARTNUMBER	$PRP@Description	$PRP@UNIT_OF_MEASURE	$CONFIGURATION@GUIDE CYLINDER<1>	$CONFIGURATION@SLIDE-TABLE<1>
3	Default	Default	99-022103	2AXIS-TRANSFER	- none -	MGPM50-100100	MXS25L-100BS
4	Normal-Normal	Normal-Normal	$D			Normal	Normal
5	Normal-Extended	Normal-Extended	$D			Normal	Extended
6	Extended-Normal	Extended-Normal	$D			Extended	Normal
7	Extended-Extended	Extended-Extended	$D			Extended	Extended

Summary of Design Table Parameters is as follows:

Summary of Design Table Parameters:		
Parameter Syntax (Header Cell)	**Legal Values (Body Cell)**	**Default if Value is Left Blank**
Parts only:		
$configuration@part_name	configuration name	not evaluated
$configuration@<feature_name>	configuration name	not evaluated
Parts and Assemblies:		
$comment	any text string	empty
$part number	any text string	configuration name
$state@feature_name	Suppressed, S Unsuppressed, U	Unsuppressed
dimension@feature	any legal decimal value for the dimension	not evaluated
$parent	parent configuration name	property is undefined
$prp@ property	any text string	property is undefined
$state@equation_number@equations	Suppressed, S Unsuppressed, U	Unsuppressed
$state@lighting_name	Suppressed, S Unsuppressed, U	Unsuppressed
$state@sketch relation@sketch name	Suppressed, S Unsuppressed, U	Unsuppressed
$user_notes	any text string	not evaluated
$color	32-bit integer specifying RGB (red, green, blue) color. See Online Help, color for more info.	zero (black)
Assemblies only:		
$show@component<instance>	Yes, Y No, N	No
$state@component<instance>	Resolved, R, Suppressed, S	Resolved
$configuration@component<instance>	configuration name	Component's "in-use" or last saved configuration. NOTE: If the component uses a derived configuration, and the value is left blank, the configuration used is linked to its parent.

To learn additional information on Design Tables, click **Help**, **SolidWorks Help** from the Menu bar menu. Click the **Contents** tab. **Expand** the Configurations folder. Click **Configurations Overview**. The Configuration Overview dialog box is displayed. Click **Manually** in the You can create configurations manually section as illustrated.

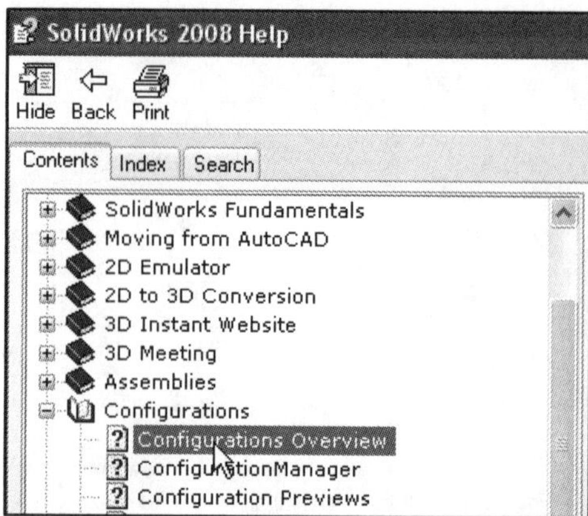

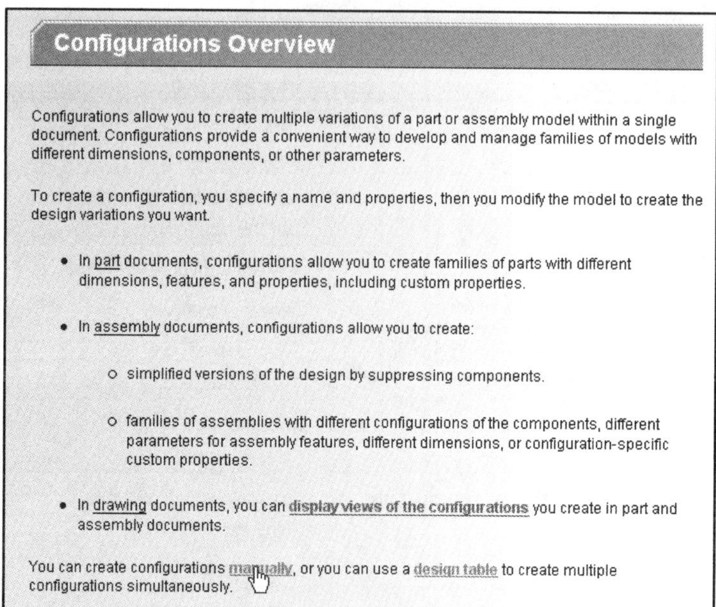
Configurations Overview

Configurations allow you to create multiple variations of a part or assembly model within a single document. Configurations provide a convenient way to develop and manage families of models with different dimensions, components, or other parameters.

To create a configuration, you specify a name and properties, then you modify the model to create the design variations you want.

- In part documents, configurations allow you to create families of parts with different dimensions, features, and properties, including custom properties.
- In assembly documents, configurations allow you to create:
  - simplified versions of the design by suppressing components.
  - families of assemblies with different configurations of the components, different parameters for assembly features, different dimensions, or configuration-specific custom properties.
- In drawing documents, you can display views of the configurations you create in part and assembly documents.

You can create configurations manually, or you can use a design table to create multiple configurations simultaneously.

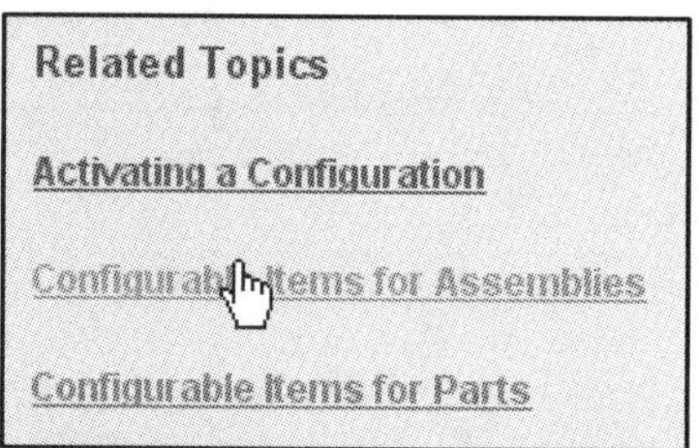

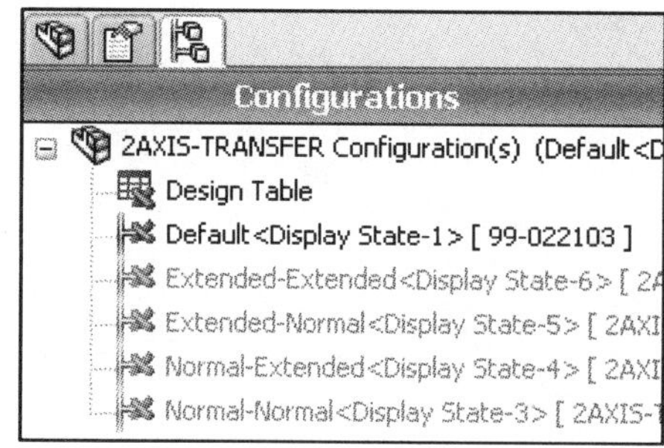

The Design Table PropertyManager is divided into three sections: *Source*, *Edit Control*, and *Options*.

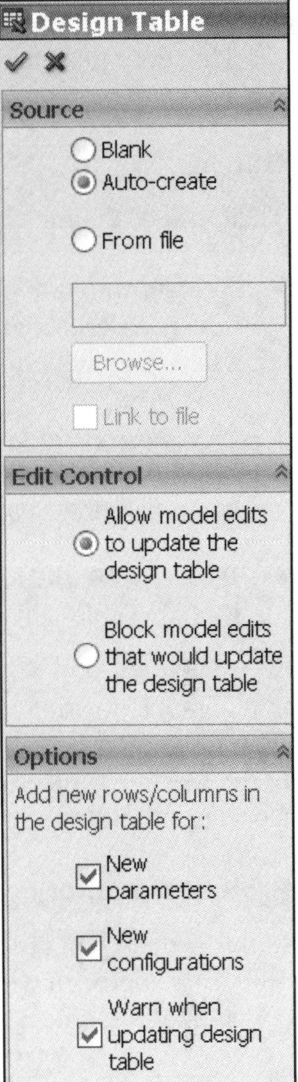

Source:

The Source dialog box provides the following options:

- *Blank*: The Blank option provides the ability to insert an empty Design Table. The designer fills in the parameters.

- *Auto-create*: Selected by default. The Auto-create option provides the ability to automatically create a new Design Table and loads all different configured parameters and values entered in the ConfigurationManager.

The Auto-create option inserts only parameters that are *different*. Example: Create two configurations. The first configuration is the Default. Insert as many parameters into the second configuration. Auto-create will then insert the parameters from the second configuration into the Design Table. The PLATE-D Design Table activity provides an example with multiple parameters.

- ***From file***: The From file option provides the ability to utilize a pre-existing Excel spreadsheet. Browse to locate the spreadsheet. Checking the Link to file check box option means that any changes made in the spreadsheet outside SolidWorks are updated in the model during the next SolidWorks session. If the Allow model edits to update the design table option is checked, the spreadsheet reflects the model changes.

Edit Control:

The Edit Control dialog box provides the following options:

- ***Allow model edits to update the design table***. This option is selected by default. If you modify the model, the changes are updated in the design table.

- ***The Block model edits that would update the design table.*** This option prohibits any changes that updates the Design Table.

Options:

Options

Add new rows/columns in the design table for:

- [x] New parameters
- [x] New configurations
- [x] Warn when updating design table

The Options dialog box provides the following options:

- ***New parameters.*** This option provides the ability to insert new rows and columns into the Design Table when you add a new parameter to the part/assembly.
- ***New configurations.*** This option provides the ability to insert new rows and columns into the Design Table when you add a new configuration to the part/assembly.
- ***Warn when updating design table.*** This option produces a warning message that the Design Table will change based on the parameters updated in the part/assembly.

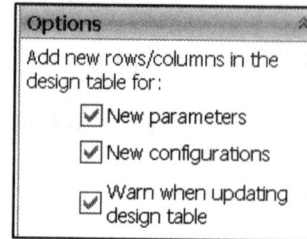

Click a position outside the Design Table to exit the EXCEL spreadsheet and to return to SolidWorks. To return to the Design Table, right-click Design Table from the ConfigurationManager. Click Edit Table.

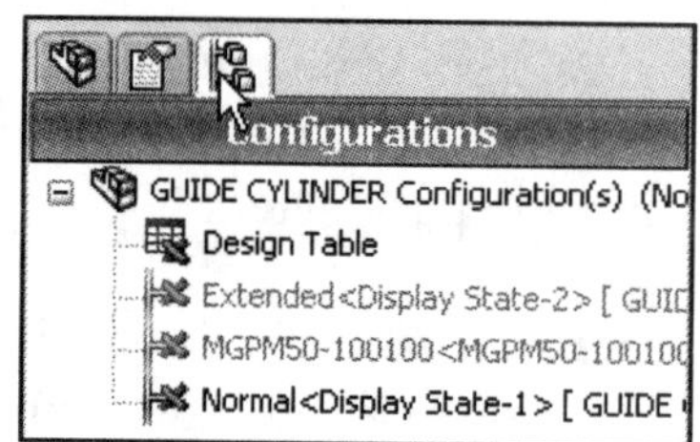

Project Summary

In this project you utilized the Top-down design assembly modeling approach with InPlace Mates and features developed In-Context to the 2AXIS-TRANSFER assembly.

The 2AXIS-TRANSFER assembly consists of: *GUIDE-CYLINDER assembly, PLATE-B part, SLIDE-TABLE assembly, and SHCSs parts.*

You utilized the Configure dimension tool to create the *Normal* and *Extended* configurations of the GUIDE-CYLINDER assembly

You utilized the Configure dimension tool to create the *Normal* and *Extended* configurations of the SLIDE-TABLE assembly.

You combined the GUIDE-CYLINDER assembly *Normal* configuration and *Extended* configuration with the SLIDE-TABLE assembly *Normal* configuration and *Extended* configuration to create four new 2AXIS-TRANSFER configurations: *Normal-Normal, Normal-Extended, Extended-Normal, Extended-Extended.*

You created the PLATE-B part In-Context of the GUIDE-CYLINDER assembly and SLIDE-TABLE assembly. Interference problems were detected and resolved before any parts were manufactured.

Questions

1. Describe the two design methods utilized in a Top-down design assembly modeling approach.

2. Define an In-context relation.

3. Describe the procedure to rename a feature, sketch or Mate name.

4. Define an InPlace Mate.

5. True or False. An InPlace Mate cannot be deleted from an assembly.

6. Describe the procedure to create a rectangular sketch centered about the part Origin. The rectangular sketch contains only one vertical and one horizontal dimension.

7. True or False. A Concentric SmartMate is created between two cylindrical faces from the same part.

8. True or False. External references cannot be redefined.

9. Identify the two components that determine the geometric and functional requirements for PLATE-B.

10. How do you redefine a component in an assembly?

11. True or False: External references defined In-context become out of context when the corresponding components are not loaded into memory.

12. Describe the procedure to block updates to a Design Table in the 2AXIS-TRANSFER assembly.

13. The GUIDE-CYLINDER has two configurations. The SLIDE-TABLE has two configurations. Describe the process of combining the GUIDE-CYLINDER configurations and the SLIDE-TABLE configurations to create the 2AXIS-TRANSFER configurations.

Notes:

Project 6

Part and Assembly Configurations, Custom Properties, Design Tables, & References

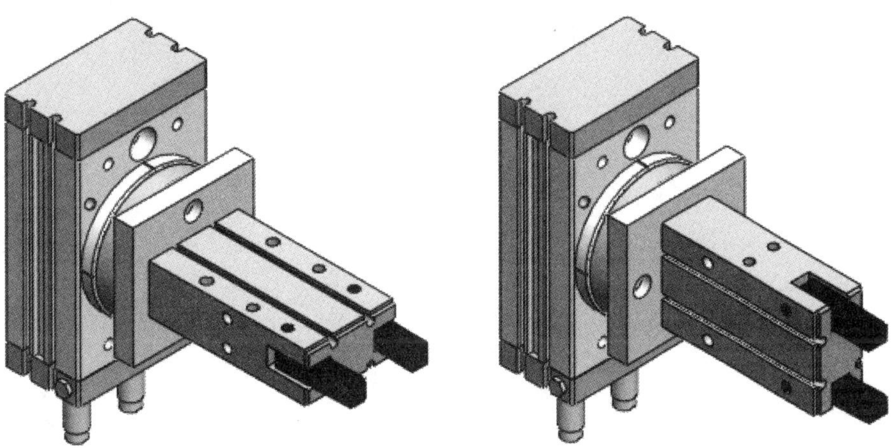

Below are the desired outcomes and usage competencies based on the completion of this project.

Project Desired Outcomes:	Usage Competencies:
• ROTARY-GRIPPER assembly.	• Ability to create seven configurations at two levels with three components. • Understanding of Design Tables.
• PLATE-C part.	• Create an Empty Part with no InPlace Mates. • Define an empty part in an assembly with Reference planes.
• ROTARY and ROTARY-GRIPPER configurations.	• Apply the Add Configuration tool and utilize the Add Configuration PropertyManager.
• PLATE-D part. • PLATE-D Design Table.	• Develop an empty part and Copy/Paste sketches from different components. • Aptitude to delete External References and InPlace mates. • Understanding of Design Tables with the ability to utilize parameters to control configurations and states.

Notes:

Project 6 – Part and Assembly Configurations, Custom Properties, Design Tables, & References

Project Objective

Create the ROTARY-GRIPPER assembly. The ROTARY-GRIPPER assembly is the third component in the 3AXIS-TRANSFER assembly.

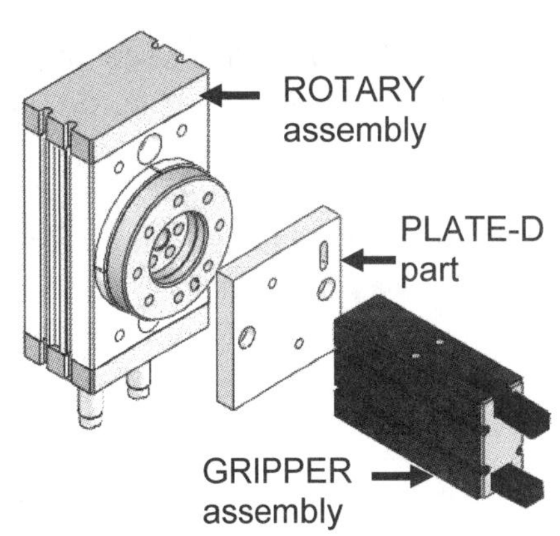

ROTARY-GRIPPER assembly

Create the PLATE-C part. Insert the PLATE-C part into the 2AXIS-TRANSFER assembly with no External References.

Create the PLATE-D part In-Context of the ROTARY and GRIPPER assembly. Delete all InPlace Mates.

Utilize the Add Configuration tool and the Design Table tool to create multi configurations in the ROTARY assembly, ROTARY-GRIPPER assembly, and the PLATE-D part.

Develop Custom Properties for the PLATE-D part.

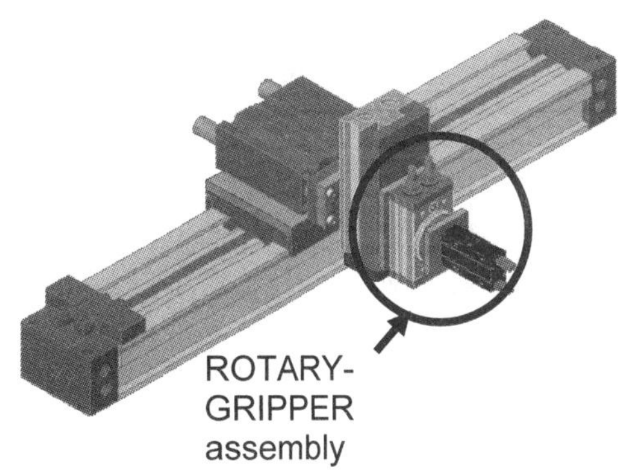

3AXIS-TRANSFER assembly

On the completion of this project, you will be able to:

- Apply Top-down and Bottom-up design assembly modeling techniques.
- Develop multi levels of configurations in an assembly with parts and sub-assemblies.
- Recognize and delete External references and InPlace Mates.
- Define an empty part in an assembly with Reference planes.
- Copy/Paste a sketch from one component to another.
- Create Configuration Specific Custom Properties and utilize SolidWorks Properties.
- Manipulate views and configurations in a drawing.

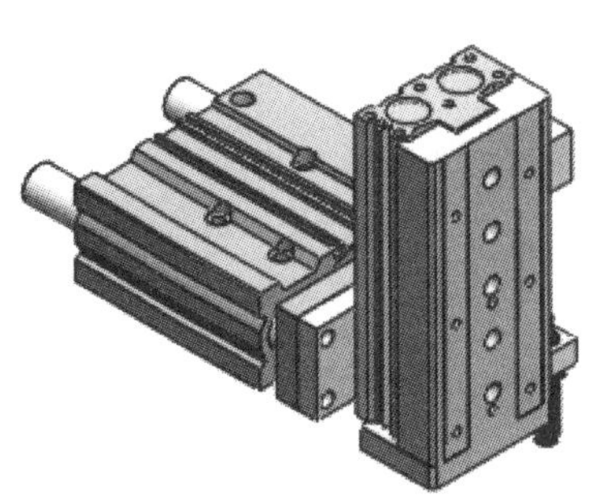

Project Overview

Develops additional skill sets in creating configurations, In-Context parts and recognizing and deleting External references and InPlace Mates.

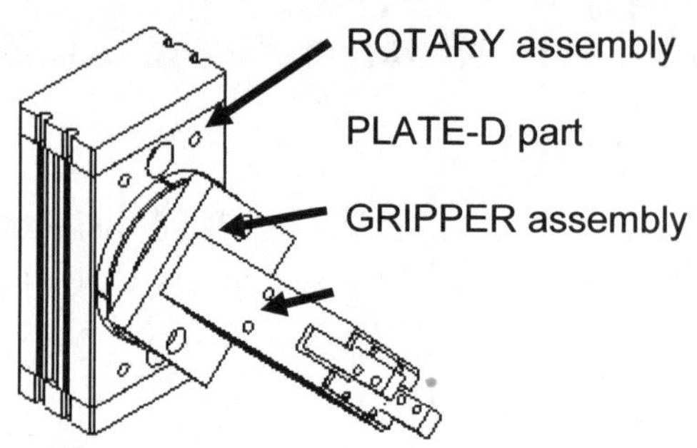

ROTARY-GRIPPER assembly

The ROTARY-GRIPPER assembly incorporates configurations at the part and sub-assembly level.

Create three new configurations for the ROTARY assembly. Utilize the Add Configuration tool, and the Design table tool to manipulate parameters and their values.

SolidWorks Properties and Custom Properties link model information to a drawing. In the next Project, apply this ability.

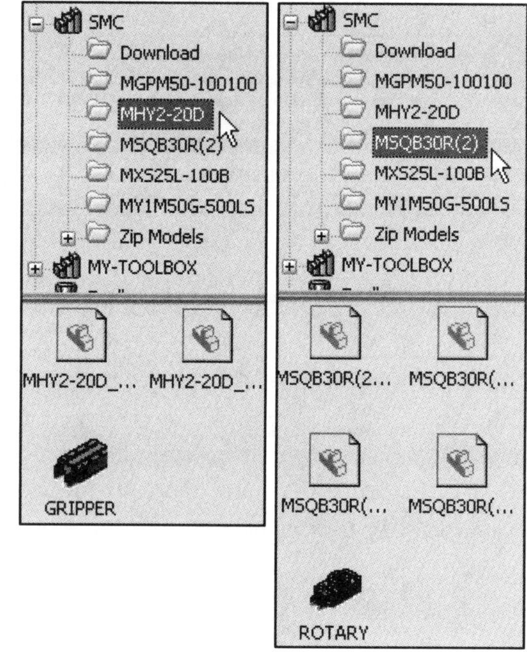

The ROTARY-GRIPPER assembly consists of the following:

- *ROTARY Assembly*
- *GRIPPER Assembly*
- *PLATE-D Part*

The ROTARY assembly and GRIPPER assembly are SMC components.

Develop the PLATE-D part In-Context of the ROTARY assembly and GRIPPER assembly.

In the initial design phase, the PLATE-C part was listed in the Assembly Layout Diagram as a component of the ROTARY-GRIPPER assembly. You encountered a situation to rethink the location of the PLATE-C part.

Create the PLATE-C part as a component in the 2AXIS-TRANSFER assembly. Utilize three Reference planes to mate PLATE-C to the 2AXIS-TRANSFER Reference planes. Obtain geometry for PLATE-C features from the SLIDE-TABLE assembly and ROTARY assembly.

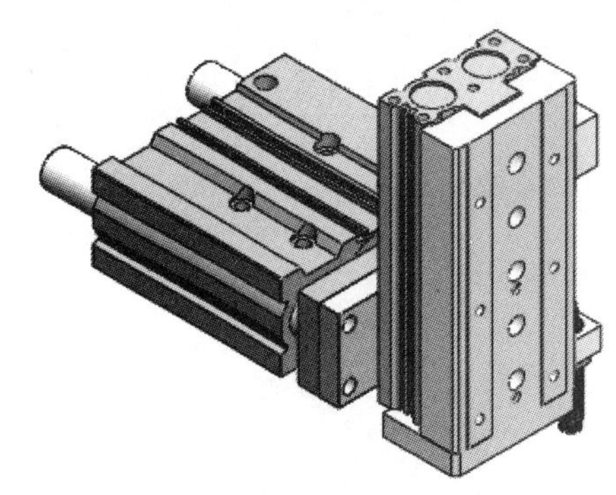

The ROTARY assembly rotates 360°. The GRIPPER assembly requires a vertical and horizontal position. The rotation of the GRIPPER assembly depends on the rotation of the ROTARY assembly.

At a 0° ROTARY position, the GRIPPER moves to a vertical position.

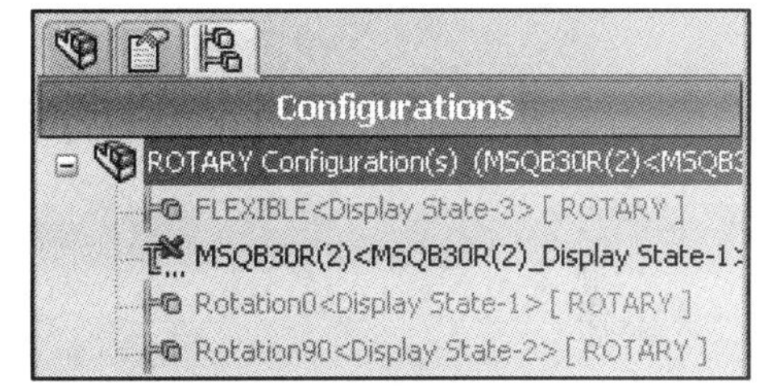

At a 90° ROTARY position, the GRIPPER moves to a horizontal position.

Begin complex configurations at the lowest assembly level. Develop the ROTARY assembly configurations. Incorporate the ROTARY configuration into the ROTARY-GRIPPER configurations.

Create three new configurations for the ROTARY assembly using the Add Configuration tool:

- *Flexible*
- *Rotation0*
- *Rotation90*

A small dowel pin slot indicates the ROTARY position.

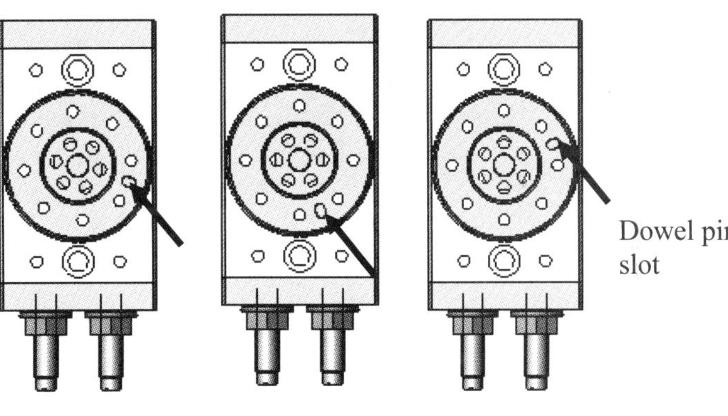

FLEXIBLE (Rotates) | Default & Rotation0 | Rotation90

ROTATRY Configurations

Create three new configurations for the ROTARY-GRIPPER assembly: *Flexible, Rotation0, Rotation90*

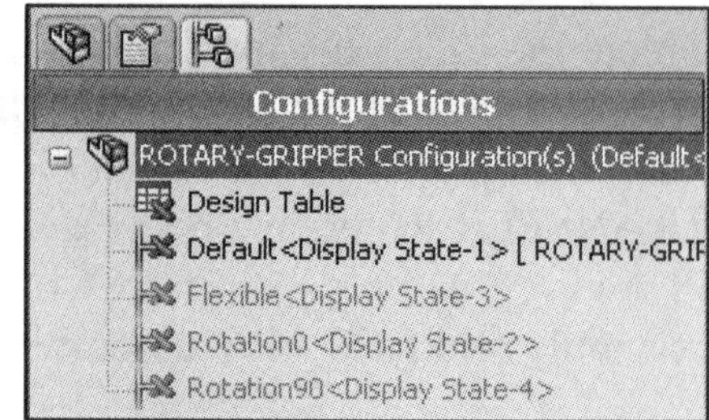

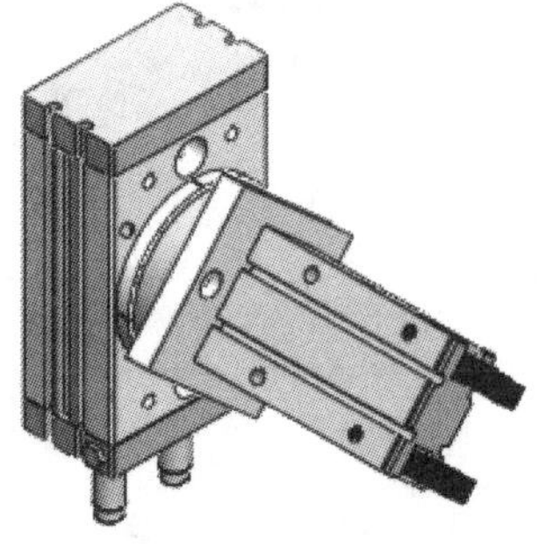
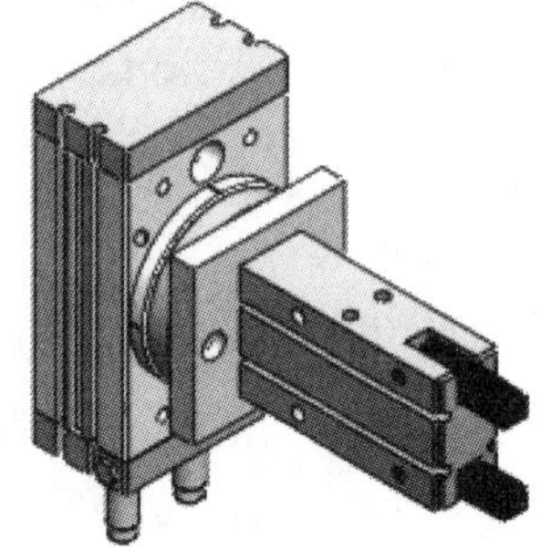
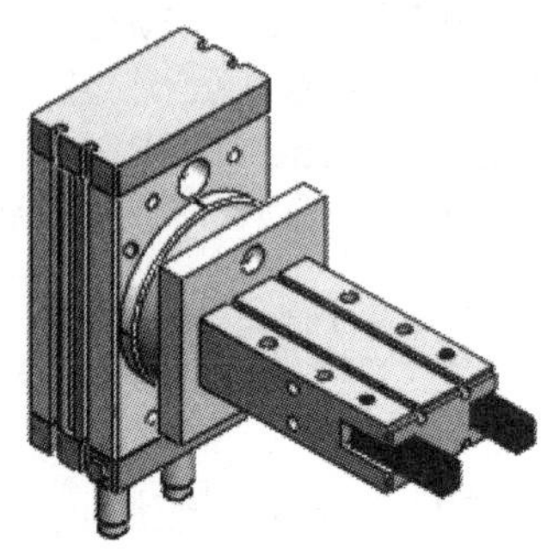

Flexible (Rotates) Rotation0 Rotation90

ROTARY-GRIPPER configurations

Create PLATE-D with configurations. Apply a design table to control the configurations, depth of the Extrude feature: *10mm, 15mm, 20mm* and Custom Properties for color.

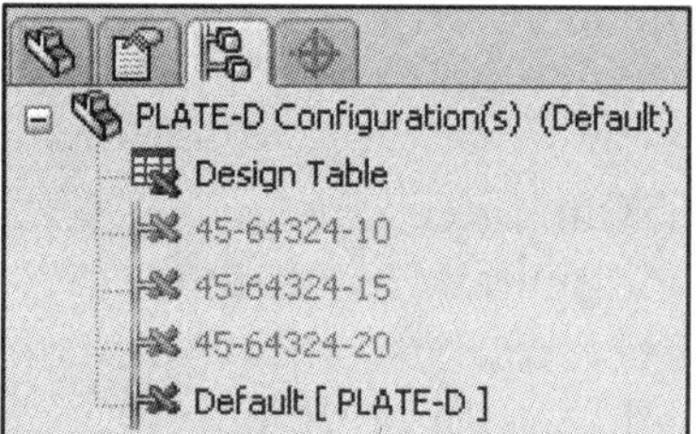

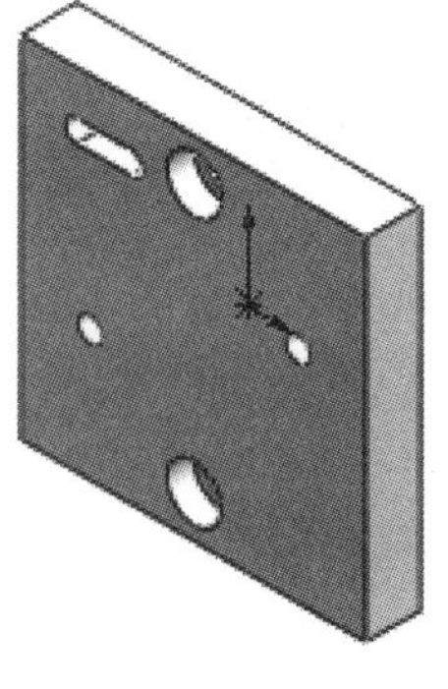
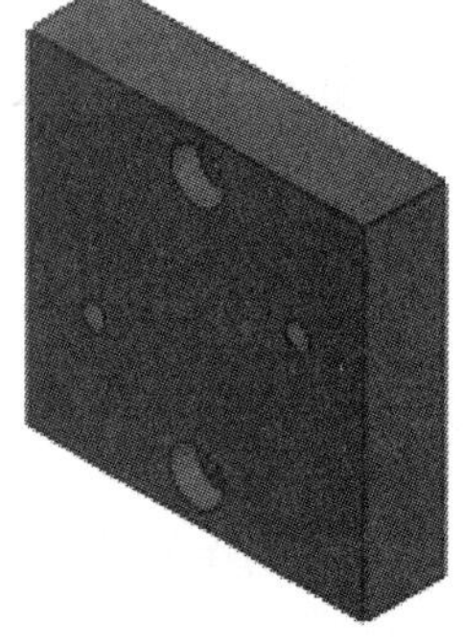
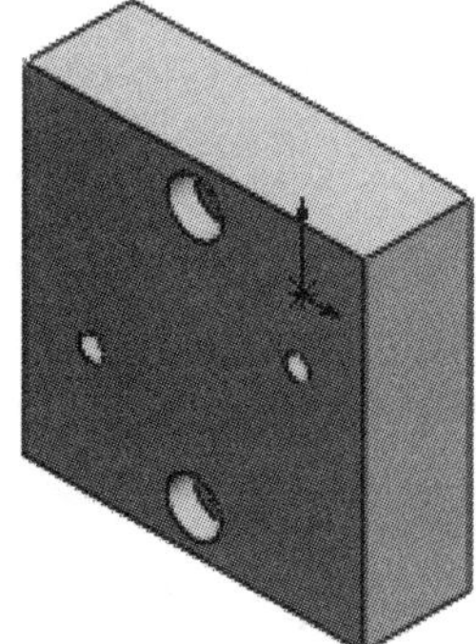

45-64324-10
10mm

45-64324-15
15mm

45-64324-20
20mm

PLATE-D Configurations

Properties are parameters defined in a single document that can be accessed and utilized by multiple documents. The PLATE-D part requires three Custom Properties:

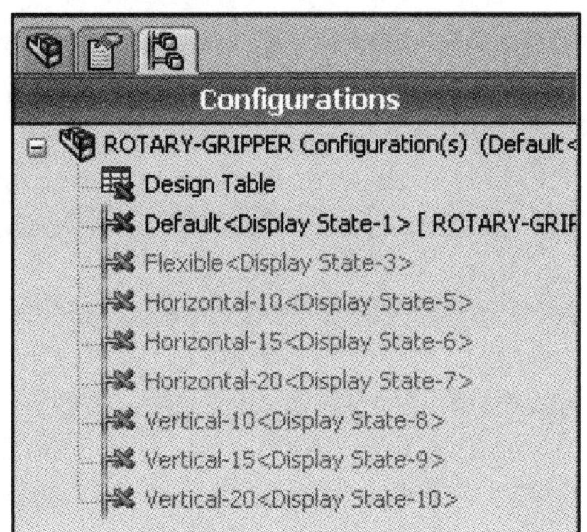

- *MASS*
- *MATERIAL*
- *DESCRIPTION*

Combine the PLATE-D configurations and modify the ROTARY-GRIPPER configurations: *Horizontal-10, Horizontal-15, Horizontal-20, Vertical-10, Vertical-15, and Vertical-20.*

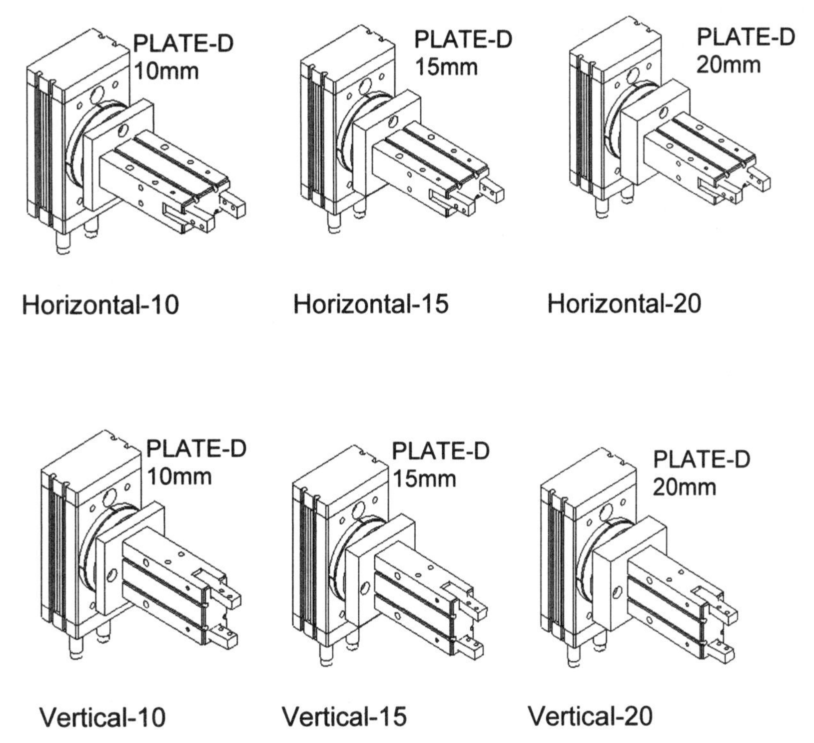

ROTARY-GRIPPER Configurations

ROTARY-GRIPPER Assembly

Create the ROTARY-GRIPPER assembly. Insert the ROTARY assembly as the first component. Modify the default orientation. Suppress the mate to rotate the component in the assembly.

Insert the GRIPPER assembly. Determine the specific features required to create the PLATE-D part using the Top-down design approach.

Create PLATE-D as a new part, In-Context of the ROTARY assembly and the GRIPPER assembly.

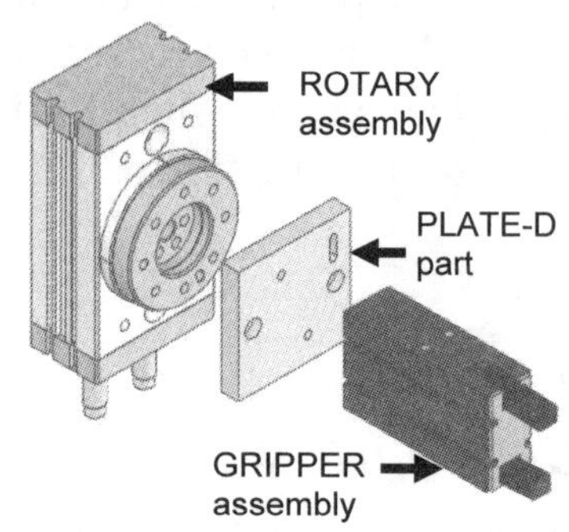

ROTARY-GRIPPER assembly

Activity: Create the ROTARY-GRIPPER Assembly

Close all documents.

1) Click **Window**, **Close All** from the Menu bar menu.

Expand the SMC folder from the Design Library.

2) **Expand** the SMC folder in the Design Library.

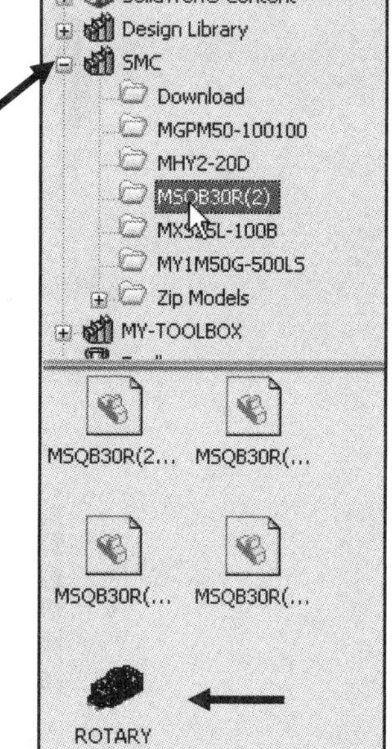

Open the ROTARY assembly.

3) Click the **MSQB30R(2)** folder.

4) Click and drag the **ROTARY** icon into the Graphic window. The ROTARY assembly is displayed.

5) Click **Yes** to rebuild.

Create a new assembly.

6) Click **Make Assembly from Part/Assembly** from the Menu bar toolbar.

7) Select the **MY-TEMPLATES** tab.

8) Double-click **ASM-MM-ANSI**. The Begin Assembly PropertyManager is displayed.

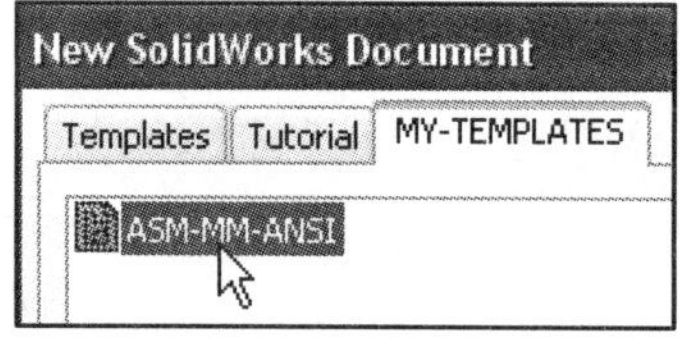

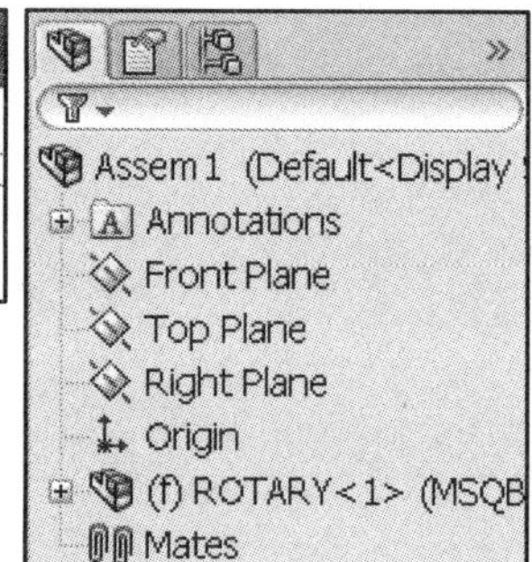

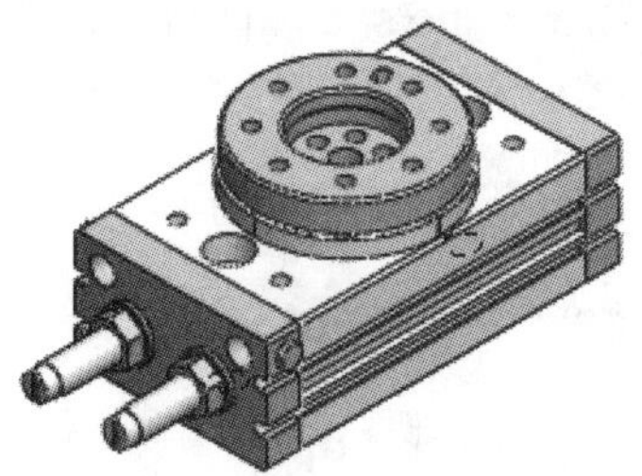

9) Click **OK** ✔ from the PropertyManager.

10) Click **Isometric** view from the Heads-up View toolbar.

Save the assembly.

11) Click **Save**.

12) Enter **ROTARY-GRIPPER** for File name in the DELIVERY-STATION folder.

13) Click **Save**. The ROTARY-GRIPPER FeatureManager is displayed.

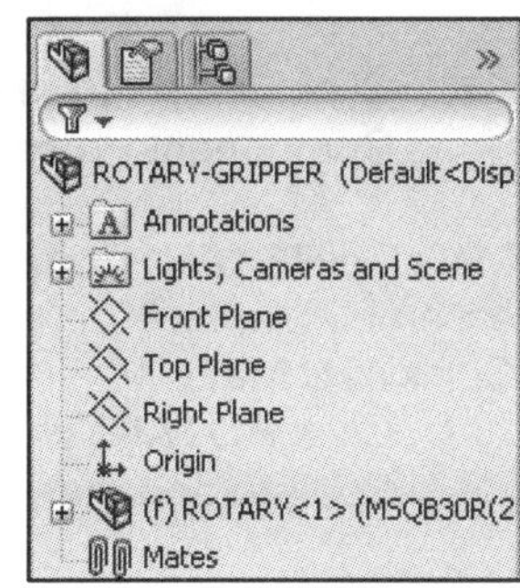

Hide the Origins.

14) Click **View**, un-check **Origins** from the Menu bar menu.

Float the ROTARY component.

15) Right-click **(f)ROTARY** from the FeatureManager.

16) Click **Float**. The ROTARY entry in the FeatureManager changes from fixed, (f) to under-defined, (-).

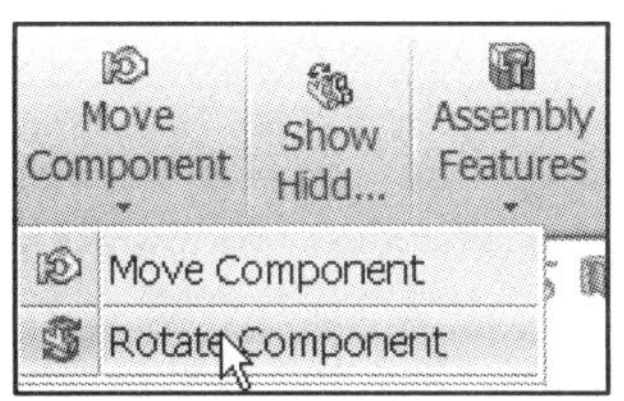

Rotate the ROTARY component.

17) Click **ROTARY** from the FeatureManager.

18) Click the **Rotate Component** tool from the Assembly Consolidated toolbar. The Rotate Component PropertyManager is displayed.

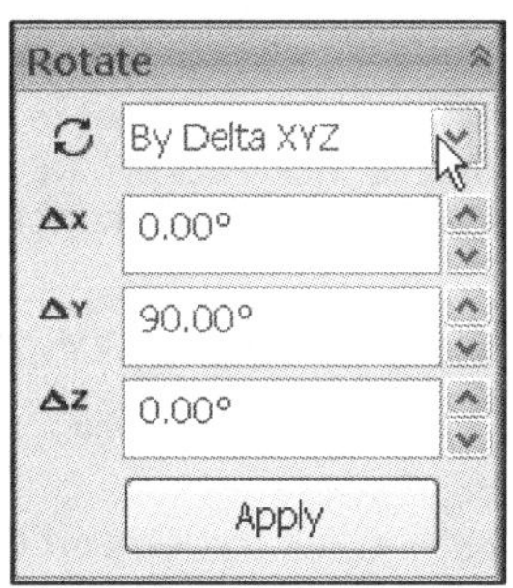

Create the first rotation.

19) Select **By Delta XYZ** from the Rotate drop-down menu.

20) Enter **0** for ΔX.

21) Enter **90°** for ΔY.

22) Enter **0** for ΔZ.

23) Click the **Apply** button. View the results

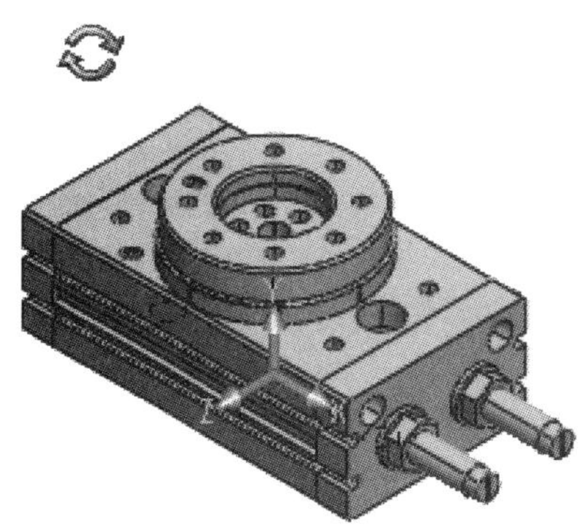

Create the second rotation.

24) Enter **0** for ΔX.

25) Enter **0** for ΔY.

26) Enter **-90°** for ΔZ.

27) Click **Apply**.

28) Click **OK** from the Rotate Component PropertyManager.

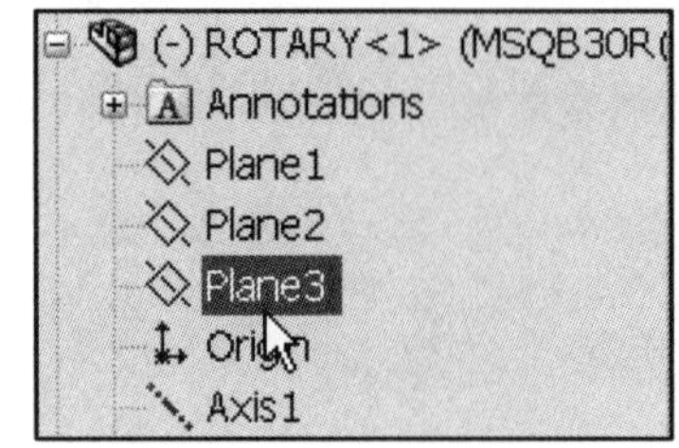

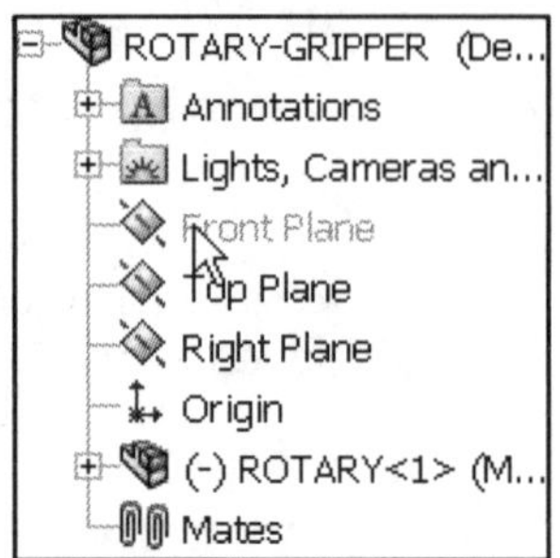

Mate the ROTARY component to the assembly planes. Create the first Coincident Mate.

29) Click **ROTARY\Plane3** from the FeatureManager.

30) Click the **Mate** tool. The Mate PropertyManager is displayed.

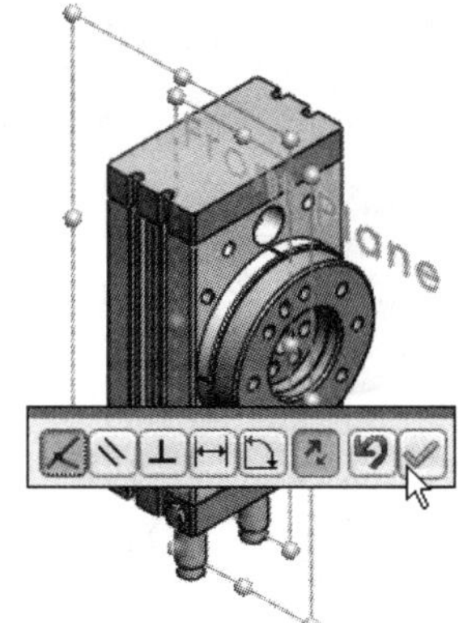

31) Click **ROTARY-GRIPPER\Front Plane** from the fly-out FeatureManager. Coincident is selected by default.

32) Click the **Green Check mark**.

Create the second Coincident Mate.

33) Click **ROTARY\Plane1** from the FeatureManager.

34) Click **ROTARY-GRIPPER\Top Plane** from the fly-out FeatureManager. Coincident is selected by default.

35) Click the **Green Check mark**.

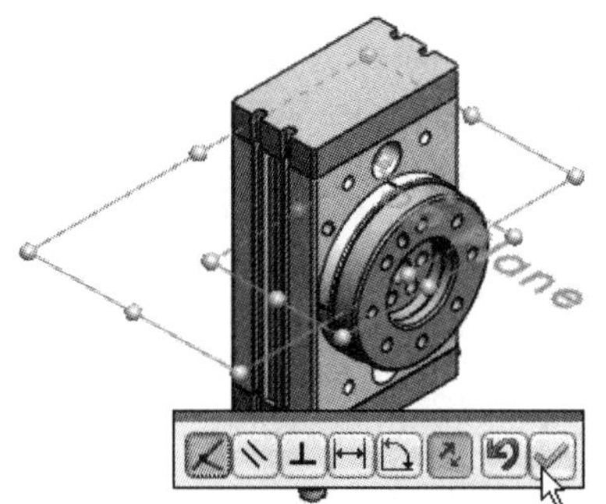

Create the third Coincident mate.

36) Click **ROTARY\Plane2** from the FeatureManager.

37) Click **ROTARY-GRIPPER\Right Plane** from the fly-out FeatureManager. Coincident is selected by default.

38) Click the **Green Check mark**.

39) Click **OK** from the Mate PropertyManager.

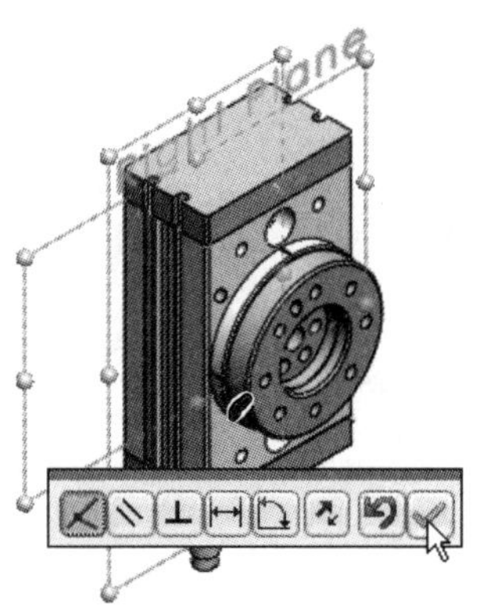

Expand the Mates folder.

40) **Expand** the Mates folder to display the three Coincident Mates. The ROTARY component is fully defined in the ROTARY-GRIPPER assembly.

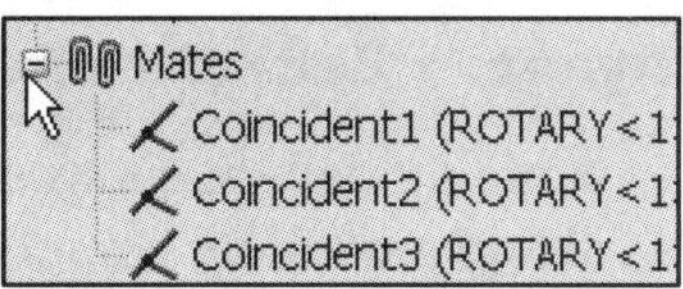

Insert the GRIPPER component using the Design Library.

41) Click the **SMC\MHY2-20D** folder.

42) Click and drag the **GRIPPER** icon into the ROTARY-GRIPPER Graphics window. Position the GRIPPER to the left of the ROTARY component as illustrated.

43) Click **Cancel** ✖ from the Insert Components PropertyManager.

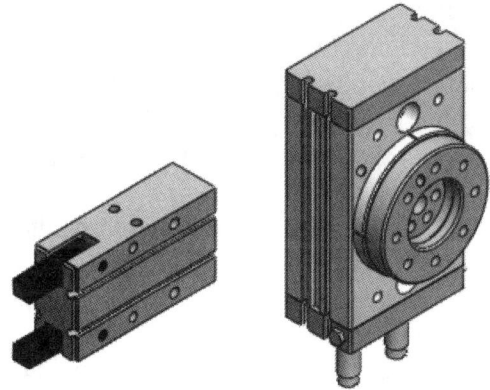

Move and Rotate the GRIPPER.

44) **Move** and **Rotate** the GRIPPER as illustrated.

Save the ROTARY-GRIPPER assembly.

45) Click **Save**.

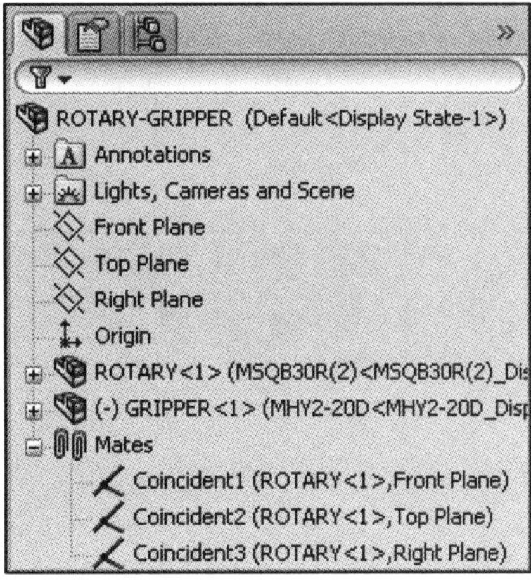

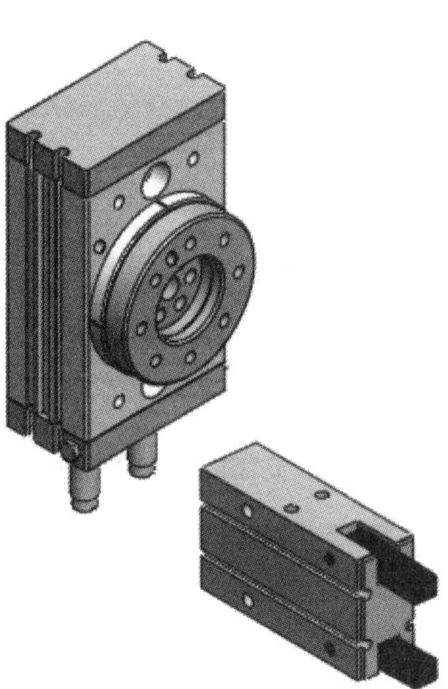

Dynamic Behavior of Components

In static modeling, components do not move. In dynamic modeling, components translate and rotate. Mates reflect the dynamic behavior of the physical components.

MSQBody

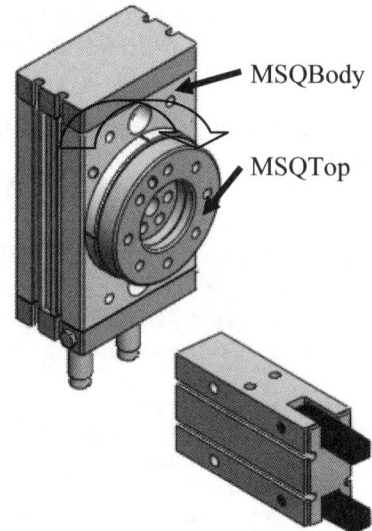

MSQTop

Investigate the dynamic behavior of the components before you assemble them. Determine the design intent of the ROTARY and GRIPPER assemblies as individual components and as a sub-assembly.

The ROTARY assembly contains the MSQTop part. Suppress the mate so the ROTARY\MSQTop part rotates about the X-axis.

The GRIPPER assembly position is dependent on the MSQTop part position.

The GRIPPER assembly requires two positions:

- *Position One at 0°*
- *Position Two at 90°*

Control the GRIPPER assembly rotation through configurations of the ROTARY assembly.

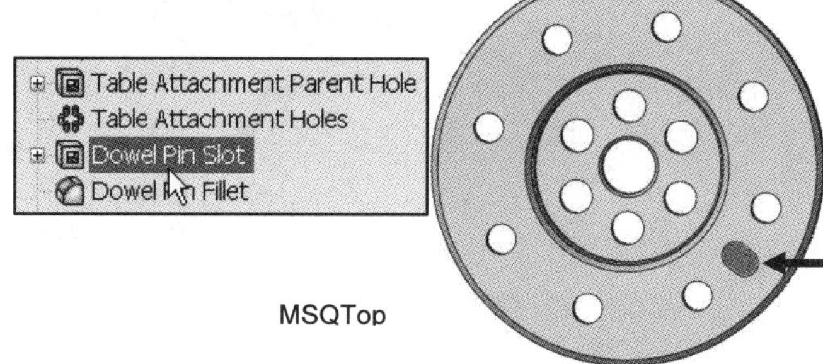

The ROTARY\MSQTop part contains an Extruded Cut feature named Dowel Pin Slot.

The Dowel Pin Slot indicates the 0° home position.

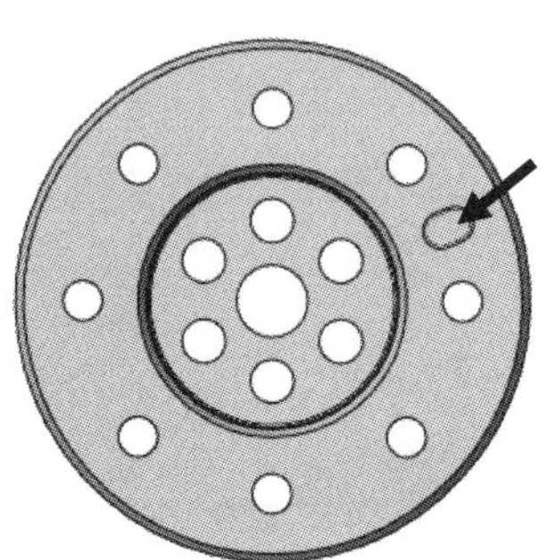

Control rotation of the ROTARY\MSQTop part. Create Coincident and Perpendicular Mates between the ROTARY\MSQBody\Front and the ROTARY\MSQTop\Side.

Activity: View the Dynamic Behavior of Components

Open the ROTARY assembly.

46) Right-click **ROTARY** from the ROTARY-GRIPPER FeatureManager.

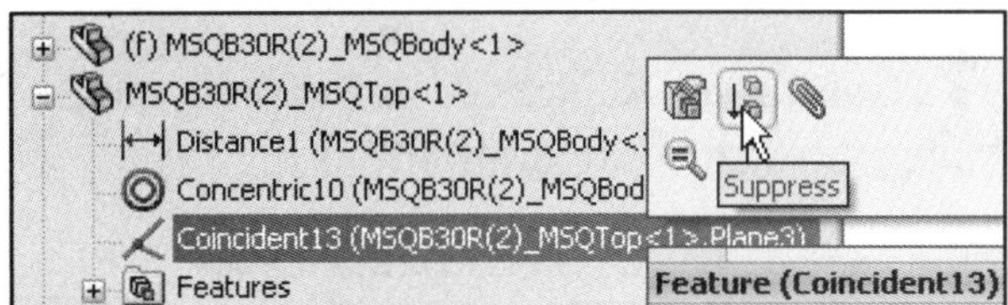

47) Click **Open Assembly** from the Context toolbar. The ROTARY assembly is displayed in the Graphics window.

48) Click **Top** view from the Heads-up View toolbar.

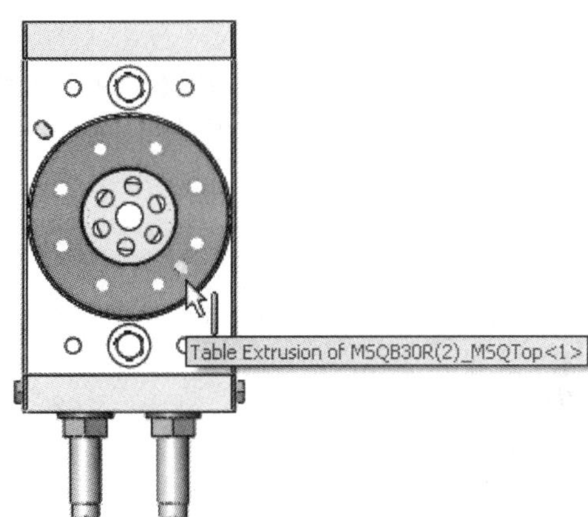

49) **Suppress** the Coincident13 mate in the ROTARY\MSQB3OR(2)_MSQTop<1> component. This provides the ability for the MSQTop<1> component to rotate.

50) Click **ROTARY\MSQB3OR(2)_MSQTop<1>** from the FeatureManager.

51) Position the **Dowel Pin Slot** approximately in the lower right corner as illustrated.

Insert a Coincident Mate between the MSQBTop and the MSQBBody.

52) **Expand** MSQBBody from the FeatureManager.

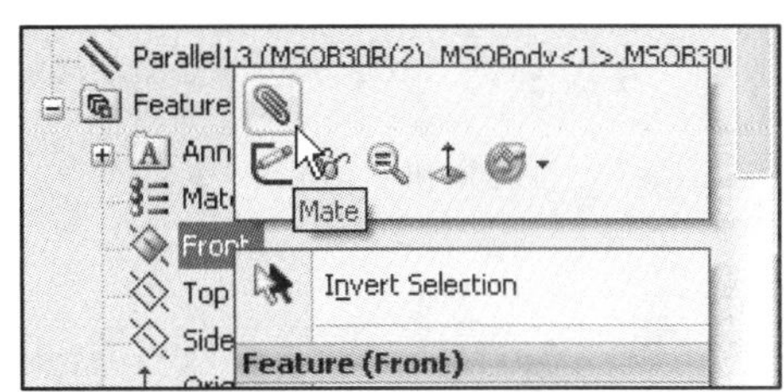

53) Right-click **MSQBody\Front**.

54) Click the **Mate** tool from the Context toolbar. The Mate PropertyManager is displayed.

55) **Expand** MSQTop from the fly-out FeatureManager.

56) Click **MSQTop\Side**. Coincident is selected by default.

57) Click the **Green Check mark**.

58) Click **OK** from the Mate PropertyManager.

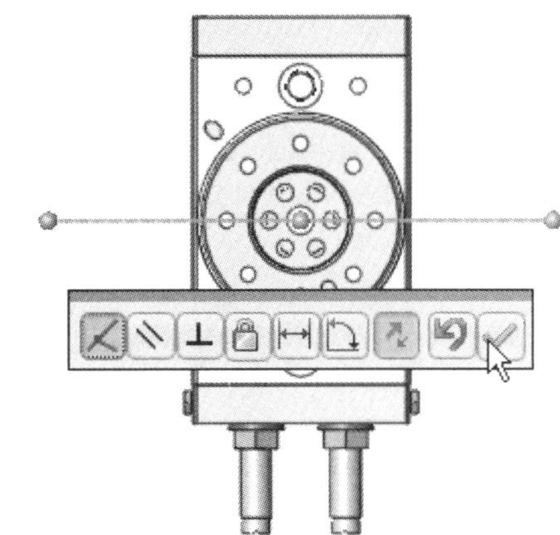

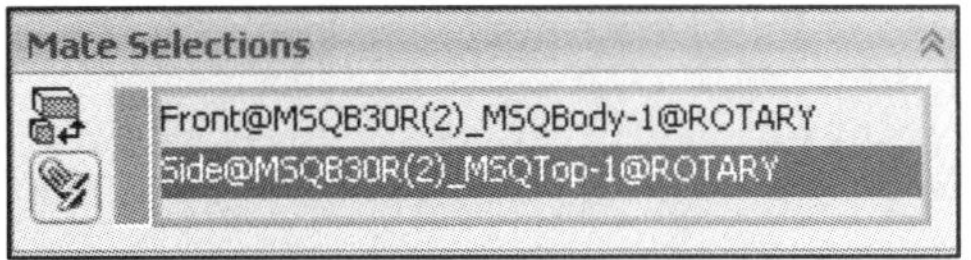

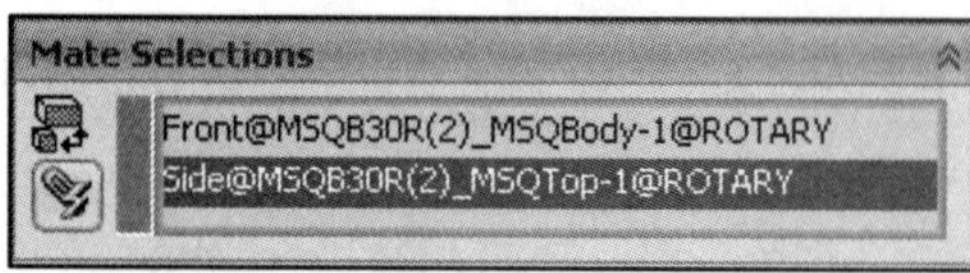

The MSQBody\Front and MSQTop\Side planes are horizontal. This is the Default and Rotation0 configuration position of the ROTARY assembly.

Control the Suppress\Un-Suppress state of Mates through configurations.

Rename and Suppress the Coincident Mate.

59) **Expand** the ROTARY/MateGroup1 folder.

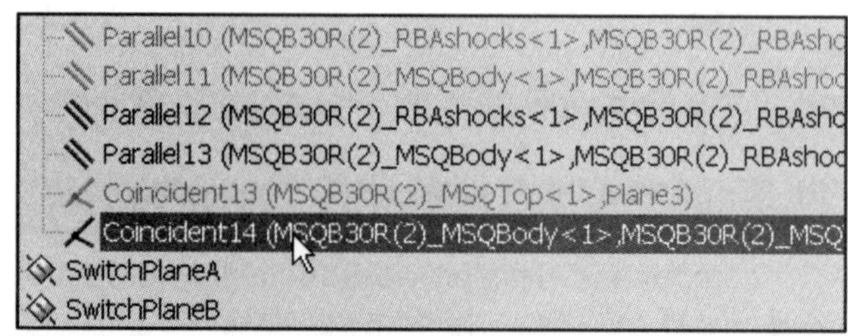

60) Double-click the **Coincident** Mate at the bottom of MateGroup1. Click the **Coincident** mate.

61) Rename to **Rotation0**.

Suppress the Mate.

62) Right-click **Rotation0**.

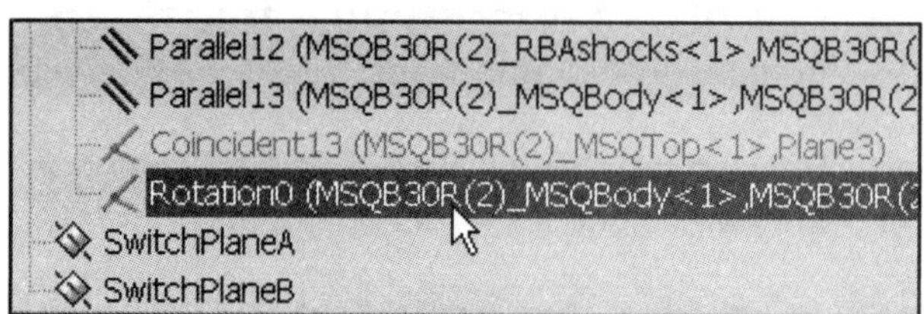

63) Click **Suppress** from the Context toolbar. The Suppressed Mate icon is displayed in light gray.

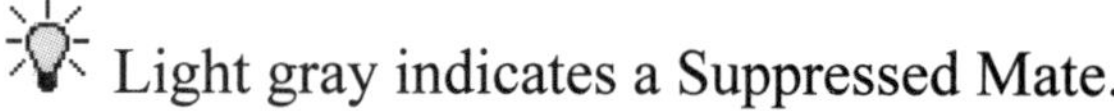

Light gray indicates a Suppressed Mate.

Insert a Perpendicular Mate.

64) Right-click **MSQBody\Front**.

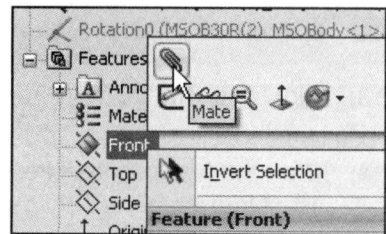

65) Click the **Mate** tool. The Mate PropertyManager is displayed.

66) Click **MSQTop\Side** from the fly-out FeatureManager.

67) Click **Perpendicular**. The Dowel Pin Slot rotates to the upper right corner. Click the **Flip** box if required.

68) Click the **Green Check mark**.

69) Click **OK** from the Mate PropertyManager.

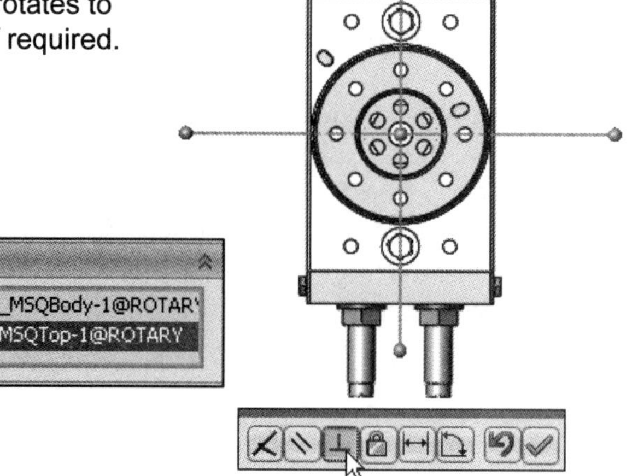

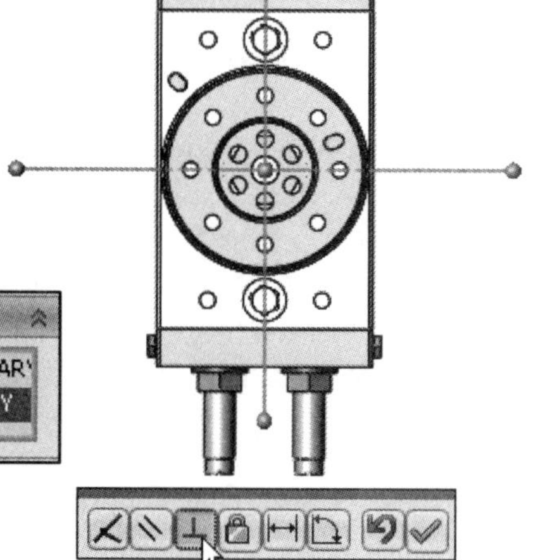

70) **Expand** ROTARY/MateGroup1.

71) Click the **Perpendicular1** Mate.

72) Rename to **Rotation90**.

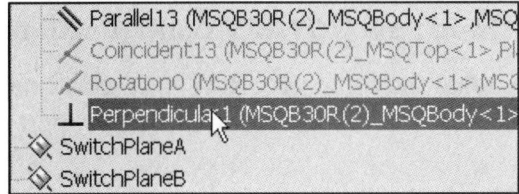

Suppress the Mate.

73) Right-click **Rotation90**.

74) Click **Suppress** from the Context toolbar.

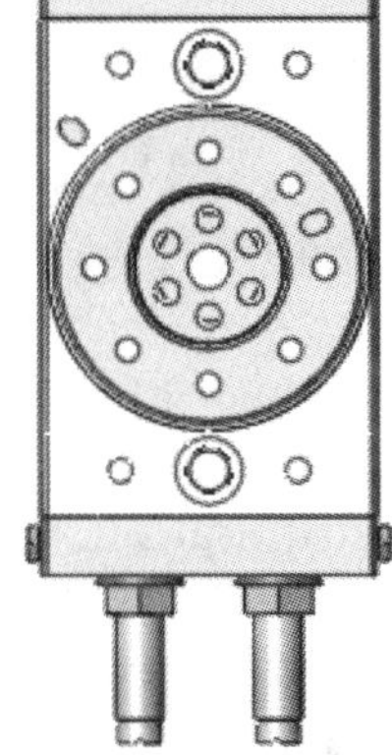

Save the ROTARY assembly.

75) Click **Save**.

In the next activity, work with the Rotation0 and Rotation90 Mates. Reposition Mates in MateGroup1 to locate quickly in the FeatureManager. Note: Rotation0 and Rotation90 contain no dependency on any other Mate.

Reposition the Mates.

76) Drag the **Rotation0** Mate from the bottom of MateGroup1 to the top of MateGroup1. The Move feature in tree ⏎ icon is displayed above the Distance1 Mate.

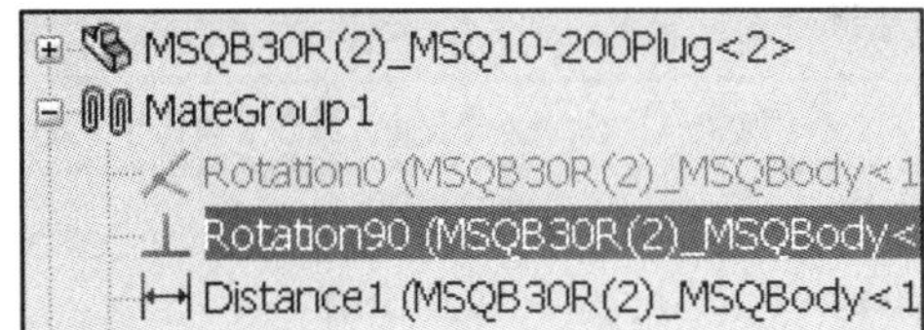

77) Repeat the above procedure for the **Rotation90** Mate.

Utilize an Angle Mate when configurations require multiple angle values. Modify the Angle value in the configuration.

In some mating situations at 180°, the Mate Alignment flips and the Mate becomes invalid. Utilize an Angle Mate to resolve this issue.

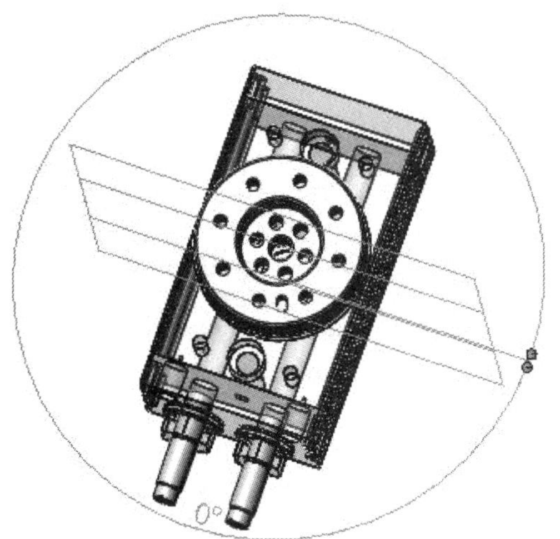

💡 As an exercise, modify the mate scheme. Replace the Rotation0 Mate and Rotation90 Mate; utilize a single Angle Mate and modify the values in the configuration.

💡 Suppress the Angle Mate in the Flexible configuration.

Three new ROTARY configurations

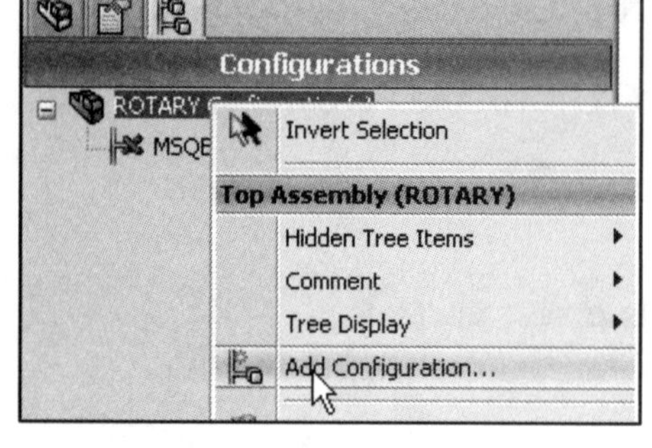

Create the three new ROTARY configurations utilizing the Add Configuration PropertyManager:

- *Rotation0*
- *Rotation90*
- *Flexible*

Suppress\Un-Suppress the Rotation0 Mate and the Rotation90 Mate to create three configurations.

Utilize a separate Flexible configuration and fixed Default configuration for additional control. Suppress the Rotation0 Mate and the Rotation90 Mate to create the Flexible configuration. Unsuppress the Rotation0 Mate to create a fixed Default configuration.

Avoid rotation when defining In-Context features. Utilize the Default configuration to create PLATE-D defined In-context of the assembly. Utilize the three new ROTARY configurations and the default configuration with the PLATE-D configurations.

Activity: Create New ROTARY Configurations: Add Configuration Tool

Modify the ROTARY (Default) configuration.

78) Right-click **Rotation0**.

79) Click **Unsuppress** from the Context toolbar. View the pin location in the Graphics window.

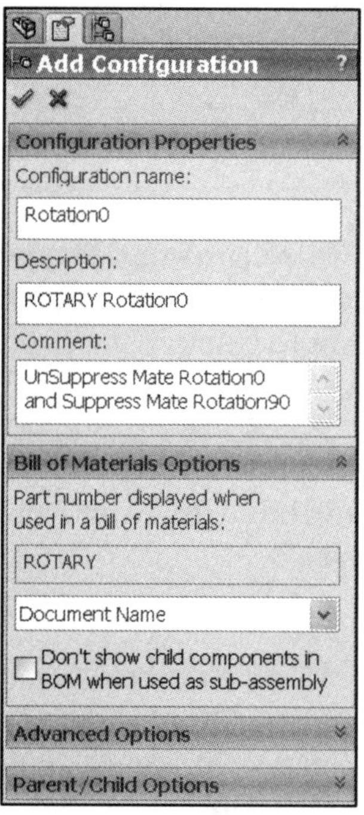

Insert the ROTARY (Rotation0) configuration.

80) Click the **ROTARY ConfigurationManager** tab.

81) Right-click **ROTARY Configuration(s)**.

82) Click **Add Configuration**. The Add Configuration PropertyManager is displayed.

83) Enter **Rotation0** for Configuration name.

84) Enter **ROTARY Rotation0** for Description.

85) Enter **UnSuppress Mate Rotation0** and **Suppress Mate Rotation90** for Comment.

86) Click **OK** from the Add Configuration PropertyManager. The Rotation0 configuration name is added to the ConfigurationManager.

Insert the ROTARY (Rotation90) configuration.

87) Right-click **ROTARY Configuration(s)**.

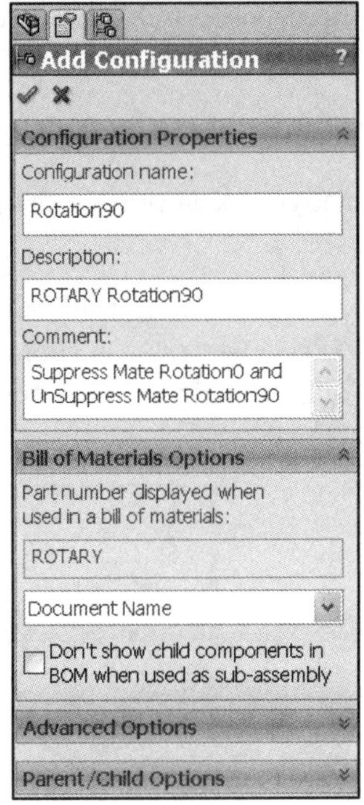

88) Click **Add Configuration**. Enter **Rotation90** for Configuration name. Enter **ROTARY Rotation90** for Description.

89) Enter **Suppress Mate Rotation0** and **UnSuppress Mate Rotation90** for Comment.

90) Click **OK** from the Add Configuration PropertyManager. The Rotation90 configuration name is added to the ConfigurationManager.

Define the Rotation90 configuration Mate state.

91) Click the **FeatureManager** tab.

92) Right-click **Rotation0** from the MateGroup1 folder.

93) Click **Suppress** from the Context toolbar.

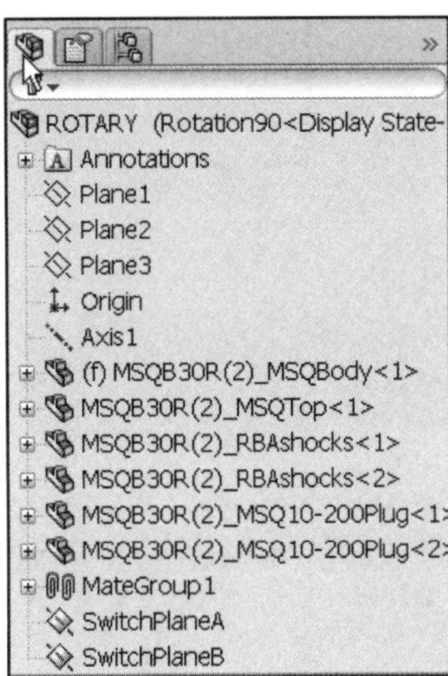

94) Right-click **Rotation90** from the MateGroup1 folder.

95) Click **UnSuppress** from the Context toolbar. The Dowel Pin Slot rotates to Position90.

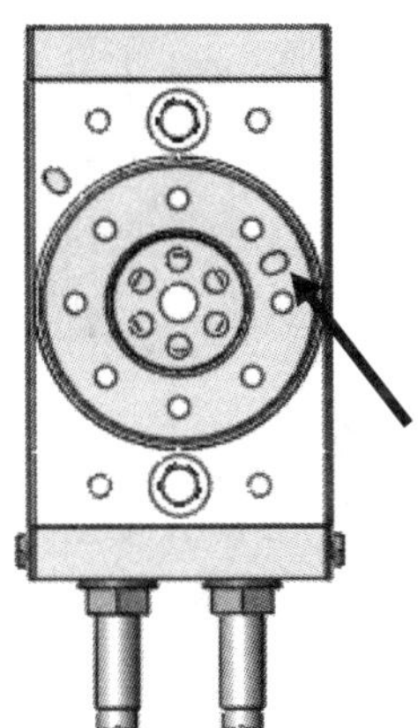

Return to the ConfigurationManager.

96) Click the **ConfigurationManager** tab.

Insert the ROTARY (Flexible) configuration.

97) Right-click **ROTARY Configuration(s).**

98) Click **Add Configuration**.

99) Enter **FLEXIBLE** for Configuration name.

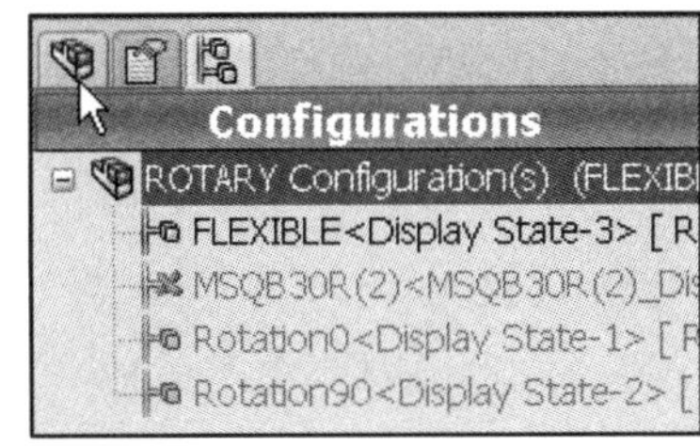

100) Enter **ROTARY Flexible** for Description.

101) Enter **Suppress Mate Rotation0** and **Suppress Mate Rotation90** for Comment.

102) Click **OK** from the Add Configuration PropertyManager. The FLEXIBLE configuration name is added to the ConfigurationManager.

Define the Flexible configuration Mate state.

103) Return to the FeatureManager.

104) Right-click **Rotation90** from the MateGroup1 folder.

105) Click **Suppress**. The Dowel Pin Slot rotates freely.

Work with multiple Mates to control configurations. Suppress related Mates. UnSuppress the Mates required to achieve dynamic behavior through the configurations.

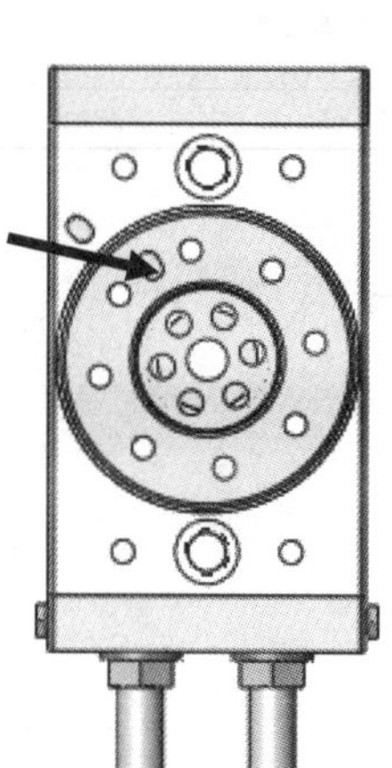

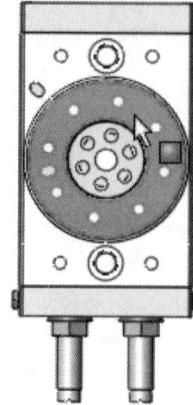

FLEXIBLE
(Rotates)

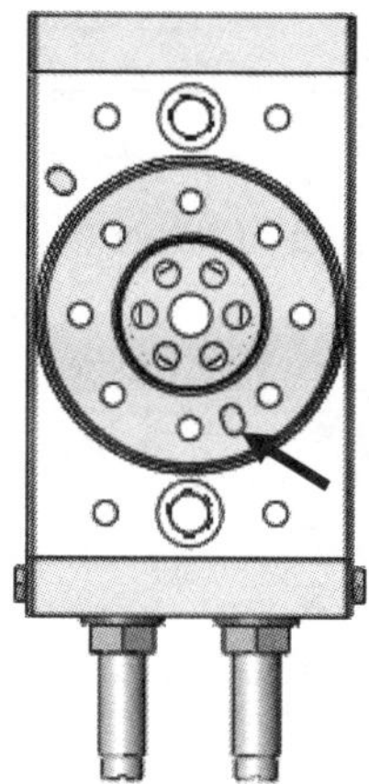

Default & Rotation0

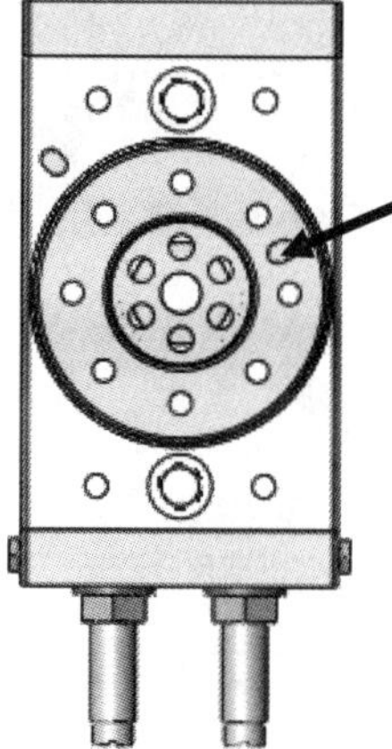

Rotation90

Example: Suppress the Rotation0 Mate and Suppress the Rotation90 Mate. UnSuppress either the Rotation0 Mate or the Rotation90 Mate. The Mates would be over defined if both the Rotation0 and the Rotation90 Mates were UnSuppressed.

Verify the ROTARY configurations.

106) Double-click **Default(MSQB3-R(2))**, **FLEXIBLE**, **Rotation0,** and **Rotation90**. The FLEXIBLE configuration rotates.

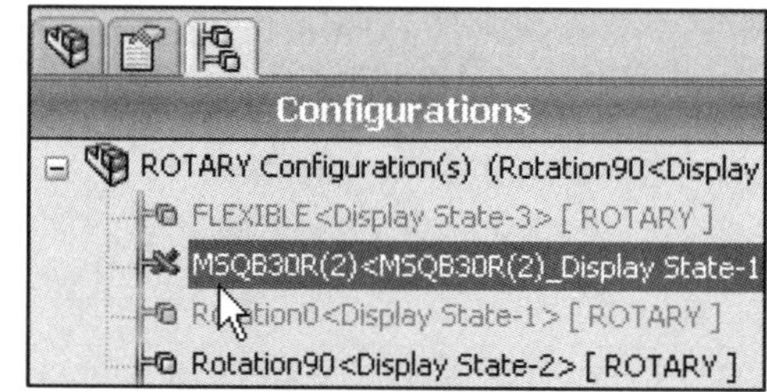

Display the Default configuration.

107) Double-click **MSQB30R(2)** from the ConfigurationManager. The Dowel Pin Slot is located in the lower right corner.

Return to the FeatureManager.

108) Click the **FeatureManager** tab.

Save the ROTARY assembly.
109) Click **Save**.

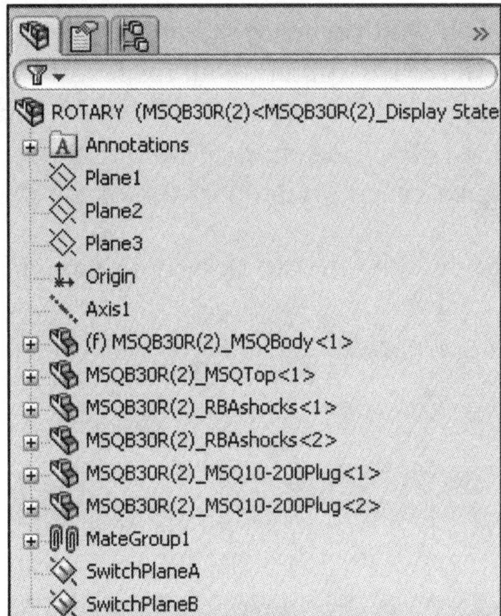

Configurations are an integral part of the design process. Define the ROTARY positions before mating the GRIPPER assembly.

Why maintain a Default(MSQB30R(2)) configuration and a Rotation0 configuration when both positions are the same? Answer: The Default(MSQB30R(2)) configuration remains a "safety fall back" configuration.

The Default(MSQB30R(2)) configuration is recognized by the members of the design team. The Rotation0 configuration affects four levels of assemblies: *ROTARY, ROTARY-GRIPPER, 3AXIS-TRANSFER*, and *DELIVERY-STATION*.

Each assembly and their components contain configurations. Issues can and will occur in the development process. The Default(MSQB30R(2)) configuration provides assistance in solving issues.

The Default(MSQB30R(2)) configuration remains a static configuration. All multiple configuration components utilize the Default(MSQB30R(2)) configuration.

Assemble the GRIPPER assembly to the ROTARY Assembly

Utilize two Coincident Mates and one Distance Mate to assemble the GRIPPER assembly to the ROTARY assembly. The ROTARY-GRIPPER assembly currently contains nine components. As components and geometry increase in complexity, utilize the FeatureManager to select planes in the mating process. Expand the sub-assembly entries to select the Planes to constrain the model.

Example: The ROTARY\MSQBody part is fixed. Mate selections to this component result in a non-rotating GRIPPER assembly. The ROTARY\MSQTop part rotates. Mate selection to this component result in a rotating GRIPPER assembly.

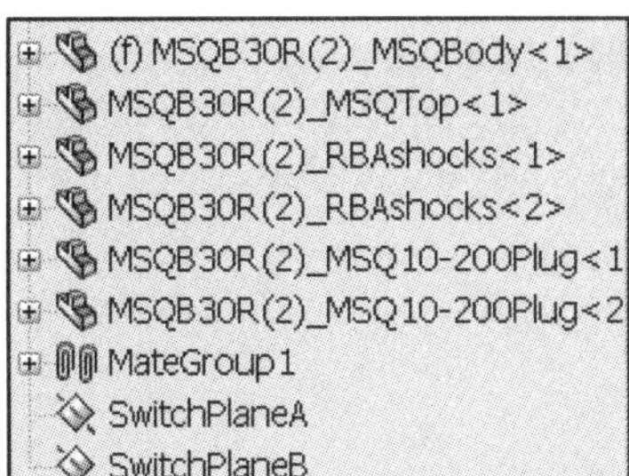

The Distance Mate mates the back face of the GRIPPER\Body part to the front face of the ROTARY\MSQTop part.

You wait for team members to provide critical dimensions for the location of the GRIPPER fingers with respect to other DELIVERY-STATION components. Allow for future design changes. Create a 10mm gap between the ROTARY assembly and the GRIPPER assembly. Note: Later you will create 15mm and 20mm gaps and adjust the gaps based on the position of the INPUT and OUTPUT components.

View the GRIPPER assembly position with the three ROTARY configurations:

- *Default*
- *Rotation0*
- *Rotation90*

The MSQTop part rotates in the ROTARY (FLEXIBLE) configuration. When the ROTARY (FLEXIBLE) configuration is inserted into the ROTARY-GRIPPER assembly, SolidWorks solves the Mates as rigid.

The MSQTop is fixed. Modify the Solve As option from Rigid to Flexible in the ROTARY Component Properties.

Activity: Assemble the GRIPPER Assembly to the ROTARY Assembly

Hide the ROTARY\MSQBody part.

110) Click **ROTARY\MSQBody** from the FeatureManager.

111) Right-click **Hide components** from the Context toolbar.

112) **Hide** the illustrated components.

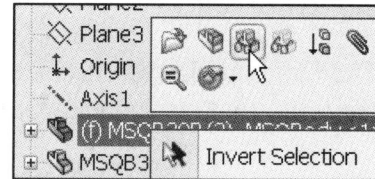

Return to the ROTARY-GRIPPER assembly.

113) Click **Windows**, **ROTARY-GRIPPER**. The ROTARY-GRIPPER FeatureManager is displayed.

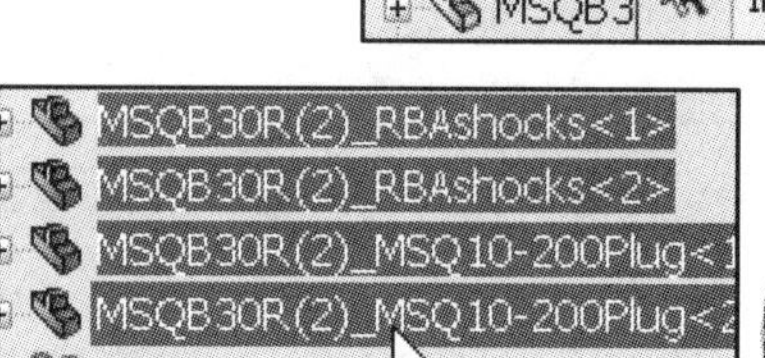

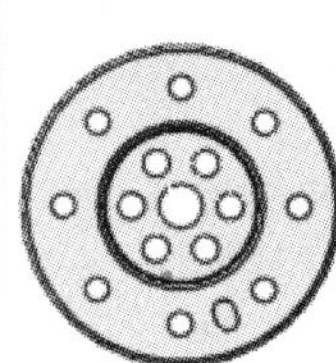

Display an Isometric view.

114) Click **Isometric** view from the Heads-up View toolbar.

Select the GRIPPER assembly.

115) Click the **right face** of the GRIPPER assembly between the two FINGERS as illustrated.

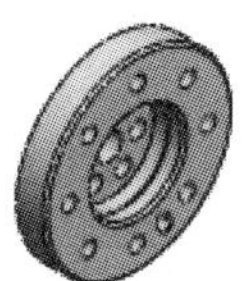

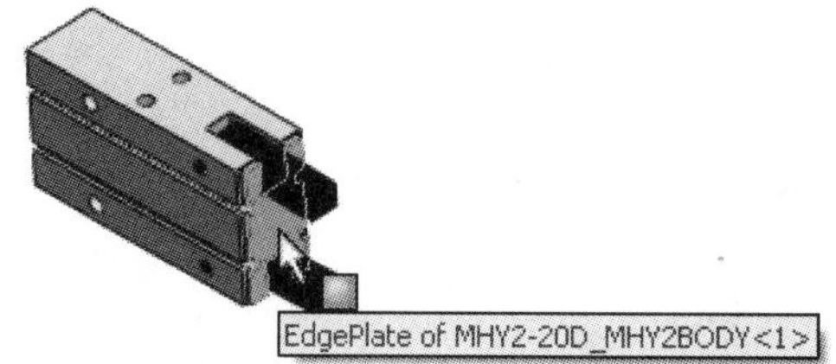

116) Click **Section view**.

117) Enter **–80** for Offset Distance.

118) Click **OK** from the Section View PropertyManager.

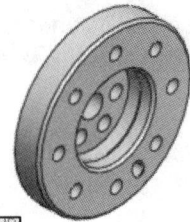

Assemble the GRIPPER assembly to the ROTARY assembly. Insert the first Coincident Mate.

119) Right-click **ROTARY/MSQTop/Front** from the FeatureManager.

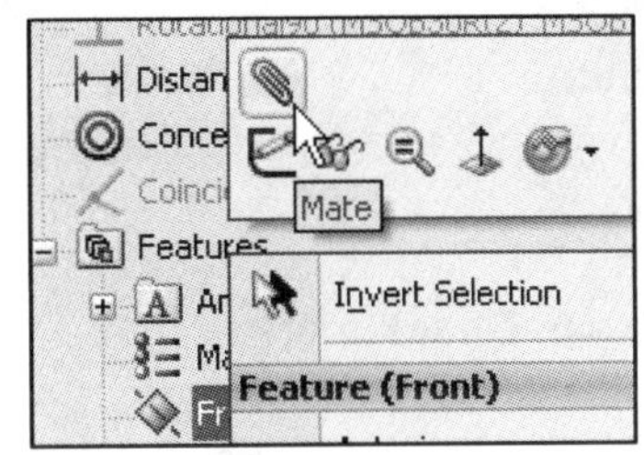

120) Click the **Mate** tool. The Mate PropertyManager is displayed.

121) Click **GRIPPER\Right** from the fly-out FeatureManager. Coincident is selected by default.

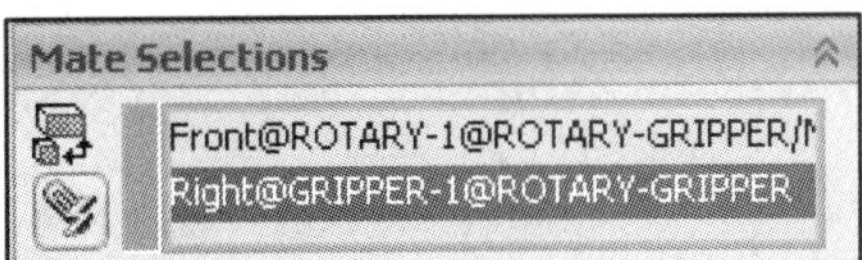

122) Click the **Green Check mark**.

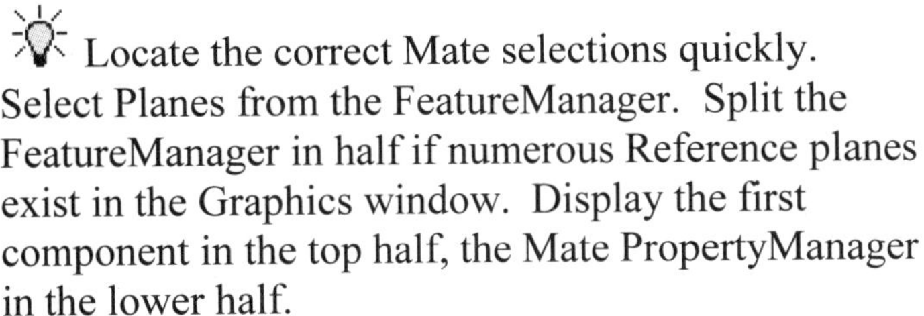
Locate the correct Mate selections quickly. Select Planes from the FeatureManager. Split the FeatureManager in half if numerous Reference planes exist in the Graphics window. Display the first component in the top half, the Mate PropertyManager in the lower half.

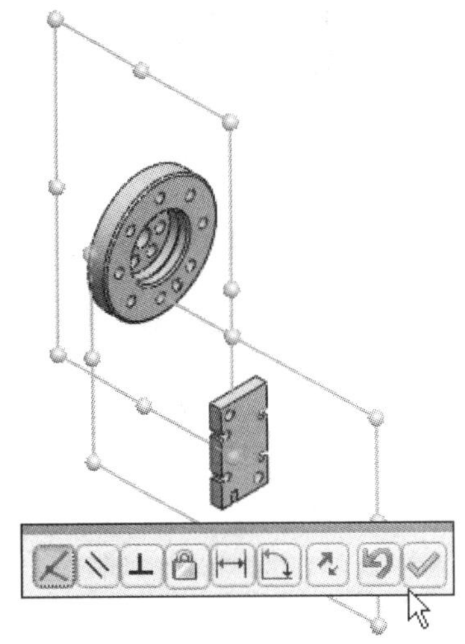

Insert the second Coincident Mate.

123) Click **ROTARY\MSQTop\Side** from the fly-out FeatureManager.

124) Click **GRIPPER\Front** from the fly-out FeatureManager. Coincident is selected by default.

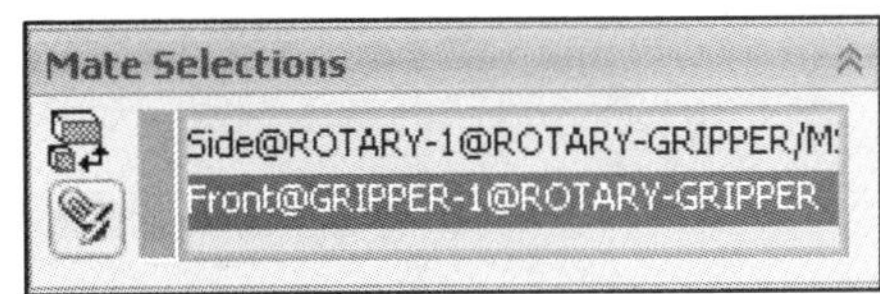

125) Click the **Green Check mark**.

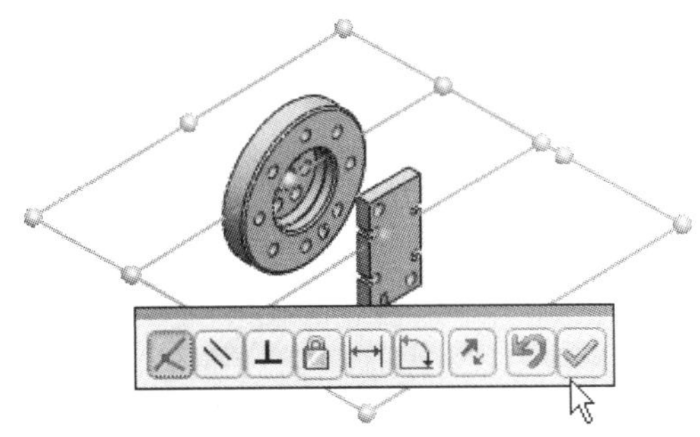

Insert a Distance Mate.

126) Click the **back face** of the GRIPPER assembly.

127) Click the **front face** of the ROTARY assembly.

128) Click **Distance**.

129) Enter **10**mm.

130) Click the **Green Check mark** ✔.

131) Click **OK** ✔ from the Mate PropertyManager.

132) Click **Isometric** view from the Heads-up View toolbar.

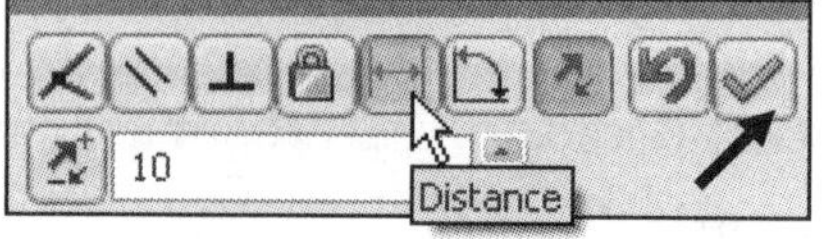

Display the Full view.

133) Click **Section view**. The GRIPPER assembly is fully defined in the ROTARY-GRIPPER assembly.

Select the ROTARY(FLEXIBLE) configuration.

134) Right-click **ROTARY** from the ROTARY-GRIPPER FeatureManager.

135) Click **Component Properties** from the Context toolbar.

136) Check the **Flexible** box as illustrated.

137) Select **FLEXIBLE** for the Referenced configuration.

138) Click **OK** from the dialog box.

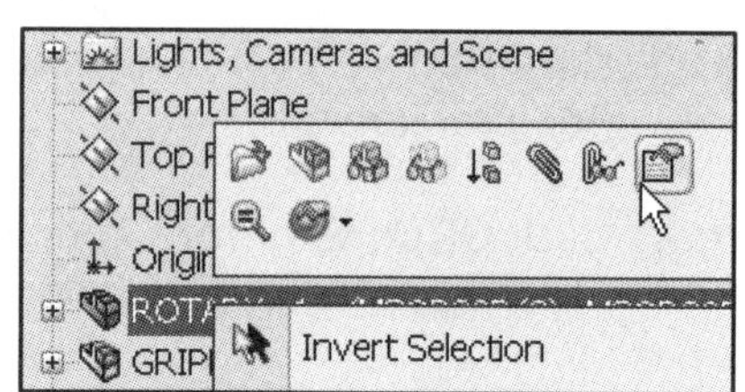

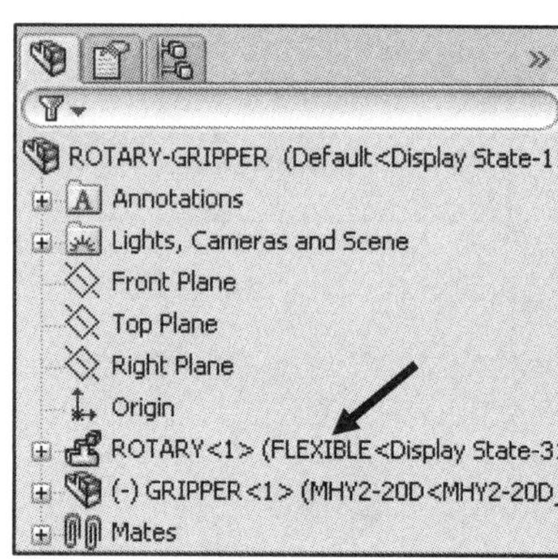

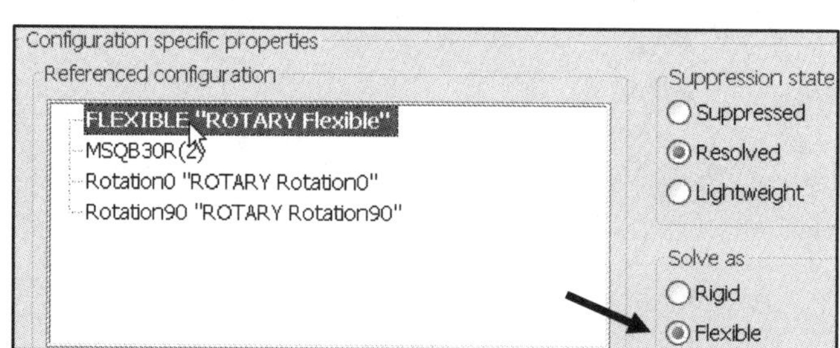

139) Drag the **GRIPPER** assembly in the ROTARY-GRIPPER Graphics window. The GRIPPER assembly is free to rotate.

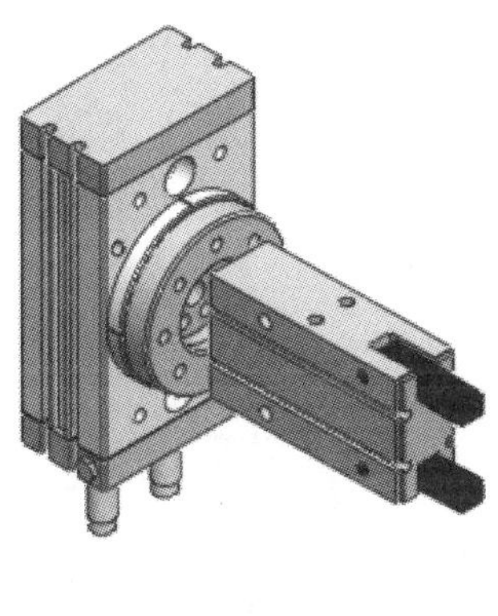

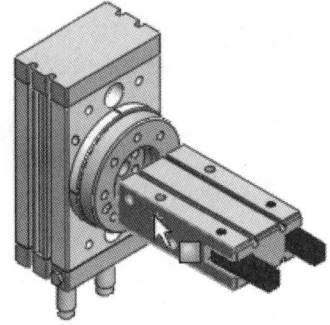

Select the ROTARY (Rotation0) configuration.

140) Right-click **ROTARY** from FeatureManager.

141) Click **Component Properties** from the Context toolbar.

142) Select **Rotation0** "ROTARY Rotation0" for the Reference configuration.

143) Click **OK**.

Select the ROTARY (Rotation90) configuration.

144) Right-click **ROTARY** from the ROTARY-GRIPPER FeatureManager.

145) Click **Component Properties** from the Context toolbar.

146) Select **Rotation90** for the Reference configuration.

147) Click **OK**.

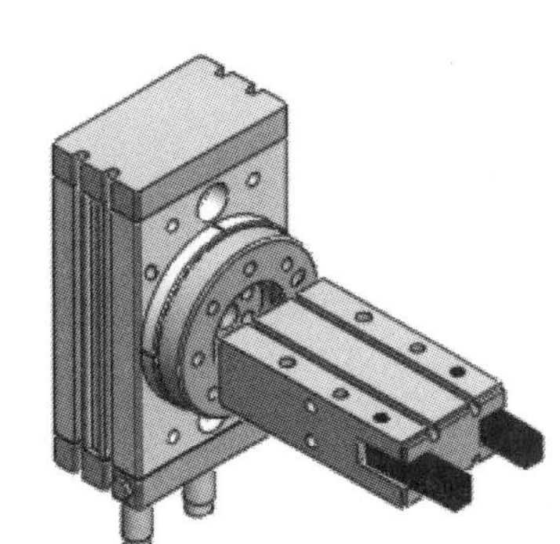

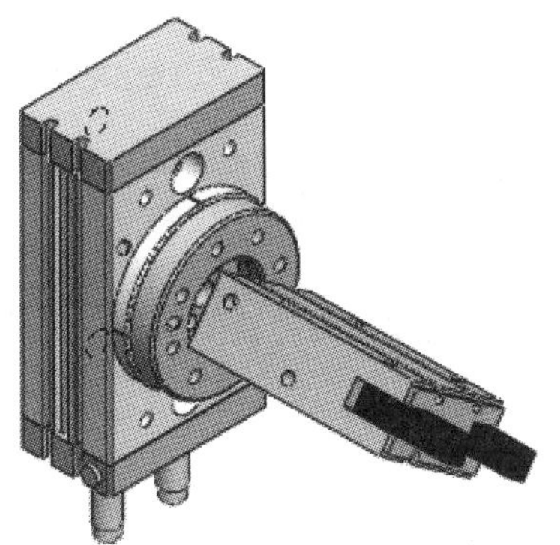

Flexible

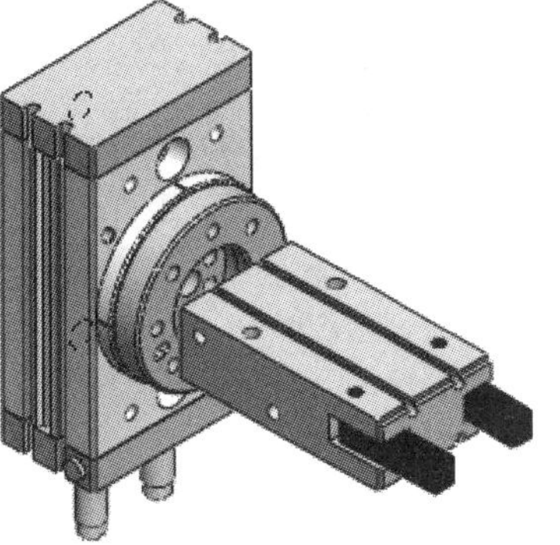

Rotation90

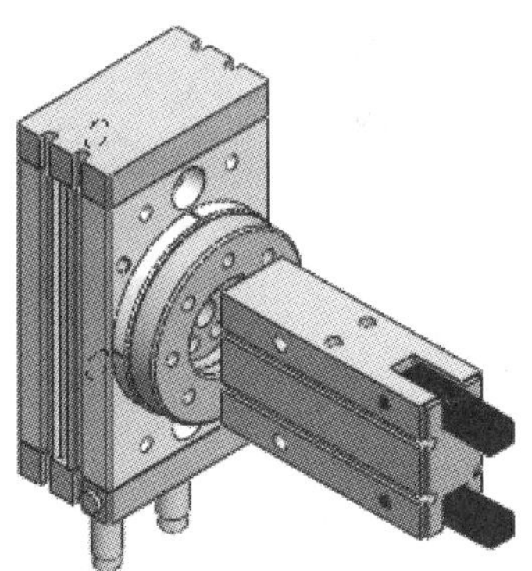

Default/Rotation0

ROTARY-GRIPPER Configurations

Return to the ROTARY(Default) configuration.

148) Right-click **ROTARY** from the ROTARY-GRIPPER FeatureManager.

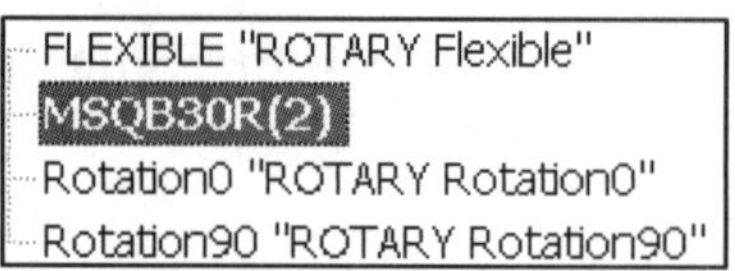

149) Click **Component Properties** from the Context toolbar.

150) Select **MSQB30R(2)**.

151) Click **OK**.

152) Click **Right** view from the Heads-up View toolbar. The default configuration of the ROTARY\MSQTop\Dowel Pin Slot is located in the lower right corner in the Graphics window.

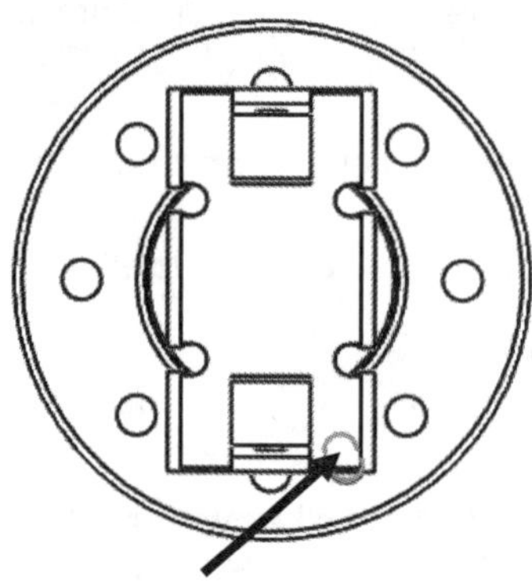

PLATE-D part with In-Context features

The ROTARY\MSQTop part contains eight, 5mm holes. The GRIPPER assembly contains two, 4mm holes. The GRIPPER assembly mounting holes do not align to the ROTARY\MSQTop part mounting holes.

Create the PLATE-D part as an interim part between the ROTARY\MSQTop part and the GRIPPER assembly. Develop the PLATE-D part In-Context of the ROTARY-GRIPPER assembly. In the first activity, create the Extruded-Base feature sketched on the front face of the ROTARY assembly. The first sketch references the circular edges of the ROTARY\MSQTop part. In the second activity, create the holes as In-Context features.

Utilize the New Part tool from the Assembly toolbar. Select the Part-MM-ANSI-AL6061 Template. The Template was created in Project 2. SolidWorks automatically selects the Sketch tool. The PLATE-D Extruded Base feature sketch is parallel to the MSQTop Plane1. The PLATE-D entry in the FeatureManager is displayed in blue.

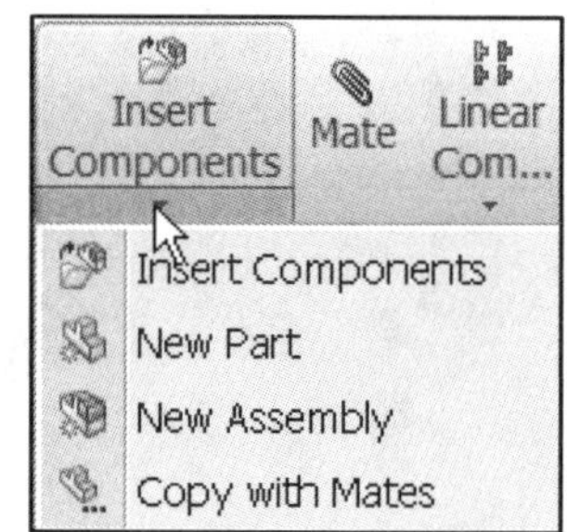

SolidWorks inserts the InPlace Mate as a Coincident Mate between the PLATE-D Front Plane and the MSQTop circular face. The InPlace Mate fully defines the PLATE-D part in the ROTARY-GRIPPER assembly.

Create the PLATE-D sketch. Sketch a horizontal centerline through the MSQTop Origin. Sketch a rectangle. The four lines of the rectangle are tangent to the MSQTop circular edge. Extrude the sketch to the back vertex of the GRIPPER assembly. The depth of the PLATE-D part references the vertex of the GRIPPER assembly.

The Extruded-Base feature of the PLATE-D part is a square shape versus a circular shape. A square flat plate shape costs less to machine than a circular flat plate shape.

You are in the ROTARY-GRIPPER assembly level.

Activity: Create the PLATE-D part In-Context to the ROTARY-GRIPPER Assembly

Hide the GRIPPER assembly.

153) Right-click **GRIPPER** from the FeatureManager.

154) Click **Hide components** from the Context toolbar.

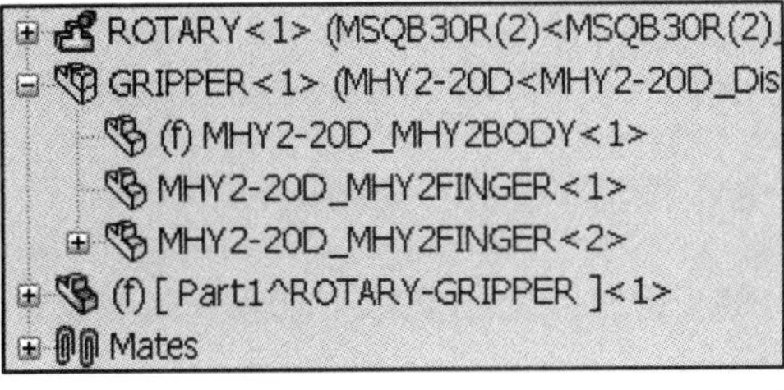

Insert the new PLATE-D part.

155) Click the **New Part** tool from the Consolidated Insert Components toolbar.

156) Double-click **PART-MM-ANSI-AL6061**. The new part is displayed in the FeatureManager design tree with a name in the form [Part*n*^*assembly_name*]. The square brackets indicate that the part is a virtual component.

The new Component Pointer icon is displayed. The default component is empty and requires a Sketch plane. The Right face is the Sketch plane.

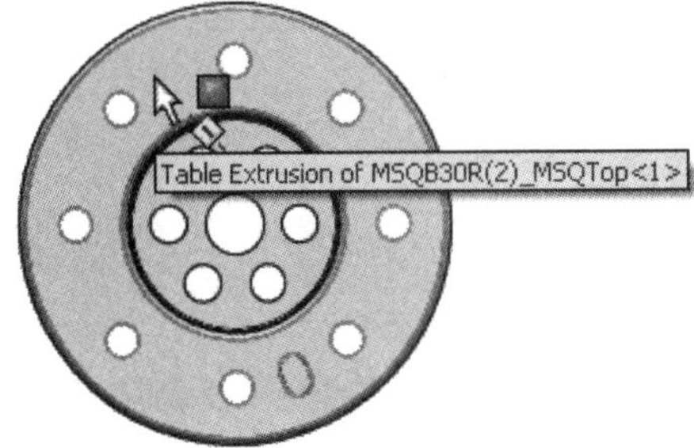

157) Click the **circular face** of MSQTop. The InPlace Mate is added to MateGroup1. The Edit Component mode is selected.

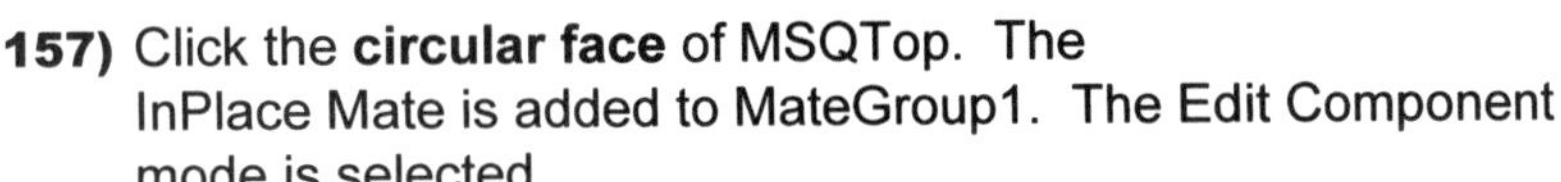

Sketch the profile.

158) Click **Right** view from the Heads-up View toolbar.

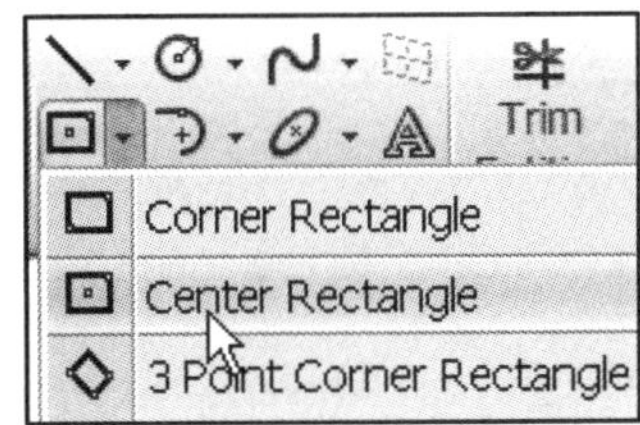

159) Display the Origin.

160) Click the **Center Rectangle** tool from the Sketch toolbar.

161) Click the **Origin**.

162) Sketch a **center rectangle** larger than the MSQTop as illustrated.

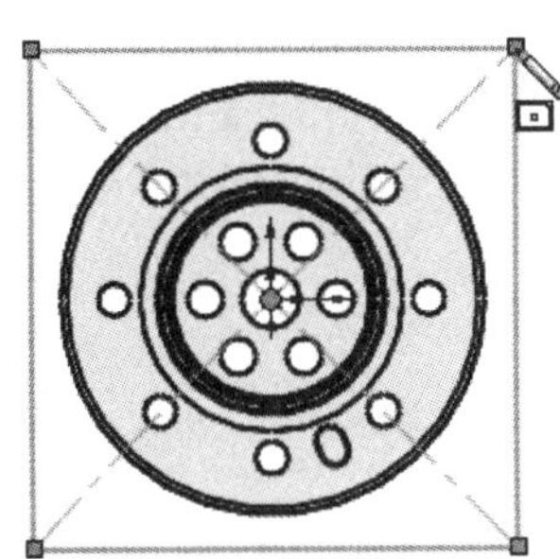

163) Right-click **Select** to deselect the sketch tool.

Select and verify reference geometry with the FeatureManager. Utilize the FeatureManager to select the MSQTop Origin. Review the entity name in the Selected Entities box, Point1@Origin@ROTARY-1@ROTARY-GRIPPER\MSQTop-1. Utilize Display/Delete Relations in the part sketch to verify the entity. The syntax is slightly different, Point1@Origin of ROTARY<1>\MSQTop<1>.

Insert an Equal relation.

164) Click the **top horizontal line** of the rectangle.

165) Hold the **Ctrl** key down.

166) Click the **right vertical line** of the rectangle.

167) Release the **Ctrl** key.

168) Right-click **Make Equal** from the Context toolbar.

Insert a Tangent relation.

169) Click the **top horizontal line** of the rectangle.

170) Hold the **Ctrl** key down.

171) Click the inside **top circular edge**.

172) Release the **Ctrl** key.

173) Right-click **Make Tangent** from the Context toolbar.

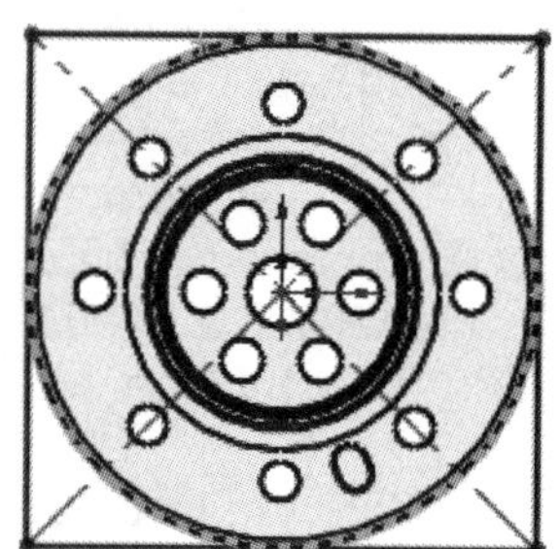

174) Click **OK** ✔ from the Properties PropertyManager. View the FeatureManager.

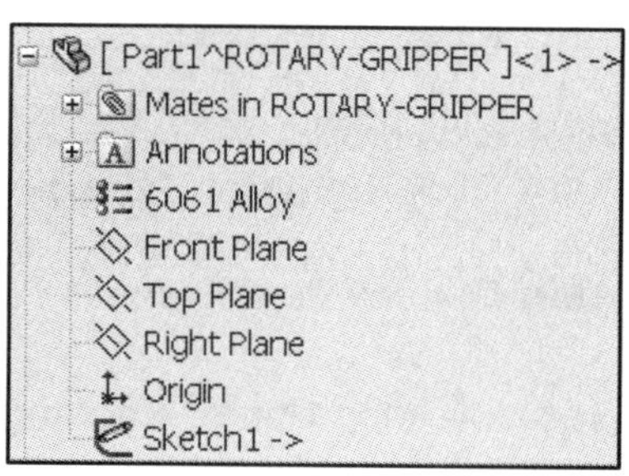

Display the GRIPPER assembly.

175) Right-click **GRIPPER** from the FeatureManager.

176) Click **Show components** from the Context toolbar.

Display an Isometric view.

177) Click **Isometric** view from the Heads-up Views toolbar.

Extrude Sketch1.

178) Click the **Extruded Boss/Base** tool from the Features toolbar.

179) Click **Up To Vertex**.

180) Click the back **Vertex** of the Gripper as illustrated.

181) Click **OK** ✔ from the Extrude PropertyManager.

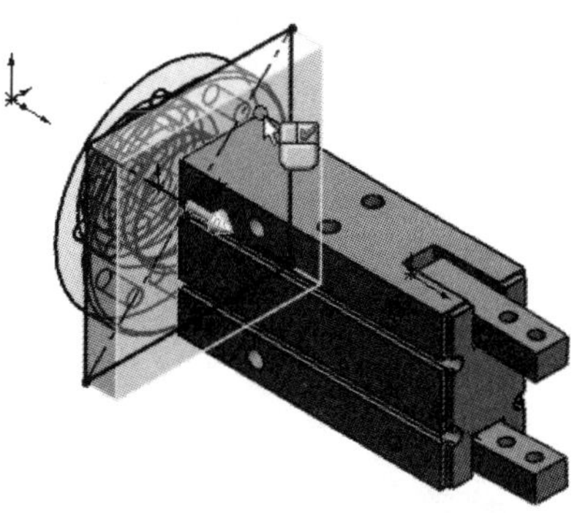

Display the virtual component.

182) Expand [Part1^ROTARY-GRIPPER]. View the results.

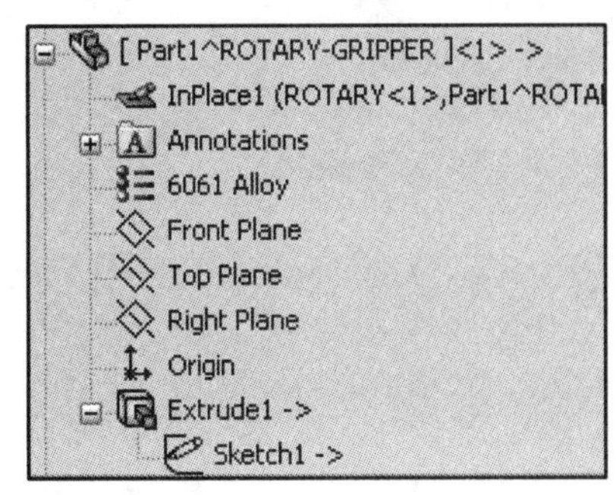

The External References "->" symbol indicates that the Extrude1 feature and Sketch1 contain solved External references.

Return to the ROTARY-GRIPPER.

183) Right-click a **position** in the Graphics window.

184) Click the **Edit Component** tool to return to the assembly.

Rename the virtual component to PLATE-D.

185) Right-click the **virtual component name**.

186) Click **Open Part** from the Context toolbar.

187) Click **Save As** from the Menu bar toolbar.

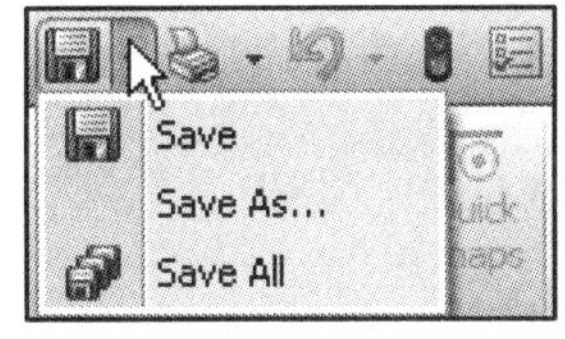

188) Click **OK**.

189) Enter **PLATE-D** in the DELIVERY STATION folder.

190) Close the part and return to the assembly.

191) Rebuild the assembly.

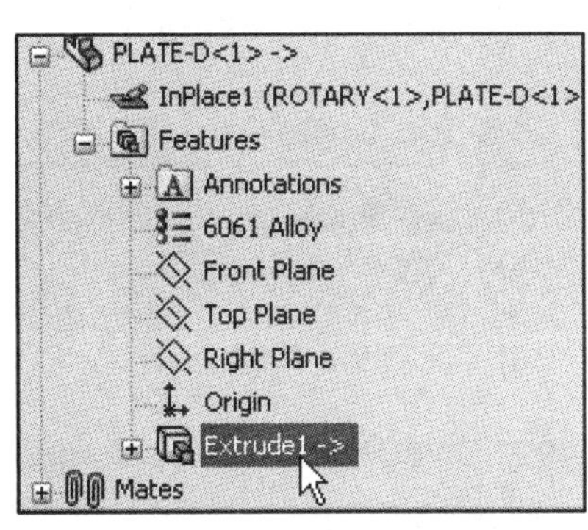

List the PLATE-D External references.

192) Right-click **Extrude1** ->.

193) Click **List External Refs**. The Referenced Entity column lists the referenced geometry from ROTARY<1>\MSQBTop<1> and GRIPPER<1>\MHY2BODY< 1>.

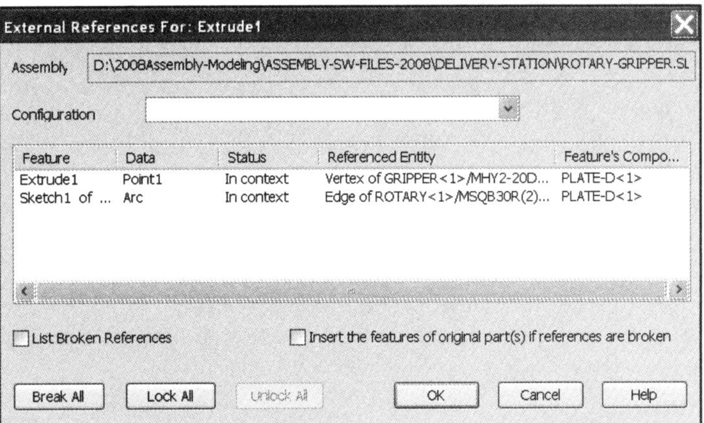

194) Click **OK**.

PLATE-D Holes

PLATE-D fastens to the ROTARY\MSQTop part and to the back face of the GRIPPER assembly. Determine the size and location of the mounting holes.

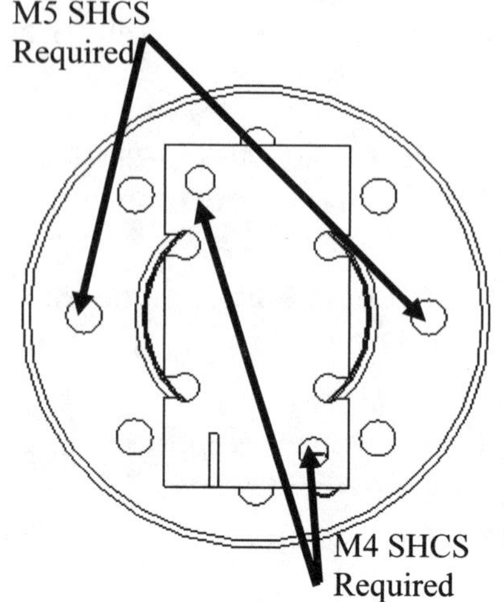

PLATE-D fastens to the GRIPPER with two 4mm SHCSs. Create the Cbores on the PLATE-D back face, in the context of the GRIPPER/BackHole1 and GRIPPER/BackHole2 features.

PLATE-D fastens to the MSQTop part with two 5mm SHCSs. Create the Cbores on the PLATE-D front face, In-Context of the MSQTop\Mounting Holes feature.

Identify your location in the ROTARY-GRIPPER assembly. The assembly window displays "PLATE-D-in-ROTARY-GRIPPER." The PLATE-D entry in the FeatureManager is displayed in blue.

Activity: Create the PLATE-D Holes with the Hole Wizard tool

Create two 5mm Cbores on the PLATE-D part In-Context to the assembly.
195) Right-click **PLATE-D**.

196) Click **Edit Part** from the Context toolbar. You are in Exit Component mode.

197) Click **Hidden Lines Visible** from the Heads-up View toolbar.

Display the Right view.
198) Click **Right** view from the Heads-up View toolbar.

Hide the GRIPPER assembly.
199) Right-click **GRIPPER** from the FeatureManager.

200) Click **Hide components** from the Context toolbar. Note: PLATE-D is in the Edit Component mode.

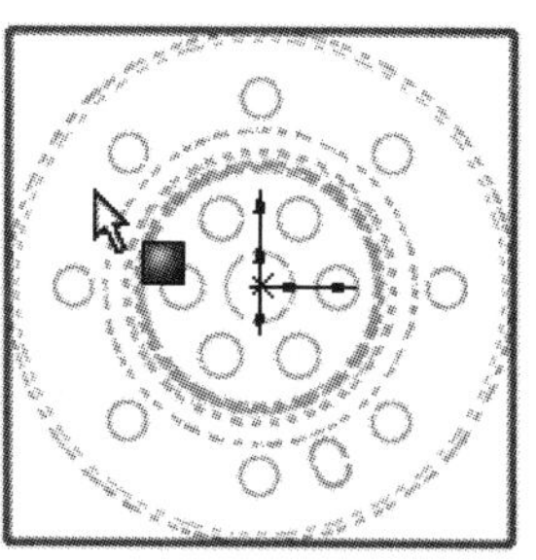

Select the Sketch Plane for the two 5mm Cbores.
201) Click the **front face of PLATE-D** on the left side as illustrated.

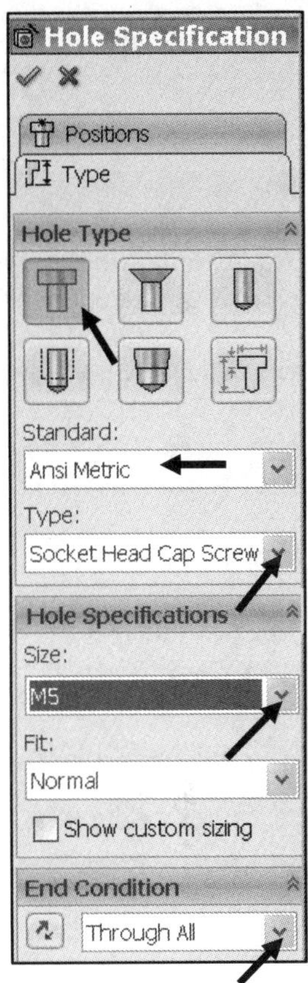

Apply the Hole Wizard tool to create the Cbore.

202) Click the **Hole Wizard** tool from the Features toolbar.

203) Click **Counterbore** for Hole Specification.

204) Select **Ansi Metric** for Standard.

205) Select **Socket Head Cap Screw** for Type.

206) Select **M5** for Size.

207) Select **Through All** for End Condition.

208) Click the **Positions** tab. The Point icon is displayed.

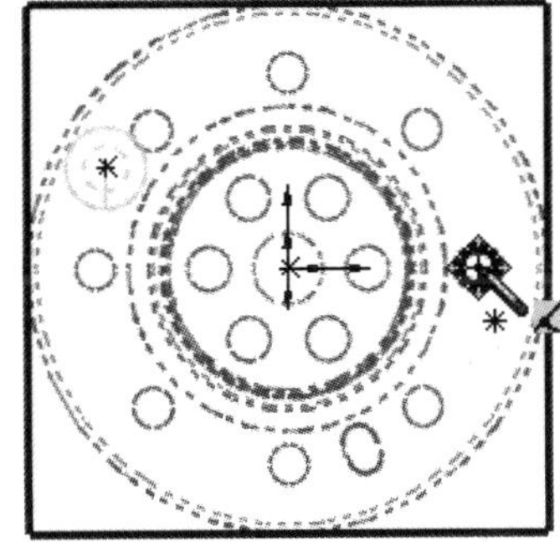

Activate the center point.

209) Drag the **mouse pointer** over the right Mounting Hole of the MSQBTop part.

210) Click a **position** on the center point for the right Mounting Hole.

Activate Filters.

211) Click **Filter Edges** and Filter **Sketch Points** from the Selection Filter toolbar.

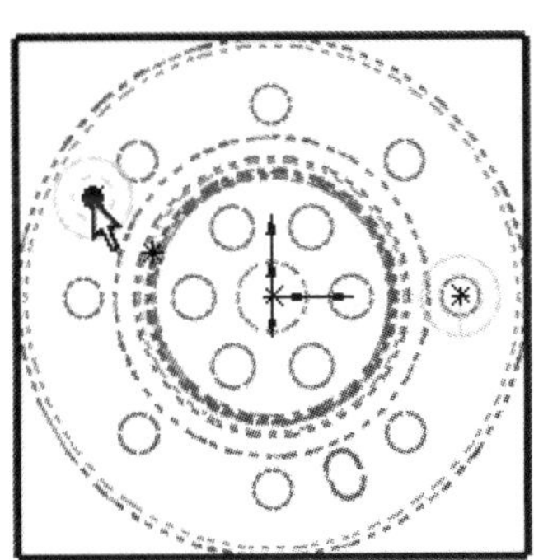

Add a Concentric relation.

212) Right-click **Select**. The Filter icon is displayed.

213) Click the **blue center point**, as illustrated.

214) Hold the **Ctrl** key down.

215) Click the **left Mounting Hole circle**.

216) Release the **Ctrl** key.

217) Right-click **Make Concentric** from the Context toolbar.

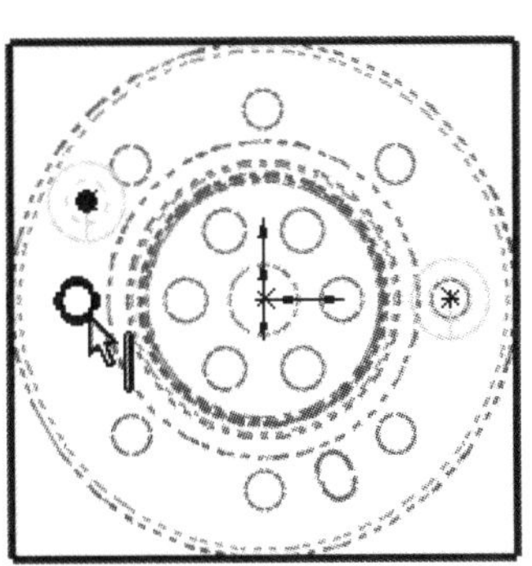

218) Click **OK** ✔ from the Properties PropertyManager.

219) Click **OK** ✔ from the Hole Position PropertyManager.

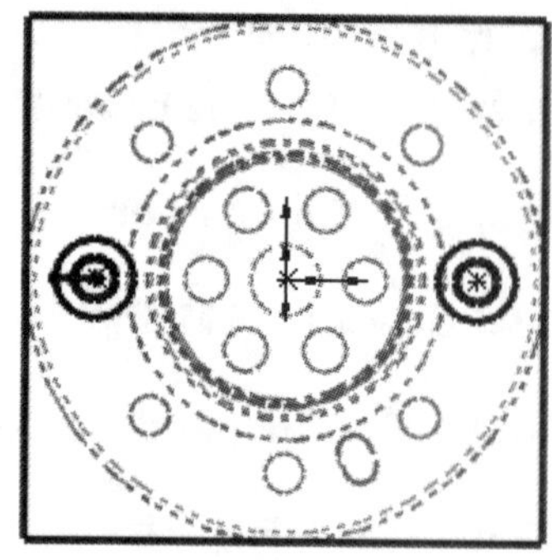

Display the GRIPPER assembly.
220) Right-click **GRIPPER** from the FeatureManager.

221) Click **Show components**.

Hide the ROTARY assembly.
222) Right-click **ROTARY** from the FeatureManager.

223) Click **Hide components**.

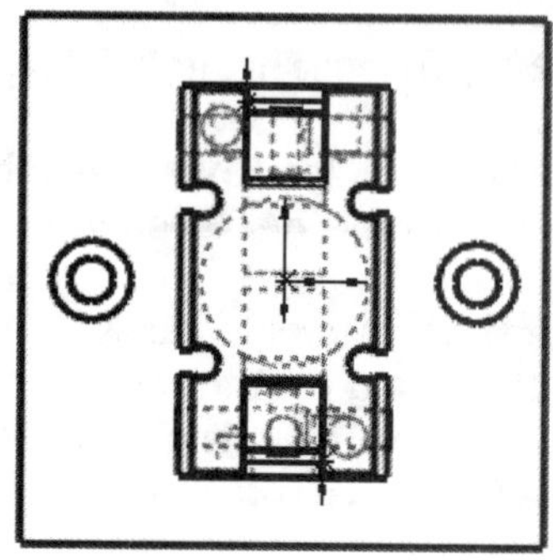

Deactivate Filters.
224) **Deactivate** all filters.

225) Click **Isometric** view.

The PLATE-D part remains in the Edit Component mode, (blue).

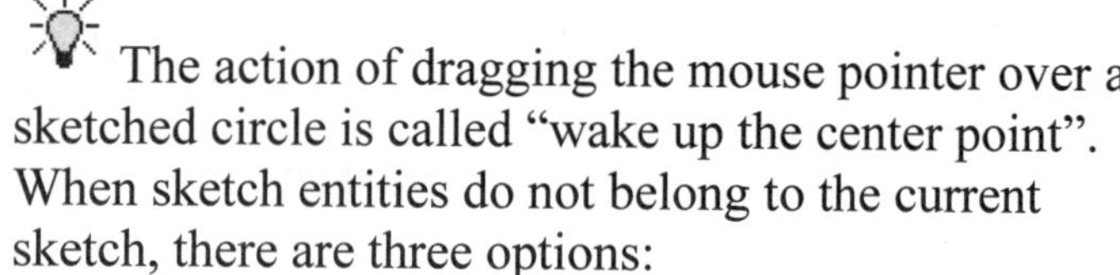

The action of dragging the mouse pointer over a sketched circle is called "wake up the center point". When sketch entities do not belong to the current sketch, there are three options:

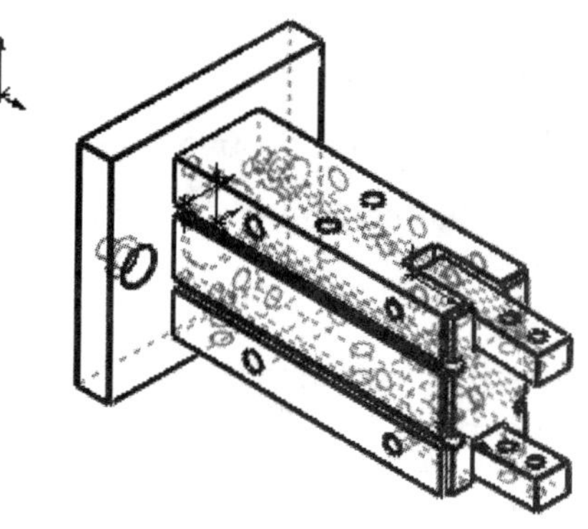

- Add a Concentric relation between the point and the circular edge.
- Add a Coincident relation between the point and the Temporary axis.
- Utilize the Sketch snaps, Center Point Snap option.

Quick Snaps/Sketch snaps are similar to the AutoCAD O-Snaps (Object Snaps). The mouse pointer snaps to specified geometry. Enable snapping or the Sketch snaps under **Options**, **System Options**, **Relations/Snaps**. Right-click **Quick Snaps** on a sketch entity to view the snap options.

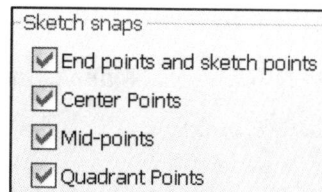

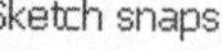

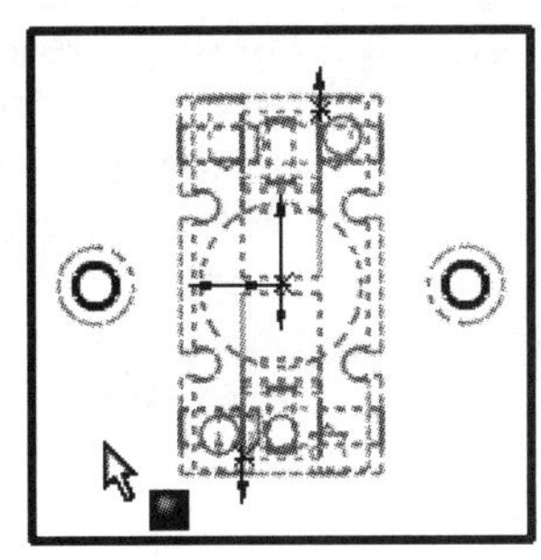

Create two 4mm Cbores on PLATE-D In-Context using Hole Wizard.

226) Click **left** view from the Heads-up View toolbar.

227) Click the **back face of PLATE-D** in the lower left corner as illustrated.

228) Click the **Hole Wizard** tool from the Features toolbar.

229) Click **Counterbore** for Hole Specification.

230) Select **Ansi Metric** for Standard.

231) Select **Socket Head Cap Screw** for Type.

232) Select **M4** for Size.

233) Select **Through all** for End Condition.

234) Click the **Positions** tab. The Point icon is displayed.

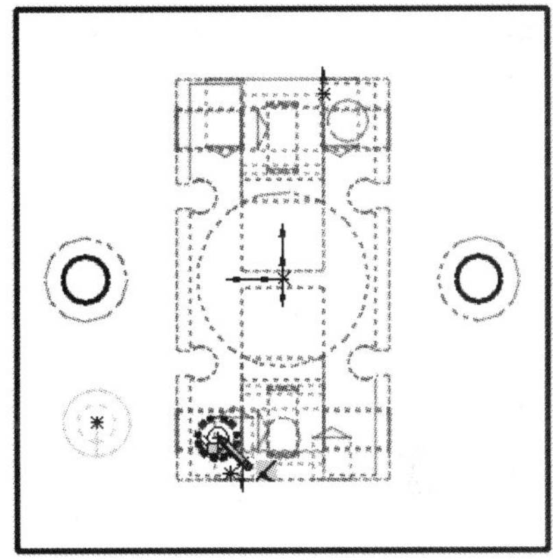

235) Click the center point of the GRIPPER\MHY2BODY**M5 x 0.8BackHole1 circle** as illustrated.

236) Click the center point of the GRIPPER\MHY2BODY**M5 x 0.8BackHole2 circle** as illustrated.

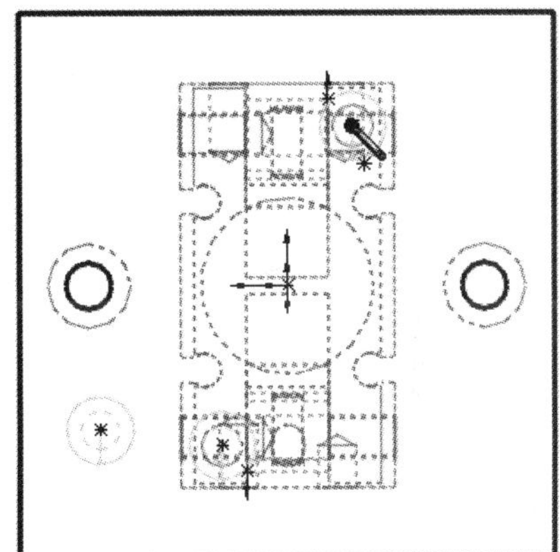

237) Right-click **Select** to deselect the Point sketch tool.

238) Click the **first point** as illustrated.

239) Right-click **Delete**.

240) Click **OK** from the Hole Position PropertyManager.

Return to the ROTARY-GRIPPER assembly.

241) Right-click **ROTARY-GRIPPER** from the Graphics window.

242) Click **Edit Assembly: ROTARY-GRIPPER.**

243) **Rebuild** the assembly.

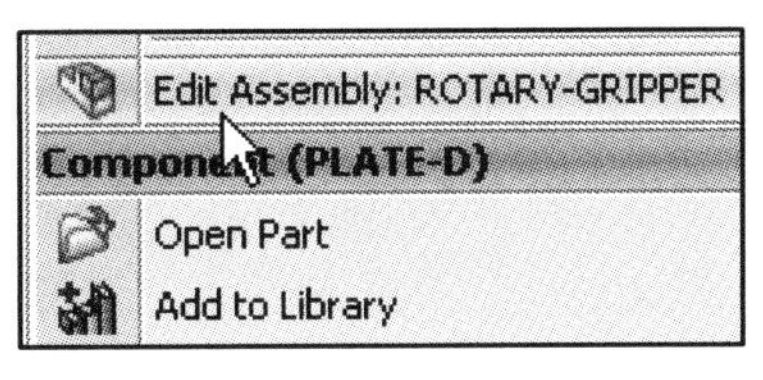

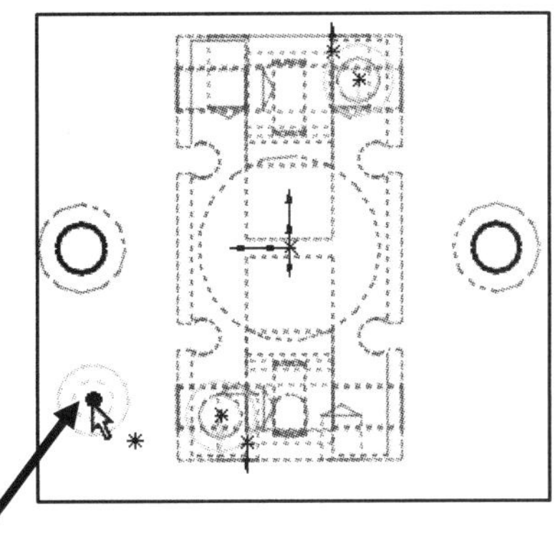

Delete point

Activity: Display Update Holders in the Assembly

Display the Update Holders.

244) Right-click the **ROTARY-GRIPPER** assembly icon.

245) Click **Show Update Holders**. The FeatureManager lists six entities.

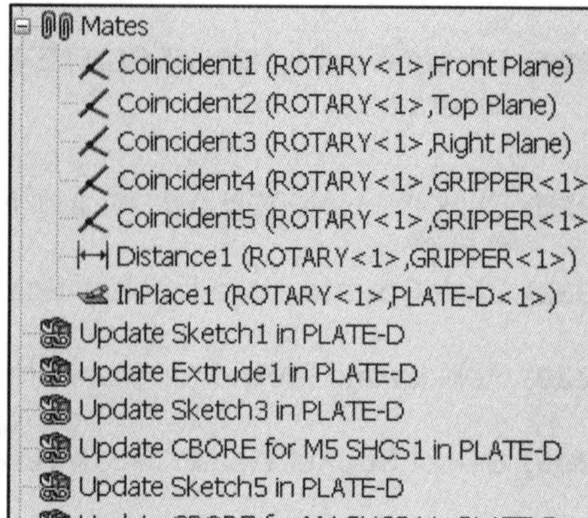

Hide the Update Holders.

246) Right-click **ROTARY-GRIPPER** from the FeatureManager.

247) Click **Hide Update Holders**.

Display the ROTARY assembly and GRIPPER assembly.

248) Show the **features** as illustrated.

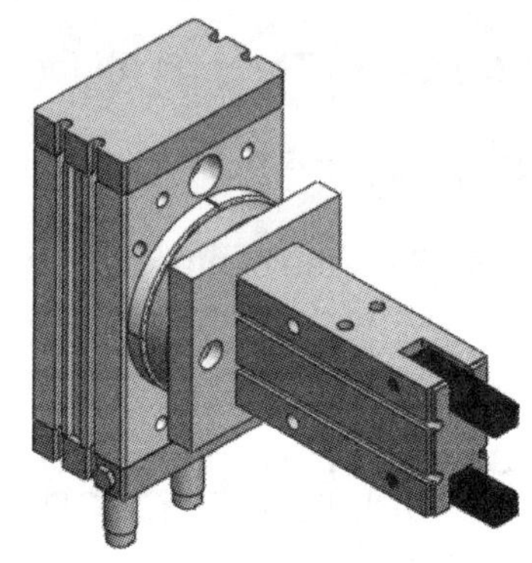

The distance between the ROTARY assembly and the GRIPPER assembly controls the depth of the PLATE-D part.

Modify the PLATE-D Distance1 Mate.

249) **Expand** ROTARY-GRIPPER/Mates.

250) Right-click **Distance1**.

251) Click **Edit Feature** from the Context toolbar.

252) Enter **30**mm for distance.

253) Click **OK** ✔ from the Distance1 PropertyManager.

254) Click **OK** ✔ from the Mate PropertyManager. View the results.

ROTARY<1> (MSQB30R(2)<MSQB30R(2)_D
GRIPPER<1> (MHY2-20D<MHY2-20D_Displ
PLATE-D<1> ->
Mates
Coincident1 (ROTARY<1>,Front Plane)
Coincident2 (ROTARY<1>,Top Plane)
Coincident3 (ROTARY<1>,Right Plane)
Coincident4 (ROTARY<1>,GRIPPER<1>)
Coincident5 (ROTARY<1>,GRIPPER<1>)
Distance1 (ROTARY<1>,GRIPPER<1>)
InPlace1 (ROTARY<1>,PLATE-D<1>)

Rename Distance1 Mate.

255) Rename **Distance1** to **Distance-PLATE-D-Depth**.

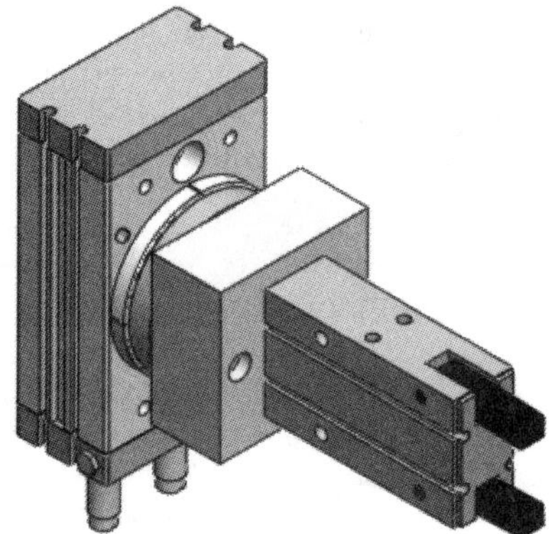

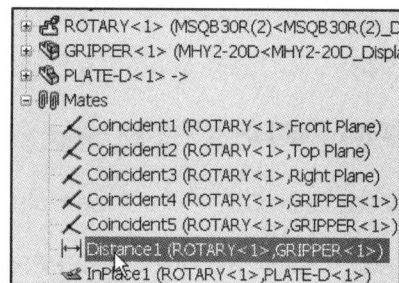

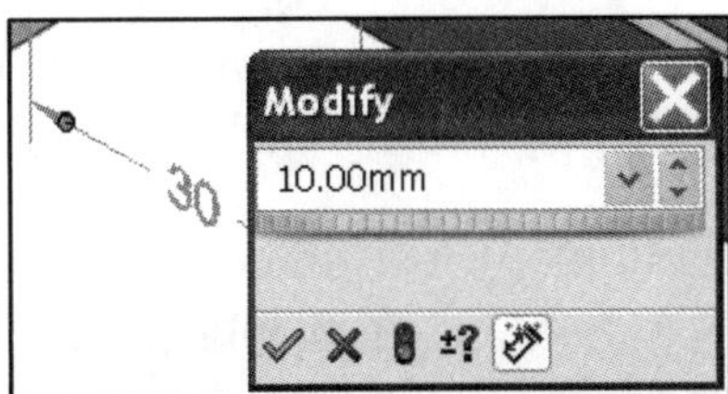

Modify PLATE-D.

256) Double-click **Distance-PLATE-D-Depth** from the FeatureManager. The 30 text dimension is displayed.

257) **Drag** the dimension off the model.

258) Double-click **30**.

259) Enter **10**mm.

260) Click **Rebuild**.

261) Click the **Green Check mark** ✔.

262) Click **OK** ✔ from the Dimension PropertyManager.

263) **Fit** the model to the Graphics window.

Save the ROTARY-GRIPPER assembly.

264) Click **Save**.

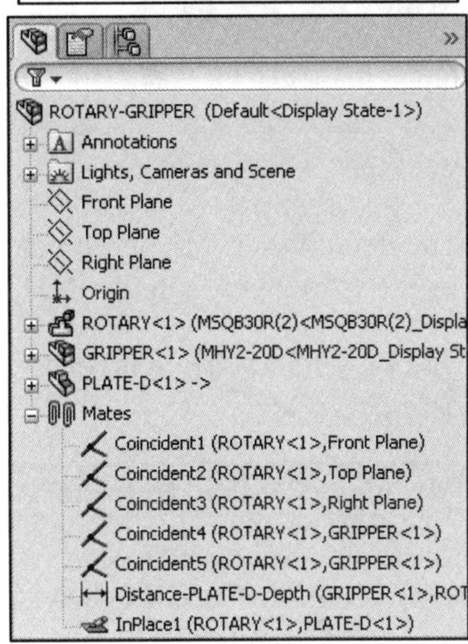

Remove External References and InPlace Mates

Review InPlace Mates and External references. The PLATE-D part references two assemblies: *GRIPPER assembly* and *ROTARY assembly*

Utilize the PLATE-D part in a future project without the GRIPPER assembly and the ROTARY assembly. Remove the PLATE-D External references. Redefine features and sketch geometry in the PLATE-D part.

Delete the InPlace1 Mate. The PLATE-D part is free to translate and rotate in the ROTARY-GRIPPER assembly without the InPlace1 Mate. Utilize three SmartMates to assemble the PLATE-D part to the ROTARY assembly. The PLATE-D part contains no External references.

The "->" symbol indicates that the features were developed in-context of another component. The ROTARY assembly and the GRIPPER assembly reside in memory in order for PLATE-D to locate the In-Context features.

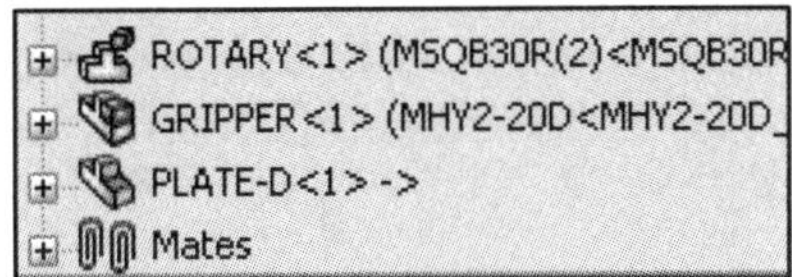

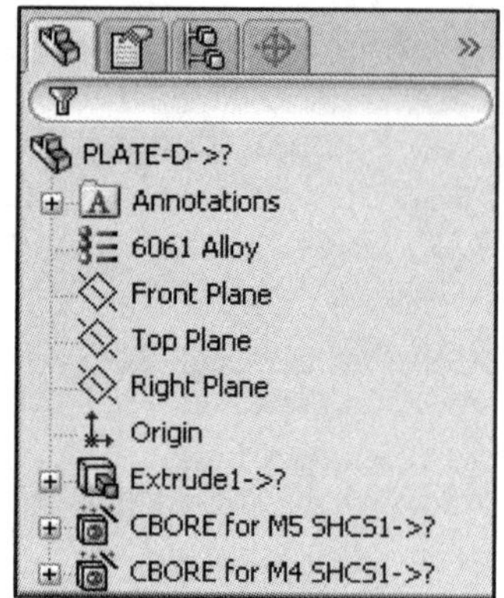

Otherwise, the features are out of context and the "->?" symbol is displayed after each feature.

Example: Close all documents. Open PLATE-D. The FeatureManager displays the out of context "->?" symbol next to the PLATE-D part icon and the three In-Context features.

Open the ROTARY-GRIPPER assembly. Rebuild PLATE-D. The FeatureManager displays the restored In-Context features with the "->" symbol.

The default view orientation of the PLATE-D part differs from its view orientation in the ROTARY-GRIPPER assembly.

The PLATE-D Origin is relative to the ROTARY-GRIPPER assembly.

Activity: Remove External References and InPlace Mates in PLATE-D

Review the External references.

265) Right-click **PLATE-D** in the Graphics window from the ROTARY-GRIPPER assembly.

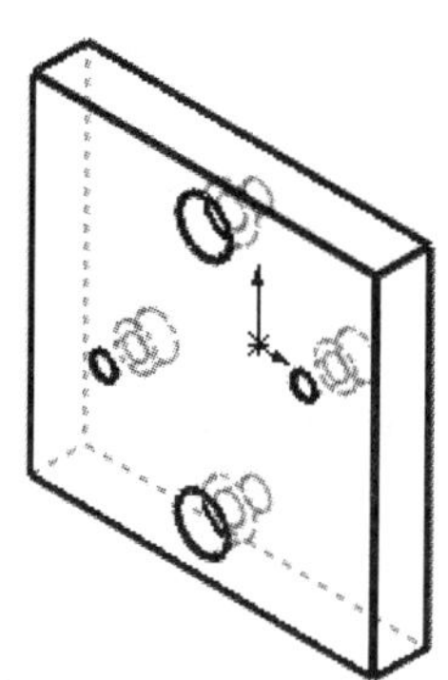

266) Click **Open Part** from the Context toolbar. PLATE-D is displayed in the Graphics window.

267) Click **Hidden Lines Visible** from the Context toolbar.

List the External references.

268) Right-click **PLATE-D** from the FeatureManager.

269) Click **List External Ref**.

270) Click the **Lock All** button.

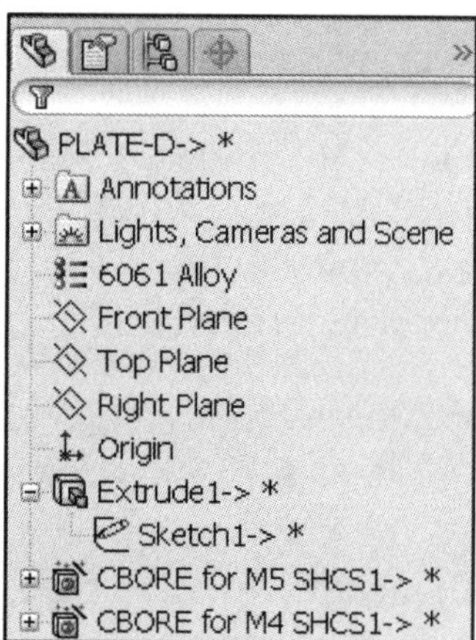

271) Click **OK**. The warning message is displayed, "All external references for the model, PLATE-D will be locked. You will not be able to add any new External references until you unlock the existing references."

272) Click **OK**. The "->*" symbol is displayed next to the part name, PLATE-D in the FeatureManager. The PLATE-D part contains External references that are locked.

Redefine Sketch1.

273) Right-click **Extrude1**->*.

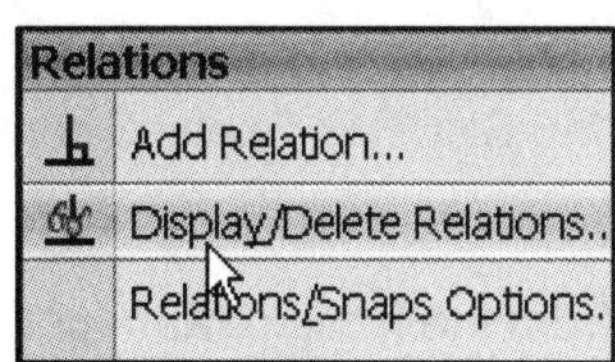

274) Click **Edit Sketch** from the Context toolbar.

275) Right-click **Display/Delete Relations** in the Graphics window.

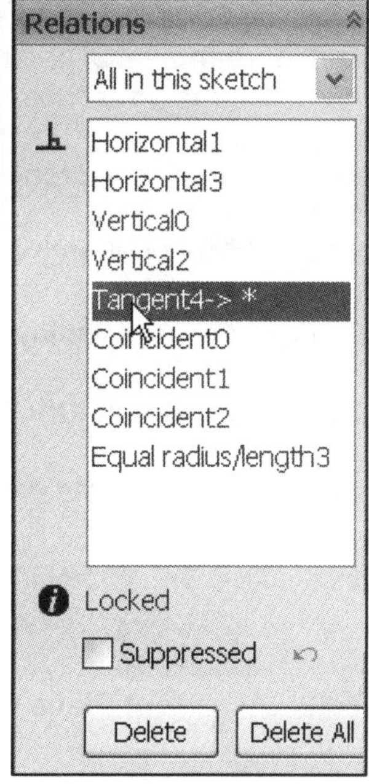

Delete the Tangent relation.

276) Click the **Tangent4 ->*** relation.

277) Click the **Delete** button. The sketch is underdefined and is displayed in blue.

Add a Horizontal dimension.

278) Click the **Smart Dimension** tool from the Sketch toolbar.

279) Click the **top horizontal line**.

280) Click a **position** for the 63 dimension above the profile. The black sketch is fully defined.

281) Click **OK** from the Dimension PropertyManager.

Exit the Sketch.

282) Click **Exit Sketch**.

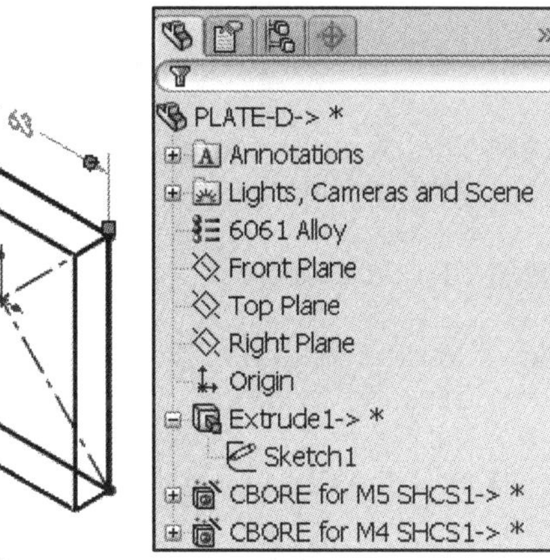

Sketch1 contains no External references. The Extrude1 feature indicates an External reference. The Depth option, Up to Vertex, references a point on the GRIPPER assembly.

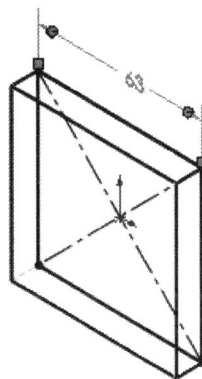

Redefine the depth of the Extrude1 feature.

283) Right-click **PLATE-D\Extrude1** from the FeatureManager.

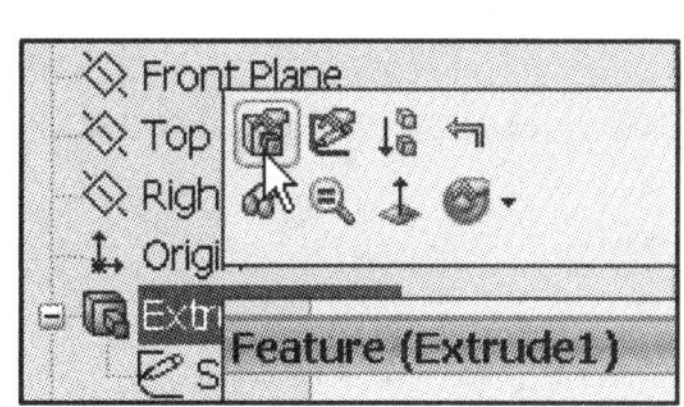

284) Click **Edit Feature** from the Context toolbar.

285) Select **Blind** from the End Condition in Direction 1.

286) Enter **10**mm for Depth.

287) Click **OK** from the Extrude1 PropertyManager. The Extrude1 feature is fully defined with no External references.

Redefine the M5 Cbores.

288) **Expand** CBORE for M5 SHCS1. Sketch3 contains an External reference.

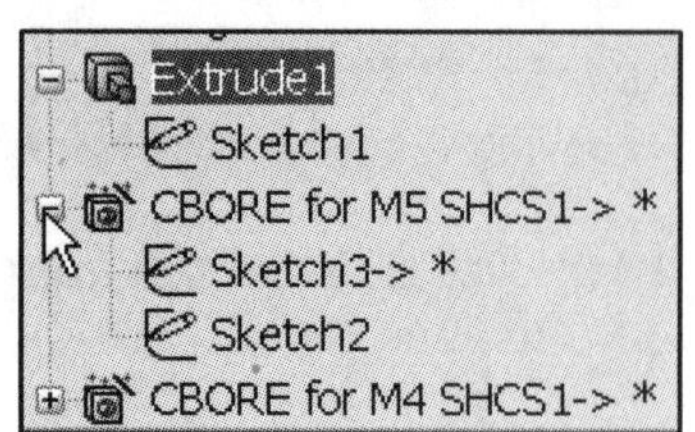

289) Right-click **Sketch3** from the FeatureManager.

290) Click **Edit Sketch** from the Context toolbar.

291) Right-click **Display/Delete Relations**.

292) Select **Concentric0** and **Concentric1** External references.

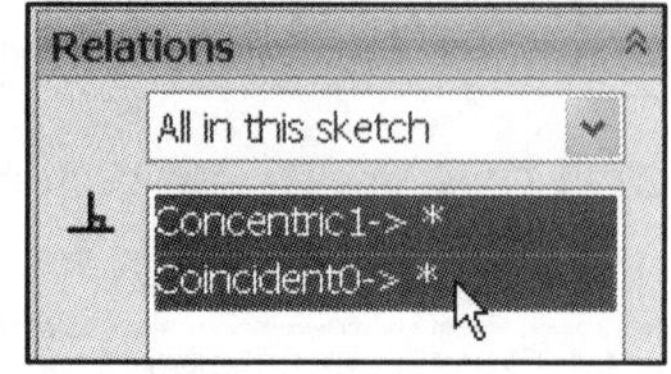

293) Click the **Delete All** button.

294) Click **OK** from the Display/Delete Relations.

Sketch a Centerline.

295) Click **Front Plane** from the FeatureManager.

296) Click **Front** view.

297) Click the **Centerline** tool from the Sketch toolbar.

298) Sketch a **horizontal centerline** from the Origin to the right vertical midpoint.

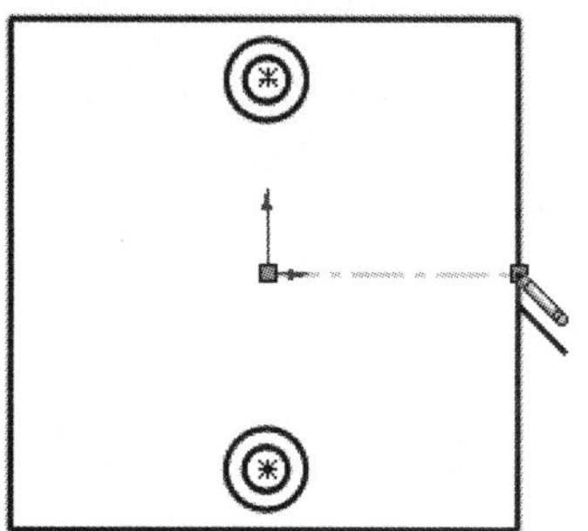

299) Right-click **Select**.

Add a Vertical relation.

300) Click the **Origin**.

301) Hold the **Ctrl** key down.

302) Click the **first point** and **second point** as illustrated. If needed insert centerpoints.

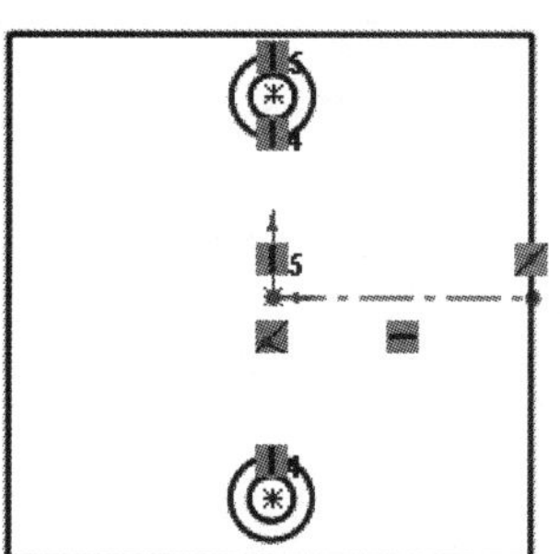

303) Release the **Ctrl** key.

304) Click **Vertical**.

Add a Symmetric relation.

305) Click the **horizontal centerline**.

306) Hold the **Ctrl** key down.

307) Click the **first point** and **second point**.

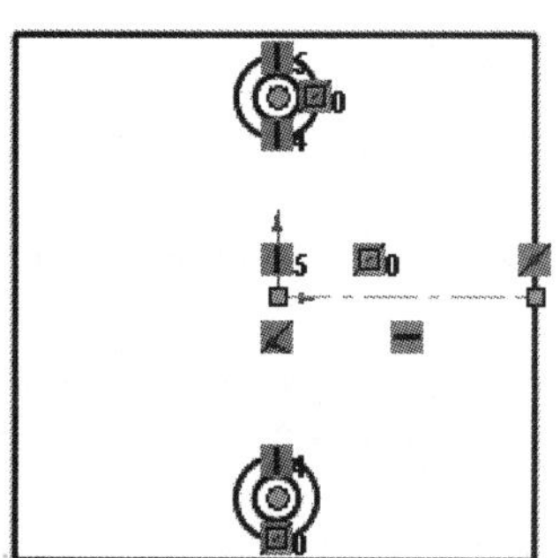

308) Release the **Ctrl** key.

309) Click **Symmetric**.

310) Click **OK** ✔ from the PropertyManager.

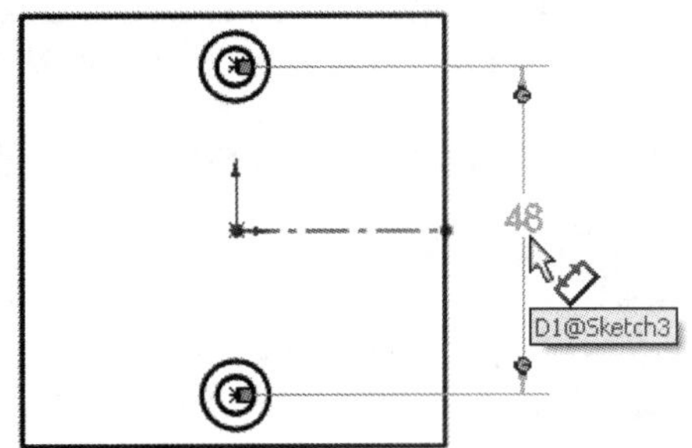

311) **Dimension** the two holes as illustrated. The Sketch is fully defined.

312) Click **Exit Sketch**.

Redefine the M4 Cbores.

313) **Expand** CBORE for M4 SHCS. Sketch5 contains the External reference.

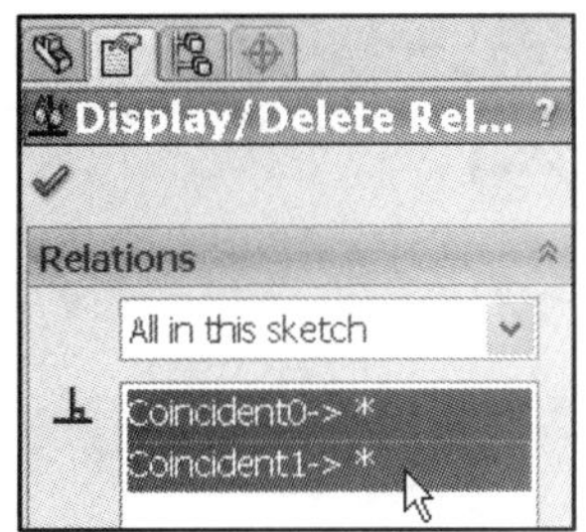

314) Right-click **Sketch5 -> ***.

315) Click **Edit Sketch** from the Context toolbar.

316) Right-click **Display/Delete Relations** in the Graphics window.

317) Click the **Delete All** button.

318) Click **OK** ✔ from the Display/Delete Relations PropertyManager.

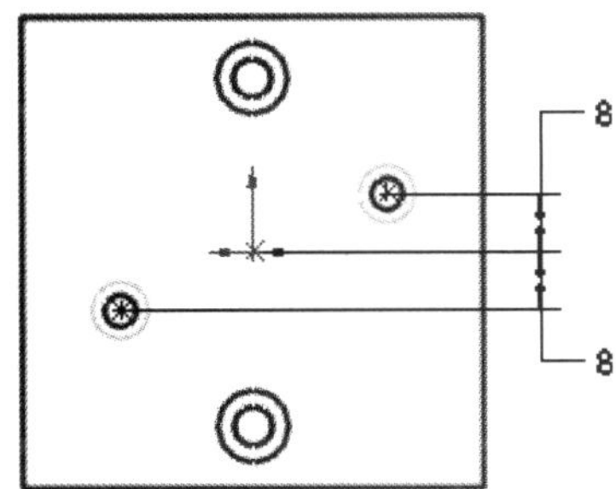

Insert dimensions. Define holes from the Origin to maintain common design intent from the GRIPPER assembly.

319) Click the **Smart Dimension** tool.

320) Create a **vertical dimension** from the Origin to the first point.

321) Accept **8**.

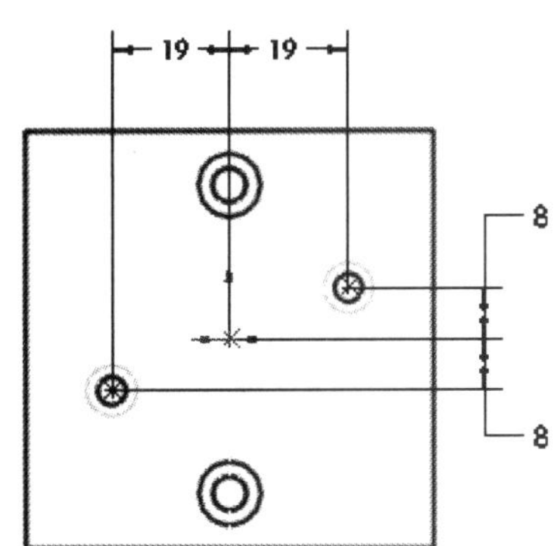

322) Create a **vertical dimension** from the Origin to the second point.

323) Accept **8**.

324) Create a **horizontal dimension** from the Origin to the first point.

325) Accept **19**.

326) Create a **horizontal dimension** from the Origin to the second point.

327) Accept **19**. The black sketch is fully defined.

328) Click **Exit Sketch**.

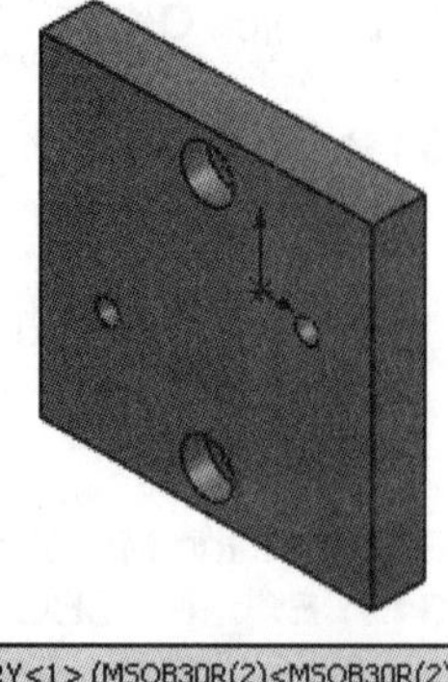

Save PLATE-D.

329) Click **Isometric** view from the Heads-up Views toolbar.

330) Click **Shaded With Edges** from the Heads-up Views toolbar.

331) Click **Save**.

Delete the InPlace1 Mate.

332) Open the **ROTARY-GRIPPER** assembly.

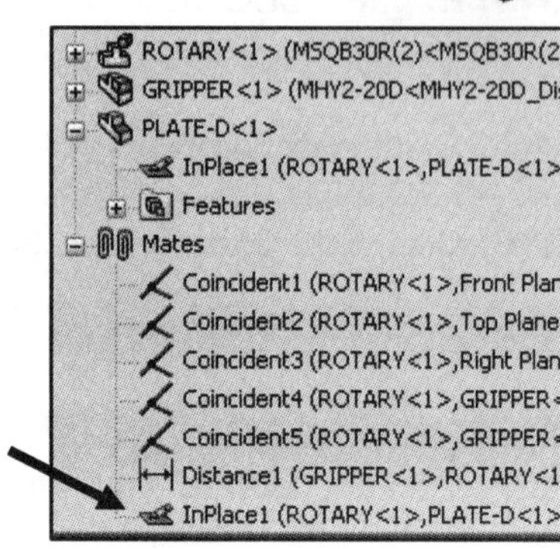

333) **Expand** the Mates folder.

334) Click **InPlace1** from the Mates folder as illustrated.

335) Press the **Delete** key.

336) Click **Yes** to confirm delete. PLATE-D is free to translate and rotate. Create three Mates to define the PLATE-D part in the ROTARY-GRIPPER assembly.

Recall that there are two methods to utilize SmartMates:

- *Alt key + Drag*
- *SmartMate tool + double-click (component to mate) + click (assembly)*

In project 4, you utilized the Alt key. As models become more complex, selecting the correct face while dragging the mouse becomes challenging. Utilize the SmartMate tool located in the Move Component PropertyManager. Double-click the required cylindrical component faces. Click the required assembly face.

Activity: Apply the SmartMate tool to PLATE-D and the ROTARY Assembly

Move the PLATE-D part.

337) Click and drag the **PLATE-D** part in the Graphics window to create an approximate 50mm gap between the ROTARY assembly and the PLATE-D part.

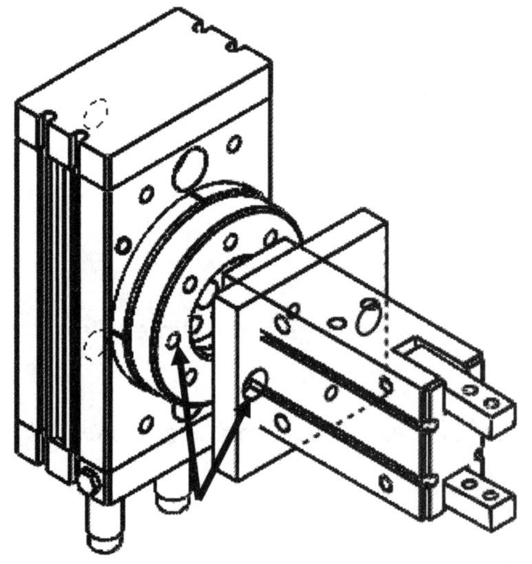

Assemble the PLATE-D part.

338) Click the **Move Component** tool. The Move Component PropertyManager is displayed.

339) Click **SmartMate** from the Move Component Property Manager.

Insert the first SmartMate.

340) Double-click the **left inside hole face** on the PLATE-D part. If needed use the Selection filter tool.

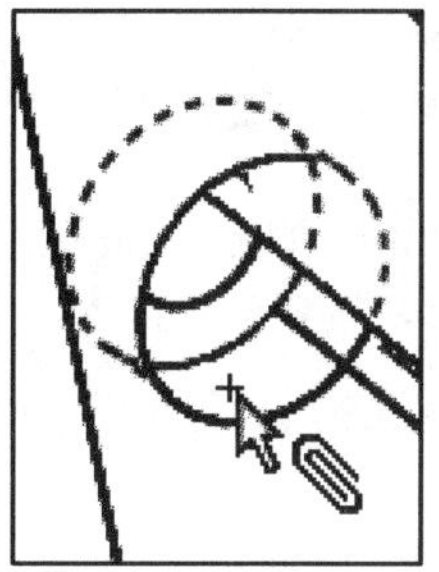

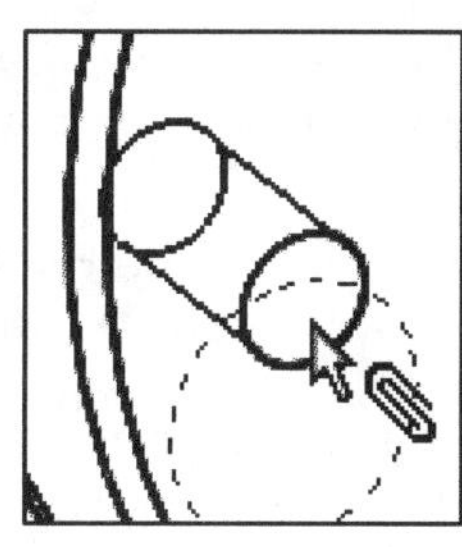

341) Click the **left hole face** of the ROTARY assembly. Concentric is selected by default.

342) Click the **Green Check mark** ✔.

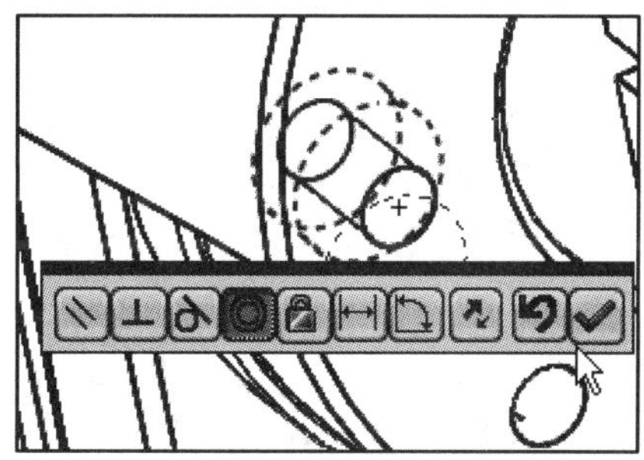

Insert the second SmartMate.

343) Double-click the **right inside hole face** on the PLATE-D part.

344) Click the **right inside hole** face on the ROTARY assembly. Concentric is selected by default.

345) Click the **Green Check mark** ✔.

Insert the third SmartMate.

346) Double-click the **back face** on the PLATE-D part.

347) Click the **front face** of the ROTARY assembly.

348) Click the **Green Check mark** ✔. Coincident is selected by default.

349) Click **OK** ✔ from the SmartMates PropertyManager.

PLATE-D contains no InPlace Mates or External references.

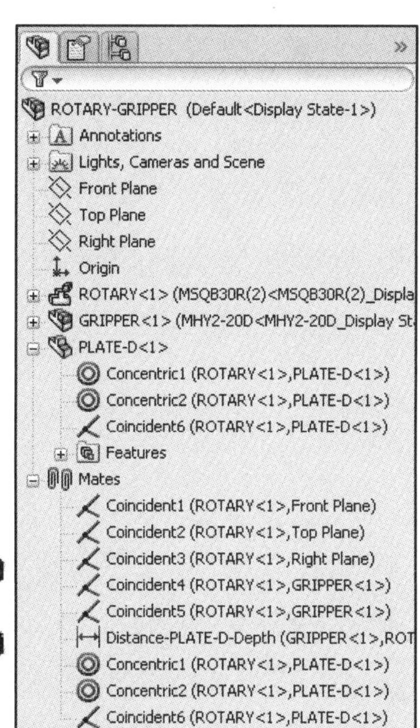

The GRIPPER assembly back face references the ROTARY assembly front face. These Mate Selections are no longer valid in the new design scheme. Redefine the Distance Mate with the PLATE-D front face.

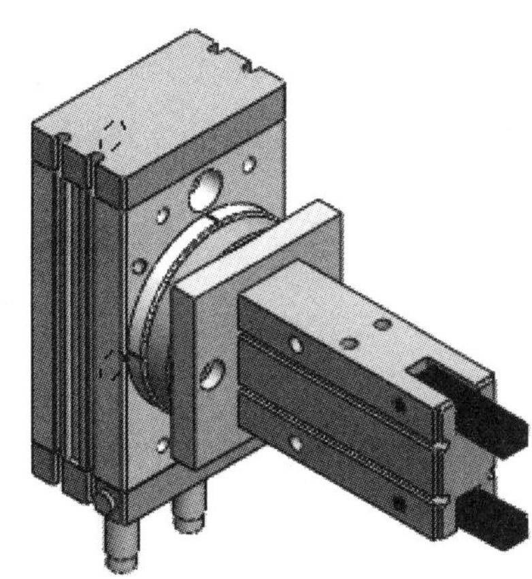

Redefine the Distance-PLATE-D-Depth Mate.

350) Right-click **Distance-PLATE-D-Depth** Mate.

351) Click **Edit Feature**. The Distance-PLATE-D-Depth PropertyManager is displayed.

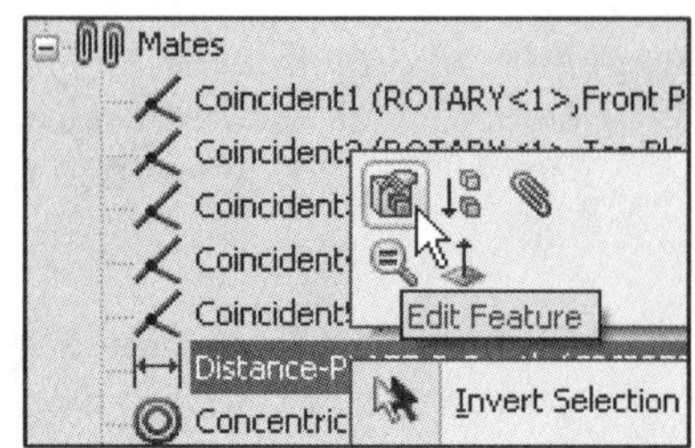

352) Right-click the **ROTARY face** reference in the Mate Selections box.

353) Click **Delete**.

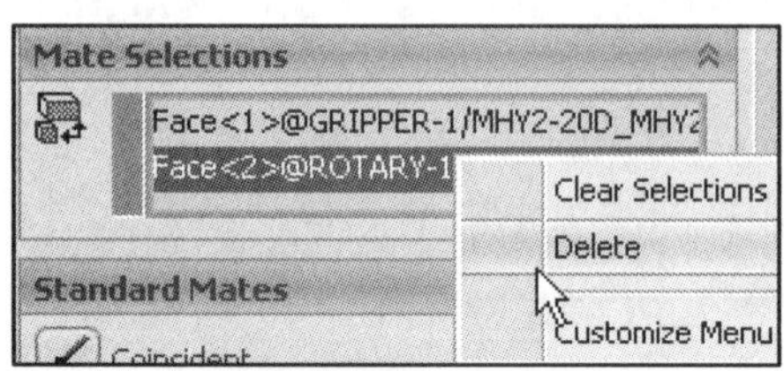

354) Click the **front face** of the PLATE-D part for the Mate Selection as illustrated in the Graphics window.

355) Click **Coincident** from the Pop-up toolbar.

356) Click the **Green Check mark** ✔.

357) Click **OK** ✔ from the Mate PropertyManager.

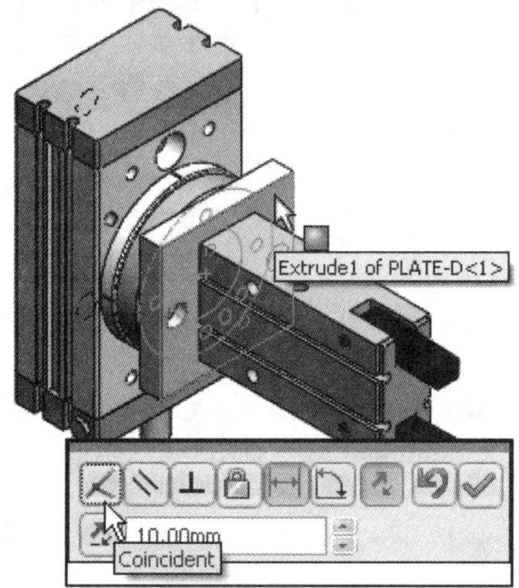

Save the ROTARY-GRIPPER assembly.

358) Click **Save**.

Close all SolidWorks documents.

359) Click **Windows**, **Close All** from the Menu bar menu.

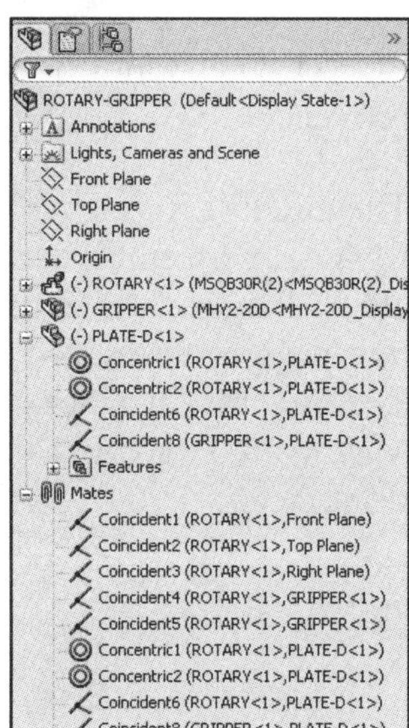

PLATE-C part

Create PLATE-C. The PLATE-C part is listed in the Assembly Layout Diagram under the ROTARY-GRIPPER assembly.

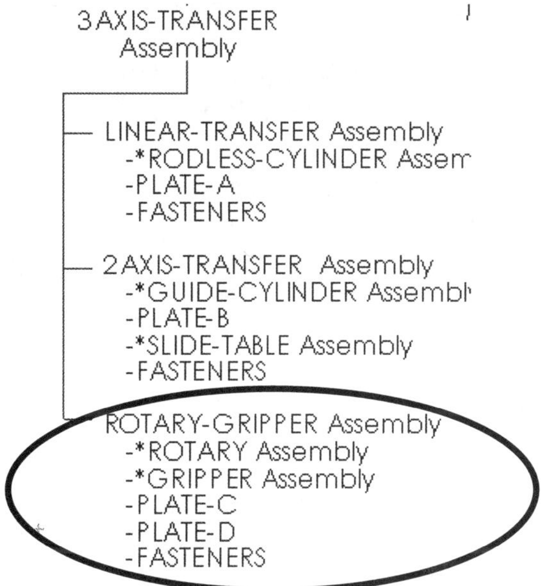

The ROTARY-GRIPPER assembly can't be directly fastened to the 2AXIS-TRANSFER assembly.

Use the PLATE-C part to assemble the ROTARY-GRIPPER assembly to the 2AXIS-TRANSFER assembly.

Review the PLATE-C design options:

1. Utilize an InPlace Mate in the ROTARY-GRIPPER assembly.

2. Utilize an InPlace Mate in the 2AXIS-TRANSFER assembly.

3. Utilize an InPlace Mate in the 3AXIS TRANSFER assembly.

4. Create an Empty Part with no InPlace Mates.

PLATE-C required between two assemblies

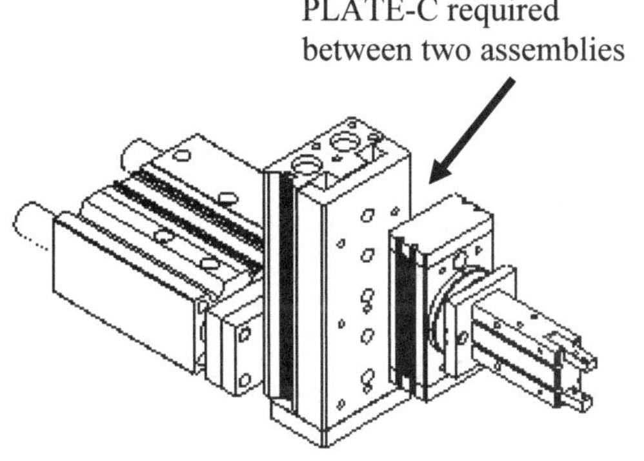

Select option 4. An Empty Part is a new part that only contains reference planes.

Option 4 creates no InPlace Mates. The three default reference planes orient to the assembly as specified.

Perform the following steps to create the PLATE-C part.

1. Create a new part, PLATE-C.

2. Utilize three Mates to assemble the PLATE-C part reference planes to the 2-AXIS-TRANSFER\SLIDE-TABLE assembly.

3. Select a PLATE-C reference plane for the base feature sketch.

Determine the size and shape of the PLATE-C part.

The 2AXIS-TRANSFER/SLIDE-TABLE assembly and ROTARY assembly determines the geometric and functional requirement for the PLATE-C part.

PLATE-C references the SLIDE-TABLE assembly geometry In-Context of the 2AXIS-TRANSFER assembly.

Create two Thru Holes on the PLATE-C part from the copied ROTARY\MountingHoles sketch geometry. Design for future changes. Create three different sets of Thru Holes on the PLATE-C part.

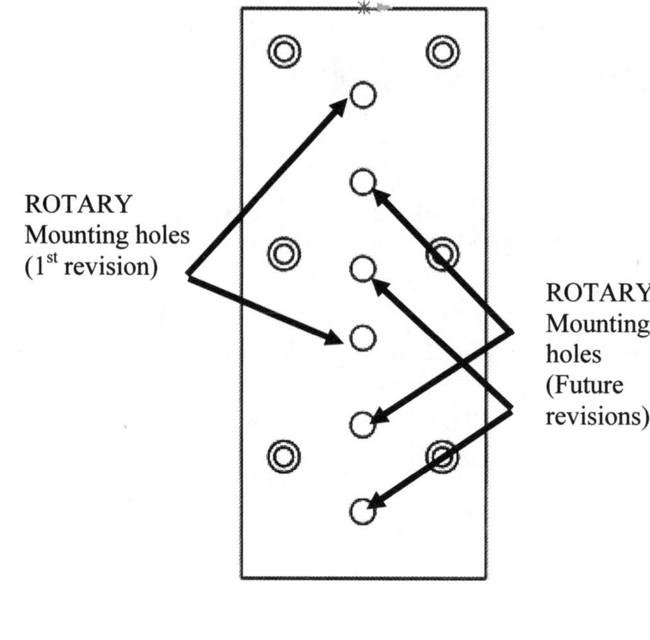

PLATE-C

Additional mounting holes provide design flexibility for manufacturing, field service and the customer.

Activity: Create the PLATE-C Part

Hide the components.

360) Open the 2AXIS-TRANSFER assembly.

361) Hold the **Ctrl** key down.

362) Select the **GUIDE-CYLINDER**, **PLATE-B**, and the **SLIDE-TABLE\MXSLBody**.

363) Release the **Ctrl** key.

364) Right-click **Hide components** from the Context toolbar.

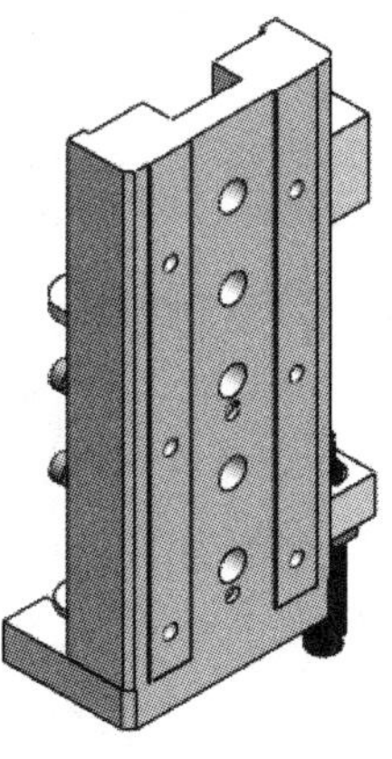

Create the PLATE-C part

365) Click **New** from the Menu bar toolbar.

366) Double-click **PART-MM-ANSI-AL6061**.

367) Click **Save**.

368) Enter **PLATE-C** for File name in the DELIVERY-STATION folder. Click **Save**. The PLATE-C FeatureManager is displayed.

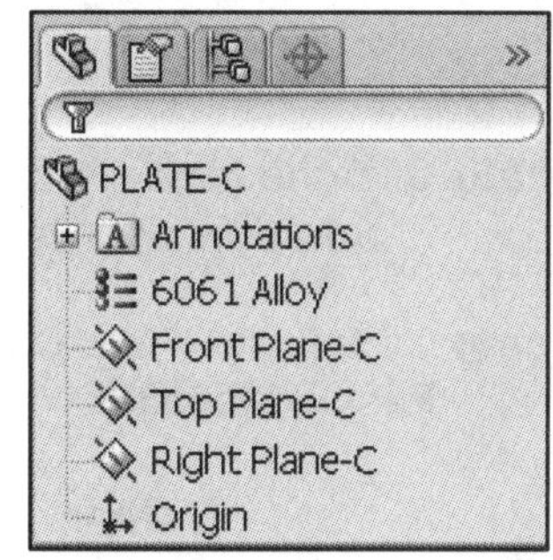

Display an Isometric view.

369) Click **Isometric** view from the Heads-up Views toolbar.

Rename the Default Reference Planes.

370) Rename **Front** to **Front-Plate-C**.

371) Rename **Top** to **Top-Plate-C**.

372) Rename **Right** to **Right-Plate-C**.

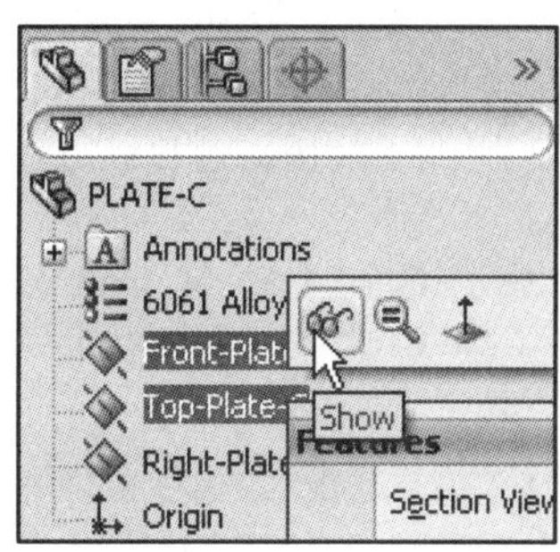

Display the Reference Planes.

373) Click **Front Plane** from the PLATE-C FeatureManager.

374) Hold the **Ctrl** key down.

375) Click **Top Plane** and **Right Plane** from the FeatureManager.

376) Release the **Ctrl** key.

377) Right-click **Show** from the Context toolbar.

Save the PLATE-C part.

378) Click **Save**.

Return to the 2AXIS-TRANSFER assembly.

379) Click **Window**, **2AXIS-TRANSFER** from the Menu bar menu.

Activity: Insert PLATE-C into the 2AXIS TRANSFER Assembly with no External References

Insert the PLATE-C part into the 2AXIS-TRANSFER assembly.

380) Click the **Insert Components** tool from the Assembly toolbar.

381) Click **PLATE-C** from the Open documents box.

382) Click a **position** to the right of the SLIDE-TABLE assembly. The PLATE-C part is added to the 2AXIS-TRANSFER FeatureManager. The PLATE-C Reference planes are not displayed. All planes are hidden.

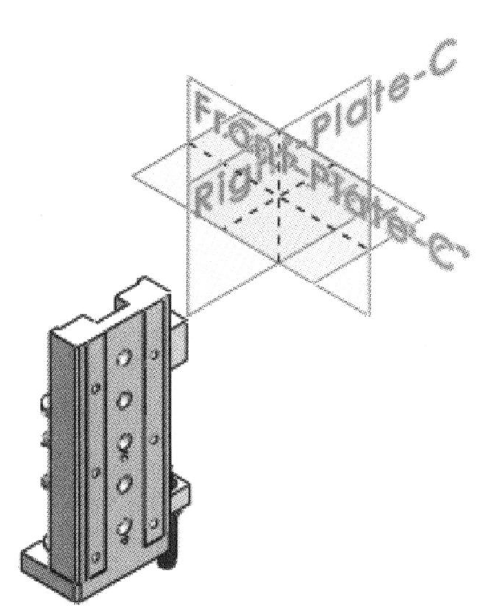

Display Planes.

383) Click **View**, check **Planes** from the Menu bar menu. Note: If needed, click the Show components tool from the Context toolbar.

Assemble PLATE-C to the SLIDE-TABLE/MXS-TABLE.

384) Right-click the **right face** of the SLIDE-TABLE/MXSL-TABLE part as illustrated.

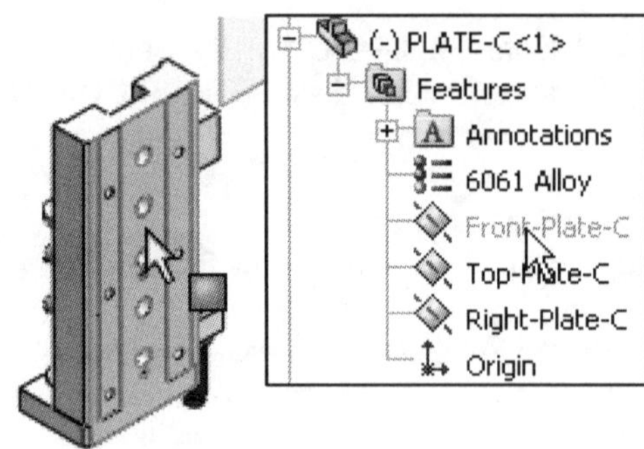

385) Click the **Mate** tool. The Mate PropertyManager is displayed.

386) Click **Front-Plate-C** from the fly-out FeatureManager.

387) Click **Aligned**. The PLATE-C Plane rotate. The Front-Plate-C Plane is Coincident with the front face of the MXSL-TABLE part. The positive side of the Front-Plate-C plane points to the right. Coincident is selected by Default.

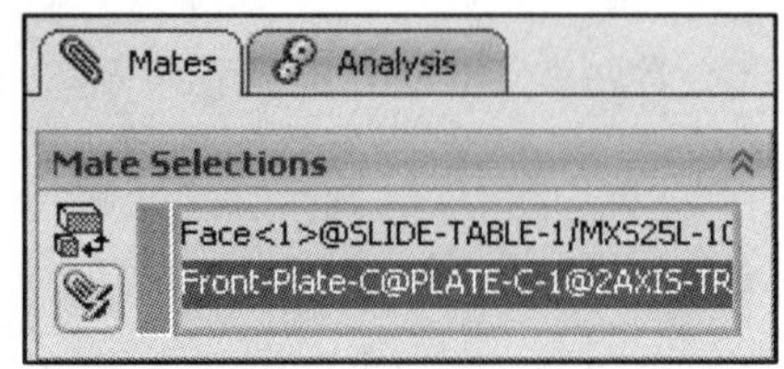

388) Click **OK** from the Coincident PropertyManager.

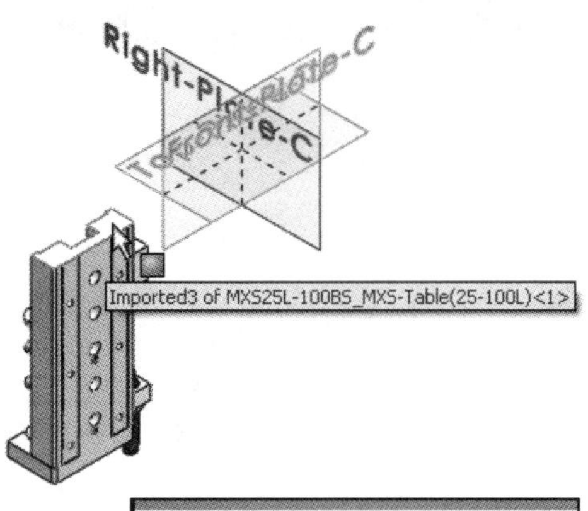

Create the second Mate.

389) Click the **top face** of the MXSL-TABLE part.

390) Click **Top-Plate-C** from the FeatureManager. Coincident is selected by default.

391) Click the **Green Check mark**.

Create the third Mate.

392) Click the **MXS-TABLE\Right Plane**.

393) Click **Right-Plate-C** from the PLATE-C. Coincident is selected by default.

394) Click the **Green Check mark**.

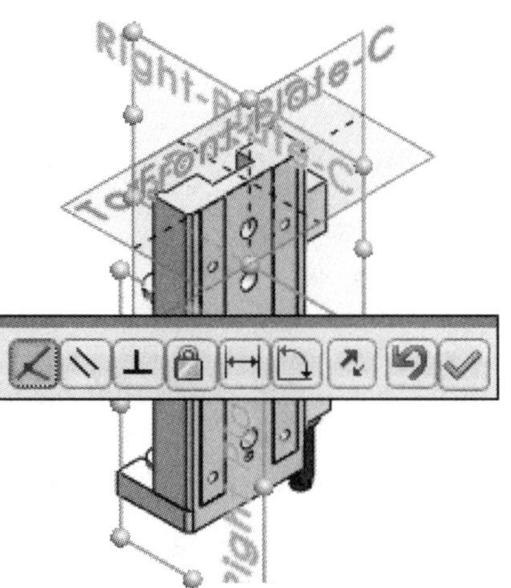

395) Click **OK** from the Mate PropertyManager.

View the three Coincident Mates.

396) **Expand** the 2AXIS-TRANSFER/Mates folder. Note: InPlace Mates are not created.

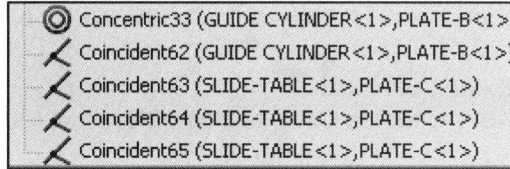

Concentric33 (GUIDE CYLINDER<1>,PLATE-B<1>)
Coincident62 (GUIDE CYLINDER<1>,PLATE-B<1>)
Coincident63 (SLIDE-TABLE<1>,PLATE-C<1>)
Coincident64 (SLIDE-TABLE<1>,PLATE-C<1>)
Coincident65 (SLIDE-TABLE<1>,PLATE-C<1>)

397) Click **Hidden Lines Visible** from the Heads-up Views toolbar.

398) **Hide** all Planes.

Select the No External References Command. Select this option to create ***NO*** External References when designing In-Context of an assembly. No In-Place mates are created when you create a new component. Also, External references are not created when you reference the geometry of other components, such as when you use the Convert Entities or Offset Entities Sketch tool or extrude Up to Vertex of another component.

Select the No External References tool.

399) Click the **No External References** tool from the Assembly toolbar. Note: The No External References tool was added to the Assembly toolbar in a previous chapter.

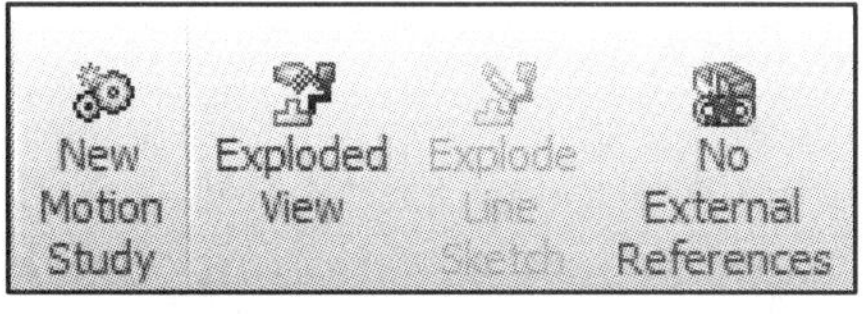

Edit the PLATE-C part In-Context of the 2AXIS-TRANSFER assembly

400) Right-click **PLATE-C** from the FeatureManager

401) Click **Edit Part** from the Context toolbar. PLATE-C is displayed in blue.

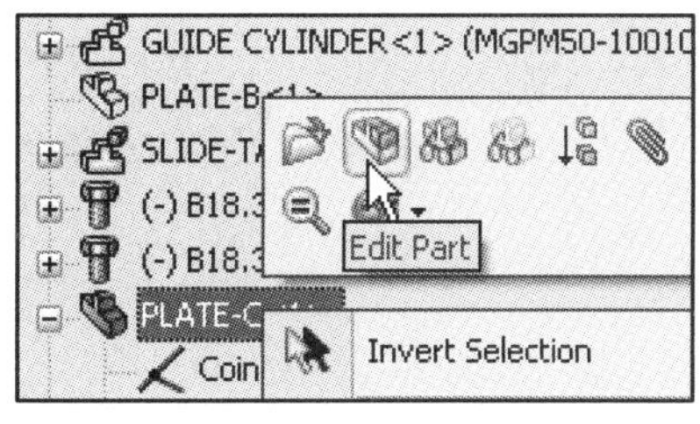

Insert a Sketch.

402) Right-click **Front Plane-C** from the FeatureManager.

403) Click **Sketch** from the Context toolbar.

404) Click the **right face** of the SLIDE-TABLE part as illustrated. Note the face feedback icon.

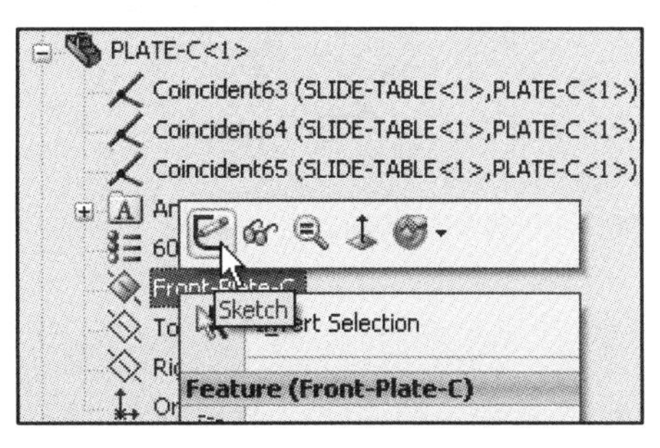

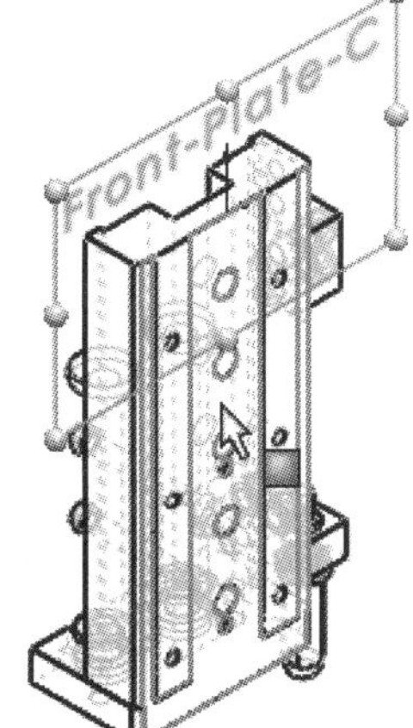

405) Click the **Corner Rectangle** tool from the Sketch toolbar.

406) Sketch a **rectangle** as illustrated. Note: *Do not select the fillet feature.*

Extrude the Sketch.

407) Click the **Extrude Boss/Base** tool from the FeatureManager toolbar.

408) Enter **15** for Depth. The direction arrow points to the right.

409) Click **OK** ✔ from the Extrude PropertyManager.

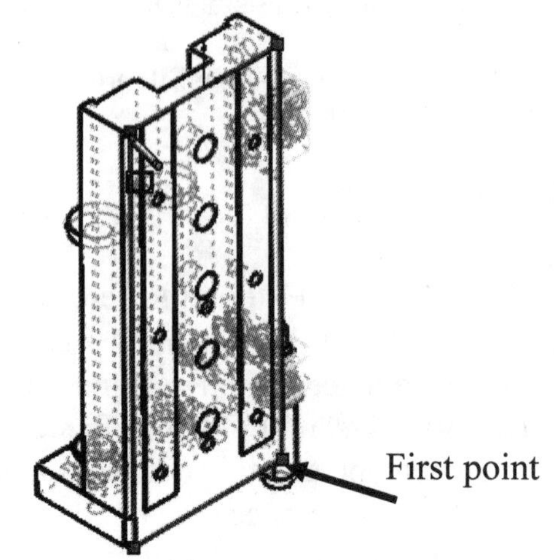

The Front-PLATE-C Plane is Extrude1 Sketch Plane. The FeatureManager lists no In-Place Mates and no External references. Sketch1 is under-defined.

Edit Component mode remains selected in the Assembly toolbar.

The PLATE-C entry in the FeatureManager is displayed in blue.

The location of the SLIDE-TABLE hole requires the Convert Entity Sketch tool. Obtain the required geometry.

Exit Edit Part and return to the 2AXIS-TRANSFER assembly.

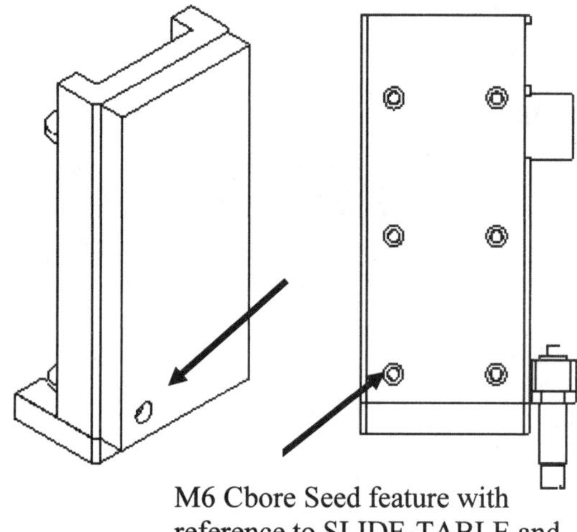

M6 Cbore Seed feature with reference to SLIDE-TABLE and Linear Pattern

Activity: Create the Cbore and the Linear Pattern Feature in PLATE-C

Insert a new Sketch.

410) Right-click the **right face** of the PLATE-C part.

411) Click **Sketch** from the Context toolbar.

Select the Edge filter.

412) Select the **Filter Edges** tool.

413) Click the **lower left circular edge**. The Imported3 of MXS25L-100BS_MXS-Table is displayed as illustrated.

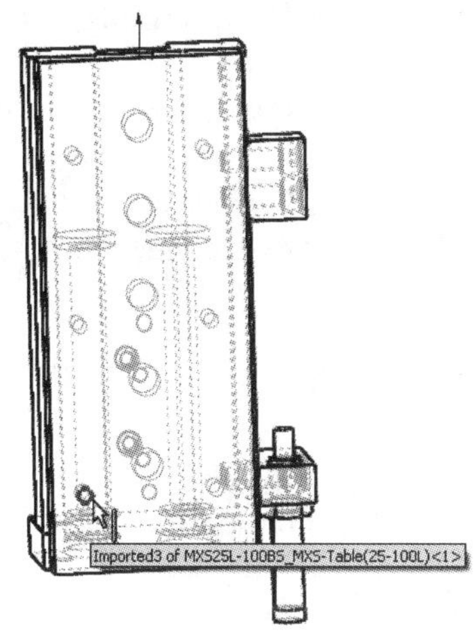

414) Click the **Convert Entities** tool from the Sketch toolbar.

415) Click **Exit Sketch**. Sketch2 is displayed. Note: Sketch2 is undefined.

Return to the assembly.

416) Click **2AXIS-TRANSFER** from the FeatureManager.

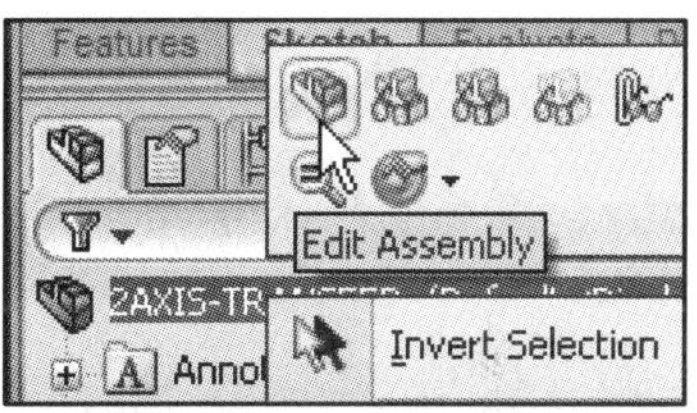

417) Click the **Edit Assembly** from the Context toolbar.

Open the PLATE-C part.

418) Right-click **PLATE-C** from the FeatureManager.

419) Click **Open Part** from the Context toolbar. The PLATE-C FeatureManager is displayed.

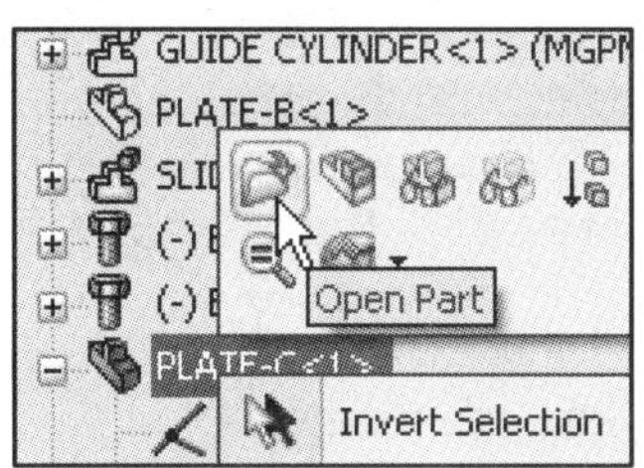

Fully define Sketch1 and Sketch2 in PLATE-C. Add Geometric relations and dimensions.

Add a Vertical relation to Sketch1.

420) Click **Isometric** view from the Heads-up Views toolbar.

421) Right-click **Sketch1**.

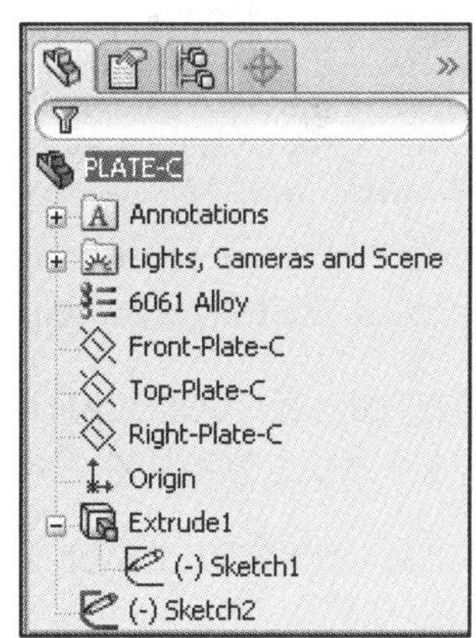

422) Click **Edit Sketch** from the Context toolbar.

423) Hold the **Ctrl** key down.

424) Click the **left** and **right** vertical lines of the rectangle.

425) Release the **Ctrl** key.

426) Click **Vertical** from the Add Relations box.

Create a Horizontal relation to Sketch1.

427) Hold the **Ctrl** key down.

428) Click the **top** and **bottom** horizontal lines of the rectangle.

429) Release the **Ctrl** key.

430) Click **Horizontal** from the Add Relations box.

431) Click **OK** from the Properties PropertyManager.

Display the Front view.
432) Click **Front** view from the Heads-up View toolbar.

Hide the Planes if needed.
433) Click **View**, uncheck **Planes** from the Menu bar menu.

Create a Midpoint relation.
434) Hold the **Ctrl** key down.

435) Click the **top horizontal line** and the **Origin**.

436) Click **Midpoint** from the Add Relations box.

437) Click **OK** from the Properties PropertyManager.

Add dimensions.
438) Click the **Smart Dimension** tool from the Sketch toolbar.

439) Add the **vertical** and **horizontal** dimension as illustrated.

440) Click **Exit Sketch** from the Sketch toolbar. Sketch1 is fully defined

Save the model.
441) Click **Save**.

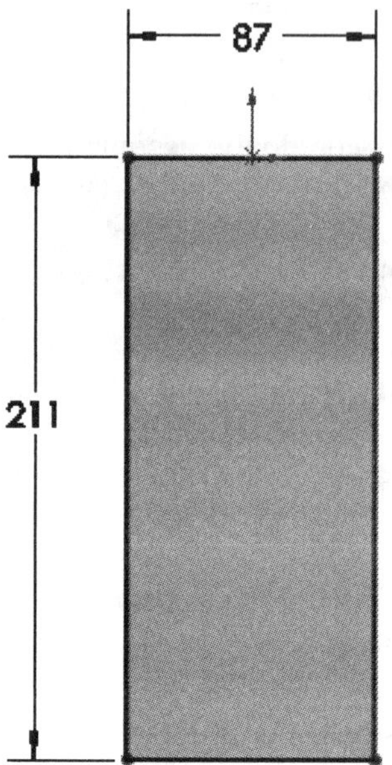

Talk to the machine shop. Identify machined components that can save money and time. Apply precision and tolerance to dimensions in the part. The values propagate to the drawing when inserted from the part.

Edit Sketch2. Sketch2 is not fully defined.
442) Right-click **Sketch2**.

443) Click **Edit Sketch** from the Context toolbar.

Add dimensions.
444) Click the **Smart Dimension** tool from the Sketch toolbar.

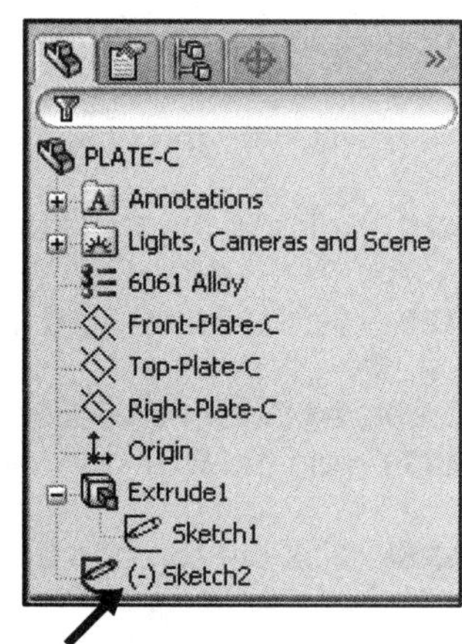

445) Insert a **vertical** and **horizontal** dimension as illustrated. The dimensions are referenced from the Origin.

446) Click **OK** from the Dimension PropertyManager.

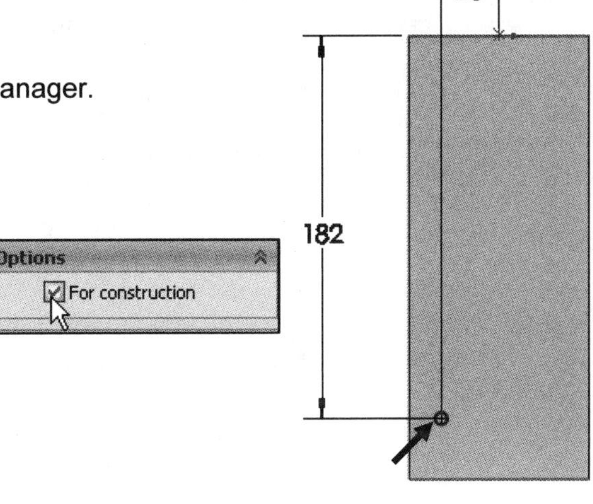

Modify geometry.

447) Click the **circular edge** of Sketch2.

448) Check the **For construction** box.

449) Click **OK** from the Circle PropertyManager.

Add a hole dimension.

450) Click the **Smart Dimension** tool from the Sketch toolbar.

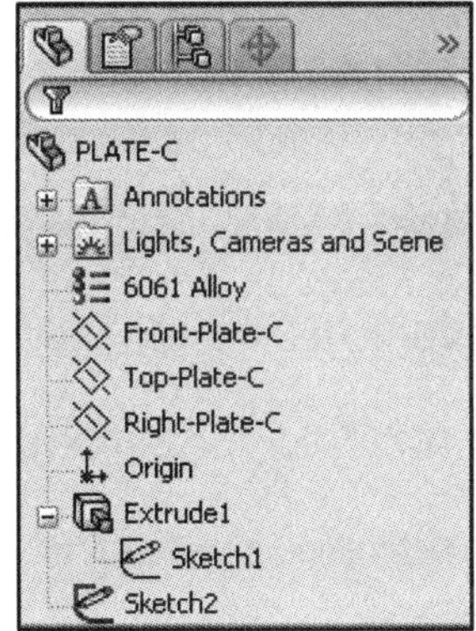

451) Insert a **diameter** dimension. The hole dimension is 6mm. Sketch2 is fully defined.

452) Click **OK** from the Dimension PropertyManager.

453) Click **Exit Sketch**. View the updated FeatureManager

Insert the Cbore seed feature. Apply the Hole Wizard tool.

454) Click **Front** View from the Heads-up View toolbar.

455) Click **Hidden Lines Visible** from the Heads-up View toolbar.

456) Click the **front face** as illustrated. Extrude1 is displayed in blue.

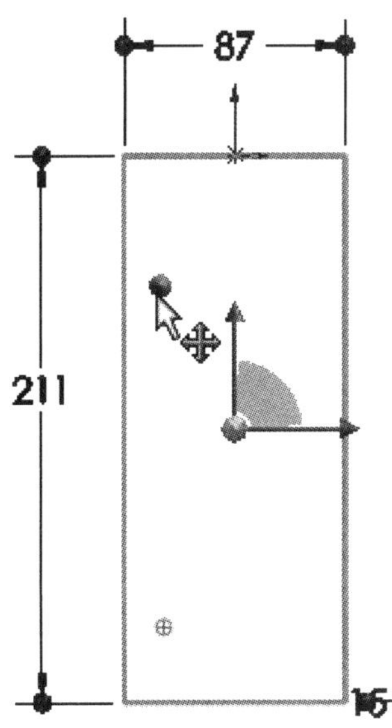

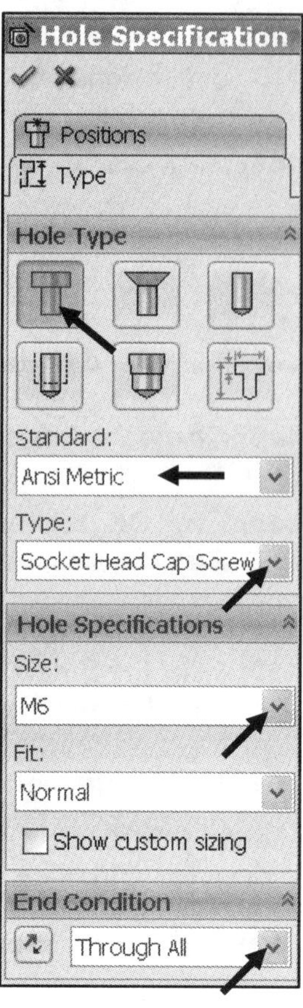

457) Click the **Hole Wizard** tool from the Feature toolbar. The Hole Specification PropertyManager is displayed.

458) Click **Counterbore** for Hole Specification.

459) Click **Ansi Metric** for Standard.

460) Click **Socket Head Cap Screw** for Type.

461) Select **M6** for Size.

462) Select **Through All** for End Condition.

463) Click the **Positions** tab. The Point icon is displayed.

464) Right-click **Select** to deselect the Point Sketch tool.

Add a Concentric relation.

465) Click the **M6 point.**

466) Hold the **Ctrl** key down.

467) Click the **centerpoint** of the construction circle.

468) Release the **Ctrl** key.

469) Click **Concentric**.

470) Click **OK** from the Properties PropertyManager.

471) Click **OK** from the Hole Position PropertyManager.

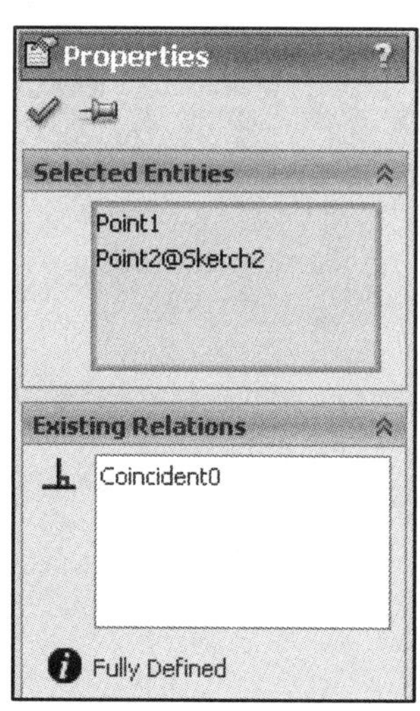

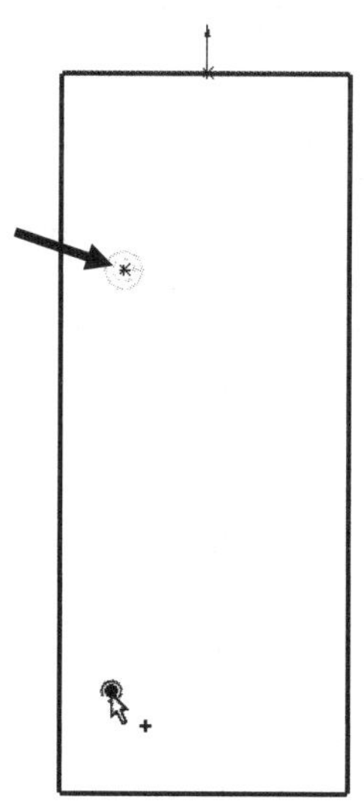

Review the SLIDE-TABLE hole locations. Double-click SLIDE-TABLE\MXSLTable\TableHoleLayout sketch. The holes are spaced 56mm x 70mm apart.

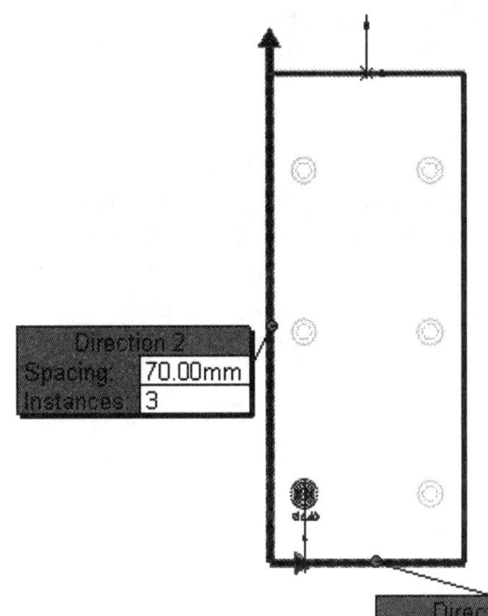

Insert a Linear Pattern feature.

472) Click the **Linear Pattern** tool from the Features toolbar.

473) Click the **bottom horizontal line** for Direction1. The arrow points to the right. If required, click the Reverse Direction button.

474) Enter **56** for Direction1.

475) Enter **2** for Number of Instances.

476) Click the **left vertical line** for Direction2. The arrow point up. If required, click the Reverse Direction button.

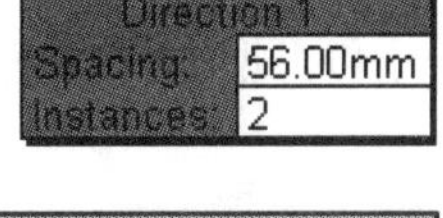

477) Enter **70** for Direction2.

478) Enter **3** for Number of Instances.

479) Check the **Geometric pattern** box. Note: CBORE for M6 is displayed in the Features to Pattern box.

480) Click **OK** from the Linear Pattern PropertyManager.

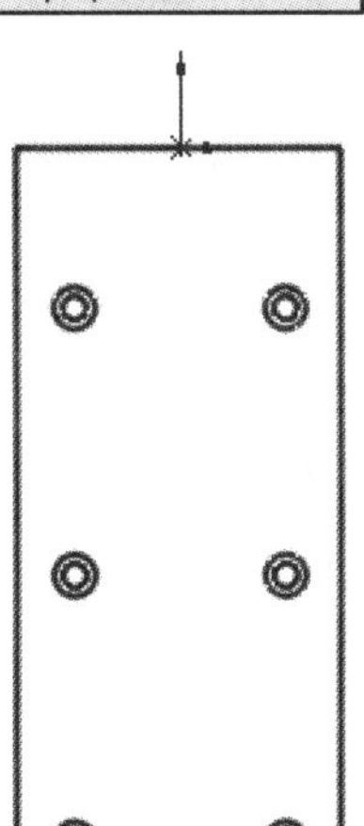

PLATE-C requires two 8.6mm holes. Copy the sketch, ROTARY\MSQBody\MountingBoreLocator to the PLATE-C part.

The dimensions, 21.55mm and 127.10mm determine the location of the first hole and the overall length of the ROTARY body. Modify the dimension values to 22mm and 127mm.

The first hole is located 22mm from the PLATE-C edge. The second hole is vertically located 84mm from the first hole.

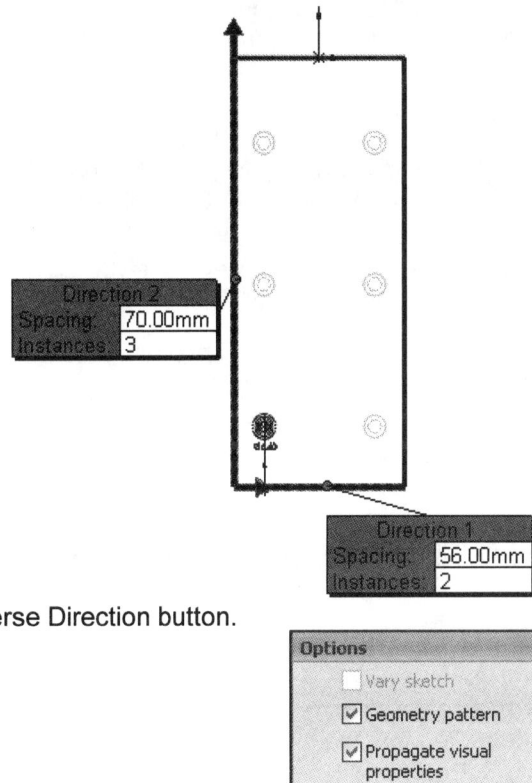

Activity: Copy a Sketch from One Component to Another

Open the ROTARY assembly.

481) Click **Open** from the Menu bar toolbar.

482) Double-click **ASSEMBLY-SW-FILES-2008\DELIVERY-STATION\ROTARY.sldasm**.

Review the ROTARY requirements.

483) Open **MSQBody** from the ROTARY FeatureManager.

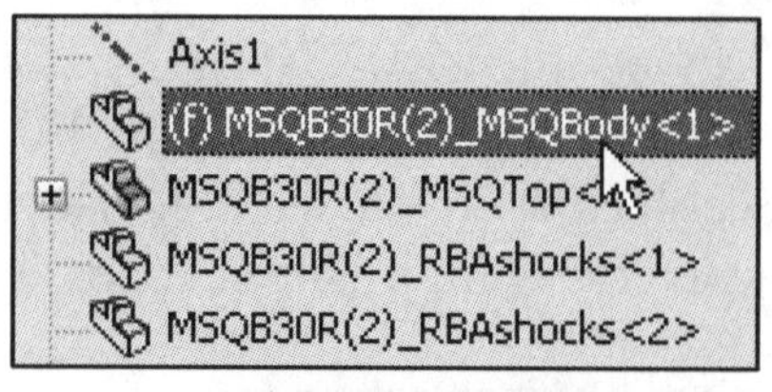

484) Click **MSQBBody\MountingBoreLocator** from the FeatureManager. View the dimensions.

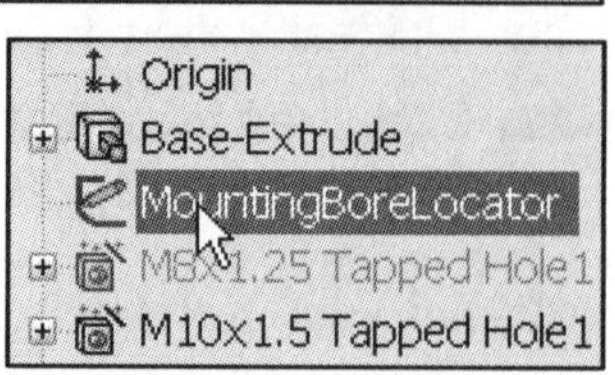

Copy the MountingBoreLocator Sketch.

485) Click **Edit**, **Copy** from the Menu bar menu.

Paste the Sketch. Return to PLATE-C

486) **Return** to PLATE-C.

487) Click **Back** view from the Heads-up View toolbar.

488) Click the **back face** of PLATE-C as illustrated.

489) Click **Edit**, **Paste** from the Menu bar menu.

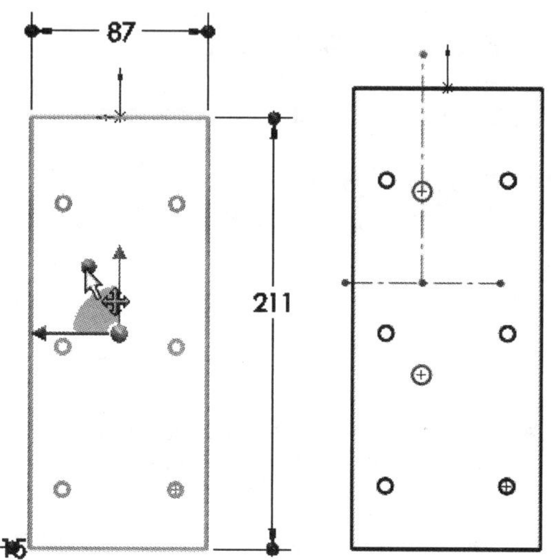

Rename the sketch.

490) Rename the sketch to **Rotary Hole Position**.

Edit the Sketch.

491) Right-click **Rotary Hole Position** from the FeatureManager.

492) Click **Edit Sketch**.

Add a Vertical relation.

493) Click the PLATE-C **Origin**.

494) Hold the **Ctrl** key down.

495) Click the **top center point**.

496) Click the **bottom center point**.

497) Release the **Ctrl** key.

498) Click **Vertical**.

499) Click **OK** from the Properties PropertyManager.

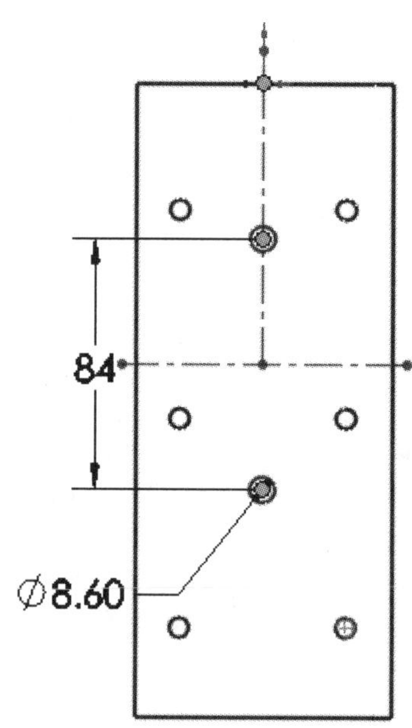

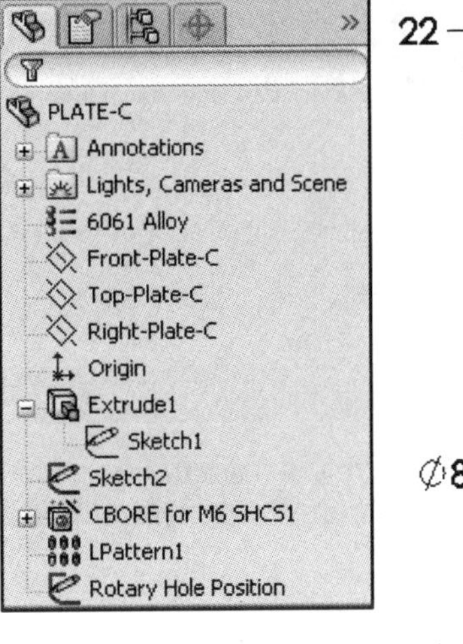

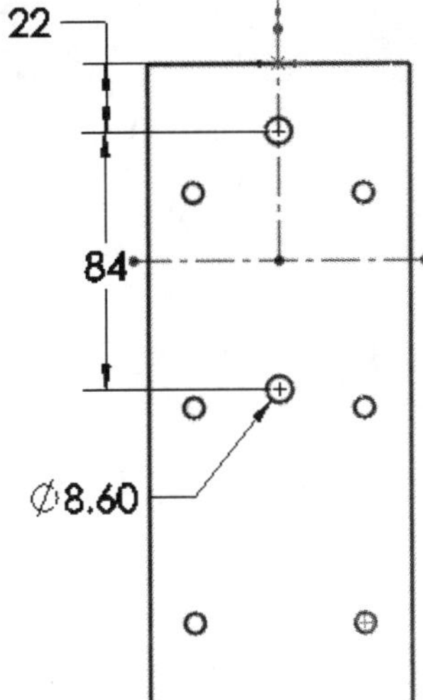

Add a vertical dimension.

500) Click the **Smart Dimension** tool from the Sketch toolbar.

501) Create a **vertical dimension** from the Origin to the top center point.

502) Enter **22**. The black sketch is fully defined.

503) Click **OK** ✓ from the PropertyManager.

504) Click **Exit Sketch**.

Use the Rotary Hole Position sketch to locate the PLATE-C M8.6 Thru Holes. Create the Thru Holes with the Hole Wizard tool. Prepare for future design changes. Create three sets of two Thru Holes with a Linear Pattern feature.

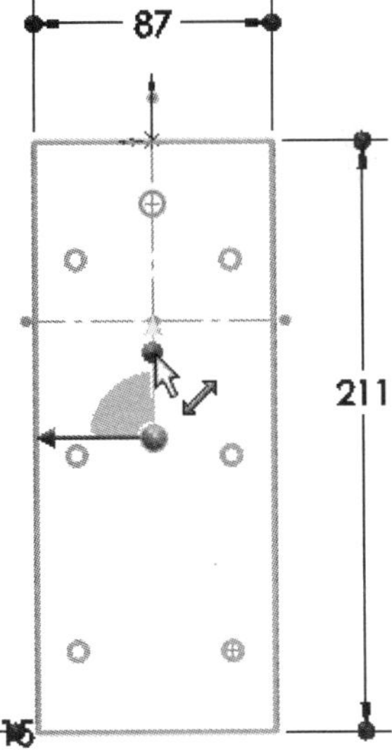

Create two holes. Apply the Hole Wizard tool.

505) Click the **back face** in between the two sketched circles as illustrated.

506) Click the **Hole Wizard** tool from the Feature toolbar.

507) Click **Hole** for Hole Specification.

508) Click **Ansi Metric** for Standard.

509) Click **Drill size** for Type.

510) Select **8.6** for Size.

511) Select **Through All** for End Condition.

512) Click the **Positions** tab. The Point icon is displayed.

513) Click the **center point** of the first sketched circle.

514) Click the **center point** of the second sketched circle. Right-click **Select**.

515) Click the **first point**.

516) Right-click **Delete**.

517) Click **OK** ✓ from the Hole Position PropertyManager.

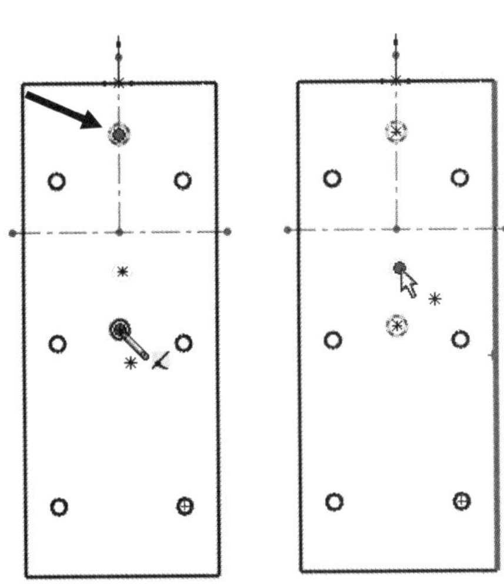

Hide the Rotary Hole Position sketch.

518) Right-click **Rotary Hole Position** from the FeatureManager.

519) Click **Hide**.

Create a Linear Pattern feature.

520) Click **8.6(8.6) Diameter Hole1** from the FeatureManager.

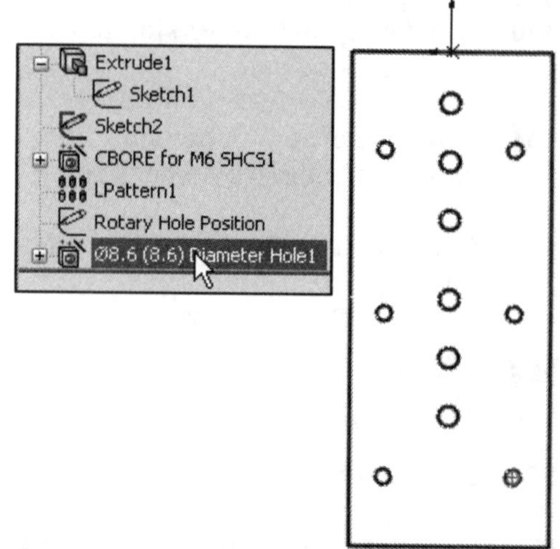

521) Click the **Linear Pattern** tool from the Feature toolbar. The Linear Pattern PropertyManager is displayed.

522) Click the **left vertical edge**. The arrow points downward. If required, click the Reverse Direction button.

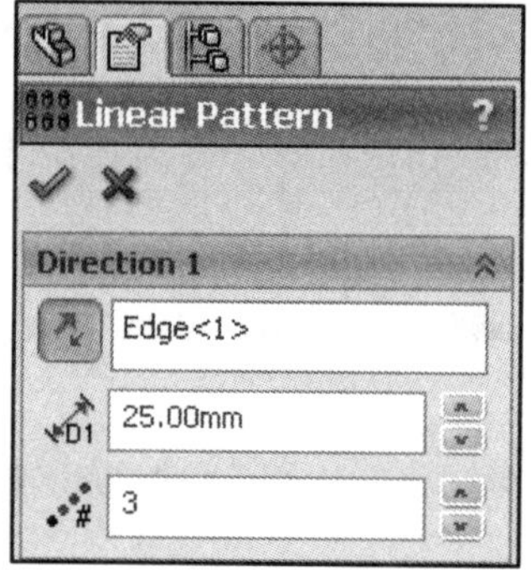

523) Enter **25** for Distance.

524) Enter **3** for Number of Instances. Click the Reverse Direction if needed.

525) Click **OK** ✔ from the Linear Pattern PropertyManager. LPattern2 is displayed.

526) Click **Front** view from the Heads-up View toolbar.

Confirm dimensions and precision when copying geometry between parts. Check the precision of the copied part.

Example 1: In inch units, the value .375 is rounded to .38. Two decimal places are selected for linear units.

Example 2: In millimeter units, the value 27.5 is rounded to 28. Zero decimal places are selected for linear units.

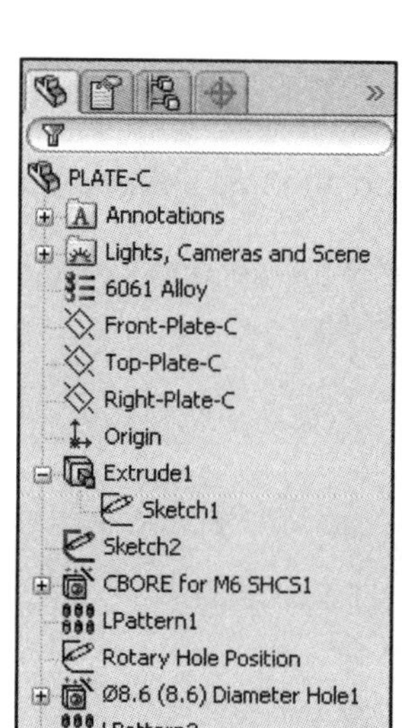

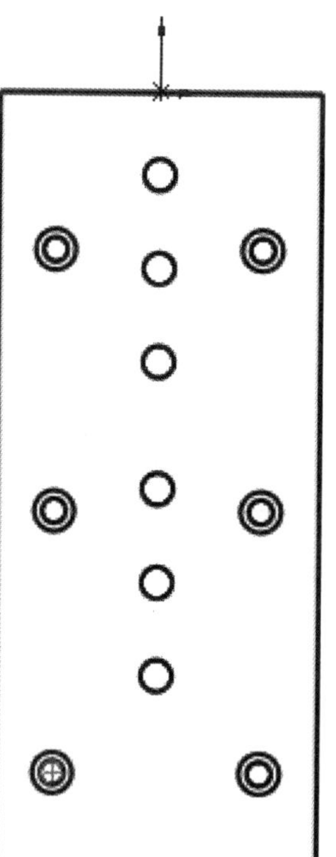

Save the PLATE-C part.

527) Click **Save**.

Open the 2AXIS-TRANSFER assembly.

528) Open the 2AXIS-TRANSFER assembly.

529) Click **Yes** to Update the assembly.

Display all Hidden Components.

530) Display all hidden components.

Save the 2AXIS-TRANSFER assembly.

531) Click **Save**.

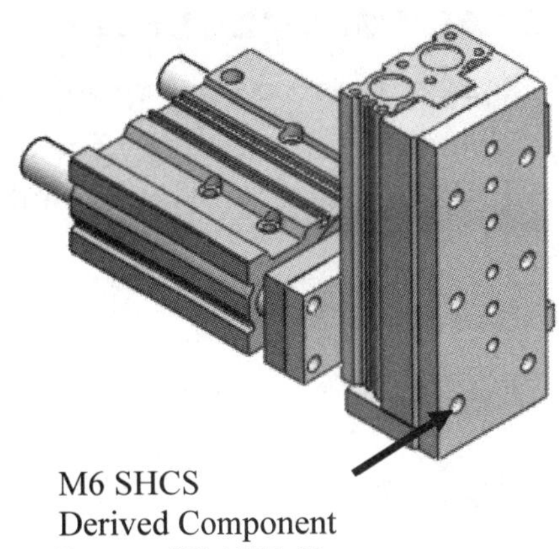

M6 SHCS
Derived Component
Pattern (PLATE-C)

Close all models.

532) Click **Windows**, **Close All** from the Menu bar menu.

Identify the fasteners for the PLATE-C part and the PLATE-D part.

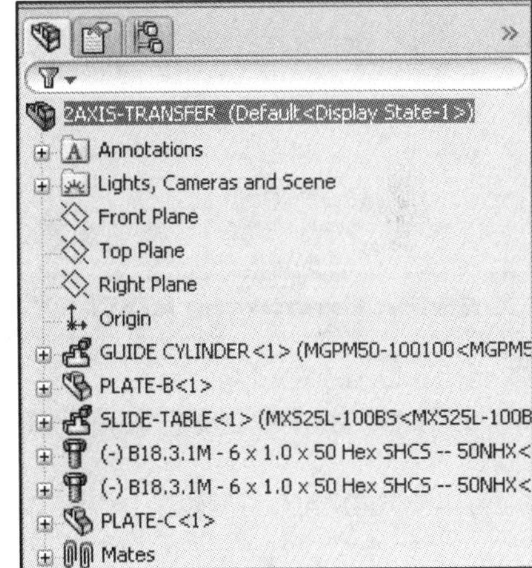

Required fasteners for the PLATE-C part:

- Six M6 SHCSs to fasten the PLATE-C part to the SLIDE-TABLE assembly.
- Two M8 SHCSs to fasten the PLATE-C part to the ROTARY assembly.

Required fasteners for the PLATE-D part:

- Two M5 SHCSs to fasten the PLATE-D part to the ROTARY assembly.
- Two M4 SHCSs to fasten to the PLATE-D part to the GRIPPER assembly.

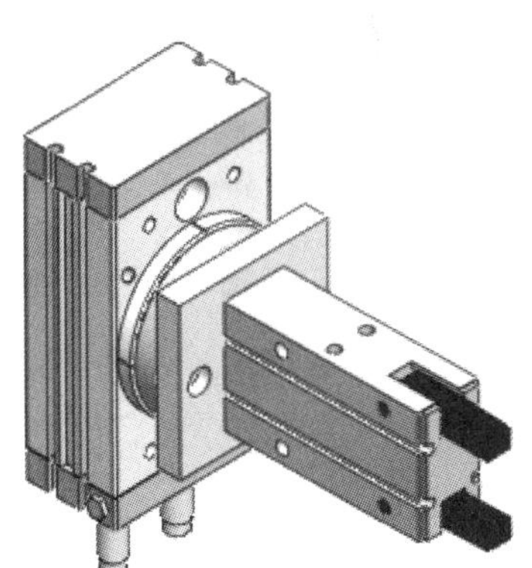

Develop the fasteners for the PLATE-D part and the PLATE-C part as an exercise.

ROTARY-GRIPPER Design Table

Create the ROTARY-GRIPPER Design Table with three configurations: *Flexible*, *Rotation0* and *Rotation90*. The configuration names refer to the position of the GRIPPER assembly. The Default is the current configuration.

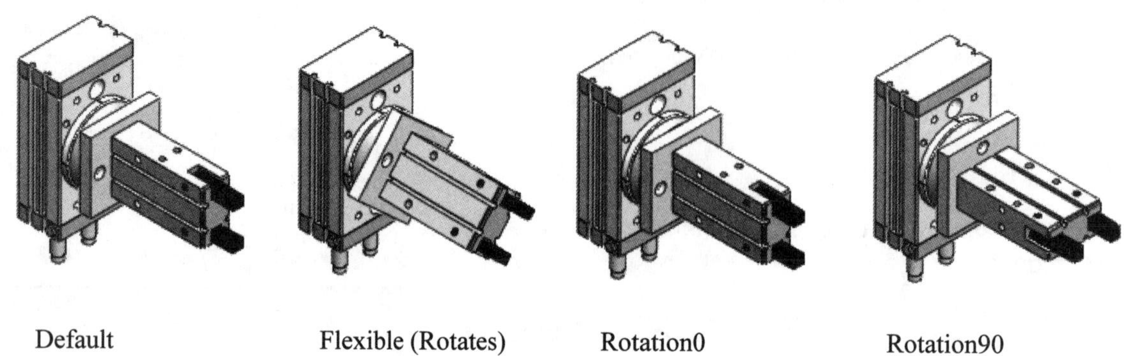

Default Flexible (Rotates) Rotation0 Rotation90

ROTARY-GRIPPER configuration

Activity: Create the ROTARY-GRIPPER Design Table

Create a Design Table.

533) **Open** the ROTARY-GRIPPER assembly.

534) Click **Insert**, **Design Table** from the Menu bar menu. The Design Table PropertyManager is displayed. Accept the defaults.

535) Click **OK** ✔ from the Design Table PropertyManager.

Enter the ROTARY-GRIPPER configuration names.

536) Enter **Rotation0** in Cell A4.

537) Enter **Flexible** in Cell A5.

538) Enter **Rotation90** in Cell A6.

Enter the ROTARY configuration parameters.

539) Enter **$Configuration@ROTARY <1>** in Cell B2.

540) **Enter** the illustrated information in Cell B3 - Cell B6.

	A	B	C	D
1	Design Table for: ROTARY-GRIPPER			
2		$Configuration@ROTARY<1>		
3	Default	MSQB30R(2)		
4	Rotation0	Rotation0		
5	Flexible	Flexible		
6	Rotation90	Rotation90		
7				
8				
9				
10				

541) Click a **position** in the Graphics window.

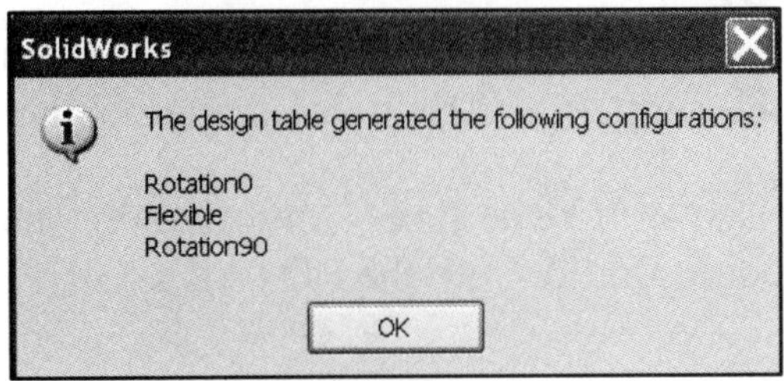

The $Configuration@ROTARY<1> utilizes the name and instance number from the FeatureManager. The values must be identical. Parameters and values are not case-sensitive.

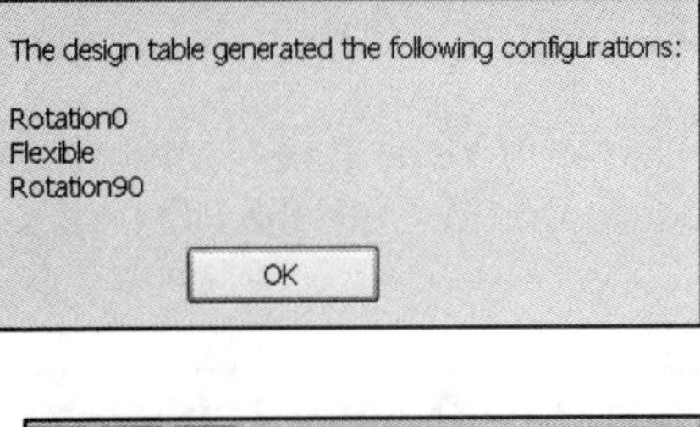

Modify the Flexible configuration.

542) Double-click **Flexible** from the ConfigurationManager.

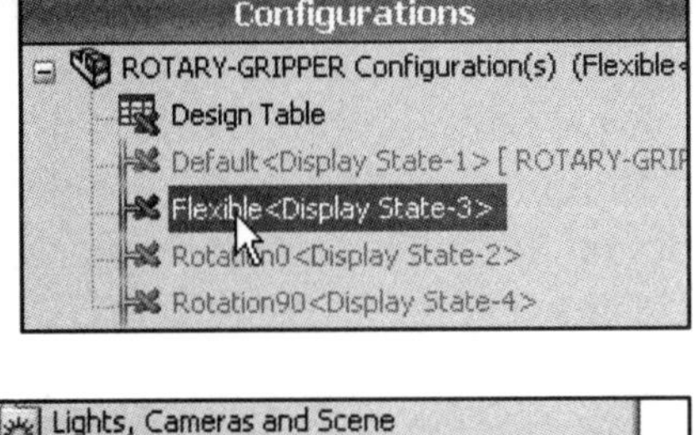

543) Right-click **ROTARY** from the FeatureManager.

544) Click **Component Properties**.

545) Check the **Flexible** box.

546) Click **OK**. The GRIPPER assembly and the PLATE-D part are free to rotate.

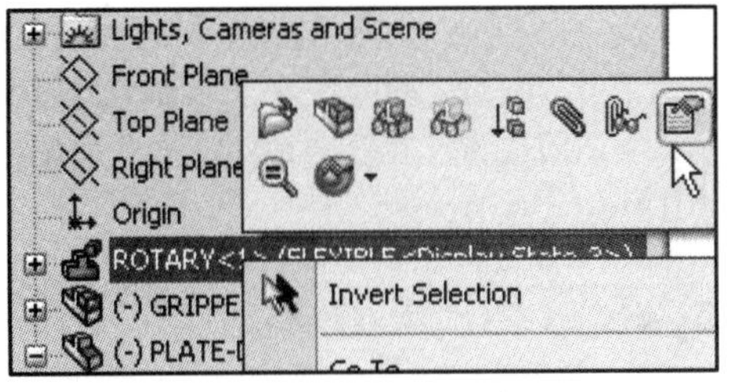

547) Click the **ConfigurationManager** icon.

Test the configurations.

548) Double-click the **Default** configuration. View the results.

549) Double-click the **Flexible** configuration. View the results.

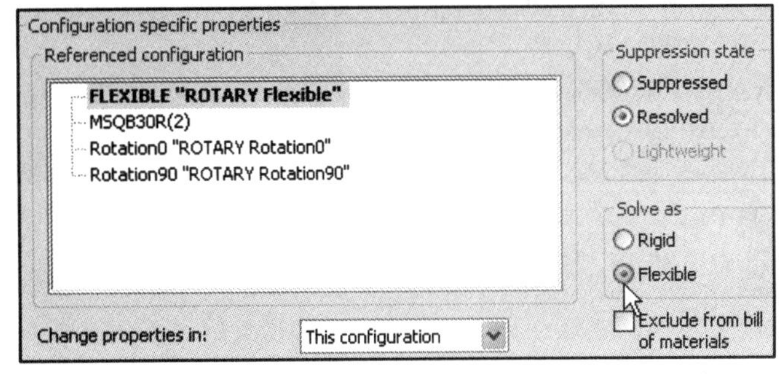

550) Double-click the **Rotation0** configuration. View the results.

551) Double-click the **Rotation90** configuration. View the results.

A Rebuild may be required to update the ROTARY-GRIPPER assembly.

Return to the Default configuration.

552) Double-click the **Default** configuration.

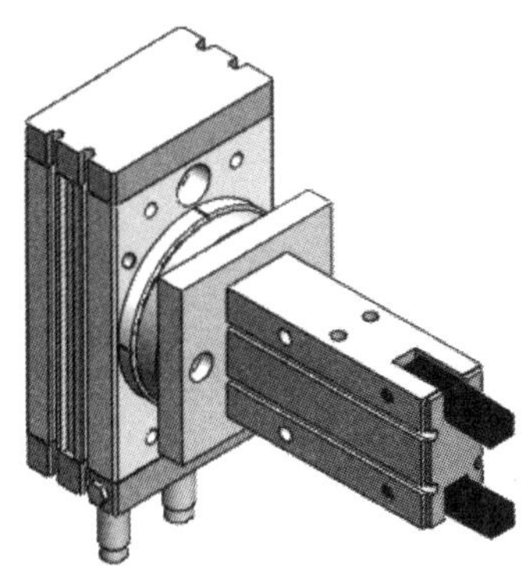

Save the ROTARY-GRIPPER assembly.

553) Click the **FeatureManager** icon.

554) Click **Isometric** view from the Heads-up Views toolbar.

555) Click **Save**.

PLATE-D requires three different material thicknesses for testing. How do you control the depth of the Extrude1 feature in the ROTARY-GRIPPER assembly?

Answer: Create three configurations in the PLATE-D part. Incorporate the PLATE-D configuration into the ROTARY-GRIPPER Design Table.

PLATE-D Design Table and Properties

Utilize the Design Table to create three configurations of the PLATE-D part. The configuration name contains a unique part number. Each configuration represents a different extruded depth. Rename the depth dimension parameter and insert the dimension parameter into the Design Table.

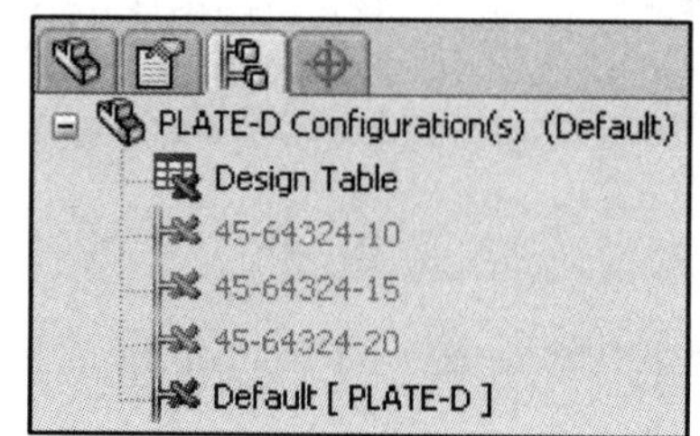

Properties are parameters defined in a single document that can be accessed and utilized by multiple documents. Parts and assemblies contain System Properties and User defined Properties.

System Properties

System Properties extract Summary Information values from the current document. System Properties are determined from the SolidWorks documents. Insert System Properties as linked Notes.

System Properties begin with the prefix SW. Set System Properties in the **File, Properties**, Summary Information dialog box.

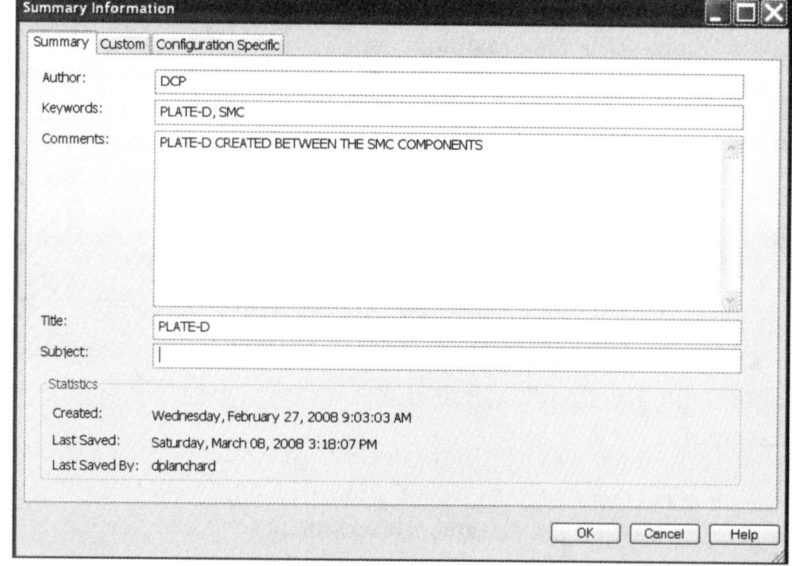

User defined Properties

There are two types of User defined Properties: *Custom Properties* and *Configuration Specific Properties*.

Custom Properties apply to all of the configurations of a part or an assembly. Configuration Specific Properties apply to only a single configuration of a part or an assembly.

Assign User defined Property values to named variables in the SolidWorks document.

The default variables are listed in the text file: SolidWorks/Lang/English/Properties.txt. Create your own User defined Property named variables.

Conserve design time. Utilize System Properties and define Custom Properties and Configuration Specific Properties in the ConfigurationManager and the Design Table.

Description
PartNo
Number
Revision
Material
Weight
Finish
StockSize
UnitofMeasure
Cost
MakeOrBuy
LeadTime
CheckedBy
CheckedDate
DrawnBy
DrawnDate
EngineeringApproval
EngAppDate
ManufacturingApproval
MfgAppDate
QAApproval
QAAppDate
Vendor
VendorNo
Client
Project
Status
DateCompleted
CompanyName
Department
Division
Group
Author
Owner
Source

User Defined Properties

PLATE-D Properties

PLATE-D requires four Configuration Specific Properties. Utilize the following PLATE-D Properties in the part drawing and assembly drawing:

- *Material*
- *Mass*
- *Description*
- *$PARTNUMBER*

The Materials Editor provides a list of predefined and user defined materials and their physical properties. Link the Material Property to the value, "SW-Material@@Default@PLATE-D.SLDPRT".

This value corresponds to the Material assigned with the Materials Editor. Link the Mass Property to the value;"SW-Mass@@Default@PLATE-D.SLDPRT". The value corresponds to the mass calculated through the Mass Properties tool. Create a new Property named Mass.

A parameter is in the form:

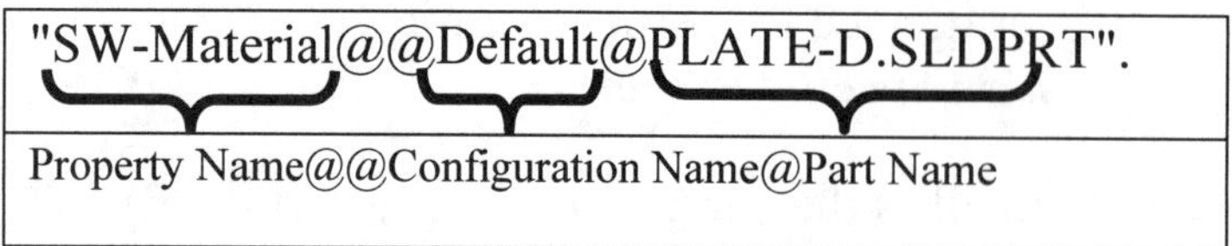

"SW-Material@@Default@PLATE-D.SLDPRT".
Property Name@@Configuration Name@Part Name

Cell entries in the Bill of Materials (BOM) are linked to Properties created in the part and assembly. Create Properties in the part with two techniques:

- *Configuration Properties*
- *Design Table*

There are three Bill of Materials Options for the part number:

- *Document Name (file name)*
- *Configuration Name*
- *User Specified Name*

The $PARTNUMBER Property contains three values in a Design Table:

- *$D Document Name (filename)*
- *$C Configuration Name*
- *User Specified Name (not shown)*

Do you notice the similarity? Answer: Values entered in the ConfigurationManager correspond to values in the Design Table and vice versa.

In the next activity, define Properties and their values by working between the Design Table and the ConfigurationManager.

Activity: Create the PLATE-D Design Table with Custom Properties

Display the PLATE-D part dimensions.

556) Open the PLATE-D part.

557) Click **Isometric** view from the Heads-up Views toolbar.

558) Drag the **Rollback bar** below the Extrude1 feature.

559) Right-click the **Annotations** folder.

560) Click **Show Feature Dimensions** as illustrated.

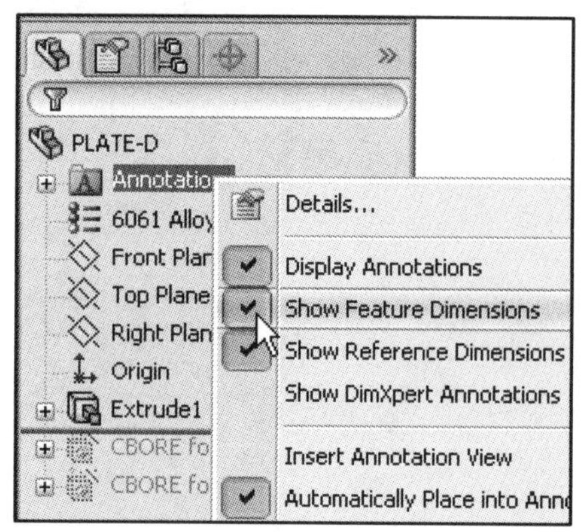

561) Click the **10** dimension text in the Graphics window. D1@Extrude1 is the name of the 10 dimension text.

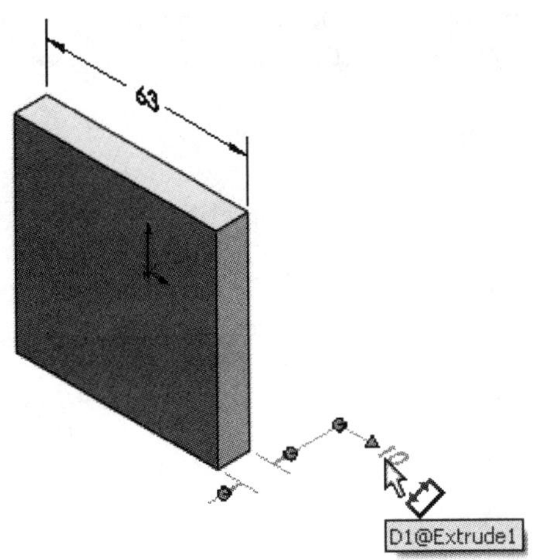

Provide additional control to clearly display feature dimensions for the Design Table. The Show Feature Dimensions option in the Annotations folder displays all feature dimensions. Only entries before the Rollback bar display feature dimensions. Position the Rollback bar to reduce the number of dimensions.

To hide unwanted individual feature dimensions, right-click on the feature entry. Click Hide All Dimensions.

To display hidden feature dimensions, right-click on the feature entry. Click Show All Dimensions.

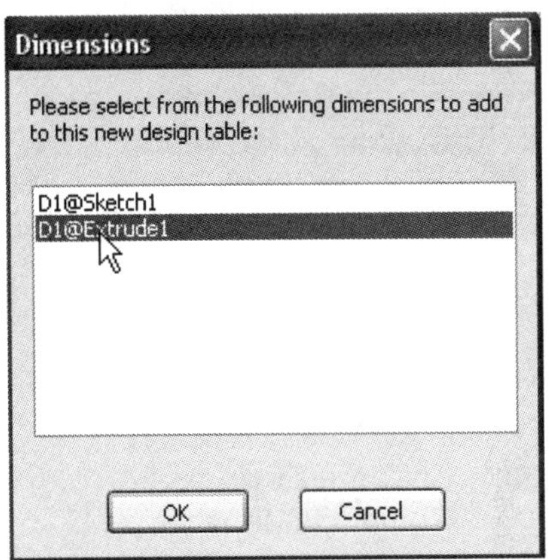

Insert a Design Table.

562) Right-click the **Annotations** folder.

563) Un-check **Show Feature Dimensions**

564) Click **Insert**, **Design Table** from the Menu bar menu. The Design Table PropertyManager is displayed. Accept the defaults.

565) Click **OK** from the Design Table PropertyManager.

566) Click **D1@Extrude1** from the Dimensions box.

567) Click **OK**. The Design Table displays the D1@Extrude1 parameter in Cell B2. The dimension value 10 is displayed in Cell B3.

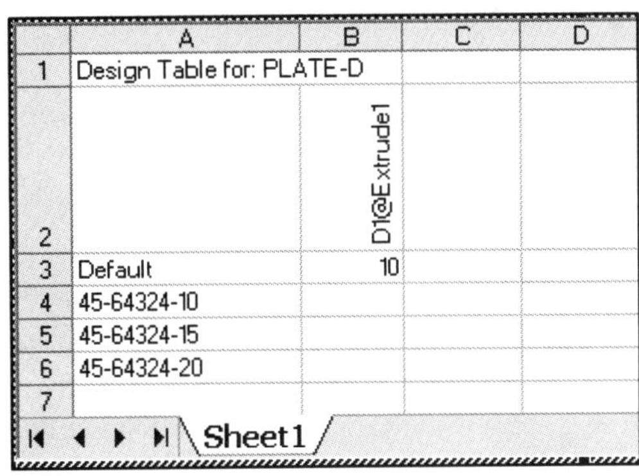

	A	B	C	D
1	Design Table for: PLATE-D			
2		D1@Extrude1		
3	Default	10		
4	45-64324-10			
5	45-64324-15			
6	45-64324-20			
7				

Sheet1

Enter the configuration names.

568) Enter **45-64324-10** in Cell A4.

569) Enter **45-64324-15** in Cell A5.

570) Enter **45-64324-20** in Cell A6.

Enter the D1@Extrude1 dimension values.

571) Enter **10** in Cell B4.

572) Enter **15** in Cell B5.

573) Enter **20** in Cell B6.

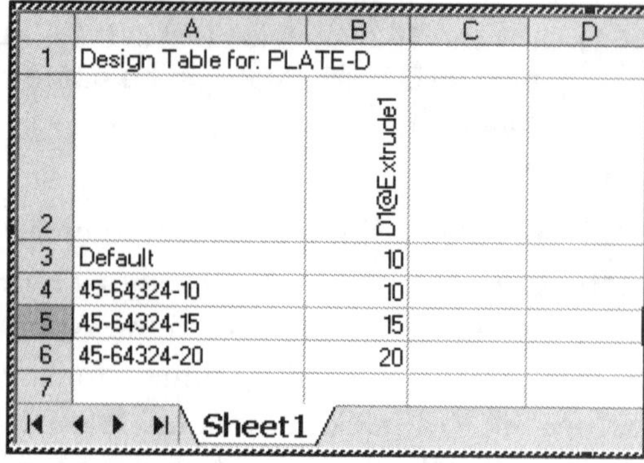

	A	B	C	D
1	Design Table for: PLATE-D			
2		D1@Extrude1		
3	Default	10		
4	45-64324-10	10		
5	45-64324-15	15		
6	45-64324-20	20		
7				

Sheet1

Create the PLATE-D configurations.

574) Click a **position** outside the Design Table.

575) Click **OK** to generate the three tables.

Restore all features.

576) Drag the **Rollback** bar to the bottom of the FeatureManager.

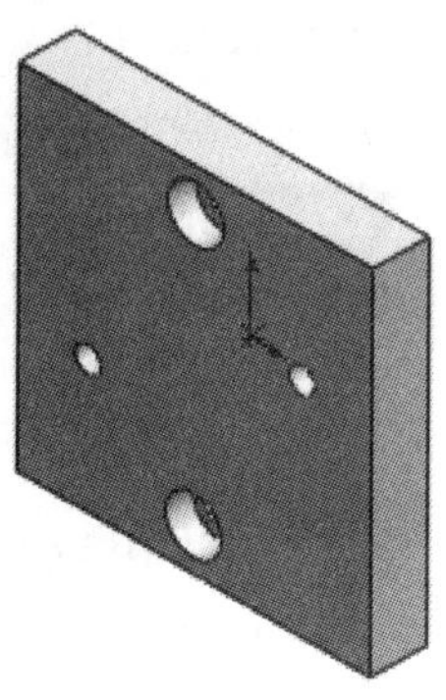

Verify the PLATE-D configurations.

577) Double-click each configuration: **45-64324-10**, **45-64324-15** & **45-64324-20** and view the results in the Graphics window.

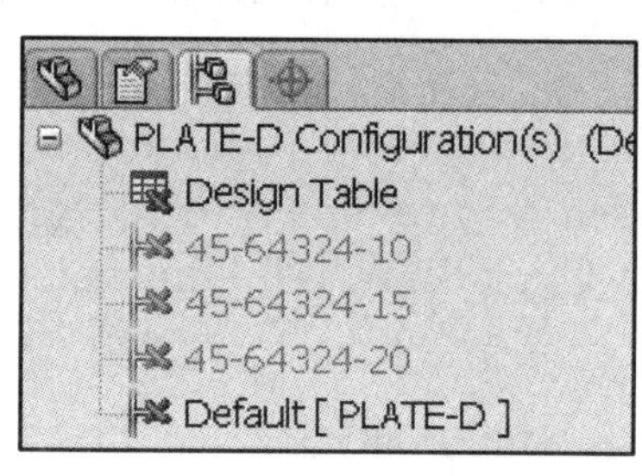

Return to the Default configuration.

578) Double-click **Default**.

579) Click the **FeatureManager** icon.

Save the PLATE-D part.

580) Click **Save**.

Display the Mass Properties.

581) Click the **Evaluate** tab from the CommandManager.

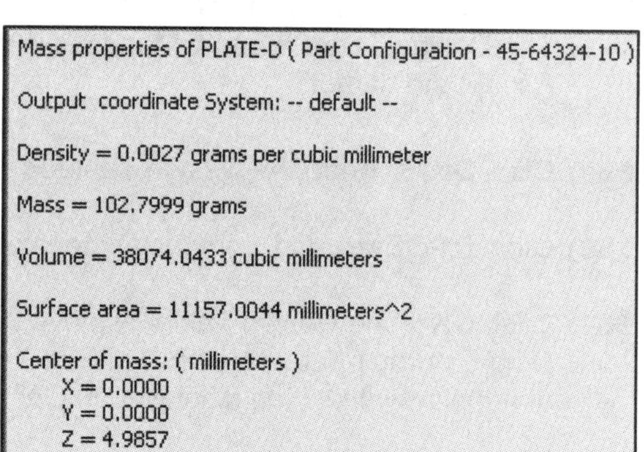

Mass properties of PLATE-D (Part Configuration - 45-64324-10)

Output coordinate System: -- default --

Density = 0.0027 grams per cubic millimeter

Mass = 102.7999 grams

Volume = 38074.0433 cubic millimeters

Surface area = 11157.0044 millimeters^2

Center of mass: (millimeters)
X = 0.0000
Y = 0.0000
Z = 4.9857

582) Click the **Mass Properties** tool from the Evaluate toolbar.

583) Click the **Options** button.

584) Click **Use custom settings**.

585) Enter **4** for Decimal Places.

586) Click **OK**. The Mass 102.7999 grams is displayed. The assigned Material determines the Density 0.0027 g/mm^3.

Close the Mass Properties dialog box.

587) Click **Close**.

Define Mass and Material in the PLATE-D ConfigurationManager. Enter and modify parameters in the ConfigurationManager and Design Table.

Always check units. Example: The volume of the PLATE-D part is measured in mm^3. Density of Aluminum is $2.700g/cm^3 = 0.0027g/mm^3$. Mass is calculated in grams. Mass = Density x Volume. Mass is multiplied by the gravitational constant of $9.8 m/s^2$ to obtain the force; weight. In the SI system, force is measured in newtons.

SolidWorks calculates the volume to be $40,634.0433mm^3$. A rough volume calculation based on overall dimensions is $65mm \times 65mm \times 10mm = 42,250mm^3$. Mass equals $(0.0027g/mm^3)(42250mm^3) = 114.08g$. So why do the calculated values differ from the SolidWorks values. Answer: The rough calculations did not account for the holes.

Add Custom Properties to the PLATE-D part.

588) Click the **ConfigurationManager** icon.

589) Right-click **Default**.

590) Click **Properties**. The Part number displayed when used in a bill of materials option displays PLATE-D.

591) Click **Custom properties**. The Configuration Specific properties are displayed in a table.

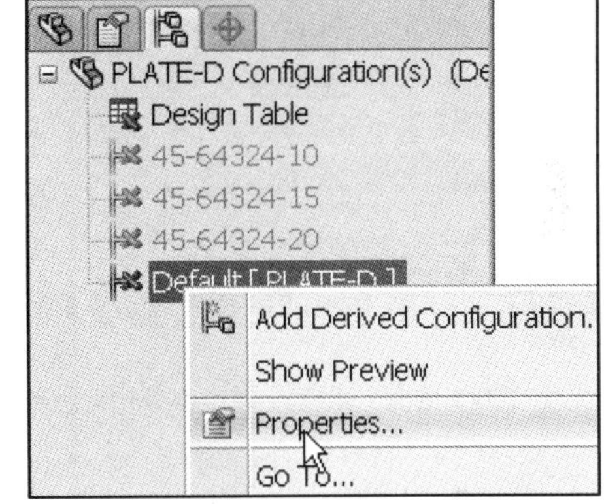

Insert the Configuration Specific Properties.

592) Click the **Configuration Specific** tab.

593) Click **inside** the Property Name box.

594) Select **Material** for Property Name from the drop-down menu.

595) Click **inside** the Value / Text Expression box.

596) Select **Material** for Value/Text Expression from the drop-down menu. SolidWorks displays the Evaluated Value, 6061 Alloy.

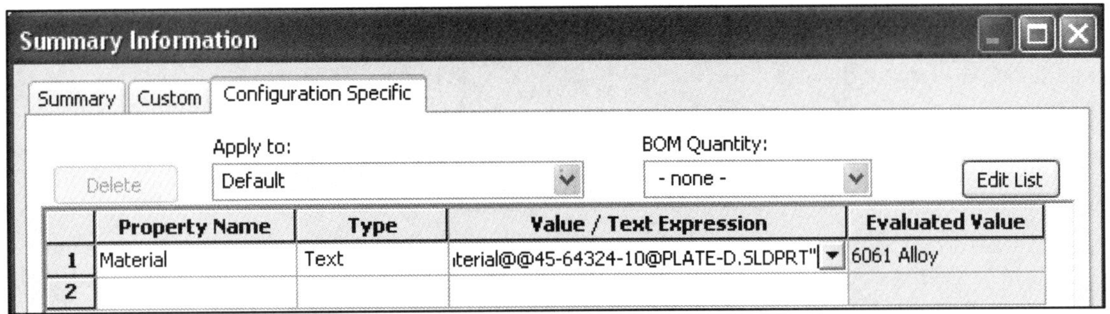

597) Click **inside** the Property Name box. Select **Description** for Property Name from the drop-down menu.

598) Click **inside** the Value / Text Expression box. Enter **PLATE-D** for the Value/Text Expression.

599) Click **inside** the Property Name box. Enter **Mass**.

600) Click **inside** the Value / Text Expression box.

601) Select **Mass** from the drop-down menu.

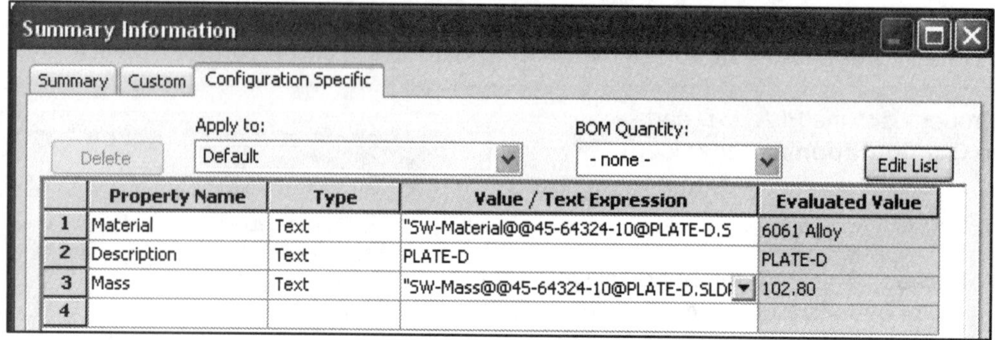

602) Click **OK** from the Summary Information dialog box.

603) Click **OK** ✔ from the Configuration PropertyManager.

Update the Design Table.

604) Right-click **Design Table**.

605) Click **Edit Table**.

606) Check the **Show unselected items again** box.

607) Click **$PRPDescription**.

608) Hold the **Ctrl** key down.

609) Click **$PRP@Mass** and **$PRP@Material**.

610) Release the **Ctrl** key.

611) Click **OK** to insert the parameters and values into the Design Table. View the updated table.

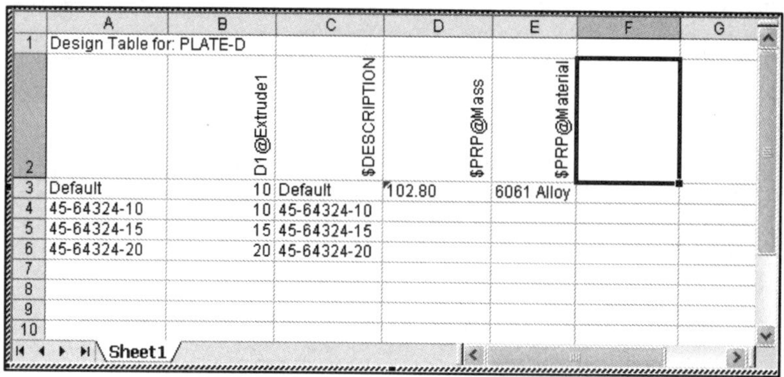

Update the Mass and Material Columns.

612) Update the **Mass** and **Material** columns in the design table as illustrated. Note: You can either apply the Mass Properties tool to calculate each PLATE-D configuration, and then enter the information into the cell or you can apply the Custom Properties tool in each configuration, this will update the design table automatically.

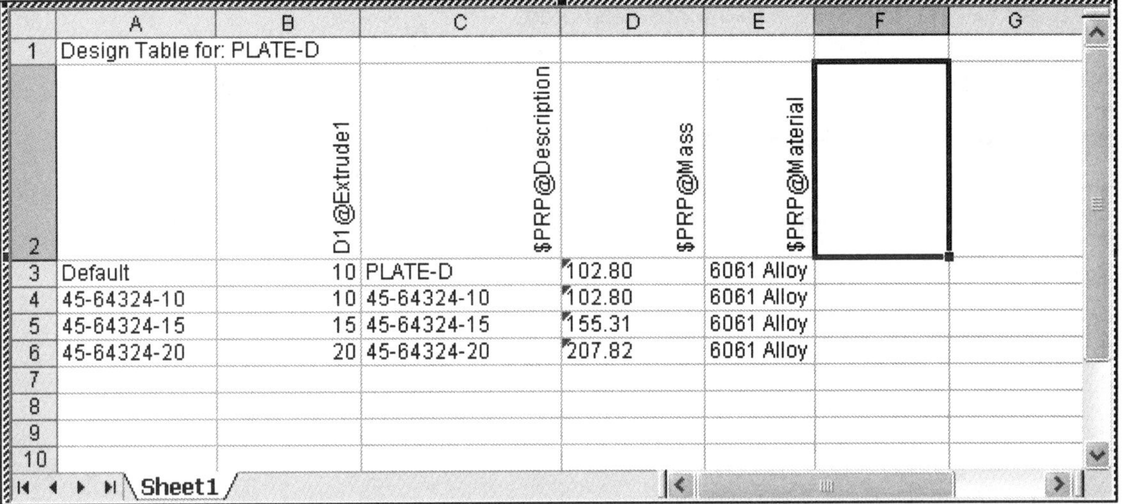

	A	B	C	D	E	F	G
1	Design Table for: PLATE-D						
2		D1@Extrude1	$PRP@Description	$PRP@Mass	$PRP@Material		
3	Default	10	PLATE-D	102.80	6061 Alloy		
4	45-64324-10	10	45-64324-10	102.80	6061 Alloy		
5	45-64324-15	15	45-64324-15	155.31	6061 Alloy		
6	45-64324-20	20	45-64324-20	207.82	6061 Alloy		
7							
8							
9							
10							

Sheet1

Return to SolidWorks.

613) Click a **position** outside the Design Table.

Review the 45-64324-10 configuration.

614) Right-click **45-64324-10** from the ConfigurationManager.

615) Click **Properties**.

616) Click **Custom properties**.

617) Click the **Configuration Specific** tab. The Description, Mass, and Material values are displayed.

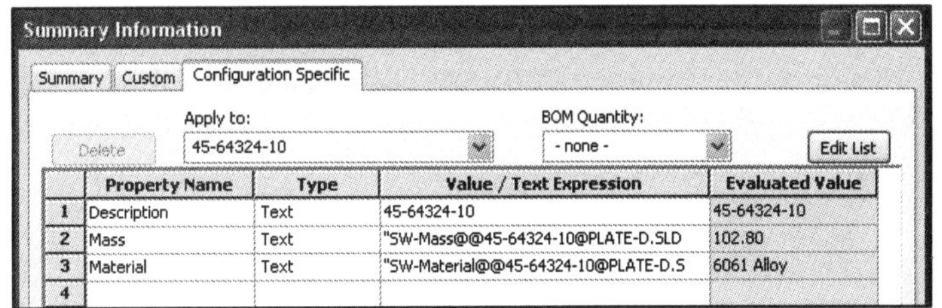

Summary Information

Summary | Custom | Configuration Specific

Apply to: 45-64324-10 BOM Quantity: - none -

Delete Edit List

	Property Name	Type	Value / Text Expression	Evaluated Value
1	Description	Text	45-64324-10	45-64324-10
2	Mass	Text	"SW-Mass@@45-64324-10@PLATE-D.SLD	102.80
3	Material	Text	"SW-Material@@45-64324-10@PLATE-D.S	6061 Alloy
4				

618) Click **OK**.

619) Click **OK** from the PropertyManager.

Return to the Design Table.

620) Right-click **Design Table**.

621) Click **Edit Table**.

622) Click **OK**.

SolidWorks updates the Description, Mass, and Material values and enters $PARTNUMBER in Cell F2. If $PARTNUMBER is not displayed, select Cell F2. Enter $PARTNUMBER.

Enter $PARTNUMBER used in the Bill of Materials.
623) Enter **$PARTNUMBER** in Cell F2 as illustrated.

624) Enter **$D** in Cell F3.

625) Enter **$C** in Cell F4 through Cell F6 for Configuration name.

	A	B	C	D	E	F
1	Design Table for: PLATE-D					
2		D1@Extrude1	$PRP@Description	$PRP@Mass	$PRP@Material	$PARTNUMBER
3	Default	10	PLATE-D	102.80	6061 Alloy	$D
4	45-64324-10	10	45-64324-10	102.80	6061 Alloy	$C
5	45-64324-15	15	45-64324-15	155.31	6061 Alloy	$C
6	45-64324-20	20	45-64324-20	207.82	6061 Alloy	$C
7						

The $user_notes parameter accepts all text values. Utilize the $user_notes parameter to enter comments that describe the Extrude1 depth in millimeters. Column B contains the values for each configuration. Enter the text, "mm Depth" in Cell I3. The EXCEL Concatenate function combines text strings into a single cell. An absolute reference to an EXCEL cell location contains the "$" symbol before the row and column entry, Example: I3.

Utilize an empty column in the Design Table to separate values not calculated by SolidWorks. If you insert additional rows and columns into the Design Table, verify that you maintained proper absolute cell references.

Enter $user_notes parameter.
626) Click **Cell G2**.

627) Enter **$user_notes**.

628) Click **Cell I3**.

629) Enter **mm Depth**.

E	F	G	H	I
$PRP@Material	$PARTNUMBER	$user_notes		
6061 Alloy	$D			mm Depth
6061 Alloy	$C			
6061 Alloy	$C			
6061 Alloy	$C			

630) Click **Cell G3**.

631) Click a **position** inside the formula bar.

632) Enter **=CONCATENATE(B3,I3)**. Click inside the H3 cell. The value, 10mm Depth is displayed in Cell G3.

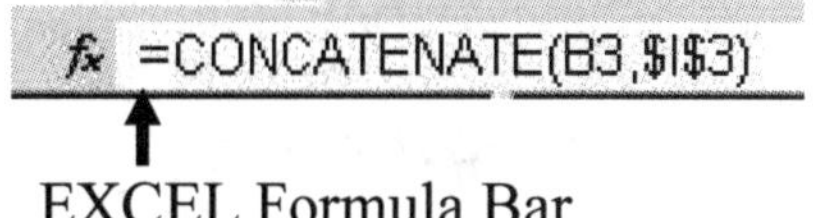

EXCEL Formula Bar

633) Copy **Cell G3** to **Cell G4 through Cell G6** as illustrated.

	A	B	C	D	E	F	G	H	I
1	Design Table for: PLATE-D								
2		D1@Extrude1	$PRP@Description	$PRP@Mass	$PRP@Material	$PARTNUMBER	$user_notes		
3	Default	10	PLATE-D	102.80	6061 Alloy	$D	10mm Depth		mm Depth
4	45-64324-10	10	45-64324-10	102.80	6061 Alloy	$C	10mm Depth		
5	45-64324-15	15	45-64324-15	155.31	6061 Alloy	$C	15mm Depth		
6	45-64324-20	20	45-64324-20	207.82	6061 Alloy	$C	20mm Depth		
7									
8									

Select Cell entries directly as function arguments. Select the Function *fx* icon. Enter CONCATENATE. Click Cell B3 for the Text1 box. Click Cell I3 for Text2. The values display to the right of the box. Modify Text2 to I3.

Utilize the "=" Shortcut key to begin a new formula. Utilize the "&" Shortcut key for the CONCATENATE function. Example: =B3&I3.

To align the text in a cell, right-click in the cell and click Format Cells. The Format Cell dialog box is displayed. Select the required conditions.

To remove a Hyperlink from a cell, right-click inside the cell, click Remove Hyperlink.

Exit the Design Table and Return to SolidWorks.
634) Click a **position** outside the Design Table.

635) Double-click the **Default** configuration.

Insert a Custom Property.
636) Right-click **Default** from the ConfigurationManager.

637) Click **Properties**.

638) Click **Custom Properties**.

639) Click the **Custom** tab.

640) Click **OK** to update.

641) Click **inside** the Property Name box.

642) Select **LeadTime** for Property Name from the drop-down menu.

643) Click **inside** the Value / Text Expression box.

644) Enter **1-2 Weeks** for the Value/Text Expression.

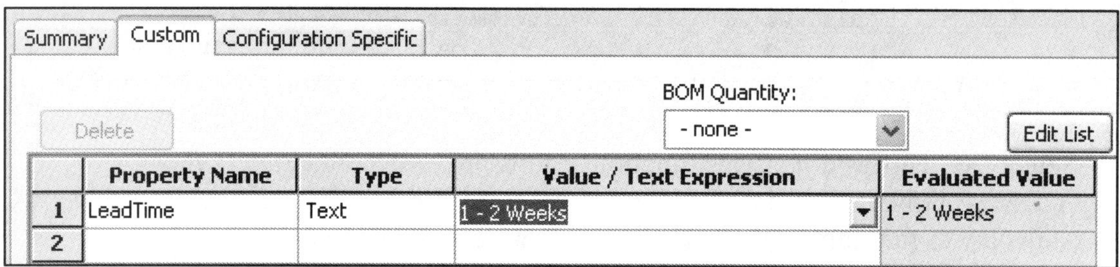

645) Click **OK**. Click **OK** from the PropertyManager.

646) **Return** to the FeatureManager.

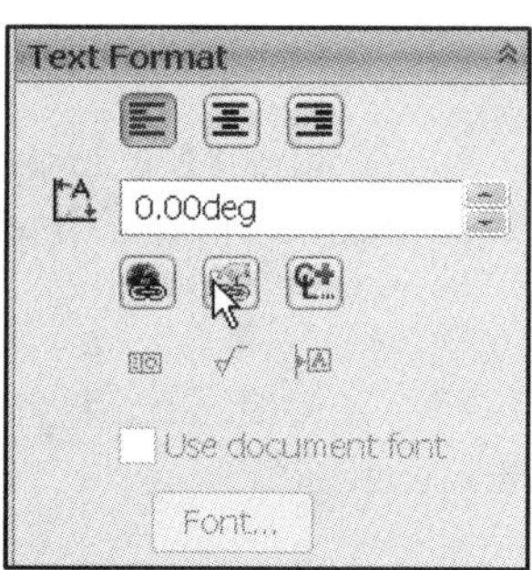

Insert a Linked Note.
647) Click **Insert**, **Annotations**, **Note** from the Menu bar menu. The Note PropertyManager is displayed.

648) Click a **position** in the lower left corner of the Graphics window.

649) Enter **Lead Time for PLATE-D**.

650) Click **Link to Property** from the Text Format box.

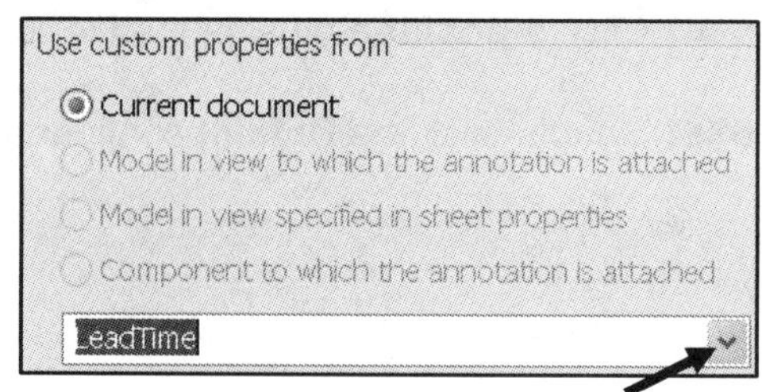

651) Select **LeadTime** from the Link to Property list.

652) Click **OK**.

653) Click **OK** ✔ from the Note PropertyManager.

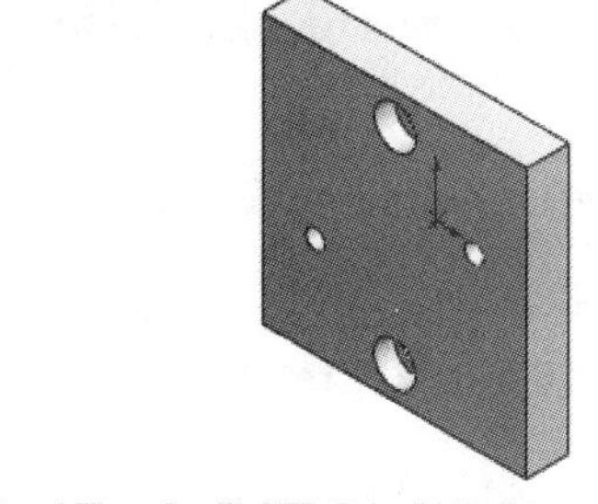

Lead Time for PLATE-D 1 - 2 Weeks

Hide Annotations

654) Right-click **Annotations** from the FeatureManager.

655) Un-check **Display Annotations**.

Save the PLATE-D part.

656) Click **Save**

The LeadTime Custom Property contains the same value across all configurations.

The ROTARY-GRIPPER assembly contains the default configuration for the PLATE-D part. How do you modify the assembly to support multiple configurations of the PLATE-D in a drawing? Answer: Utilize a Design Table.

Edit the ROTARY-GRIPPER Design Table

The ROTARY-GRIPPER incorporates PLATE-D configurations and ROTARY configurations. Edit the ROTARY-GRIPPER Design Table. Delete the *Rotation0* and *Rotation90* configuration.

Insert six ROTARY-GRIPPER configurations to define the horizontal and vertical position.

Utilize the three PLATE-D configurations: *45-64324-10, 45-64324-15*, and *45-64324-20*.

Activity: Edit the ROTARY-GRIPPER Design Table

Open the ROTARY-GRIPPER assembly.

657) Click **Window**, **ROTARY-GRIPPER**. The ROTARY assembly and PLATE-D part are set to the Default configurations.

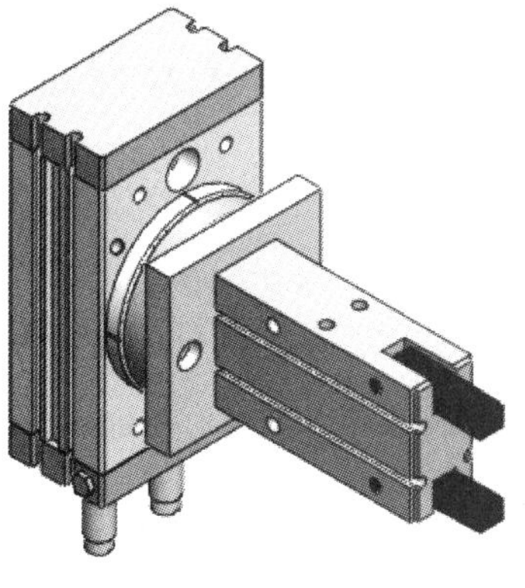

Edit the Design Table.

658) Right-click **Design Table** from the ConfigurationManager.

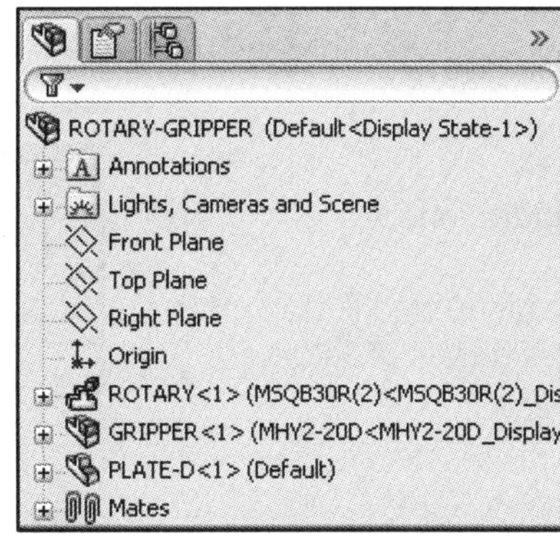

659) Click **Edit Table**.

660) Click **OK**.

661) Delete the *Rotation0* and *Rotation90* configuration. Select **Row 4** and **Row 6** as illustrated.

662) Right-click **Delete**.

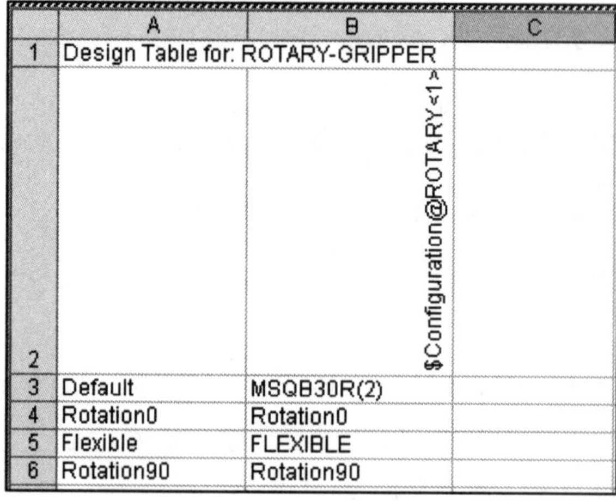

	A	B	C
1	Design Table for: ROTARY-GRIPPER		
2		$Configuration@ROTARY<1>	
3	Default	MSQB30R(2)	
4	Rotation0	Rotation0	
5	Flexible	FLEXIBLE	
6	Rotation90	Rotation90	

Insert six new configuration names.

663) Enter **Horizontal-10** in Cell A5.

664) Enter **Horizontal-15** in Cell A6.

665) Enter **Horizontal-20** in Cell A7.

666) Enter **Vertical-10** in Cell A8.

667) Enter **Vertical-15** in Cell A9.

668) Enter **Vertical-20** in Cell A10.

Insert parameters and values.

669) Enter **ROTATION90** in Cell B5.

670) Copy **Cell B5** to Cell B6-B7.

671) Enter **ROTATION0** in Cell B8.

672) Copy **Cell B8** to Cell B9-B10.

673) Enter **$Configuration@PLATE-D<1>** in Cell C2.

674) Enter **45-64324-10** in Cell C5.

675) Enter **45-64324-15** in Cell C6.

676) Enter **45-64324-20** in Cell C7.

677) Copy **Cell C5-C7** to Cell C8-C10.

678) Click a **position** in the Graphics window to exit the Design Table.

	A	B	C
1	Design Table for: ROTARY-GRIPPER		
2		$Configuration@ROTARY<1>	$Configuration@PLATE-D<1
3	Default	MSQB30R(2)	Default
4	Flexible	FLEXIBLE	Default
5	Horizontal-10	Rotation90	45-64324-10
6	Horizontal-15	Rotation90	45-64324-15
7	Horizontal-20	Rotation90	45-64324-20
8	Vertical-10	Rotation0	45-64324-10
9	Vertical-15	Rotation0	45-64324-15
10	Vertical-20	Rotation0	45-64324-20

679) Click **OK** to generate configurations.

680) Click **Yes** to delete the Rotation0 and Rotation90 configurations from the ConfigurationManager.

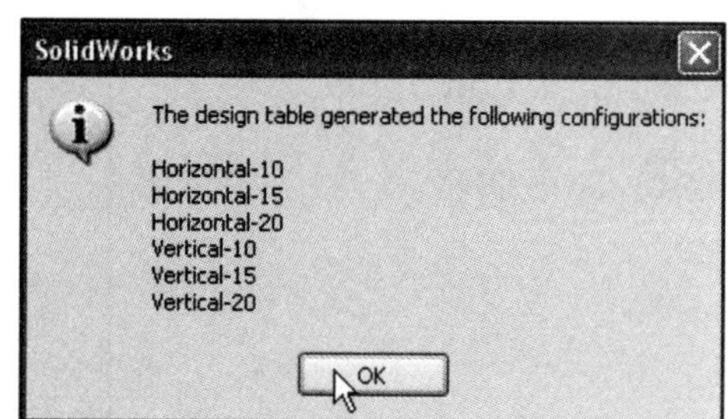

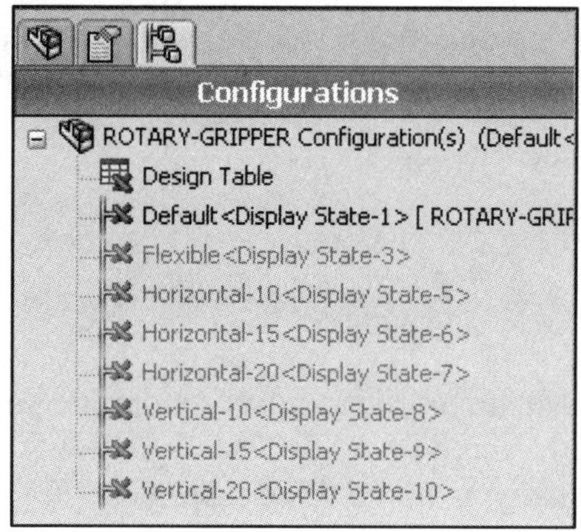

View the six ROTARY-GRIPPER configurations.

681) Double-click **Horizontal-10**, **Horizontal-15**, **Horizontal-20**, **Vertical-10**, **Vertical-15,** and **Vertical-20**. Note: The Flexible configuration is in the Flexible state.

Return to the Default configuration.

682) Double-click the **Default** configuration.

683) Click the **FeatureManager** icon.

Save the ROTARY-GRIPPER assembly.

684) Click **Save**.

Close the ROTARY-GRIPPER assembly.

685) Click **File**, **Close** from the Menu bar menu.

686) Close all models.

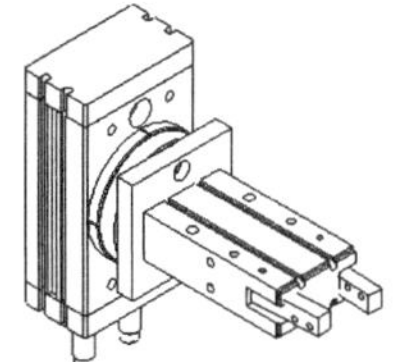
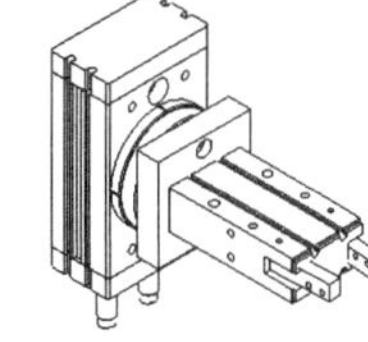
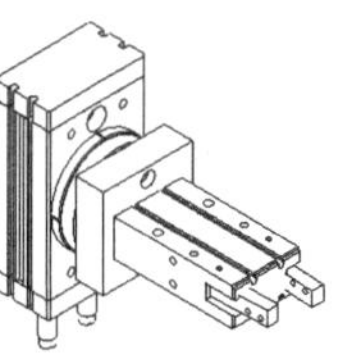

Horizontal-10 Horizontal-15 Horizontal-20

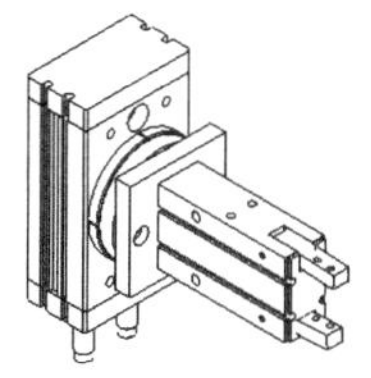
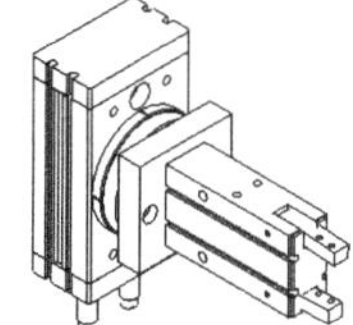
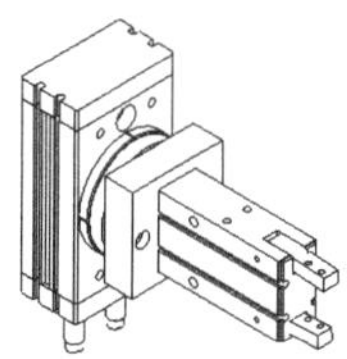

Vertical-10 Vertical-15 Vertical-20

PLATE-D configuration incorporated into ROTARY-GRIPPER configurations

Activity: Edit the PLATE-D part and Design Table

Display PLATE-D in an Isometric view.

687) Open PLATE-D.

688) Click **Isometric** view from the Heads-up View toolbar. PLATE-D is in the Default configuration.

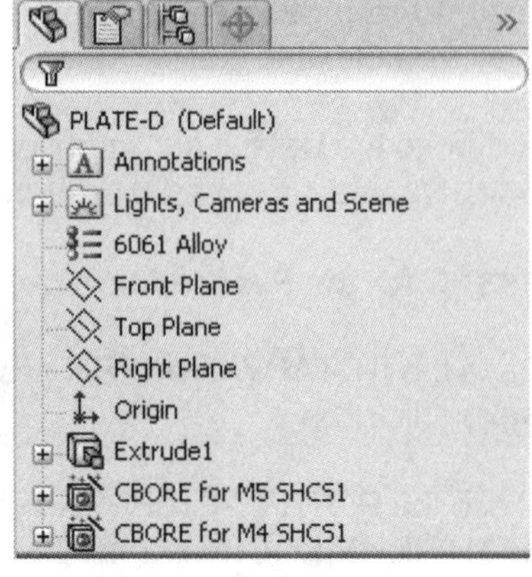

Manufacturing requires a drawing of the three PLATE-D configurations. Do you create three separate drawings?

Answer: No. Create the configurations in a Design Table and then utilize the configurations in a multi-sheet drawing.

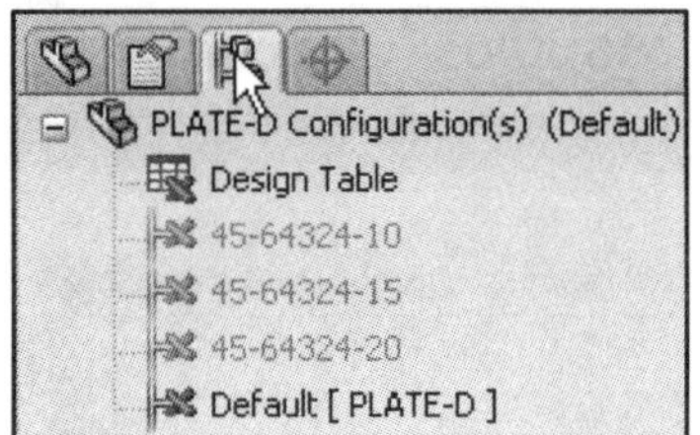

689) Right-click the **front face** of PLATE-D. This is your Sketch plane.

690) Click **Sketch** from the Context toolbar. The Sketch toolbar is displayed.

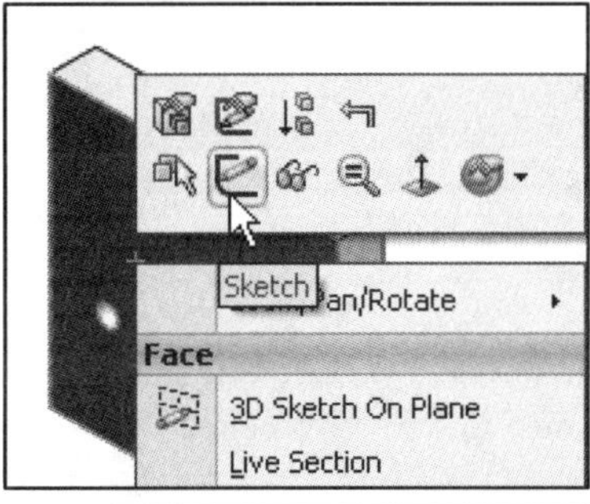

Sketch a Rectangle.

691) Click **Front** view from the Heads-up View toolbar.

692) Click **Hidden Lines Removed** from the Heads-up View toolbar.

693) Click the **Corner Rectangle** tool from the Sketch toolbar.

694) Sketch a **rectangle** in the upper left corner as illustrated.

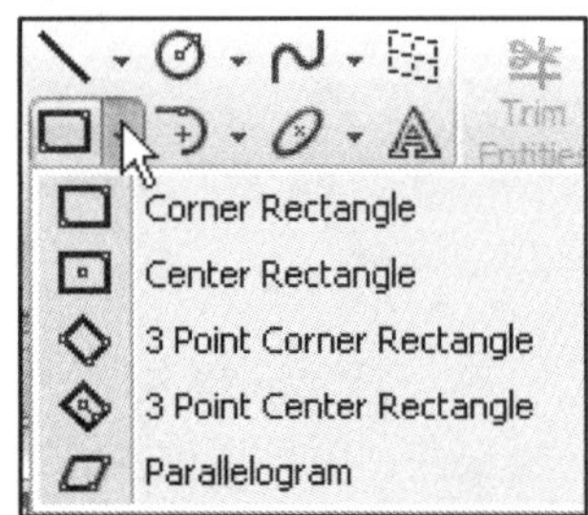

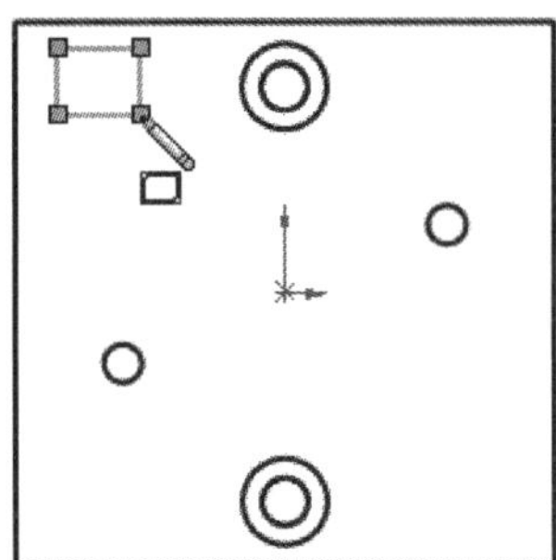

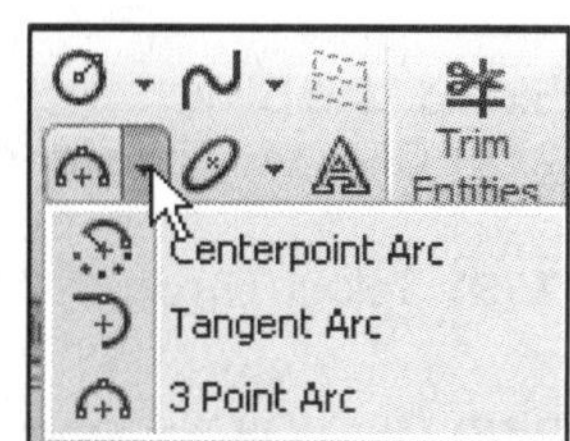

695) Click the **Trim Entities** tool from the Sketch toolbar. The Trim PropertyManager is displayed.

696) Click **Trim to closest**.

697) Select the **two vertical lines** to be removed.

698) Click **OK** from the Trim PropertyManager.

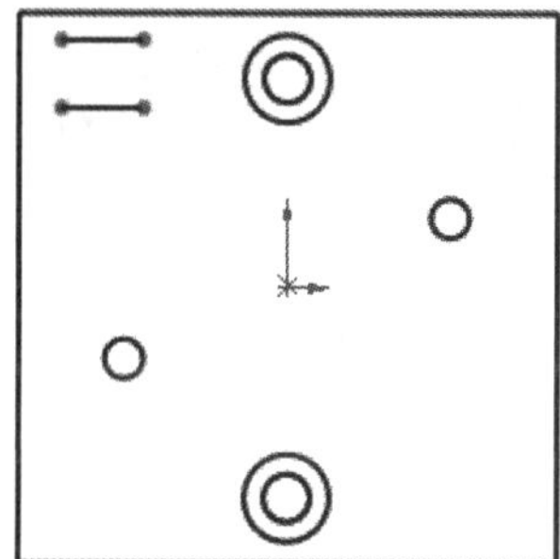

699) Click the **Tangent Arc** tool from the Consolidated Sketch toolbar.

700) Sketch **two arcs** on each end of the two horizontal lines.

701) Click the **Centerline** tool from the Consolidated Sketch toolbar.

702) Sketch three **centerlines** as illustrated.

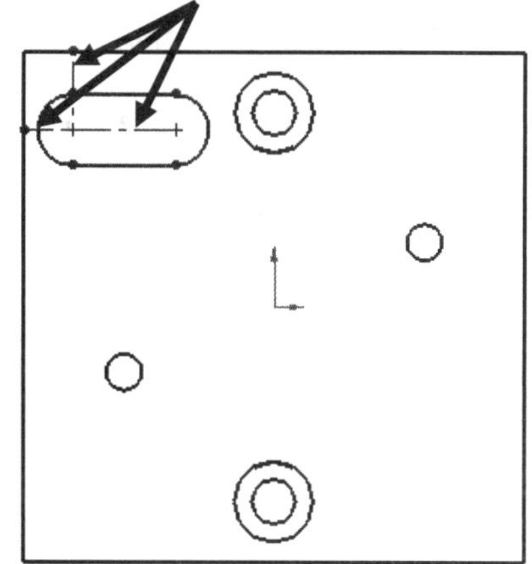

Add an Equal relation.

703) Right-click **Select**.

704) Select the **vertical centerline**.

705) Hold the **Ctrl** key down.

706) Click the **two horizontal centerlines**.

707) Release the **Ctrl** key.

708) Click **Equal**.

709) Click **OK** from the Properties PropertyManager.

Dimension the Sketch.

710) Click the **Smart Dimension** tool.

Insert a horizontal dimension.

711) Enter **10**. The All Configurations option is selected by default.

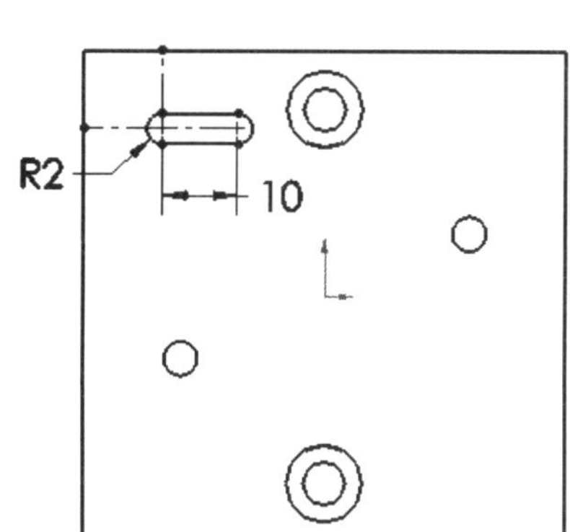

Insert a radial dimension.

712) Enter **2**. The All Configurations option is selected by default.

713) Click **OK** from the Dimension PropertyManager.

Extrude the Sketch.
714) Click the **Extruded Cut** tool from the Feature toolbar.

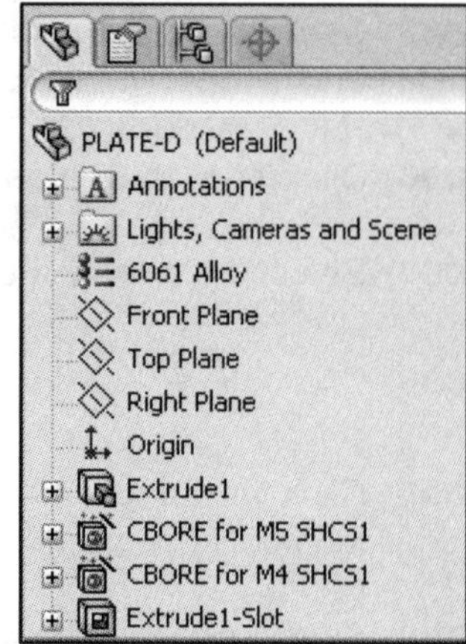

715) Select **Through All** for Depth.

716) Click **OK** from the Extrude PropertyManager. Extruded2 is displayed.

Rename the feature.
717) Rename **Extrude2** to **Extrude1-Slot**.

Control the Suppressed/Unsuppressed state of the Extrude1-Slot feature through Feature Properties and the $State parameter in the Design Table.

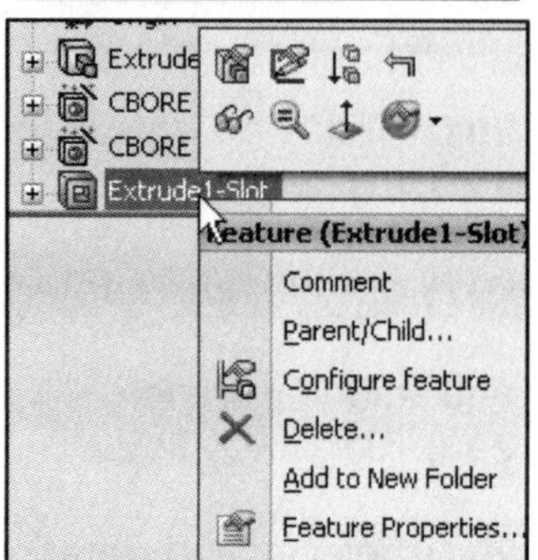

Suppress the Extrude1-Slot feature through Feature Properties.
718) Right-click **Extrude1-Slot**.

719) Click **Feature Properties**.

720) Select **All Configurations** from the drop-down menu.

721) Click the **Suppressed** check box.

722) Click **OK** from the Features Properties dialog box.

Edit the PLATE-D Design Table.
723) Right-click **Design Table** from the ConfigurationManager.

724) Click **Edit Table**.

725) Select **$COLOR** from the Parameters box.

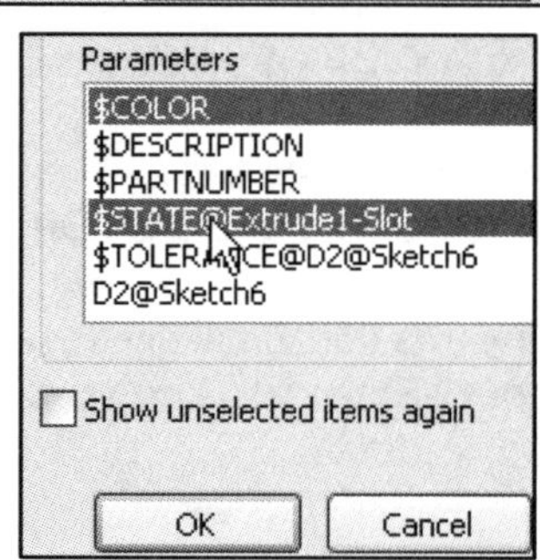

726) Hold the **Ctrl** key down.

727) Select **$STATE@Extrude1-Slot**.

728) Release the **Ctrl** key.

729) Click **OK**.

SolidWorks inserts the $COLOR parameter into Cell C2. The value 14933469 indicates the default light gray part color. The $COLOR parameter controls part color. The value in each cell represents the 32-bit integer specifying RGB (red, green & blue).

	A	B	C	D	E
1	Design Table for: PLATE-D				
2		D1@Extrude1	$COLOR	$STATE@Extrude1-Slot	
3	Default	10	14933469	S	
4	45-64324-10	10	14933469	S	
5	45-64324-15	15	14933469	S	
6	45-64324-20	20	14933469	S	
7					
8					

The $STATE@Extrude1-Slot parameter controls the Suppressed/Unsuppressed feature state.

S indicates the feature is suppressed.

U indicates the feature is unsuppressed.

	A	B	C	D
1	Design Table for: PLATE-D			
2		D1@Extrude1	$COLOR	$STATE@Extrude1-Slot
3	Default	10	14933469	U
4	45-64324-10	10	0	S
5	45-64324-15	15	255	S
6	45-64324-20	20	65280	S
7				

Modify the $COLOR values.

730) Enter **0** in Cell C4 (black).

731) Enter **255** in Cell C5 (red).

732) Enter **65280** in Cell C6 (green).

Modify the STATE values.

733) Enter **U** in Cell D3.

The Extrude1-Slot is Un-Suppressed in the Default Configuration. The Extrude1 Slot is Suppressed in the other configurations.

Additional integer color values are located in the SW help, Colors, Parameter in design tables.

Update the three PLATE-D configurations.

734) Click a **position** outside the Design Table.

735) Click **Shaded With Edges**.

Verify the three configurations.

736) Double-click **45-63424-10**, **45-63424-15** & **45-63424-20**. A different color is displayed.

Return to the Default Configuration.
737) Click **Default**.

738) Click the **FeatureManager** icon.

Save the PLATE-D part.
739) Click **Isometric** view.

740) Click **Save**.

741) **Close** all documents.

Project Summary

In this project, you utilized a Top-down design assembly modeling approach with In-Context features. You developed the ROTARY-GRIPPER assembly. The PLATE-D part was developed In-Context of the ROTARY assembly and GRIPPER assembly.

You utilized a Bottom-up design assembly modeling approach to model the PLATE-C part. PLATE-C was created as an empty part and assembled to the 2AXIS-TRANSFER assembly.

The InPlace Mates and External references were redefined in the PLATE-D part.

You developed three configurations for the ROTARY assembly: *Flexible*, *Rotation0*, and *Rotation90*.

You developed six configurations for the ROTARY-GRIPPER assembly: *Horizontal-10, Horizontal-15, Horizontal-20, Vertical-10, Vertical-15,* and *Vertical-20*

You developed three configurations for the PLATE-D part: *45-63424-10, 45-63424-15, and 45-63424-20*

Material, Mass and Description were developed as Configuration Specific Properties in the ConfigurationManager. The $PARTNUMBER, $COLOR and $STATE parameters were inserted into the PLATE-D Design Table.

Utilize the configurations and parameters defined in this project in the 3AXIS-TRANSFER Bill of Materials. Combine the LINEAR-TRANSFER assembly, 2AXIS-TRANSFER assembly and the ROTARY-GRIPPER assembly to complete the 3AXIS-TRANSFER assembly in the new Project.

Questions

1. Identify the two components that determine the geometric and functional requirements for the PLATE-D part.

2. True or False. The small dowel pin slot on the ROTARY assembly moves linearly along the Right plane of the assembly.

3. Utilize a ____________ to create 100 PLATE-D configurations.

4. True or False. A drawing contains only one configuration of a part or assembly.

5. Describe the two modeling methods that are utilized to create the ROTARY-GRIPPER assembly.

6. True or False. Suppressed Mates are not loaded into memory.

7. Describe the process to split the FeatureManager and to display the reference planes from two different components.

8. True or False. Mates in SolidWorks guarantee that a component can be physically assembled in your factory.

9. What does the "->"symbol and "->?" symbol indicate after a feature entry in the FeatureManager?

10. True or False. Configuration names entered in a Design Table are displayed in the ConfigurationManager.

11. Describe the components that determine the geometric and functional requirements for the PLATE-C part.

12. Mass, Density and Volume are calculated utilizing what tool ________________________?

13. Describe the difference between a Custom Property and a Configuration Specific Property.

14. Identify the location in the FeatureManager to assign Material to a part.

15. Describe the differences between System Properties and User defined Properties.

16. $COLOR and $STATE are two parameters defined in a Design Table. Where do you locate other SolidWorks parameters and their syntax?

Notes:

Project 7

Assembly Drawings with Revision Table and Bill of Materials

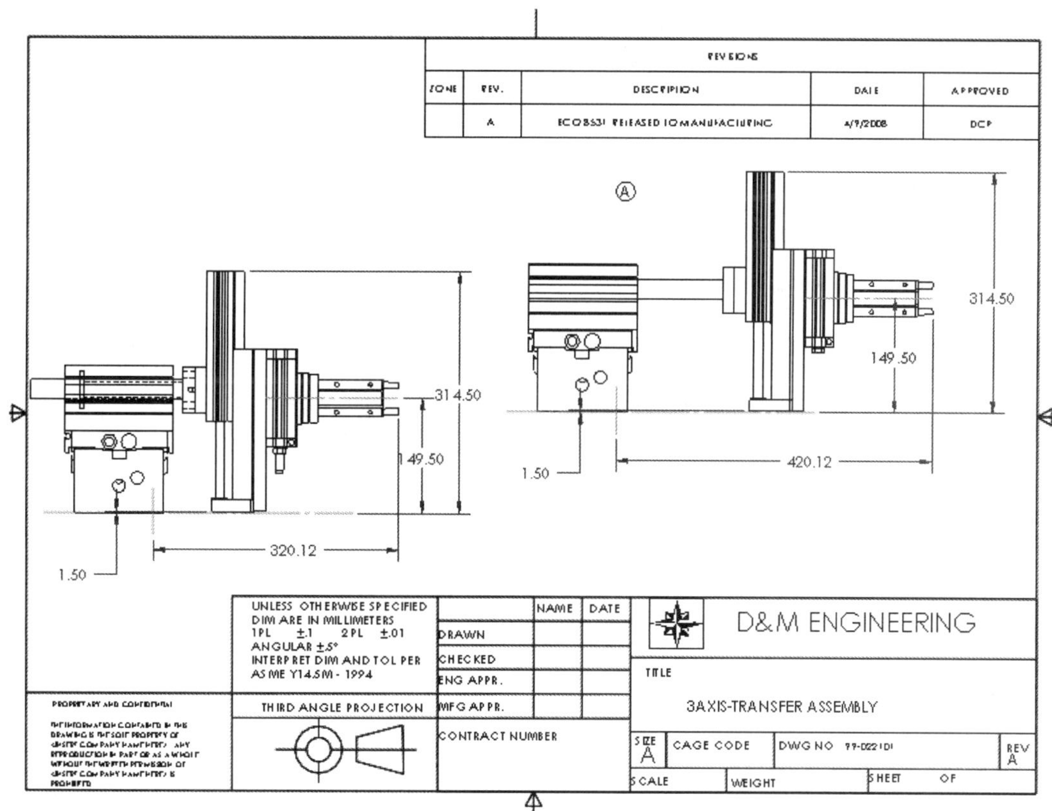

Below are the desired outcomes and usage competencies based on the completion of this Project. An assembly drawing refers to a SolidWorks drawing that contains a SolidWorks assembly.

Project Desired Outcomes:	Usage Competencies:
• 3AXIS-TRANSFER assembly.	• Apply final configurations to create the 3AXIX-TRANSFER assembly from the: 2AXIS-TRANSFER, LINEAR-TRANSFER, and ROTARY-GRIPPER.
• 3AXIS-TRANSFER drawing. • Sheet1: Two views. • Sheet2: Exploded Isometric view. • Sheet3: Two views.	• Knowledge of Custom Properties in a part/assembly and Linked Notes in a drawing.
	• Ability to create an Assembly drawing using multiple configurations and multiple sheets.
	• Knowledge to incorporate an Exploded View, Bill of Materials, Revision table, and more.

Notes:

Project 7 – Assembly Drawings with Revision Tables and Bill of Materials

Project Objective

Create the 3AXIS-TRANSFER assembly. Utilize the Configure Component tool to create eight position configurations and a Fastener configuration using the following assemblies: *LINEAR-TRANSFER, 2AXIS-TRANSFER,* and the *ROTARY-GRIPPER.*

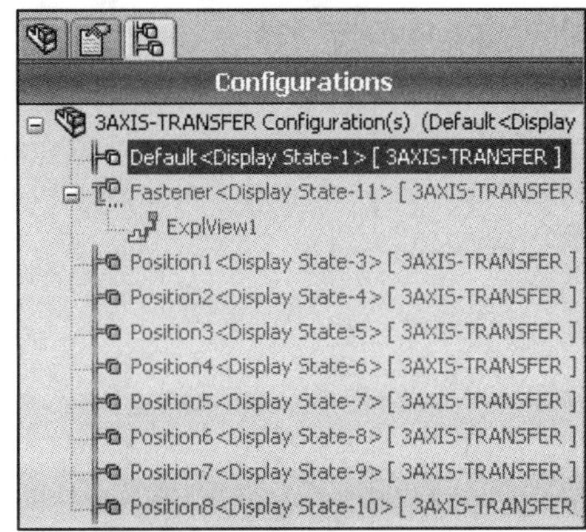

Create the 3AXIS-TRANSFER drawing. Insert Fasteners into the 3AXIS-TRANSFER assembly. Insert Custom Properties to the components in the 3AXIS-TRANSFER assembly. Apply the Replace Component tool to the 3AXIS-TRANSFER assembly. Develop an Exploded View, Linked Notes, Revision Table, and Bill of Materials in the 3AXIS-TRANSFER drawing.

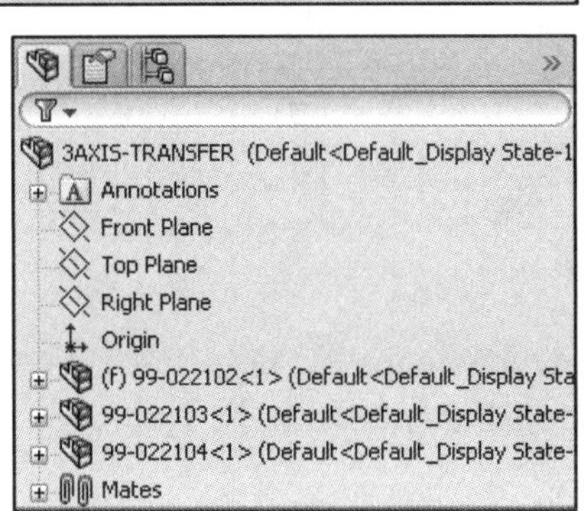

On the completion of this project, you will be able to:

- Apply the Configure Component tool at two levels for nine components.
- Apply the View Palette and the Model Items tool to insert a Front and Isometric view.
- Develop a multi-sheet assembly drawing with Driven dimensions and Link Properties
- Define Custom Properties utilized in a Bill of Materials.
- Apply the Replace Component tool.
- Create and insert an Exploded View.
- Recognize and redefine various created configurations in a drawing view.
- Insert a Revision Table.
- Insert a Revision Property from the part as a Linked Note in the drawing.
- Apply SolidWorks Explorer.

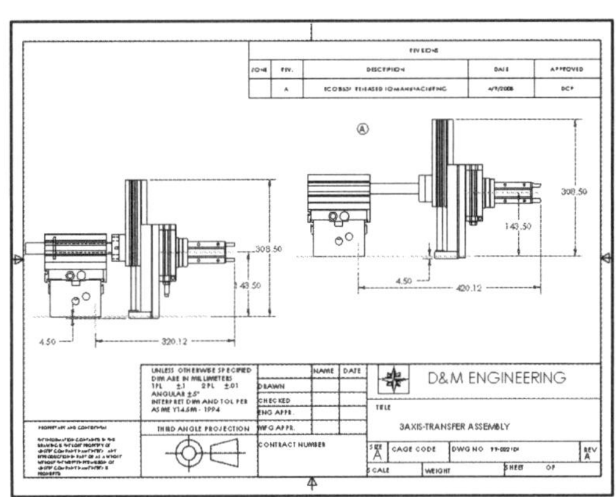

Develop modeling skill and speed. Project 7 primarily utilizes the Context menu and the CommandManager to execute the tools in the Assembly toolbar, Features toolbar, and View Layout toolbar.

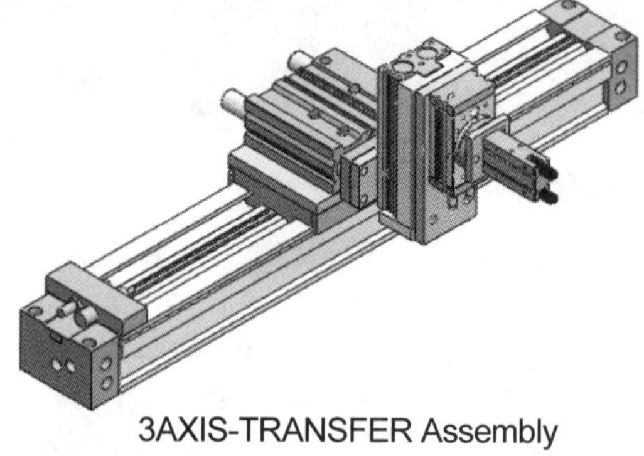

3AXIS-TRANSFER Assembly

Project Overview

Create the 3AXIS-TRANSFER assembly. The 3AXIS-TRANSFER assembly contains three sub-assemblies which you created in previous Projects:

- *LINEAR-TRANSFER assembly*
- *2AXIS-TRANSFER assembly*
- *ROTARY-GRIPPER assembly*

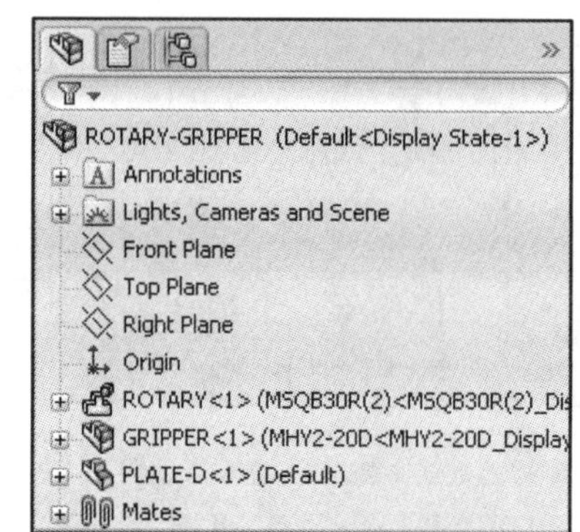

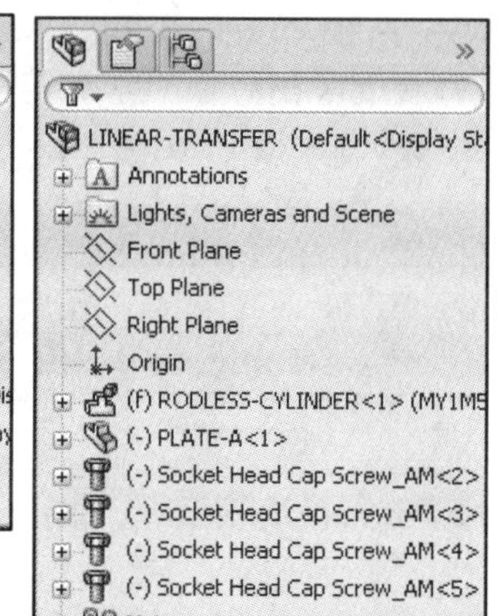

Create new configurations of the 3AXIS-TRANSFER assembly using the Configure Component tool.

Add Fasteners. Modify PLATE-A. Replace existing components with the Replace Component tool.

Create an Exploded 3AXIS-TRANSFER assembly configuration.

Create the 3AXIS-TRANSFER drawing with multiple sheets and drawing views in various configurations.

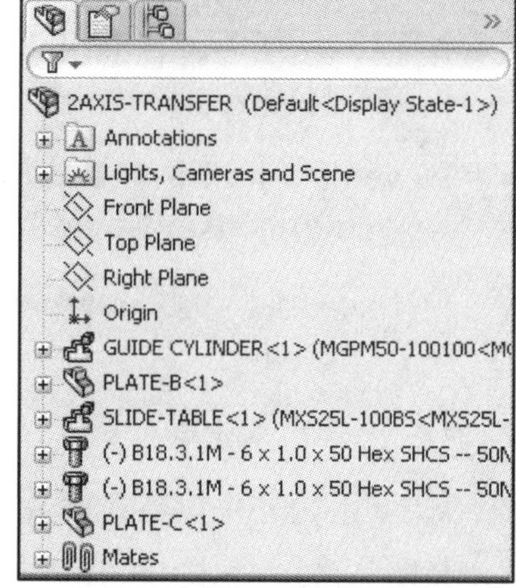

If you did not complete the assemblies in the previous chapters, the completed assemblies: *LINERAR-TRANSFER*, *2AXIS-TRANSFER*, and the *ROTARY-GRIPPER* are located in the DeliveryStation-Project7 folder in the CD of the book. Work from the DeliveryStation-Project7 folder to create the 3AXIS-TRANSFER assembly in this Project.

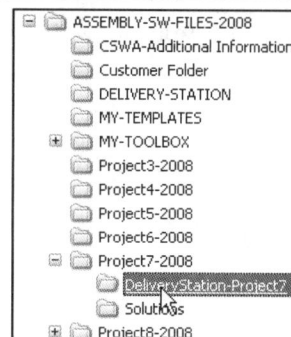

ASSEMBLY-SW-FILES-2008
CSWA-Additional Information
Customer Folder
DELIVERY-STATION
MY-TEMPLATES
MY-TOOLBOX
Project3-2008
Project4-2008
Project5-2008
Project6-2008
Project7-2008
DeliveryStation-Project7
Solutions
Project8-2008

The 3AXIS-TRANSFER drawing includes three sheets:

- *Sheet1*
- *Sheet2*
- *Sheet3*

Sheet1: Contains the Front view with two configurations. Insert Driven dimensions with Custom Properties. Apply the Revision Table tool. Work between the part, assembly, and drawing.

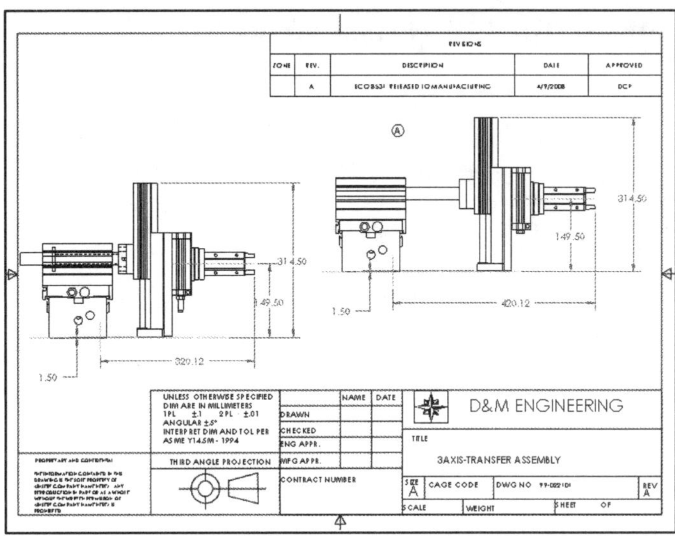

Sheet2: Contains an Exploded Isometric View of the 3AXIS-TRANSFER assembly and the Fastener configuration. Insert a Bill of Materials and utilize Custom Properties. Apply the AutoBalloon tool.

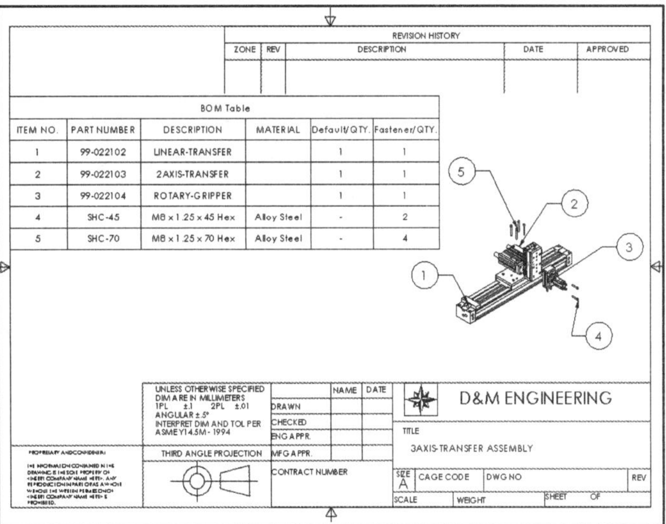

BOM Table

ITEM NO.	PART NUMBER	DESCRIPTION	MATERIAL	Default/QTY.	Fastener/QTY.
1	99-022102	LINEAR-TRANSFER		1	1
2	99-022103	2AXIS-TRANSFER		1	1
3	99-022104	ROTARY-GRIPPER		1	1
4	SHC-45	M8 x 1.25 x 45 Hex	Alloy Steel	-	2
5	SHC-70	M8 x 1.25 x 70 Hex	Alloy Steel	-	4

Sheet3: Contains a Top view off of the Sheet and a Section view of the 3AXIS-TRANSFER assembly.

Modify the Section view properties to display the 3AXIS-TRANSFER assembly components with Custom Properties.

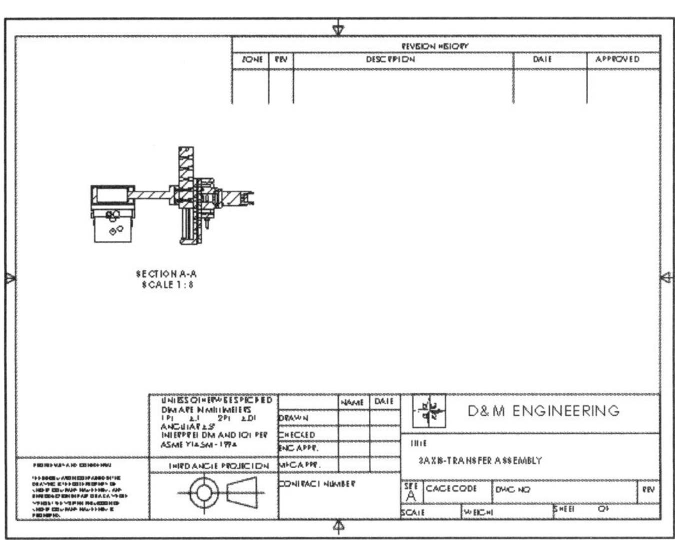

3AXIS-TRANSFER Assembly

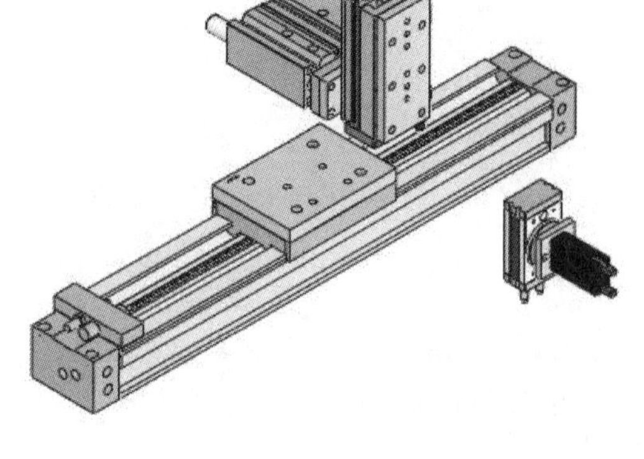

At this time, the 3AXIS-TRANSFER assembly consists of three sub-assemblies. The three sub-assemblies are:

1. *LINEAR-TRANSFER assembly*

2. *2AXIS-TRANSFER assembly*

3. *ROTARY-GRIPPER assembly*

Each sub-assembly contains multiple configurations. Set each sub-assembly to its Default configuration.

Remember, If you did not complete all of the assemblies in the previous chapter, the completed assemblies: *LINERAR-TRANSFER*, *2AXIS-TRANSFER*, and the *ROTARY-GRIPPER* are located in the DeliveryStation-Project7folder in the CD of the book. Work from this folder to create the 3AXIS-TRANSFER assembly and drawing. Note: ***Set all models to their Default configurations.***

Insert and assemble the *LINEAR-TRANSFER* assembly to the *3AXIS-TRANSFER* assembly. Mate the Front, Top and Right Planes to orient the *LINEAR-TRANSFER* assembly.

Insert and assemble the *2AXIS-TRANSFER* assembly. Insert and assemble the *ROTARY-GRIPPER* assembly.

The assemblies utilized in this project contain numerous sub-assemblies. To avoid problems with memory and referenced document locations, close any existing SolidWorks session you have open and start a new one.

An assembly contains absolute references to its components. An absolute reference is the complete path name. Example: E:\ASSEMBLY-SW-FILES-2008\PROJECT7-2008\DeliveryStation-Project7\PLATE-A.sldprt. The individual component does not have references back to the assembly. When an assembly document opens, the referenced documents of the assembly load into memory. SolidWorks searches for referenced documents in the following order:

- SolidWorks documents loaded into Random Access Memory (RAM).
- Paths specified in the System Options, File Locations, Folders list.
- Last accessed path you specified to open the document.

- Last accessed path SolidWorks utilized to open the document.
- The path referenced by the parent document.
- SolidWorks prompts you to browse and locate the document.

Review additional information on search order in On-line help\Search\File Reference Locations.

Activity: Copy and Open the Project7 models

Copy the Project7-2008 folder .

1) Copy the **Project7-2008 folder** from the CD in the book to the ASSEMBLY-SW-FILES-2008 folder.

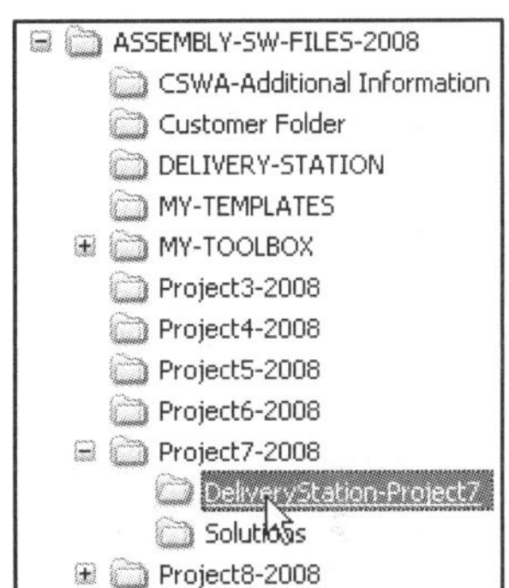

Open the LINEAR-TRANSFER assembly.

2) Double-click **ASSEMBLY-SW-FILES-2008\Project7-2008\DeliveryStation-Project7\LINEAR-TRANSFER** assembly. The LINEAR-TRANSFER assembly is displayed.

Review the LINEAR-TRANSFER assembly configurations.

3) Click the **ConfigurationManager** icon.

4) Double-click each **configuration**. View the results.

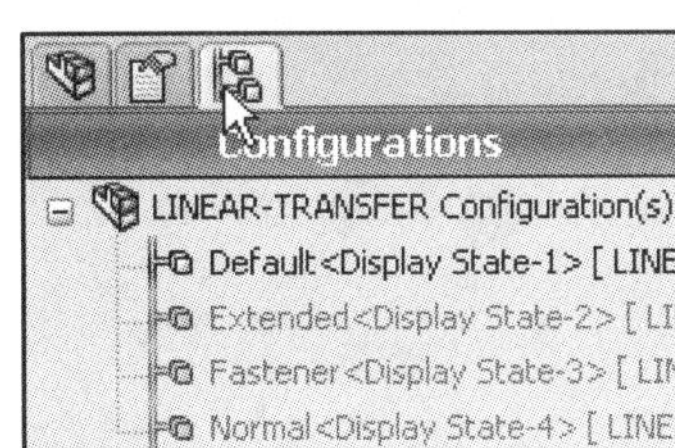

Return to the Default configuration.

5) Double-click the **Default** configuration.

Return to the FeatureManager.

6) Click the **FeatureManager** icon.

Open the 2AXIS-TRANSFER assembly.

7) Double-click **ASSEMBLY-SW-FILES-2008\Project7-2008\DeliveryStation-Project7\2AXIS-TRANSFER** assembly.

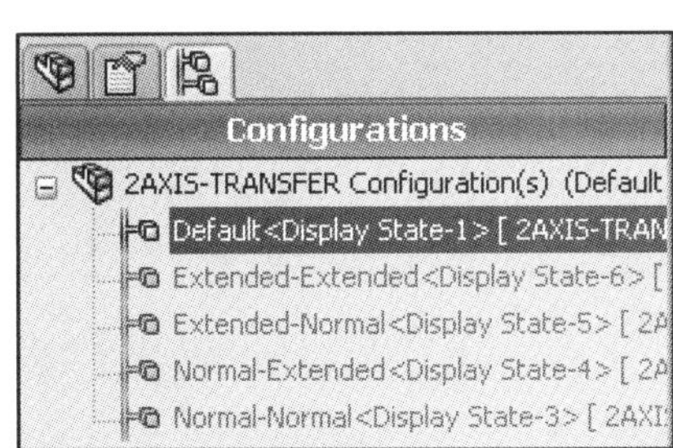

Review the configurations.

8) Click the **ConfigurationManager** icon.

9) Double-click each **configuration**. View the results.

Return to the Default configuration.

10) Double-click the **Default** configuration.

Return to the FeatureManager.

11) Click the **FeatureManager** icon.

Open the ROTARY-GRIPPER.

12) Double-click **ASSEMBLY-SW-FILES-2008\Project7-2008\DeliveryStation-Project7\ROTARY-GRIPPER** assembly.

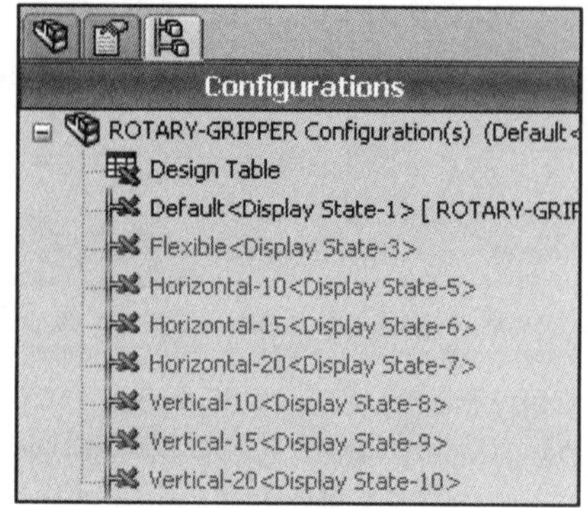

Review the configurations.

13) Click the **ConfigurationManager** icon.

14) Double-click each **configuration** as displayed.

Return to the Default configuration.

15) Double-click the **Default** configuration.

Return to the FeatureManager.

16) Click the **FeatureManager** icon.

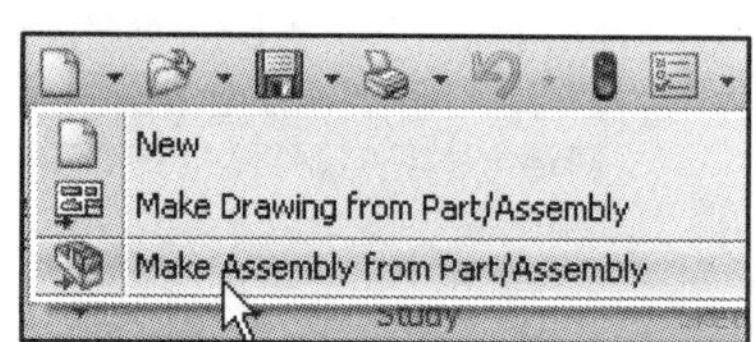

Create a new assembly from the LINEAR-TRANSFER assembly.

17) Click **Window**, **Tile Horizontally** from the Menu bar menu.

18) Click inside the **LINEAR-TRANSFER** Graphics window.

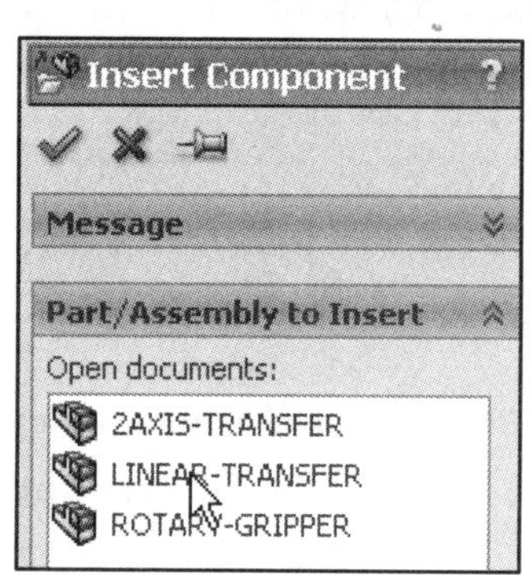

19) Click **Make Assembly From Part/Assembly** from the Menu bar toolbar.

20) Click the **MY-TEMPLATES** tab.

21) Double-click **ASM-MM-ANSI**. The Begin Assembly PropertyManager is displayed.

22) Click **LINEAR-TRANSFER** in the Open documents box.

23) Click **OK** from the Begin Assembly PropertyManager.

Save the 3AXIS-TRANSFER assembly.

24) Click **Save**.

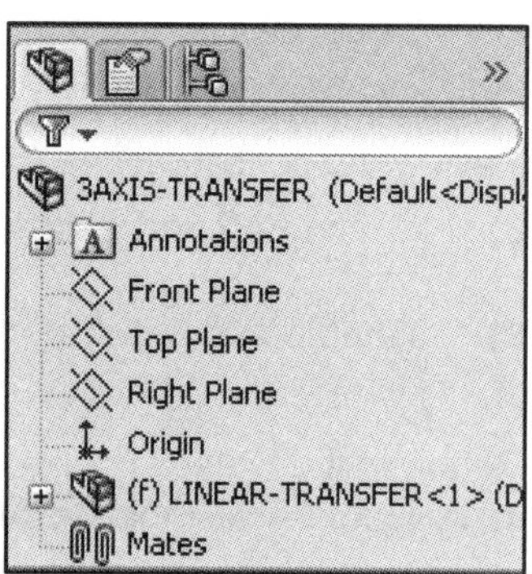

25) Select **DeliveryStation-Project7** for Save in folder.

26) Enter **3AXIS-TRANSFER** for File name.

27) Click **Save**. View the FeatureManager.

Float the LINEAR-TRANSFER component.

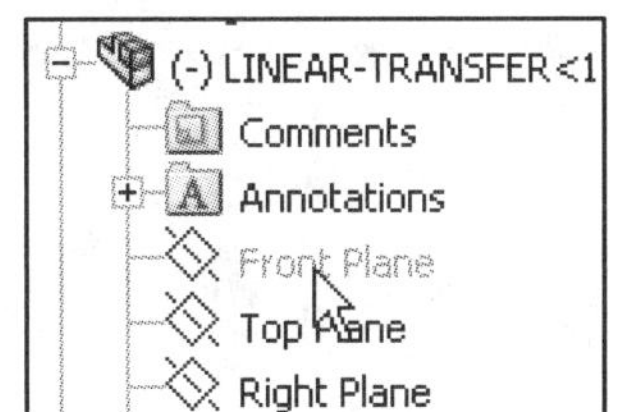

28) Right-click **LINEAR-TRANSFER** from the FeatureManager.

29) Click **Float**.

If needed, hide the Origins.

30) Click **View**, uncheck **Origins** from the Menu bar menu.

Mate the 3AXIS-TRANSFER component. Insert a Coincident Mate.

31) Right-click the 3AXIS-TRANSFER **Front Plane**.

32) Click the **Mate** tool from the Context toolbar.

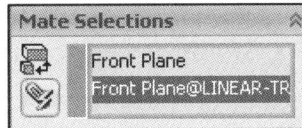

33) Click the **LINEAR-TRANSFER Front Plane** from the fly-out FeatureManger. Coincident is selected by default.

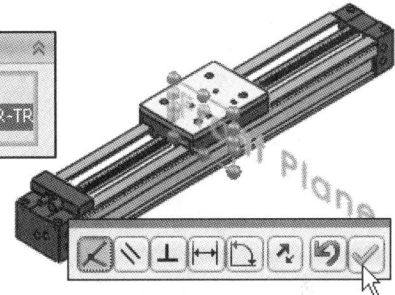

34) Click the **Green Check mark**.

Insert a second Coincident Mate.

35) Click the **3AXIS-TRANSFER Right Plane**.

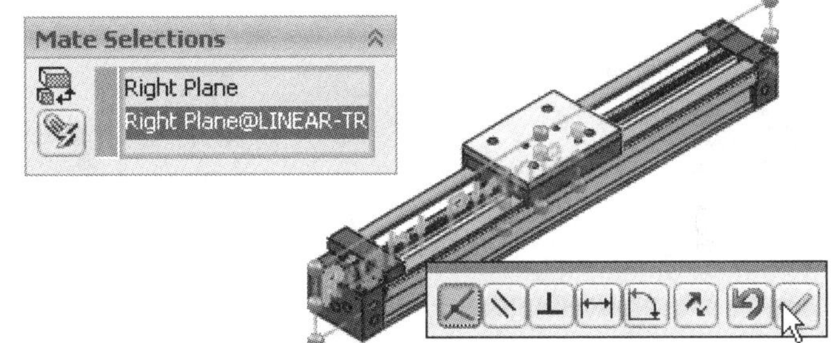

36) Click the **LINEAR-TRANSFER Right Plane** from the fly-out FeatureManager. Coincident is selected by default.

37) Click the **Green Check mark**.

Insert a thrid Coincident Mate.

38) Click the **3AXIS-TRANSFER Top Plane**.

39) Click the **LINEAR-TRANSFER bottom left face** as illustrated. Coincident is selected by default.

40) Click the **Green Check mark**.

41) Click **OK** from the Mate PropertyManager.

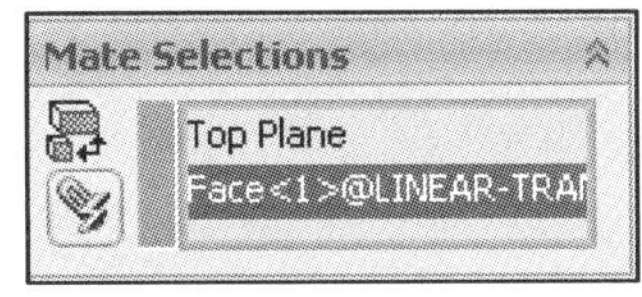

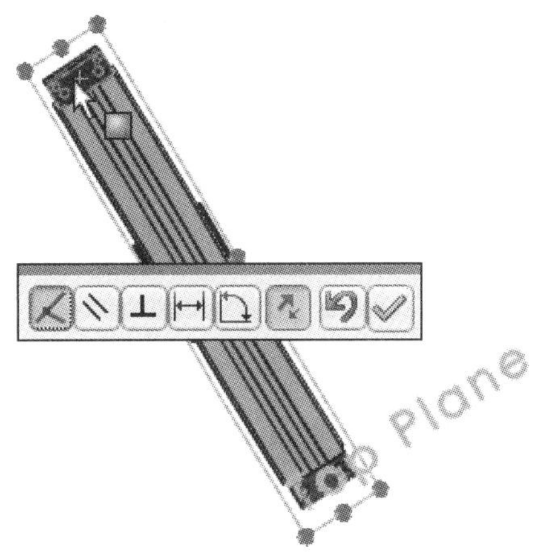

Display the open documents.

42) Click **Isometric** view from the Heads-up View toolbar.

43) Click **Save**.

44) Click **Windows**, **Tile Horizontally** from the Menu bar menu.

Insert the 2AXIS-TRANSFER component.

45) Click and drag the **2AXIS-TRANSFER** icon from the top of the FeatureManager to the right of the LINEAR-TRANSFER component as illustrated. _Do not select the Origin_.

Insert the ROTARY-GRIPPER component.

46) Click and drag the **ROTARY-GRIPPER** icon from the top of the FeatureManager to the right of the the 3AXIS-TRANSFER assembly. _Do not select the Origin_.

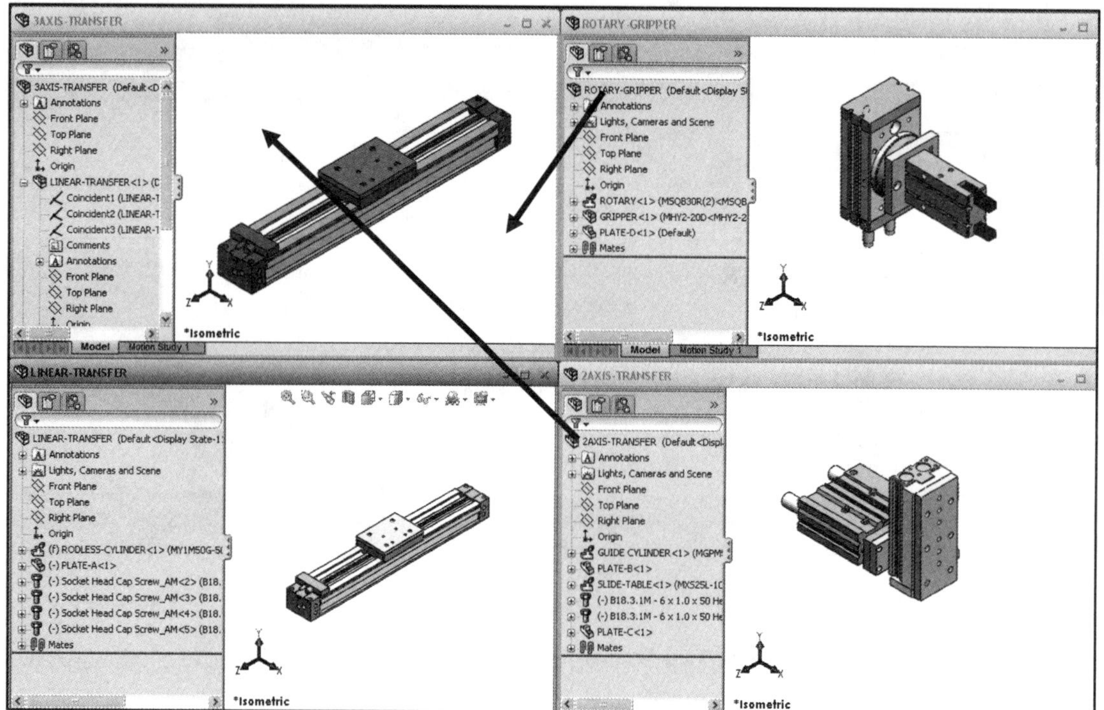

Maximize the assembly.

47) **Maximize** the **3AXIS-TRANSFER** Graphics window.

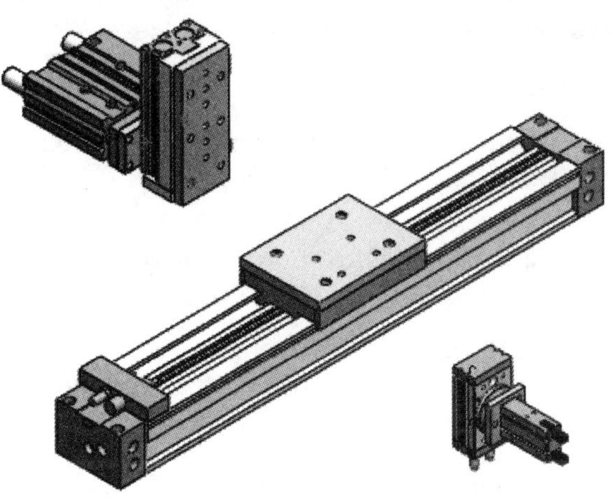

Fit all components in the Graphics window.

48) Press the **f** key.

Save the 3AXIS-TRANSFER assembly.

49) Click **Save**.

Hide the ROTARY-GRIPPER component.

50) Right-click the **ROTARY-GRIPPER** component from the FeatureManager.

51) Click the **Hide components** tool from the Context toolbar.

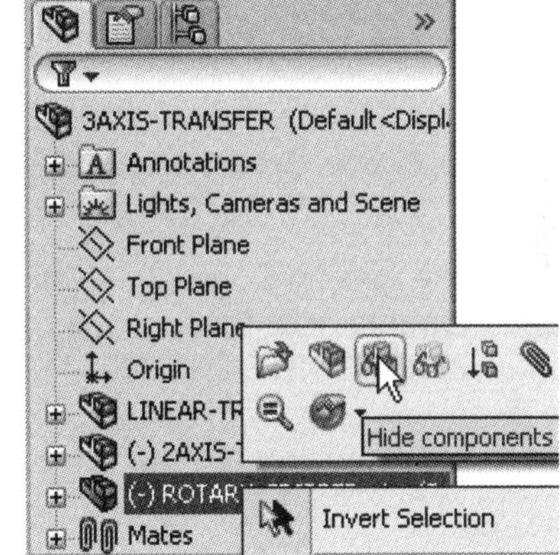

Window-select a component in the Graphics window to save mouse travel time to the FeatureManager. To Window-select a component, click the upper left corner, drag the mouse pointer and click the lower right corner. Right-click a position in the Graphics window.

Select the Component options such as Move or Hide. Utilize the Ctrl key to select multiple separate areas in the Graphics window.

Move the the 2AXIS-TRANSFER component.

52) Click and drag the **2AXIS-TRANSFER** sub-assembly above the LINEAR-TRANSFER sub-assembly as illustrated.

Prepare for SmartMates. **Zoom in** and **rotate** the model before selecting the SmartMate geometry. For Concentric SmartMates, orient the model to view the inside cylindrical face.

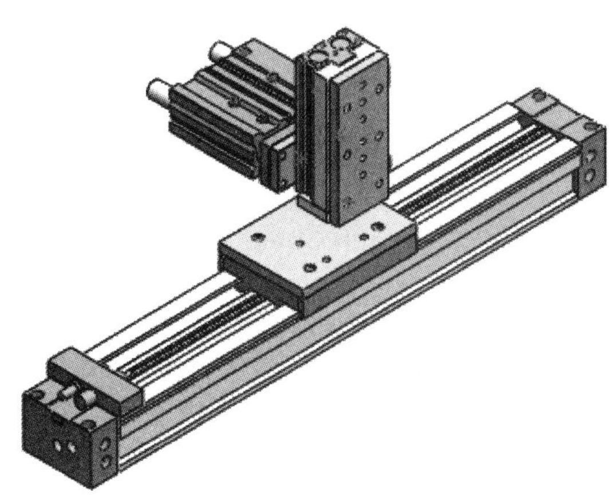

Activity: Insert SmartMates between the 2AXIS-TRANSFER and LINEAR-TRANSFER Assembly

Insert three SmartMates.

53) Right-click the **Move Component** tool from the Graphics window.

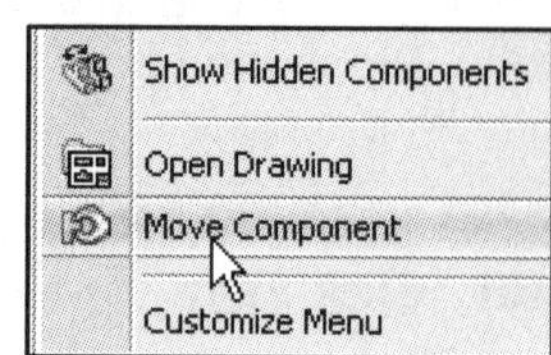

54) Click **SmartMate** from the Move Component PropertyManager.

Insert the first Concentric SmartMate.

55) Double-click the **bottom left Cbore cylindrical face** of the GUIDE-CYLINDER.

56) Click the **bottom left M8 Thru hole cylindrical face** of PLATE-A. Do not select the Cbore face of the PLATE-A part.

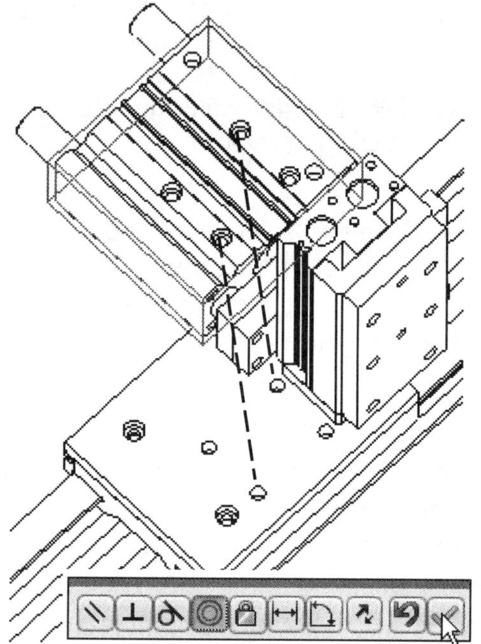

57) Click the **Green Check mark**.

Insert the second Concentric SmartMate.

58) Double-click the **top left Cbore cylindrical face** of the GUIDE-CYLINDER.

59) Click the **top left M8 Thru hole cylindrical face** of the PLATE-A part.

60) Click the **Green Check mark**.

Insert a Coincident SmartMate.

61) Double-click the **bottom face** of the GUIDE-CYLINDER.

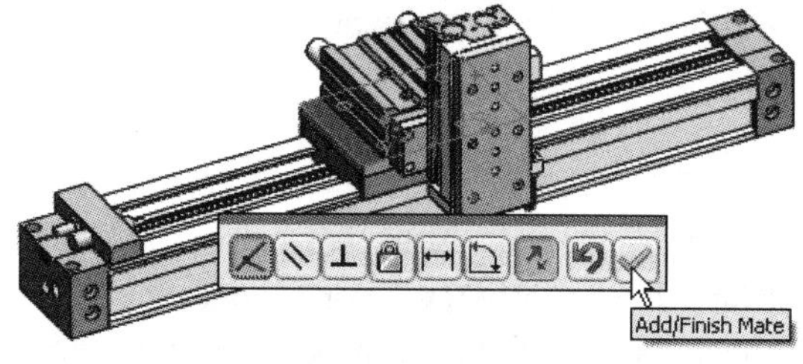

62) Click the **top face** of PLATE-A. The 2AXIS-TRANSFER component is fully defined.

63) Click the **Green Check mark**.

64) Click **OK** from the SmartMate PropertyManager. View the created Mates.

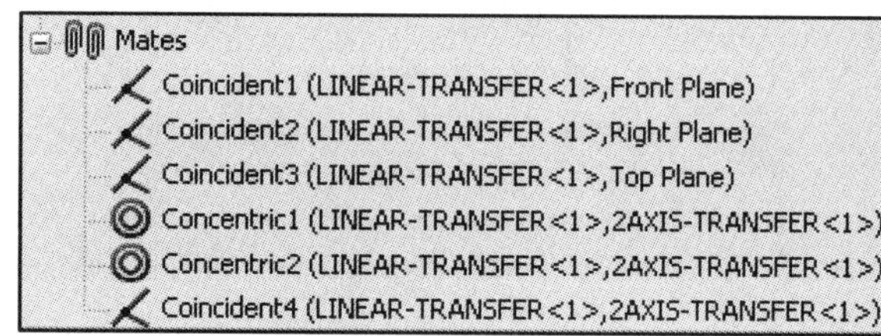

Save the 3AXIS-TRANSFER assembly.

65) Click **Isometric** view.

66) Click **Save**.

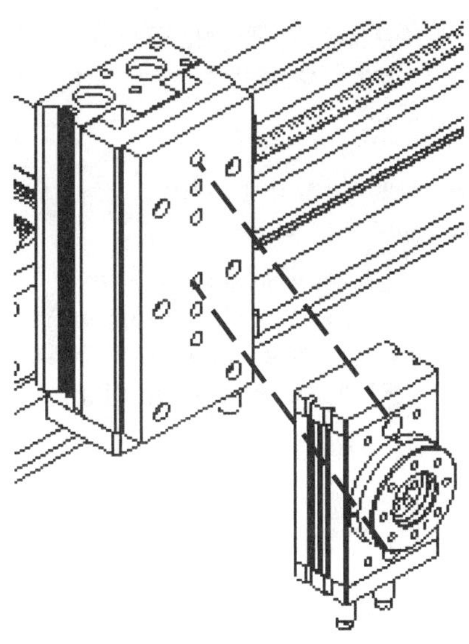
GRIPPER assembly hidden for clarity

Display the ROTARY-GRIPPER assembly.

67) Right-click **ROTARY-GRIPPER** from the FeatureManager.

68) Click the **Show components** tool from theContext toolbar.

Move the ROTARY-GRIPPER component.

69) Click and drag the **ROTARY-GRIPPER** component to the right of the 2AXIS-TRANSFER component.

70) **Zoom in** on PLATE-C and the ROTARY assembly.

Insert three SmartMates.

71) Click the **Move Component** tool from the Assembly toolbar.

72) Click **SmartMate** from the Move Component PropertyManager.

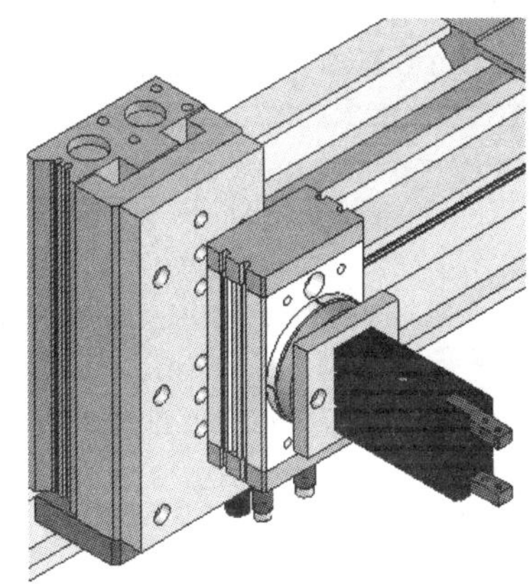

Insert the first Concentric SmartMate.

73) Double-click the **top inside Cbore cylindrical face** of the ROTARY assembly.

74) Click the **top M8.6 Thru Hole cylindrical face** of the PLATE-C part.

75) Click the **Green Check mark** .

Insert the second Concentric SmartMate.

76) Double-click the **bottom inside Cbore cylindrical face** of the ROTARY assembly.

77) Click the **fourth M8.6Thru Hole cylindrical face** of the PLATE-C part.

78) Click the **Green Check mark** .

Insert a Coincident SmartMate.

79) Double-click the **back face** of the ROTARY assembly. Click the **top face** of the PLATE-C part.

80) Click the **Green Check mark** .

81) Click **OK** from the SmartMate PropertyManager. The ROTARY-GRIPPER component is fully defined.

Save the 3AXIS-TRANSFER assembly.

82) Click **Isometric** view from the Heads-up View toolbar

83) Click **Save**.

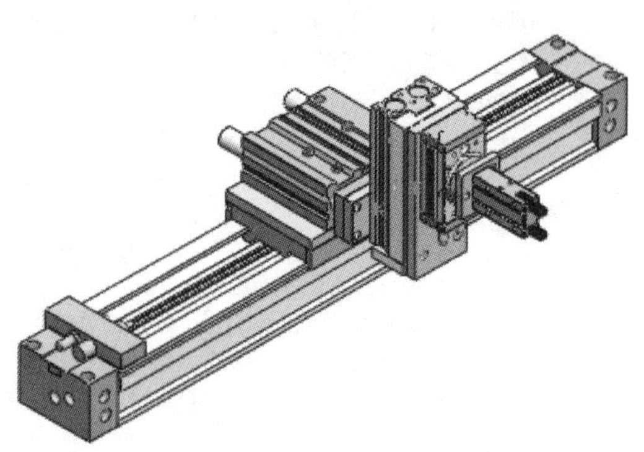

View the FeatureManager.

84) **Expand** the Mates folder. View the created mates. You have completed the 3AXIS-TRNASFER configuration.

3AXIS-TRANSFER Configurations

Apply the Configure Component tool to create multiple configurations of the 3AXIS-TRANSFER assembly

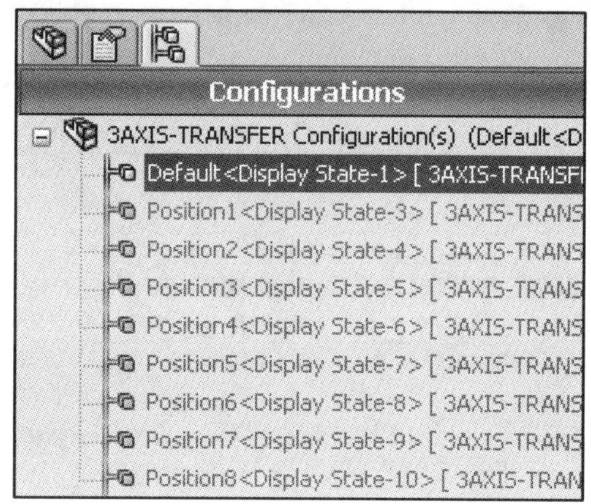

In previous Projects, you applied the Configure Component, Configure dimension, Add Configuration, and Design Table tools to create configurations.

Apply the Configure Component tool in the next step to create eight configurations of the 3AXIS-TRANSFER assembly: *Position1, Position2, Position3, Position4, Position5, Position6, Position7, Position8.*

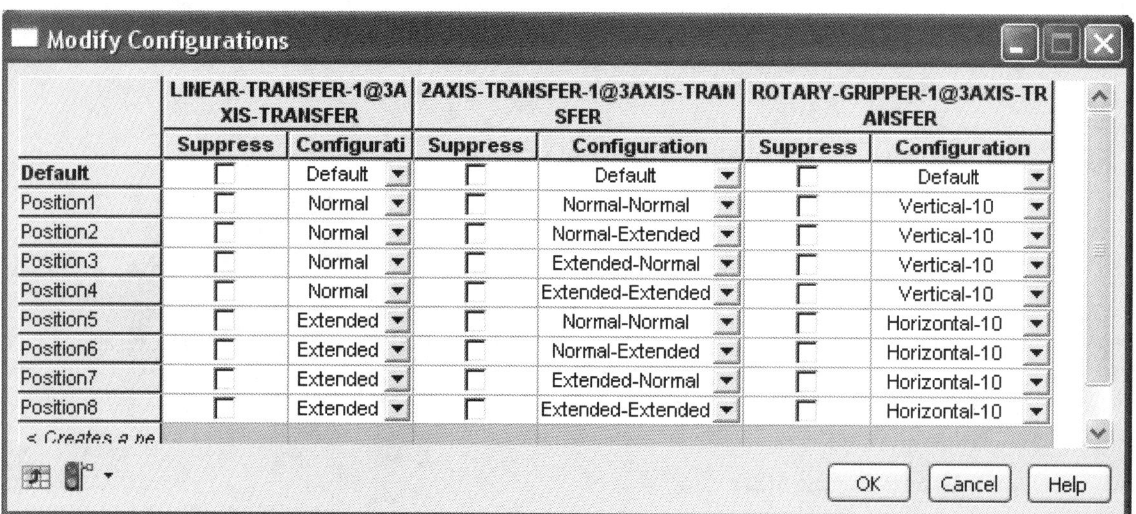

Modify Configurations

	LINEAR-TRANSFER-1@3AXIS-TRANSFER		2AXIS-TRANSFER-1@3AXIS-TRANSFER		ROTARY-GRIPPER-1@3AXIS-TRANSFER	
	Suppress	Configurati	Suppress	Configuration	Suppress	Configuration
Default	☐	Default	☐	Default	☐	Default
Position1	☐	Normal	☐	Normal-Normal	☐	Vertical-10
Position2	☐	Normal	☐	Normal-Extended	☐	Vertical-10
Position3	☐	Normal	☐	Extended-Normal	☐	Vertical-10
Position4	☐	Normal	☐	Extended-Extended	☐	Vertical-10
Position5	☐	Extended	☐	Normal-Normal	☐	Horizontal-10
Position6	☐	Extended	☐	Normal-Extended	☐	Horizontal-10
Position7	☐	Extended	☐	Extended-Normal	☐	Horizontal-10
Position8	☐	Extended	☐	Extended-Extended	☐	Horizontal-10
< Creates a ne						

OK Cancel Help

Activity: Create the 3AXIS-TRANSFER Assembly Configurations

Create the 3AXIS-TRANSFER Assembly Configurations.

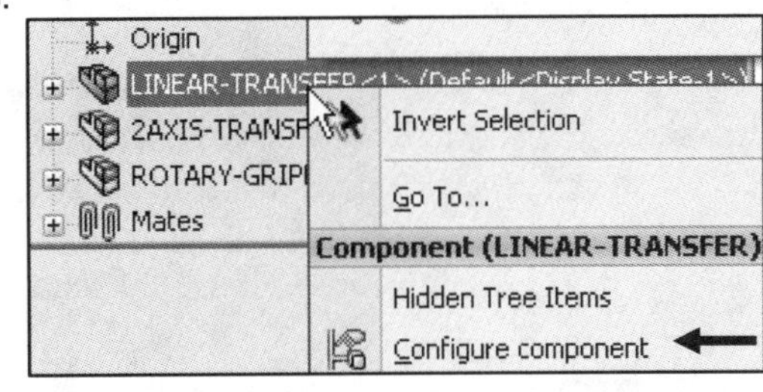

85) Right-click **LINEAR-TRANSFER** from the FeatureManager.

86) Click **Configure component.** The Modify Configurations dialog box is displayed. Remember, the Modify Configurations dialog box facilitates creating and modifying configurations for commonly configured parameters in parts and assemblies. You can add, delete, and rename configurations, and change which configuration is active.

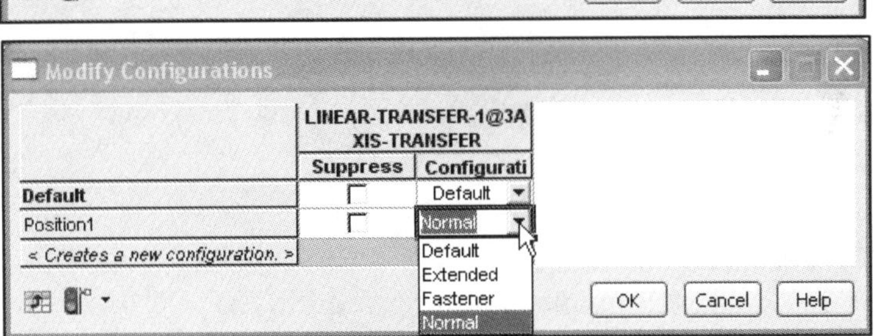

87) Click inside the **Creates a new configuration** box.

88) Enter the first configuration. Enter **Position1**.

89) Click the **Tab** key.

90) Select **Normal** from the drop-down configuration menu for the LINEAR-TRANSFER assembly.

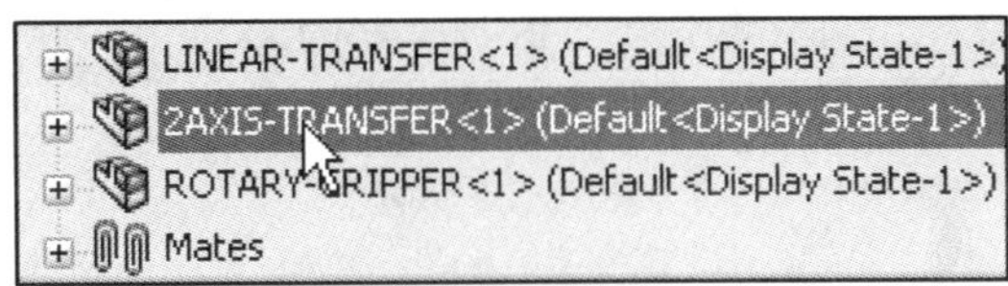

91) Double-click **2AXIS-TRANSFER** in the FeatureManager.

92) Select **Normal-Normal** for the 2AXIS-TRANSFER configuration.

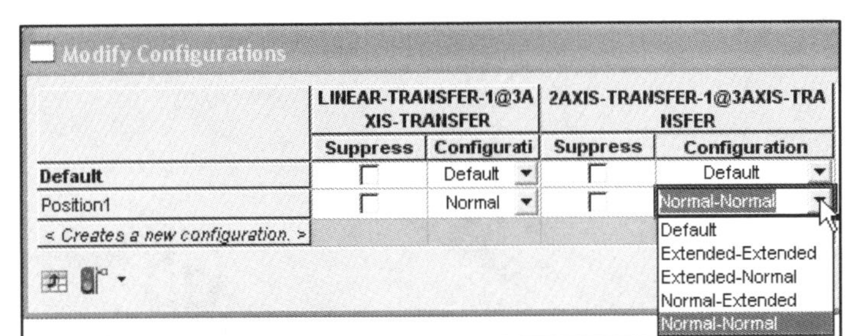

93) Double-click **ROTARY-GRIPPER** from the FeatureManager.

94) Select **Vertical-10** for the ROTARY-GRIPPER configuration. Note: Apply the 10mm PLATE in all ROTARY-GRIPPER configurations.

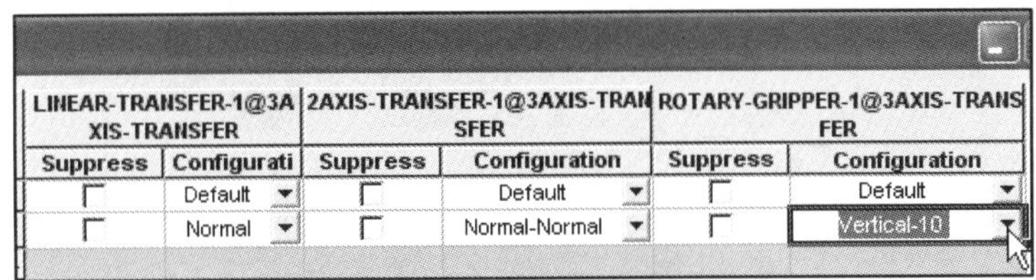

95) **Repeat** this process to create the following Modify Configurations dialog box for the 8 new configurations.

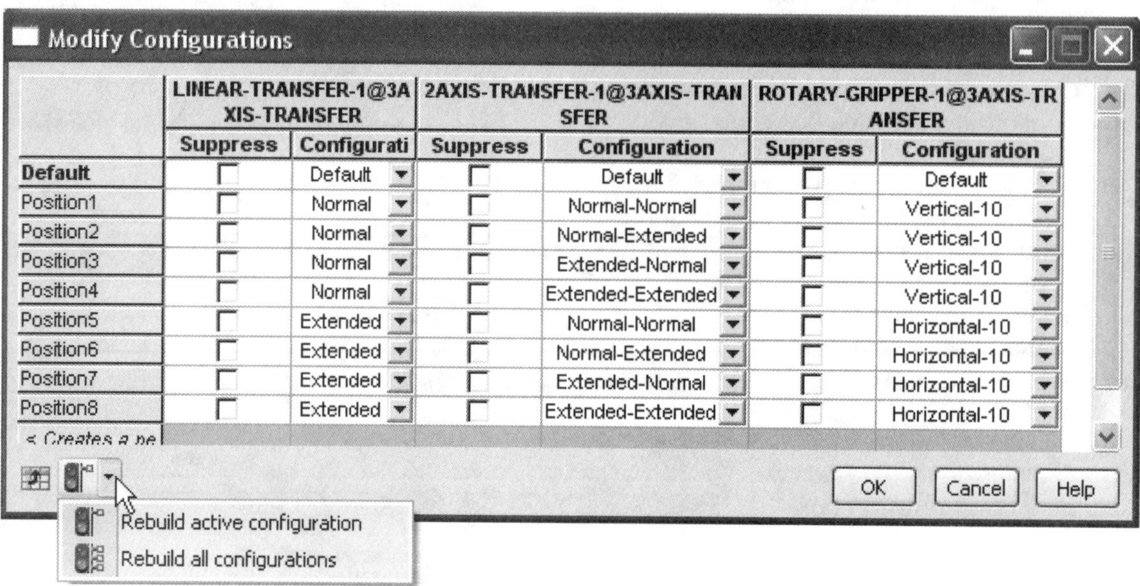

	LINEAR-TRANSFER-1@3AXIS-TRANSFER		2AXIS-TRANSFER-1@3AXIS-TRANSFER		ROTARY-GRIPPER-1@3AXIS-TRANSFER	
	Suppress	Configurati	Suppress	Configuration	Suppress	Configuration
Default	☐	Default	☐	Default	☐	Default
Position1	☐	Normal	☐	Normal-Normal	☐	Vertical-10
Position2	☐	Normal	☐	Normal-Extended	☐	Vertical-10
Position3	☐	Normal	☐	Extended-Normal	☐	Vertical-10
Position4	☐	Normal	☐	Extended-Extended	☐	Vertical-10
Position5	☐	Extended	☐	Normal-Normal	☐	Horizontal-10
Position6	☐	Extended	☐	Normal-Extended	☐	Horizontal-10
Position7	☐	Extended	☐	Extended-Normal	☐	Horizontal-10
Position8	☐	Extended	☐	Extended-Extended	☐	Horizontal-10
< Creates a ne						

Rebuild all configurations.

96) Click the **Rebuild all configurations** tool.

97) Click **OK** from the Modify Configurations dialog box.

View the created configurations.

98) Click the **ConfigurationManager** tab.

99) **Double-click** each configuration. View the results

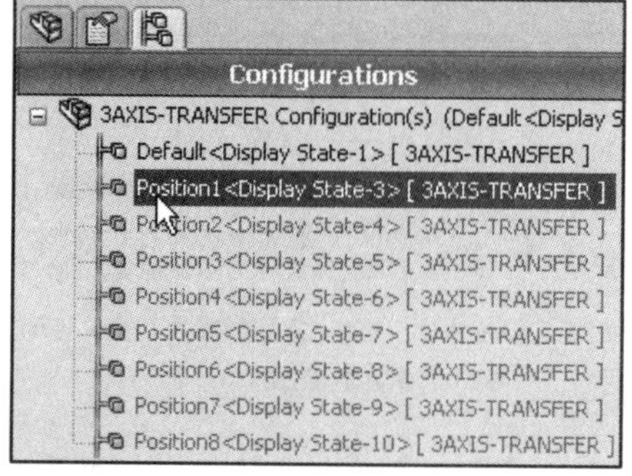

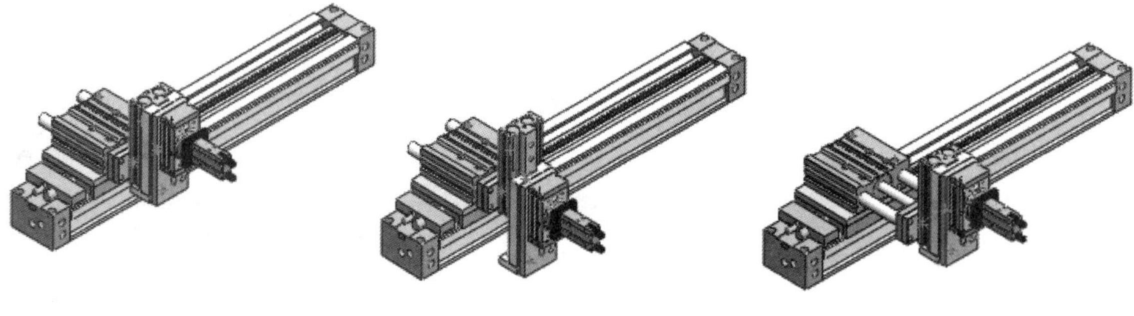

Position1 Position2 Position3

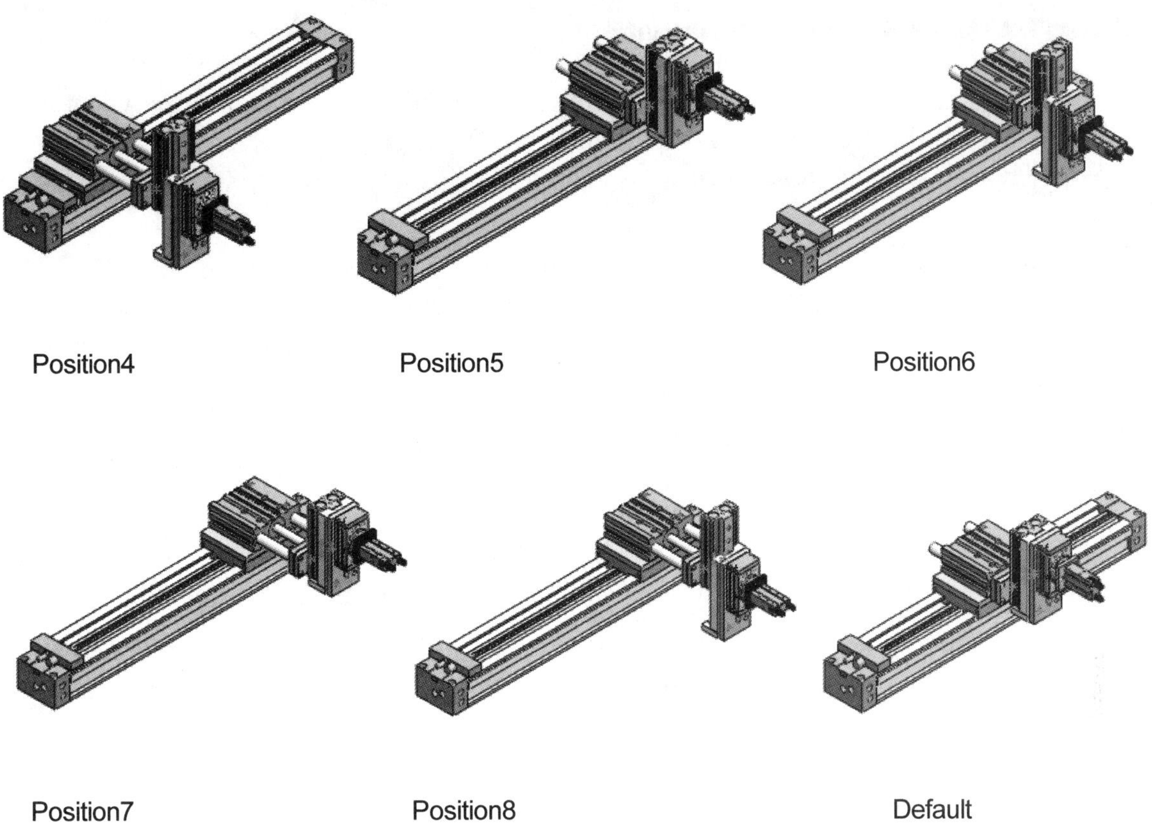

Return to the Default configuation.

100) Double-click the **Default** configuration.

Return to the FeatureManager.

101) Click the **FeatureManager** tab.

Save the 3AXIS-TRANSFER assembly.

102) Click **Save**.

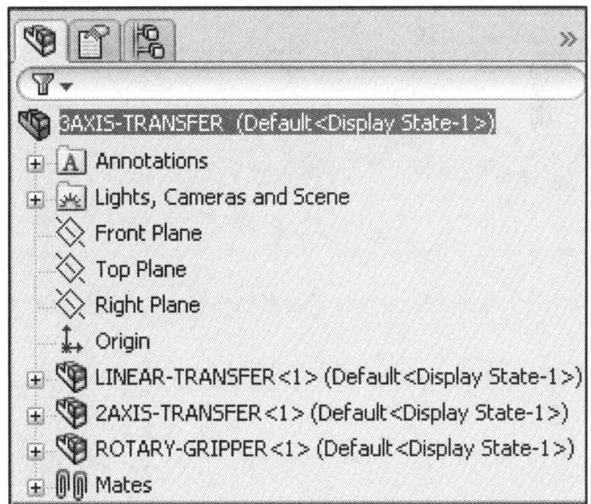

3AXIS-TRANSFER Assembly Drawing

Assembly drawings illustrate how to assemble components in manufacturing. Assembly drawings contain Section views to display internal details and Exploded Views with a Bill of Materials for item identification.

Utilize assembly drawings as working drawings. When you begin an assembly, in addition begin an assembly drawing. As the assembly develops, the drawing also develops. Assembly drawings determine potential problems between components early in the design process.

Develop the 3AXIS-TRANSFER assembly drawing. The 3AXIS-TRANSFER assembly drawing consists of three Sheets.

- Sheet1: Contains two Front views in different configurations with Driven dimensions of the assembly. Apply the Revision Table tool with Custom Properties.
- Sheet2: Contains an Isometric Exploded View in the Fastener configuration with a Bill of Materials using Custom Properties and Notes. Apply the Balloon tool.
- Sheet3: Contains a Top and Section view with Custom Properties.

Activity: Create the 3AXIS-TRANSFER Drawing: Sheet1

Create a new 3AXIS-TRANSFER drawing.

103) Click **Make Drawing from Part/Assembly** from the Menu bar toolbar.

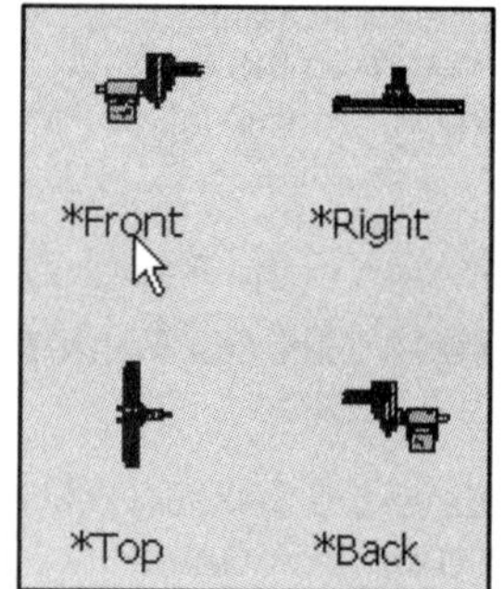

104) Click the **MY-TEMPLATES** tab. Double-click **A-ANSI-MM**. The Model View PropertyManager is displayed. Insert the the Front view using the View Palette. The View Palette is located in the Task Pane.

Insert the Front View.

105) Click the **View Palette** icon located in the Task Pane.

106) Click and drag the ***Front** view into the active Sheet.

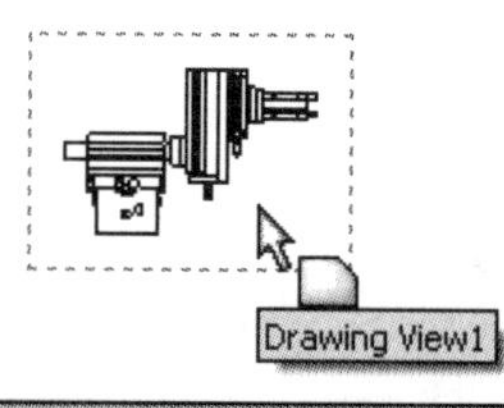

107) Click **OK** from the Projected View PropertyManager. Drawing View1 is created.

108) Click **inside** the view bounday of the Front View as illustrated. The Drawing View1 PropertyManager is displayed.

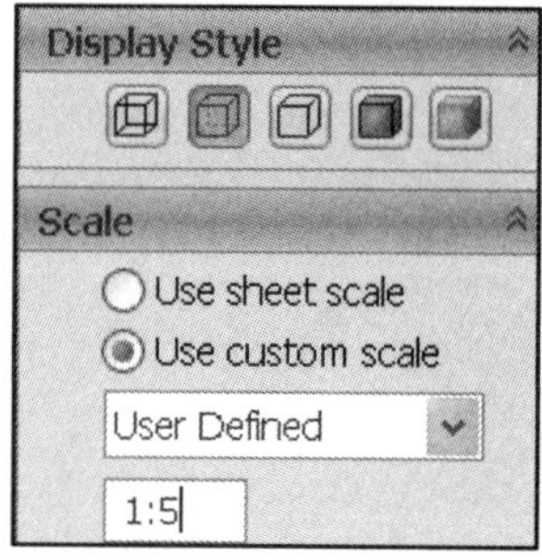

109) Click **Hidden Lines Visible** for Display Style.

110) Click **Use custom scale**. Select **User Defined**.

111) Enter **1:5** for Sheet Scale.

112) Click **OK** ✔ from the Drawing View1 PropertyManager.

Expand the FeatureManager.

113) Expand Drawing View1 from the FeatureManager.

114) Expand 3AXIS-TRANSFER from the FeatureManager. View the sub-assemblies.

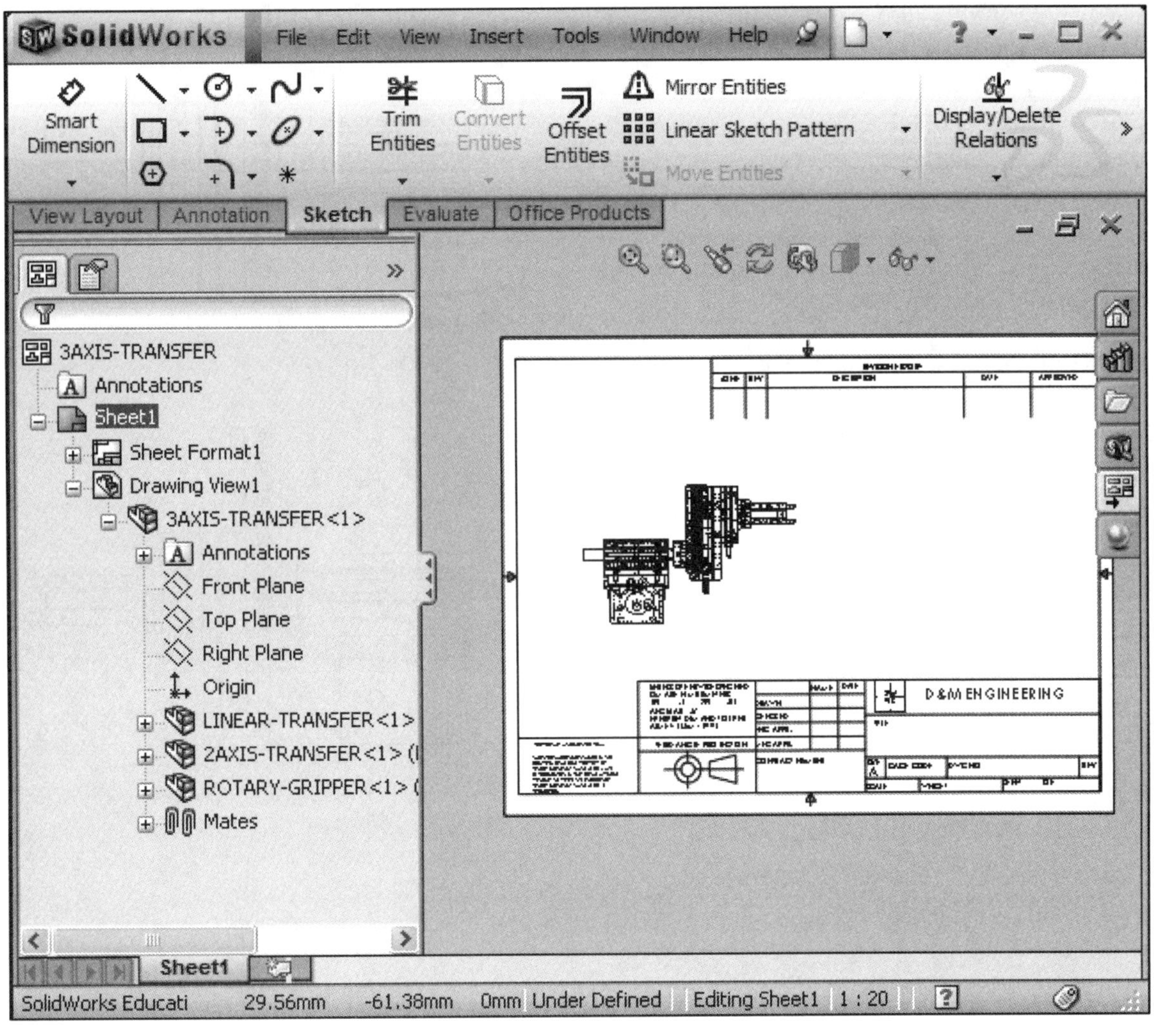

Select the Position2 configuration.

115) Right-click inside the **Front view** boundary.

116) Click **Properties**. Select **Position2** from the Configuration information drop-down menu.

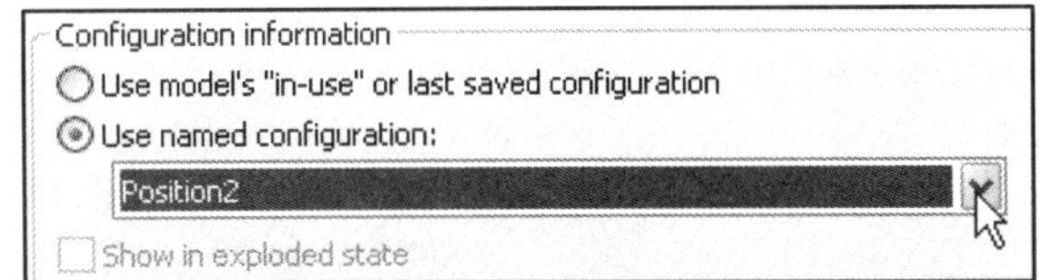

117) Click **OK**.

118) Click **Hidden Lines Removed** for Display Style.

119) Click **OK** from the Drawing View1 PropertyManager.

Utilize sketched centerlines to reference dimensions in drawing views. Sketched geometry in a drawing resides with the current view. A green view boundary indicates the current view.

Select the Drawing view.
120) Click inside the **Front view** boundary.

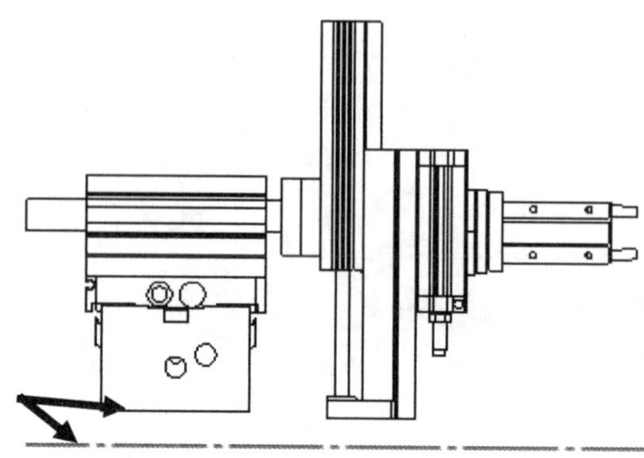

Sketch the first Centerline.

121) Click the **Centerline** tool from the Sketch toolbar.

122) Sketch a **horizontal centerline** below the profile lines as illustrated.

123) Right-click **select** to deselect the sketch tool.

Add a Collinear relation.
124) Click the **bottom horizontal line** of the LINEAR-TRANSFER assembly.

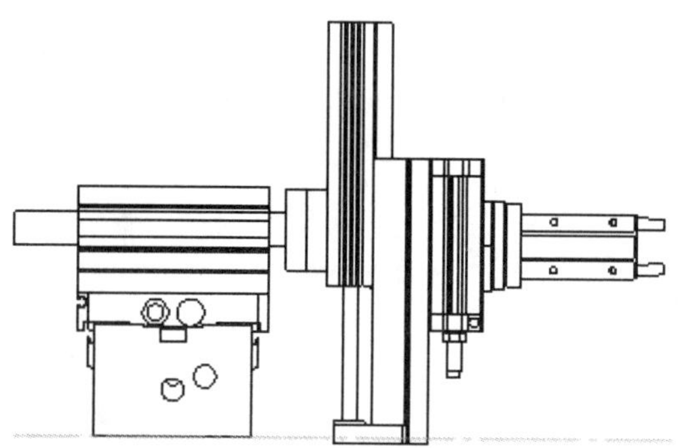

125) Hold the **Ctrl** key down.

126) Click the **horizontal centerline**.

127) Release the **Ctrl** key.

128) Click **Collinear**.

129) Click **OK** from the Properties PropertryManager .

Sketch the second Centerline.

130) Click the **Centerline** tool from the Sketch toolbar.

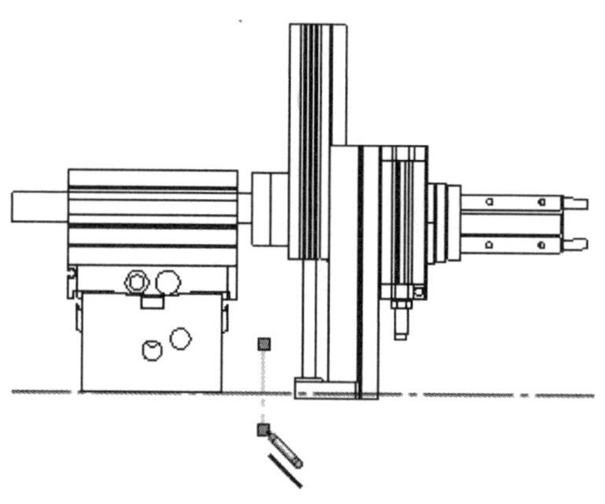

131) Sketch a **vertical centerline** on the right side of the LINEAR-TRANSFER assembly as illustrated.

132) Right-click **Select** to deselect the sketch tool.

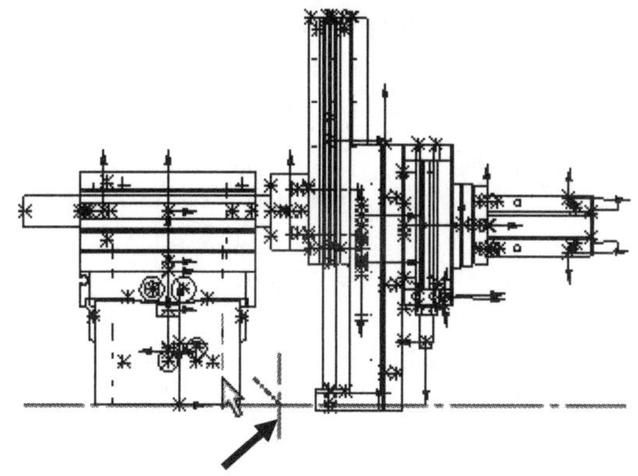

Activate Temporary Axis and Origins.

133) Click **View**, check **Origins**.

134) Click **View**, check **Temporary Axis**.

Add a Collinear relation.

135) Click the **Temporary Axis of the right Mounting Hole** of the LINEAR-TRANSFER assembly.

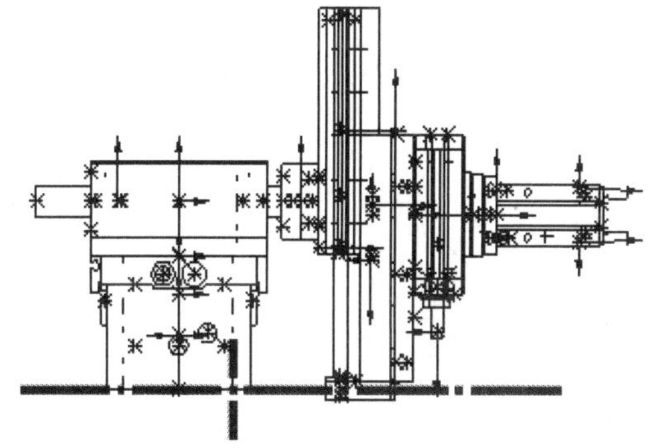

136) Hold the **Ctrl** key down.

137) Click the **vertical centerline**.

138) Release the **Ctrl** key.

139) Click **Collinear**.

140) Click **OK** from the Properties PropertyManager.

Deactivate the Temporary Axis.

141) Click **View**, uncheck **Temporary Axis**.

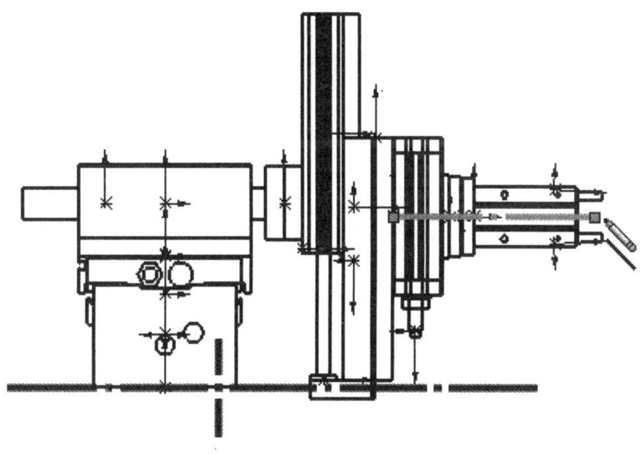

Create the third Centerline.

142) Click the **Centerline** tool from the Sketch toolbar.

143) Sketch a **horizontal centerline** from the Origin of the ROTARY assembly to the right of the GRIPPER FINGERS part as illustrated. Note: The centerline is vertical to the right endpoint of the Gripper.

144) Right-click **Select**.

Add a Vertical relation.

145) Click the **right endpoint** of the centerline.

146) Hold the **Ctrl** key down.

147) Click the **end vertex** of the GRIPPER FINGER part.

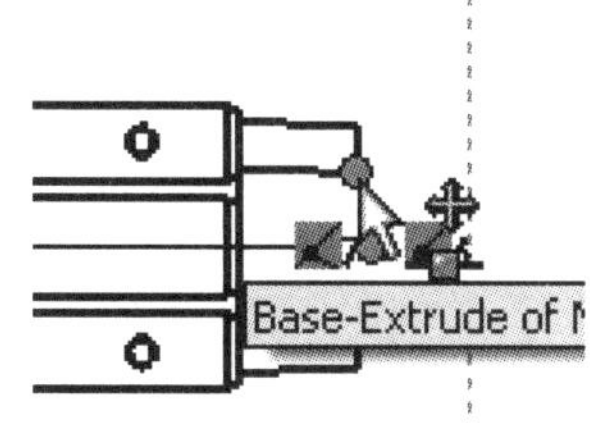

148) Release the **Ctrl** key.

149) Click **Vertical**.

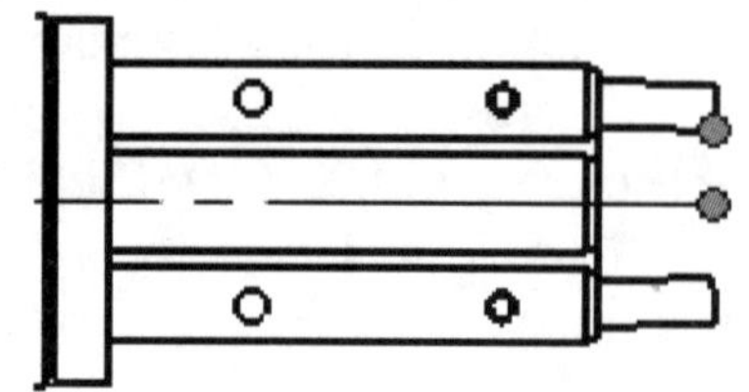

150) Click **OK** from the Properties PropertyManager.

151) Deactivate the Origins.

Three Driven Dimensions reference the three centerlines in the front view.

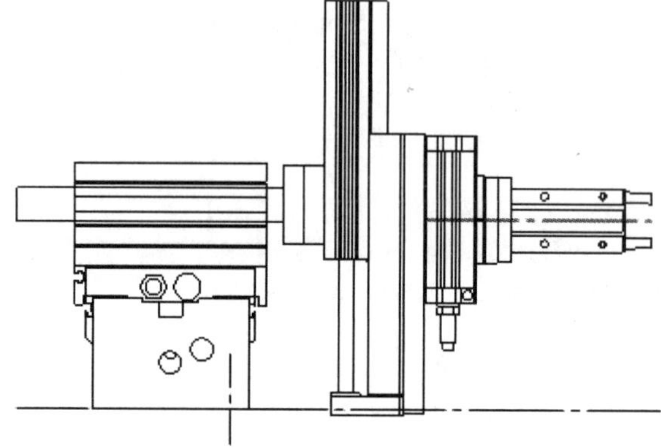

Driven Dimensions are dimensions controlled by other dimensions and conditions of a component. Driven dimensions cannot be modified. Driven Dimensions created in the next steps utilize a sketched centerline and a vertex, origin or edge of a component.

Add Driven Dimensions.

152) Click the **Smart Dimension** tool from the Sketch toolbar.

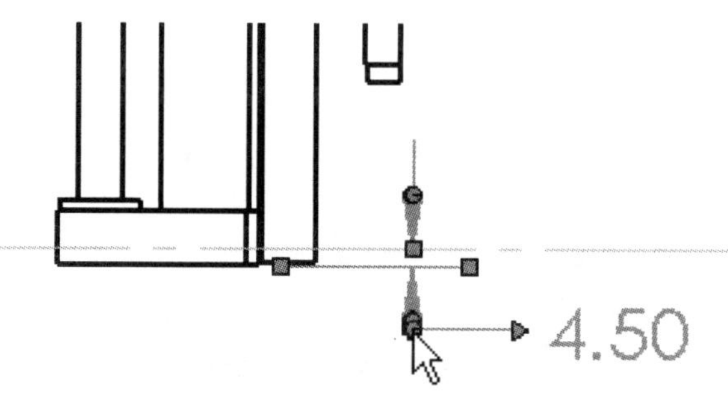

153) Click the **bottom horizontal centerline** and the **bottom edge** of the SLIDE-TABLE assembly.

154) Click a **position** below the horizontal centerline.

155) Check the **Make this dimension diven** box.

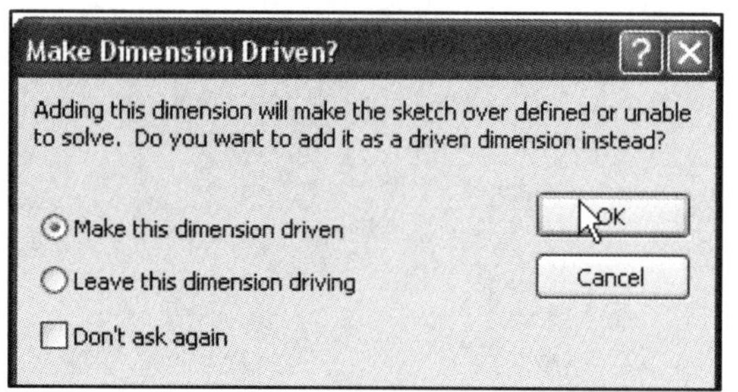

156) Click **OK**. The 4.50 Driven dimension is displayed.

157) Click **OK** from the Dimension PropertyManager.

You encounter a design issue. There is an interference of 4.50mm between the MOUNTING-PLATE part and the SLIDE-TABLE assembly.

Do you raise the RODLESS-CYLINDER component? Answer: No. This option is too expensive. Do you design a new component? Answer: No. This option will take too much time.

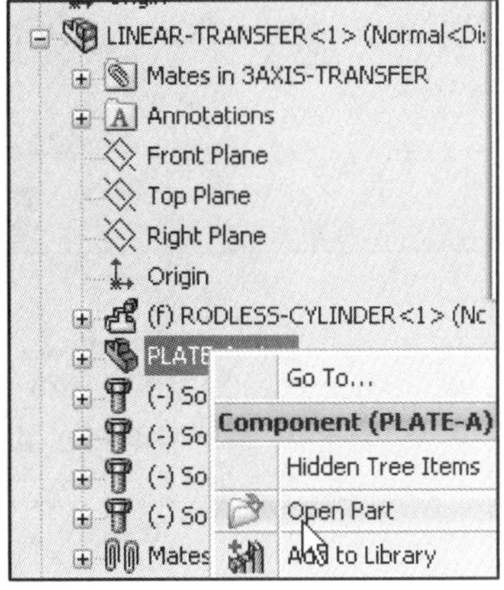

Do you modify the PLATE-A part? Answer: Yes. Increase the thickness of the PLATE-A part to raise the SLIDE-TABLE assembly.

The depth of the PLATE-A part is 15mm. Apply 21mm for the new depth to ensure clearance. Note: The PLATE-A part has not been released to Manufacturing. You do not need to modify the revision number.

Modify the PLATE-A part.

158) Right-click **PLATE-A** from the 3AXIS-TRANSFER\LINEAR-TRANSFER FeatureManager.

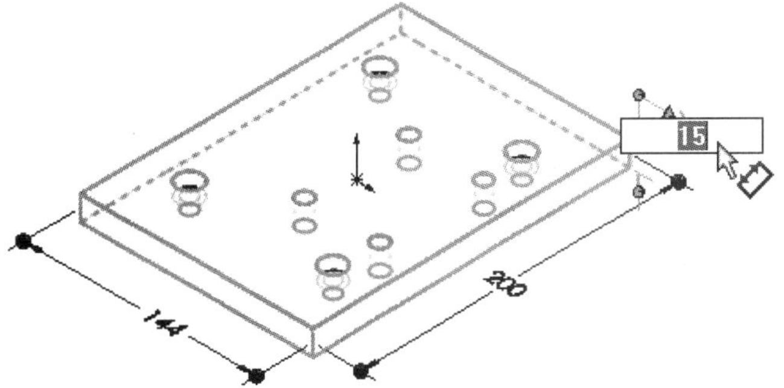

159) Click **Open Part**. The PLATE-A part is displayed in the Graphics window.

160) Double-click **Extrude1** from the FeatureManager.

161) Click **15**.

162) Enter **21** for Depth.

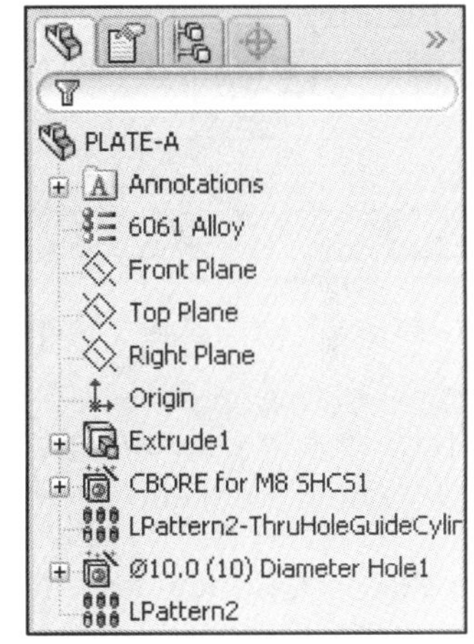

Save the PLATE-A part.

163) Click **Save**.

Close the PLATE-A part.

164) **Return** to the drawing. Note the illustrated Driven dimension.

165) Click **File**, **Close** from the Menu bar menu.

The PLATE-A design changes from 15mm to 21mm affects other components in the assembly.

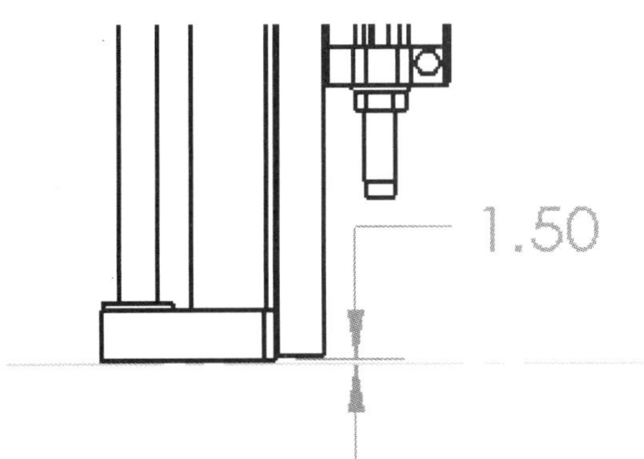

What components are affected? Answer: Review the following Design Change Task List table.

Design Change Task List:	
Task:	**Action:**
Identify the assembly and related components affected by the part.	PLATE-A is a component of the LINEAR-TRANSFER assembly.
Identify other assemblies that utilize the part.	PLATE-A is not used in any other assemblies.
Identify all the configurations that utilize this part. Does the design change affect different configuration or suppressed components?	The Fastener configuration contains the hardware. Increase the fastener length to accommodate the increased PLATE-A thickness.
Review your company's Engineering Change Order (ECO) process. Identify the parts, assemblies and drawings that require a revision change.	PLATE-A has not been released to manufacturing. No revision change is required.

Activity: Search for a Part : SolidWorks Explorer

Determine where the PLATE-A part is used in the LINEAR-TRANSFER assembly.

Open SolidWorks Explorer.

166) Click **Tools**, **SolidWorks Explorer** from the Menu bar menu.

167) Click **Cancel** from the PDMWorks dialog box.

168) Enter **PLATE-A** in the Search box. Press the enter key. SolidWorks provides Document Types and Seach Locations. Click each type and location to determine where PLATE-A is used.

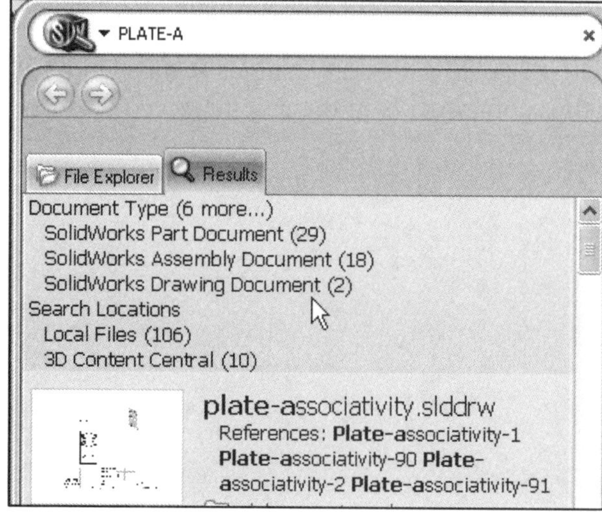

You can either located the LINEAR-TRANSFER assembly where the PLATE-A part is located using SolidWorks Explorer as illustrated, or open the LINEAR-TRANSFER assembly directly for the folder. In this exercise, close SolidWorks Explorer and open the LINEAR-TRANSFER folder directly.

Close the SolidWorks Explorer dialog box and return to the drawing.

169) Click **Close**. The drawing is displayed.

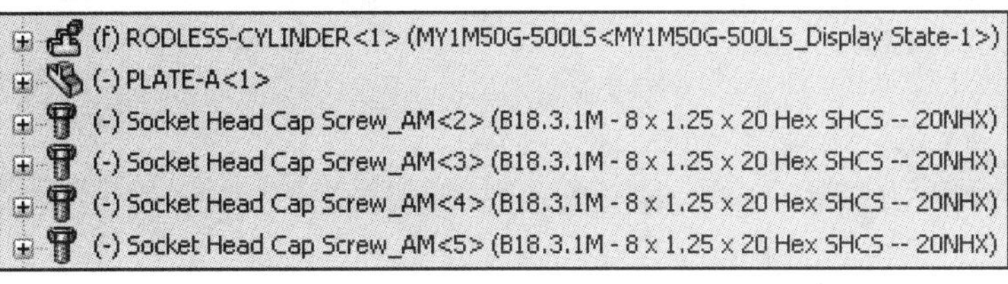

As an exercise at the end of this Project, open the LINEAR-TRANSFER assembly from the 3AXIS-TRANSFER drawing. Double-click the Fastener configuration. Display the Fastener FeatureManager. The configuration contains the four B18.3.1M-8x1.25x20 SHCS in the Unsuppressed state.

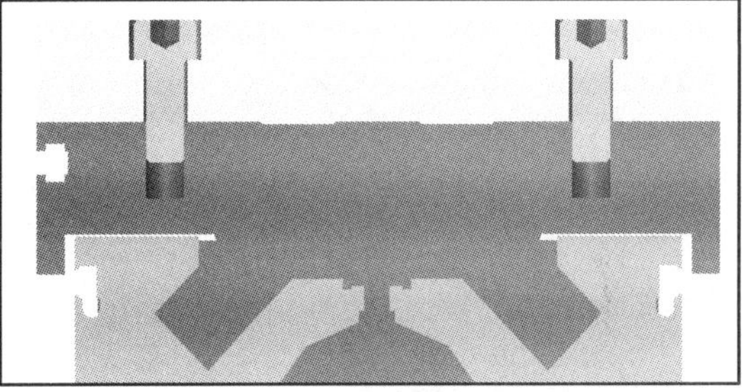

The M8x1.25x20 SHCSs are too short for the 21mm PLATE-A part. Utilize the Replace Component tool located in the FeatureManager. Replace the SHCSs as an exercise. Return to the Default configuration. Close the assembly and return to drawing.

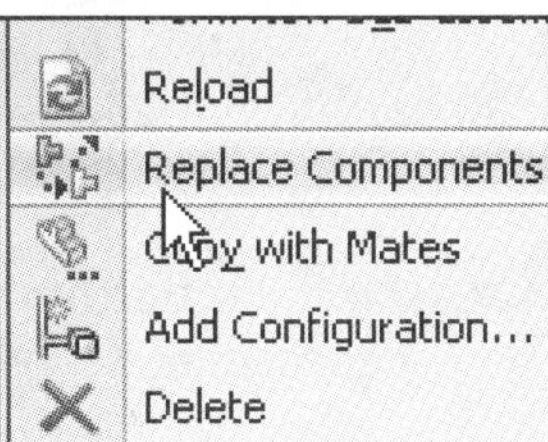

Update the drawing.

170) **Rebuild** the models. The Driven dimension displays 1.50. There is a 1.50mm clearance.

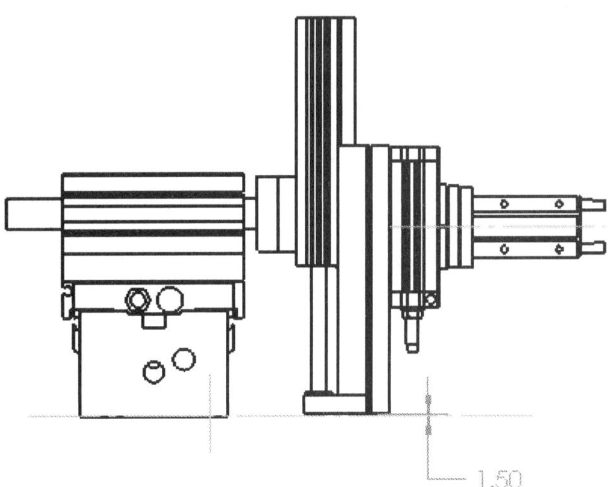

Activate the the Front view.

171) Click inside the **Front view** boundary. The Drawing View1 PropertyManager is displayed.

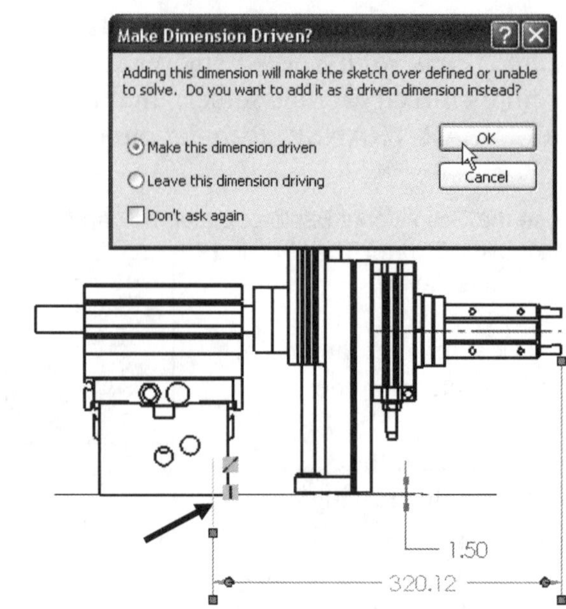

Add Driven Dimensions.

172) Click the **Smart Dimension** tool from the Sketch toolbar.

Add the second horizontal linear dimension.

173) Click the left **vertical centerline**. Click the **bottom right vertex** of the GRIPPER FINGER part.

174) Check the **Make this dimension driven** box.

175) Click **OK**.

176) Drag the **320.12 dimension** text below the 1.50 text.

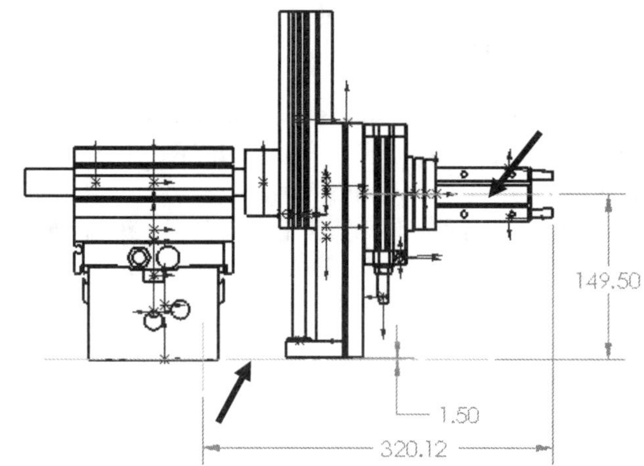

Add the first vertical linear dimension.

177) Click **View**, check **Origins**.

178) Click the **bottom horizontal centerline**.

179) Click the **horizontal centerline** between the GRIPPER fingers as illustrated.

180) Check the **Make this dimension driven** box.

181) Click **OK**. 149.50 is displayed.

182) Click **View**, uncheck **Origins**.

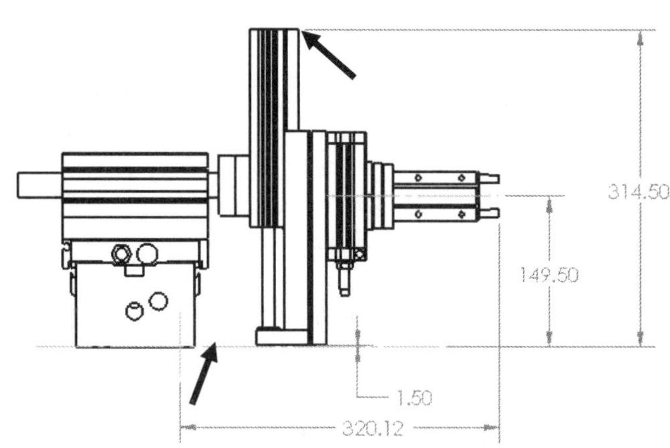

Add the second vertical linear dimension.

183) Click the **bottom horizontal centerline**.

184) Click the **right top vertex** of the SLIDE-TABLE assembly.

185) Check the **Make this dimension driven** box. 314.50 is displayed.

186) Click **OK**. Click **OK** ✔ from the Dimension PropertyManager

Copy the view.

187) Click **Drawing View1** from the FeatureManager.

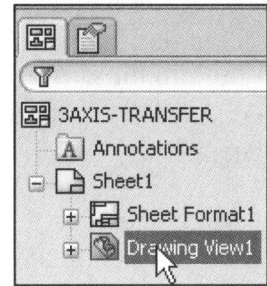

188) Press **Ctrl + C**. Click a **position** in the upper right corner of Sheet1.

189) Press **Ctrl + V**.

3AXIS-TRANSFER
Annotations
Sheet1
Sheet Format1
Drawing View1

190) Right-click inside **Drawing View2**.

191) Click **Properties**.

192) Select **Position4** from the Configuration information box.

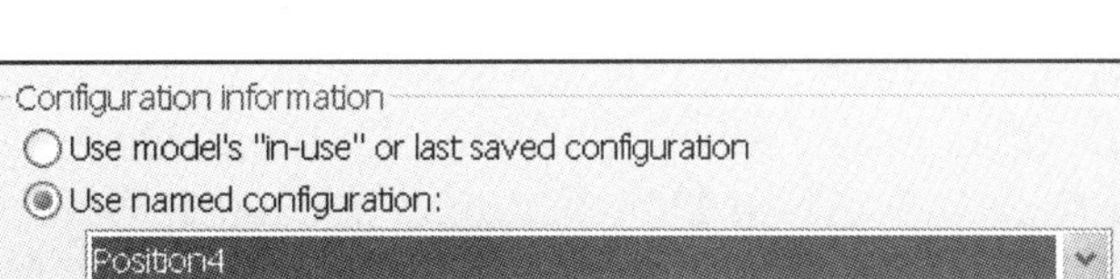

193) Click **OK**. Click **OK** ✔ from the Drawing View2 PropertyManager.

194) Click and drag the **views** to fit Sheet1 as illustrated.

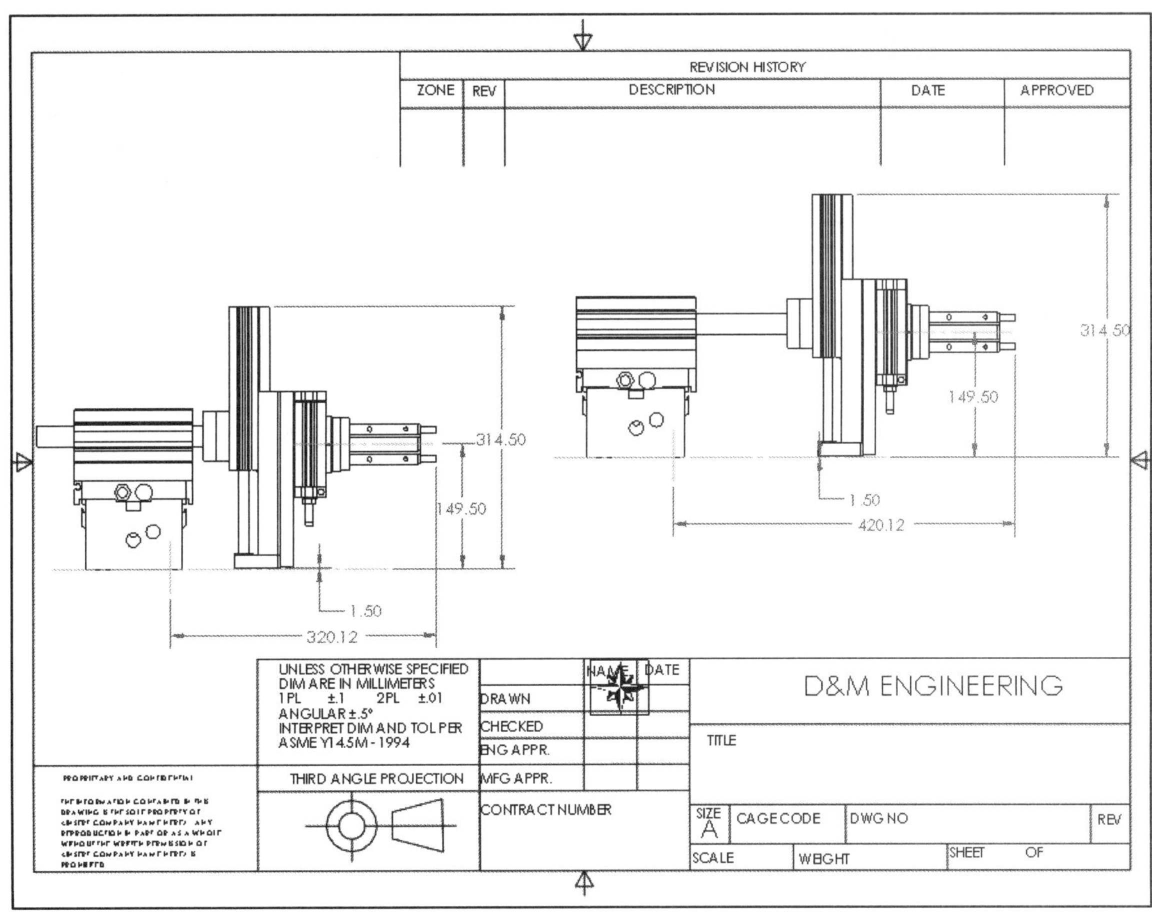

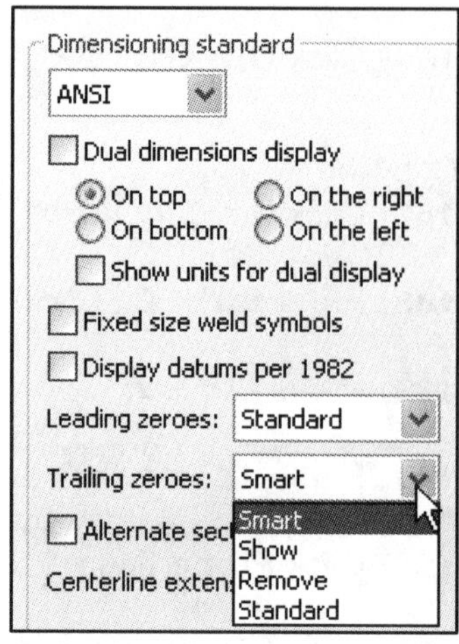

If the dimension values remain unchanged, select Rebuild. If the dimension values are not correct after rebuild, return to the assembly and double-click the specific configuration. Return to the drawing and issue the Rebuild again.

Utilize Sheet1 as a working drawing to calculate interference and view potential issues between configurations. Display dimensions with 2-place decimal precision for calculations.

For a millimeter component drawing, remove the trailing zeros in accordance with ASME Y14.5 Types of Decimal Dimensions. Utilize the Tools, Options, Document Properties, ANSI Dimensioning standard. Select Trailing Zeros, Remove option.

Review the types of decimal dimensions for millimeter and inch units:

<table>
<tr><th colspan="4">TYPES of DECIMAL DIMENSIONS (ASME Y14.5M):</th></tr>
<tr><th>Description:</th><th>Example: MM</th><th>Description:</th><th>Example: INCH</th></tr>
<tr><td>Dimension is less than 1mm.
Zero precedes the decimal point.</td><td>0.9
0.95</td><td>Dimension is less than 1 inch.
Zero is not used before the decimal point.</td><td>.5
.56</td></tr>
<tr><td>Dimension is a whole number.
Display no decimal point.
Display no zero after decimal point.</td><td>19</td><td rowspan="2">Express dimension to the same number of decimal places as its tolerance.
Add zeros to the right of the decimal point.
If the tolerance is expressed to 3 places, then the dimension contains 3 places to the right of the decimal point.</td><td rowspan="2">1.750</td></tr>
<tr><td>Dimension exceeds a whole number by a decimal fraction of a millimeter.
Display no zero to the right of the decimal.</td><td>11.5
11.51</td></tr>
</table>

The Tolerance Display Inch and Metric table illustrates the rules for Unilateral, Bilateral and Limit Tolerance.

Tolerance Display for Inch and Metric DIMENSIONS (ASME Y14.5M)		
Display:	**Metric:**	**Inch:**
Unilateral Tolerance	$36^{0}_{-0.5}$	$1.417^{+.005}_{-.000}$
Bilateral Tolerance	$36^{+0.25}_{-0.50}$	$1.417^{+.010}_{-.020}$
Limit Tolerance	14.50 11.50	.571 .463

Activity: Modify the Title Block: Sheet1

Modify the Title Block.

195) Right-click a **position** in the Graphics window. Note: Do not select inside a drawing view.

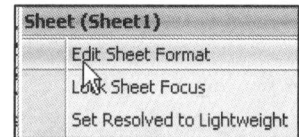

196) Click **Edit Sheet Format**.

197) **Zoom in** on the lower right hand corner of the Title block.

198) Double-click **<COMPANY NAME>**.

199) Enter your company name. Example: **D&M ENGINEERING**. The Formatting dialog box provides the ability to modify the font display and style. The Note PropertyManager provides the ability to to insert a Note, or to edit an existing note, balloon note, or revision symbol. Click the question mark in the PropertyManager to view additional information.

200) Click **OK** from the Note PropertyManager..

Enter a Note for the drawing name.

201) Click the **Note** tool from the Annotation toolbar.

202) Click a **position** in the TITLE Block as illustrated.

203) Select **16** for Font size.

204) Enter **3AXIS-TRANSFER ASSEMBLY**.

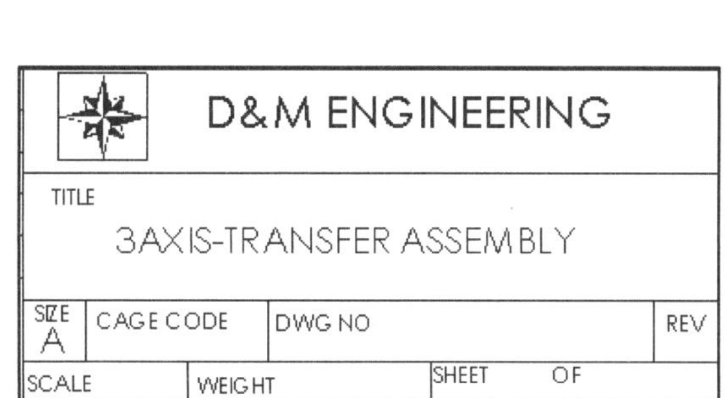

205) Click **OK** from the Note PropertyManager.

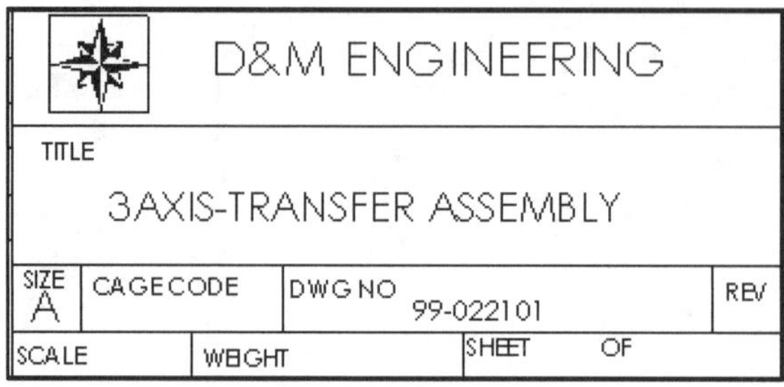

Activity: Create a Linked Note: Sheet1

Create a Linked Note.

206) Click the **Note** tool from the Annotation toolbar.

207) Click a **position** below the DWG NO. text.

208) Click the **Link to Property** tool. The Link to Property dialog box is displayed.

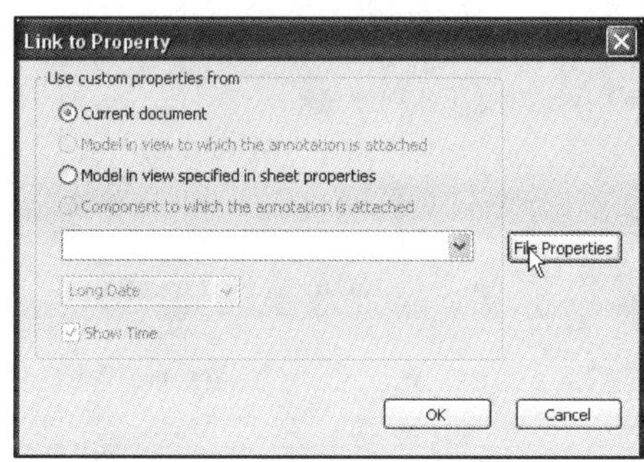

209) Click the **File Properties** button.

210) Click the **Custom** tab.

211) Click inside the **Property Name** box.

212) Enter **DWG. NO**.

213) Click inside the **Value/Text Expresion** box.

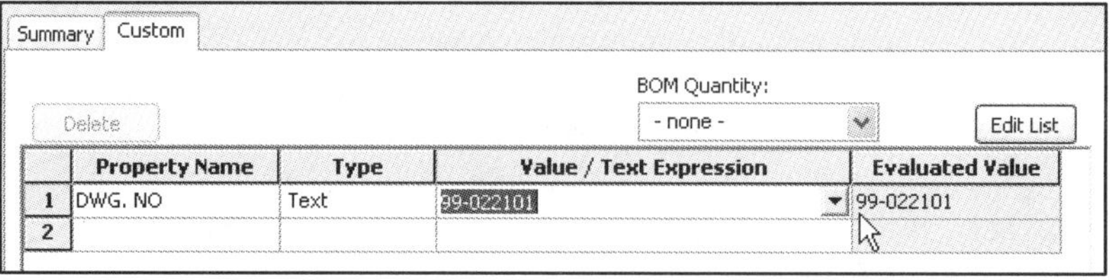

214) Enter **99-0022101**.

215) Click **OK**.

216) Select **SW-File Name** from the Link to Property drop-down menu.

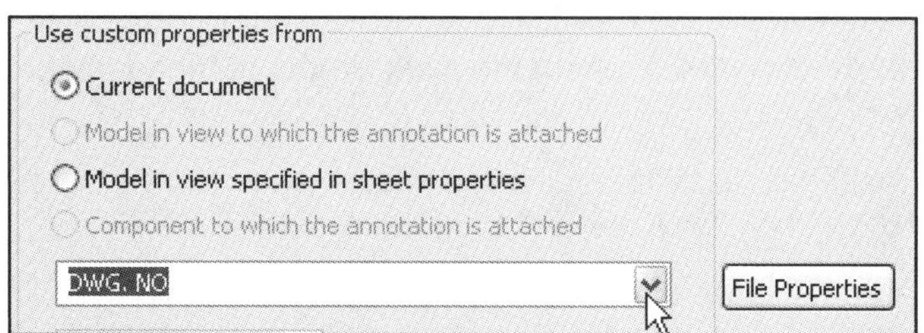

217) Click **OK**. View the inserted linked note. Modify the font to fit the text box.

218) Click **OK** from the Note PropertyManager.

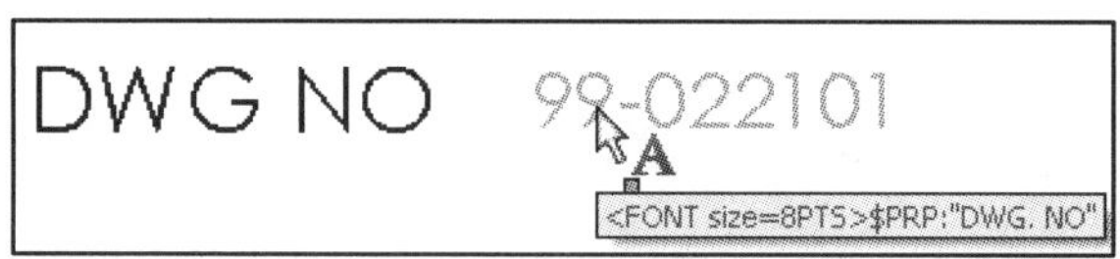

The drawing requires a revision letter. Control the revision letter with a Custom Property. Develop Custom Properties and Revision Tables later in this project.

Return to normal mode.

219) Press the **f** key to fit the sheet to the Graphics window.

220) Right-click **Edit Sheet**.

Sheet (Sheet Format1)
Edit Sheet
Add Sheet...
Copy

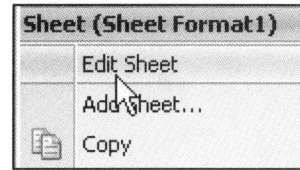

Save the 3AXIS-TRANSFER drawing.

221) Click **Save**.

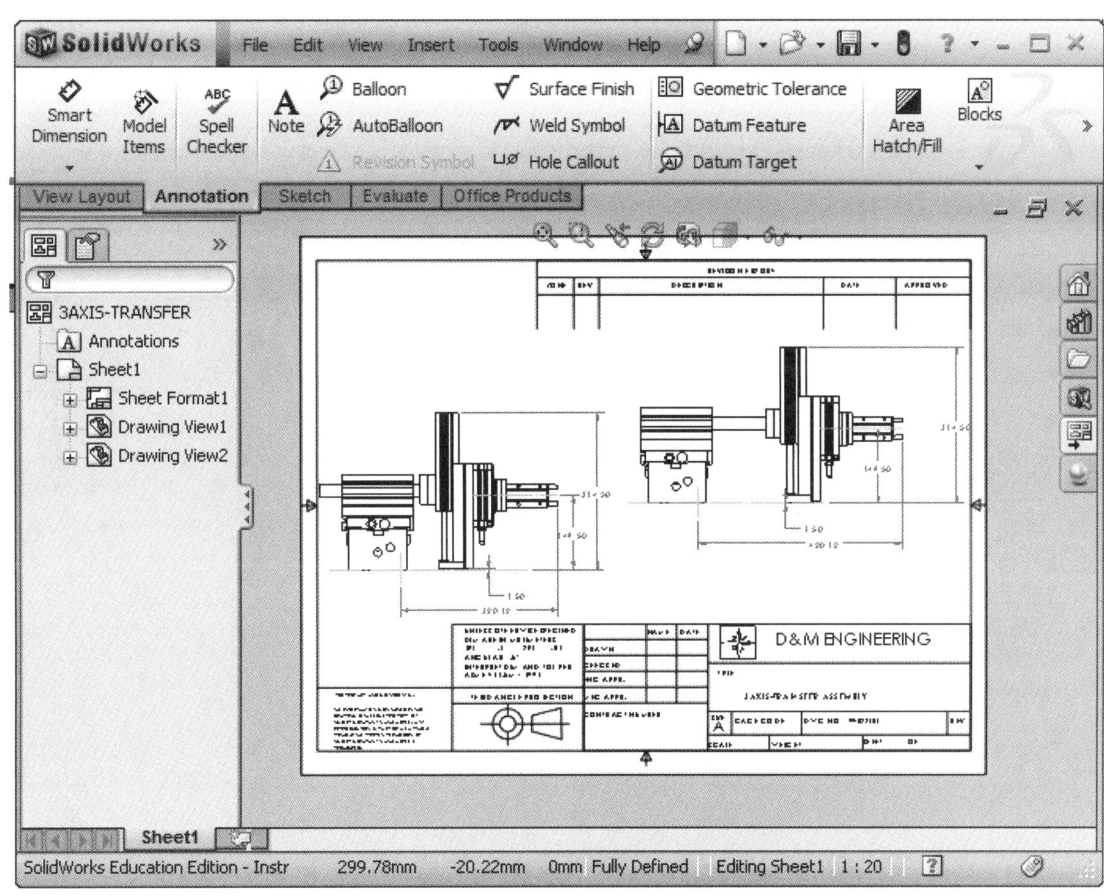

Activity: Add a Sheet - Insert an Isometric view

Add Sheet2.

222) Right-click the **Sheet1** tab.

223) Click **Add Sheet**. Sheet2 is displayed

You can add a Sheet to an active drawing by clicking the add Sheet tab in the bottom left corner of the drawing.

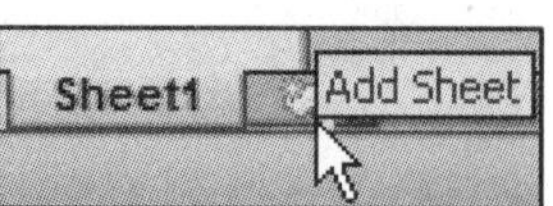

Select the Sheet Format.

224) Click **OK**.

225) Click the **Browse** button.

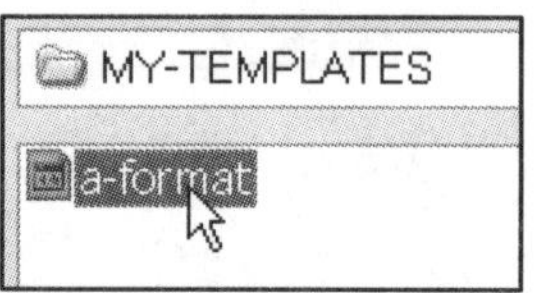

226) Double-click **MY-TEMPLATES\a-format.slddrt.**

227) Click **OK**.

Set the Sheet Scale.

228) Right-click **Properties** in Sheet2.

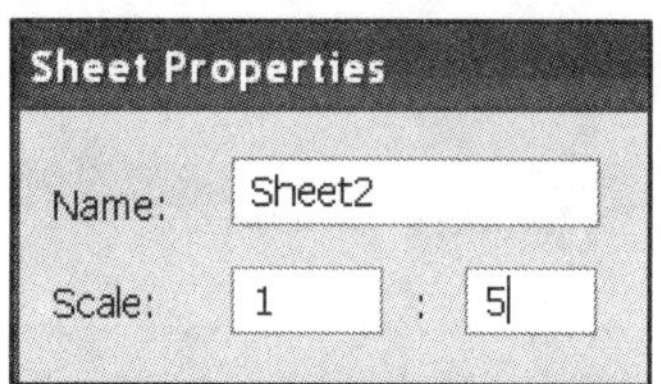

229) Enter **1:5** for Scale.

230) Click **OK** from the Sheet Properties box. View the updated FeatureManager.

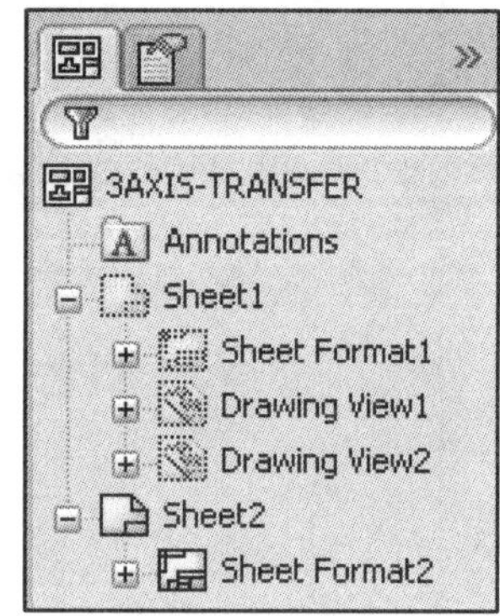

Insert an Isometric view.

231) Click the **Model View** tool from the View Layout toolbar. The Model View PropertyManager is displayed.

232) Click **3AXIS-TRANSFER** from the Insert document box.

233) Click **Next**.

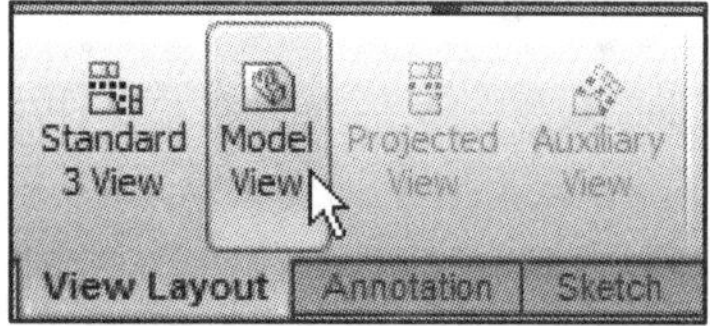

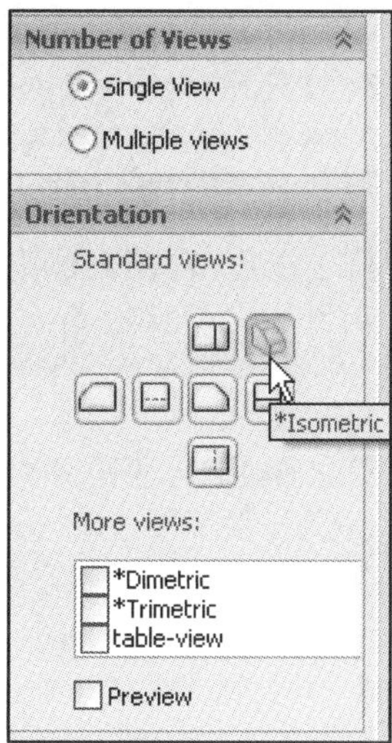

234) If required, click ***Isometric** from the Orientation list. Note: If needed, modify the drawing view scale to 1:5.

235) Click a **position** on the right side of Sheet2.

236) Click **OK** from the Model View PropertyManager.

Select the Default configuration.

237) Right-click **Properties** inside the Drawing View3 view boundary.

238) Select **Default** from the Used name configuration drop-down menu.

239) Click **OK**.

240) Click **OK** from the Drawing View3 PropertyManager

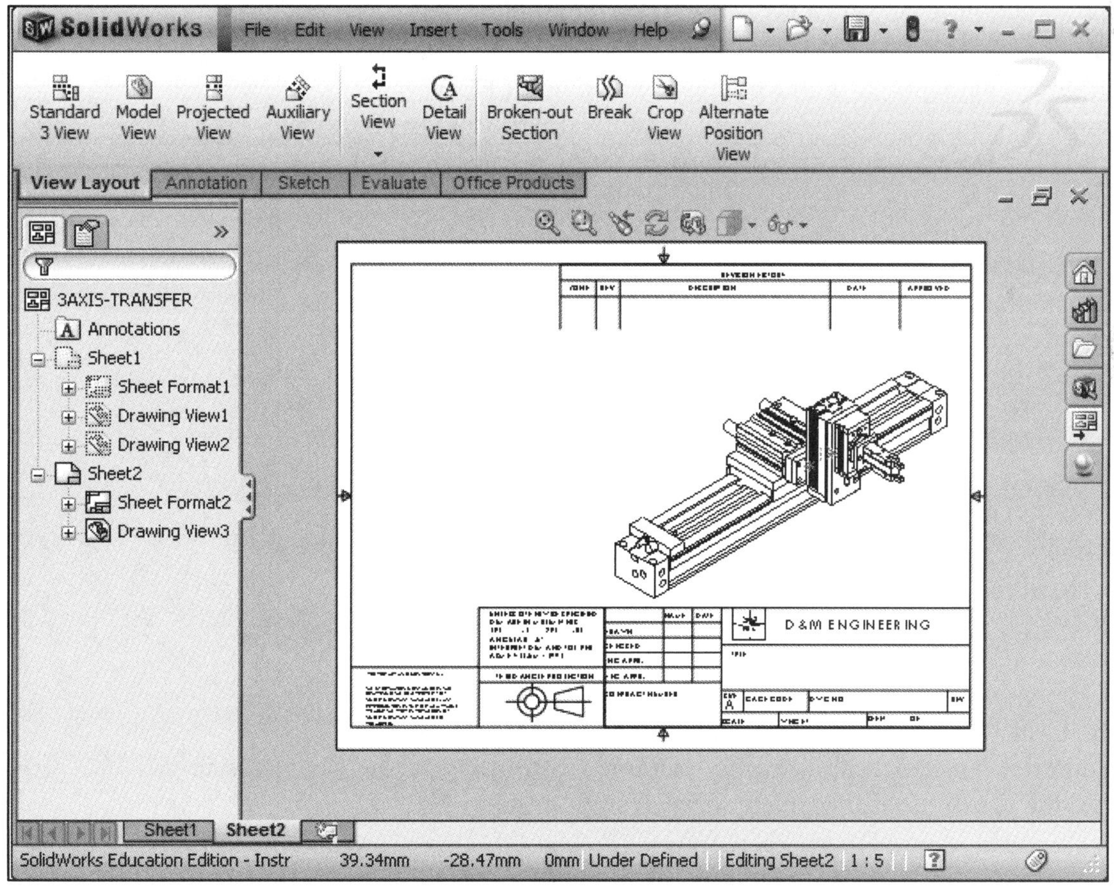

Rename the Drawing View3.
241) Rename Drawing View3 to **BOM-VIEW**.

Bill of Materials

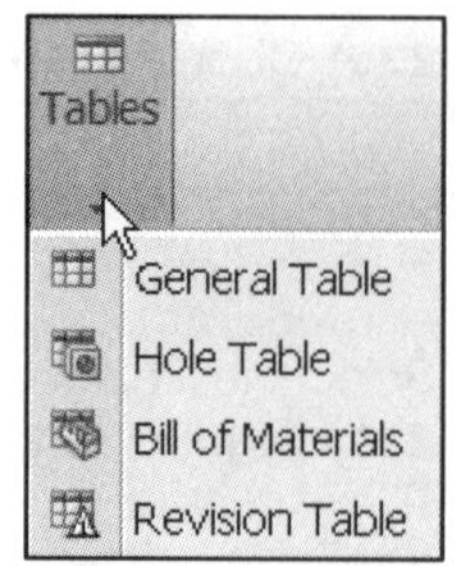

The Bill of Materials (BOM) is a table that lists essential information on the components in an assembly. Insert a Bill of Materials (BOM) into the 3AXIS-TRANSFER drawing, Sheet2.

The BOM is linked to the Custom Properties of the 3AXIS-TRANSFER components. There are two options to create a BOM in the drawing: *Table* option and the *Excel* spreadsheet option. Investigate the *Table* option in this activity.

The first BOM Table inserted into the 3AXIS-TRANSFER drawing requires additional work. Information is missing. Utilize Component Properties to define the majority of information located in the BOM.

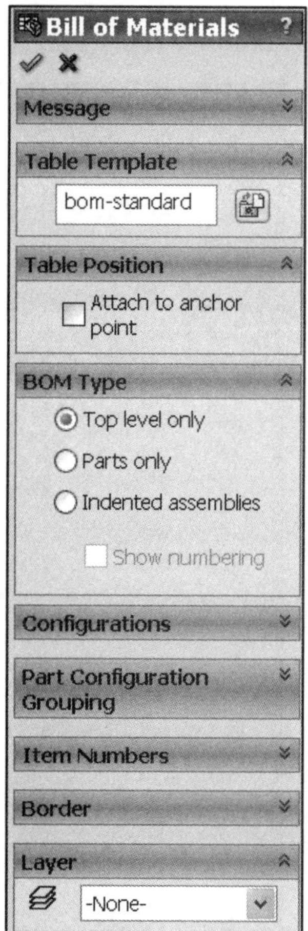

The foundation for the BOM is the BOM Template. The foundation for the BOM is the BOM template. The template contains the major column headings. The default BOM template, bom-standard.sldbomtbt contains the following column headings: *ITEM NO., PART NUMBER, DESCRIPTION, QTY. (QUANTITY).*

The SolidWorks\lang\<language> folder contains additional BOM templates:

- MATERIAL.
- STOCK-SIZE.
- VENDOR.
- WEIGHT.

The bom-all.sldbomtbt contains the default column headings. A BOM template also contains User Defined Custom headings. The User Defined Custom headings are linked to Custom Properties in the part or assembly. Define Custom Properties with the ConfigurationManager or a Design Table.

The BOM Table Anchor point locates the BOM at a corner of the drawing. The BOM Table moves when the Attach to anchor option is unchecked. The BOM Type contains three options:

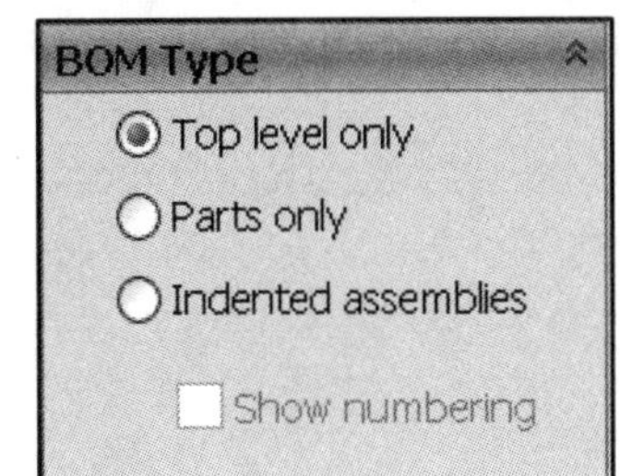

- **Top level only**: List parts and sub-assemblies, but not sub-assembly components.
- **Parts only**: Does not list sub-assemblies. Lists sub-assembly components as individual items.
- **Indented assemblies**: Lists sub-assemblies. Indents sub-assembly components below their sub-assemblies. Select Show numbering to display item numbers for sub-assembly components.

Summary Table:

Utilize the **Top level only** option (for assemblies that contain sub-assemblies) to display the highest level components in the FeatureManager.

ITEM NO.	PART NUMBER
1	99-022102
2	99-022103
3	99-022104

Utilize the **Parts only** option to display the parts in an assembly.

ITEM NO.	PART NUMBER
1	50GF
2	50GR
3	45-63421
4	50M

Utilize the **Indented assemblies** option to display lower level components indented in the BOM.

ITEM NO.	PART NUMBER
1	99-022102
	015081
	50
	50FL
2	99-022013
	015082

By default, the component order in the assembly determines its ITEM NO. in the BOM.

The occurrence of the same component in an assembly defines the value in the QTY column. The PART NUMBER column in the BOM is the SolidWorks document name entered in the File name box,

The DESCRIPTION column is the text entered in the Description box. The Description box is blank for the Project 6 components. Define Description as a Custom Property in the next section.

Create a Top level only Bill of Materials with the SolidWorks BOM Template, bom-material.sldbomtbt for Sheet2.

Add additional components and configurations to the assembly. Update the drawing. Modify the BOM to display other parameters in Sheet2.

Activity: Create a Top-level only Bill of Materials: Sheet2

Insert the default Bill of Materials.

242) Click inside the **Isometric view boundary** of Sheet2.

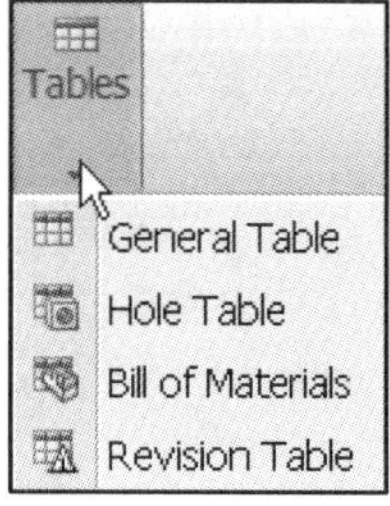

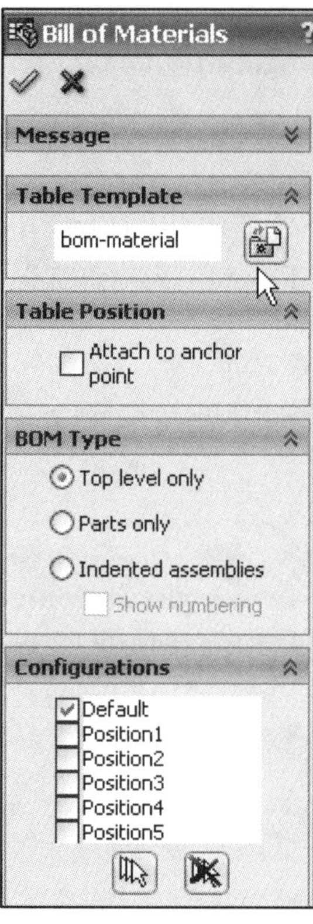

243) Click **Tables**, **Bill of Materials** from the Annotation toolbar.

244) Double-click **bom-material.sldbomtbt** from the SolidWorks\lang\english folder.

245) Click **Top level only** for BOM Type.

246) Check **Default** in the Configurations box. Uncheck all other Configurations.

247) Click **OK** ✓ from the Bill of Materials PropertyManager.

248) Click a **position** on the upper left corner of the sheet.

249) Click **OK** ✓ from the Bill of Materials PropertyManager.

250) Click a **position** in the Sheet.

Save the drawing.

251) Click **Save**.

ITEM NO.	PART NUMBER	DESCRIPTION	MATERIAL	Default/QTY.
1	LINEAR-TRANSFER			1
2	2AXIS-TRANSFER			1
3	ROTARY-GRIPPER			1

View the BOM

252) Click and drag the **BOM** to view. **Modify** the Isometric view scale if needed.

Information in the current BOM is incomplete. The Custom Properties in the components are linked to the PART NUMBER, DESCRIPTION, MATERIAL, and QTY. columns in the BOM. Create additional Custom Properties in the components to complete the BOM in the drawing.

Activity: Create Custom Properties for the BOM Components: Sheet2

Create Custom Properties for the Listed Components.

253) Right-click **LINEAR-TRANSFER** from the drawing FeatureManager.

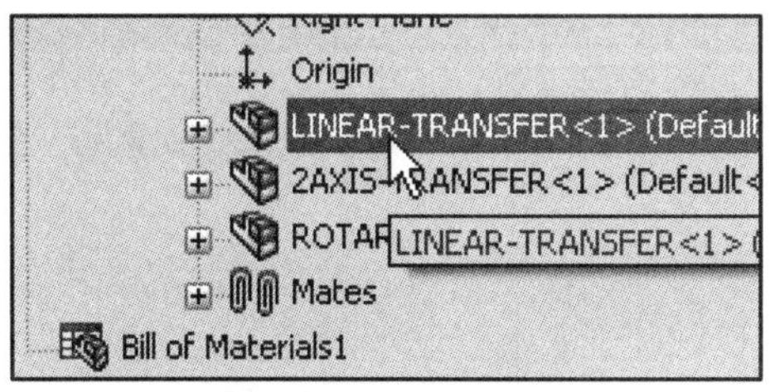

254) Click the **Open Assembly** tool from the Context toolbar.

255) Click the **Configuration** tab. Note Default is the active configuration.

256) Right-click the **Default** configuration.

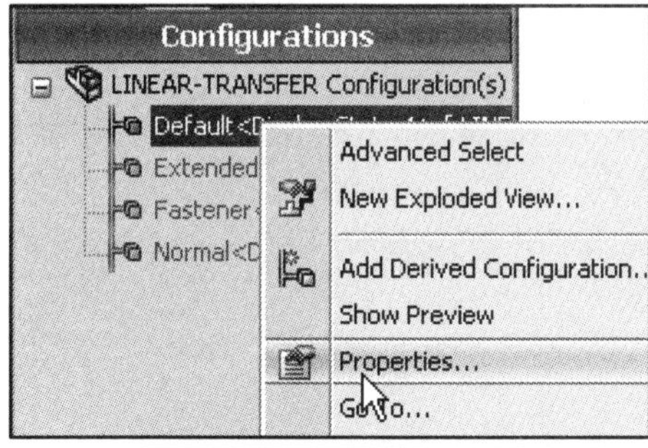

257) Click **Properties**.

258) Select **User Specified Name** from the drop-down menu.

259) Enter **99-022102**.

260) Click the **Custom Properties** button. The Summary Information dialog box is displayed.

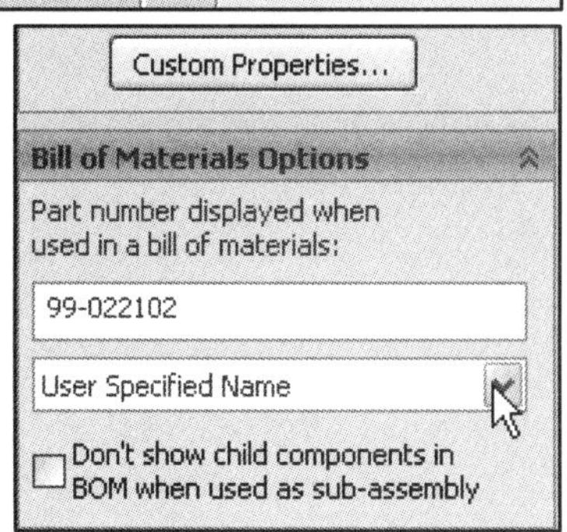

261) Click inside the **Property Name box**.

262) Select **Description**.

263) Click inside the **Value / Text Expression** box.

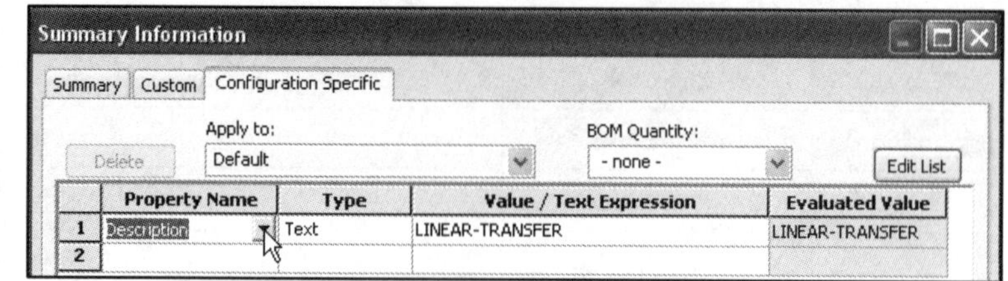

264) Enter **LINEAR-TRANSFER**. View the Summary Information dialog box.

265) Click **OK** from the Summary Information dialog box.

266) Click **OK** from the PropertyManager.

Return to the FeatureManager.
267) Click the **FeatureManager** tab.

268) **Save** the model.

269) **Return** to the 3AXIS-TRANSFER drawing. View the updated model.

270) **Perform the same procedure as above** to obtain the illustrated Bill of Materials. The PART NUMBER and DESCRIPTION are displayed for the three sub-components in the 3AXIS-TRANSFER assembly.

ITEM NO.	PART NUMBER	DESCRIPTION	MATERIAL	Default/QTY.
1	99-022102	LINEAR-TRANSFER		1
2	99-022103	2AXIS-TRANSFER		1
3	99-022104	ROTARY-GRIPPER		1

Fasteners

The 3AXIS-TRANSFER assembly requires two sets of SHCSs. The GUIDE-CYLINDER assembly requires four, M10x1.5x70 SHCSs. The ROTARY assembly requires two, M8 x 1.25 x 45 SHCSs. Utilize Custom Properties to add PART NUMBER and DESCRIPTION to the BOM.

The BOM updates to reflect the two components added at the top-level assembly. Modify the "Default" configuration name to a numeric part number. Insert MATERIAL as a Custom Property.

An interference issue exists between the GUIDE-CYLINDER and the M10 SHCSs. Modify the M10 x 1.5 x 70 Hex SHCSs to M8 x 1.25 x 70 Hex SHCSs. Utilize Replace Components to modify all four instances in one operation. The M8 x 1.25 x 70 Hex SHCS part is in a closed state in order to be utilized with Replace Components. The BOM updates to reflect the new component.

Changing four M10 x 1.5 x 70 Hex SHCSs to four M8 x 1.25 x 70 Hex SHCSs is an exercise in the Replace Components option.

How could you have avoided inserting the wrong size fastener? Answer: Utilize the Measure tool to determine the SHCS diameter. Work between the part, assembly, drawing and BOM in the next activities.

Activity: Insert Fasteners from the MY-TOOLBOX Folder

Open the assembly.

271) Right-click **Open 3axis-transfer.sldasm** from the Isometric drawing view. The default configuration is selected.

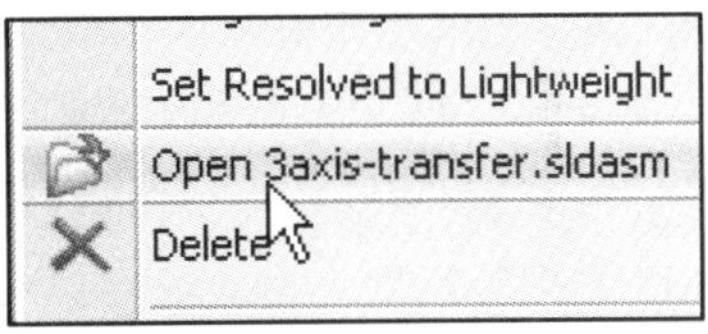

Open the SHCS.

272) Click **Open** from the Menu bar toolbar.

273) Double-click **MY-TOOLBOX\SHCS\B18.3.1M-8 x 1.25 x 45 Hex SHCS**.

Display the models.

274) Click **Window**, **Tile Horizontally** from the Menu bar menu.

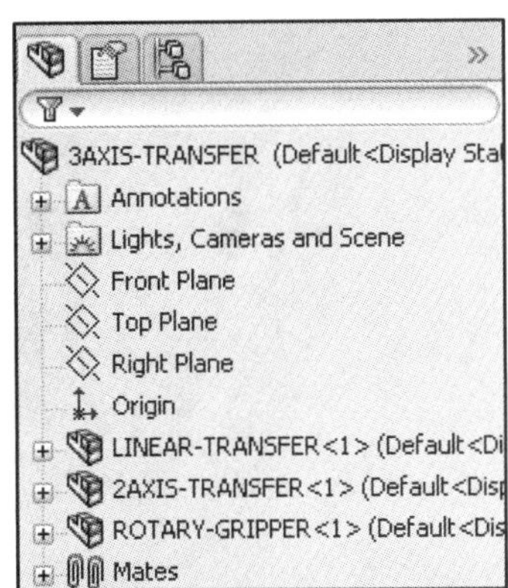

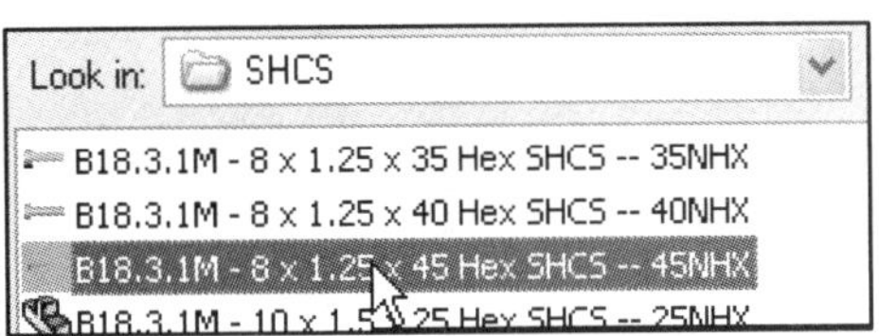

275) **Zoom in** on the circular edge of the SHCS.

276) **Zoom in** on the inside circular edge of the top Cbore of the ROTARY assembly.

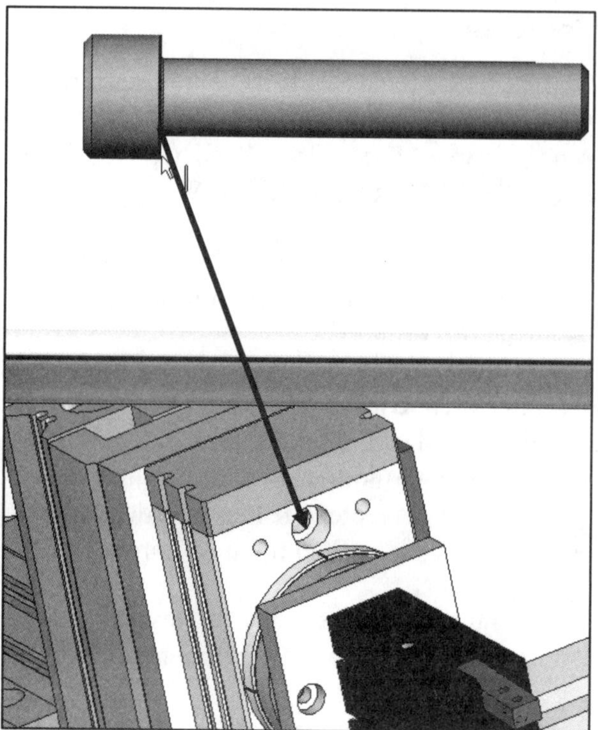

Insert the first M8x1.25x45 Hex SHCS.

277) Click and drag the **SHCS circular edge** to the top ROTARY Cbore inside circular edge.

Insert the second M8x1.25x45 Hex SHCS.

278) Click and drag the **SHCS circular edge** to the bottom ROTARY Cbore inside circular edge.

Close the SHCS Graphics window.

279) Click **Close**.

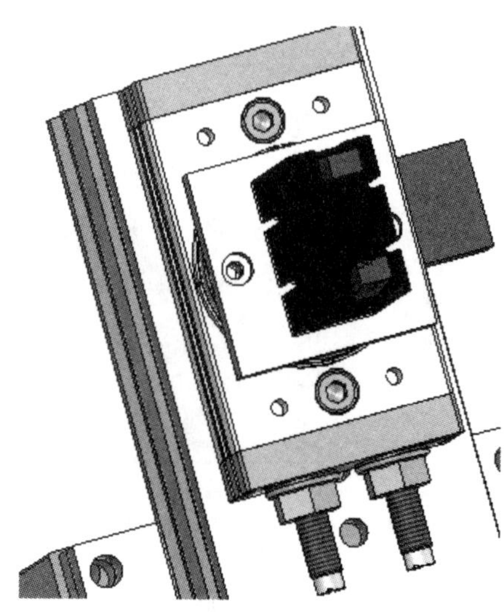

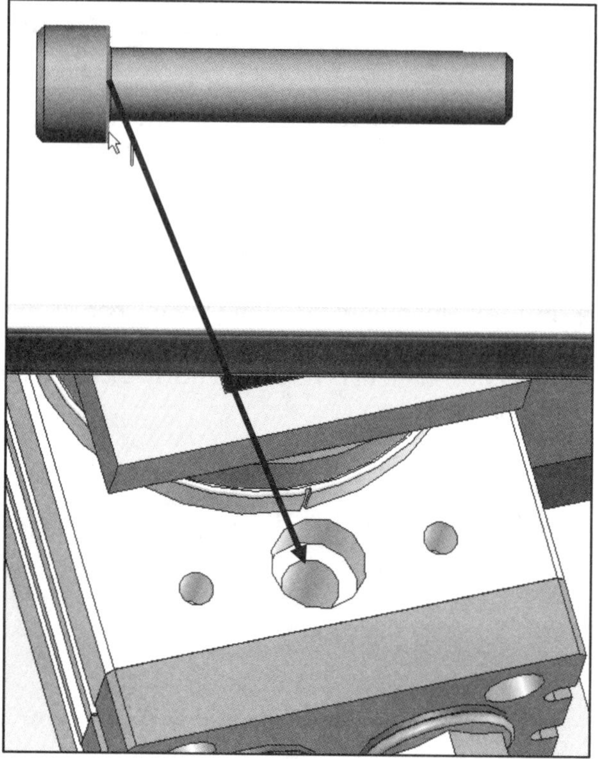

Open the SHCS.

280) Click **Open** from the Menu bar toolbar.

281) Double-click **MY-TOOLBOX\SHCS\B18.3.1M-10 x 1.5 x 70 Hex SHCS**.

Display the models.

282) Click **Window**, **Tile Horizontally**.

283) **Zoom in** on the circular edge of the SHCS.

284) **Zoom in** on the circular edge of the front Cbore of the GUIDE-CYLINDER assembly.

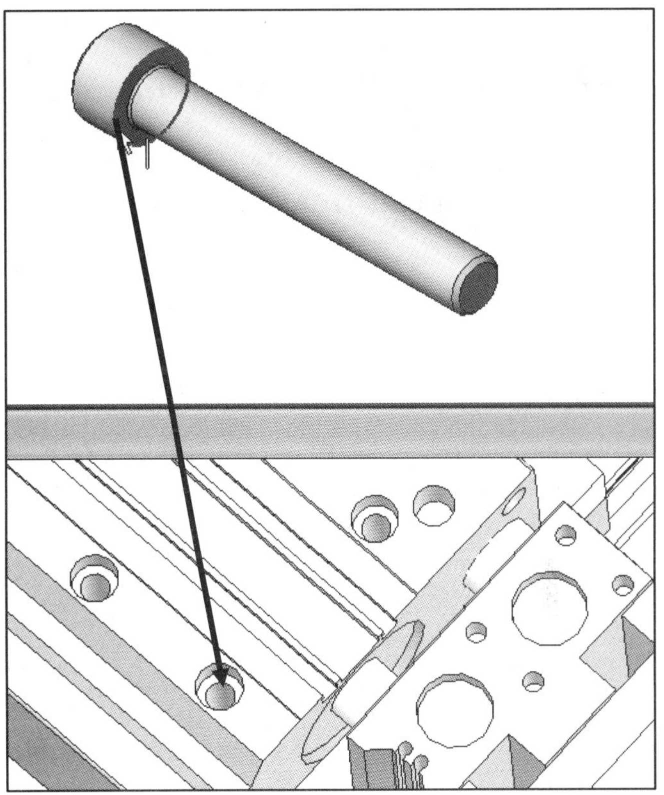

Insert the first M10 x 1.5 x 70 Hex SHCS.

285) Click and drag the **SHCS circular edge** to the front, right GUIDE-CYLINDER Cbore inside circular edge.

286) Repeat the above process for the second, third, and forth **B18.3.1M-10 x 1.5 x 70 Hex SHCSs**.

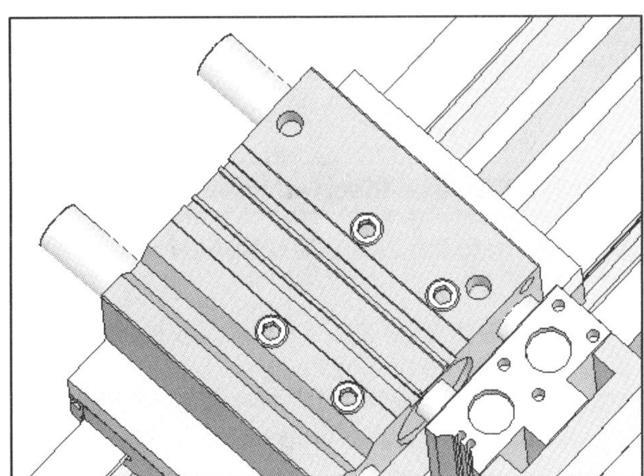

Close the SHCS.

287) Click **Close**.

Save the assembly.

288) Click **Save**. View the updated FeatureManager.

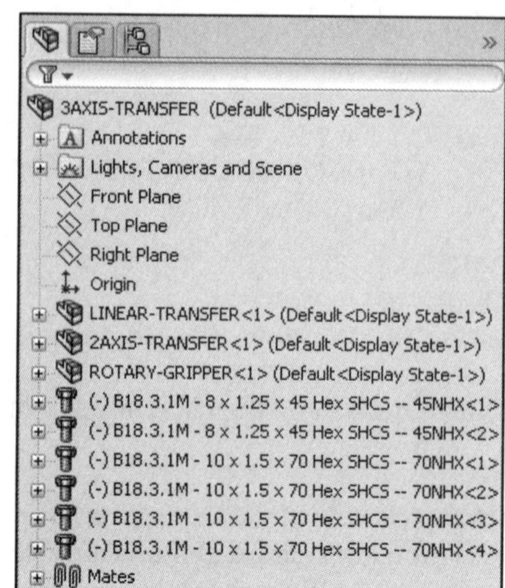

Update the Bill of Materials.

289) Return to the **3AXIS-TRANSFER Drawing, Sheet2**. The Bill of Materials is updated with the SHCS.

290) **Modify** the Bill of the Matierals to reflect the below illustration with Part Numbers and Descriptions. Note: Open the 3AXIS-TRANSFER assembly from the drawing. Open the needed part. Click the ConfigurationManager tab. Use the Properties tool. Modify the Part Number and Description from the Configuration Properties PropertyManager and Custom Properties dialog box.

ITEM NO.	PART NUMBER	DESCRIPTION	MATERIAL	Default/QTY.
1	99-022102	LINEAR-TRANSFER		1
2	99-022103	2AXIS-TRANSFER		1
3	99-022104	ROTARY-GRIPPER		1
4	SHC-45	M8 x 1.25 x 45 Hex		2
5	SHC-70	M10 x 1.5 x 70 Hex		4

Activity: Replace Inserted Fasteners (Components)

291) **Return** to the 3AXIS-TRANSFER assembly.

Replace the B18.3.1M-10 x 1.5 x 70 Hex SHCS components in the assembly.

292) Click the first **B18.3.1M-10 x 1.5 x 70 Hex SHCS** from the FeatureManager.

293) Hold the **Ctrl** down key.

294) Click the other **three B18.3.1M-10 x 1.5 x 70 Hex SHCS**.

295) Release the **Ctrl** key.

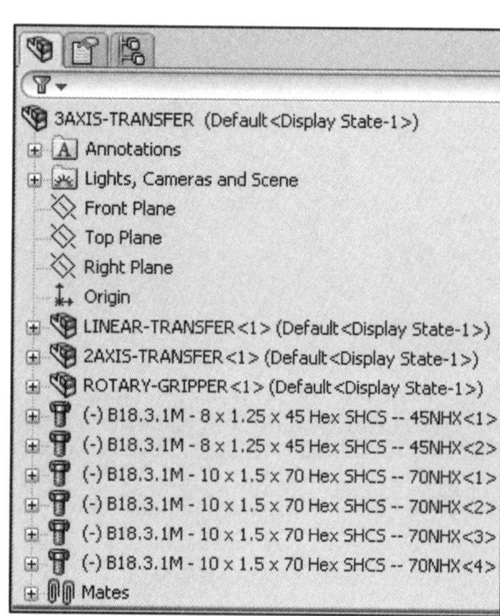

296) Right-click **Replace Components**. The Replace PropertyManager is displayed. The selected components are displayed in the Selection box.

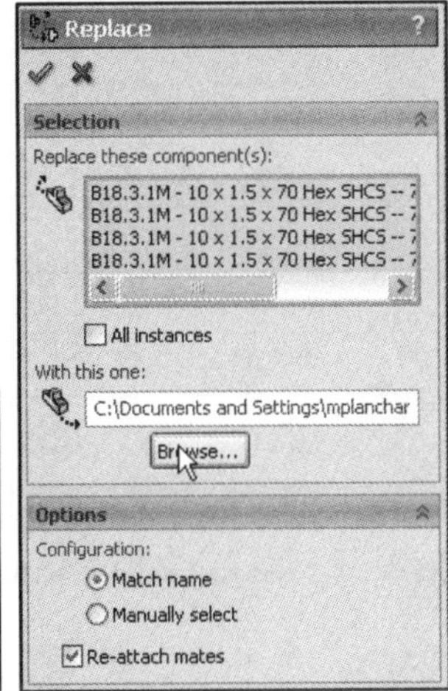

Select the replacing component.

297) Click the **Browse** button.

298) Double-click **B18.3.1M-8 x 1.25 x 70 Hex SHCS**.

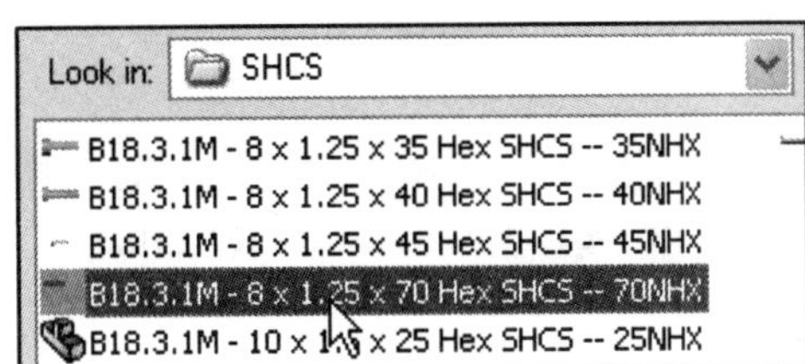

299) Click **OK** from the Replace PropertyManager. View the information in the Mated Entities PropertyManager.

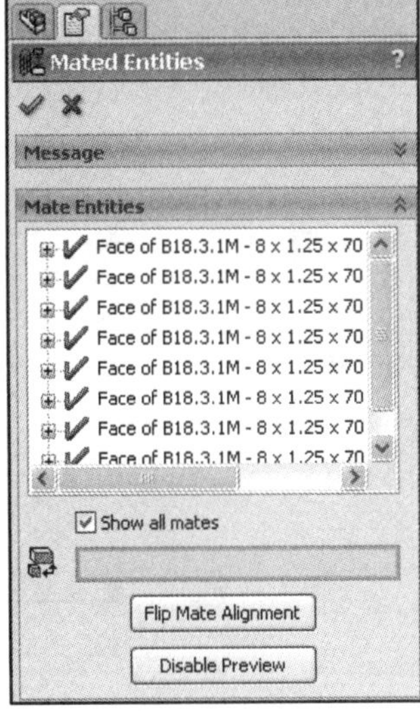

300) Click **OK** from the Mated Entities PropertyManager. View the updated 3AXIS-TRANSFER FeatureManager.

Save the 3AXIS-TRANSFER assembly.

301) Click **Save**.

The FeatureManager contains the four new B18.3.1M-8 x 1.25 x 70 Hex SHCSs.

Update the Bill of Materials. Return to the 3AXIS-TRANSFER drawing.

302) Press **Ctrl+Tab** to display the 3AXIS-TRANSFER drawing, Sheet2. View the updated Bill of Materials.

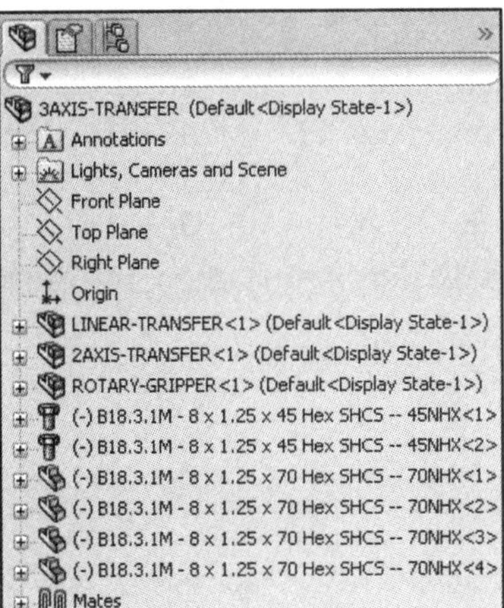

ITEM NO.	PART NUMBER	DESCRIPTION	MATERIAL	Default/QTY.
1	99-022102	LINEAR-TRANSFER		1
2	99-022103	2AXIS-TRANSFER		1
3	99-022104	ROTARY-GRIPPER		1
4	SHC-45	M8 x 1.25 x 45 Hex		2
5	Default			4

Enter Custom Properties. Modify the PART NUMBER, DESCRIPTION, and MATERIAL as illustrated in the below Bill of Materials.

Open the needed part. Click the ConfigurationManager tab. Apply the Properties tool. Modify the Part Number, Description, and Material from the Configuration Properties PropertyManager and the Custom Properties dialog box. Apply Material in the FeatureManager of the part.

ITEM NO.	PART NUMBER	DESCRIPTION	MATERIAL	Default/QTY.
1	99-022102	LINEAR-TRANSFER		1
2	99-022103	2AXIS-TRANSFER		1
3	99-022104	ROTARY-GRIPPER		1
4	SHC-45	M8 x 1.25 x 45 Hex	Alloy Steel	2
5	**SHC-70**	M8 x 1.25 x 70 Hex	Alloy Steel	4

Fastener Configuration

Develop a new configuration named Fastener in the 3AXIS-TRANSFER assembly.

The Fastener configuration contains the six SHCSs. Apply the Configure component tool.

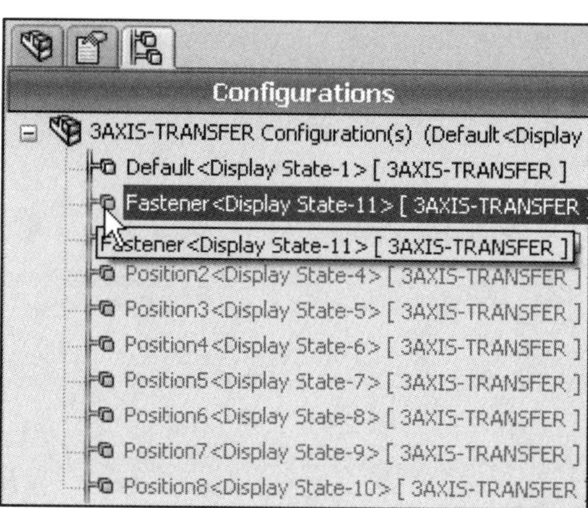

Activity: Create the 3AXIS-TRANSFER Assembly Fastener Configuration

Create the Fastener configuration

303) **Open** the 3AXIS-TRANSFER assembly from the drawing, Sheet2.

304) Right-click **LINEAR-TRANSFER** in the 3AXIS-TRANSFER assembly FeatuerManager.

305) Click **Configure component**. The Modify Configuration dialog box is displayed.

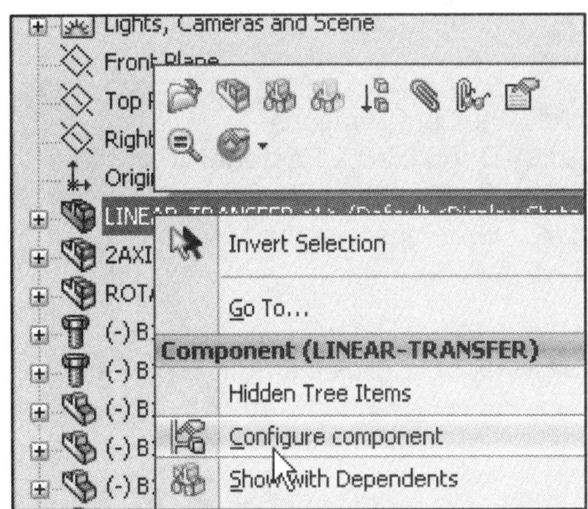

306) Double-click **2AXIS-TRANSFER** from the FeatureManager.

307) Double-click the **ROTRARY-GRIPPER** from the FeatuerManger.

308) Double-click the **six SCHS** from the FeatureManager.

309) Click inside the **Creates a new configuration** box.

310) Enter **Fastener**. Accept the default configurations.

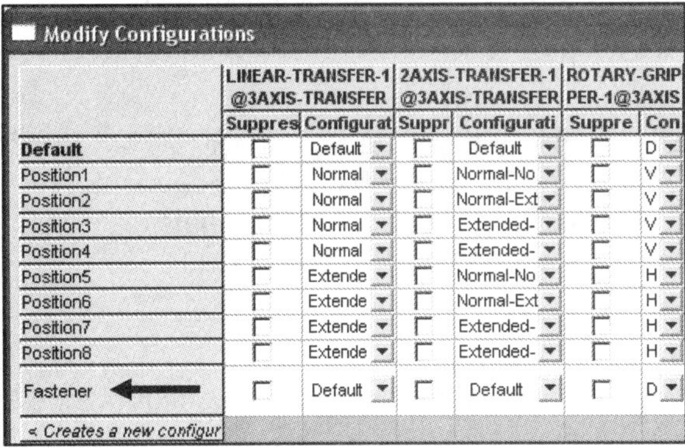
Modify Configurations

	LINEAR-TRANSFER-1 @3AXIS-TRANSFER		2AXIS-TRANSFER-1 @3AXIS-TRANSFER		ROTARY-GRIP PER-1@3AXIS	
	Suppres	Configurat	Suppr	Configurati	Suppre	Con
Default	☐	Default	☐	Default	☐	D
Position1	☐	Normal	☐	Normal-No	☐	V
Position2	☐	Normal	☐	Normal-Ext	☐	V
Position3	☐	Normal	☐	Extended-	☐	V
Position4	☐	Normal	☐	Extended-	☐	V
Position5	☐	Extende	☐	Normal-No	☐	H
Position6	☐	Extende	☐	Normal-Ext	☐	H
Position7	☐	Extende	☐	Extended-	☐	H
Position8	☐	Extende	☐	Extended-	☐	H
Fastener	☐	Default	☐	Default	☐	D
« Creates a new configur						

311) Check the **Suppress** boxes in each column for the six SCHS components. Do not check the suppress box for the Fastener configuration as illustrated. Note: The six SCHC fasteners are suppressed in all configurations, except the Fastener configuration.

	LINEAR-TRANSFER-1 @3AXIS-TRANSFER		2AXIS-TRANSFER-1 @3AXIS-TRANSFER		ROTARY-GRIP PER-1@3AXIS		B18.3.1M - 8 x 1.25 x 45 Hex	
	Suppres	Configurat	Suppr	Configurati	Suppre	Con	Suppr	Configura
Default	☐	Default	☐	Default	☐	D	☑	Preview
Position1	☐	Normal	☐	Normal-No	☐	V	☑	Preview
Position2	☐	Normal	☐	Normal-Ext	☐	V	☑	Preview
Position3	☐	Normal	☐	Extended-	☐	V	☑	Preview
Position4	☐	Normal	☐	Extended-	☐	V	☑	Preview
Position5	☐	Extende	☐	Normal-No	☐	H	☑	Preview
Position6	☐	Extende	☐	Normal-Ext	☐	H	☑	Preview
Position7	☐	Extende	☐	Extended-	☐	H	☑	Preview
Position8	☐	Extende	☐	Extended-	☐	H	☑	Preview
Fastener	☐	Default	☐	Default	☐	D	☐	Preview

	B18.3.1M - 8 x 1.25 x 45 Hex		B18.3.1M - 8 x 1.25 x 70 Hex		B18.3.1M - 8 x 1.25 x 70 Hex		B18.3.1M - 8 x 1.25 x 70 Hex		B18.3.1M - 8 x 1.25 x 70 Hex SHCS --	
	Suppre	Configur	Suppr	Configu	Suppre	Configu	Suppr	Configur	Suppr	Configurat
Default	☑	Previe	☑	Defaul	☑	Defaul	☑	Default	☑	Default
Position1	☑	Previe	☑	Defaul	☑	Defaul	☑	Default	☑	Default
Position2	☑	Previe	☑	Defaul	☑	Defaul	☑	Default	☑	Default
Position3	☑	Previe	☑	Defaul	☑	Defaul	☑	Default	☑	Default
Position4	☑	Previe	☑	Defaul	☑	Defaul	☑	Default	☑	Default
Position5	☑	Previe	☑	Defaul	☑	Defaul	☑	Default	☑	Default
Position6	☑	Previe	☑	Defaul	☑	Defaul	☑	Default	☑	Default
Position7	☑	Previe	☑	Defaul	☑	Defaul	☑	Default	☑	Default
Position8	☑	Previe	☑	Defaul	☑	Defaul	☑	Default	☑	Default
Fastener	☐	Previe	☐	Defaul	☐	Defaul	☐	Default	☐	Default

312) Click **Rebuild all configuration**.

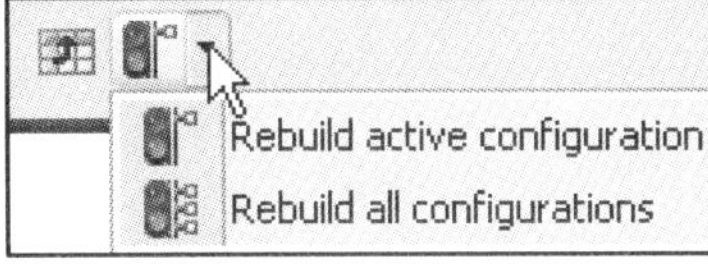

313) Click **OK.**

314) Click **Save**. You just created the Fastener configuration.

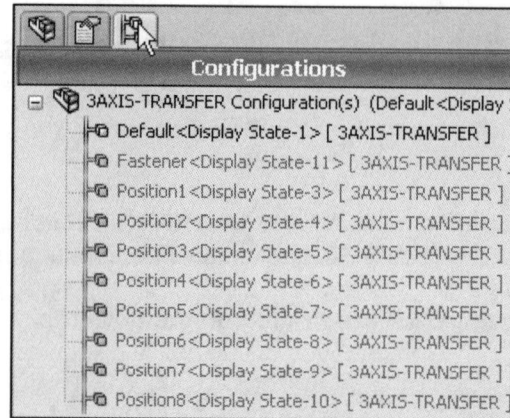

View the configurations

315) Double click **Fastener** from the ConfigurationManager. View the SHCSs in the Graphics window.

Return to the Default configuration.

316) Double-click **Default**. The Fastener are suppressed.

Update the Bill of Materials.

317) Return to the 3AXIS-TRANSFER drawing, Sheet2.

Display the BOM PropertyManager.

318) Click the **Bill of Materials header** as illustrated. The Bill of Materials PropertyManager is displayed.

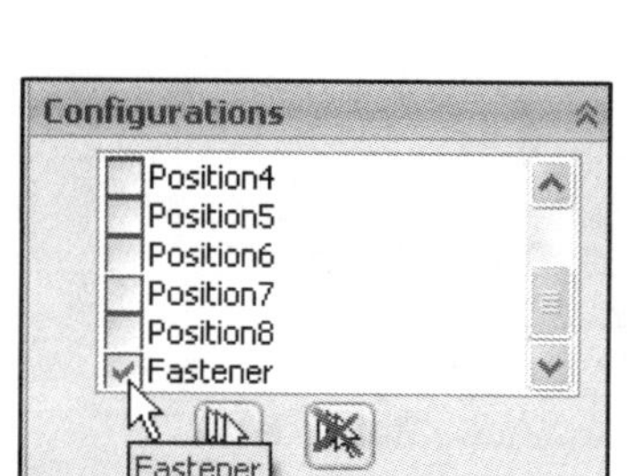

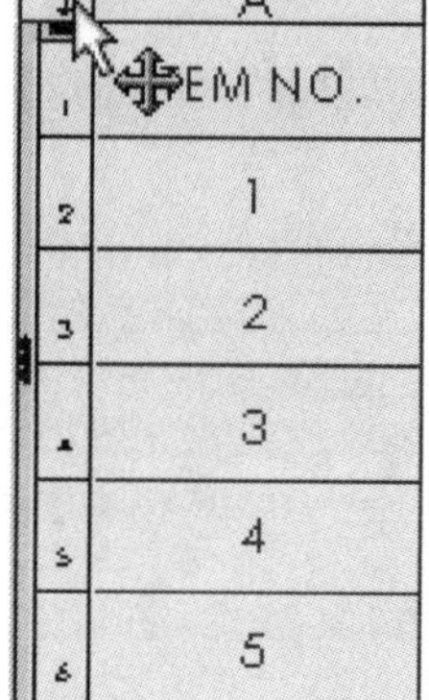

Modify the configurations.

319) Check **Fastener** from the Configurations box.

320) Click **OK** from the Bill of Material PropertyManager. View the updated BOM.

ITEM NO.	PART NUMBER	DESCRIPTION	MATERIAL	Default/QTY.	Fastener/QTY.
1	99-022102	LINEAR-TRANSFER		1	1
2	99-022103	2AXIS-TRANSFER		1	1
3	99-022104	ROTARY-GRIPPER		1	1
4	SHC-45	M8 x 1.25 x 45 Hex	Alloy Steel	-	2
5	SHC-70	M8 x 1.25 x 70 Hex	Alloy Steel	-	4

Additional information on Editing Bill of Materials Tables

Hovering over a cell displays the Editing Table icon. Click a cell to display the Context toolbar.

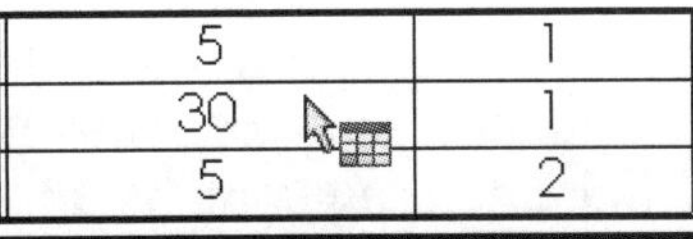

The toolbar's buttons reflect the available options for the type of table and selections, (rows, column, and cells).

To access a table's PropertyManager, click the move table icon in the upper left corner or Right-click the table, and click Properties from the Pop-up menu.

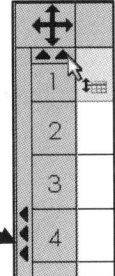

Click the vertical arrows as illustrated to insert a row. Click the Horizontal arrows as illustrated to insert a column.

The Table Properties option returns you to the BOM PropertyManager.

The Insert tool provides the ability to insert a column to the Right or Left side of the selected column or a Row above or below the selected row.

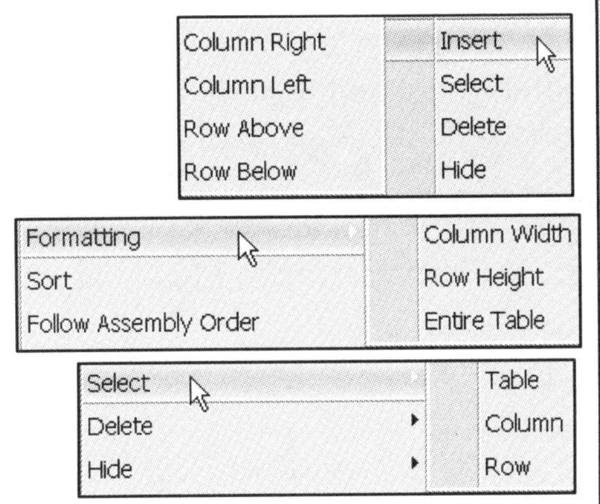

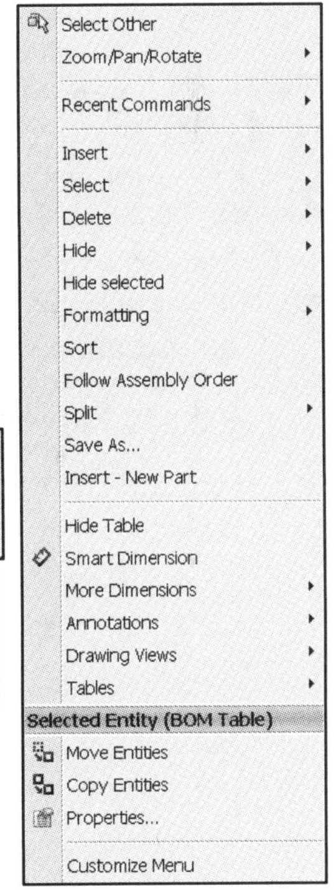

The Select tool provides the ability to select a Table, Column, or Row.

The Formatting tool provides the ability to format the width of a column, the height of a row, or the entire table.

The Formatting Entire Table tool displayed the Entire Table dialog box.

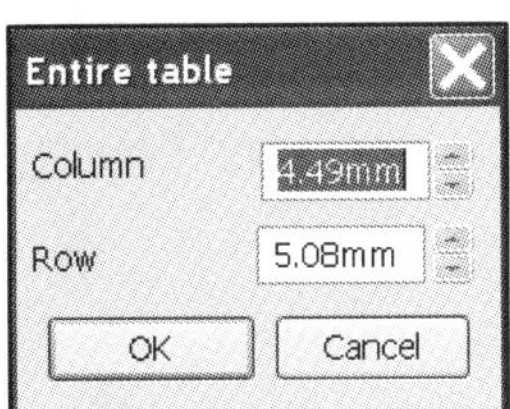

Exploded View

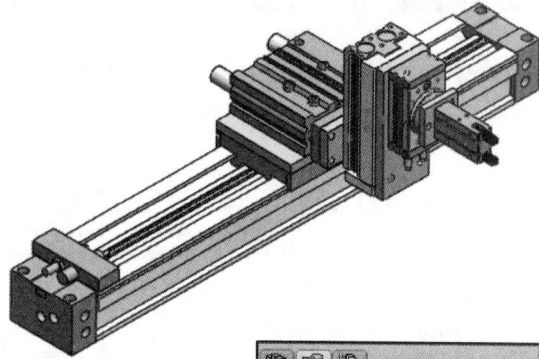

The Exploded View illustrates how to assemble the components in an assembly. Create an Exploded View with multi-steps. Click and drag components in the Graphics window. Explode the 3AXIS-TRANSFER assembly with a multi step procedure.

The Manipulator icon indicates the direction to explode. Select an alternate component edge for the explode direction. Drag the component in the Graphics window or enter an exact value in the Explode distance box. In this activity, manipulate the top-level components in the assembly.

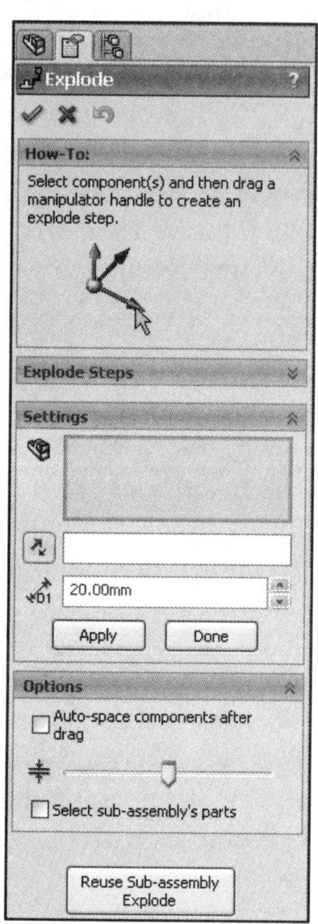

In the section, create Exploded views for each sub-assembly and utilize the Re-use sub-assembly Explode option in the top level assembly.

Access the Explode view option as follows:

- Right-click the configuration name in the ConfigurationManager. Click New Explode View.
- Click the Exploded View tool from the Assembly toolbar.
- Select Insert, Exploded View from the Menu bar menu.

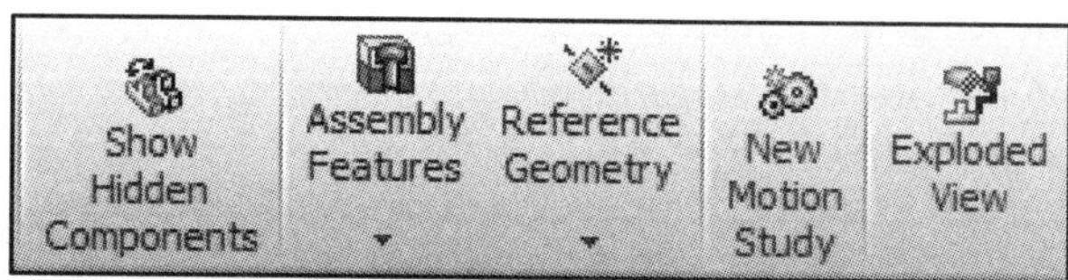

Activity: Create the 3AXIS TRANSFER Assembly Exploded View

Insert an Exploded View.

321) **Open** the to the 3AXIS TRANSFER assembly from the drawinging.

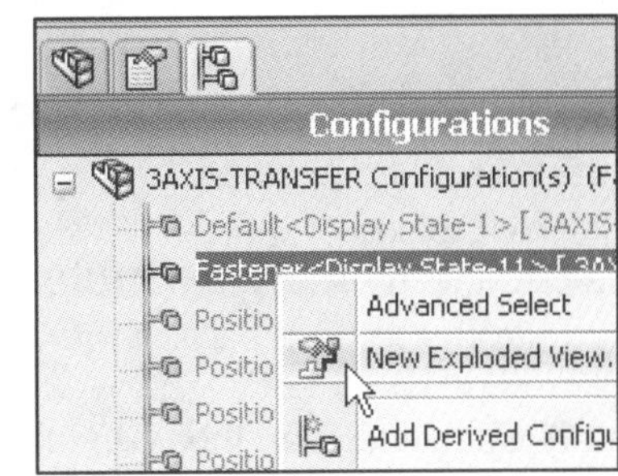

322) Click the **ConfigurationManager** tab.

323) Double-click the **Fastener** configuration from the ConfigurationManager.

324) Right-click **New Exploded View**. The Explode PropertyManager is displayed.

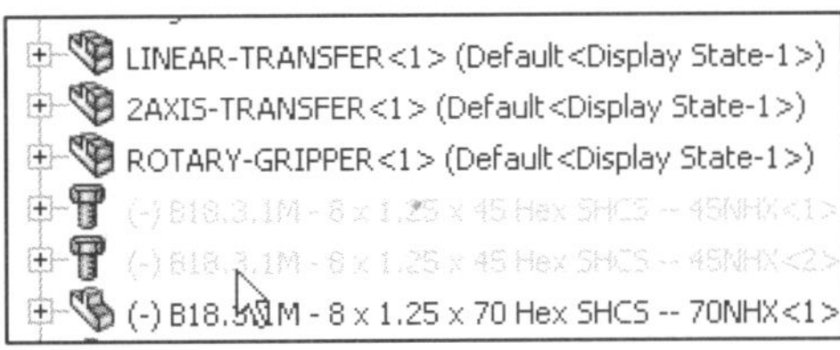

Create Explode Step 1.

325) Click the first **B18.3.1M-8x1.25x45 Hex** from the fly-out FeatureManager.

326) Hold the **Ctrl** key.

327) Click the **second B18.3.1M-8x1.25x45 Hex** from the fly-out FeatureManager.

328) Release the **Ctrl** key.

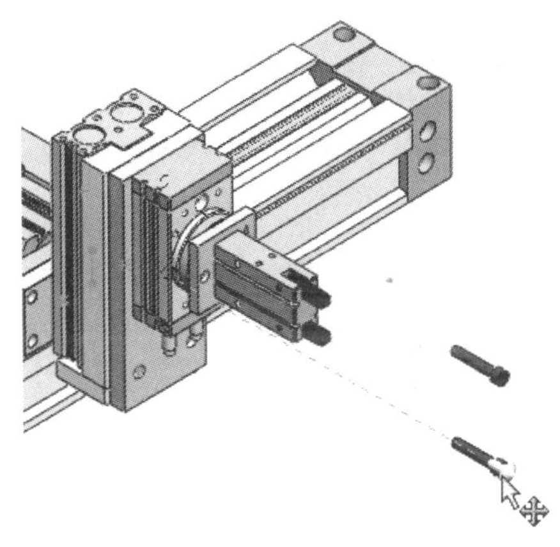

329) Click and drag the red/yellow **Manipulator** arrow to the right as illustrated.

330) Click **Done**. Explode Step1 is created.

Create Explode Step 2.

331) Click the first **B18.3.1M-8x1.25x70 Hex SHCS** from the FeatureManager.

332) Hold the **Ctrl** key down.

333) Click the second, third and forth **B18.3.1M-8x1.25x70 Hex SHCSs**.

334) Release the **Ctrl** key.

335) Click and drag the green/yellow **Manipulator** arrow above the GUIDE-CYLINDER.

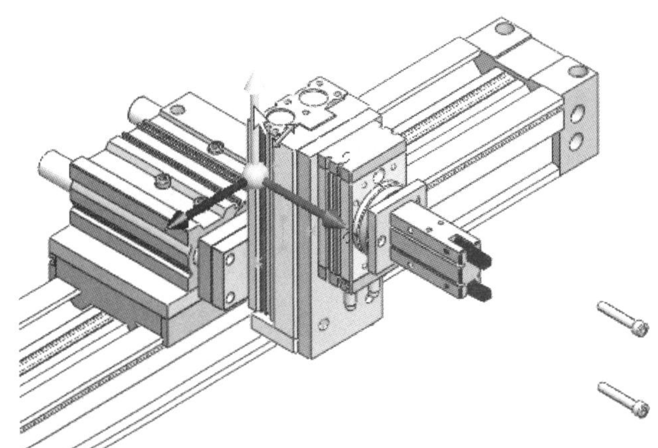

336) Click **Done**. Explode Step2 is created.

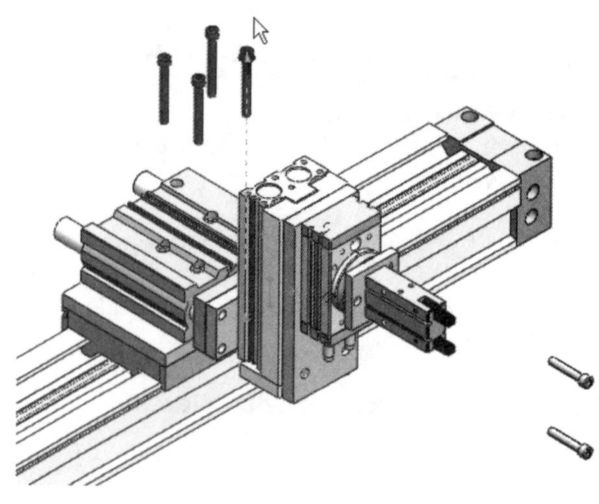

Create Explode Step3.

337) Click the **ROTARY-GRIPPER** assembly from the FeatureManager.

338) Click and drag the red/yellow **Manipulator** arrow to the right as illustrated.

339) Click **Done**. Explode Step3 is created.

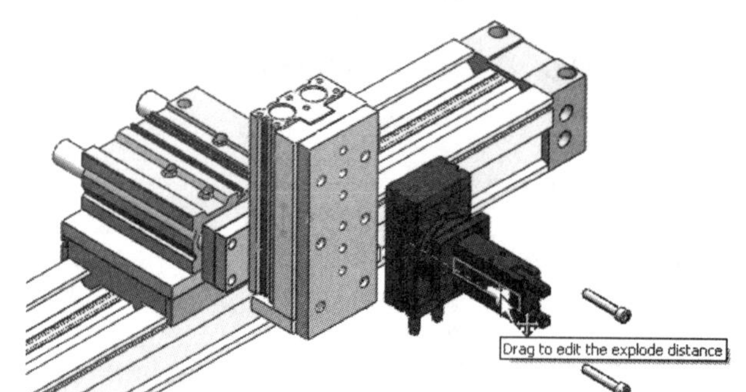

Create Step 4.

340) Click the 2AXIS-TRANSFER assembly from the fly-out FeatureManager.

341) Click and drag the green/yellow **Manipulator** arron above the LINEAR-TRANSFER assembly.

342) Click **Done**. Explode Step4 is created.

343) Click **OK** ✓ from the Explode PropertyManager.

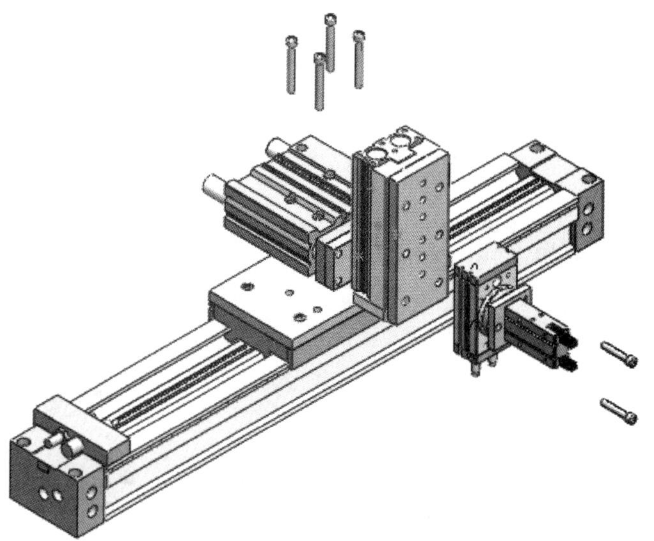

Collapse the Exploded View.

344) **Expand** the Fastener configuration.

345) Right-click **ExplView1**.

346) Click **Collapse**. View the model in the Graphics window.

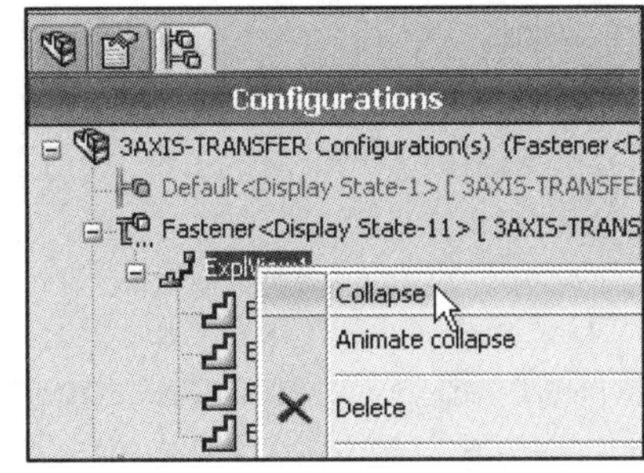

Return to the 3AXIS-TRANSFER Default assembly.

347) Double-click the **Default** configuration from the ConfigurationManager.

Save the 3AXIS-TRANSFER assembly.

348) Click **Save**.

Return to the 3AXIS-TRANSFER drawing, Sheet2.

349) Press **Ctrl+Tab**.

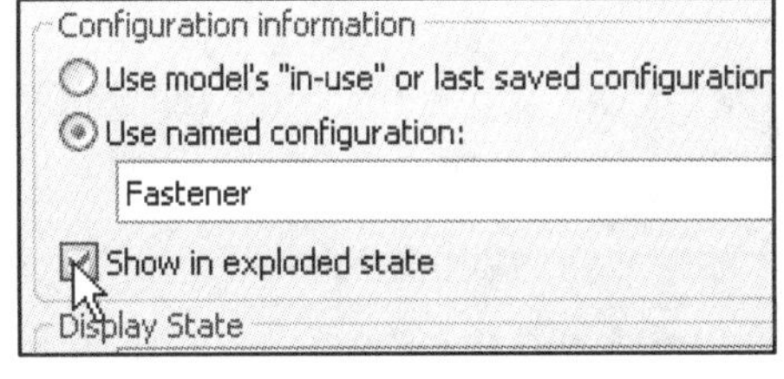

Display the Exploded View.

350) Click inside the **Isometric** view.

351) Right-click **Properties**.

352) Select **Fastener** from the Use named configuration drop-down menu.

353) Check the **Show in exploded state** box.

354) Click **OK** from the Drawing View Properties dialog box.

Modify the Scale.

355) Check the **Use custom scale** box.

356) Enter **1:15.**

357) Click **OK** ✔ from the PropertyManager.

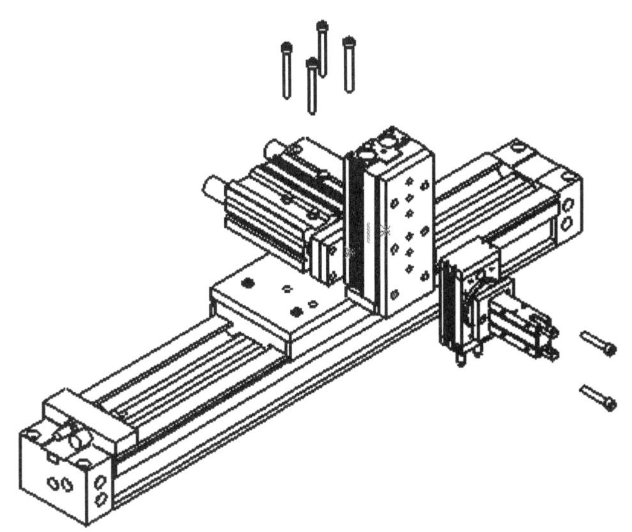

Drawing - Balloons

The 3AXIS-TRANSFER drawing, Sheet2 contains an Exploded Isometric view in the Fastener configuration. Apply Balloon annotations to label components in an assembly. The Balloon contains the Item Number listed in the Bill of Materials.

A Balloon displays different end conditions based on the arrowhead geometry reference. Drag the endpoint of the arrowhead to modify the attachment and the end condition.

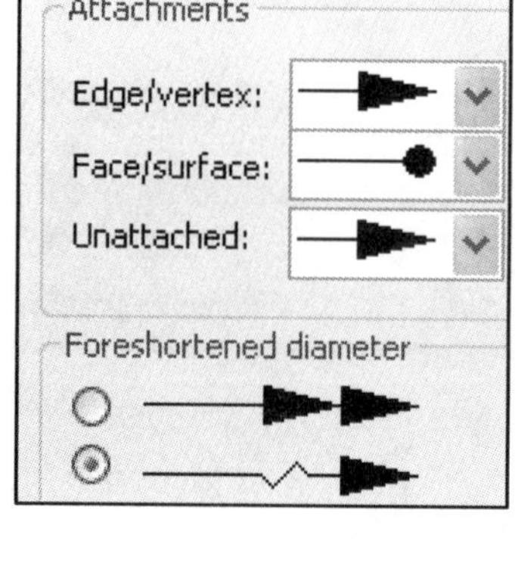

There are three attachment types:

- *Edge – arrowhead*
- *Face – dot*
- *No Reference – question mark*

View mouse pointer feedback to distinguish between a vertex in the model and the attachment point in a Balloon.

The attachment point displays the Note icon for a Balloon and the Point icon for point geometry.

The Document Template, Document Properties, Balloons option defines the default arrow style and Balloons options.

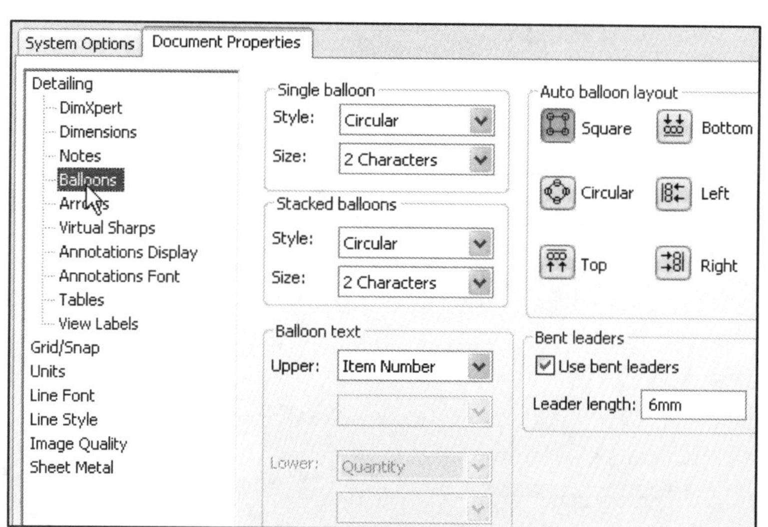

The Balloons option controls the Single balloon, Stacked balloons, Balloon text, Bent leaders, and Auto Balloon Layout options.

The Auto Balloon Layout option determines the display of the Balloons. Square Layout is the default.

The Top Layout displays the Balloons horizontally aligned above the model. The Left Layout displays the Balloon vertically aligned to the left of the model.

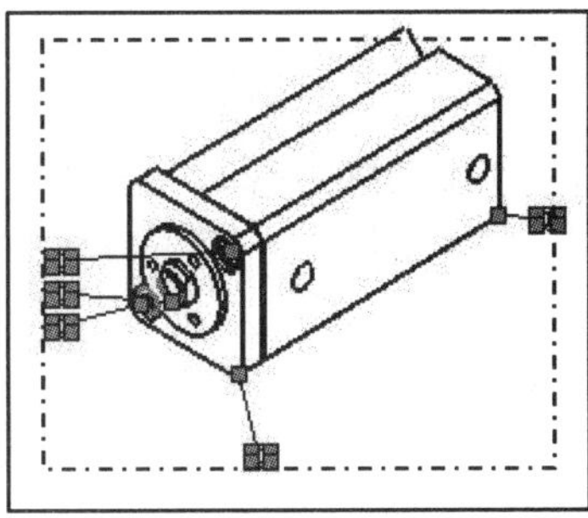
Square (Default)

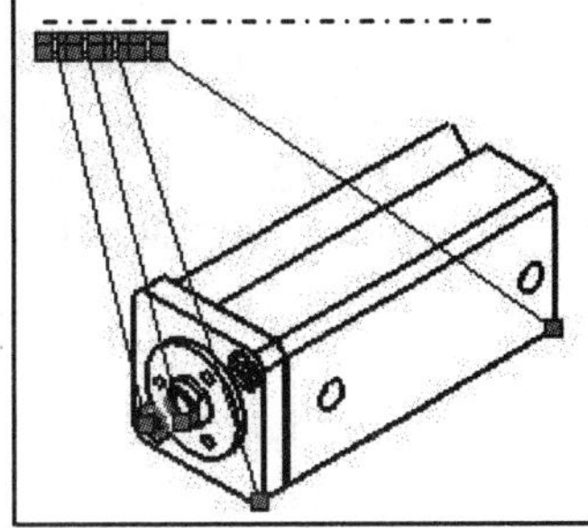
Top Layout

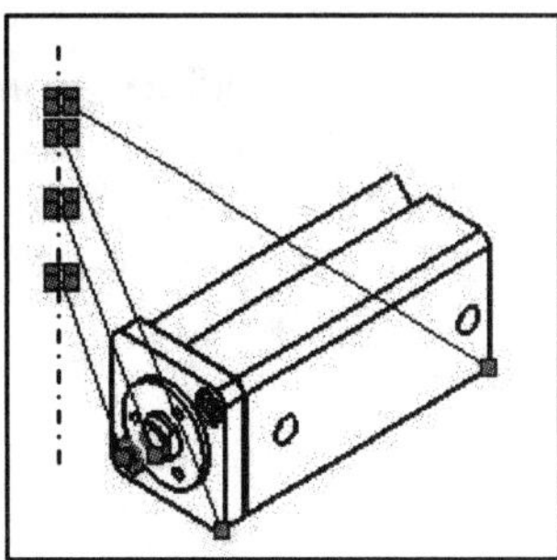
Left Layout

Modify the selected Balloon with Balloon Properties. The Circular Split Line Style displays the Item Number in the Upper portion of the circle and the Quantity in the Lower portion of the circle.

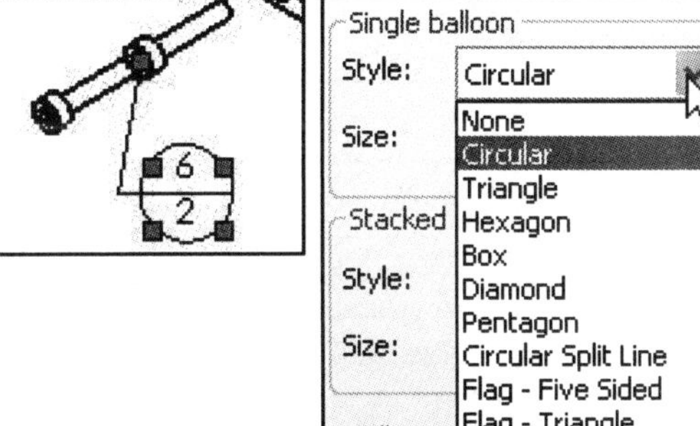

Select the Balloon option from the Annotations toolbar. Right-click Annotations in the Graphics window, or select Insert, Annotations from the Menu bar menu.

The Balloon option inserts a single item with a leader.

The Auto Balloon option inserts Balloons based on the view boundary and the BOM type.

The Stacked Balloon option contains multiple item numbers with a single leader.

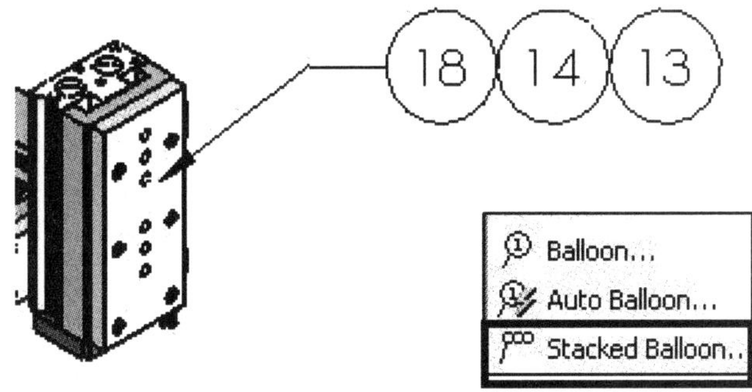

Activity: Apply the AutoBallon Tool: Sheet2

Insert Balloons to Label each component.

358) Click **inside** the Isometric Exploded View.

359) Click the **Annotation** tab in the CommandManager.

360) Click the **AutoBalloon** tool from the Annotation toolbar. The Auto Balloon PropertyManager is displayed. Accept the default settings. Five balloons are displayed in the Isometric view.

361) Click **OK** ✔ from the Auto Balloon PropertyManager.

ITEM NO.	PART NUMBER	DESCRIPTION	MATERIAL	Default/QTY.	Fastener/QTY.
1	99-022102	LINEAR-TRANSFER		1	1
2	99-022103	2AXIS-TRANSFER		1	1
3	99-022104	ROTARY-GRIPPER		1	1
4	SHC-45	M8 x 1.25 x 45 Hex	Alloy Steel	-	2
5	SHC-70	M8 x 1.25 x 70 Hex	Alloy Steel	-	4

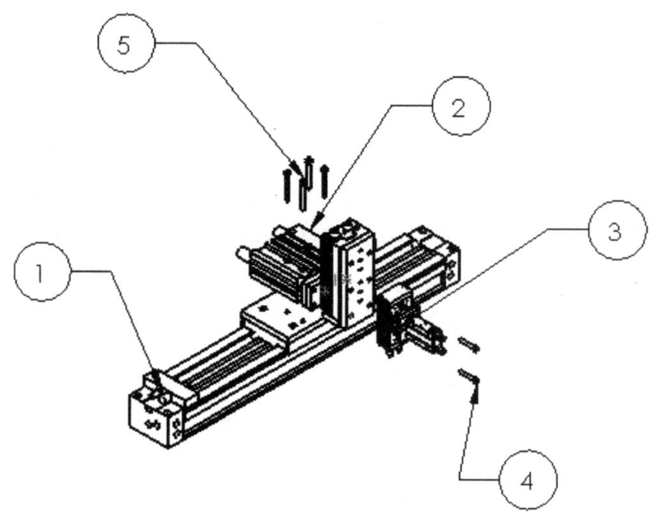

Modify the Balloons.

362) **Window-select** the five Balloons. The Balloon PropertyManager is displayed.

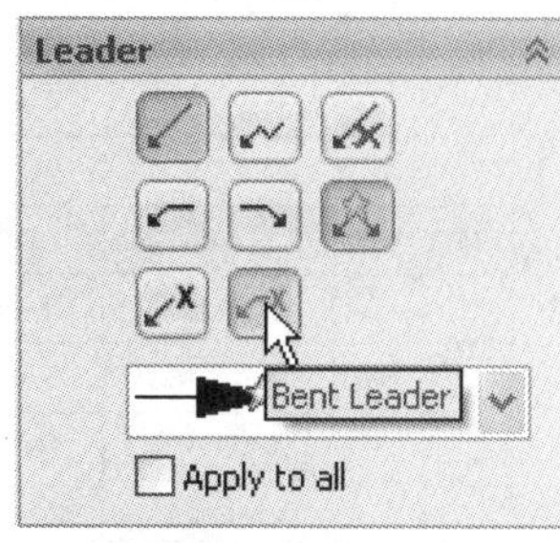

363) Click the **More Properties** button.

364) Click **Bent Leader** from the Leader box.

Modify the font.

365) Uncheck **Use document's font**.

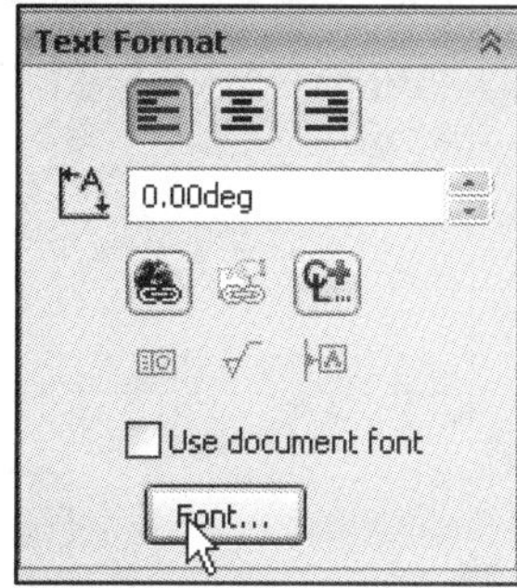

366) Click **Font**.

367) Enter **4**mm for font height.

368) Click **OK** from the Font dialog box.

Modify the arrowhead.

369) Click **Balloon 1**.

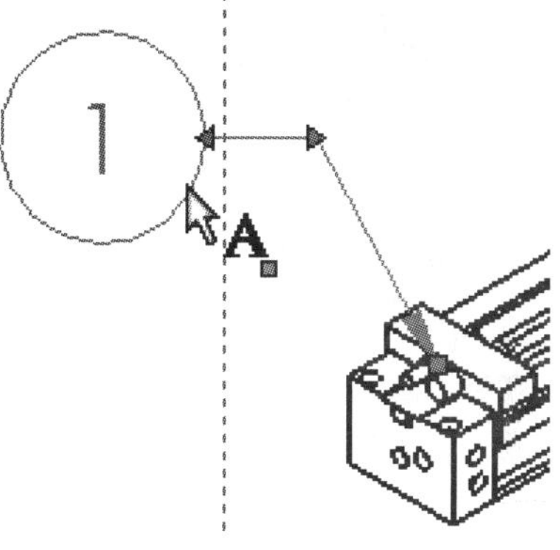

370) Drag the **arrowhead** to the middle edge as illustrated.

371) Drag each **Balloon** into position. Leave space between Balloon numbers.

372) Click **OK** ✔.

Save the 3AXIS-TRANSFER drawing.

373) Click **Save**.

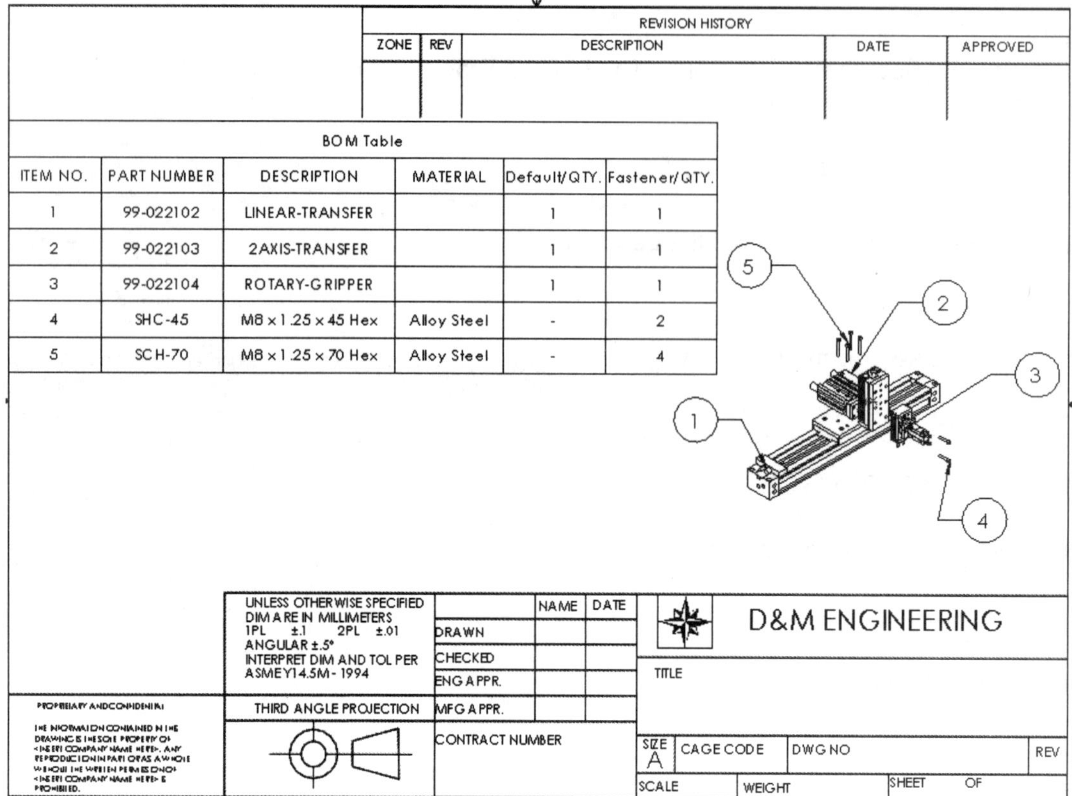

ITEM NO.	PART NUMBER	DESCRIPTION	MATERIAL	Default/QTY.	Fastener/QTY.
1	99-022102	LINEAR-TRANSFER		1	1
2	99-022103	2AXIS-TRANSFER		1	1
3	99-022104	ROTARY-GRIPPER		1	1
4	SHC-45	M8 x 1.25 x 45 Hex	Alloy Steel	-	2
5	SCH-70	M8 x 1.25 x 70 Hex	Alloy Steel	-	4

Custom Properties

Add the Description Custom Property to the Title block, Sheet2.

374) **Zoom in** on the lower right hand corner of the Title block.

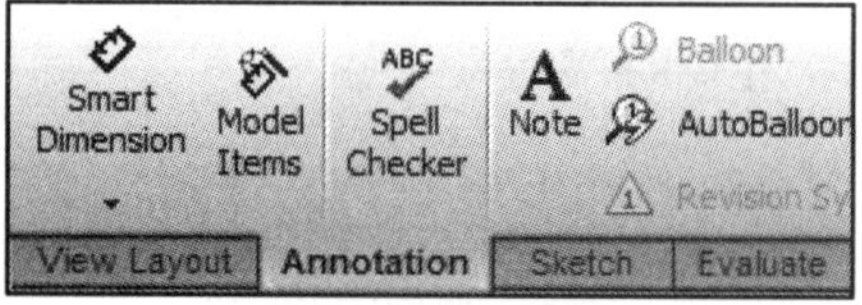

Insert a Linked Note for Description.

375) Click the **Note** tool from the Annotation toolbar.

376) Click a **position** to the right of TITLE text.

377) Click **Link to Property**.

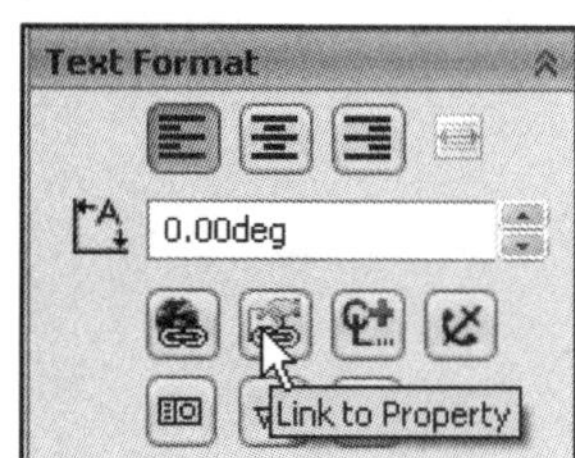

378) Click the **File Properties** button.

379) Click **inside** the Property Name box.

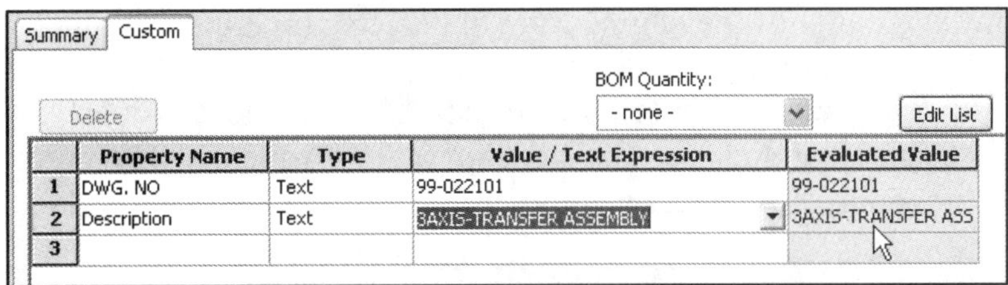

380) Select **Description** from the drop-down menu.

381) Click **inside** the Value / Text Expression box.

382) Enter **3AXIS-TRANSFER Assembly**

383) Click **OK**.

384) Select **Description** from the drop-down menu.

385) Click **OK** from the Link to Properties box.

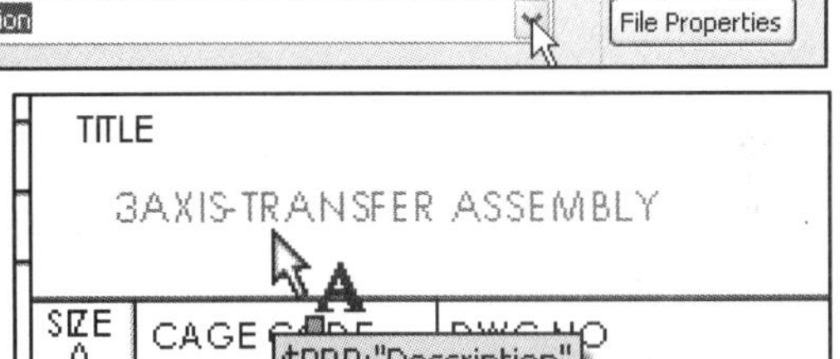

386) **OK** from the Note PropertyManger.

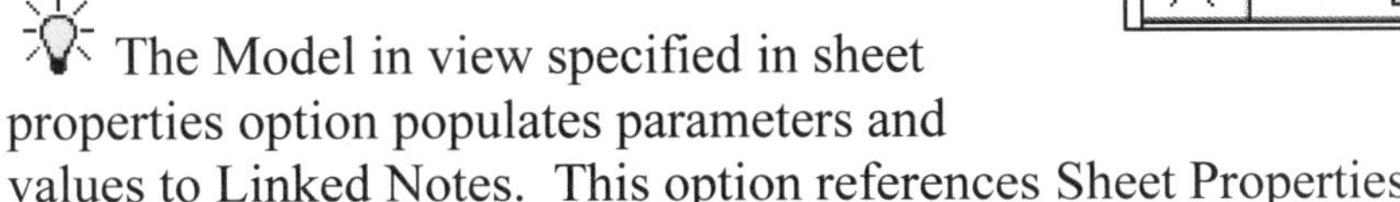

The Model in view specified in sheet properties option populates parameters and values to Linked Notes. This option references Sheet Properties.

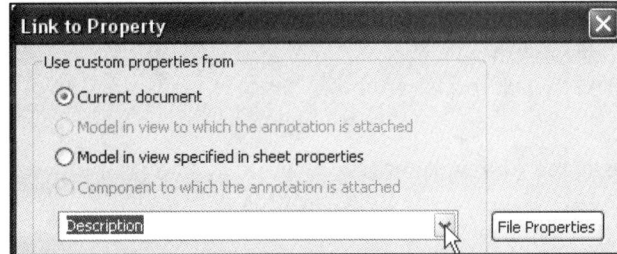

Revision Table

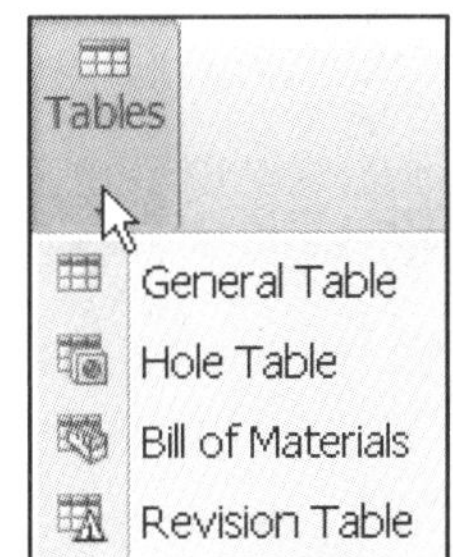

The Revision Table lists the Engineering Change Order (ECO) in the top right section of the drawing. An ECO documents changes that occur to a component. The Engineering department maintains each ECO with a unique document number. In this project, the ECO 8531 releases the drawing to manufacturing.

The current Revision block on the drawing was imported from AutoCAD. Delete the current Revision block lines and text. Utilize the Insert, Tables, Revision option to create a Revision Table or click Revision Table from the Annotation toolbar from the CommandManager. The default columns are as follows: Zone, Rev, Description, Date, and Approved.

The Zone column utilizes the row letter and column number contained in the drawing border. Position the REV letter in the Zone area. Enter the Zone letter/number. Enter a Description that corresponds to the ECO number. Modify the date if required. Enter the initials/name of the engineering manager who approved the revision.

The REV. column in the Revision Table is a Sheet Property. Create a Linked Note in the Title block and utilize the Revision Sheet Property. The current Revision of the drawing corresponds to the letter in the last row of the Revision Table.

Activity: Create a Revision Table: Sheet1

Activate Sheet1.
387) Click the **Sheet1** tab. Sheet1 is displayed.

Edit the Sheet Format.
388) Right-click in the **Graphics window**.

389) Click **Edit Sheet Format**.

Delete the current Revision Table created in the Autocad format.
390) Zoom in on the upper right corner of the Sheet Format.

391) Window-select the Revision Table. The Note PropertyManager is displayed.

REVISION HISTORY				
ZONE	REV	DESCRIPTION	DATE	APPROVED

392) Press the **Delete** key.

Return to the drawing sheet.
393) Right-click in the **Graphics window**.

394) Click **Edit Sheet**.

Fit the drawing to the Graphics window.
395) Press the **f** key.

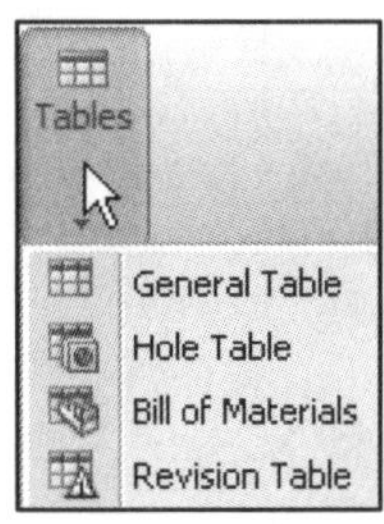

Insert a Revision Table.

396) Click the **Revision Table** tool from the Annotation toolbar in the CommandManager. The Revision Table PropertyManager is displayed.

397) Select the **standard revision** Table Template.

398) Click the **Circle Revision** Symbol Shape.

399) Check the **Enable symbol when adding new revision** box.

400) Click **OK**.

401) Drag the **Revision Table** downward to the inside upper right sheet boundary.

The Enable symbol when adding new revision option displays the Revision Symbol on the mouse pointer when you execute the Add Revision command. Position the revision symbol on the drawing that corresponds to the change.

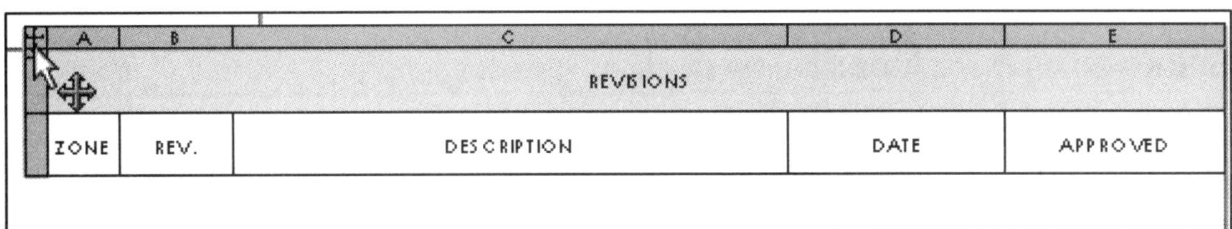

Insert the First row in the Revision Table.

402) Right-click the **Revision Table**.

403) Click **Revisions**, **Add Revision**. The Revision letter, A and the current date are displayed in the Revision Table. The Revision Symbol is displayed on the mouse pointer.

Revisions | Insert | Add Revision

Position the Revision Symbol.

404) Click a **position** in the Front view: Drawing View2

405) Click **OK** from the Revision Symbol PropertyManager.

Edit the Revision Table.
406) Double-click the **text box** under the Description column.

407) Enter **ECO 8531 RELEASED TO MANUFACTURING** for DESCRIPTION.

408) Click **outside** of the table.

409) Double-click the **text box** under the APPROVED column.

410) Enter Documentation Control Manager's Initials, Example: **DCP**.

411) Click **outside** of the table.

REVISIONS				
ZONE	REV.	DESCRIPTION	DATE	APPROVED
	A	ECO 8531 RELEASED TO MANUFACTURING	4/9/2008	DCP

Edit the Sheet Format.
412) Right-click a **position** in the Sheet boundary.

413) Click **Edit Sheet Format**.

Activity: Insert a Linked Note for Revision: Sheet1

Insert a Linked Note for Revision.

414) Click **Note** A from the Annotation toolbar.

415) Click a **position** below the REV text in the Title block.

416) Click **Link to Property**.

417) Select **Revision** from the drop-down list.

418) Click **OK**.

419) Click **OK** from the Note PropertyManager.

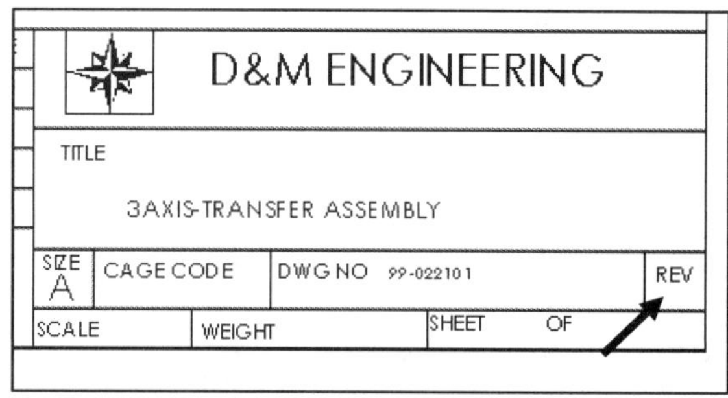

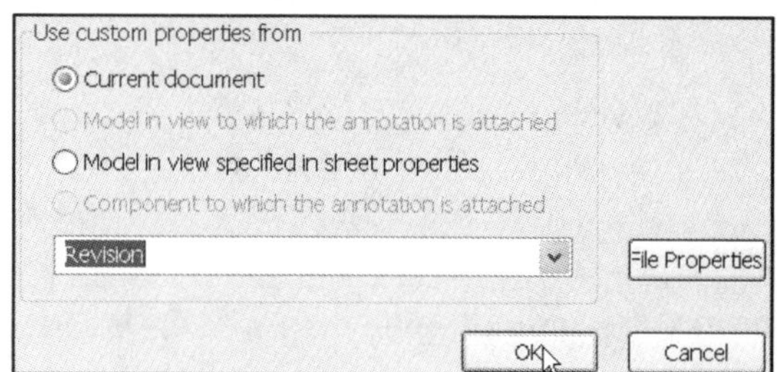

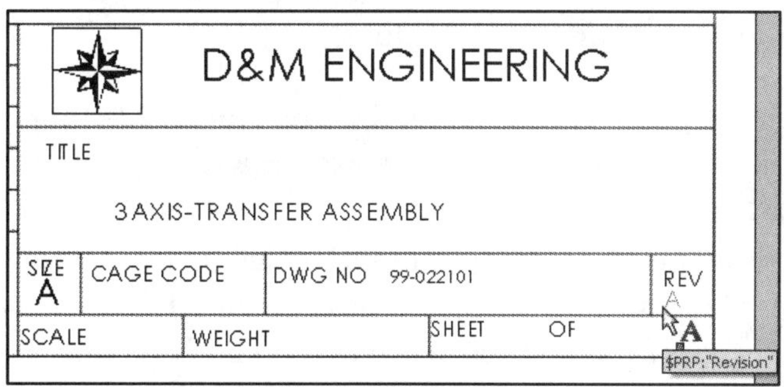

Return to the drawing sheet.

420) Right-click a **position** in the sheet boundary.

421) Right-click **Edit Sheet**.

Save the drawing.

422) Click **Save**.

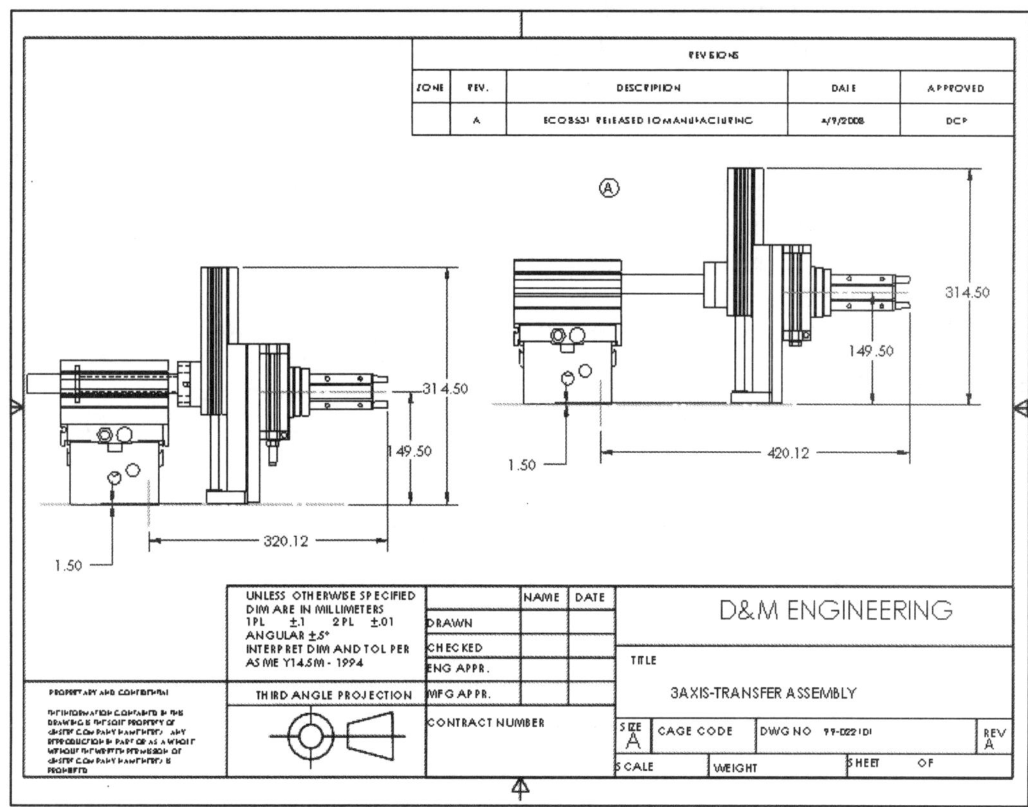

The File Properties button in the Link to Property box lists the Custom Properties of the sheet and their current values.

Insert the next revision in the Revision Table to increment the REV. text in the Title block. The Revision Table example shows how to control a REV. value through the drawing Sheet Properties.

Companies also control the REV. value by combining a Revision Custom Property in the part and a Linked Note in the drawing. PDM systems control document revisions based on the Revision rules in your company's engineering documentation practices.

Only Sheet1 displays the current REV. You will have to update the Title block in every sheet. Is there a more efficient method to control notes in the Title block? Answer: Yes. Develop a Sheet Format with Drawing Specific SolidWorks Properties and Custom Properties.

The default A-size SolidWorks Sheet Format contains Custom Properties defined in the Title block. Set Drawing Specific System Properties: SW-Sheet Name, SW-Sheet Scale SW-Sheet Format Size and SW-Template Size in the Sheet Properties dialog box.

The following Drawing Specific SolidWorks Properties exist only in a drawing:

Drawing Specific:	
SW-Sheet Name	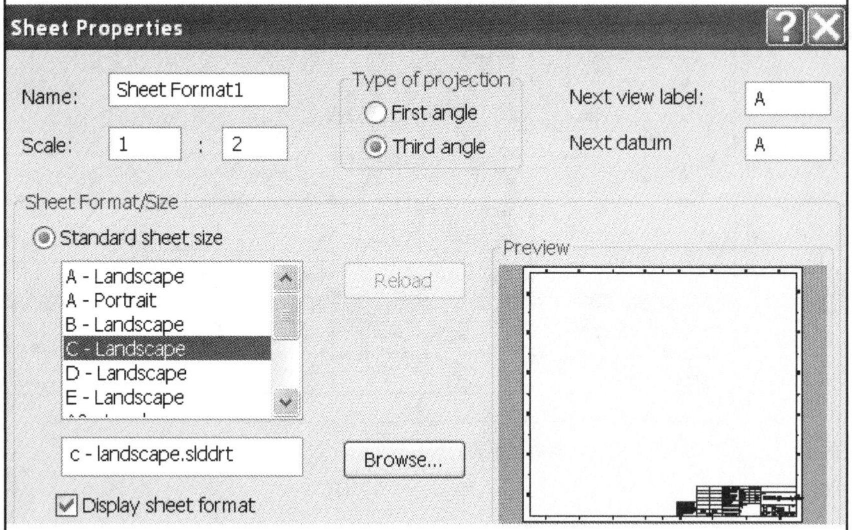 Sheet Properties Name: Sheet Format1 Scale: 1 : 2 Type of projection: First angle / Third angle Next view label: A Next datum: A Sheet Format/Size Standard sheet size A - Landscape A - Portrait B - Landscape C - Landscape D - Landscape E - Landscape Reload Preview c - landscape.slddrt Browse... Display sheet format
SW-Sheet Scale	
SW-Sheet Format Size	
SW-Template Size	
SW-Current Sheet	Determined from the current sheet selected in the drawing and the total number of sheets selected in the drawing.
SW-Total Sheet	

Creating customized Drawing Templates and Sheet Formats requires an understanding of SolidWorks Properties and Custom Properties.

Customized Drawing Templates and Sheet Formats save you set-up time in every drawing and on every sheet.

Utilize Online help, customize, sheet formats for additional information.

Refer to **Drawing and Detailing with SolidWorks 2008**, Project 2 for step-by-step instructions on creating Drawing Templates and Sheet Formats.

A .pdf file of Project 1& 2 is available at the publisher's website, www.schroff.com.

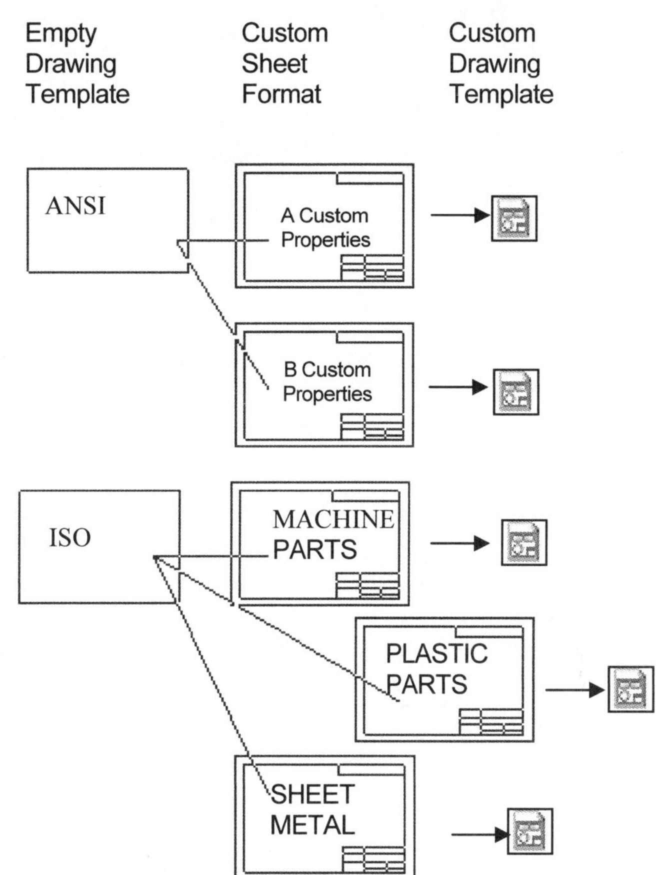

Drawing View Properties

The Drawing View Properties dialog box controls the display of edges and components. Utilize the Show/Hide option to display individual edges or components. Utilize the Drawing View Properties Show Hidden Edges and Hide/Show Components for efficient control.

Utilize a Design Table and the $Show@configuration<instance> parameter to Show/Hide a component. The values for the $Show parameter are Y for Show and N for Hide.

Activity: Apply Drawing View Properties: Sheet1

Drawing View Properties – Show Hidden Edges.

423) Click the **Sheet1** tab.

424) Click **inside** DrawingView1.

425) Right-click **Properties**.

426) Click the **Show Hidden Edges** tab.

427) Click the **MGPRod** component from the Graphics window as illustrated.

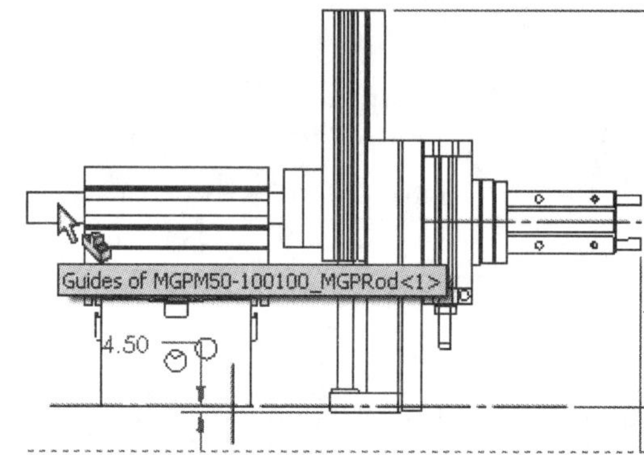

428) Click **Apply** from the Drawing View Properties box. The hidden edges of the MGPRod part inside the GUIDE-CYLINDER assembly are displayed.

429) Click **OK** from the Drawing View Properties box. View the results.

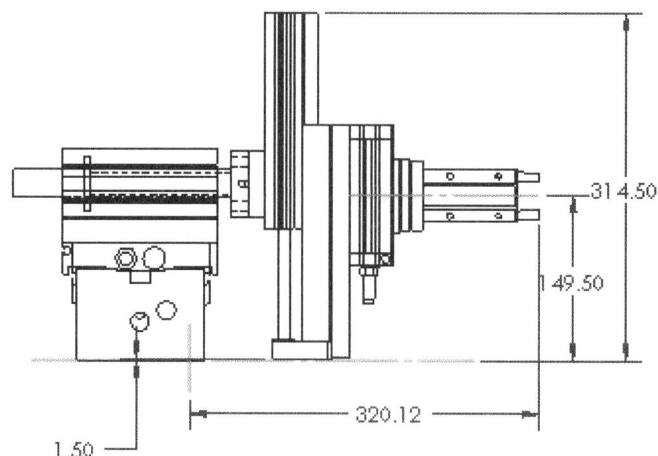

Hide two RBAshocks components.

430) Click **inside** DrawingView2, Position4.

431) Right-click **Properties**.

432) Click the **Hide/Show Components** tab.

433) Click the **RBAshocks<1>** component at the bottom of the ROTARY assembly as illustrated. Click Yes.

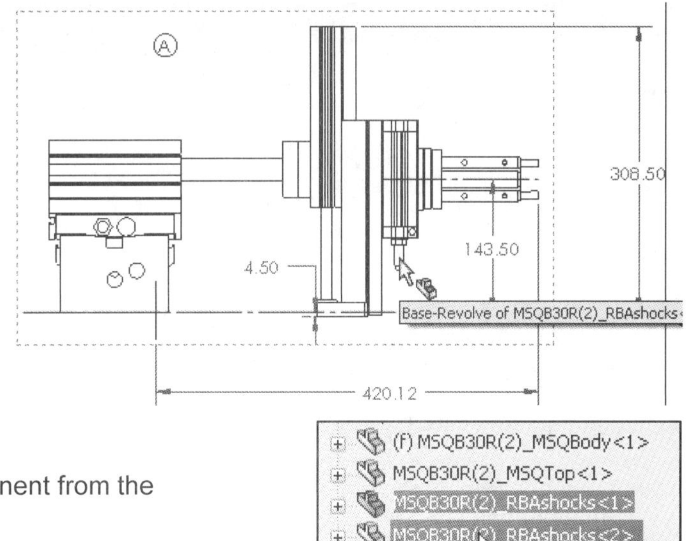

434) Click the **RBAshocks<2>** component from the FeatureManager.

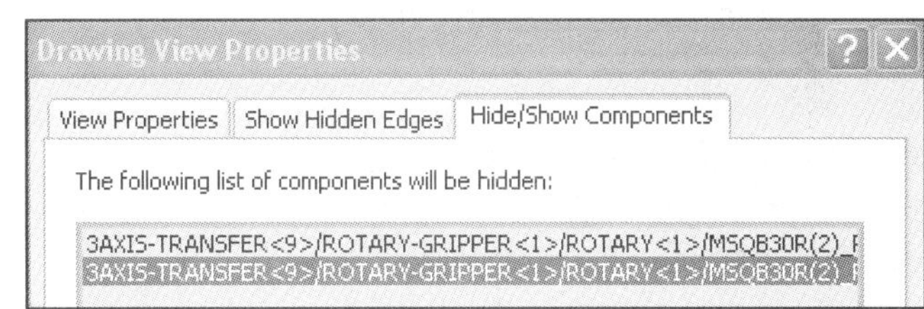

435) Click **Apply**.

436) Click **OK**.

Note: If components are difficult to select, utilize the FeatureManager to select components for a specific drawing view.

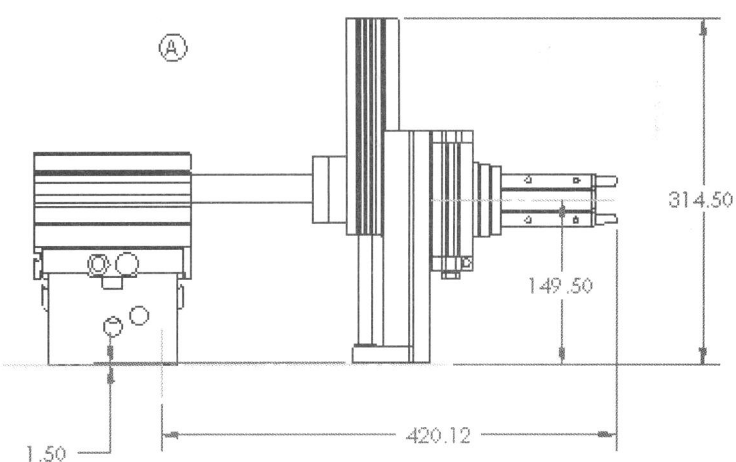

Activity: Create the 3AXIS-TRANSFER Drawing: Sheet3

Add Sheet3.

437) Click the **Sheet1** tab.

438) Right-click **Add Sheet**.

439) Click **OK**.

Select the Sheet Format.

440) Click the **Browse** button.

441) Double-click MY-TEMPLATES**a-format.slddrt.**

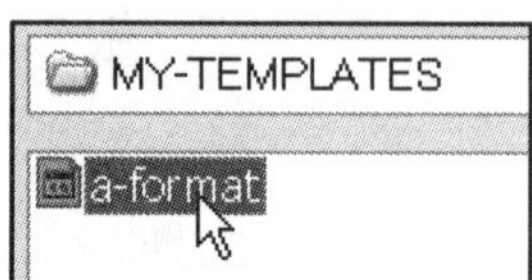

442) Click **OK** from the Sheet Properties box. Sheet3 is added to the drawing.

Copy DrawingView1 from Sheet1 to Sheet3.

443) Click inside the **DrawingView1** view boundary.

444) Press **Ctrl + C**.

Paste DrawingView1 from Sheet1.

445) Click a **position** on the left side of Sheet3 inside the sheet boundary.

446) Press **Ctrl + V**. Drawing View3 is created.

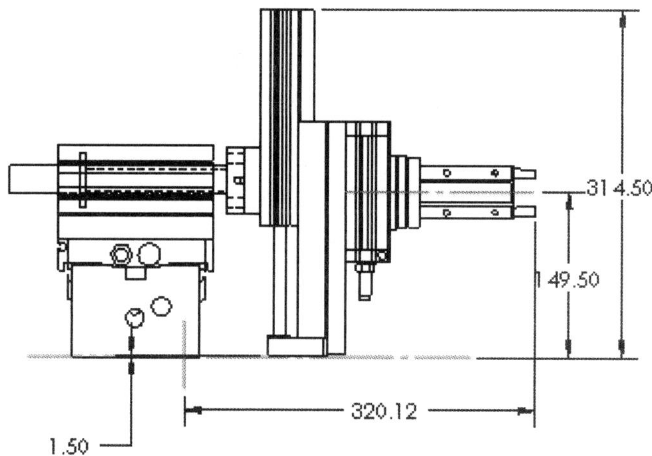

Delete the dimensions.

447) **Delete** the driven dimensions in Drawing View3 on Sheet3.

448) Click ***Top** for View Orientation.

449) Modify the scale to **1: 8**.

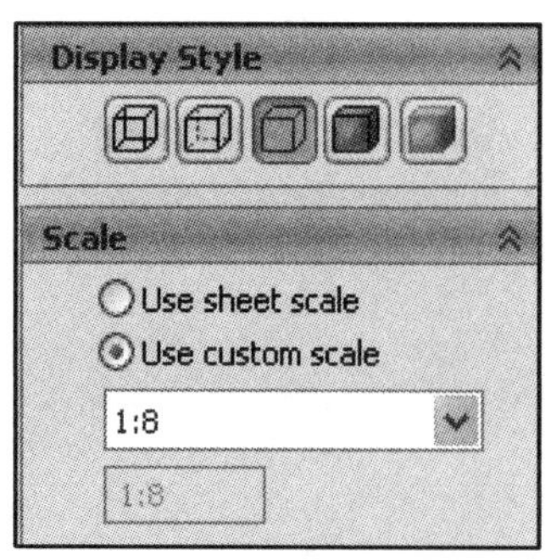

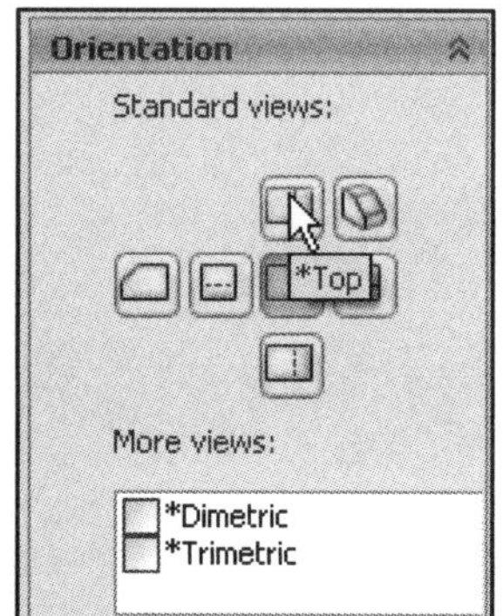

450) Drag the **view boundary** above the sheet boundary.

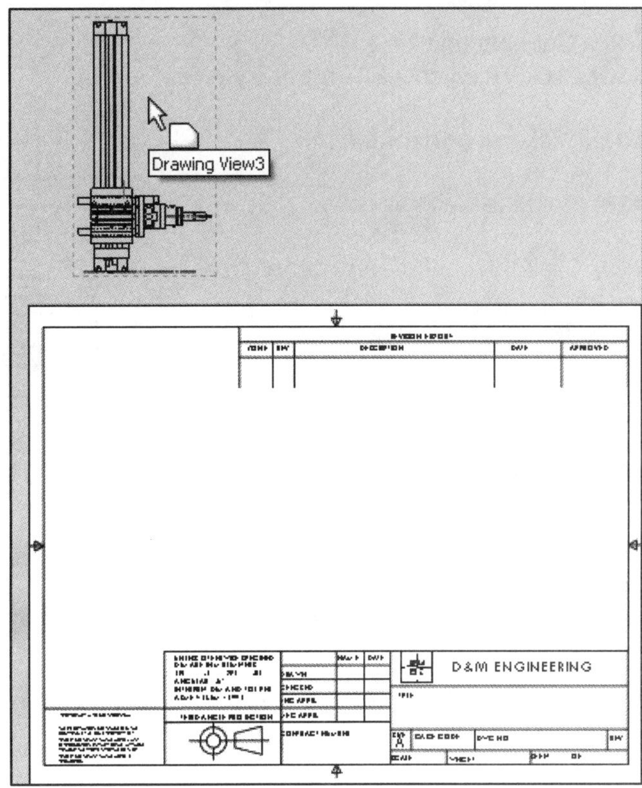

Insert a line.

451) The view boundary is selected. Click the **Line** tool from the Sketch toolbar.

452) Sketch a **horizontal line** below the top view inside the view boundary. Note: *The length of the horizontal line must be longer than the profile.*

453) Right-click **inside** the view boundary.

454) Click **Properties**.

455) Select **Position4** for use named configuration.

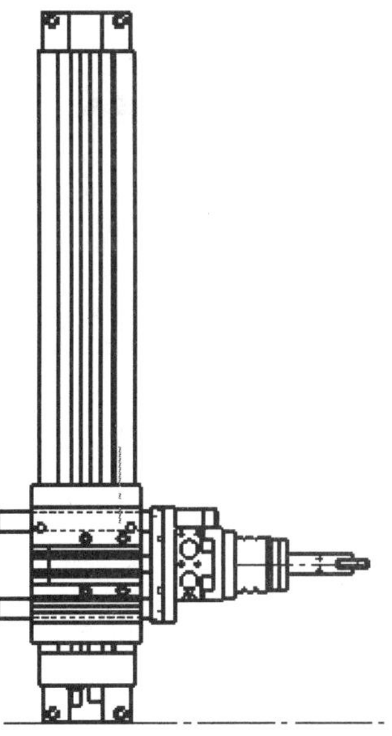

Add a Collinear relation.

456) Click **View**, check **Temporary Axes**.

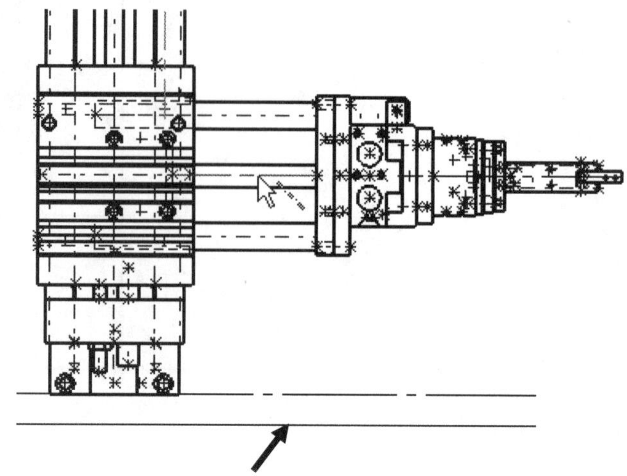

457) Click the **horizontal line**.

458) Hold the **Ctrl** key down.

459) Click the center **Temporary Axes**.

460) Release the **Ctrl** key.

461) Click **Collinear**.

462) Click **OK** from the Properties PropertyManager.

Hide the Temporary Axes.

463) Click **View**, uncheck **Temporary Axes**.

Activity: Create a Section View: Sheet3

Insert the Section view.

464) Click the **horizontal** line.

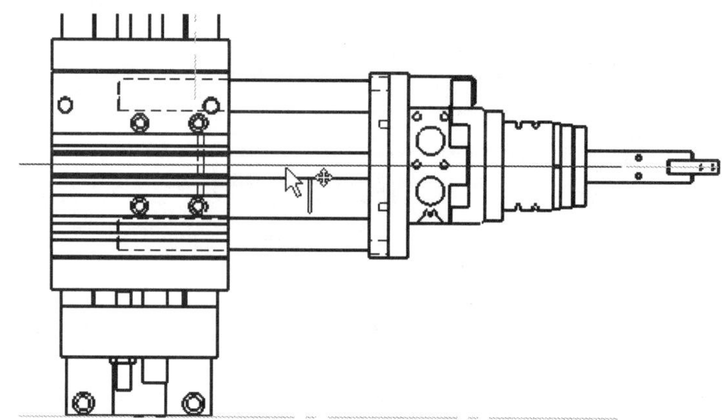

Fit the drawing to the screen.

465) Press the **f** key.

466) Click the **Section View** tool from the View Layout toolbar.

467) Click **OK** to the message, Do you want this to be a partical section view. Flip direction if required.

468) Click **OK** from the Section Scope box.

469) Click a **position** below the Top view inside the sheet boundary.

470) Click **OK** from the Section View A-A PropertyManager.

471) Add the Title: **3AXIS-TRANSFER** in the Title block. Note: Apply the Note tool.

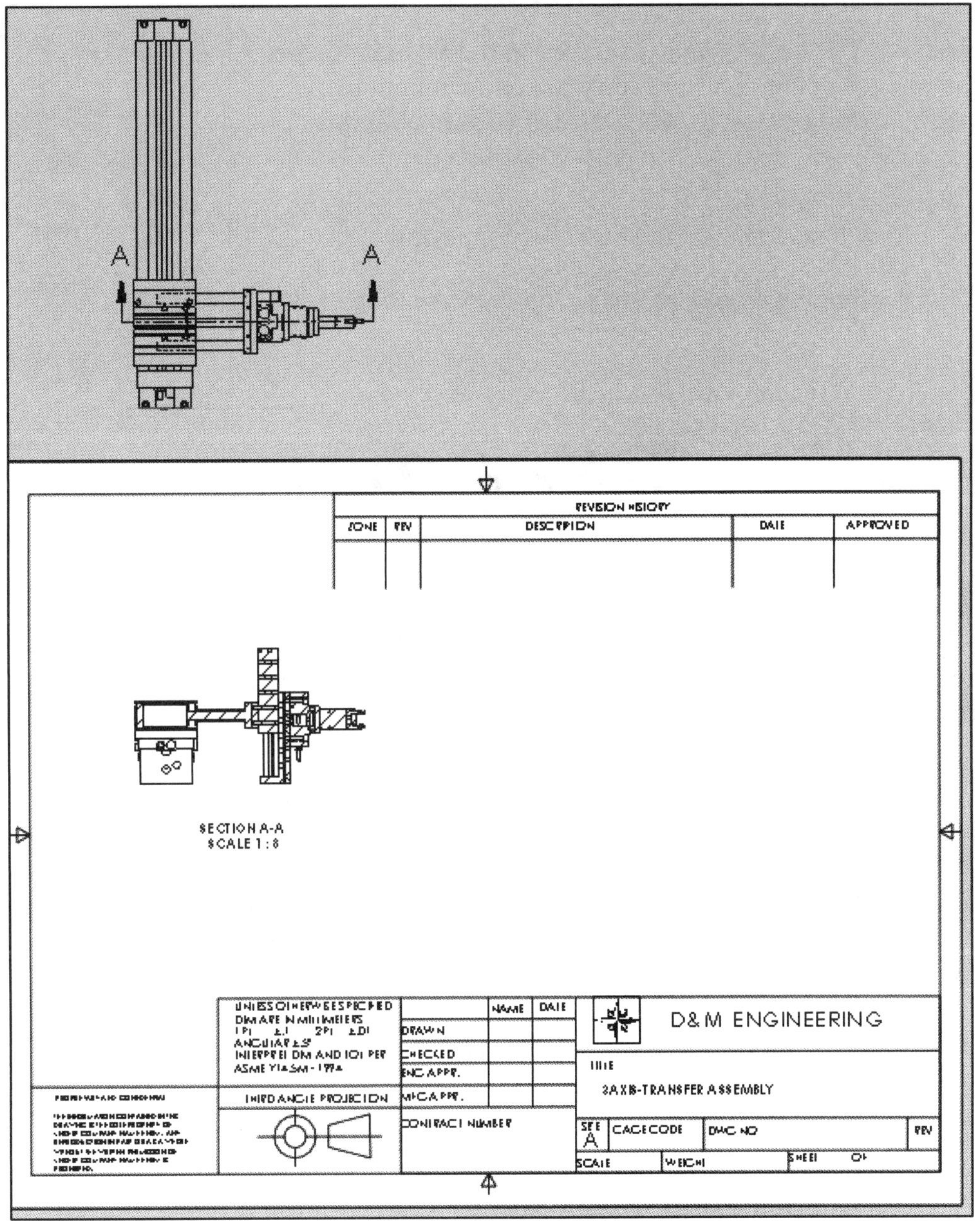
A
A
REVISION HISTORY
ZONE
REV
DESCRIPTION
DATE
APPROVED
SECTION A-A
SCALE 1 : 8
NAME
DATE
DRAWN
CHECKED
ENG APPR.
MFG APPR.
THIRD ANGLE PROJECTION
CONTRACT NUMBER
D&M ENGINEERING
TITLE
3AXIS-TRANSFER ASSEMBLY
SIZE
A
CAGE CODE
DWG NO
REV
SCALE
WEIGHT
SHEET
OF

The Section Scope, Select Other option, toggles through components. The components displayed in the Section Scope box contain no section lines. Modify the Drawing View Properties, Section Scope to select the entire sub-assembly.

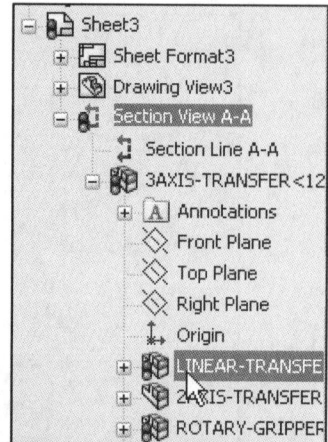

Modify the Section Properties.

472) Right-click **Properties** in the Section view boundary.

473) Click the **Section Scope** tab in the Drawing View Properties box.

474) Expand the **Section View A-A** in the FeatureManager.

475) Click the **LINEAR-TRANSFER** assembly.

476) Click **OK**.

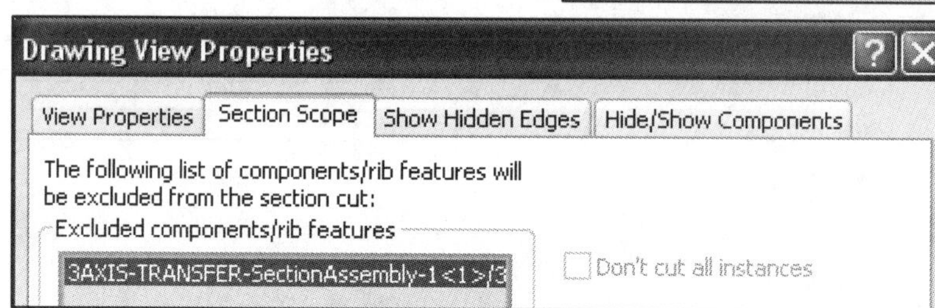

Save the drawing.

477) Click **Save**.

The Auto hatching option causes the hatch lines to alternate between the mating components. The default hatch pattern is Steel.

Modify the hatch pattern in the assembly by assigning the Aluminum material in the part. Why return to the part when you can edit the hatch pattern in the drawing? Answer: You are required to create component drawings of the PLATE-A, PLATE-B, PLATE-C, and PLATE-D parts.

Activity: Copy a SolidWorks Part / Assembly - SolidWorks Explorer

Close all documents.

478) Click **Windows**, **Close All** from the Menu bar menu.

Save PLATE-A.SLDPRT part as 45-63421-A.SLDPRT.

479) Click **Tools**, **SolidWorks Explorer** from the Menu bar menu.

480) Click **Cancel** from the PDMWorks dialog box.

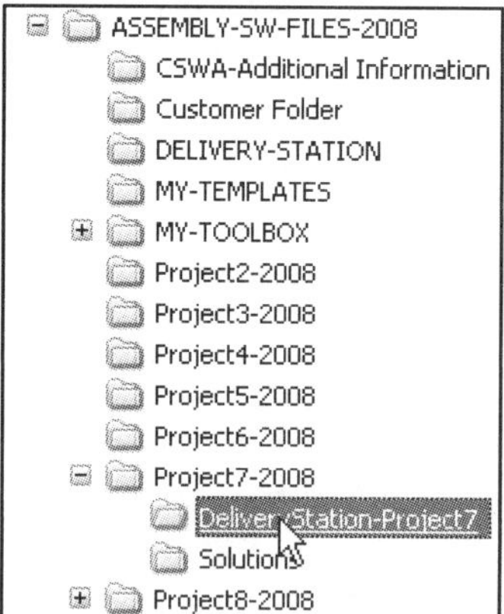

481) Browse to the DeliveryStation-Project7 folder.

482) Click **PLATE-A**.

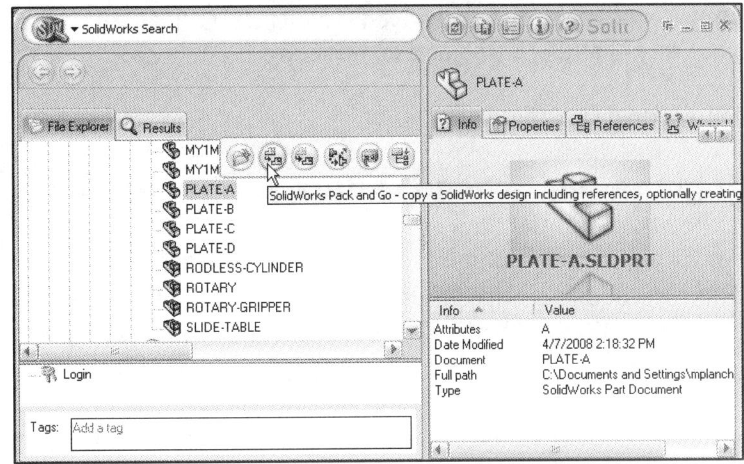

Copy the PLATE-A.SLDPRT part as 45-63421-A.SLDPRT.

483) Click the **SolidWorks Pack and Go** icon as illustrated.

484) Double-click the column **PLATE-A-SLDPRT**. The Rename Save To Names box is displayed.

485) Enter **45-63421-A.SLDPRT**.

486) Click **OK**.

487) Click **Save**. You just saved PLATE-A as 45-63421-A using SolidWorks Explorer.

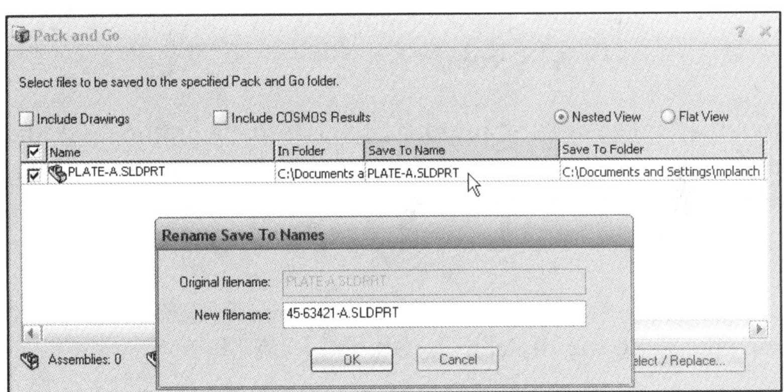

Save an Assembly with the references. Save the GUIDE CYLINDER assembly in the DeliveryStation-Project7 folder.

488) Click the **GUIDE CYLINDER**.

489) Click the **SolidWorks Pack and Go** icon as illustrated.

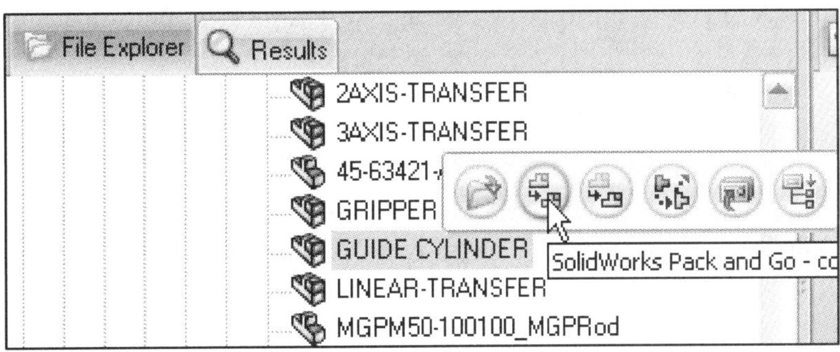

490) Double-click the column **GUIDE CYLINDER.SLDASM**. The Rename Save To Names box is displayed.

491) Enter **99-101456.SLDASM**.

492) Click **OK** from the Rename Save To Names dialog box.

493) Click **OK**.

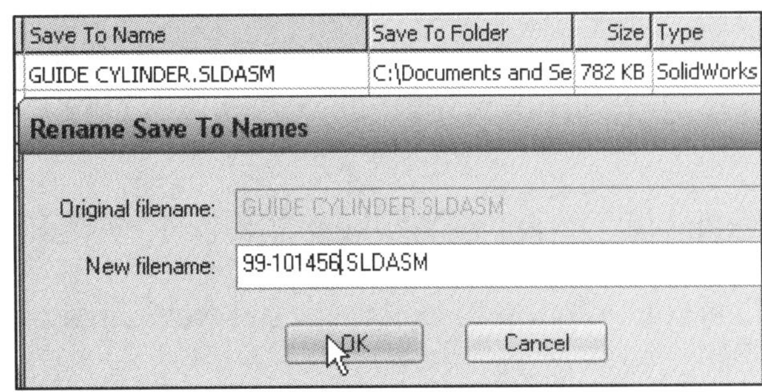

494) Click **Save.** You just saved the GUIDE CYLINDER assembly as 99-101456.SLDASM with all of its references and components.

495) Close SolidWorks Explorer.

Engineering Change Orders and Revisions

An Engineering Change Order (ECO) documents changes that occur to a component. The Engineering department maintains each ECO with a unique document number, Example: 0845. The ECO describes the design change, the affected departments, implementation strategy and the required signoff signatures.

When Engineering issues an ECO that affects a drawing, the drawing revision, located in the Title block, is incremented. In a letter revision system, Revision A becomes Revision B. In a number revision system, Revision 1 becomes Revision 2. In a letter/number revision system A1 becomes A2.

In a manual system or automated 2D drafting application, the ECO process affected the drawing. In SolidWorks, the part, assembly and drawing share a common file structure. Your company requires copies of all modified documents on released products in manufacturing. You do not have a Product Data Management (PDM) system.

The PLATE-A requires an etched number on the corner top face. The ECO documents the change to the PLATE-A part and PLATE-A drawing.

The documentation control manager makes a decision not to "up-rev" the LINEAR-TRANSFER assembly. There are no PLATE-A parts in inventory. You do not have to address the assembly revision or parts in stock.

Note: The term up-rev means to increment the revision number or letter of a document. Companies up-rev under different conditions. Example: Company A chooses to up-rev a sub-assembly every time a change is made to a part contained within that assembly. Company B chooses not to up-rev the sub-assembly if the overall form, fit and function of the part does not change. Luckily, you work for Company B.

The automotive, aerospace, medical and many other industries are required by law to document all engineering changes. Keeping track of these changes is the responsibility of all engineers and designers.

You must decide what enhancements to incorporate into your engineering documentation practices.

Example: Option 1: You keep the old Revisions table and utilize Notes to enter text.

Example: Option 2: Delete the old Revisions table and utilize Insert, Table, Revision Table.

Companies have various methods for updating and documenting revisions in a drawing. Utilize the following Revision Procedure Task List to stimulate questions.

Revision Procedure Task List:
Obtain an understanding of how engineering, manufacturing, quality assurance, marketing, field service and the customer work with parts, assemblies, drawings and revisions in your company.
Develop an example assembly, not tied to a current product delivery schedule. Evaluate scenarios for: • A part revision. • An assembly revision. • A drawing revision. • A Bill of Material revision. • Addition/Deletion of a part. • Addition/Deletion of a sub-assembly. • Addition/Deletion of a configuration.
Create benchmark assemblies, parts and drawings to test new revisions of software.
Research PDM software applications.
Ask other users, either at a local meeting or online, about their revision procedures.

SolidWorks modifies the document structure with every major release. As a result, older versions of SolidWorks cannot open documents created in a newer version. When you open an assembly file in a newer release, SolidWorks updates the document structure in the assembly and the referenced components.

This process takes time. The Tools, Conversion Wizard option performs the task of converting older version files to new version files in bulk. Once you convert the assembly files and the related components, the documents cannot be opened at the older version.

Project Summary

In this project, you completed the 3AXIS-TRANSFER assembly with nine different configurations.

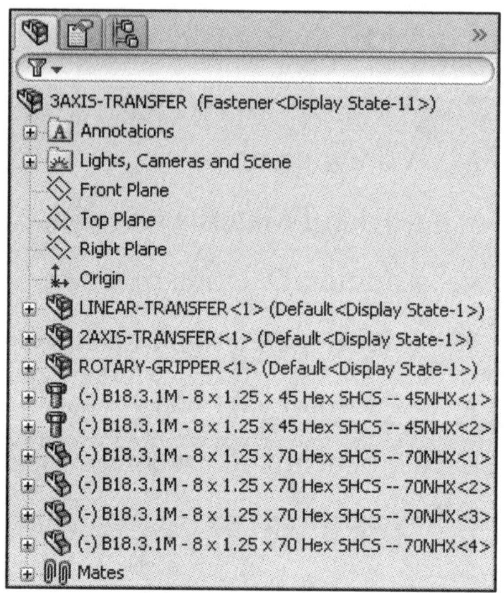

You create the 3AXIS-TRANSFER drawing with three sheets. Each drawing sheet displayed different configurations and views.

You added fasteners to the 3AXIS-TRANSFER assembly and created an Exploded View.

Custom Properties controlled the values displayed in the Bill of Materials and in the drawing Title block.

The Bill of Materials contains multiple options to display Top level, Parts only or Indented. Determine the Bill of Material Type before you insert balloons or edit the BOM in the drawing.

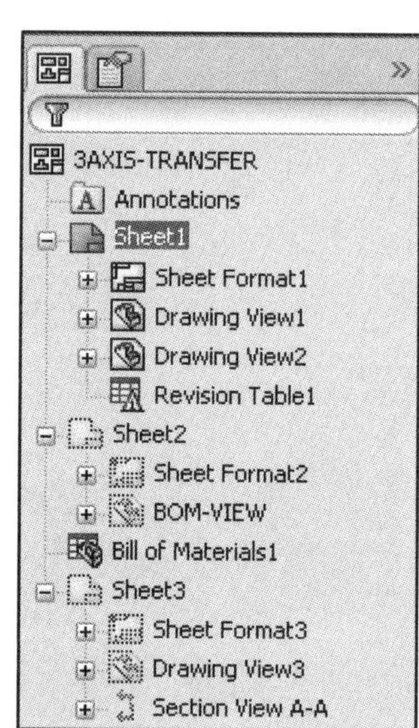

The more parameters and values you create in the part/assembly, the more time you will save in the BOM, Title block and other drawing views and annotations.

Revisions are an integral part of the engineering process. Engineering Change Orders track all revisions. Update all related documents when a change occurs.

You explored a Revision Table and a Revision Custom Property in the part as two separate methods to control the REV letter in the drawing Title block.

You copied a SolidWorks Part and Assembly with references using SolidWorks Explorer.

Questions:

1. Each component in an assembly has ____________ degrees of freedom.
2. Identify a method to remove degrees of freedom in an assembly.
3. True or False. A Design Table is used to create multiple configurations in an assembly.
4. True or False. A Design Table is used to create multiple configurations in a part.
5. True or False. A Design Table is used to create multiple configurations in a drawing.
6. Describe the (f) symbol functionality in the FeatureManager.
7. Describe the procedure to create an Exploded View.
8. Describe the function of a Balloon annotation.
9. True or False. The PART NO. Property in the default Bill of Materials is determined by the file name.
10. The ITEM NO. order in the default Bill of Materials is determined by the component order in the Assembly FeatureManager. Explain the process to modify the order.
11. Describe the procedure to add additional Properties, such as DESCRIPTION, to the Bill of Materials.
12. Describe the procedure to add additional Properties, such as REV, to the Title Block of a drawing.
13. Describe the function of the $STATE variable in the Design Table.
14. A drawing can contain multiple configurations of a _____________ and an ____________.
15. Describe the consequence of an ECO on a SolidWorks drawing.
16. Identify the location of the Revision Table.
17. Identify the document that defines the part material.

Notes:

Project 8

Top-down design, Layout Sketches, Blocks, Motion, and more

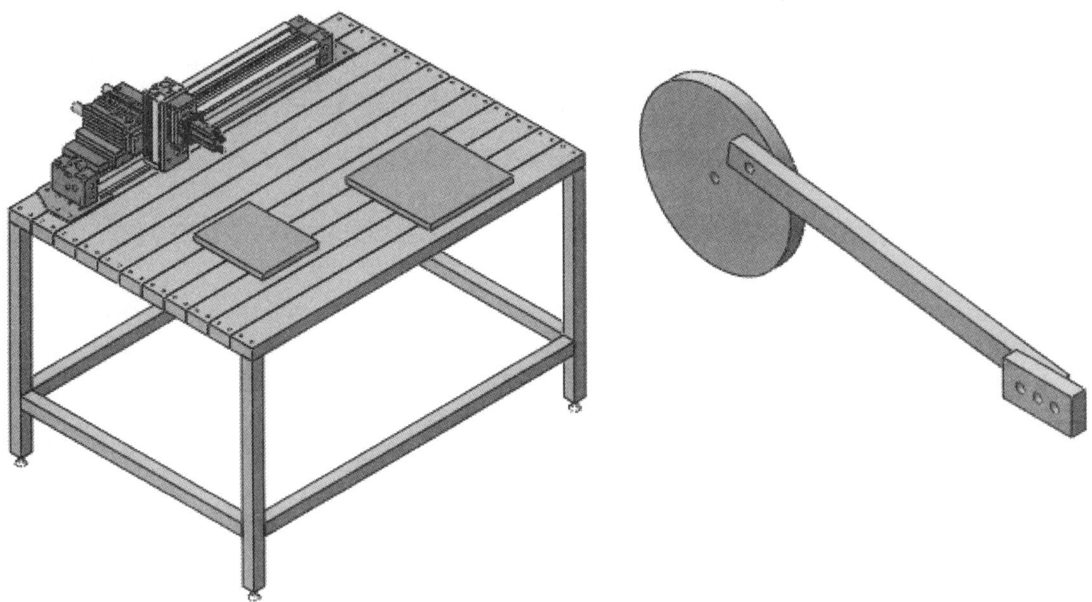

Below are the desired outcomes and usage competencies based on the completion of this Project.

Project Desired Outcomes:	Usage Competencies:
• DELIVERY-STATION Assembly.	• Top-down design from a Sketch in an Assembly.
• Link Values and Equations.	• Define Link Values and Equations to control relations in a sketch.
• INPUT-BASE-PART. • INPUT Assembly.	• Reuse and Reorder components.
• Layout Based Assembly Design with Blocks.	• Applied the Component Pattern and Mirror Component tool along with the Explode Line Sketch, Join feature, and Split feature.
• Motion Studies.	• Apply the following Motion Study tools: Linear motor, Rotary motor, and gravity.

Notes:

Project 8 – Top-down design, Layout Sketches, Blocks, Motion, and more

Project Objective

Create the DELIVERY-STATION assembly utilizing the Top-down design assembly modeling approach.

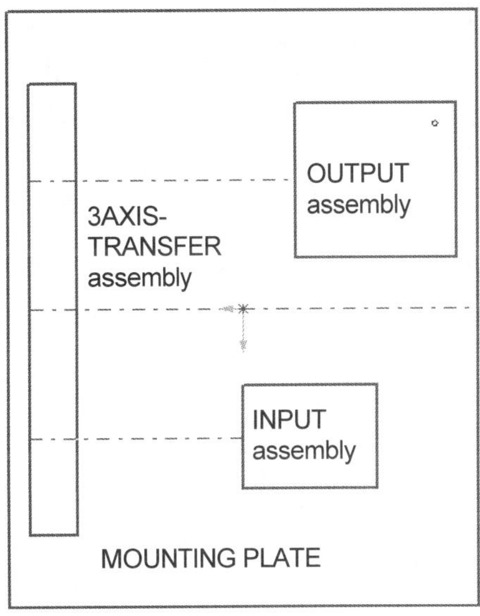

DELIVERY-STATION Layout sketch

In this Project, use the models in the Project8-2008 folder provided on the CD in the book.

The INPUT assembly contains the INPUT-BASE-PLATE part. The DELIVERY-STATION assembly contains the INPUT assembly.

The INPUT-BASE-PLATE part is created In-Context of the assembly.

The INPUT assembly is created In-Context of the DELIVERY-STATION assembly. Reorder the INPUT-BASE-PLATE part.

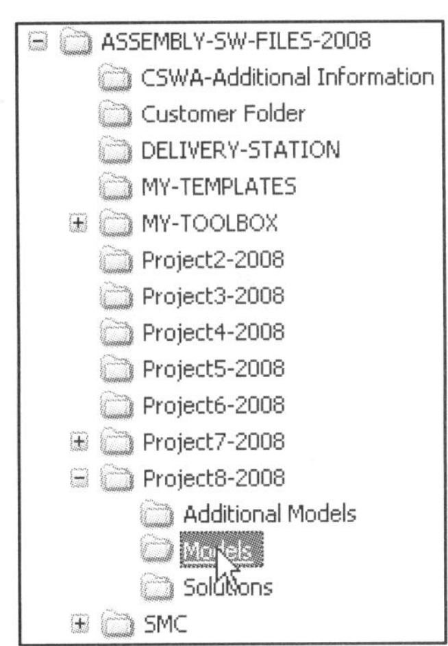

On the completion of this project, you will be able to:

- Understand the two methods to create a Top-down design assembly modeling approach:
  - **Method 1**: An individual sketch in the assembly created from a sketch or imported geometry.
  - **Method 2**: A Layout Sketch using the Layout tools to understand motion between components utilizing blocks.
- Define Link Value and Equations to control relations in a sketch.
- Utilize Convert Entities and build relationships from the Layout sketch to components developed in the context of the assembly.
- Recognize Edit Component while working in a multi-level environment between assembly, sub-assembly and part.
- Reuse component geometry with Component Pattern and Mirror Components.
- Create Motion Studies using the following tools: Linear motor, Rotary motor, and gravity.

Product Specification

You are on the final design phase of the DELIVERY-STATION assembly project. Your manager temporarily assigned your colleagues to a different project. You are required to keep the DELIVERY-STATION assembly project on track and to update the product specification. Review the preliminary product specification and utilize a Top-down design assembly modeling approach.

Major design requirements in the Top-down design assembly modeling approach translate into assemblies, sub-assemblies and components. You do not need all of the required component design details. Individual relationships are required.

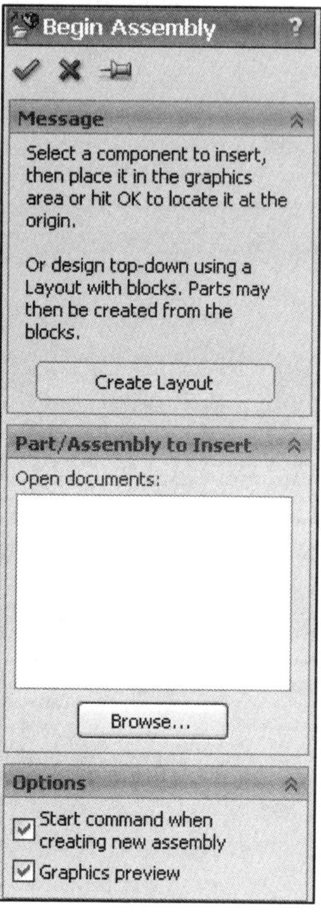

There are two methods to create a Top-down design assembly modeling approach:

- **Method 1**: An individual sketch in the assembly created from a sketch or imported geometry.
- **Method 2**: A Layout Sketch using the Layout tools to understand motion between components utilizing blocks.

Consider the following questions in a preliminary design product specification:

What are the major components in the design of the DELIVERY-STATION assembly?

- *3AXIS-TRANSFER assembly*
- *INPUT assembly*
- *OUTPUT assembly*
- *MOUNTING-PLATE part*

What are the key design constraints of the DELIVERY-STATION assembly?

- INPUT assembly, BASE PLATE part: 250mm x 200mm x 20mm
- OUTPUT assembly, BASE PLATE part: 300mm x 200mm x 20mm
- Location of the GRIPPER fingers for the INPUT assembly
- Location of the GRIPPER fingers for the OUTPUT assembly
- Displacement between the INPUT pick point and the OUTPUT place point: 500mm in the x direction, 100mm in the y direction and 100mm in the z direction.

- How does each part relate to the other parts? From past experience and discussions with the engineering department:
  - A 40mm minimum physical gap is required between the OUTPUT assembly and the outside edge of the MOUNTING PLATE part.
  - A 100mm x 400mm minimum area is required on both sides of the 3AXIS-TRANSFER assembly.
  - The 100mm x 400mm area is utilized to fasten switches and valves for the SMC components.
- How will the customer use the product?
- The customer does not disclose the specific usage of the DELIVERY-STATION assembly. The customer is in a very competitive market.
- What is the most cost-effective material for the product?
- Aluminum is the most cost-effective material. Aluminum is also strong, relatively easy to fabricate, corrosion resistant and is non-magnetic.

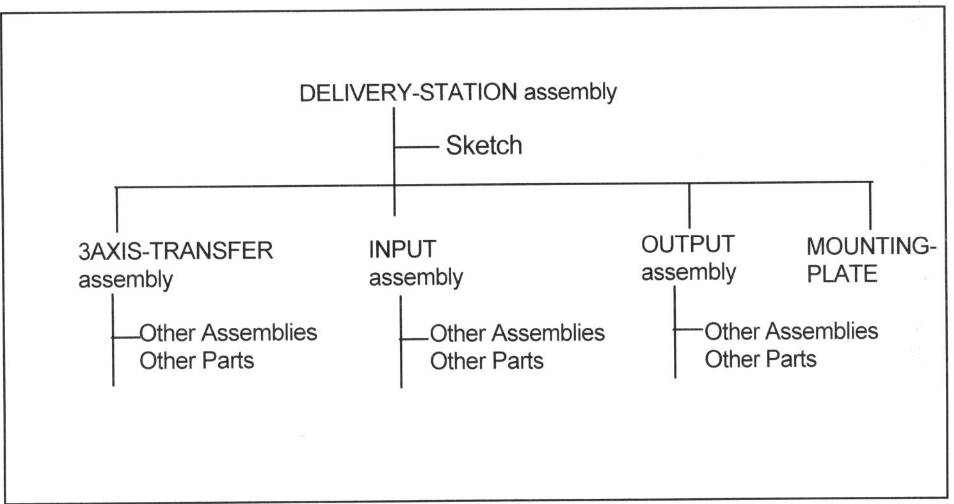

Incorporate the design specifications into the DELIVERY-STATION assembly. Use a sketch. The sketch represents components with sketched geometry, reference geometry and dimensions. Verify geometry relationships in the sketch.

How do you know when an assembly requires an initial sketch? How large is a large assembly that requires an initial sketch? Answer: Although there is no direct answer, ask questions in the beginning of a design to determine if an assembly is a candidate for an initial sketch.

The follow table lists questions to ask at the beginning of the design process.

Assembly candidate for an initial sketch:
Does the assembly contain new components that require modeling?
Does the assembly require design constraints between components to be determined?
Are major sub-assemblies modular?
Will sub-assemblies be developed in a team environment?
Does the top-level assembly require a majority of new models?
Are you working in a large assembly environment with hundreds of components?

A an initial sketch in an assembly provides information on how each component interacts with the other. Utilize an initial sketch to extract information and to build new parts in the DELIVERY-STATION assembly.

Insure that the DELIVERY-STATION maintains the required minimum 40mm spatial gap between the internal components and the MOUNTING-PLATE part outside edges. How do you design for future revisions?

Answer: Through Link Values and Equations.

Link Values and Equations

Define equal relations between dimensions with Link Values. A Link Value requires a shared parameter name.

Create mathematical relations between model dimensions, using dimension names as variables. Mathematical expressions that define relationships between parameters and/or dimensions are called Equations. When using equations in an assembly, you can set equations between parts, between a part and a sub-assembly, with mating dimensions, and so on. You can use the following as variables in equations: *Dimension names, Global variables, Linked dimension names*

Equations use shared names to control dimensions. Use Equations to connect values from sketches, features, patterns and various parts in an assembly. Use Link Values within the same part. Use Equations in different parts and assemblies.

Activity: Create Link Values and Equations in the DELIVERY-STATION

Open the Link Value-Equations assembly from the Project8-2008\Models folder. Note: This assembly represents the sketch of the DELIVERY-STATION.

1) Click **Open** for the Menu bar menu.

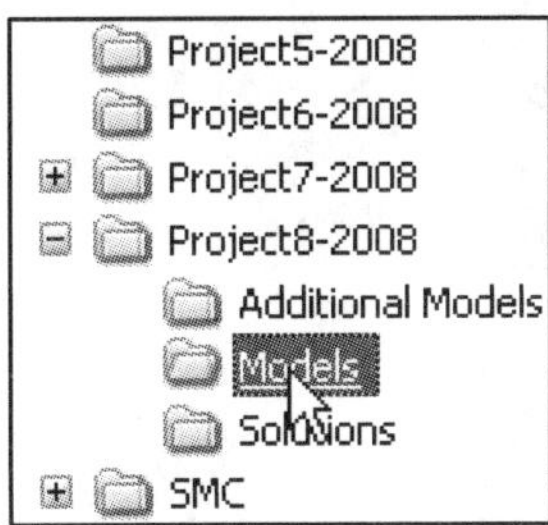

2) Double-click the **Link Value-Equations** assembly from the Project8-2008\Models folder. The Link Value-Equations FeatureManager is displayed. Sketch1 represents the positions of the components.

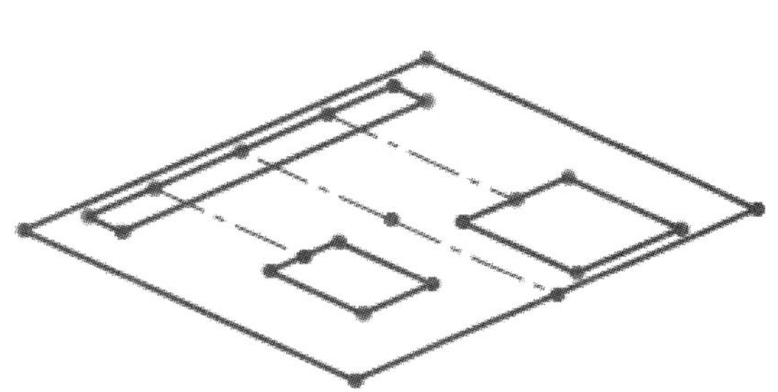

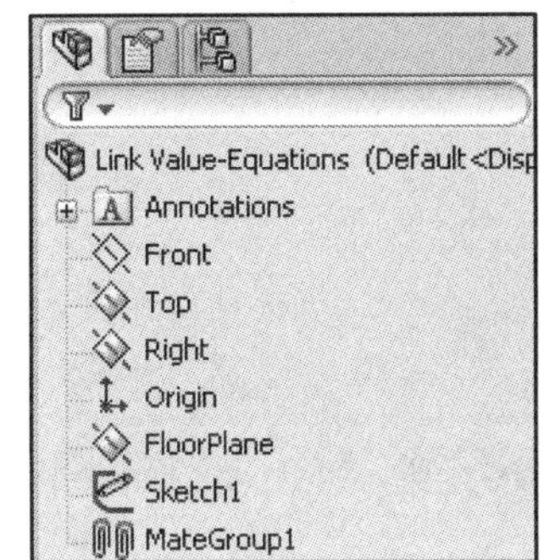

Display the Dimensions.

3) Right-click **Annotations** from the FeatureManager.

4) Click **Show Feature Dimensions**.

5) Click **Top** view from the Heads-up View toolbar. If needed, click View, All Annotations from the Menu bar menu. The dimensions are displayed.

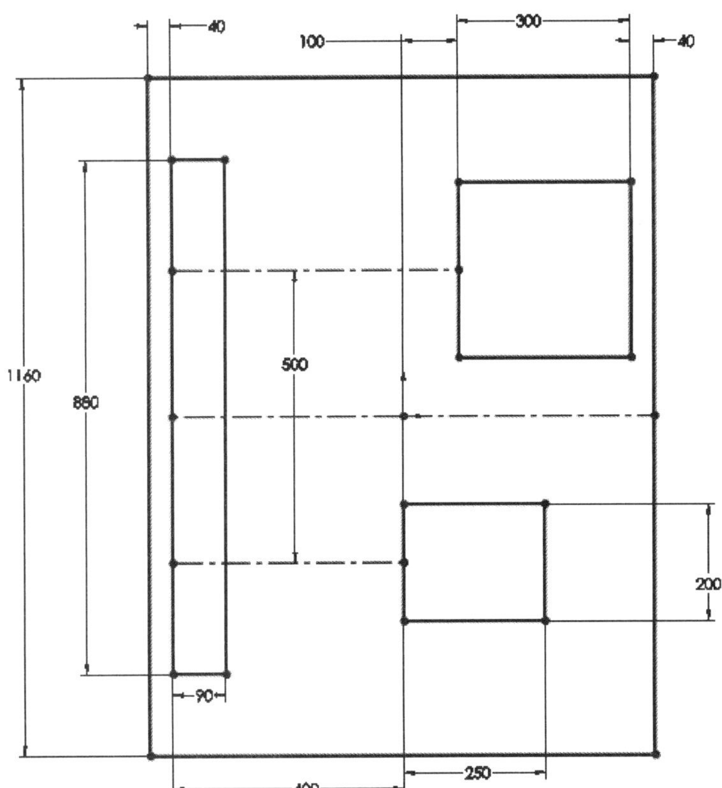

Create Link Values.

6) Right-click on the top right horizontal dimension **40**.

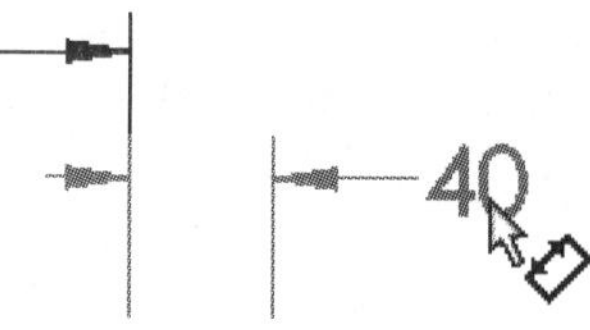

7) Click **Link Values**. The Shared Values dialog box is displayed.

8) Enter **gap** for Name in the Shared Values box.

9) Click **OK** from the Shared Values box.

10) Right click on the left horizontal dimension **40**.

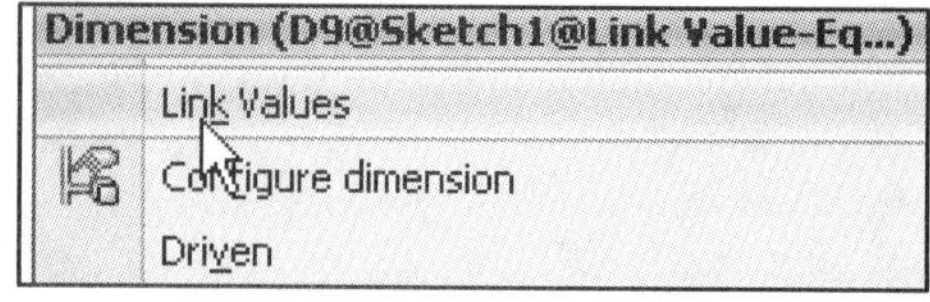

11) Click **Link Values**.

12) Click the **drop-down arrow** from the Name text box.

13) Select **gap**.

14) Click **OK** from the Shared Values box.

Verify the Link Values.

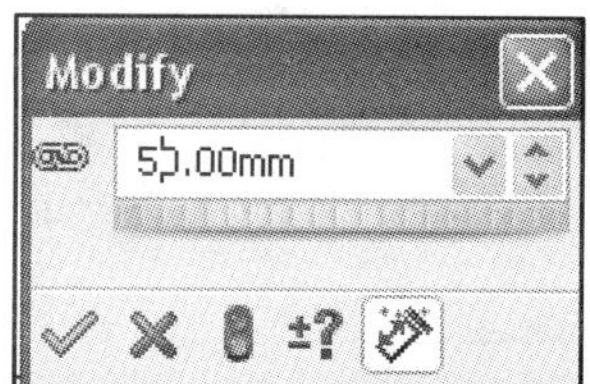

15) Double-click the left **40** dimension.

16) Enter **50**.

17) Click **Rebuild** in the Modify dialog box. The two Link Values change. Return to the original value.

18) Enter **40**.

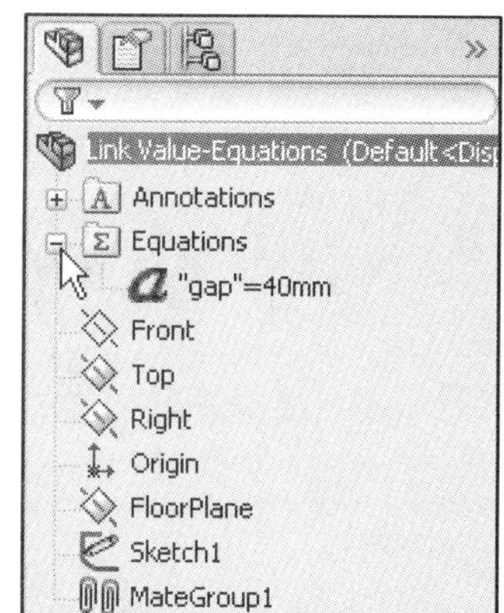

19) Click the **Green Check mark**. All Link Values are equal to 40.

Each dimension has a unique parameter name. Utilize the parameter names as Equation variables. The default parameter names display the sketch, feature or part. Rename parameters for clarity when creating numerous equations.

View the dimension name for hole spacing.

20) Click the vertical dimension **880** in the Graphics window. The Dimension PropertyManager is displayed. The dimension name is mounthole_spacing@Sketch1.

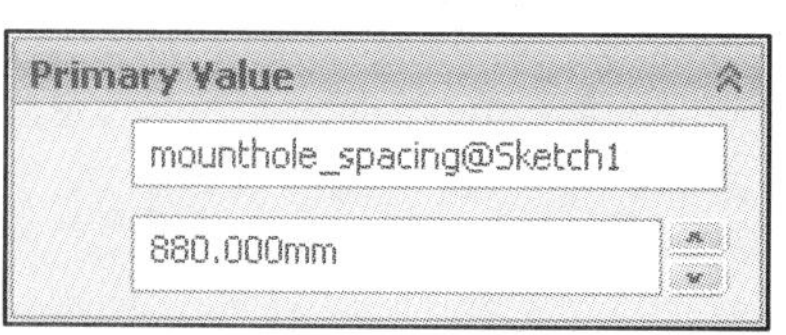

View the dimension Name for the height.

21) Click the vertical dimension **1160** in the Graphics window. The Dimension PropertyManager is displayed. The dimension name is mountplate_height@Sketch1.

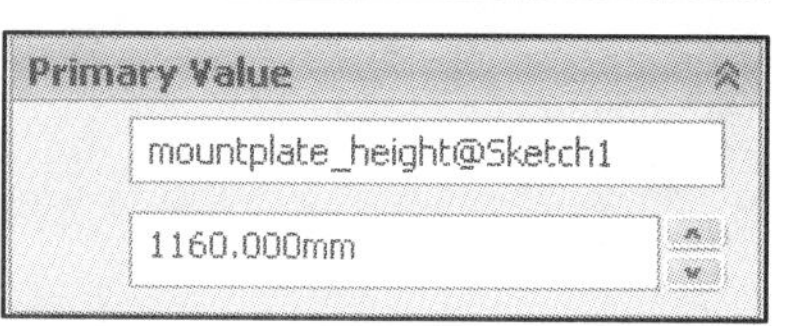

22) Click **OK** from the Dimension PropertyManager.

Display the dimension Name.

23) Position the **mouse pointer** over the 1160 dimension and the 880 dimension to display the full name.

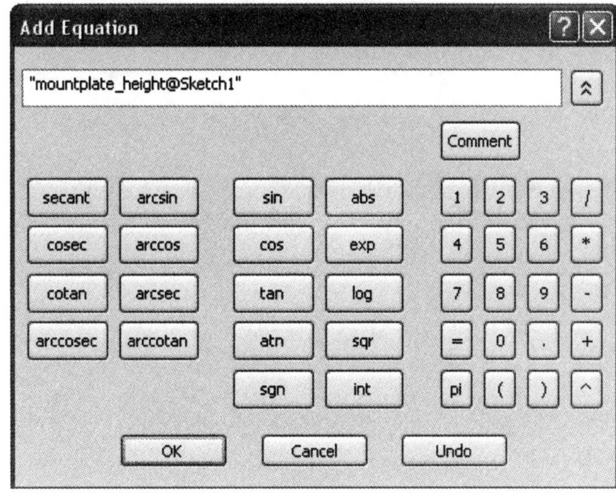

Add an Equation for the Layout sketch.

24) Right-click **Equations** from the FeatureManager.

25) Click **Add Equation**. The Add Equation dialog box is displayed.

Create the first half of Equation1.

26) Click the mountplate_height dimension, **1160**. The variable "mountplate_height@Sketch1" is added to the equation text box.

Create the second half of Equation1.

27) Enter **Equals** = from the keypad. Click mounthole_spacing dimension, **880**. The variable "mounthole_spacing@Sketch1" is added to the equation text box.

28) Enter + 2 * (from the keypad.

29) Click gap, **40**. The variable "gap@Sketch1" is added to the equation text box.

30) Enter + 1 0 0) from the keypad.

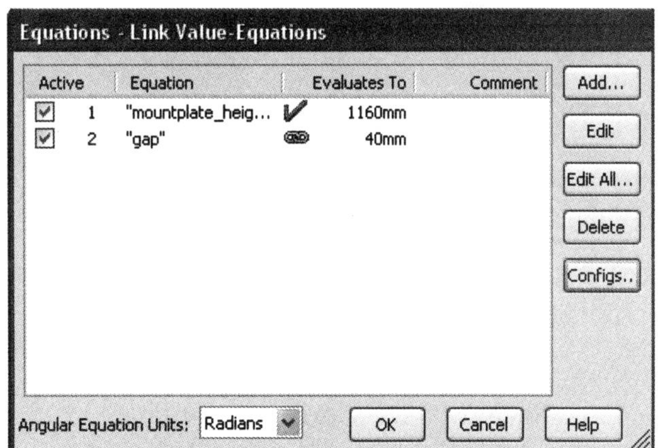

Display Equation1.

31) Click **OK** from the Add Equation box. The Equations – Link Value-Equations dialog box contains the complete equation.

A large green check mark ✔ indicates that the Equation is solved. The chain link symbol indicates a Link Value.

Return to the assembly.

32) Click **OK** from the Equations box.

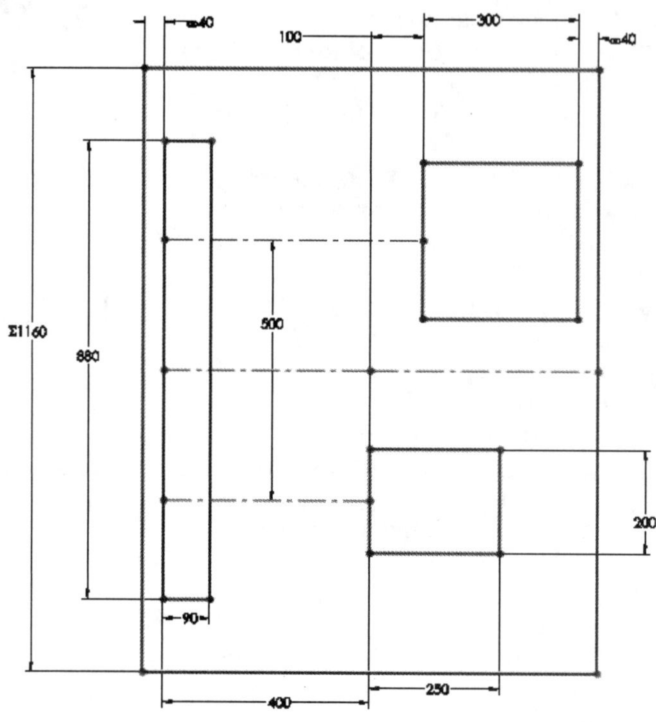

Modify Equation1.

33) Double-click the **880** mounthole_spacing dimension.

34) Enter **980**.

35) Click **Rebuild**.

36) Double click the gap dimension, **40**.

37) Enter **50**.

38) Click **Rebuild**.

Return to the original dimensions.

39) Enter **40** for Gap.

40) Click **Rebuild**.

41) Enter **880** for the mounthole_spacing.

42) Click **Rebuild**.

43) Click **OK** ✓.

The Equation maintains the design intent of the assembly.

💡 Dimensions driven by an Equation are preceded with the red Equation symbol n. Link Values are preceded with the red Link ∞ symbol.

Display the Isometric view and hide all dimensions.

44) Click the **Isometric** view.

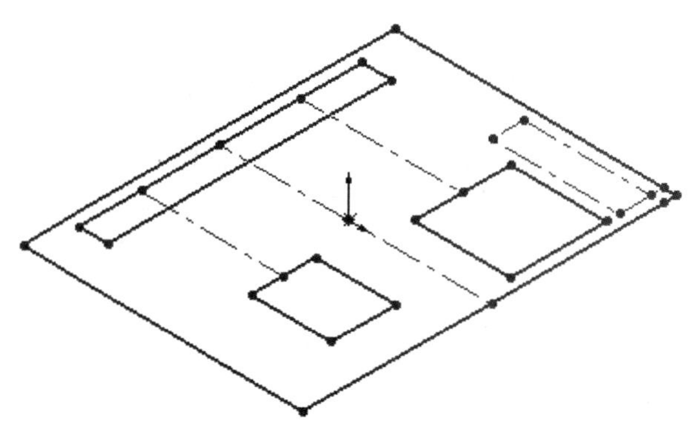

Hide all dimensions.

45) Right-click **Annotations** from the FeatureManager.

46) Uncheck **Show Feature Dimensions**.

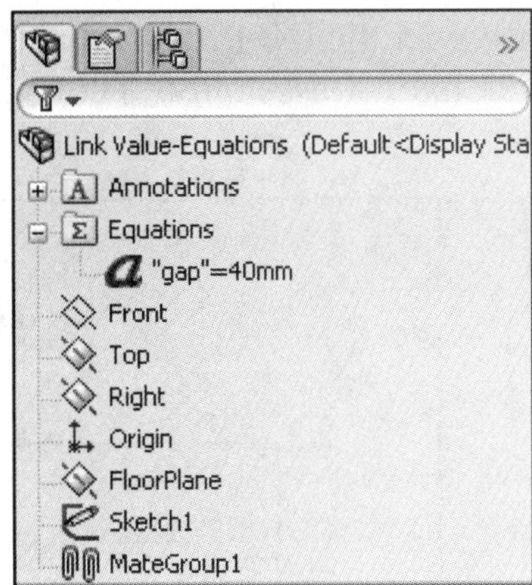

Save the assembly.

47) Click **Save**. The Link Value-Equations assembly is the Layout sketch for the Delivery Station.

Find the file references. Save both the assembly and the referenced components when you exit SolidWorks. When components reference the Layout sketch, open the assembly before opening individual components in a new session of SolidWorks.

Input Assembly and Reordering Components

The INPUT assembly contains the INPUT-BASE-PLATE part. The DELIVERY-STATION assembly contains the INPUT assembly.

Create the INPUT-BASE-PLATE part In-Context of the assembly.

Create the INPUT assembly In-Context of the DELIVERY-STATION assembly. Reorder the INPUT-BASE-PLATE part.

Move the INPUT-BASE-PLATE part into the INPUT assembly. The INPUT-BASE-PLATE part moves down one level in the DELIVERY-STATION assembly.

Reordering assemblies and parts removes InPlace Mates. Reordering creates both over defined and under defined Mates.

Determine component location in the assembly early in the design process to avoid problems.

Create empty parts and sub-assemblies to determine and organize the assembly layout structure.

Avoid future Mate issues. Test the Mates for all related components and assembly features that you reorder.

Reordering components in an assembly can be confusing. Evaluate the reordering procedure for the INPUT assembly.

Reorder the INPUT-BASE-PLATE part from the DELIVERY-STATION assembly to the INPUT assembly. The INPUT-BASE-PLATE part is at the second level.

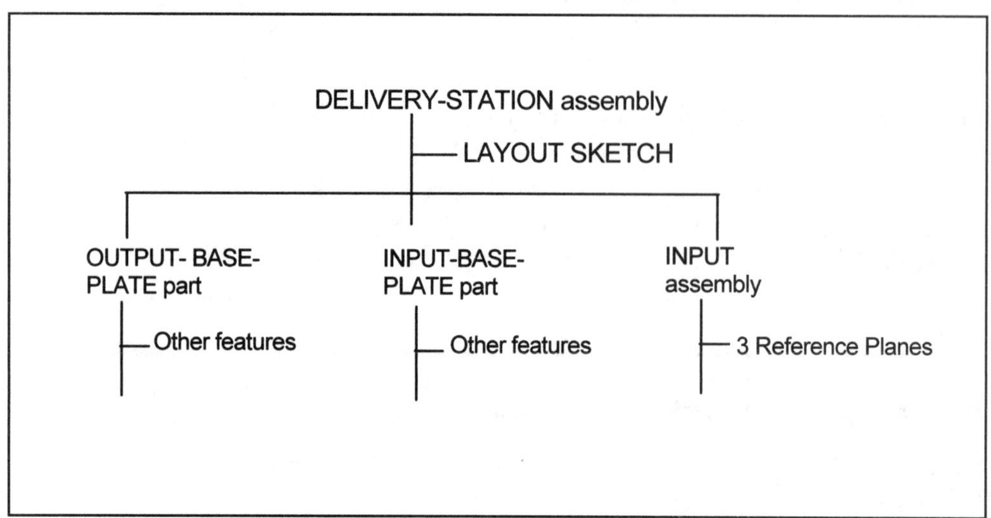

Drag the component to a new location to reorder the component in the FeatureManager. Utilize Tools, Reorganize Components when reordering multiple components in one operation.

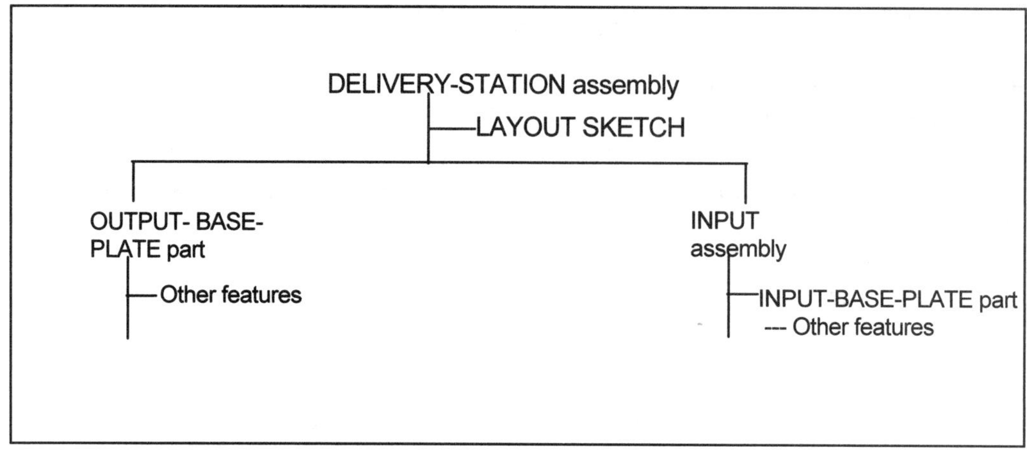

Activity: Create the INPUT-BASE-PLATE Part

Utilize the New Part tool from the Assembly toolbar. Select the Part-MM-ANSI-AL6061 Template. The Template was created in Project 2. SolidWorks automatically selects the Sketch tool.

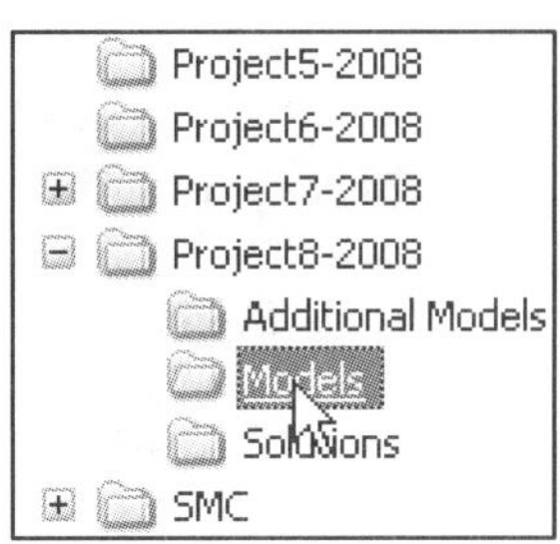

Open the Reorder Assembly.

48) Click **Open** from the Menu bar menu.

49) Double-click the **Reorder** assembly from the Project8-2008\Models folder. The FeatureManager is displayed.

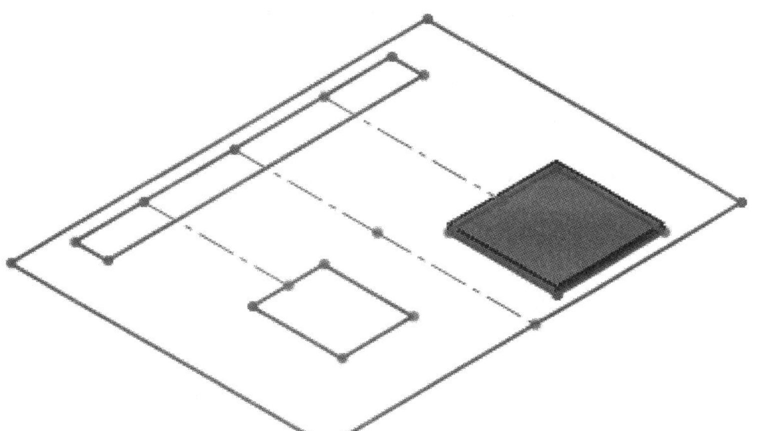

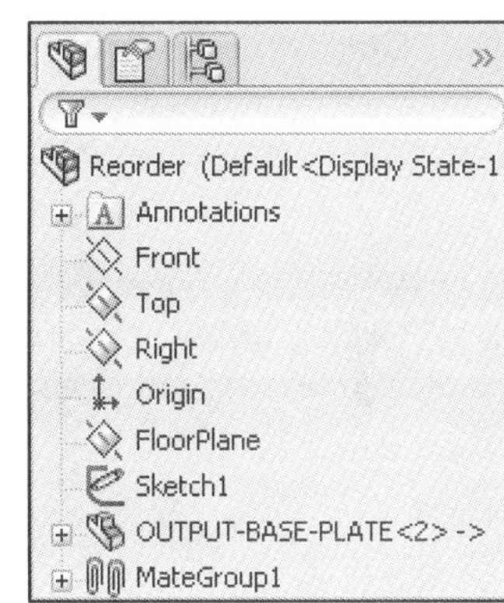

Insert a new Part.

50) Click **New Part** from the Consolidated Insert Components toolbar.

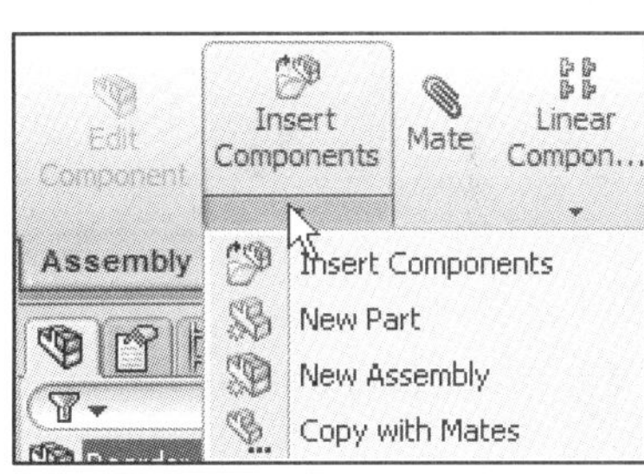

51) Double-click **PART-MM-ANSI-AL6061** from the MY-TEMPLATES tab. The new part is displayed in the FeatureManager design tree with a name in the form [Part#^*assembly_name*]. The square brackets indicate that the part is a virtual component. The new Component Pointer icon is displayed. The default component is empty and requires a Sketch plane.

52) Click the **Top Plane** from the FeatureManager.

53) Right-click **[Part1^reorder]** from the FeatureManager.

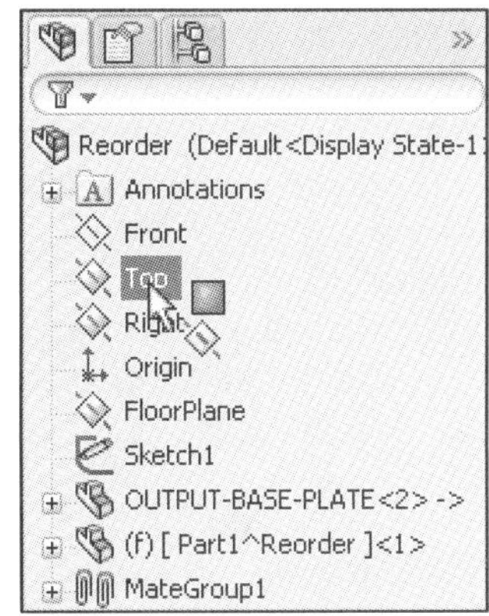

54) Click **Save Part(in External File)**. The Part FeatureManager is displayed. The Save As dialog box is displayed.

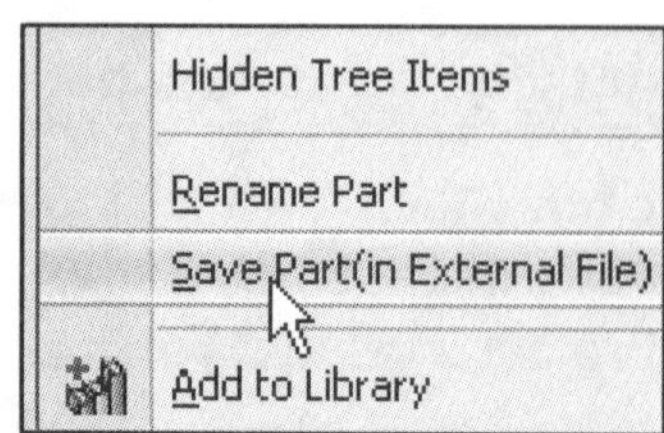

Save the Part.

55) Click **inside** the File Name box.

56) Enter **INPUT-BASE-PLATE**.

57) Click the **Same As Assembly** button.

58) Click **OK**. You return to the Assembly FeatureManager. The New part is renamed. Note: You are in the Edit Component mode.

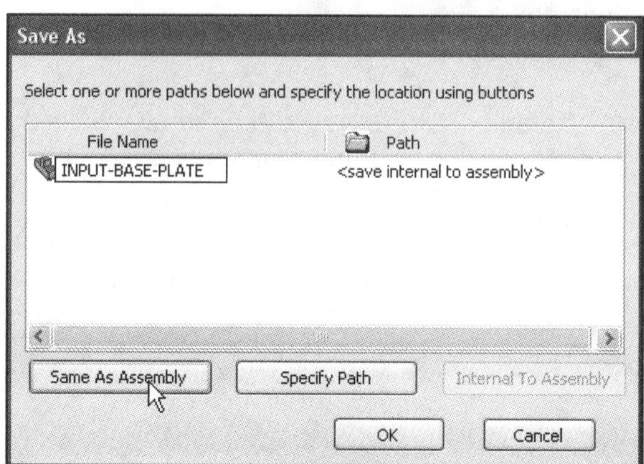

Convert existing outside edges form the sketch.

59) Click a **line segment** from the 200mm x 250mm rectangle as illustrated.

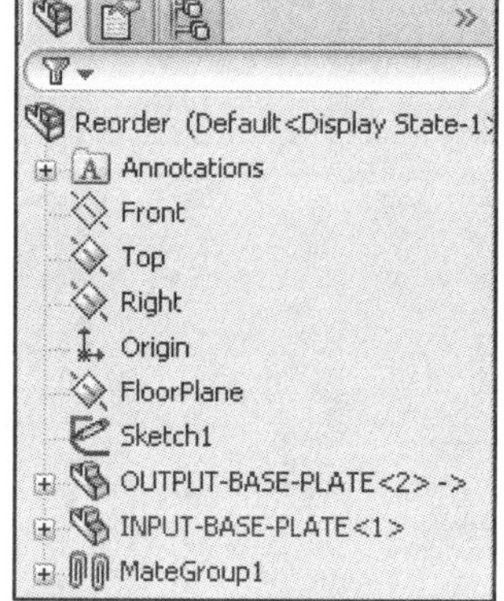

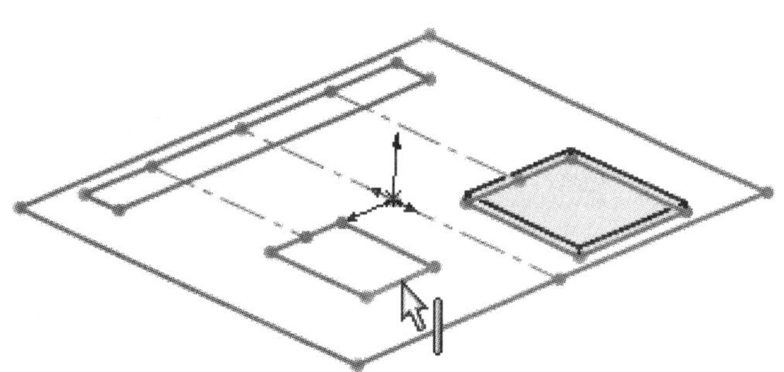

60) Click the **Convert Entities** Sketch tool. The Resolve Ambiguity dialog box is displayed.

61) Click **closed contour**.

62) Click **OK**. The current sketch is the outside perimeter of the small left box.

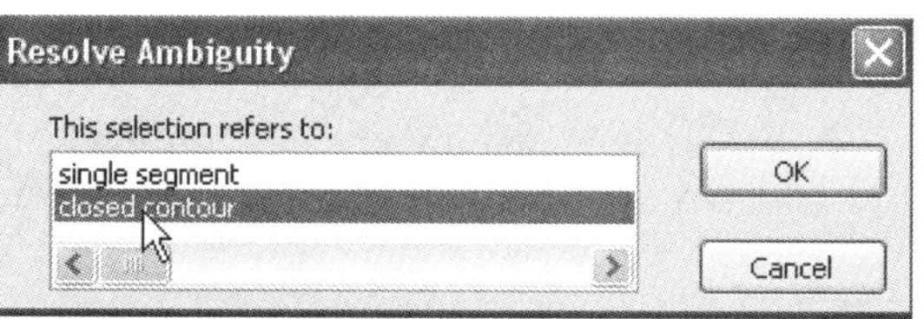

Extrude Sketch1.

63) Click the **Extruded Boss/Base** feature. The Extrude PropertyManager is displayed. Blind is the default End Condition.

64) Enter **20** for Depth. Note: The Extrude direction is upwards.

65) Click **OK** from the Extruded PropertyManager.

66) Click **Edit Component** from the Features toolbar.

67) **Rebuild** the assembly.

Save the Assembly.
68) Click **Save**.

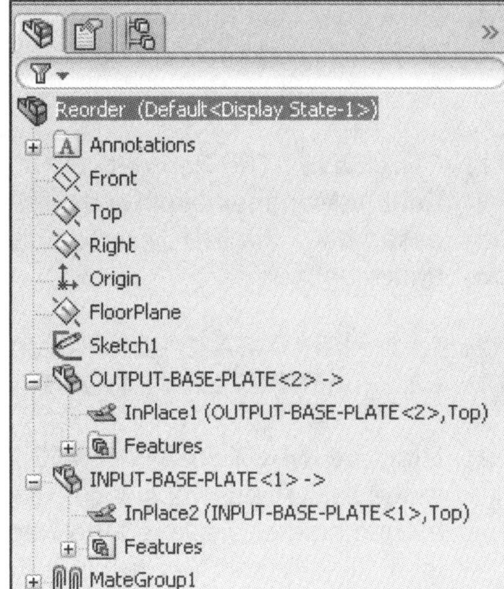

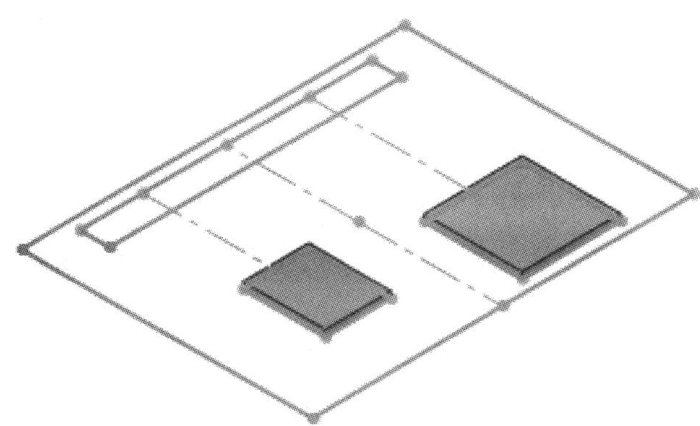

Activity: Insert a New Assembly – Reorder Components

Insert a New Assembly called INPUT.
69) Click **New Assembly** from the Consolidated Insert Components toolbar.

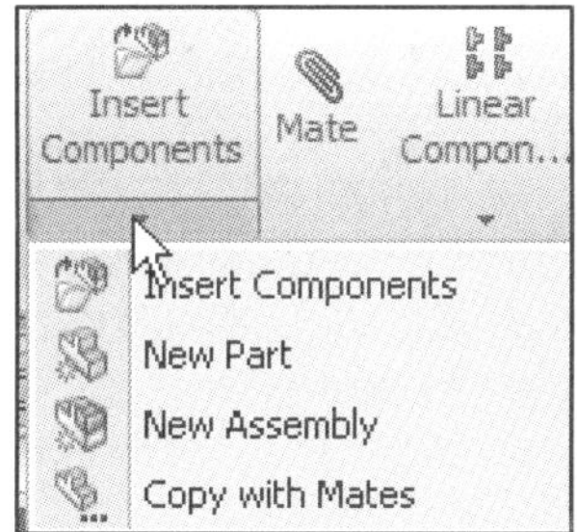

70) Double-click **ASM-MM-ANSI** from the MY-TEMPLATES tab. The new assembly is displayed in the FeatureManager. The square brackets indicate that the part is a virtual component.

Save the Assembly.
71) Right-click **[Assem1^Reorder]**.

72) Click **Save Assembly(in External File)**. The Save As dialog box is displayed.

73) Click **inside** the File Name box.

74) Enter **INPUT**.

75) Click the **Same As Assembly** button.

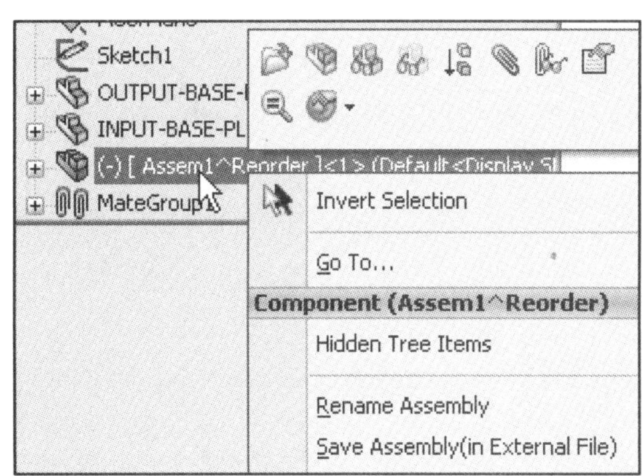

76) Click **OK**. You return to the Assembly FeatureManager. The New assembly is renamed.

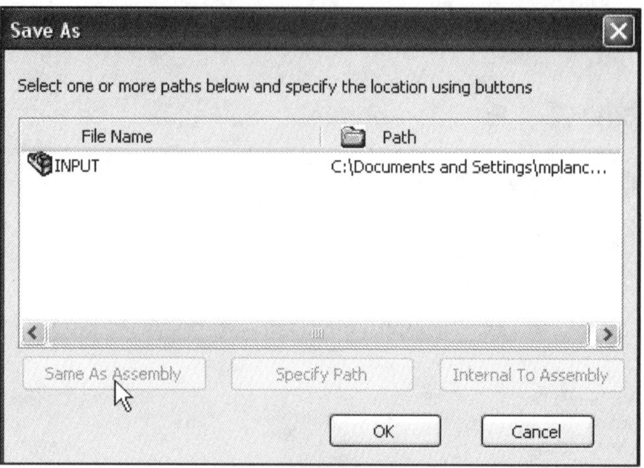

77) Click **Save**. The Reorder FeatureManager displays the INPUT assembly. The INPUT assembly is under-defined.

Reorder the INPUT-BASE-PLATE part.

78) Click the **INPUT-BASE-PLATE** icon.

79) Drag the **INPUT-BASE-PLATE** icon to the INPUT assembly icon. The mouse pointer displayed the Reorder icon. The Assembly Structure Editing dialog box is displayed.

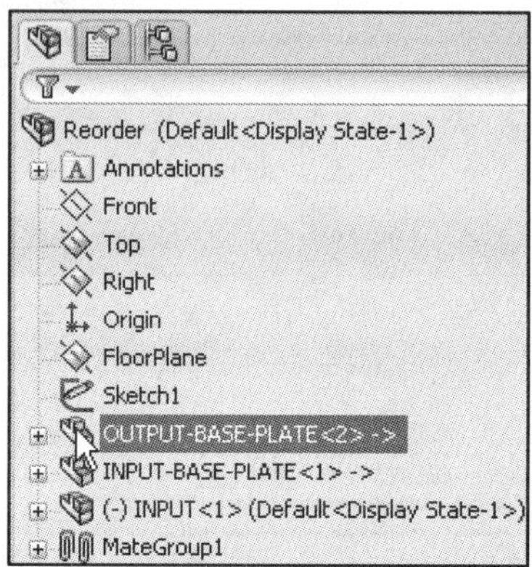

80) Click the **Move** button. View the results.

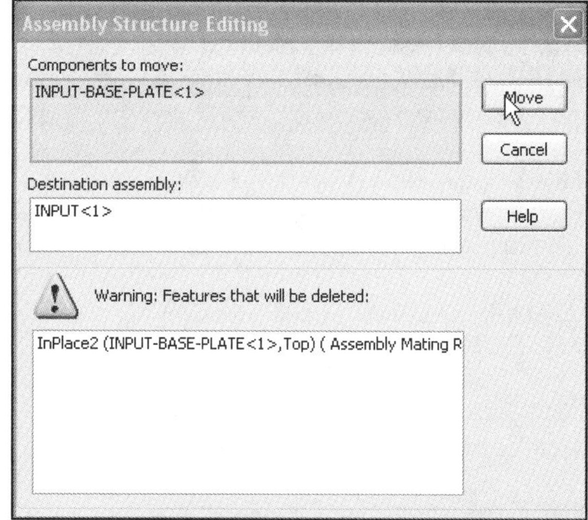

81) **Expand** the INPUT assembly in the FeatureManager. View the new location of the INPUT-BASE-PLATE model.

The Reorder command modifies the InPlace Mate reference from the INPUT-BASE-PLATE part to the INPUT assembly. The INPUT-BASE-PLATE part is under defined.

Edit the INPUT Assembly.

82) Right-click **INPUT** from the FeatureManager.

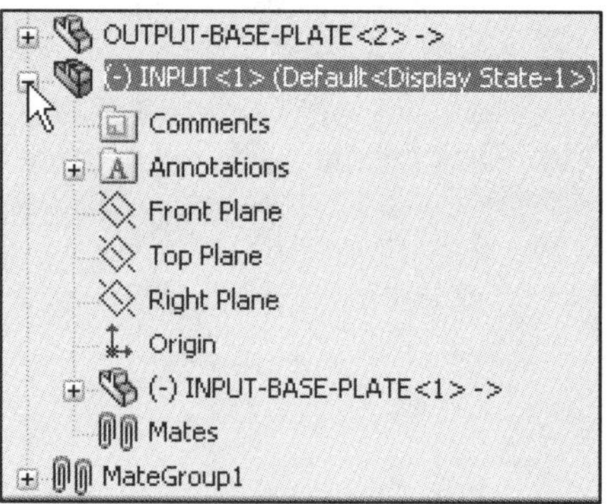

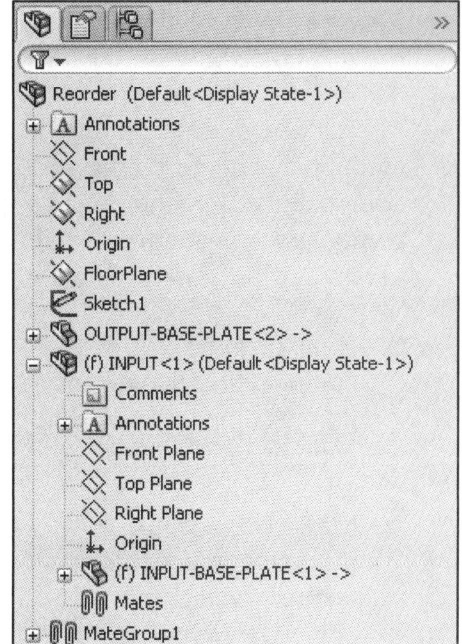

83) Click **Edit Assembly**. The Assembly is displayed in blue. You are now working in the INPUT assembly.

84) Click **Isometric** view.

Fix the INPUT-BASE-PLATE.

85) Right-click **INPUT-BASE-PLATE** from the FeatureManager.

86) Click **Fix** to locate the INPUT-BASE-PLATE part with respect to the INPUT assembly Origin.

87) Click **Edit Component**.

Fix the INPUT Assembly.

88) Right-click **INPUT** from the FeatureManager.

89) Click **Fix**.

Save the assembly.

90) Click **Save**.

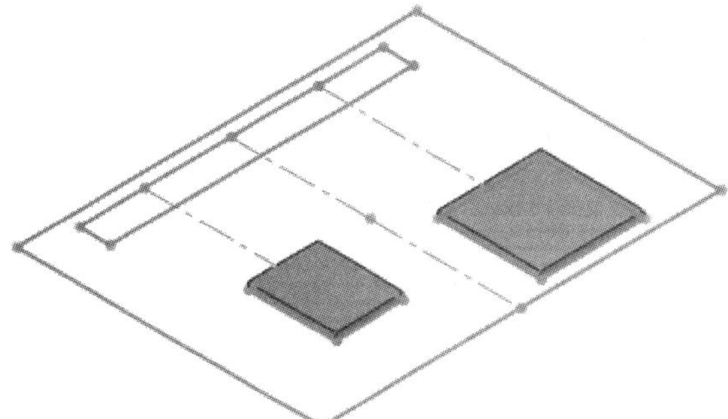

Reusing Components: Component Pattern and Mirror Component

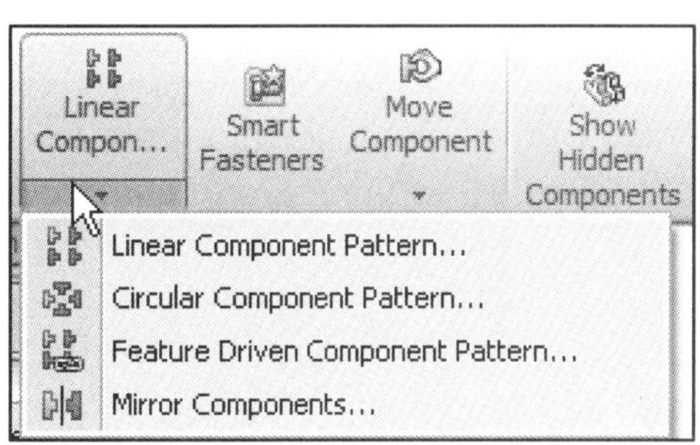

The Assembly toolbar provides the following Pattern and mirror tools:

- *Linear Component Pattern.* The Linear Component Pattern tool provides the ability to create a linear pattern of components in an assembly in one or two directions.

- *Circular Component Pattern.* The Circular Component Pattern tool provides the ability to create a circular pattern of components in an assembly.

- *Feature Driven Component Pattern.* The Feature Driven Component Pattern tool provides the ability to create a pattern of components based on an existing pattern.

- *Mirror Components.* The Mirror Components tool provides the ability to create new components by mirroring an existing part or sub-assembly components. The new components can either be a copy or a mirror of the original components. A mirrored component is sometimes called a "right-hand" version of the original "left-hand" version as illustrated. Some important items to note include:

  - If the original components change, so do the copied or mirrored components.
  - Mates between the original components can be preserved in the copied or mirrored components.
  - Configurations in the original components appear in the copied or mirrored components.
  - You can copy custom properties from the original component when you create a mirrored component.

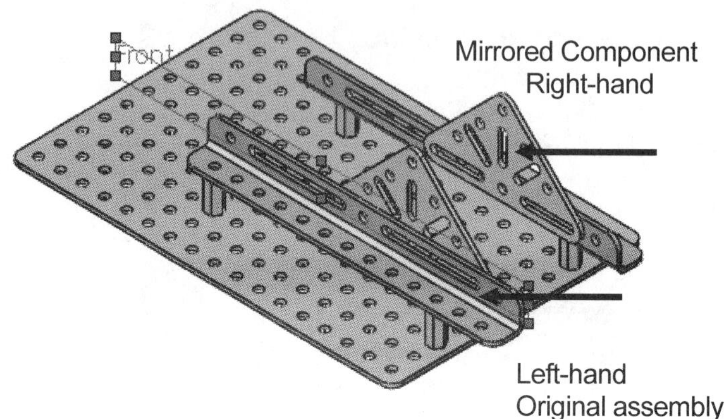

Example of Mirrored component has left/right hand option.

The difference between a component that you copy and one that you mirror is described as follows:

- *Copy*: No new documents are created. The geometry of the copied component is identical to the original component; only the orientation of the component is different.

- *Mirror*: A new document is created. The geometry of the new component is mirrored; thus it is different from the original component.

You utilized the Linear Component Pattern tool and the Feature Driven Component Pattern tool in the 3AXIS-TRANSFER assembly.

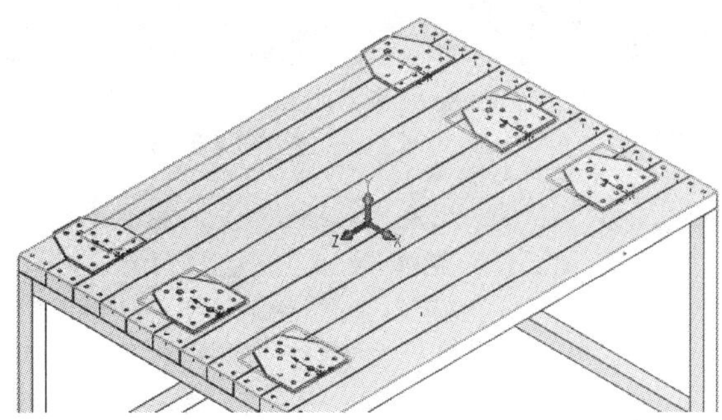

Example of a Component Pattern, Linear Pattern option

The Mirror Components tool reuses existing parts and assemblies. There are two options for Mirror Components:

- Mirrored component has left/right hand option.
- Instanced component is used on both sides option.

Utilize the second option in the next activity.

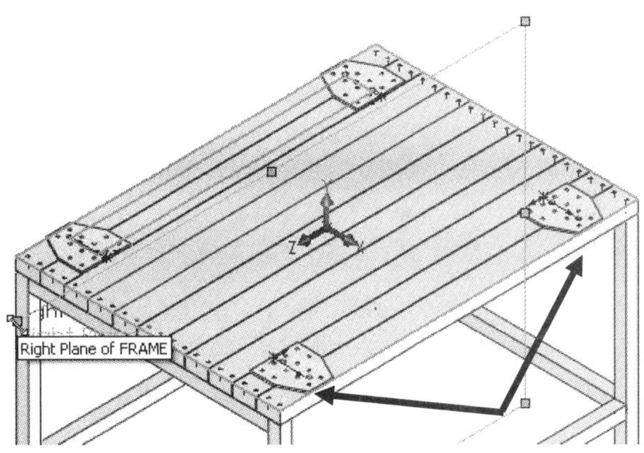

Example of Instanced component, used on both sides.

The Selections box requires a mirror plane. Select the Right Plane.

The Components to Mirror box lists a check box before the component name.

When the box is checked, the mirrored component has a left/right hand version. When the box is unchecked, SolidWorks creates an instanced component.

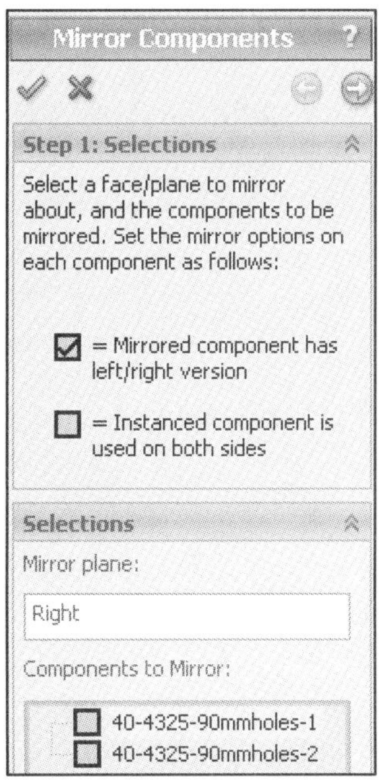

The mirrored components are free to translate and rotate.

To fully define a mirror component, insert Mates between the components and the assembly.

Activity: Reuse Components: Apply the Mirror Components Tool

Open the Frame assembly.

91) Click **Open** from the Menu bar menu.

92) Double-click the **Frame** assembly from the Project8-2008\Models folder. The FeatureManager is displayed. View the features in the FeatureManager.

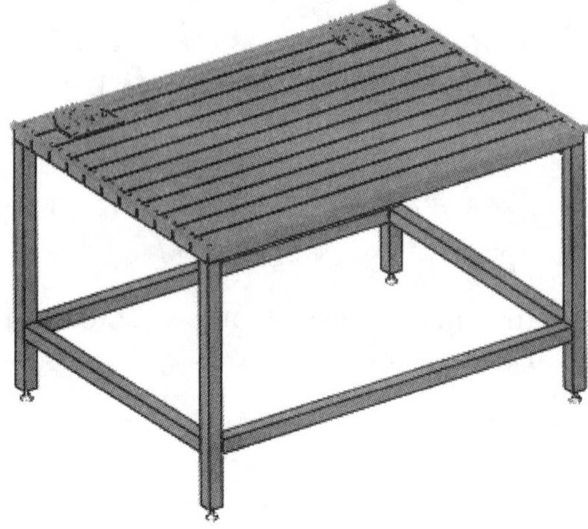

Mirror the two 40-4325-14mm-holes.

93) Click **40-4325-14mm-holes<1>** from the FeatureManager

94) Hold the **Ctrl** key down.

95) **Expand** LocalLPattern1.

96) Click the **40-4325-14mm-holes<2>** from the FeatureManager.

97) Release the **Ctrl** key.

98) Click **Mirror Components** from the Consolidated Linear Component Pattern toolbar. The Mirror Components PropertyManager is displayed.

99) Click **Right Plane** from the fly-out FeatureManager.

100) Click **Next** from the Mirror Components PropertyManager.

101) Click **OK** ✓ from the Mirror Components PropertyManager.

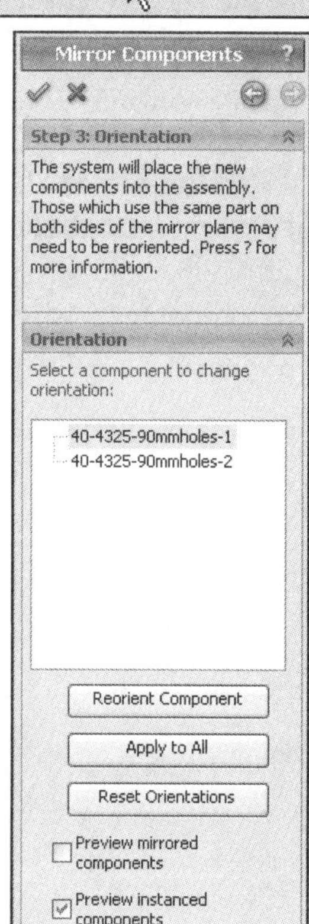

Two additional instances are mirrored and are displayed in the FeatureManager. The components 40-4325-14mm-holes<3> and 40-4325-14mm-holes<4> require additional Coincident Mates.

 Insert Mates as an exercise.

For now, suppress the two instances.

A quick mating technique is to utilize the Fix option for the components listed in the Components to Mirror box. Why is the Fix option not a good modeling technique in this project?

Answer: The FRAME sub-assembly and top level DELIVERY-STATION assembly utilize Layout sketches. If the Layout dimensions change, the position of the mirrored components remains the same.

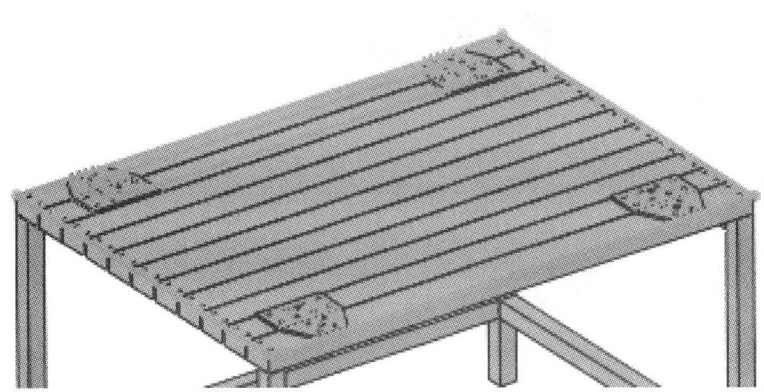

Suppress the Mirror Components.

102) Click **40-4325-14mm-holes<3>**.

103) Hold the **Ctrl** key down.

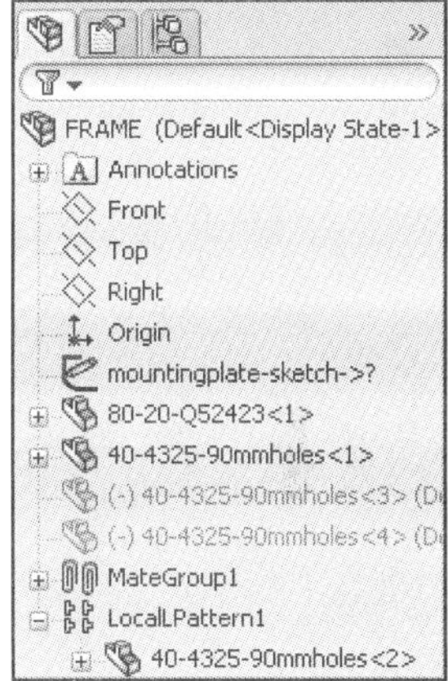

104) Click **40-4325-14mm-holes<4>**.

105) Release the **Ctrl** key.

106) Right-click **Suppress**.

Save the FRAME assembly.

107) Click **Save**.

Close all models.

108) Click **Window**, **Close All**.

Insert the DELIVERY-STATION Assembly

You are now at the last step of the project. Insert the 3AXIS-TRANSFER assembly into the DELIVERY-STATION assembly. Mate the Tapped Holes.

Save memory. Load the 3AXIS-TRANSFER assembly in Lightweight mode.

Resolve the LINEAR-TRANSFER assembly to obtain the Mate references from the Cbore mounting holes.

The 3AXIS-TRANSFER assembly fastens to the JOINING-PLATE part. The 3AXIS-TRANSFER\99-022013\015801\MY1M2104HeadCover part contains the Cbore hole features required to assemble the JOINING-PLATE.

Activity: Insert the DELIVERY-STATION Assembly

Open the DELIVERY-STATION assembly. Remember, in this Project, use the models from the Project8-2008\Models folder which you copied for the CD in the book.

109) Click **Open** from the Menu bar toolbar.

110) Double-click **DELIVERY-STATION** from the Project8-2008\Models folder. The FeatureManager is displayed.

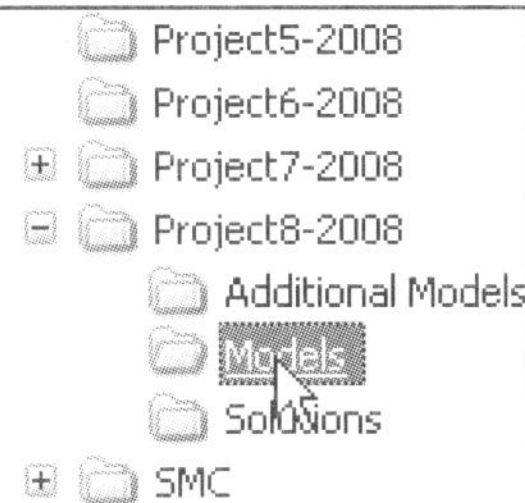

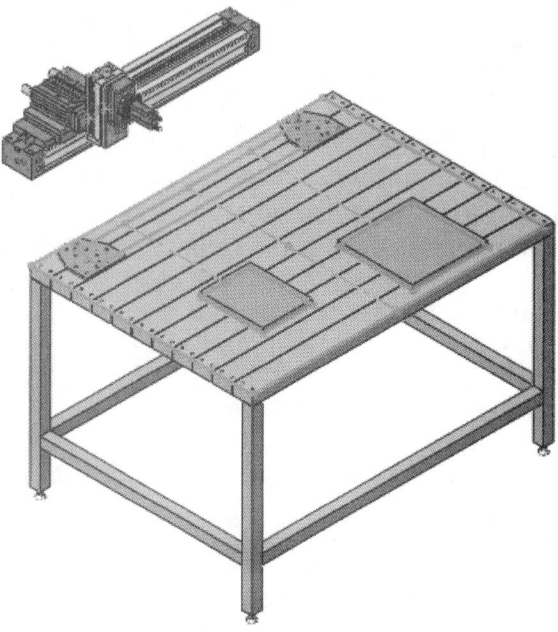

Insert the 3AXIS-TRANSFER assembly.

111) Click the **Insert Components** tool from the Assembly toolbar. The Insert Components PropertyManager is displayed.

112) Click **Browse**.

113) Click **3AXIS-TRANSFER** from the Project8-2008\Models folder.

114) Check the **Lightweight** box.

115) Click the **Position1** configuration.

116) Click **Open**.

117) Click a **position** above the DELIVERY-STATION. View the results

Know your level in the assembly and the component that makes sense for mating.
The MY1M2104 HeadCover contains the holes to fasten to the JOINING-PLATE parts.

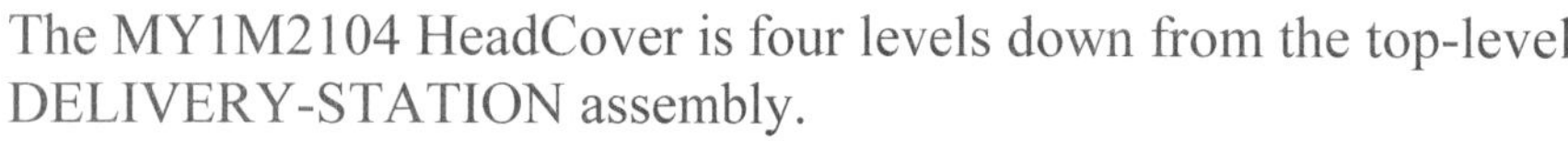

The MY1M2104 HeadCover is four levels down from the top-level DELIVERY-STATION assembly.

Locate the MY1M2104 HeadCover<1> part.

118) Expand 3AXIS-TRANSFER assembly.

119) Expand LINEAR-TRANSFER assembly.

120) Expand RODLESS-CYLINDER assembly.

121) Expand MY1M2104HeadCover<1>.

122) Double-click **Mount_CBore** from the FeatureManager. The Cbore diameter is 17mm.

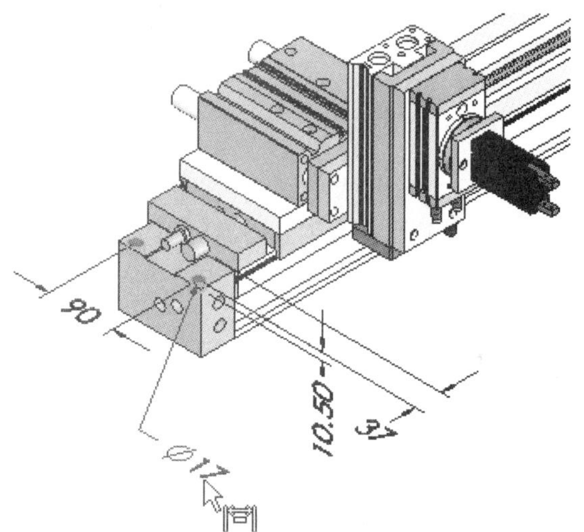

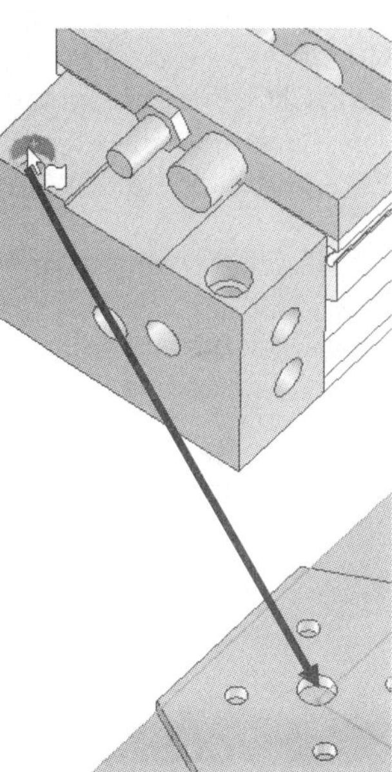

Assemble the 3AXIS-TRANSFER assembly to the DELIVERY-STATION assembly. Insert a Concentric SmartMate.

123) Hold the **Alt** key down.

124) Click the **left CBore face** of the 3AXIS-TRANSFER assembly\99-022013/015801MY1M2104HeadCover.

125) Drag the left CBore face to the **left face** of the 40-4325-14mm-holes part M14 Tapped Hole. Concentric is selected by default.

126) Release the **Alt** key

127) Click the **Green Check mark** ✓.

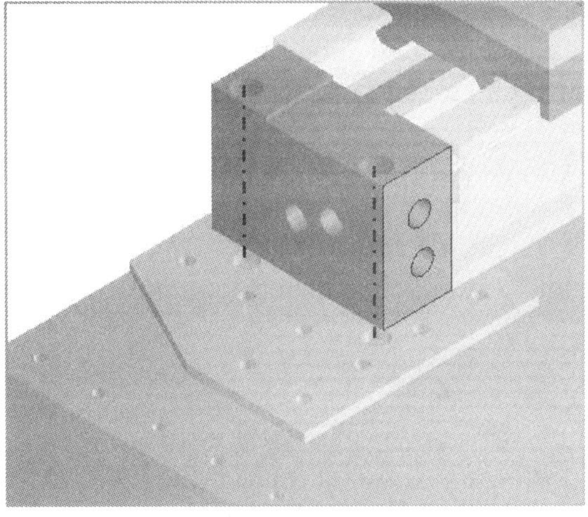

Insert the second Concentric SmartMate.

128) Hold the **Alt key** down.

129) Click the **right Cbore face** of the 3AXIS-TRANSFER assembly\99-022013\015801\MY1M2104HeadCover part.

130) Drag the right CBore face to the **right face** of the 40-4325-14mm-holes part M14 Tapped Hole. Concentric is selected by default.

131) Click the **Green Check mark** ✓.

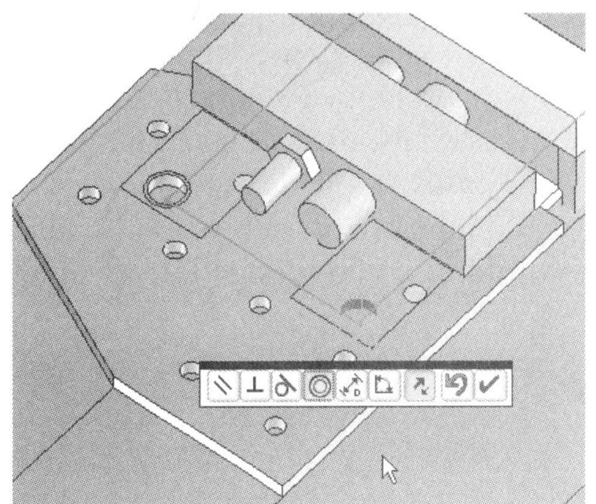

Create a Coincident Mate.

132) Click the **bottom face** of the 3AXIS-TRANSFER assembly\99-022102\015801\MY1M2104HeadCover part.

133) Click the **Mate** tool.

134) Click the **top face** of the 40-4325-90mm-holes part. Coincident is selected by default.

135) Click the **Green Check mark** ✓.

136) Click **OK** ✓ from the Mate PropertyManager.

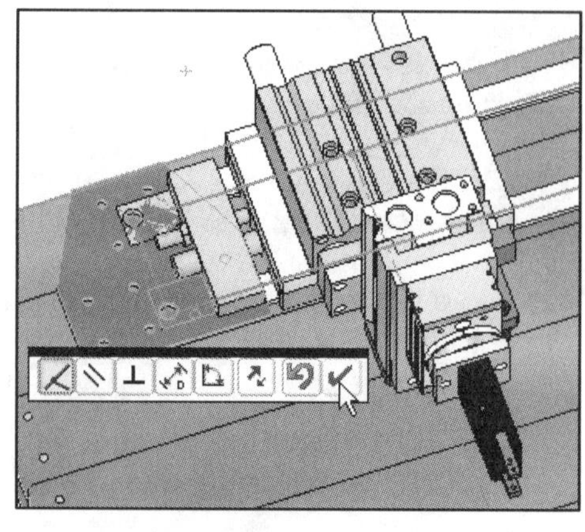

AssemblyXpert

The AssemblyXpert tool provides the ability to analyzes performance of assemblies and suggests possible actions you can take to improve performance.

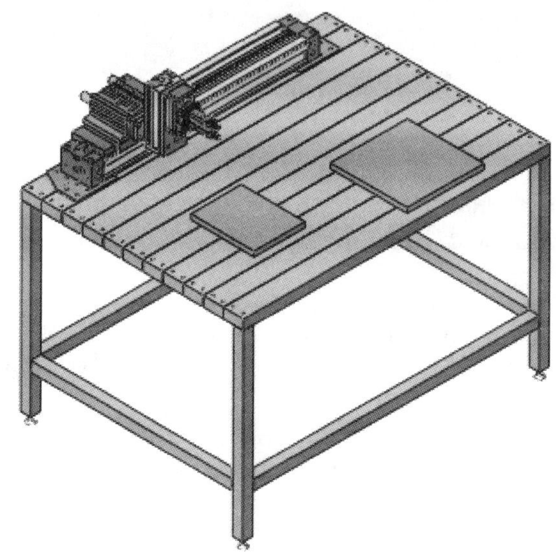

This is useful when you work with large and complex assemblies. In some cases, you can select to have the software make changes to your assembly to improve performance.

The AssemblyXpert tool has performance limitations at this time. Although the conditions identified by AssemblyXpert can degrade assembly performance, they are not errors. It is important that you weigh recommendations of the AssemblyXpert against your design intent. In some cases, implementing the recommendation would improve assembly performance, but would compromise your design intent.

Activity: Apply the AssemblyXpert Tool

Apply the AssemblyXpert tool.

137) Click **AssemblyXpert** from the Evaluate tab in the CommandManager. View the results. View the Status and Descriptions provided. Explore the More Information links.

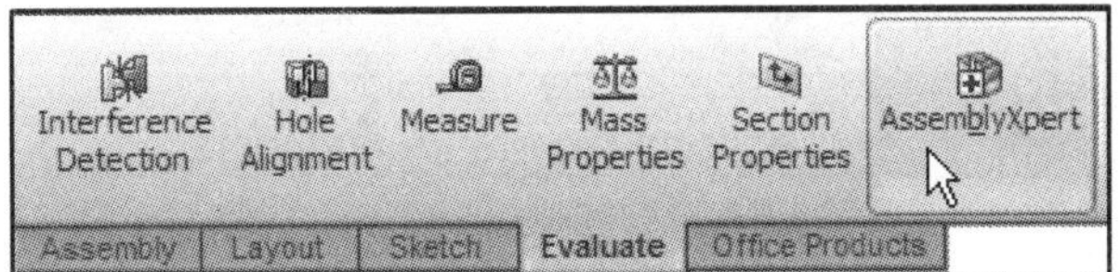

138) Click **OK**.

139) Click **Save**.

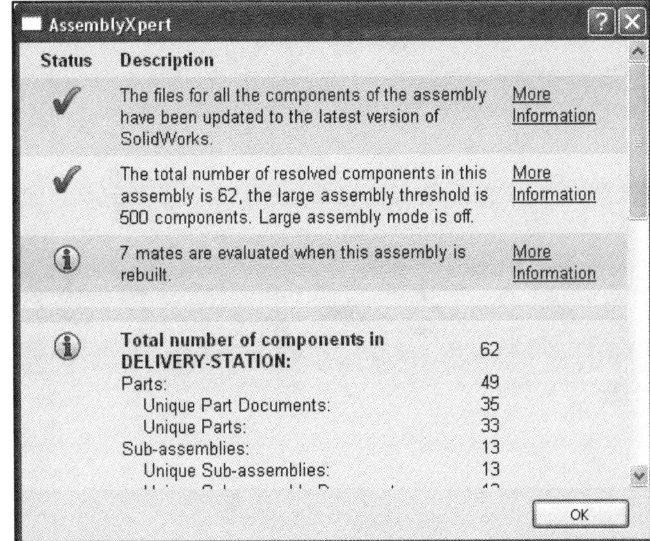

AssemblyXpert
Status
Description
The files for all the components of the assembly have been updated to the latest version of SolidWorks.
More Information
The total number of resolved components in this assembly is 62, the large assembly threshold is 500 components. Large assembly mode is off.
More Information
7 mates are evaluated when this assembly is rebuilt.
More Information
Total number of components in DELIVERY-STATION: 62
Parts: 49
Unique Part Documents: 35
Unique Parts: 33
Sub-assemblies: 13
Unique Sub-assemblies: 13
OK

You have completed your tasks for the DELIVERY-STATION assembly. The completion of the project depends on your colleagues to design additional assemblies. It is time to move to another project. But wait. Remember, the next engineer who works on the DELIVERY-STATION assembly will handle the INPUT and OUTPUT assemblies and load hundreds of components into memory.

How can you assist your colleagues to select and show components in the assembly? Answer: Insert an assembly envelope into the DELIVERY-STATION assembly.

Layout-based Assembly Design

As stated earlier, there are two methods to create a Top-down design assembly modeling approach:

- **Method 1**: An individual sketch in the assembly created from a sketch or imported geometry.
- **Method 2**: A Layout Sketch using the Layout tools to understand motion between components utilizing blocks

In this section, you will apply Method 2.

Enhancements in 2008, provides the ability to create, edit, and delete parts and blocks at any point in the design cycle without any history-based restrictions. This is particularly useful during the conceptual design process, when you frequently experiment with and make modification to the assembly structure, and components.

In the next activity, explore Layout-based assembly design with motion.

Activity: Layout-based Assembly Design – Motion – Example 1

Open the Layout Assembly with Blocks.

140) Click **Open** from the Menu bar toolbar.

141) Double-click **Layout** assembly from the Project8-2008\Models folder. View the FeatureManager. Block B translates vertically and represents the motion of the Linear Transfer assembly.

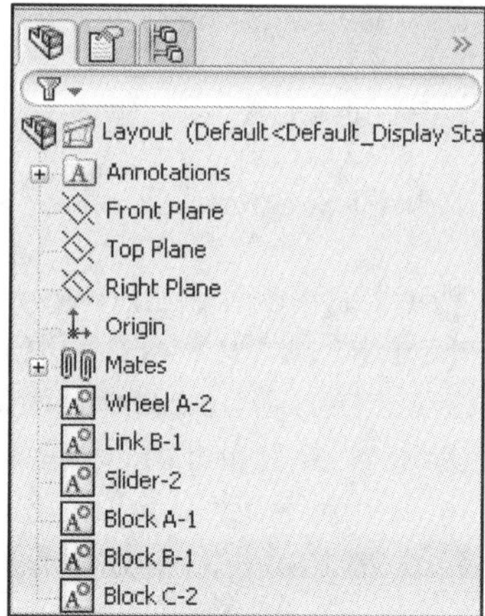

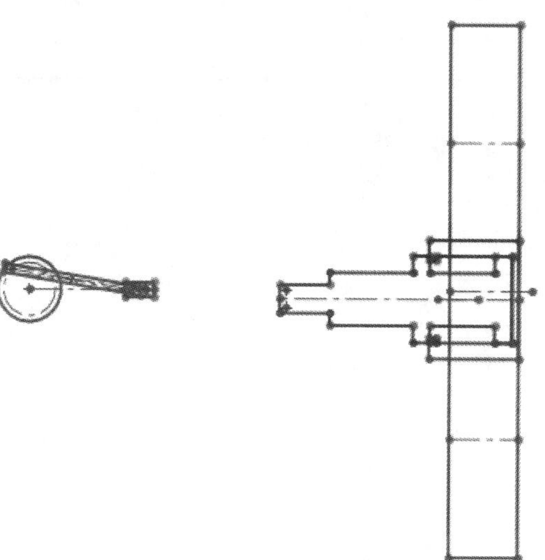

142) Click the **Layout** tool from the Layout tool bar in the CommandManager. Remember, block B translates vertically and represents the motion of the Linear Transfer assembly.

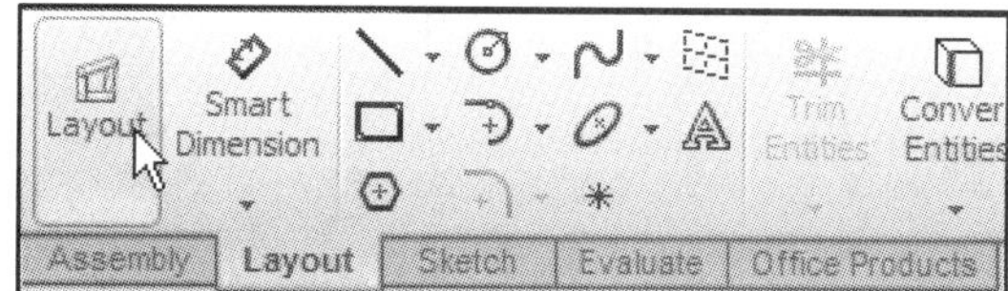

143) Drag **Block B** vertically. Note: Block C translates horizontally and represents the motion of the 2AXIS-TRANSFER assembly.

144) Drag **Block C** horizontally a few mm's.

145) **Return** Block B and Block C to their original positions.

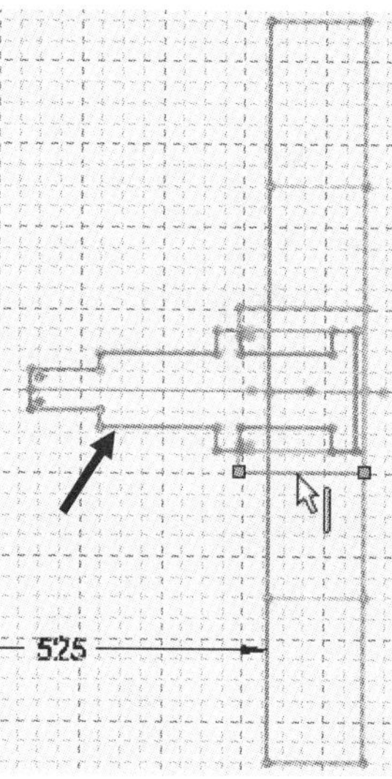

146) Click the **Insert Block** tool from the Layout toolbar. The Insert Block PropertyManager is displayed.

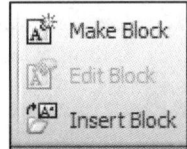

147) Click the **Browse** button. Browse to the **Project8-2008\Models** folder.

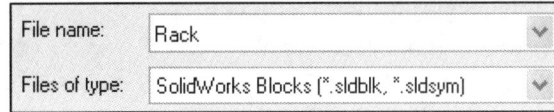

148) Double-click **Rack**. Rack is displayed in the Blocks to Insert box.

149) Click a **position** at the midpoint of the end of the Slider block as illustrated.

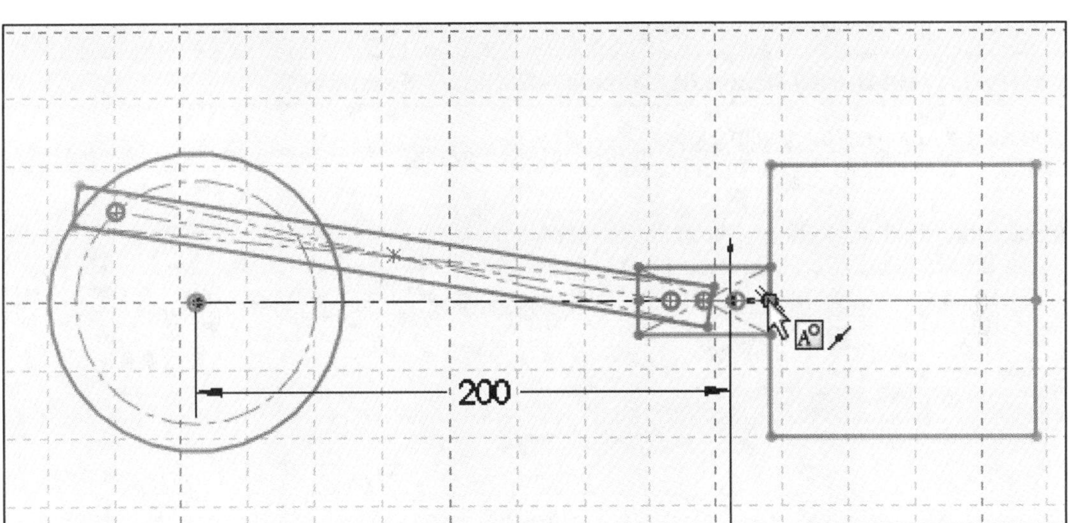

150) Click **OK** from the Insert Block PropertyManager.

Insert a Collinear Geometric relation.

151) Click the **horizontal centerline** of the Rack.

152) Hold the **Ctrl** key down.

153) Click the **horizontal centerline** in the Layout sketch.

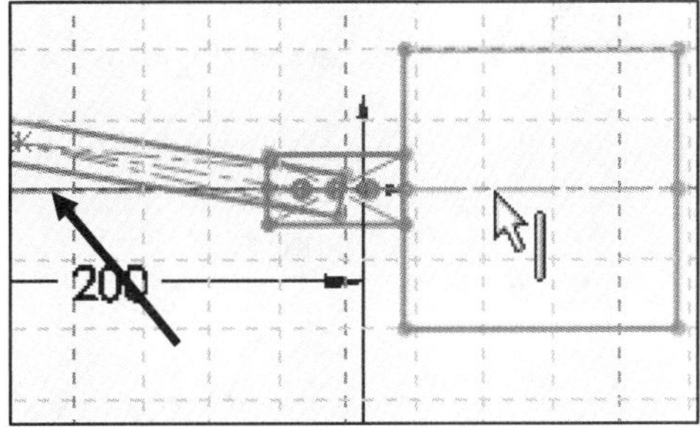

154) Release the **Ctrl** key.

155) Click **Collinear**.

156) Click **OK** from the Properties PropertyManager. Verify the Rack motion relative to the Wheel.

157) Click and drag the **wheel** counterclockwise.

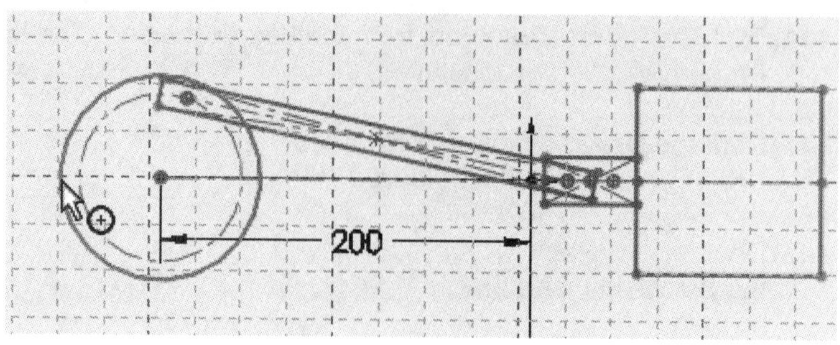

Exit the Layout Sketch.

158) Click the **Layout** tool from the Layout tool bar in the CommandManager. Verify the motion of the other components with the Rack.

159) **Close** all models. Do not save.

Activity: Layout-based Assembly Design – Motion – Example 2

Open the Layout Assembly with Blocks.

160) Click **Open** from the Menu bar toolbar.

161) Double-click the **Wheel-Slider** assembly from the Project8-2008\Models folder. View the FeatureManager.

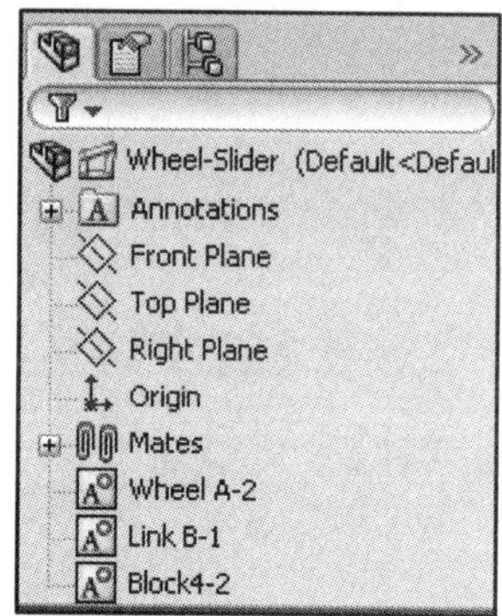

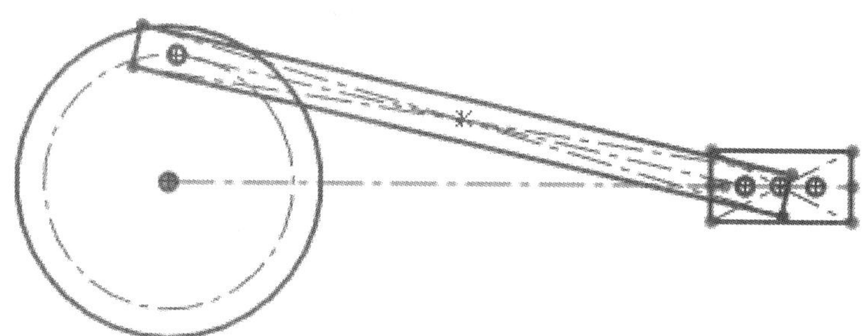

Create a Base feature for Wheel A-2.

162) Click the **Wheel A-2** block from the FeatureManager.

163) Click the **Make Part From Block** tool from the Layout toolbar in the CommandManager. The Make Part from Block PropertyManager is displayed. Accept the default settings.

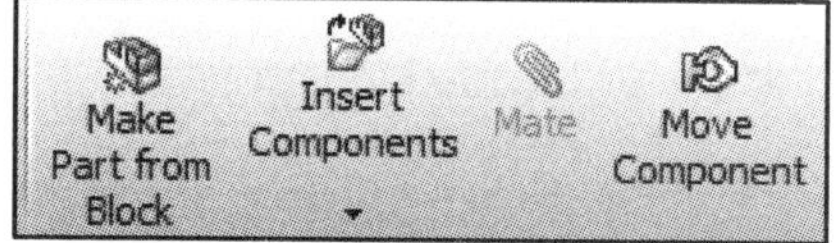

164) Click **OK** from the Make Part from Block PropertyManager. The New SolidWorks Document dialog box is displayed.

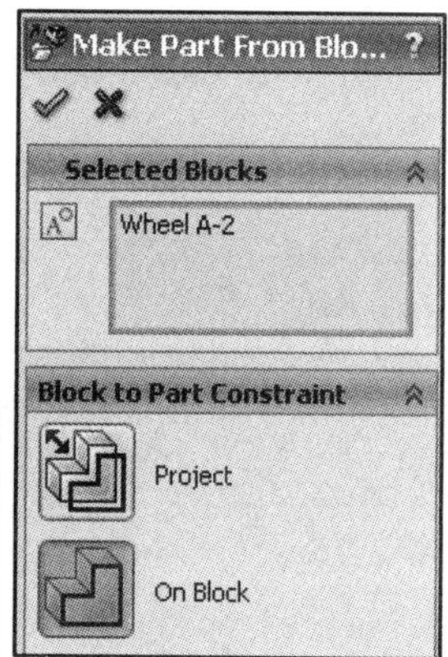

165) Select the **MY-TEMPLATES** tab. Note: This tab and template was created in Project 2.

166) Double-click **PART-MM-ANSI-AL6061**.

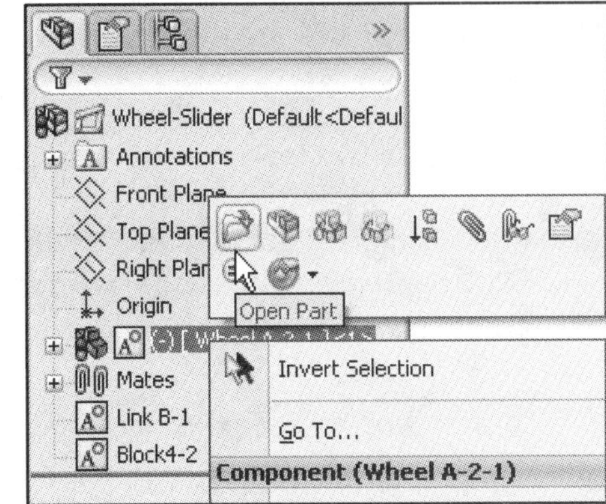

167) Right click **Wheel A** from the FeatureManager.

168) Click **Open Part** from the Context toolbar. The Part FeatureManager is displayed.

169) Click **Sketch1** from the FeatureManager.

170) Click **Extrude Boss/Bass** from the Features toolbar. The Extrude PropertyManager is displayed.

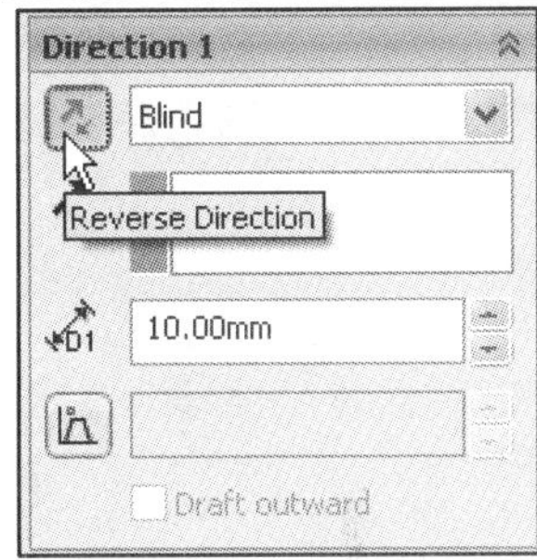

171) Click the **Reverse** Direction arrow.

172) Enter **10** for Depth. Blind is the default End Condition in Direction 1.

173) Click **OK** from the Extrude PropertyManager.

174) **Close** the part.

175) Click **Yes** to rebuild. The Wheel-Slider assembly is displayed.

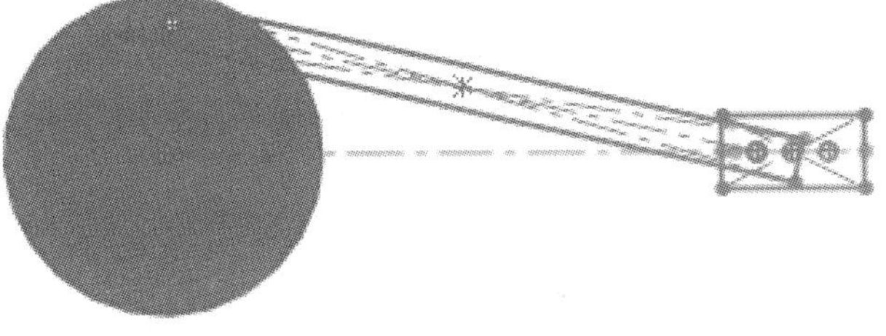

176) Click **Link B-1** from the FeatureManager.

177) Click the **Make Part from Block** tool from the Layout toolbar in the CommandManager. The Make Part from Block PropertyManager is displayed. Accept the default settings.

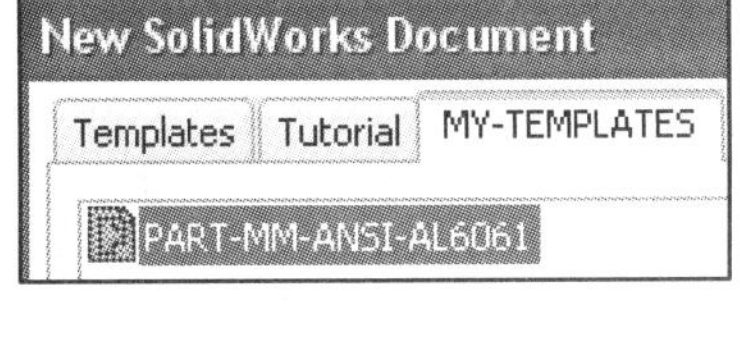

178) Click **OK** from the Make Part from Block PropertyManager. The New SolidWorks Document dialog box is displayed.

179) Select the **MY-TEMPLATES** tab.

180) Double-click **PART-MM-ANSI-AL6061**.

181) Right-click **Link B-1** from the FeatureManager.

182) Click **Edit Part** from the Context toolbar. The Link B-1 FeatureManager is displayed in blue.

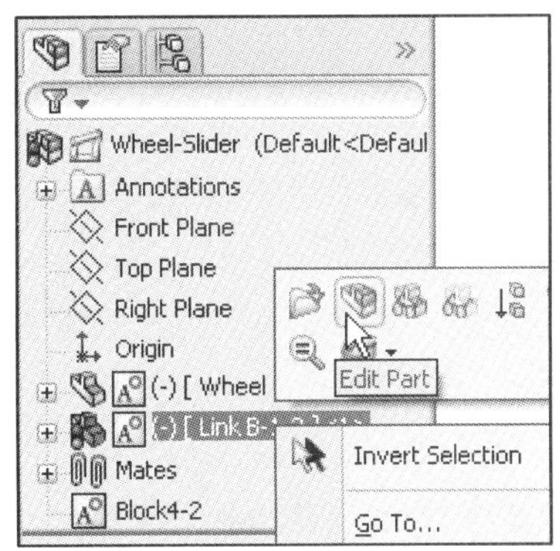

183) **Expand** Link B-1 in the FeatureManager.

Create a Base feature in-context.

184) Click **Sketch1** from the FeatureManager.

185) Click **Extrude Boss/Bass** from the Features toolbar. The Extrude PropertyManager is displayed. Blind is the default End Condition in Direction 1.

186) Enter **10** for Depth.

187) Click **OK** ✓ from the Extrude PropertyManager.

188) Click **Edit Component** to return to the Wheel Slider Assembly.

189) Click **Isometric** view. View the results.

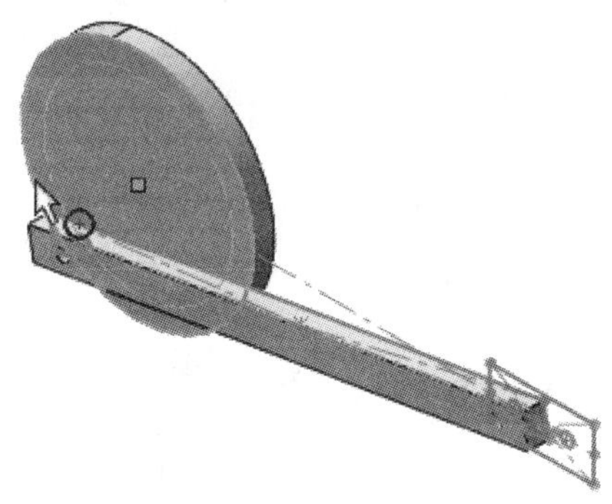

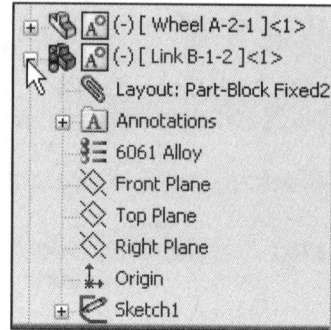

190) Drag **Wheel A** counterclockwise. View the results.

Insert a new part into the assembly. Extrude with a different Start Condition.

191) Click **Block 4-2** from the FeatureManager.

192) Click the **Make Part from Block** tool from the Layout toolbar in the CommandManager. The Make Part from Block PropertyManager is displayed. Accept the default settings.

193) Click **OK** ✓ from the Make Part from Block PropertyManager. The New SolidWorks Document dialog box is displayed.

194) Select the **MY-TEMPLATES** tab.

195) Double-click **PART-MM-ANSI-AL6061**.

196) Right-click **Block 4-2** from the FeatureManager.

197) Click **Edit Part**. The Block 4-2 FeatureManager is displayed in blue.

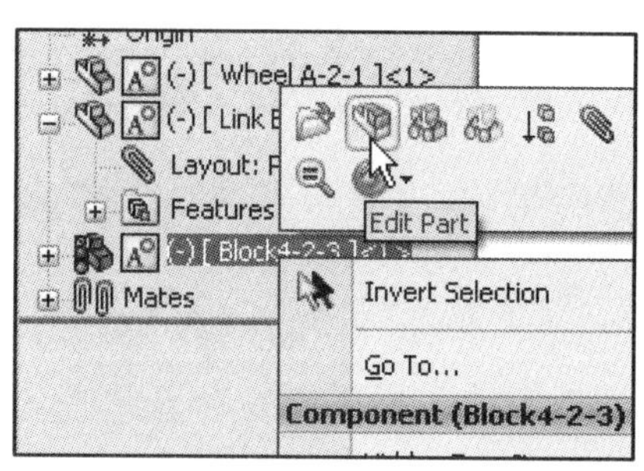

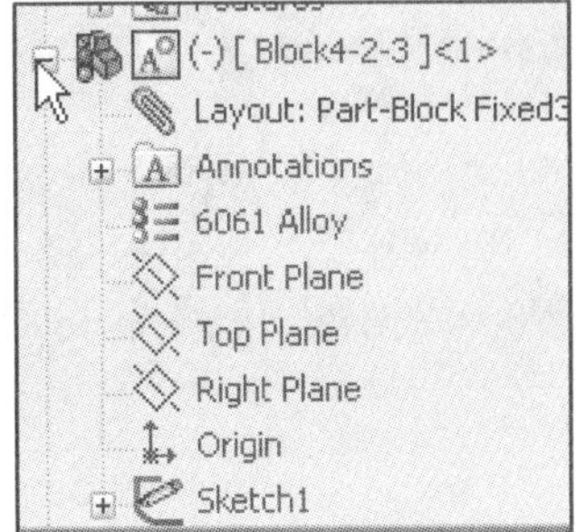

198) Expand Block4-2 in the FeatureManager.

199) Click **Sketch1**.

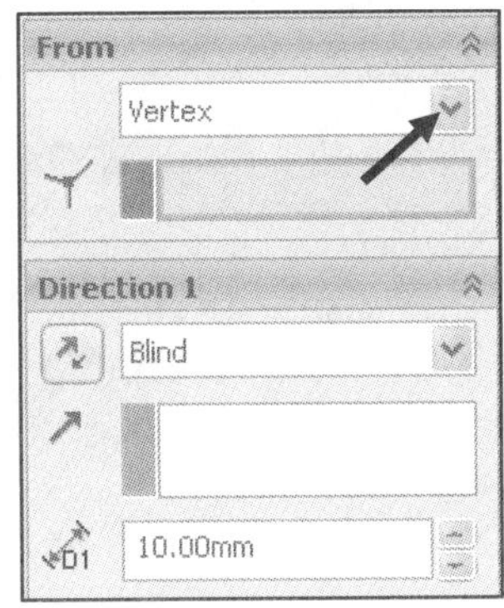

Create a Base feature in-context.

200) Click **Extrude Boss/Bass** from the Features toolbar. The Extrude PropertyManager is displayed. Blind is the default End Condition in Direction 1.

201) Select **Vertex** for Start Condition.

202) Enter **10** for Depth.

203) Click **OK** from the Extrude PropertyManager. View the results.

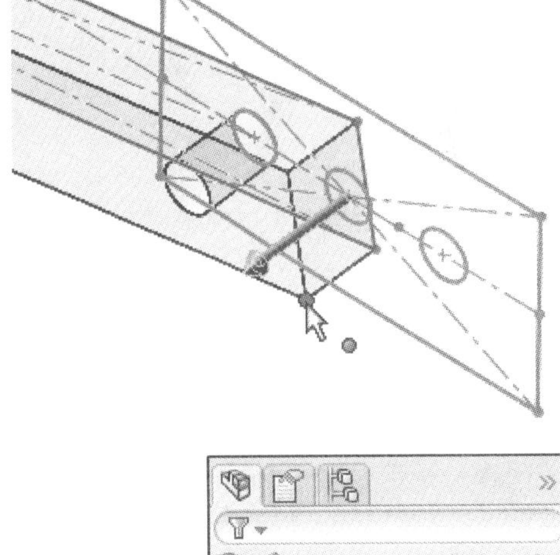

204) Click **Edit Component** to return to the Wheel Slider Assembly.

Deactivate displayed sketches.

205) Click **View**, uncheck **Sketches** from the Menu bar menu.

206) Click **Isometric** view. View the results.

207) Close the model. Do not save.

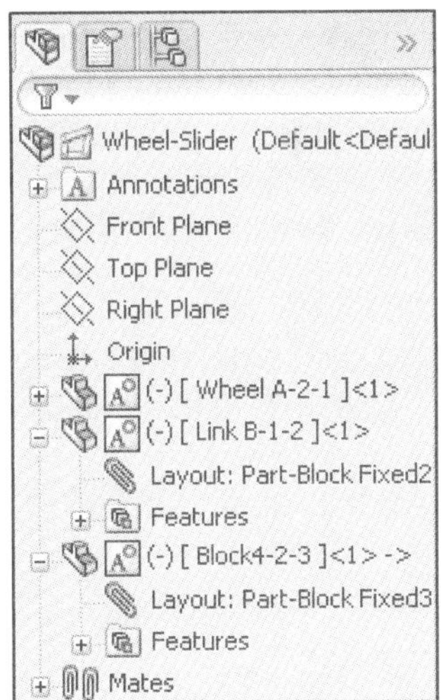

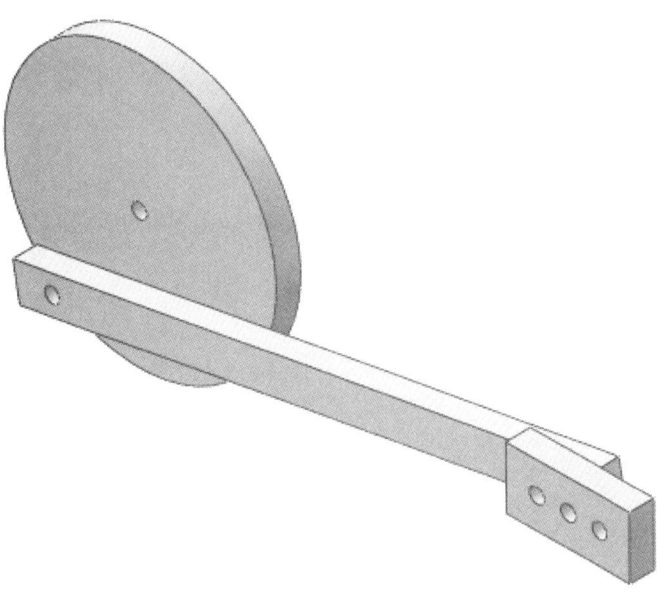

Envelopes

An assembly envelope is an assembly component that utilizes its volume to determine the position of other components in the assembly.

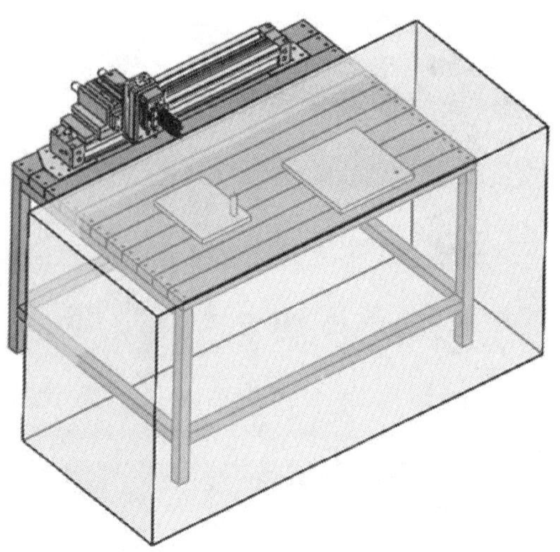

Utilize an envelope to modify the visibility of assembly components and to select components for suppress, copy resolve, delete and other editing operations.

As a solid reference component, an envelope plays no role in the Bill of Materials, Mass Properties or other global assembly operations.

SolidWorks displays envelope components in a light blue transparent color in Shaded view mode.

The FeatureManager contains the envelope entry that defines its geometry. The CommandManager contains the envelope configuration that defines selection criteria.

Additional Assembly Modeling tools: Join, Split, and Explode Line Sketch

The following assembly modeling tools are for information only, they are not related to the DELIVERY-STATION project. Additional assembly modeling information is available in Online help and the SolidWorks Reference Guide.

Join Feature

The Join feature combines multiple components in an assembly into a single part. Utilize the Join feature with casting and plastic applications. Explore the Join feature with the COSMOSXpress analysis tool.

Approximate an analysis with COSMOSXpress by combining parts in an assembly with the Join feature. This method is a good first analysis approach if the components utilize the same material.

To perform the analysis, execute the Join feature In-Context of the CRANK-ORG assembly. Combine the BASE part and the HANDLE part to create the JOIN-CRANK part. Analyze the JOIN-CRANK part with COSMOSXpress.

The COSMOSXpress command is located in the Evaluate toolbar. The COSMOSXpress tool is visible in the part document.

Activity: Join Feature and COSMOSXpress

Open the CRANK-ORG assembly.

208) Click **Open** from the Menu bar toolbar.

209) Double-click the **crank-org** assembly from the Project8-2008\Additional-Models folder. The CRANK-ORG assembly contains the BASE part and the HANDLE part. The handle part is free to rotate around the vertical axis of the base part.

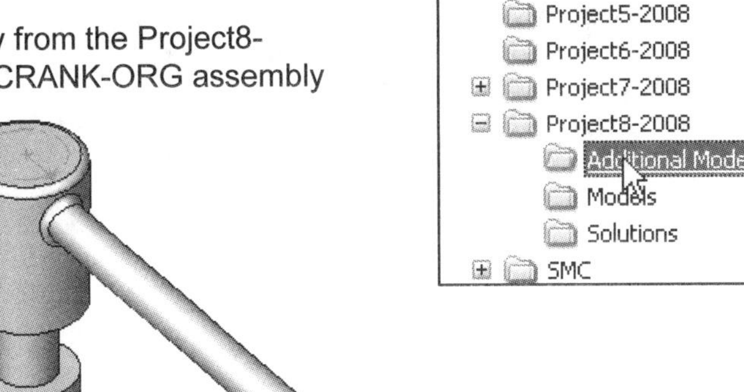

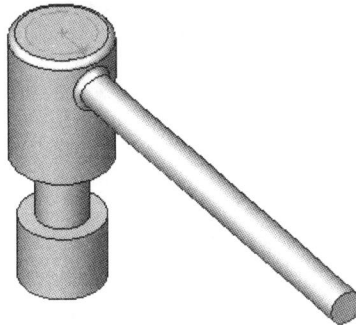

Insert a new part into the CRANK-ORG assembly.

210) Click **New Part** from the Consolidated Insert Components toolbar as illustrated. The New SolidWorks Document dialog box is displayed.

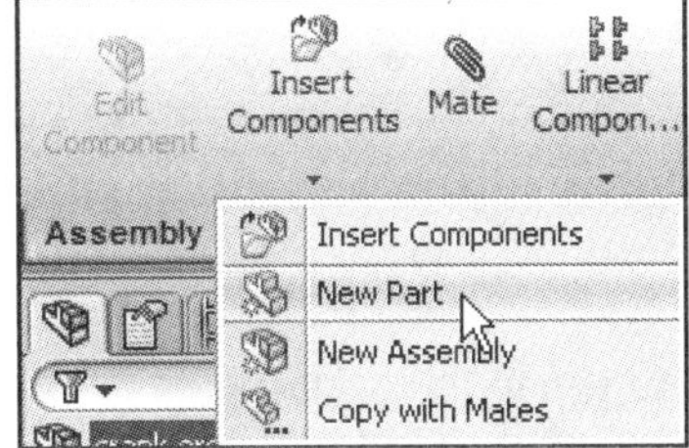

211) Select the **MY-TEMPLATES** tab. Note: This tab and template was created in Project 2.

212) Double-click **PART-MM-ANSI-AL6061**. The new part is displayed in the FeatureManager design tree with a name in the form [Part#^*assembly_name*]. The square brackets indicate that the part is a virtual component. The new Component Pointer icon is displayed. The default component is empty and requires a Sketch plane

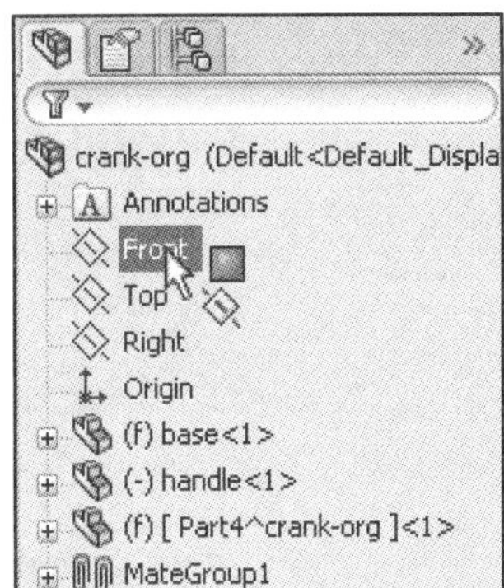

213) Click **Front Plane** from the FeatureManager. Right-click **[Part#^crank-org]** from the FeatureManager.

214) Click **Save Part(in External File)**. The Part FeatureManager is displayed. The Save As dialog box is displayed.

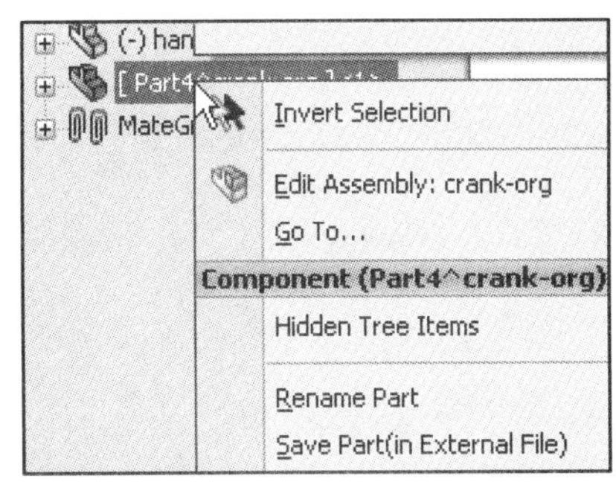

Save the Part.

215) Click **inside** the File Name box.

216) Enter **JOIN-CRANK**.

217) Click the **Same As Assembly** button.

218) Click **OK**. You return to the Assembly FeatureManager. The New part is renamed. Note: You are in the Edit Component mode.

219) Click the **Exit Sketch** tool.

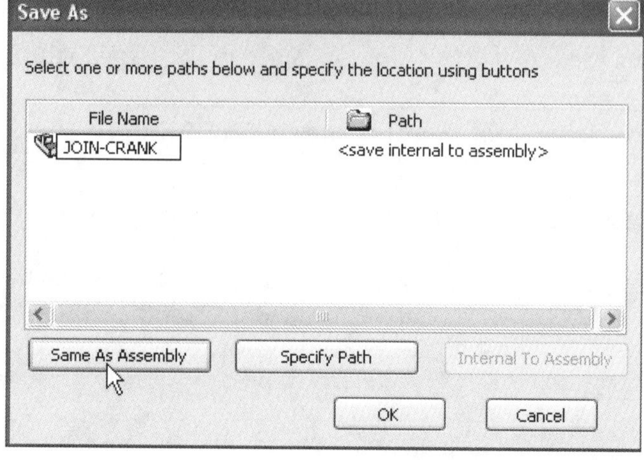

Insert the Join feature into the JOIN-CRANK part.

220) Click **Insert**, **Features**, **Join** from the Menu bar menu. The Join PropertyManager is displayed.

221) Click **base** from the crank-org fly-out FeatureManager.

222) Click **handle** from the crank-org fly-out FeatureManager.

223) Check the **Hide parts** box.

224) Click **OK** from the Join Property Manager.

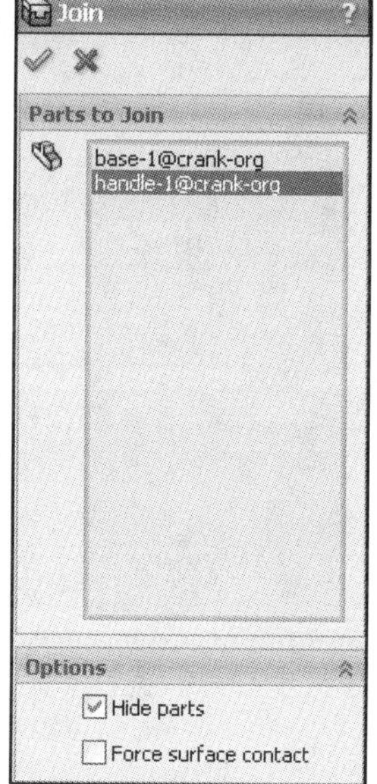

Return to the crank-org assembly.

225) Click **Edit Component**.

Open the **JOIN-CRANK** part.

226) Right-click **JOIN-CRANK** from the FeatureManager.

227) Click **Open Part from the Context toolbar**. The Part FeatureManager is displayed.

Run a COSMOSXpress Analysis.

228) Click the **COSMOSXpress Analysis Wizard** tool from the Evaluate tab in the CommandManager. The Welcome tab is displayed.

229) Click **Next>.**

230) Select **Alloy Steel** from the Material list.

231) Click **Apply**.

232) Click **Next>**. View the Restraint screen.

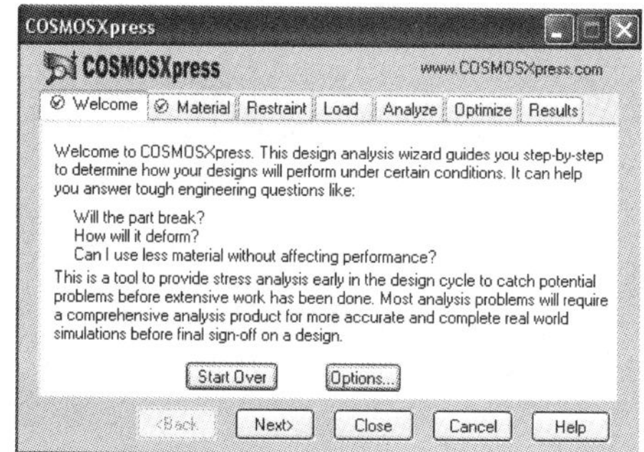

233) Click **Next>.**

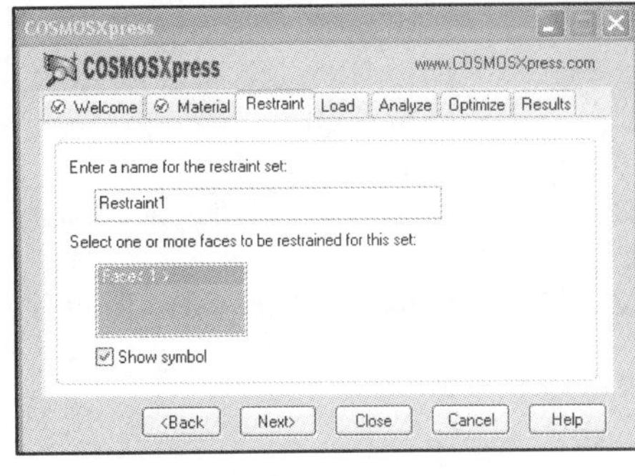

234) Click the base **bottom circular face** for the Restraint. Face<1> is displayed.

235) Click **Next>**.

236) Click **Next>**. The Load tab is displayed.

237) Click **Next>**.

238) Click **Force**.

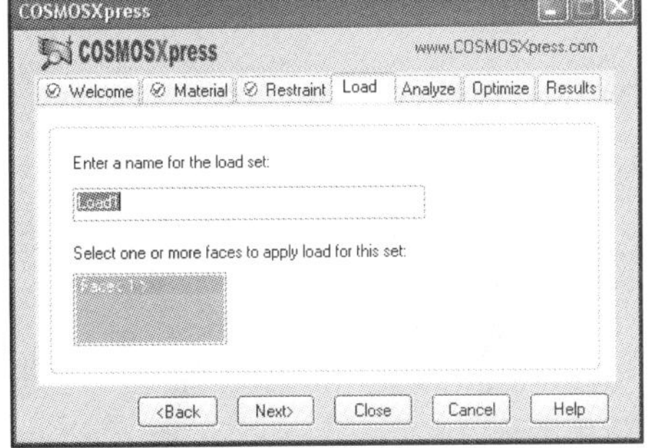

239) Click **Next>**.

240) Click the **handle circular face** to apply a load. Face<1> is displayed.

241) Click **Next>**.

242) Enter **100 N** for the vertical force.

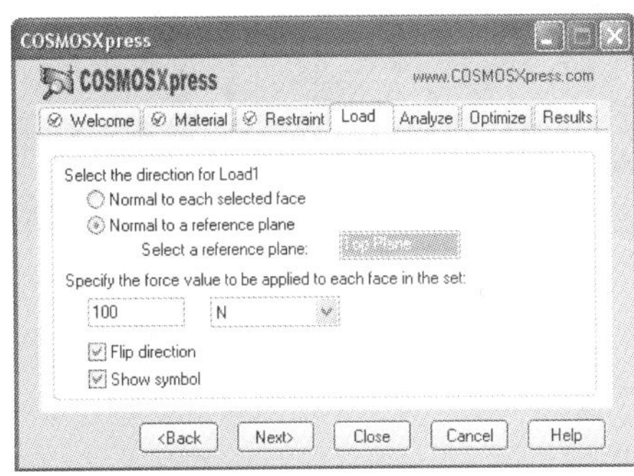

243) Check the **Normal to a reference plane** box.

244) Click **Top Plane** from the FeatureManager.

245) Check the **Flip direction** box. The direction arrows point downwards.

246) Click **Next>**.

247) Click **Next>**.

248) Click **Next>**.

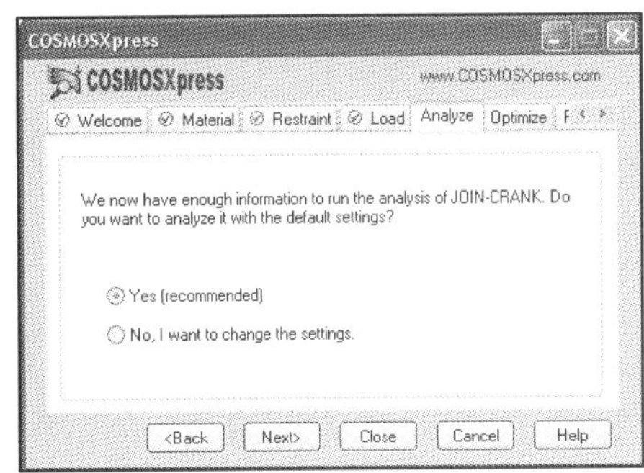

Run the first Analysis.

249) Click **Run** from the Analyze tab to review the FOS. The FOS is 8.21.

250) Click **Next>**.

251) Check **No**. Do you want to optimize this design?

252) Click **Next>**.

253) Check the **Show me the Stress distribution in the model** box.

254) Click **Next>**. Review the stress distribution.

255) Click **Close**.

256) Click **Yes** to save data.

257) **Close** all models.

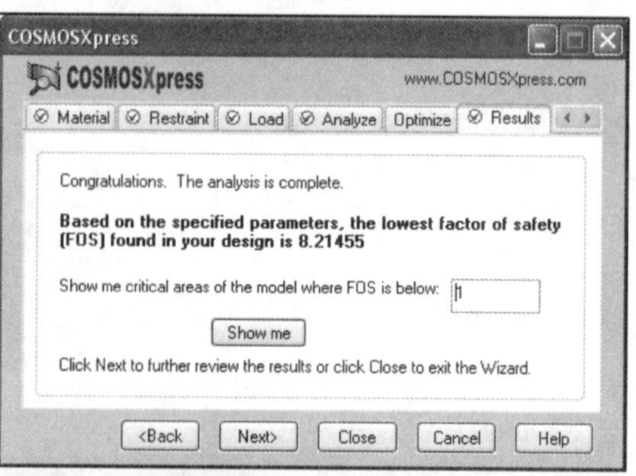

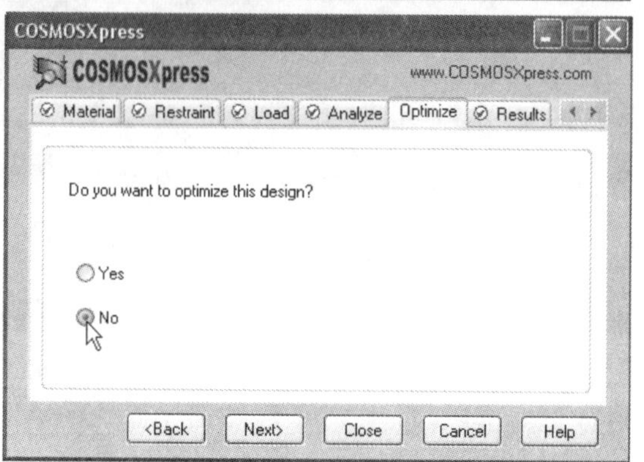

As an exercise, modify the force on the handle part to obtain a FOS between 3 and 6. Rerun COSMOSXpress. Click **COSMOSXpress Analysis Wizard** from the Evaluate toolbar. Click **Update** from the Analyze tab.

Refer to the COSMOSXpress Online tutorial or **Engineering Design with SolidWorks 2008** for additional examples.

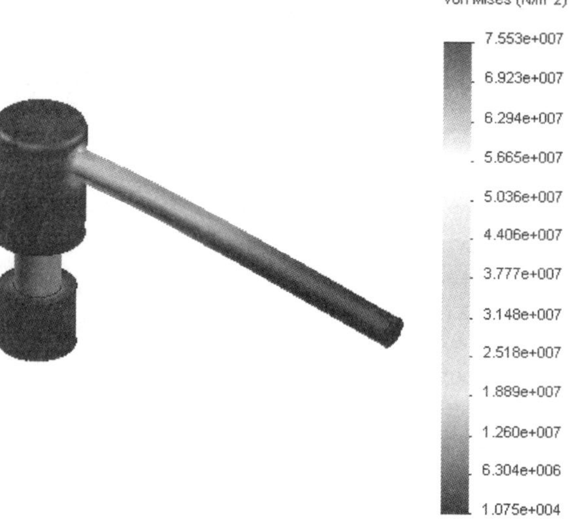

Tips on performing analysis. You are dealing with thousands or millions of equations. Every analysis situation is unique.

- Utilize symmetry. If a part is symmetric about a plane, one half of the model is required for analysis. If a part is symmetric about two planes, one fourth of the model is required for analysis.
- Suppress small fillets and detailed features in the part.

- Avoid parts that have aspect ratios over 100.
- Utilize consistent units.
- Estimate an intuitive solution based on the fundamentals of stress analysis techniques.
- Factor of Safety is a guideline for the designer. The designer is responsible for the safety of the part.

Split feature

The Split feature is utilized to break a single solid body into multiple bodies. To create a Split feature perform the following steps:

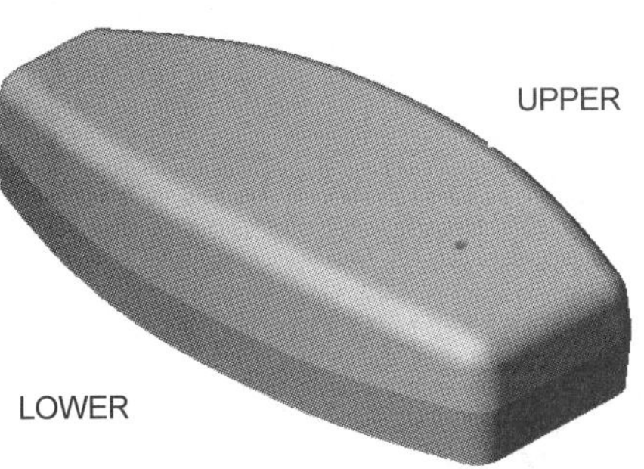

CASE Part

1. Select the Split feature.
2. Select a plane or curve for the Trim Tool.
3. Select the bodies to form individual parts.
4. Name the parts.

Create Assembly tool

The Create Assembly tool builds a new assembly from the parts developed in the Split feature. To utilize the Create Assembly tool perform the following steps:

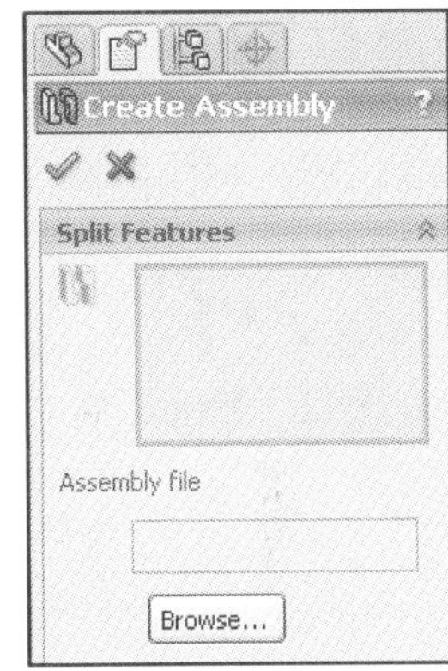

1. Select Insert, Features, Create Assembly.
2. Select the Split feature.
3. Enter a new assembly file name.

The assembly contains the parts developed with the Split feature.

The CASE part is available in the Project8-Additional-Models folder.

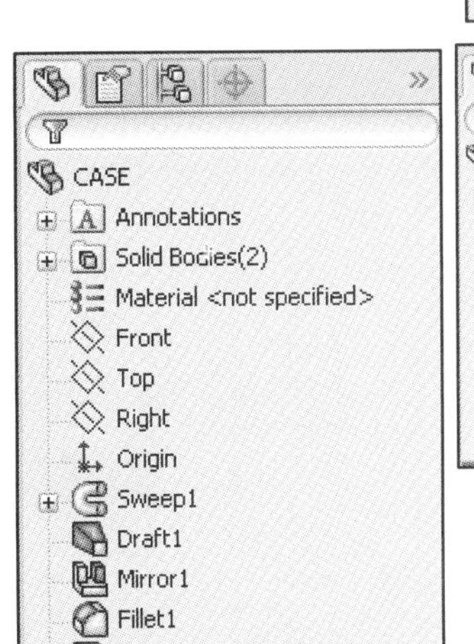

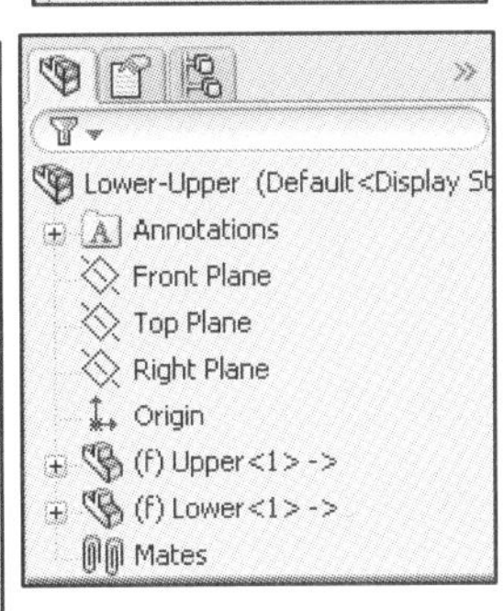

Exploded Line Sketch

The Exploded Line Sketch tool is a 3D sketch added to an Exploded View in an assembly. The explode lines indicate the relationship between components in the assembly.

Create an Exploded View. Apply the Exploded Line Sketch tool between selected components.

The 4Bar Linkage Assembly contains five components - three links and two joints. Utilize an Exploded Line Sketch to specify how to assemble the three links.

Activity: Create an Exploded View: 4Bar Linkage Assembly

Create an Exploded View.

258) Click **Open** from the Menu bar menu.

259) Double-click the **4-Bar-Linkage assembly** from the Project8-2008\Additional-Models folder.

260) Click the **Exploded View** tool from the Assembly toolbar. The Exploded PropertyManager is displayed.

4-Bar-Linkage (option1<option1_D
Annotations
Front
Top
Right
Origin
(f) joint-english<1>
joint-english<2>
(-) link-english<1> (2in)
(-) link-english<2> (4.5in)
(-) link-english<3> (7in)
MateGroup1

Create Exploded Step1.

261) Click the **lower joint** part as illustrated.

262) Drag the **blue/yellow arrow** as illustrated.

263) Click **Done**.

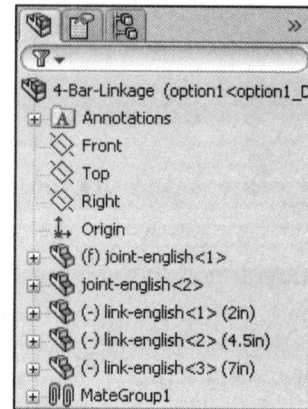

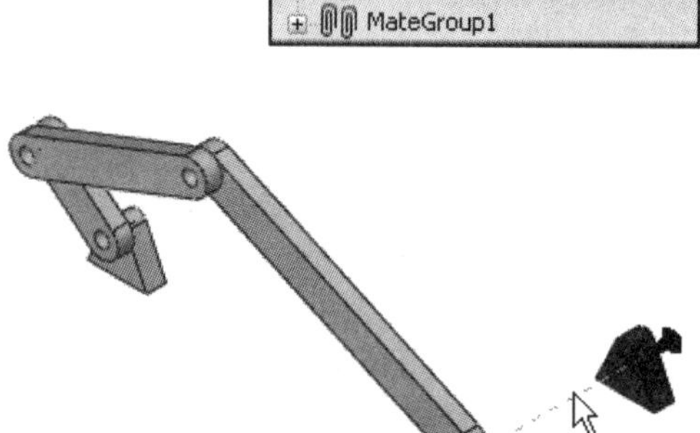

Create Exploded Step2.

264) Click the **upper link** part as illustrated.

265) Drag the **blue/yellow arrow** as illustrated.

266) Click **Done**.

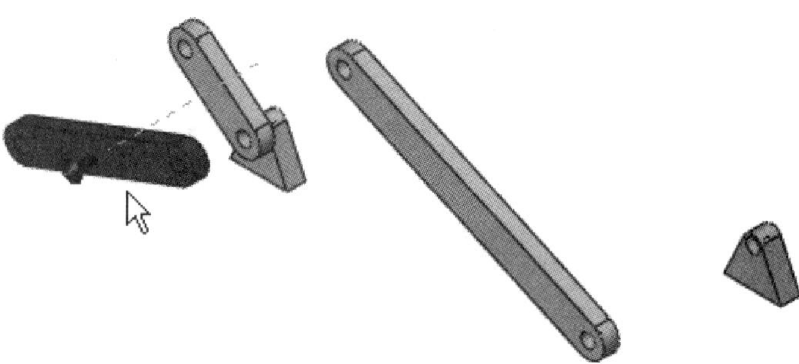

Create Exploded Step3.

267) Click the **upper joint** part as illustrated.

268) Drag the **blue/yellow arrow** as illustrated.

269) Click **Done**.

270) Click **OK** from the Explode PropertyManager.

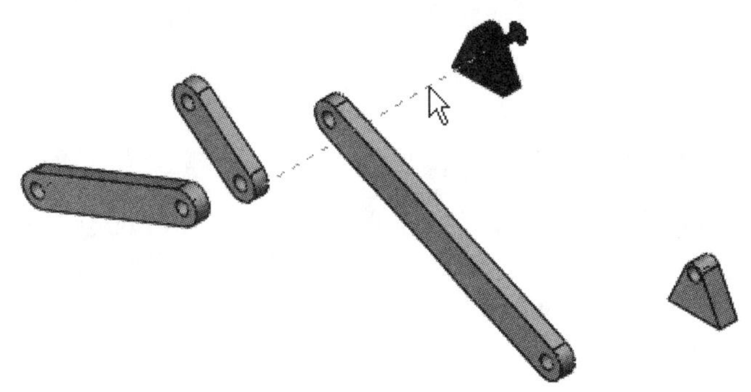

Activity: Create an Explode Line Sketch

Apply the Explode Line Sketch tool.

271) Click the **Explode Line Sketch** tool from the Assembly toolbar. The Route Line PropertyManager is displayed.

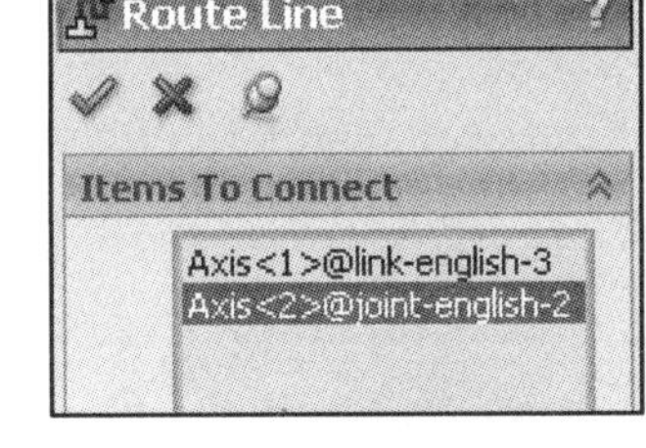

272) **Zoom in** on the link-english part and joint-english part as illustrated.

273) Click the **axis** from the link-english right hole.

274) Click the **axis** from the joint-english hole. The direction arrow points towards the back.

275) Click **OK** Route Line PropertyManager.

276) Repeat the **Explode Line Sketch** three times between the remaining components.

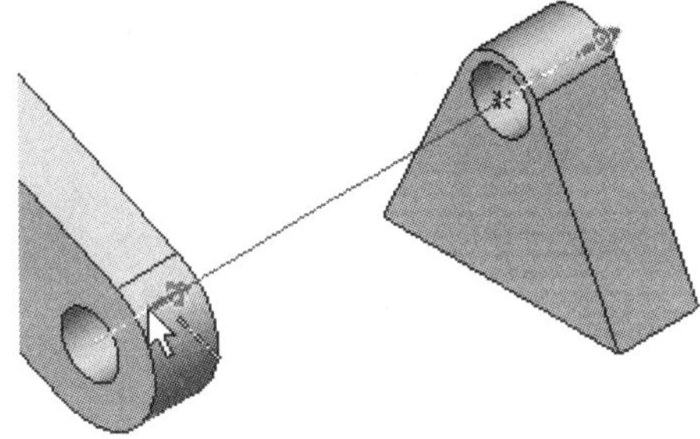

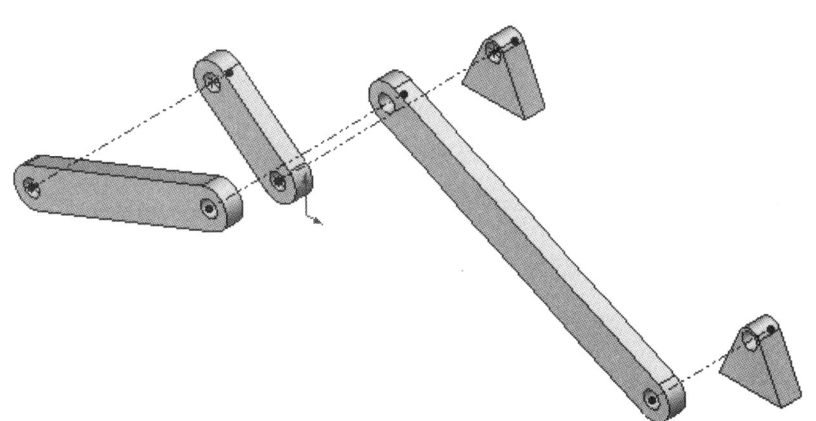

277) **Rebuild** the model.

278) Click **Isometric** view.

279) Click **Save**.

280) Click **Window**, **Close All** from the Menu bar menu.

Motion Study - Physical Simulation Tool

The New Motion Study tool provides the ability to generate graphical simulations of motion and visual properties of your active assembly. The New Motion Study tool does not modify your original assembly model or its properties. The study just displays the assembly model changes based on simulation elements you add.

The Motion Studies tool uses the MotionManager, a timeline-based interface, and provides access to the following functionality:

- *All levels*. Change viewpoints, display properties, and create distributable animations displaying your assembly in motion.
- *Assembly Motion*. Available in core SolidWorks. Animate assemblies by adding motors to drive them, or decide how the assembly should look at various times, set key points, and the Assembly Motion application computes the sequences needed to go from one position to the next.
- *Physical Simulation*. Available in core SolidWorks. Provides the ability to simulate the effects of motors, springs, dampers, and gravity on assemblies, also contains all the tools available in Assembly Motion. Physical Simulation combines simulation elements, motors, gravity, springs, and contacts with SolidWorks tools such as mates and Physical Dynamics to move the components of your assembly, while taking into account their mass properties.
- *COSMOSMotion*. Only available in SolidWorks office premium. Provides the ability to simulate, analyze, and output the effects of simulation elements, forces, springs, dampers, friction, etc. on your assembly. COSMOSMotion also contains all the tools available in Physical Simulation.

Assembly Motion

There are two types of animation supported in Assembly Motion, *motor-based* and *key frame-based*. In Motor-based animations define the type of motor and how it drives the assembly.

In Key frame-based animation, position the timebar along the timeline to define where you want the animation to end, and position the assembly components in the Graphics window where you want them to be at the time indicated by the position of the timebar.

Displayed to the right of the MotionManager FeatureManager design tree is the timeline. The timeline is the temporal interface for the animation, it displays the times and types of animation events in the Motion Study.

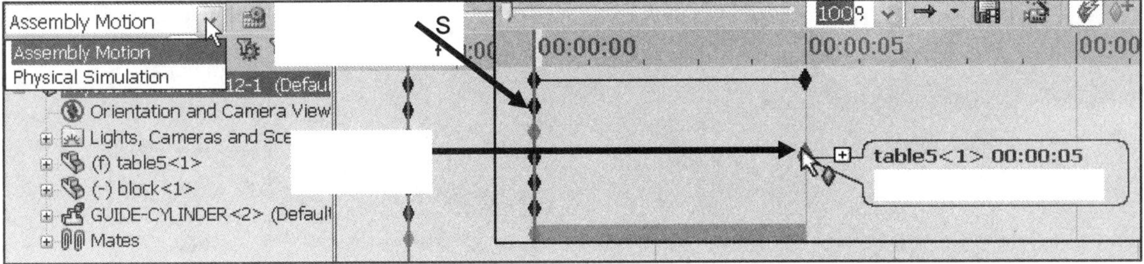

Animation Wizard

The Animation Wizard tool provides the ability to rotate parts or assemblies or explode or collapse assemblies using a simple wizard format. The following selections are available:

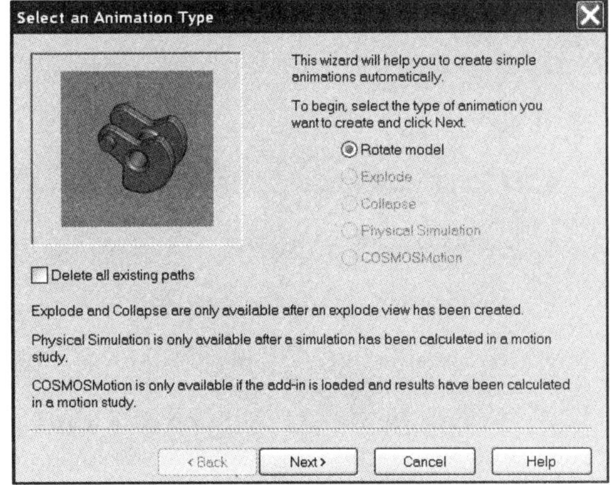

- ***Select an axis of rotation:*** Provides the ability to select the *X-axis*, *Y-axis*, or *Z-axis*.

- ***Number of rotations***: Provides the ability to enter the desired number of rotations either Clockwise or Counterclockwise.

- ***Set the duration of the animation***. Provides the ability to set the duration of the animation in seconds.

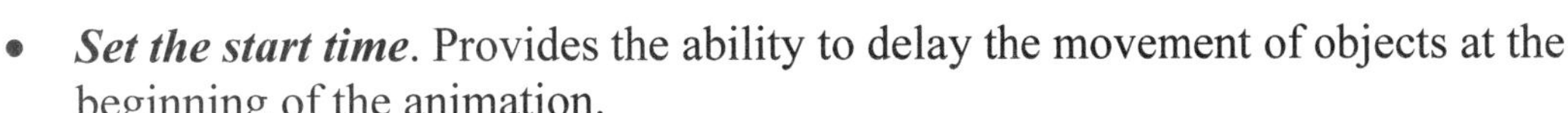

- ***Set the start time***. Provides the ability to delay the movement of objects at the beginning of the animation.

To apply the Animation Wizard in the Explode and Collapse option, you must first create an Exploded view of the assembly.

Physical Simulation

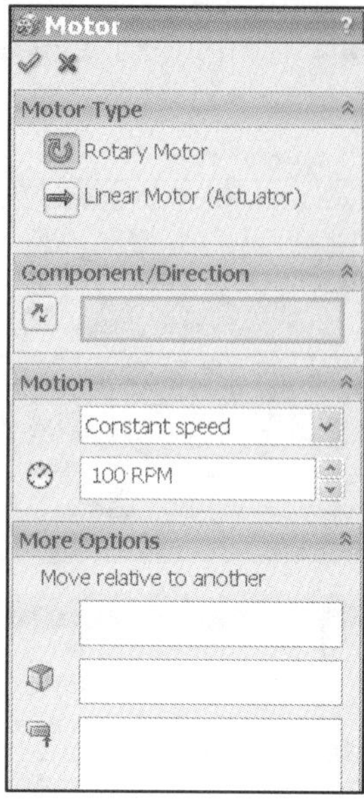

Physical Simulation provides the ability to simulate the effects of motors, springs, and gravity on your assemblies. When you record a simulation, the affected components move to a new location in the assembly. Physical Simulation uses the following options. *Linear Motor*, *Rotary Motor*, *Springs*, *3D Contacts*, and *Gravity*.

Linear / Rotary Motor tool

The Linear / Rotary Motor tool simulates elements that move components around an assembly. The Linear / Rotary Motor tool uses the Motor PropertyManager. The Motor PropertyManager provides the following selections:

- ***Motor Type***. Select Linear or Rotary.
- ***Motor Direction***. Select the component the motor will act on.
- ***Motion***. Select the type of motion to apply with the motor, and the corresponding value. The available options are:
  - **Constant speed**. The motor's value will be constant.
  - **Distance**. The motor will operate only for the set distance.
  - **Oscillating**. Set the amplitude and frequency.
  - **Interpolated**. Select the item to interpolate, *Displacement*, *Velocity*, *Acceleration*.
  - **Formula**. Select the type of formula to apply, *Displacement*, *Velocity*, *Acceleration*, and enter the formula.
  - ***More Options***. Provides the ability to set motion relative to another part, and to select components for Load-bearing Faces/Edges to transfer them to a COSMOSWorks analysis.

Spring

The Spring tool simulates elements that move components around an assembly using Physical Simulation. Physical Simulation combines simulation elements with other tools such as Mates and Physical Dynamics to move components within the components degrees of freedom. The Spring PropertyManager provides the following selections:

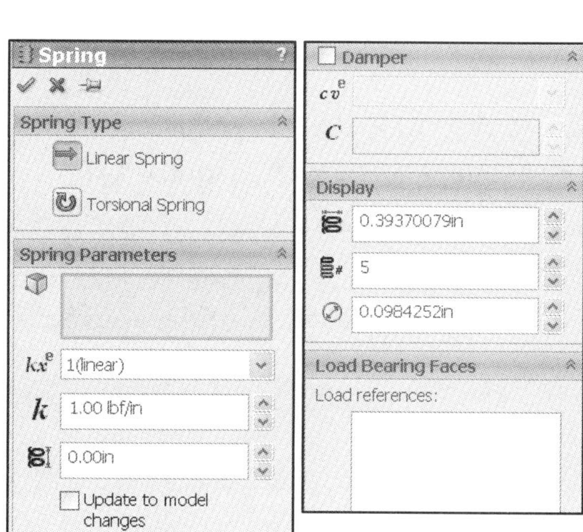

- *Spring Type*. Select Linear Spring or Torsional Spring. Note: Linear Spring is only available in Physical Simulation and COSMOSMotion. Torsional Spring is only available in COSMOSMotion.
- *Spring Parameters*. Select the following options:
    - **Spring Endpoints**.
    - **Exponent of Spring Force Expression**.
    - **Spring Constant**.
    - **Free Length**. The initial distance is the distance between the parts as currently displayed in the Graphics window.
    - **Update to model changes**. Provides the ability to have the free length dynamically update to model changes while the PropertyManager is open.
- **Damper**. Provides two options: Exponent of Damper Force Expression, and Damping Constant.
- **Display**. Provides three options: Coil Diameter, Number of Coils, and Wire Diameter.
- **Load Bearing Faces**. Select components for Load-bearing Faces/Edges to transfer them to a COSMOSWorks analysis.

3D Contact

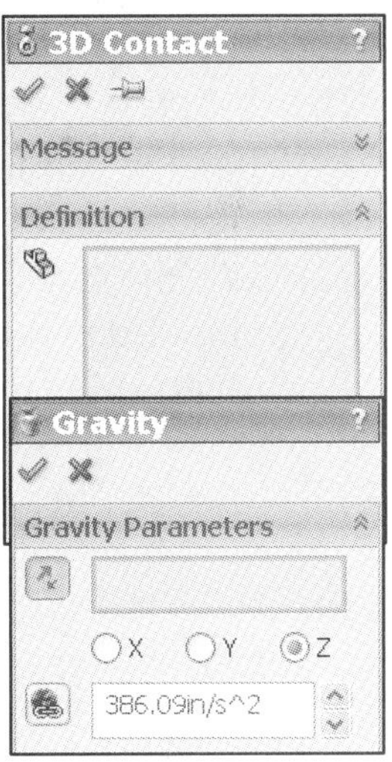

The 3D Contact tool is only available in Physical Simulation and COSMOSMotion. See SolidWorks Help for additional information.

Gravity

The Gravity tool is a simulation element that moves components around an assembly by inserting a simulated gravitational force. The Gravity tool is only available in Physical Simulation and COSMOSMotion.

The Gravity tool uses the Gravity PropertyManager. The Gravity PropertyManager provides the following options:

- *Gravity Parameters*. Provides the ability to set a Direction Reference for gravity.
- **Numeric gravity value**. Default is standard gravity.

Activity: Create a Motion Study – Example 1

Perform a Motion Study with an assembly using the linear motor and gravity options.

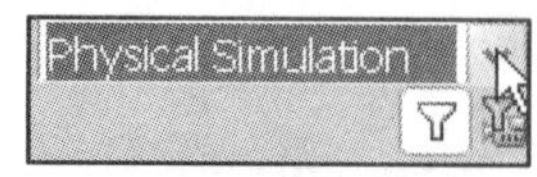

281) Open **Physical Simulation-1** from the SolidWorks Project8-2008\Additional-Models folder.

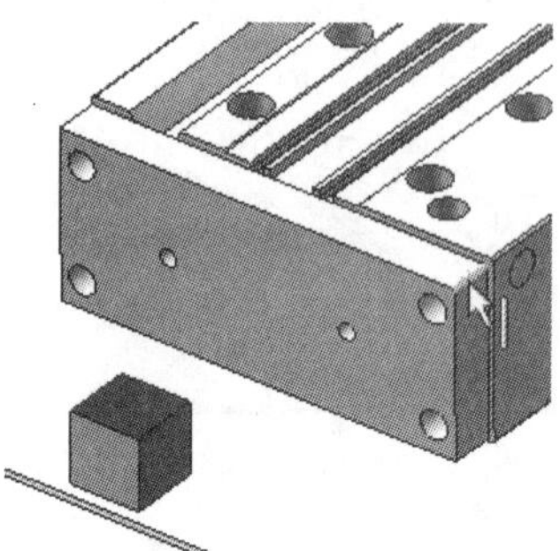

282) Click the **Motion Study1** tab in the lower left corner of the Graphics window.

283) Select **Physical Simulation** for Study type.

284) Click the **linear right front edge** Plate of MGPRod<1> as illustrated.

285) Click the **Motor** tool from the Physical Simulation toolbar. The Motor PropertyManager is displayed. Edge<1>@GUIDE-CYLINDER is displayed in the Motor direction box.

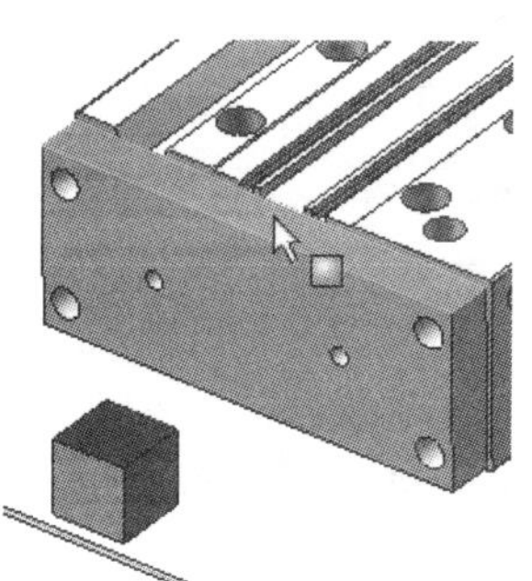

286) Click **Linear Motor**.

287) Click the **Reverse Direction** button. The direction arrow points to the front. Accept the defaults.

288) Click **OK** from the Motor PropertyManager.

289) Click the **top face** of the block part as illustrated.

290) Click the **Gravity** tool from the Physical Simulation toolbar. The Gravity PropertyManager is displayed. The direction arrow points downward. If required, click the Reverse Direction button.

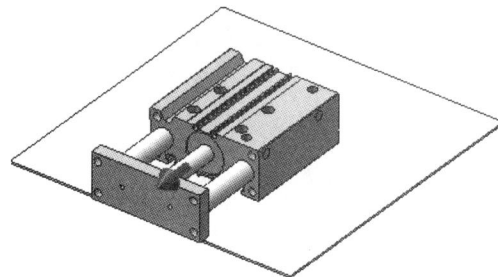

291) Click **OK** from the Gravity PropertyManager.

292) Click **Calculate** from the Physical Simulation toolbar. The piston moves and pushes the block of the table.

To create a new Motion Study, click **Insert, New Motion Study** from the Menu bar menu.

Close the Motion Study.

293) Click the **Model tab** to return to SolidWorks.

294) **Close** the model.

Activity: Create a Motion Study – Example 2

Insert a Rotary Motor Physical Simulation.

295) Open the **LINKAGE** assembly from the Project8-2008\Additional-Models folder. The LINKAGE FeatureManager is displayed.

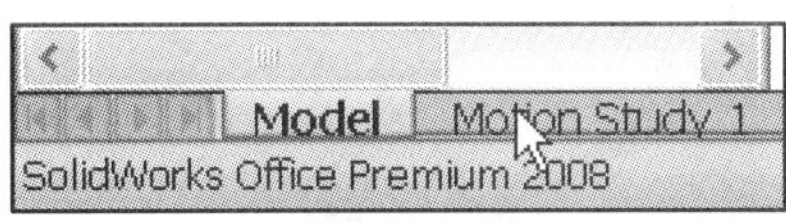

296) Click the **Motion Study 1** tab located in the bottom left corner of the Graphics window. The MotionManager is displayed.

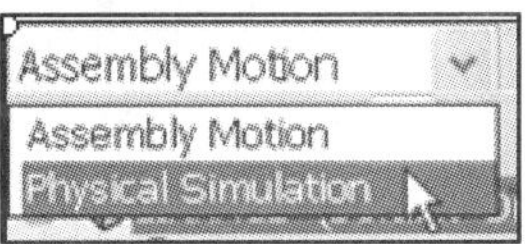

297) Select **Physical Simulation** for Type of study from the MotionManager drop-down menu.

298) Click **Motor** from the MotionManager. The Motor PropertyManager is displayed.

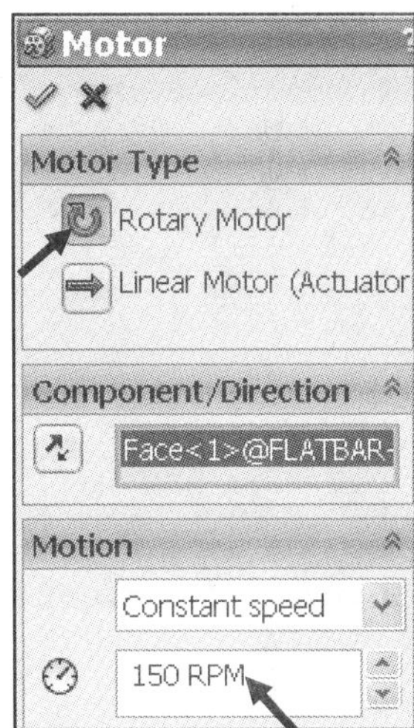

299) Click the **Rotary Motor** box.

300) Click the **FLATBAR front face** as illustrated. A red Rotary Motor icon is displayed. The red direction arrow points counterclockwise.

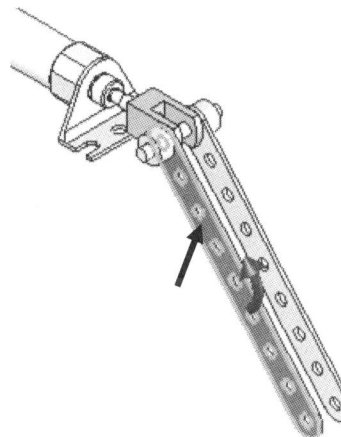

301) Enter **150 RPM** for speed in the Motion box.

302) Click **OK** from the Motor PropertyManager.

Record the Simulation.

303) Click **Calculate**. The FLATBAR rotates in a counterclockwise direction for a set period of time. View the simulation.

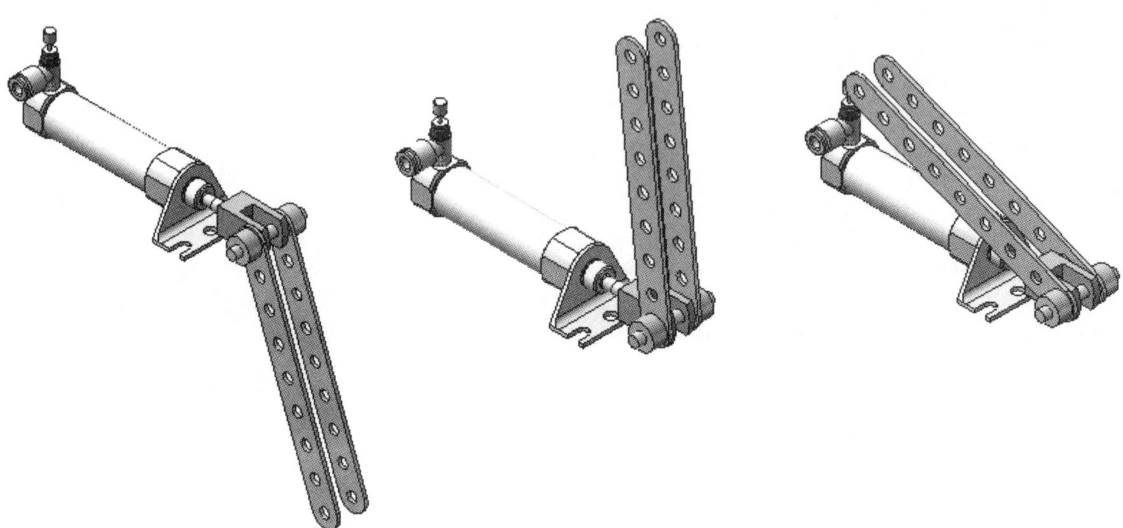

Linear Assembly Physical Simulation

Save the simulation in an AVI file to the SW-TUTORIAL-2008 folder.

304) Click **Save Animation**.

305) Click **Save** from the Save Animation to File dialog box. View your options.

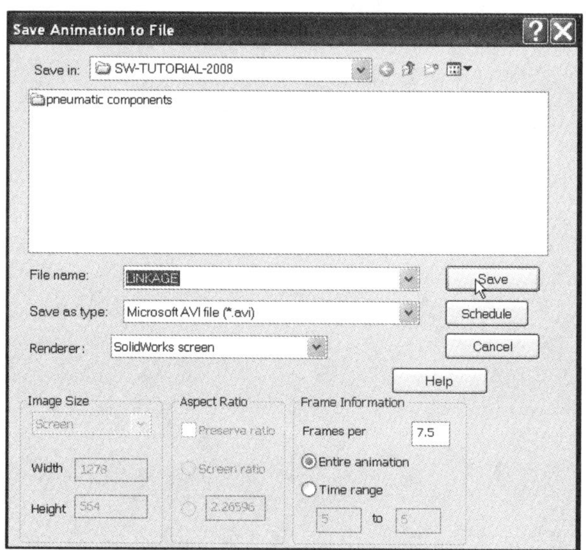

306) Click **OK** from the Video Compression box.

Close the Motion Study and return to SolidWorks.

307) Click the **Model** tab location in the bottom left corner of the Graphics window.

Fit the assembly to the Graphics window.

308) Press the **f** key.

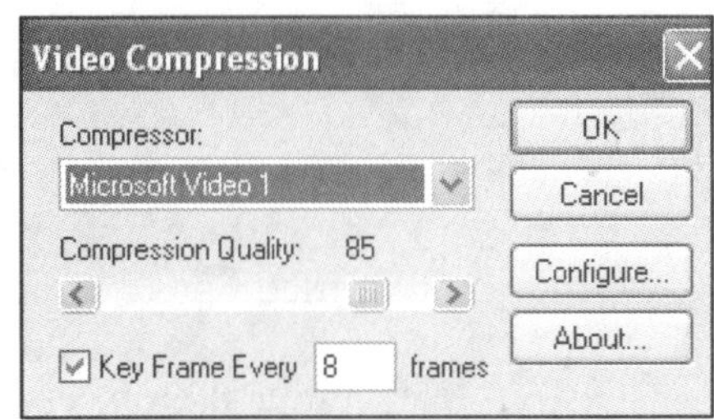

Save the LINKAGE assembly.

309) Click **Save**.

Exit SolidWorks.

310) Click **Windows**, **Close All** from the Menu bar.

Project Summary

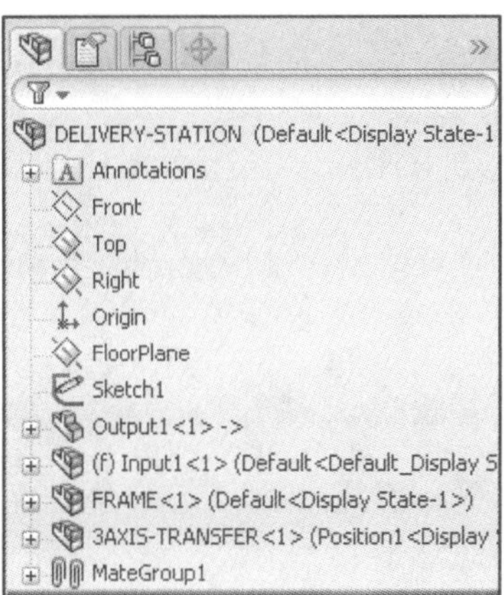

You created the DELIVERY-STATION assembly utilizing the Top-down design assembly modeling approach.

In this Project, you applied models from the Project8-2008 folder provided on the CD in the book.

The INPUT assembly contained the INPUT-BASE-PLATE part. The DELIVERY-STATION assembly contained the INPUT assembly. The INPUT-BASE-PLATE part was created In-Context of the assembly.

You created the INPUT-BASE-PLATE part and reordered components in the assembly.

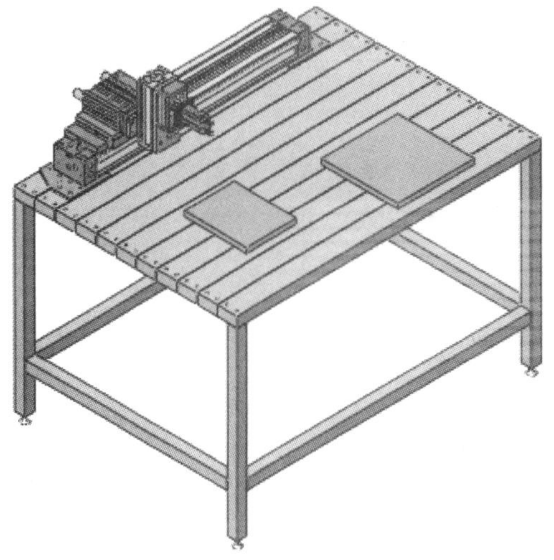

You created Link Values and applied Equations to control relationships.

You applied the Component Pattern and Mirror Components tool.

The Explode Line Sketch, Join feature, and Split feature were explored as additional assembly modeling tools.

You also created two Motion Studies using the Linear motor, Rotary motor, and gravity options.

You applied a Layout-based assembly design with blocks to create motion, the AssemblyXpert tool, and learned about assembly envelopes.

Engineers and designers study hard, work diligently and gain knowledge from their experiences. Parts, assemblies and drawings are only a portion of this project. In an engineering environment, you must also work with your engineering colleagues, other departments and the customer to complete a successful project.

Questions

1. Describe the Top-down design approach to assembly modeling.
2. Describe two methods to create a Top-down design assembly.
3. Describe a Layout sketch.
4. True or False. Centerlines cannot exist in a Layout sketch.
5. True or False. A Layout sketch exists only in a part.
6. How do you create a new part in the context of an assembly?
7. Explain the differences between a Link Value and an Equation.
8. Explain the procedure to edit an Equation.
9. Identify the location in the assembly to position the Layout sketch.
10. True or False. Only AutoCAD 2D geometry can be imported into SolidWorks.
11. Why set the Default Part template before importing an AutoCAD Solids assembly?
12. Describe the types of Component Patterns you can create in an assembly.
13. Identify the two major options available in Mirror Component.
14. True of False. A Mirror Component creates a component that is fully defined in the assembly.
15. Define an envelope.
16. Why would you utilize an envelope in a large assembly?
17. Identify two locations to activate Large Assembly Mode.
18. How does the Assembly Statistics tool assist you when you are creating an assembly?
19. Identify the procedure to create a new sub-assembly by utilizing components in the FeatureManager.
20. Describe how Assembly Features differ from features developed in a part.
21. An Explode View contains an __________________ to indicate how components are assembled together.

Appendix

Engineering Changer Order (ECO)

D&M

Engineering Change Order

ECO # ______________
Page 1 of __

	☐	Hardware		Author
	☐	Software		Date
Product Line	☐	Quality		Authorized Mgr.
	☐	Tech Pubs		Date
Change Tested By				

Reason for ECO(Describe the existing problem, symptom and impact on field)

D&M Part No.	Rev From/To	Part Description	Description	Owner

ECO Implementation/Class			Departments	Approvals	Date		
All in Field	☐		Engineering				
All in Test	☐		Manufacturing				
All in Assembly	☐		Technical Support				
All in Stock	☐		Marketing				
All on Order	☐		DOC Control				
All Future	☐						
Material Disposition			ECO Cost				
Rework	☐		DO NOT WRITE BELOW THIS LINE(ECO BOARD ONLY)				
Scrap	☐		Effective Date				
Use as is	☐		Incorporated Date				
None	☐		Board Approval				
See Attached	☐		Board Date				

This text follows the ASME Y14 Engineering Drawing and Related Documentation Practices for drawings. Display of dimensions and tolerances are as follows:

<table>
<tr><th colspan="4">TYPES of DECIMAL DIMENSIONS (ASME Y14.5M)</th></tr>
<tr><th>Description:</th><th>UNITS: MM</th><th>Description:</th><th>UNITS: INCH</th></tr>
<tr><td>Dimension is less than 1mm.
Zero precedes the decimal point.</td><td>0.9
0.95</td><td>Dimension is less than 1 inch.
Zero is not used before the decimal point.</td><td>.5
.56</td></tr>
<tr><td>Dimension is a whole number.
Display no decimal point.
Display no zero after decimal point.</td><td>19</td><td rowspan="2">Express dimension to the same number of decimal places as its tolerance.
Add zeros to the right of the decimal point.
If the tolerance is expressed to 3 places, then the dimension contains 3 places to the right of the decimal point.</td><td rowspan="2">1.750</td></tr>
<tr><td>Dimension exceeds a whole number by a decimal fraction of a millimeter.
Display no zero to the right of the decimal.</td><td>11.5
11.51</td></tr>
</table>

<table>
<tr><th colspan="3">TABLE 1

TOLERANCE DISPLAY FOR INCH AND METRIC DIMENSIONS (ASME Y14.5M)</th></tr>
<tr><th>DISPLAY:</th><th>UNITS:
INCH:</th><th>UNITS:
METRIC:</th></tr>
<tr><td>Dimensions less than 1</td><td>.5</td><td>0.5</td></tr>
<tr><td>Unilateral Tolerance</td><td>$1.417^{+.005}_{-.000}$</td><td>$36^{0}_{-0.5}$</td></tr>
<tr><td>Bilateral Tolerance</td><td>$1.417^{+.010}_{-.020}$</td><td>$36^{+0.25}_{-0.50}$</td></tr>
<tr><td>Limit Tolerance</td><td>.571
.463</td><td>14.50
11.50</td></tr>
</table>

SolidWorks Keyboard Shortcuts

Listed below are the pre-defined keyboard shortcuts in SolidWorks:

Action:	**Key Combination:**
Model Views	
Rotate the model horizontally or vertically:	**Arrow** keys
Rotate the model horizontally or vertically 90 degrees.	**Shift** + **Arrow** keys
Rotate the model clockwise or counterclockwise	**Alt** + left of right **Arrow** keys
Pan the model	**Ctrl** + **Arrow** keys
Zoom in	**Shift + z**
Zoom out	**z**
Zoom to fit	**f**
Previous view	**Ctrl + Shift + z**
View Orientation	
View Orientation menu	**Spacebar**
Front view	**Ctrl + 1**
Back view	**Ctrl + 2**
Left view	**Ctrl + 3**
Right view	**Ctrl + 4**
Top view	**Ctrl + 5**
Bottom view	**Ctrl + 6**
Isometric view	**Ctrl + 7**
NormalTo view	**Ctrl + 8**
Selection Filters	
Filter edges	**e**
Filter vertices	**v**
Filter faces	**x**
Toggle Selection Filter toolbar	**F5**
Toggle selection filters on/off	**F6**
File menu items	
New SolidWorks document	**Ctrl + n**
Open document	**Ctrl + o**
Open From Web Folder	**Ctrl + w**
Make Drawing from Part	**Ctrl + d**
Make Assembly from Part	**Ctrl + a**
Save	**Ctrl +s**
Print	**Ctrl + p**
Additional shortcuts	
Access online help inside of PropertyManager or dialog box	**F1**
Rename an item in the FeatureManager design tree	**F2**
Rebuild the model	**Ctrl + b**
Force rebuild – Rebuild the model and all its features	**Ctrl + q**
Redraw the screen	**Ctrl + r**
Cycle between open SolidWorks document	**Ctrl + Tab**

Line to arc/arc to line in the Sketch	**a**
Undo	**Ctrl + z**
Redo	**Ctrl + y**
Cut	**Ctrl + x**
Copy	**Ctrl + c**
Additional shortcuts	
Paste	**Ctrl + v**
Delete	**Delete**
Next window	**Ctrl + F6**
Close window	**Ctrl + F4**
Selects all text inside an Annotations text box	**Ctrl + a**

In the Sketch, the Esc key unselects geometry items currently selected in the Properties box and Add Relations box. In the model, the Esc key closes the PropertyManager and cancels the selections.

Windows Shortcuts

Listed below are the pre-defined keyboard shortcuts in Microsoft Windows:

Action:	Keyboard Combination:
Open the Start menu	Windows Logo key
Open Windows Explorer	Windows Logo key + E
Minimize all open windows	Windows Logo key + M
Open a Search window	Windows Logo key + F
Open Windows Help	Windows Logo key + F1
Select multiple geometry items in a SolidWorks document	Ctrl key (Hold the Ctrl key down. Select items.) Release the Ctrl key.

CSWA Certification - Introduction

SolidWorks Corporation offers two levels of certification representing increasing levels of expertise in 3D CAD design as it applies to engineering: Certified SolidWorks Associate CSWA, and the Certified SolidWorks Professional CSWP.

The CSWA certification indicates a foundation in and apprentice knowledge of 3D CAD design and engineering practices and principles. The main requirement for obtaining the CSWA certification is to take and pass the three hour, seven question on-line proctored exam at a Certified SolidWorks CSWA Provider, "university, college, technical, vocational, or secondary educational institution" and to sign the SolidWorks Confidentiality Agreement.

Passing this exam provides students the chance to prove their knowledge and expertise and to be part of a world wide industry certification standard.

 You can either take the exam in SolidWorks 2007 or SolidWorks 2008.

Intended Audience

The intended audience for the CSWA exam is anyone with a minimum of 6 - 9 months of SolidWorks experience and basic knowledge of engineering fundamentals and practices. SolidWorks recommends that you review their SolidWorks Tutorials on Parts, Assemblies, Drawings, and COSMOSXpress as a prerequisite and have at least 45 hours of classroom time learning SolidWorks or using SolidWorks with basic engineering design principles and practices.

To prepare for the CSWA exam, it is recommended that you first perform the following:

- Take a CSWA exam preparation class or review a text book written for the CSWA exam.
- Complete the SolidWorks Tutorials
- Practice creating models from the isometric working drawings sections of any Technical Drawing or Engineering Drawing Documentation text books.
- Complete the sample CSWA exam in a timed environment, available at www.solidworks.com/cswa.

Additional references to help you prepare are as follows:

- SolidWorks Users Guide, SolidWorks Corporation, 2007.
- Official Certified SolidWorks Associate Exam Book, Delmar Thomson 2007.
- Bertoline, Wiebe, Miller, Fundamentals of Graphics Communication, Irwin, 1995.

- Hibbler, R.C, Engineering Mechanics Statics and Dynamics, 8th ed, Prentice Hall, Saddle River, NJ.
- Hoelscher, Springer, Dobrovolny, Graphics for Engineers, John Wiley, 1968.
- Jensen, Cecil, Interpreting Engineering Drawings, Glencoe, 2002.
- Jensen & Helsel, Engineering Drawing and Design, Glencoe, 1990.
- Lieu, Sorby, Visualization, Modeling, and Graphics for Engineering, Delmar Thomson, 2007.
- Madsen, David, Engineering Drawing and Design, Delmar Thomson, 2007.
- Planchard & Planchard, Drawing and Detailing with SolidWorks, SDC Pub., Mission, KS 2007.

CSWA Exam Content

The CSWA V1, (Version 1) exam is split into five categories. Questions on the timed exam are provided in a random manor. The following information provides general guidelines for the content likely to be included on the exam. However, other related topics may also appear on any specific delivery of the exam. In order to better reflect the contents of the exam and for clarity purposes, the guidelines below may change at any time without notice.

Basic Theory and Drawing Theory (2 Questions - Total 10 Points)

- Identify and apply basic concepts in SolidWorks
- Recognize 3D modeling techniques:
  - Understand how parts, assemblies, and drawings are related
  - Identify the feature type, parameters, and dimensions
  - Identify the correct standard reference planes: Top, Right, and Front
  - Determine the design intent for a model
- Identify and understand the procedure for the following:
  - Assign and edit material to a part
  - Apply the Measure tool to a part or an assembly
  - Locate the Center of mass, and Principal moments of inertia relative to the default coordinate location, Origin.

- Calculate the overall mass and volume of a part

- Recognize and know the function and elements of the Part and Assembly FeatureManager design tree:
    - Sketch status
    - Component status and properties
    - Display Pane status
    - Reference configurations

- Identify the default Sketch Entities from the Sketch toolbar: Line, Rectangle, Circle, etc.

- Identify the default Sketch Tools from the Sketch toolbar: Fillet, Chamfer, Offset Entities, etc.

- Identify the available SolidWorks File formats for input and export:
    - Save As type for a part, assembly, and drawing
    - Open File of different formats

- Use SolidWorks Help:
    - Contents, Index, and Search tabs

- Identify the process of creating a simple drawing from a part or an assembly:
    - Knowledge to insert and modify the 3 Standard views
    - Knowledge to add a sheet and annotations to a drawing

- Recognize all drawing name view types by their icons:
    - Model, Projected, Auxiliary, Section, Aligned, Detail, Standard, Broken Section, Break, Crop, and Alternate Position

- Identify the procedure to create a named drawing view:
    - Model, Projected, Auxiliary, Section, Aligned, Detail, Standard, Broken Section, Break, Crop, and Alternate Position

- Specify Document Properties:
    - Select Unit System
    - Set Precision

Part Modeling (1 Question - Total 30 Points)

- Read and understand an Engineering document:
    - Identify the Sketch plane, part Origin location, part dimensions, geometric relations, and design intent of the sketch and feature
- Build a part from a detailed dimensioned illustration using the following SolidWorks tools and features:
    - 2D & 3D sketch tools
    - Extruded Boss/Base
    - Extruded Cut
    - Fillet
    - Mirror
    - Revolved Base
    - Chamfer
    - Reference geometry
    - Plane
    - Axis
    - Calculate the overall mass and volume of the created part
- Locate the Center of mass for the created part relative to the Origin

Advanced Part Modeling (1 Question -Total 20 Points)

- Specify Document Properties
- Interpret engineering terminology:
    - Create and manipulate a coordinate system

- Build an advanced part from a detailed dimensioned illustration using the following tools and features:
  - 2D & 3D Sketch tools
  - Extruded Boss/Base
  - Extruded Cut
  - Fillet
  - Mirror
  - Revolved Boss/Base
  - Linear & Circular Pattern
  - Chamfer
  - Revolved Cut
- Locate the Center of mass relative to the part Origin
- Create a coordinate system location
- Locate the Center of mass relative to a created coordinate system

Assembly Modeling (1 Question - Total 30 Points)

- Specify Document Properties
- Identify and build the components to construct the assembly from a detailed illustration using the following features:
  - Extruded Boss/Base
  - Extruded Cut
  - Fillet
  - Mirror
  - Revolved Boss/Base
  - Revolved Cut
  - Linear Pattern

  - Chamfer
  - Hole Wizard
- Identify the first fixed component in an assembly
- Build a bottom-up assembly with the following Standard mates:
  - Coincident, Concentric, Parallel, Perpendicular, Tangent, Angle, and Distance
  - Aligned, Anti-Aligned options
- Apply the Mirror Component tool
- Locate the Center of mass relative to the assembly Origin
- Create a coordinate system location
- Locate the Center of mass relative to a created coordinate system
- Calculate the overall mass and volume for the created assembly
- Mate the first component with respect to the assembly reference planes

Advanced Modeling Theory and Analysis (2 Questions - Total 10 Points)

- Understand the procedure and process to apply COSMOSXpress to a simple part
- Understand the functions and differences of the following SolidWorks analysis tools:
  - COMSMOSXpress, COSMOSWorks Designer, COSMOSWorks Professional, COSMOSMotion, & COSMOSFloWorks

Why the CSWA exam?

The CAD world has many different certifications available. Some of these certifications are sponsored by vendors and some by consortiums of different vendors. Regardless of the sponsor of the certifications, most CAD professionals today recognize the need to become certified to prove their skills, prepare for new job searches, and to learn new skill, while at their existing jobs.

Specifying a CSWA or CSWP certification on your resume is a great way to increase your chances of landing a new job, getting a promotion, or looking more qualified when representing your company on a consulting job.

How to obtain your CSWA Certification?

SolidWorks Corporation requires that you take and pass the 3 hour on-line proctored exam in a secure environment at a designated CSWA Provider and to sign the SolidWorks Confidentiality Agreement. A CSWA Provider can be a university, college, technical, vocational, or secondary educational institution. Contact your local SolidWorks Value Added Reseller (VAR) or instructor for information on CSWA Providers.

There are five key categories in the CSWA exam. The minimum passing grade is 70 out of 100 points. There are two questions in both the Basic Theory and Drawing, and Advanced Modeling Theory and Analysis Categories, (multiple choice, single answer) and one question in each of the Part modeling, Advanced Part Modeling and Analysis, and the Assembly Modeling categories. The single questions are on an in-depth illustrated dimension model. All questions are in a multiple choice single answer format.

How to prepare to pass the CSWA exam?

Taking a SolidWorks class at a university, college, technical, vocational, or secondary educational institution or time in industry using SolidWorks does not mean that you will automatically pass the CSWA exam. In fact, the CSWA exam purposefully attempts to make the questions prove that you know the material well by making you apply the concepts in a real world situation. The CSWA exam questions tend to be a fair amount more involved than just creating a single sketch, part, or simple assembly. The exam requires that you know and apply the knowledge to different scenarios.

How does an institution become a CSWA Provider?

A Certified SolidWorks Associate CSWA Provider is any university, college, technical, vocational, or secondary educational institution. All CSWA Providers must complete the CSWA Provider application. The educational institution provides the following to administer the CSWA exam:

- Valid SolidWorks Maintenance agreement
- Recommended computer hardware with the required internet access
- Printer for CSWA certificates
- Proctor to administer the CSWA exam
- Completed CSWA Provider application www.solidworks.com/cswa
- Reviewed CSWA “Terms and Conditions” document

Educational institution instructors or administrators should contact their Value Added Reseller for additional information.

Exam day

Candidates must acknowledge the SolidWorks CSWA Certification and Confidentiality Agreement online at the authorized CSWA Provider site prior to taking the exam. Candidates will not be able to proceed with the exam and a refund will not be provided. Signing this legal agreement is required to be officially certified.

Gather personal information prior to exam registration:

- Legal name (from government issued ID)
- Social Security or passport number
- CSWA Certification exam event code from the Provider
- Valid email address
- Method of payment

Students will not be able to use notes, books, calculators, PDA's, cell phones, or materials not authorized by a SolidWorks Certified Provider or SolidWorks during the exam.

The CSWA exam, at this time, is provided in the following languages: English, French, German, Italian, Spanish, Chinese-Simplified, Chinese-Traditional, Korean, Japanese, and Brazilian Portuguese.

Exams may contain non-scored items to collect performance data on new items. Non-scored items are not used in determining the passing score nor are reported in a subsection of the score report. All non-scored items are randomly placed in the exam with sufficient time calculated and given to complete the entire exam.

At the completion of the computer-based on-line exam, candidates receive a score report along with a score breakout by exam section and the passing score for the given exam. Note: All students are required to sign and return all supplied papers/notes that were taken during the exam to the onsite proctor before leaving the testing room.

What do I get when I pass the exam?

After a candidate passes the CSWA exam and signs the required agreements, the SolidWorks Provider will print on-site the CSWA Certification certificate identifying the candidate's CSWA Career Certification ID and valid certification date.

Certified candidates are authorized to use the appropriate CSWA SolidWorks certification logo indicating certification status. Prior to use, they must read and acknowledge the SolidWorks Certification Logo Agreement. Logos can be downloaded through the CSWA Certification Tracking System.

The CSWA Certification Tracking System provides a record of both exam and certification status. Candidates and certification holders are expected to keep contact information up to date for receiving notifications from SolidWorks.

Helpful On-Line Information

The SolidWorks URL: http://www.solidworks.com contains information on Local Resellers, Solution Partners, Certifications, SolidWorks users groups, and more.

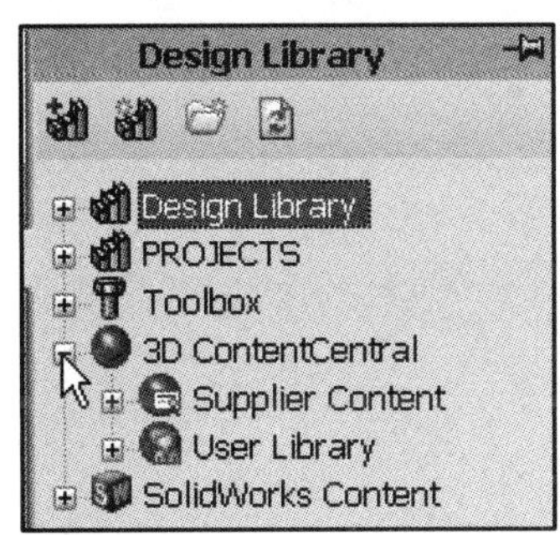

Access 3D ContentCentral using the Task Pane to obtain engineering electronic catalog model and part information.

Use the SolidWorks Resources tab in the Task Pane to obtain access to Customer Portals, Discussion Forums, User Groups, Manufacturers, Solution Partners, Labs, and more.

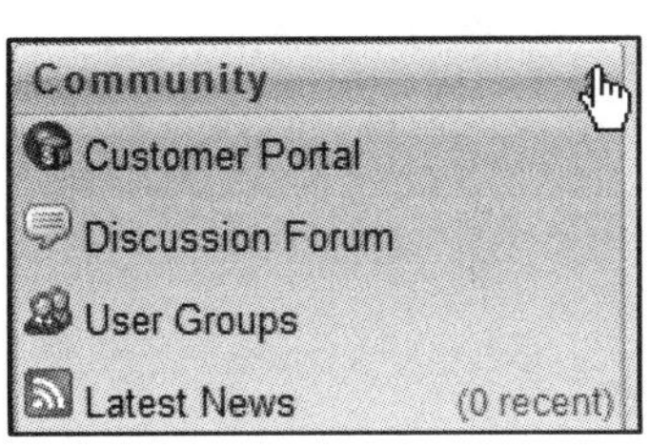

Helpful on-line SolidWorks information is available from the following URLs:

- http://www.dmeducation.net

  Information on the CSWA Certification, software updates, design tips, and new book releases.

- http://www.mechengineer.com/snug/

  News group access and local user group information.

- http://www.nhcad.com

  Configuration information and other tips and tricks.

- http://www.solidworktips.com

  Helpful tips, tricks on SolidWorks and API.

- http://www.topica.com/lists/SW

  Independent News Group for SolidWorks discussions, questions and answers.

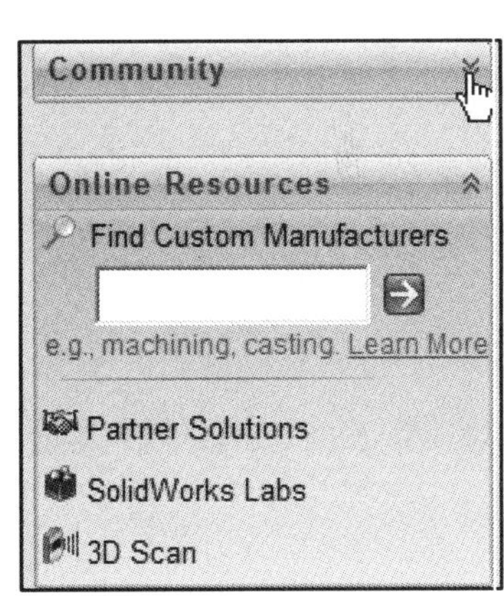

Certified SolidWorks Professionals (CSWP) URLs provide additional helpful on-line information.

- http://www.scottjbaugh.com Scott J. Baugh
- http://www.3-ddesignsolutions.com Devon Sowell
- http://www.zxys.com Paul Salvador
- http://www.mikejwilson.com Mike J. Wilson

Notes:

INDEX

C

D

N

O

P

Notes:

Notes:

Notes:

Notes:

Notes:

Notes:

Notes:

Notes:

Notes:

Notes:

Notes:

Notes: